EXPERIMENTAL STRESS ANALYSIS

[*A Textbook for Engineering Students*]

By

Dr. Sadhu Singh

Ex-Director (Colleges)

Punjab Technical University, Jalandhar - 144 011

Formerly

Professor and Head, Mechanical Engineering Department

&

Dean, Faculty of Engineering and Technology

G.B. Pant University of Agriculture & Technology,

Pantnagar-263145

KHANNA PUBLISHERS

Operational Office

B-35/9, G.T. Karnal Road, Industrial Area,

(Near Telephone Exchange), Delhi-110033

Phones : 011-27224179, 0114-45033189 • *Mob*. 09811541460

email : contactus@khannapublishers.in

Published by :

Romesh Chander Khanna & Vineet Khanna
for **KHANNA PUBLISHERS**
2-B, Nath Market, Nai Sarak,
Delhi-110 006 (India)

Website : www.khannapublishers.in

Hologram & Description

To all readers of our books, from yourself if being defrauded by pirates to prevent, please make sure that there is an Hologram on the cover of our books with the below specifications. If you find any book without Hologram and Description, please mail us at **contactus@khannapublishers.in**

Thanking you

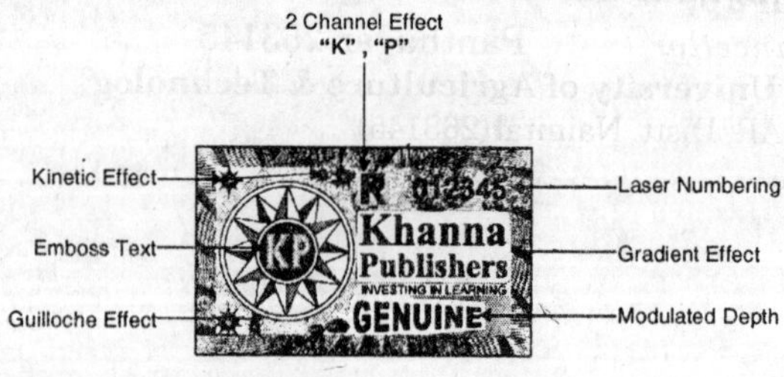

ISBN No. 978-81-7409-182-3

First Edition : 1981
Fourth Edition
Thirteenth Reprint : 2020 (November)

Price : **₹ 399.00**

Forward

I am very happy to know that Dr. Sadhu Singh, Professor of Mechanical Engineering of this University, has written a Textbook on Experimental Stress Analysis. This is a relatively new subject not only for Indian Universities but also for many universities all over the world. This book, as far I know, is the first one of its kind, written on this subject by an Indian author.

The coverage of various aspects of this subject, varying from theory to practice, is quite comprehensive. The book, apart from providing up-to-date information on various topics relevant to Stress Analysis, also contains a selected bibliography at the end of each chapter. Undoubtedly, this book will be of immense use to Undergraduate and Postgraduate students of Engineering and hopefully, it will also help the research workers in pursuing their work with the consciousness of advanced work already done in the field.

I congratulate Dr. Singh for writing a book on this new and developing subject and hope that the engineering students, research workers and teachers will find it very useful.

Anand Sarup,
Vice Chancellor
G.B. Pant University of Agriculture & Technology
PANTNAGAR, Distt. Nainital (263145)
U.P. INDIA

Preface

A course on '*Experimental Stress Analysis*' is now being offered to students in Mechanical, Production, Civil and Aeronautical Engineering both at the undergraduate and the postgraduate levels. The need for a book covering the various aspects of Experimental Stress Analysis has been felt since long.

This book has been written to serve as a textbook on Experimental Stress Analysis. An essential feature of the book in hand is its completeness in respects. A reasonably deep coverage is presented on each topic incorporating the latest information available. A number of problems have been solved in each chapter with a purpose to illustrate the fundamental principles of various methods of stress analysis. At the end of each chapter, quiz questions, numerous exercises and references have been added for practice and further reading.

The book consists of eighteen chapters. The first chapter outlines the basic principles of elasticity. In chapters two to five, strain gauges of different types, strain rosettes, circuits for measuring static and dynamic strains, instrumentation and transducer applications of strain gauges have been discussed. Semiconductor strain gauges have been discussed in chapter six. Chapters seven and eight deal with the two and three dimensional photoelastic methods. In chapters nine and ten photoelastic coatings and brittle lacquer coatings have been discussed in detail. The scattered light method of photoelasticity has been dealt with in brief in chapter seven. Chapter twelve deals with the grid method of strain analysis and the moire methods of strain analysis have been discussed in chapter thirteen. Model laws have been dealt with in chapter fourteen and the analogous methods in chapter fifteen.

Chapter 16 is on Numerical Method followed by Photo-Holo-Elasticity nd Photo-Orthotropic Elasticity.

A special advantage of the book is its presentation, which is simple and thorough. The material embodied has been carefully chosen from various research journals and books and assimilated by the author over the past many years. It is hoped that the book will be appreciated for the immense value it has for the readers.

I wish to record my sincere thanks to the Society for Experimental Stress Analysis (SESA), USA ; Joint British Society for Stress Analysis (JBSSA), Uk ; British Society for Strain Measurements (ASME), USA and the Japanese Society of Mechanical Engineers (JSME), Japan ; whose valuable literature in their journals was consulted during the preparation of this book. Thanks are also due to M/s Photoelastic Inc. ; Vishay Intertechnology, Inc. ; BLH Electronics ; Magnaflux Corporation ; Ailtech and Micro-Measurements of USA ; Tinsely Telcon Ltd., UK ; CIBAGIEGY of India Ltd. ; Electronics Corporation of India Limited, Hyderabad & Motwane Private Ltd., Bombay. They were very kind in sending their literature on the various instruments manufactured by them.

I am very grateful to Sh. Anand Sarup, Vice Chancellor, G.B. Pant Krishi Evam Praudyogik Vishwavidyalaya, Pantnagar, for writing a beautiful foreward to the book. I am also thankful to my many friends and colleagues from whom I received constant encouragement and suggestions during the writing of this book.

Obviously, I shall be failing in my duty if I did not thank and express my gratitude to my wife Mrs. Manjit and the Children, Kamal, Gudia &Rinku, without whose patience and cooperation this work would not have been possible.

Suggestions for the improvement of the book shall be highly appreciated and acknowledged.

—Dr. Sadhu Singh

Dedicated to the loving sweet memory of my mother who could not see what I am today

Contents

List of Symbols

a	amplitude of light wave, area, radius
A	area
a, b	semi-axes of light ellipse
b	radius
B_x, B_y, B_z	body force components
C	relative stress optic coefficient, velocity of light in vacuum
C_1, C_2	stress-optic coefficients
C	constant, capacitance, torsional rigidity, correction factor
C	coefficient of sensitivity
C_ν	Poisson's ratio mismatch correction factor
D_0	fog density of a photographic film
e	error
E	emf or voltage, exposure, magnitude of light vector, modulus of elasticity
E_e	electric field strength
E_0	exposure inertia for photographic film
E_s	secant modulus
f_τ	frequency
f_ε, f_σ	material normal strain and stress fringe values respectively
f_c	material shear stress fringe value
F_e, F_σ	model strain and stress fringe values respectively
F	force, gauge factor
g	acceleration due to gravity
G	shear modulus
h	thickness
i	current
I	current, intensity of light, moment of inertia, stress-invariant
J	polar moment of inertia, strain invariant
k	dielectric constant, resistance per unit length, stiffness
K	bulk modulus, brittle-coating strength ratio
K	transverse sensitivity factor, coating sensitivity
l, L	length
m	integer
M	magnification factor, moment
n	integer, refractive index
N	fringe order, rpm, number of turn, force per unit length
p	pressure, pitch of moire grating
P	load, power
q, Q	charge
Q	figure of merit, apparent strain
r	radius, resistance ratio
R	radius, resistance, relative retardation, reflection coefficient
s	distance, arc length

S	sensitivity index, standard deviation, strain sensitivity surface for
t	time
T	period, temperature, torque transmission cofficient, boundary stress, uniform membrane tension
u, v	secondary principal axes
$u, v, w,$	or
u_x, u_y, u_z	Cartesian components of displacement
v_x, v_y	velocity components
V	volume
w	width, plate deflection
x, y, z	Cartesian coordinates
X	reactance
Z	impedance
$\alpha, \beta, \gamma, \theta, \phi$	angles
α, β	coefficients of thermal expansion
γ	shear strain, specific weight, temperature coefficient of resistivity
δ	deflection, displacement, linear phase difference
Δ	relative phase difference, retardation
ε	normal strain
η	non-linear term
λ	wavelength, Lame's constant
ν	Poisson's ratio
π	piezoresistive proportionality constant, pi
ρ	resistivity coefficient, density, radius
σ	normal stress
τ	shear stress
$\sigma_1, \sigma_2, \sigma_3$	principal stresses
$\sigma'_1, \sigma'_2, \sigma'_3$	secondary principal stresses
ϕ	Airy's stress function, velocity potential
ψ	stream function
ω	angular velocity, vorticity
Ω	body force potential
μ	permeability

SUPERSCRIPTS

c	coating
E	Eulerian
L	Lagrangian
s	specimen
u	ultimate

SUBSCRIPTS

a	apparent
c	calibration, circular
d	dark field

e	entering, equivalent
f	fractional, final
g	gauge
G	galvanometer
H	hydrostatic
i	initial
l	light field, leaving
L	lead wire
m	model
ma	modified apparent
n	normal
p	prototype, plane, plate
s	strip coating, series, shear
sh	shunt
t	true
σ	stress
ε	strain

1

Basic Concepts of Elasticity

1.1 Introduction

In this chapter, we shall study the basic concepts of the theory of elasticity which would be helpful in understanding the methods of experimental stress analysis. We shall not derive the basic equations of elasticity but present them to the reader for reference. For the derivation of these equations the reader may consult the references given at the end of the book.

1.2 Concept of Stress

Two types of forces acting on a body may be distinguished as internal or external. The internal forces are the reactive forces which are set up in the body due to externally applied forces. The internal forces are numerically equal to the external forces. The internal force set up in the body per unit area is called stress. The external forces may be classified as surface or body forces. The surface forces are the forces distributed over the surface or boundary of the body. These forces arise either due to pressure exerted by one body on the other or due to hydraulic or atmospheric pressure. The surface forces are described in terms of forces per unit area and as such are called applied stresses. If $\Delta \overline{F}$ is the force acting on an elementary area ΔA, then the components of the surface forces along the three co-ordinate axes x, y, z are represented by S_x, S_y and S_z respectively, such that

$$\left.\begin{aligned} S_x &= \underset{\Delta A \to 0}{\text{Limit}} \frac{\Delta \overline{F}_x}{\Delta A} \\ S_y &= \underset{\Delta A \to 0}{\text{Limit}} \frac{\Delta \overline{F}_y}{\Delta A} \\ S_z &= \underset{\Delta A \to 0}{\text{Limit}} \frac{\Delta \overline{F}_z}{\Delta A} \end{aligned}\right\} \quad \text{...(1.1)}$$

The body forces on the other hand act throughout the body and are designated as forces per unit volume or mass. Gravitational force, electromagnetic force, centrifugal force and inertia force are some of the examples of body forces. Likewise, the body forces are represented by B_x, B_y and B_z such that

$$\left.\begin{aligned} B_x &= \lim_{\Delta V \to 0} \frac{\Delta \overline{F}_x}{\Delta V} \\ B_y &= \lim_{\Delta V \to 0} \frac{\Delta \overline{F}_y}{\Delta V} \\ B_z &= \lim_{\Delta V \to 0} \frac{\Delta \overline{F}_z}{\Delta V} \end{aligned}\right\} \qquad \text{...(1.2a)}$$

or

$$\left.\begin{aligned} B_x &= \lim_{\Delta m \to 0} \frac{\Delta \overline{F}_x}{\Delta m} \\ B_y &= \lim_{\Delta m \to 0} \frac{\Delta \overline{F}_y}{\Delta m} \\ B_z &= \lim_{\Delta m \to 0} \frac{\Delta \overline{F}_z}{\Delta m} \end{aligned}\right\} \qquad \text{...(1.2b)}$$

where ΔV and Δm are the elementary volume ana elementary mass respectively.

After we have understood the various types of forces to which a body may be subjected to, we now bring about the concept of stress. To do this, let us select an arbitrary system of co-ordinates, and divide the body by an arbitrary plane. If we reject one part of the body and replace the remaining part by the action of the forces distributed through the cross-section of the body, then the force $\Delta \overline{F}$ acting in an arbitrary direction on the area ΔA is as shown in Fig. 1.1. The normal component of this force is $\Delta \overline{F}_n$ along the unit normal $\overline{n}$ and the total component of this force lying in the plane of the area ΔA is $\Delta \overline{F}_s$. Choosing only two orthogonal directions S_1 and S_2 in the plane of the area ΔA, the components of total shear force $\Delta \overline{F}_s$ are $\Delta \overline{F}_{s1}$ and $\Delta \overline{F}_{s2}$. The normal component of stress at point o is defined as :

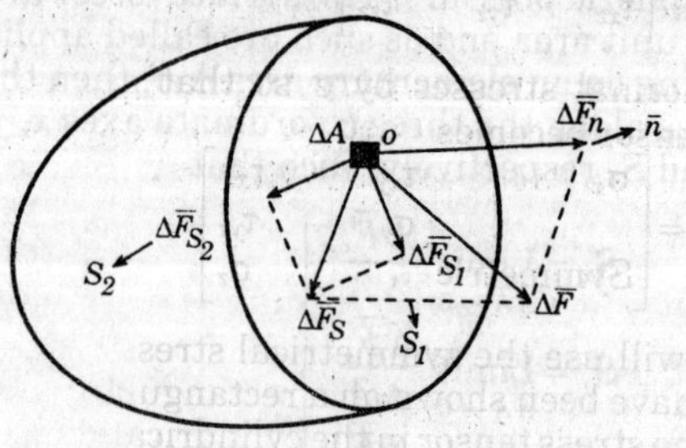

Fig. 1.1 Resolution of a force into normal and shear components.

$$\sigma = \lim_{\Delta A \to 0} \frac{\Delta \overline{F}_n}{\Delta A} \qquad \text{...(1.3)}$$

and the shear stresses are defined as :

$$\left.\begin{aligned}\tau_{s1} &= \underset{\Delta A \to 0}{\text{Limit}} \frac{\Delta \overline{F}_{s1}}{\Delta A} \\ \tau_{s2} &= \underset{\Delta A \to 0}{\text{Limit}} \frac{\Delta \overline{F}_{s2}}{\Delta A}\end{aligned}\right\} \quad \text{...(1.4)}$$

Thus we see that at a point on a plane there are three stress components, one normal and two shear. If a different plane is passed through the same point in the body, then the above stresses will be different.

Since in addition to magnitude and direction, a plane of reference must also be specified for the stress, therefore, stress is a tensor quantity.

The state of stress at any given point of a continuous body is determined entirely by the components of stress in three mutually perpendicular planes which pass through the chosen point. The planes are usually taken perpendicular to the co-ordinate directions of some orthogonal co-ordinate system. The stress components at a point can be conveniently represented by a double subscript system ; the first subscript denoting the direction of the outward drawn normal and the second subscript the direction in which the stress is measured. Thus the stress tensor τ_{ij} in rectangular Cartesian co-ordinates can be written as :

$$\tau_{ij} = \begin{bmatrix} \tau_{xx} & \tau_{xy} & \tau_{xz} \\ \tau_{yx} & \tau_{yy} & \tau_{yz} \\ \tau_{zx} & \tau_{zy} & \tau_{zz} \end{bmatrix}$$

By taking moments about the three different axes it can be shown that $\tau_{ij} = \tau_{ji}$, $i \neq j$, $i, j = x, y, z$, *i.e.* the stress tensor is symmetric in nature. Therefore, the above stress tensor can be written as :

$$\tau_{ij} = \begin{bmatrix} \tau_{xx} & \tau_{xy} & \tau_{xz} \\ \tau_{xy} & \tau_{yy} & \tau_{yz} \\ \tau_{xz} & \tau_{yz} & \tau_{zz} \end{bmatrix}$$

Denoting the normal stresses by σ so that $\sigma_x = \tau_{xx}$, $\sigma_y = \tau_{yy}$ and $\sigma_z = \tau_{zz}$, the stress tensor becomes

$$\tau_{ij} = \begin{bmatrix} \sigma_x & \tau_{xy} & \tau_{xz} \\ & \sigma_y & \tau_{yz} \\ \text{Symmetric} & & \sigma_z \end{bmatrix} \quad \text{...(1.5)}$$

Henceforth we will use the symmetrical stress tensor only. These stress components have been shown on a rectangular parallelopiped in Fig. 1.2. Similarly the stress tensor in the cylindrical (r, θ, z) co-ordinate system may be written as

$$\tau_{ij} = \begin{bmatrix} \sigma_r & \tau_{r\theta} & \tau_{rz} \\ & \sigma_\theta & \tau_{\theta z} \\ \text{Symmetric} & & \sigma_z \end{bmatrix} \quad \text{...(1.6)}$$

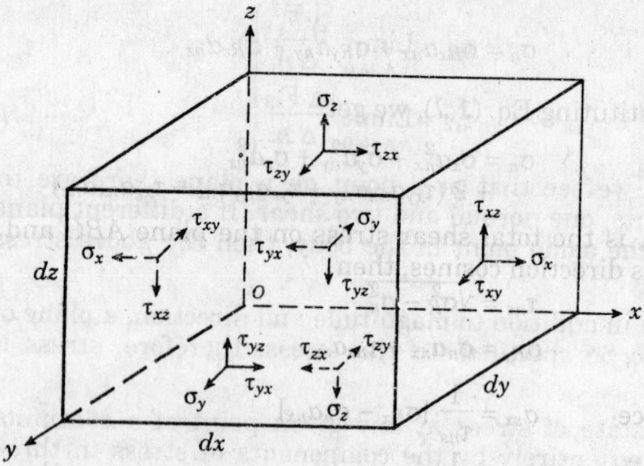

Fig. 1.2 Cartesian components of stress acting on the faces of an elementary parallelopiped.

1.3 Transformation of Stress Components

If we know the stresses on three mutually perpendicular elementary areas, we can always determine the resultant stress σ_R which acts on any area passing through the same point. Consider a body under a generalised state of stress. If we cut from this body an elementary tetrahedron and represent the stresses acting on its faces as shown in Fig. 1.3, then by resolving the forces acting on the faces of the tetrahedron along the three axes, the stress components σ_{Rx}, σ_{Ry} and σ_{Rz} on the face ABC, whose direction cosines are a_{nx}, a_{ny}, a_{nz} become,

$$\left.\begin{aligned}\sigma_{Rx} &= \sigma_x a_{nx} + \tau_{xy} a_{ny} + \tau_{xz} a_{nz}\\ \sigma_{Ry} &= \tau_{xy} a_{nx} + \sigma_y a_{ny} + \tau_{yz} a_{nz}\\ \sigma_{Rz} &= \tau_{xz}\, a_{nx} + \tau_{yz} a_{ny} + \sigma_z a_{nz}\end{aligned}\right\} \quad ...(1.7)$$

and
$$\sigma_R^2 = \sigma_{Rx}^2 + \sigma_{Ry}^2 + \sigma_{Rz}^2 \quad ...(1.8)$$

The normal stress σ_n on the face ABC whose normal is $\bar{n}$, then becomes

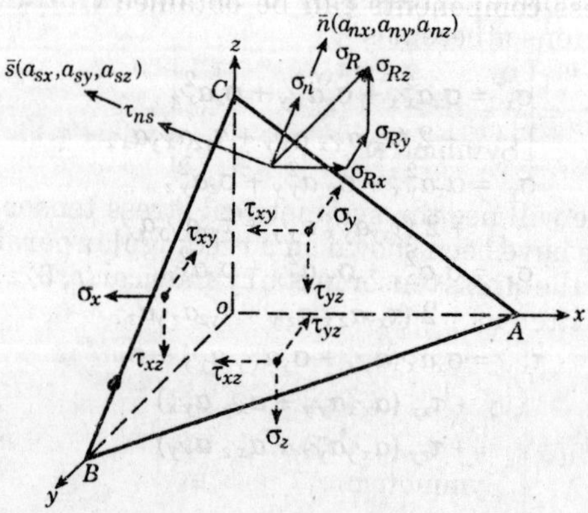

Fig.1.3 Stresses acting on the faces of an elementary tetrahedron.

$$\sigma_n = \sigma_{Rx} a_{nx} + \sigma_{Ry} a_{ny} + \sigma_{Rz} a_{nz}$$

Substituting Eq. (1.7), we get

$$\sigma_n = \sigma_x a_{nx}^2 + \sigma_y a_{ny}^2 + \sigma_z a_{nz}^2 + 2\,(\tau_{xy} a_{nx} a_{ny} + \tau_{yz} a_{ny} a_{nz} + \tau_{xz} a_{nx} a_{nz}) \qquad ...(1.9)$$

If τ_{ns} is the total shear stress on the plane ABC and a_{sx}, a_{sy} and a_{sz} are its direction cosines, then

$$\tau_{ns} = \sqrt{\sigma_R^2 - \sigma_n^2} \qquad ...(1.10)$$

Also $\quad \sigma_{R_x} = \sigma_n a_{nx} + \tau_{ns} a_{sx}$

$$\left.\begin{aligned} \text{Hence} \quad a_{sx} &= \frac{1}{\tau_{ns}} [\sigma_{Rx} - \sigma_n a_{nx}] \\ &= \frac{1}{\tau_{ns}} [(\sigma_x - \sigma_n)\, a_{nx} + \tau_{xy}\, a_{ny} + \tau_{xz}\, a_{nz})] \\ \text{Similarly} \quad a_{sy} &= \frac{1}{\tau_{ns}} [\tau_{xy} a_{nx} + (\sigma_y - \sigma_n)\, a_{ny} + \tau_{yz} a_{nz}] \\ a_{sz} &= \frac{1}{\tau_{ns}} [\tau_{xz} a_{nx} + \tau_{yz} a_{ny} + (\sigma_z - \sigma_n)\, a_{nz}] \end{aligned}\right] \qquad ...(1.11)$$

Sometimes it is desired to express the stress component referred to a new co-ordinate system $x'\ y'\ z'$ obtained by a rotation of the co-ordinate system xyz about the origin o, then the direction cosines are determined by the following array of terms :

	x	y	z
x'	$a_{x'x}$	$a_{x'y}$	$a_{x'z}$
y'	$a_{y'x}$	$a_{y'y}$	$a_{y'z}$
z'	$a_{z'x}$	$a_{z'y}$	$a_{z'z}$

where $a_{i'j} = \cos(i', j)$; $i' = x', y', z'$; $j = x, y, z$

The new stress components can be obtained from the following equations

$$\left.\begin{aligned} \sigma_x' &= \sigma_x a_{x'x}^2 + \sigma_y a_{x'y}^2 + \sigma_z a_{x'z}^2 \\ &\quad + 2\,(\tau_{xy} a_{x'x}\, a_{x'y} + \tau_{yz} a_{x'y} a_{x'z} + \tau_{xz} a_{x'x} a_{x'z}) \\ \sigma_y' &= \alpha_x a_{y'x}^2 + \sigma_y\, a_{y'y}^2 + \sigma_z a_{y'z}^2 \\ &\quad + 2\,(\tau_{xy} a_{y'x}\, a_{y'y} + \tau_{yz} a_{y'y} a_{y'z} + \tau_{xz} a_{y'x} a_{y'z}) \\ \sigma_z' &= \sigma_x a_{z'x}^2 + \sigma_y\, a_{z'y}^2 + \sigma_z a_{z'z}^2 \\ &\quad + 2\,(\tau_{xy} a_{z'x}\, a_{z'y} + \tau_{yz} a_{z'y} a_{z'z} + \tau_{xz} a_{z'x} a_{z'z}) \\ \tau_{x'y'} &= \sigma_x a_{x'x} a_{y'x} + \sigma_y a_{x'y}\, a_{y'y} + \sigma_z a_{x'z}\, a_{y'z} \\ &\quad + \tau_{xy}\, (a_{x'x} a_{y'y} + a_{x'y}\, a_{y'x}) \\ &\quad + \tau_{zy}\, (a_{x'y} a_{y'z} + a_{x'z}\, a_{y'y}) \end{aligned}\right\}$$

$$
\left.
\begin{aligned}
&+ \tau_{xz}\,(a_{x'x}a_{y'z} + a_{x'z}\,a_{y'x}) \\
\tau_{y'z'} &= \sigma_x a_{y'x}a_{z'x} + \sigma_y a_{y'y}a_{z'y} + \sigma_z a_{y'z}a_{z'z} \\
&+ \tau_{xy}\,(a_{y'x}a_{z'y} + a_{y'y}a_{z'x}) \\
&+ \tau_{yz}\,(a_{y'y}a_{z'z} + a_{y'z}a_{z'y}) \\
&+ \tau_{xz}\,(a_{y'x}a_{z'z} + a_{y'z}a_{z'x}) \\
\tau_{x'z'} &= \sigma_x a_{z'x}a_{x'x} + \sigma_y a_{z'y}a_{x'y} + \sigma_z a_{z'z}a_{x'z} \\
&+ \tau_{xy}\,(a_{z'x}a_{x'y} + a_{z'y}a_{x'x}) \\
&+ \tau_{yz}\,(a_{z'y}a_{x'z} + a_{z'z}a_{x'y}) \\
&+ \tau_{xz}\,(a_{z'z}a_{x'x} + a_{z'x}a_{x'z})
\end{aligned}
\right\} \quad \text{...(1.12)}
$$

A plane which is equally inclined to the three axes of reference is called the octahedral plane and the normal and shearing stresses acting on this plane are called the octahedral stresses.

1.4 Principal Stresses

The importance of stress transformation is that they can be used to determine the planes on which the shear stress is zero and the normal stress is maximum, *i.e.* the principal planes. It can be shown that the principal stresses are the roots of the cubic equations,

$$\sigma^3 - I_1\,\sigma^2 + I_2\,\sigma - I_3 = 0 \quad \text{...(1.13)}$$

where

$$
\left.
\begin{aligned}
I_1 &= \sigma_x + \sigma_y + \sigma_z \\
I_2 &= \sigma_x\sigma_y + \sigma_y\sigma_z + \sigma_x\sigma_z - \tau_{xy}^2 - \tau_{yz}^2 - \tau_{xz}^2 \\
I_3 &= \sigma_x\sigma_y\sigma_z - \sigma_x\,\tau_{yz}^2 - \sigma_y\,\tau_{xz}^2 - \sigma_z\,\tau_{xy}^2 \\
&+ 2\,\tau_{xy}\,\tau_{yz}\,\tau_{xz}
\end{aligned}
\right\} \quad \text{...(1.14)}
$$

are the three stress invariants.

The solution of Eq. (1.13) may be obtained by a hit and trial method or a numerical technique like the Newton-Raphson method.

If σ_1, σ_2 and σ_3 are the three principal stresses, then the principal directions can be obtained as follows :

$$
\left.
\begin{aligned}
a_{nx1} &= \frac{A_1}{\sqrt{(A_1^2 + B_1^2 + C_1^2)}} \\
a_{ny1} &= \frac{B_1}{\sqrt{(A_1^2 + B_1^2 + C_1^2)}} \\
a_{nz1} &= \frac{C_1}{\sqrt{(A_1^2 + B_1^2 + C_1^2)}}
\end{aligned}
\right\} \quad \text{...(1.15)}
$$

where
$$A_1 = \begin{vmatrix} \sigma_y - \sigma_1 & \tau_{yz} \\ \tau_{yz} & \sigma_z - \sigma_1 \end{vmatrix}$$

$$B_1 = -\begin{vmatrix} \tau_{xy} & \tau_{yz} \\ \tau_{xz} & \sigma_z - \sigma_1 \end{vmatrix}$$

$$C_1 = \begin{vmatrix} \tau_{xy} & \sigma_y - \sigma_1 \\ \tau_{xz} & \tau_{yz} \end{vmatrix}$$

Similarly, the direction cosines of σ_2 and σ_3 can be determined.

1.5 Equilibrium Equations

By considering the equilibrium of forces acting on an elementary rectangular parallelopiped (Fig. 1.4) cut from a body subjected to generalised state of stress and noting that the stress tensor is symmetric, it can be shown that the following equilibrium equations hold good.

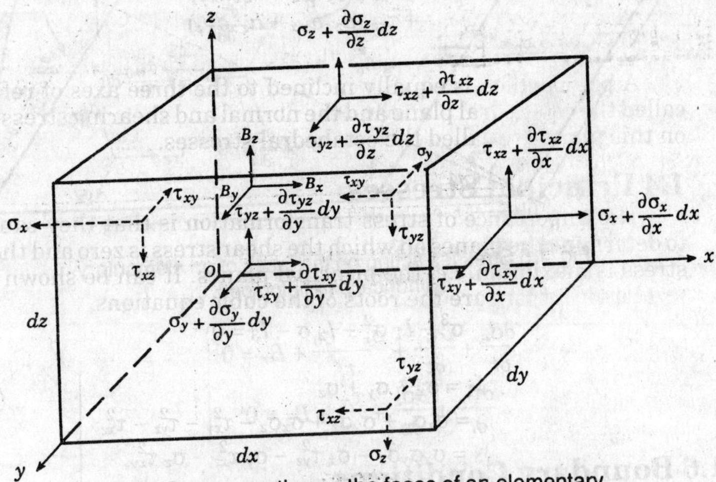

Fig. 1.4 Stresses acting on the faces of an elementary rectangular parallelopiped.

$$\left.\begin{aligned} \frac{\partial \sigma_x}{\partial x} + \frac{\partial \tau_{xy}}{\partial y} + \frac{\partial \tau_{xz}}{\partial z} + B_x = 0 \\ \frac{\partial \tau_{xy}}{\partial x} + \frac{\partial \sigma_y}{\partial y} + \frac{\partial \tau_{yz}}{\partial z} + B_y = 0 \\ \frac{\partial \tau_{xz}}{\partial x} + \frac{\partial \tau_{yz}}{\partial y} + \frac{\partial \sigma_z}{\partial z} + B_z = 0 \end{aligned}\right\} \quad ...(1.16)$$

When dealing with bodies which have rotational symmetry it is usually convenient to use cylindrical co-ordinates. By considering the equilibrium of forces acting on an elementary cylindrical parallelopiped as shown in Fig. 1.5, we get

$$\left.\begin{aligned} \frac{\partial \sigma_r}{\partial r} + \frac{1}{r}\frac{\partial \tau_{r\theta}}{\partial \theta} + \frac{\partial \tau_{rz}}{\partial z} + \frac{\sigma_r - \sigma_\theta}{r} + B_r = 0 \\ \frac{\partial \tau_{r\theta}}{\partial r} + \frac{1}{r}\frac{\partial \sigma_\theta}{\partial \theta} + \frac{\partial \tau_{\theta z}}{\partial z} + \frac{2\tau_{r\theta}}{r} + B_\theta = 0 \\ \frac{\partial \tau_{rz}}{\partial r} + \frac{1}{r}\frac{\partial \tau_{\theta z}}{\partial \theta} + \frac{\partial \sigma_r}{\partial z} + \frac{\tau_{rz}}{r} + B_z = 0 \end{aligned}\right\} \quad ...(1.17)$$

For problems having axial symmetry $\tau_{\theta z} = \tau_{r\theta} = 0$ and Eqs. (1.17) reduce to

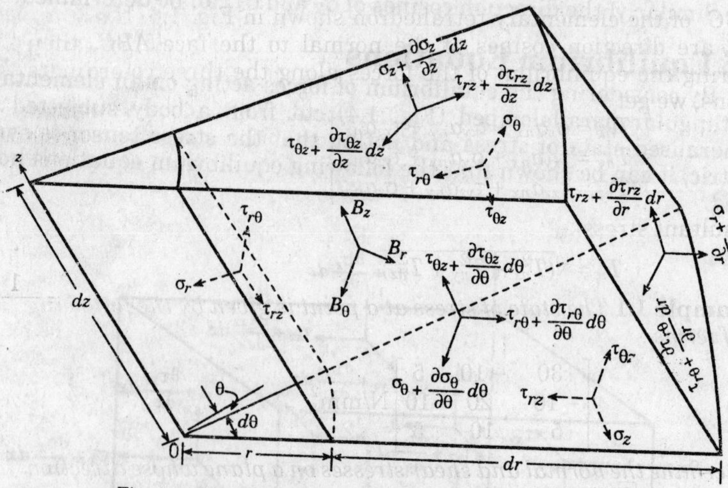

Fig. 1.5 Stresses acting on the faces of an elementary cylindrical parallelopiped.

$$\left.\begin{aligned}\frac{\partial \sigma_r}{\partial r} + \frac{\partial \tau_{rz}}{\partial z} + \frac{\sigma_r - \sigma_\theta}{r} + B_r = 0 \\ \frac{\partial \tau_{rz}}{\partial r} + \frac{\partial \sigma_z}{\partial z} + \frac{\tau_{rz}}{r} + B_z = 0\end{aligned}\right\} \qquad ...(1.18)$$

1.6 Boundary Conditions

The equations of equilibrium must be satisfied by the components of stress at every point in a body including all points on the boundary. Let T_{nx}, T_{ny} and T_{nz} be the components of the boundary stresses on the

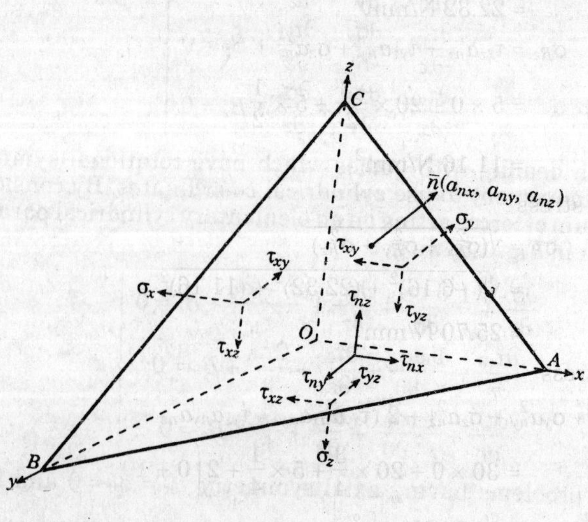

Fig. 1.6 Boundary stresses acting on the face *ABC* of an elementary tetrahedron.

face ABC of the elementary tetrahedron shown in Fig. 1.6. If a_{nx}, a_{ny} and a_{nz} are direction cosines of the normal to the face ABC, then considering the equilibrium of the forces along the three co-ordinate directions, we get

$$\left.\begin{aligned} T_{nx} &= \sigma_x a_{nx} + \tau_{xy} a_{ny} + \tau_{xz} a_{nz} \\ T_{ny} &= \tau_{xy} a_{nx} + \sigma_y a_{ny} + \tau_{yz} a_{nz} \\ T_{nz} &= \tau_{xz} a_{nx} + \tau_{yz} a_{ny} + \sigma_z a_{nz} \end{aligned}\right\} \quad \text{...(1.19)}$$

Resultant stress

$$T_n = \sqrt{(T_{nx}^2 + T_{ny}^2 + T_{nz}^2)}$$

Example 1.1 *The state of stress at a point is given by the following array of terms :*

$$\begin{bmatrix} 30 & -10 & 5 \\ -10 & 20 & 10 \\ 5 & 10 & 5 \end{bmatrix} \text{N/mm}^2$$

Determine the normal and shear stresses on a plane whose direction cosines are, 0, $\frac{\sqrt{3}}{2}$, 1/2. Also determine the direction of the shear stress.

Solution. $\sigma_{Rx} = \sigma_x a_{nx} + \tau_{xy} a_{ny} + \tau_{xz} a_{nz}$

$$= 30 \times 0 - 10 \times \frac{\sqrt{3}}{2} + 5 \times \frac{1}{2}$$

$$= -6.16 \text{ N/mm}^2$$

$$\sigma_{Ry} = \tau_{xy} a_{nx} + \sigma_y a_{ny} + \tau_{yz} a_{nz}$$

$$= -10 \times 0 + 20 \times \frac{\sqrt{3}}{2} + 10 \times \frac{1}{2}$$

$$= 22.32 \text{ N/mm}^2$$

$$\sigma_{Rz} = \tau_{xz} a_{nx} + \tau_{yz} a_{ny} + \sigma_z a_{nz}$$

$$= 5 \times 0 + 20 \times \frac{\sqrt{3}}{2} + 5 \times \frac{1}{2}$$

$$= 11.16 \text{ N/mm}^2$$

Resultant stress

$$\sigma_R = \sqrt{(\sigma_{Rx}^2 + \sigma_{Ry}^2 + \sigma_{Rz}^2)}$$

$$= \sqrt{[(-6.16)^2 + (22.32)^2 + (11.16)^2]}$$

$$= 25.70 \text{ N/mm}^2$$

Normal stress

$$\sigma_n = \sigma_x a_{nx}^2 + \sigma_y a_{ny}^2 + \sigma_z a_{nz}^2 + 2\,(\tau_{xy} a_{nx} a_{ny} + \tau_{yz} a_{ny} a_{nz} + \tau_{xz} a_{nx} a_{nz})$$

$$= 30 \times 0 + 20 \times \frac{3}{4} + 5 \times \frac{1}{4} + 2\left(0 + 10 \times \frac{\sqrt{3}}{2} \times \frac{1}{2} + 0\right)$$

$$= 24.91 \text{ N/mm}^2$$

Shear stress :

$$\tau_{ns} = \sqrt{(\sigma_R^2 - \sigma_n^2)}$$
$$= \sqrt{(25.70)^2 - (24.91)^2}$$
$$= 6.34 \text{ N/mm}^2$$

The direction cosines of shear stress are :

$$a_{sx} = \frac{1}{\tau_{ns}} [\sigma_{Rx} - \sigma_n a_{nx}]$$
$$= \frac{1}{6.34} [-6.16 - 24.91 \times 0] = -0.9720$$
$$a_{sy} = \frac{1}{\tau_{ns}} [\sigma_{Ry} - \sigma_n a_{ny}]$$
$$= \frac{1}{6.34}\left[22.32 - 24.91 \times \frac{\sqrt{3}}{2}\right] = 0.1180.$$
$$a_{sz} = \frac{1}{\tau_{ns}} [\sigma_{Rz} - \sigma_n a_{nz}]$$
$$= \frac{1}{6.34}\left[11.16 - 24.91 \times \frac{1}{2}\right] = -0.2043$$

Example 1.2 *The state of stress at a point is given by the following stress components ;*

$$\sigma_x = 200,\ \sigma_y = 100,\ \sigma_z = 50$$
$$\sigma_{xy} = 30,\ \tau_{yz} = 20 \text{ and } \tau_{xz} = 40 \text{ N/mm}^2$$

Determine the principal stresses and principal planes.

Solution. $I_1 = \sigma_x + \sigma_y + \sigma_z$

$$= 200 + 100 + 50 = 350$$
$$I_2 = \sigma_x\sigma_y + \sigma_y\sigma_z + \sigma_x\sigma_z - \tau_{xy}^2 - \tau_{yz}^2 - \tau_{xz}^2$$
$$= 200 \times 100 + 100 \times 50 + 200 \times 50 - 900 - 400 - 1600$$
$$= 32{,}100$$
$$I_3 = \sigma_x\sigma_y\sigma_z - \sigma_x\tau_{yz}^2 - \sigma_y\tau_{xz}^2 - \sigma_z\tau_{xy}^2 + 2\,\tau_{xy}\tau_{yz}\tau_{xz}$$
$$= 200 \times 100 \times 50 - 200 \times 400 - 100 \times 1600$$
$$- 50 \times 90 + 2 \times 30 \times 20 \times 40$$
$$= 763{,}000$$

The principal stresses are the roots of the equation

$$f(\sigma) = \sigma^3 - 350\,\sigma^2 + 32{,}100\,\sigma - 763{,}000 = 0$$

We shall determine the solution of this equation by Newton-Raphson method.

Let $\sigma = 90 \text{ N/mm}^2$

$$f'(\sigma) = 3\sigma^2 - 700\,\sigma + 32{,}100$$

First iteration gives,

$$\sigma = 90 - \frac{f(90)}{f'(90)}$$

$$= 90 - \frac{20{,}000}{-6600} = 93.03$$

Second iteration gives,

$$\sigma = 93.03 - \left(\frac{-704.625}{-7057.25}\right)$$

$$= 92.93 \text{ N/mm}^2$$

So we take one root equal to 92.93 N/mm^2. Dividing the cubic equation by $(\sigma - 92.93)$, we get the quadratic equation, $\sigma^2 - 257.07\,\sigma + 8210.485 = 0$. The roots of this equation are 219.69 and 37.37. Hence the principal stresses become,

$$\sigma_1 = 219.69 \text{ N/mm}^2$$

$$\sigma_2 = 92.93 \text{ N/mm}^2$$

$$\sigma_3 = 37.37 \text{ N/mm}^2$$

The direction cosines of σ_1 are obtained as follows :

$$A_1 = \begin{vmatrix} \sigma_y - \sigma_1 & \tau_{yz} \\ \tau_{yz} & \sigma_y - \sigma_1 \end{vmatrix} = \begin{vmatrix} -119.69 & 20 \\ 20 & -169.69 \end{vmatrix} = 19910.96$$

$$B_1 = -\begin{vmatrix} \tau_{xy} & \tau_{yz} \\ \tau_{xz} & \sigma_z - \sigma_1 \end{vmatrix} = -\begin{vmatrix} 30 & 20 \\ 40 & -169.69 \end{vmatrix} = -5890.7$$

$$C_1 = \begin{vmatrix} \tau_{xy} & \sigma_y - \sigma_1 \\ \tau_{xz} & \tau_{yz} \end{vmatrix} = \begin{vmatrix} 30 & -119.69 \\ 40 & 20 \end{vmatrix} = 5387.6$$

$$K_1 = \sqrt{(A_1^2 + B_1^2 + C_1^2)}$$

$$= \sqrt{(19910.96)^2 + (-5890.7)^2 + (5387.6)^2}$$

$$= 21450$$

$$a_{nx1} = \frac{A_1}{K_1} = \frac{19910.96}{21450} = 0.9280$$

$$a_{ny1} = \frac{B_1}{K_1} = \frac{-5890.7}{21450} = -0.2746$$

$$a_{nz1} = \frac{C_1}{K_1} = \frac{5387.6}{21450} = 0.2511$$

Similarly the direction cosines for σ_2 and σ_3 can be obtained as

$$a_{nx2} = -0.3160,\ a_{ny2} = 0.9380,\ a_{nz2} = 0.1425$$

$$a_{nx3} = -0.1963,\ a_{ny3} = 0.2114,\ a_{nz3} = 0.9574$$

Example 1.3 *The stress components at a point are given by :*

$$\sigma_x = 20, \sigma_y = 10, \sigma_z = 15$$

$$\tau_{xy} = 5, \tau_{yz} = 4, \tau_{xz} = 3 \text{ N/mm}^2$$

with reference to x, y, z co-ordinates system. If this co-ordinate system is rotated about the z-axis in the anti-clockwise direction through 45°, determine the new stress components.

Solution. As shown in Fig. 1.7, the direction cosines are

	x	y	z
x'	$\frac{1}{\sqrt{2}}$	$\frac{1}{\sqrt{2}}$	0
y'	$-\frac{1}{\sqrt{2}}$	$\frac{1}{\sqrt{2}}$	0
z'	0	0	1

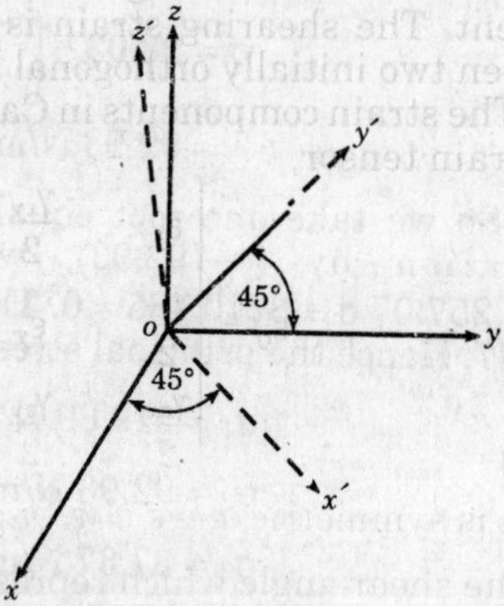

Fig. 1.7

$$\sigma_{x'} = \sigma_x a_{x'x}^2 + \sigma_y a_{x'y}^2 + \sigma_z a_{x'z}^2$$
$$+ 2\,(\tau_{xy} a_{x'x} a_{x'y} + \tau_{yz} a_{x'y} a_{x'z} + \tau_{xz} a_{x'x} a_{x'z})$$
$$= 20 \times \frac{1}{2} + 10 \times \frac{1}{2} + 15 \times 0 + 2\,(5 \times \frac{1}{2} + 0 + 0)$$
$$= 20 \text{ N/mm}^2$$

Similarly $\sigma_y' = 10 \text{ N/mm}^2$

$$\sigma_{z'} = 15 \text{ N/mm}^2$$

$$\tau_{x'y'} = \sigma_x a_{x'x}\, a_{y'x} + \sigma_y a_{x'y}\, a_{y'y} + \sigma_z a_{x'z} a_{y'z}$$
$$+ \tau_{xy}\,(a_{x'x} a_{y'y} + a_{x'y} a_{y'x}) + \tau_{yz}\,(a_{x'y} a_{y'z} + a_{x'z} a_{y'y})$$
$$+ \tau_{xz}\,(a_{x'x}\, a_{y'z} + a_{x'z}\, a_{y'x})$$
$$= 20 \times \frac{1}{\sqrt{2}} \left(-\frac{1}{\sqrt{2}} \right) + 10 \times \frac{1}{\sqrt{2}} \times \frac{1}{\sqrt{2}} + 0$$
$$+ 5 \left(\frac{1}{\sqrt{2}} \times \frac{1}{\sqrt{2}} - \frac{1}{\sqrt{2}} \times \frac{1}{\sqrt{2}} \right) + 0 + 0$$
$$= -5 \text{ N/mm}^2$$

Similarly $\tau_{y'z'} = 0.707 \text{ N/mm}^2$, $\tau_{x'z'} = 4.949 \text{ N/mm}^2$

1.7 Concept of Strain

The displacements of the different points of a material body consist of two parts, rigid body displacements and deformation. The first corresponds to a translation or rotation of the body as a whole, or combination of this and the second corresponds to displacements of material points relative to each other, that enters the definition of strain. The state of deformation in the neighbourhood of a point of a continuous body is determined by six components of strain, three normal and three shear. Physically, the normal strain is the change in length of a small line segment divided by the original length of the segment. The shearing strain is visualized as the decrease in angle between two initially orthogonal line segments as a result of deformation. The strain components in Cartesian co-ordinate system constitute the strain tensor,

$$\varepsilon_{ij} = \begin{Bmatrix} \varepsilon_x & \dfrac{\gamma_{xy}}{2} & \dfrac{\gamma_{xz}}{2} \\ \dfrac{\gamma_{yx}}{2} & \varepsilon_y & \dfrac{\gamma_{yz}}{2} \\ \dfrac{\gamma_{zx}}{2} & \dfrac{\gamma_{zy}}{2} & \varepsilon_z \end{Bmatrix} \quad \text{...(1.20)}$$

which is symmetric, *i.e.* $\varepsilon_{ij} = \varepsilon_{ji}$, $i \neq j$ and $\gamma_{ij} = 2\,\varepsilon_{ij}$, $i \neq j$, and $i, j = x, y, z$.

γ_{ij} is the shear angle which represents the total decrease of right angle between two line segments initially perpendicular to each other.

The components of rotation tensor are :

$$w_{ij} = \begin{bmatrix} 0 & w_{xy} & w_{xz} \\ w_{yx} & 0 & w_{yz} \\ w_{zx} & w_{zy} & 0 \end{bmatrix} \quad \text{...(1.21)}$$

which is skew symmetric, *i.e.* $w_{ij} = -w_{ji}$, $i \neq j$ and $i, j = x, y, z$.

If u_x, u_y and u_z are the components of the displacement field, then

$$\left.\begin{aligned} w_{xy} &= \frac{1}{2}\left(\frac{\partial u_x}{\partial y} - \frac{\partial u_y}{\partial x}\right) \\ w_{yz} &= \frac{1}{2}\left(\frac{\partial u_y}{\partial z} - \frac{\partial u_z}{\partial y}\right) \\ w_{xz} &= \frac{1}{2}\left(\frac{\partial u_x}{\partial z} - \frac{\partial u_z}{\partial x}\right) \end{aligned}\right\} \quad \text{...(1.22)}$$

so that the components of the rigid body rotations are :

$$\left.\begin{aligned} \delta\,\phi_x &= -w_{yz} \\ \delta\phi_y &= w_{xz} \\ \delta\phi_z &= -w_{xy} \end{aligned}\right\} \quad \text{...(1.23)}$$

and the angle of rotation becomes,

$$\delta\phi = \delta\,\phi_x\,\hat{i} + \delta\,\phi_y\,\hat{j} + \delta\,\phi_z\,\hat{k} \quad \text{...(1.24)}$$

The components of strain tensor in Cartesian co-ordinates are :

$$\left.\begin{aligned}
\varepsilon_x &= \frac{\partial u_x}{\partial x}\\
\varepsilon_y &= \frac{\partial u_y}{\partial y}\\
\varepsilon_z &= \frac{\partial u_z}{\partial z}\\
\gamma_{xy} &= \frac{\partial u_x}{\partial y} + \frac{\partial u_y}{\partial x}\\
\gamma_{yz} &= \frac{\partial u_y}{\partial z} + \frac{\partial u_z}{\partial y}\\
\gamma_{xz} &= \frac{\partial u_x}{\partial z} + \frac{\partial u_z}{\partial x}
\end{aligned}\right\} \qquad \text{...(1.25)}$$

Similarly the components of strain tensor in cylindrical co-ordinates (r, θ, z) can be written as :

$$\left.\begin{aligned}
\varepsilon_r &= \frac{\partial u_r}{\partial r}\\
\varepsilon_\theta &= \frac{1}{r}\frac{\partial u_\theta}{\partial \theta} + \frac{u_r}{r}\\
\varepsilon_z &= \frac{\partial u_z}{\partial z}\\
\gamma_{r\theta} &= \frac{1}{r}\frac{\partial u_r}{\partial \theta} + \frac{\partial u_\theta}{\partial r} - \frac{u_\theta}{r}\\
\gamma_{\theta z} &= \frac{\partial u_\theta}{\partial z} + \frac{1}{r}\frac{\partial u_z}{\partial \theta}\\
\gamma_{rz} &= \frac{\partial u_r}{\partial z} + \frac{\partial u_z}{\partial r}
\end{aligned}\right\} \qquad \text{...(1.26)}$$

1.8 Transformation of Strain Components

The strain components may be transformed from one coordinate system to another in the same manner as the stress components. Thus, for example, for transformation from old co-ordinate system *xyz* to the new system *x′ y′ z′*, we have

$$\left.\begin{aligned}
\varepsilon_{x'} &= \varepsilon_x a_{x'x}^2 + \varepsilon_y a_{x'y}^2 + \varepsilon_z a_{x'z}^2 + \gamma_{xy} a_{x'x}\, a_{x'y}\\
&\quad + \gamma_{yz}\, a_{x'y}\, a_{x'z} + \gamma_{xz}\, a_{x'x}\, a_{x'z}\\
\frac{\gamma_{x'y'}}{2} &= \varepsilon_x\, a_{x'x}\, a_{y'x} + \varepsilon_y\, a_{x'y}\, a_{y'y} + \varepsilon_z\, a_{x'z}\, a_{y'z}\\
&\quad + \frac{\gamma_{xy}}{2}\,(a_{x'x}\, a_{y'y} + a_{x'y}\, a_{y'x})\\
&\quad + \frac{\gamma_{yz}}{2}\,(a_{x'y}\, a_{y'z} + a_{x'z}\, a_{y'y})\\
&\quad + \frac{\gamma_{xz}}{2}\,(a_{x'x}\, a_{y'z} + a_{x'z}\, a_{y'x})
\end{aligned}\right] \qquad \text{....(1.27)}$$

and so on.

The normal and shearing strains on any plane can be determined in the same manner as explained for stresses in Art. 1.3.

1.9 Principal Strains

The principal strains are the roots of the cubic equation

$$\varepsilon^3 - J_1\varepsilon^2 + J_2\,\varepsilon - J_3 = 0 \qquad \text{...(1.28)}$$

where

$$\left.\begin{aligned} J_1 &= \varepsilon_x + \varepsilon_y + \varepsilon_z \\ J_2 &= \varepsilon_x\varepsilon_y + \varepsilon_y\varepsilon_z + \varepsilon_x\varepsilon_z - \frac{1}{4}\,(\gamma_{xy}^2 + \gamma_{yz}^2 + \gamma_{xz}^2) \\ J_3 &= \varepsilon_x\varepsilon_y\varepsilon_z - \frac{1}{4}\,(\varepsilon_x\gamma_{yz}^2 + \varepsilon_y\,\gamma_{xz}^2 + \varepsilon_z\,\gamma_{xy}^2 - \gamma_{xy}\,\gamma_{yz}\,\gamma_{xz}) \end{aligned}\right\} \qquad \text{...(1.29)}$$

are the three strain invariants.

Eq. (1.28) may be solved by a hit-and-trial method or any numerical technique like the Newton-Raphson method.

1.10 Strain Compatibility Equations

For a given displacement field, a unique strain field can be computed. However, for a given strain field, the corresponding displacements are not necessarily unique and continuous, unless certain conditions are satisfied by the strain components. These conditions are known as the compatibility equations, expressed as :

$$\left.\begin{aligned} \frac{\partial^2\gamma_{xy}}{\partial x\partial y} &= \frac{\partial^2\varepsilon_x}{\partial y^2} + \frac{\partial^2\varepsilon_y}{\partial x^2} \\ \frac{\partial^2\gamma_{yz}}{\partial y\partial z} &= \frac{\partial^2\varepsilon_y}{\partial z^2} + \frac{\partial^2\varepsilon_z}{\partial y^2} \\ \frac{\partial^2\gamma_{xz}}{\partial x\partial z} &= \frac{\partial^2\varepsilon_x}{\partial z^2} + \frac{\partial^2\varepsilon_z}{\partial x^2} \\ \frac{2\,\partial^2\varepsilon_x}{\partial y\partial z} &= \frac{\partial}{\partial x}\left(-\frac{\partial\gamma_{yz}}{\partial x} + \frac{\partial\gamma_{xz}}{\partial y} + \frac{\partial\gamma_{xy}}{\partial z}\right) \\ \frac{2\,\partial^2\varepsilon_y}{\partial x\partial z} &= \frac{\partial}{\partial y}\left(-\frac{\partial\gamma_{xz}}{\partial y} + \frac{\partial\gamma_{xy}}{\partial z} + \frac{\partial\gamma_{yz}}{\partial x}\right) \\ \frac{2\,\partial^2\varepsilon_z}{\partial x\partial y} &= \frac{\partial}{\partial z}\left(-\frac{\partial\gamma_{xy}}{\partial z} + \frac{\partial\gamma_{yz}}{\partial x} + \frac{\partial\gamma_{xz}}{\partial y}\right) \end{aligned}\right\} \qquad \text{...(1.30)}$$

1.11 Stress-Strain Relations

For a homogeneous, isotropic and linear material the stress-strain relations may be expressed as :

$$\begin{Bmatrix} \sigma_x \\ \sigma_y \\ \sigma_z \\ \tau_{xy} \\ \tau_{yz} \\ \tau_{xz} \end{Bmatrix} = \begin{bmatrix} \lambda + 2G & \lambda & \lambda & 0 & 0 & 0 \\ & \lambda + 2G & \lambda & 0 & 0 & 0 \\ & & \lambda + 2G & 0 & 0 & 0 \\ & \text{Symmetric} & & G & 0 & 0 \\ & & & & G & 0 \\ & & & & & G \end{bmatrix} \begin{Bmatrix} \varepsilon_x \\ \varepsilon_y \\ \varepsilon_z \\ \gamma_{xy} \\ \gamma_{yz} \\ \gamma_{xz} \end{Bmatrix} \qquad \text{...(1.31)}$$

where λ is the Cauchy's constant and G is the shear modulus. If E and ν is the modulus of elasticity and Poisson's ratio respectively, then

$$G = \frac{E}{2(1+\nu)} \quad \text{...(1.32)}$$

$$\lambda = \frac{E_\nu}{(1+\nu)(1-2\nu)} \quad \text{...(1.33)}$$

The stress-strain relations can now be expressed as :

$$\left.\begin{aligned} \varepsilon_x &= \frac{1}{E}[\sigma_x - \nu(\sigma_y + \sigma_z)] \\ \varepsilon_y &= \frac{1}{E}[\sigma_y - \nu(\sigma_x + \sigma_z)] \\ \varepsilon_z &= \frac{1}{E}[\sigma_z - \nu(\sigma_x + \sigma_y)] \\ \gamma_{xy} &= \tau_{xy}/G \\ \gamma_{yz} &= \tau_{yz}/G \\ \gamma_{xz} &= \tau_{xz}/G \end{aligned}\right\} \quad \text{...(1.34)}$$

1.12 Two-Dimensional Analysis

1.12.1 Stress analysis

For two-dimensional problems the stress transformation equations from the old xy co-ordinate system to the new $x'y'$ co-ordinate system become,

$$\left.\begin{aligned} \sigma_{x'} &= \sigma_x \cos^2\theta + \sigma_y \sin^2\theta + 2\,\tau_{xy} \sin\theta\cos\theta \\ \sigma_{y'} &= \sigma_x \sin^2\theta + \sigma_y \cos^2\theta - 2\,\tau_{xy} \sin\theta\cos\theta \\ \tau_{x'y'} &= -\sigma_x \sin\theta\cos\theta + \sigma_y \sin\theta\cos\theta + \tau_{xy}(\cos^2\theta - \sin^2\theta) \end{aligned}\right\} \quad \text{...(1.35)}$$

where θ is the angle between the x' and x axes.

The principal stresses are the roots of the equation,

$$\sigma_i^2 - \sigma_i(\sigma_x + \sigma_y) - \tau_{xy}^2 + \sigma_x\,\sigma_y = 0.$$

Hence
$$\sigma_{1,2} = \left(\frac{\sigma_x + \sigma_y}{2}\right) \pm \frac{1}{2}\sqrt{(\sigma_x - \sigma_y)^2 + 4\tau_{xy}^2} \quad \text{...(1.36)}$$

and the principal directions are given by

$$\tan 2\theta_1 = \frac{2\,\tau_{xy}}{\sigma_x - \sigma_y},\ \theta_2 = 90° + \theta_1 \quad \text{...(1.37)}$$

The Mohr's circle for the two-dimensional state of stress may be drawn as shown in Fig. 1.8.

1.12.2 Strain analysis

For two-dimensional problems the strain transformation equations from xy co-ordinate system to $x'y'$ co-ordinate system become,

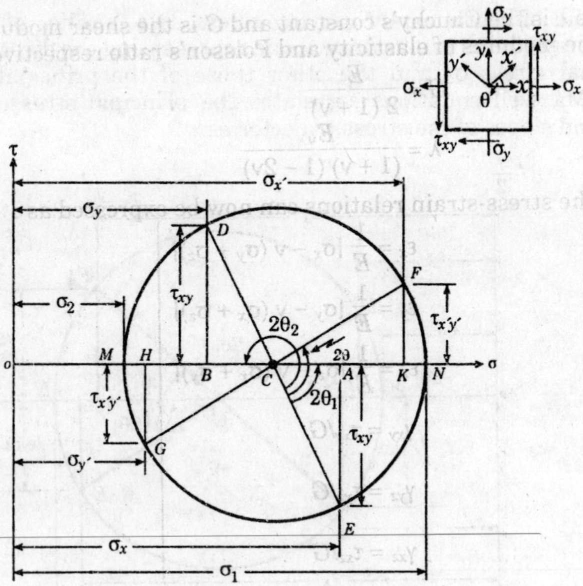

Fig. 1.8 Mohr-s circle for two-dimensional state of stress.

$$\left.\begin{aligned}\varepsilon_{x'} &= \varepsilon_x \cos^2\theta + \varepsilon_y \sin^2\theta + \gamma_{xy}\sin\theta\cos\theta \\ \varepsilon_{y'} &= \varepsilon_x \sin^2\theta + \varepsilon_y \cos^2\theta - \gamma_{xy}\sin\theta\cos\theta \\ \gamma_{x'y'} &= -\varepsilon_x\sin\theta\cos\theta + \varepsilon_y\sin\theta\cos\theta + \frac{\gamma_{xy}}{2}(\cos^2\theta - \sin^2\theta)\end{aligned}\right\} \quad ...(1.38)$$

where θ is the angle between the x and x' axes.

The principal strains are the roots of the equation,

$$\varepsilon_i^2 - \varepsilon_i(\varepsilon_x + \varepsilon_y) - \frac{\gamma_{xy}^2}{4} + \varepsilon_x\varepsilon_y = 0$$

Hence $$\varepsilon_{1,2} = \left(\frac{\varepsilon_x + \varepsilon_y}{2}\right) \pm \frac{1}{2}\sqrt{(\varepsilon_x - \varepsilon_y)^2 + \gamma_{xy}^2} \quad ...(1.39)$$

and the principal directions are given by

$$\tan 2\theta_1 = \frac{\gamma_{xy}}{\varepsilon_x - \varepsilon_y}, \quad \theta_2 = 90° + \theta_1 \quad ...(1.40)$$

The Mohr's circle for the two-dimensional state of strain may be drawn as shown in Fig. 1.9.

1.13 Lame-Maxwell Equations

A stress trajectory is a line tangent to which at every point coincides with the directions of one of the principal stresses. Since the two principal stresses at every point are mutually perpendicular, therefore, in a field of continuously varying stress, two families of orthogonal stress trajectories can be drawn, one representing the directions of the principal stress σ_1 and the other those of the principal stress σ_2. Lame-Maxwell equations correlates the principal stresses with the radii and slopes of the stress trajectories.

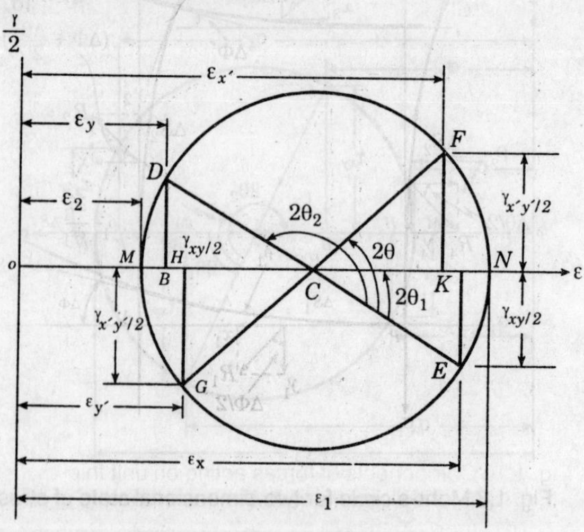

Fig. 1.9 Mohr's circle for two-dimensional state of strain.

Consider two elementary arcs of lengths Δs_1 and Δs_2 located at a point P in a two-dimensional state of stress which are bounded by stress trajectories as shown in Fig. 1.10. Let ρ_1 and ρ_2 be the radii of curvature of the stress trajectories in the directions of σ_1 and σ_2 respectively at the point P. ρ_1 and ρ_2 are taken positive if the tangents to the stress trajectories rotate counter-clockwise as S_1 and S_2 increase.

Now $$\frac{CB}{PA} = \frac{\Delta s_1'}{\Delta s_1} = \frac{(\rho_1 - \Delta s_2)\,\Delta\phi'}{\rho_1\,\Delta\phi} = 1 - \frac{\Delta s_2}{\rho_1}$$

Hence $$\Delta s_1' = \Delta s_1\left(1 - \frac{\Delta s_2}{\rho_1}\right) \qquad [\because \Delta\phi' \approx \Delta\phi]$$

Also $$\frac{AB}{PC} = \frac{\Delta s_2'}{\Delta s_2} = \frac{(\rho_2 + \Delta s_1)\,\Delta\theta'}{\rho_2\,\Delta\theta} = 1 + \frac{\Delta s_1}{\rho_2}$$

Hence $$\Delta s_2' = \Delta s_2\left(1 + \frac{\Delta s_1}{\rho_2}\right) \qquad [\because \Delta\theta' \approx \Delta\theta]$$

Components of forces on unit thickness of the elements of the stress trajectories along the x-direction are given by,

$$X_1 = \sigma_2\,\Delta s_1 \sin\frac{\Delta\phi}{2} = \sigma_2\,\Delta s_1\,\frac{\Delta\phi}{2}$$

$$= \sigma_2\,\Delta s_1\,\frac{\Delta s_1}{2\rho_1} = \sigma_2\,\frac{\Delta s_1^2}{2\rho_1}\left[\because \sin\frac{\Delta\phi}{2} \approx \frac{\Delta\phi}{2}\right]$$

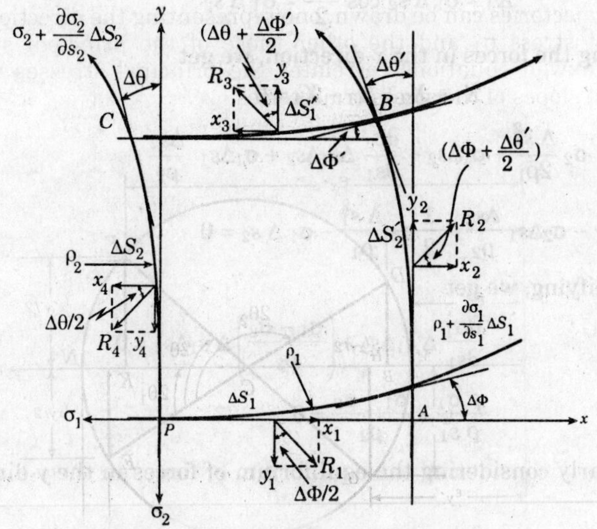

Fig. 1.10 Components of forces acting on unit thickness of the elements of stress trajectories.

$$X_2 = \left(\sigma_1 + \frac{\partial \sigma_1}{\partial s_1}\,\Delta s_1\right)\Delta s_2{}'\cos\left(\Delta\phi + \frac{\Delta\theta'}{2}\right)$$

$$= \left(\sigma_1 + \frac{\partial \sigma_1}{\partial s_1}\,\Delta s_1\right)\Delta s_2\left(1 + \frac{\Delta s_1}{\rho_2}\right)$$

$$\left[\because\ \cos\left(\Delta\phi + \frac{\Delta\theta'}{2}\right) \approx 1\right]$$

$$= \left(\sigma_1 + \frac{\partial \sigma_1}{\partial s_1}\,\Delta s_1\right)\Delta s_2 + \left(\sigma_1 + \frac{\partial \sigma_1}{\partial s_1}\,\Delta s_1\right)\Delta s_2\,\frac{\Delta s_1}{\rho_2}$$

$$= \sigma_1\,\Delta s_2 + \frac{\partial \sigma_1}{\partial s_1}\,\Delta s_1\,\Delta s_2 + \sigma_1\,\Delta s_2\,\frac{\Delta s_1}{\rho_2}$$

(Neglecting terms containing $\Delta s_1^2 \,.\, \Delta s_2$)

$$X_3 = \left(\sigma_2 + \frac{\partial \sigma_2}{\partial s_2}\,\Delta s_2\right)\Delta s_{1'}\sin\left(\Delta\theta + \frac{\Delta\phi'}{2}\right)$$

$$= \left(\sigma_2 + \frac{\partial \sigma_2}{\partial s_2}\,\Delta s_2\right)\Delta s_1\left(1 - \frac{\Delta s_2}{\rho_1}\right)\left(\Delta\theta + \frac{\Delta\phi}{2}\right)$$

$$= \left(\sigma_2 + \frac{\partial \sigma_2}{\partial s_2}\,\Delta s_2\right)\Delta s_1\left(1 - \frac{\Delta s_2}{\rho_1}\right)\left(\frac{\Delta s_2}{\rho_2} + \frac{\Delta s_1}{2\,\rho_1}\right)$$

$$= \sigma_2\,\Delta s_1\,\frac{\Delta s_2}{\rho_2} + \frac{1}{2}\,\sigma_2\,\frac{\Delta s_1^2}{\rho_1}$$

(Neglecting small quantities)

$$X_4 = \sigma_1 \Delta s_2 \cos \frac{\Delta \theta}{2} = \sigma_1 \Delta s_2$$

Adding the forces in the x-direction, we get

$$X_1 + X_2 - X_3 - X_4 = 0$$

or
$$\sigma_2 \frac{\Delta s_1^2}{2\rho_1} + \sigma_1 \Delta s_2 + \frac{\partial \sigma_1}{\partial s_1} \Delta s_1 \Delta s_2 + \sigma_1 \Delta s_1 \frac{\Delta s_2}{\rho_2}$$

$$- \sigma_2 \Delta s_1 \frac{\Delta s_2}{\rho_2} - \frac{1}{2} \sigma_2 \frac{\Delta s_1^2}{\rho_1} - \sigma_1 \Delta s_2 = 0$$

Simplifying, we get

$$\frac{\partial \sigma_1}{\partial s_1} \Delta s_1 \Delta s_2 + \left(\frac{\sigma_1 - \sigma_2}{\rho_2} \right) \Delta s_1 \Delta s_2 = 0$$

or
$$\frac{\rho \sigma_1}{\rho s_1} + \frac{\sigma_1 - \sigma_2}{\rho_2} = 0$$

Similarly considering the equilibrium of forces in the y-direction, we get

$$\frac{\partial \sigma_2}{\partial s_2} + \frac{\sigma_1 - \sigma_2}{\rho_1} = 0$$

Hence, the Lame-Maxwell equations become,

$$\left.\begin{aligned} \frac{\rho \sigma_1}{\rho s_1} + \frac{\sigma_1 - \sigma_2}{\rho_2} = 0 \\ \frac{\partial \sigma_2}{\partial s_2} + \frac{\sigma_1 - \sigma_2}{\rho_1} = 0 \end{aligned}\right\} \qquad \text{...(1.41)}$$

Integrating Eqs. (1.41), we get

$$\left.\begin{aligned} (\sigma_1)_i = (\sigma_1)_0 - \int_0^i \left(\frac{\sigma_1 - \sigma_2}{\rho_2} \right) ds_1 \\ (\sigma_2)_i = (\sigma_2)_0 - \int_0^i \left(\frac{\sigma_1 - \sigma_2}{\rho_1} \right) ds_2 \end{aligned}\right\} \qquad \text{...(1.42)}$$

where 0 and i denotes initial and any point on the stress trajectory respectively.

1.14 Equations of Equilibrium in Terms of Principal Stresses

Now
$$\left.\begin{aligned} \sigma_x = \frac{1}{2} [(\sigma_1 + \sigma_2) + (\sigma_1 - \sigma_2) \cos 2\theta] \\ \sigma_y = \frac{1}{2} [(\sigma_1 + \sigma_2) - (\sigma_1 - \sigma_2) \cos 2\theta] \\ \tau_{xy} = \frac{1}{2} (\sigma_1 - \sigma_2) \sin 2\theta \end{aligned}\right] \qquad \text{...(1.43)}$$

where θ is the angle between the x-axis and the direction σ_1.

Substituting these values in the equilibrium Eq. (1.16) in two-dimensions when $\sigma_z = \tau_{yz} = \tau_{xz} = 0$ and the body forces are zero, we obtain

$$\frac{\partial}{\partial x}(\sigma_1+\sigma_2)+\frac{\partial}{\partial x}(\sigma_1-\sigma_2)\cos 2\theta-2(\sigma_1-\sigma_2)\sin 2\theta\frac{\partial\theta}{\partial x}$$
$$+\frac{\partial}{\partial y}(\sigma_1-\sigma_2)\sin 2\theta+2(\sigma_1-\sigma_2)\cos 2\theta\frac{\partial\theta}{\partial y}=0 \quad ...(1.44a)$$

$$\frac{\partial(\sigma_1+\sigma_2)}{\partial y}-\frac{\partial(\sigma_1-\sigma_2)}{\partial y}\cos 2\theta+2(\sigma_1-\sigma_2)\sin 2\theta\frac{\partial\theta}{\partial y}$$
$$+\frac{\partial(\sigma_1-\sigma_2)}{\partial x}\sin 2\theta+2(\sigma_1-\sigma_2)\cos 2\theta\frac{\partial\theta}{\partial x}=0 \quad ...(1.44b)$$

These are the equations of equilibrium for the two mutually perpendicular directions inclined at an angle θ to the principal stresses.

1.15 Equations of Equilibrium Along Lines of Maximum Shear Stress

A line of maximum shear stress is a line which is tangential at every point to one of the two directions in which the shear stress is a maximum. Since the maximum shear stress at any point acts at 45° to the directions of the principal stresses, the lines of maximum shear stress form two orthogonal families which are 45° to the stress trajectories as shown in Fig. 1.11.

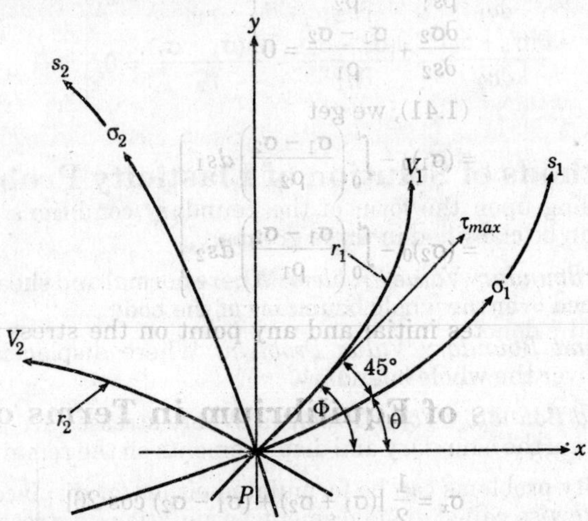

Fig. 1.11 Lines of maximum shear stress and stress trajectories.

Let ν_1 and ν_2 represent the directions of maximum shear stress and S_1 and S_2 the stress trajectories corresponding to σ_1 and σ_2 respectively.

Let σ_1 make an angle θ with the x-axis at the point P, ϕ be the angle between ν_1 and x-axis. We have

$$\theta = \phi - 45°$$

Hence $\dfrac{\partial \theta}{\partial x} = \dfrac{\partial \phi}{\partial x}, \dfrac{\partial \theta}{\partial y} = \dfrac{\partial \phi}{\partial y}$

and
$$\cos 2\theta = \cos (2\phi - 90°) = \sin 2\phi$$
$$\sin 2\theta = \sin (2\phi - 90°) = -\cos 2\phi$$

If the x-axis is taken along the v_1 direction,

then
$$\phi = 0$$
and
$$\cos 2\theta = \sin 2\phi = 0$$
$$\sin 2\theta = -\cos 2\phi = -1$$

Substituting these values in Eqs. (1.44), we get

$$\frac{\partial (\sigma_1 + \sigma_2)}{\partial v_1} + 2 (\sigma_1 - \sigma_2) \frac{\partial \phi}{\partial v_1} - \frac{\partial (\sigma_1 - \sigma_2)}{\partial v_2} = 0$$

$$\frac{\partial (\sigma_1 + \sigma_2)}{\partial v_2} - 2 (\sigma_1 - \sigma_2) \frac{\partial \phi}{\partial v_2} - \frac{\partial (\sigma_1 - \sigma_2)}{\partial v_1} = 0$$

Since $\dfrac{\partial \phi}{\partial v_1} = \dfrac{1}{r_1}$

and $\dfrac{\partial \phi}{\partial v_2} = \dfrac{1}{r_2}$, hence, we get

$$\left.\begin{aligned} \frac{\partial(\sigma_1 + \sigma_2)}{\partial v_1} - \frac{\partial(\sigma_1 - \sigma_2)}{\partial v_2} + \frac{2 (\sigma_1 - \sigma_2)}{r_1} = 0 \\ \frac{\partial(\sigma_1 + \sigma_2)}{\partial v_2} - \frac{\partial(\sigma_1 - \sigma_2)}{\partial v_1} - \frac{2 (\sigma_1 - \sigma_2)}{r_2} = 0 \end{aligned}\right] \quad ...(1.45)$$

1.16 Methods of Solution of Elasticity Problems

Depending upon the form of the boundary conditions, elasticity problems can be classified in three groups.

1. *First Boundary Value Problem.* Where normal and shear stresses are prescribed over the whole boundary of the body.

2. *Second Boundary Value Problem.* Where displacements are prescribed over the whole boundary.

3. *Mixed Boundary Value Problem.* Where stresses are prescribed on some part of the boundary and displacements on the remaining part.

Elasticity problems can be formulated either for displacements or stresses, likewise called, displacement formulation or stress formulation respectively. However, these direct methods of solving elasticity problems are too complicated to yield practical results.

In order to simplify the solution methods, inverse and semi-inverse methods are resorted to. In the inverse methods, a judicious guess of the solution is made and is checked against the basic equations and boundary conditions. If all conditions are satisfied the solution is the correct one ; otherwise, corrections are made and a revised solution is checked in the same manner.

In the semi-inverse method, some of the unknowns are guessed and a simplified group of equations is solved for the remaining unknowns. These educated guesses are based on experience, intution, solutions of similar problems or experiments.

The solutions of the elasticity problems may be obtained by using stress functions, complex potentials, Fourier transform method, conformal transformation method, Cauchy integral method, Real potential method and numerical methods, etc.

1.17 Plane Stress

If the stress components σ_z, τ_{xz} and τ_{yz} are a zero, then the state of stress is called plane stress with respect to the *xoy* plane. Thus for the plane stress case,

$$\sigma_x, \sigma_y, \tau_{xy} = f(x, y) \qquad ...(1.46)$$

and the governing equations of elasticity become,

(*i*) Equilibrium equations

$$\left.\begin{aligned}\frac{\partial \sigma_x}{\partial x} + \frac{\partial \tau_{xy}}{\partial y} + B_x = 0\\ \frac{\partial \tau_{xy}}{\partial x} + \frac{\partial \sigma_y}{\partial y} + B_y = 0\end{aligned}\right] \qquad ...(1.47)$$

(*ii*) Strain-displacement relations

$$\left.\begin{aligned}\varepsilon_x = \frac{\partial u_x}{\partial x}, \quad \varepsilon_y = \frac{\partial u_y}{\partial y}, \quad \varepsilon_z = \frac{\partial u_z}{\partial z},\\ \gamma_{xy} = \frac{\partial u_x}{\partial y} + \frac{\partial u_y}{\partial x}\end{aligned}\right] \qquad ...(1.48)$$

(*iii*) Stress-strain relations

$$\left.\begin{aligned}\varepsilon_x &= \frac{1}{E}[\sigma_x - \nu\sigma_y]\\ \varepsilon_y &= \frac{1}{E}[\sigma_y - \nu\sigma_x]\\ \varepsilon_z &= -\frac{\nu}{E}[\sigma_x + \sigma_y]\\ \gamma_{xy} &= \tau_{xy}/G\end{aligned}\right\} \qquad ...(1.49)$$

(*iv*) Strain-compatibility equation

$$\frac{\partial^2 \gamma_{xy}}{\partial x \partial y} = \frac{\partial^2 \varepsilon_x}{\partial y^2} + \frac{\partial^2 \varepsilon_y}{\partial x^2} \qquad ...(1.50)$$

(*v*) Equilibrium equations in terms of displacements.

Substituting Eqs. (1.48) and (1.49) in Eq. (1.47), we get

$$\left.\begin{aligned}\nabla^2 u_x + \left(\frac{1}{1-2\nu}\right)\frac{\partial}{\partial x}\left(\frac{\partial u_x}{\partial x} + \frac{\partial u_y}{\partial y}\right) + \frac{B_x}{G} = 0\\ \nabla^2 u_y + \left(\frac{1}{1-2\nu}\right)\frac{\partial}{\partial y}\left(\frac{\partial u_x}{\partial x} + \frac{\partial u_y}{\partial y}\right) + \frac{B_y}{G} = 0\end{aligned}\right\} \qquad ...(1.51)$$

where $$\nabla^2 = \frac{\partial^2}{\partial x^2} + \frac{\partial^2}{\partial y}.$$

(*vi*) Stress-compatibility equation

Substituting Eqs. (1.49) in (1.50), we get

$$2\,(\sigma_x + \sigma_y) = -(1 + \nu)\left(\frac{\partial B_x}{\partial x} + \frac{\partial B_y}{\partial y}\right) \quad ...(1.52)$$

(*vii*) Boundary conditions

$$\left.\begin{aligned} T_x &= \sigma_x a_{nx} + \tau_{xy}\, a_{ny} \\ T_y &= \tau_{xy} a_{nx} + \sigma_y a_{ny} \end{aligned}\right\} \quad ...(1.53)$$

1.18 Plane Strain

When the length of the member in the z-direction is either very large so that no displacement is possible or the displacements along the z-axis are otherwise prevented so that $\varepsilon_z = \gamma_{yz} = \gamma_{xz} = 0$, then the state of strain is said to be plane strain with respect to the *xoy* plane. In this case

$$\varepsilon_x,\ \varepsilon_y,\ \gamma_{xy} = f(x, y) \quad ...(1.54)$$

and the governing equations become,

(*i*) Equilibrium equations

$$\left.\begin{aligned} &\frac{\partial \sigma_x}{\partial x} + \frac{\partial \tau_{xy}}{\partial y} + B_x = 0 \\ &\frac{\partial \tau_{xy}}{\partial x} + \frac{\partial \sigma_y}{\partial y} + B_y = 0 \\ &\frac{\partial \sigma_z}{\partial z} + B_z = 0 \end{aligned}\right\} \quad ...(1.55)$$

(*ii*) Strain displacement relations

$$\left.\begin{aligned} &\varepsilon_x = \frac{\partial u_x}{\partial x},\ \varepsilon_y = \frac{\partial u_y}{\partial y},\ \gamma_{xy} = \frac{\partial u_x}{\partial y} + \frac{\partial u_y}{\partial x} \\ &\varepsilon_z = \gamma_{yz} = \gamma_{xz} = 0 \end{aligned}\right\} \quad ...(1.56)$$

(*iii*) Stress-strain relations

Now $$\varepsilon_z = \frac{1}{E}\,[\sigma_z - \nu\,(\sigma_x + \sigma_y)] = 0$$

or $$\sigma_z = \nu\,(\sigma_x + \sigma_y).$$

Hence
$$\left.\begin{aligned} \varepsilon_x &= \left(\frac{1+\nu}{E}\right)[\sigma_x - \nu\,(\sigma_x + \sigma_y)] \\ \varepsilon_y &= \left(\frac{1+\nu}{E}\right)[\sigma_y - \nu\,(\sigma_x + \sigma_y)] \\ \gamma_{xy} &= \tau_{xy}/G \end{aligned}\right\} \quad ...(1.57)$$

(*iv*) Strain compatibility equation

$$\frac{\partial^2 \gamma_{xy}}{\partial x \partial y} = \frac{\partial^2 \varepsilon_x}{\partial y^2} + \frac{\partial^2 \varepsilon_y}{\partial x^2} \quad ...(1.58)$$

(*v*) Equilibrium equations in terms of displacements

$$\left.\begin{aligned}\nabla^2 u_x + \left(\frac{1}{1-2\nu}\right)\frac{\partial}{\partial x}\left(\frac{\partial u_x}{\partial x} + \frac{\partial u_y}{\partial y}\right) + \frac{B_x}{G} = 0 \\ \nabla^2 u_y + \left(\frac{1}{1-2\nu}\right)\frac{\partial}{\partial y}\left(\frac{\partial u_x}{\partial x} + \frac{\partial u_y}{\partial y}\right) + \frac{B_y}{G} = 0\end{aligned}\right\} \quad ...(1.59)$$

(*vi*) Stress-compatibility equation

$$\nabla^2 (\sigma_x + \sigma_y) = -\left(\frac{1}{1-\nu}\right)\left(\frac{\partial B_x}{\partial x} + \frac{\partial B_y}{\partial y}\right) \quad ...(1.60)$$

(*vii*) Boundary conditions

$$\left.\begin{aligned}T_x = \sigma_x a_{nx} + \tau_{xy}\, a_{ny} \\ T_y = \tau_{xy}\, a_{nx} + \sigma_y\, a_{ny}\end{aligned}\right\} \quad ...(1.61)$$

1.19 Airy's Stress Functions and Biharmonic Equation

1.19.1 Cartesian Co-ordinates

Suppose that there exists a body force potential V such that

$$B_x = \frac{\partial V}{\partial x}, \qquad B_y = \frac{\partial V}{\partial y}$$

Define
$$\left.\begin{aligned}\sigma_x = \frac{\partial^2 \phi}{\partial x^2} - V \\ \sigma_x = \frac{\partial^2 \phi}{\partial y^2} - V \\ \tau_{xy} = -\frac{\partial^2 \phi}{\partial x \partial y}\end{aligned}\right\} \quad ...(1.62)$$

where ϕ is the Airy's stress function, then the stress components given by Eqs. (1.62) satisfy the equilibrium equations in two dimensions, and on substitution into the stress compatibility Eqs. (1.52 and 1.60), yield the Biharmonic equation,

$$\nabla^4 \phi = (1-\nu)\, \nabla^2 V \quad ...(1.63)$$

for the plane stress case, and

$$\nabla^4 \phi = \left(\frac{1-2\nu}{1-\nu}\right) \nabla^2 V \quad ...(1.64)$$

for the plane strain case respectively,

where
$$\nabla^4 = \nabla^2 \,.\, \nabla^2 = \frac{\partial^4}{\partial x^4} + \frac{2\partial^4}{\partial x^2 \partial y^2} + \frac{\partial^4}{\partial y^4}$$

If the body force potential V is zero, then the Eqs. (1.63) and (1.64) reduce to

$$\nabla^4 \phi = 0 \quad ...(1.65)$$

1.19.2. Polar Co-ordinates

In Polar co-ordinates (r, θ), we define

$$\left.\begin{aligned}\sigma_r &= \frac{1}{r^2}\frac{\partial^2\phi}{\partial\theta^2}+\frac{1}{r}\frac{\partial\phi}{\partial r}\\ \sigma_\theta &= \frac{\partial^2\phi}{\partial r^2}\\ \tau_{r\theta} &= -\frac{\partial}{\partial r}\left(\frac{1}{r}\frac{\partial\phi}{\partial\theta}\right)\end{aligned}\right\} \qquad ...(1.66)$$

The biharmonic equation in the absence of body forces become,

$$\nabla^4\phi = \nabla^2 . \nabla^2\phi = \left(\frac{\partial^2}{\partial r^2}+\frac{1}{r}\frac{\partial}{\partial r}+\frac{1}{r^2}\frac{\partial^2}{\partial\theta^2}\right)$$
$$\times\left(\frac{\partial^2\phi}{\partial r^2}+\frac{1}{r}\frac{\partial\phi}{\partial r}+\frac{1}{r^2}\frac{\partial^2\phi}{\partial\theta^2}\right)=0 \qquad ...(1.67)$$

1.20 Some Useful Results

Now we present some of the useful results which would be helpful in understanding the concepts of experimental stress analysis.

1.20.1 Circular Disc Under Diametral Compression

The stresses in a circular disc of diameter D and loaded in diametral compression by a force P as shown in Fig. 1.12 are given by,

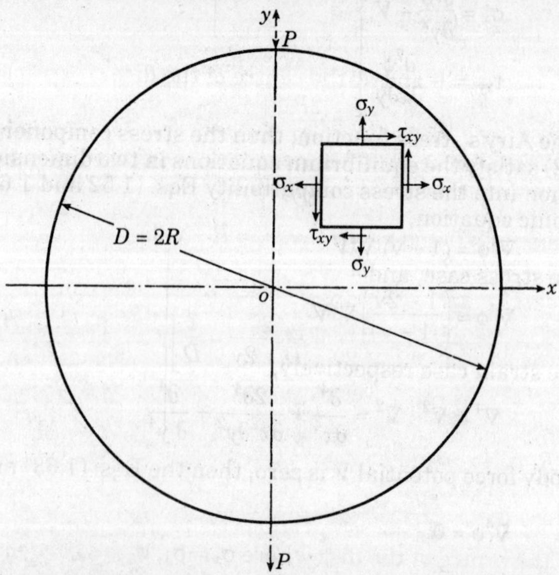

Fig. 1.12 Circular disc under diametral compression.

$$\left.\begin{aligned}
\sigma_x &= \frac{-2P}{\pi}\left[\frac{(R-y)\,x^2}{r_1^4}+\frac{(R+y)\,x^2}{r_2^4}-\frac{1}{D}\right]\\
\sigma_y &= \frac{-2P}{\pi}\left[\frac{(R-y)^3}{r_1^4}+\frac{(R+y)^3}{r_2^4}-\frac{1}{D}\right]\\
\tau_{xy} &= \frac{-2P}{\pi}\left[\frac{(R-y)^2\,x}{r_1^4}-\frac{(R+y)^2\,x}{r_2^4}\right]
\end{aligned}\right\} \quad \text{...(1.68)}$$

where

$$r_1^2 = x^2 + (R-y)^2$$

$$r_2^2 = x^2 + (R+y)^2$$

$$2R = D$$

On the x-axis, $y = 0$ and

$$r_1 = r_2 = \sqrt{x^2 + R^2}$$

Hence

$$\left.\begin{aligned}
\sigma_x &= \frac{2P}{\pi D}\left[\frac{D^2-4x^2}{D^2+4x^2}\right]^2\\
\sigma_y &= \frac{-2P}{\pi D}\left[\frac{4D^2}{(D^2+4x^2)^2}-1\right]\\
\tau_{xy} &= 0
\end{aligned}\right\} \quad \text{...(1.69)}$$

At $x = \pm R$, $\sigma_x = \sigma_y = 0$ and at the centre of the disc

$$\left.\begin{aligned}
(\sigma_x)_{x=y=0} &= \frac{2P}{\pi D}\\
(\sigma_y)_{x=y=0} &= \frac{-6P}{\pi D}
\end{aligned}\right\} \quad \text{...(1.70)}$$

On the y-axis, $x = 0$ and $r_1 = R - y$, $r_2 = R + y$. Hence

$$\left.\begin{aligned}
\sigma_x &= \frac{2P}{\pi D}\\
\sigma_y &= \frac{-2P}{\pi}\left[\frac{2}{D-2y}+\frac{2}{D+2y}-\frac{1}{D}\right]\\
\tau_{xy} &= 0
\end{aligned}\right\} \quad \text{...(1.71)}$$

For $y = \pm R$, $\sigma_y \to \infty$ and at $x = y = 0$

$$\sigma_y = \frac{-6P}{\pi D}$$

Hence at the centre of the disc where $\sigma_x = \sigma_1$, $\sigma_y = \sigma_2$, we obtain

$$\sigma_1 - \sigma_2 = \frac{8P}{\pi D} \quad \text{...(1.72)}$$

This result will be useful while calibrating photoelastic models by using a circular disc under diametral compression.

1.20.2 Stress in a thin plate with a circular hole under uniaxial tension

For a thin plate of infinite dimensions containing a circular hole of radius a and subjected to uniaxial tension σ_0, the stresses at a point P as shown in Fig. 1.13 are given by

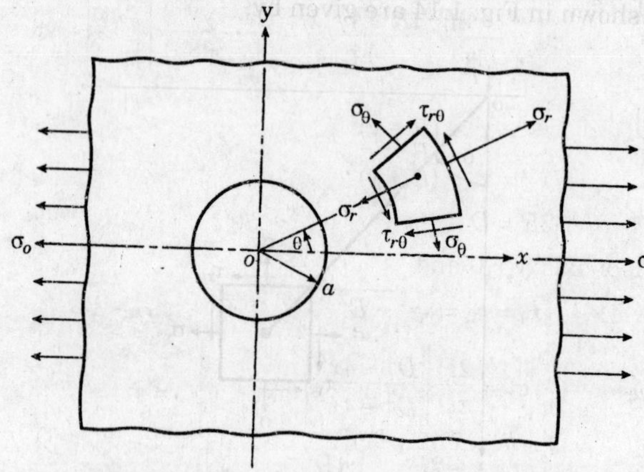

Fig. 1.13 Infinite plate with a circular hole subjected to uniaxial tension.

$$\left.\begin{aligned}\sigma_r &= \frac{\sigma_0}{2}\left(1-\frac{a^2}{r^2}\right)+\frac{\sigma_0}{2}\left(1+\frac{3a^4}{r^4}-\frac{4a^2}{r^2}\right)\cos 2\theta \\ \sigma_\theta &= \frac{\sigma_0}{2}\left(1-\frac{a^2}{r^2}\right)-\frac{\sigma_0}{2}\left(1+\frac{3a^4}{r^4}\right)\cos 2\theta \\ \tau_{r\theta} &= -\frac{\sigma_0}{2}\left(1-\frac{3a^4}{r^4}+\frac{2a^2}{r^2}\right)\sin 2\theta\end{aligned}\right\} \quad \text{...(1.73)}$$

For $\theta = \frac{\pi}{2}, \frac{3\pi}{2}$ we get

$$\sigma_\theta = \frac{\sigma_0}{2}\left(2+\frac{a^2}{r^2}+\frac{3a^4}{r^4}\right) \quad \text{...(1.74}a\text{)}$$

and for $r = a$ leads to,

$$(\sigma_\theta)_{\max} = 3\,\sigma_0$$

For $\theta = 0, \pi$, we get

$$\sigma_\theta = \frac{\sigma_0}{2}\left[\frac{a^2}{r^2}-\frac{3a^4}{r^4}\right] \quad \text{...(1.74}b\text{)}$$

and for $r = a$ leads to,

$$(\sigma_\theta)_{\min} = -\sigma_0$$

For $\frac{r}{a} = 10$, the difference between σ_θ and σ_0 is 0.515 per cent, which is negligible for all practical purposes.

1.20.3 Concentrated load acting on the free surface of a semi-infinite plate

The stresses in a semi-infinite plate subjected to a concentrated load P as shown in Fig. 1.14 are given by,

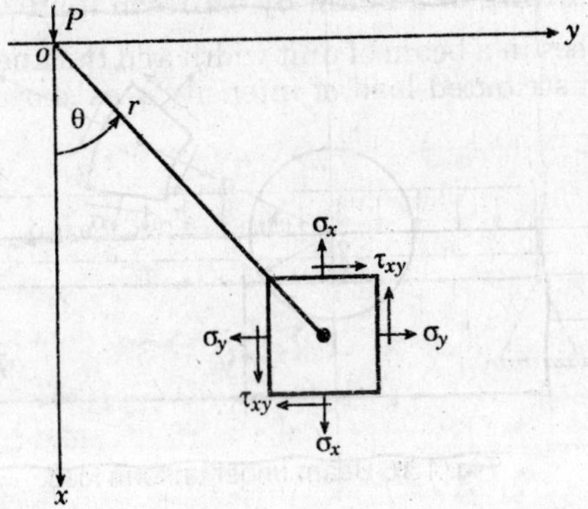

Fig. 1.14 Concentrated load on a semi-infinite plate.

$$\left.\begin{aligned} \sigma_x &= \frac{-2P}{\pi r}\cos^3\theta = \frac{-2Px^3}{\pi (x^2+y^2)^2} \\ \sigma_y &= \frac{-2P}{\pi r}\sin^2\theta\cos\theta = \frac{-2Pxy^2}{\pi (x^2+y^2)^2} \\ \tau_{xy} &= \frac{-2P}{\pi r}\sin\theta\cos^2\theta = \frac{-2Px^2y}{\pi (x^2+y^2)^2} \end{aligned}\right\} \quad \text{...(1.75)}$$

Under the load, $y = 0$ and

$$\sigma_x = \frac{-2P}{\pi x}, \; \sigma_y = \tau_{xy} = 0 \quad \text{...(1.76)}$$

Eq. (1.76) can also be used for calibrating a photoelastic model.

1.20.4 Bending of a cantilever loaded at the end

The stresses in a cantilever of depth $2c$ and unit width, carrying an end load P shown in Fig. 1.15 are given by,

$$\left.\begin{aligned} \sigma_x &= -\frac{P_{xy}}{I}, \; \sigma_y = 0 \\ \tau_{xy} &= -\frac{P}{2I}(c^2 - y^2) \end{aligned}\right\} \quad \text{...(1.77)}$$

where $I = \frac{2}{3}c^3$ is the moment of inertia for the cantilever.

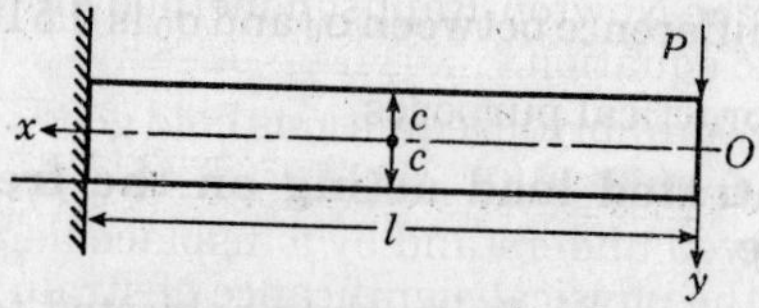

Fig. 1.15 Cantilever loaded at the end.

1.20.5 Bending of a beam by uniform load

The stresses in a beam of unit width and thickness $2c$, subjected to a uniformly distributed load of intensity q as shown in Fig. 1.16 are given by,

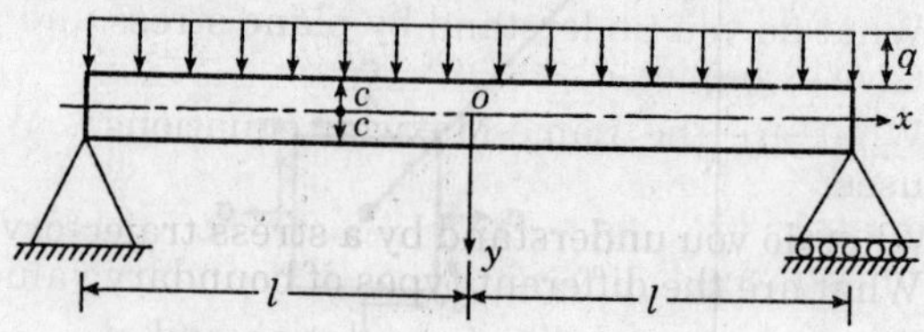

Fig. 1.16 Beam under uniform load.

$$\left.\begin{aligned}\sigma_x &= \frac{q}{2I}(l^2 - x^2)\,y + \frac{q}{I}\left(\frac{y^3}{3} - \frac{c^2 y}{5}\right)\\ \sigma_y &= \frac{-q}{2I}\left(\frac{y^3}{3} - c^2 y + \frac{2}{3}c^3\right)\\ \tau_{xy} &= \frac{-q}{2I}\,x\,(c^2 - y^2)\end{aligned}\right\} \qquad ...(1.78)$$

where $I = \frac{2}{3}c^3$.

The corresponding results from strength of materials are,

$$\left.\begin{aligned}\sigma_x &= \frac{q}{2I}(l^2 - x^2)y, \quad \sigma_y = 0\\ \tau_{xy} &= \frac{-q}{2I}\,x\,(c^2 - y^2)\end{aligned}\right\} \qquad ...(1.79)$$

1.21 Quiz Questions

1. Differentiate between internal and external forces.
2. Differentiate between (*i*) stress and pressure (*ii*) surface and body forces.
3. Explain how stress is a tensor quantity ?
4. How many independent stress components are there at a point in a body subjected to generalised state of stress ?
5. Write the law of transformation for stress components.
6. What do you understand by principal stresses and principal planes ?

7. Explain the Newton-Raphson method for obtaining the roots of a cubic equation.
8. Does the equilibrium equations hold good in the plastic range also ? Comment.
9. What do you understand by a displacement field ?
10. What is the physical significance of strain components ?
11. Explain the meaning of small deformation and affine deformation.
12. What do you understand by stress and strain invariants ?
13. Explain the necessity of compatibility equations.
14. What is the generalised Hooke's law ?
15. How many independent elastic constants are there for an isotropic, linear and homogeneous material ?
16. What do you understand by plane stress and plane strain ? Give examples.
17. What are the Lame-Maxwell equations ? What are their uses?
18. What do you understand by a stress trajectory ?
19. What are the different types of boundary value problems ?
20. What are the various formulation and solution methods for elasticity problems ?
21. How would you obtain stresses from Airy's stress function ?
22. What do you mean by the Biharmonic equation ?
23. Write the Biharmonic equation for the plane stress and plane strain cases in the presence of body force potential.
24. How much is the maximum shear stress at the centre of a circular disc loaded in diametral compression ?
25. What is the value of the maximum stress-concentration factor in an infinite plate with a circular hole under uniaxial tension ?

EXERCISES

1.1 The state of stress at a point of interest in a solid body is defined by :

$$[\tau_{ij}] = \begin{bmatrix} 30 & 50 & 60 \\ 50 & 20 & 0 \\ 60 & 0 & 10 \end{bmatrix} \text{N/mm}^2$$

Determine the principal stresses and their directions.

1.2 The state of stress at a point is given by :

$$[\tau_{ij}] = \begin{bmatrix} 10 & -60 & -40 \\ -60 & 20 & -20 \\ -40 & -20 & 30 \end{bmatrix} \text{N/mm}^2$$

Determine (*a*) the principal stresses (*b*) the Octahedral stress components and (*c*) the spherical and deviator stress tensors.

1.3 The state of stress at a point is given by

$$[\tau_{ij}] = A\begin{bmatrix} \frac{3}{2}x^2y^2 & -xy^3 & 0 \\ -xy^3 & \frac{1}{4}y^4 & 0 \\ 0 & 0 & 0 \end{bmatrix}$$

where A is a parameter depending on the load. Show that the equations of equilibrium are satisfied.

1.4 Prove the following relationships :

(a) $(\sigma_n)_{oct} = \frac{1}{3}(\sigma_1 + \sigma_2 + \sigma_3)$

(b) $9\,\tau_{oct}^2 = (\sigma_1 - \sigma_2)^2 + (\sigma_2 - \sigma_3)^2 + (\sigma_3 - \sigma_1)^2$

(c) $9\,\tau_{oct}^2 = 2I_1^2 - 6I_2$

(d) $\tau_{oct}^2 = \frac{2}{3}I'_2$.

where I_1 and I_2 are the first and second stress invariants and I_2' is the second deviator stress invariant.

1.5 The stress tensor at a point with respect to xyz co-ordinate system is given by :

$$[\tau_{ij}] = \begin{bmatrix} 150 & 80 & 60 \\ 80 & 200 & 40 \\ 60 & 40 & 100 \end{bmatrix} \text{N/mm}^2$$

If the co-ordinate axes are rotated about the z-axis by 30° in the anti-clockwise direction, determine the new stress tensor.

1.6 The state of stress at a point is given by,

$\sigma_x = 20$, $\sigma_y = 10$, $\sigma_z = -15$, $\tau_{xy} = 30$, $\tau_{yz} = 10$, $\tau_{xz} = -20$ N/mm^2

Determine the normal and shearing stresses on a plane and the direction of shear stress, if the normal to the plane is given by

$$2x - y + 3z = 9$$

1.7 The state of strain at a point of interest in a solid is defined by the following matrix. Determine the principal strains and principal directions.

$$[\varepsilon_{ij}] = \begin{bmatrix} 2.74 & -2.12 & 4.07 \\ -2.12 & -3.69 & -3.02 \\ 4.07 & -3.02 & 5.05 \end{bmatrix} \times 10^{-4}$$

1.8 The components of a strain tensor at a point are :

$$[\varepsilon_{ij}] = \begin{bmatrix} 3 & 5 & 8 \\ 5 & 1 & 0 \\ 8 & 0 & 2 \end{bmatrix} \times 10^{-3}$$

Determine the new strain tensor obtained by rotation of the axes about the z-axis by 45° in the anti-clockwise direction.

1.9 If a state of plane strain exists in the neighbourhood of a point of interest in a solid and that

$$\varepsilon_x = 2 + C_1(x^2 + y^2) + (x^4 + y^4)$$

$$\varepsilon_y = 3 + (x^2 + y^2) + (x^4 + y^4)$$

$$\gamma_{xy} = 4 + C_2\, xy\, (x^2 + y^2 + 6)$$

Determine the values of constants C_1 and C_2 in order that these equations should represent a compatible state of strain.

1.10 Show that the elastic constants are related as follows :

$$\lambda = K - \frac{2}{3}G = \frac{2\,G\nu}{1-2\nu}\quad G = \frac{3\,KE}{9K-E} = \frac{\lambda\,(1-2\nu)}{2\nu}$$

1.11 The state of stress at a point is defined by,

$$[\tau_{ij}] = C\begin{bmatrix} y^2 + \nu\,(x^2 - y^2) & -2\nu\,xy & 0 \\ -2\,\nu\,xy & x^2 + \nu\,(y^2 - x^2) & 0 \\ 0 & 0 & \nu\,(x^2 + y^2) \end{bmatrix}$$

where C is a constant and the body force is negligible. Does this represent a true state of stress ?

1.12 If $\phi = \frac{p}{8c^3}\,[x\,(y^3 - 3c^2y - 2c^3) - \frac{1}{5}y^3\,(y^2 - 2c^2)]$ is appropriate as a stress function, determine the stress field it generates. If this is to represent the stress distribution in a cantilever of unit thickness occupying $x > 0$, $-c \geq y \geq c$ and supporting a uniform pressure at its top edge $y = c$, determine the stress components.

1.13 Determine the constants A, B, C, D and E in

$$\phi = x^2\,(Ay^3 + By + C) + Dy^3 + Ey^5$$

in order that it shall represent the stress distribution in the beam shown in Fig. 1.16.

1.14 If $\phi = \left(Ar^3 + \frac{B}{r} + Cr + Dr\ln r\right)\sin\theta$ is suitable as an Airy stress function for the bending of a curved bar by a force at the end, determine the values of A, B, C and D.

1.15 Given that $\phi = r\theta\,(A\sin\theta + B\cos\theta)$ is suitable as a stress function, determine the nature of the stress field it generates, A and B are constants.

1.16 A circular disc of 10 cm diameter is loaded in diametral compression by a load of 1.5 kg. Plot the variation of stresses along the diameter perpendicular to the line of action of the load.

1.17 A thin plate of infinite dimensions contains a circular hole of 2 cm radius and is pulled in uniaxial tension so that the uniform stress in the plate is 20 N/mm^2. Plot the variation of hoop stress σ_0 on the hole boundary and at $\theta = 90°$.

1.18 A concentrated load of 1 kN is applied at a point on the free surface of a semi-infinite plate. Determine the stresses at a point (3, 2).

1.19 Derive equilibrium equations in Cartesian co-ordinates.

1.20 Derive Lame-Maxwell equations. What are the uses of these equations ?

2

Strain Gauges

2.1 Introduction

A strain gauge may be defined as any instrument or device that is employed to measure the linear deformation over a given gauge length, occurring in the material of a structure during the loading of the structure. This definition is quite broad, in fact it covers the range of instruments included between the linear scale and the precise optical and electrical gauges now available. The many types of strain gauges available are quite varied, both in application and in the principles involved in their magnification systems. Depending upon the magnification system, the strain gauges may be classified as follows :

1. Mechanical.
   (*a*) Wedge and Screw
   (*b*) Lever—simple and compound
   (*c*) Rack and pinion
   (*d*) Combination of lever and rack and pinion
   (*e*) Dial indicators.
2. Optical.
3. Interferometric type.
4. Electrical.
   (*a*) Inductance
   (*b*) Capacitance
   (*c*) Resistance
   (*d*) Piezoelectric and piezoresistive.
5. Magnetic.
6. Acoustical.
7. Pneumatic.
8. Scratch type.
9. Photostress gauge.

In this chapter we shall study all these types of gauge except the electrical and magnetic gauges, which have been described in the next chapter. The photostress gauge has been discussed in the chapter on photoelastic coatings.

2.2 Characteristic of a Strain Gauge

A strain gauge has the following four basic characteristics :

1. *Gauge length.* The gauge size for a mechanical strain gauge is characterized by the distance between the two knife edges in contact with the specimen and by the width of the movable knife edge. The gauge length becomes more important when measuring non-linear strains, which should be as small as possible in that case.

2. *Sensitivity.* It is the smallest value of strain which can be read on the scale associated with the strain gauge. Sensitivity can be defined in two ways :

(*i*) Deformation sensitivity

$$= \frac{\text{Smallest reading of scale}}{\text{Multiplication factor}}$$

(*ii*) Strain sensitivity

$$= \frac{\text{Deformation sensitivity}}{\text{Base length}}$$

3. *Range.* This represents the maximum strain which can be recorded without resetting or replacing the strain gauge. The range and sensitivity are inter-related since very sensitive gauges respond to small strains with appreciable deflections and the range is usually limited to the full scale deflection of the indicator. Therefore, it becomes essential to make a compromise between range and sensitivity of a gauge to obtain reasonable performance for both of these categories.

4. *Accuracy of repeatability.* Sensitivity does not ensure accuracy. Usually the very sensitive instruments are quite prone to errors unless they are employed with the utmost care. One of the problems of repeatability of an instrument is the existence of friction at the pivot points. Inaccuracies may also result from backlash in gear train, temperature changes, wear in the mechanism, slippage or deflection of the components. A desirable instrument design would use components that are as light in weight as possible so that the forces required to support and move the components are as small as possible.

Before selecting a particular type of gauge the following factors must also be carefully evaluated :

1. Readability.
2. Ease of mounting.
3. Required operator skill.
4. Weight.
5. Frequency response.
6. Cost.

2.3 Mechanical Strain Gauges

Depending upon the manner of obtaining the magnification, the mechanical gauges can be classified as :

1. Wedge and screw magnification.
2. Simple mechanical lever magnification.
3. Compound magnification system.
4. Compound lever magnification.
5. Magnification by rack and pinion.
6. Combined lever, rack and pinion magnification.

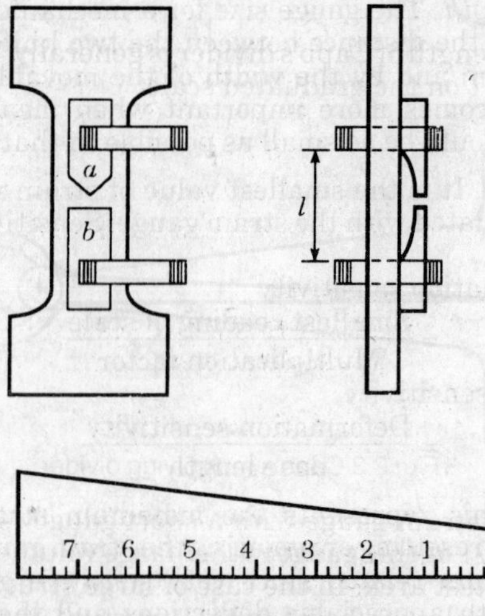

Fig. 2.1 The wedge gauge.

1. **Wedge and screw magnification.** The wedge gauge is simply a triangular plate with its longer sides related by a 1 : 10 slope as shown in Fig. 2.1. When inserted between two shoulders clipped to the test specimen, extensions could be detected to the nearest 0.05 mm. A single screw extensometer which is one of the pioneer instruments used for measurement of strain in actual structure is the Howard (1885) strain gauge shown in Fig. 2.2. The magnification in this instrument is accomplished solely by a screw micrometer *a*, which measures the relative motion of two coaxial tubes *b*, each provided with a conical contact point *c*. The contact points are inserted in prepared holes marking a known gauge length on the structure. In this extensometer, measurements can be made to the nearest 0.0025 mm with a probable accuracy of 0.005 mm under normal operating conditions.

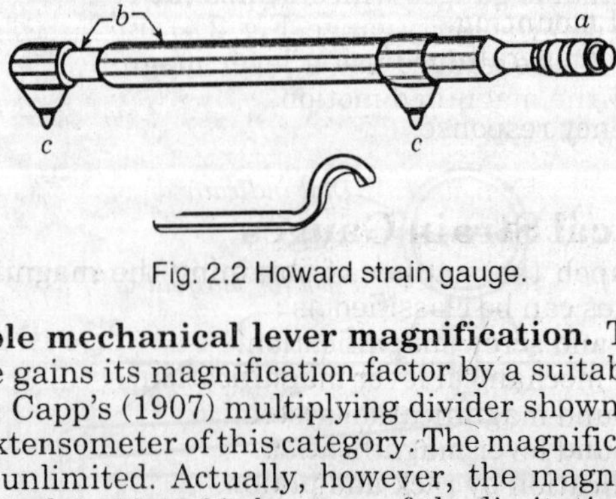

Fig. 2.2 Howard strain gauge.

2. **Simple mechanical lever magnification.** The simple lever strain gauge gains its magnification factor by a suitable positioning of the fulcrum. Capp's (1907) multiplying divider shown in Fig. 2.3 is an important extensometer of this category. The magnification of this type of gauge is unlimited. Actually, however, the magnification ratio is perhaps limited to 10 to 20, because of the limitations placed on the gauge by size and weight. The strain magnification can be increased either by increasing the gauge length or by increasing the leverage

ratio. The gauge length of Capp's divider is generally 5 cm and the strain is magnified 10 : 1 on the graduated scale.

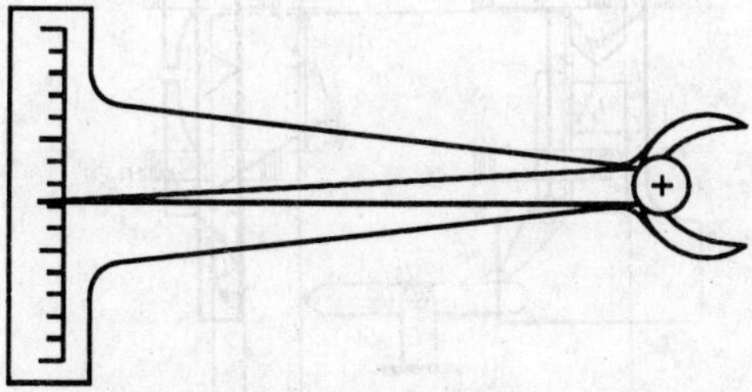

Fig. 2.3 Capp's multiplying divider.

Simple lever strain gauge with a short gauge length and a microscope is also used. For this gauge rather large volume must be available directly over the test area. In the case of large structures, for securing the gauge, small holes are bored in the structure, into which is secured a yoke to hold the strain gauge in position during the loading of the structure. In the application of these gauges to small structures, spring clams or *C* clamps are frequently used. For strain measurements on inner surfaces of small structures, the clearance may be insufficient for the gauge and all its auxiliary equipment.

Because of the above limitations, this type of gauge is now rarely used in stress analysis. Capp's divider is generally used for the determination of the yield point and the yield strength of materials in routine inspection tension tests. Although intended for qualitative indication of yield point rather than quantitative strain measurement, it is of interest for its simplicity.

3. **Compound magnification system.** To meet the demand for greater sensitivity, while retaining the advantage of relative case of applying the mechanical gauge, mechanical magnification is used. Two commercially available gauges which utilize the compound magnification are illustrated by the Berry gauge (Fig. 2.4) and Tinius Olsen strain gauge (Fig. 2.5). These gauges use a lever magnification with a dial indicator to show the magnified motion.

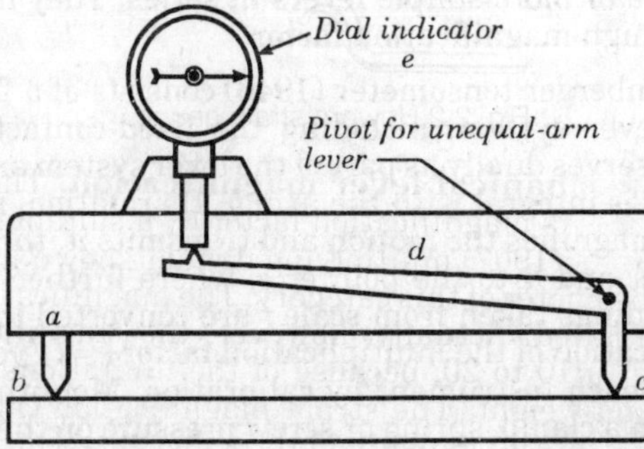

Fig. 2.4 The Berry strain gauge.

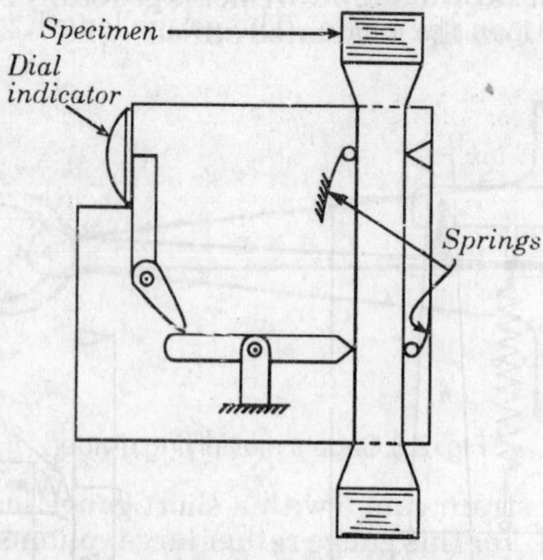

Fig. 2.5 The Tinius Olsen strain gauge.

The Berry (1910) strain gauge consists of a frame *a* with two conically pointed contact points. One point *b* is rigidly fixed to the frame, while the other *c* is pivoted from the frame and is integral with a lever arm, *d,* which alone magnifies the strain about 5 : 1. A screw micrometer or dial indicator *e* is used to measure the motion of the arm, thus permitting measurements of strain to the nearest 0.005 mm with a 0.025 mm micrometer. However variations of micrometer contact pressure and seating of the conical points in holes, making the gauge length, probably reduce the accuracy to about 0.015 mm.

The Tinius Olsen extensometer is a very compact and convenient instrument for laboratory use. This combines lever and an indicator in which the strain in the 5 cm gauge length may be read to the nearest 0.0025 mm. The knife contacts, acting on opposite sides of the specimen, give an average of the strain values on the two sides with only one gauge reading. A cantilever spring acting on the specimen opposite each knife edge provides the necessary mounting force and contact pressure.

4. **Compound lever magnification.** Two gauges of this category are Huggenberger strain gauge (Fig. 2.6) and the Porter Lipp strain gauge (Fig. 2.7). In these instruments the magnification system is composed of two or more simple levers in series. They have relatively small size and high magnification factor.

The Huggenberger tensometer (1946) consists of a frame *C* which supports the lever system, including the fixed-contact point *a* and rhomb *b* which serves dually as part of the lever system and as a contact point. Rhomb *b* is integral with the arm *h*. Its rotation, resulting from the motion Δl, magnifies the motion and transmits it, through link *d* in a knife edges *m* and *n* to the pointer *e*, where further magnification occurs. The readings taken from scale *f* are converted to actual strain values by application of the multiplication factor ($= l_1 l_2 / a_1 a_2$), which is established for each instrument by calibration. Mounting may be accomplished with a clamp, spring or screw pressure on the frame to hold points *a* and *b* in contact with the test piece. However, a spring pressure mounting is most desirable. The magnification may vary from 300 to 2000 depending upon the model. The gauge length varies from 12.5 to 25 mm.

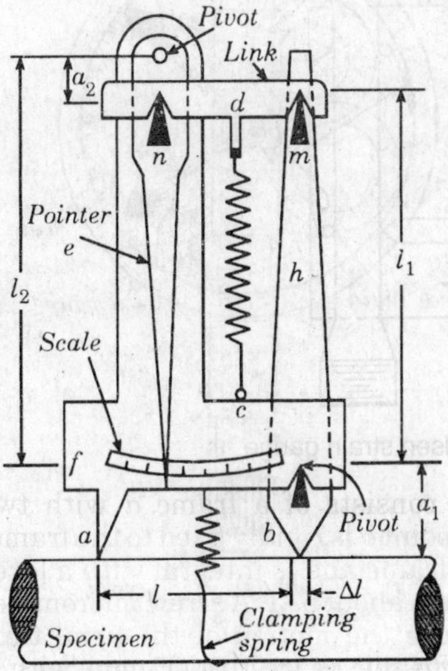

Fig. 2.6 Huggenberger tensometer.

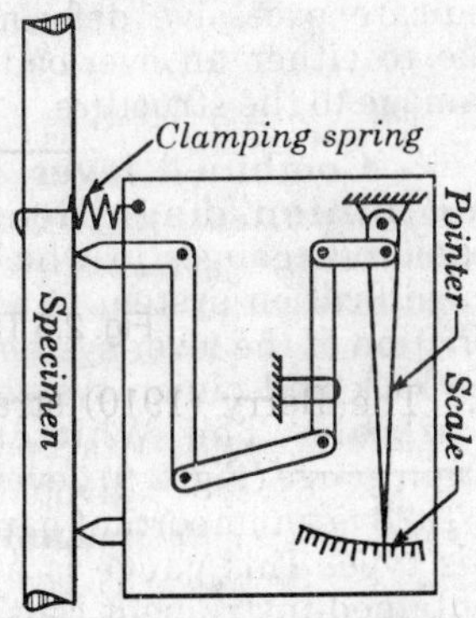

Fig. 2.7 Porter-Lipp strain gauge.

The Porter-Lipp gauge is similar to the Huggenberger strain gauge. For many applications its compactness and extreme light weight would prove advantageous. The gauge length of this gauge is 25 mm and magnification 300.

Because of their design and construction, these type of gauges are very sensitive to any vibrations that may occur in the structure under test. The natural frequency of these gauges is rather low, hence almost any structural vibration renders the readings questionable. Size of these gauges also limits their application. However, these gauges have the advantage that the magnification system and indicator are both contained in the gauge. These gauges are of the direct reading type and are rugged in construction and can be used under adverse conditions. Strains in structures outside the laboratory like bridges under actual loading conditions can be measured.

5. **Magnification by rack and pinion.** The rack and pinion principle along with various types of gear trains is employed in gauges in which the magnification system is incorporated in an indicating dial. In general a dial indicator consists of an encased gear train actuated by a rack cut in the spindle, which follows the motion to be measured. A spring imposes sufficient spindle force to maintain a reasonably uniform and positive contact with the moving part. The gear train terminates with a light weight pointer which indicates spindle travel on a graduated dial. Lost motion in the gear train is minimized by the positive force of a small coil spring. The dial gauge extensometer as

shown in Fig. 2.8 is the most popular gauge of this type used in a material testing laboratory. The Ames and Federal dials are of this type. Dial gauge indicators are frequently attached permanently to a structure to indicate the deflection on deformation obtained under working conditions. These gauges then indicate excessive deformation due to either an overload or a damage to the structure.

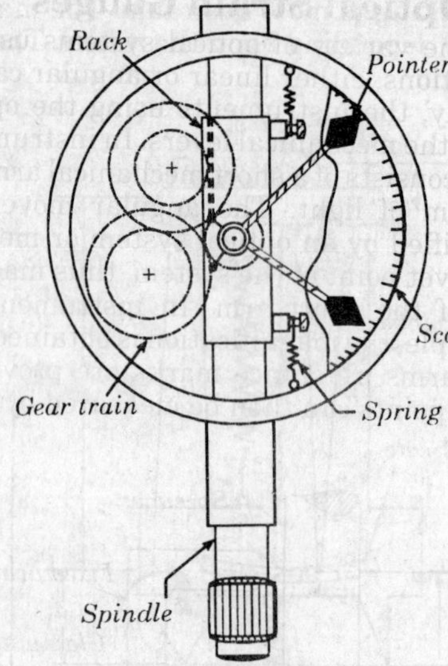

Fig. 2.8 Dial gauge indicator.

3. **Combined lever, rack and pinion magnification.** Numerous gauges in which the magnification system is a combination of the lever system and the rack and pinion system are available. The Whittemore strain gauge (Fig. 2.9) developed in 1928 is an important gauge of this type. This gauge is a self-contained instrument consisting essentially of two frame members A bound together by two elastic hinges B for parallel frictionless motion. One 45° conical contact point C is attached to each frame member. For strain measurements, the contact points are inserted into drilled holes defining a predetermined gauge length. Motion between the two frame members, or strain, is measured directly with a dial indicator. Certain undesirable features of these type of gauges are, size and attachment methods. These gauges are ruggedly encased and well suited for handling.

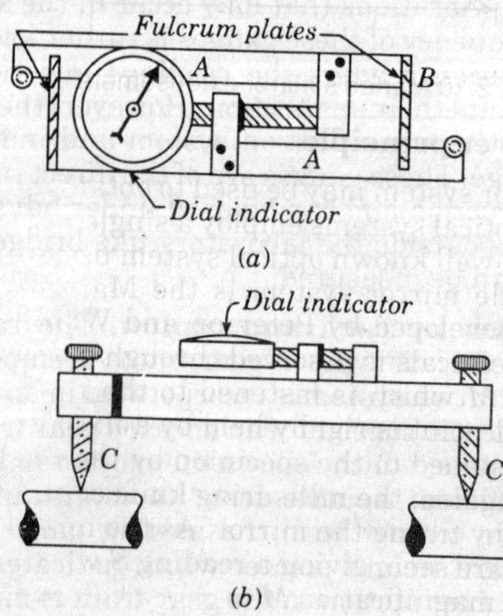

Fig. 2.9 The Whittemore strain gauge.

2.4 Optical Strain Gauges

The variety of optical systems used to measure elongations and deflections, either linear or angular can be classified into two groups, namely, the instruments using the optical lever principle and those using the mechanical levers. In instruments using the optical lever, the lever consists of a short mechanical arm holding a mirror which reflects a beam of light. The angular movement of the reflected beam is magnified by an optical system or measured at a large distance from the pivot point of the system, thus magnifying the displacement of the end of the short arm. In instruments employing mechanical lever principle, the magnification is obtained by solid levers. At the end of the long arms, reference marks are provided. The relative movement of these points can then be measured by optical or other means.

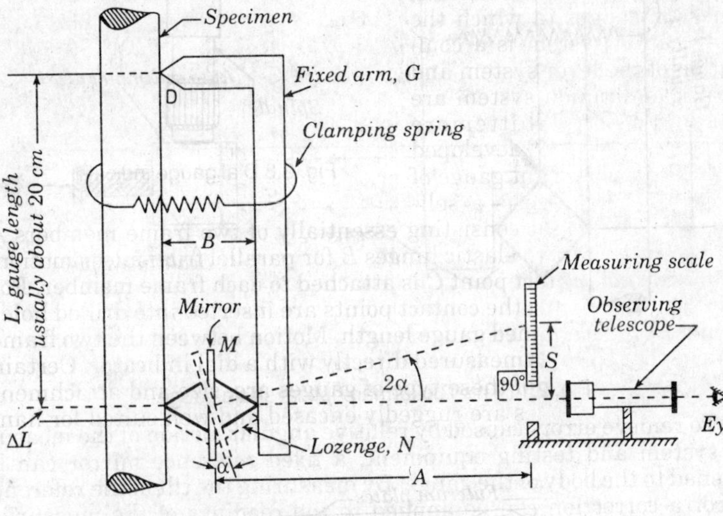

Fig. 2.10 Marten's mirror extensometer.

2.4.1 Optical lever principle

A variety of mirror system may be used to obtain optical magnification. Generally the optical systems employ a single mirror, two mirrors or three mirrors. The well known optical system used in a strain gauge working on the single mirror system is the Marten's mirror extensometer (Fig. 2.10) developed by Peterson and Wahl in 1936. In this extensometer the fixed scals is observed through a telescope by means of the tilting mirror M which is fastened to the rotatable knife edge (lozenge) whose pivot point is rigidly held by a fixed arm D. The other end of this arm is fastened to the specimen by the fixed knife edge B. As the specimen elongates, the measuring knife edge will rotate about its pivot point, thereby tilting the mirror. As the mirror tilts, different portions of the scale are seen, giving a reading S which is a measure of the angle of tilt. The magnification M is

$$M = \frac{S}{\Delta L} = \frac{A \tan 2\alpha}{B \sin \alpha} \approx \frac{2A}{B} \qquad ...(2.1)$$

(within 10% accuracy) provided the rotation of the mirror is less than approximately 10 degree. The distance B is usually 5 mm with A 250 times B, giving a magnification of 500. This instrument is extremely sensitive and by using a telescope, readings may be estimated to 1/10 mm which corresponds to a length change of approximately 0.0002 mm.

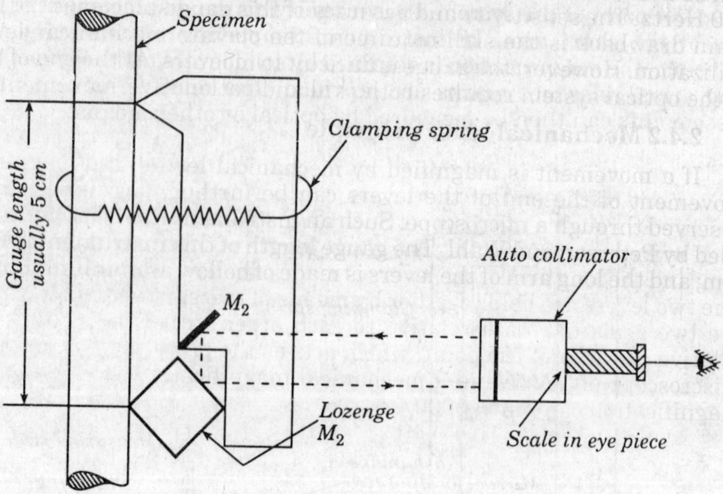

Fig. 2.11 The Tuckerman optical strain gauge.

To remove errors caused by relative angular motion of the measuring system and testing equipment, a fixed reference mirror can be fastened to the body of the gauge. By measuring the tilt of the reference mirror a correction can be applied to the readings of the measuring mirror. However, the error due to linear displacement of the mirror remains. An improvement over the two-mirror system has been made by Tuckerman, by using the three-mirror system. This gauge now known as the Tuckerman strain gauge (Fig. 2.11) is the most outstanding and was developed in 1922. In this instrument, the relative rotation between the fixed mirror M_1 and the movable mirror lozenge M_2 is measured with a autocollimator, thus eliminating the effect of specimen rotation. The optical principle of this gauge is shown in Fig. 2.12. Let us trace a ray of light originating at point F on the autocollimator. After the light passes through the lens of the autocollimator, it emerges as a beam parallel to the axis of the autocollimator. The light then strikes and reflects from mirror M_1 which in reality is a roof edge prism. The light is further reflected by mirror M_2, which is attached to the rotating knife edge, back into the autocollimator lens, which focusses the image on the reticule plane. The image of point F on the reticule plane occurs at point C. A record image produced by a second ray of light will occur at point B on the other side of F. Since the section containing point B is the only visible portion of the reticule, B is the image which is seen. When the angle between the mirrors is equal to 90°, both B and C will be exactly on F. If this angle is reduced further, C will come into the visible range and B will move out of the visible range. The gauge is calibrated by an interferometer. The sensitivity of the Tuckerman gauge is 2μ cm/cm, and the accuracy is quoted at ± 0.1% of full scale deflections. This gauge is not subjected to extraneous vibrations and can be used for measurement of dynamic strains and cyclic strains upto 180 Hertz. The sensitivity and accuracy of this gauge are very high. Its main drawback is the skill required of the operator for its successful utilization. However, the gauge is difficult to mount, and the alignment of the optical system requires both skill and patience.

2.4.2 Mechanical lever principle

If a movement is magnified by mechanical levers, the magnified movement of the end of the levers can be further magnified if it is observed through a microscope. Such an instrument has been built and used by Peterson and Wahl. The gauge length of this instrument is 2.54 mm; and the long arm of the levers is made of hollow aluminium tubing. The two levers are held together by means of two springs which permit the two arms to rotate relative to each other without altering their relative distance at the point, which acts as the pivot point. By using a miscroscope of 100 X and a mechanical magnification of 50, the total magnification can reach 5000.

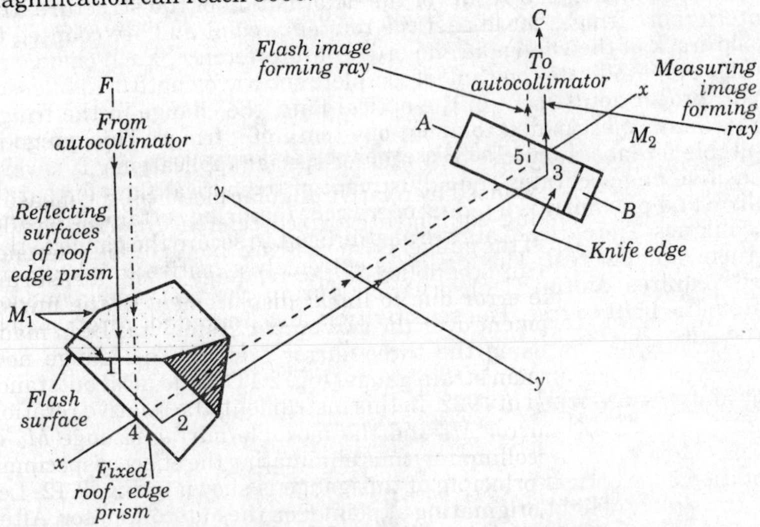

Fig. 2.12 Optical principle of Tuckerman gauge.

Instead of observing the movement of the levers, it is possible to record their relative movement by means of a variable slit which they actuate. A beam of light is passed through the slit and directed to a photoelectric cell. As the gap opening changes, the amount of light reaching the cell varies, causing a varying intensity in the current generated by the cell. The intensity is electronically amplified and measured. Gadd and Van Degrift, instead of using one gap, placed gratings of alternate transparent and opaque points at the end of the levers in such a way that one grating moved in front of the other. In this manner, they obtained a large number of slits varying in identical manner. This system has the advantage of using a wider beam which can be uniformly distributed over the whole surface of the cell. A magnification of 30,000 is claimed for this system.

2.5 Interferometric Strain Gauge

2.5.1 Vose Interferometer

If the displacement to be measured is a minute quantity, then the interference fringes produced by optical flats may be used. By using optical flats, dimensional changes of the order of the wavelength of monochromatic light can be measured. An application of this principle by R.V. Vose (1935) to the measurement of lateral strains is indicated in Fig. 2.13. The gauge is essentially composed of two optical flats, secured to the structure either directly in a frame or through leverage system. The monochromatic light is introduced into the system by means of a half silvered mirror, and the interference is observed, using a telescope, through the back side of the mirror. These optical flats must be so adjusted that the interference fringes are clearly defined and are not too close together for ease of observation. Cross-hairs are usually scratched on the surface of one optical flat for reference. As the optical flats move apart, as a result of the deformation of the structure, the interference fringes move past the reference point and are counted to keep track of the change in the order of interference. Each change in fringe order indicates one half of complete one wavelength of light used. With proper adjustment of the optical flats, the change in the fringe order may be estimated to about one-tenth of a fringe. This gauge is suitable for laboratory use only and for special applications. It is very sensitive and accurate. The adjustment of the optical flats for parallelism and proximity is a tedius operation, requiring certain skills and techniques. The optical flats are also difficult to secure the gauge to the structure under test. This gauge is extremely sensitive to vibrations and requires continual observation during the test and a monochromatic light source. The sensitivity is also limited for direct measurements.

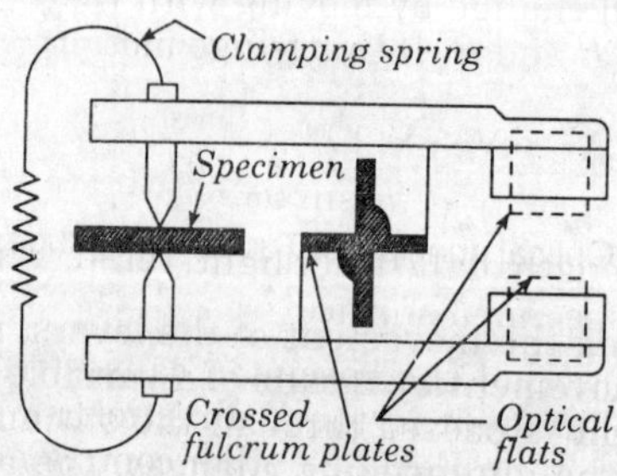

Fig. 2.13 Vose Interferometric strain gauge.

2.5.2 Sharpe interferometer

The interferometric strain gauge (ISG) developed by W.N. Sharpe, Jr. in 1968 is an optical technique for measuring strain by observing the motion of interference fringes generated by coherent light incident on closely spaced reflecting surfaces. These reflecting surfaces are ruled or impressed directly onto the surface of interest. The result is a strain gauge integral with a sample that has a short gauge length and requires no mechanical or electrical contact. This type of gauge has been used primarily for large plastic strain measurement and as a standard to evaluate other strain measuring techniques.

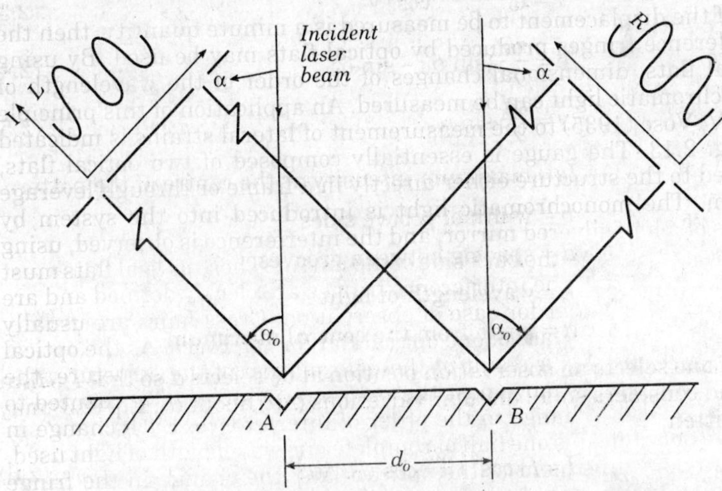

Fig. 2.14 Principle of Sharpe interferometric strain gauge.

In the double groove interference method (Fig. 2.14) two wedge shaped grooves are ruled onto screens L and R located symmetrically at an angle α_0. The grooves are very shallow (on the order of 2.5 microns deep), thus, the light reflected from the sides is spread by diffraction effects, the zeroth order at α_0. Because A and B are close enough (on the order of 0.125 mm) together for their diffraction patterns to overlap and the laser light is coherent, the interference frings pattern is formed at L and R. If the distance d_0, between A and B changes the fringe pattern at L and R will change by moving with respect to some fixed observation position at L and R. If this fringe motion is N_L and N_R the simple equation

$$\varepsilon = \left(\frac{N_L + N_R}{2}\right) \frac{\lambda}{d_0 \sin \alpha_0} \quad ...(2.2)$$

in which λ is the wavelength of the laser light, relates the fringe motion to the strain ε, on the specimen surface.

Any rigid body motion of the specimen causes fringe motion not related to strain. Displacement in the X-direction and rotation about the Z-axis are averaged out in Eq. (2.2), other components of rigid body motion do not average out and may lead to errors in measurement. Displacement in the Y-direction is the most damaging.

To get observable fringe patterns, the surface of the specimen must be smooth, a mechanical polish with buffing wheels and rouge is quite satisfactory. The grooves can be ruled onto the specimen with a wedge shaped diamond, or a Vicker's hardness tester diamond may be used to impress indentations into the surface. The ISG may be used on other materials by vapour depositing a thin metal coating on the specimen and ruling the grooves onto the coating. For small strain, the intensity I, of the fringe pattern is given by

$$I = I_0 \frac{\sin^2 \beta}{\beta^2} \cos^2 \gamma \qquad ...(2.3)$$

where $$\beta = \frac{\pi b}{\lambda} (\sin \alpha_0 - \sin \alpha) \qquad ...(2.4)$$

and $$\gamma = \frac{\pi d}{\lambda} \sin \alpha \qquad ...(2.5)$$

I_0 = maximum intensity at the centre of the pattern

b = width of groove sides

d = spacing between grooves

λ = wavelength of light

α = angle from the central maximum

If one selects an observation position at α_0 selects d so that $I = I_0$ at α_0, and considers small angular variations ($\Delta\alpha$) about α_0, Eq. (2.3) may be written,

$$I \approx I_0 \cos^2 \left(\frac{\pi d}{\lambda} \cos \alpha_0 . \Delta\alpha \right) \qquad ...(2.6)$$

For strain measurement, one fixes the observation position at α_0 and monitors the intensity changes as d changes. Eq. (2.3) becomes

$$I = I_0 \cos^2 \left(\frac{\pi d}{\lambda} \sin \alpha_0 \right) \qquad ...(2.7)$$

The intensity has a minimum whenever

$$\frac{\pi d}{\lambda} \sin \alpha_0 = \left(m + \frac{1}{2} \right), m = 0, \pm 1, \pm 2, ... \qquad ...(2.8)$$

which is the basis for Eq. (2.2), where strain is measured by counting the number of fringes passing the observation positions.

Define a gauge factor

$$F = \frac{d_0 \sin \alpha_0}{\lambda} \qquad ...(2.9)$$

and since $\frac{d}{d_0} = 1 + \varepsilon$, Eq. (2.7), becomes

$$I = I_0 \cos^2 \pi F (1 + \varepsilon) \qquad ...(2.10)$$

Now choose F so that $I = I_0/2$ when $\varepsilon = 0$. F can be selected by small angular variation about α_0, this affects the maximum intensity only slightly. This choice requires that

$$F = p/4$$

where $p = \pm 1, \pm 2, ...$

In practice p is a large integer (on the order of 750), and Eq. (2.10) finally becomes,

$$I = I_0 \cos^2 \pi \left(\frac{D}{4} + F\,\varepsilon\right) \qquad ...(2.11)$$

Sensitivity

The sensitivity S of the strain measurement is derived by evaluating the slope of the intensity curve at $\varepsilon = 0$. From Eq. (2.11).

$$S = \pi I_0 F \qquad ...(2.12)$$

α_0 cannot be increased beyond 70°, but F can be made large by increasing the gauge length d_0 or using light with a shorter wavelength.

Linearity

Expanding Eq. (2.11) about the mid-point of the cosine squared intensity function, we get

$$I = \frac{I_0}{2} - \pi I_0 F\,\varepsilon + \frac{2}{3}\pi^3 I_0 F^3 \varepsilon^3 + I_0\, 0\,(\varepsilon^5) \qquad ...(2.13)$$

For small strains, the non-linear contribution to the intensity is $\frac{2}{3}\pi^2 F^2 \varepsilon^2$. For 1 percent deviation, using $F = 200$, the gauge is linear for $\varepsilon \approx \pm 450$ μ strain.

Range

The range would normally be taken as the linear region of operation, but this is obviously restrictive. From Eq. (2.11) the range corresponds to $\Delta m = \frac{1}{2}$ or $\varepsilon \approx 1250$ με. A simple way of extending the range is simply to rezero the system by moving the photodetector back to the starting position.

2.5.3 Diffraction Strain Gauge

The diffraction strain gauge developed by Pryor and North in 1971, consists of two blades that are bonded or welded to the component as shown in Fig. 2.15. The two blades are separated by a distance b to form a narrow aperture and are fixed to the specimen along the edges to give a gauge length l. A beam of collimated monochromatic light from a helium-neon laser is directed on to the aperture to produce a diffraction pattern that can be observed as a line of dots on a screen a distance R from the aperture. When the distance R to the screen is very large compared with the aperture width b, the distribution of the intensity I of light in the diffraction pattern is

$$I = A_o^2 \frac{\sin^2 \beta}{\beta^2} \qquad ...(2.14)$$

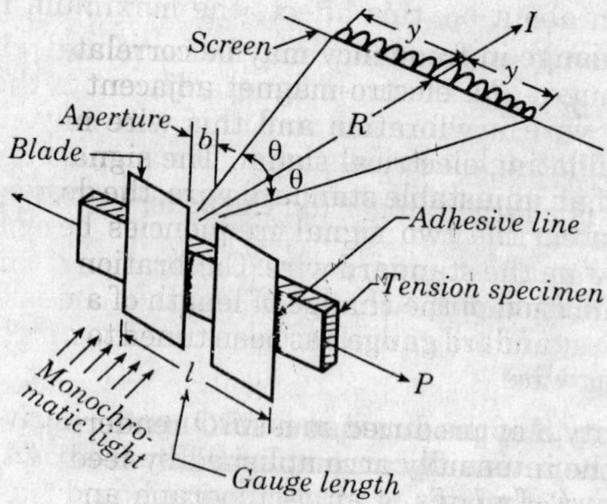

Fig. 2.15 Diffraction strain gauge.

where A_0 = amplitude of light on the centre line of the pattern ($\theta = 0$)

$$\beta = \frac{\pi b}{\lambda} \sin \theta \qquad ...(2.15)$$

For y to be small, $\sin \theta$ is small so that $\sin \theta = \frac{y}{R}$ and we get

$$\beta = \frac{\pi b}{\lambda} \cdot \frac{y}{R} \qquad ...(2.16)$$

$$I = 0 \text{ when } \sin \beta = 0 \text{ or } \beta = n\pi,\ n = 1, 2, 3, ...$$

and
$$b = \frac{\lambda R n}{y} \qquad ...(2.17)$$

where n = order of extinction in the diffraction pattern at the point having y as its position.

As the specimen is strained, the deformation results in a change in the aperture width $\Delta b = \varepsilon l$ and a corresponding change in the diffraction pattern. The magnitude of this strain ε can be determined from Eq. (2.17) and measurements from the two diffraction patterns. After deformation

$$b + \Delta b = \frac{\lambda R n^*}{y_1}$$

and before deformation

$$b = \frac{\lambda R n^*}{y_0}$$

$$\therefore \quad \varepsilon = \frac{\Delta b}{l} = \frac{\lambda R n^*}{l} \left(\frac{y_0 - y_1}{y_0 y_1} \right) \qquad ...(2.18)$$

2.6 Acoustical Strain Gauge

The vibrating wire or acoustical gauge consists essentially of a steel wire tensioned between two supports a predetermined distance apart. Variation of the distance alters the natural frequency of vibration of the wire and this change in frequency may be correlated with the change in strains causing it. An electro-magnet adjacent to the wire may be used to set the wire in vibration and this wire movement will then generate an oscillating electrical signal. The signal may be compared with the pitch of an adjustable standard wire, the degree of adjustment necessary to match the two signal frequencies being provided by a tensioning screw on the standard wire. Calibration of this screw allows a direct determination of the change of length of a measuring gauge to be made once the standard gauge has been tuned to match the frequency of the measuring wire.

The visual display produced or a *CRO* renders adjustment easier. Tuning is now more usually accomplished by feeding the two signals into the two pairs of plates of an oscillograph and making use of the Lissajous figure formation to balance the frequencies. Matching of the tones is simplified and made more accurate by tuning out the beats which results when the vibration frequencies of two wires are nearly the same, which can be compared by using earphones.

The fundamental frequency of a stretched wire may be estimated from the expression

$$f = \frac{1}{2L}\sqrt{\frac{P}{m}} = \frac{1}{2L}\sqrt{\frac{(E\,\delta L)/L}{m}\,A} \qquad ...(2.19)$$

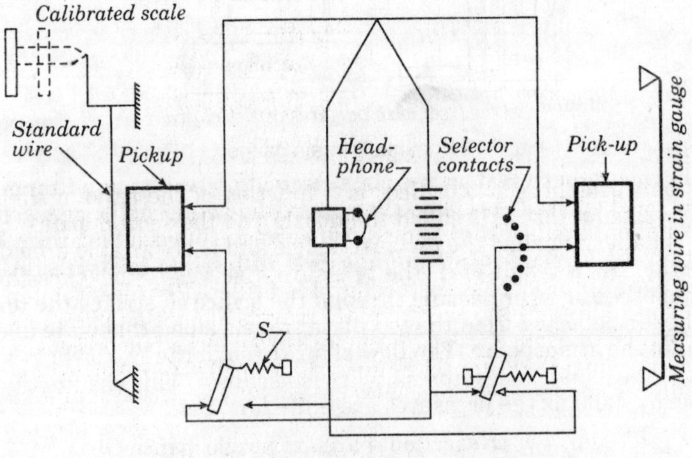

Fig. 2.16 Acoustical strain gauge.

where A = cross-sectional area of vibrating wire

E = Young's modulus of wire material

L = length of vibrating wire

m = mass per unit length of the wire

P = tensioning force in the wire

δL = increment in length of the vibrating wire.

Fig. 2.16 shows an acoustical gauge developed by Dr. O. Schaeff about 1933. The sensitivity of this gauge is very high, with possible determinations of displacement of the order of 0.25 μ cm. The range is limited to about 1/1000 of the wire length. The gauge is temperature sensitive unless the thermal coefficients of expansion of the base and wire are closely matched over the temperature range encountered during a test.

2.7 Pneumatic Strain Gauge

The principle of operation of an air or pneumatic gauge depends upon the relative discharge of air between a fixed orifice and a variable orifice. Fig. 2.17 shows a pneumatic gauge. Air under constant pressure H, flows through two orifices placed in series. The pressure h which

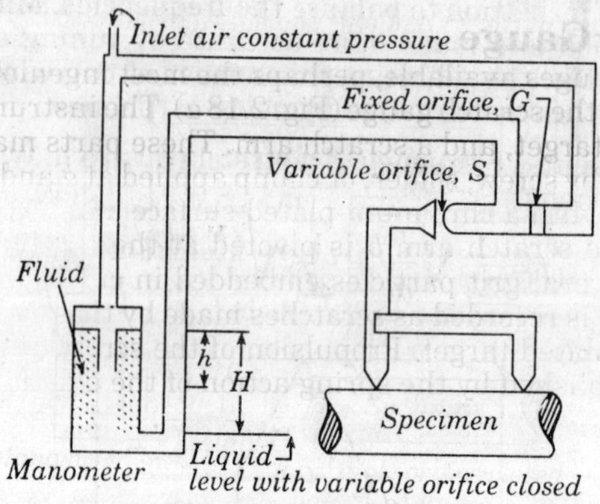

Fig. 2.17 Pneumatic strain gauge.

prevails between these two orifices is a function of the ratio of their areas. The fixed orifice G is called the nozzle and the second orifice S, which is smaller, is called the exhaust orifice and is of variable area of cross-section. As a result of it, the pressure h serves to measure the dimension of S. Air after passing through the orifice G, strikes the top plate. The air deflected from the top plate travels along this plate and is vented to the atmosphere. The flow of air through the two orifices in series must be equal if incompressibility is assumed. This assumption is practically valid as the pressures are quite low. Let,

A_G = cross-sectional area of nozzle orifice G

A_S = cross-sectional area of discharge orifice S

C_G, C_S = coefficients of contraction for the orifices

ρ = density of air

g = acceleration due to gravity.

Since the flow through each orifice is the same, hence

$$C_G A_G \sqrt{\frac{2g(H-h)}{\rho}} = C_S A_S \sqrt{\frac{2gh}{\rho}} \qquad ...(2.20)$$

when $\quad C_S = C_G = C$, then

$$h = \frac{H}{1 + (A_S/A_G)^2} \qquad ...(2.20)$$

When the specimen is loaded, the distance between the two gauge points changes. This elongation is transmitted through the lever system to the pneumatic gauge, where it changes the gap between orifice S and the top plate, thus changing the area A_S in direct proportion to the strain. From Eq. (2.20) it is obvious that the manometer reading varies as a quadratic function of the strain. However, it has an inflection point when $h/H = 3/4$ or $A_S/A_G = 0.58$. Hence, for values in this neighbourhood, the relation is very nearly linear. Multiplication factors of 100,000 are possible with this type of pneumatic amplification.

2.8 Scratch Gauge

Of all the gauges available, perhaps the most ingenious because of its simplicity, is the scratch gauge (Fig. 2.18 *a*). The instrument consists of two parts ; a target, and a scratch arm. These parts may be secured to the test piece by screw, solder, or clamp applied at g and e. The target is a small plate with a chromium-plated surface and includes a raised clip arm '*a*'. The scratch arm b is pivoted at the elastic hinge C and carries, at f, several grit particles embedded in cured rubber. Motion between e and g is recorded as scratches made by the grit particles f on the chromium plated target. Propulsion of the scratch arm across the target is accomplished by the spring action of the elastic hinge C. The

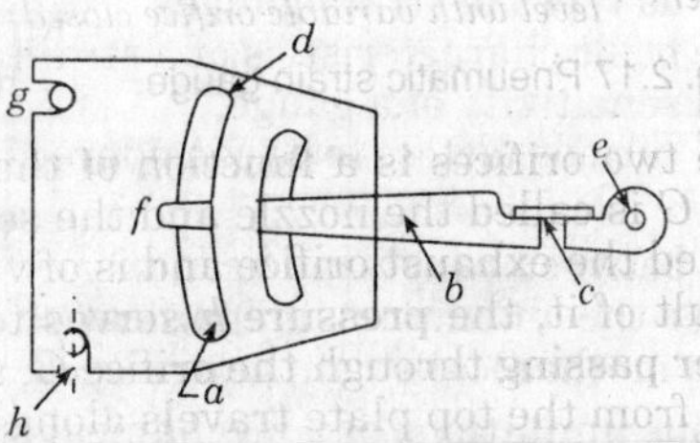

(*a*) Scratch recording system.

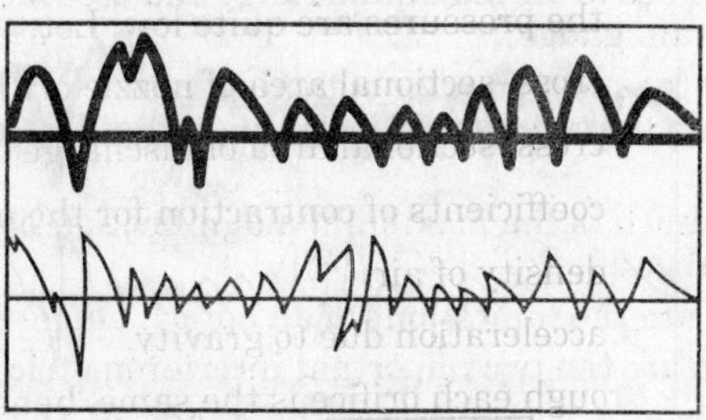

(*b*) Magnified strain record.

Fig. 2.18 Scratch gauge.

cross motion is regulated by the pressure of clip a on arm b. This pressure develops sufficient static friction to restrain the arm, but cross motion is permitted by the smaller sliding friction, which results from relative motion of the target and arm as the test piece is strained. The rate of the scratch arm cross travel is a function of the sliding motion occurring, rather than of time. It can be controlled by variation of the clip pressure and the thickness of the spring hinge. The several grit particles scratch patterns of varying depth, depending on the alignment of target and arm. Of course, the most clearly defined pattern is used for interpreting the record. The base line is established by moving the arm across the target while the test piece is in an unloaded condition. The measurements of deformation indicated by the scratches on the target, is accomplished by means of a microscope. Fig. 2.18 (*b*) shows the strain record.

This gauge is used for measuring deformation of rail-road rails because of the load caused by a passing train. Strain measurements can be made inside pressure vessels, inside moving mechanisms, under water etc. Dynamic strains pattern on analysis can be separated into various harmonics of a vibratory deformation. However, this gauge cannot be applied to small structures or finished surfaces, and extreme care has to be exercised in measuring the scratch record to obtain any degree of precision. The gauge is also little affected by its own inertia forces. Readings may be estimated to 0.0025 mm.

2.10 Quiz Questions

1. Define a strain gauge.
2. List the various types of strain gauges.
3. What are the basic characteristics of a strain gauge ?
4. Define strain sensitivity of a gauge.
5. What are the various factors to be considered before selecting a gauge ?
6. Differentiate between range and accuracy.
7. How much is the maximum magnification which can be obtained by a mechanical strain gauge ?
8. List the various limitations of a mechanical strain gauge.
9. Name most popular mechanical strain gauges.
10. How much is the maximum range and accuracy of a mechanical strain gauge ?
11. Name the most popular optical gauges.
12. Explain the two ways of obtaining magnification by an optical gauge.
13. How much is the maximum magnification obtainable by an optical gauge ?
14. What are the limitations of an optical gauge ?
15. Which are the two important interferometric strain gauges?
16. How would you increase the range of the Sharpe interferometric strain gauge ?
17. How much is the maximum range of an interferometric gauge ?

18. Write an equation for the fundamental frequency of a stretched wire.
19. What are Lissajous figures ?
20. What are the advantages of an acoustical gauge ?
21. How much is the maximum magnification obtainable by a pneumatic gauge ?
22. List the important advantages of a scratch gauge.
23. What are the limitations of scratch gauge ?
24. Name the various gauges which can be used for measuring dynamic strain.

EXERCISES

2.1 Write a short account of the various types of strain gauges. Give their special advantages and limitations.

2.2 What are the various types of mechanical strain gauges ? Explain Huggenberger tensometer in detail.

2.3 What are the basic characteristics of a strain gauge ? Which factors should be considered while selecting a strain gauge?

2.4 What is the necessity of a compound magnification in a strain gauge ? Explain some of the important gauges using compound magnification.

2.5 What are the various types of optical strain gauges ? Explain the Tuckerman gauge in detail.

2.6 What are the advantages and limitations of an optical strain gauge ? How do you define the magnification of an optical gauge ?

2.7 Explain the construction and working of the Vose interferometer. How strain can be measured with this interferometer ?

2.8 Explain the construction and working of the Sharpe interferometer in detail.

2.9 Explain the construction and working of the following gauges:
(*a*) Acoustical strain gauge,
(*b*) Pneumatic strain gauge,
(*c*) Scratch gauge,
(*d*) Diffraction strain gauge.

2.10 List the various requirements of a gauge to be suitable for measuring dynamic strain. Which of the gauges can be used for measuring dynamic strain ? Explain their working briefly.

2.11 A scratch gauge with a gauge length of 500 mm is employed to measure a strain which varies from 0 to 500 μcm/cm. Determine the total range of motion of the scratch recorded on the target plate. If the target place is magnified 10 times in a microscope and the range of motion is measured with a filar unit accurate to ± 0.002 mm, determine the expected error.

2.12 A helium-neon laser ($\lambda = 6328$ Å) is used to illuminate a diffraction-type strain gauge with a gauge length of 25 mm. The diffraction pattern is displayed on a screen which is located 2 m from the aperture. The initial aperture width is 0.1 mm.

(*a*) Determine the intensity of diffraction pattern.

(*b*) Determine the new aperture width and intensity for a strain of 600 μcm/cm.

2.13 In a Huggenberger tensometer $a_1 = 40$ mm, $a_2 = 80$ mm, $l_1 = 400$ mm, $l_2 = 480$ mm. Determine (*a*) the magnification factor for the tensometer and (*b*) movement of the indicating pointer if gauge length is 500 mm and tensometer is used to measure a strain of 2000 μ cm/cm.

3

Electrical Strain Gauges

3.1 Introduction

An electrical strain gauge is a device in which a change in length produces a change in some electrical characteristics of the gauge.

The electrical strain gauges may be classified as follows :

(*a*) The inductance or magnetic strain gauges.
(*b*) The capacitance strain gauge.
(*c*) The electrical resistance strain gauges.

Out of these three types of gauges, the resistance strain gauges (RSG) have become more popular and reliable. Hence, in this chapter, we shall study the first two types of gauges briefly and lay more emphasis on the resistance gauges.

The inductance type of strain gauges in which the strain is measured as a change in the magnetic field, was developed as a strain gauge about 1930 by Shamberger. Since then this gauge has been used for various applications, particularly in motion measurements. An important application of inductance type of gauge is the linear variable differential transformer, developed by Schaevitz about 1947.

The capacitance type of gauges have found very little use as strain gauges and are not commercially available. However, these type of gauges have found applications as transducers to measure pressure, force and displacement.

In 1856 Lord Kelvin reported that the electrical resistance of certain wires varied with the tension to which the wires were subjected. Bridgeman in 1923 confirmed Kelvin's results in a series of tests involving wires under hydrostatic pressure. Little use was made of this knowledge until after 1930, when attempts were made to apply the phenomenon of strain sensitivity in wires to the actual measurement of strain in other bodies. The first use of this principle for strain measurements was made by Carlson and Eaton about 1931. A non-metallic, unbonded resistance gauge was however developed and used by Mc-Collum and Peters in 1924. A non-metallic, bonded resistance gauge was developed by Bloach in 1935.

The bonded wire metallic strain gauge was developed independently and almost simultaneously in 1938 by Simmons at the

California Institute of Technology and Ruge at the Massachusetts Institute of Technology, now commercially known as the SR 4 gauges, and marketed by Baldwin-Lima-Hamilton Corporation of U.S.A. Since then the activity in this field has been on the increase and a lot of improvements have been made in these gauges. During the 1950's considerable attention was given to the foil-type strain gauges. Much of the credit for development and acceptance of this type of gauge goes to Bean, Saunders and Roe. Currently the foil gauges have largely displaced the wire gauges.

A uniquely constructed weldable wire-filament strain gauge has been developed recently for application in many hostile environments and installation by Ailtech (U.S.A.).

3.2 Inductance Strain Gauges

An electric inductance gauge is a device in which the mechanical quantity to be measured produces a change in the magnetic field, and, hence in the impedance, of a current-carrying coil. The impedance of a coil depends on its inductance and on its effective resistance, and either or both of these quantities can be made sensitive to the mechanical quantity being measured. The inductance which is changed can be either the self inductance of the coil or its mutual inductance with respect to another coil. Depending upon the method of varying the impedance, electric-inductance gauges may be classified as follows :

1. *Variable-air-gap gauges.* In which the reluctance of the magnetic field is varied by changing the air gap.

2. *Movable-core solenoid gauges.* In which the reluctance of the magnetic circuit is varied by changing the position of the iron core in the coil.

3. *Eddy current gauges.* In which the losses in the magnetic circuit are varied by changing the thickness or position of the high-loss element inserted in the magnetic field.

4. *Magnetostriction gauges.* In which the reluctance of the magnetic circuit is varied by changing the stress in the magnetic core of the coil.

The impedance of a coil to the passage of alternating current is given by the expression :

$$Z = \sqrt{(2\pi f L)^2 + R^2} \qquad \text{...(3.1)}$$

where
Z = impedance in ohms
f = frequency in hertzs
L = inductance of the coil in henrys
R = resistance component in ohms.

In general, R is negligible as compared to L and the impedance varies almost in proportion to the inductance. The inductance of a variable-air-gap gauge is given by

$$L = \frac{8.1026\,N^2}{\dfrac{l_i}{\mu_{a_i}} + \dfrac{l_a}{a_a}} \times 10^{-8} \qquad \text{...(3.2)}$$

N = number of turns.

l_i = length of iron magnetic circuit, cm

l_a = length of air gap, cm

μ = permeability of magnetic material at the maximum alternating flux density

a_i = cross-section of iron, cm^2

a_a = cross-section of air gap, cm^2

If the value of μ is sufficiently large, then $\frac{l_i}{\mu a_i}$ is negligible as compared to $\frac{l_a}{a_a}$ and we find that

$$L = \frac{a_a}{l_a} \times 8.1026\, N^2 \times 10^{-8} \quad \text{...(3.3)}$$

The relationship between the voltage applied across a coil and the flux density in its core is

$$E = 0.10667\, BaNf \times 10^{-8}$$

where E = voltage

B = flux density in lines per square cm

a = cross section of core, cm^2.

Thus, we find that under ideal conditions, the impedance of an iron-core coil varies inversely with the length of the air gap in the magnetic circuit. If the motion to be measured is a large percentage of the initial air gap, very large changes in impedance can be produced and large amounts of electric energy become available. Therefore, the variable-air-gap gauge is one of the best-known methods of converting small motions into high energy electric signals. For large motions, it is more advisable to use the moving-core solenoid. Eddy-current gauges find applications in special fields, such as the measurement of motion and of the thickness of nonferrous sheets Magnetostriction effect is small in most commercial magnetic irons but is large in nickel and some nickel-iron and cobalt-iron alloys. Fig. 3.1 shows circuits for some of these gauges. These gauges are placed in one arm of an inductance bridge with either a voltmeter or *CRO* to indicate the out-of-balance potential to the bridge. The bridge is supplied with an alternating current of about 1000 hertzs for static strain measurements. For dynamic strains, the frequency of current source must be 20 to 30 times the frequency of the strain being measured. One serious difficulty is that magnetic forces set up across the air gap frequently give rise to serious vibrations in the structure. These gauges cannot be applied to light structures. Large strains can not be measured as the strain-inductance relationship is linear only over a small range of strain. These gauges are weighty, bulky and susceptible to magneto-mechanical resonance.

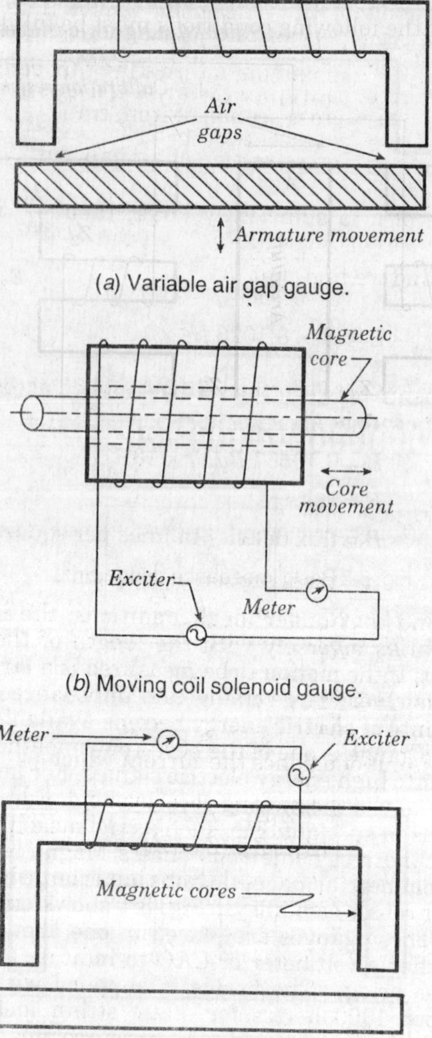

(*a*) Variable air gap gauge.

(*b*) Moving coil solenoid gauge.

(*c*) Eddy current gauge.

Fig. 3.1 Inductance strain gauges.

Fig. 3.2 shows the basic impedance bridge circuit. E_1 and E_2 are the laminated iron cores and A is the armature. When the armature A moves the air gap between A and E_1 increases and that between A and E_2 decreases or *vice versa*. This changes the reluctance of the magnetic paths in E_1 and E_2 and consequently changes the impedance of the two e wound on them. Let Z_1, Z_2, Z_3 and Z_4 be the impedance e coils and balancing elements. Z_5 is the impedance of the t circuit. In order to reduce the voltage across Z_5 to zero, both ve and the reactive components of the bridge legs must be . Both of the following conditions must be fulfilled :

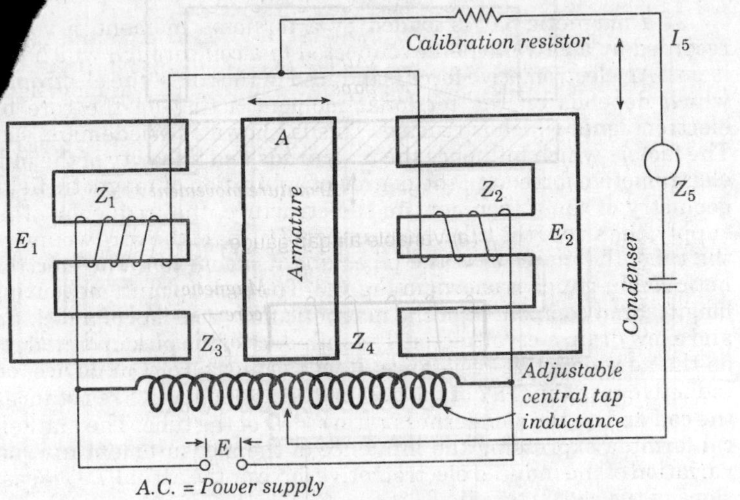

Fig. 3.2 Basic impedance bridge circuit.

$$\frac{R_1}{R_2} = \frac{R_3}{R_4} \qquad ...(3.5)$$

and

$$\frac{X_1}{X_2} = \frac{X_3}{X_4}$$

when the bridge is out of balance the current which passes through the instrument is given by,

$$I_5 = \frac{\left[\dfrac{Z_1 Z_4 - Z_2 Z_3}{(Z_1 + Z_2)(Z_3 + Z_4)}\right] E}{Z_5 + \dfrac{1}{\dfrac{1}{Z_1} + \dfrac{1}{Z_2}} + \dfrac{1}{\dfrac{1}{Z_3} + \dfrac{1}{Z_4}}} \qquad ...(3.6)$$

Maximum power to the instrument is obtained when $I_5^2 R_5$ is a maximum.

Let $Z_5 = R_5 + jX_5$

and

$$\frac{1}{\dfrac{1}{Z_1} + \dfrac{1}{Z_2}} + \frac{1}{\dfrac{1}{Z_3} + \dfrac{1}{Z_4}} = A + jB$$

Maximum power will be obtained when

$$R_5 = A \text{ and } X_5 = -B$$

The condition $X_5 = -B$ is satisfied by the use of the c in series with Z_5. The condition $R_5 = A$ may be satisfiec choice of the instrument or else by using a matching tra operate the instrument circuit.

3.2.1 Electromagnetic strain gauge

If a magnetic bar is loaded by a torsional moment, a vo recorded by a galvanometer connected to a coil through which t is put. An electromotive force is induced in the coil of the electrom which depends on the torsional moment acting on the core of electromagnet which is twisted. This is known as Wiedemann's effect. The factors which influence the magnitude and linearity of the induced electromotive force are : the degree of saturation of magnetic field, the geometry of the attachment to the structure, the frequency of power supply, the size of the tube, the number of turns of the wire wound round the tube, the material of the pipes and its condition. The electromagnetic strain-gauge is shown in Fig. 3.3. The pick up unit, measuring the longitudinal component of the magnetic flow, consists of a pick up coil and a low drain a.c. voltmeter. The influence of the pick up unit depends on the non-inductive resistance R_m of the measurement device, on the inductive resistance wl of the coil, on the non-inductive resistance R_c of the coil and on the slenderness ratio $r = lD$ of the tube. The mathematical formula expressing the influence of the measurement unit on the variation of the induced electromotive force or the actual, *i.e.*, measured slope of the characteristic $K_m{}'$ is

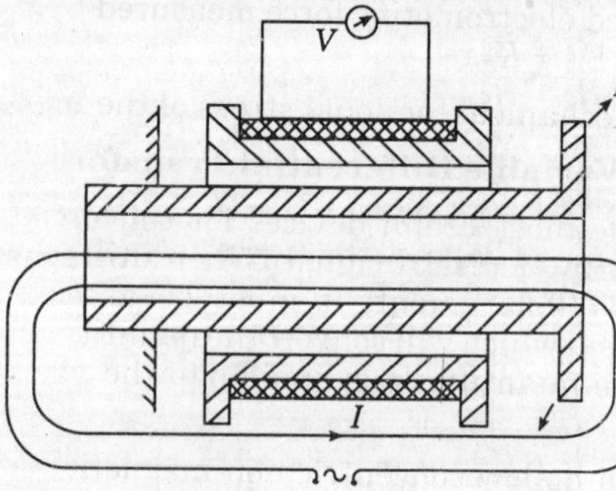

Fig. 3.3 Electromagnetic strain gauge (Wiedemann's effect).

$$K_m{}' = K_0 \frac{R_m}{R_c} \frac{x}{1 + \left[\dfrac{wl}{R_c}\right]^2} \quad ...(3.7)$$

where K_0 = ideal slope of the characteristic, for $r = 0.8$.

x = ratio of induced electromotive force for general r to the voltage E_m for $r = 0.8$.

The inductance *e*, increases in proportion with the number of turns N,

coils which ar

of the gaug

$$e = -N\frac{\partial\phi}{\partial t} \times 10^{-8} \text{ volts} \qquad ...(3.8)$$

instrument

the resisti ongitudinal component of the magnetic flow.

balanced ise the intensity of the magnetic field H is a function of i, the and the size of the wire, *i.e.*,

$H = f(D, i)$, it is permissible to write

$\phi = A\varphi\,(D, i_m \cos wt)$, owing to the fact that

$i = i_m \cos wt$, where A is the area of cross-section of the wire.

Now
$$\frac{\partial\phi}{\partial t} = wA\,\frac{\partial\varphi\,(D, i_m \cos wt)}{\partial\,(wt)}$$

from which, after due substitution

$$e = -NwA\,\frac{\partial\phi}{\partial\,(wt)} \times 10^{-8} \qquad ...(3.9)$$

For D = 2 mm to 20 mm the relationship of the stress in the tube is practically linear so that

$$K_m = K_0\,\frac{R_m}{R}\cdot\frac{1}{1+\left[\frac{wl}{R}\right]^2}\,\frac{xDN}{1000}\,\varphi(f) \qquad ...(3.10)$$

and the induced electromotive force measured by the voltmeter is

$$E_m = K_m\tau \qquad ...(3.11)$$

where τ = mechanical torsional stress of the torsion pipe.

3.2.2 Linear Variable Differential Transformer (LVDT)

It is one of the most useful devices for converting a mechanical displacement into an electrical signal. When utilizing it in measurement other than displacement, it must be associated with some auxiliary mechanism which will convert the quantity into displacement proportional to the quantity. It is similar to the variable-inductance transducer.

It consists of a hollow concentric non-magnetic form (Fig. 3.4) on which are mounted three windings, one primary and two secondaries. The position of the core placed within the coil form determines the relative mutual coupling, and thus voltage developed, between the primary winding and each of the secondary or output windings. When the a.c. voltage is impressed across the primary winding and the output of the two secondary windings connected in series opposition, the net output voltage is the difference of these two voltages and is a direct measure of the displacement of the core. As the core is moved from the balance or null position, the voltage induced in that secondary coil toward which the core is moved, increases, whereas in the other secondary coil it decreases. Motion of the core in the opposite direction produces a similar voltage but of opposite phase. The output voltage characteristics of the LVDT are shown in Fig. 3.5. While the output voltage magnitudes are ideally the same for equal core displacements on either side of the null balance, the phase relation existing between power source and output changes 180° through null. It is therefore possible through phase determination to distinguish between outputs resulting from displacements on each side of null. This is generally operated on linear range and as such is commercially known as linear-variable differential transformer.

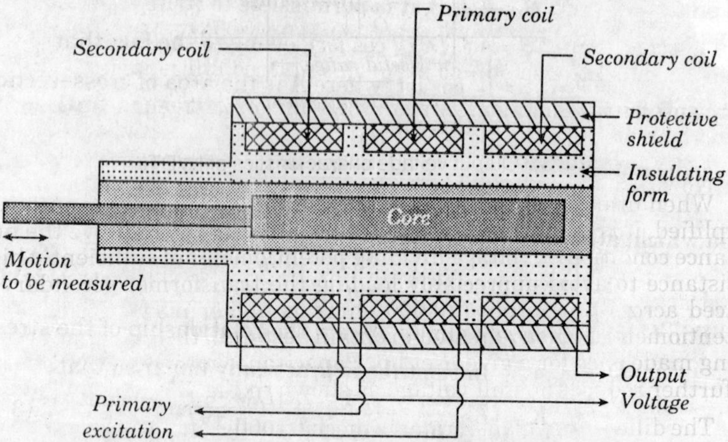

Fig. 3.4 Construction of linear variable differential transformer.

The input voltage is limited by current carrying ability of the primary coil. They are generally made to operate upto 6.3 volts and draw less than one watt of power. Higher exciting frequencies provide increased sensitivity. But in order to maintain linearity, they are designed for a specific input frequency. The exciting frequency is referred to as the carrier frequency. A minimum ratio of 10 : 1 between carrier and signal frequencies is a limit.

The sensitivity defined in terms of millivolts output per volt input per 0.025 mm core displacement increases with frequency and number of turns and is dependent upon exciting voltage. The number of turns are limited by the solenoid effect on the core. Input harmonics resulting from adjacent metallic materials, magnetic or non-magnetic will hinder obtaining the sharp null balance position.

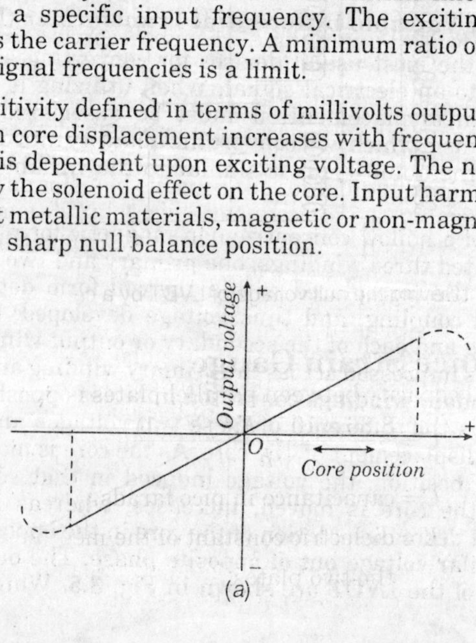

(a)

where

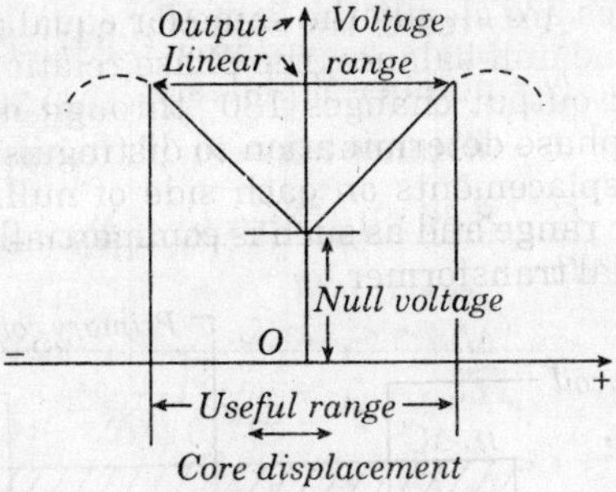

(b)

Fig. 3.5 Output voltage characteristics of LVDT.

When utmost sensitivity is desired and the transformer output is amplified, it is necessary to use external circuitary to improve the null balance condition. A voltage dividing potentiometer of sufficiently high resistance to avoid appreciably loading the transformer secondary is placed across the output (20,000 ohms or higher may be used). The potentiometer is then adjusted to obtain best null, the adjustment only being made once for a given set up. Capacitance may be added by trial to further reduce the null voltage as shown in Fig. 3.6.

The differential transformer is mechanically simple and is a rather rugged electrical pick up. It is insensitive to temperature changes and can not be overloaded mechanically. It is reusable and is of reasonable cost. However, due to the appreciable mass of the core, its use is restricted in dynamic measurements.

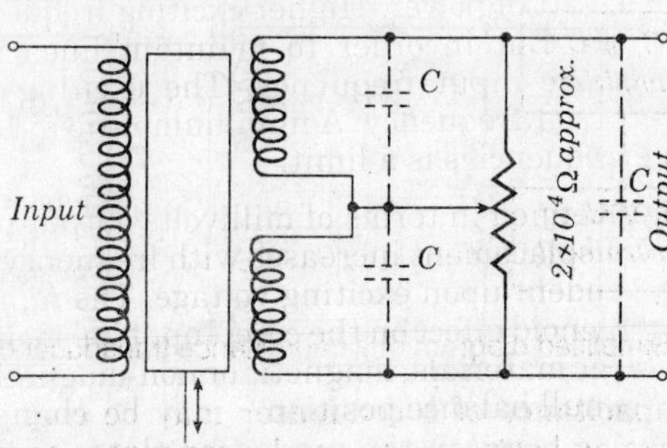

Fig. 3.6 Improving the null voltage of LVDT by a capacitance.

3.3 Capacitance Strain Gauge

The electrical capacity between parallel plates is given by :

$$C = \frac{8.86 \times 10^{-3}\, KA\, (N-1)}{h} \qquad ...(3.12)$$

where C = capacitance in pico farads.

K = dielectric constant of the medium between the two plates

A = area of one side of the plates, mm^2
N = number of plates
h = distance between plates, mm.

Now $$\frac{C}{dh} = \frac{8.86 \times 10^{-3}\, KA\,(N-1)}{h^2} = -\frac{C}{h}$$

Strain $$\varepsilon = \frac{\Delta h}{l_0}$$

Hence $$\varepsilon = \frac{h}{l_0}\,\frac{\Delta C}{C} \qquad \text{...(3.13)}$$

where l_0 is the gauge length.

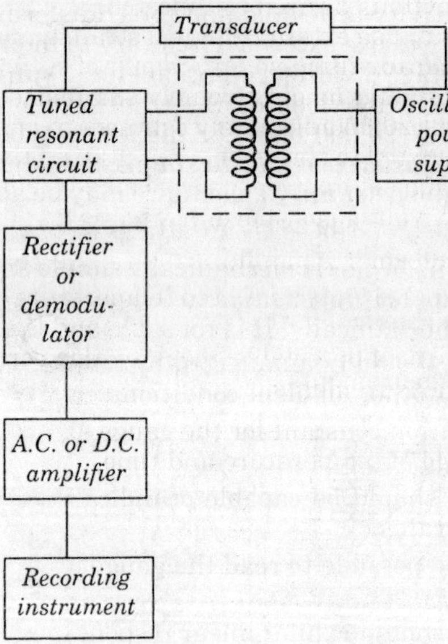

Fig. 3.7 Simplified diagram of a capacitance transducer circuit.

Thus the capacitance of a condenser may be changed either by changing the spacing between the condenser plates or the condenser plate area may be changed. The variation in the capacitance because of a change in the plate spacing is linear over a change of only small fraction of the total spacing while the change in capacitance resulting from a change in area is linear for large changes in the plate area. Two types of cirçuits may be used to measure the change in capacitance of a gauge. In the first method, a capacitance bridge is supplied with an a.c., the out-of-balance of the bridge, because of a change in the capacitance of the gauge, is measured by either a voltmeter or CRO. In the second method, the capacitance gauge may be placed in a circuit, oscillating at resonance. As the capacitance of the condenser changes as a result of strain, the frequency of oscillation of the circuit changes. The output of this resonant circuit is passed through a discriminator, the variation in frequency is indicated on the screen of CRO. The first method employs an amplitude-modulated signal, while the second method uses a frequency-modulated signal. A simplified diagram of a capacitance transducer circuit is shown in Fig. 3.7.

Capacitance gauges are small in size and they have excellent high-frequency response and high temperature resistance, as well as good linearity resolution and ability to measure both static and dynamic quantities. These gauges are sensitive to temperature, vibrations, have high impedance output and complexity of associated electronic equipment. Dielectric, mounting and clamping difficulties make this gauge not too desirable.

3.4 Electrical Resistance Strain Gauges

In the electrical resistance strain gauges the displacement or strain is measured as a function of the resistance change produced by the displacement in the gauging circuit. An ideal strain gauge should have the following basic characteristics :

1. The gauge should be of extremely small size (gauge length and width) so as to adequately estimate strain at a point.
2. The gauge should be of significant mass to permit the recording of dynamic strains.
3. The gauge should be easy to attach to the member being analysed and easy to handle.
4. The strain sensitivity and accuracy of the gauge should be sufficiently high.
5. The gauge should be unaffected by temperature, vibration, humidity or other ambient conditions.
6. The calibration constant for the gauge should be stable over a wide range of temperature and time.
7. The gauge should be capable of indicating both static and dynamic strains.
8. It should be possible to read the gauge either on location or remotely.
9. The gauge should exhibit linear response to strain.
10. The gauge and the associated equipment should be available at a reasonable cost.
11. The gauge should be suitable for use as a sensing element or other transducer systems.

3.5 Types of Resistance Strain Gauges

There are basically four types of electrical resistance strain gauges as classified below :

1. Unbonded gauges :
   (*a*) Non-metallic
   (*b*) Metallic
2. Bonded gauges
   (*a*) Non-metallic
   (*b*) Metallic
      (*i*) Wire type

(*ii*) Foil type.

3. Weldable gauges.
4. Piezoresistive gauges.

1. (*a*) **Unbonded Non-Metallic Gauges.** The unbonded non-metallic gauge is a mechanically actuated gauge that contains a resistance element so arranged that when one part of the gauge is displaced with respect to another there is developed a change in pressure on the measuring element of the gauge. This change in pressure changes the resistance of the element which may be recorded by electrical means. A gauge of this type was developed in 1923 and 1924 by McCollum and Peters and is shown in Fig. 3.8. This gauge is composed of a series of carbon plates arranged in a stack. The stack is so adjusted that a displacement of one part of the gauge relative to another changes the pressure, on the stack of plates. When the strain is applied in the structure to which the gauge is attached, the change in length is communicated to the carbon-plate stack. This change in length requires a change in pressure in the stack, and the resistance of the stack changes.

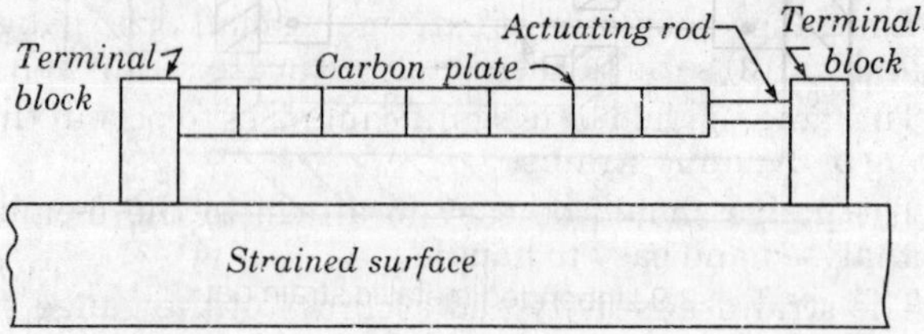

Fig. 3.8 Unbonded non-metallic strain gauge.

With an increase in pressure, the areas of contact between the plates are enlarged and new areas come into contact, thus decreasing the resistance of the element. If the pressure is released, the areas of contact are reduced, and some of the areas lose contact, thus increasing the resistance of the element. If the pressure becomes excessive, so that the elastic limit of the carbon in the gauges is exceeded or the carbon is even crushed, or if the plates are allowed to shift in the lateral direction with respect to each other, the results become erratic. Besides these difficulties, there is a further defect of mechanical friction and hystertsis in the mechanical parts of the gauge.

Gauges of this kind have been used to determine displacements, loads and strains in flexible cables, airplanes, bridges, vibrating members, dynamometers and pressure gauges. However, with the advancement of metallic gauges the usefulness of these type of gauges has reduced materially.

1. (*b*) **Unbonded-Metallic Gauges.** The principle of the unbonded-metallic gauges is based on the change in electrical resistance of a metallic wire due to the change in tension of the wire. The first device of this kind was designed by Carlson and Eaton in 1930. This type of gauge is constructed by winding wire in three coils, the first providing a coil unaffected by the gauge motion, and the other two having tensions altered by the gauge motion, each in an opposite manner. The whole is mounted in a sleeve that allows only longitudinal movement. The coils

are placed under initial tension into a four arm Wheatstone bridge. As the compressive strain is applied, the prestrain would simply be relieved and the unbonded element would remain taut. For the gauge to register compressive strains, the initial assembly must include a built-in tensile prestrain in the coils greater than the maximum compressive strain to be measured. A gauge of this type is shown in Fig. 3.9. These type of gauges are rarely used for experimental stress analysis. However, these type of gauges have been incorporated into accelerometers and pressure pickups.

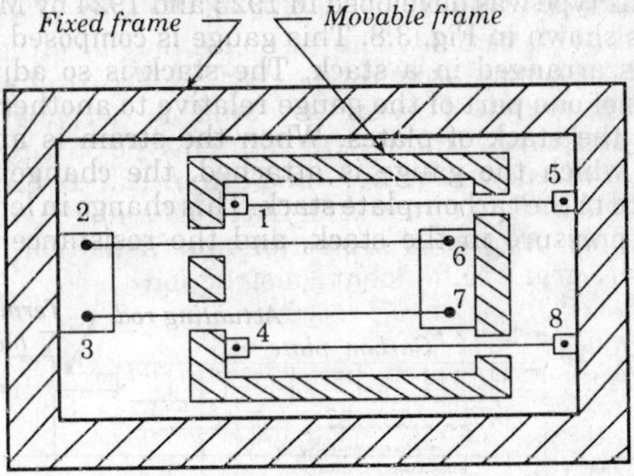

Fig. 3.9 Unbonded metallic strain gauge.

2. (*a*) **Bonded Non-Metallic Gauges.** A strain gauge using direct bonding of a non-metallic resistor element to a material in which the strain is so to be measured was reported by Bloach in 1935. In this gauge a carbon coating is applied directly to the surface of the structure in which strain is to be measured. For metallic structures the surface is first coated with a non-conducting material. If the underlying surface of such a coating is stretched, the carbon particles would move apart, and the under-coating is compressed, the particles would move closer together, and the resistance will change. This resistance change can be interpreted in terms of strain.

Generally these type of gauges are made by impregnating carbon particles in plastic sheets. These sheets are then cut into strips about 6 mm wide and 25 mm long. On each end of the strip a silver band is plated so that lead wires may be attached (Fig. 3.10). The gauge is bonded directly to the surface to be strained with a common glue.

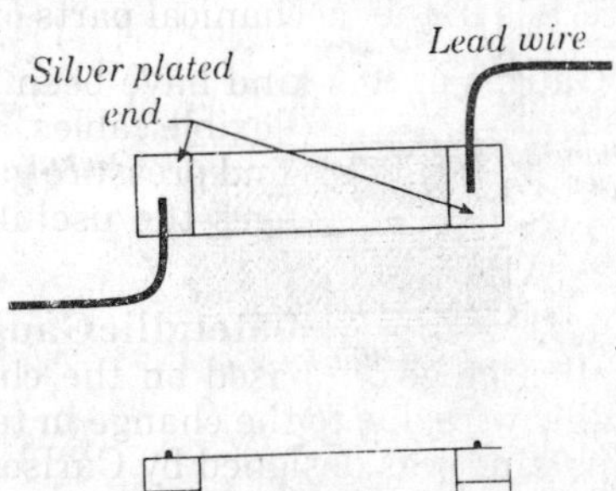

Fig. 3.10 Bonded non-metallic strain gauge.

The sensitivity and resistance of the gauge are affected by temperature and humidity. This gauge is of rugged construction and can withstand rough handling. However, the cross-sensitivity of the gauge is quite high.

2. (*b*) **Bonded Metallic Gauges.** The bonded metallic type of strain gauge consists of a length of a strain-sensitive conductor mounted on a small piece of paper or plastic backing. In use this gauge is cemented to the surface of the structural member to be tested. These gauges may be either of the wire or foil type. In the case of wire strain gauges, the filament consists of a long length of wire in the form of a grid fixed in place with a suitable cement. The wire grid may be either of the flat type (Fig. 3.11 *a*) or wrap-around type (Fig. 3.11 *b*). After attaching the lead wires to the two ends of the grid, a second piece of paper is cemented over the wire as a cover. In the wrap around type of wire gauges, the strain-sensitive wire is wound around a cylindrical core in the form of a close-wound helix. This core is then flattened and cemented between layers of paper for purpose of protection and insulation. Fig. 3.11 (*c*) shows a flat wire grid free filament construction.

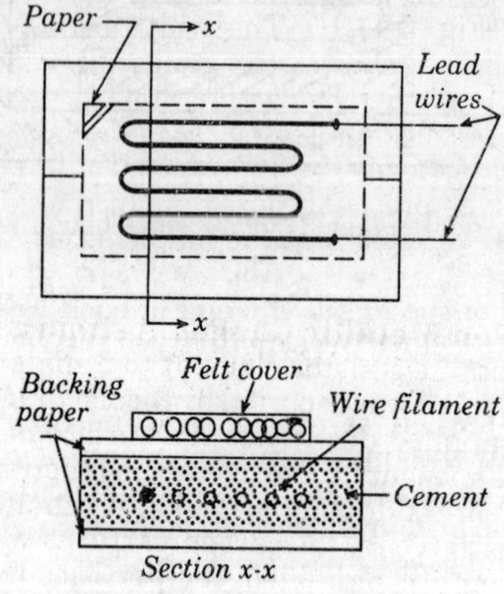

(*a*) Bonded wire flat grid gauge.

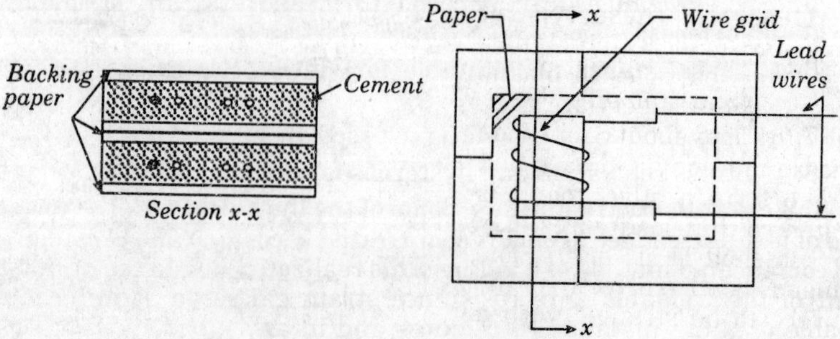

(*b*) Bonded wire wrap-around gauge.

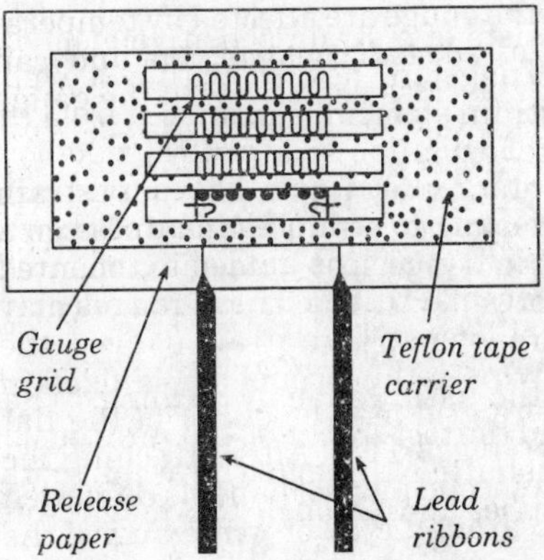

(*c*) Flat wire grid free filament construction.

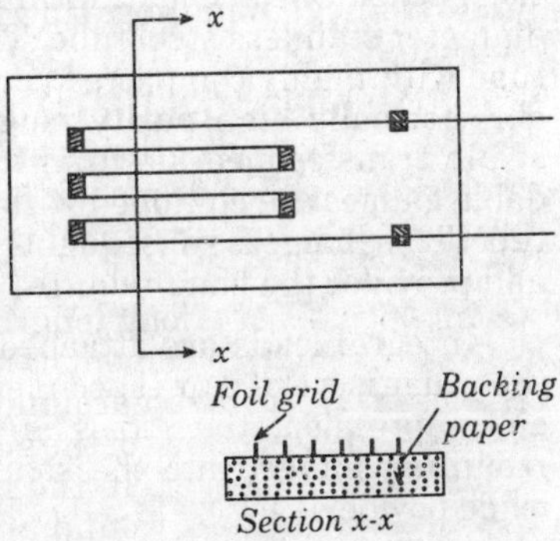

(*d*) Bonded flat foil grid gauge.

Fig. 3.11 Types of bonded metallic gauges.

The foil type of strain gauge has a grid made from a very thin strain-sensitive foil (Fig. 3.11 *d*). The width of foil is very large as compared to the thickness so that the gauge provides a much larger area for cementing the gauge. The gauge configuration is obtained by printing the desired pattern on a sheet of foil with acid resistant ink and subsequently etching away the unprotected metal. Another method of manufacture involves precision punching of the gauges from a foil sheet. The foil type of gauges have the following advantages over the wire type gauges :

1. The width of the foil at the end of each loop can be greatly increased to reduce the sensitivity of the gauge to transverse strains.
2. The cross-section of the gauge conductor is rectangular, resulting in the high ratio of surface area to cross-section area. This increases heat dissipation and avoids adhesion between the grid and the backing material.
3. The gauge factor is higher by 4 to 10 per cent than other gauges.
4. These gauges are easier to manufacture.
5. These gauges can be used to measure strain on curved surfaces.
6. These gauges are suitable for static and dynamic strain measurements.
7. They have very good fatigue properties.
8. Stress relaxation and hysterisis is very less in these gauges.

3. **Weldable strain gauges.** Some of the limitations of the bonded type of metallic gauges are their comparatively costly, time consuming and complicated method of bonding. This realization led to the development of the weldable wire resistance strain gauge—a strain gauge capable of being installed in minutes and in any environment. This unique technique, utilizing capacitive discharge spot welding equipment eliminates the need for all bonding materials.

The weldable strain gauge consists of a strain sensitive element, the Nickel Chrome or Platinum Tungsten, housed within a small diameter stainless steel tube. The strain element is insulated from the tube with highly compacted ceramic insulation or metallic oxide powder, normally high purity magnesium oxide, which also serves as a strain transfer medium from the housing to strain element. The weldable gauges are equipped with a thin flange spot welded to the strain tube. This flange is subsequently spotwelded to the structure under test and provides the bond required to transfer strain.

Integral leads are attached to the basic gauge by welding. When the gauge is welded to a specimen and the test specimen put into tension or compression, the stress is transmitted through the weld to the mounting flange, into the strain tube, and through the magnesium oxide powder.

The basic construction of a quarter-bridge or half-bridge, self-temperature compensated gauge is shown in Fig. 3.12 and includes integral metal sheathed or flexible lead wire configurations. This gauge construction provides inherent mechanical and environmental protection for both the main filament and lead wires and is used over a broad temperature range from cryogenic to 65°C. Weldable strain gauges can be used for a wide range of static and dynamic measurement applications. Their rugged construction and positive attachment make it possible to measure strain at high or low temperatures and in severe environments, including shock and vibration, steam, salt water, chemicals, and other corrosive atmospheres.

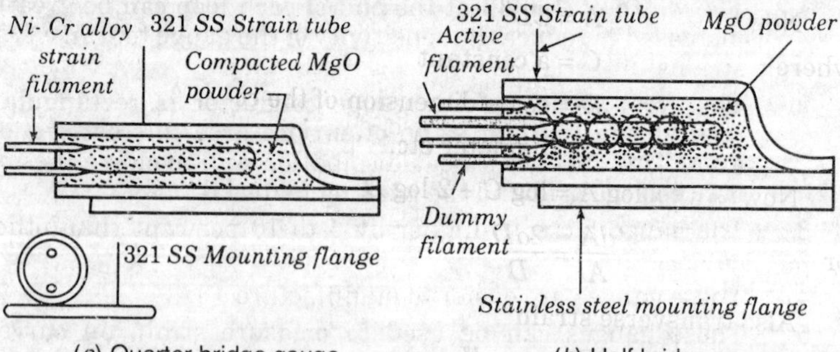

(a) Quarter bridge gauge. (b) Half bridge gauge.

Fig. 3.12 Weldable strain gauges.

4. **Piezo-resistive strain gauges.** Crystals of silicon, germanium, quartz and Rochelle salt show a change in resistance when deformed by applying pressure. This effect can be utilized to measure strain. Such like gauges are called piezo-resistance strain gauges. We shall discuss these gauges in details in chapter 6.

3.6 Selection of Gauges

The following factors should be considered while selecting a strain gauge :

1. Gauge material.
2. Carrier material.

3. Grid geometry.
4. Grid configuration.
5. Gauge factor.
6. Gauge size.
7. Gauge resistance.
8. Cross-sensitivity.
9. Lead-out method.
10. Gauge material form.
11. Adhesive used.
12. Type of strain to be measured.
13. Operating temperature.
14. Environmental condition.

3.7 Gauge Factor

The resistance R of a straight conductor of length L, area of cross-section A and resistivity ρ is given by

$$R = \frac{\rho L}{A} \qquad \text{...(3.14)}$$

If the conductor is stretched, its length will increase and area of cross-section will decrease ; this will result in a change of resistance R. Taking log of both sides of Eq. (3.14), we get

$$\log R = \log \rho + \log L - \log A$$

Differentiating, we get

$$\frac{dR}{R} = \frac{d\rho}{\rho} + \frac{dL}{L} - \frac{dA}{A}$$

Now $\qquad A = CD^2$

where $\qquad C$ = a constant

D = some dimension of the conductor like width, diameter etc.

Now $\qquad \log A = \log C + 2 \log D$

or $$\frac{dA}{A} = \frac{2dD}{D}$$

Also transverse strain

$$\frac{dD}{D} = -\nu \frac{dL}{L}$$

where ν is the Poisson's ratio for the conductor material.

Hence, we find that

$$\frac{dR}{R} = \frac{d\rho}{\rho} + \frac{dL}{L} + 2\frac{\nu dL}{L}$$

$$= \frac{d\rho}{\rho} + (1 + 2\nu)\frac{dL}{L}$$

Now $\qquad \frac{dL}{L} = \varepsilon$, longitudinal strain

Hence $$\frac{dR}{R} = \frac{d\rho}{\rho} + (1 + 2\nu)\,\varepsilon$$

or $$\frac{dR/R}{\varepsilon} = \frac{d\rho/\rho}{\varepsilon} + (1 + 2\nu) \qquad ...(3.15)$$

The term on the left hand side of Eq. (3.15) which represents the change in resistance per unit resistance per unit strain is defined as the gauge factor and is denoted by F. Therefore, Eq. (3.15) may be written as :

$$F = \frac{d\rho/\rho}{\varepsilon} + (1 + 2\nu) \qquad ...(3.16)$$

The term $(d\rho/\rho)/\varepsilon$ is positive for most materials and nearly zero for some ; in a few cases it is negative. The value of Poisson's ratio is nearly 0.3 for most of the materials. Therefore, if we take the value of the first term on the right hand side to be equal to zero, the value of gauge factor should be equal to 1.6 for most of the materials. However, due to the effect of the first term on the right hand side of Eq. (3.16), the value of gauge factor ranges from + 4 to – 12 for most of the materials, with a most common value of approximately 2.0 for the materials generally used for strain gauge construction.

3.8 Materials for Gauges

A good gauge material should have the following qualities :

1. High gauge factor
2. High resistance
3. Low temperature sensitivity
4. High electrical stability
5. High yield point stability
6. High endurance limit
7. Good workability
8. Good solderability and workability
9. Low hysteresis
10. Good corrosion resistance
11. Low thermal e.m.f. when joined with other metals.

The important properties of the most commonly used materials for strain gauges are given in Table 3.1.

3.9 Carrier Materials

A strain-gauge grid is normally supported on some form of carrier material. This provides the necessary electrical insulation between the grid and the material to be tested, dimensional stability, and also provides some degree of mechanical protection for the delicate sensing element. A good carrier material should have the following desirable characteristics :

1. Minimum thickness
2. High mechanical strength
3. High dielectric strength
4. Minimum temperature restrictions
5. Good adherence to cement used
6. Non-hygroscopic.

Table 3.1. Properties of Strain Gauge Materials

Gauge material	*Composition*	*Gauge Factor F*	*Coefficient of expension $\times 10^6$*	*Temperature coefficient $\Delta R/R/C°$*	*Poisson's ratio υ*	*Maximum strain %*	*Temperature range C°*	*Remarks*
Constantan (Copel, Advance)	Cu = 0.55 Ni = 0.45	2.1	15.5	0.00001	0.28	15	– 100 to 300	Self compensated. Excellent linearity, Suitable for static strain measurements.
Iso-elastic (Elinvar)	Ni = 0.36 Cr = 0.08 Fe = 0.52 Mo = 0.04	3.5	8	0.0002	0.36	2	– 50 to 300	Preferred for dynamic strain measurements. Unsuitable in magnetic fields.
Nichrome (Karma and Evanohm)	Ni = 0.75 Fe = 0.12 Cr = 0.11 Mn = 0.02	2.5	10	0.00002	0.36	5	– 270 to 850	Suitable also for dynamic strain measurement and preferred for high temperature measurements.
Manganin	Cu = 0.84 Mn = 0.12 Ni = 0.04	0.47	19	0.00001		—	—	Low gauge factor. Not recommended for use.
Chromel-C	Ni = 0.60 Fe = 0.24 Cr = 0.16	2.5	13	0.0004	0.30	—	—	—

Gauge material	*Composition*	*Gauge Factor F*	*Coefficient of expansion × 10^6*	*Temperature coefficient Δ R/R/C°*	*Poisson's ratio υ*	*Maximum strain %*	*Temperature range C°*	*Remarks*
Monel	Ni = 0.67 Cu = 0.33	19	14	0.002	—	—	—	High temperature coefficient
Invar	Fe = 0.64 Ni = 0.36	19	10	0.002	—	—	—	High gauge factor
Platinum	—	4.8	9	0.003	—	5	600 to 800	Very costly. Rerely used
Platinum-Iridium	Pt = 0.80 Ir = 0.20	6	9	0.001	—	—	—	—
Gold	—	3.2	14	0.0035	—	—	—	Very costly. Rarely used
Phosphor-Bronze	Sn = 0.05 P = 0.01 Cu = 0.94	1.93	17	0.002	0.34	—	—	—
Soft iron	—	4.2	10.5	0.005	0.30	—	—	—
Carbon	—	20	—	- 0.0005	—	—	—	—
Nickel	—	- 12	13	0.006	0.32	—	—	—

Table 3.2. Properties of Carrier Materials for Strain-Gauges

Backing material	*Suitable for type of gauge*	*Suitable adhesive*	*Temperature Range, C°*	*Maximum strain %*	*Electrical Insulation*	*Remarks*
Paper	Wire or foil	Nitrocellulose (Ducos, Durotix)	– 50 to 50	1	Fair	Suitable for use at room temperature and easy to install.
Resin-impregnated Paper. Cellulose Fibres	Wire or foil	Phenolic (Bakelite)	– 50 to 50	2	Good	—do—
Epoxy resin (Polyimide)	Foil	Cyanoacrylate	– 270 to 120	2	Excellent	Suitable for post yield gauges upto 15% strain
Epoxy/fibre glass	Foil	Phenolic	– 270 to 300	—	Excellent	Suitable for moderate temperature and dynamic strains
Ceramic	Free filament wire	Ceramic cements (Forta fix, Rokide etc)	– 200 to 600	—	Excellent	Suitable for high temperature gauges and dynamic strain measurements

The carrier materials may be classified into two categories ; permanent, those become an integral part of the gauge during the manufacturing process, and temporary which can be separated from the sensing element during the installation process. Permanent carriers are generally manufactured from organic materials. The properties of some of the most commonly used carrier materials are given in Table 3.2.

The permanent carriers, in addition to supporting the gauge, provide insulation between the gauge grid and the specimen surface. These carriers are very thin, usually 0.025 mm or less and are flexible enough to maintain intimate mechanical contact with the specimen regardless of the surface contours. Organic carrier systems are produced as cast film or as laminated construction. In the cast film types, a resin is coated and cured directly on the foil without the use of any reinforcing materials. The construction results in a thin, flexible backing capable of high elongation measurements with temperature limits of resin employed. Laminated carriers are constructed of resin impregnated paper or cloth which is transferred to the foil or wire filament and bonded under heat and pressure. Gauges constructed in this manner are generally utilized for high temperature applications and in the manufacture of precision transducers. Many commercial gauges are manufactured with an additional layer of organic material applied over the top of the sensing element. This technique improves the temperature range, extends the fatigue life and provides chemical and mechanical protection for the sensing grid.

Temporary carriers are used where environmental conditions are not suitable to the organic carriers. The stripable carrier is removed during the installation process. This improves the mechanical and thermal contact with the specimen with a minimum increase in specimen stiffness.

3.10 Bonding Cements

The bondable strain gauges are attached to the test specimen by some form of cement or adhesive. A number of bonding cements are available which require various detailed techniques for their use. The following are the desirable characteristics of the bonding cements :

1. High mechanical strength
2. High creep resistance
3. High dielectric strength
4. Minimum temperature restrictions
5. Good adherence giving shear strength of 10.5 to 14 N/mm^2
6. Minimum moisture absorption
7. Ease of application
8. Low setting time.

Nitrocellulose binders, in combination with thin-paper reinforcement serve fairly well as bonding materials upto about 80°C. Phenolic resins are unusual in that their tightly cross-linked structure does not appreciably soften at high temperatures. For this reason, phenolic or 'Bakelite' gauges have long been used when operating temperatures will extend to 200 to 300°C, even though these resins become rather brittle after exposure to high temperature. Certain epoxy, polyimide and polyimide resins are also suitable for long time exposure to these temperatures, with good short term performance to over 300°C. Modern elevated temperature strain-gauges therefore usually employ these resin systems as binders with glass-fibre paper or cloth reinforcement. Because of the wide variation in properties obtainable with different resin and hardener combinations, epoxy resins have become a very important class of strain-gauge adhesives. Phenolics are still used occasionally, and some polyimides are used for temperatures over about 300°C. Fast-cure adhesives such as the cyanoacrylates are very popular for routine stress analysis work. This adhesive is commonly referred to as a contact-setting adhesive.

At about 300° to 700°C, organic plastics oxidize, and soften rapidly. Therefore, strain gauges operating above these temperatures are usually installed with spraying inorganic (ceramic) bonding agents or flame-spraying aluminium oxide onto prepared metal surfaces using a special spray gun. This patented process is known as 'Rokide' and is used for free filament gauges equipped with removable carriers. Advantages offered by this method are : no cure cycle, reduction of installation time and improved mechanical cure adhesives such as the cyanoacrylates are very popular for resistant to nuclear radiation and are particularly suited for vacuum installations where outgassing is prohibited. The properties of most commonly used bonding cements are given in Table 3.3.

3.11 Lead Wire System and Materials

The lead wire system used to transmit electrical signal from the strain gauge to the monitoring instrument or device is as important, to the accuracy and integrity of the strain measurements, as the gauge itself. The entire lead wire network, including the joint or connection between the wire and the strain gauge, must perform satisfactorily under all environment conditions to which the gauge is subjected. The lead wire system should not introduce significant resistance, cause any resistance change, or generate and transmit electrical signals that are not related to strain gauge output. Lead wire systems vary in complexity from simple solder connections between integral gauge leads and insulated main lead wires to multi-wire conductors or ribbons.

Terminals used in strain gauge installations generally are either bondable or weldable. Bondable types consist of copper or beryllium-copper terminals attached to flexible carriers. This style of terminal can be bonded to the specimen at the same time the gauge is applied using the same adhesives and bonding techniques. Weldable terminals are used in high temperature installations. These terminals are usually nickel or nickel plated stainless steel. Connections can also be made by brazing with silver alloy solder provided that the alloy used can withstand the test temperature.

Table 3.3. Properties of Bonding Cements for Strain Gauges

Item	*Organic*							*Ceramic*			
	One component			*Two components (Chemical setting type)*				*Drying heat curing*	*Chemical setting heat curing*	*Molten spray*	*Sintered at high temperature*
	Soluble	*Thermoplastic*	*Pressure sensitive*	*Room temperature curing type*		*Hot setting type*					
Base	Nitro-cellulose	Shellac	Acrylate	Polyester (acrylic)	Epoxy	Epoxy	Phenolic	Silicate	Phosphate	Refractory oxide	Glass
Cement	Duco	De-Khotinsky	—	Eastman—910 Cyanoacrylate	EPY –150	Epy –400	Bakelite	RX–1	AL-P1 PBX	Rokide A & C	I6 AC
Curing temperature (C°)	20 to 60	125	20	20	20	100 to 200	140 to 200	110	300 to 600	None	900
Curing pressure (kg/cm²)	0.007 to 0.035	0.035	0.035	0.035 to 0.07	0.035 to 0.07	0.035 to 0.21	0.07 to 0.35	None	None	None	None
Curing time (Hr)	12 to 48	When cool	—	3 to 15 min	10 to 50	2 to 10	1 to 4	1	1	None	0.5
Maximum operating temperature (C°)	60	40	80	80	80	180	180	250	300 to 800	300 to 800	800
Strain gauge compatibility	Paper	All	Except paper	All	All	All	Only phenolic backed	Stripable and ceramic insulated			
Specimen material compatibility	All except plastics, soluble in acetone	All except some plastics				All except some plastics and reactive metals		All except some Plastics and reactive metals		All except some plastics	All metals that will stand cure temperature

Table 3.3 (Continued)

Strain limit (%)	10 at room $\frac{1}{3}$ at − 150°C	2 to 3	2 to 3	2	2	2	2 to 3	$\frac{1}{2}$	$\frac{1}{2}$	2	$\frac{1}{2}$
Electrical insulation	Excellent						Excellent upto 150°C and poor in 200 to 250°C	Deteriorates with increase in temperature		Excellent but deteriorates at high temperature	Excellent
Humidity Resistance	Fair, absorbs upto 2% water	Good	Moisture sensitive	Fair absorbs upto 0.3% water	Good absorbs upto 0.1% water	Good absorbs upto 0.1% water	Fair, absorbs upto 0.2% water	Poor, hygroscopic soluble in water	Fair, hygroscopic	Good, porous and somewhat hygroscopic	Excellent
Remarks	Suitable for static strain measurement. Requires water proofing.	Suitable for static strain measurements	Injurious to health	Does not keep well. Store in a cool place. Gives an instantaneous bond	Store in a cool place. Toxic	Toxic	Keeps well	High temperature cements			

Copper is the most widely used conductor material because of its low resistivity. Copper, however, has a large temperature coefficient of resistance, is strain sensitive and has poor fatigue and corrosion resistance. Whenever solid copper wire or ribbon is used as an intermediate lead between a gauge tab and a remote terminal, a strain relief loop is required. Standard copper conductors are recommended as main lead wires where motion between the lead and the specimen is anticipated. The use of tinned, plated, or metal-clad solid and standard copper conductors greatly improves the corrosion resistance and increases the operating temperature limit of the wire. Nickel chromium alloys such as Nichrome or Karma are used as conductor materials for high temperature applications. Lead wire or ribbon made of these materials is stable to 370°C and serviceable to about 900°C for dynamic applications. The high resistivity of these alloys limits their use to short lengths at the higher limits of the operating temperature. Beryllium copper is another alloy used as conductor material in either the clad or plated form. This is particularly useful in dynamic applications where strain relief loops cannot be used or where the leads must be bonded directly to the test surface for mechanical reasons.

Lead wires require insulation for which a number of insulating materials suitable for strain gauge work are available. Among these are polyvinylchloride (PVC), Polyethylene, Irradiated-Polyethylene and Nylon. PVC is a rugged, reliable insulation used for general purpose applications where operating temperatures are within the range of – 73° to 65°C. Polyethylene is used for temperature upto 95°C, Irradiated-polyethylene can withstand temperature upto 200°C. Nylon, because of its superior mechanical behaviour in the extreme cold, is best suited for applications in the cryogenic temperature range. Teflon, because of its resistance to mechanical and chemical damage and its wide temperature range (–73° to 260°C) is the most popular insulating material. Polyimide film is wrapped and bonded on conductors to provide a tough, flexible insulation capable of withstanding temperatures upto 420°C. Conductors covered with natural or synthetic rubber materials such as neoprene or silicon are generally selected for use on installations requiring long term exposure to weather environments and immersion in oil or concrete. Rubber insulation has a high resistance to moisture penetration.

When temperature above the range of the organic materials are involved then the lead wire is covered with glass or quartz fibre sleeving. If sleeving is used, it is often impregnated with silicon resin to bond it to the conductor and reduce the tendency to unravel. Ceramic beads made of high purity alumina or magnesium oxide are also used as high temperature insulators.

The lead wire can be attached to the strain-gauge by soldering, brazing or welding. Solder is the material most widely used to join lead conductors to strain gauges. Eutectic solders, alloys of lead, tin, silver or antimony, are designed for abrupt transition from a solid to a liquid state at one atmosphere. The choice of a solder for a particular application is usually determined by the melting point which should be at least 15°C higher than the test temperature.

Structurally sound, electrically reliable, solder or brazed joints cannot be obtained unless surfaces of the mating conductors are clean and free of all oxides. In addition to the solvent removal of oily contaminates and the mechanical abrarison required to remove the oxides, the use of a flux is necessary, during the final forming of the joint. Flux is designed to promote melting and retard the instantaneous forming of oxides during the soldering process. Flux residues should be thoroughly removed upon completion of the joining process. The lead wires of gauges used in high temperature tests can be attached by welding.

3.12 Protective Coatings

Strain gauge installation require various degrees of protection to avoid gauge instability and mechanical damage. Gauges are easily degraded by any chemical attack. Moisture, fingerprints flux residues, etc. are all detrimental. While it is often practical, in the laboratory, to operate fully encapsulated gauges without additional protection, open faced gauges should always have a suitable coating applied as soon possible after installation. Factors influencing the selection of a coating are : the test environment, the test duration, and the accuracy requirements. Coatings used for protecting the gauge installation should not appreciably stiffen the specimen. A large number of commercial coating products are available. We shall describe few of these coatings which have been found to be compatible with the gauge system.

Microcrystalline wax is one of the first coating material used in gauge work. The wax has to be melted and the specimen preheated before application. A wax coating is a most effective barrier to water or humidity but provides very little mechanical protection. Wax coatings are generally limited to use within a temperature range of –73° to 65°C.

Plastic coatings such as liquid vinyls or flexible spray resins systems are resistant to many solvents, chemicals, and in some degree, oil and grease. Vinyl coatings are particularly useful where operation is in the cryogenic temperature range. Epoxy coatings have a higher operating temperature limit than vinyls.

Silicon base materials provide good protection against chemicals and moisture and can be used at temperature upto 425°C. Silicons may convert to harmless silica when upper temperature limits are exceeded.

Synthetic rubber coatings, including neoprene, polysulphides, butyl polymers and room temperature vulcanizing type silicon rubber offer excellent mechanical and environmental protection against moisture, fresh and salt water immersion and spray. The operating temperature range of these materials varies between –73° to + 230°C, depending upon the polymer selected.

Metal foil tapes used in combination with Teflon padding and one or more of the materials described above can be used to protect the gauge against mechanical damage and moisture.

The following precautions should be observed while applying coatings :

1. For long term test, or in particularly hostile environments, carefully clean the surface before applying any protective coating.
2. When several layers of coating are required, extend each overcoat beyond the previous layer.
3. Before applying any protective coating to an unprotected installation which has been exposed to high humidity, dry the installation thoroughly by heating.
4. Generally, a thick coating offers a more difficult path for moisture absorption than a thin one.

3.13 Strain Gauge Application Techniques

A strain gauge can only give best results if it is bonded to the test piece in such a maner so that the strain experienced by the gauge grid is precisely the same as the strain of the test specimen. To achieve this the proper installation of gauge is very important. In fact the bonding technique depends upon the type of gauge and the cement to be used, which is supplied by the manufacturer. Hence the instructions as per manufacturers catalogue should be followed. However, the following steps, in general, may be followed while applying the strain gauge to the test specimens :

1. Surface preparation.
2. Gauge perparation.
3. Adhesive preparation.
4. Gauge installation.
5. Lead wire connection.
6. Environmental protection.

Fig. 3.13 shows a gauge installation technique and Fig. 3.14 shows a proper lead wire layout.

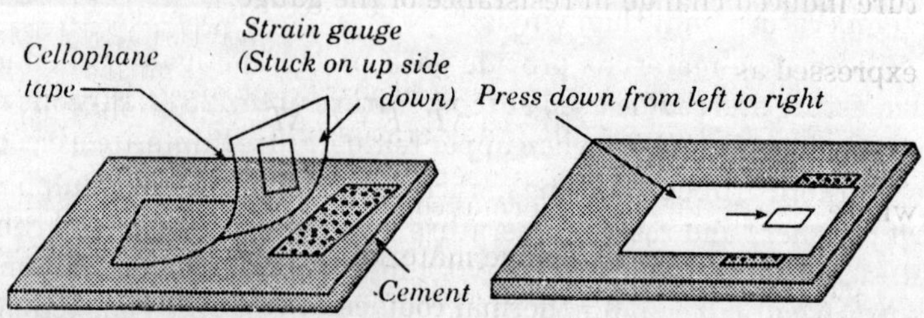

Fig. 3.13 Gauge installation.

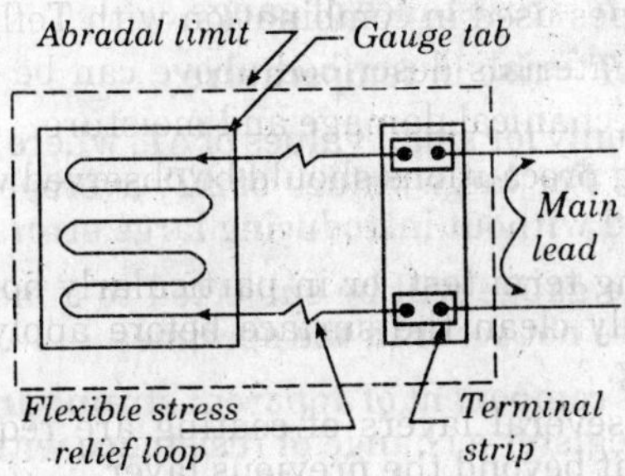

Fig. 3.14 Lead-wire layout method (Post-yield gauge).

3.14 Temperature Compensation

The ideal strain gauge would change resistance in accordance with stress-producing deformations in the structural surface to which it was bonded and for no other reason. Unfortunately, gauge resistance is affected by many other factors, out of which temperature is very important.

The total indicated strain occurring at a point in a structure is made up of mechanical strain and apparent strain. The mechanical strain is that produced by external forces. The apparent strain is the portion of the total indicated strain induced by thermal effects including expansion of the base metal, expansion of the gauge metal and change in electrical resistance of the gauge. Thus, when the ambient temperature increases (say), then

1. The gauge grid will elongate so that $\frac{\Delta l}{l} = \alpha \,.\, \Delta T$.
2. The base material on which the gauge is mounted will elongate so that $\frac{\Delta l}{l} = \beta \,.\, \Delta T$.
3. The resistance of the gauge metal will increase because of the influence of the temperature coefficient of resistivity of the gauge material so that $\frac{\Delta R}{R} = \gamma \,.\, \Delta T$.

The combined effect of these three factors will produce a temperature induced change in resistance of the gauge, $\left(\frac{\Delta R}{R}\right)_{\Delta T}$ which may be expressed as :

$$\left(\frac{\Delta R}{R}\right)_{\Delta T} = (\beta - \alpha)\, \Delta T \,.\, F + \gamma \,.\, \Delta T \qquad \text{...(3.17)}$$

where α = thermal coefficient of expansion of the gauge material

β = thermal coefficient of expansion of the base material

γ = temperature coefficient of resistivity of the gauge material

F = gauge factor

R = resistance of gauge

ΔT = rise in temperature.

Eq. (3.17) holds only for small values of ΔT, where α, β and γ can be considered constant. For large values of ΔT, average values of these factors might be used without introducing large errors.

If $\alpha \neq \beta$, then the gauge will be subjected to a mechanical strain, $(\beta - \alpha)\,\Delta T$, which does not occur in the specimen.

If $\alpha = \beta$, then this component of apparent strain vanishes. However, the gauge will still register a change of resistance with temperature if γ is not zero. In order to prevent significant errors due to this effect, some form of "temperature compensation" is usually employed when strain gauges are used in applications where the steady state or static component of strain must be measured. Currently available methods of compensation for the apparent strain include the use of a dummy or compensating strain gauge, self-temperature compensating (STC) gauge, compensation by dissimilar or similar gauges in the Wheatstone bridges and compensation by computation.

1. **Compensating Dummy Gauge.** The earliest form of temperature compensation makes use of the electrical bridge circuit in which the active gauge is connected to balance out unwanted temperature induced resistance change. This is usually called the "compensating dummy" arrangement. The "dummy gauge" identical to the active gauge in type and lot number, is mounted on an unstressed piece of the specimen material and placed in the same thermal environment as the active gauge. The active and compensating gauges are then connected as adjacent arms of the bridge circuit in the readout instrument. Effects common to both gauges will preserve bridge-balance conditions, and no output signal results. Since only the active gauge is exposed on mechanical or thermal strain caused by specimen stress, bridge unbalance is proportional to the magnitude of specimen stress producing strain. The method fails entirely if the temperature does not vary in an identical fashion at both gauge locations.

2. **Self-temperature Compensated Gauge.** The terms "temperature compensated" is applied to strain gauges in which the resistance change due to temperature is equal to zero. Self-temperature compensated gauges will perform properly only when used on materials having the specific value of thermal expansion coefficient for which they are designed. *STC* gauges can be obtained for use on materials having thermal expansion coefficients from zero to 25 ppm/°C.

Two methods are used for obtaining self-temperature compensation. In the first method, self-temperature compensation is created by altering the temperature coefficient of resistance of the grid material so that, when mounted on materials having a certain thermal expansion coefficient, the apparent strain will be a suitably low value. This is done, in most cases, by special selection or thermal processing of the grid alloy. The two principal classes of strain-gauge alloys susceptible to such treatment are Constantan and Karma. The second method includes forming a grid with two lengths of gauge wires joined suitably in series (Fig. 3.15) so that the resultant apparent strain is zero.

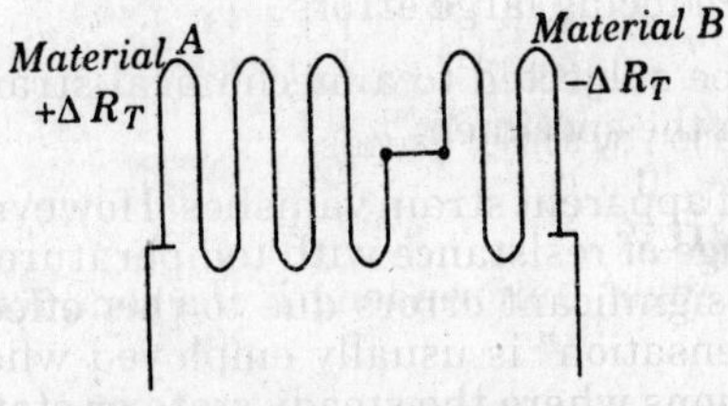

Fig. 3.15 Dual-element self-temperature compensated gauge.

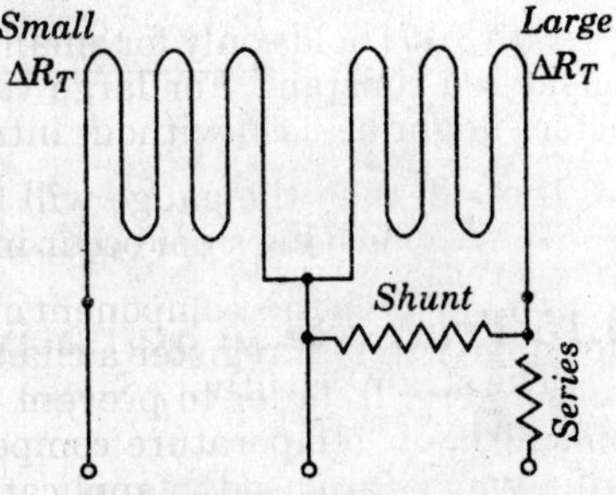

Fig. 3.16 Compensation by dissimilar gauges.

3. **Compensation by Dissimilar Gauges.** Compensation of the temperature effect in a bridge network is accomplished by putting dissimilar gauges into adjacent bridge arms as shown in Fig. 3.16. The gauge in the first arm should have a relatively small temperature effect in the same direction. With proper, fixed series and shunt resistances for the gauge in the second arm, it is possible to obtain an overall temperature effect for the second arm, that is equal to that of the first arm. Hence, the temperature effects of the two arms will cancel each other with a relatively small loss in the strain sensitivity of the network.

This method would appear to have a better chance of success than the self-temperature compensated gauge because the relative resistance of the filament is not critical. It will always be possible after a gauge has been made, to select the fixed resistances for proper compensation. Furthermore, compensation over a greater temperature range might be achieved by adjusting the fixed resistance as temperature increases. In this case, temperature would not have to be known very accurately.

4. **Compensation by Similar Gauges.** Best possible temperature compensation is obtained for unpredictable effects as for predictable effects with two similar gauges in adjacent arms of a Wheatstone bridge. However, this circuit arrangement eliminates the hydrostatic component of stress from the reading and only the shear component of stress is reflected. Hence, the gauges should be arranged so as to pick up the greatest signal from the shear component of stress. This means that one gauge should be positioned in the direction of the maximum principal strain, the other in the direction of minimum principal strain (Fig. 3.17). This method is likely to give best results when the direction of the principal strains is known.

5. **Compensation by Computation.** By knowing the temperature characteristics of a strain gauge and the base metal, and if the temperature can be observed separately, a correction can be calculated theoretically from Eq. (3.17) and applied to the observed strain.

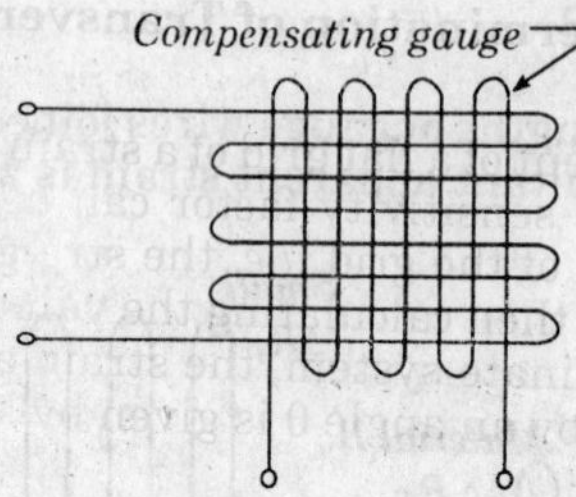

Fig. 3.17 Compensation by similar gauges.

3.15 Transverse Sensitivity

The strain sensitivity S_A of a single, uniform length of a conductor is given by

$$S_A = \frac{\Delta R/R}{\varepsilon}$$

where ε is the uniform strain along the conductor and in the direction of the conductor. Whenever the conductor is wound into a strain-gauge grid, certain effects take place which alter to a certain degree this value of sensitivity of the gauge. The change is introduced by the end loops, which are transverse to the straight portion of the grid. Thus the gauge in addition to measuring the strain along its axis also measures the strain transverse to it. This affect is reflected as an error in the strain gauge reading. This is known as the transverse or cross-sensitivity of the gauge. Now

Axial (parallel) strain sensitivity

$$S_{11} = \frac{\Delta R/R}{\varepsilon_x} \text{ when } \varepsilon_y = 0 \qquad ...(3.19)$$

Normal (perpendicular) strain sensitivity

$$S_{\perp} = \frac{\Delta R/R}{\varepsilon_y} \text{ when } \varepsilon_x = 0 \qquad ...(3.20)$$

Transverse sensitivity factor K is defined as

$$K = \frac{S_{\perp}}{S_{||}} = \frac{\left.\dfrac{\Delta R/R}{\varepsilon_y}\right|_{\varepsilon_x = 0}}{\left.\dfrac{\Delta R/R}{\varepsilon_x}\right|_{\varepsilon_y = 0}} \qquad ...(3.21)$$

Gauge factor F as specified by the manufacturer is

$$F = \frac{\Delta R/R}{\varepsilon_x} \text{ when } \varepsilon_y = -0.285\ \varepsilon_x \qquad ...(3.22)$$

assuming that the gauge has been calibrated on steel whose Poisson's ratio is 0.285.

3.15.1 Theoretical Determination of Transverse Sensitivity Factor

Consider the single element of a flat grid of a strain gauge as shown in Fig. 3.18. The transverse sensitivity factor can be determined by computing R in each portion of the grid (*i.e.* the straight part and the loop), adding the two R's and then calculating the value of K as defined above. Using principal coordinate system, the strain along the loop of wire at any position located by an angle θ is given by :

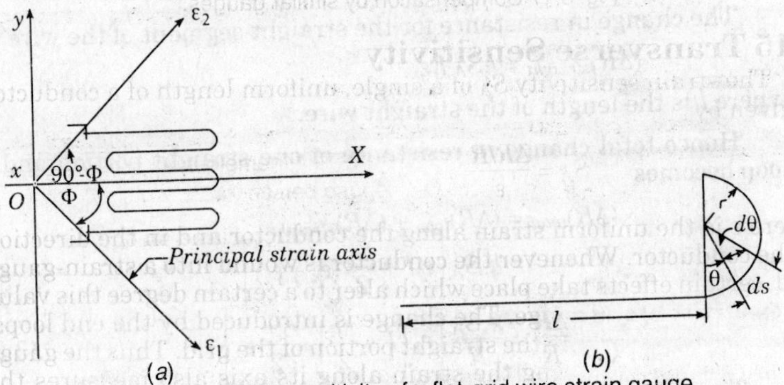

Fig. 3.18 Transverse-sensitivity of a flat-grid wire strain gauge.

$$\varepsilon_\theta = \frac{1}{2}(\varepsilon_1 + \varepsilon_2) + \frac{1}{2}(\varepsilon_1 - \varepsilon_2)\cos 2(\theta + \phi) \quad \text{...(3.23)}$$

Let $\varepsilon_H = \frac{1}{2}(\varepsilon_1 + \varepsilon_2)$, hydrostatic component of strain

$\varepsilon_S = \frac{1}{2}(\varepsilon_1 - \varepsilon_2)$, shear component of strain,

where ϕ is the angle between the direction of measurement and direction of algebraically larger principal strain ε_1.

Then $$\varepsilon_\theta = \varepsilon_H + \varepsilon_S \cos 2(\theta + \phi) \quad \text{...(3.24)}$$

The corresponding change in resistance along the length ds becomes,

$$d(\Delta R) = \varepsilon_\theta S_A \, dR$$
$$= \varepsilon_\theta S_A \, . \, kds$$
$$= \varepsilon_\theta S_A \, . \, (k.rd\theta)$$

where dR = resistance of length $ds = rd\theta$

k = resistance of the wire per unit length

r = radius of the loop

S_A = strain sensitivity of the wire material.

Therefore, the total change in resistance of the semi-circular loop becomes,

$$(\Delta R)_{loop} = k\, S_A \,.\, r \int_0^{\pi} [\varepsilon_H + \varepsilon_S \cos 2\,(\theta + \phi)]\, d\theta$$

$$= k\,.\,S_A\,.\,r\,[\pi\varepsilon_H]$$

$$= k\,.\,S_A\,.\,r\pi\left(\frac{\varepsilon_1 + \varepsilon_2}{2}\right)$$

$$= k\,S_A\,.\,r\,.\,\pi\left(\frac{\varepsilon_x + \varepsilon_y}{2}\right) \qquad [\because \varepsilon_1 + \varepsilon_2 = \varepsilon_x + \varepsilon_y]$$

The change in resistance for the straight segment of the wire is

$$(\Delta R)_{straight} = kS_A\, l\, \varepsilon_x$$

where l is the length of the straight wire.

Hence total change in resistance of one straight portion and one loop becomes

$$(\Delta R)_{total} = (\Delta R)_{loop} + (\Delta R)_{straight}$$

$$= k\,S_A\left[\varepsilon_x l + \frac{\pi r}{2}(\varepsilon_x + \varepsilon_y)\right] \qquad ...(3.25)$$

$$\frac{\Delta R}{R} = \frac{k.S_A}{R}\left[\varepsilon_x\left(l + \frac{\pi r}{2}\right) + \frac{\pi r}{2}\varepsilon_y\right] \qquad ...(3.25a)$$

Transverse sensitivity factor

$$K = \frac{\left.\dfrac{\Delta R/R}{\varepsilon_y}\right|_{\varepsilon_x = 0}}{\left.\dfrac{\Delta R/R}{\varepsilon_x}\right|_{\varepsilon_y = 0}} = \frac{\dfrac{\pi r}{2}}{l + \dfrac{\pi r}{2}} \qquad ...(3.26)$$

If there are m straight lengths in the flat grid and n semicircular loops, then we find that

$$K = \frac{\dfrac{n\pi r}{2}}{ml + \dfrac{n\pi r}{2}} \qquad ...(3.27)$$

For the gauge shown in Fig. 3.18 (a), $m = 6$, $n = 5$. Hence

$$K = \frac{\dfrac{5\pi r}{2}}{6l + \dfrac{5\pi r}{2}} \qquad ...(3.28)$$

It can be seen that the transverse sensitivity factor K is solely dependent on the geometry of the grid and is independent of the biaxiality of the strain field.

3.15.2 Corrections for Transverse Sensitivity

From Eq. (3.26), we find that

$$1 - K = 1 - \frac{\pi r/2}{l + \dfrac{\pi r}{2}} = \frac{l}{l + \dfrac{\pi r}{2}}$$

or $$l + \frac{\pi r}{2} = \frac{l}{1-K}$$

or $$\frac{\pi r}{2} = \frac{Kl}{1-K}$$

Hence Eq. (3.25) becomes

$$(\Delta R)_{total} = k.S_A\left[\left(\frac{l}{1-K}\right)\varepsilon_x + \left(\frac{Kl}{1-K}\right)\varepsilon_y\right]$$

$$= k.S_A\left(\frac{l}{1-K}\right)[\varepsilon_x + K\varepsilon_y]$$

Total length of wire $= l + \pi r$.

Hence total resistance of wire

$$R = k\,(l + \pi r)$$

$$= k\left(l + \frac{2Kl}{1-K}\right)$$

$$= kl\left(\frac{1+K}{1-K}\right)$$

$$\therefore \quad \frac{(\Delta R)_{total}}{R} = \frac{S_A}{(1+K)}(\varepsilon_x + \varepsilon_y) \qquad ...(3.29)$$

(*a*) **Uniaxial strain field.** Let ν be the Poisson's ratio of the material of the test specimen, so that under uniaxial tension along the *x*-axis, the transverse strain along the *y*-axis is

$$\varepsilon_y = -\nu\,\varepsilon_x$$

Substituting in Eq. (3.29), we get

$$\frac{\Delta R}{R} = \frac{S_A\,\varepsilon_x}{1+K}(1 - \nu K) \qquad ...(3.30)$$

During calibration of the strain gauge by the manufacturer, let ν_0 be the Poisson's ratio of the material on which the gauge was calibrated and *F* is the gauge factor specified by the manufacturer, then Eq. (3.30) can be written as,

$$\frac{\Delta R}{R} = \frac{S_A\varepsilon_x}{(1+K)}(1 - \nu_0 K)$$

$$= \varepsilon_x \,.\, F$$

Hence $$F = \frac{S_A}{(1+K)}(1 - \nu_0 K) \qquad ...(3.31)$$

or $$S_A = \frac{F\,(1+K)}{(1 - \nu_0 K)} \qquad ...(3.32)$$

Substituting in Eq. (3.30), we get

$$\varepsilon_x = \frac{\Delta R}{R}\cdot\frac{1}{S_A}\left(\frac{1+K}{1-\nu K}\right)$$

$$= \left(\frac{\Delta R}{R} \cdot \frac{1}{F}\right)\left(\frac{1 - \nu_0 K}{1 - \nu K}\right) \qquad \text{...(3.33)}$$

The first factor $(\Delta R/R)/F$ in Eq. (3.33) represents the reading which would be obtained if the transverse sensitivity effects are ignored. The second term $\left(\frac{1 - \nu_0 K}{1 - \nu K}\right)$ represents the correction factor. The strain readings may be corrected either by knowing the value of F and K as given by the manufacturer, or by using a corrected value of F, while setting the gauge factor of the measuring instrument.

$$F_{corrected} = F\left(\frac{1 - \nu K}{1 - \nu_0 K}\right) \qquad \text{...(3.34)}$$

Apparent strain $\quad \varepsilon_{xa} = (\Delta R/R)/F \qquad$ ...(3.35)

True strain $\quad \varepsilon_{xt} = (\Delta R/R)/F_{corrected} \qquad$ ...(3.36)

where the subscripts 'a' and 't' stand for apparent and true.

Error

$$e = \frac{\varepsilon_{xa} - \varepsilon_{xt}}{\varepsilon_{xt}}$$

$$= \frac{\varepsilon_{xa}}{\varepsilon_{xt}} - 1$$

$$= \left(\frac{1 - \nu K}{1 - \nu_0 K}\right) - 1$$

$$= \frac{K(\nu_0 - \nu)}{(1 - \nu_0 K)} \qquad \text{...(3.37)}$$

(*i*) When the gauge is calibrated on steel ($\nu_0 = 0.285$) and used on aluminium ($\nu = 0.33$), then

$$e = \frac{K(0.285 - 0.33)}{(1 - 0.285\,K)} = \frac{-0.045\,K}{1 - 0.285\,K}$$

(*ii*) When the gauge is calibrated on steel ($\nu_0 = 0.285$) and used on cast iron ($\nu = 0.26$), then

$$e = \frac{0.025\,K}{1 - 0.285\,K}$$

Hence the error may be positive or negative depending upon the material of the specimen.

(*b*) **Biaxial strain field.** To make strain measurements in biaxial strain field, we require two strain gauges, one in the x-direction and the other in the y-direction. The apparent strains measured by the two gauges will be,

$$\varepsilon_{xa} = \frac{(\Delta R/R)_{x\text{-}gauge}}{F}$$

$$\varepsilon_{ya} = \frac{(\Delta R/R)_{y\text{-}gauge}}{F}$$

Now $$\left(\frac{\Delta R}{R}\right)_{x\text{-}gauge} = \frac{F}{(1 - \nu_0 K)}\left[\varepsilon_{xt} + K\,\varepsilon_{yt}\right]$$

$$\left(\frac{\Delta R}{R}\right)_{y\text{-}gauge} = \frac{F}{(1 - \nu_0 K)} [\varepsilon_{yt} + K\,\varepsilon_{xt}]$$

$$\left.\begin{aligned} \varepsilon_{xa} &= \frac{\varepsilon_{xt} + K\,\varepsilon_{yt}}{1 - \nu_0\,K} \\ \varepsilon_{ya} &= \frac{\varepsilon_{yt} + K\,\varepsilon_{xt}}{1 - \nu_0\,K} \end{aligned}\right\} \quad \text{...(3.38)}$$

Solving for the true strains, we get

$$\left.\begin{aligned} \varepsilon_{xt} &= \left(\frac{1 - \nu_0\,K}{1 - K^2}\right)(\varepsilon_{xa} - K\,\varepsilon_{ya}) \\ \varepsilon_{yt} &= \left(\frac{1 - \nu_0\,K}{1 - K^2}\right)(\varepsilon_{ya} - K\,\varepsilon_{xa}) \end{aligned}\right\} \quad \text{...(3.39)}$$

The errors in strains become,

$$\begin{aligned} e_x &= \frac{\varepsilon_{xa} - \varepsilon_{xt}}{\varepsilon_{xt}} \\ &= \frac{\varepsilon_{xa}}{\varepsilon_{xt}} - 1 \\ &= \frac{1}{\varepsilon_{xt}}\left(\frac{\varepsilon_{xt} + K\,\varepsilon_{yt}}{1 - \nu_0\,K}\right) - 1 \\ &= \left(\frac{1}{1 - \nu_0\,K}\right)\left(1 + K\frac{\varepsilon_{yt}}{\varepsilon_{xt}}\right) - 1 \\ &= \frac{K\left(\nu_0 + \dfrac{\varepsilon_{yt}}{\varepsilon_{xt}}\right)}{(1 - \nu_0\,K)} \end{aligned} \quad \text{...(3.40)}$$

$$\begin{aligned} e_y &= \frac{\varepsilon_{ya} - \varepsilon_{yt}}{\varepsilon_{yt}} \\ &= \frac{1}{\varepsilon_{yt}}\left(\frac{\varepsilon_{yt} + K\varepsilon_{xt}}{1 - \nu_0\,K}\right) - 1 \\ &= \frac{K\left(\nu_0 + \dfrac{\varepsilon_{xt}}{\varepsilon_{yt}}\right)}{(1 - \nu_0\,K)} \end{aligned} \quad \text{...(3.41)}$$

When the gauge is calibrated on steel ($\nu_0 = 0.285$) and used on steel with biaxial stress field, then

$$e_x = \frac{K\left(0.285 + \dfrac{\varepsilon_{yt}}{\varepsilon_{xt}}\right)}{(1 - 0.285\,K)}$$

$$e_y = \frac{K\left(0.285 + \dfrac{\varepsilon_{xt}}{\varepsilon_{yt}}\right)}{(1 - 0.285\,K)}$$

(*c*) **Hydrostatic strain field.** For hydrostatic state of strain

$$\varepsilon_x = \varepsilon_y = \varepsilon_H$$

Hence $\dfrac{\Delta R}{R} = F \,.\, \varepsilon_H \left(\dfrac{1 + K}{1 - \nu_0 K}\right)$

and the true hydrostatic strain becomes,

$$\varepsilon_{Ht} = \frac{\Delta R}{R}\,\frac{1}{F}\left(\frac{1 - \nu_0 K}{1 + K}\right)$$

$$= \varepsilon_{Ha}\left(\frac{1 - \nu_0 K}{1 + K}\right) \quad ...(3.42)$$

Similarly the true hydrostatic stress becomes,

$$\sigma_{Ht} = \sigma_{Ha}\left(\frac{1 - \nu_0 K}{1 + K}\right) \quad ...(3.43)$$

Error $\quad e = \dfrac{K\,(1 + \nu_0)}{(1 - \nu_0 K)} \quad ...(3.44)$

(*d*) **Pure shear**

Here $\quad \varepsilon_x = -\,\varepsilon_y = \varepsilon_S.\quad$ Hence,

$$\frac{\Delta R}{R} = F \,.\, \varepsilon_S \left(\frac{1 - K}{1 - \nu_0 K}\right)$$

and the true shear strain becomes,

$$\varepsilon_{St} = \frac{\Delta R}{R}\,.\,\frac{1}{F}\left(\frac{1 - \nu_0 K}{1 - K}\right)$$

$$= \varepsilon_{Sa}\left(\frac{1 - \nu_0 K}{1 - K}\right) \quad ...(3.45)$$

Similarly, the true shear stress becomes,

$$\sigma_{St} = \sigma_{Sa}\left(\frac{1 - \nu_0 K}{1 - K}\right) \quad ...(3.46)$$

Error $\quad e = \dfrac{K\,(\nu_0 - 1)}{(1 - \nu_0 K)} \quad ...(3.47)$

3.15.3 Determination of Poisson's ratio

By definition

$$\text{Poisson's ratio} = \frac{\text{Lateral strain}}{\text{Longitudinal strain}}$$

or $\quad \nu = -\,\dfrac{\varepsilon_{yt}}{\varepsilon_{xt}}$

$$= \frac{-(1-\nu_0 K)(\varepsilon_{xa} - K\varepsilon_{ya})/(1-K^2)}{(1-\nu_0 K)(\varepsilon_{ya} - K\varepsilon_{xa})/(1-K^2)}$$

$$= \frac{-\varepsilon_{xa} + K\varepsilon_{ya}}{\varepsilon_{ya} - K\varepsilon_{xa}} \qquad \text{...(3.48)}$$

where ε_{xa} and ε_{ya} are the measured or apparent maximum and minimum principal strains, respectively, in a uniaxial stress field.

3.15.4 Error in stresses

(*a*) In a biaxial strain field the errors in strains from Eqs. (3.40) and (3.41) are,

$$\left.\begin{aligned} e_x &= \frac{\varepsilon_{xa} - \varepsilon_{xt}}{\varepsilon_{xt}} = \frac{K\left(\nu_0 + \dfrac{\varepsilon_{yt}}{\varepsilon_{xt}}\right)}{(1-\nu_0 K)} \\ e_y &= \frac{\varepsilon_{ya} - \varepsilon_{yt}}{\varepsilon_{yt}} = \frac{K\left(\nu_0 + \dfrac{\varepsilon_{xt}}{\varepsilon_{yt}}\right)}{(1-\nu_0 K)} \end{aligned}\right\} \qquad \text{...(3.49)}$$

and the true strains from Eq. (3.39) are,

$$\left.\begin{aligned} \varepsilon_{xt} &= \frac{(1-\nu_0 K)(\varepsilon_{xa} - K\varepsilon_{ya})}{(1-K^2)} \\ \varepsilon_{yt} &= \frac{(1-\nu_0 K)(\varepsilon_{ya} - K\varepsilon_{xa})}{(1-K^2)} \end{aligned}\right\} \qquad \text{...(3.50)}$$

Now

$$\left.\begin{aligned} \sigma_{xt} &= \frac{E}{(1-\nu^2)}(\varepsilon_{xt} + \nu\,\varepsilon_{yt}) \\ \sigma_{yt} &= \frac{E}{(1-\nu^2)}(\varepsilon_{yt} + \nu\,\varepsilon_{xt}) \end{aligned}\right\} \qquad \text{...(3.51)}$$

True stress ratio,

$$K_{\sigma_t} = \frac{\sigma_{xt}}{\sigma_{yt}} = \frac{\varepsilon_{xt} + \nu\,\varepsilon_{yt}}{\varepsilon_{yt} + \nu\,\varepsilon_{xt}} \qquad \text{...(3.52)}$$

or

$$\frac{\varepsilon_{xt}}{\varepsilon_{yt}} = \frac{K_{\sigma_t} - \nu}{1 - \nu K_{\sigma t}} \qquad \text{...(3.53)}$$

Apparent stresses are

$$\left.\begin{aligned} \sigma_{xa} &= \frac{E}{1-\nu^2}(\varepsilon_{xa} + \nu\,\varepsilon_{ya}) \\ \sigma_{ya} &= \frac{E}{1-\nu^2}(\varepsilon_{ya} + \nu\,\varepsilon_{xa}) \end{aligned}\right\} \qquad \text{...(3.54)}$$

Apparent stress ratio :

$$K_{\sigma a} = \frac{\sigma_{xa}}{\sigma_{ya}} = \frac{\varepsilon_{xa} + \nu\,\varepsilon_{ya}}{\varepsilon_{ya} + \nu\,\varepsilon_{xa}} \qquad \text{...(3.55)}$$

Substituting Eq. (3.53) in (3.49), we find that

$$\left.\begin{aligned} e_x &= \frac{K\left(\nu_0 + \dfrac{1 - \nu K_{\sigma t}}{K_{\sigma t} - \nu}\right)}{(1 - \nu_0 K)} \\ e_y &= \frac{K\left(\nu_0 + \dfrac{K_{\sigma t} - \nu}{1 - \nu K_{\sigma t}}\right)}{(1 - \nu_0 K)} \end{aligned}\right\} \quad \text{...(3.56)}$$

and

$$\left.\begin{aligned} \varepsilon_{xa} &= (1 + e_x)\,\varepsilon_{xt} \\ \varepsilon_{ya} &= (1 + e_y)\,\varepsilon_{yt} \end{aligned}\right\} \quad \text{...(3.57)}$$

Error in $\sigma_{xt} = \dfrac{\sigma_{xa} - \sigma_{xt}}{\sigma_{xt}}$

$$= \frac{\varepsilon_{xa} + \nu\,\varepsilon_{ya} - \varepsilon_{xt} - \nu\,\varepsilon_{yt}}{\varepsilon_{xt} + \nu\,\varepsilon_{yt}}$$

Using Eq. (3.57), the error becomes

$$= \frac{e_x\,\varepsilon_{xt} + \nu\,e_y\,\varepsilon_{yt}}{\varepsilon_{xt} + \nu\,\varepsilon_{yt}}$$

$$= \frac{e_x \dfrac{\varepsilon_{xt}}{\varepsilon_{yt}} + \nu\,e_y}{\dfrac{\varepsilon_{xt}}{\varepsilon_{yt}} + \nu}$$

Substituting the value of e_x and e_y from Eq. (3.56) and $\dfrac{\varepsilon_{xt}}{\varepsilon_{yt}}$ from Eq. (3.53), we get

Error in $\sigma_{xt} = \dfrac{K\,(1 + \nu_0\,K_{\sigma t})}{K_{\sigma t}\,(1 - \nu_0\,K)}$ ...(3.58)

Similarly error in σ_{yt}

$$= \frac{K\,(\nu_0 + K_{\sigma t})}{(1 - \nu_0\,K)} \quad \text{...(3.59)}$$

Error in $K_{\sigma t} = \dfrac{K_{\sigma a} - K_{\sigma t}}{K_{\sigma t}}$

Using Eqs. (3.52) and (3.55), the error in $K\sigma_t$ becomes

$$= \frac{(e_x - e_y)\,(1 - \nu^2)}{\left(\dfrac{\varepsilon_{yt}}{\varepsilon_{xt}} + e_y\,\dfrac{\varepsilon_{yt}}{\varepsilon_{xt}} + \nu + \nu\,e_x\right)\left(\dfrac{\varepsilon_{xt}}{\varepsilon_{yt}} + \nu\right)}$$

Using Eqs. (3.56) and (3.53), we get

$$= \frac{K\,(1 - K_{\sigma t}^2)}{K_{\sigma t}\,(1 + K_{\sigma t})} \quad \text{...(3.60)}$$

Substituting the values of ε_{xt} and ε_{yt} from Eq. (3.50) in (3.52), we get

$$K_{\sigma t} = \frac{\varepsilon_{xa}\,(1 - \nu K) + \varepsilon_{ya}\,(\nu - K)}{\varepsilon_{ya}\,(1 - \nu K) + \varepsilon_{xa}\,(\nu - K)}$$

$$= \frac{K_{\sigma a} - K}{1 - K_{\sigma a}\,K} \qquad \ldots(3.61)$$

(*b*) Let $\varepsilon_{1a}, \varepsilon_{2a}$ = Principal strains neglecting transverse sensitivity errors.

σ_{1a}, σ_{2a} = Principal stresses neglecting transverse sensitivity errors.

ν_a, ν = Apparent and true values of Poisson's ratio respectively.

Then for a uniaxial state of stress, where $\sigma_y = \tau_{xy} = 0$ and σ_x direction is known, we have, by using a single gauge,

$$\sigma_{1t} = E\,\varepsilon_{1t}$$

$$\varepsilon_{2t} = -\,\nu\,\varepsilon_{1t}$$

$$\varepsilon_{2a} = -\,\nu_a\,\varepsilon_{1a}$$

$$\sigma_{1a} = E\,\varepsilon_{1a}$$

Now
$$\varepsilon_{1t} = \left(\frac{1 - \nu_0 K}{1 - K^2}\right)(\varepsilon_{1a} - K\,\varepsilon_{2a}) \qquad \ldots(3.62)$$

Hence
$$\sigma_{1t} = E\,\varepsilon_{1a}\left(\frac{1 - \nu_0 K}{1 - K^2}\right)\left(1 - K\,\frac{\varepsilon_{2a}}{\varepsilon_{1a}}\right)$$

$$= \sigma_{1a}\left(\frac{1 - \nu_0 K}{1 - K^2}\right)(1 + \nu_a K)$$

Now
$$\nu_a = \frac{\nu - K}{1 - \nu K} \qquad \ldots(3.63)$$

$\therefore$
$$\sigma_{1t} = \sigma_{1a}\left(\frac{1 - \nu_0 K}{1 - K^2}\right)\left[1 + K\left(\frac{\nu - K}{1 - \nu K}\right)\right]$$

$$= \sigma_{1a}\left(\frac{1 - \nu_0 K}{1 - \nu K}\right) \qquad \ldots(3.64)$$

or
$$\frac{\sigma_{1t}}{\sigma_{1a}} = \frac{1 - \nu_0 K}{1 - \nu K}$$

Hence the error in σ_{1t} due to transverse sensitivity becomes

$$\Delta_1 = \frac{\sigma_{1a} - \sigma_{1t}}{\sigma_{1a}} = \frac{K\,(\nu_0 - \nu)}{(1 - \nu K)} \approx K\,(\nu_0 - \nu) \qquad \ldots(3.65)$$

where νK has been neglected as compared to 1 in the denominator.

(*c*) For an isotropic state of stress, $\sigma_x = \sigma_y = \sigma_1 = \sigma_2$ and $\tau_{xy} = 0$. Again using a single gauge and noting that in this case,

$$\sigma_1 = \sigma_2 = \frac{E\,\varepsilon}{1 - \nu}$$

where ε is the strain in any direction.

From Eq. (3.62), we have

$$\varepsilon_t = \frac{\varepsilon_a (1 - \nu_0 K)(1 - K)}{(1 - K^2)} \qquad \text{...(3.66)}$$

$$\sigma_{1a} = \left(\frac{E}{1 - \nu}\right)\varepsilon_a$$

$$\sigma_{1t} = \frac{\sigma_{1a}(1 - \nu_0 K)}{(1 + K)}$$

Then $$\Delta_1 = 1 - \frac{\sigma_{1t}}{\sigma_{1a}} = \frac{K(1 + \nu_0)}{(1 + K)} \qquad \text{...(3.67)}$$

(*d*) Two element rectangular rosette

$$\sigma_{1t} = \frac{E}{1 - \nu^2}(\varepsilon_{1t} + \nu\,\varepsilon_{2t})$$

$$\sigma_{2t} = \frac{E}{1 - \nu^2}(\varepsilon_{2t} + \nu\,\varepsilon_{1t})$$

Let $$K\varepsilon_a = \frac{\varepsilon_{2a}}{\varepsilon_{1a}} \text{ and } W = \frac{1 - \nu_0 K}{1 - K^2}$$

Then $$\varepsilon_{1t} = W(\varepsilon_{1a} - K\,\varepsilon_{2a})$$

$$\varepsilon_{2t} = W(\varepsilon_{2a} - K\,\varepsilon_{1a})$$

Also $$\sigma_{1a} = \frac{E}{1 - \nu^2}(\varepsilon_{1a} + \nu\,\varepsilon_{2a})$$

Hence $$\Delta_1 = \frac{\sigma_{1a} - \sigma_{1t}}{\sigma_{1a}}$$

$$= \frac{\varepsilon_{1a} + \nu\,\varepsilon_{2a} - W(\varepsilon_{1a} - K\,\varepsilon_{2a}) - \nu\,W(\varepsilon_{2a} - K\,\varepsilon_{1a})}{(\varepsilon_{1a} + \nu\,\varepsilon_{2a})}$$

$$= \frac{(1 - W + \nu\,WK) + K_{\varepsilon a}(\nu + WK - \nu W)}{(1 + \nu\,K\,\varepsilon_a)}$$

Neglecting K^2 with respect to 1, $W \approx (1 - \nu_0 K)$

Hence $$\Delta_1 = \frac{(\nu_0 K + \nu K - \nu\nu_0 K^2) + K_{\varepsilon a}(K - \nu_0 K^2 + \nu\,\nu_0 K)}{(1 + \nu\,K_{\varepsilon a})}$$

$$\approx \frac{K}{1 + \nu K_{\varepsilon a}}[\nu_0 + \nu + K_{\varepsilon a} + \nu\,\nu_0\,K_{\varepsilon a}]$$

$$= K\left[\frac{\nu + K_{\varepsilon a}}{1 + \nu\,K_{\varepsilon a}} + \nu_0\right] \qquad \text{...(3.68)}$$

Similarly error in σ_{2t} becomes

$$\Delta_2 = \frac{\sigma_{2a} - \sigma_{2t}}{\sigma_{2a}}$$

$$= K\left[\frac{1 + \nu\,K_{\varepsilon a}}{\nu + K_{\varepsilon a}} + \nu_0\right] \qquad \text{...(3.69)}$$

3.15.5 Mohr's circle method for transverse sensitivity corrections

Let A = distance from origin to centres of concentric Mohr circles

B = radius of strain or stress circle

K_σ, K_ε = ratio of principal stresses and strains respectively

r = relative resistance change, $\Delta R/R$

ϕ = angle between direction of measurement and direction of algebraically larger principal stress or strain

Δ, Δ' = derived gauge factors replacing F, K and ν_0.

Subscripts a = apparent

ma = modified apparent

t = true

l, c = longitudinal and transverse (cross) directions on calibration bar

1, 2 = principal directions on investigated component, also number of gauge in coaxial pair.

(*a*) **Concentric circles.** It is known that stress and strain circles can be plotted concentrically if the stress and strain origins are plotted at different points of the abscissa in the Mohr diagram and if appropriate scale factors are introduced. The same technique can be used for the circles of "apparent" and of "true" values of strain and stress.

The parametric equations of the various concentric circles are (Fig. 3.19).

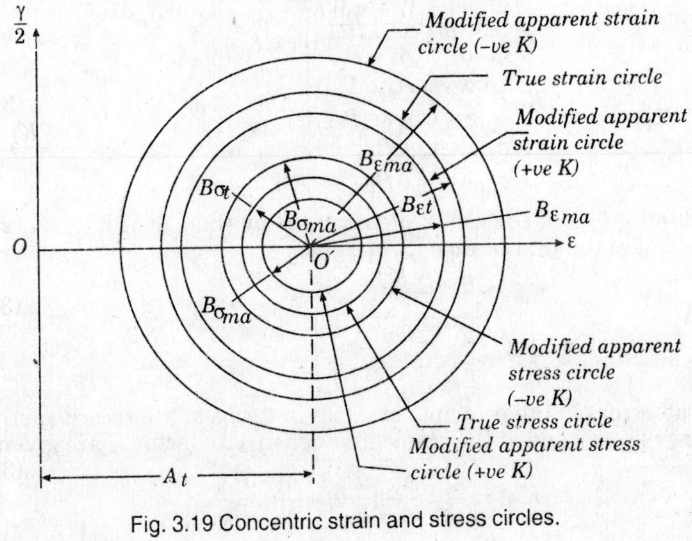

Fig. 3.19 Concentric strain and stress circles.

$$\left.\begin{aligned} \varepsilon_t &= A_t + B_{\varepsilon t} \cos 2\phi \\ \varepsilon_a &= A_a + B_{\varepsilon a} \cos 2\phi \\ \varepsilon_{ma} &= A_t + B_{\varepsilon ma} \cos 2\phi \end{aligned}\right\} \qquad \text{...(3.70)}$$

$$\left.\begin{aligned} \sigma_t &= \frac{1-\nu}{E} = A_t + B_{\sigma t} \cos 2\phi \\ \sigma_a &= \frac{1-\nu}{E} = A_a + B_{\sigma a} \cos 2\phi \\ \sigma_{ma} &= \frac{1-\nu}{E} = A_t + B_{\sigma ma} \cos 2\phi \end{aligned}\right\} \qquad \text{...(3.71)}$$

with

$$\left.\begin{aligned} \frac{A_a}{A_t} &= \frac{1+K}{1-\nu_0 K} \\ \frac{B_{\varepsilon a}}{B_{\varepsilon t}} &= \frac{B_{\sigma a}}{B_{\sigma t}} = \frac{1-K}{1-\nu_0 K} \\ \frac{B_{\sigma t}}{B_{\varepsilon t}} &= \frac{1-\nu}{1+\nu} \\ \frac{B_{\varepsilon ma}}{B_{\varepsilon t}} &= \frac{B_{\sigma ma}}{B_{\sigma t}} = \frac{1-K}{1+K} \end{aligned}\right] \qquad \text{...(3.72)}$$

It is seen from Eq. (3.72) that the "modified apparent" circles have a larger radius than the "true" circles, if K has a negative value. The significance of the "modified" apparent circles lies in the fact that

$$\frac{A_a}{A_t} = \frac{A_a}{A_{ma}} = \frac{B_{\sigma a}}{B_{\sigma ma}} = \frac{B_{\varepsilon a}}{B_{\varepsilon ma}} = \frac{\varepsilon_a}{\varepsilon ma} = \frac{1+K}{1-\nu_0 K} \qquad \text{...(3.73)}$$

so that εma is proportional to ε_a whilst sharing with ε_t the constant value A_t.

(*b*) **Corrections for transverse sensitivity.** From Eq. (3.71), we have

$$\left.\begin{aligned} K_{\sigma t} &= \frac{\sigma_{1t}}{\sigma_{2t}} = \frac{A_t + B_{\sigma t}}{A_t - B_{\sigma t}} \\ K_{\sigma a} &= \frac{\sigma_{1a}}{\sigma_{2a}} = \frac{A_a + B_{\sigma a}}{A_a - B_{\sigma a}} \\ \frac{\sigma_{1a}}{\sigma_{1t}} &= \frac{A_a + B_{\sigma a}}{A_t + B_{\sigma t}} \end{aligned}\right\} \qquad \text{...(3.74)}$$

Elimination of the constants A and B by the use of Eqs. (3.72) or (3.73) and of the first of Eqs. (3.74), gives

$$K_{\sigma t} = \frac{K_{\sigma a} - K}{1 - K_{\sigma a} K}$$

and

$$\frac{\sigma_{1a} - \sigma_{1t}}{\sigma_{1t}} = \frac{K(1+\nu_0 K_{\sigma t})}{K_{\sigma t}(1-\nu_0 K)} \qquad \text{...(3.75)}$$

The errors in the principal stresses in terms of the recorded strain readings ε_{1a}, ε_{2a} and of the transverse sensitivity factor K are given by

$$K_{\varepsilon a} = \frac{\varepsilon_{2a}}{\varepsilon_{1a}} = \frac{A_a - B_{\varepsilon a}}{A + B_{\varepsilon a}} = \frac{A_t - B_{\varepsilon ma}}{A_t + B_{\varepsilon ma}}$$

$$\frac{\sigma_{1a} - \sigma_{1t}}{\sigma_{1a}} = 1 - \left(\frac{A_t + B_{\sigma t}}{A_t + B_{\sigma ma}}\right)\left(\frac{1 - \nu_0 K}{1 + K}\right) \qquad ...(3.76)$$

Elimination of A_t by means of the first of these equations, insertion of Eq. (3.72), and omission of terms in K^2, since K is usually small, leads to,

$$\frac{\sigma_{1a} - \sigma_{1t}}{\sigma_{1a}} = K\left[\frac{K_{\varepsilon a} + \nu}{1 + \nu K_{\varepsilon a}} + \nu_0\right] \qquad ...(3.77)$$

(*c*) **Calibration.** If two identical gauges, l and c, are affixed in longitudinal and transverse directions on the calibration bar strained in pure bending, then the concentric circle method leads at once from Eq. (3.72) to,

$$\left.\begin{aligned}
2A_t &= \varepsilon_{lt} + \varepsilon_{ct} = \varepsilon_{lma} + \varepsilon_{cma} \\
&= \left(\frac{1 - \nu_0 K}{1 + K}\right)(\varepsilon_{la} + \varepsilon_{ca}) \\
&= \left(\frac{1 - \nu_0 K}{1 + K}\right). 1/F \,.\, (r_l + r_c) \\
2B_{\varepsilon t} &= \varepsilon_{lt} - \varepsilon_{ct} \\
&= \left(\frac{1 - \nu_0 K}{1 - K}\right)(\varepsilon_{la} - \varepsilon_{ca}) \\
&= \left(\frac{1 - \nu_0 K}{1 - K}\right). 1/F \,.\, (r_l - r_c)
\end{aligned}\right] \qquad ...(3.78)$$

Hence, if ε_{lt} and ε_{ct} are measured separately by extensometer during calibration or if $\nu_0 = -\dfrac{\varepsilon_{ct}}{\varepsilon_{lt}}$ of the calibration bar is known and ε_{lt} measured, then all the ratios of Eq. (3.72) can be calculated from the calibration strain gauge readings, ε_{la} and ε_{ca}, except the ratio $B_{\sigma t}/B_{\varepsilon t}$, which must be determined on the actual test object. It is thus not necessary to determine K explicitly for each gauge batch. In fact it will lead to increased precision in measurement evaluation if calibration is used to determine the factors,

$$\Delta = \frac{1 - \nu_0 K}{F(1 + K)} \quad \text{and} \quad \Delta' = \frac{1 - \nu_0 K}{F(1 - K)} \qquad ...(3.79)$$

instead of the gauge factor, F, and the transverse sensitivity K. From Eq. (3.79) or (3.78) with $\varepsilon_{ct} = -\nu_0\, \varepsilon_{lt}$, we also obtain,

$$K = \frac{\Delta' - \Delta}{\Delta' + \Delta} = \frac{\nu_0 + r_c/r_l}{1 - \nu_0 r_c/r_l} \qquad ...(3.80)$$

Hence if Δ and Δ' are indicated on the gauge packet instead of F, K and ν_0 the strain gauge user can decide for himself whether correction is worthwhile for his purpose or whether $\Delta \approx \Delta' \approx 1/F$ will suffice.

(*d*) **Measurements in biaxial strain fields.** For an orthogonal pair affixed in arbitrary directions p, q, the line pq on the circle diagram (Fig. 3.20) applies. From Fig. 3.20 and Eqs. (3.70) and (3.72), it follows that

$$\varepsilon_{pt},\ \varepsilon_{qt} = OO \pm \frac{1}{2} PQ$$

$$= \frac{1}{2}(\varepsilon_{pt} + \varepsilon_{qt}) \pm \frac{1}{2}(\varepsilon_{pt} - \varepsilon_{qt})$$

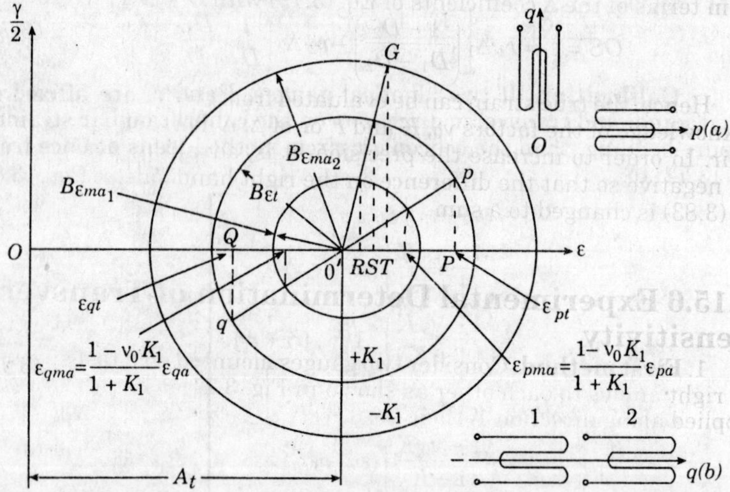

Fig. 3.20 Strain circles of a point in biaxial strain field. (*a*) Orthogonal pair, (*b*) Coaxial pair.

$$= \frac{1}{2}(\varepsilon_{pma} + \varepsilon_{qma}) \pm \frac{1}{2}\left(\frac{1 + K_1}{1 - K_1}\right)(\varepsilon_{pma} - \varepsilon_{qma})$$

$$= \frac{1}{2}\left(\frac{1 - \nu_0 K_1}{1 + K_1}\right)(\varepsilon_{pa} + \varepsilon_{qa}) \pm \frac{1}{2}\left(\frac{1 - \nu_0 K_1}{1 - K_1}\right)(\varepsilon_{pa} - \varepsilon_{qa})$$

$$= \frac{1}{2}\Delta(r_p + r_q) \pm \frac{1}{2}\Delta'(r_p - r_q) \qquad \text{...(3.81)}$$

Here the true strains are obtained from the gauge reading r_p and r_q if Δ and Δ' are known or have been calibrated as described above.

Results from a coaxial gauge pair with transverse sensitivity factors K_1 and K_2 affixed in an arbitrary direction, *q*, may be represented in Fig. 3.20 by the line *O′G*. Fig. 3.20 has been drawn for positive K_1 and negative K_2. If both are assumed positive, then in Fig. 3.20.

$$OS = \varepsilon_t = \varepsilon_{1ma} + RS = \varepsilon_{2ma} + TS$$

with
$$\frac{RS}{TS} = \frac{O'S - O'R}{O'S - O'T} = \frac{B\varepsilon_t - B_{\varepsilon ma1}}{B_{\varepsilon 1} - B_{\varepsilon ma1}} = C$$

RS and *TS* can be eliminated from the last two equations to give,

$$OS = \varepsilon_{1ma}\left(\frac{1}{1 - C}\right) - \varepsilon_{2ma}\left(\frac{C}{1 - C}\right)$$

Insertion of the ratio $B_{\varepsilon ma}/B_{\varepsilon t}$ from Eq. (3.72) and of $\varepsilon_a/\varepsilon_{ma} = \dfrac{1+K}{1-\nu_0 K}$ from Eq. (3.73) and Eq. (3.70) results in

$$OS = \varepsilon_t - \varepsilon_{1a} = \frac{(1-\nu_0 K_1)\,K_2}{(K_1 - K_2)} + \varepsilon_{2a}\,\frac{(1-\nu_0 K_2)\,K_1}{(K_1 - K_2)} \qquad \text{...(3.82)}$$

or in terms of the Δ coefficients of Eq. (3.79) with $D = \Delta/\Delta'$, we get

$$OS = \varepsilon_t = r_1\,\Delta_1\left(\frac{1-D_2}{D_1 - D_2}\right) - r_2\,\Delta_2\left(\frac{1-D_1}{D_1 - D_2}\right) \qquad \text{...(3.83)}$$

Hence, the true strain can be evaluated from the readings and from a knowledge of the factors ν_0, K and F or of Δ, Δ' for each gauge in the pair. In order to increase the precision, it is, advantageous to choose K_2 negative so that the difference on the right hand side of Eqs. (3.82) or (3.83) is changed to a sum.

3.15.6 Experimental Determination of Transverse Sensitivity

1. **First method.** Consider two gauges mounted on a test specimen at right angles to each other as shown in Fig. 3.21. When the stress is applied along direction 1, then

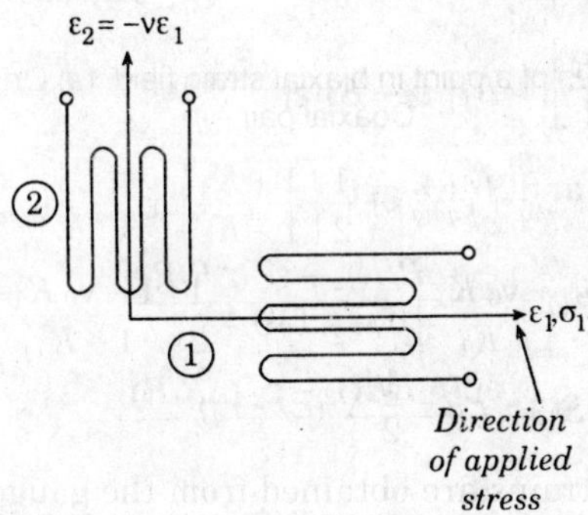

Fig. 3.21

$$\left(\frac{\Delta R}{R}\right)_1 = S_{\parallel}\,\varepsilon_1 + S_{\perp}\,\varepsilon_2$$

$$= S_{\parallel}\,\varepsilon_1 - \nu S_{\perp}\,\varepsilon_1$$

$$= \varepsilon_1\,(S_{\parallel} - \nu S_{\perp})$$

and $$\left(\frac{\Delta R}{R}\right)_2 = \varepsilon_1\,(S_{\perp} - \nu S_{\parallel})$$

Solving for $S_{\parallel}$ and $S_{\perp}$, we get

$$S_\perp = \frac{\left(\dfrac{\Delta R}{R}\right)_2 + \nu \left(\dfrac{\Delta R}{R}\right)_1}{\varepsilon_1 (1 - \nu^2)}$$

$$S_{||} = \frac{\left(\dfrac{\Delta R}{R}\right)_1 + \nu \left(\dfrac{\Delta R}{R}\right)_2}{\varepsilon_1 (1 - \nu^2)}$$

Thus $$K = \frac{S_\perp}{S_{||}} = \frac{\left(\dfrac{\Delta R}{R}\right)_2 + \nu \left(\dfrac{\Delta R}{R}\right)_1}{\left(\dfrac{\Delta R}{R}\right)_1 + \nu \left(\dfrac{\Delta R}{R}\right)_2}$$

$$= \frac{\nu + X}{1 + \nu X} \qquad \text{...(3.84)}$$

where $X = (\Delta R/R)_2/(\Delta R/R)_1$.

2. **Second method.** Two gauges with known K's and two gauges of unknown K's are mounted side by side along the principal axes 1 and 2 in a uniaxial stress field. The readings on test gauges are given by

$$\left(\frac{\Delta R}{R}\right)_1 = S_{||}\, \varepsilon_1 + S_\perp\, \varepsilon_2$$

$$\left(\frac{\Delta R}{R}\right)_2 = S_{||}\, \varepsilon_2 + S_\perp\, \varepsilon_1$$

Solving for $S_{||}$ and $S_\perp$ we get

$$S_{||} = \frac{\varepsilon_2\, (\Delta R/R)_2 - \varepsilon_1\, (\Delta R/R)_1}{\varepsilon_2^2 - \varepsilon_1^2}$$

$$S_\perp = \frac{\varepsilon_1\, (\Delta R/R)_2 - \varepsilon_2\, (\Delta R/R)_1}{\varepsilon_1^2 - \varepsilon_2^2}$$

Thus $$K = \frac{S_\perp}{S_{||}} = \frac{[\varepsilon_1\, (\Delta R/R)_2 - \varepsilon_2\, (\Delta R/R)_1]/(\varepsilon_1^2 - \varepsilon_2^2)}{[\varepsilon_2\, (\Delta R/R)_2 - \varepsilon_1\, (\Delta R/R)_1]/(\varepsilon_2^2 - \varepsilon_1^2)}$$

$$= \frac{\varepsilon_2 - X\varepsilon_1}{X\varepsilon_2 - \varepsilon_1} \qquad \text{...(3.85)}$$

For reference gauges

$$\varepsilon_1^* = \frac{K^*\, (\Delta R/R)_2^* - (\Delta R/R)_1^*}{S_{||}^*\, (K^{*2} - 1)}$$

$$\varepsilon_2^* = \frac{(\Delta R/R)_2^* - K^*\, (\Delta R/R)_1^*}{S_{||}^*\, (1 - K^{*2})}$$

If $\varepsilon_2 = \varepsilon_2^*,\ \varepsilon_1 = \varepsilon_1^*,$ then

$$K = \frac{(K^* - X^*) - X\,(K^*X^* - 1)}{X\,(K^* - X^*) - (K^*X^* - 1)} \qquad \text{...(3.86)}$$

where K^* is the known cross-sensitivity and

$$X^* = (\Delta R/R)_2^*/(\Delta R/R)_1^*.$$

3. **Third method.** The strain along any direction q inclined at an angle θ is given by

$$\varepsilon_q = \varepsilon_1 \cos^2\theta + \varepsilon_2 \sin^2\theta$$

Now $\qquad \varepsilon_2 = -\nu\,\varepsilon_1$

Hence $\qquad \varepsilon_q = \varepsilon_1 (\cos^2\theta - \nu \sin^2\theta)$

$$\frac{\cos^2\theta}{\sin^2\theta} = \nu \quad \text{or } \tan\theta = \sqrt{\frac{1}{\nu}}, \text{ then } \varepsilon_q = 0$$

Thus by mounting two identical gauges in the p and q directions as shown in Fig. 3.22, we can compute K from their readings. For this case then

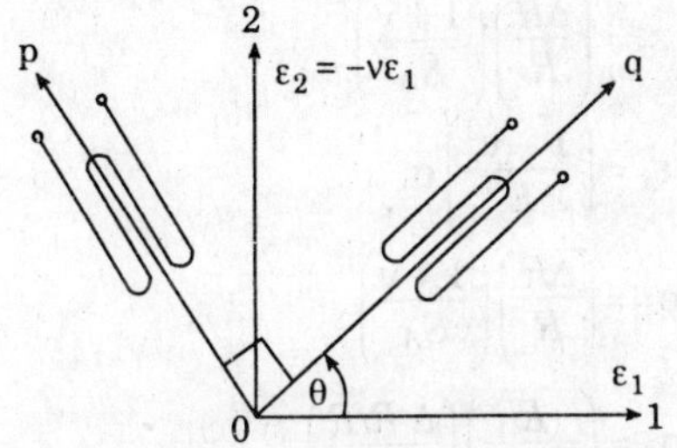

Fig. 3.22

$$\left(\frac{\Delta R}{R}\right)_q = 0 + S_\perp\,\varepsilon_p$$

$$\left(\frac{\Delta R}{R}\right)_p = S_\parallel\,\varepsilon_p + 0$$

$$\therefore \qquad K = \frac{S_\perp}{S_\parallel} = (\Delta R/R)_q/(\Delta R/R)_p \qquad \text{...(3.87)}$$

When $\varepsilon_q \neq 0$, then

$$S_\perp = \frac{\left(\frac{\Delta R}{R}\right)_p - \left(\frac{\varepsilon_p}{\varepsilon_q}\right)\left(\frac{\Delta R}{R}\right)_q}{(\varepsilon_q - \varepsilon_p^2/\varepsilon_q)}$$

$$S_\parallel = \frac{(\Delta R/R)_p - (\varepsilon_q/\varepsilon_p)\,(\Delta R/R)_q}{(\varepsilon_q - \varepsilon_q^2/\varepsilon_p)}$$

$$\therefore \qquad K = \frac{S_{\perp}}{S_{\parallel}} = \frac{\varepsilon_p \,.\, X - \varepsilon_q}{\varepsilon_p - \varepsilon_q X} \qquad \text{...(3.88)}$$

where $\qquad X = (\Delta R/R)_q/(\Delta R/R)_p$

3.16 The Stress Gauge

A modified strain gauge, with a specially designed grid to produce the proper transverse sensitivity, is known as a stress gauge.

In a biaxial stress field, we have

$$\sigma_x = \frac{E}{1 - \nu^2} (\varepsilon_x + \nu \, \varepsilon_y)$$

Also the output of a gauge having strain sensitivity S_A and transverse sensitivity K is given by,

$$\frac{\Delta R}{R} = \frac{S_A}{(1 + K)} (\varepsilon_x + K \, \varepsilon_y)$$

If $\qquad K = \nu$, then

$$\frac{\Delta R}{R} = \frac{S_A}{(1 + \nu)} (\varepsilon_x + \nu \, \varepsilon_y)$$

so that $\qquad \varepsilon_x + \nu \, \varepsilon_y = \left(\frac{\Delta R}{R}\right)\left(\frac{1 + \nu}{S_A}\right)$

But $\qquad \varepsilon_x + \nu \, \varepsilon_y = \left(\frac{1 - \nu^2}{E}\right) \sigma_x$

$$\therefore \qquad \left(\frac{1 - \nu^2}{E}\right) \sigma_x = \left(\frac{\Delta R}{R}\right)\left(\frac{1 + \nu}{S_A}\right)$$

or $\qquad \sigma_x = \left(\frac{E}{1 - \nu}\right)\left(\frac{\Delta R/R}{S_A}\right)$

or $\qquad \sigma_x \propto \frac{\Delta R}{R} \qquad \text{...(3.89)}$

i.e. the change in resistance of the gauge per unit resistance is directly proportional to the stress applied. Hence, the gauge will straight away measure stress.

3.16.1 Grid Forms

The following types of grid forms can be used for the stress gauge :

1. Grid of straight parallel portions connected by semicircular end loops (Fig. 3.23).

Let $\qquad r$ = radius of the semi-circular end loop

$\qquad = y/2$, half the distance between straight portions of wire

$\qquad l$ = length of straight wire.

For this type of gauge

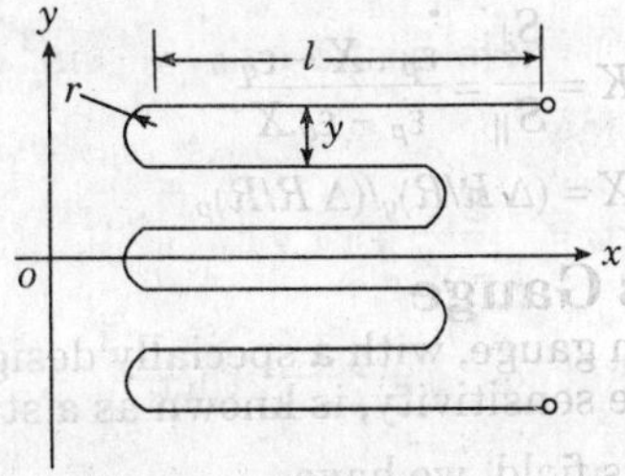

Fig. 3.23

$$K = \frac{\pi r/2}{l + \frac{\pi r}{2}}$$

This grid will perform the function of a stress gauge, when

$$\frac{\pi r/2}{l + \frac{\pi r}{2}} = \nu$$

or
$$\frac{r}{l} = \frac{2}{\pi}\left(\frac{\nu}{1-\nu}\right) \qquad ...(3.90)$$

2. **V-type grid.** For the V-type grid as shown in Fig. 3.24, we have

$$\varepsilon_{(\theta+\phi)} = \varepsilon_1 \cos^2(\theta+\phi) + \varepsilon_2 \sin^2(\theta+\phi)$$

$$\varepsilon_{(\theta-\phi)} = \varepsilon_1 \cos^2(\theta-\phi) + \varepsilon_2 \sin^2(\theta-\phi)$$

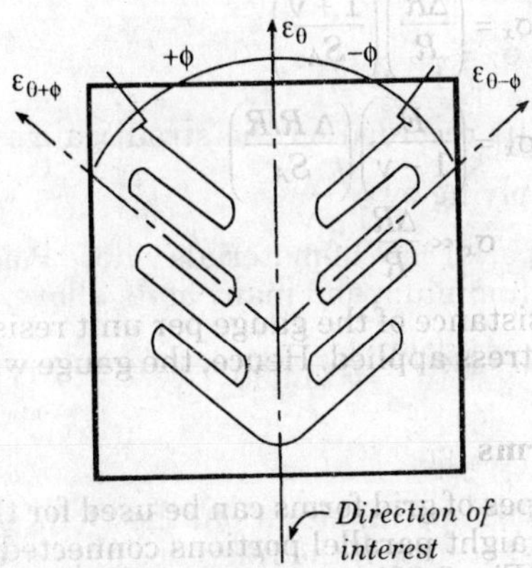

Fig. 3.24 Commercial stress gauge (V-type grid).

$$\therefore\ \varepsilon_{(\theta+\phi)} + \varepsilon_{(\theta-\phi)} = \varepsilon_1 [\cos^2(\theta+\phi) + \cos^2(\theta-\phi)]$$
$$+ \varepsilon_2 [\sin^2(\theta+\phi) + \sin^2(\theta-\phi)]$$
$$= 2[(\varepsilon_1 \cos^2\theta + \varepsilon_2 \sin^2\theta)\cos^2\phi$$
$$+ (\varepsilon_1 \sin^2\theta + \varepsilon_2 \cos^2\theta)\sin^2\phi]$$

$$= 2\,[\varepsilon_\theta \cos^2\phi + \varepsilon_{(\theta+90°)} \sin^2\phi]$$

Also by Hooke's law

$$\sigma_\theta = \frac{E}{1-\nu^2}\,[\varepsilon_0 + \nu\,\varepsilon_{(\theta+90°)}]$$

If $\tan^2\phi = \nu$ so that $\cos^2\phi = \frac{1}{1+\nu}$, then

$$\varepsilon_{(\theta+\phi)} + \varepsilon_{(\theta-\phi)} = \frac{1}{1+\nu}\,[\varepsilon_\theta + \nu\,\varepsilon_{(\theta+90°)}]$$

or $\frac{1}{2}\,(\varepsilon_{(\theta+\phi)} + \varepsilon_{(\theta-\phi)}) = \frac{1}{1+\nu}\,[\varepsilon_\theta + \nu\,\varepsilon_{(\theta+90°)}]$

Now $\frac{1}{2}\,(\varepsilon_{(\theta+\phi)} + \varepsilon_{(\theta-\phi)})$ is the average strain indicated by the two elements of the *V*-grid gauge. Also

$$\sigma_\theta = \left(\frac{E}{1-\nu}\right)\cdot\frac{1}{2}\,[\varepsilon_{(\theta+\phi)} + \varepsilon_{(\theta-\phi)}]$$

$$= \left(\frac{E}{1-\nu}\right)\left(\frac{\Delta R}{R}\cdot\frac{1}{F}\right)$$

Hence multiplying gauge reading by $\left(\frac{E}{1-\nu}\right)$, we can get the value of σ_θ. The stress gauge will thus give σ_θ directly with a single gauge. If $\theta = 0°$ then $\varepsilon_\phi = \varepsilon_{-\phi}$,

so that $$\sigma_1 = \frac{E}{1-\nu}\,.\,\varepsilon_\phi \qquad ...(3.91)$$

The value of ε_ϕ is recorded on the strain gauge and converted to σ_1 directly by multiplying by $\frac{E}{1-\nu}$.

3. For the special case of materials whose Poisson's ratio is 1/3, such as aluminium and many of its alloys,

$$\sqrt{\nu} = \sqrt{\frac{1}{3}} = \tan 30°$$

Hence $\phi = 30°$.

Therefore, for this special situation, the Delta strain rosette can also be a Delta stress rosette if the reference axes are rotated through 30° and the gauges are connected successively in pairs in series as shown in Fig. 3.25.

3.16.2 Conventional Gauge as a Stress Gauge

In a biaxial strain field

$$\sigma_1 = \frac{E}{1-\nu^2}\,(\varepsilon_1 + \nu\,\varepsilon_2) \qquad ...(3.92)$$

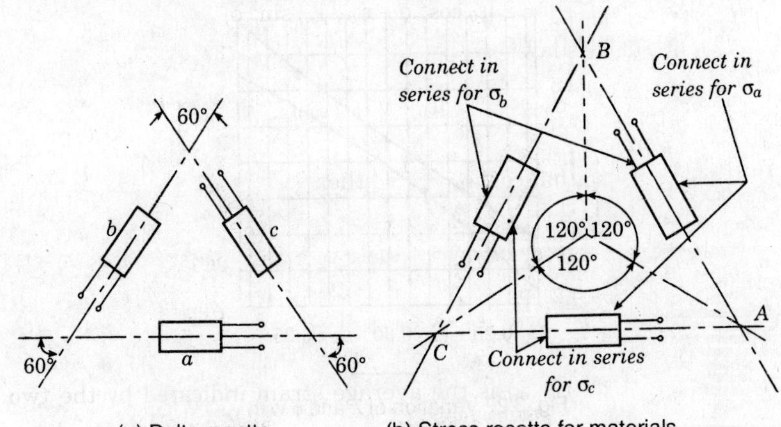

(a) Delta rosette (b) Stress rosette for materials with $\nu = 1/3$

Fig. 3.25

Also $$\varepsilon_\phi = \varepsilon_1 \cos^2 \phi + \varepsilon_2 \sin^2 \phi$$

where ϕ is the angle between the gauge axis and the maximum principal stress (Fig. 3.26).

$$\varepsilon_\phi = \cos^2 \phi \, (\varepsilon_1 + \varepsilon_2 \tan^2 \phi)$$

If $\tan^2 \phi = \nu$ then $\cos^2 \phi = \dfrac{1}{1+\nu}$

$$\therefore \quad \varepsilon_\phi = \frac{1}{1+\nu}(\varepsilon_1 + \nu\, \varepsilon_2) \qquad \text{...(3.93)}$$

Dividing Eq. (3.92) by (3.93), we get

$$\frac{\sigma_1}{\varepsilon_\phi} = \frac{E}{1-\nu}$$

or $$\sigma_1 = \left(\frac{E}{1-\nu}\right) \varepsilon_\phi = \lambda E \, \varepsilon_\phi \qquad \text{...(3.94)}$$

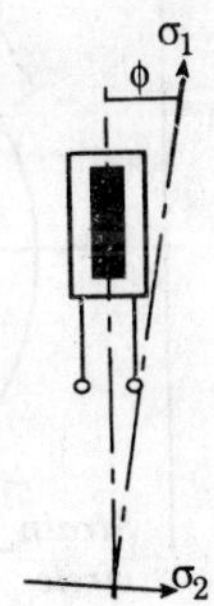

Fig. 3.26 Strain gauge mounted for direct indication of stress.

where $\lambda = \dfrac{1}{1-\nu}$ and is called the biaxial coefficient for modulus of elasticity.

Also $$\varepsilon_\phi = \frac{\Delta R/R}{F}$$

The variation of λ and ϕ with ν is shown in Fig. 3.27. Fig. 3.28 shows concentric Mohr's stress and strain circles.

$$\frac{\text{Radius of stress circle}}{\text{Radius of strain circle}} = \frac{R_\sigma}{R_\varepsilon} = \frac{1-\nu}{1+\nu} = \cos \phi = 2 \tan^{-1} \sqrt{\nu}$$

The following inaccuracies are associated with the use of a conventional strain gauge as a stress gauge.

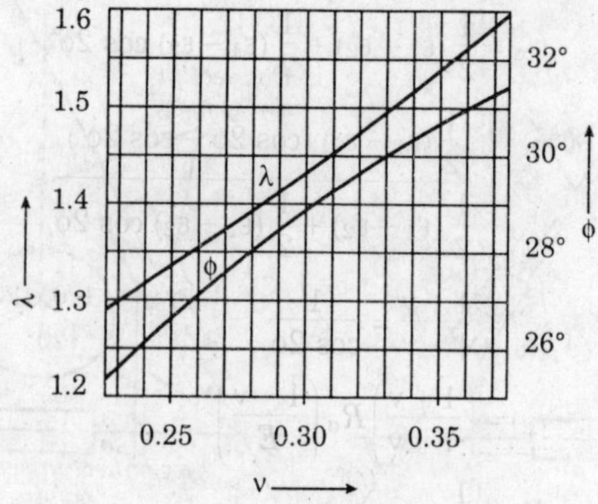

Fig. 3.27 Variation of λ and φ with ν.

(*a*) Error due to mounting the gauge at an angle φ′ instead of φ (Fig. 3.29).

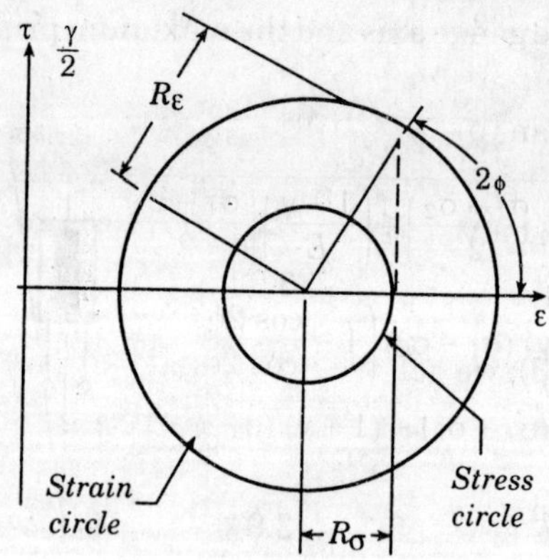

Fig. 3.28 Concentric Mohr's stress and strain circles.

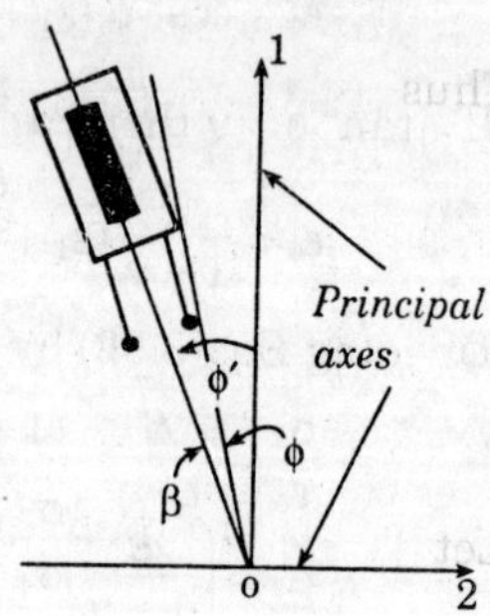

Fig. 3.29 Mounting error determination.

The error *e* as a fraction of the true maximum principal stress is,

$$e = \frac{\sigma_1 - \sigma_1'}{\sigma_1}$$

Now $\sigma_1 \propto \varepsilon_\phi$

and $\sigma'_1 \propto \varepsilon_\phi'$

$$\therefore \qquad e = \frac{\varepsilon_\phi - \varepsilon_\phi'}{\varepsilon_\phi}$$

Now $$\varepsilon_\phi = \frac{1}{2}(\varepsilon_1 + \varepsilon_2) + \frac{1}{2}(\varepsilon_1 - \varepsilon_2)\cos 2\phi$$

$$\varepsilon'_{\phi} = \frac{1}{2}(\varepsilon_1 + \varepsilon_2) + \frac{1}{2}(\varepsilon_1 - \varepsilon_2)\cos 2\phi'$$

$$e = \frac{\frac{1}{2}(\varepsilon_1 - \varepsilon_2)(\cos 2\phi - \cos 2\phi')}{\frac{1}{2}(\varepsilon_1 + \varepsilon_2) + \frac{1}{2}(\varepsilon_1 - \varepsilon_2)\cos 2\phi}$$

Also $$\frac{R_\varepsilon}{R_\sigma} = \frac{1+\nu}{1-\nu} = \frac{1}{\cos 2\phi}$$

$$\therefore \quad \frac{1}{2}(\varepsilon_1 - \varepsilon_2) = \left(\frac{1+\nu}{1-\nu}\right) R_\sigma \left(\frac{1-\nu}{E}\right)$$

But $$R_\sigma = \frac{1}{2}(\sigma_1 - \sigma_2)$$

$$\therefore \quad \frac{1}{2}(\varepsilon_1 - \varepsilon_2) = \left(\frac{1+\nu}{E}\right)\left(\frac{\sigma_1 - \sigma_2}{2}\right)$$

Also $$\frac{1}{2}(\varepsilon_1 + \varepsilon_2) = \left(\frac{1-\nu}{E}\right)\left(\frac{\sigma_1 + \sigma_2}{2}\right)$$

Thus $$e = \frac{\left(\frac{1+\nu}{E}\right)\left(\frac{\sigma_1 - \sigma_2}{2}\right)(\cos 2\phi - \cos 2\phi')}{\left(\frac{1-\nu}{E}\right)\left(\frac{\sigma_1 + \sigma_2}{2}\right) + \left(\frac{1+\nu}{E}\right)\left(\frac{\sigma_1 - \sigma_2}{2}\right)\cos 2\phi}$$

$$= \frac{(1+\nu)(\sigma_1 - \sigma_2)\left(1 - \frac{\cos 2\phi'}{\cos 2\phi}\right)\cos 2\phi}{(1-\nu)(\sigma_1 + \sigma_2) + (1+\nu)(\sigma_1 - \sigma_2)\cos 2\phi}$$

Let $m = \frac{\sigma_2}{\sigma_1}$, then

$$e = \frac{(1-m)\left(1 - \frac{\cos 2\phi'}{\cos 2\phi}\right)}{2}$$

Also $$\frac{\cos 2\phi'}{\cos 2\phi} = \frac{\cos 2\phi \cos 2\beta - \sin 2\phi \sin 2\beta}{\cos 2\phi}$$

If $\cos 2\beta \approx 1$, then

$$\frac{\cos 2\phi'}{\cos 2\phi} = 1 - \tan 2\phi \sin 2\beta$$

Now $$\tan 2\phi = \frac{2\sqrt{\nu}}{1-\nu}$$

$$e = (1-m)\left(\frac{\sqrt{\nu}}{1-\nu}\sin 2\beta\right) \qquad \text{...(3.96)}$$

If $\nu = 0.285$, then

$$e = 0.747\,(1 - m)\sin 2\beta \qquad ...(3.97)$$

(*b*) Error due to transverse sensitivity of gauge.

Now
$$\frac{\Delta R}{R} = F\varepsilon$$
$$= S_{||}\,\varepsilon_{1t} + S_{\perp}\,\varepsilon_{2t}$$

For uniaxial strain during calibration

$$\varepsilon_{2t} = -\nu_0\,\varepsilon_{1t}$$

$$\therefore \quad \frac{\Delta R}{R} = S_{||}\,\varepsilon_1\,(1 - \nu_0 K)$$

$$F = S_{||}\,(1 - \nu_0 K)$$

and
$$\frac{\Delta R}{R} = S_{||}\,(1 - \nu_0 K)\,\varepsilon_{1a}$$
$$= F\,\varepsilon_{1a}$$

Now
$$\varepsilon_{1a} = \frac{\varepsilon_{1t} + K\,\varepsilon_{2t}}{1 - \nu_0 K}$$

To determine the error when a strain gauge is used to indicate a principal stress in a biaxial stress field, we have

$$\varepsilon_{1t} = \frac{\sigma_{1t}\,(1 - \nu)}{E}$$

$$\varepsilon_{2t} = \frac{\sigma_{2t}\,(1 - \nu)}{E}$$

and
$$\varepsilon_{1a} = \frac{\sigma_{1a}\,(1 - \nu)}{E}$$

$$\sigma_{1a} = \frac{\sigma_{1t} + K\,\sigma_{2t}}{1 - \nu_0 K}$$

Error
$$e = \frac{\sigma_{1a} - \sigma_{1t}}{\sigma_{1t}}$$
$$= \left(\frac{\sigma_{1t} + K\,\sigma_{2t}}{1 - \nu_0 K} - \sigma_{1t}\right)\frac{1}{\sigma_{1t}}.$$
$$= \frac{\sigma_{1t} + K\,\sigma_{2t}}{\sigma_{1t}\,(1 - \nu_0 K)} - 1$$

If $\dfrac{\sigma_{2t}}{\sigma_{1t}} = m$, then

$$e = \frac{1 + mK}{1 - \nu_0 K} - 1 = \frac{K\,(m + \nu_0)}{1 - \nu_0 K} \qquad ...(3.98)$$

3.16.3 Plane shear gauge

For two gauges oriented at θ_A and θ_B with respect to the x-axis as shown in Fig. 3.30, the strains measured by the gauges are given by

$$\varepsilon_A = \frac{\varepsilon_x + \varepsilon_y}{2} + \frac{\varepsilon_x - \varepsilon_y}{2} \cdot \cos 2\theta_A + \frac{\gamma_{xy}}{2} \sin 2\theta_A$$

$$\varepsilon_B = \frac{\varepsilon_x + \varepsilon_y}{2} + \frac{\varepsilon_x - \varepsilon_y}{2} \cdot \cos 2\theta_B + \frac{\gamma_{xy}}{2} \sin 2\theta_B$$

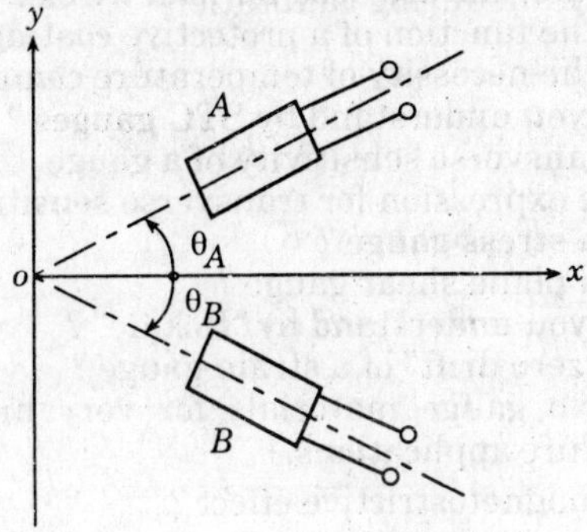

Fig. 3.30 Plane-shear gauge.

Solving for γ_{xy} we get

$$\gamma_{xy} = \frac{2(\varepsilon_A - \varepsilon_B) - (\varepsilon_x - \varepsilon_y)(\cos 2\theta_A - \cos 2\theta_B)}{\sin 2\theta_A - \sin 2\theta_B}$$

If the two gauges are oriented such that

$$\cos 2\theta_A = \cos 2\theta_B$$

then, we get $$\gamma_{xy} = \frac{2(\varepsilon_A - \varepsilon_B)}{\sin 2\theta_A - \sin 2\theta_B} \quad ...(3.99)$$

Since the cosine is an even function, $\theta_A = -\theta_B$ for $\cos 2\theta_A$ to be equal to $\cos 2\theta_B$. For $\theta_A = 45°$, Eq. (3.99) reduces to

$$\gamma_{xy} = \varepsilon_A - \varepsilon_B \quad ...(3.100)$$

Thus the shearing strain γ_{xy} can be measured with a two-element rectangular rosette by orienting the gauges at 45° and −45° with respect to the x-axis and connecting them into the adjacent arms of the Wheatstone bridge. Such a gauge is called a plane-shear gauge.

3.17 Quiz Questions

1. Name the different types of electrical strain gauges.
2. What do you mean by SR-4 gauges ?
3. What is Wiedemann's ffect ?
4. What is LVDT ?
5. Wh; capacitance gauges have not become popular ?
6. Name different types of electrical resistance strain gauges.
7. Dif rentiate between bonded and unbonded gauges.
8. What are the advantages of a free filament gauge ?

9. What is a weldable gauge ? What are its advantages ?
10. Write the expression for gauge-factor. Why gauge factor is nearly 2 for most of the materials used for gauge construction?
11. Name the materials used for metallic gauges.
12. What is the function of a carrier material ?
13. Name bonding cements suitable for room temperature applications.
14. Which materials are used for lead wires ?
15. What is the function of a protective coating ?
16. What is the necessity of temperature compensation ?
17. What do you understand by STC gauges ?
18. Define transverse sensitivity of a gauge.
19. Write the expression for transverse sensitivity of a gauge.
20. What is a stress gauge ?
21. What is a plane shear gauge ?
22. What do you understand by "Rokide" ?
23. What is "zero drift" of a strain gauge ?
24. Name two gauge materials for very high and very low temperature applications.
25. What is magnetostrictive effect ?

EXERCISES

3.1 What are the different types of electrical strain gauges ? Describe a capacitance strain gauge and give its uses and limitations.

3.2 What are the different types of resistance strain gauges ? What are their advantages over other types of gauges ? Why foil type of gauges are preferred over wire type of gauges ?

3.3 What are the various criterias for gauge selection ? Which type of gauges you would recommend for high temperature strain measurements ? How would you compensate for temperature changes ?

3.4 Write short notes on the following :
(*i*) Inductance strain gauge,
(*ii*) Electromagnetic strain gauge,
(*iii*) Weldable strain gauge.

3.5 Describe in detail the principle of working, uses and limitations of a linear variable differential transformer.

3.6 What are the different types of materials used for metallic resistance strain gauges ? Give their properties in brief.

3.7 What are the different types of carrier materials used for strain gauges ? What are the functions of a carrier material?

3.8 What are the characteristics of a good bonding cement ? What are the various cements available for bonding strain gauges?

3.9 Write short notes on the following :
(*i*) Lead wire materials,
(*ii*) Protective coatings.

3.10 What is the necessity of temperature compensation ? How this can be achieved ?

3.11 Derive an expression for the gauge factor of an electrical conductor of length L, cross-sectional area A, resistance R and resistivity ρ. Why for some materials the value of gauge factor is far away from the normal value of 2.0 ?

3.12 What do you understand by transverse sensitivity of a strain gauge ? Derive an expression to determine the transverse sensitivity of a strain gauge.

3.13 Determine the transverse sensitivity factor for a strain gauge fabricated from Constantan alloy with $S_A = 2.11$ if it has been calibrated and found to exhibit a gauge factor $F = 2.04$.

3.14 Develop an expression for K in terms of Poisson's ratio of the specimen material and the ratio of the outputs from the two strain gauges oriented in the axial and transverse directions.

3.15 A value of $K = 0.03$ was obtained for a gauge by assuming $\nu = 0.30$ for the specimen material. If true value of ν was 0.29, determine the percentage error introduced in the determination of K.

3.16 Determine the percentage error introduced by neglecting transverse sensitivity if a strain gauge having $F = 2.12$, $S_{||} = 2.12$, $S_{\perp} = 0.0191$, $K = 0.9\%$ is used to determine the longitudinal strain in a steel beam having $\nu = 0.30$.

3.17 Determine the percentage error introduced by neglecting transverse sensitivity if a strain gauge having $F = 2.10$, $S_{||} = 2.10$, $S_{\perp} = -0.0063$, $K = -0.3\%$ is used to measure the maximum tensile strain on the surface of a circular steel shaft having $\nu = 0.30$ when subjected to a pure torque.

3.18 Determine the percentage error introduced by neglecting transverse sensitivity if a strain gauge having $F = 2.06$, $S_{||} = 2.07$, $S_{\perp} = 0.0228$ and $K = 1.1\%$ is used to measure the maximum tensile strain on the outside surface of a thin-walled cylindrical pressure vessel ($\nu = 0.30$) which is being subjected to an internal gas pressure.

3.19 A single strain gauge is mounted to measure the axial strain in a simple tensile member. If the recorded strain is 450 μm/m, what is the axial stress if (*a*) the member is of steel with $E_{steel} = 210$ GPa, (*b*) the member is of aluminium with $E_{al} = 70$ GPa. Gauge factor = 2.

3.20 A simple tension member, area of cross-section 125 mm^2 subjected to an axial load of 25 kN. Strains of 1620 and − 460 μm/m are measured in the axial and transverse directions respectively. Assuming that elastic conditions prevail, determine the value of Young's modulus and Poisson's ratio.

3.21 A single strain gauge is to be used to determine the principal stress at a given point. $F = 1.98, K = 0.035$, $E = 70$ GPa, $\nu = 0.33$, (*a*) Find the angle at which the gauge must be mounted, (*b*) The gauge is read on a standard indicator with the gauge factor control set at 1.98, the reading obtained was 800 μm/m. What is the principal stress ?

3.22 A strain gauge is used to measure the strain at the edge of a circular hole of radius 25 mm on a wide plate. The plate is under uniaxial tension in the *y*-direction and the gauge is placed along the *x*-direction, at 90° to *y*. What is the maximum gauge length if the maximum error due to the length effect is to be limited to 5% ? What is the error if a gauge length of 3 mm is used ? Take $\nu = 0.30$.

3.23 The transverse sensitivity of a strain gauge is 0.04. If the resulting error when it is used to measure strains on steel ($\nu = 0.30$) under the conditions, (*a*) uniaxial strain, (*b*) biaxial compression, $\varepsilon_x = \varepsilon_y$, (*c*) pure shear, $\varepsilon_x = -\varepsilon_y$. What is the error when two identical gauges are used to find the Poisson's ratio in a uniaxial tension test ?

3.24 A steel bar in Uniaxial tension has two strain gauges fixed on its surface, one in the direction of the load and the other in the transverse direction. When the stress in the steel bar is 70 MPa, the relative change in resistance are 0.69×10^{-3} for the longitudinal gauge and -0.195×10^{-3} for the transverse gauge. Find the gauge factor and the transverse sensitivity if $E = 210$ GPa.

3.25 Calculate the transverse sensitivity of the following two gauges : (*a*) grid 3 mm long, 25 mm wide, 48 strands, (*b*) grid 25 mm long, 3 mm wide, 6 strands. For each gauge, calculate (*i*) the gauge factor, in simple tension, on a steel bar of $\nu = 0.30$, if the gauge factor for a single strand is 2.05, (*ii*) if the nominal gauge factor for both gauges is given by manufacturer as equal to 2. Find the true gauge factor when they are used on a steel shaft in torsion (pure shear, *i.e.* $\varepsilon_x = -\varepsilon_y$) and when they are fixed on a steel bar in simple tension, at 90° to the direction of the load, (*iii*) what is the error in the measured strain if the nominal gauge factor is used ?

3.26 Derive expression for the error introduced in stresses due to transverse sensitivity in a biaxial stress field.

3.27 Explain the Mohr's circle method for transverse sensitivity corrections.

3.28 Explain the different experimental methods for determining transverse sensitivity of a gauge.

3.29 What is a stress gauge ? How a conventional gauge can be used as a stress gauge ?

3.30 (*a*) How various grid forms can be used as a stress gauge ?
(*b*) How two gauges can be used as a plane shear gauge ?

3.31 A strain gauge is mounted at 30° from the longitudinal axis of a tensile specimen. Including the effects of transverse sensitivity, calculate the strain indicated by the gauge if P = 1 kN, A = 5 cm^2, ν = 0.30, K = 0.02, F = 2, E = 210 GPa.

3.32 Two gauges are mounted on a tensile test piece, one in the direction of the stress field, the other at right angles to this direction. The gauge in the direction of the stress field indicates a strain of 500 μm/m. If ν = 0.32, K = 0.035, what reading should the transverse gauge exhibit ? What is the maximum stress in the piece, if E = 210 GPa.

3.33 A cylindrical steel tank 125 cm is diameter has a wall thickness of 6 mm and is subjected to an internal pressure of 2.5 N/mm^2. Calculate the expected strain reading from a gauge used as a maximum principal stress gauge.

4

Strain Rosettes

4.1 Introduction

When the state of strain at a point and the direction of principal strains is known, then the strain gauges can be oriented along these directions, and strain measurements may be made. However, when the state of strain is not known, then three or more gauges may be used at the point to determine the state of strain at the point. The resulting configuration is termed a strain rosette. Strain-rosette analysis is the art of arranging strain gauges as rosettes at a number of points on the object to be investigated, taking the measurements, and computing the state of stress at these points.

Strain rosette analysis is based on the assumptions of isotropic, homogeneous and linear material and of strain gradients so small that the strains can be considered as substantially uniform over the area covered by the rosette gauges. In this chapter, we shall study strain rosettes of various configurations currently in use.

4.2 Strain Rosette Configurations

The strain gauges may be arranged in the following ways to obtain strain rosettes :

1. Two gauge rosette.
2. Rectangular rosette.
   (*a*) Three element ;
   (*b*) Four element.
3. Delta or Equiangular rosette.
4. T-Delta rosette.

Fig. 4.1 shows the configuration of the currently available strain rosettes. In the two-gauge rosette the gauges 1 and 2 are arranged at 0° at 90° respectively. In the rectangular rosette the gauges 1, 2 and 3 are arranged at 0°, 45° and 90° respectively. Delta rosette has gauges 1, 2, 3 arranged at 0°, 60° and 120° respectively, whereas in the T-delta, the gauges 1, 2, 3, 4 are arranged at 0°, 60°, 120° and 90° respectively.

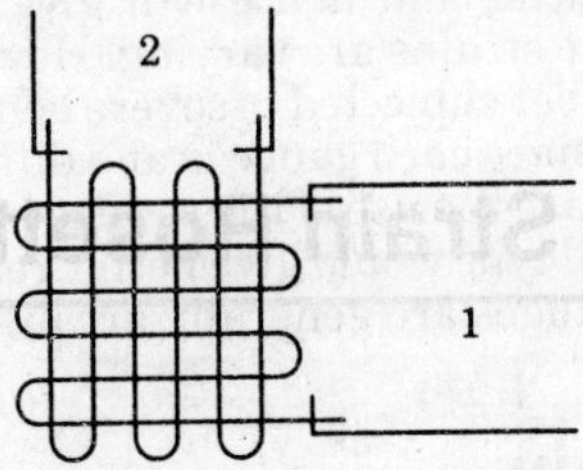

(*a*) Two-gauge rosette

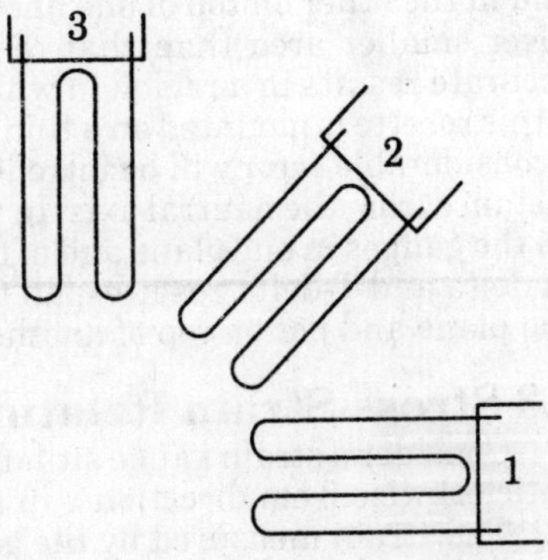

b (*i*) Three gauges rectangular rosette

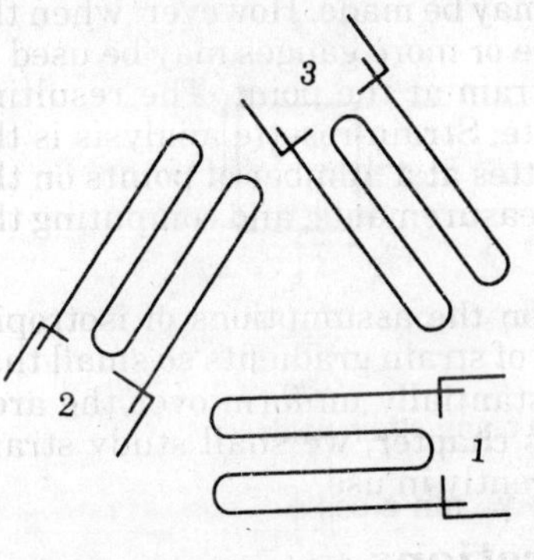

(*c*) Delta rosette

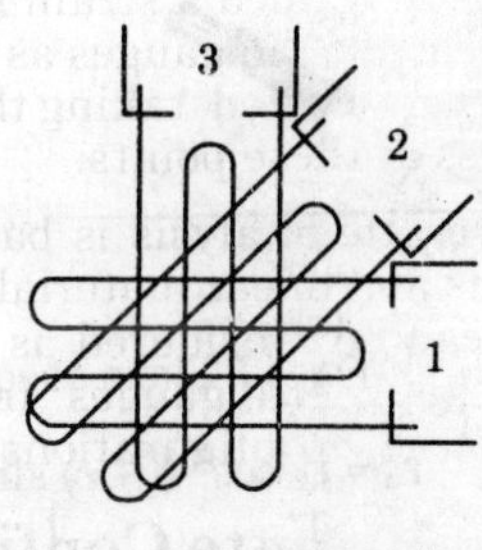

b (*ii*) Three gauge rectangular rosette

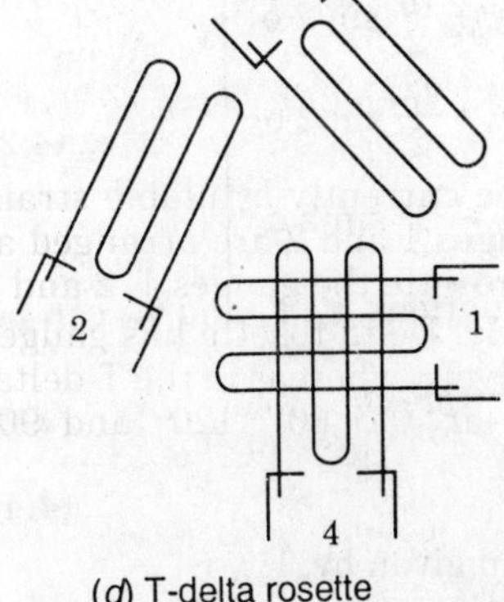

(*d*) T-delta rosette

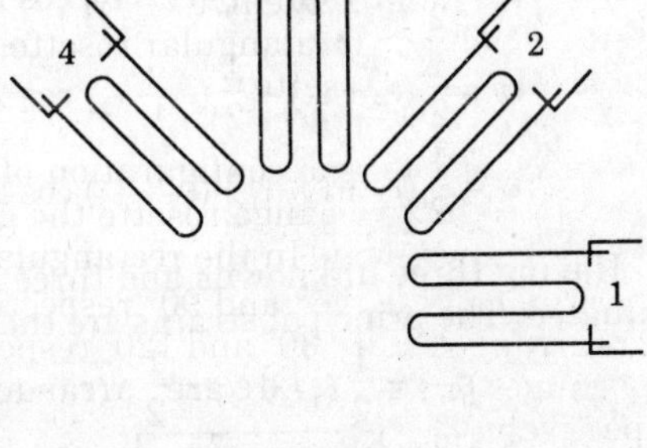

b (*iii*) Four gauge rectangular rosette.

Fig. 4.1 Strain rosette configurations.

In one form of the rectangular rosette the gauges are in one plane and in the other on top of one another. The rosette in the first case will cover smaller area than that of the latter and hence will give more accurate results in a region in which the strains are varying. However, if this rosette is mounted on a thin member subjected to severe bending, a considerable error will be introduced since each gauge is at a different distance from the neutral axis. In this case the use of the rosette having all the gauges in one plane and of the foil type would give better results. In delta and T-delta rosettes, all the gauges are generally arranged in one plane and not on top of another.

4.3 Stress-Strain Relationship

Consider a strain gauge situated at an angular position ϕ measured anticlockwise from direction x in a plane-strain field as shown in Fig. 4.2. The strain measured by the gauge is given by

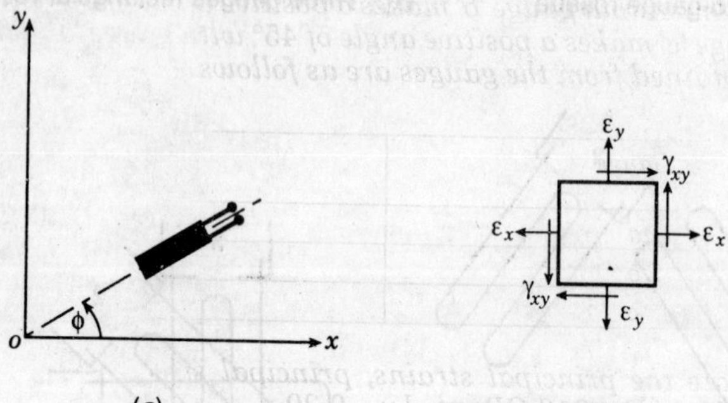

Fig. 4.2 Strain gauge in a plane-strain field.

$$\varepsilon_\phi = \varepsilon_x \cos^2\phi + \varepsilon_y \sin^2\phi + \gamma_{xy}\sin\phi\cos\phi$$
$$= \frac{1}{2}(\varepsilon_x + \varepsilon_y) + \frac{1}{2}(\varepsilon_x - \varepsilon_y)\cos 2\phi + \frac{\gamma_{xy}}{2}\sin 2\phi \quad ...(4.1)$$

Eq. (4.1) contains three unknowns, ε_x, ε_y and γ_{xy} and therefore three strains ε_a, ε_b and ε_c are required along three directions a, b and c to determine the state of strain at a point. Hence

$$\left.\begin{aligned}
\varepsilon_a &= \frac{1}{2}(\varepsilon_x + \varepsilon_y) + \frac{1}{2}(\varepsilon_x - \varepsilon_y)\cos 2\phi_a + \frac{\gamma_{xy}}{2}\sin 2\phi_a \\
\varepsilon_b &= \frac{1}{2}(\varepsilon_x + \varepsilon_y) + \frac{1}{2}(\varepsilon_x - \varepsilon_y)\cos 2\phi_b + \frac{\gamma_{xy}}{2}\sin 2\phi_b \\
\varepsilon_c &= \frac{1}{2}(\varepsilon_x + \varepsilon_y) + \frac{1}{2}(\varepsilon_x - \varepsilon_y)\cos 2\phi_c + \frac{\gamma_{xy}}{2}\sin 2\phi_c
\end{aligned}\right\} \quad ...(4.2)$$

Having three unknowns and three equations, ε_x, ε_y and γ_{xy} can be evaluated. The principal strains are then

$$\varepsilon_{1,2} = \frac{1}{2}(\varepsilon_x + \varepsilon_y) \pm \frac{1}{2}\sqrt{(\varepsilon_x - \varepsilon_y)^2 + \gamma_{xy}^2} \quad ...(4.3)$$

and

$$\gamma_{max} = \sqrt{(\varepsilon_x - \varepsilon_y)^2 + \gamma_{xy}^2} \quad ...(4.4)$$

The principal strain directions are then given by

$$\tan 2\phi_1 = \frac{\gamma_{xy}}{\varepsilon_x - \varepsilon_y}$$

or
$$\phi_1 = \frac{1}{2}\tan^{-1}\left(\frac{\gamma_{xy}}{\varepsilon_x - \varepsilon_y}\right) \qquad \text{...(4.5)}$$

where ϕ_1 is the angle between the principal strain ε_1 and x-axis.

The principal stresses then become

$$\left.\begin{aligned} \sigma_1 &= \frac{E}{1-\nu^2}(\varepsilon_1 + \nu\,\varepsilon_2) \\ \sigma_2 &= \frac{E}{1-\nu^2}(\varepsilon_2 + \nu\,\varepsilon_1) \end{aligned}\right\} \qquad \text{...(4.6)}$$

Example 4.1 *Three strain gauges are applied to an area at a point in such a manner that gauge 'b' makes a positive angle of 30° with gauge 'a', and gauge 'c' makes a positive angle of 45° with gauge 'b'. The strain readings obtained from the gauges are as follows :*

Gauge	*Strain μm/m*
a	*– 600*
b	*300*
c	*400*

Calculate the principal strains, principal stresses and principal directions. Take E = 210 GPa and $\nu = 0.30$.

Solution. Selecting x-axis in the direction of gauge '*a*'

$$\phi_a = 0°,\ \phi_b = 30°,\ \phi_c = 75°$$

Now
$$\varepsilon_\phi = \frac{1}{2}(\varepsilon_x + \varepsilon_y) + \frac{1}{2}(\varepsilon_x - \varepsilon_y)\cos 2\phi + \frac{\gamma_{xy}}{2}\sin 2\phi$$

Hence
$$-600 \times 10^{-6} = \varepsilon_x$$

$$300 \times 10^{-6} = 0.75\,\varepsilon_x + 0.25\,\varepsilon_y + 0.433\,\gamma_{xy}$$

$$400 \times 10^{-6} = 0.067\,\varepsilon_x + 0.933\,\varepsilon_y + 0.25\,\gamma_{xy}$$

Solving for ε_x, ε_y and γ_{xy}, we get

$$\varepsilon_x = -600 \times 10^{-6}$$

$$\varepsilon_y = 9.1132 \times 10^{-6}$$

$$\gamma_{xy} = 1726.84 \times 10^{-6}$$

$$\varepsilon_{1,2} = \frac{1}{2}(\varepsilon_x + \varepsilon_y) \pm \frac{1}{2}\sqrt{(\varepsilon_x - \varepsilon_y)^2 + \gamma_{xy}^2}$$

$$= \frac{1}{2}(-600 + 9.1132)\,10^{-6}$$

$$\pm \frac{1}{2} \times 10^{-6} \sqrt{(-600 - 9.1132)^2 + (1726.84)^2}$$

$$= 620.12 \times 10^{-6}, -1211 \times 10^{-6}$$

$$\tan 2\phi_1 = \frac{\gamma_{xy}}{\varepsilon_x - \varepsilon_y}$$

$$= \frac{1726.84}{-600 - 9.1132} = \frac{1726.84}{-609.1132}$$

$$= -2.835$$

$$\phi_1 = 144.715°$$

$$\phi_2 = 234.715°$$

$$\sigma_1 = \frac{E}{1 - \nu^2} (\varepsilon_1 + \nu\, \varepsilon_2)$$

$$= \frac{210 \times 10^9}{1 - (0.3)^2} (620.12 - 0.3 \times 1211) \times 10^{-6}$$

$$= 59.266 \text{ MPa}$$

$$\sigma_2 = \frac{E}{1 - \nu^2} (\varepsilon_2 + \nu\, \varepsilon_1)$$

$$= \frac{210 \times 10^9}{1 - (0.3)^2} (-1211 + 0.3 \times 620.12) \times 10^{-6}$$

$$= -236.53 \text{ MPa}$$

4.4 Computation of Strain Rosette Data

The computation method to be adopted for the strain rosette data depends upon the following factors :

(*i*) The accuracy required.
(*ii*) The amount of rosette analysis contemplated.
(*iii*) The speed of analysis required.
(*iv*) Requirements as to permanent records for future checks on calculation.
(*v*) The preference and aptitude of the individual.

The following methods are available for computing the strain rosette data :

1. Analytical solutions.
2. Graphical solutions.
3. Semi-graphical or vectorial layout method.
4. Nomographic solutions.
5. Geometrical computer.

We shall discuss only the first three methods in detail. For the last two methods the reader may consult the references given at the end of this book.

4.4.1 Analytical Solutions

(*a*) **The Two-Gauge Rosette.** This rosette is suitable only when the directions of principal strain are known. The gauge '*a*' is arranged along the maximum strain direction chosen along the *x*-axis so that $\phi_a = 0°$ and the gauge '*b*' is set along the minimum strain direction so that $\phi_b = 90°$ (Fig. 4.3).

Now $$\varepsilon_\phi = \frac{1}{2}(\varepsilon_x + \varepsilon_y) + \frac{1}{2}(\varepsilon_x - \varepsilon_y)\cos 2\phi + \frac{\gamma_{xy}}{2}\sin 2\phi$$

$\therefore$ $$\varepsilon_a = \varepsilon_x$$

$$\varepsilon_b = \varepsilon_y$$

Hence $\varepsilon_1 = \varepsilon_a$, $\varepsilon_2 = \varepsilon_b$, $\gamma_{max} = \varepsilon_a - \varepsilon_b$ ...(4.7)

$$\sigma_1 = \frac{E}{1-\nu^2}(\varepsilon_a + \nu\,\varepsilon_b) \quad ...(4.8)$$

$$\sigma_2 = \frac{E}{1-\nu^2}(\varepsilon_b + \nu\,\varepsilon_a)$$

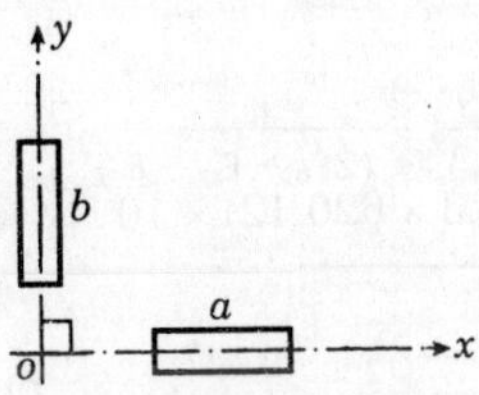

Fig. 4.3 Two-gauge rosette.

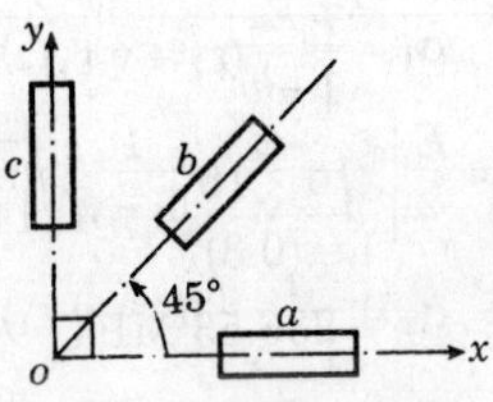

Fig. 4.4 Rectangular three element rosette.

$$\tau_{max} = \frac{E}{2(1+\nu)}(\varepsilon_a - \varepsilon_b)$$

(*b*) **The Rectangular Rosette.** (*i*) *Three Element Rosette.* For the three element rectangular rosette as shown in Fig. 4.4.

$$\phi_a = 0°,\ \phi_b = 45°,\ \phi_c = 90°$$

Now $$\varepsilon_\phi = \frac{1}{2}(\varepsilon_x + \varepsilon_y) + \frac{1}{2}(\varepsilon_x - \varepsilon_y)\cos 2\phi + \frac{\gamma_{xy}}{2}\sin 2\phi$$

$\therefore$ $$\varepsilon_a = \varepsilon_x$$

$$\varepsilon_b = \frac{1}{2}(\varepsilon_x + \varepsilon_y) + \frac{1}{2}\gamma_{xy}$$

$$\varepsilon_c = \varepsilon_y$$

Solving for ε_x, ε_y and γ_{xy}, we get

$$\left.\begin{aligned} \varepsilon_x &= \varepsilon_a \\ \varepsilon_y &= \varepsilon_c \\ \gamma_{xy} &= 2\,\varepsilon_b - (\varepsilon_a + \varepsilon_c) \end{aligned}\right\} \quad ...(4.9)$$

The principal strains are given by

$$\varepsilon_{1,2} = \frac{1}{2}(\varepsilon_x + \varepsilon_y) \pm \frac{1}{2}\sqrt{(\varepsilon_x - \varepsilon_y)^2 + \gamma_{xy}^2}$$
$$= \frac{1}{2}(\varepsilon_a + \varepsilon_c) \pm \frac{1}{2}\sqrt{(\varepsilon_a - \varepsilon_c)^2 + (2\,\varepsilon_b - \varepsilon_a - \varepsilon_c)^2} \quad \text{...(4.10)}$$

Maximum shear strain becomes

$$\gamma_{max} = \sqrt{(\varepsilon_x - \varepsilon_y)^2 + \gamma_{xy}^2}$$
$$= \sqrt{(\varepsilon_a - \varepsilon_c)^2 + (2\varepsilon_b - \varepsilon_a - \varepsilon_c)^2} \quad \text{...(4.11)}$$

The principal strain directions are :

$$\phi_1 = \frac{1}{2}\tan^{-1}\left(\frac{\gamma_{xy}}{\varepsilon_x - \varepsilon_y}\right)$$
$$= \frac{1}{2}\tan^{-1}\left(\frac{2\,\varepsilon_b - \varepsilon_a - \varepsilon_c}{\varepsilon_a - \varepsilon_c}\right) \quad \text{...(4.12)}$$
$$\phi_2 = 90° + \phi_1$$

The principal stresses are then obtained from,

$$\sigma_1 = \frac{E}{1 - \upsilon^2}(\varepsilon_1 + \upsilon\,\varepsilon_2)$$
$$= \frac{E}{2}\left[\frac{\varepsilon_a + \varepsilon_c}{1 - \nu} + \frac{1}{1 + \nu}\sqrt{(\varepsilon_a - \varepsilon_c)^2 + (2\varepsilon_b - \varepsilon_a - \varepsilon_c)^2}\right] \quad \text{...(4.13)}$$
$$\sigma_2 = \frac{E}{1 - \nu^2}(\varepsilon_2 + \nu\,\varepsilon_1)$$
$$= \frac{E}{2}\left[\frac{\varepsilon_a + \varepsilon_c}{1 - \nu} - \frac{1}{1 + \nu}\sqrt{(\varepsilon_a - \varepsilon_c)^2 + (2\varepsilon_b - \varepsilon_a - \varepsilon_c)^2}\right]$$

The maximum shear stress is then

$$\tau_{max} = \frac{E}{2\,(1 + \nu)}\gamma_{max}$$
$$= \frac{E}{2\,(1 + \nu)}\sqrt{(\varepsilon_a - \varepsilon_c)^2 + (2\,\varepsilon_b - \varepsilon_a - \varepsilon_c)^2} \quad \text{...(4.14)}$$

Example 4.2 *The following readings of strain were obtained on a rectangular strain rosette mounted on aluminium for which E = 70 GPa,* $\nu = 0.32$, $\varepsilon_a = 285 \times 10^{-6}$, $\varepsilon_0 = 65 \times 10^{-6}$, $\varepsilon_c = 102 \times 10^{-6}$. *Determine the principal strains, principal strain directions, principal stresses and maximum shear stress.*

Solution. For a three-element rectangular rosette, we have

$$\varepsilon_{1,2} = \frac{1}{2}(\varepsilon_a + \varepsilon_c) \pm \frac{1}{2}\sqrt{(\varepsilon_a - \varepsilon_c)^2 + (2\,\varepsilon_b - \varepsilon_a - \varepsilon_c)^2}$$

$$= \frac{1}{2}\left[(285 + 102) \pm \sqrt{(285 - 102)^2 + (130 - 285 - 102)^2}\right] \times 10^{-6}$$

$$= 351.25 \times 10^{-6},\ 35.75 \times 10^{-6}$$

$$\gamma_{max} = \sqrt{(\varepsilon_a - \varepsilon_c)^2 + (2\,\varepsilon_b - \varepsilon_a - \varepsilon_c)^2}$$
$$= 315.5 \times 10^{-6} \text{ rad.}$$
$$\phi_1 = \frac{1}{2} \tan^{-1}\left(\frac{2\,\varepsilon_b - \varepsilon_a - \varepsilon_c}{\varepsilon_a - \varepsilon_c}\right)$$
$$= \frac{1}{2} \tan^{-1}\left(\frac{130 - 285 - 102}{285 - 102}\right)$$
$$= \frac{1}{2} \tan^{-1}(-1.4037)$$
$$\phi_1 = -(27° \; 16')$$
$$\phi_2 = -(117° \; 16')$$
$$\sigma_1 = \frac{E}{1 - \nu^2}(\varepsilon_1 + \nu\,\varepsilon_2)$$
$$= \frac{70 \times 10^9}{1 - (0.32)^2}(351.25 + 0.32 \times 35.75) \times 10^{-6}$$
$$= 28.285 \text{ MPa}$$
$$\sigma_2 = \frac{E}{1 - \nu^2}(\varepsilon_2 + \nu\,\varepsilon_1)$$
$$= \frac{70 \times 10^9}{1 - (0.32)^2}(35.75 + 0.32 \times 351.25) \times 10^{-6}$$
$$= 11.553 \text{ MPa}$$
$$\tau_{max} = \frac{E}{2(1 - \nu)}\gamma_{max} = \frac{70 \times 10^9}{2(1 + 0.32)} \times 315.5 \times 10^{-6}$$
$$= 8.365 \text{ MPa}$$

(*ii*) *Four-element Rosette.* The four element rectangular rosette is shown in Fig. 4.5.

Here $\phi_a = 0°$, $\phi_b = 45°$, $\phi_c = 90°$ and $\phi_d = 135°$.

Now $\varepsilon_\phi = \frac{1}{2}(\varepsilon_x + \varepsilon_y) + \frac{1}{2}(\varepsilon_x - \varepsilon_y)\cos 2\phi + \frac{\gamma_{xy}}{2}\sin 2\phi$

$$\therefore \quad \varepsilon_a = \varepsilon_x$$
$$\varepsilon_b = \frac{1}{2}(\varepsilon_x + \varepsilon_y + \gamma_{xy})$$
$$\varepsilon_c = \varepsilon_y$$
$$\varepsilon_d = \frac{1}{2}(\varepsilon_x + \varepsilon_y - \gamma_{xy})$$

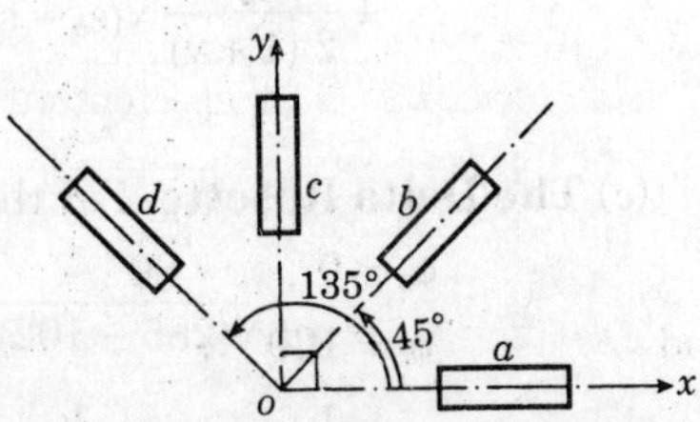

Fig. 4.5 Rectangular four element rosette.

Solving for ε_x, ε_y and γ_{xy}, we get

$$\left.\begin{aligned} \varepsilon_x &= \varepsilon_a \\ \varepsilon_y &= \varepsilon_c \\ \gamma_{xy} &= \varepsilon_b - \varepsilon_d \end{aligned}\right\} \quad \text{...(4.15)}$$

The principal strains are given by

$$\varepsilon_{1,2} = \frac{1}{2}(\varepsilon_x + \varepsilon_y) \pm \frac{1}{2}\sqrt{(\varepsilon_x - \varepsilon_y)^2 + \gamma_{xy}^2}$$

$$= \frac{1}{2}(\varepsilon_a + \varepsilon_c) \pm \frac{1}{2}\sqrt{(\varepsilon_a - \varepsilon_c)^2 + (\varepsilon_b - \varepsilon_d)^2} \quad \text{...(4.16)}$$

Maximum shear strain

$$\gamma_{max} = \sqrt{(\varepsilon_x - \varepsilon_y)^2 + \gamma_{xy}^2}$$

$$= \sqrt{(\varepsilon_a - \varepsilon_c)^2 + (\varepsilon_b - \varepsilon_d)^2} \quad \text{...(4.17)}$$

Maximum principal strain direction is

$$\phi_1 = \frac{1}{2}\tan^{-1}\left(\frac{\gamma_{xy}}{\varepsilon_x - \varepsilon_y}\right)$$

$$= \frac{1}{2}\tan^{-1}\left(\frac{\varepsilon_b - \varepsilon_d}{\varepsilon_a - \varepsilon_c}\right) \quad \text{...(4.18)}$$

The principal stresses are then obtained from

$$\sigma_1 = \frac{E}{1 - \nu^2}(\varepsilon_1 + \nu\,\varepsilon_2)$$

$$\sigma_2 = \frac{E}{1 - \nu^2}(\varepsilon_2 + \nu\,\varepsilon_1)$$

$$\therefore\ \sigma_{1,2} = \frac{E}{2}\left[\frac{\varepsilon_a + \varepsilon_c}{1 - \nu} \pm \frac{1}{1 + \nu}\sqrt{(\varepsilon_a - \varepsilon_c)^2 + (\varepsilon_b - \varepsilon_d)^2}\right]$$

or $$\sigma_{1,2} = \frac{E}{2}\left[\frac{\varepsilon_a + \varepsilon_b + \varepsilon_c + \varepsilon_d}{2(1 - \nu)} \pm \frac{1}{1 + \nu}\sqrt{(\varepsilon_a - \varepsilon_c)^2 + (\varepsilon_b - \varepsilon_d)^2}\right]$$

or $$\sigma_{1,2} = \frac{E}{2}\left[\frac{\varepsilon_b + \varepsilon_d}{1 - \nu} \pm \frac{1}{1 + \nu}\sqrt{(\varepsilon_a - \varepsilon_c)^2 + (\varepsilon_b - \varepsilon_d)^2}\right] \quad \text{...(4.19)}$$

Maximum shear stress is then given by

$$\tau_{max} = \frac{E}{2(1 + \nu)}\gamma_{max}$$

$$= \frac{E}{2(1 + \nu)}\sqrt{(\varepsilon_a - \varepsilon_c)^2 + (\varepsilon_b - \varepsilon_d)^2} \quad \text{...(4.20)}$$

(*c*) **The Delta Rosette.** For the delta rosette as shown in Fig. 4.6,

$$\phi_a = 0°,\ \phi_b = 60°$$

and $$\phi_c = 120°$$

Now $$\varepsilon_\phi = \frac{1}{2}(\varepsilon_x + \varepsilon_y) + \frac{1}{2}(\varepsilon_x - \varepsilon_y)\cos 2\phi + \frac{1}{2}\gamma_{xy}\sin 2\phi$$

$$\therefore \quad \varepsilon_a = \varepsilon_x$$

$$\varepsilon_b = \frac{1}{4}(\varepsilon_x + 3\,\varepsilon_y + 3\,\gamma_{xy})$$

$$\varepsilon_c = \frac{1}{4}(\varepsilon_x + 3\,\varepsilon_y - 3\,\gamma_{xy})$$

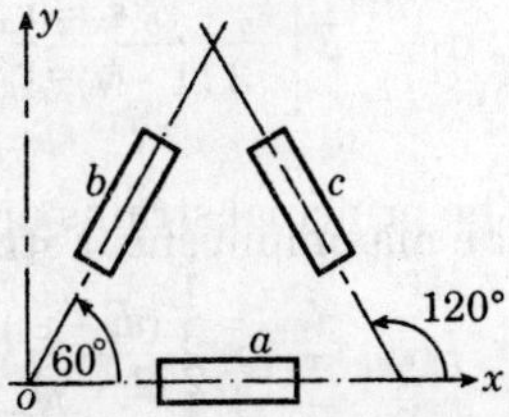

Fig. 4.6 Delta rosette.

Solving for ε_x, ε_y and γ_{xy}, we get

$$\varepsilon_x = \varepsilon_a$$

$$\varepsilon_y = \frac{1}{3}(-\varepsilon_a + 2\,\varepsilon_b + 2\,\varepsilon_c) \qquad \text{...(4.21)}$$

$$\gamma_{xy} = \frac{2}{\sqrt{3}}(\varepsilon_b - \varepsilon_c)$$

The principal strains are given by

$$\varepsilon_{1,2} = \frac{1}{2}(\varepsilon_x + \varepsilon_y) \pm \frac{1}{2}\sqrt{(\varepsilon_x - \varepsilon_y)^2 + \gamma_{xy}^2}$$

$$= \frac{\varepsilon_a + \varepsilon_b + \varepsilon_c}{3} \pm \sqrt{\left(\varepsilon_a - \frac{\varepsilon_a + \varepsilon_b + \varepsilon_c}{3}\right)^2 + \left(\frac{\varepsilon_b - \varepsilon_c}{\sqrt{3}}\right)^2} \qquad \text{...(4.22)}$$

and maximum shear strain

$$\gamma_{max} = \sqrt{(\varepsilon_x - \varepsilon_y)^2 + \gamma_{xy}^2}$$

$$= 2\sqrt{\left(\varepsilon_a - \frac{\varepsilon_a + \varepsilon_b + \varepsilon_c}{3}\right)^2 + \left(\frac{\varepsilon_b - \varepsilon_c}{\sqrt{3}}\right)^2} \qquad \text{...(4.23)}$$

The principal strain directions are

$$\phi_1 = \frac{1}{2}\tan^{-1}\left(\frac{\gamma_{xy}}{\varepsilon_x - \varepsilon_y}\right)$$

$$= \frac{1}{2}\tan^{-1}\left[\frac{\frac{1}{\sqrt{3}}(\varepsilon_b - \varepsilon_c)}{\varepsilon_a - \frac{\varepsilon_a + \varepsilon_b + \varepsilon_c}{3}}\right] \qquad \text{...(4.24)}$$

$$\phi_2 = 90° + \phi_1$$

The principal stresses are given by

$$\sigma_1 = \frac{E}{1 - \nu^2}(\varepsilon_1 + \nu\,\varepsilon_2)$$

$$\sigma_2 = \frac{E}{1 - \nu^2}(\varepsilon_2 + \nu\,\varepsilon_1)$$

$$\therefore \sigma_{1,2} = E\left[\frac{\varepsilon_a + \varepsilon_b + \varepsilon_c}{3\,(1-\nu)} \pm \frac{1}{1+\nu}\sqrt{\left(\varepsilon_a - \frac{\varepsilon_a + \varepsilon_b + \varepsilon_c}{3}\right)^2 + \left(\frac{\varepsilon_b - \varepsilon_c}{\sqrt{3}}\right)^2}\right] \quad ...(4.25)$$

and the maximum shear stress

$$\tau_{max} = \frac{E}{2\,(1+\nu)}\,\gamma_{max}$$

$$= \frac{E}{1+\nu}\sqrt{\left(\varepsilon_a - \frac{\varepsilon_a + \varepsilon_b + \varepsilon_c}{3}\right)^2 + \left(\frac{\varepsilon_b + \varepsilon_c}{\sqrt{3}}\right)^2} \quad ...(4.26)$$

Example 4.3 *A delta rosette yields the following strain indications:* $\varepsilon_a = -845$ *μm/m ;* $\varepsilon_b = 1220$ *μm/m* and $\varepsilon_c = 710$ *μm/m.*

Calculate the maximum principal strain direction, the principal stresses and the maximum shear stress.

E = 200 GPa, ν = 0.285.

Solution. For a delta rosette

$$\varepsilon_x = \varepsilon_a = -845 \text{ μm/m}$$

$$\varepsilon_y = \frac{1}{3}\,(-\varepsilon_a + 2\,\varepsilon_b + 2\,\varepsilon_c)$$

$$= \frac{1}{3}\,(845 + 2440 + 1420)$$

$$= 1568.33 \text{ μm/m}$$

$$\gamma_{xy} = \frac{2}{\sqrt{3}}\,(\varepsilon_b - \varepsilon_c)$$

$$= \frac{2}{\sqrt{3}}\,(1220 - 770)$$

$$= 588.90 \text{ μ rad.}$$

The principal strains become

$$\varepsilon_{1,\,2} = \frac{1}{2}\,(\varepsilon_x + \varepsilon_y) \pm \frac{1}{2}\sqrt{(\varepsilon_x - \varepsilon_y)^2 + \gamma_{xy}^2}$$

$$= \frac{1}{2}\,[(-845 + 1568.33)$$

$$\pm \sqrt{(-845 - 1568.33)^2 + (588.90)^2}]$$

$$= 1603.73 \text{ μ m/m}; -880.41 \text{ μm/m}$$

$$\gamma_{max} = \sqrt{(\varepsilon_x - \varepsilon_y)^2 + \gamma_{xy}^2}$$

$$= \sqrt{(-845 - 1568.33)^2 + (588.90)^2}$$

$$= 2484.14 \text{ μ rad.}$$

Maximum principal strain direction is

$$\phi_1 = \frac{1}{2}\tan^{-1}\left(\frac{\gamma_{xy}}{\varepsilon_x - \varepsilon_y}\right)$$

$$= \frac{1}{2}\tan^{-1}\left(\frac{588.90}{-845 - 1568.33}\right)$$

$$= \frac{1}{2}\tan^{-1}(-0.24402)$$

$$= -6.85° = -(6° - 51')$$

The principal stresses then become

$$\sigma_1 = \frac{E}{1-\nu^2}(\varepsilon_1 + \nu\,\varepsilon_2)$$

$$= \frac{200 \times 10^9}{1-(0.285)^2}(1603.75 - 0.285 \times 880.41)\,10^{-6}$$

$$= 294.482 \text{ MPa}$$

$$\sigma_2 = \frac{E}{1-\nu^2}(\varepsilon_2 - \nu\,\varepsilon_1)$$

$$= \frac{200 \times 10^9}{1-(0.285)^2}(-880.41 + 0.285 \times 1603.73)\,10^{-6}$$

$$= -92.154 \text{ MPa}$$

$$\tau_{max} = \frac{E}{2(1+\nu)}\gamma_{max}$$

$$= \frac{200 \times 10^9 \times 2484.14 \times 10^{-6}}{2(1+0.285)} = 193.32 \text{ MPa}$$

(*d*) **The T-Delta Rosette.** In the T-delta rosette as shown in Fig. 4.7,

$$\phi_a = 0°,\ \phi_b = 60°,\ \phi_c = 120°$$

and $\phi_d = 90°$.

Now

$$\varepsilon_\phi = \frac{1}{2}(\varepsilon_x + \varepsilon_y) + \frac{1}{2}(\varepsilon_x - \varepsilon_y)\cos 2\phi + \frac{1}{2}\gamma_{xy}\sin 2\phi$$

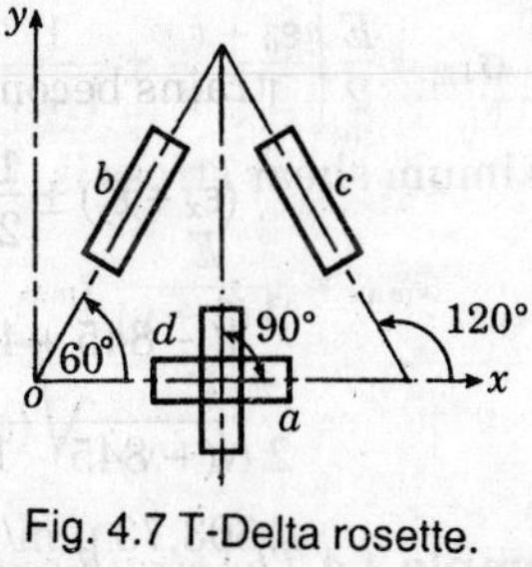

Fig. 4.7 T-Delta rosette.

Hence $\varepsilon_a = \varepsilon_x$

$$\varepsilon_b = \frac{1}{4}(\varepsilon_x + 3\varepsilon_y + 3\,\gamma_{xy})$$

$$\varepsilon_c = \frac{1}{4}(\varepsilon_x + 3\varepsilon_y - 3\,\gamma_{xy})$$

$$\varepsilon_d = \varepsilon_y$$

Solving for ε_x, ε_y and γ_{xy}, we get

$$\varepsilon_x = \varepsilon_a$$

$$\varepsilon_y = \varepsilon_d$$

$$\gamma_{xy} = \frac{2}{\sqrt{3}}(\varepsilon_b - \varepsilon_c)$$

The principal strains are given by

$$\varepsilon_{1,2} = \frac{1}{2}(\varepsilon_x + \varepsilon_y) \pm \frac{1}{2}\sqrt{(\varepsilon_x - \varepsilon_y)^2 + \gamma_{xy}^2}$$

$$= \frac{1}{2}(\varepsilon_a + \varepsilon_d) \pm \frac{1}{2}\sqrt{(\varepsilon_a - \varepsilon_d)^2 + \frac{4}{3}(\varepsilon_b - \varepsilon_c^2)} \quad \text{...(4.28)}$$

$$\gamma_{max} = \sqrt{(\varepsilon_x - \varepsilon_y)^2 + \gamma_{xy}^2}$$

$$= \sqrt{(\varepsilon_a - \varepsilon_d)^2 + \frac{4}{3}(\varepsilon_b - \varepsilon_c)^2} \quad \text{...(4.29)}$$

The maximum principal strain direction is

$$\phi_1 = \frac{1}{2}\tan^{-1}\left(\frac{\gamma_{xy}}{\varepsilon_x - \varepsilon_y}\right)$$

$$= \frac{1}{2}\tan^{-1}\left[\frac{\frac{2}{\sqrt{3}}(\varepsilon_b - \varepsilon_c)}{\varepsilon_a - \varepsilon_d}\right] \quad \text{...(4.30)}$$

The principal stresses are then obtained from

$$\sigma_1 = \frac{E}{1-\nu^2}(\varepsilon_1 + \nu\,\varepsilon_2)$$

$$\sigma_2 = \frac{E}{1-\nu^2}(\varepsilon_2 + \nu\,\varepsilon_1)$$

or

$$\sigma_{1,2} = \frac{E}{2}\left[\frac{\varepsilon_a + \varepsilon_d}{1-\nu} \pm \frac{1}{1+\nu}\sqrt{(\varepsilon_a - \varepsilon_d)^2 + \frac{4}{3}(\varepsilon_b - \varepsilon_c)^2}\right] \quad \text{...(4.31)}$$

and maximum shear stress is

$$\tau_{max} = \frac{E}{2(1+\nu)}\gamma_{max}$$

$$= \frac{E}{2(1+\nu)}\sqrt{(\varepsilon_a - \varepsilon_d)^2 + \frac{4}{3}(\varepsilon_b - \varepsilon_c)^2} \quad \text{...(4.32)}$$

Example 4.4 *The strain readings as measured by a T-delta rosette at a point in a stressed body are given by : $\varepsilon_a = 225\ \mu\ m/m$, $\varepsilon_b = 305\ \mu\ m/m$, $\varepsilon_c = -294\ \mu\ m/m$, and $\varepsilon_d = -65\ \mu\ m/m$. Determine the principal stresses, maximum principal stress direction and maximum shear stress. $E = 200$ GPa, $\nu = 0.30$.*

Solution. For the T-delta rosette

$$\varepsilon_x = \varepsilon_a = 225 \ \mu \text{ m/m}$$

$$\varepsilon_y = \varepsilon_d = -65 \ \mu \text{ m/m}$$

$$\gamma_{xy} = \frac{2}{\sqrt{3}}(\varepsilon_b - \varepsilon_c)$$

$$= \frac{2}{\sqrt{3}}(305 + 274)$$

$$= 668.59 \ \mu \text{ rad.}$$

Maximum principal stress direction

$$\phi_1 = \frac{1}{2}\tan^{-1}\left[\frac{\frac{2}{\sqrt{3}}(\varepsilon_b - \varepsilon_c)}{\varepsilon_a - \varepsilon_d}\right]$$

$$= \frac{1}{2}\tan^{-1}\frac{\frac{2}{\sqrt{3}}(305 + 274)}{225 + 65}$$

$$= \frac{1}{2}\tan^{-1}[2.30548]$$

$$= 33.27°$$

$$= 33° \ 16'$$

$$\sigma_{1,2} = \frac{E}{2}\left[\frac{\varepsilon_a + \varepsilon_d}{1 - \nu} \pm \frac{1}{1 + \nu}\sqrt{(\varepsilon_a - \varepsilon_d)^2 + \frac{4}{3}(\varepsilon_b - \varepsilon_c)^2}\right]$$

$$= \frac{200 \times 10^9}{2}\left[\frac{225 - 65}{1 - 0.30} \pm \frac{1}{1 + 0.30}\sqrt{(225 + 65)^2 + \frac{4}{3}(305 + 274)^2}\right]$$

$$= 78.915 \text{ MPa}, \ -33.201 \text{ MPa}$$

$$\tau_{max} = \frac{\sigma_1 - \sigma_2}{2} = \frac{78.915 - 33.201}{2}$$

$$= 56.058 \text{ MPa}$$

(*e*) **Some Simplifications in Rosette Analysis.** The strain rosette analysis has the following advantages :

(*i*) Extreme simplicity and speed of application.

(*ii*) Possibility of allowing for transverse effects.

(*iii*) No requirements for additional equipment.

(*iv*) The possibility of training relatively unskilled persons to use the method.

However the data to be handled is quite large and in order to simplify the computation of rosette analysis, the following simplifications may be made

Now $$\varepsilon_{1,2} = \frac{1}{2}(\varepsilon_x + \varepsilon_y) \pm \frac{1}{2}\sqrt{(\varepsilon_x - \varepsilon_y)^2 + \gamma_{xy}^2}\,.$$

If we define,

Table 4.1. Analytical Solutions for Strain Rosettes

Names 1	*Two gauge* 2	*Rectangular three element* 3		*Rectangular four element* 4	*Delta or Equiangular* 5	*T-Delta* 6
Configuration	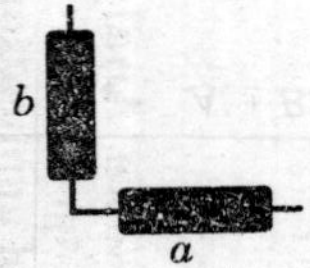	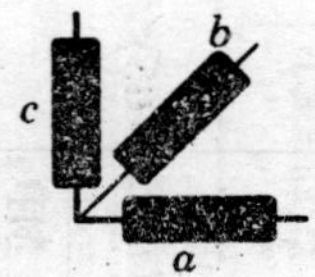		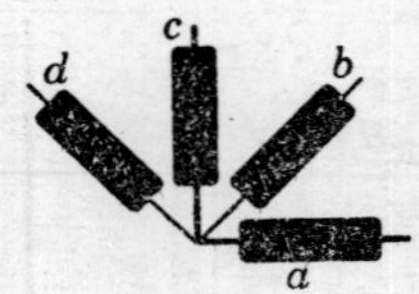	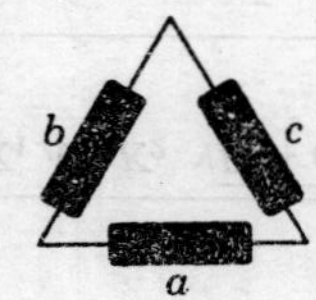	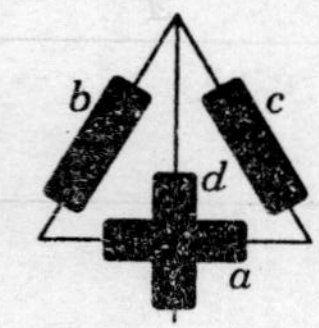
$\phi_a - \phi_b$	90°	45°		45°	60°	60°
$\phi_a - \phi_c$	—	90°		90°	120°	120°
$\phi_a - \phi_d$	—	—		135°	—	90°
A	$\frac{1}{2}(\varepsilon_a + \varepsilon_b)$	$\frac{1}{2}(\varepsilon_a + \varepsilon_c)$		$\frac{1}{2}(\varepsilon_a + \varepsilon_c)$	$\frac{1}{2}(\varepsilon_a + \varepsilon_b + \varepsilon_c)$	$\frac{1}{2}(\varepsilon_a + \varepsilon_d)$
			or	$\frac{1}{2}(\varepsilon_b + \varepsilon_d)$		
			or	$\frac{1}{4}(\varepsilon_a + \varepsilon_b + \varepsilon_c + \varepsilon_d)$		
B	$\frac{1}{2}(\varepsilon_a - \varepsilon_b)$	$\frac{1}{2}(\varepsilon_a - \varepsilon_c)$		$\frac{1}{2}(\varepsilon_a - \varepsilon_c)$	$\varepsilon_a - \frac{1}{3}(\varepsilon_a + \varepsilon_b + \varepsilon_c)$	$\frac{1}{2}(\varepsilon_a - \varepsilon_d)$

1	2	3	4	5	6
C	Zero	$\varepsilon_b - \frac{1}{2}(\varepsilon_a + \varepsilon_c)$	$\frac{1}{2}(\varepsilon_b - \varepsilon_d)$	$\frac{1}{\sqrt{3}}(\varepsilon_b - \varepsilon_c)$	$\frac{1}{\sqrt{3}}(\varepsilon_b - \varepsilon_c)$
Principal strains $\varepsilon_{1,2}$	$A \pm B$	$A \pm \sqrt{B^2 + C^2}$			
Max. shearing strain, γ_{max}	$2B$	$2\sqrt{B^2 + C^2}$			
Max. principal direction, $\tan 2\phi_1$	Zero	$\frac{C}{B}$			
Principal stresses, $\sigma_{1,2}$	$A' \pm B'$	$A' \pm \sqrt{B'^2 + C'^2} = K_1 A \pm K_2 \sqrt{B^2 + C^2}$			
Max. shear stress, τ_{max}	B'	$\sqrt{B'^2 + C'^2}$, $A' = K_1 A$, $B' = K_2 B$, $C' = K_2 C$, $K_1 = \frac{E}{1-\nu}$, $K_2 = \frac{E}{1+\nu}$			

$$A = \frac{1}{2}(\varepsilon_x + \varepsilon_y)$$

$$B = \frac{1}{2}(\varepsilon_x - \varepsilon_y)$$

$$C = \frac{1}{2}\gamma_{xy}$$

then
$$\varepsilon_{1,2} = A \pm \sqrt{B^2 + C^2} \quad \text{...(4.33)}$$

$$\frac{\gamma_{max}}{2} = \sqrt{B^2 + C^2} \quad \text{...(4.34)}$$

$$\phi_1 = \frac{1}{2}\tan^{-1}\frac{C}{B} \quad \text{...(4.35)}$$

$$\sigma_{1,2} = E\left[\frac{A}{1-\nu} \pm \frac{1}{1+\nu}\sqrt{B^2 + C^2}\right]$$

$$= A' \pm \sqrt{B'^2 + C'^2} \quad \text{...(4.36)}$$

$$K_1 A \pm K_2 \sqrt{B^2 + C^2}$$

where
$$A' = \frac{AE}{1-\nu} = K_1 A$$

$$B' = \frac{BE}{1+\nu} = K_2 B \quad \text{...(4.37)}$$

$$C' = \frac{CE}{1+\nu} = K_2 C$$

and
$$K_1 = \frac{E}{1-\nu}$$

$$K_2 = \frac{E}{1+\nu}.$$

The values of *A, B, C* for the various rosettes are given in Table 4.1. The table also summarizes the equations required to find the principal strains, maximum shearing strain, principal stresses, maximum shearing stress and the angle of the maximum principal stress direction.

Example 4.5 *The strain measurements at a point with an equiangular rosette gave the following readings :*

$\varepsilon_a = 500\ \mu\ m/m$, $\varepsilon_b = 380\ \mu\ m/m$, $\varepsilon_c = 200\ \mu\ m/m$.

Determine the principal strains, principal stresses and maximum shear stress at the point. $E = 210$ *GPa*, $\nu = 0.286$.

Solution. For an equiangular rosette

$$A = \frac{1}{3}(\varepsilon_a + \varepsilon_b + \varepsilon_c)$$

$$= \frac{1}{3}(500 + 380 + 200)$$

$$= 360\ \mu\ \text{m/m}$$

$$B = \varepsilon_a - \frac{1}{3}(\varepsilon_a + \varepsilon_b + \varepsilon_c)$$

$$= 500 - 360$$

$$= 140\ \mu\ \text{m/m}$$

$$C = \frac{1}{\sqrt{3}}(\varepsilon_b - \varepsilon_c)$$

$$= \frac{1}{\sqrt{3}}(380 - 200)$$

$$= 103.92\ \mu\ \text{m/m}$$

$$K_1 = \frac{E}{1-\nu} = \frac{210 \times 10^9}{1 - 0.286}$$

$$= 294.11764\ \text{GPa}$$

$$K_2 = \frac{E}{1+\nu} = \frac{210 \times 10^9}{1 + 0.286}$$

$$= 163.29704\ \text{GPa}$$

$$A' = K_1 A = 105.88\ \text{MPa}$$

$$B' = K_2 B = 22.86\ \text{MPa}$$

$$C' = K_2 C = 16.97\ \text{MPa}$$

$$\varepsilon_{1,2} = A \pm \sqrt{B^2 + C^2}$$

$$= 534.35\ \mu\ \text{m/m},\ 185.65\ \mu\ \text{m/m}$$

$$\sigma_{1,2} = A' \pm \sqrt{B'^2 + C'^2}$$

$$= 134.35\ \text{MPa},\ 77.41\ \text{MPa}$$

$$\tau_{max} = \sqrt{B'^2 + C'^2}$$

$$= 28.47\ \text{MPa}$$

$$\tan 2\phi_1 = \frac{C}{B} = \frac{103.92}{140}$$

$$= 0.7422857$$

$$\phi_1 = 18° - 17'$$

4.4.2 Graphical Solutions

(*a*) **Determination of principal strains from measured strains.** Graphical methods have been presented by Murphy, Hoff and others, for the determination of principal strains from three measured strains. We will discuss here the Murphy' method.

Consider that σ_1, σ_2 and ε_1, ε_2 are the principal stresses and strains respectively at a point. Let σ_a, σ_b, σ_c ; ε_a, ε_b, ε_c are the stresses and strains respectively in the *a*, *b* and *c* directions as shown in Fig. 4.8. Let primed subscripts indicate directions at right angles to those of the unprimed subscripts. Let ϕ_a, ϕ_b and ϕ_c be the angles between the *a, b* and *c* directions respectively and the direction of σ_1. Then, we have

$$\sigma_a = \frac{1}{2}(\sigma_1 + \sigma_2) + \frac{1}{2}(\sigma_1 - \sigma_2)\cos 2\phi_a$$

$$\sigma_{a'} = \frac{1}{2}(\sigma_1 + \sigma_2) - \frac{1}{2}(\sigma_1 - \sigma_2)\cos 2\phi_a$$

Applying Hooke's law to both sides of these equations, we get

$$\varepsilon_a + \nu\,\varepsilon_{a'} = \frac{1}{2}(1+\nu)(\varepsilon_1 + \varepsilon_2) + \frac{1}{2}(1-\nu)(\varepsilon_1 - \varepsilon_2)\cos 2\phi_a$$

$$\varepsilon_{a'} + \nu\,\varepsilon_a = \frac{1}{2}(1+\nu)(\varepsilon_1 + \varepsilon_2) - \frac{1}{2}(1-\nu)(\varepsilon_1 - \varepsilon_2)\cos 2\phi_a$$

Solving the equations to eliminate $\varepsilon_{a'}$, we have

$$\varepsilon_a = \frac{1}{2}(\varepsilon_1 + \varepsilon_2) + \frac{1}{2}(\varepsilon_1 - \varepsilon_2)\cos 2\phi_a \qquad ...(4.38)$$

Similarly for the *b* and *c* directions ;

$$\varepsilon_b = \frac{1}{2}(\varepsilon_1 + \varepsilon_2) + \frac{1}{2}(\varepsilon_1 - \varepsilon_2)\cos 2\phi_b$$

$$\varepsilon_c = \frac{1}{2}(\varepsilon_1 + \varepsilon_2) + \frac{1}{2}(\varepsilon_1 - \varepsilon_2)\cos 2\phi_c$$

These equations suggest that a Mohr's circle construction is possible for the strains. In Fig. 4.8, direction '*a*' is $\phi_b - \phi_a$ clockwise from *b* and direction '*c*' is $\phi_c - \phi_b$ counter clockwise from *b*.

The following is the step-by-step procedure involved in Murphy's construction of the strain circle (Fig. 4.9).

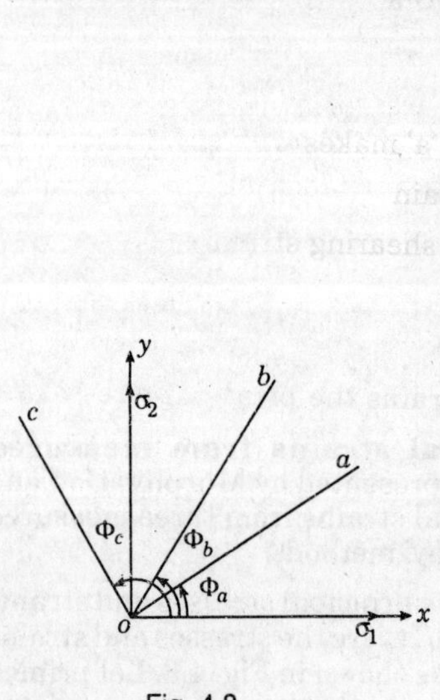

Fig. 4.8

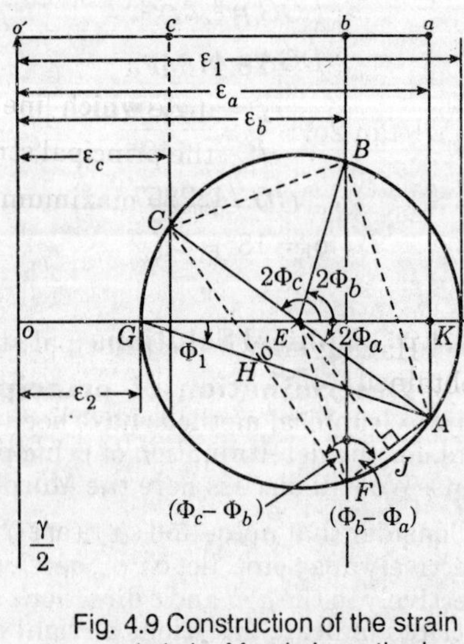

Fig. 4.9 Construction of the strain circle by Murphy's method.

1. To the line OO' draw the perpendicular $O'a$.
2. Lay off on the line $O'a$ the strains, ε_a, ε_b and ε_c to a suitably chosen scale from O'.
3. Through the points a, b and c representing the strains ε_a, ε_b and ε_c drop the perpendiculars as aA, bF and cC.
4. From any convenient point F on bF, lay off lines corresponding to the gauging lines of the strain rosette and maintaining the same directional sense as in the rosette. The lines representing the rosette intersect aA and cC at the point A and C respectively.
5. Erect perpendicular bisectors JE and HE to the lines FA and FC respectively. The point E, where these perpendicular bisectors intersect, will be the centre of the Mohr's strain circle.
6. Describe a circle with center at E and passing through the points A, F and C.
7. From A, B and C draw radii to E. Draw the line OE perpendicular to OO'. These radii must have the same angular orientation sense as the corresponding gauging lines of the strain rosette.

From the construction, we see that

$$\varepsilon_a = OE + EA \cos 2\,\phi_a$$

$$\varepsilon_b = OE + EB \cos 2\,\phi_b$$

$$\varepsilon_c = OE + EC \cos 2\,\phi_c$$

Hence $OE = \frac{1}{2}(\varepsilon_1 + \varepsilon_2)$ and $EA = EB = EC = \frac{1}{2}(\varepsilon_1 - \varepsilon_2)$; and that the angles $2\,\phi_a$, $2\,\phi_b$ and $2\,\phi_c$ are double the angles of Eqs. (4.38).

Also $OD = \varepsilon_1$

$OG = \varepsilon_2$

$\angle DGA = \phi_1$

= angle which line 'a' makes with the direction of the principal strain

$GD = \gamma_{max}$ = maximum shearing strain

$= \varepsilon_1 - \varepsilon_2$.

Having known the principal strains the principal stresses can be obtained from :

$$\sigma_1 = \frac{E}{1-\nu^2}(\varepsilon_1 + \nu\,\varepsilon_2)$$

$$\sigma_2 = \frac{E}{1-\nu^2}(\varepsilon_2 + \nu\,\varepsilon_1)$$

If we join *AB*, *FE* and *BC*, then in triangles *AEB* and *AFB*, arc *AB* is common. Since $\angle AFB = (\phi_b - \phi_a)$, therefore $\angle AEB = 2(\phi_b - \phi_a)$. Similarly $\angle BEC = 2(\phi_c - \phi_b)$.

(*b*) **The rectangular rosette.** For the rectangular rosette $\phi_c - \phi_b = 90° - 45° = 45°$. Following the procedure as outlined in the foregoing article, we can draw the Mohr's circle (Fig. 4.10), so that $\varepsilon_1 = OD$, $\varepsilon_2 = OG$, $\gamma_{max} = GD$, $\phi_1 = \angle DGA$. Then the principal stresses can be evaluated for the given material. We shall illustrate this solution by an example.

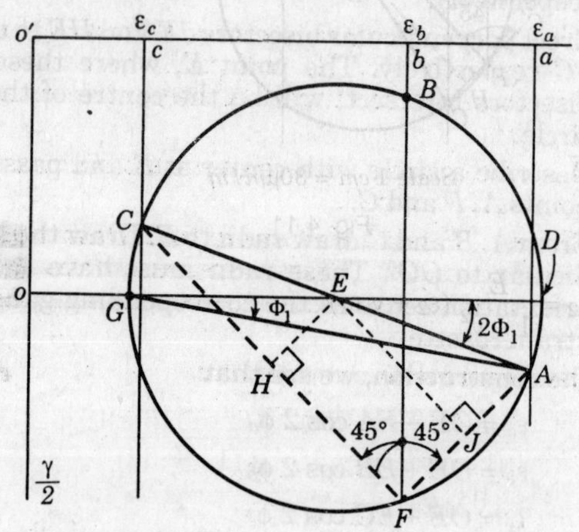

Fig. 4.10 Graphical solution of rectangular rosette.

Example 4.6 *Solve example 4.2 by using Murphy's graphical construction.*

Solution. We have $\varepsilon_a = 285\ \mu$ m/m, $\varepsilon_b = 65\ \mu$ m/m, $\varepsilon_c = 102\ \mu$ m/m. Choose a scale of 1 cm = 30 μ m/m. Take *O′a* = 9.5 cm, *O′b* = 2.167 cm, *O′c* = 3.4 cm. Draw perpendicular *aA*, *bB* and *cC*, on *O′a*. Choose any point *F* on *bB*. Make $\angle BFA = 45°$ and $\angle BFC' = 45°$ as shown in Fig. 4.11. Produce *C′F* to intersect *cC* at point *C*. Draw the right bisectors of *FA* and *FC* to intersect at *B*. With *E* as centre and *EA* = *EC* = *EF* as radii, draw the circle. Join *GA*. Then $OD = \varepsilon_1 = 11.7$ cm = 351 μ m/m, $OG = \varepsilon_2 = 1.2$ cm = 36 μ m/m, $GH = \gamma_{max} = 10.5$ cm = 315 μ rad.

$$\angle DGA = \phi_1 = (-27° 20')$$

Then
$$\sigma_1 = \frac{E}{1-\nu^2}(\varepsilon_1 + \nu\,\varepsilon_2)$$

$$= \frac{70 \times 10^9}{1-(0.32)^2}(351 + 0.32 \times 36)\,10^{-6}$$

$$= 28.27 \text{ MPa}$$

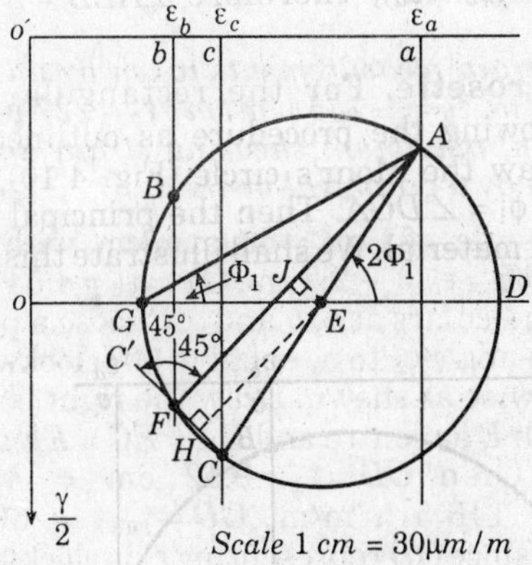

Scale 1 cm = 30μm/m

Fig. 4.11

$$\sigma_2 = \frac{E}{1-\nu^2}(\varepsilon_2 + \nu\,\varepsilon_1)$$

$$= 11.57 \text{ MPa}$$

$$\tau_{max} = \frac{E}{2(1+\nu)}\gamma_{max} = \frac{70 \times 10^9 \times 315 \times 10^{-5}}{2(1+0.32)}$$

$$= 8.35 \text{ MPa}$$

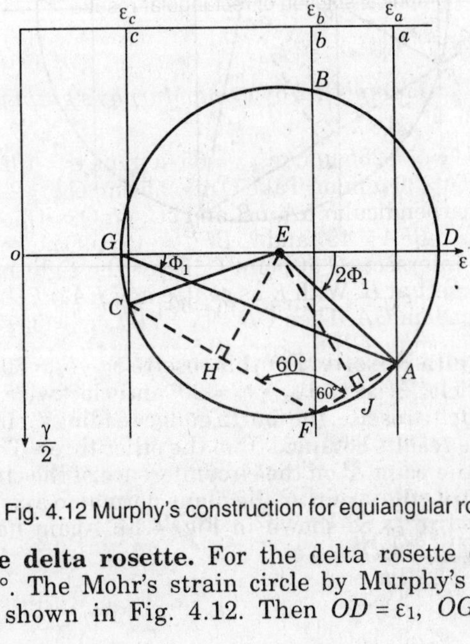

Fig. 4.12 Murphy's construction for equiangular rosette.

(*c*) **The delta rosette.** For the delta rosette $\phi_b - \phi_a = 60°$ and $\phi_c - \phi_b = 60°$. The Mohr's strain circle by Murphy's method may be drawn as shown in Fig. 4.12. Then $OD = \varepsilon_1$, $OG = \varepsilon_2$, $GH = \gamma_{max}$,

$\angle DGA = \phi_1$. The sense of ϕ_1 is the same as that of ε_1, *i.e.* OD from EA, *i.e.* anti-clockwise as in Fig. 4.12.

Example 4.7 *The strain measurements taken by an equiangular rosette are :* $\varepsilon_a = 374\ \mu\ m/m$, $\varepsilon_b = -135\ \mu\ m/m$; $\varepsilon_c = 227\ \mu\ m/m$. *Determine the principal strain, maximum shearing strain and maximum principal strain direction by a graphical method.*

Solution. Choose a scale, of 1 cm = 50 μ cm/cm, with O' as origin, take $O'a = \varepsilon_a = 7.48$ cm, $O'b = \varepsilon_b = -2.7$ cm, $O'c = \varepsilon_c = 4.54$ cm as shown in Fig. 4.13. Draw perpendiculars at a, b and c. Choose a point F on the perpendicular at b. Make angle ϕ_b to ϕ_a equal to 60° clockwise and ϕ_b to ϕ_c equal to 60° anti-clockwise as shown. Draw the right bisectors of FA and FC to meet at E. With E as centre and $EA = EC = EF$ as radii draw the circle. Join GA. Then $OD = \varepsilon_1 = 9.12$ cm = 456 μ m/m, $OG = \varepsilon_2 = -2.93$ m = – 146.5 μ m/m, $GD = \gamma_{max}$ = 602.5 μ rad., $\angle DGA = \phi_1 = -(21°\ 48')$, since OD representing ε_1 is clockwise from EA.

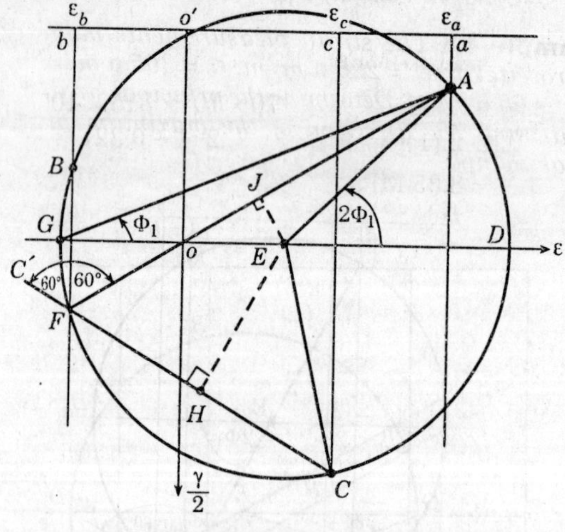

Fig. 4.13 Scale 1 cm = 50 μ m/m

(*d*) **The T-delta Rosette.** For this rosette $\phi_b - \phi_a = 60°$ clockwise, $\phi_c - \phi_b = 60°$, anticlockwise and $\phi_d - \phi_b = 30°$ anti-clockwise. This rosette is similar to the delta rosette, the fourth gauge reading ε_d simply serving as a check on the results obtained from the other three. The projection on the ε axis of the point A' on the circumference of the circle opposite to that representing the strain on the plane normal to axis '*a*', *i.e.* point A, must be equal to ε_d as shown in Fig. 4.14. Again here, $OD = \varepsilon_1$, $OG = \varepsilon_2$, $GD = \gamma_{max}$, $\angle AED = 2\ \phi_1$.

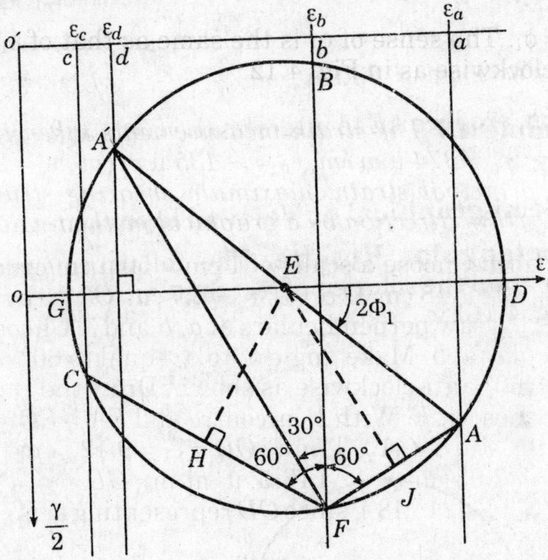

Fig. 4.14 Murphy's construction for T-delta rosette.

Example 4.8 *The strain measurements made at a point with a T-delta rosette are $\varepsilon_a = 225\ \mu\ m/m$, $\varepsilon_b = 305\ \mu\ m/m$, $\varepsilon_c = -274\ \mu\ m/m$ and $\varepsilon_d = -65\ \mu m/m$. Determine the principal strains, maximum shearing strain and the direction of the maximum principal strain by a graphical method.*

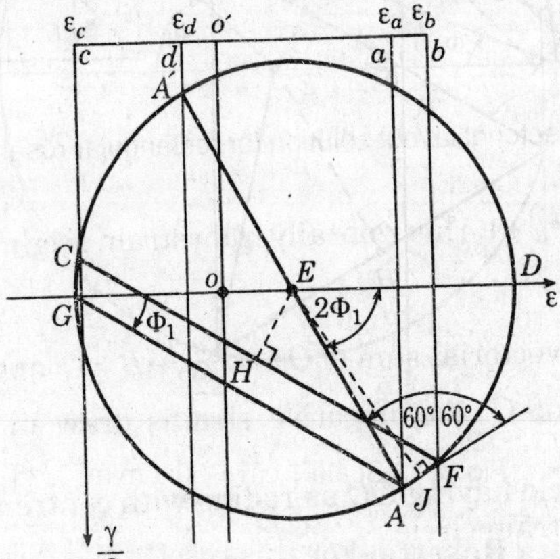

Fig. 4.15 Scale 1 cm = 100 μ m/m.

Solution. Choose a scale of 1 cm = 100 μ m/m. Take $O'a$ = 2.25 cm, $O'b$ = 3.05 cm, $O'c$ = − 2.74 cm and $O'd$ = − 0.65 cm. Draw perpendiculars at O', a, b, c and d. Take a point F on the perpendicular at b. Make angle of 60° as shown in Fig. 4.15. Draw right bisectors of FA and FC to intersect at E. With E as centre and $EA = EF = EC$ as radii draw the circle. Draw EO perpendicular to OO'. Then $OD = \varepsilon_1$ = 4.45 cm = 445 μ m/m, $OG = \varepsilon_2$ = − 2.85 cm = − 285 μ m/m,

$GD = \gamma_{max} = 7.30$ cm $= 730$ μ rad, $\phi_1 = \frac{1}{2} \angle AED = 33°$. To check the construction, produce AE to intersect the circle at A', where the perpendicular at d meets.

4.4.3 Semi-graphical or Vertical layout method

(*a*) **Rectangular Rosette.** The following procedure may be adopted to obtain the solution of rectangular rosette by vectorial layout method (Fig. 4.16).

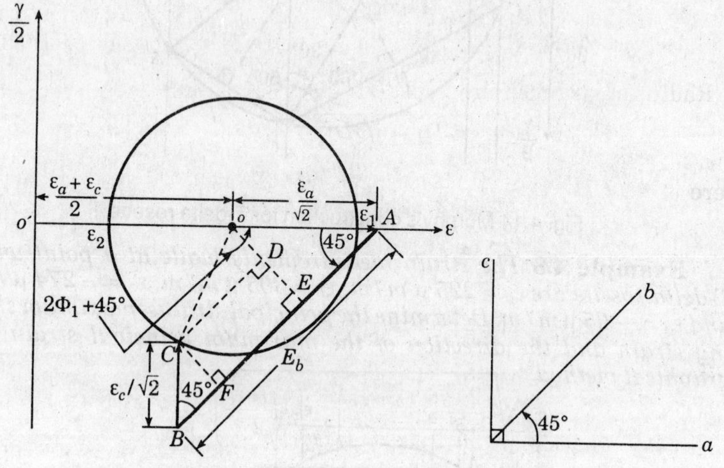

Fig. 4.16. Vectorial layout solution for rectangular rosette.

1. Layout $\frac{1}{2}(\varepsilon_a + \varepsilon_c)$ horizontally from strain origin O' and mark O.
2. Construct vectorial sum of $OA = \frac{\varepsilon_a}{\sqrt{2}}$, $AB = \varepsilon_b$ and $BC = \frac{\varepsilon_c}{\sqrt{2}}$ to obtain point C. For negative strains draw in the reverse direction.
3. Draw a circle having OC as radius with centre at O. This is the Mohr strain circle.
4. Measure $\angle COA$, the angle from radius line to OC to abscissa ε in counter clockwise direction, and deduct 45° to determine $2\phi_1$, which is twice of the angle of maximum principal stress with the gauge line '*a*'. Knowing ϕ_1, the direction of other stresses namely minimum principal stress and maximum shearing stress can be determined.
5. Draw Mohr stress circle by common origin method, where radius of stress circle is obtained from multiplying strain circle radius by $(1 - \nu)/(1 + \nu)$.

$$\text{Stress scale} = \frac{E}{(1-\nu)} \times \text{Strain scale} \qquad \text{...(4.39)}$$

Once the stress scale is determined, σ_1, σ_2 and τ_{max} are read from the graph and multiplied by the stress scale to find their magnitudes.

Proof. For a rectangular rosette

$$\tau_{max} = \pm \frac{\sqrt{2}\,E}{2\,(1+\nu)} \sqrt{(\varepsilon_b - \varepsilon_a)^2 + (\varepsilon_b - \varepsilon_c)^2}$$

$$\sigma_{1,2} = \frac{E}{2}\left[\frac{\varepsilon_a + \varepsilon_c}{1-\nu} \pm \frac{\sqrt{2}}{1+\nu} \sqrt{(\varepsilon_b - \varepsilon_a)^2 + (\varepsilon_b - \varepsilon_c)^2}\right].$$

$$\tan 2\,\phi_1 = \frac{2\,\varepsilon_b - \varepsilon_a - \varepsilon_c}{\varepsilon_a - \varepsilon_c}$$

Radius of strain circle

$$OC = r_\varepsilon = \pm \sqrt{(CD)^2 + (OD)^2}$$

where $$CD = \varepsilon_b - \frac{\varepsilon_a}{2} - \frac{\varepsilon_c}{2}$$

$$= \frac{2\,\varepsilon_b - \varepsilon_a - \varepsilon_c}{2} \qquad [\because CD = FE = AB - AE - BF]$$

$$OF = \frac{\varepsilon_a}{2} - \frac{\varepsilon_c}{2} = \frac{\varepsilon_a - \varepsilon_c}{2} \qquad [\because OD = OE - DE]$$

$$\therefore \qquad r_\varepsilon = \pm \sqrt{\left(\frac{2\,\varepsilon_b - \varepsilon_a - \varepsilon_c}{2}\right)^2 + \left(\frac{\varepsilon_a - \varepsilon_c}{2}\right)^2}$$

$$= \pm \frac{\sqrt{2}}{2} \sqrt{(\varepsilon_b - \varepsilon_a)^2 + (\varepsilon_b - \varepsilon_c)^2}$$

Radius of stress circle

$$r_\sigma = \pm \left(\frac{1-\nu}{1+\nu}\right) \frac{\sqrt{2}}{2} \sqrt{(\varepsilon_b - \varepsilon_a)^2 + (\varepsilon_b - \varepsilon_c)^2}$$

To obtain τ_{max} we multiply r_σ by stress scale.

$$\tau_{max} = \pm \left(\frac{E}{1-\nu}\right) \times \left(\frac{1-\nu}{1+\nu}\right) \times \frac{\sqrt{2}}{2} \sqrt{(\varepsilon_b - \varepsilon_a)^2 + (\varepsilon_b - \varepsilon_c)^2}$$

Also $\sigma_{1,2} = \sigma_H \pm \tau_{max}$

where $\sigma_H = \dfrac{E}{1-\nu}\left(\dfrac{\varepsilon_a + \varepsilon_c}{2}\right)$ is the hydrostatic stress component.

$$\sigma_{1,2} = \frac{E}{1-\nu}\left(\frac{\varepsilon_a + \varepsilon_c}{2}\right) \pm \frac{\sqrt{2}\,E}{2\,(1+\nu)} \sqrt{(\varepsilon_b - \varepsilon_a)^2 + (\varepsilon_b - \varepsilon_c)^2}$$

$$\tan \angle COD = \frac{CD}{OD} = \frac{2\,\varepsilon_b - \varepsilon_a - \varepsilon_c}{\varepsilon_a - \varepsilon_c}$$

$$\angle COA = \angle COD + \angle AOD = \angle COD + 45°$$

$$\angle COA = 2\phi_1 + 45°.$$

Example 4.9 *Determine the magnitude and the direction of the principal stresses and maximum shearing stress by the vectorial layout method for $\varepsilon_a = 200\ \mu\ m/m$, $\varepsilon_b = -300\ \mu\ m/m$, $\varepsilon_c = 200\ \mu\ m/m$ of a rectangular strain rosette. Assume E = 210 GPa and ν = 0.30.*

Solution. $OA = \dfrac{\varepsilon_a}{\sqrt{2}} = \dfrac{200}{\sqrt{2}}$

$$= 141.4\ \mu\ \text{m/m}$$

$$O'O = \frac{\varepsilon_a + \varepsilon_c}{2} = \frac{200 + 200}{2} = 200\ \mu\ \text{m/m}$$

$$Bc = \frac{\varepsilon_c}{\sqrt{2}} = \frac{200}{\sqrt{2}} = 141.4\ \mu\ \text{m/m}$$

$$AB = \varepsilon_b = 300\ \mu\ \text{m/m}.$$

Draw the vectorial layout diagram as shown in Fig. 4.17, by choosing a scale of 1 cm = 10 μ m/m.

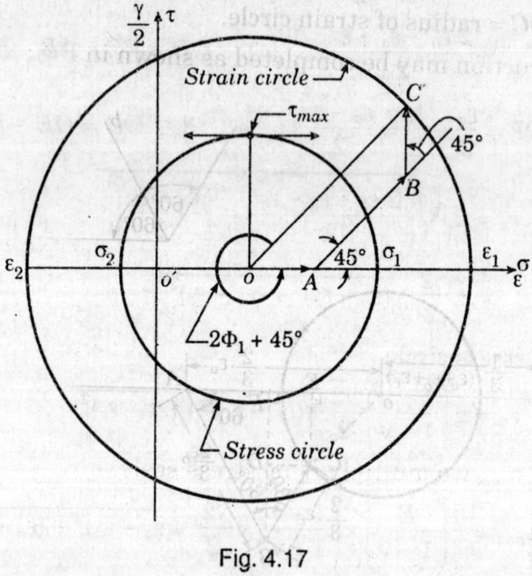

Fig. 4.17

From the figure,

$$2\ \phi_1 + 45° = 315°$$

∴ $\phi_1 = 135°$ counterclockwise from gauge '*a*'.

Now $\dfrac{1 - \nu}{1 + \nu} = \dfrac{1 - 0.3}{1 + 0.3} = 0.538$

∴ $r_\sigma = 0.538\ r_\varepsilon$

$$\text{Stress scale} = \left(\frac{210 \times 10^9}{1 - 0.3}\right) 100 \times 10^{-6} = 30\ \text{MPa}$$

Since $r_\varepsilon = OC = 5.1$ cm. Hence $r_\sigma = 0.538 \times 5.1 = 2.74$ cm

$\sigma_1 = 4.8 \times 30 = 144$ MPa, 135° C.C.W. from gauge a.

$\sigma_2 = -0.7 \times 30 = -21$ MPa 45° C.C.W. from gauge a.

$\tau_{max} = \pm 2.74 \times 30 = \pm 82.2$ MPa in the direction of gauge a.

(*b*) **Equiangular rosette.** In this case, take

$$O'O = \frac{1}{3}(\varepsilon_a + \varepsilon_b + \varepsilon_c)$$

$$OA = \frac{2}{3}\varepsilon_a$$

$$AB = \frac{2}{3}\varepsilon_b$$

$$BC = \frac{2}{3}\varepsilon_c$$

OC = radius of strain circle.

The construction may be completed as shown in Fig. 4.18.

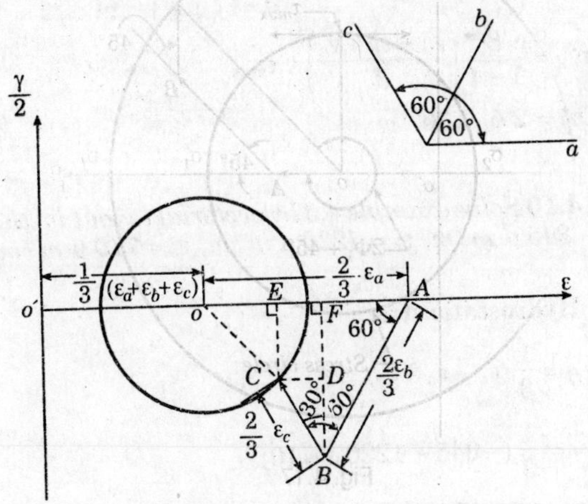

Fig. 4.18 Vectorial layout solution for equiangular rosette.

Proof. $OC = \sqrt{(OE)^2 + (EC)^2}$

$$OE = OA - EF - FA = OA - CD - FA$$

$$= \frac{2}{3}\left(\varepsilon_a - \frac{\varepsilon_c}{2} - \frac{\varepsilon_b}{2}\right)$$

$$= \frac{1}{3}(2\varepsilon_a - \varepsilon_c - \varepsilon_b)$$

$$= \left(\varepsilon_a - \frac{\varepsilon_a + \varepsilon_b + \varepsilon_c}{3}\right)$$

$$EC = FD = FB - DB.$$

$$= \frac{2}{3}\left[\frac{\sqrt{3}}{2}\,\varepsilon_b - \frac{\sqrt{3}}{2}\,\varepsilon_c\right]$$

$$= \frac{\varepsilon_b - \varepsilon_c}{\sqrt{3}}$$

$$OC = r_\varepsilon = \sqrt{\left(\varepsilon_a - \frac{\varepsilon_a + \varepsilon_b + \varepsilon_c}{3}\right)^2 + \left(\frac{\varepsilon_b - \varepsilon_c}{\sqrt{3}}\right)^2}$$

= Radius of strain circle

Radius of stress circle

$$r_\sigma = \left(\frac{1-\nu}{1+\nu}\right) r_\varepsilon$$

Stress scale

$$= \left(\frac{E}{1-\nu}\right) \times \text{Strain scale}$$

$$\tau_{max} = \left(\frac{E}{1+\nu}\right)\sqrt{\left(\varepsilon_a - \frac{\varepsilon_a + \varepsilon_b + \varepsilon_c}{3}\right)^2 + \left(\frac{\varepsilon_b - \varepsilon_c}{\sqrt{3}}\right)^2}$$

$$\sigma_{1,2} = \frac{E}{1-\nu}\left(\frac{\varepsilon_a + \varepsilon_b + \varepsilon_c}{3}\right) \pm \tau_{max}$$

$$\angle COA = 2\,\phi_1 + 30°.$$

Example 4.10 *Solve example 4.3 by vectorial layout method, where we have* $\varepsilon_a = -845\ \mu\ m/m$, $\varepsilon_b = 1220\ \mu\ m/m$, $\varepsilon_c = 710\ \mu\ m/m$, $E = 210$ *GPa*, $\nu = 0.285$.

Solution. Hydrostatic strain

$$\varepsilon_H = \frac{1}{3}(\varepsilon_a + \varepsilon_b + \varepsilon_c)$$

$$= \frac{1}{3}(-845 + 1220 + 710)$$

$$= 361.67\ \mu\ \text{m/m}$$

$$\frac{2}{3}\,\varepsilon_a = -\frac{2}{3} \times 845 = -563.33\ \mu\ \text{m/m}$$

$$\frac{2}{3}\,\varepsilon_b = \frac{2}{3} \times 1220 = 813.33\ \mu\ \text{m/m}$$

$$\frac{2}{3}\,\varepsilon_c = \frac{2}{3} \times 710 = 473.33\ \mu\ \text{m/m}$$

Choose a scale of 1 cm = 200 μ m/m, so that $O'O = 1.8$ cm, $OA = -2.81$ cm, $AB = 4.06$ cm, $BC = 2.36$ cm. Then complete the construction as shown in Fig. 4.19.

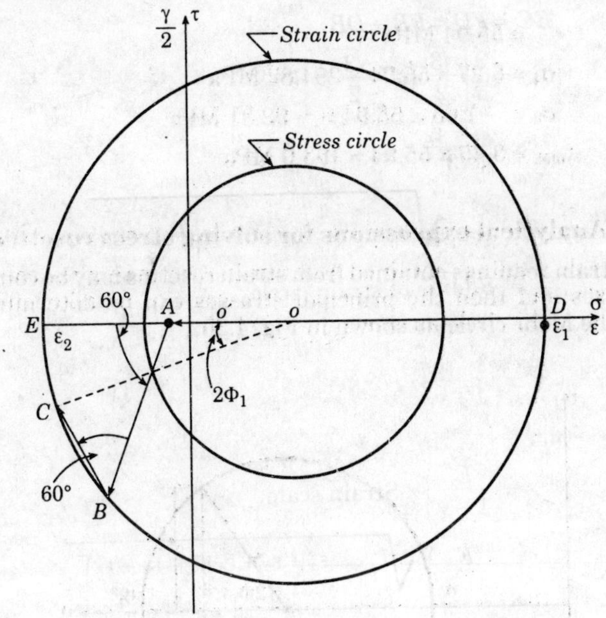

Scale 1 cm = 200 μ strain

Fig. 4.19

From the figure,

$$O'D = \varepsilon_1 = 8 \text{ cm}$$
$$= 1600 \ \mu \text{ m/m}$$
$$O'E = \varepsilon_2 = 4.4 \text{ cm}$$
$$= 880 \ \mu \text{ m/m}$$
$$\gamma_{max} = 2r_\varepsilon = 12.4 \text{ cm}$$
$$= 2380 \ \mu \text{ rad.}$$
$$\phi_1 = -(6° \ 51')$$
$$r_\varepsilon = 6.2 \text{ cm}$$
$$r_\sigma = \left(\frac{1-\nu}{1+\nu}\right) r_\varepsilon$$
$$= \left(\frac{1-0.285}{1+0.285}\right) 6.2$$
$$= 3.45 \text{ cm}$$

$$\text{Stress scale} = \left(\frac{E}{1-\nu}\right) \times \text{Strain scale}$$
$$= \left(\frac{200 \times 10^9}{1-0.285}\right) \times 200 \times 10^{-6}$$

$$= 55.94 \text{ MPa}$$

$$\sigma_1 = 5.27 \times 55.94 = 294.82 \text{ MPa}$$

$$\sigma_2 = -1.65 \times 55.94 = -92.31 \text{ MPa}$$

$$\tau_{max} = 3.45 \times 55.94 = 193.0 \text{ MPa}$$

4.4.4 Analytical expressions for solving stress rosettes

The strain readings obtained from strain rosettes may be converted into stresses and then the principal stresses can be determined by drawing the Mohr circle as shown in Fig. 4.20.

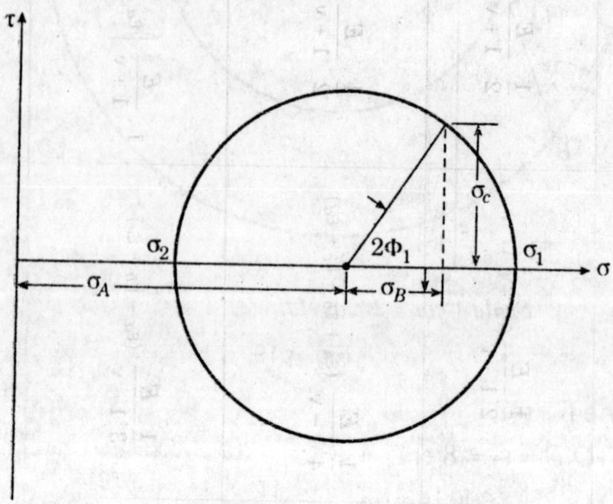

Fig. 4.20

$$\sigma_{1,2} = \sigma_A \pm \sqrt{\sigma_B^2 + \sigma_C^2}$$

$$\tan 2\phi_1 = \frac{\sigma_C}{\sigma_B} \quad \text{...(4.40)}$$

For example for a three-gauge rectangular rosette,

$$\sigma_A = \frac{1}{2} \cdot \left(\frac{E}{1-\nu}\right) \cdot (\varepsilon_a + \varepsilon_c)$$

$$\sigma_B = \frac{1}{2} \cdot \left(\frac{E}{1+\nu}\right) \cdot (\varepsilon_a - \varepsilon_c)$$

$$\sigma_C = 1 \cdot \left(\frac{E}{1+\nu}\right)\left(\varepsilon_b - \frac{\varepsilon_a + \varepsilon_c}{2}\right)$$

so that $\sigma = k \cdot f \cdot \varepsilon$

where k and f are constants. The analytical expressions for various rosettes are given in Table 4.2.

Table 4.2. Analytical expressions for strain rosettes

Type of rosette	*Space diagram*	σ_A	σ_B	σ_C
Rectangular 3-element	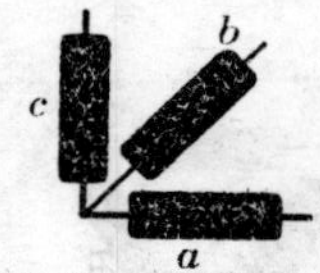	$\frac{1}{2}\cdot\frac{E}{1-\nu}(\varepsilon_a+\varepsilon_c)$	$\frac{1}{2}\cdot\frac{E}{1+\nu}(\varepsilon_a-\varepsilon_c)$	$1\cdot\frac{E}{1+\nu}\left(\varepsilon_b-\frac{\varepsilon_a+\varepsilon_c}{2}\right)$
Rectangular 4-element	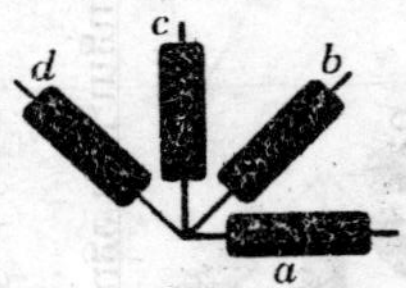	$\frac{1}{4}\cdot\frac{E}{1-\nu}(\varepsilon_a+\varepsilon_b+\varepsilon_c+\varepsilon_d)$	$\frac{1}{2}\cdot\frac{E}{1+\nu}(\varepsilon_a-\varepsilon_c)$	$\frac{1}{2}\cdot\frac{E}{1+\nu}(\varepsilon_b-\varepsilon_d)$
Equiangular		$\frac{1}{3}\cdot\frac{E}{1-\nu}(\varepsilon_a+\varepsilon_b+\varepsilon_c)$	$1\cdot\frac{E}{1+\nu}\left(\varepsilon_a-\frac{\varepsilon_a+\varepsilon_b+\varepsilon_c}{3}\right)$	$1\cdot\frac{E}{1+\nu}\left(\frac{\varepsilon_b-\varepsilon_c}{\sqrt{3}}\right)$
T-Delta	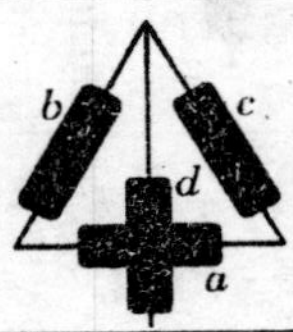	$\frac{1}{2}\cdot\frac{E}{1-\nu}(\varepsilon_a+\varepsilon_d)$	$1\cdot\frac{E}{1+\nu}\left(\frac{\varepsilon_a-\varepsilon_d}{2}\right)$	$1\cdot\frac{E}{1+\nu}\left(\frac{\varepsilon_b-\varepsilon_c}{\sqrt{3}}\right)$

Table 4.3. Analytical expressions for stress rosettes

Type of rosette	*Space diagram*	*Hydrostatic stress*, σ_H	*Shear stress*, σ_s
Rectangular 3-element	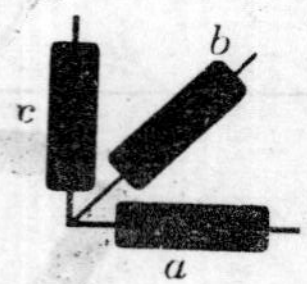	$\frac{\sigma_a + \sigma_c}{2}$	$\frac{1}{2}\sqrt{(\sigma_a - \sigma_c)^2 + [2\sigma_b - (\sigma_a + \sigma_c)]^2}$
Rectangular 4-element	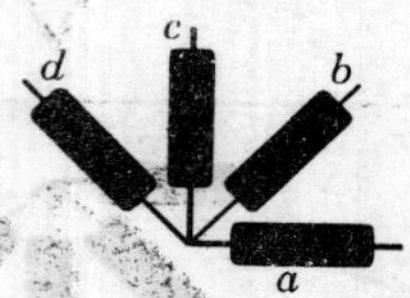	$\frac{\sigma_a + \sigma_b + \sigma_c + \sigma_d}{4}$	$\frac{1}{2}\sqrt{(\sigma_a - \sigma_c)^2 + (\sigma_b - \sigma_d)^2}$
Equiangular		$\frac{\sigma_a + \sigma_b + \sigma_c}{3}$	$\sqrt{\left(\sigma_a - \frac{\sigma_a + \sigma_b + \sigma_c}{3}\right)^2 + \left(\frac{\sigma_b - \sigma_c}{\sqrt{3}}\right)^2}$
T-Delta	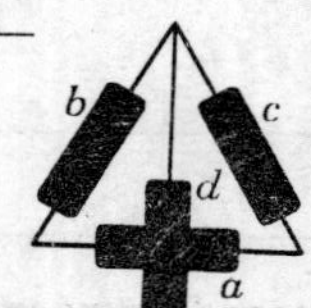	$\frac{\sigma_a + \sigma_d}{2}$	$\sqrt{\left(\frac{\sigma_a - \sigma_d}{2}\right)^2 + \left(\frac{\sigma_b - \sigma_c}{\sqrt{3}}\right)^2}$

If stress rosettes are used instead of strain rosettes, then principal stresses may be obtained from Table 4.3 by using the expression,

$$\sigma_{1,2} = \sigma_H \pm \sigma_S \quad ...(4.41)$$

where σ_H is the hydrostatic stress component and σ_S is the shear stress component.

4.4.5 Plotting of stress rosette readings

The stress rosette readings may be plotted as shown in Fig. 4.21 in the following manner :

1. From the observations for σ_H and using the lower scale plot a point P on the abscissa. This corresponds to the centre of the Mohr's circle and the equivalent stress value can be read on the upper scale.

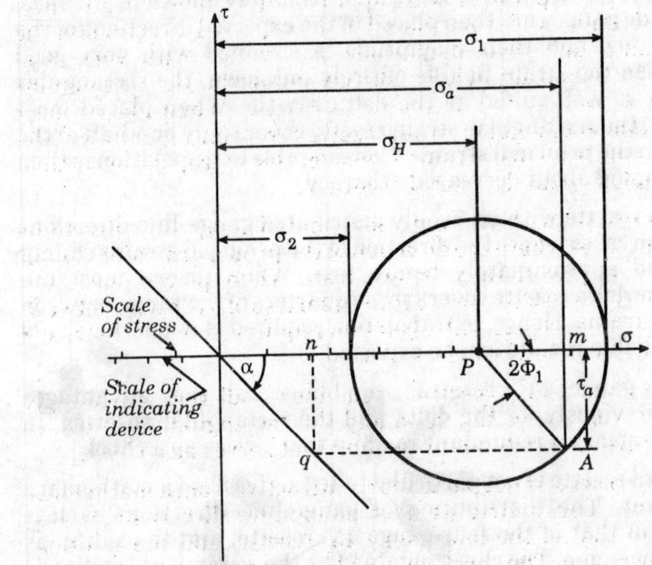

Fig. 4.21

2. To locate the second point, two steps are used :

The co-ordinate in the direction parallel to the abscissa is established by marking the reading corresponding to σ_a on the lower scale, *e.g.* point m. The co-ordinate in the direction parallel to the ordinate is found by marking off on the lower scale of the abscissa the reading corresponding to $(\sigma_b - \sigma_d)$ or $(\sigma_c - \sigma_b)$ depending upon the rosette arrangement, at point n and then drawing a line nq parallel to the ordinate and intersecting the inclined line at q. The distance of point q from the abscissa corresponds to the shear co-ordinate τ_a, of the point which we are trying to establish. Therefore, if one draws a line through q parallel to the abscissa, its intersection with the ordinate through m will establish the point A on the circumference of Mohr's circle.

If we now draw the circle, its intersections with the abscissa will give the values of the principal stresses (upper scale), and the angle between the abscissa and the radius to point A will be twice the angle of reference. The values of τ_a and $\tan\alpha$ are given later on.

Type of rosette	*Rectangular 3-element*	*Rectangular 4-element*	*Delta*	*T-Delta*
τ_a	$\sigma_b - \dfrac{\sigma_a + \sigma_c}{2}$	$\dfrac{\sigma_b - \sigma_d}{2}$	$\dfrac{\sigma_c - \sigma_b}{\sqrt{3}}$	$\dfrac{\sigma_c - \sigma_b}{\sqrt{3}}$
$\tan\alpha$	1	$\dfrac{1}{2}$	$\dfrac{1}{\sqrt{3}}$	$\dfrac{1}{\sqrt{3}}$

4.5 Comparison of Strain Rosettes

The rectangular strain rosette is particularly suited when the directions of the principal strains are approximately known in advance. The two outside gauges are then placed in the expected directions of the principal strains, and their magnitude is obtained with very good accuracy. When the strain field is entirely unknown, the rectangular rosette is not so well suited as the delta rosette. When placed most unfavourably, the rectangular strain rosette covers only one-half of the range between the principal strains. Considerable extrapolation is then required, bringing about decreased accuracy.

The delta rosette with its evenly distributed gauge-line directions is best suited in cases where the direction of the principal strains cannot be established approximately before test. When placed most unfavourably, the delta rosette covers three quarters of the range between the principal strains. Hence, extrapolation required is not serious, and reasonably reliable results can be expected.

The four-gauge 45° rosette combines all the advantages enumerated previously for the delta and the rectangular rosettes. In addition, it furnishes a redundant reading that serves as a check.

The T-delta rosette is not particularly attractive from a mathematical stand point. The distribution of gauge-line directions is less favourable than that of the four-gauge 45° rosette, and the solutions are more cumbersome. The check obtained by the redundant reading is also not readily interpreted.

4.6 Effect of Transverse Sensitivity Errors in Strain Rosettes

In an arbitrary stress field at a free surface the strain in any direction ϕ is given by

$$\varepsilon_\phi = \varepsilon_x \cos^2\phi + \varepsilon_y \sin^2\phi + \frac{1}{2}\gamma_{xy}\sin 2\phi \qquad \ldots(4.42)$$

The stresses in the x and y directions are related to the strains by

$$\sigma_x = \frac{E}{1-\nu^2}(\varepsilon_x - \nu\,\varepsilon_y)$$

$$\left.\begin{aligned}\sigma_y &= \frac{E}{1-\nu^2}(\varepsilon_y + \nu\,\varepsilon_x)\\ \tau_{xy} &= \frac{E}{2(1+\nu)}\gamma_{xy}\end{aligned}\right\} \quad ...(4.43)$$

The principal stresses are related to these stresses by

$$\sigma_{1,2} = \frac{\sigma_x + \sigma_y}{2} \pm \sqrt{\left(\frac{\sigma_x - \sigma_y}{2}\right)^2 + \tau_{xy}^2} \quad ...(4.44)$$

The apparent strain Q_ϕ recorded by a strain gauge placed along the direction ϕ is

$$Q_\phi = \frac{\varepsilon_\phi + K\,\varepsilon_{(\phi+90°)}}{1 - \nu_0 K} \quad ...(4.45)$$

The true strains ε_a, ε_b and ε_c are

$$\left.\begin{aligned}\varepsilon_a &= W\,(Q_a - K\,Q_c)\\ \varepsilon_b &= W\,[(1+K)\,Q_b - K\,(Q_a + Q_c)]\\ \varepsilon_c &= W\,[Q_c - K\,Q_a]\end{aligned}\right\} \quad ...(4.46)$$

where $W = \dfrac{1 - \nu_0 K}{1 - K^2}$

$$Q_a = \frac{(\Delta R/R)_a}{F}$$

$$Q_b = \frac{(\Delta R/R)_b}{F}$$

$$Q_c = \frac{(\Delta R/R)_c}{F}$$

where F is the gauge factor specified by the manufacturer and K is the transverse sensitivity (sometimes given by the manufacturer in terms of an auxiliary gauge factor b, $K = \dfrac{1}{b}$).

Substituting Eq. (4.42) in (4.45), we get

$$Q_\phi = \frac{1}{1 - \nu_0 K}\left\{\varepsilon_x(\cos^2\phi + K\sin^2\phi) + \varepsilon_y(\sin^2\phi + K\cos^2\phi) + \frac{1}{2}\gamma_{xy}(1-K)\sin 2\phi\right\} \quad ...(4.47)$$

(*a*) **Rectangular rosette (3-element).** For the three-element rectangular rosette the apparent strains Q_a, Q_b, Q_c are measured in the directions $\phi = 0°$, $45°$ and $90°$. Then from Eq. (4.47), we get

$$Q_a = \frac{1}{1 - \nu_0 K}(\varepsilon_x + K\,\varepsilon_y)$$

$$Q_b = \frac{1}{2(1 - \nu_0 K)}\{(1+K)(\varepsilon_x + \varepsilon_y) + \gamma_{xy}(1-K)\} \quad ...(4.48)$$

$$Q_c = \frac{1}{1 - \nu_0 K} \{\varepsilon_y + K \varepsilon_x\}$$

Then $$\sigma_{1,2} = \frac{E(1 - \nu_0 K)}{2} \left\{ \frac{Q_a + Q_c}{(1 - \nu)(1 + K)} \right.$$

$$\left. \pm \frac{1}{(1 + \nu)(1 - K)} \sqrt{(Q_a - Q_c)^2 + (Q_a + Q_c - 2Q_b)^2} \right\} \quad ...(4.49)$$

$$\tau_{max} = \frac{E(1 - \nu_0 K)}{2(1 + \nu)(1 - K)} \sqrt{(Q_a - Q_c)^2 + (Q_a + Q_c - 2Q_b)^2} \quad ...(4.50)$$

$$\phi_1 = \frac{1}{2} \tan^{-1} \left\{ \frac{2Q_b - Q_a - Q_c}{Q_a - Q_c} \right\} \quad ...(4.51)$$

Eqs. (4.49) and (4.50) may be written as

$$\sigma_{1,2} = \left(\frac{1 - \nu_0 K}{1 + K}\right) \left\{ \frac{E}{(1 - \nu)} \left(\frac{Q_a + Q_c}{2}\right) \right\}$$

$$\pm \left(\frac{1 - \nu_0 K}{1 - K}\right) \left(\frac{E}{1 + \nu}\right) \sqrt{\left(\frac{Q_a - Q_c}{2}\right)^2 + \left(Q_b - \frac{Q_a + Q_c}{2}\right)^2}$$

$$= \left(\frac{1 - \nu_0 K}{1 + K}\right) K_1 A \pm \left(\frac{1 - \nu_0 K}{1 - K}\right) K_2 \sqrt{B^2 + C^2} \quad ...(4.52)$$

where $$K_1 = \frac{E}{1 - \nu}, \; K_2 = \frac{E}{1 + \nu}$$

$$A = \frac{Q_a + Q_c}{2}, \; B = \frac{Q_a - Q_c}{2}, \; C = Q_b - \frac{Q_a + Q_c}{2}$$

Also $K_1 A = \sigma_{Ha}$ = apparent hydrostatic stress

$K_2 \sqrt{B^2 + C^2} = \sigma_{sa}$ = apparent pure shear stress.

$$\therefore \quad \sigma_{1,2} = \left(\frac{1 - \nu_0 K}{1 + K}\right) \sigma_{H_a} \pm \left(\frac{1 - \nu_0 K}{1 - K}\right) \sigma_{sa} \quad ...(4.53)$$

Hence to account for transverse sensitivity, the apparent component of the hydrostatic stress must be multiplied by $\left(\frac{1 - \nu_0 K}{1 + K}\right)$ and the apparent component of the pure shear stress by $\left(\frac{1 - \nu_0 K}{1 - K}\right)$, where $\nu_0 = 0.285$.

Similarly $$\tau_{max} = \left(\frac{1 - \nu_0 K}{1 - K}\right) \sigma_{sa} \quad ...(4.54)$$

If the transverse sensitivity K is ignored the calculated principal stresses would be

$$\sigma'_{1,2} = K_1 A \pm K_2 \sqrt{B^2 + C^2}$$

Hence the error would be

$$e = \frac{\sigma_{1,2} - \dot{\sigma}_{1,2}}{\sigma_{1,2}}$$

$$= \frac{\left[\left(\frac{1-\nu_0 K}{1+K}\right) K_1 A \pm \left(\frac{1-\nu_0 K}{1-K}\right) K_2 \sqrt{B^2+C^2}\right] - \left[K_1 A \pm K_2 \sqrt{B^2+C^2}\right]}{\left[\left(\frac{1-\nu_0 K}{1+K}\right) K_1 A \pm \left(\frac{1-\nu_0 K}{1-K}\right) K_2 \sqrt{B^2+C^2}\right]}$$

$$= \frac{K_1 A\,[(1-\nu_0 K)(1-K) - (1-K^2)] \pm K_2 \sqrt{B^2+C^2}\,[(1-\nu_0 K)(1+K) - (1-K^2)]}{(1-\nu_0 K)(1-K) K_1 A \pm (1-\nu_0 K) K_2 \sqrt{B^2+C^2}}$$

$$= \frac{-K_1 A K (1+\nu_0)(1-K) \pm K_2 K (1-\nu_0)(1+K)\sqrt{B^2+C^2}}{(1-\nu_0 K)\left[(1-K) K_1 A \pm (1+K) K_2 \sqrt{B^2+C^2}\right]} \quad ...(4.56)$$

The denominator of this expression obviously vanishes when the principal stresses, for which the error is sought, equals zero. However, if we look for the error in the numerically larger (non-zero) principal stress, then Eq. (4.56) is simply

$$e = \frac{-K_1 A K (1+\nu_0)(1-K) \pm K_2 K (1-\nu_0)(1+K)\sqrt{B^2+C^2}}{(1-\nu_0 K)\left[(1-K) K_1 A \pm (1+K) K_2 \sqrt{B^2+C^2}\right]} \quad ...(4.57)$$

and has a maximum value when $\sqrt{B^2+C^2} = 0$, so that

$$e = -\frac{K(1+\nu_0)}{(1-\nu_0 K)}$$

$$= -\frac{1.285\,K}{(1-0.285\,K)} \quad ...(4.58)$$

Now from Eq. (4.52) we find that $\sqrt{B^2+C^2} = 0$ when $Q_a = Q_b = Q_c$, that is, when there exists a state of equal biaxial stress.

(*b*) **Rectangular Rosette (Mohr's Circle Method).** If Q_a, Q_b, Q_c and Q_d are the measured values of strains and ε_a, ε_b, ε_c and ε_d are the true strains, then

$$\varepsilon_a + \varepsilon_c = \varepsilon_b + \varepsilon_d \quad ...(4.59)$$

Also

$$\varepsilon_a = W(Q_a - KQ_c) \quad ...(4.60)$$

$$\varepsilon_c = W(Q_c - KQ_a) \quad ...(4.61)$$

$$\varepsilon_b = W(Q_b - KQ_d)$$

$$\varepsilon_d = W(Q_b - KQ_b)$$

From Eq. (4.92), we have

$$\varepsilon_d = \varepsilon_a + \varepsilon_c - \varepsilon_b$$

$$= W(Q_d - KQ_b)$$

$$\therefore \quad Q_d = \frac{\varepsilon_d}{W} + KQ_b$$

$$= \frac{\varepsilon_a + \varepsilon_c - \varepsilon_b}{W} + KQ_b$$

$$= \frac{Q_b(1-\nu_0 K) - (1-K^2)\,\varepsilon_b}{K(1-\nu_0 K)} \qquad \ldots(4.62)$$

Also $$\varepsilon_b = W\left\{Q_b - K\left(\frac{\varepsilon_a + \varepsilon_c - \varepsilon_b}{W} + KQ_b\right)\right\}$$

$$= WQ_b - K\left\{W(Q_a - KQ_c) + W(Q_c - KQ_a) - \varepsilon_b\right\} - WK^2 Q_b$$

or $$\varepsilon_b = \left(\frac{1-\nu_0 K}{1-K^2}\right)\left\{(1+K)\,Q_b - K(Q_a + Q_c)\right\} \qquad \ldots(4.63)$$

To study the effect of cross-sensitivity errors on principal stresses for rectangular rosettes, suppose we have the measured values Q_a, Q_b and Q_c, then a Mohr's circle of strain can be drawn passing through points A', B' and C' (Fig. 4.22). This can be done by drawing any temporary horizontal line OX as the strain axis. The three strains are laid off along this line from an original point O. By drawing the verticals through these points and selecting any point B' on the vertical through Q_b we can draw two lines at 45° to the vertical intersecting the other two verticals at A' and C'. The circle drawn through A', B' and C' is the required circle. From Eqs. (4.60), (4.61) and (4.63) we can obtain the true values ε_a, ε_b and ε_c so that a Mohr's circle for the true strain can be drawn passing through points A, B and C as in Fig. 4.22. The effect of the cross-sensitivity error may be understood as the change of CA to become $C'A'$ in both direction and magnitude, as measured by the angle θ_1 and the difference $C'A' - CA$.

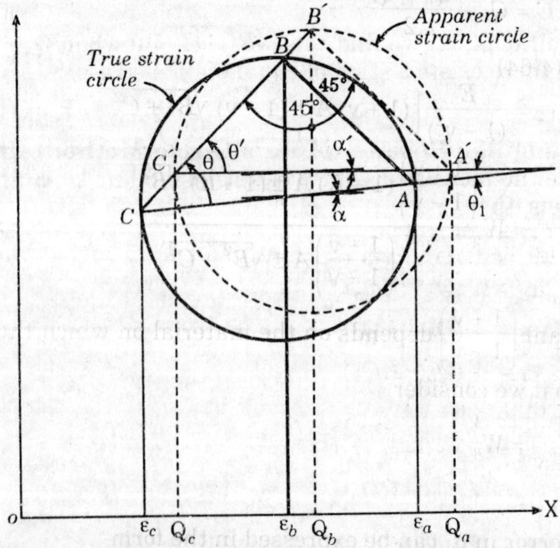

Fig. 4.22 Mohr's circle construction of true and recorded strains rectangular rosette.

The principal strains are :

$$\varepsilon_{1,2} = \frac{\varepsilon_a + \varepsilon_c}{2} \pm \frac{1}{2}\sqrt{2\,(\varepsilon_a - \varepsilon_b)^2 + 2\,(\varepsilon_b - \varepsilon_c)^2}$$

Also
$$Q_{1,2} = \frac{Q_a + Q_c}{2} \pm \frac{1}{2}\sqrt{2\,(Q_a - Q_b)^2 + 2\,(Q_b - Q_c)^2} \qquad ...(4.64)$$

But from Eqs. (4.60) and (4.61)

$$\varepsilon_a + \varepsilon_c = \frac{1 - \nu_0 K}{1 + K}\,(Q_a + Q_c) \qquad ...(4.65)$$

Also
$$\varepsilon_a - \varepsilon_b = W\,(1 + K)\,(Q_a - Q_b) \qquad ...(4.66)$$

$$\varepsilon_b - \varepsilon_c = W\,(1 + K)\,(Q_b - Q_c) \qquad ...(4.67)$$

$$\therefore \quad \varepsilon_{1,2} = \frac{W}{2}\Big[(Q_a + Q_c)\,(1 - K) \pm \sqrt{2}\,(1 + K)\sqrt{(Q_a - Q_b)^2 + (Q_b - Q_c)^2}\Big] \qquad ...(4.68)$$

Now
$$\sigma_{1,2} = \frac{E}{1 - \nu^2}\,(\varepsilon_1 + \nu\,\varepsilon_2)$$

$$= \frac{EW}{(1 - \nu^2)}\,[(1 + \nu)\,(1 - K)\,A \pm (1 - \nu)\,(1 + K)\,\sqrt{B^2 + C^2}] \qquad ...(4.69)$$

where
$$A = \frac{Q_a + Q_c}{2}$$

$$B = \frac{Q_a - Q_c}{2}$$

$$C = Q_b - \frac{Q_a + Q_c}{2}$$

From Eq. (4.64)

$$\sigma_{1,2} = \frac{E}{(1 - \nu^2)}\Big[(1 + \nu)\,A \pm (1 - \nu)\,\sqrt{B^2 + C^2}\Big] \qquad ...(4.70)$$

$$\therefore \quad \frac{\sigma_{1,2}}{\sigma_{1,2}} = W\,\frac{\left(\dfrac{1 + \nu}{1 - \nu}\right)(1 - K)\,A \pm (1 + K)\,\sqrt{B^2 + C^2}}{\left(\dfrac{1 + \nu}{1 - \nu}\right)A \pm \sqrt{B^2 + C^2}}$$

The constant $\left(\dfrac{1 + \nu}{1 - \nu}\right)$ depends on the material on which the gauge is mounted, so if we consider

$$\frac{1 + \nu}{1 - \nu} = W_m$$

Then the error in σ_1 can be expressed in the form

$$e_1 = \frac{W_m\,A\,[1 - W\,(1 - K)] + \sqrt{B^2 + C^2}\,[1 - (1 + K)\,W]}{W_m\,A + \sqrt{B^2 + C^2}} \qquad ...(4.71)$$

and as a good approximation, considering $W_m \approx 1$, then

$$e_1 \approx K \frac{W_m A - \sqrt{B^2 + C^2}}{W_m A + \sqrt{B^2 + C^2}} \quad \text{...(4.72)}$$

Similarly

$$e_2 \approx K \frac{W_m A + \sqrt{B^2 + C^2}}{W_m A - \sqrt{B^2 + C^2}} \quad \text{...(4.73)}$$

The error in the direction is,

$$\alpha + \alpha' = \theta_1$$

where $\theta_1 = \theta' - \theta$

and $\tan \theta = \frac{BA}{BC} = \frac{\varepsilon_a - \varepsilon_b}{\varepsilon_b - \varepsilon_c}$

Also from Fig. 4.22,

$$\tan \theta' = \frac{Q_a - Q_b}{Q_b - Q_c}$$

Using Eqs. (4.66) and (4.67)

$$\tan \theta = \frac{Q_a - Q_b}{Q_b - Q_c} = \tan \theta'$$

or $\theta_1 = 0$

This means that transverse sensitivity errors have no effect on the principal directions.

Example 4.11 *The apparent strains measured by a rectangular rosette are : $Q_a = -1000$ μ/cm, $Q_b = 327$ μ/cm and $Q_c = 200$ μ/cm. The transverse sensitivity of gauges is one percent and the Poisson's ratio of the material on which the rosette is mounted is 0.30. Calculate the principal stresses with and without considering the effect of transverse sensitivity and the errors in principal stresses. E = 210 GPa.*

Solution. $\sigma_{1,2} = \left(\frac{1 - \nu_0 K}{1 + K}\right) \sigma_{Ha} \pm \left(\frac{1 - \nu_0 K}{1 - K}\right) \sigma_{sa}$

where $\sigma_{Ha} = K_1 A$

$$K_1 = \frac{E}{1 - \nu}$$

$$A = \frac{Q_a + Q_c}{2}$$

$$\sigma_{sa} = K_2 \sqrt{B^2 + C^2}, \; K_2 = \frac{E}{1 + \nu}$$

$$B = \frac{Q_a - Q_c}{2}$$

$$C = Q_b - \frac{Q_a + Q_c}{2}$$

Here $K = 0.01, \nu_0 = 0.285$

$$\nu = 0.30$$

$$E = 210 \text{ GPa}$$

$$\frac{1 - \nu_0 K}{1 + K} = \frac{1 - 0.285 \times 0.01}{1 + 0.01}$$

$$= 0.9872772$$

$$\frac{1 - \nu_0 K}{1 - K} = \frac{1 - 0.285 \times 0.01}{1 - 0.01}$$

$$= 1.0072222$$

$$K_1 = \frac{210}{1 - 0.3}$$

$$= 300 \text{ GPa}$$

$$K_2 = \frac{210}{1 + 0.3}$$

$$= 161.54 \text{ GPa}$$

$$A = \frac{-1000 + 200}{2}$$

$$= -400 \ \mu/\text{cm}$$

$$B = \frac{-1000 - 200}{2}$$

$$= -600 \ \mu/\text{cm}$$

$$C = 327 - \frac{-1000 + 200}{2}$$

$$= 727 \ \mu/\text{cm}$$

$$\sigma_{Ha} = -300 \times 10^9 \times 400 \times 10^{-6}$$

$$= -120 \text{ MPa}$$

$$\sigma_{Sa} = 161.54 \times 10^9 \times 10^{-6} \sqrt{(600)^2 + (727)^2}$$

$$= 152.27 \text{ MPa}$$

$$\sigma_{1,2} = -0.9872772 \times 120 \pm 1.0072222 \times 152.27$$

$$= 34.89, \ -271.84 \text{ MPa}$$

Neglecting transverses sensitivity, the stresses are :

$$\dot{\sigma}_{1,2} = \sigma_{Ha} \pm \sigma_{Sa}$$

$$= -120 \pm 152.27$$

$$= 32.27, -272.27 \text{ MPa}$$

Error in σ_1 is $e_1 = \dfrac{\sigma_1 - \dot{\sigma}_1}{\sigma_1}$

$$= \frac{34.89 - 32.27}{32.27}$$

$$= 8.138\%$$

Error in σ_2 is $e_2 = \dfrac{\sigma_2 - \dot{\sigma}_2}{\dot{\sigma}_2}$

$$= \frac{-271.84 + 272.27}{-272.27}$$

$$= -0.157\%.$$

Example 4.12 *The gauge readings taken with a rectangular rosette are : $Q_a = 600\ \mu/cm$, $Q_b = 300\ \mu/cm$, $Q_c = -200\ \mu/cm$. The test material is steel with $E = 200$ GPa, $V = 0.30$ and the gauges have a transverse sensitivity $K = 3$ percent. Determine the error in principal stresses by neglecting the effect of transverse sensitivity by drawing Mohr's circle.*

Solution. $W = \dfrac{1 - \nu_0 K}{1 - K^2}$

$$= \frac{1 - 0.285 \times 0.03}{1 - (0.03)^2}$$

$$= 0.99234$$

$$\varepsilon_a = W\,(Q_a - K\,Q_c)$$

$$= 0.9923\,(600 + 0.03 \times 200)$$

$$= 539.45\ \mu/\text{cm}$$

$$\varepsilon_b = W\,[(1 + K)\,Q_b - K\,(Q_a + Q_c)]$$

$$= 0.99234\,[(1 + 0.03)\,300 - 0.03\,(600 - 200)]$$

$$= 294.72\ \mu/\text{cm}$$

$$\varepsilon_c = W\,(Q_c - K\,Q_a)$$

$$= 0.99234\,(-200 - 0.03 \times 600)$$

$$= -216.33\ \mu/\text{cm}$$

Scale of stain is 1 cm = 50 μ/cm

Scale of stress $= \left(\dfrac{E}{1 - \nu}\right) 50 \times 10^{-6}$

$$= \frac{200 \times 10^9 \times 50 \times 10^{-6}}{1 - 0.30}$$

$$= 14.28 \text{ MPa}$$

Radius of stress circle

$$= \left(\frac{1 - \nu}{1 + \nu}\right) \times \text{radius of strain circle } r_\varepsilon \text{ or } r_Q.$$

Radius of apparent stress circle

$$r_\sigma = \left(\frac{1-0.3}{1+0.3}\right) r_Q$$

$$= \frac{0.7}{1.3} \times 8.25 = 4.44 \text{ cm}$$

Radius of true stress circle

$$r_\sigma = \frac{0.7}{1.3} \times r_\varepsilon$$

$$= \frac{0.7}{1.3} \times 8.35$$

$$= 4.496 \text{ cm}$$

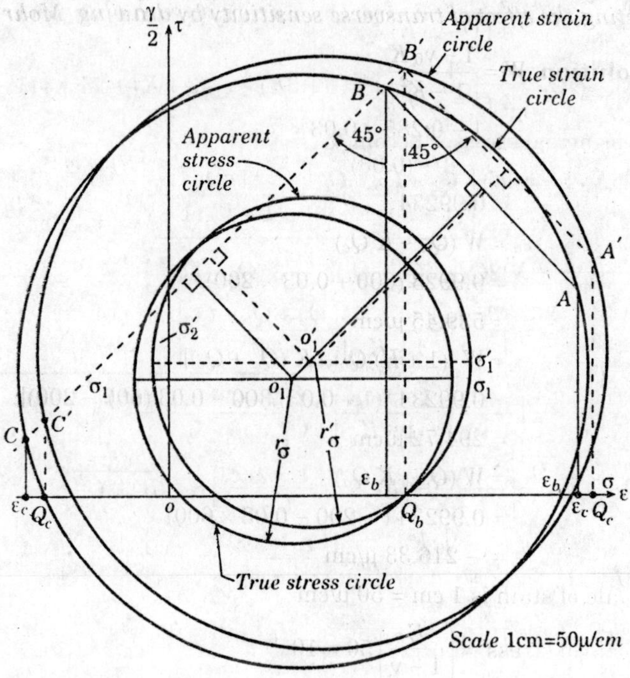

Fig. 4.23

From Fig. 4.23, we have

$$\sigma_1 = 8.45 \times 14.28 = 120.71 \text{ MPa}$$

$$\sigma_2 = -0.42 \times 14.28 = -6.0 \text{ MPa}$$

$$\sigma_1 = 8.30 \times 14.28 = 118.57 \text{ MPa}$$

$$\sigma_2 = -0.7 \times 14.28 = -10.0 \text{ MPa}$$

Error in σ_1 is $e_1 = \dfrac{\sigma_1 - \sigma_1}{\sigma_1} = -1.8\%$

Error in σ_2 is $e_1 = \dfrac{\sigma_1 - \dot{\sigma}_2}{\sigma_2} = -40\%$

The exact solution is

$$\dot{\sigma}_1 = 120.57 \text{ MPa}, \ \sigma_2 = -6.29 \text{ MPa}$$

$$\sigma_1 = 119.84 \text{ MPa}, \ \sigma_2 = -9.83 \text{ MPa}$$

(*c*) **Delta rosette.** For the delta rosette the apparent strains are :

$$Q_a = \frac{1}{1 - \nu_0 K} [\varepsilon_x + K \varepsilon_y]$$

$$Q_b = \frac{1}{4(1 - \nu_0 K)} [\varepsilon_x (1 + 3K) + \varepsilon_y (3 + K) + \sqrt{3} \gamma_{xy} (1 - K)]$$

$$Q_c = \frac{1}{4(1 - \nu_0 K)} [\varepsilon_x (1 + 3K) + \varepsilon_y (3 + K) + \sqrt{3} \gamma_{xy} (1 - K)]$$

The principal stresses become

$$\sigma_{1,2} = \frac{E(1 - \nu_0 K)}{3} \left[\frac{Q_a + Q_b + Q_c}{(1 + K)(1 - \nu)} \pm \frac{1}{(1 - K)(1 + \nu)} \times \sqrt{\{2Q_a - (Q_b + Q_c)\}^2 + 3(Q_a - Q_c)^2} \right]$$

$$= \frac{E}{1 - \nu} \left(\frac{1 - \nu_0 K}{1 - K} \right) \left[\frac{Q_a + Q_b + Q_c}{3} \right] \pm \left(\frac{E}{1 + \nu} \right) \left(\frac{1 - \nu_0 K}{1 - K} \right) \sqrt{\left\{ \frac{2 Q_a - (Q_b + Q_c)}{3} \right\}^2 + \left(\frac{Q_a - Q_c}{\sqrt{3}} \right)^2}$$

$$= \left(\frac{1 - \nu_0 K}{1 + K} \right) K_1 A \pm \left(\frac{1 - \nu_0 K}{1 - K} \right) K_2 \sqrt{B^2 + C^2}$$

$$= \left(\frac{1 - \nu_0 K}{1 + K} \right) \sigma_{Ha} \pm \left(\frac{1 - \nu_0 K}{1 - K} \right) \sigma_{sa} \qquad \text{...(4.74)}$$

where $K_1 = \dfrac{E}{1 - \nu}, \ K_2 = \dfrac{E}{1 + \nu}$

$$A = \frac{Q_a + Q_b + Q_c}{3}, \ \sigma_{Ha} = K_1 A$$

$$B = \frac{2 Q_a - Q_b - Q_c}{3}, \ C = \frac{Q_a - Q_c}{\sqrt{3}}$$

$$\sigma_{sa} = K_2 \sqrt{B^2 + C^2}$$

$$\tau_{\max} = \left(\frac{1 - \nu_0 K}{1 - K} \right) \sqrt{B^2 + C^2} \qquad \text{...(4.75)}$$

$$\phi_1 = \frac{1}{2} \tan^{-1} \frac{C}{B}.$$

The errors may be evaluated in the same manner as for the rectangular rosette.

If b is the auxiliary gauge factor then the transverse sensitivity K for the equiangular rosette is

$$K = \frac{3}{2b - 1} \quad \text{...(4.76)}$$

Example 4.13 *The apparent strain readings obtained by an equiangular rosette are :*

$Q_a = 500\ \mu/cm$, $Q_b = 380\ \mu/cm$, $Q_c = 200\ \mu/cm$.

$E = 210\ GPa$, $\nu = 0.286$

auxiliary gauge factor $b = 75$. Determine the errors in principal stresses by neglecting the effect of transverse sensitivity.

Solution. $K = \dfrac{3}{2b - 1} = \dfrac{3}{2 \times 75 - 1} = 0.02$

$$K_1 = \frac{E}{1 - \nu} = \frac{210}{1 - 0.286} = 294.11 \text{ GPa}$$

$$K_2 = \frac{E}{1 + \nu} = \frac{210}{1 + 0.286}$$

$$= 163.29 \text{ GPa}$$

$$A = \frac{1}{3}(Q_a + Q_b + Q_c)$$

$$= \frac{1}{3}(500 + 380 + 200) = 360\ \mu/\text{cm}.$$

$$B = \frac{2\,Q_a - Q_b - Q_c}{3}$$

$$= \frac{2 \times 500 - 380 - 200}{3} = 140\ \mu/\text{cm}$$

$$C = \frac{Q_a - Q_c}{\sqrt{3}}$$

$$= \frac{500 - 200}{3} = 173.2\ \mu/\text{cm}$$

$$\sigma_{Ha} = K_1 A = 105.88 \text{ MPa}$$

$$\sigma_{Sa} = K_2 \sqrt{B^2 + C^2} = 36.37 \text{ MPa}$$

$$W_1 = \frac{1 - \nu_0 K}{1 + K}$$

$$= \frac{1 - 0.285 \times 0.02}{1 + 0.02} = 0.9748032$$

$$W_2 = \frac{1 - \nu_0 K}{1 - K}$$

$$= \frac{1 - 0.285 \times 0.02}{1 - 0.02} = 1.0145918$$

$$\sigma_{1,2} = W_1\, \sigma_{Ha} \pm W_2\, \sigma_{Sa}$$

$$= 140.11,\ 66.32 \text{ MPa}$$

$$\tau_{max} = 368.98 \text{ kg/cm}^2$$

$$\phi_2 = \frac{1}{2} \tan^{-1} \frac{C}{B} = 25.52°$$

Neglecting transverse sensitivity

$$\dot{\sigma}_{1,2} = \sigma_{Ha} \pm \sigma_{Sa}$$

$$= 142.25,\ 69.51 \text{ MPa}$$

$$\text{Error in } \sigma_1 \text{ is } e_1 = \frac{\sigma_1 - \dot{\sigma}_1}{\dot{\sigma}_1} = -1.50\%$$

$$\text{Error in } \sigma_2 \text{ is } e_2 = \frac{\sigma_2 - \dot{\sigma}_2}{\dot{\sigma}_2} = -4.60\%$$

4.7 Three Dimensional Strain Rosette

To completely define the strain situation at interior points in solids, three normal strains and six shearing strains must be known. Since there are only three independent shearing strains, only six independent strain components are required. Therefore, it is necessary to use at least six strain gauges in the rosette to measure normal strains from which the required shearing strain components could be computed. The relative directions of the six normal strains measured with the rosette are shown in Fig. 4.24, where x^*, y^* and z^* are orthogonal, x' in plane of $z^* - x^*$, y'' in plane of $y^* - z^*$ and x'' in plane of $x^* - y^*$.

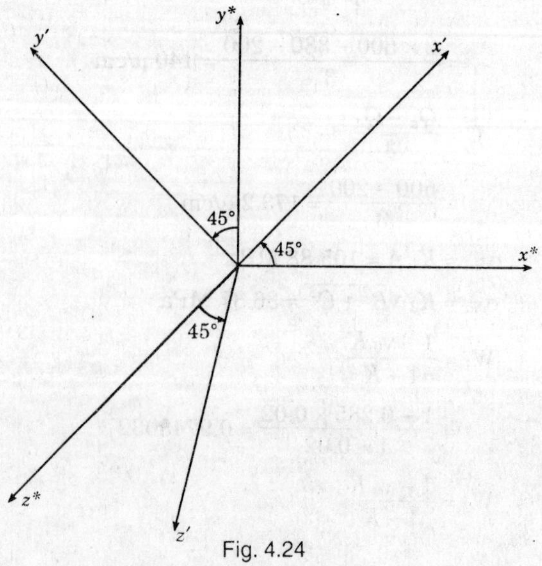

Fig. 4.24

Now

$$\varepsilon_{xx'} = \varepsilon_{xx^*} a^2_{x'x^*} + \varepsilon_{yy^*} a^2_{x'y^*} + \varepsilon_{zz^*} a^2_{x'z^*} + \gamma_{xy^*} a_{x'x^*} a_{x'y^*} + \gamma_{yz^*} a^*_{x'y} a_{x'z^*} + \gamma_{zx^*} a_{x'z^*} z_{x'x^*}$$

$$\varepsilon_{yy''} = \varepsilon_{xx^*} a^2_{y''x^*} + \varepsilon_{yy^*} a^2_{y''y^*} + \varepsilon_{zz^*} a^2_{y''z^*} + \gamma_{xy^*} a_{y''x^*} a_{y''y^*} + \gamma_{yz^*} a_{y''y^*} a_{y''z^*} + \gamma_{zx^*} a_{y''z^*} a_{y''x^*}$$

$$\varepsilon_{xx''} = \varepsilon_{xx^*} a^2_{x'''x^*} + \varepsilon_{yy^*} a^2_{x'''y^*} + \varepsilon_{zz^*} a^2_{x'''z^*} + \gamma_{xy^*} a_{x'''x^*} a_{x'''y^*} + \gamma_{yz^*} a_{x'''y^*} a_{x'''z^*} + \gamma_{zz^*} a_{x'''x^*} a_{x'''x^*}$$

	x^*	y^*	z^*
x'	0.707	0	0.707
y'	0	1	0
z'	– 0.707	0	0.707

	x^*	y^*	z^*
x''	1	0	0
y''	0	0.707	0.707
z''	0	–0.707	0.707

	x^*	y^*	z^*
x'''	0.707	0.707	0
y'''	– 0.707	0.707	0
z'''	0	0	1

$$\left.\begin{aligned} \varepsilon_{xx'} &= \frac{1}{2}\left(\varepsilon_{xx^*} + \varepsilon_{zz^*} + \gamma_{zx^*}\right) \\ \varepsilon_{yy''} &= \frac{1}{2}\left(\varepsilon_{yy^*} + \varepsilon_{zz^*} + \gamma_{yz^*}\right) \\ \varepsilon_{xx'''} &= \frac{1}{2}\left(\varepsilon_{xx^*} + \varepsilon_{yy^*} + \gamma_{xy^*}\right) \end{aligned}\right\} \quad ...(4.77)$$

All of the normal strains in Eqs. (4.77) are measured by the individual gauges of the three dimensional rosette, so the shearing strains components in each equation may be found. Therefore all strain components for the orientation of the (*) co-ordinate system are known. The rosette configuration is shown in Fig. 4.25.

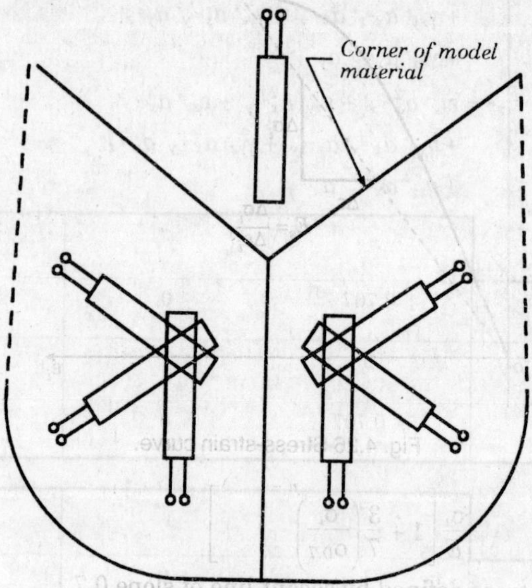

Fig. 4.25 Three dimensional rosette configuration.

4.8 Reduction of Strain Rosette in the Plastic Range

Since the rosette gauge equations are based solely on geometrical and strain considerations, the presence of permanent strains does not alter them or affect the results obtained. For a biaxial stress condition, the equations for the principal stresses in terms of the principal strains are

$$\left.\begin{aligned}\sigma_1 &= \frac{E_s}{1-\nu^2}(\varepsilon_1 + \nu\,\varepsilon_2)\\ \sigma_2 &= \frac{E_s}{1-\nu^2}(\varepsilon_2 + \nu\,\varepsilon_1)\end{aligned}\right\} \quad \text{...(4.78)}$$

where $\nu = \frac{1}{2} - \frac{E_s}{2E}(1 - 2\mu)$ is a variable Poisson's ratio.

E_s = secant modulus

σ_1 = equivalent uniaxial stress

$$= \frac{\sqrt{3}}{2}\,\tau_{oct} = \sqrt{\sigma_1^2 + \sigma_2^2 - \sigma_1\,\sigma_2} \quad \text{...(4.79)}$$

Now Rambery-Osgood equation is

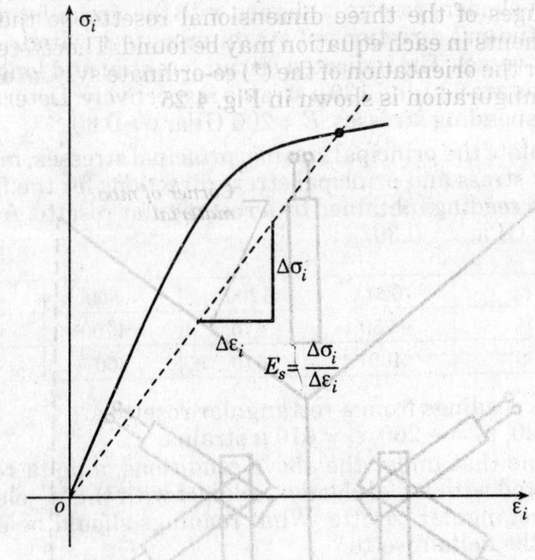

Fig. 4.26 Stress-strain curve.

$$\varepsilon_i = \frac{\sigma_i}{E}\left[1 + \frac{3}{7}\left(\frac{\sigma_i}{\sigma_{0.7}}\right)^{n-1}\right] \qquad ...(4.80)$$

where $\sigma_{0.7}$ = stress defined by secant line of slope $0.7\,E$.

$$\therefore \qquad \varepsilon_s = \frac{\sigma_i}{\varepsilon_i} = \frac{E}{1 + \frac{3}{7}\left(\frac{\sigma_i}{\sigma_{0.7}}\right)^{n-1}} \qquad ...(4.81)$$

These equations must be solved simultaneously to determine the values of σ_1 and σ_2.

4.9 Quiz Questions

1. Define a strain rosette.
2. What is the function of the fourth gauge in T-delta rosette ?
3. What are the advantages of strain rosettes ?
4. What is the relationship between the stress scale and strain scale ?
5. Write the relationship between auxiliary gauge factor and transverse sensitivity factor for a rectangular and equiangular rosette.
6. What is a three-dimensional strain rosette ?

EXERCISES

4.1 What do you understand by a strain rosette ? What are the different types of strain rosette configurations currently in use ? Discuss their uses and limitations.

4.2 A two-element rosette is aligned with the circumferential and longitudinal directions of strain in a steel cylindrical pressures vessel. The indicated circumferential and longitudinal strains are 620 and 130 μ strains respectively. Determine the corresponding stresses. E = 200 GPa, ν = 0.30.

4.3 Calculate the principal strains, principal stresses, maximum shear stress and principal stress directions for the following strain readings obtained by a rectangular rosette. Assume E = 200 GPa, ν = 0.30.

ε_a	620	1200	– 800	– 1100
ε_b	– 250	470	– 1700	– 1450
ε_c	400	670	860	– 840

4.4 Strain readings from a rectangular rosette are : $\varepsilon_a = 620$, $\varepsilon_b = -200$, $\varepsilon_c = 410$ μ strains.
Assume that under the above conditions, a delta rosette is mounted with its 'a' element aligned with the 'a' element of the rectangular rosette. What readings should be expected from the delta rosette ?

4.5 The measured specific resistance changes by a rectangular rosette are :

$$\left(\frac{\Delta R}{R}\right)_a = 10 \times 10^{-4}\ \Omega/\Omega, \quad \left(\frac{\Delta R}{R}\right)_b = 8 \times 10^{-4}\ \Omega/\Omega$$

$$\left(\frac{\Delta R}{R}\right)_c = 4 \times 10^{-4}\ \Omega/\Omega$$

$F = 2.0$, $K = +0.012$, $E = 70$ GPa,

$\nu = 0.34$

Determine the principal strains, principal stresses and directions.

4.6 Three gauges are mounted on a test specimen to form a rectangular rosette. The gauge factor given by the manufacturer is 2.0. With this factor on a null balance strain indicator, the readings taken were as given below.

(a) What is the true strain in direction 'b' ?

(b) Find the magnitude and direction of the principal stresses.

$Q_a = 130$ μ m/m, $Q_b = -70$ μ m/m

$Q_c = 700$ μ m/m

$E = 70$ GPa, $\nu = 0.30$

$F = 2.0$, $K = +0.03$.

4.7 Two gauges are mounted on steel at right angles to form a biaxial strain gauge. $F = 3.5$, $K = 0.03$, $E = 200$ GPa and $\nu = 0.285$. With the gauge factor set at 3.5, gauge 1 reads 700 μ m/m and gauge 2 reads 300 μ m/m. Find the stresses in the 1 and 2 directions.

4.8 A rectangular rosette is mounted on steel (E = 200 GPa, ν = 0.285). The gauge factors given by the manufacturer are F = 2.09, K = 0.02. The gauge readings taken were :

Q_a = 750 μ m/m, Q_b = 1000 μ m/m

Q_c = – 200 μ m/m.

Find the principal stresses in magnitude and direction.

4.9 Three gauges were mounted at 0°, 90° and – 135° with the x-axis on a steel plate (E = 210 GPa, ν = 0.30). The gauge factor given on the package was F = 1.83 and the cross-sensitivity of this type is known to be – 0.02. The strain indicator was read with the gauge factor control set at 1.83. Readings obtained were :

Q_a = – 1000 μ m/m, Q_b = – 1000 μ m/m

Q_c = – 1000 μ m/m

Find principal stresses and directions.

4.10 A rectangular rosette is mounted on steel. The gauge factor given by the manufacturer is 2.0. With this factor set on a null balance strain indicator, the readings taken were as given below. (a) What is the true strain in the direction of gauge 'c' ? (b) Find the magnitude and direction of the principal stresses.

Q_a = 500 μm/m, Q_b = – 700 μm/m

Q_c = 700 μm/m

E = 210 GPa, ν = 0.285, K = 0.02.

4.11 A delta rosette yields the following strain indications. ε_a = – 845 μ m/m, ε_b = 1220 μ m/m, ε_c = 710 μ m/m. Calculate the angle from the axis of gauge 'a' to the maximum principal stress, the maximum principal stress and the maximum shear stress. E = 200 GPa, ν = 0.285.

4.12 The strain readings obtained from an equiangular rosette are:

$\varepsilon_a = 357 \times 10^{-6}$ μ m/m , $\varepsilon_b = -254 \times 10^{-6}$ m/m and

$\varepsilon_c = 312 \times 10^{-6}$ m/m. Determine the principal stresses.

E = 200 GPa, ν = 0.30

4.13 A rectangular rosette, when mounted on a structural member, produces the following strain indications with the application of load : ε_a = 1680 μ m/m, ε_b = – 1110 μ m/m, ε_c = 620 μ m/m. Calculate the maximum normal stress, maximum shear stress and the angle between gauge 'a' and the principal axis. E = 200 GPa and ν = 0.30.

4.14 For a delta rosette with gauge readings Q_a = 315 μ m/m, Q_b = – 20 μ m/m, Q_c = 950 μ m/m, calculate the true maximum and minimum principal strains if ν = 0.33 and K = 0.025 for each gauge.

4.15 Calculate the principal strains and stresses and their directions and the maximum shear stress in a steel plate in the following cases : (E = 200 GPa and ν = 0.30)

(*a*) Rectangular rosette

$\varepsilon_a = 250\ \mu$ m/m, $\varepsilon_b = -160\ \mu$ m/m

$\varepsilon_c = -50\ \mu$ m/m

(*b*) Delta rosette

$\varepsilon_a = -250\ \mu$ m/m, $\varepsilon_b = 250\ \mu$ m/m

$\varepsilon_c = -200\ \mu$ m/m.

4.16 The strain readings obtained at a point by a rectangular rosette are :

$\varepsilon_a = -1300\ \mu$ m/m, $\varepsilon_b = 0$, $\varepsilon_c = 1600\ \mu$ m/m

Determine the principal strains, maximum shearing strain and maximum principal strain direction by using Murphy's graphical construction method.

4.17 The strains measured at a point by an equiangular rosette are : $\varepsilon_a = 1300\ \mu$ m/m , $\varepsilon_b = 0$, $\varepsilon_c = 1600\ \mu$ m/m. Determine the principal strains, maximum shearing strain and the direction of the maximum principal strain.

4.18 Two gauges are mounted parallel to the principal stress axes on steel (E = 200 GPa, ν = 0.3). The gauges which have a transverse sensitivity of 3%, give readings of Q_a = 600 μ m/m, Q_b = − 200 μm/m, calculate the errors in principal stresses by neglecting the effect of transverse sensitivity.

5

Strain Gauge Circuits, Instrumentation and Transducers

5.1 Introduction

Having simulated the mechanical strain by a strain gauge in the form of an electrical signal, we are faced with the problem of measuring this quantity. The measurement of strain is the act of a quantitative comparison between a predetermined strain standard and the unknown magnitude of strain. The simplest measuring system consists basically of three functional units as shown in Fig. 5.1.

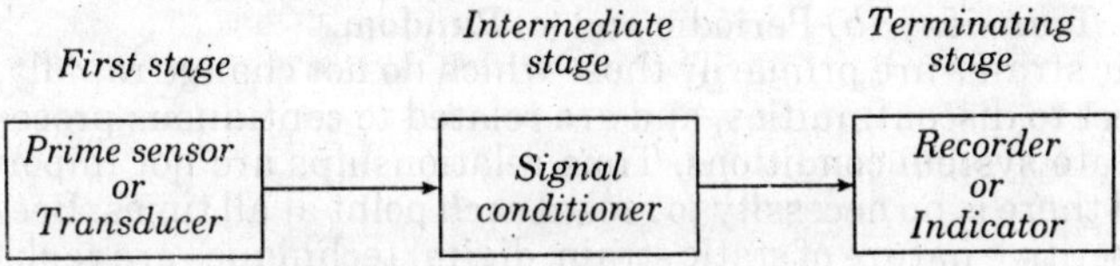

Fig. 5.1 Basic measuring system.

The first stage or primary detector system senses the desired input signal with the exclusion of all others and provides an analogous output signal. It receives the input quantity by self-generation or voltage or current conversion and produces a second physical quantity capable of amplification. For strain measurements, these include, resistance, capacitance, inductance, piezoresistive and piezoelectric strain gauges.

The intermediate stage modifies transduced signal into form usable by final stage and may perform one or more basic operations, such as selective filtering, integration, differentiation, telemetering, amplifying and matching. For strain measurements, we have either an amplifier or a chopper.

The terminating stage provides an indication or recording in form which may be evaluated by an unaided human sense or by a controller. The readout may be analogue, digital or recording type. The analogue indicators are of the moving pointer and scale, moving scale and index, and light beam and scale types. Digital indicators are of the numbered drum devices or electronic digital readouts of the null balance type. The analogue recorders are of the digital printing, inked pen and chart, *x-y* plotters, light beam and photographic film and magnetic tapes.

Fig. 5.2 shows a block diagram of the general measuring system.

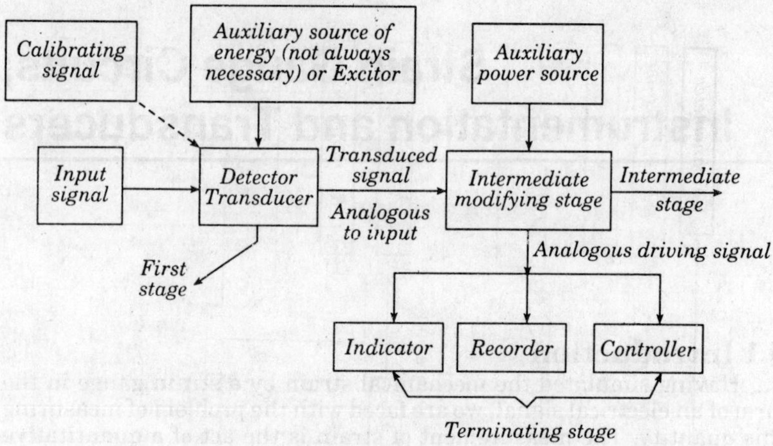

Fig. 5.2 Generalized measuring system.

There are basically two types of strains to be measured :

(*i*) Static (*ii*) Dynamic

(*a*) Transient, (*b*) Periodic and (*c*) Random.

Static strains are primarily those which do not change rapidly, are not subject to discontinuities, and are related to continuous process or steady state system conditions. Time relationships are not important at all and there is no necessity to record each point at all times. Because of the repetitive nature of static strain, digital techniques are replacing the analogue ones.

Dynamic strains contain rapid fluctuations of both periodic and random nature. The amplitudes of these rapid fluctuations may be systematic and ordered or arbitrary and unstable in nature.

The two basic circuits used for strain measurements are the Wheatstone bridge and the potentiometer (POT). The Wheatstone bridge circuit is preferred for the static strain measurements and the POT for dynamic strains only. Both of these circuits may be operated either on D.C. or A.C. A complete strain gauge instrumentation diagram is shown in Fig. 5.3. In this chapter we shall study the basic circuits, related instrumentation and the transducer applications of strain gauges.

5.2 Basic Circuits (Constant Voltage Type)

There are two types of circuits used for strain measurements.

(*i*) The Wheatstone bridge
  (*a*) Null balance type
  (*b*) Out-of-balance type.

(*ii*) Potentiometer.

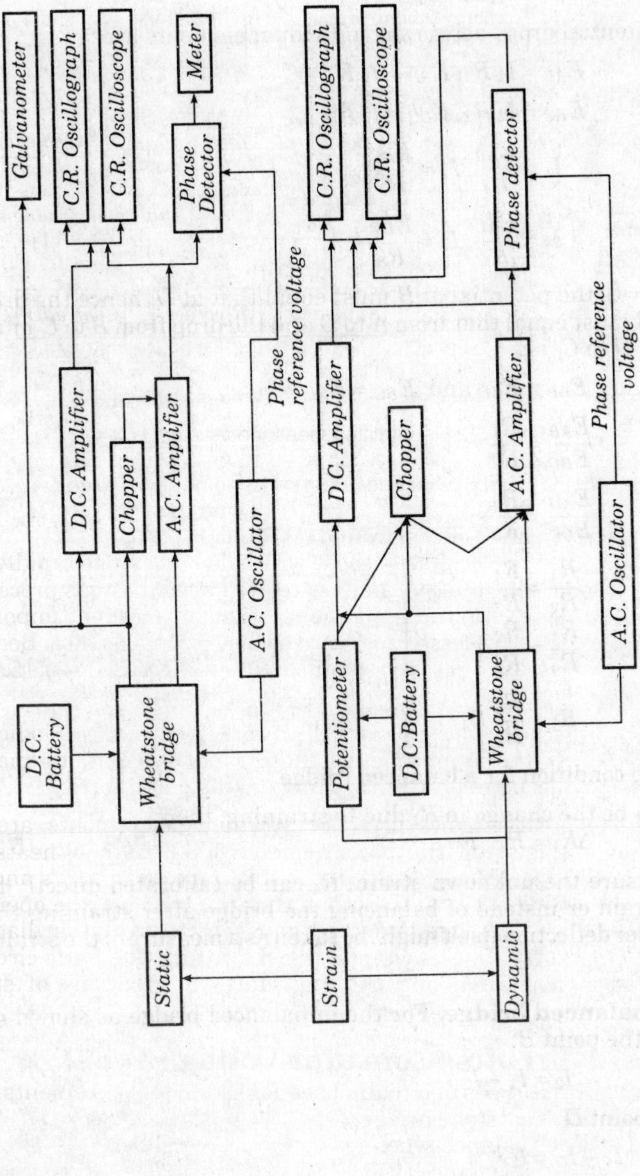

Fig. 5.3 Strain gauge instrumentation diagram.

5.2.1 The Wheatstone bridge circuit

(*a*) **Balanced bridge.** Fig. 5.4 shows the basic circuit for the Wheatstone bridge. For a balanced bridge the current I_G through the galvanometer is zero.

Hence $I_1 = I_2, I_4 = I_3$

The potential drops across the individual elements are :

$$E_{AB} = I_1 R_1, E_{AD} = I_4 R_4$$

$$E_{BC} = I_2 R_2, E_{DC} = I_3 R_3$$

Hence $$I_1 = \frac{E_{AB}}{R_1}, I_2 = \frac{E_{BC}}{R_2}$$

$$I_4 = \frac{E_{AD}}{R_4}, I_3 = \frac{E_{DC}}{R_3}$$

If $E_{BD} = 0$, the potential at B must equal that at D, hence the drop from A to B must equal that from A to D and the drop from B to C must be equal to D to C, *i.e.*

$$E_{AB} = E_{AD} \text{ and } E_{BC} = E_{DC}$$

$$\therefore \quad \frac{E_{AB}}{E_{BC}} = \frac{R_1}{R_2}$$

and $$\frac{E_{AD}}{E_{DC}} = \frac{R_4}{R_3}$$

$$\therefore \quad \frac{R_1}{R_2} = \frac{R_4}{R_3}$$

or $$\frac{R_1}{R_4} = \frac{R_2}{R_3}$$

or $$R_1 = \frac{R_2}{R_3} R_4 \qquad \ldots(5.1)$$

which is the condition for a balanced bridge.

Let ΔR_1 be the change in R_1 due to straining, then

$$\Delta R_1 = R_1 \,.\, F \,.\, \varepsilon \qquad \ldots(5.2)$$

To measure the unknown strain, R_4 can be calibrated directly in terms of strain or instead of balancing the bridge after straining the galvanometer deflection itself might be taken as a measure of the strain.

(*b*) **Unbalanced bridge.** For the unbalanced bridge as shown in Fig. 5.5, at the point B.

$$I_2 = I_1 + I_G$$

At the point D

$$I_4 - I_G = I_2$$

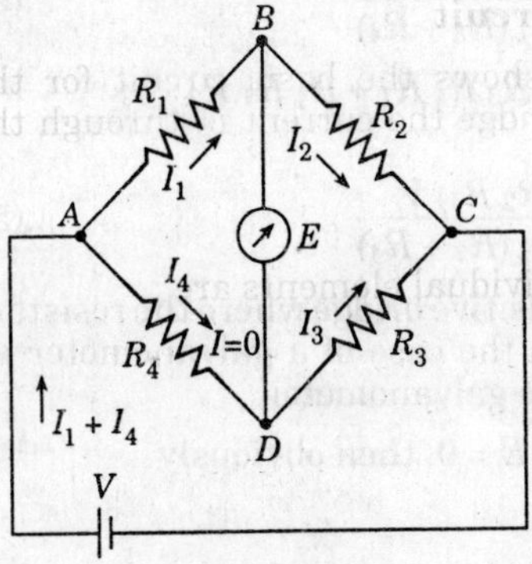

Fig. 5.4 Wheatstone bridge circuit.

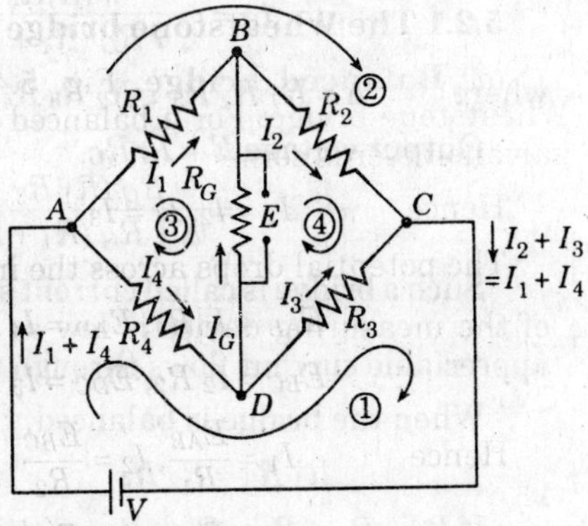

Fig. 5.5 Unbalanced Wheatstone bridge circuit.

Considering circuits (1), (2), (3) and (4) and applying Kirchhoff's law, we get

1. $$I_4 R_4 + I_3 R_3 = V$$

or $$I_4 R_4 + R_3 (I_4 - I_G) = V \quad ...(5.3)$$

2. $$I_1 R_1 + I_2 R_2 = V$$

or $$I_1 R_1 + R_2 (I_1 + I_G) = V \quad ...(5.4)$$

3. $$I_1 R_1 - I_G R_G - I_4 R_4 = 0 \quad ...(5.5)$$

4. $$I_2 R_2 + I_G R_G - I_3 R_3 = 0$$

or $$R_2 (I_1 + I_G) + I_G R_G - R_3 (I_4 - I_G) = 0 \quad ...(5.6)$$

From Eq. (5.5), we have

$$I_4 = \frac{I_1 R_1 - I_G R_G}{R_4}$$

Substituting in Eq. (5.3), we get

$$\left(\frac{I_1 R_1 - I_G R_G}{R_4}\right)(R_3 + R_4) - R_3 I_G = V$$

or $$I_1 \frac{R_1}{R_4} (R_3 + R_4) - \frac{I_G R_G}{R_4} (R_3 + R_4) - I_G R_3 = V \quad ...(5.7)$$

From Eq. (5.4), we have

$$I_1 (R_1 + R_2) + I_G R_2 = V$$

$$\therefore \quad I_1 = \frac{V - I_G R_2}{R_1 + R_2}$$

Substituting in Eq. (5.7), we get

$$\left[\frac{V - I_G R_2}{R_1 + R_2}\right] \frac{R_1}{R_4} (R_3 + R_4) - \frac{I_G R_G}{R_4} (R_3 + R_4) - I_G R_3 = V$$

Simplifying, we get

$$I_G = \frac{V(R_1R_3 - R_2R_4)}{\Delta + R_G(R_1 + R_2)(R_3 + R_4)} \qquad ...(5.8)$$

where $\Delta = R_1 R_2 R_3 + R_2 R_3 R_4 + R_3 R_4 R_1 + R_4 R_1 R_2$

Output voltage $E = I_G R_G$

$$= \frac{R_G(R_1 R_3 - R_2 R_4) V}{\Delta + R_G(R_1 + R_2)(R_3 + R_4)} \qquad ...(5.9)$$

Such a bridge is called current sensitive bridge where the resistance of the measuring device is low as in the case of a galvanometer and appreciable current flows through the galvanometer.

When the bridge is balanced, *i.e.* $E = 0$, then obviously

$$R_1 R_3 = R_2 R_4$$

If $R_1 = R_2 = R_3 = R_4 = R$ and the resistance of only one gauge changes by a small amount ΔR, then

$$I_G = \frac{\Delta R.V}{4R(R + R_G)} = \frac{F\varepsilon V}{4(R + R_G)} \qquad ...(5.10)$$

Output voltage across the load resistance is

$$E = \frac{F\varepsilon VR_G}{4(R + R_G)} \qquad ...(5.11)$$

The open-circuit output voltage (for $R_G = \infty$) can be obtained by taking the limit of E as R_G approaches ∞.

$$E_0 = \underset{R_G \to \infty}{\text{Limit}}\, E = \frac{\frac{d}{dR_G}(F\varepsilon VR_G)}{\frac{d}{dR_G}[4(R + R_G)]} = \frac{VF\varepsilon}{4} \qquad ...(5.12)$$

This is the maximum attainable output voltage from the bridge circuit with a resistance change in only one leg. Therefore, the load resistance should be considerably higher than the gauge resistance in order to develop an appreciable fraction of the available signal.

Eq. (5.9) can be written as

$$E = \frac{(R_1 R_3 - R_2 R_4) V}{\frac{\Delta}{R_G} + (R_1 + R_2)(R_3 + R_4)}$$

Since R_G is very large as in the case of an oscilloscope $\frac{\Delta}{R_G} \to 0$ and, we get

$$E = \frac{(R_1 R_3 - R_2 R_4) V}{(R_1 + R_2)(R_3 + R_4)} \qquad ...(5.13)$$

Now if R_1 changes by an amount ΔR_1, then

$$\frac{E + \Delta E}{V} = \frac{(R_1 + \Delta R_1) R_3 - R_2 R_4}{[(R_1 + \Delta R_1) + R_2](R_3 + R_4)}$$

$$= \frac{(1 + \Delta R_1/R_2) - (R_2 R_4/R_1 R_3)}{(1 + \Delta R_1/R_1 + R_2/R_1)(1 + R_4/R_3)} \quad ...(5.14)$$

If initially it is assumed that the resistances were equal so that $E = 0$, then

$$\frac{\Delta E}{V} = \frac{\Delta R_1/R_1}{2(2 + \Delta R_1/R_1)} = \frac{\Delta R_1/R_1}{4 + 2(\Delta R_1/R_1)} \quad ...(5.15)$$

The variation of $\frac{\Delta E}{V}$ with $\frac{\Delta R_1}{R_1}$ has been shown in Fig. 5.6. When all the resistances change, then

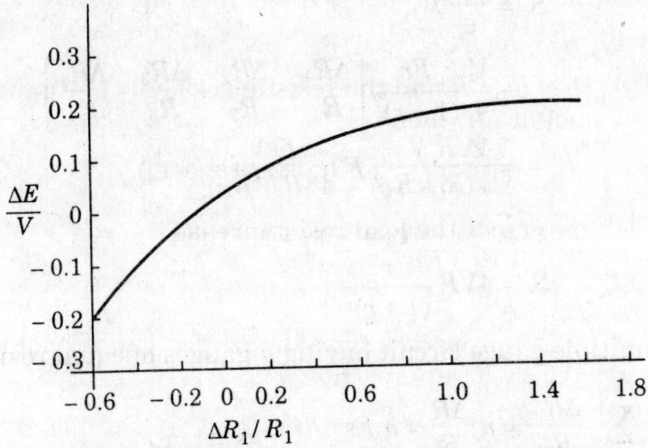

Fig. 5.6 Variation of output voltage with change in resistance of one leg of a voltage sensitive Wheatstone bridge.

$$\frac{E + \Delta E}{V} = \frac{(R_1 + \Delta R_1)(R_3 + \Delta R_3) - (R_2 + \Delta R_2)(R_4 + \Delta R_4)}{[(R_1 + \Delta R_1) + (R_2 + \Delta R_2)][(R_3 + \Delta R_3) + (R_4 + \Delta R_4)]}$$

For initial value of $E = 0$, we get

$$\frac{\Delta E}{V} = \frac{A}{B}(1 - \eta)$$

where $A = R_1 R_3 (\Delta R_1/R_1 - \Delta R_2/R_2 + \Delta R_3/R_3 - \Delta R_4/R_4)$

$$B = \frac{R_1 R_3 (R_1 + R_2)^2}{R_1 R_2}$$

or $$\frac{\Delta E}{V} = \frac{R_1 R_2}{(R_1 + R_2)^2}[\Delta R_1/R_1 - \Delta R_2/R_2 + \Delta R_3/R_3 - \Delta R_4/R_4](1 - \eta) \quad ...(5.16)$$

$$= \frac{r}{(1 + r)^2} F(\varepsilon_1 - \varepsilon_2 + \varepsilon_3 - \varepsilon_4)(1 - \eta) \quad ...(5.17)$$

where $r = R_2/R_1$

$$\eta = \frac{1}{1 + \dfrac{r + 1}{\dfrac{\Delta R_1}{R_2} + \dfrac{\Delta R_4}{R_4} + r\left(\dfrac{\Delta R_2}{R_2} + \dfrac{\Delta R_3}{R_3}\right)}}$$

If the non-linear term is ignored, when strains are less than about 5%, then

$$\frac{\Delta E}{V} = \frac{r}{(1+r)^2} F(\varepsilon_1 - \varepsilon_2 + \varepsilon_3 - \varepsilon_4) \quad ...(5.18)$$

Eq. (5.18) shows that the unbalance of the bridge is proportional to the sum of strains in opposite arms and to the difference of strains in adjacent arms.

(*c*) **Circuit Sensitivity.** The circuit sensitivity S_c of the bridge circuit is defined as :

$$S_c = \frac{\Delta E}{\varepsilon}$$

$$= \frac{V}{\varepsilon} \frac{Fr}{(1+r)^2} \left[\frac{\Delta R_1}{R_1} - \frac{\Delta R_2}{R_2} + \frac{\Delta R_3}{R_3} - \frac{\Delta R_4}{R_4} \right]$$

$$= \frac{V}{\varepsilon} \frac{r}{(1+r)^2} F(\varepsilon_1 - \varepsilon_2 + \varepsilon_3 - \varepsilon_4) \quad ...(5.19)$$

If $\varepsilon_1 = -\varepsilon_2 = \varepsilon_3 = -\varepsilon_4 = \varepsilon$, then

$$S_c = 4VF \frac{r}{(1+r)^2} \quad ...(5.20)$$

In a multiple gauge circuit having n gauges of equal resistance,

$$\sum_{m=1}^{m=n} \frac{\Delta R_m}{R_m} = n \frac{\Delta R}{R} = n F\varepsilon$$

$$\therefore \quad S_c = Vn F \frac{r}{(1+r)^2} \quad ...(5.21)$$

The circuit sensitivity depends upon the values of $\frac{r}{(1+r)^2}$ as shown in Fig. 5.7, which is maximum at $r = 1$.

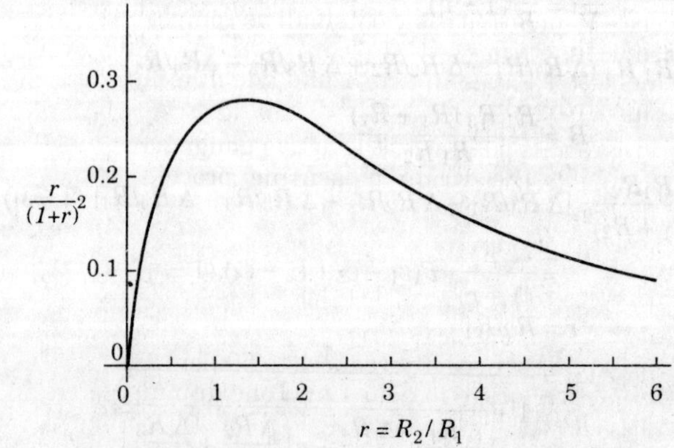

Fig. 5.7 Effect of R_2/R_1 ratio on sensitivity of a Wheatstone bridge with constant supply voltage.

(*d*) **Sensitivity analysis.** (*i*) One active gauge, *e.g.* $R_1 = R_g$ (Fig. 5.8).

Now $\quad R_g R_3 = R_2 R_4$

$$V = I_g (R_1 + R_2) = I_g R_g (1 + r)$$

where I_g is the current flowing through the active gauge. Circuit sensitivity becomes

$$S_c = \left(\frac{r}{1+r}\right) I_g R_g F$$

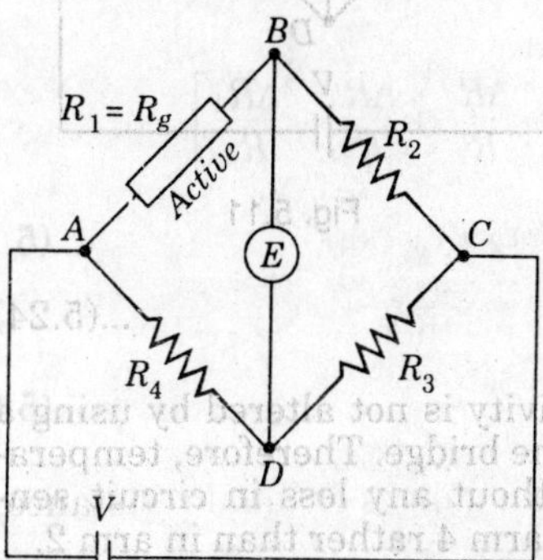

Fig. 5.8

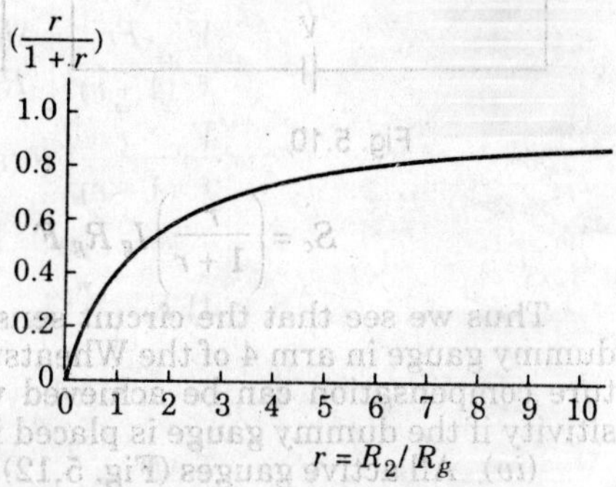

Fig. 5.9 Effect of R_2/R_g ratio on the sensitivity of a bridge with a constant gauge current.

The circuit sensitivity depends upon the ratio $\left(\frac{r}{1+r}\right)$ which has been shown in Fig. 5.9. It can be seen from Fig. 5.9 that the circuit sensitivity is 0.9 at $r = 0$, 0.909 at $r = 10$ and 0.99 for $r = 100$. Thus we can conclude that we can limit $r = 9$, because beyond this ratio the increase in circuit sensitivity is very small as compared to the tremendous increase in the ratio *r*.

(*ii*) One active gauge in arm 1 and one dummy gauge in arm 2 (Fig. 5.10).

A dummy gauge is similar to the active gauge but is not subjected to any load during the strain measuring process. Thus for $R_1 = R_2 = R_g$, $r = 1$.

Hence $\quad V = 2 I_g R_g$

$$S_c = \frac{1}{2} I_g R_g F \qquad \text{...(5.23)}$$

Hence the circuit sensitivity reduces to 50 per cent.

(*iii*) One active gauge in arm 1 and one dummy gauge in arm 4 (Fig. 5.11).

Here $\quad R_1 = R_4 = R_g$

Now $\quad V = I_g (R_1 + R_2) = I_g R_g (1 + r)$

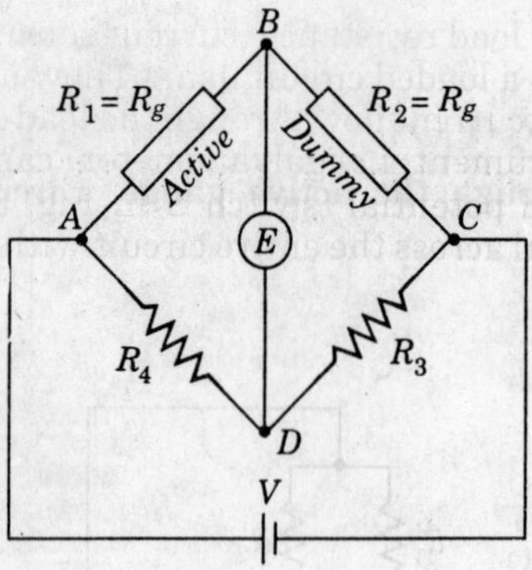

Fig. 5.10

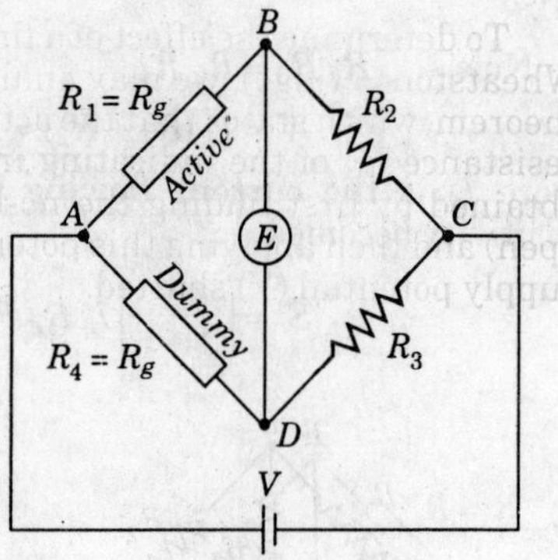

Fig. 5.11

$$S_c = \left(\frac{r}{1+r}\right) I_g R_g F \qquad \text{...(5.24)}$$

Thus we see that the circuit sensitivity is not altered by using a dummy gauge in arm 4 of the Wheatstone bridge. Therefore, temperature compensation can be achieved without any loss in circuit sensitivity if the dummy gauge is placed in arm 4 rather than in arm 2.

(*iv*) All active gauges (Fig. 5.12).

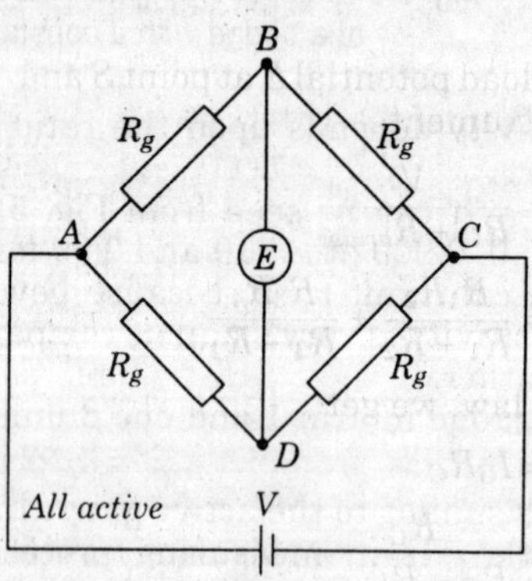

Fig. 5.12

In this case, $R_1 = R_2 = R_3 = R_4 = R_g$

and hence $r = 1$

$$V = 2\, I_g R_g$$

$$S_c = 2\, I_g R_g F \qquad \text{...(5.25)}$$

Thus the circuit sensitivity becomes 200 per cent. Out-of-balance method is more suitable for dynamic strain measurements.

5.2.2 Effect of a Finite Load Resistance

To determine the effect of a finite load resistance (current sensitive Wheatstone bridge), we may analyze a loaded circuit using Thevenin's theorem, which states that the actual current flow through the load (the resistance R_G of the indicating instrument, *i.e.* galvanometer) can be obtained by first finding the no-load potential (switch S in Fig. 5.13 open) and then applying this potential across the entire circuit with the supply potential (V) shorted.

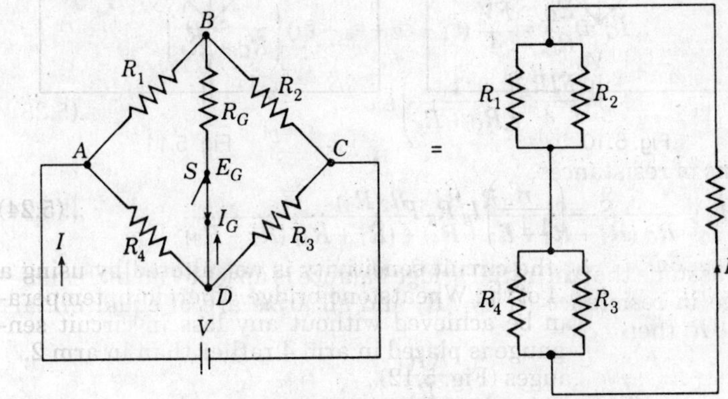

Fig. 5.13 Bridge circuit with load resistance.

We apply the no-load potential E at point S and compute the current flow through the instrument.

$$I_G = \frac{V}{R_G + R_{bridge}}$$

$$R_{bridge} = \frac{R_1R_2}{R_1 + R_2} + \frac{R_3R_4}{R_3 + R_4}$$

Applying Ohm's law, we get

$$E_G = I_G R_G$$

or
$$E_G = \frac{R_G}{R_G + R_{bridge}} \cdot V$$

where E_G is the potential across the indicating instrument.

The factor $\frac{R_G}{R_G + R_{bridge}}$ is the factor by which the open circuit (or no-load potential) voltage V is reduced, due to the load resistance R_G. For the special case of $R_1 = R_2 = R_3 = R_4 = R_g$,

$$E_G = \frac{FV}{4}(\varepsilon_1 - \varepsilon_2 + \varepsilon_3 - \varepsilon_4)\left(\frac{R_G}{R_G + R_g}\right)$$

$$= \frac{FIR_g}{4}(\varepsilon_1 - \varepsilon_2 + \varepsilon_3 - \varepsilon_4)\left(\frac{R_G}{R_G + R_g}\right) \quad ...(5.26)$$

where I is the total battery current.

Now $\varepsilon_1 - \varepsilon_2 + \varepsilon_3 - \varepsilon_4 = \varepsilon$ is the net strain affecting the bridge.

$$\therefore \quad E_G = \frac{FIR_g}{4} \times \frac{R_G}{R_G + R_g} \times \varepsilon \quad ...(5.27)$$

The output of the bridge is often measured by using a current sensitive instrument (galvanometer), for this case, we can write

$$I_G = \frac{E_G}{R_G} = \frac{FV}{4}(\varepsilon_1 - \varepsilon_2 + \varepsilon_3 - \varepsilon_4)\left(\frac{1}{R_G + R_g}\right)$$

$$= \frac{FIR_g}{4}\left(\frac{1}{R_G + R_g}\right)\varepsilon \quad ...(5.28)$$

or in terms of resistances,

$$I_G = \frac{I\,(R_1 R_3 - R_2 R_4)}{R_G\,(R_1 + R_2 + R_3 + R_4) + (R_1 + R_4)\,(R_2 + R_3)} \quad ...(5.29)$$

If we assume that an initial bridge balance is upset by an incremental change in resistance R_1 by ΔR_1 and all arms are of equal initial resistance R, then

$$\frac{\Delta I_G}{I} = \frac{\dfrac{\Delta R_1}{R_1}}{4\left[1 + \dfrac{R_G}{R}\right] + \left[2 + \dfrac{R_G}{R}\right]\left(\dfrac{\Delta R_1}{R}\right)} \quad ...(5.30)$$

The variation of $\Delta I_G/I$ with $\Delta R_1/R$ for $\dfrac{R_G}{R} = 0.5$, 1 and 2 is shown in Fig. 5.14.

Example 5.1 *A Wheatstone bridge using four 120 Ω gauges of gauge factor 2.0 is used so that the current through the gauge is to be held to 20 mA. Find the sensitivity of this circuit, when (i) a Cathode-ray oscilloscope is used as an indicator, and (ii) a low impedance microammeter of 120 Ω resistance is used.*

Solution. (*i*) The circuit sensitivity of the Wheatstone bridge having one active arm when using a C.R.O. is given by

$$S_c = \left(\frac{r}{1+r}\right) I_g R_g F$$

$$= \frac{1}{2} \times 20 \times 10^{-3} \times 120 \times 2$$

$$= 2400 \times 10^{-3} \text{ volts/(m/m)}$$

(*ii*) When the micrometer of 120 Ω resistance is used, then

$$S_c = \left(\frac{r}{1+r}\right) I_g R_g F \left(\frac{1}{R_G + R_g}\right)$$

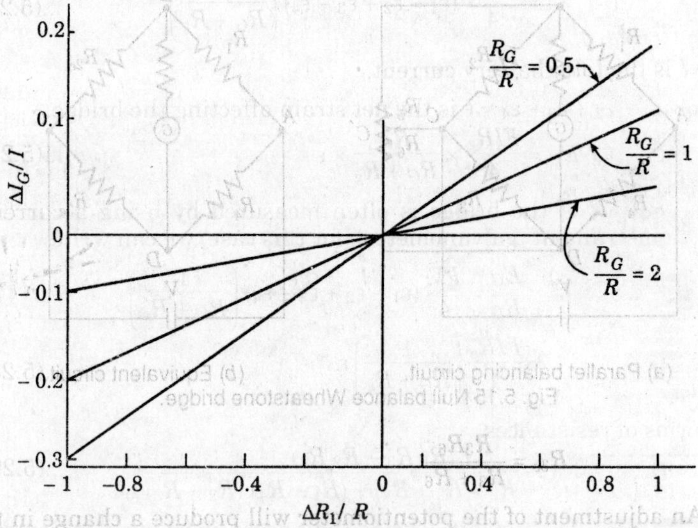

Fig. 5.14

$$= \frac{1}{2} \times 20 \times 10^{-3} \times 120 \times 2 \left(\frac{1}{120 + 120} \right)$$

$$= 10 \times 10^{-3} = 0.01\ \mu\text{A}/(\mu\text{m/m}).$$

5.2.3 Null-Balance Bridges

In static applications it is possible to employ a null balance bridge where the resistance of one or more arms in the bridge is changed to match the effect of the change in resistance of the active gauge. The null-balance system is usually more accurate than the direct-readout bridge and requires less expensive equipment for its operation. A relatively simple null-balance type of Wheatstone bridge is shown in Fig. 5.15 (*a*). A slide wire resistance potentiometer is placed across the bridge from *B* to *D* and the point *C* is connected to a point *C′* on the balance resistor. Assume that initially the bridge is balanced with active gauge in arm 1 so that $R_1 R_3 = R_2 R_4$ and $R_5 = R_6$. The meter *G* is at null or zero voltage. Now consider a resistance change in R_1, which upsets this balance, causing a voltage indication on meter *G*. The slide wire on the potentiometer is adjusted, making $R_5 \neq R_6$, untill the bridge is again balanced. The potentiometer adjustment, which is calibrated, is proportional to the resistance change in the active gauge. Thus the mechanical movement of the potentiometer serves as the readout means, and the voltage is measured only to establish a zero or null point.

Now the equivalent resistances are

$$R_{2e} = \frac{R_2 R_5}{R_2 + R_5}$$

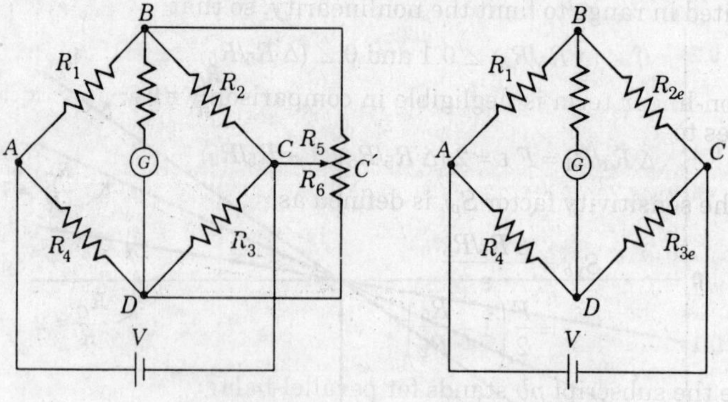

(*a*) Parallel balancing circuit. (*b*) Equivalent circuit.

Fig. 5.15 Null balance Wheatstone bridge.

$$R_{3e} = \frac{R_3 R_6}{R_3 + R_6}$$

An adjustment of the potentiometer will produce a change in the resistances of R_5 and R_6 equal to ΔR_5 and ΔR_6, so that $\Delta R_5 = -\Delta R_6$, since the total resistance of potentiometer remains constant.

The change in equivalent resistances become,

$$\Delta R_{2e}/R_{2e} = \frac{[R_2 (R_5 + \Delta R_5)/(R_2 + R_5 + \Delta R_5)] - R_2 R_5/(R_2 + R_5)}{R_2 R_5/(R_2 + R_5)}$$

$$= (\Delta R_5/R_5)/[1 + (R_5/R_2)\ (1 + \Delta R_5/R_5)]$$

$$\Delta R_{3e}/R_{3e} = (\Delta R_6/R_6)/[1 + (R_6/R_3)\ (1 + \Delta R_6/R_6)]$$

Hence by using an active gauge in arm 1 and a dummy gauge in arm 4, the change in voltage output becomes,

$$\Delta E = [V R_1 R_{2e}/(R_1 + R_{2e})^2]\ [\Delta R_1/R_1 - \Delta R_{2e}/R_{2e} - \Delta R_{3e}/R_{3e}] = 0$$

$$\Delta R_1/R_1 = F\varepsilon = \Delta R_{2e}/R_{2e} - \Delta R_{3e}/R_{3e}$$

$$= (\Delta R_5/R_5)/[(1 + R_5/R_2)\ (1 + \Delta R_5/R_5)] - (\Delta R_6/R_6)/[(1 + R_6/R_3)\ (1 + \Delta R_6/R_6)]$$

For an initially balanced bridge,

when $R_5 = R_6,\ R_2 = R_3$

and $\Delta R_5 = -\Delta R_6$, we get

$$\Delta R_1/R_1 = F\varepsilon$$

$$= \frac{2\ (1 + R_5/R_2)\ (\Delta R_5/R_5)}{1 + 2\ (R_5/R_2) + (R_5/R_2)^2\ [1 - \Delta R_5/R_5)^2]} \qquad \text{...(5.31)}$$

Eq. (5.31) indicates that the strain reading ε obtained by using a parallel-balance circuit is nonlinear in terms of the adjustment of R_5

and R_6 due to the presence of $(\Delta R_5/R_5)^2$ term. If the value of $(\Delta R_5/R_5)$ is limited in range to limit the nonlinearity, so that

$$0 \angle (\Delta R_5/R_5) \angle 0.1 \text{ and } 0 \angle (\Delta R_5/R_5)^2 \angle 0.01$$

the non-linear term is negligible in comparison with 1 and Eq. (5.31) reduces to

$$\Delta R_1/R_1 = F\,\varepsilon = 2\,(\Delta R_5/R_5)/(1 + R_5/R_2) \quad ...(5.32)$$

The sensitivity factor S_{pb} is defined as

$$S_{pb} = \frac{\Delta R_5/R_5}{\varepsilon} = \frac{F}{2}\left(1 + \frac{R_5}{R_2}\right) \quad ...(5.33)$$

where the subscript pb stands for parallel-balance.

5.2.4 Temperature Compensation

If the strain gauge is placed in arm 1 then the dummy gauge can be placed either in arm 2 or arm 4 of the Wheatstone bridge to achieve temperature compensation. Since $\frac{R_1}{R_4} = \frac{R_2}{R_3}$ or $\frac{R_1}{R_2} = \frac{R_4}{R_3}$, therefore, if R_1 increases by an amount ΔR_1 then R_2 also increases by an amount ΔR_2 due to temperature rise. Since $R_1 \approx R_2$, hence $(R_1 + \Delta R_1) \approx (R_2 + \Delta R_2)$. Similarly

$$\frac{R_1 + \Delta R_1}{R_4 + \Delta R_4} = \frac{R_2}{R_3}$$

or

$$\frac{R_1 + \Delta R_1}{R_2 + \Delta R_2} = \frac{R_4}{R_3}$$

The ratio is undisturbed because the numerator and denominator of the L.H.S. are increased by the same proportion. Since the presence of a dummy gauge in arm 2 reduces the circuit sensitivity by 50% and in arm 4, has no effect on circuit sensitivity, hence it is advisable to use the dummy gauge in arm 4 to obtain temperature compensation. In case of bending loads,

$$\frac{R_1 + \Delta R_1}{R_2 - \Delta R_2} \neq \frac{R_4}{R_3}$$

when two adjacent arms are active,

and

$$\frac{R_1 + \Delta R_1}{R_2 - \Delta R_2} = \frac{R_4 - \Delta R_4}{R_3 + \Delta R_3}$$

When four arms are active.

5.2.5 Balancing Techniques

For a balanced bridge, *i.e.* when no current flows through the galvanometer G, we have (Fig. 5.16).

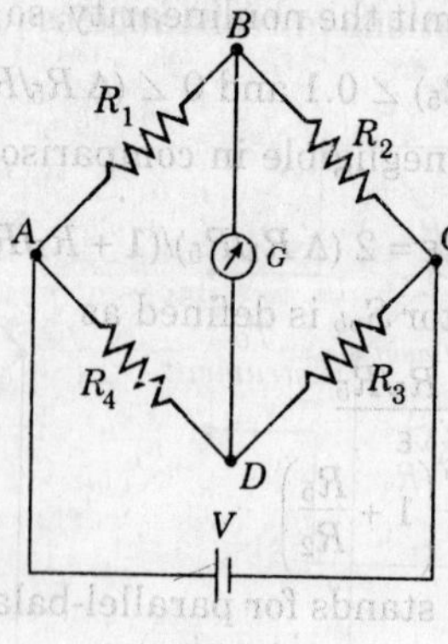

Fig. 5.16

$$\frac{R_1}{R_2} = \frac{R_4}{R_3}$$

It is impractical to satisfy this condition perfectly by the proper selection of four gauges or resistors. This problem is more pronounced in the case of torque measurement on rotating shafts. Hence some devices must be evolved to balance the bridge initially. An ideal balancing technique would have all the following attributes :

(*i*) Span–provision for balancing out the greatest resistive unbalance likely to be encountered.

(*ii*) Resolution–within 20 strain for torque telemetering applications and 1 μ strain or less for load cell applications.

(*iii*) Suitability for use with gauges with 120 Ω to 1000 Ω resistance.

(*iv*) Mechanical robustness.

(*v*) Perfect temperature stability.

(*vi*) Ease and convenience of installation and use.

(*vii*) Cheapness.

(*viii*) No effect on gauge factor.

There are four methods for balancing of Wheatstone bridges as discussed below :

1. **Series Resistor Balancing Method.** By connecting an appropriate low value of resistance in series with one gauge (*e.g.* gauge 4) as shown in Fig. 5.17, the resistance of that bridge arm is altered to give electrical balance of the bridge. In practice two resistors are put in series. Out of which one is the primary series resistance R_{sp} for course adjustment and the other is the fine series resistance R_{sf} (having resistance of $\frac{1}{20}$th of R_{sp} per unit length) for fine adjustment of bridge balance. The resistances are fabricated from a short length of resistance wire, about 12.7 mm and soldered across adjacent tags of a section of printed circuits connecting strip. Differential series balancing may also be used as shown in Fig. 5.18. This method is however less frequently

used to obtain initial balance because of the difficulty in obtaining the small and precise variations in resistance required.

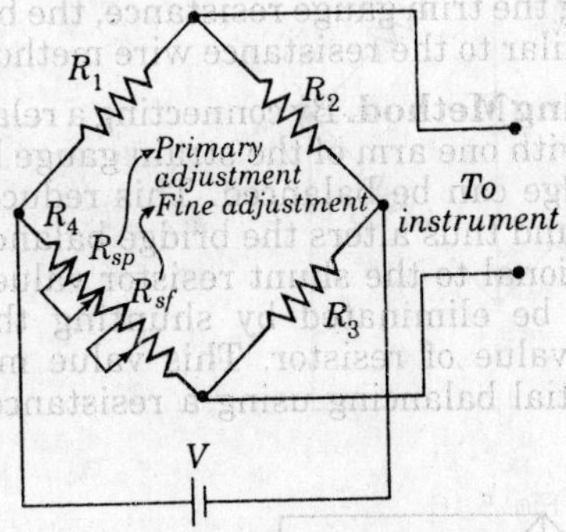

Fig. 5.17 Balancing by means of series resistor.

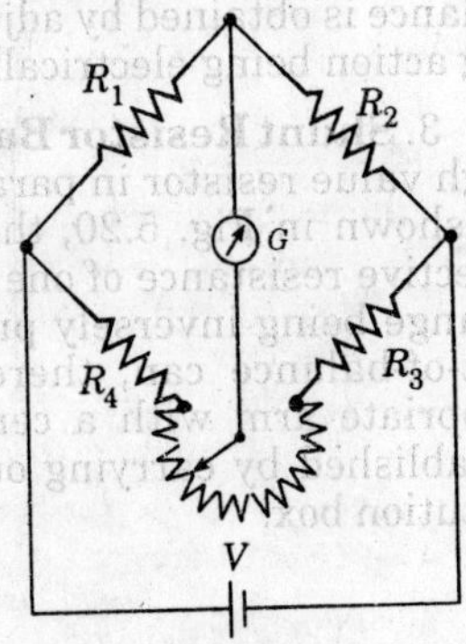

Fig. 5.18 Differential series balance.

2. **Trim Gauge Balancing Method.** The trim gauge is a low value resistor similar in construction to a foil strain gauge. In place of the grid, however, it has (theoretically) a non-strain-sensitive resistance element, usually in the form of a ladder network (Fig. 5.19). The resistance of the trim gauge can be adjusted by altering this resistance element. Typical methods include cutting sections of the ladder out with

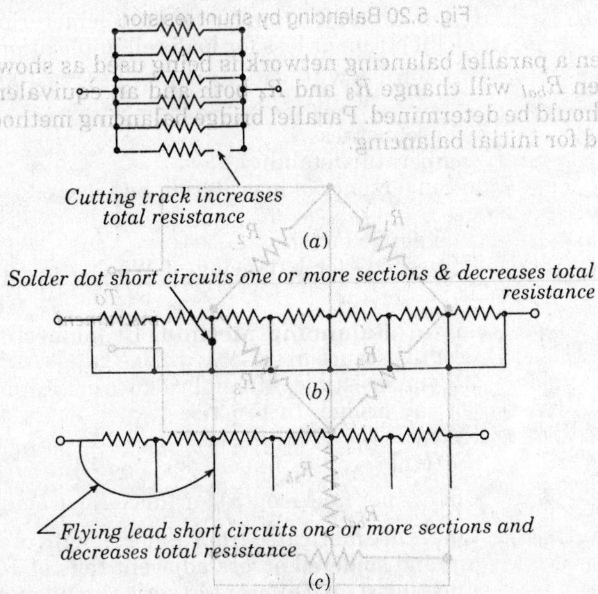

Fig. 5.19 Trim gauge circuits.

a sharp blade (Fig. 5.19 *a*), shorting sections out with a solder dot (Fig. 5.19 *b*), and soldering a flying contact lead to one of several tapping points (Fig. 5.19 *c*). It is bonded to the specimen in the same manner as a strain gauge and wired into one corner of the bridge circuit. Bridge balance is obtained by adjusting the trim gauge resistance, the balancing action being electrically similar to the resistance wire method.

3. **Shunt Resistor Balancing Method.** By connecting a relatively high value resistor in parallel with one arm of the strain gauge bridge as shown in Fig. 5.20, the bridge can be balanced. This reduces the effective resistance of one arm and thus alters the bridge balance, the change being inversely proportional to the shunt resistor value. Any out-of-balance can, therefore, be eliminated by shunting the appropriate arm with a certain value of resistor. This value may be established by carrying out initial balancing using a resistance substitution box.

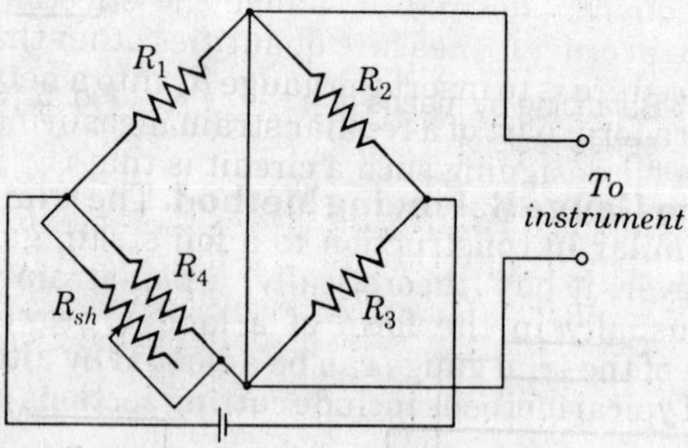

Fig. 5.20 Balancing by shunt resistor.

When a parallel balancing network is being used as shown in Fig. 5.21, then R_{bal} will change R_3 and R_4 both and an equivalent bridge circuit should be determined. Parallel bridge balancing method is often preferred for initial balancing.

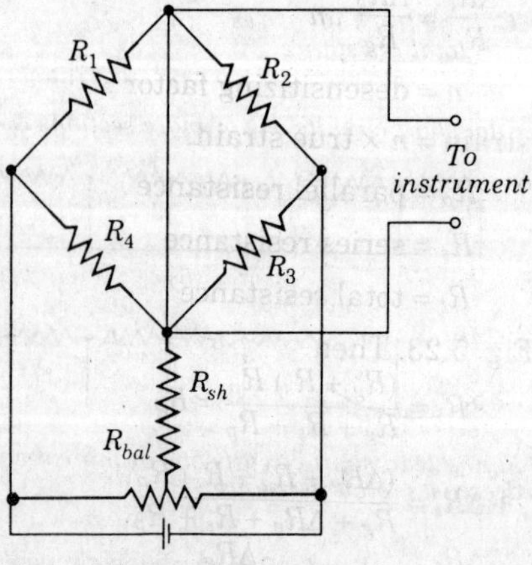

Fig. 5.21 Differential shunt balance.

4. **Altering Gauge Resistance Method.** Another method of balancing is to alter the actual resistance of one of the gauges. This may be achieved by slightly abrading the gauge grid surface, thus reducing the cross-sectional area of the element slightly and increasing its resistance. This technique is, of course, only applicable to gauges having exposed grids. Methods of abrading include gently rubbing with a soft pencil-eraser and wiping with a cotton bud loaded with metal polish, or fine pumice powder. After balancing, the "Doctored" gauge must be thoroughly cleaned with solvent and neutralizer. When carrying out the balancing operation it is preferable that some form of wide range indicating instrument be used to show the initial polarity to unbalance any magnitude after each wipe. The two great drawbacks of this method are the possibility of damage to the gauge and possible loss of long term stability due to contamination of gauge, despite thorough cleaning.

5.2.6 Individual strain gauge desensitization

It is frequently desired to change the effective gauge factor of a strain gauge in order to measure quantities other than pure strain. The general procedure is to insert the gauge R_g into a network of resistances which in turn form part of a regular strain measuring circuit (Fig. 5.22). The criteria for designing such a circuit is that

$$R_t = R_g \quad \text{...(5.34)}$$

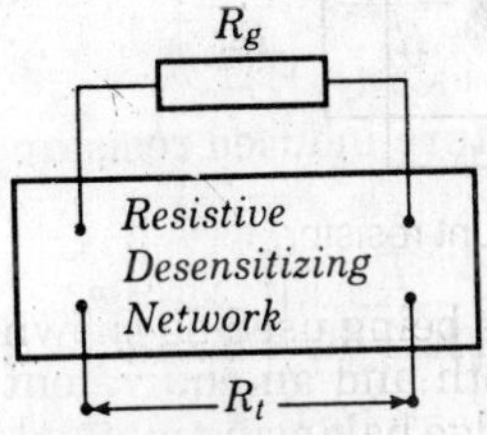

Fig. 5.22

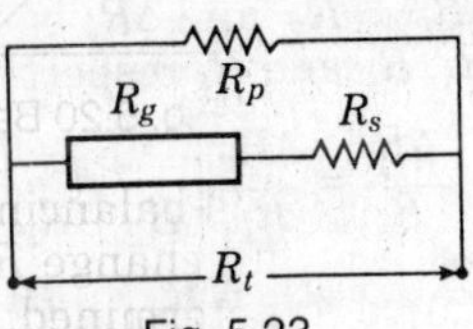

Fig. 5.23

so that

$$\frac{\Delta R_t}{R_t} = \frac{\Delta R_g}{R_g} \,.\, n \quad \text{...(5.35)}$$

where n = desensitizing factor

or Indicated strain = $n \times$ true strain.

Let R_p = parallel resistance

R_s = series resistance

R_t = total resistance

as shown in Fig. 5.23. Then

$$R_t = \frac{(R_g + R_s)\, R_p}{R_g + R_s + R_p} = R_g \quad \text{...(5.36)}$$

$$R_t + \Delta R_t = \frac{(\Delta R_g + R_g + R_s)\, R_p}{R_g + \Delta R_g + R_s + R_p}$$

or

$$\frac{\Delta R_t}{R_t} = (1 + \eta) n \,.\, \frac{\Delta R_g}{R_g} \quad \text{...(5.37)}$$

where $\eta =$ non-linearity factor

$$= \sqrt{n}\,(1 - \sqrt{n})\,.\,\frac{\Delta R_g}{R_g} \qquad ...(5.38)$$

If non-linearity is negligible, then

$$\frac{R_p}{R_g} = \frac{1}{1 - \sqrt{n}} \qquad ...(5.39)$$

$$\frac{R_s}{R_g} = \frac{1 - \sqrt{n}}{\sqrt{n}} \qquad ...(5.40)$$

To determine the error on n made by using resistances R_p and R_g which are slightly different from the specified value and based on a nominal value of R_g instead of an actually measured value, we proceed as follows :

Eliminating R_g from Eqs. (5.39) and (5.40) and differentiating, we get

$$\frac{\Delta n}{n} = 2\left(\frac{1-\sqrt{n}}{1+\sqrt{n}}\right)\left(\frac{\Delta R_p}{R_p} - \frac{\Delta R_s}{R_s}\right) \qquad ...(5.41)$$

$$\left(\frac{\Delta n}{n}\right)_{max} = 2\left(\frac{1-\sqrt{n}}{1+\sqrt{n}}\right)\left(\frac{\Delta R_p}{R_p} + \frac{\Delta R_s}{R_s}\right) \qquad ...(5.42)$$

$$\left(\frac{\Delta n}{n}\right)_{total\ max} = 2\left(\frac{1-\sqrt{n}}{1+\sqrt{n}}\right)\left(\frac{2\,\Delta R_g}{R_g} + \frac{\Delta R_p}{R_p} + \frac{\Delta R_s}{R_s}\right) \qquad ...(5.43)$$

If ΔR_g, ΔR_p and ΔR_s be the temperature-induced resistance changes in R_g, R_p and R_s respectively, then

$$\frac{\Delta R_t}{R_t} = \frac{\Delta R_p}{R_p}\left(\frac{R_g + R_s}{R_p + R_g + R_s}\right) + \frac{\Delta R_s}{R_s}\left(\frac{R_s}{R_g + R_s}\right)\left(\frac{R_p}{R_p + R_g + R_s}\right) + \frac{\Delta R_g}{R_g}\left(\frac{R_g}{R_g + R_s}\right)\left(\frac{R_p}{R_p + R_g + R_s}\right) \qquad ...(5.44)$$

Extra component caused by the presence of R_p and R_s may be expressed as:

$$\left(\frac{\Delta R}{R}\right)_{extra} = \frac{\Delta R_t}{R_t} - \frac{\Delta R_g}{R_g} \qquad ...(5.45)$$

$$= (1 - \sqrt{n})\left[\frac{\Delta R_p}{R_p} + \sqrt{n}\,\frac{\Delta R_s}{R_s} - (1 + \sqrt{n})\,\frac{\Delta R_g}{R_g}\right] \qquad ...(5.46)$$

If $\Delta T =$ temperature difference between operating and reference temperature.

$\alpha_p, \alpha_s =$ resistance temperature coefficient of R_p and R_s respectively.

then
$$\left(\frac{\Delta R_t}{R_t}\right)_{extra} = (1 - n)\left[\frac{1 + \dfrac{\alpha_s}{\alpha_p}\sqrt{n}}{1 + \sqrt{n}}\,\alpha_p\,.\,\Delta T - \frac{\Delta R_g}{R_g}\right] \qquad ...(5.47)$$

If $\alpha_p = \alpha_s$, then

$$\left(\frac{\Delta R_t}{R_t}\right)_{extra} = (1-n)\,\Delta T\left(\alpha_p - \frac{1}{\Delta T}\frac{\Delta R_g}{R_g}\right) \quad ...(5.48)'$$

$\frac{1}{\Delta T} \cdot \frac{\Delta R_g}{R_g}$ represents the combined effect of temperature on actual gauge installation.

5.3 Calibration Methods

Necessity of calibration

1. By knowing the output of a constant voltage or constant gauge current bridge circuit and sensitivity (units of deflection/mV or/μA) of the indicator, the indicator deflection can be related to strain. This is the method generally used for designing strain gauge circuits and selecting recording or indicating equipment. However, it is not suitable for final calibration of system, since with this method the final accuracy of the system would depend upon the accuracy with which all of the parameters involved could be measured and held constant during the period of test. Hence a handy, reliable, and direct calibration is extremely important.

2. Since the final output of the strain amplifiers is an electrical signal whose magnitude depends on the strain to which the gauge is subjected, the strain appears as nothing more than a wave or series of waves on an oscilloscope screen, and some means of judging its absolute magnitude must be provided. The following methods may be used for calibrating a strain gauge :

1. **Electrical calibration.** (*a*). **Static Strain Calibration**

First Method : Shunt resistor. The strain-gauge resistance in one leg of the Wheatstone bridge circuit is shunted by an open-circuited resistor of considerably high value as shown in Fig. 5.24.

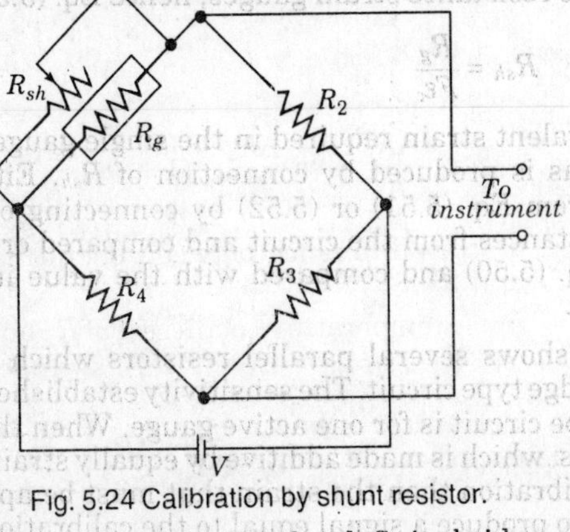

Fig. 5.24 Calibration by shunt resistor.

When this resistor circuit is closed, a definite bridge unbalance will result. This bridge unbalance can be looked upon as a synthetic, controlled strain, and as such it will appear on the oscilloscope screen. Noting the height of the wave from the calibrating strain makes it possible to determine the factor relating strain to displacement of CRO electron beam.

Let R_g = gauge resistance, ohms

R_{sh} = shunt resistance, ohms

After the shunt resistor circuit is closed, the resistance of the gauge becomes, $\dfrac{R_g R_{sh}}{R_g + R_{sh}}$.

Therefore, the change in gauge resistance is

$$\Delta R_g = R_g - \frac{R_g R_{sh}}{R_g + R_{sh}}$$

$$= \frac{R_g^2}{R_g + R_{sh}}$$

$$\therefore \quad \frac{\Delta R_g}{R_g} = \frac{R_g}{R_g + R_{sh}}$$

or $$F\varepsilon_e = \frac{R_g}{R_g + R_{sh}}$$

$$\therefore \quad \varepsilon_e = \frac{1}{F}\left(\frac{R_g}{R_g + R_{sh}}\right) \qquad ...(5.49)$$

or $$F = \frac{1}{\varepsilon_e}\left(\frac{R_g}{R_g + R_{sh}}\right) \qquad ...(5.50)$$

or $$R_{sh} = \frac{R_g\,(1 + F\varepsilon e)}{F\,\varepsilon e} \qquad ...(5.51)$$

Since the quantity $F\varepsilon_e$ is commonly smaller then 0.005 for conventional metallic resistance strain gauges, hence Eq. (5.51) reduces to

$$R_{sh} = \frac{R_g}{F\varepsilon_e} \qquad ...(5.52)$$

ε_e is the equivalent strain required in the single gauge to produce the same signal as is produced by connection of R_{sh}. Either R_{sh} can be determined from Eq. (5.51) or (5.52) by connecting or disconnecting different resistances from the circuit and compared or F can be calculated from Eq. (5.50) and compared with the value indicated by the manufacturer.

Fig. 5.25 shows several parallel resistors which can be used to calibrate a bridge type circuit. The sensitivity established by calibration of a bridge-type circuit is for one active gauge. When the output of two or more gauges, which is made additive by equally straining the gauges is used for calibration then the strain that must be applied to each of the n gauges to produce a signal equal to the calibration signal is

$$\varepsilon_e = \frac{R_g}{F\,(R_g + R_{th})} \cdot \frac{1}{n} \qquad ...(5.53)$$

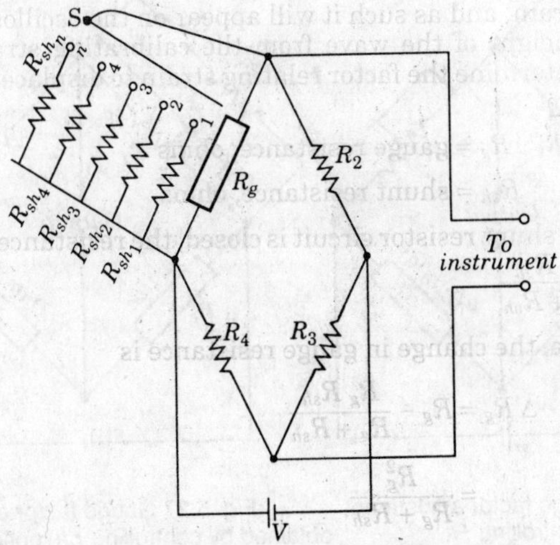

Fig. 5.25 Calibration by several parallel resistors.

Second method. The bridge shown in Fig. 5.26 will be balanced when $R_1 = R_2$. Shunting R_1 with a calibration resistance R_c produces an unbalance which is analogous to the resistance in the active gauge produced by strain.

$$\varepsilon = \frac{1}{F}\frac{\Delta R_1}{R_1} = \frac{R_1}{F(R_1 + R_c)}$$

Now $\qquad R_c \gg R_1$ so that

$$\varepsilon \approx \frac{1}{R_c}\left(\frac{R_1}{F}\right) \qquad ...(5.54)$$

In order that ε be a function of only R_c, the ratio $\frac{R_1}{F}$ must be a constant or R_1 must be directly proportional to F. This can be accomplished by using a linearly graduated dial to control a linearly variable resistor R_1. A circuit can be designed so that the graduations on the dial represent gauge factor directly. Then in use, if one sets the dial at the gauge factor of the active gauge, a preselected strain can be simulated by shunting the adjusted R_1 with a preselected R_c. The output from the bridge can then be used to calibrate a recording instrument.

Third Method. The resistances R_1 and R_2 are fixed, but R_1 is a potentiometer connected into the bridge (Fig. 5.27) so that the calibration resistor can be shunted across r, a portion of R_1. Simulated strain is

$$\varepsilon = \frac{1}{F}\cdot\frac{\Delta R_1}{R_1} = \frac{r^2}{FR_1(r + R_c)} \approx \frac{r^2}{FR_1R_c}$$

If $R_c >> r$ then

$$\varepsilon \propto r^2 \qquad ...(5.55)$$

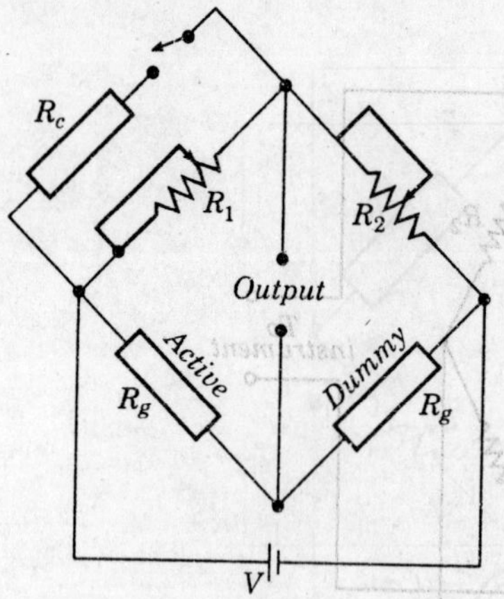

Fig. 5.26 Gauge factor adjustment by controlling R_1.

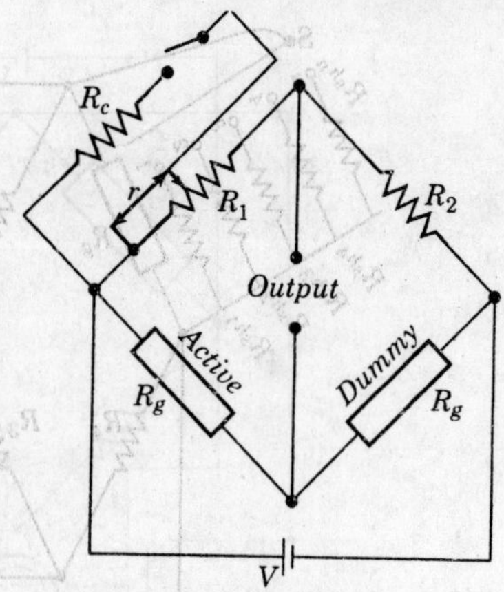

Fig. 5.27 Gauge factor adjustment obtained by controlling r.a potion of R_1.

To obtain direct reading gauge factor adjustment, the ratio $\frac{r^2}{F}$ must be a constant, k. If R_1 were a nonlinear potentiometer with r equal to the square root of angular position, and if r were controlled by a linear turns counting dial, a circuit could be designed so that graduations on the dial represented gauge factor. However, potentiometers with

$\frac{r}{R_{max}} = \sqrt{\frac{\theta}{\theta_{max}}}$, where θ equals angular position are expensive.

(*b*) **Dynamic Calibration.** Dynamic calibration is obtained by replacing the manual calibration switch with an electrically driven switch, often referred to as a chopper, which makes and breaks the contact 60 to 100 times per second. When displayed on a CRO screen or recorded, the trace obtained is found to be a square wave. The step in the trace represents the equivalent strain calculated from Eq. (5.49).

2. Mechanical Calibration

First Method. This method consists in mounting a pair of gauges on a cam deflected cantilever beam as shown in Fig. 5.28. These strain gauges are mounted in the adjacent legs of the Wheatstone bridge. Each time the cantilever suffers maximum deflection from the cam, the strain gauges will undergo corresponding changes in resistance. This change will unbalance the bridge and show on the oscilloscope as a calibrating pulse. The calibrating strain can be computed from the flexure formula.

Calibrating strain

$$\varepsilon_c = \frac{Pld}{2EI} \quad ...(5.56)$$

where P = force exerted by the cam

l = distance of the strain gauges from the cam centre

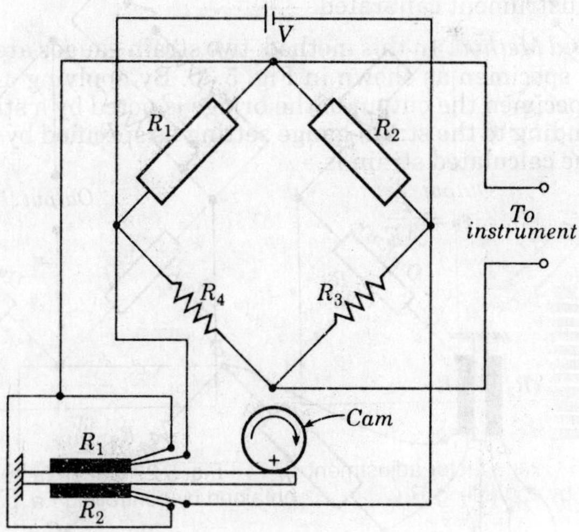

Fig. 5.28 Mechanical calibration using a cantilever.

d = depth of cantilever beam.

Also $$\varepsilon_c = \frac{3\delta l d}{2L^3} \quad \text{...(5.57)}$$

where δ = deflection of the free end of the cantilever

L = length of the cantilever.

Knowing δ, l, d and L, ε_c can be evaluated and the CRO trace can be calibrated accordingly. As there are two active gauges the output has to be halved.

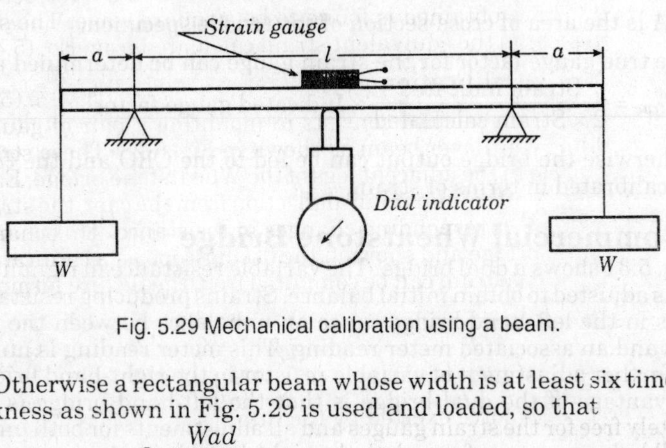

Fig. 5.29 Mechanical calibration using a beam.

Otherwise a rectangular beam whose width is at least six times the thickness as shown in Fig. 5.29 is used and loaded, so that

$$\varepsilon_c = \frac{Wad}{2EI} \quad \text{...(5.58)}$$

The value of ε_c may be determined as a function of meter reading and the instrument calibrated.

Second Method. In this method, two strain gauges are cemented on a tensile specimen as shown in Fig. 5.30. By applying a load P to the tensile specimen the output of the bridge is noted by a strain indicator corresponding to the strain gauge setting as specified by the manufacturer. The calculated strain is,

$$\varepsilon_c = \frac{P}{AE}$$

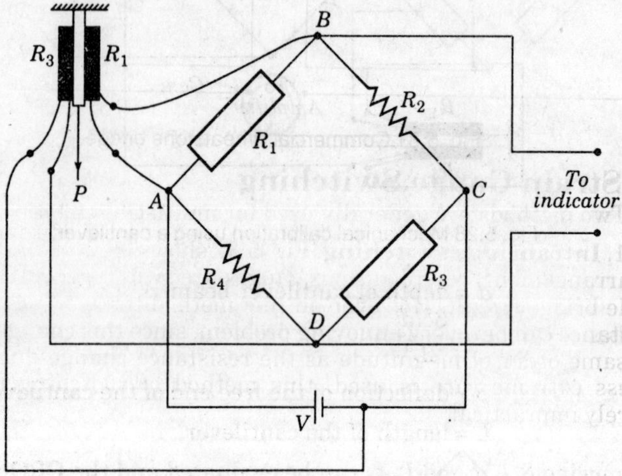

Fig. 5.30 Mechanical calibration.

where A is the area of cross-section of the tensile specimen.

The true gauge factor for the strain gauge can be determined as :

$$F_{true} = \frac{\text{Strain indicated}}{2 \times \text{Strain calculated}} \times \text{Indicated gauge factor} \quad ...(5.59)$$

Otherwise the bridge output can be fed to the CRO and the trace can be calibrated in terms of strain.

5.4. Commercial Wheatstone Bridge

Fig. 5.31 shows a dual bridge. The variable resistance in right hand bridge is adjusted to obtain initial balance. Strains producing resistance changes in the left-hand bridge cause an unbalance between the two bridges and an associated meter reading. This meter reading is nulled out by further adjustment of variable resistor in the right-hand bridge. The advantage of the dual bridge is that the left-hand bridge is left completely free for the strain gauges and all adjustments for both initial and null balance are performed on the right-hand bridge.

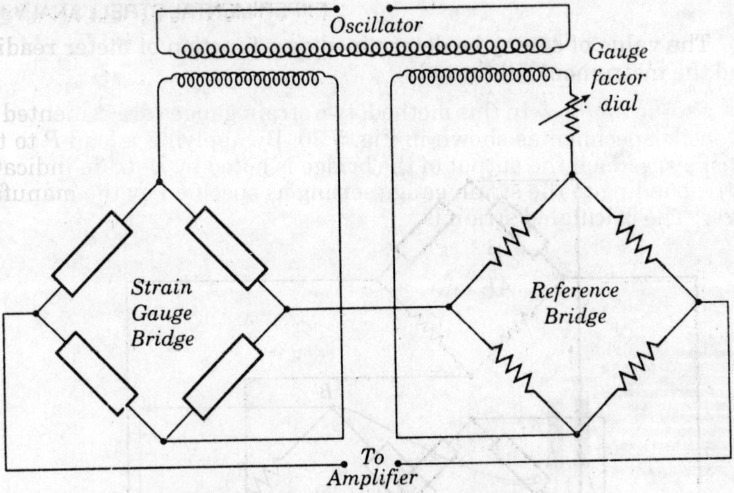

Fig. 5.31 Commercial Wheatstone bridge.

5.5 Strain Gauge Switching

Two methods are generally used for multistrain gauge switching.

1. **Intrabridge switching.** Fig. 5.32 shows an intrabridge switching arrangement, where various gauges are switched into and out of a single bridge circuit. However, in this method the variation in switch resistance can be a very annoying problem, since this change may be of the same order of magnitude as the resistance change due to strain. Unless extreme care is used, this method of switching may prove entirely impractical.

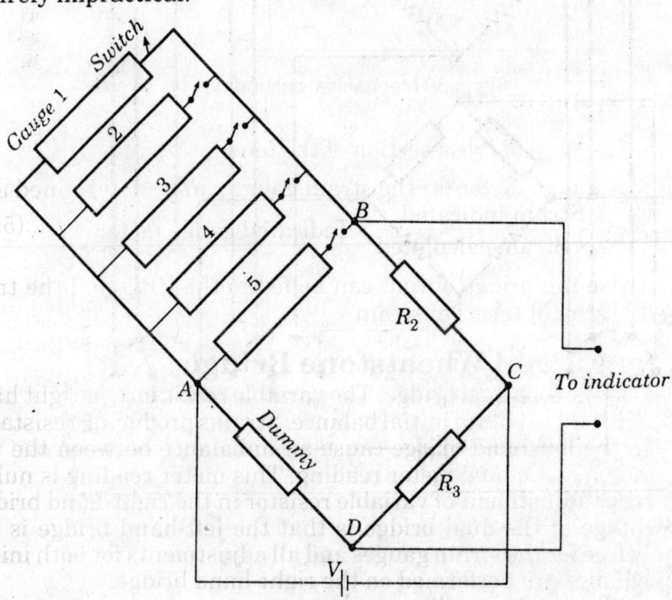

Fig. 5.32 Intrabridge switching.

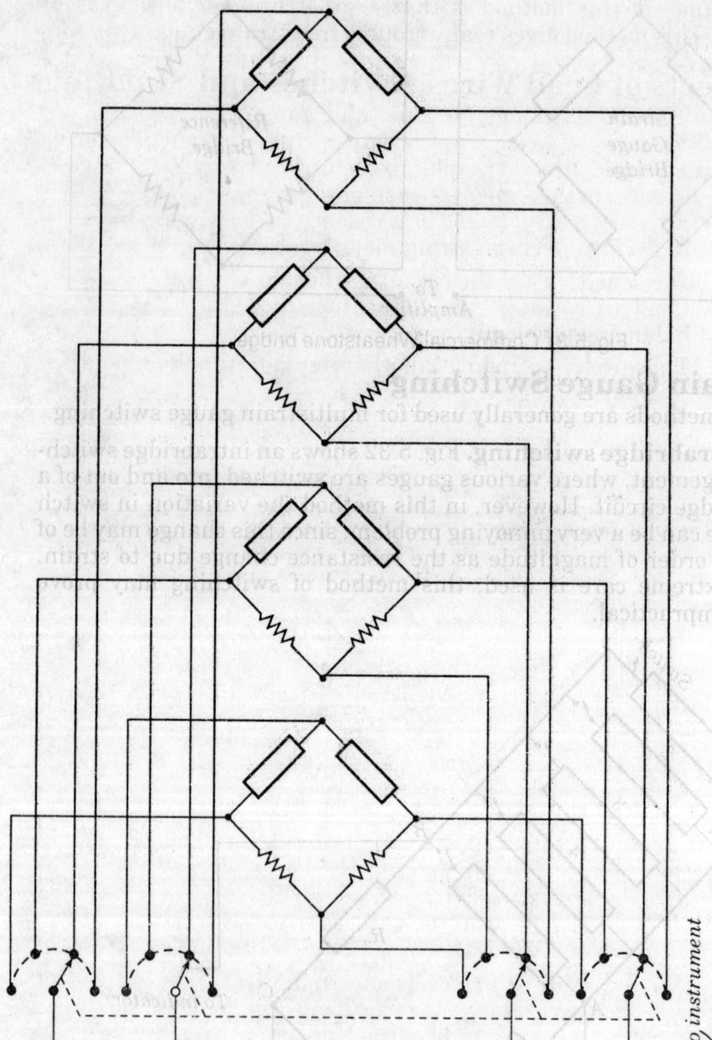

Fig. 5.33 Interbridge switching

2. **Interbridge switching.** Fig. 5.33 shows an interbridge switching arrangement where the switch connections are entirely outside the bridge and complete bridges are switched into and out of the measuring system. In this case the variations in switch resistance do not alter bridge balance. However, this may alter bridge sensitivity slightly. The disadvantage of this method is that a great number of gauges are required. This method gives really trouble free strain gauge switching.

5.6 Effects of Lead Wires, Switches and Slip Rings

As the resistance change for a metallic gauge is very small, anything producing resistance change is extremely important. The bridge includes lead-wires, switches, soldered joints and may also have slip rings. We now discuss the effect of each of these components.

(*a*) *Effect of lead wires.* The presence of lead wires have the following effects on strain measurements :

(*i*) The sensitivity of the circuit is affected.

(*ii*) Lead wires affect the calibration procedure and increase balancing problems.

(*iii*) These may introduce another temperature-compensation problem.

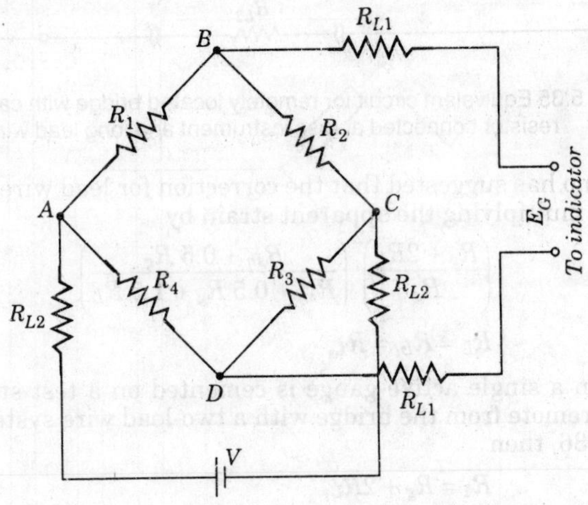

Fig. 5.34 Bridge circuit showing lead wire resistance.

For a remote recording bridge as shown in Fig. 5.34, the lead wire resistance will be in series with the recording equipment and the power supply. Therefore, the only effects of the lead wire resistance will be (*i*) to change the load resistance associated with the measuring instrument from R_G to $R_G + 2R_{L1}$, and (*ii*) to change the resistance in series with the power supply (V) from R_{bridge} to $R_{bridge} + 2R_{L_2}$. Since R_G is very large as compared to $2\,R_{L_1}$ for an instrument of the voltage sensitive (*i.e.* high impedance) type, therefore, $2R_{L_1}$ should be ignored for such an instrument. Therefore, no corrections are necessary for strain measurements.

The calibration of this bridge can be accomplished by paralleling a calibration resistor R_{sh} across $R_1 = R_g$ (say). In this case the analysis remains unchanged. However, in practice it is sometimes convenient to calibrate the system by placing the calibration resistor at the instrument location as shown in Fig. 5.35. In this case the calibration resistor is in parallel with $R_g + R_{L_1} + R_{L_2}$; hence equivalent strain

$$\varepsilon_e = \frac{(R_g + R_{L_1} + R_{L_2})^2}{FR_g\,(R_g + R_{sh} + R_{L_1} + R_{L_2})} \qquad \text{...(5.60)}$$

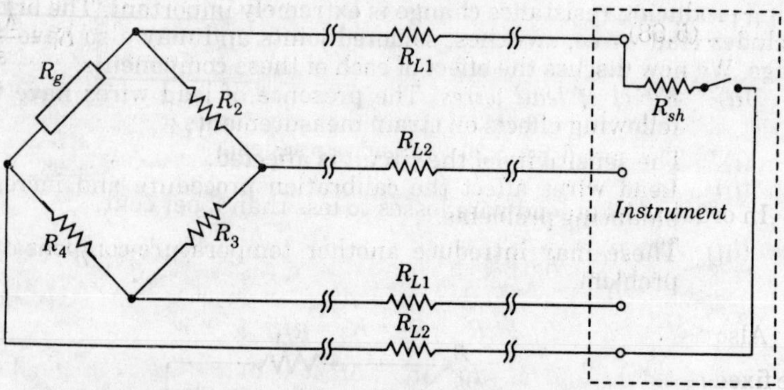

Fig. 5.35 Equivalent circuit for remotely located bridge with calibration resistor connected across instrument and long lead wire.

Perino has suggested that the correction for lead wire error can be made by multiplying the apparent strain by

$$\left(\frac{R_g + 2R_L}{R_g}\right)^2 \left(\frac{R_{sh} + 0.5\,R_g}{R_{sh} + 0.5\,R_g + 1.5\,R_L}\right) \qquad \text{...(5.61)}$$

where $\quad R_L = R_{L_1} = R_{L_2}$

When a single active gauge is cemented on a test structure at a location remote from the bridge with a two-lead wire system as shown in Fig. 5.36, then

$$R_1 = R_g + 2R_{L_1}$$

Also
$$\frac{\Delta R_1}{R_1} = \frac{\Delta R_g}{R_g + 2R_{L_1}} = \frac{\Delta R_g/R_g}{1 + 2R_{L_1}/R_g}$$

$$= \frac{\Delta R_g}{R_g}(1 - K_L) \qquad \text{...(5.62)}$$

where $\quad K_L$ = signal loss factor

$$= \frac{2R_{L_1}/R_g}{1 + 2R_{L_1}/R_g}$$

$$\approx \frac{2R_{L_1}}{R_g} \text{ if } \frac{2R_{L_1}}{R_g} << 1 \qquad \text{...(5.63)}$$

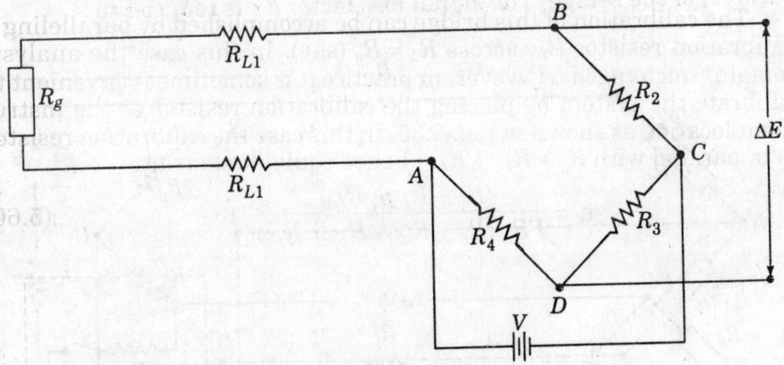

Fig. 5.36 Two lead wire system.

In order to limit lead-wire losses to less than 2 per cent,

$$\frac{R_{L_1}}{R_g} \leq 0.01$$

Also as $\quad R_1 = R_g + 2R_{L_1}$; $R_2 = R_3 = r\,R_g$

are fixed resistors, and $R_4 = R_g$, $\Delta R_2 = \Delta R_3 = 0$, hence the initial balance condition $R_1R_3 = R_2R_4$ is not satisfied. However, if $\frac{R_{L_1}}{R_g} > 0.02$ and if a shunt balancing method is used, the range of the balance potentiometer is exceeded and initial balance of the bridge cannot be achieved.

Further the output voltage due to resistance changes in arms R_1 and R_4 is given by

$$\Delta E = V.\frac{r}{(1+r)^2}\left(\frac{\Delta R_1}{R_1} - \frac{\Delta R_4}{R_4}\right)$$

If the gauges are subjected to temperature difference ΔT at the same time that the active gauge is subjected to a strain ε, then

$$\Delta E = V \cdot \frac{r}{(1+r)^2}\left[\left(\frac{\Delta R_g}{R_g + 2R_{L_1}}\right)_{\varepsilon} + \left(\frac{\Delta R_g}{R_g + 2R_{L_1}}\right)_{\Delta T} - \left(\frac{2\,\Delta R_{L_1}}{R_g + 2R_{L_1}}\right)_{\Delta T} - \left(\frac{\Delta R_g}{R_g}\right)_{\Delta T}\right] \quad ...(5.64)$$

Thus temperature compensation is not achieved in the Wheatstone bridge as the second and fourth terms in the bracketed quantity are not equal.

The detrimental effects of long lead wires can be minimized by using the three-lead-wire system shown in Fig. 5.37, where both the active and dummy gauges are placed at the remote location. One of the three wires is used to transfer terminal A of the bridge to the remote location.

It is not considered a lead wire since it is not within either arm R_1 or arm R_4 of the bridge. The signal loss factor K_L is reduced to

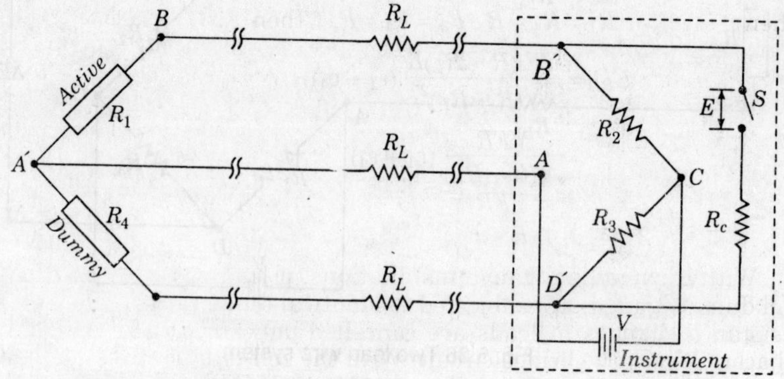

Fig. 5.37 Three lead wire system.

$$K_L = \frac{R_L/R_g}{1 + R_L/R_g}$$

$$\approx \frac{R_L}{R_g} \text{ if } \frac{R_L}{R_g} << 1 \qquad ...(5.65)$$

The bridge retains the initial balance capability since the resistance of both arms R_1 and R_4 is increased by R_L. With the three lead-wire system, Eq. (5.64) becomes,

$$\Delta E = V\frac{r}{(1+r)^2}\left[\left(\frac{\Delta R_g}{R_g + R_L}\right)_\varepsilon + \left(\frac{\Delta R_g}{R_g + R_L}\right)_{\Delta T} + \left(\frac{\Delta R_L}{R_g + R_L}\right)_{\Delta T} - \left(\frac{\Delta R_g}{R_g + R_L}\right)_{\Delta T} - \left(\frac{\Delta R_L}{R_g + R_L}\right)_{\Delta T}\right]$$

$$= V\frac{r}{(1+r)^2}\left(\frac{\Delta R_g}{R_g + R_L}\right)_\varepsilon \qquad ...(5.66)$$

Thus temperature compensation is achieved.

If two active gauges are used at the site and the bridge is completed at the recorder, then

$$\Delta E_{AB} = \frac{(R_4 + R_L)\,(\Delta R_1 + \Delta R_L)}{(R_1 + R_4 + 2R_L)^2}\cdot V$$

$$= \frac{(R_4 + R_L)\,\Delta R_1}{(R_1 + R_4 + 2R_L)^2}\cdot V$$

$$= \frac{(R_4 + R_L)\,R_1\,F\varepsilon}{(R_1 + R_4 + 2R_L)^2}\,V \qquad ...(5.67)$$

and $$E_{BD} = \left[\frac{(R_4 + R_L)\, R_1 F_1\, \varepsilon_1}{(R_1 + R_2 + 2R_L)^2} - \frac{(R_1 + R_L)\, R_4 F_4\, \varepsilon_4}{(R_1 + R_4 + 2R_L)^2}\right] V$$

when $R_1 = R_4 = R$; $F_1 = F_4 = F$, then

$$E_{BD} = \frac{VF\,(R + R_L)R}{4\,(R + R_L)^2}\,(\varepsilon_1 - \varepsilon_4)$$

$$= \frac{VFR}{4\,(R + R_L)}\,(\varepsilon_1 - \varepsilon_4)$$

$$= \frac{VFR}{4\,(R + R_L)}\,.\,\varepsilon_{net} \quad \text{...(5.68)}$$

With conventional gauge installations, if lead wires of the active and dummy gauges are subjected to identical temperature conditions, resistance changes in leads are cancelled out, since they appear in adjacent legs of the bridge circuit. With the self-temperature compensated gauge, however, only one pair of lead wire is required, and since they are connected in one leg of the bridge, variations in their resistance will be indicated. This problem can be eliminated by placing one lead in one bridge leg and the other lead in the adjacent leg as shown in Fig. 5.38. The temperature variations in the battery lead and its resultant resistance changes will not effect the balance of the bridge.

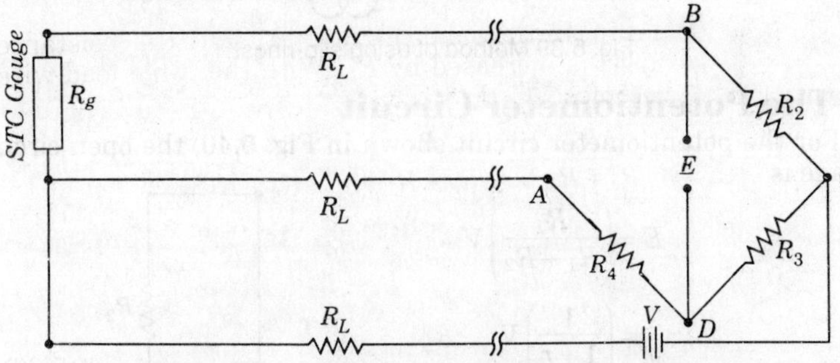

Fig. 5.38 Eliminating lead errors in employing a single STC gauge (Three-wire system).

(*b*) *Effect of Switches.* When the number of gauges is large, it is not economically feasible to employ a separate recording instrument for each gauge. Instead, a single recording system is used, and the gauges are switched in and out of the instrument system. Two methods of switching as discussed in Art. 5.5 may be used. In the interbridge switching method, if the switching resistance is not negligible, the switch resistance adds to ΔR_g to produce an error in the strain measurement. In the intrabridge switching, the switch is not located in the arms of the bridge and the switching resistance is not particularly important.

(*c*) *Effect of Slip Rings.* Slip rings are employed to provide lead wire connections when strain gauges are used on rotating machinery. Dirt collecting on the slip rings and brush jump tends to generate electrical noise. The use of multiple brushes in parallel helps to minimize the noise, however, the resistance changes between the rings and the brushes are usually so large that slip rings are recommended for use in the arm of the bridge. Instead, a complete bridge should be assembled on the rotating member as shown in Fig. 5.39, and the slip rings should be used to connect the bridge to the power supply and recording instrument, thereby minimizing the effects of slip-ring resistance changes on the strain measurements.

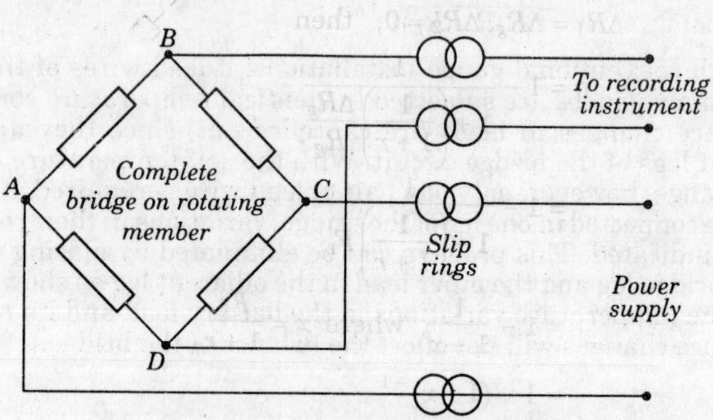

Fig. 5.39 Method of using slip-rings.

5.7 The Potentiometer Circuit

For the potentiometer circuit shown in Fig. 5.40, the open circuit voltage is

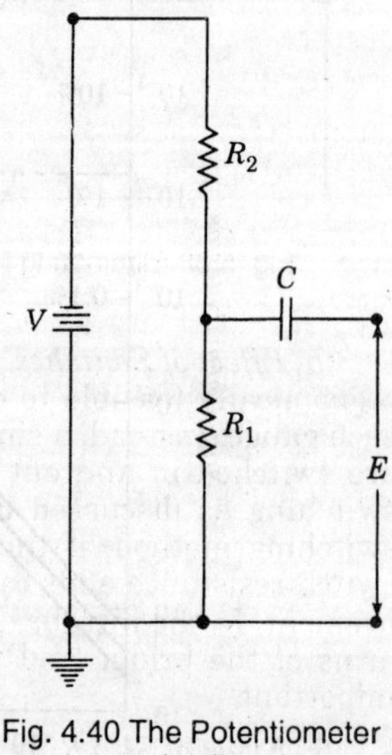

Fig. 4.40 The Potentiometer circuit.

$$E = \left(\frac{R_1}{R_1 + R_2}\right) V$$

$$= \left(\frac{1}{1+r}\right) V$$

where $r = R_2/R_1$

When R_1 increases by ΔR_1 and R_2 by ΔR_2, then the output voltage becomes,

$$E + \Delta E = \left(\frac{R_1 + \Delta R_2}{R_1 + \Delta R_1 + R_2 + \Delta R_2}\right) V$$

$$\therefore \quad \Delta E = \left(\frac{R_1 + \Delta R_1}{R_1 + \Delta R_1 + R_2 + \Delta R_2} - \frac{R_1}{R_1 + R_2}\right) V$$

$$= \frac{r}{(1+r)^2}\left(\frac{\Delta R_1}{R_1} - \frac{\Delta R_2}{R_2}\right)(1-\eta)\,V \qquad \text{...(5.69)}$$

where the non-linear term η is expressed as

$$\eta = 1 - \frac{1}{1+\left(\frac{1}{1+r}\right)\left(\frac{\Delta R_1}{R_1} + r\frac{\Delta R_2}{R_2}\right)} \qquad \text{...(5.70)}$$

If $R_1 = R_g$, $R_2 = R_b$, ballast resistor so that

$$\Delta R_1 = \Delta R_g,\ \Delta R_2 = 0, \quad \text{then}$$

$$\eta = 1 - \frac{1}{1+\left(\frac{1}{1+r}\right)\frac{\Delta R_g}{R_g}}$$

$$= 1 - \frac{1}{1+\left(\frac{1}{1+r}\right)F\varepsilon}$$

$$= 1 - \frac{1}{1+x}, \text{ where } x = \frac{F\varepsilon}{1+r}$$

$$= 1-(1+x)^{-1}$$

$$= 1 - 1 + x - x^2 + x^3 - x^4 + \ldots\ldots$$

$$= x - x^2 + x^3 - x^4 + \ldots.. \qquad \text{...(5.71)}$$

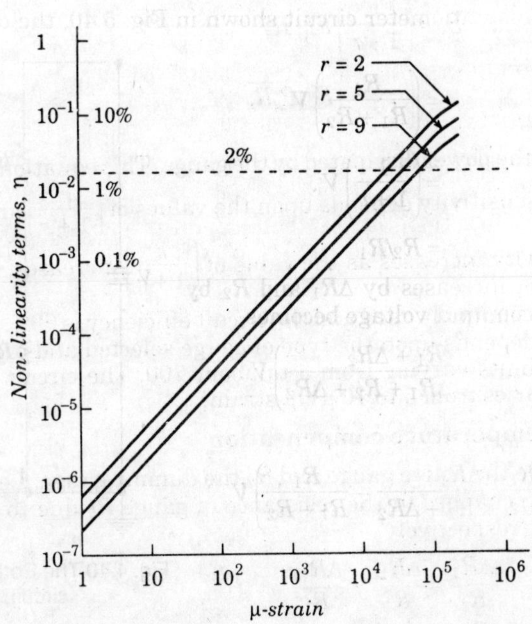

Fig. 5.41 Dependence of the non-linearity term η on strain level.

Range : The range of the potentiometer circuit depends upon the error which can be tolerated due to the non-linearities introduced by the circuit. In Fig. 5.41 the non-linear term η is given as a function of strain for various values of r. From the figure it can be seen that the error introduced by the nonlinearity term is sufficiently small to be negligible for strains below 1 per cent. Increasing the value of r decreases the error due to circuit non-linearities.

Sensitivity. The sensitivity of the potentiometer circuit is defined as the ratio of the output voltage divided by the strain, *i.e.*

$$S_c = \frac{\Delta E}{\varepsilon} \quad ...(5.72)$$

$$= \frac{r}{(1+r)^2}\left(\frac{\Delta R_1}{R_1} - \frac{\Delta R_2}{R_2}\right)\frac{V}{\varepsilon} \quad \text{when } \eta << 1 \quad ...(5.73)$$

If $R_1 = R_g,\ \Delta R_1 = \Delta R_g,$

$R_2 = R_b,\ \Delta R_2 = 0,$ then

$$S_c = \frac{r}{(1+r)^2} \cdot \frac{\Delta R_g}{R_g} \frac{V}{\varepsilon}$$

$$= \frac{r}{(1+r)^2} F\varepsilon \cdot \frac{V}{\varepsilon} = \frac{r}{(1+r)^2} FV \quad ...(5.74)$$

This equation shows that the circuit sensitivity depends upon the ratio r and the supply voltage V. Now

$$V = I_g\,(R_g + R_b) = I_g\,R_g\,(1+r) = \sqrt{P_g\,R_g}\,(1+r) \quad ...(5.75)$$

$$\therefore \quad S_c = \left(\frac{r}{1+r}\right) FI_g\,R_g$$

$$= \left(\frac{r}{1+r}\right) F\sqrt{P_g R_g} \quad ...(5.76)$$

where P_g is the power dissipated by the gauge. This equation shows that the circuit sensitivity depends upon the values of $\left(\frac{r}{1+r}\right)$ and $F\sqrt{P_g R_g}$.

The sensitivity increases as the value of $\left(\frac{r}{1+r}\right)$ increases. Values of r about 9 are commonly used and the circuit efficiency is 90%. The values of $F\sqrt{P_g\,R_g}$ depends upon the type of gauge selected and can be varied over wide limits varying from 3 to about 700. The circuit sensitivity generally varies from 5 to 10 $\mu V/\mu$ strain.

5.7.1 Temperature compensation

Let R_1 be the active gauge and R_2 the dummy gauge. Let $\Delta R_{1\varepsilon}$ and ΔR_{1T} be the changes in the resistance of gauge R_1 due to strain and temperature respectively.

$$\frac{\Delta R_1}{R_1} = \frac{\Delta R_{1\varepsilon}}{R_1} + \frac{\Delta R_{1T}}{R_1}$$

If ΔR_{2T} be the change in resistance due to temperature of gauge R_2, then

$$\frac{\Delta R_2}{R_2} = \frac{\Delta R_{2T}}{R_2}$$

$$\therefore \quad \Delta E = \frac{r}{(1+r^2)}\left[\frac{\Delta R_{1\varepsilon} + \Delta R_{1T}}{R_1} - \frac{\Delta R_{2T}}{R_2}\right](1-\eta)\, V$$

If $R_1 = R_2 = R_g$ then $\Delta R_{1T} = \Delta R_{2T}$ and the temperature terms cancel out and we get

$$\Delta E = \frac{1}{4}\left(\frac{\Delta R_{1\varepsilon}}{R_1}\right)(1-\eta)V$$

$$= \frac{1}{4}\,.\,F\,.\,\varepsilon\,(1-\eta)\,V \approx \frac{1}{4}F\varepsilon V$$

$$= \frac{1}{4}F\varepsilon\, 2I_g R_g = \frac{1}{2}F\varepsilon\, I_g R_g$$

$$= \frac{1}{2}F\varepsilon\sqrt{P_g R_g} \qquad \text{...(5.78)}$$

For two active gauges having equal strains of opposite sign, we get

$$\Delta E = \frac{r}{(1+r)^2}\,.\,2\left(\frac{\Delta R_g}{R_g}\right)V$$

$$= \frac{1}{4}\,.\,2F\varepsilon\, 2I_g R_g$$

$$= I_g R_g\,.\,F\varepsilon$$

$$= \sqrt{P_g R_g}\,.\,F\varepsilon \qquad \text{...(5.79)}$$

5.7.2 Calibration

Calibration of the potentiometer circuit may be achieved either by placing a shunt resistance across the strain gauge or the ballast resistance R_2. For the first method as shown in Fig. 5.42, the equivalent resistance of the strain gauge becomes,

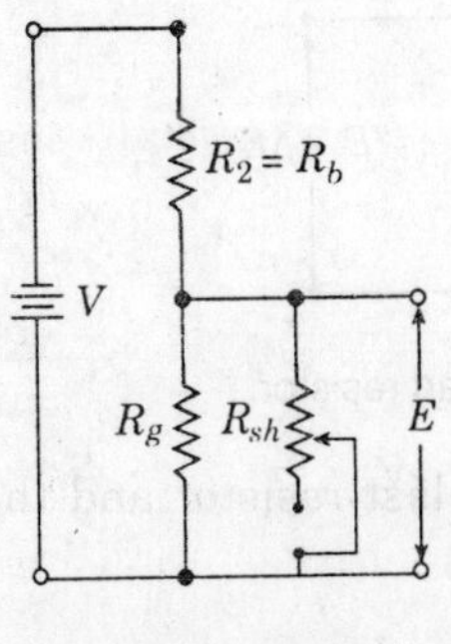

Fig. 5.42 Calibration of potentiometer by a shunt resistor across the gauge.

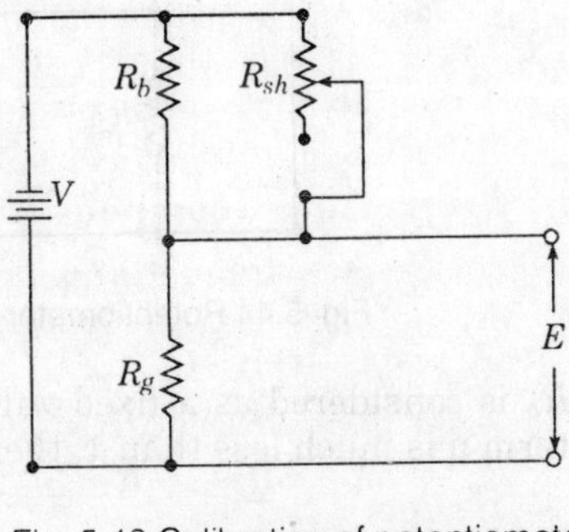

Fig. 5.43 Calibration of potentiometer by a shunt resistor across the ballast resistor.

$$R_e = \frac{R_g\, R_{sh}}{R_g + R_{sh}}$$

Now $$\Delta R_g = R_g - \frac{R_g\, R_{sh}}{R_g + R_{sh}}$$

$$= \frac{R_g^2}{R_g + R_{sh}}$$

$$\frac{\Delta R_g}{R_g} = \frac{R_g}{R_g + R_{sh}} = R\, \varepsilon_e$$

$$\therefore \quad R_{sh} = \frac{R_g\,(1 - F\varepsilon_e)}{F\varepsilon_e} \qquad \text{...(5.80)}$$

where ε_e is the equivalent strain.

For the second method as shown in Fig. 5.43 the size of the calibration shunt resistor can be calculated from

$$R_{sh} = \frac{R_b\,(R_b - F_\varepsilon\, R_g)}{F_\varepsilon\, R_g} \qquad \text{...(5.81)}$$

Since $F_\varepsilon << 1$ and $R_g << R_b$, hence

$$R_{sh} = \frac{R_b^2}{F_\varepsilon R_g} = \left(\frac{R_b}{R_g}\right)^2 \cdot \frac{R_g}{F_\varepsilon} \qquad \text{...(5.82)}$$

5.7.2 Effect of the resistance of the measuring instrument

Let R_m be the resistance of the measuring instrument. The equivalent resistance R_s of the strain gauge becomes (Fig. 5.44).

$$R_e = \frac{R_g R_m}{R_g + R_m}$$

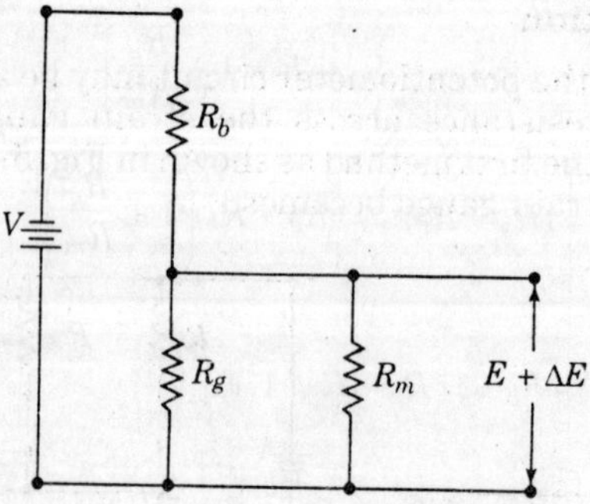

Fig. 5.44 Potentiometer with load resistor.

If R_b is considered as a fixed value ballast resistor and the non-linear term η is much less than 1, then

$$\Delta E\,|_{R_m} = \frac{r}{(1+r)^2} \cdot \frac{\Delta R_e}{R_e} \cdot V$$

$$= \frac{R_b\, R_e}{(R_b + R_e)^2} \cdot \frac{\Delta R_e}{R_e} \cdot V$$

For the open circuit, *i.e.* infinite resistance for the measuring instrument

$$\Delta E\ |_{R_m = \infty} = \frac{R_b\, R_g}{(R_b + R_g)^2} \cdot \frac{\Delta R_g}{R_g} \cdot V$$

Now

$$R_b R_e/(R_b + R_e)^2 = [R_b\, R_g\, R_m/(R_g + R_m)] \times [1/\{R_b + R_g\, R_m/(R_g + R_m)\}]^2$$

$$= R_b R_g R_m\ (R_g + R_m)/[R_b\ (R_g + R_m) + R_g\, R_m]^2$$

$$= R_b R_g\ (1 + R_g/R_m)/[R_g + R_b\ (1 + R_g/R_m)]^2$$

and $\Delta R_e/R_e = \Delta[R_g R_m/(R_g + R_m)]/[R_g R_m/(R_g + R_m)]$

$$= \frac{[(R_g + \Delta R_g)\, R_m/(R_g + \Delta R_g + R_m)] - R_g R_m/(R_g + R_m)}{R_g\, R_m/(R_g + R_m)}$$

$$= \frac{[(R_g + \Delta R_g)/(R_g + \Delta R_g + R_m)] - R_g/(R_g + R_m)}{R_g/(R_g + R_m)}$$

$$= (\Delta R_g/R_g)/(1 + R_g/R_m)$$

$$\therefore\ \Delta E\,|_{Rm} = R_b\, R_g\ (\Delta R_g/R_g)\ V/[(R_g + R_b)\ (1 + R_g/R_m)]^2$$

$$\Delta E\,|_{Rm} - \Delta E\,|_{R_m = \infty} = R_b R_g\, .\, (\Delta R_g/R_g) V/[R_g + R_b\ (1 + R_g R_m)]^2$$

$$- R_b R_g\, .\, (\Delta R_g/R_g)\ V/(R_b + R_g)^2$$

$$= \frac{R_b R_g}{(R_b + R_g)^2} \cdot \frac{\Delta R_g}{R_g} \cdot V \cdot \left[\frac{(R_b + R_b)^2}{\left[R_g + R_b\left(1 + \frac{R_g}{R_m}\right)\right]^2} - 1\right]$$

$$= \Delta E\ |_{R_m = \infty} \times \left[\frac{(R_b + R_g)^2 - \left\{R_g + R_b\left(1 + \frac{R_g}{R_m}\right)\right\}^2}{\left\{R_g + R_b\left(1 + \frac{R_g}{R_m}\right)\right\}^2}\right]$$

$$= \Delta E\ |_{R_m = \infty} \times \left[\frac{\left\{2R_g + R_b\left(2 + \frac{R_g}{R_m}\right)\right\}\left\{-R_b\,\frac{R_g}{R_m}\right\}}{\left\{R_g + R_b\left(1 + \frac{R_g}{R_m}\right)\right\}^2}\right]$$

Loss factor

$$K_L = \frac{\Delta E|_{R_m=\infty} - \Delta E|_{R_m}}{\Delta E|_{R_m=\infty}}$$

$$= \frac{2r\dfrac{R_g}{R_m}\left[1 + r\left(1 + \dfrac{R_g}{2R_m}\right)\right]}{\left[1 + r\left(1 + \dfrac{R_g}{R_m}\right)\right]^2} \quad ...(5.83)$$

where $r = \dfrac{R_b}{R_g}$

The signal loss factor depends upon the value of ratio r and the ratio of $\dfrac{R_g}{R_m}$. The variation of loss factor K_L with $\dfrac{R_g}{R_m}$ is shown in Fig. 5.45 for $r = 2$, 5 and 10. The loss in sensitivity is less than 2% if $\dfrac{R_m}{R_g} \approx 100$, *i.e.* for $R_g = 120\ \Omega$, $R_m = 12{,}000\ \Omega$.

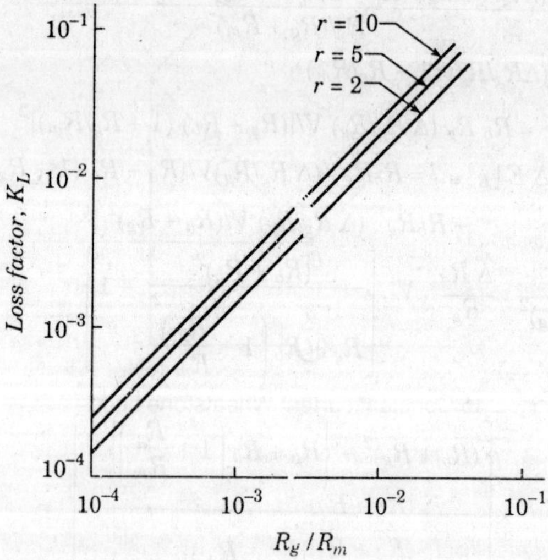

Fig. 5.45 Loss factor K_L as a function of R_g/R_m.

5.8 Constant-Current Circuits

Upto now we have discussed the Wheatstone and Pot circuits driven by a constant voltage source which ideally remains constant with change in resistance of the circuit. The output of these circuits is non-linear and the non-linearity factor η increases as $\Delta R/R$ increases. To improve upon the circuit performance a constant current source instead of the constant voltage source may be used. A constant-current power supply is a high impedance device (of the order of 1 to 10 MΩ) which changes output voltage with changing resistive load to maintain a constant current.

5.8.1 Wheatstone bridge circuit

Consider the constant-current source Wheatstone bridge circuit as shown in Fig. 5.46. At point A

$$I = I_1 + I_2$$

Also $\quad V_{AB} = I_1 R_1$

$$V_{AD} = I_2 R_4$$

The output voltage E from the bridge can be expressed as

$$E = V_{BD} = V_{AB} - V_{AD}$$

$$= I_1 R_1 - I_2 R_4$$

For the balanced bridge under no-load conditions,

$$E = 0$$

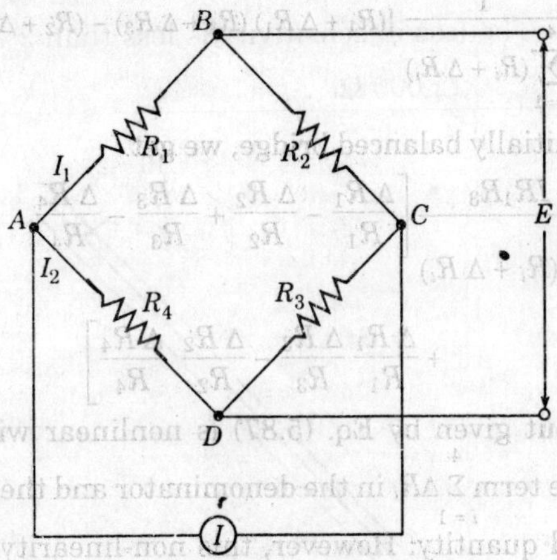

Fig. 5.46 Constant current Wheatstone bridge circuit.

...(5.84)

Hence $\quad I_1 R_1 = I_2 R_4$

Now $\quad V_{AC} = I_1 (R_1 + R_2)$

$$= I_2 (R_3 + R_4)$$

Hence $\quad \dfrac{I_1}{I_2} = \left(\dfrac{R_3 + R_4}{R_1 + R_2}\right)$

or $\quad 1 + \dfrac{I_1}{I_2} = 1 + \dfrac{R_3 + R_4}{R_1 + R_2}$

$$\frac{I_1 + I_2}{I_2} = \frac{R_1 + R_2 + R_3 + R_4}{R_1 + R_2}$$

$$\therefore \qquad I_2 = \left(\frac{R_1 + R_2}{R_1 + R_2 + R_3 + R_4}\right) I$$

and

$$I_1 = \left(\frac{R_3 + R_4}{R_1 + R_2 + R_3 + R_4}\right) I$$

Thus the output voltage becomes

$$E = \frac{I\,(R_1 R_3 - R_2 R_4)}{(R_1 + R_2 + R_3 + R_4)} \qquad ...(5.85)$$

When the bridge is balanced, $E = 0$ we get

$$R_1 R_3 = R_2 R_4 \qquad ...(5.86)$$

If the resistances R_1, R_2, R_3 and R_4 change by the amounts $\Delta R_1, \Delta R_2, \Delta R_3$ and ΔR_4, the output voltage $E + \Delta E$ measured with a very high impedance meter is

$$E + \Delta E = \frac{1}{\sum_{i=1}^{4} (R_i + \Delta R_i)} [(R_1 + \Delta R_1)(R_3 + \Delta R_3) - (R_2 + \Delta R_2)(R_4 + \Delta R_4)]$$

For an initially balanced bridge, we get

$$\Delta E = \frac{I R_1 R_3}{\sum_{i=1}^{4} (R_i + \Delta R_i)} \left[\frac{\Delta R_1}{R_1} - \frac{\Delta R_2}{R_2} + \frac{\Delta R_3}{R_3} - \frac{\Delta R_4}{R_4} + \frac{\Delta R_1}{R_1}\frac{\Delta R_3}{R_3} - \frac{\Delta R_2}{R_2}\frac{\Delta R_4}{R_4}\right] \qquad ...(5.87)$$

The output given by Eq. (5.87) is nonlinear with respect to ΔR because of the term $\sum_{i=1}^{4} \Delta R_i$ in the denominator and the last two terms in the bracketed quantity. However, this non-linearity is much smaller than the constant voltage source circuit. Let $R_1 = R_4 = R_g$, $R_2 = R_3 = rR_g$, $\Delta R_2 = \Delta R_3 = 0$, *i.e.* R_1 is an active gauge and R_4 is temperature-compensating dummy gauge, then $\Delta R_1 = \Delta R_g$, $\Delta R_4 = 0$, Eq. (5.87) then reduces to

$$\Delta E = \frac{Ir R_g}{2(1 + r) + \dfrac{\Delta R_g}{R_g}} \cdot \frac{\Delta R_g}{R_g} \qquad ...(5.88)$$

$$= \frac{IrR_g}{2(1 + r)} \cdot \frac{\Delta R_g}{R_g} \cdot (1 - \eta)$$

where the non-linear term η, is

$$\eta = \frac{\Delta R_g / R_g}{2(1 + r) + \Delta R_g / R_g} = \frac{F\varepsilon}{2(1 + r) + F\varepsilon} \qquad ...(5.89)$$

The nonlinear term can be minimised by increasing r as is obvious from Eq. (5.89). Generally r is taken to be equal to 9.

5.8.2 Potentiometer circuit

Consider the constant-current potentiometer circuit shown in Fig. 5.47. When a very high impedance meter is placed across resistance R_1, the output is

$$E = IR_1$$

When resistances R_1 and R_2 change by ΔR_1 and ΔR_2, then output voltage becomes

$$E + \Delta E = I(R_1 + \Delta R_1)$$

Thus

$$\Delta E = I(R_1 + \Delta R_1) - IR_1$$

$$= IR_1 \cdot \frac{\Delta R_1}{R_1} \quad ...(5.90)$$

When $R_1 = R_g$ then Eq. (5.90) becomes

$$E = IR_g F_\varepsilon$$

Therefore, the output voltage is linear with respect to resistance change ΔR and strain ε.

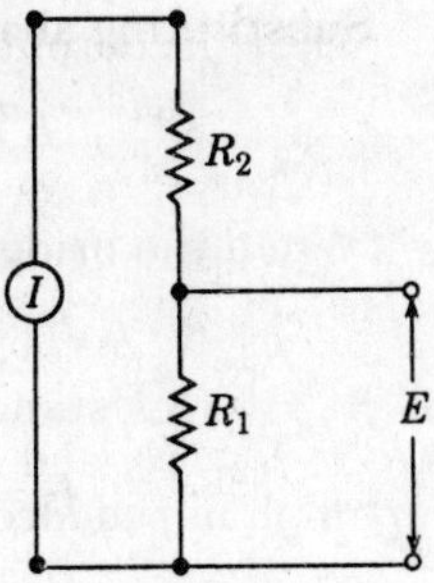

Fig. 5.47 Constant current potentiometer circuit.

Circuit sensitivity

$$S_c = \frac{\Delta E}{\varepsilon} = IR_g F \quad ...(5.91)$$

$$= \sqrt{P_g R_g}\, F \quad \text{when } I = I_g \quad ...(5.92)$$

It can be easily seen that the circuit sensitivity of the constant current is higher than that of the constant-voltage circuit.

5.9 Alternating Current Bridges

(*a*) **Balanced Bridge.** Consider the A.C. bridge as shown in Fig. 5.48. Applying Kirchhoff's law, we have

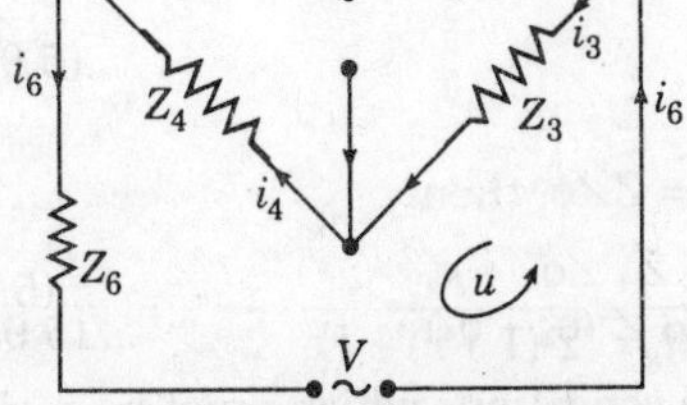

Fig. 5.48 A.C. bridge circuit.

$$Z_6 i_6 + Z_3 i_3 + Z_4 i_4 = V$$

$$Z_2 i_2 + Z_5 i_5 - Z_3 i_3 = 0$$

$$Z_1 i_1 - Z_4 i_4 - Z_5 i_5 = 0$$

and

$$i_6 - i_2 - i_3 = 0$$

$$i_2 - i_1 - i_5 = 0$$

$$i_1 + i_4 - i_6 = 0.$$

According to Maxwell, we assume a hypothetical 'cyclic' current flowing in each mesh of the network, such that the current in each branch is the difference of the 'cyclic' currents in the adjacent meshes. Thus

$$u(Z_6 + Z_2 + Z_4) - vZ_3 - \omega Z_5 = V$$
$$v\,(Z_2 + Z_5 + Z_3) - uZ_3 - \omega Z_5 = 0$$
$$\omega\,(Z_1 + Z_4 + Z_5) - u\,Z_4 - vZ_5 = 0$$

which reduces the number of equations from 6 to 3.

Now $\quad i_5 = v - \omega \;$ or $v = i_5 + \omega$

Substituting above, we get

$$u\,(Z_3 + Z_4 + Z_6) - \omega\,(Z_3 + Z_4) - i_5Z_3 = V$$
$$-\,uZ_3 + \omega(Z_2 + Z_3) + i_5\,(Z_2 + Z_3 + Z_5) = 0$$
$$-\,uZ_4 + \omega(Z_1 + Z_4) - i_5\,Z_5 = 0$$

$$\therefore \qquad i_5 = \frac{\begin{vmatrix} Z_3 + Z_4 + Z_6 & -(Z_3 + Z_4) & V \\ -Z_3 & Z_2 + Z_3 & 0 \\ -Z_4 & Z_1 + Z_4 & 0 \end{vmatrix}}{\begin{vmatrix} Z_3 + Z_4 + Z_6 & -(Z_3 + Z_4) & -Z_3 \\ -Z_3 & Z_2 + Z_3 & Z_2 + Z_3 + Z_5 \\ -Z_4 & Z_1 + Z_4 & -Z_5 \end{vmatrix}}$$

$$= V\,\frac{-Z_3\,(Z_1 + Z_4) + Z_4\,(Z_2 + Z_3)}{D}$$

$$= V\,\frac{(Z_2Z_4 - Z_1Z_3)}{D} \qquad \text{...(5.94)}$$

where D represents the denominator.

When the bridge is balanced, $i_5 = 0$

Hence $\quad Z_1Z_3 = Z_2Z_4 \qquad$ ...(5.95)

or $\quad (R_1 + jX_1)\,(R_3 + jX_3) = (R_2 + jX_2)\,(R_4 + jX_4)$

$$(R_1R_3 - X_1X_3) + j\,(R_1X_3 + R_3X_1)$$
$$= (R_2R_4 - X_2X_4) + j\,(R_2X_4 + R_4X_2)$$

$$\therefore\; R_1R_3 - X_1X_3 = R_2R_4 - X_2X_4$$
$$R_1X_3 + R_3X_1 = R_2X_4 + R_4X_2$$

$$\therefore \qquad R_1R_3 = R_2R_4$$

or $\quad R_1 = \dfrac{R_2R_4}{R_3} \qquad$ ...(5.96)

$$X_1X_3 = X_2X_4$$

or $\quad X_1 = \dfrac{X_2X_4}{X_3} \qquad$ ...(5.97)

If we have impedance operator $Z = Z\angle\phi$, then

$$Z_1\angle\phi_1\, Z_3\angle\phi_3 = Z_2\angle\phi_2\, Z_4\angle\phi_4$$

or $\quad Z_1\,Z_2\angle\,(\phi_1 + \phi_3) = Z_2\,Z_4\angle\,(\phi_2 + \phi_4) \qquad$ ...(5.98)

Thus there are really two balance conditions which must be satisfied simultaneously in the four arm impedance bridge.

(*i*) $Z_1Z_3 = Z_2Z_4$ for magnitude balance, or

$$\frac{Z_1}{Z_2} = \frac{Z_4}{Z_3}$$

(*ii*) $\phi_1 + \phi_3 = \phi_2 + \phi_4$ for phase-angle balance or $\phi_1 - \phi_4 = \phi_2 - \phi_3$.

(*b*) **Unbalanced Bridge.** For the A.C. bridge as shown in Fig. 5.49,

$$E_{12} = \frac{Z_1}{Z_1 + Z_2} V$$

$$E_{14} = \frac{Z_4}{Z_3 + Z_4}$$

At balance $E_{12} = E_{14}$ so that

$$\frac{Z_1}{Z_1 + Z_2} = \frac{Z_4}{Z_3 + Z_4}$$

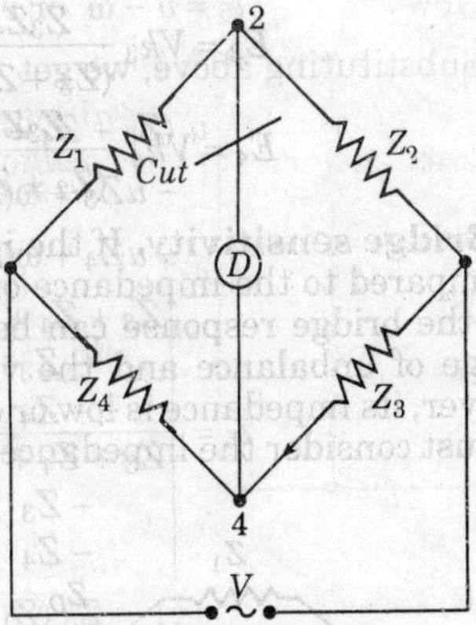

Fig. 5.49 Unbalanced A.C. bridge.

Now if the bridge is unbalanced due to change in Z_1 by an amount ΔZ_1 then the open circuit voltage of unbalance appearing at a cut in the detector branch (*i.e.* between points 2 and 4) would be

$$E = E_{12} - E_{14}$$

$$= V\left[\frac{Z_1 + \Delta Z_1}{Z_1 + \Delta Z_1 + Z_2} - \frac{Z_4}{Z_4 + Z_3}\right]$$

$$= V\left[\frac{Z_1\left(1 + \dfrac{\Delta Z_1}{Z_1}\right)}{(Z_1 + Z_2)\left(1 + \dfrac{\Delta Z_1}{Z_1 + Z_2}\right)} - \frac{Z_4}{Z_4 + Z_3}\right]$$

$$= \frac{VZ_1}{(Z_1 + Z_2)}\left[\frac{1 + \dfrac{\Delta Z_1}{Z_1}}{1 + \dfrac{\Delta Z_1}{Z_1 + Z_2}} - 1\right]$$

$$= \frac{VZ_1}{(Z_1 + Z_2)}\left[\left(1 + \frac{\Delta Z_1}{Z_1}\right)\left\{1 - \frac{\Delta Z_1}{Z_1 + Z_2} + \frac{(\Delta Z_1)^2}{(Z_1 + Z_2)^2}\right\} - 1\right]$$

$$= \frac{VZ_2 \,.\, \Delta Z_1}{(Z_1 + Z_2)^2}$$

by neglecting $(\Delta Z_1)^2$ and higher order terms.

If $\quad k_1 = \dfrac{\Delta Z_1}{Z_1}$ then

$$E_1 = Vk_1 \frac{Z_1 Z_2}{(Z_1 + Z_2)^2} \qquad \text{...(5.99)}$$

Similarly for impedance changes in other arms, we can write that

$$\left.\begin{aligned} E_2 &= Vk_2 \frac{Z_1 Z_2}{(Z_1+Z_2)^2},\ k_2 = \frac{\Delta Z_2}{Z_2} \\ E_3 &= Vk_3 \frac{Z_3 Z_4}{(Z_3+Z_4)^2},\ k_3 = \frac{\Delta Z_3}{Z_3} \\ E_4 &= Vk_4 \frac{Z_3 Z_4}{(Z_2+Z_4)^2},\ k_4 = \frac{\Delta Z_4}{Z_4} \end{aligned}\right\} \qquad \text{...(5.100)}$$

Bridge sensitivity. If the impedance of the detector is very high as compared to the impedance of the bridge arms connected across it, then the bridge response can be determined directly in terms of the voltage of unbalance and the voltage sensitivity of the detector. If, however, its impedance is low or comparable to that of the bridge arms, we must consider the impedance of the entire circuit.

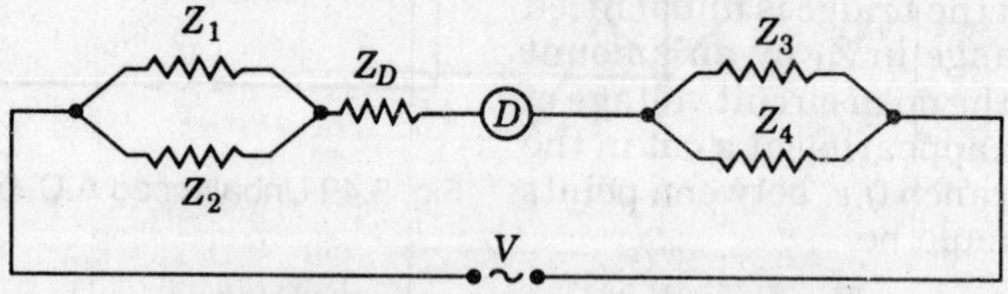

Fig. 5.50 Equivalent circuit for a.c. bridge

Assuming that the impedance of the source is negligible, we have, from Thevenin's theorem, that the voltage of unbalance acts in the equivalent circuit as shown in Fig. 5.50. For high impedance detector, let $Z_2 = KZ_1$, the voltage in the detector branch becomes

$$E = V \cdot k_1 \frac{KZ_1^2}{(1+K)^2 Z_1^2} = Vk_1 \frac{K}{(1+K)^2}$$

For E to be maximum,

$$\frac{dE}{dK} = 0$$

$$\therefore \qquad Vk_1 \cdot \frac{(1+K)^2 - 2K(1+K)}{(1+K)^4} = 0 \qquad \text{...(5.101)}$$

or $\qquad K = 1$

Hence $\qquad Z_1 = Z_2$

Similarly $Z_3 = Z_4$. If we interchange the detector and voltage source, we can show that $Z_1 = Z_4$ and $Z_2 = Z_3$ for maximum sensitivity.

Thus maximum open-circuit voltage will occur in the detector branch of circuit if $Z_1 = Z_2 = Z_3 = Z_4$ or the sensitivity will be maximum if the impedances of the bridge arms are equal.

E (for bridge ratio K)

$$= E \text{ (for equal arm bridge)} \times \frac{4K}{(1+K)^2} \qquad ...(5.102)$$

Balancing method. For A.C. bridges, balancing has to be provided for both the resistance and reactance. Fig. 5.51 shows how this can be achieved. Balance is accomplished by alternately adjusting the resistance and reactive balance controls, each time reducing bridge output, until proper balance is finally achieved.

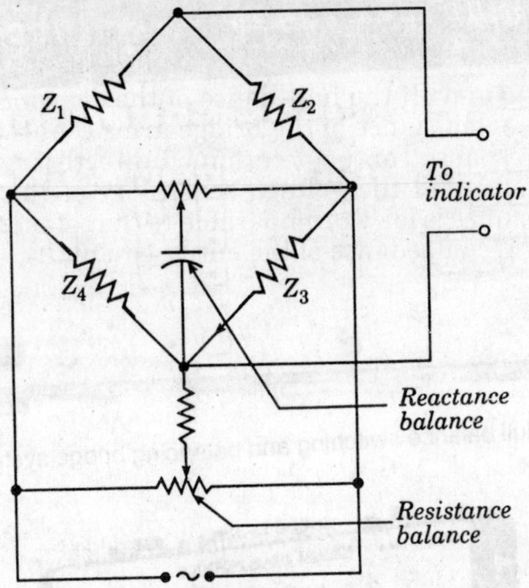

Fig. 5.51 Circuit arrangement for balancing an A.C. bridge.

5.10 Associated Instrumentation

5.10.1. Static strains

For most analysis work, static strains may be measured by a Wheatstone bridge. The bridge may be either operated on D.C. or A.C. When A.C. is employed then a carrier system has to be used. Generally null balance system is preferred over the out-of-balance method because the null balance system is more accurate than the direct readout and is less expensive. The earlier commercial strain indicators use a reference bridge circuit to provide the null-balance system as shown in Fig. 5.31. With commercial strain indicators, the adjustment resistance gives a direct readout in strain. A commercial null-balance system is shown in Fig. 5.52 (*a*) and (*b*). These models can operate either on A.C. or battery. Fig. 5.53 shows a direct readout amplifier and junction box. Switching and balancing units are available for multiple gauge installations (Fig. 5.54).

In recent years, high quality, low cost, integrating digital voltmeters have become available and have led to the development of static data-logging systems. With such systems, the output signals from several gauges are measured with the integrating digital voltmeter and automatically recorded in digital form on either punched or magnetic tape for processing with relatively simple computer programs. Fig. 5.55 shows a direct-digital-readout strain indicator. These units are more costly but they are more flexible and easier to use. Their output can be connected to an oscilloscope for dynamic applications.

(*a*) Null balance switching and balancing bridge system.

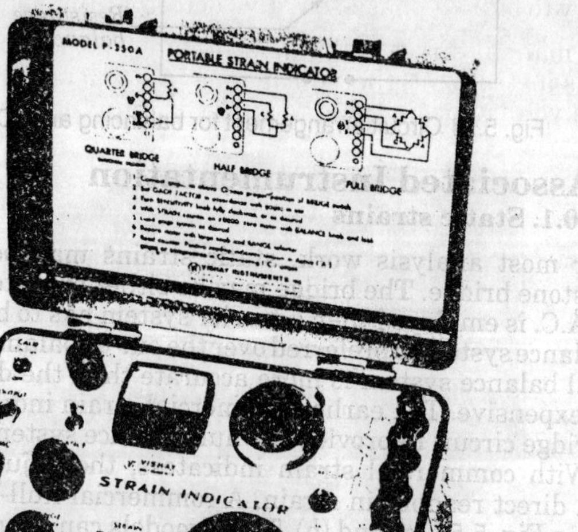

Fig. 5.52 (*b*) Null balance type strain indicator.
(*Courtesy*: Strain sert Company, USA)

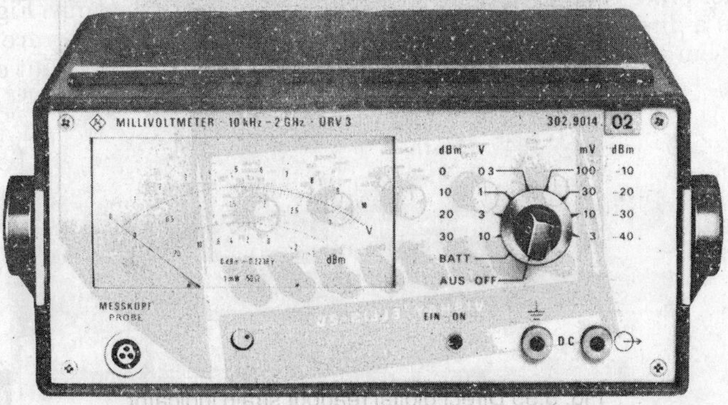

Fig. 5.53 Direct readout amplifier and junction box.

In the manual null-balance strain indicators the output from each gauge is recorded manually on a data sheet. The data are usually processed by hand or with a simple programmable calculator. Fig. 5.56 shows a typical strain indicator system. Fig. 5.57 shows the D.C. operation of the Wheatstone bridge and Fig. 5.58 shows the A.C. operation. Fig. 5.59 shows an automatically balanced bridge of the null-balance type generally used for static strain measurements. In order to keep track of the sign of the strain affecting the bridge, it is necessary to build a phase-sensitive detector into the rectifying circuit.

The manual direct reading strain indicator is shown in Fig. 5.60. With this instrument, the Wheatstone bridge is initially balanced and then the voltage output due to strain is amplified and read out on a

Fig. 5.54 Switching and balancing unit.

Fig. 5.55 Direct digital readout strain indicator.

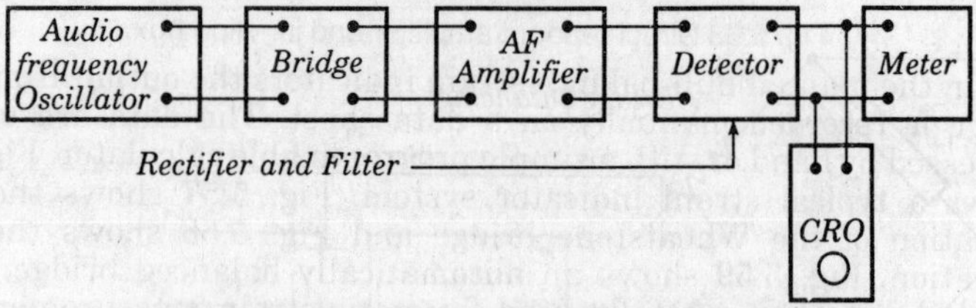

Fig. 5.56 A typical strain indicating system.

digital voltmeter. When relatively large strain-gauge installations are used to analyse a problem then automatic data-acquisition systems should be employed. The automatic data-acquisition system consists of four basic sub-system which include the controller, the signal conditioner-scanner, the analog-to-digital converter and the readout devices. The signal conditioner-scanner consists of the power supply, the Wheatstone bridges and the switches used to connect a large number of gauges in turn to the single voltage recording instrument. Each bridge has a small control panel with a balance adjustment, a span adjustment and a calibration switch. The output from the Wheatstone

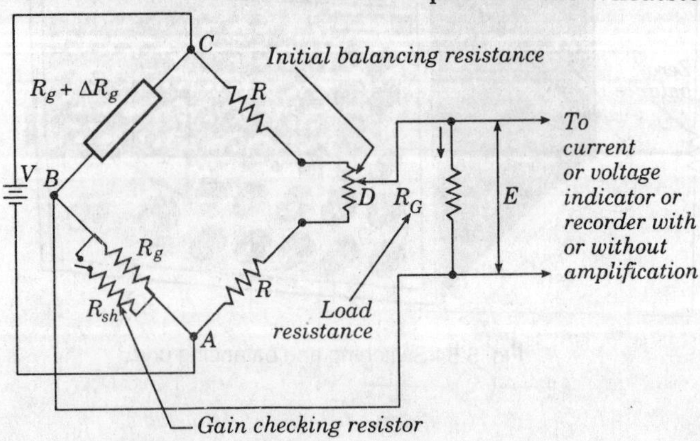

Fig. 5.57 D.C. operation of Wheatstone bridge.

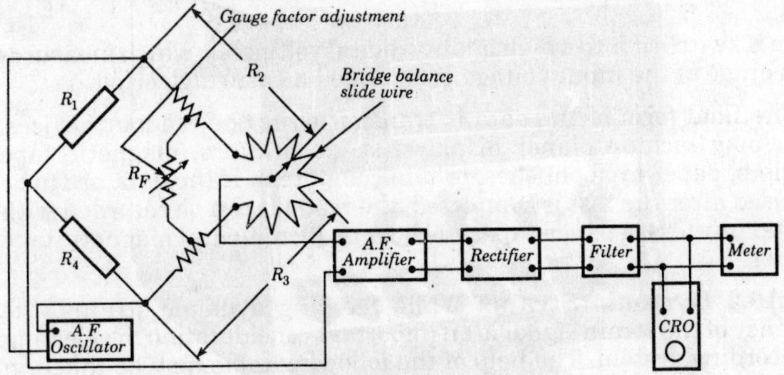

Fig. 5.58 Static strain a.c. amplifier indicator system.

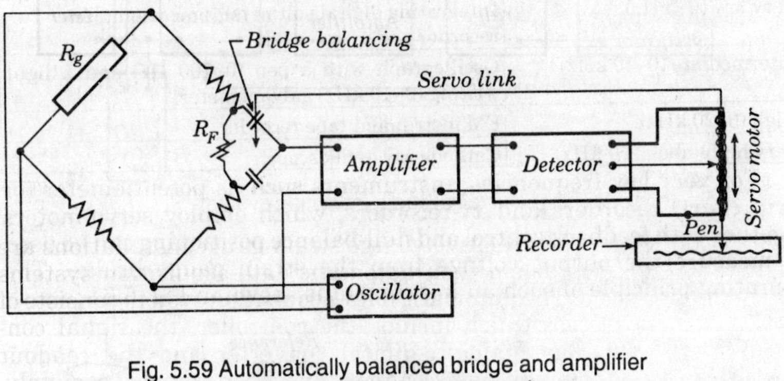

Fig. 5.59 Automatically balanced bridge and amplifier system for recording static strain.

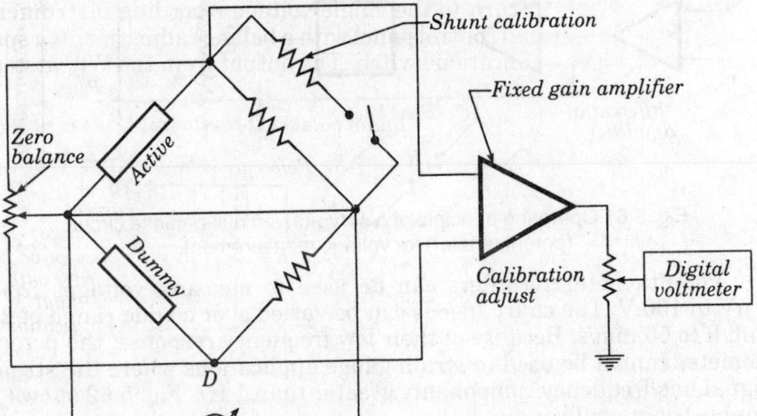

Fig. 5.60 Direct reading digital strain indicator.

bridge is switched into a high quality digital voltmeter, which measures the average of the input voltage over a fixed measuring period.

The final form of the data is transmitted to the readout devices, which may include planer displays, strips printers, magnetic tape recorders, paper tape punches, or minicomputers. If the data are to be processed after the test is completed, the readout can be recorded with a digital printers, a paper-tape punch, or an incremental magnetic tape recorder.

5.10.2 Dynamic Strains While recoding dynamic strains, the frequency of the strain signal is an important consideration in selecting the recording system. The help of the following table may be taken in selecting the recording system depending upon the strain frequency.

Frequency Range	*Recording System*
Very low (0–3 Hz)	Integrating digital voltmeter, potentiometer recorder and *xy*-recorder.
Intermediate (0–10 kHz)	Oscillograph with a pen (0–100 Hz) and a light writing (0–10 kHz) galvanometer.
High (0–20 kHz)	FM instrument tape recorder.
Very high (above 20 kHz)	Cathode ray oscilloscope.

For very low frequencies, instruments such as potentiometer (or strip chart) recorders and *xy*-recorders, which employ servo-motors together with feedback control and null-balance positioning can be used to measure the output voltage from the strain gauge bridge. The operating principle of such an instrument is shown in Fig. 5.61.

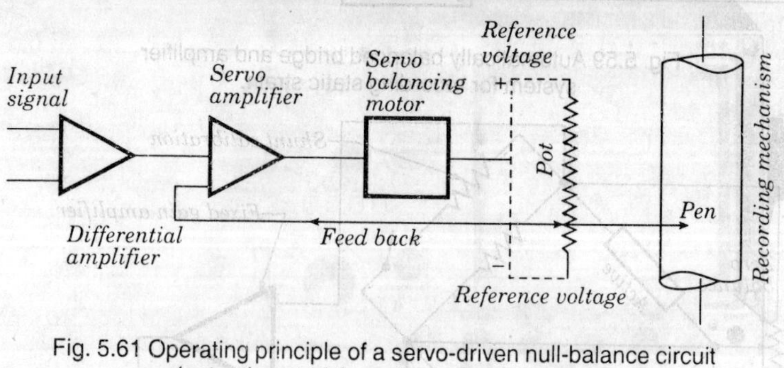

Fig. 5.61 Operating principle of a servo-driven null-balance circuit (potentiometer) for voltage measurement.

Potentiometer recorders can be used to measure voltages from 1 μV to 100 V. The chart speeds can be varied over a wide range of 25 mm/h to 50 mm/s. Because of their low frequency response, the potentiometer cannot be used in strain gauge applications where the strain signal has frequency components greater than 1 Hz. Fig. 5.62 shows a double beam oscilloscope.

The *xy*-recorder shown in Fig. 5.63 is very similar to the strip chart recorder except that it simultaneously records one voltage along the *x*-axis and another along the *y*-axis. This can record voltages from about 5 μV to 100 V. Slewing speeds of the pen can be from 500 to 750 mm/s.

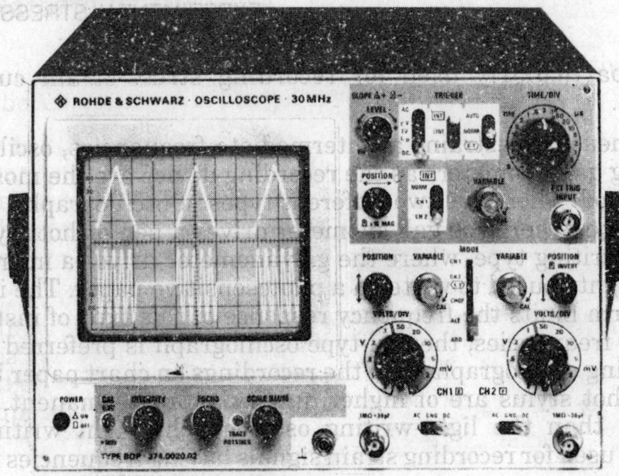

Oscilloscope BOP

♦ DC to 30 MHz/1 mV

- 2-channel oscilloscope
- Deflection factor 1 mV/div to 2 V/div
- Display modes CH1, CH2, CHOP, ALT, ADD and X-Y
- Timebase 20 ns/div to 0.5 s/div
- Auto-fix triggering
- Rectangular tube, no-parallax internal graticule

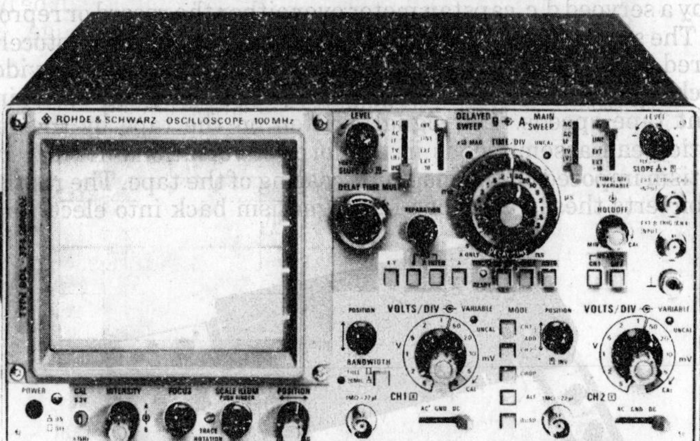

Oscilloscope BOL

♦ DC to 100 MHz/2 mV

- 4-channel oscilloscope, 8-trace display
- Deflection factor 2 mV/div to 5 V/div
- Display modes CH1, CH2, CHOP, ALT, QUAD, ADD and X-Y
- Timebase A: 2 ns/div to 0.5 s/div
  B: delayed, 2 ns/div to 50 ms/div
- Auto-fix triggering

Fig. 5.62

This is particularly used for recording stress-strain curves for materials.

For measuring strains at intermediate frequencies, oscillographs employing galvanometers as the recording device are the most widely used method. There are two different types of oscillographs, the pen-writing type, where the galvanometer drives a pen or hot stylus, and the light-writing type, where the galvanometer drives a mirror and a beam of light is used to write on a photosensitive paper. The inertia of the pen arm limits the frequency response of this type of instrument. For lower frequencies, the pen-type oscillograph is preferred over the light writing oscillograph since the recordings on chart paper by either a pen or hot stylus are of higher quality, more permanent and less expensive than the light-writing oscillograph. Light writing oscillograph is used for recording strain signals having frequencies from d.c. to 10 kHz.

For recording strains at high frequencies magnetic-tape analog-data recording systems are used. Data recorded and stored on magnetic tape are usually played back and displayed on an oscillograph. By varying the tape speed during playback, the time base can be extended or compressed. Information stored on magnetic tape can be reliably retrieved any number of times and different analysis made. Fig. 5.64 shows the schematic sketch for a magnetic tape recorder. In a magnetic tape recorder, the tape (12.7 to 25.4 mm wide) is driven at a constant speed by a servoed d.c. capstan motor over either the record or reproduce heads. The speed of the capstan motor is monitored with a photocell and compared with the frequency from a crystal oscillator to provide the feedback signal in a closed loop servosystem designed to maintain constant tape speeds. The signal written on the tape by the record magnetic head assemblies is in the form of variations in the level of magnetism imposed on the magnetic coating of the tape. The reproduce head converts these variations in magnetism back into electrical signals.

Fig. 5.63 X-Y Recorder.
(*Courtesy*: Hewlett Packard, Palo Alto, California, USA)

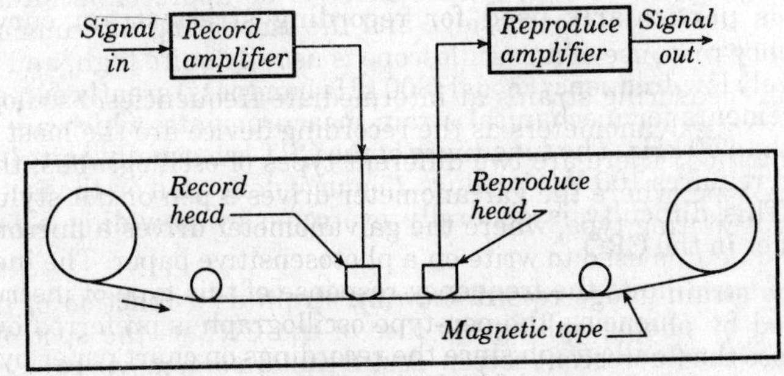

Fig. 5.64 Magnetic tape recorder.

Most instrument tape systems can be used in either direct recording or frequency modulation (FM) modes. With direct recording, the intensity of magnetization on the tape is proportional to the instantaneous amplitude of the input signal. Direct recording is usually limited to audio recording where the human ear, on playback, can average the amplitude errors or to recordings where the signal frequency and not the signal amplitude is of primary importance.

With FM recording, a carrier oscillator is frequency modulated by the input signal. The oscillator has a centre frequency which corresponds to a zero input signal. Deviations from the centre frequency are proportional to the input signal. The polarity of the input signal determines the direction of deviation FM recording preserves the d.c. component in the signal and is much more accurate than direct recording. Fig. 5.65 shows a basic FM system.

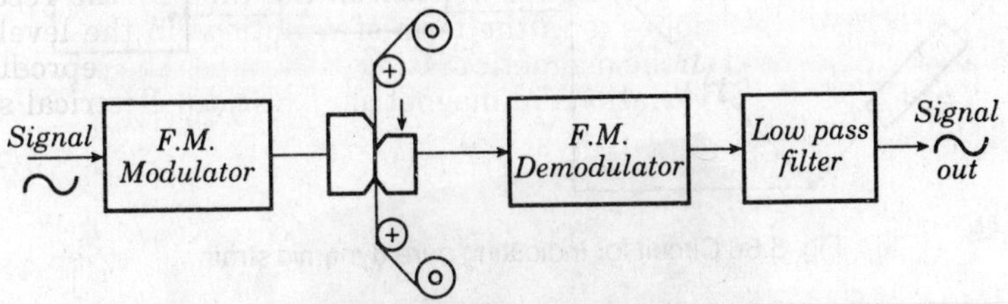

Fig. 5.65 Basic F.M. system.

Very high frequency recording can be accomplished with cathode ray oscilloscopes which have bandwidths upto 500 MHz. The CRO is, in effect, a voltmeter which can be employed to measure transient voltage signals. The heart of the CRO is the cathode ray tube (CRT). The stream of electrons permits the CRT to be employed as a dynamic voltmeter with an inertialess indicating system. Now-a-days, storage oscilloscopes are available which retain the display the image of an electrical wave-form on the tube face after the waveform ceases to exist. The stored display can be instantaneously erased to ready the tube for display of the next waveform.

For dynamic strain-gauge applications, the CRO is an ideal voltage-measuring equipment. The input impedance of the instrument is quite high (about 1 MΩ) ; thus, there is no appreciable interaction between the Wheatstone bridge and the measuring instrument. The frequency response of an oscilloscope is usually quite high, and even a relatively low-frequency model (800 kHz bandpass) greatly exceeds the requirements for mechanical strain measurements, which are rarely more than 50 kHz. The sensitivity of the CRT is normally quite low and it often requires 100 V to produce 25 mm of deflection on the face of the tube. This difficulty is generally overcome by providing a built in amplifier in the CRO.

The strain gauge record showing strain as a function of time is obtained by photographing the face of the CRT as the spot of light traverses the fluorescent screen. A still camera or a movie camera may be used to obtain a permanent strain signal record.

A chopper is a switch (electronic and mechanical) which alternates between the bridge output and a short circuit from 60 to 100 times per record. The chopper output is a square wave.

Fig. 5.66 shows a system for indicating pure dynamic strain on CRO. Fig. 5.67 shows the chopper system for indicating static, dynamic and combined strains and Fig. 5.68 with FM output.

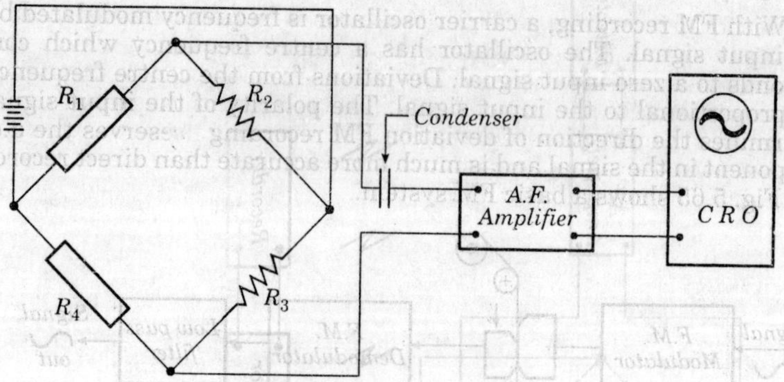

Fig. 5.66 Circuit for indicating pure dynamic strain.

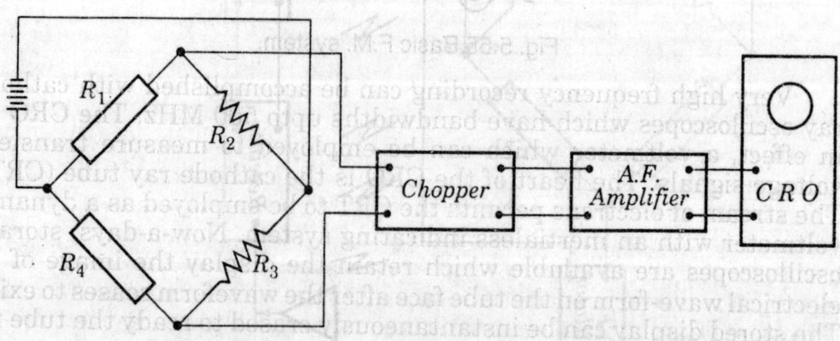

Fig. 5.67 Chopper system for indicating static, dynamic and combined strains.

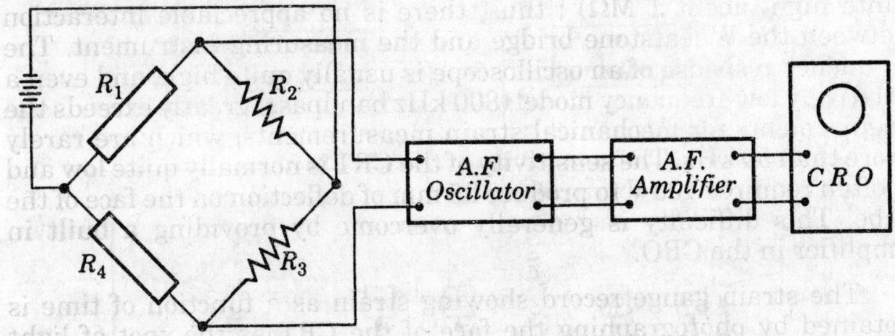

Fig. 5.68 Frequency modulated strain indicating system.

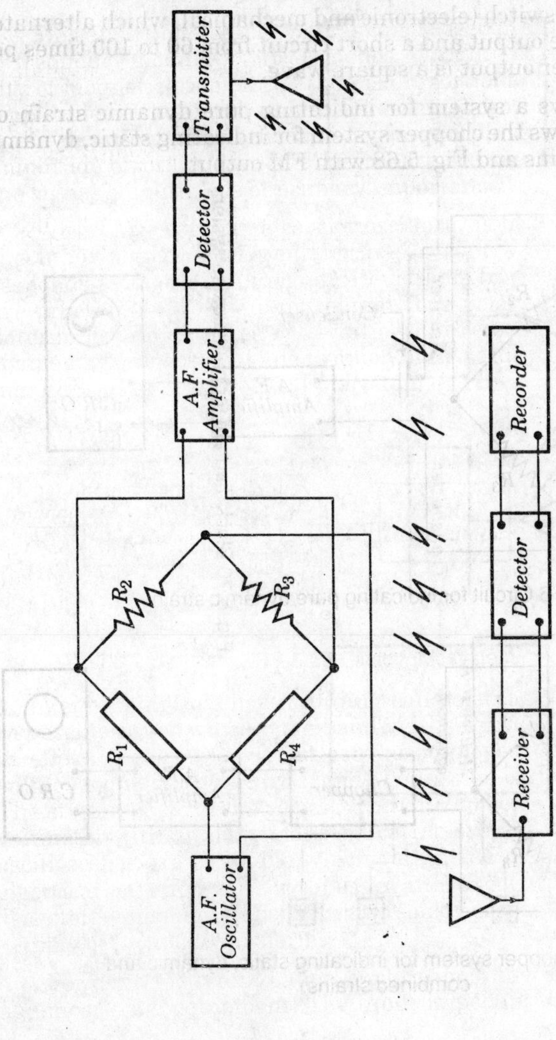

Fig. 5.69 Block diagram for single channel radio telemetry system.

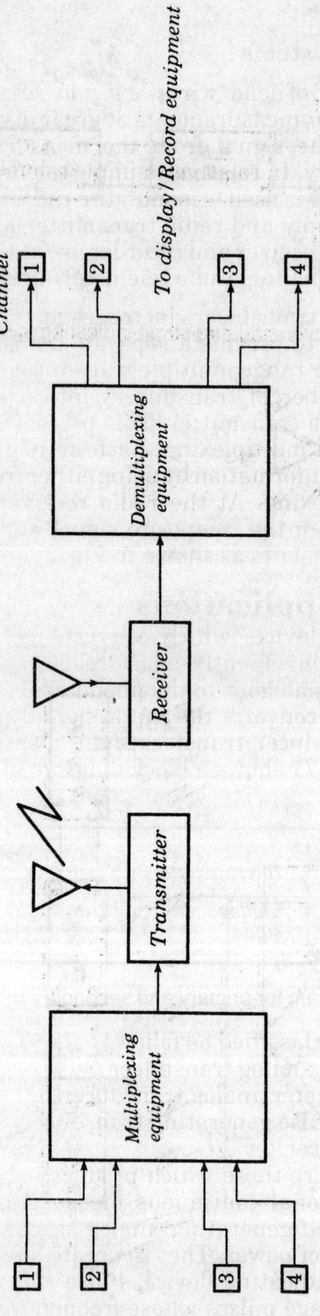

Fig. 5.70 Block diagram for multiplexing system.

5.10.3 Telemetry Systems

To preclude the use of lead wires, *e.g.*, on rotating machinery, measurements in space, or measurements at great distances, it is often necessary to transmit the signal from the measuring point to the recording site by telemetry. In relatively simple telemetry systems, the output from a single bridge is used to modulate a radio signal. The strain gauge, bridge, power supply and radio transmitter are located at the measuring point and the receiver and recorder are at the recording site. Fig. 5.69 shows a single channel radio telemetering system.

When the number of transducers increases at the measuring site, it becomes less practical to provide a separate transmitter for each ; therefore, most of the long range multiple transducer systems combine the signals from a number of transducers into a single signal for transmission by one radio transmitter. This process of combining the different signals is called multiplexing. Each individual signal in the group retains its original information by using either frequency-division or time-division multiplexing. At the radio receiver, the individual signals are separated from the composite signal and recorded on individual recording instruments as shown in Fig. 5.70.

5.11 Transducer Applications

A transducer is a device, which converts phenomenon to be measured into a more conveniently measureable quantity, which is directly proportional or analogous to the phenomenon to be measured. The primary transducer converts the input signal into displacement and the secondary transducer transforms the displacement into an analogous voltage. Fig. 5.71 shows a block diagram of a transducer.

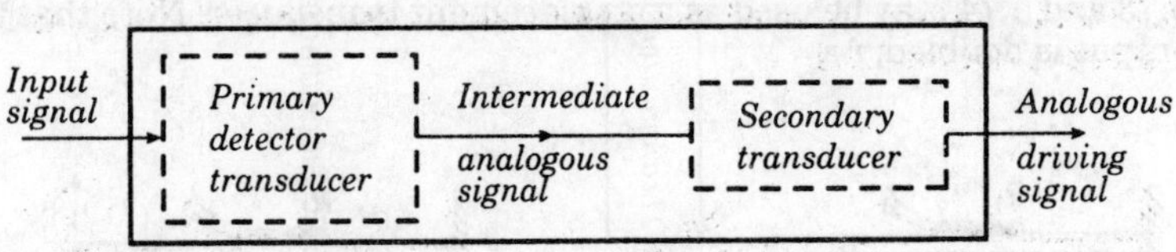

Fig. 5.71 Block diagram for primary and secondary transducers.

Transducers may be classified as follows :

1. Self-generating analog transducer.
2. Variable parameter analog transducer.
3. Frequency or pulse generating transducer.
4. Digital transducer.

Analog transducers are those which produce an electrical output signal that is a proportional continuous measurement of the input parameter variations. Self-generating analog transducers do not require any outside source of power. They generate sufficient voltage or current to operate the indicating device. Pulse rate transducers are those which produce voltage pulses whose frequency or random pulse generating rate is proportional to the input parameter variations. Digital transducers are those which produce a unique coded current or voltage form for each discrete value sensed. Fig. 5.72 shows the block diagrams for voltage generating and variable parameter transducers.

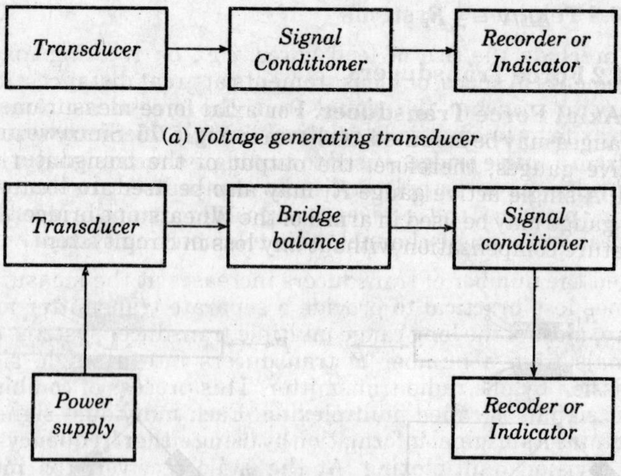

(a) Voltage generating transducer

(b) Variable parameter transducer

Fig. 5.72 Block diagrams for strain gauge transducers.

Strain gauge transducers may be classified as follows :

1. Force and displacement transducers.
2. Torque transducer.
3. Pressure transducer.
4. Velocity and acceleration transducers.

5.11.1 Displacement Transducers

Resistance strain gauges mounted on a member as shown in Figs. 5.73 and 5.74 may be used as a displacement transducer. Note that the output is doubled, *i.e.*

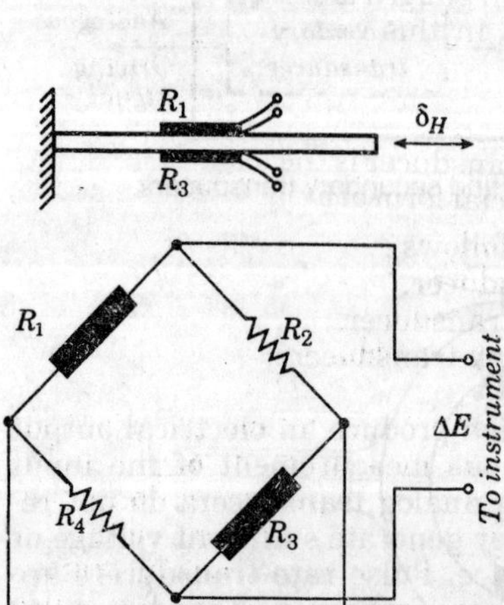

Fig. 5.73 Longitudinal displacement transducer.

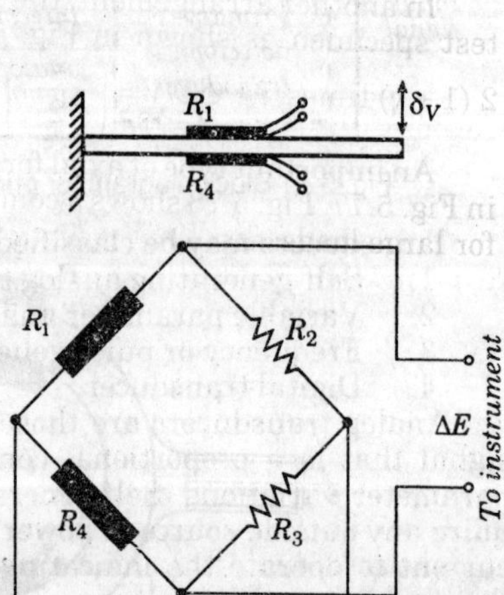

Fig. 5.74 Transverse displacement transducer.

$$\Delta E/V = \frac{1}{2} F\varepsilon$$

5.11.2 Force Transducers

(*a*) **Axial Force Transducer.** For axial force measurements the strain gauges may be mounted as shown in Fig. 5.75. Since we are using two active gauges, therefore, the output of the transducer will be doubled. A single active gauge R_1 may also be used. In that case the dummy gauge may be used in arm 4 of the Wheatstone bridge to obtain temperature compensation without any loss in circuit sensitivity.

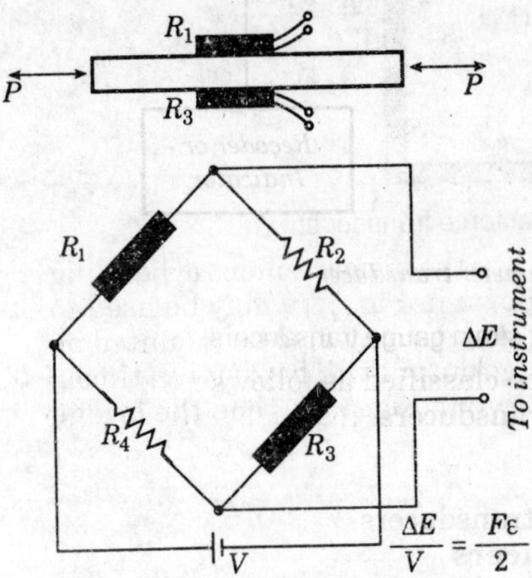

Fig. 5.75 Axial force transducer.

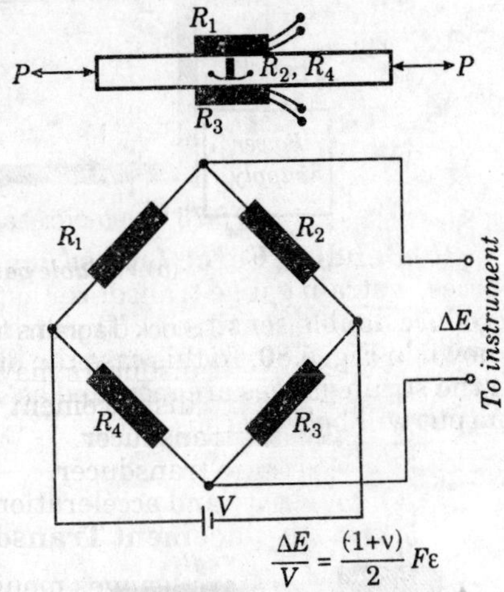

Fig. 5.76 Axial force transducer.

In another arrangement, the strain gauges may be mounted on the test specimen as shown in Fig. 5.76. In this case the output will be 2 (1 + ν) times, *i.e.* $\Delta E/V = \left(\frac{1+\nu}{2}\right) F\varepsilon$.

An important type of axial force transducer is the load cell as shown in Fig. 5.77. Fig. 5.78 shows a commercial form of axial force transducer for large loads.

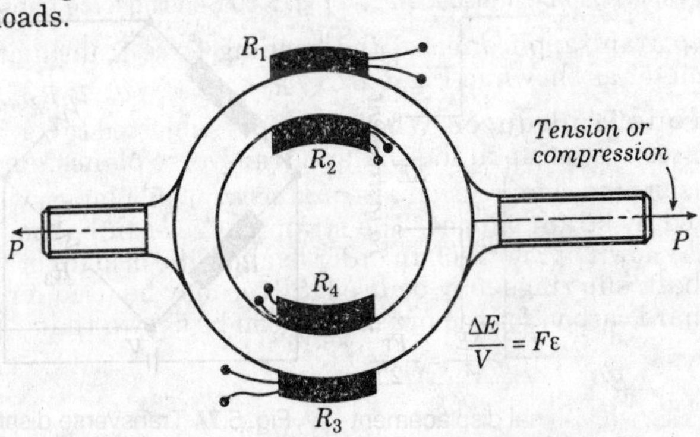

Fig. 5.77 Ring gauge force transducer.

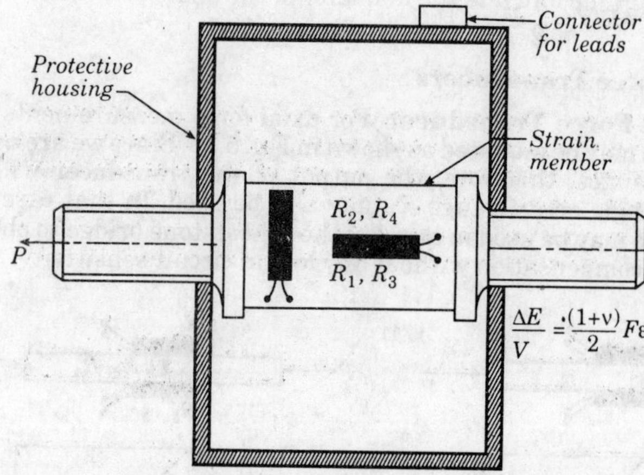

Fig. 5.78 Commercial axial force transducer.

(*b*) **Bending Force Transducer.** For the measurement of bending forces, a strain gauge transducer as shown in Fig. 5.79 may be used to produce double sensitivity. The strain gauges may also be mounted as shown in Fig. 5.80. In this case the bridge output will be 2 (1 + ν) times. If the strain gauges are mounted as shown in Fig. 5.81, then the bridge output will be 4 times.

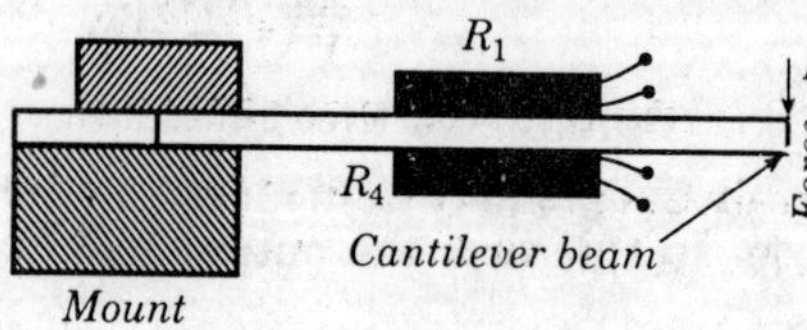

Fig. 5.79 Bending force transducer.

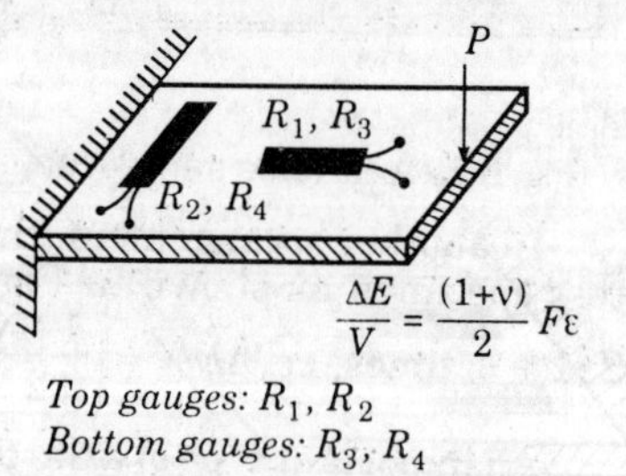

Fig. 5.80 Bending force transducer.

An important application of the bending force transducer is the micro-ammeter as shown in Fig. 5.82.

(*c*) **Torque Transducer.** When a shaft is subjected to torsion then shear stresses are set up in the shaft on transverse planes. As a result of this, tension and compression are produced on 45° planes, which can be measured by strain gauges. The strain gauges can be mounted on the shaft as shown in Fig. 5.83. In order to allow the bridge rotate along with the shaft, slip rings may be used. Silver may be used for the slip rings and hard carbon for the brushes. It can be shown that

$$\Delta E/V = \frac{16F(1+\nu)T}{\pi d^3 E}$$

where T is the torque and d is the diameter of the shaft.

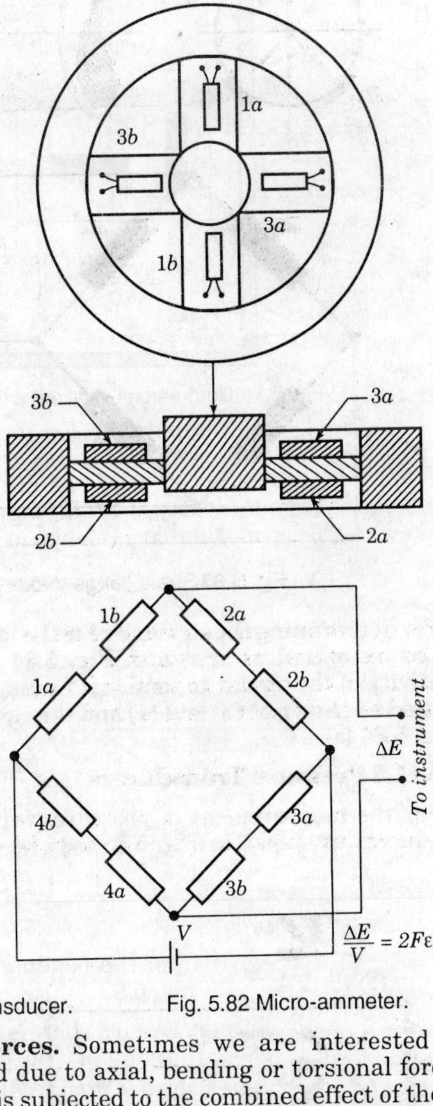

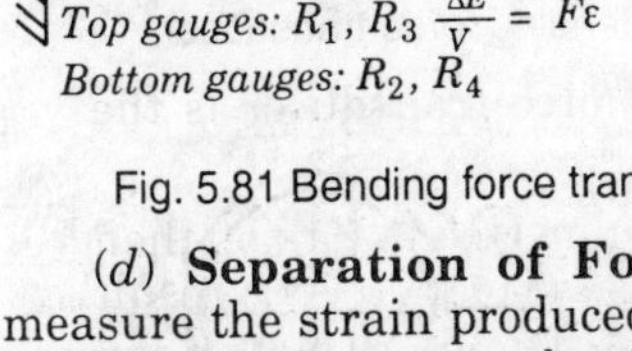

Fig. 5.81 Bending force transducer.

Fig. 5.82 Micro-ammeter.

(*d*) **Separation of Forces.** Sometimes we are interested to measure the strain produced due to axial, bending or torsional forces separately, when a member is subjected to the combined effect of these forces. For example, consider a circular tube subjected to axial tension and simultaneously subjected to bending and torsion as shown in Fig. 5.84 (*a*). To determine the strains and stresses produced in the tube due to the combined effect of these forces, a rectangular rosette may be mounted on the tube at the desired cross-section and the strains indicated by the three gauges measured. From these strain readings, the principal strains, principal stresses etc. can be evaluated.

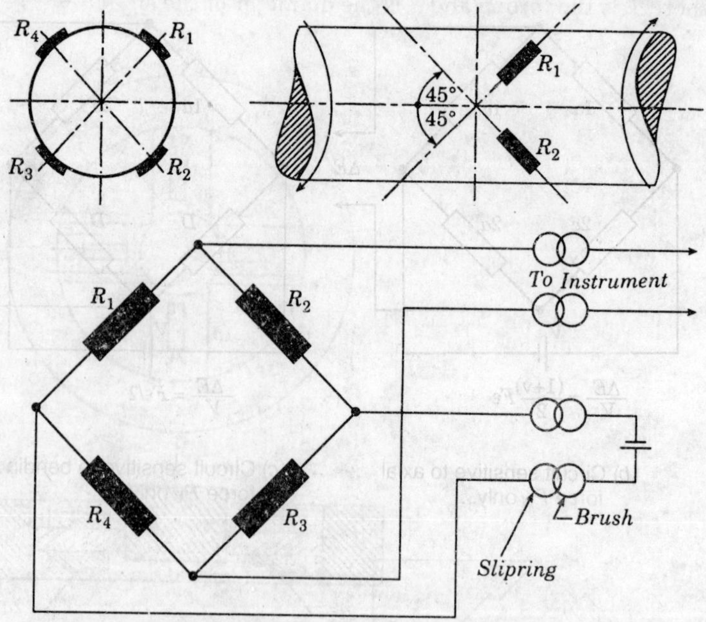

Fig. 5.83 Strain gauge torque transducer.

For determining the strains due to the individual effects, the gauges may be connected as shown in Fig. 5.84 (*b*) to (*d*). To increase the sensitivity of the circuit to torsional forces, the strain rosettes may be mounted as shown at (3) and (4) and the circuit may be made as shown in Fig. 5.84 (*e*).

5.11.3 Pressure Transducers

For the measurement of pressure, various types of strain gauge transducers as shown in Fig. 5.85 may be used. Fig. 5.85 (*a, i* and *ii*)

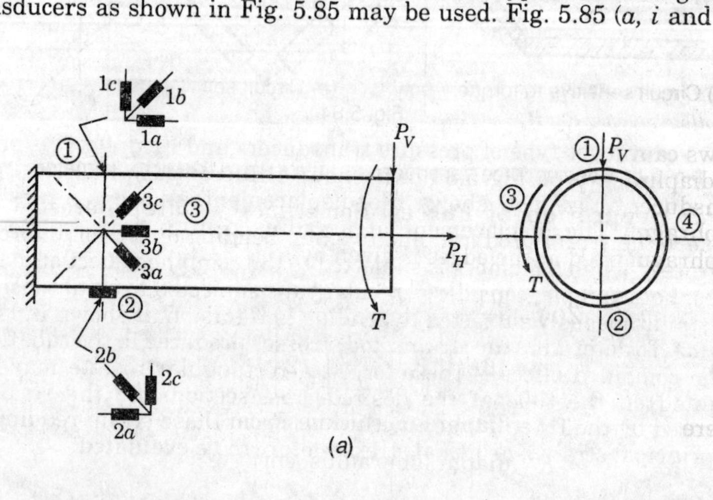

(*a*)

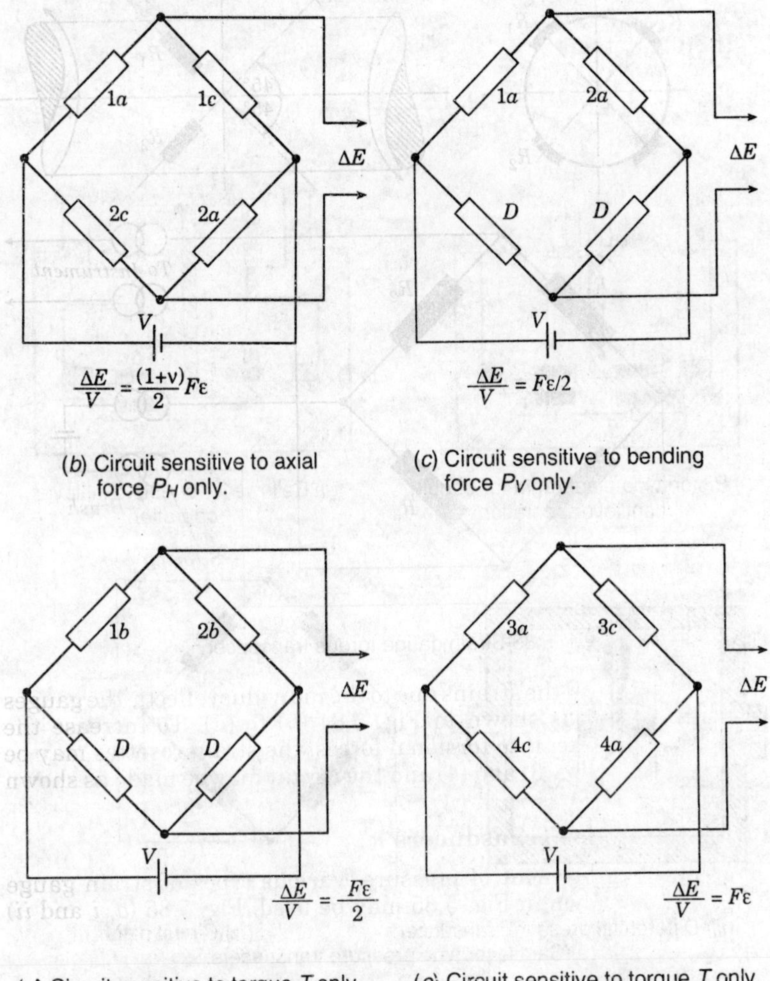

(*b*) Circuit sensitive to axial force P_H only.

(*c*) Circuit sensitive to bending force P_V only.

(*d*) Circuit sensitive to torque *T* only.

(*e*) Circuit sensitive to torque *T* only.

Fig. 5.84

shows cantilever type of pressure transducers and Fig. 5.85 (*b*) shows the diaphragm type. Fig. 5.85 (*a-iii*) shows a differential type of pressure transducer. Fig. 5.86 shows the displacement and strains in the diaphragm. The displacement at a radius *r* from the centre of a diaphragm fixed at the edges is given by,

$$Z(r) = \frac{3(1-\nu^2)\,(R^2 - r^2)^2\,\Delta p}{16Et^3\left[1 + \left(\dfrac{Z(r)}{t}\right)^2 \Big/ 2\right]} \text{ cm}$$

where t = diaphragm thickness, cm

R = diaphragm radius, cm

p = pressure difference.

If $Z(0) \leq \dfrac{t}{4}$ then

If $$Z(0) = \frac{3(1 - \nu^2)\, R^4 \, . \, \Delta p}{16\, Et^3} \text{ cm} \qquad \ldots(5.103)$$

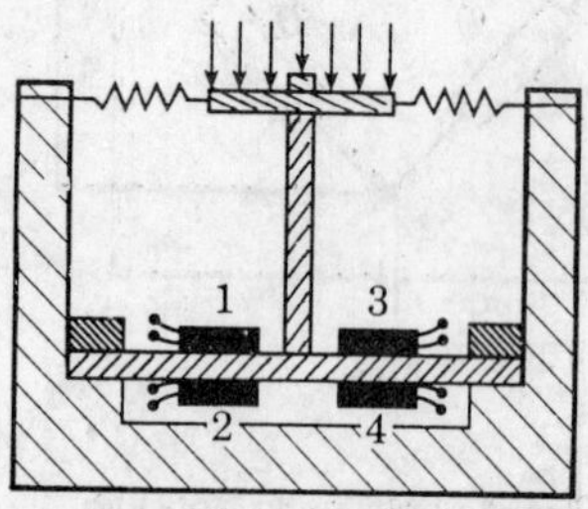

(*i*) Piston type diaphragm for double cantilever operation.

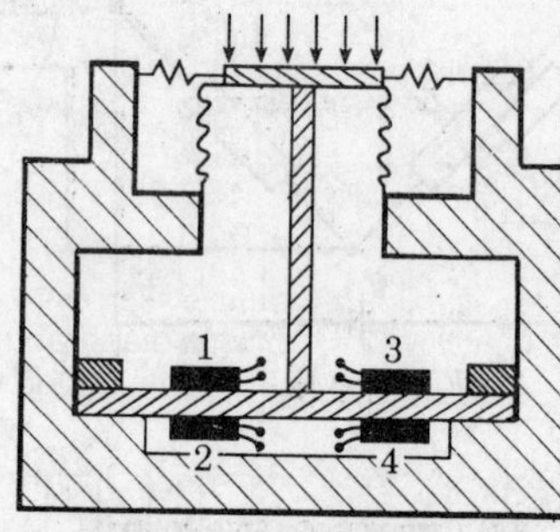

(*ii*) Bellows for double cantilever operation.

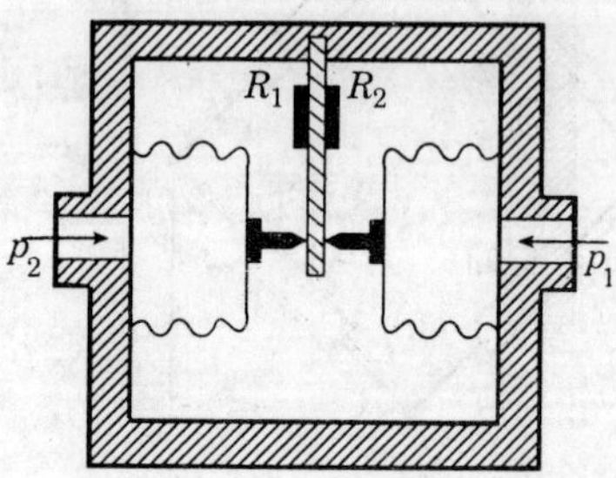

(*iii*) Differential pressure transducer.

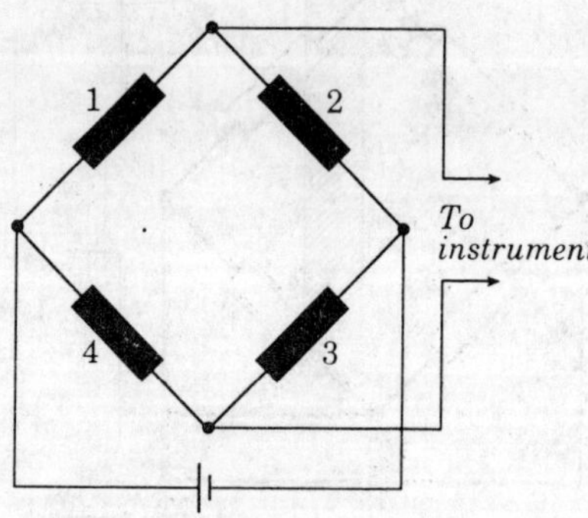

(*iv*) Circuit diagram.

(*a*) Cantilever type pressure transducers.

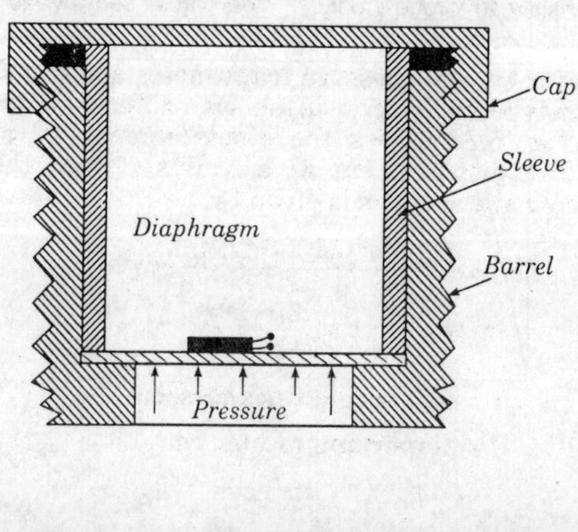

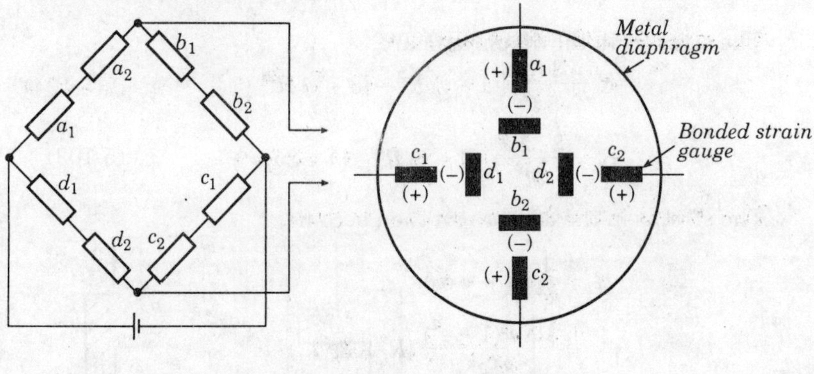

(*b*) Thin diaphragm pressure gauge.

Fig. 5.85 Strain gauge pressure transducers.

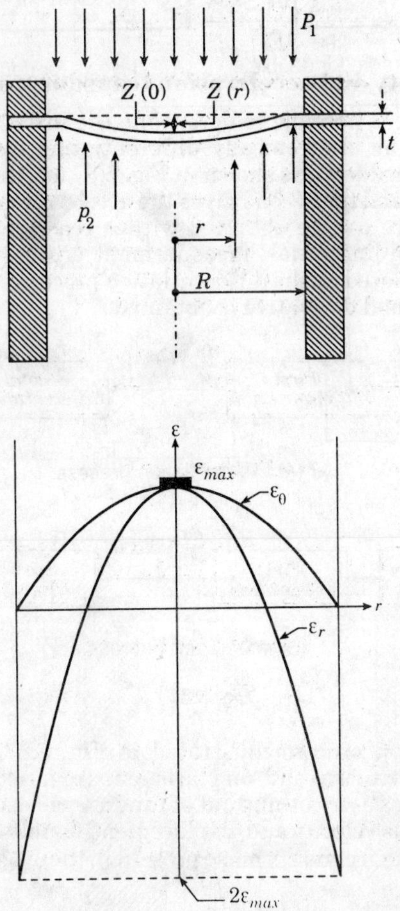

Fig. 5.86 Displacement and strain in the diaphragm.

The stresses in the diaphragm are

$$\sigma_r = \frac{3\,\Delta p}{8\,t^2}\,[(1+\nu)\,R^2 - (3+\nu)\,R^2] \qquad \text{...(5.104)}$$

$$\sigma_\theta = \frac{3\,.\,\Delta P}{8t^2}\,[(1+\nu)\,R^2 - (1+3\nu)\,r^2]$$

The strains in the diaphragm then become,

$$\left.\begin{aligned} \varepsilon_r &= \frac{1}{E}\,(\sigma_r - \nu\,\sigma_\theta) \\ &= \frac{3\,\Delta P(1-\nu^2)}{8Et^2}\,[R^2 - 3r^2] \\ \varepsilon_\theta &= \frac{1}{E}\,(\sigma_\theta - \nu\,\sigma_r) \\ &= \frac{3\,\Delta P(1-\nu^2)}{8Et^2}\,[R^2 - r^2] \end{aligned}\right\} \qquad \text{...(5.105)}$$

5.11.4 Velocity and acceleration transducers

In principle it is possible to determine the instantaneous velocity and acceleration by electronically differentiating the output from a displacement transducer. As shown in Fig. 5.87 (*a*), the first derivative gives the velocity and the second gives the acceleration. Generally, only the first derivative can be obtained with a reasonable degree of accuracy. Small non-linearities, measurement errors and noise in the signal get accumulated by the differentiation process, resulting in large errors when a second derivative is obtained.

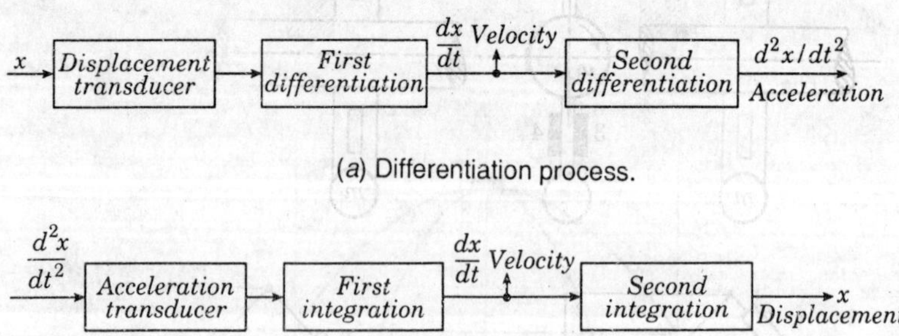

(*a*) Differentiation process.

(*b*) Integration process.

Fig. 5.87

The integration process illustrated in Fig. 5.87 (*b*) enables the determination of velocity and displacement from acceleration. Since integration involves a smoothing out of random variations, this process gives instantaneous velocity and displacement signals that are relatively free from any high frequency noise present in the original acceleration signal.

(*a*) **Angular velocity and acceleration transducer.** Angular velocity can be measured by using a force transducer. The normal acceleration of a point on a rotating body may be written as :

$$a_n = r\omega^2$$

where a_n = normal acceleration of a point.

r = radius of curvature of the path traversed by the point.

ω = the angular velocity of the rotating body on which the point is located.

Now according to Newton's second law of motion,

$$F_n = ma_n$$

where F_n = normal force applied to produce normal acceleration a_n in mass m.

Hence $$\omega^2 = \frac{a_n}{r} = \frac{F_n}{mr} \qquad \text{...(5.106)}$$

Fig. 5.88 shows how two spherical masses can be attached to a rotating shaft and instrumented with bonded strain gauges to measure the angular velocity of the shaft. Two masses are used in order not to unbalance the shaft. The gauges are mounted back to back on the connecting links so that strain due to tangential forces, which will cause bending of these links, will be cancelled.

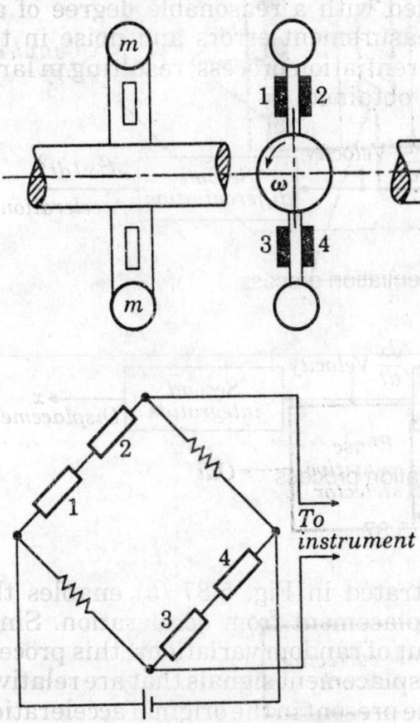

Fig. 5.88 Angular velocity strain gauge transducer.

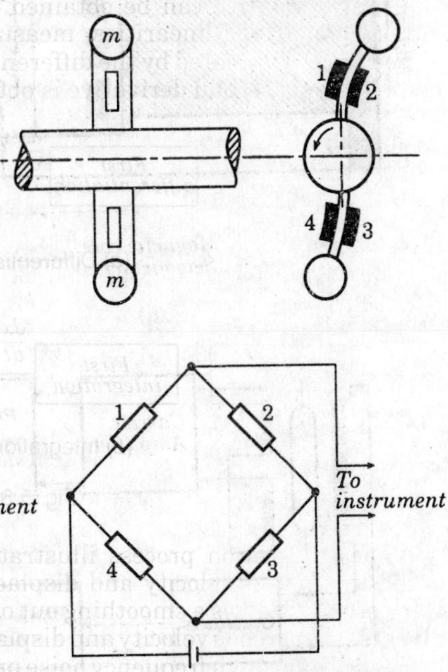

Fig. 5.89 Angular acceleration strain gauge transducer.

Now angular acceleration α is related to the tangential acceleration (a_t) of a point on a rotating body by the equation

$$a_t = r\alpha$$

Also $$F_t = m.a_t$$

Hence $$\alpha = \frac{a_t}{r} = \frac{F_t}{mr} \qquad ...(5.107)$$

Fig. 5.89 shows two masses mounted on a rotating shaft and instrumented with bonded strain gauges to determine angular acceleration. This arrangement cancels out any strain signals due to normal forces.

(*b*) **Linear acceleration transducer.** Fig. 5.90 (*a*) shows a differential transformer accelerometer of the seismic type and Fig. 5.90 (*b*) the electrical circuitry. Seismic accelerometers of this type are capable of zero frequency response. Because of the relatively large mass and dimensions, the natural frequency of this instrument is generally low. However, this offers less resistance to motion, better resolution and higher output than the variable resistance type gauges.

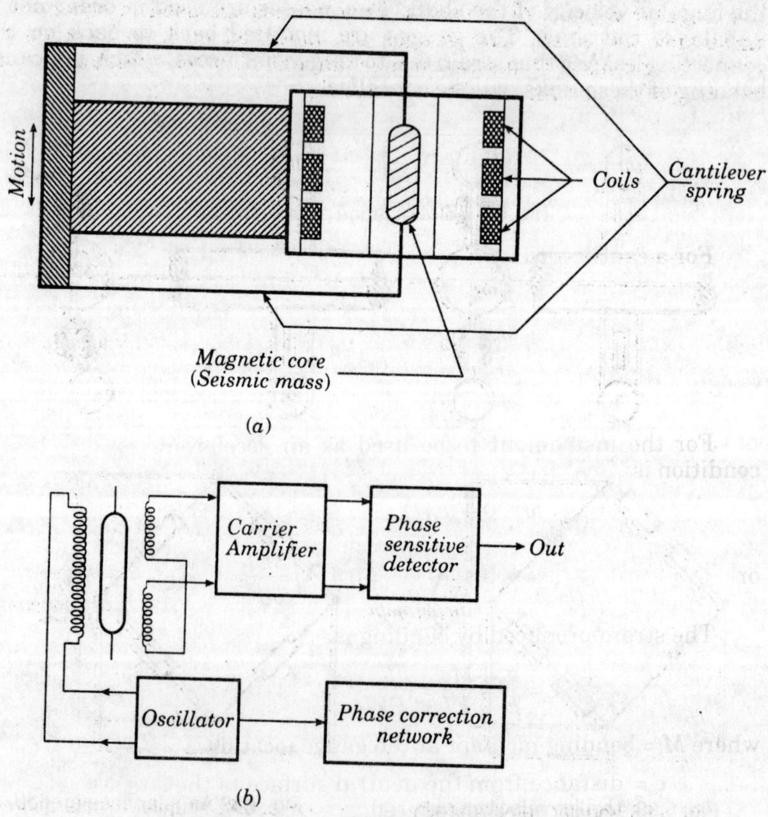

Fig. 5.90 Differential transformer accelerometer.

Fig. 5.91 shows a bonded resistance strain gauge type accelerometer. The spring constant k of the system is given by,

$$k = \frac{\text{Force } (F)}{\text{Unit deflection } (x)}$$

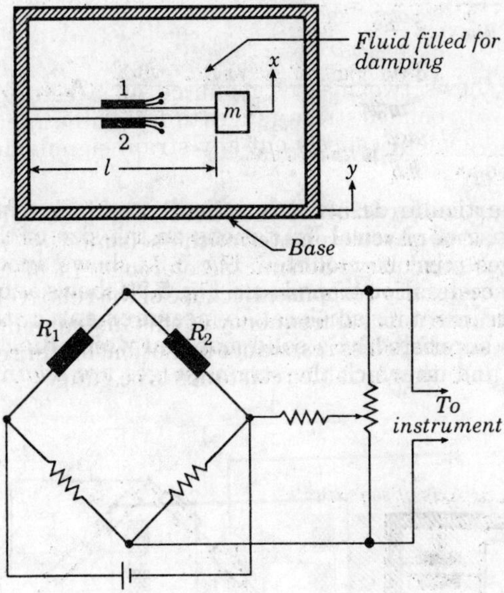

Fig. 5.91 Strain gauge accelerometer.

For a cantilever beam

$$x = \frac{Fl^3}{3EI}$$

$$\therefore \qquad k = \frac{3EI}{l^3}$$

For the instrument to be used as an accelerometer, the design condition is

$$w \leq 0.4\, w_n$$

or $$w \leq 0.4 \sqrt{\frac{k}{m}} = 0.4 \sqrt{\frac{3EI}{ml^3}}$$

The strain produced by bending is

$$\varepsilon = \frac{\sigma}{E} = \frac{Mc}{EI} = \frac{Flc}{EI}$$

where M = bending moment at the gauge location

c = distance from the neutral surface to the surface on which the strain is measured.

Now $$z = \frac{w^2 y}{w_n^2}$$

where $$z = x - y$$

$$\therefore \quad \frac{w^2 y}{w_n^2} = \frac{1}{3}\frac{Fl^3}{EI} = \frac{1}{3}\frac{\varepsilon l^2}{c}$$

or $$\varepsilon = \frac{3\,(w^2 y)c}{w_n^2 l^2} = \frac{3\,(w^2 y)\,cm}{kl^2} = \frac{mcl}{EI} \times \text{Acc. base}$$

or $$\frac{\varepsilon}{\text{Acc. base}} = \frac{mcl}{EI}\ \mu\ \text{m/m/m/s}^2 \qquad \text{...(5.108)}$$

With this particular design it is difficult to obtain a high natural frequency because of physical limitations on the size of the beam on which the gauges must be mounted. Fig. 5.92 shows another type of bonded gauges acceleration transducer. Fig. 5.93 shows another design of a seismic instrument for acceleration measurement. In this case the seismic mass is supported by a solid material which functions as the spring support and on which the strain gauges are mounted. In this case

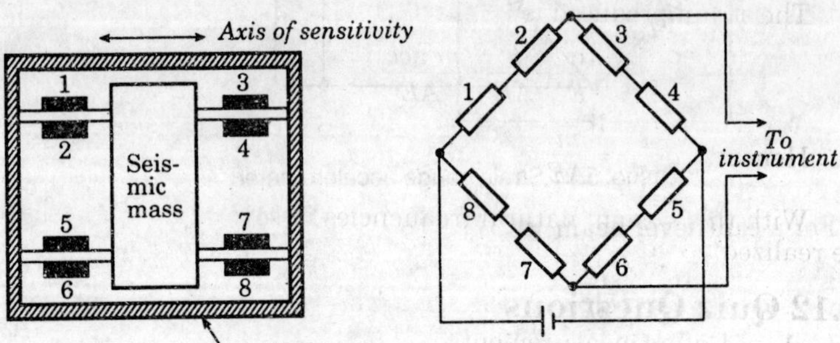

Fig. 5.92 Strain gauge accelerometer.

$$k = \frac{F}{x} = \frac{F}{\varepsilon l} = \frac{FE}{\sigma l}$$

$$= \frac{F}{Fl/AE} = \frac{AE}{l}$$

Now $$w_n = \sqrt{\frac{k}{m}} = \sqrt{\frac{AE}{ml}}$$

If the device is to function as an accelerometer

$$w \le 0.2\, w_n$$

or $$w_n \ge 5\, w$$

Hence $\sqrt{\dfrac{AE}{ml}} \geq 5w$

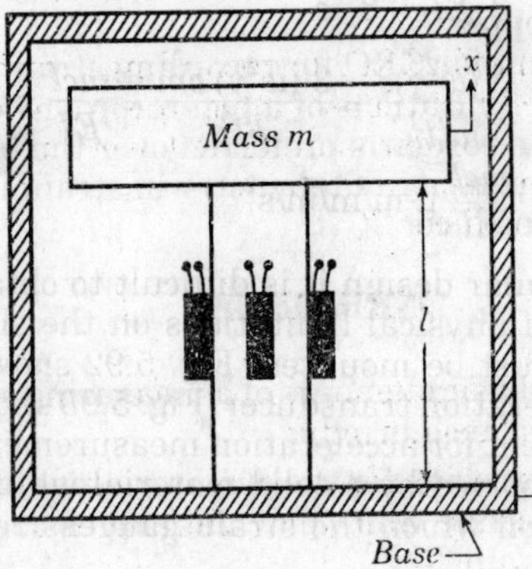

Fig. 5.93 Seismic acceleration transducer.

The strain produced is

$$\varepsilon = \frac{\sigma}{E} = \frac{F}{AE} = \frac{m \text{ acc.}}{AE}$$

Hence $\dfrac{\varepsilon}{\text{acc.}} = \dfrac{m}{AE}$

With this design, natural frequencies of several thousand Hz can be realized.

5.12 Quiz Questions

1. Define measurement.
2. Write the condition for a balanced Wheatstone bridge.
3. How much is the maximum value of the ratio of gauge resistance to the resistance of the adjoining arm for maximum circuit sensitivity of a Wheatstone bridge ?
4. What is a dumy gauge ?
5. What is a compensating and an active gauge ?
6. Differentiate between null and out-of-balance bridge.
7. What is gauge desensitization ?
8. What is the necessity of calibration ?
9. What is the function of the reference bridge in the commercial Wheatstone bridge ?
10. Differentiate between interbridge and intrabridge switching.
11. What is the advantage of three lead wire system ?
12. Out of the Wheatstone bridge and Potentiometer circuits which one do you prefer for (a) static strain (a) dynamic strain measurements ?

13. What is the effect of the resistance of the measuring instrument on the bridge performance ?
14. Is non-linearity more in case of voltage sensitive or current sensitive circuits ?
15. What is the basic difference between D.C. and A.C. bridges ?
16. What is a chopper ?
17. When do we prefer CRO for recording strain ?
18. What are the limitations of a pen recorder ?
19. Why hot pen recorder is preferred over the inked type ?
20. What is the necessity of telemetry in strain measurement ?
21. What is a transducer ?

EXERCISES

5.1 What are the basic elements of a measuring system ? Discuss the function of each briefly.

5.2 Derive an expression for the output voltage of an unbalanced Wheatstone bridge. Show how this expression can be used for measuring strain ?

5.3 Define circuit sensitivity of the Wheatstone bridge and make an analysis for circuit sensitivity of bridge bringing out clearly the important conclusions.

5.4 Why a null-balance bridge is preferred over the out-of-balance type ? Derive an expression for the sensitivity of a null balance bridge.

5.5 What are the essential requirements of a balancing technique ? Discuss the different ways in which you can balance a bridge.

5.6 Write short notes on :
(*a*) Strain gauge desensitization
(*b*) Temperature compensation
(*c*) Switching methods and
(*d*) Telemetry system.

5.7 Discuss the various methods of calibrating a strain gauge.

5.8 Discuss the effects of lead wires, switches and slip rings on the performance of the Wheatstone bridge.

5 9 (*a*) Derive an expression for the sensitivity of a potentiometer circuit.
(*b*) How a potentiometer can be calibrated ?

5.10 Why constant current circuits are preferred over the constant voltage type ?

5.11 Discuss the associated instrumentation for measuring (*a*) static strains (*b*) dynamic strains.

5.12 A foil strain gauge has a gauge factor of 2.02 and a resistance of 120 Ω. If a calibration resistor of 400,000 Ω is shunted across the gauge, what equivalent strain would be indicated?

5.13 Two gauges are mounted on a simple tensile specimen of steel. One is mounted axially and the other transversely. The two gauges are connected in adjacent arms of a bridge. If the total bridge readout (based on single gauge calibration) is 720 μ strain, what is the axial stress ?

$E = 200$ GPa, $\nu = 0.30$.

5.14 Four strain gauges are mounted on a simple flat tensile specimen arranged for complete temperature compensation and maximum strain sensitivity. When connected in the four arms of a bridge circuit, an 800,000 Ω calibration resistor is shunted across one of the gauges. Gauge resistances are each 120 Ω and the gauge factors are 2. If the strain indicator reading is 150 divisions when the calibration switch is thrown and 250 divisions when the load is applied, what is the axial strain in the specimen ?

5.15 A four-arm strain gauge bridge is mounted on a steel shaft ($E = 200$ GPa, $\nu = 0.3$) so that two gauges sense maximum tensile strain and the other two sense maximum compressive strain. The gauges are arranged to yield maximum strain output due to torque. If the strain indicator reading is 1500 μ strain, determine the maximum stresses in the shaft.

5.16 Four strain gauges are mounted on a beam to provide maximum sensitivity of bending. All gauges have a gauge factor of 2.08 and a resistance of 120 Ω. A 700,000 Ω precision resistor is shunted across one of the gauges for calibration. If the strain indicator reads 180 divisions when the calibration switch is closed and 300 divisions when load is applied to the beam, what bending strain is measured ?

5.17 A resistance type bridge circuit is made up of the following resistances, $R_1 = 9800\ \Omega$, $R_2 = 8800\ \Omega$, $R_3 = 8500\ \Omega$, $R_4 = 9000\ \Omega$ (*i*) If the bridge is of the voltage sensitive type and if the input voltages is 12 V, what should be the meter reading ?

5.18 In a Wheatstone bridge circuit $R_1 = 400\ \Omega$, $R_2 = 350\ \Omega$, $R_3 = 500\ \Omega$ and $R_4 = 300\ \Omega$. If the resistance R_1 is shunted, determine the value of shunt resistance for null in the circuit.

5.19 Compute the values of V and R_b in a potentiometer circuit from the following data. Assume circuit efficiency to be 90%.

R_g, Ω	120	350	1000
F	2.0	2.0	3.5
I_g, mA	30	60	100

5.20 Four strain gauges, connected to a Wheatstone bridge are fixed to a bar under simple tension to make a load cell. Show the orientation of the gauges in order to obtain maximum sensitivity and to cancel any bending components that may appear due to slight eccentricity in loading.

5.21 One strain gauge is connected to form a potentiometer circuit with a ballast resistor of 2000 Ω. The gauge resistance is 10,000 Ω and F = 2.0. The maximum current through the gauge is 15 mA and a CRO of sensitivity 10 mm/mV is connected to the gauge terminals. The strain gauge is fixed to a vibrating beam and subjected to a cyclic strain amplitude of 1000 μ strain. Determine (*a*) the maximum input voltage to the potentiometer, (*b*) the CRO trace deflection.

5.22 In a bridge $R_2 = R_g$ = 350 Ω and F = 2.05, R_c = 100 kΩ. If the recording instrument is operated during the period of time when the switch is closed, and instrument deflection d_c = 1.5 cm will be recorded. Calculate the strain when the strain pulse produces an instrument deflection d = 2.25 cm.

5.23 What is a transducer ? What are the basic elements of a transducer and how do you classify them ?

5.24 Write explanatory notes on the following :
(*a*) Pressure transducers
(*b*) Velocity and acceleration transducers.

5.25 Design a torque transducer. Provide for temperature compensation and maximum circuit sensitivity.

6

Semi-conductor Strain Gauges

A. Piezoresistive Gauges

6.1 Introduction

A semiconductor may be defined as an electrical conductor that has a conductivity intermediate between that of an insulator and that of a conductor, like metals. The conductivity of semiconductors may be changed radically by small changes in its physical condition.

The piezoresistive effect, which refers to the phenomenon in which the change in resistance of a semiconducting material accompanies deformation was demonstrated by Smith in 1954 on Silicon and Germanium. Manson and Thurston in 1957 reported the use of semiconductors for strain gauges based upon the piezoresistive effect. Commercial piezoresistive strain gauges became available by 1960, particularly by the efforts of Bell Telephone labs, USA. The piezoresistive strain gauges are very useful for static strain measurements.

6.2 Semiconductor Materials

Semiconductor materials may be classified as :

1. *Monoatomic elements*—These are single crystals like Germanium, Boron, Silicon, Selenium, Tellurium, Grey Tin, Diamond and Arsenic, Antimony and Phosphorus in certain forms.

2. *Ionic crystals*—These are the compounds in which atoms are held mainly by electrostatic or coulomb binding, *e.g.*, sodium chloride, potassium chloride, zinc oxide, cuprous oxide and cadmium sulphide etc.

3. *Valence crystals*—These are the compounds like silicon carbide, Indium Antimonide, Barium Titanate, Gallium Arsenide and Indium Phosphide etc.

All semiconducting materials are crystalline in nature with few exceptions like selenium and some liquids. Most semiconductors have a negative temperature coefficient of electrical resistance. Generally semiconductors are obtained by adding controlled amount of impurity when the insulators are grown and the final product acts as a conductor at room temperature. The degree of electrical behaviour sensitivity falls rapidly with increasing impurity content.

6.3 Semiconductor Gauges

The strain sensitivity or gauge factor F is defined as

$$F = \frac{(\Delta R/R)}{(\Delta L/L)} = 1 + 2\nu + \frac{(\Delta\rho/\rho)}{(\Delta L/L)}$$

$$= 1 + 2\nu + m \qquad ...(6.1)$$

where $m = (\Delta\rho/\rho)/(\Delta L/L)$

L = length of gauge

R = resistance

ρ = specific resistance.

The term m accounts for the "piezoresistive effect" and the term $(1 + 2\nu)$ arises due to the "dimensional effect". For most metals $\nu = 0.3$, so that

$$F = 1.6 + m \qquad ...(6.2)$$

The factor m varies from 0.4 to 1.9 for most of the alloys commonly used for metallic strain gauges so that the value of gauge factor varies from 2 to 3.5. This value of gauge factor is comparatively low. Attempts have been made to improve upon this value. With the rapid progress of semiconductors after 1950, semiconductor strain gauges made from *n*- and *p*-type silicon have become commercially available with gauge factors of ± 130. The values of m_{max} and F for *p*- and *n*-type silicon and germanium are given in Table 6.1.

Table 6.1 Maximum Value of m at Room Temperatures

Material	*p-silicon*	*n-silicon*	*p-germanium*	*n-germanium*
m_{max}	+175	−133	+102	−157
F	+100 to 170	−100 to 140	+102	−150

The negative values of F would permit the side-by-side use of *p*-silicon and *n*-silicon gauges, connected in adjacent arms of a bridge circuit.

6.4 Construction of Semiconductor Gauges

6.4.1 Gauge materials and manufacture

Semiconductor gauges are produced from single-crystal silicon or germanium. The majority of gauges are cut from ingots of roughly cylindrical shape, which have been grown by a special, doping process. Prior to cutting, the pure material is doped with the exact amount of foreign impurity atoms required for the particular purpose. Since the electrical conductivity of the doped materials varies with the degree of doping, the type of semiconductor material is usually described by its characteristic conductivity, and by the conduction mechanism. Since single crystals are anisotropic, the orientation of the cut with respect to the crystal axes must also be specified.

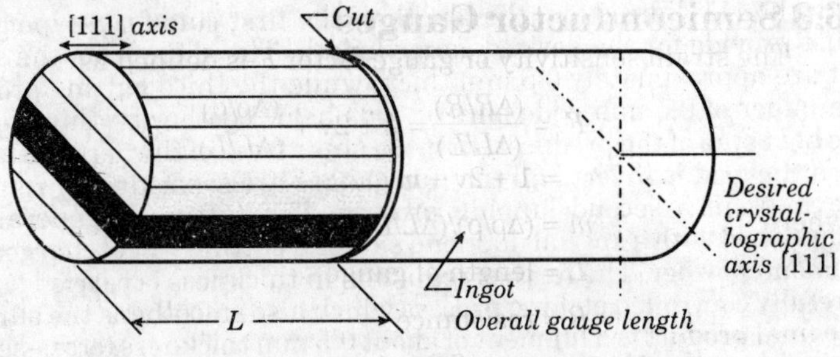

(a) Sawing of silicon ingots

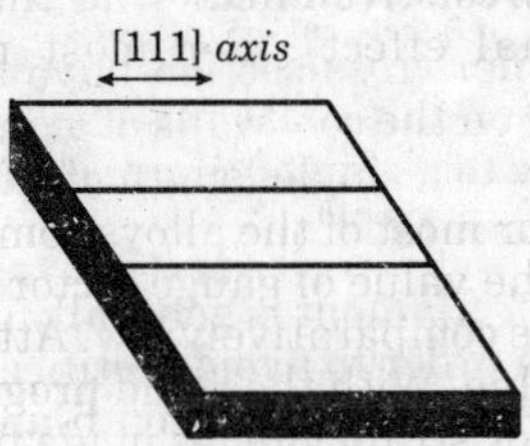

(b) Oriented slices

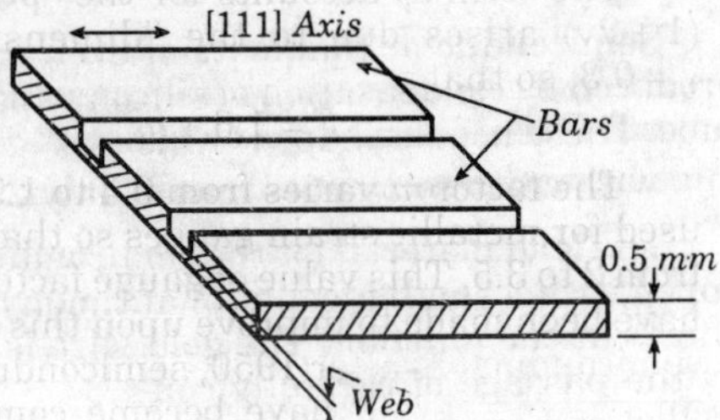

(c)

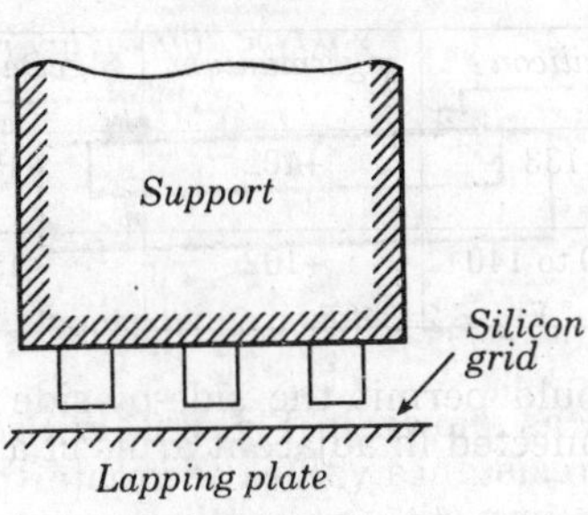

(d)

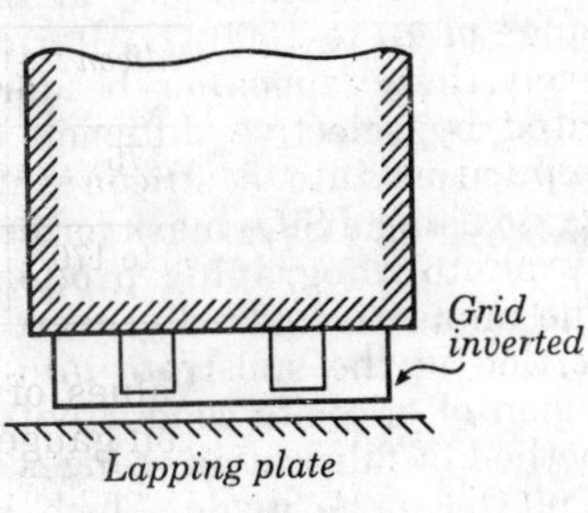

(e)

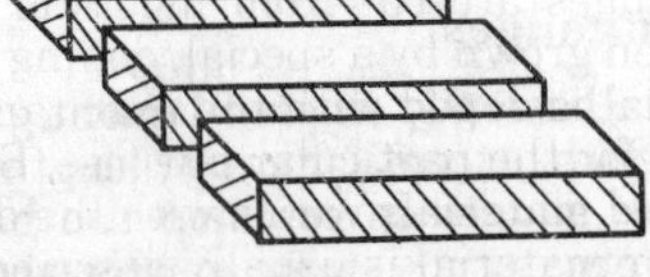

(f) Semiconductor filaments

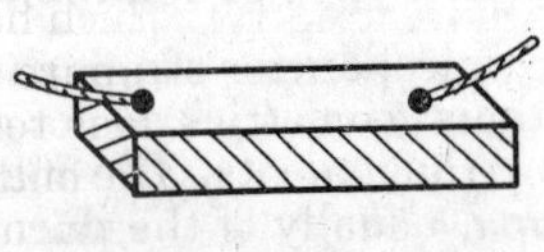

(g) Individual filaments with contacts applied

Fig. 6.1 Manufacture of silicon strain gauges.

The process of manufacture of silicon type of gauges is shown in Fig. 6.1. Since the direction of the ingot axis of the silicon is identical with the [111] direction, the length of the first cuts for *p*-type gauges must provide for the desired gauge length. The slices from the second cut are approximately 0.5 mm thick, while the third cutting produced a number of 0.5 mm wide bars or rods held together by thin webs. In the next step of the producer, first the outer faces of the bars are lapped, then the grid is invert and the raw gauges are separated by removing the webs in a second lapping process. The cutting is generally accomplished with a special diamond saw or a cutting wheel charged with diamond powder. The further reduction in thickness is carried out by a carefully controlled etching process which also smoothens the surfaces. The final product is a filament of about 0.5 mm thickness (cross-sectional area 2.5×10^{-9} m^2) which is appreciably stronger, more flexible and therefore, less delicate in handling than thickner filaments.

Semiconductor filaments of even smaller cross-section have been produced by condensation of silicon vapour on the cool walls of a quartz tube. These needle shaped "whiskers" grow to a single length of 5 to 15 mm with cross-sectional areas of only 2 to 5×10^{-10} m^2.

The lead material for the semiconductor filament is generally gold, doped with a small amount of antimony, in order to avoid rectification effects at the junction. The gold wire is welded to the silicon filament by the passage of carefully controlled current from two carbon electrodes. Typically, a semiconductor gauge may be 0.01 mm thick, 3 mm long and 0.1 mm wide, with a resistance in the range of 10 to 1000 Ω. Alternatively, these gauges may be fabricated by selective diffusion of impurities into a silicon substrate using a SiO_2 mask formed by photolithographic process. The impurities added convert a portion of the substrate into a region of opposite conductivity type as shown in Fig. 6.2. With this method of fabrication, gauges with resistance values of greater than 5000 Ω can be made. Much higher impurity concentrations, while retaining high resistance value, can be achieved through the process of masked ion implantation. Such a method appears to have considerable advantages in fabricating silicon gauges having a nearly temperature-invariant gauge factor and resistance.

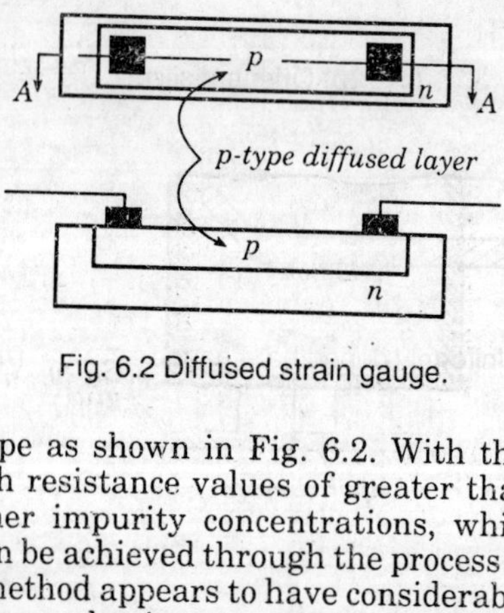

Fig. 6.2 Diffused strain gauge.

6.4.2 Types of semiconductor gauges

Semiconductor strain gauges are basically single-filament gauges and their geometries do not differ much, except for gauge lengths and lead arrangements. The majority of gauges in common use have a backing, usually of the phenolic or epoxy type, some gauges are also encapsulated in a plastic material. Unbacked gauges are much more delicate and should be used only sparingly. Some gauges are also

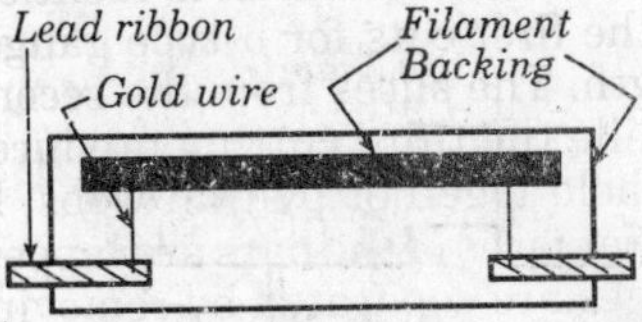

(*a*) Encapsulated gauge

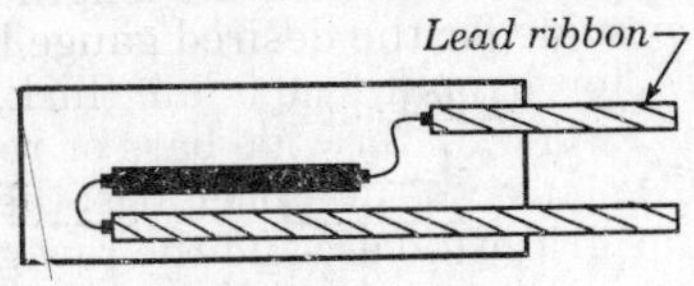

(*b*)

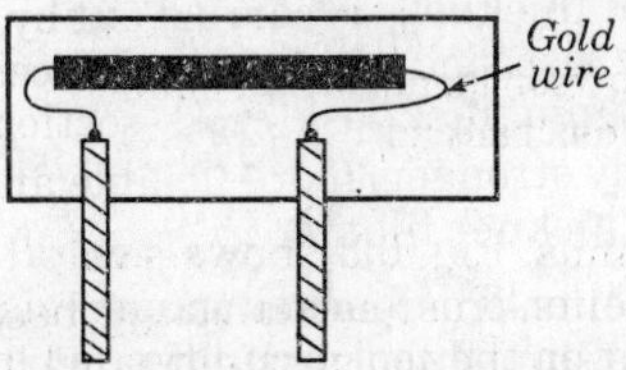

(*c*)

(*d*) Encapsulated dual element gauge compensated for apparent strain (tension).

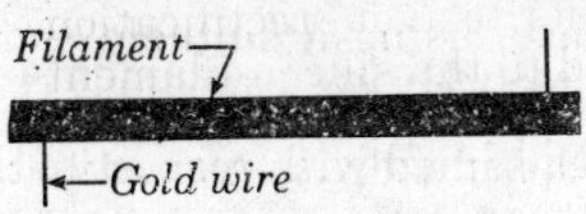

(*e*)

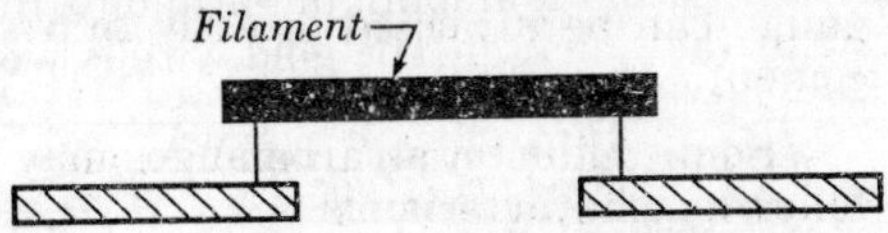

(*f*) Bare gauge

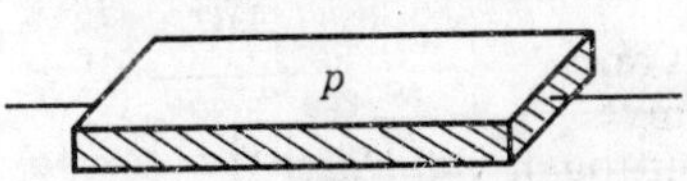

(*g*)

(*g*) Uniformly doped bare gauge

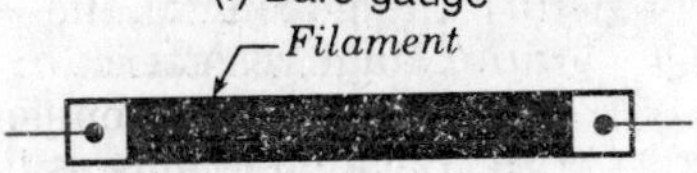

(*h*)

(*h*) Plated/soldered end or welded lead gauge.

(*i*) U-gauge etched type

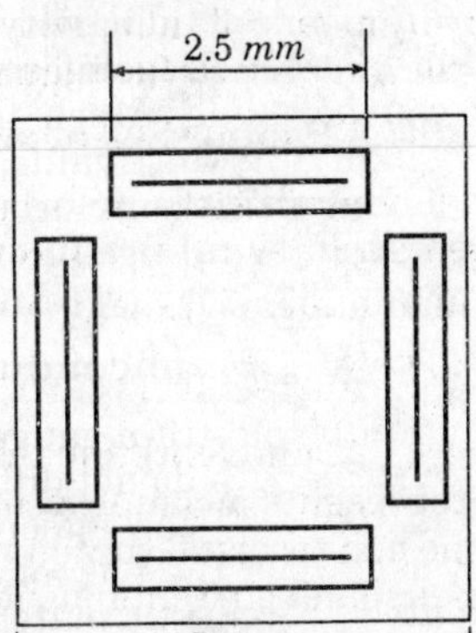

(*j*) Load wafer

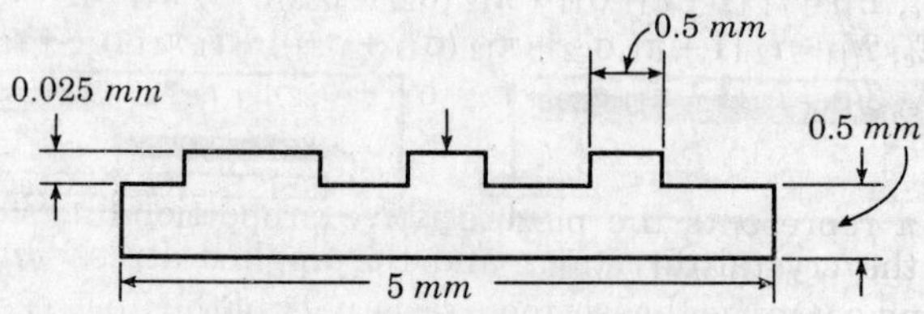

(k)

Fig. 6.3 Semiconductor strain gauge configurations. $a \rightarrow d$ with backing, $e \rightarrow i$ without backing.

bonded to weldable stainless-steel shims. Fig. 6.3 shows several common semiconductor gauge arrangements. The backed gauges usually have nickel-plated copper ribbon leads, or printed circuit type soldering tabs. With the unbacked gauges the gold wires are several centimetres long for ease of handling. Both the uniformly doped bar-type gauge and the diffused gauge are commercially available with backing material to facilitate attachment to a surface. Alternatively, an unbonded-type gauge can be attached directly to a surface, using a suitable epoxy cement.

Semiconductor strain-gauges may be classified with respect to the following characteristics :

(*i*) Filament material, *i.e.* *p*- or *n*-type
(*ii*) Gauge factor
(*iii*) Gauge length
(*iv*) Gauge resistance
(*v*) Temperature compensation, if any
(*vi*) Backing or encapsulation, if any
(*vii*) Bonding techniques, *i.e.* cementing or welding
(*viii*) Lead geometry

While bonding unbacked gauges a precoat of cement should be applied on the test specimen and the gold wires should preferably be welded. While handling the gauge should be manouvred into position only by means of their gold wire leads and no pressure should be applied by the tweezer to the filament.

6.4.3 Properties of semiconductor strain gauges

1. **Sensitivity.** In an anisotropic semiconductor the electric field strength E_e (V/m) is a function of the three-dimensional distributions of current density i (A/m^2) and stress σ (N/m^2).

$$E_e = E_e\,(i_1\,;\,i_2\,;\,i_3\,;\,\sigma_{11}\,;\,\sigma_{22}\,;\,\sigma_{33}\,;\,\sigma_{12}\,;\,\sigma_{23}\,;\,\sigma_{13}) \qquad ...(6.3)$$

where 1, 2 and 3 are the three spatial axes. The general expression for E_e represents a complex tensor relationship, but with the symmetries of the cubic crystal configurations of silicon and germanium, the three-dimensional current density pattern can be represented by

$$\left.\begin{aligned} E_e, 1/\rho &= i_1\,[1 + \pi_{11}\,\sigma_{11} + \pi_{12}\,(\sigma_{22} + \sigma_{33})] + i_2\,\pi_{44}\,\sigma_{12} + i_3\,\pi_{44}\,\sigma_{13} \\ E_e, 2/\rho &= i_2\,[1 + \pi_{11}\sigma_{22} + \pi_{12}\,(\sigma_{11} + \sigma_{33})] + i_1\,\pi_{11}\,\sigma_{12} + i_3\,\pi_{44}\,\sigma_{23} \\ E_e, 3/\rho &= i_3\,[1 + \pi_{11}\,\sigma_{33} + \pi_{12}\,(\sigma_{11} + \sigma_{22})] + i_1\,\pi_{44}\,\sigma_{13} + i_2\,\pi_{44}\,\sigma_{23} \end{aligned}\right\} \quad ...(6.4)$$

where π represents the piezoresistive proportionality constants between the crystal directions and the applied stress components in m^2/N and ρ (Ωm) is the isotropic resistivity of the unstressed material. The proportionality constants are characterized by the direction of the field potential, the direction of the current flow and the directions of the applied stress field according to the following array :

Voltage direction	*Current direction*	*Stress components*					
		σ_{11}	σ_{22}	σ_{33}	σ_{23}	σ_{13}	σ_{12}
E_e, 1	i_1	π_{11}	π_{12}	π_{12}	0	0	0
E_e, 2	i_2	π_{12}	π_{11}	π_{12}	0	0	0
E_e, 3	i_3	π_{12}	π_{12}	π_{11}	0	0	0
E_e, 2 E_e, 3	i_3, i_2	0	0	0	π_{44}	0	0
E_e, 3 E_e, 1	i_1, I_3	0	0	0	0	π_{44}	0
E_e, 1 E_e, 2	i_2, i_1	0	0	0	0	0	π_{44}

The typical values for highly doped *p*- and *n*-type silicon and germanium are listed in Table 6.2.

Table 6.2 Properties of Silicon and Germanium

Property	*Units*	*Multiply by*	*p-Si*	*n-Si*	*p-Ge*	*n-Ge*
Crystal orientation	—	—	[111]	[100]	[111]	[111]
Young's modulus	N/m^2	10^{10}	18.7	13	15.5	15.5
Poisson's ratio	—	—	0.180	0.278	0.156	0.156
Unstrained resistivity	Ωm	10^{-2}	7.8	11.7	15.0	16.6
π_{11}	m^2/N	10^{-10}	+ 0.66	−10.22	−1.06	−0.52
π_{12}	m^2/N	10^{-10}	−0.11	+5.34	+0.50	−0.55
π_{44}	m^2/N	10^{-10}	+13.81	−1.36	+9.86	−13.87
m_g	—	—	+175	−133	+102	−157

If the applied stress σ, the potential E_e and the current i are not along the crystal axis, then Eq. (6.4) may be modified as

$$\begin{aligned} E_e, g &= i_g\,(1 + \sigma_g\,\{\pi_{11} + 2\,(\pi_{44} + \pi_{12} - \pi_{11})\,[\cos^2(g, 1)\cos^2(g, 2) \\ &\quad + \cos^2(g, 1)\cos^2(g, 3) + \cos^2(g, 2)\cos^2(g, 3)]\}) \\ &= i_g\,(1 + \sigma_g\pi_g) \end{aligned} \quad ...(6.5)$$

where E_e, g, i_g, σ_g = potential, current density and stress along the gauge direction g, respectively

$$\pi_g = \pi_{11} + 2(\pi_{44} + \pi_{12} - \pi_{11})[\cos^2(g, 1)\cos^2(g, 2) + \cos^2(g, 1)\cos^2(g, 3) + \cos^2(g, 2)\cos^2(g, 3)]$$

= effective longitudinal coefficient

and cos (g, 1), cos (g, 2) and cos (g, 3) are direction cosines of π_g with respect to the crystal axes.

Since $\cos^2(g, 1)\cos^2(g, 2) + \cos^2(g, 2)\cos^2(g, 3) + \cos^2(g, 1)\cos^2(g, 3)$ has a maximum for $\cos(g, 1) = \cos(g, 2) = \cos(g, 3) = \frac{1}{\sqrt{3}}$, this means that, $(\pi_{44} + \pi_{12} - \pi_{11}) > 0$

and the maximum piezoresistive effect occurs along a crystal direction designated [111] for the p-type silicon. For, $(\pi_{44} + \pi_{12} - \pi_{11}) < 0$

the maximum occurs along a crystal axis [100] *e.g.* for the n-type silicon. It is seen (Fig. 6.4) that p-type silicon and n-type germanium has its maximum resistivity in the [111] crystal direction, while n-type silicon is most sensitive in the [100] direction. Now we shall discuss certain particular cases.

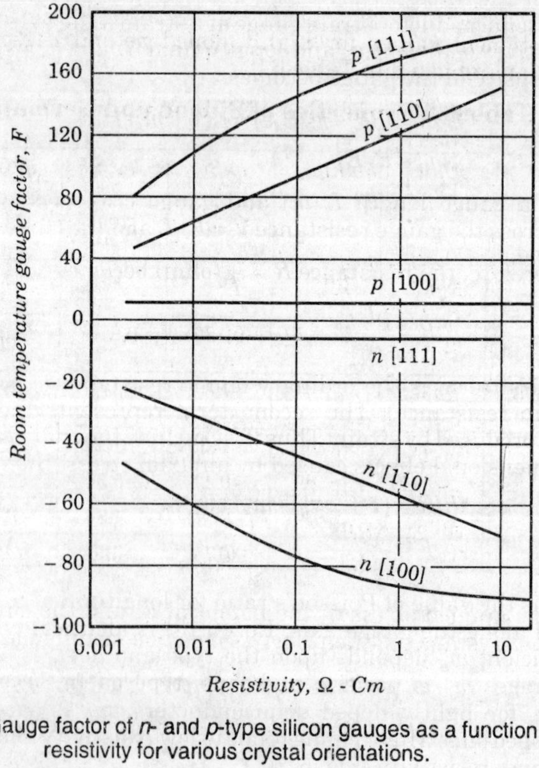

Fig. 6.4 Gauge factor of n- and p-type silicon gauges as a function of resistivity for various crystal orientations.

(*i*) Current density and uniaxial stress along the same crystal axis.

$$E_e/\rho = i\,(1 + \pi_{11}\sigma) \quad \text{...(6.6)}$$

(*ii*) Current and uniaxial stress along two orthogonal crystal axes.

$$E_e/\rho = i\,(1 + \pi_{12}\sigma) \quad \text{...(6.7)}$$

(*iii*) Current along one crystal axis, and pure shear stress operating in a plane normal to this axis.

$$E_e/\rho = i \quad \text{...(6.8)}$$

i.e. no effect on resistance.

(*iv*) Shear stress operating in a plane defined by two crystal axes, and current flowing along one of these. Then the effect along the other is

$$E_e/\rho = i\,\pi_{44}\,\tau \quad \text{...(6.9)}$$

(*v*) At hydraulic pressure p (N/m^2), we have

$$E_e/\rho = i\,\{1 + p\,(\pi_{11} + 2\,\pi_{12})\}$$

For a semiconductor strain gauge at a strain ε and with longitudinal piezoresistive coefficient π_g and longitudinal Young's modulus E_g, the current density in the gauge becomes,

$$E_e/\rho = i\,(1 + \pi_g\,E_g\varepsilon) = i\,(1 + m_g\varepsilon) \quad \text{...(6.11)}$$

where $m_g = \pi_g\,E_g$

With a gauge length $L\,(m)$ and gauge cross-section A (m^2) the voltage across the gauge resistance $V = E_e\,L$ and the current through it $I = i_A$. Therefore, the resistance $R = \dfrac{V}{I}$ (ohm) becomes

$$R = \frac{\rho L}{A}\,(1 + m_g\varepsilon) \quad \text{...(6.12)}$$

The first term is the ordinary ohmic resistance of the gauge (*i.e.* zero strain resistance). The second term represents the piezo-resistance, *i.e.* produced by strain. Thus if we include the change of resistance due to dimensional effects caused by uniaxial stress, then

$$\Delta R/R = (1 + 2\,\nu_g + m_g)\,\varepsilon$$

or

$$F = \frac{\Delta R/R}{\varepsilon} = 1 + 2\,\nu_g + m_g \quad \text{...(6.13)}$$

where ν_g is the value of Poisson's ratio for longitudinal uniaxial stress computed along the gauge axis. Eq. (6.13) is identical with Eq. (6.1). The coefficient m_g depends upon the type and degree of doping. For p-type gauges m_g is positive and for n-type gauges m_g is negative. Moreover, for lightly doped semiconductors, m_g is larger than for heavily doped ones. High doping tends to low resistivity and light doping tends in high resistivity (Fig. 6.5).

The orientation dependence of the piezoresistive strain effect is also shown in Fig. 6.6, where the gauge factor is plotted on polar coordinates as a function of orientation for a [110] plane p-type silicon.

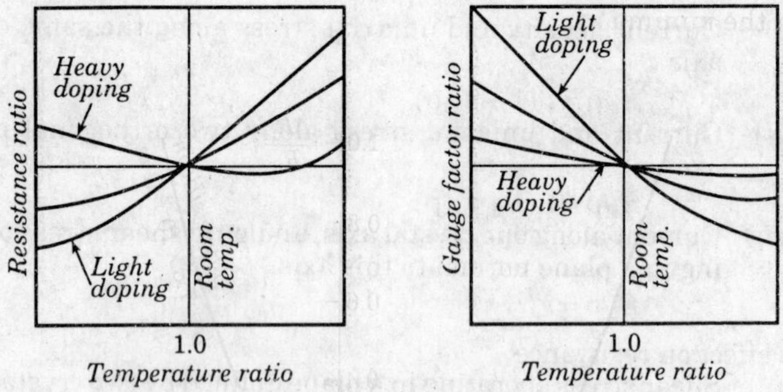

(*a*) (*b*)

Fig. 6.5 Variation with temperature of (*a*) resistance and (*b*) gauge factor of *p*-type silicon at various degrees of doping.

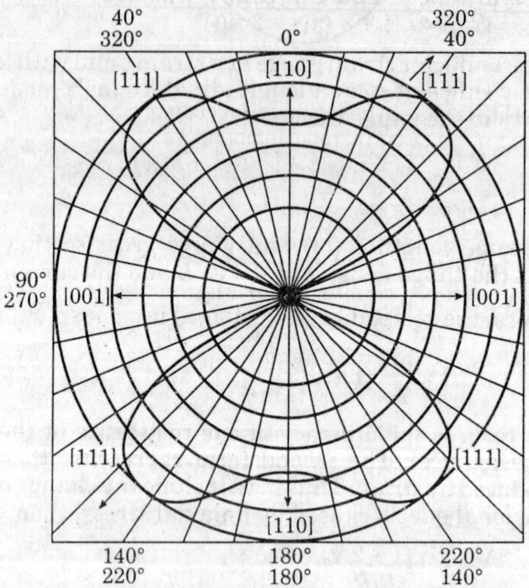

Fig. 6.6 Polar graph showing the variation in gauge factor with orientation for a [110] plane of *p*-type silicon.

2. **Linearity.** These strain gauges depend strongly on strain levels and are distinctly non-linear. The relative resistance change at constant temperature may be written as

$$\Delta R/R_0 = C_1\,\varepsilon + C_2\,\varepsilon^2 + C_3\,\varepsilon^3 + \ldots \qquad \ldots(6.14)$$

where C_1, C_2, C_3,....., are constants, R_0 is the unstrained gauge resistance and $\varepsilon = \Delta L/L$ the strain. At normal temperature levels the contribution from the strain-cubed term will be less than 1% and can thus be neglected. Eq. (6.14) is, therefore, represented by the parabola of Fig. 6.7 with the minima at,

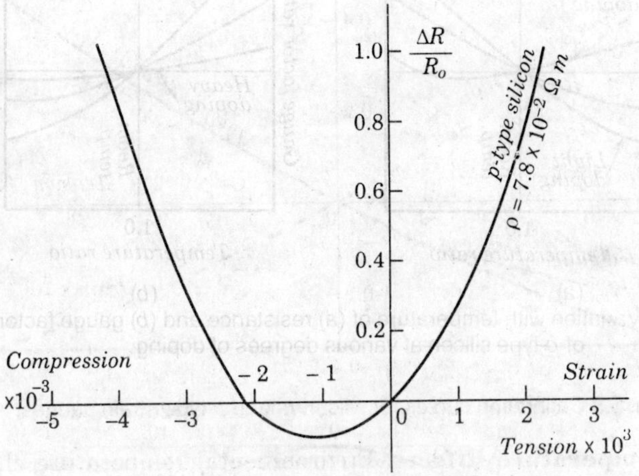

Fig. 6.7 Relative resistance change as a function of highly doped *p*-type silicon at room temperature.

$$x_m = -\frac{C_1}{2C_2}$$
$$y_m = -C_1^2/4C_2 \qquad \text{...(6.15)}$$

The lightly doped *p*-type silicon, for instance, at room temperature obeys the expression

$$\Delta R/R_0 = +175\,\varepsilon + 72625\,\varepsilon^2$$
$$\rho = 7.8 \times 10^{-2}\ \Omega\ \text{m} \qquad \text{...(6.16)}$$

where $C_1 = +175$ is the slope of the tangent of the curve at zero strain

$$F = \frac{\Delta R/R_0}{\varepsilon} = +175 \text{ for } \varepsilon \to 0 \qquad \text{...(6.17)}$$

In order to reduce the errors caused by non-linearity, semi-conductor strain gauges are now produced from heavily doped materials of low resistivity. As shown in Fig. 6.8, we have

$$\Delta R/R_0 = +120\,\varepsilon + 4000\,\varepsilon^2 \text{ for } p\text{-type silicon}$$
$$\text{and } \rho = 2 \times 10^{-4}\ \Omega\ \text{m} \qquad \text{...(6.18)}$$

$$\Delta R/R_0 = -110\varepsilon + 10{,}000\,\varepsilon^2 \text{ for } n\text{-type silicon}$$
$$\text{and } \rho = 3.1 \times 10^{-4}\ \Omega\text{m} \qquad \text{...(6.19)}$$

The higher non-linearity of *n*-type silicon makes it desirable to use *p*-type in applications where linearity is important. However, the temperature compensation properties of *n*-type silicon gauges makes it particularly useful when large temperature variations are encountered.

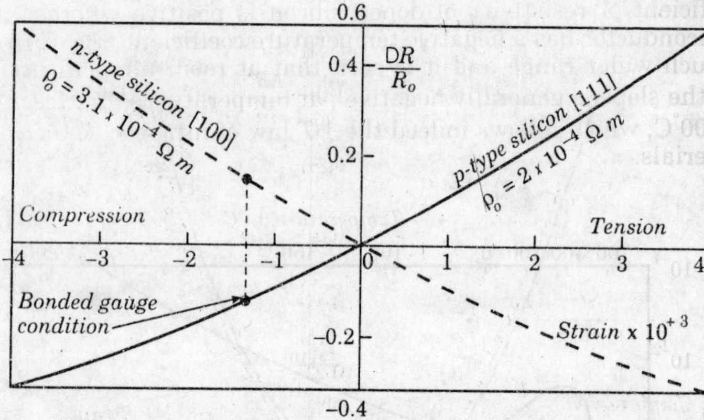

Fig. 6.8 Calibration curves for silicon *n*- and *p*-type strain gauges.

3. **Temperature Effects.** Environmental temperature changes affect the resistance and the sensitivity of semiconductor strain gauges which depends on the level of doping. Fig. 6.9 shows the resistance variations ΔR_T at various temperatures T (°C) with respect to room temperature resistance R_0 of unbonded silicon gauges with different room temperature resistivities ρ_0. At low degrees of doping (*i.e.* at high resistivities) the temperature coefficients $\Delta R_T/R_0$ are large but for heavily doped *p*- and *n*-type silicon gauges at resistivity levels below,

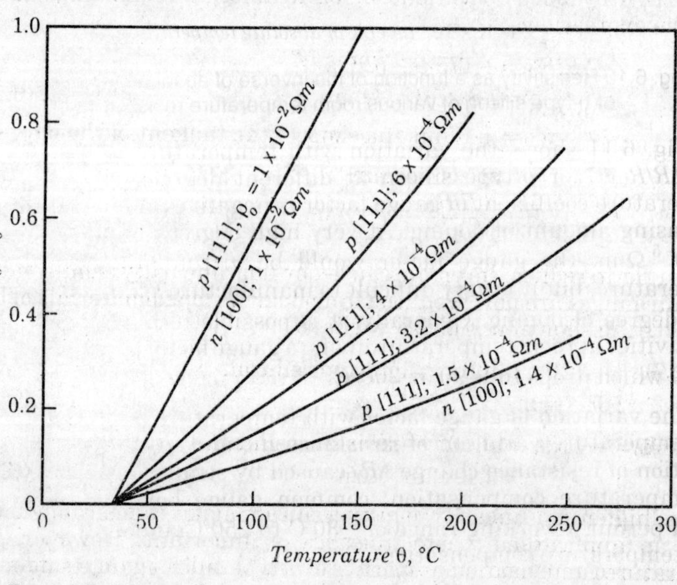

Fig. 6.9 Relative resistance variation with temperature of *p*- and *n*-type silicon of various room temperature resistivities.

say 2×10^{-4} Ω m, the resistance variation between room temperature and 200°C is less than 20%. It can be noticed that the temperature coefficient of resistivity of doped silicon is positive whereas a pure semiconductor has a negative temperature coefficient. Fig. 6.10 shows a much wider range and it is seen that at room temperature below 0°C the slope is generally negative ; at temperatures, in excess of 300 to 400°C, which follows indeed the $1/T$ law of intrinsic semiconductor materials.

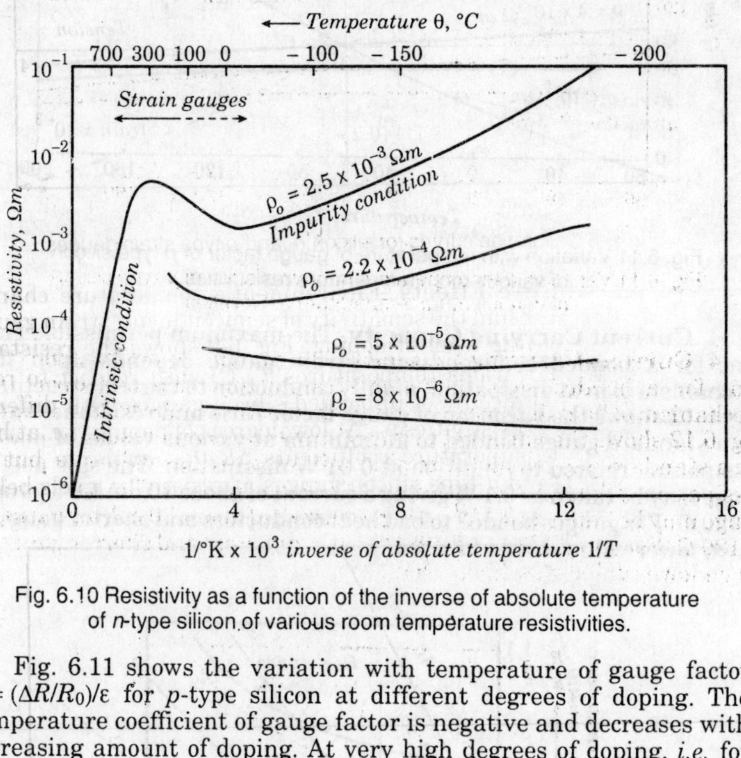

Fig. 6.10 Resistivity as a function of the inverse of absolute temperature of *n*-type silicon of various room temperature resistivities.

Fig. 6.11 shows the variation with temperature of gauge factor $F = (\Delta R/R_0)/\varepsilon$ for *p*-type silicon at different degrees of doping. The temperature coefficient of gauge factor is negative and decreases with increasing amount of doping. At very high degrees of doping, *i.e.* for $\rho_0 \approx 0^{-5}$ Ω m, the gauge factor would be virtually independent of temperature, but it is very difficult to manufacture strain gauges with high degree of doping. Generally, it is possible to have 2×10^{-4} Ω m resistivities at room temperature giving a gauge factor of approximately + 120 which drops to + 90 at 200°C.

The variation of gauge factor with temperature depends upon (*a*) the temperature variation of resistance R_0, and (*b*) the temperature variation of resistance change ΔR_ε caused by strain ε. Without regard to temperature compensation, common gauge bonding techniques would permit a working range of – 80°C to 250°C and – 40°C to 100°C with temperature compensation.

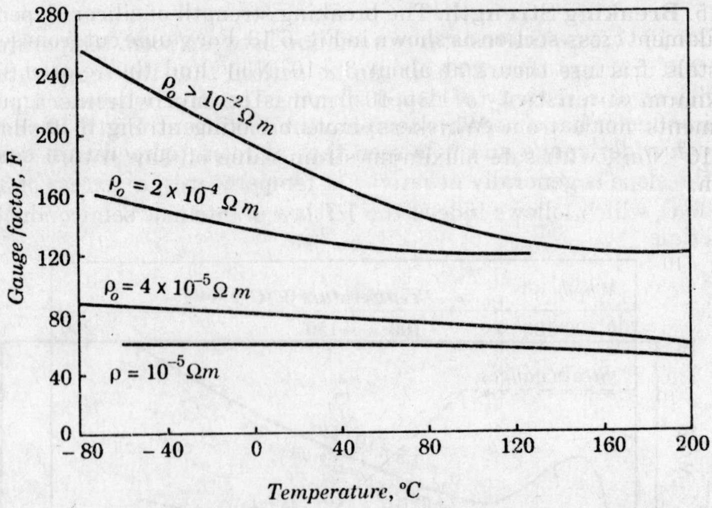

Fig. 6.11 Variation with temperature of gauge factor of *p*-type silicon of various room temperature resistivities.

4. **Current Carrying Capacity.** The maximum permissible current for a bonded semiconductor strain gauge depends upon the mechanism of heat dissipation, mainly conduction to the test structure. Fig. 6.12 shows the variation of gauge factor ratio and resistance ratio for a standard gauge bonded to aluminium at various values of power dissipation, related to condition at 0.01 W dissipation. The safe useful range may be taken as 0.1 W giving a current of about 30 mA for a gauge of 120 Ω. For gauges bonded to bad heat conductors and shorter gauges, much lower value should be used.

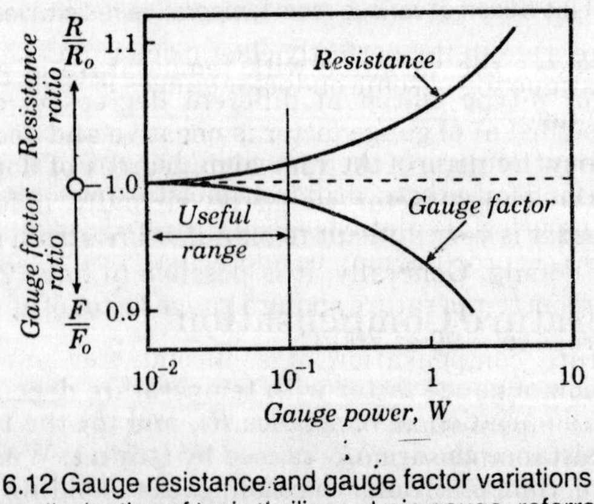

Fig. 6.12 Gauge resistance and gauge factor variations with power dissipation of typical silicon strain gauge, referred to conditions at 10^{-2} W dissipation.

5. **Breaking Strength.** The breaking strength of silicon depends on filament cross-section as shown in Fig. 6.13. For gauge cut from solid crystals, fracture occurs at about 3×10^8 N/m^2 and the related safe maximum strain is 1 to 1.5×10^{-3} m/m. The much thinner gauge filaments made from 'Whiskers' have breaking strength of about 2×10^9 N/m^2, with safe maximum strain value of, say, 4 to 5×10^{-3} m/m.

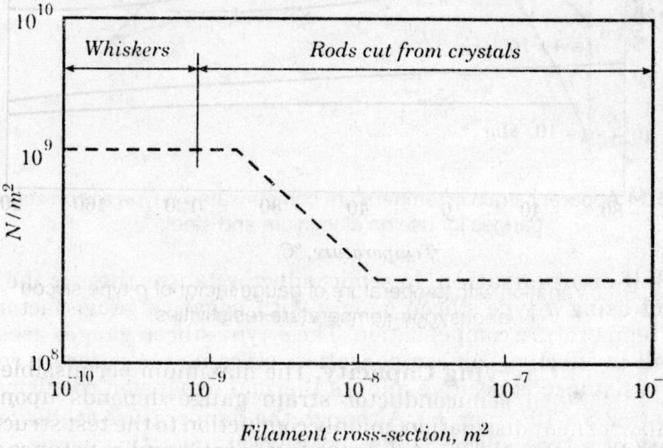

Fig. 6.13 Average breaking stress at room temperature of silicon filaments at various cross-sections.

6. **Hysteresis and Creep.** Semiconductor filament cannot be held responsible for any hysteresis or creep errors experienced in practical gauge installations. Any such effects are a function of the less perfect gauge backing and the cement and the maximum operational temperature of bonded gauges.

7. **Fatigue.** Due to the perfectly elastic deformation of the silicon filament the fatigue life of semiconductor gauges is higher than that of wire and foil gauges.

8. **Humidity.** Because of their much higher strain sensitivity than that of the wire and foil gauges, drift from moisture absorption and noise generated by imperfect insulation of lead wire are less important. Some technique for waterproofing may be adopted as for wire gauges.

6.5 Temperature Compensation

Temperature compensation of semiconductor gauges may be achieved in two ways :

(*i*) Self-compensation,

(*ii*) Circuit compensation.

The first method is effective over a limited temperature range and employs selected material gauges, the second comprises the use of dummy gauges, *p-n* combinations and temperature sensitive resistors.

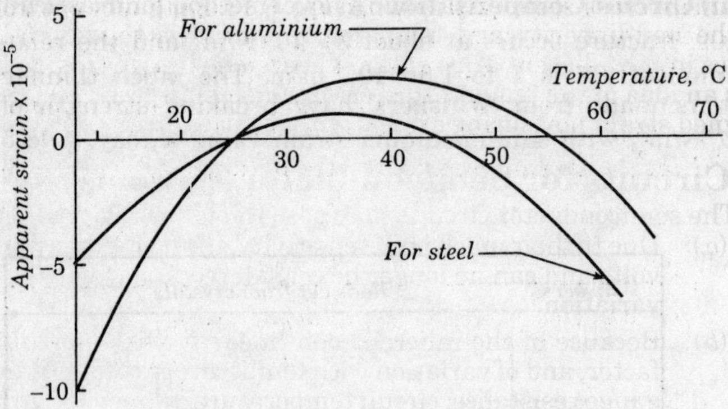

Fig. 6.14 Apparent strain in temperature compensated n-type silicon strain gauges for use on aluminium and steel.

(*i*) **Self-compensation.** In semiconductor gauges there is the possibility of using n-type silicon gauges with negative gauge factors to achieve temperature compensation. The p-type silicon gauges does not lend itself to effective self-compensation, since its temperature coefficient of resistance is positive and its thermal expansion coefficient is very low ($\approx 2.5 \times 10^{-6}$ per °C). Although the temperature coefficient of resistivity of n-type silicon is also positive, its negative gauge factor permits effective compensation at temperature upto about 70°C. Fig. 6.14 shows typical error curves of apparent strain caused by temperature effects in n-type silicon gauges bonded to aluminium and steel.

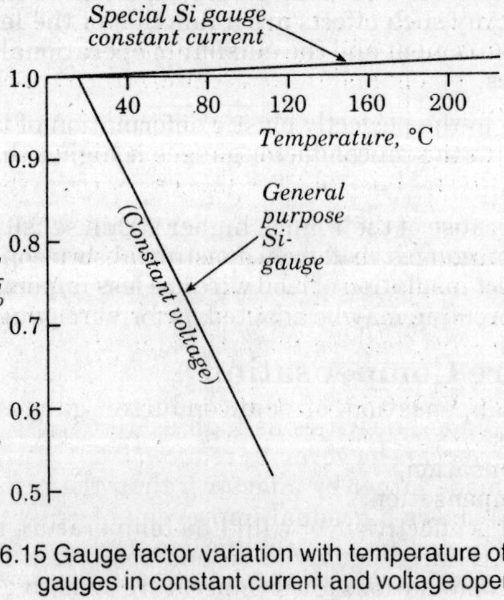

Fig. 6.15 Gauge factor variation with temperature of silicon strain gauges in constant current and voltage operation.

(ii) **Circuit Compensation.** A novel method for drastically reducing the non-linearity and temperature effects is to use both *p*-type gauges in the adjacent arms of the Wheatstone bridge circuit. Fig. 6.15 gives an idea of the temperature error which may occur in a carelessly designed strain measuring system with semiconductor strain gauges.

6.6 Circuits for Semiconductor Strain Gauges

The semiconductor circuits may pose the following problems :

(*a*) Due to their much high sensitivity, the output may be several volts and can no longer be considered linear with resistance variation.

(*b*) Because of the inherent non-linearity with strain of gauge factor, and of variation with temperature of gauge factor and gauge resistance, circuit temperature compensation becomes essential.

1. **Bridge Non-linearity.** The initially balanced (*i.e.* $R_1 R_3 = R_2 R_4$) bridge of Fig. 6.16 (*a*) has one active arm R_1. The bridge output voltage E_0 at a finite resistance change is given by,

$$E_0 = V\left\{\frac{\Delta R_1}{1+[\Delta R_1/(R_1+R_4)]} \times \frac{R_2}{(R_1+R_4)\,(R_2+R_3)}\right\}$$

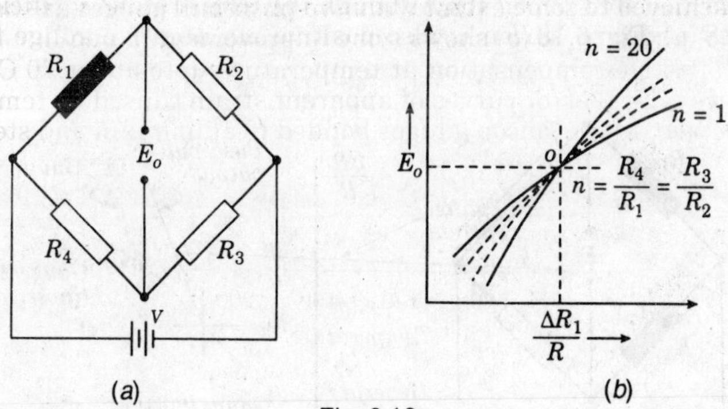

Fig. 6.16

For $$R_1 = R_2 = R_3 = R_4 = R$$

$$\frac{E_0}{V} = \frac{\frac{1}{2}(\Delta R/R)}{2 + (\Delta R/R)}$$

This may lead to non-linearities as high as 10 to 20%. The large deviations from linearity can, however, be reduced if the two resistances R_3 and R_4 are both made larger by a factor n than the resistances R_1 and R_2. Fig. 6.16 (*b*) shows a gradual improvement of linearity with increasing factor n. The non-linearity of this gauge type and that of the Wheatstone bridge circuit 'bulge' in opposite directions, good compensation can be achieved by a suitable choice of n.

(*i*) *Using Shunt resistance.* Fig. 6.17 (*a*) shows a bridge with a resistance R_{sh} in parallel to the gauge resistance R_g, where $R = \dfrac{R_g R_{sh}}{R_g + R_{sh}}$. Fig. 6.17 (*b*) shows that the linearity of this circuit is improved at small R_{sh}/R_g ratios, but loss in sensitivity is quite severe.

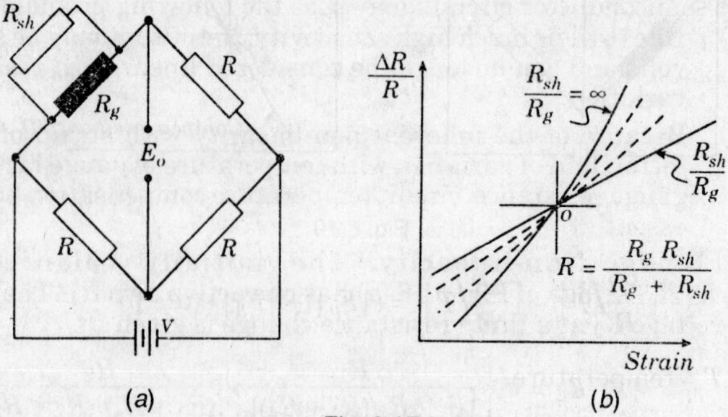

Fig. 6.17

(*ii*) *Using push-pull gauges.* Compensation of gauge non-linearity can be achieved to some extent with two push-pull gauges as shown in Fig. 6.18 (*a*). Fig. 6.18 (*b*) shows some improvement in non-linearity.

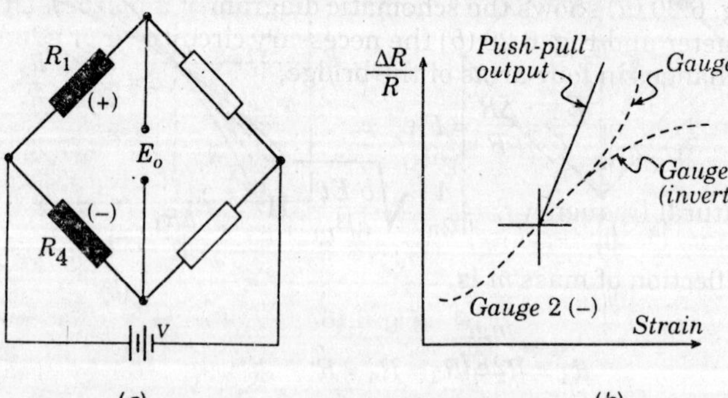

Fig. 6.18

(*iii*) *Using p–and n-type pairs.* By mounting side by side a *p*- and *n*-type gauges (*i.e.* both in tension or compression), the non-linearity can be improved as shown in Fig. 6.19.

2. **Circuit temperature compensation.** Circuit temperature compensation may be obtained by employing *p*- and *n*-type gauges mounted side by side on the test structure and connecting them in adjacent arms of the bridge circuit. In *p*-type silicon both the gauge factor and its temperature coefficient are positive, while *n*-type silicon has a negative gauge factor and a positive temperature coefficient of gauge factor. Temperature compensation occurs for

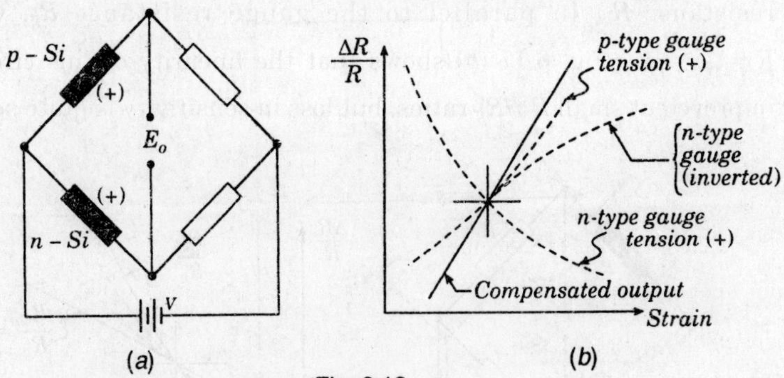

Fig. 6.19

$$\left(\frac{\Delta R}{R}/T\right)_p - \left(\frac{\Delta R}{R}/T\right)_n = (|F_p| - |F_n|)\,(\alpha - \beta) \qquad ...(6.20)$$

where T = temperature

α = coefficient of thermal expansion of the test structure

β = coefficient of thermal expansion of the silicon gauge (2.5×10^{-6} per °C)

6.7 Piezoresistive Accelerometer

Fig. 6.20 (*a*) shows the schematic diagram of a piezoresistive accelerometer and Fig. 6.20 (*b*) the necessary circuitry. For equal resistance changes in four arms of the bridge,

$$\frac{E_0}{V} = \frac{\Delta R}{R} = F\,\varepsilon$$

$$\text{Natural frequency } f_n = \frac{1}{2\pi}\sqrt{\frac{b\,Et^3}{6l^3 m}}\ \text{Hz} \qquad ...(6.21)$$

Deflection of mass m is,

$$x = \frac{mgl^3}{2EI}$$

$$= \frac{6mg}{Eb}\left(\frac{l^3}{t^3}\right)$$

$$= \varepsilon\left(\frac{l^2}{t}\right)\text{cm} \qquad ...(6.22)$$

Strain at the surface to which elements are bonded,

$$\varepsilon = \frac{mgl}{Ebt^2} \qquad ...(6.23)$$

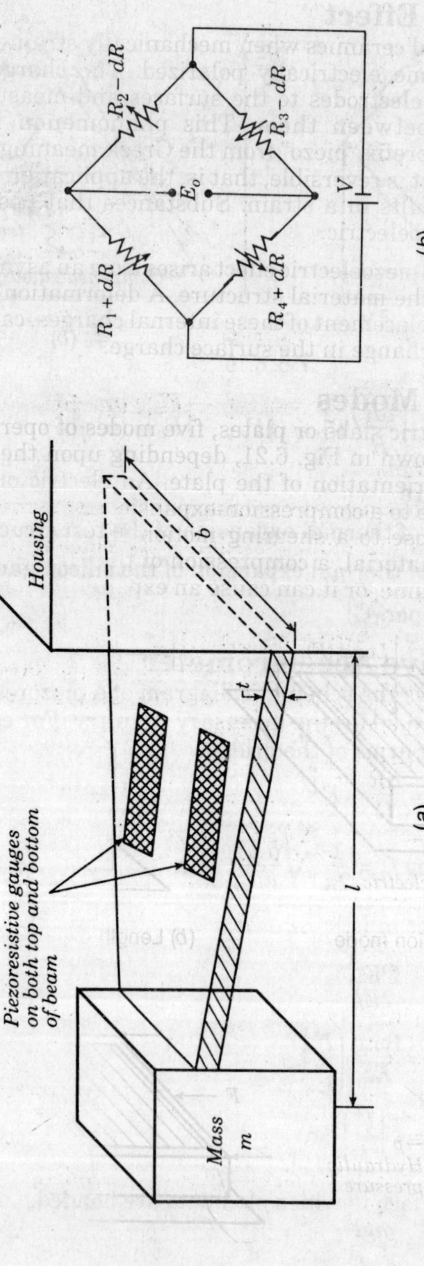

Fig. 6.20 Piezoresistive accelerometer.

B. Piezoelectric Gauges

6.8 Piezoelectric Effect

Certain crystals and ceramics when mechanically strained in particular directions become electrically polarized. The charge can be measured by applying electrodes to the surfaces and measuring the potential difference between them. This phenomenon is called piezoelectric effect the prefix "piezo" from the Greek meaning to press. It is found that the effect is reversible, that is, the application of an emf between the plates results in a strain. Substances that possess this property are called piezoelectric.

Fundamentally the piezoelectric effect arises from an asymmetrical charge distribution in the material structure. A deformation of lattice results in a relative displacement of these internal charges, causing the substance to exhibit a change in the surface charge.

6.9 Deformation Modes

In single piezoelectric slabs or plates, five modes of operation can be distinguished as shown in Fig. 6.21, depending upon the material and crystallographic orientation of the plate. An electric output can arise either in response to a compression-expansion motion [Figs. 6.21 (*a*) to (*c*)], or in response to a shearing motion [Fig. 6.21 (*d*) to (*e*)]. Depending upon the material, a compression of the plate can cause a change of the plate volume, or it can cause an expansion of the plate in

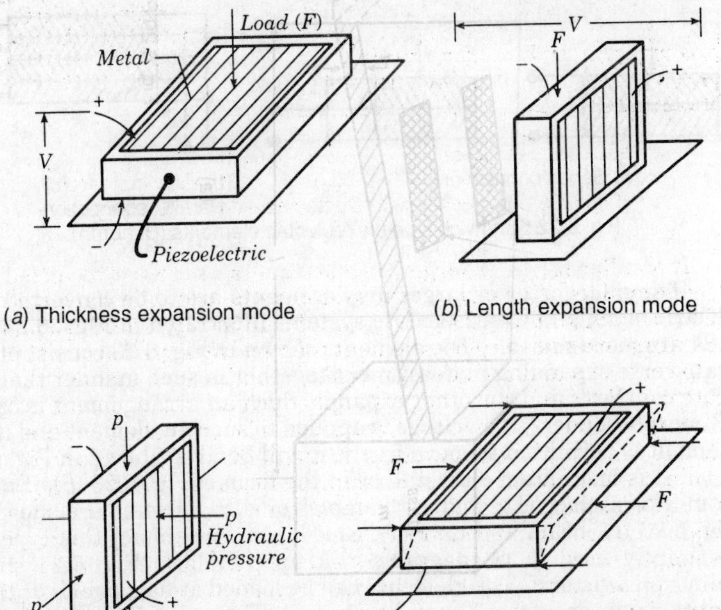

(*a*) Thickness expansion mode

(*b*) Length expansion mode

(*c*) Volume expansion mode

(*d*) Thickness shear mode

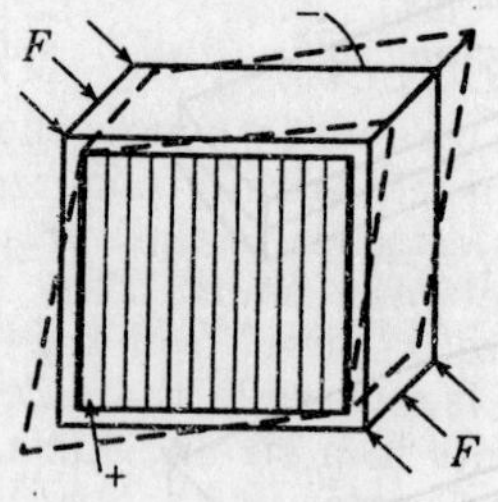

(*e*) Face shear mode

Fig. 6.21 Deformation modes of single piezoelectric materials.

other directions (transverse expansion) so that the plate volume remains constant. The deformation of discs, cylinders and tubes can be derived from these basic cases. Length-expander mode is of primary interest for strain gauge applications.

Piezoelectric crystals can be stacked or sandwiched as shown in Fig. 6.22, which can be operated in the compression-expansion mode. The elements may be connected in series, leaving to higher output voltage for the same force, or in parallel resulting in lower output impedance than a single element.

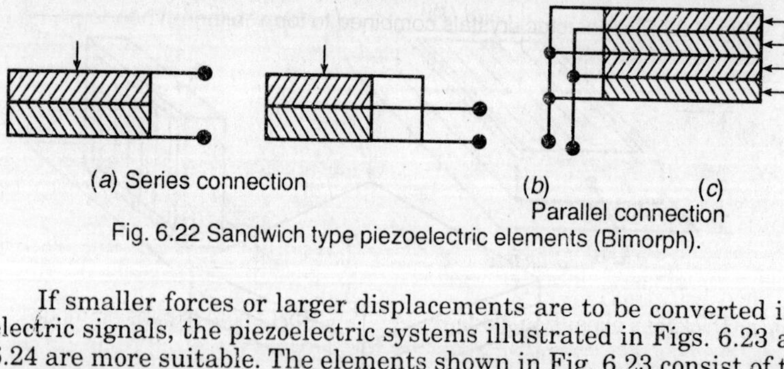

(*a*) Series connection (*b*) (*c*) Parallel connection

Fig. 6.22 Sandwich type piezoelectric elements (Bimorph).

If smaller forces or larger displacements are to be converted into electric signals, the piezoelectric systems illustrated in Figs. 6.23 and 6.24 are more suitable. The elements shown in Fig. 6.23 consist of two transverse expanding plates cement together in such manner that one plate contracts and the other expands. Such an arrangement is called "Bimorph Bender". If a voltage is applied to such an element and if the element is permitted to move freely, it will bend as shown in Fig. 6.23 (*a*), if it is made from a crystal, or in the form of Fig. 6.23 (*b*), if made from a piezoelectric ceramic. Examples of such systems are shown in Fig. 6.23 (*c*), beam and 6.23 (*d*), cantilever. Systems of this type are frequently used in phonagraph pick up cartidges. Fig. 6.24 shows "bimorph twisters". The elements can be loaded at four points or three points or an end torque may be applied. The twisting motion of the bimorph gives rise to output voltage.

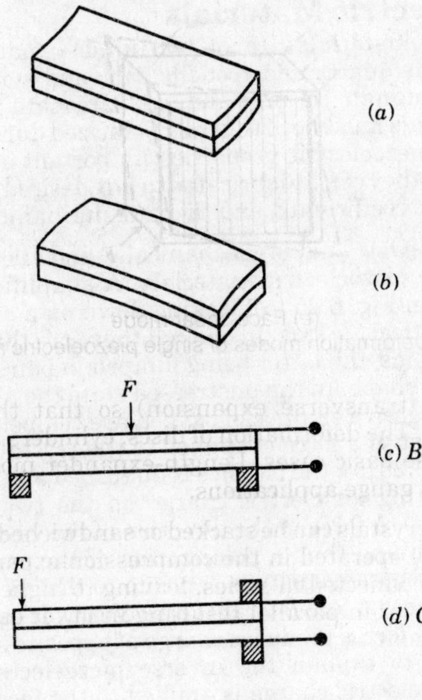

Fig. 6.23 Piezoelectric crystals combined to form "bimorph benders".

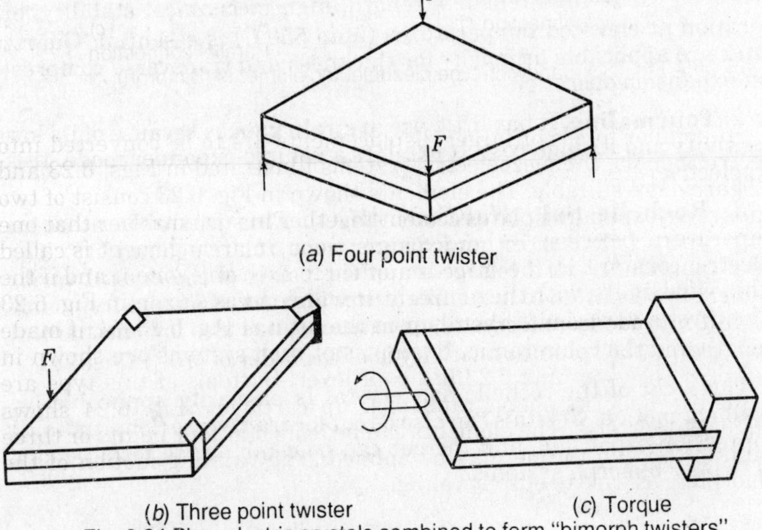

Fig. 6.24 Piezoelectric crystals combined to form "bimorph twisters".

6.10 Piezoelectric Materials

Piezoelectric materials are of two kinds : naturally occurring materials, such as quartz and rochelle salt, and synthetic materials such as barium titanate ceramic and lead zirconate titanate ceramic. The latter materials must be artificially polarized during fabrication in order to exhibit piezoelectric properties. Important advantages of the ceramics are that they can be fabricated to any desired shape, they have large piezoelectric coefficients, and they are mechanically very stable.

1. **Quartz (SiO_2).** This is mechanically and thermally the most stable among the piezoelectric materials. A simplified model of this crystal is shown in Fig. 6.25 (*a*), looking down on a crystal cell in the direction of the optical (Z) axis. In one cell there are three silicon atoms and six oxygen atoms, the latter being lumped in pairs, thus constituting the hexagonal shape. In the unstressed state the 4 positive charges of silicon and 2 negative charges of oxygen are compensated and there is no external effect. If a force is applied to the crystal in the direction of the x-axis [Fig. 6.25 (*b*)] the balance is disturbed and the cell becomes polarized, generating an electric charge on the two faces A and B (longitudinal effect). A force in the direction of the y-axis [Fig. 6.25 (*c*)] causes a distortion and thus a polarization of the crystal cell, which leads to a charge whose polarity is opposite to that of Fig. 6.25 (*b*), on the same crystal faces A and B (transverse effect). It can be easily seen that reversal of the forces produces charge of opposite sign. This model can also be used to explain the inverse piezoelectric effect, when assuming that an electric charge is applied to the faces A and B thus causing contraction or expansion of the crystal cell. Since there is symmetry in the Z-direction, no polarization occurs with forces applied in the direction of the Z -axis. The internal electric losses in quartz are small and volume resistivity is higher than $(10^{14})\ \Omega$ cm. Because of its relatively small piezoelectric effects, its applications are restricted to such uses where high tensile strength, high mechanical stability, or operation at elevated temperatures (upto 550°C) is essential. Quartz plates are applicable primarily for thickness and transverse compression-expansion operation.

2. **Tourmaline.** It has little use in strain gauges because of its low sensitivity and its high cost. It exhibits a volume-expander mode. It is pyroelectric.

3. **Rochelle Salt ($NaKC_4O_6 . 4H_2O$).** This is stable at room temperature between 35 and 85 per cent relative humidity. The dielectric constant in the direction of the x-axis of the crystal varies within wide limits, with the temperature ; also the resonance frequency of the crystal varies with the temperature. It has also low mechanical strength and the volume resistivity is of the order of $(10^{12})\ \Omega$ cm.

The x-cut of the rochelle salt crystal is primarily applicable for face-shear motion. Crystals can also be cut for transverse (longitudinal) compression-expansion, and the cut can be combined to form bender and twister bimorph systems.

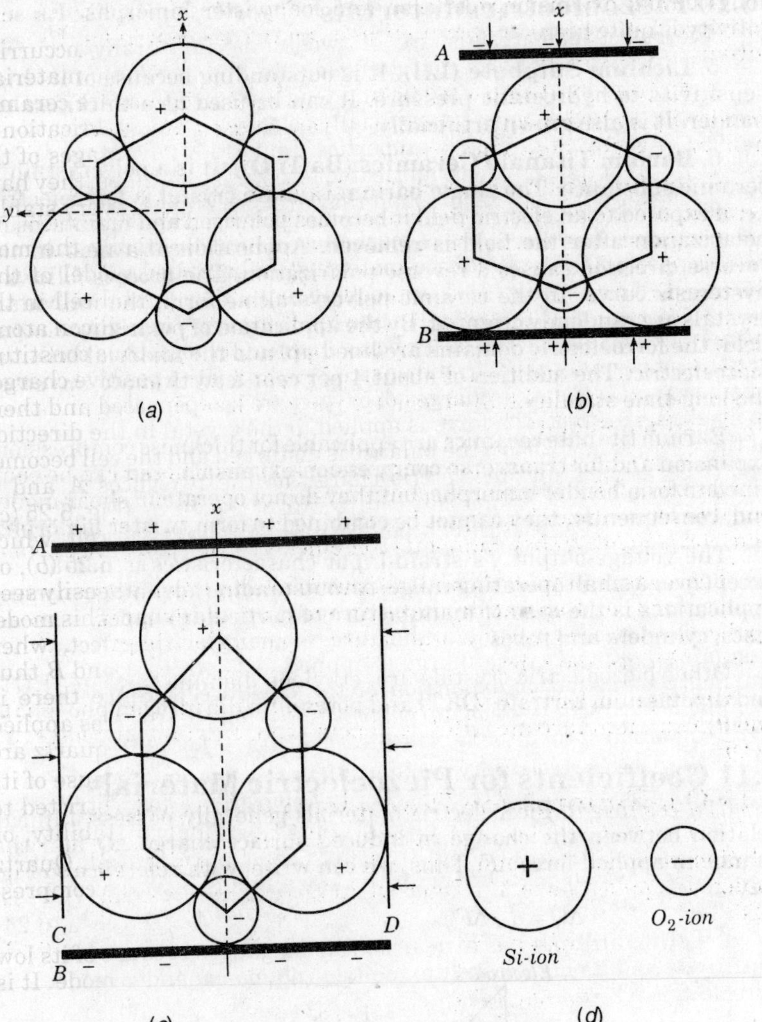

Fig. 6.25 Loading of quartz crystal.

4. **Ammonium Dihydrogen Phosphate** (**ADP, NH_4, H_2PO_4**) This is an artificial crystal which is similar to rochelle salt in many respects but has a higher thermal stability and lower permittivity. It is stable upto a temperature of 180°C, but is used, with an upper limit of 125°C. It operates satisfactorily in a range from zero to 94 per cent relative humidity. Its insulation resistance is relatively low and decreases by about an order for every 20°C temperature increase. The volume resistivity is considerably lower than that of the other substances ; it is about $(10^{10})\ \Omega$ cm and decreases strongly with increasing temperature and impurities content.

The material (primarily the Z-cut) is applicable for face shear and longitudinal expansion operation and for twister bimorphs. Its sensitivity is quite high.

5. **Lithium Sulphate (LH).** It is outstanding because of its high sensitivity to hydrostatic pressure. It can be used at a thickness expander. It is also grown artificially.

6. **Barium Titanate Ceramics (Ba Ti O_3).** It is a polycrystalline ceramic substance. The single barium titanate crystal is ferroelectric, *i.e.* if exposed to an electric field it becomes polarised and maintains its polarization after the field is removed. Application of a field in the reverse direction causes a reverse polarization. The process follows a hysteresis curve. In the ceramic polycrystalline form, the individual crystals are randomly oriented. By the application of polarizing electric field, the ferroelectric domains are lined up, and the material becomes piezoelectric. The addition of about 4 per cent lead titanate increases the long-time stability.

Barium titanate ceramics are applicable for thickness compression-expansion and for transverse compression-expansion, and can be combined to form bender bimorphs, but they do not operate in shear modes and, consequently, they cannot be combined to form twister bimorphs.

The voltage-output v's strain-input characteristics is non-linear, except over a small operating range. An outstanding advantage in many applications is the ease of manufacture of particular shapes, such as, discs, cylinders and tubes.

Other piezoelectric crystals are, ethylene diamine tartrate (EDT) and dipotassium tartrate (DKT) and potassium dihydrogen phosphate (KDP).

6.11 Coefficients for Piezoelectric Materials

(*i*) *d-coefficient.* Piezoelectric materials generally possess a linear relation between the change in induced surface charge ΔQ and the change in applied force ΔF. Thus, we can write, with reference to Fig. 6.26.

$$\Delta Q = d \,.\, \Delta F \qquad ...(6.24)$$

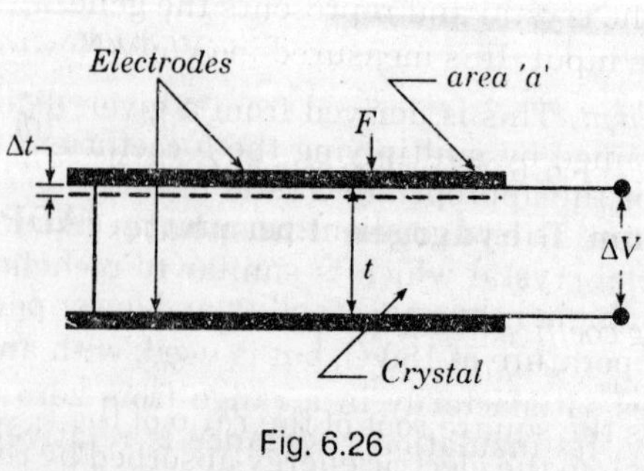

Fig. 6.26

$$\Delta F = \Delta\, a \times E \times \frac{\Delta t}{t} \qquad ...(6.25)$$

where a = area of crystal

t = thickness of crystal

E = Young's modulus

d = constant for the material that expresses its charge sensitivity and may be termed the piezoelectric constant. It is measured in Coulombs/Newton.

(ii) g-coefficient. The change in potential between the plates can be calculated by assuming that the arrangement behaves like a parallel-plate capacitor of capacitance C given by

$$C = \frac{\varepsilon_r \varepsilon_0 a}{t} \quad \text{...(6.26)}$$

where a = area (cm^2)

t = plate separation or thickness of crystal (cm)

ε_r = relative permittivity (dielectric constant)

Since $\Delta V = \frac{\Delta Q}{C}$

Hence output voltage

$$\Delta V = \frac{d\ \Delta F}{\left(\frac{\varepsilon_r \varepsilon_0 a}{t}\right)} \text{ volts} \quad \text{...(6.27)}$$

where $\varepsilon_0 = 8.85 \times 10^{-12}$

$$\therefore \quad \Delta V = \frac{dt\ \Delta F}{\varepsilon a} \quad \text{...(6.28)}$$

where $\varepsilon = \varepsilon_r\ \varepsilon_0$ = absolute dielectric constant

or $\Delta V = g\ .\ t\ .\ \Delta F$ ...(6.29)

where $g = \frac{d}{\varepsilon a}$

is a constant of the crystal and represents the generated emf gradient per unit pressure input. It is measured in (V/m)/(Newtons/m^2).

(iii) h-coefficient. This is derived from a given deformation of the crystal. It is obtained by multiplying the g-coefficient by the Young's modulus valid for the appropriate crystal orientation of the material, and thus measures the emf gradient per unit mechanical deformation or (V/m)/(mm).

(iv) Coupling coefficient—k

$$k = \sqrt{hd} \quad \text{...(6.30)}$$

It represents the square root of the ratio of the mechanical energy stored in a crystal, to the electric energy absorbed by the crystal and is thus a measure of the efficiency of the crystal as an energy converter.

Properties of piezoelectric materials and coefficients are given in Table 6.3.

Table 6.3. Piezoelectric Constants

Material	Orientation	Relative dielectric constant	d-coeff. $\times 10^{12}$ coulombs per Newton	g-coeff. $(V/m)/(N/m)^2 \times 10^2$	k-coeff.	Safe stress $N/m^2 \times 10^{-6}$	Young's modulus E $N/m^2 \times 10^{-9}$	Resis-tivity $m \times 10^{-9}$	Safe temp. °C
Quartz	Thickness expansion 0°–x cut	4.5	2.3	58	11	98	80	> 1000	550
	Length expansion 0°–x cut	4.5	2.3	58	10	98	80	> 1000	550
Tour-maline	Thickness expansion 0°–Z cut	6.6	1.9	33	10	—	160	> 100	—
Rochelle salt	Length expansion 45°–x cut	350	275	90	73	14.7	19.7	> 10	45
ADP	Length expansion 45°–Z cut	15.3	24	177	28	20.6	19.3	> 0.1	125
LH	Thickness expansion 0°–Y cut	10.3	13.5	14.8	—	—	—	> 10	75
Barium titanate	Parallel to polarization	1200	140	13	46	80	110	> 100	—
Lead zir-conateti-tanate	Parallel to polarization	1600	105	7.2	20	—	55	> 30	250

6.12 Piezoelectric Strain Gauge

If a thin slab of a piezoelectric material with an active length-expander mode is cemented to a structure under stress, the strain in the structure is transmitted to the slab and a charge is generated across the crystal. The output voltage can be computed from the h-coefficient of the length-expander mode of the piezoelectric material,

$$h = gE \text{ (V/m)/(m/m)} \quad ...(6.31)$$

The output voltage is, therefore,

$$V = h\varepsilon t = g\,E\varepsilon t \text{ volts} \quad ...(6.32)$$

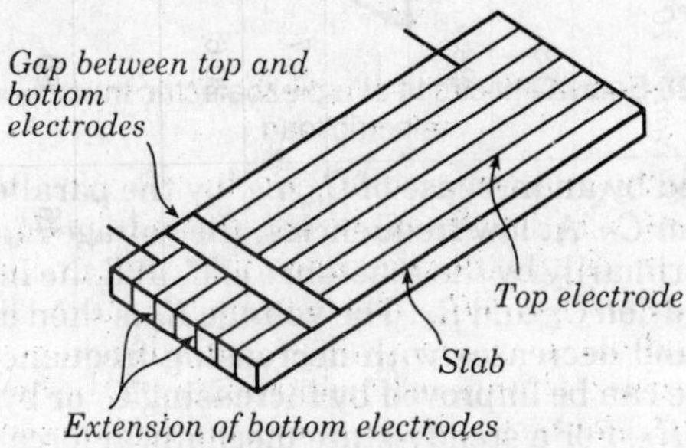

Fig. 6.27 Piezoelectric strain gague.

The output from piezoelectric strain gauge is several hundred times higher than the wire resistance gauges and are, therefore, of considerable interest. They are, however, only suitable for dynamic strain measurements, and calibration requires dynamic equipment. A commercial barium titanate strain gauge is shown in Fig. 6.27. These gauges are very useful for the measurement of dynamic strain in steam turbine blades, sensing elements for pressure transducers for the measurement of high dynamic pressure. The advantages of these gauges are :

(*i*) The crystals are cheap.
(*ii*) Light weight.
(*iii*) Highly sensitive to small strains.
(*iv*) Self-generating.
(*v*) Specially suitable to sense resonances in high frequency range.

6.13 Equivalent Circuit and Frequency Response

The equivalent circuit of a piezoelectric input transducer is shown in Fig. 6.28. C_c is the capacitance of the piezoelectric element and R_c its leakage resistance. The resistance between the terminals is, in general, determined by the load resistance R_L . C_L is the capacitance of the load plus that of the connecting cables. At medium and high frequencies, the voltage E_0 across the load is determined primarily by the capacitances C_c and C_L. These capacitances form a voltage divider, the voltage E_0 is $\frac{EC_c}{(C_c + C_L)}$, independent of the frequency. If the output voltage is large,

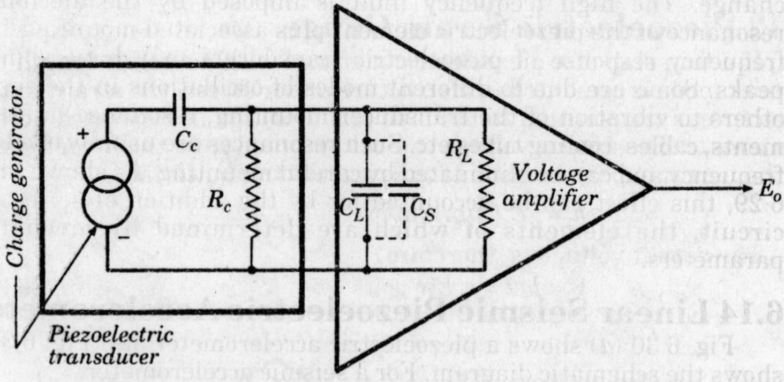

Fig. 6.28 Equivalent circuit of a piezoelectric transducer and electric load.

it can be reduced by an increase of C_L, *i.e.* by the parallel connection of a shunt capacitor C_S. At low frequencies, the voltage E_0 across the load is determined primarily by the reactance of C_c and the impedance of the parallel combination C_L and R_L. The voltage E_0 is then dependent upon the frequency and decreases with decreasing frequency. The low frequency response can be improved by increasing C_c or by increasing the load resistance R_L. For a steady-state mechanical force the transducer furnishes no output voltage. To overcome this difficulty the crystal is driven by an electric oscillator at its resonance frequency, and the applied voltage or current is measured. If mechanical stress is applied to the crystal, its resonance frequency or its power absorption will

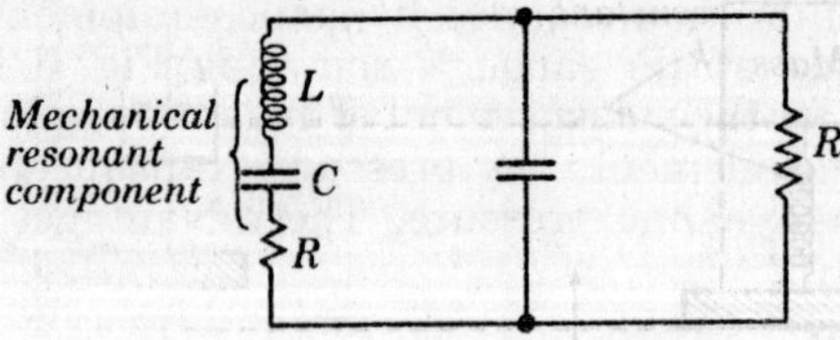

(*a*) Circuit model.

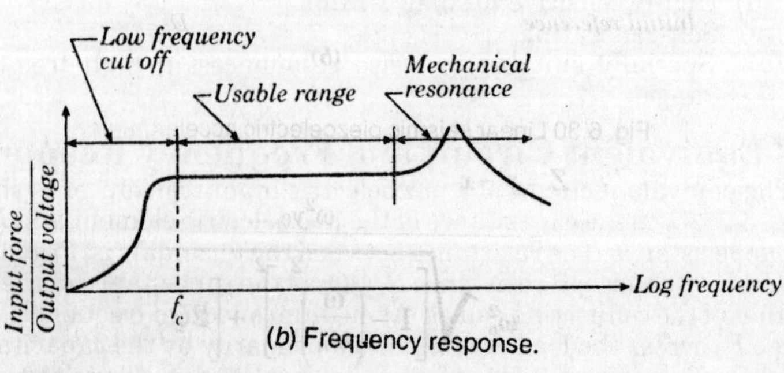

(*b*) Frequency response.

Fig. 6.29 Frequency response of a piezoelectric transducer.

change. The high frequency limit is imposed by the mechanical resonance of the piezoelectric element plus associated mountings. The frequency response of piezoelectric transducers may have spurious peaks. Some are due to different modes of oscillations in the crystal, others to vibration of the transducer mounting, resonance in attachments, cables, cooling tubes etc. Such resonances are usually of a lower frequency and can be eliminated by careful mounting. As shown in Fig. 6.29, this effect can be accounted for by the addition of series *RLC* circuit, the elements of which are determined by mechanical parameters.

6.14 Linear Seismic Piezoelectric Accelerometer

Fig. 6.30 (*a*) shows a piezoelectric accelerometer and Fig. 6.30 (*b*) shows the schematic diagram. For a seismic accelerometer,

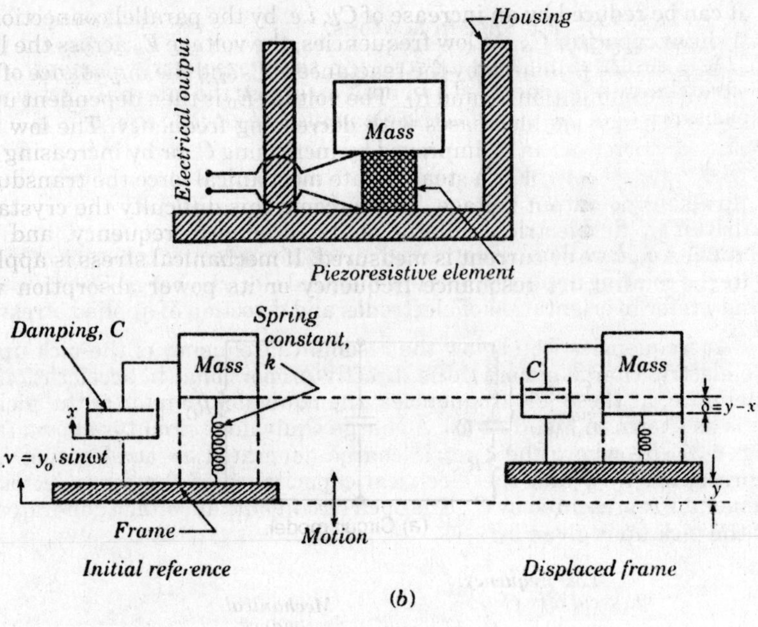

Fig. 6.30 Linear seismic piezoelectric accelerometer.

$$Z = y - x$$

$$\approx \frac{\omega^2 y_0}{\omega_n^2 \sqrt{\left[1-\left(\frac{\omega}{\omega_n}\right)^2\right]^2 + \left[2\zeta\frac{\omega}{\omega_n}\right]^2}}$$

$$\approx y_0 \text{ when } \omega >> \omega_n$$

$$\approx \frac{\omega^2 y_0}{\omega_n^2} \text{ when } \omega << \omega_n \qquad ...(6.33)$$

$$= \text{Maximum acceleration of base}/\omega_n^2.$$

For the piezoelectric accelerometer the differential equation of equilibrium is

$$L(\dot{q}_2 - \dot{q}_1) + Rq_2 + \frac{1}{C} q_2 = 0 \qquad ...(6.34)$$

where q is the charge, L the inductance, R the resistance, and C the capacitance. Assuming linear elastic characteristics of the piezoelectric element, the force F and deflection δ are related by

$$\delta = \frac{F}{k}$$

where k = stiffness of the piezoelectric element in newtons/metre

F = force in newtons.

As a result of mechanical stress in the piezoelectric element, an electric charge q is generated and built up across the internal electrical capacitance C_c of the piezoelectric element. The electric charge is given by

$$q = A\delta = \frac{AF}{k} \text{ coulombs}$$

where $A = d_{ij}\, k$ coulombs/metre and d_{ij} the piezoelectric constant of the material relating applied stress to generated electric charge. Subscripts i and j refer to orientation of electrodes and direction of applied stress.

At frequencies well below the resonance frequency of the pick up, the electric charge generated is directly proportional to acceleration. Therefore, at these low frequencies, the equivalent circuit of the pick up is as shown in Fig. 6.31 (*a*). A charge equivalent circuit is shown in Fig. 6.31 (*b*), where the electric charge generated by acceleration is represented by q and the electrical capacitance of the piezoelectric element is represented by C_c. The open circuit output voltage generated by the pick up is given by

$$K_0 = \frac{q}{C_c} \text{ volts}$$

The charge equivalent circuit of Fig. 6.31 (*a*) is equivalent to the voltage equivalent circuit of Fig. 6.31 (*b*). A charge accelerometer symbolized by a voltage source E_{oc}, and two capacitors, C_c and C_s (C_c = accelerometer capacitance, C_s = cable capacitance) is connected to an operational amplifier that has capacitive feed back [Fig. 6.31 (*c*)]. E_0 represents the output voltage. The input voltage E_{in} is related to the generator voltage E_{oc} by the equation

$$E_{in} = E_{oc}\left(\frac{C_c}{C_c + C_s}\right)$$

and the gain of the amplifier is given by

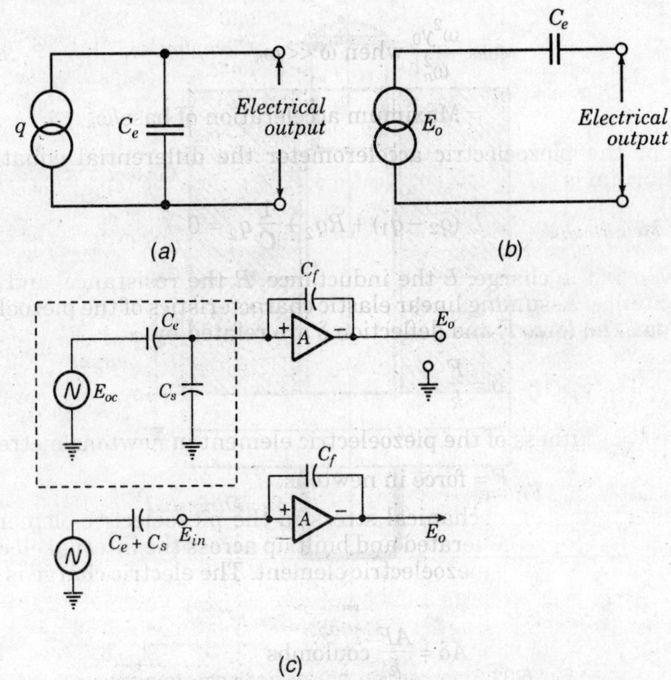

Fig. 6.31 Simplified equivalent circuit for piezoelectric seismic accelerometer.

$$\frac{E_\theta}{E_{in}} = \frac{C_e + C_s}{C_f}$$

$$E_0 = E_{oc} \frac{C_e}{C_f}$$

Now $\quad E_{oc} = \dfrac{Q}{C_e}$

where Q is the charge on capacitor C_e

so that $\quad E_0 = \dfrac{Q}{C_f}$

A compression-type piezoelectric accelerometer (Fig. 6.32) consists of a frame to which is fastened two piezoelectric discs with a metallic disc in between. The mass and the frame are bonded to these discs by electrically conducting cement. Acceleration in the direction of motion causes compressive or tensile forces on the piezoelectric element. The piezoelectric elements are electrically connected so as to add the electric charges which are created by each element when compressed. The resonance frequency of the pick up is

$$f_n = \frac{1}{2\pi} \sqrt{\frac{k}{m}} \text{ Hz} \qquad \text{...(6.35)}$$

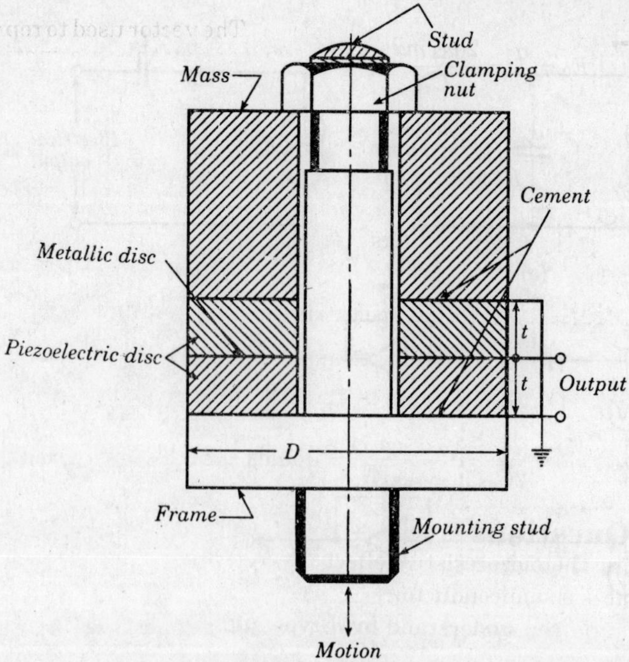

Fig. 6.32 Compression type piezoelectric transducer.

where $$k = \frac{E\pi D^2}{8t} \text{ Newtons/metre}$$

D = diameter of disc

t = thickness of each disc.

Total charge q generated by both discs due to vibration at frequencies far below the resonance frequency f_n is

$$q = 2d_{33}\, F \text{ coulombs}$$

where d_{33} = piezoelectric constant of the piezoelectric material

or $$q = 2d_{33}\, mx$$

where m is the mass (kg) and x, applied acceleration (m/s^2)

The electrical capacitance C_e of the pick up is given by

$$C_e = \frac{\varepsilon_0 \pi D^2}{2t} \text{ farads}$$

where ε_0 = dielectric constant of the piezoelectric material in farads/metre.

The open circuit voltage E_0 generated at frequencies well below f_n is

$$E_0 = \frac{q}{C_e} = \frac{2d_{33}\, m\ddot{x}}{C_e}$$

$$= \frac{4d_{33}\, mt\ddot{x}}{E_0\, \pi D^2}$$

$$= \frac{4d_{33}\, mi\ddot{x}}{\pi D^2} \text{ Volts} \qquad ...(6.36)$$

where $g_{33} = \frac{d_{33}}{\varepsilon_0}$ is the piezoelectric constant relating open circuit voltage to applied stress.

The electrical energy generated by the pick up is given by

$$= \frac{q^2}{2C_e} = \frac{(2\, d_{33}\, m\ddot{x})^2\, t}{\varepsilon_0 \pi D^2} \text{ Joules} \qquad ...(6.37)$$

6.15 Quiz Questions

1. Define the piezoresistive effect.
2. What is a semiconductor ?
3. What do you understand by n-type and p-type semiconductor?
4. What is the order of the gauge factor for a semiconductor gauge ?
5. Define 'sensitivity' of a piezoresistive gauge.
6. What do you understand by doping ?
7. Why the gauge factor of a semiconductor gauge is very high as compared to metallic gauges ?
8. Define the piezoelectric effect.
9. Write the expression for the output voltage of a piezo-electric gauge.
10. Why piezoelectric accelerometer is preferred over the piezoresistive type ?

EXERCISES

6.1 What is a semiconductor ? What are the different semi-conductor materials ?

6.2 What are the different materials used for semiconductor strain gauges ? How these gauges are manufactured ?

6.3 Discuss the important properties of piezoresistive strain gauges.

6.4 How temperature compensation can be achieved by using piezoresistive strain gauges ?

6.5 Describe the construction and working of a piezoresistive accelerometer.

6.6 Describe the piezoelectric effect. How piezoelectric gauges compare with piezoresistive gauges ?

6.7 Discuss the various deformation modes in piezoelectric materials. How these modes can be used for strain measurements ?

6.8 Write a brief account of the various piezoelectric materials.

6.9 Discuss the various coefficients for piezoelectric materials.

6.10 Describe the working of piezoelectric strain gauges. What are the advantages of these gauges ?

6.11 Describe the construction and working of a linear seismic piezoelectric accelerometer.

7

Two-Dimensional Photoelasticity

7.1 Introduction

The photoelastic method depends upon the property of certain transparent solids by which they become doubly refractive under the action of stress, the magnitude of the optical effect bearing a definite relation to that of the stress. The optical phenomenon, known as the "photo-elastic effect" was first discovered by Sir David Brewster in 1816 in sheets of stressed glass. Brewster, however, did not succeed in obtaining a uniform stress in his model and was not able to make any quantitative estimate of the relation between the stress and the optical effect produced. In 1820 Biot demonstrated that a strip of glass became doubly reflecting when set into a state of longitudinal vibrations and Fresnel attempted to measure the changes in the velocities of the two oppositely polarized rays in glass without any decisive results. Neumann presented the first theory of the photoelastic effect in 1841 and expressed the velocities of the two waves in terms of the three principal strains in the medium. In 1853, Maxwell presented a theory in which the velocities were related to the principal stresses. Both these theories produced relations of precisely similar form and were equally applicable to an isotropic linear and elastic material under any system of combined stress.

The first numerical determination of the stress-optical coefficients of several materials were made by Wertheim in 1854, followed by Mach in 1872 and Kerr in 1888. More accurate determinations were made by Pockets in 1902 and between 1902 and 1912 by Filon. Mesnager in 1912 carried out the most successful of the attempts to determine the stresses in an actual engineering structure by using the photoelastic effect in a glass model of a bridge. In 1911, Coker discovered xylonite an alternative photoelastic material to glass and began an extensive series of investigations into the stress-distribution in various engineering components. During the first quarter of the twentieth century, Coker and Filon met together and while working at the Cambridge University, made a break through by using the recently developed transparent plastics, for photoelasticity. By 1935, the photoelastic method has reached within the range of ordinary stress analysis laboratories. During this period various investigations on similar lines were being carried out by Baud and Heymans in U.S.A., Mesnager in France,

Schultz in Germany and Tuzi in Japan. In this chapter we shall study this method in detail.

7.2 The Nature of Light

Various theories about the nature of light have been put forward. In the seventeenth century Huygens (1629–1695) attempted to explain the optical effects associated with thin films, lenses and prisms with a wave theory. In this theory, light is considered as a transverse disturbance in a hypothetical medium of zero mass, called the ether. At the same time Newton (1642–1727) proposed his corpuscular theory, in which light is visualized as a stream of small but swift particles (corpuscles) emanating from shining bodies in all directions, travelling at the speed of light. The next major step in the evolution of the theory of light was due to Maxwell (1831–1879), who presented the electromagnetic wave theory. Here light is an electromagnetic disturbance, propagating through space, represented by two vectors (electric and magnetic) mutually perpendicular and perpendicular to the direction of wave propagation. The most recent theory is the wave-mechanics or quantum theory, which is a combination of the first two theories. The photoelastic effect can be conveniently explained by adopting either the wave theory or the electromagnetic theory. However, we shall follow the wave theory of light to explain all the photoelastic phenomenon.

7.3 Wave Theory of Light

Light is usually defined as radiation that can effect the human eye. The broad spectrum of electromagnetic radiation extends from cosmic rays at line end to radio waves at the other. The visible range of the spectrum is a small band extending from 4000 Å to 7500 Å and centred about a wavelength of approximately 5500 Å. The eye is most sensitive to the central colours (*i.e.* green and of 5500 Å, wavelength). All these waves travel with the same velocity of 3×10^{10} cm/sec and are transverse in nature, having random vibrations of various amplitudes, directions and frequencies. Light from a source that emits a continuous spectrum with equal energy for every wavelength is called *white light*. Light of a single wavelength is called *monochromatic light*.

Electromagnetic waves can be one, two or three dimensional according to the number of dimensions in which they propagate energy. The locus of points on different radial lines from the source exhibiting the same disturbance at a given instant of time, is a surface known as a *wavefront*. For an optically homogeneous and isotropic medium, the direction of light propagation is at right angles to the wavefront. A line normal to the wavefront, indicating the direction of propagation of the waves, is called a *ray*.

Any beam of "ordinary light" contains a vast number of elementary waves the directions of whose light vectors are distributed at random in the plane normal to the direction of propagation. A beam of light in which some system is introduced into the orientations of the vectors is said to be polarised. If all the waves have their light vectors in the same direction, the light is said to be *plane polarized*. The plane of polarization being defined as the plane containing the magnetic vectors *OH* and the direction of propagation *OX* (Fig. 7.1). The plane containing the electric vectors OE and the direction OX is frequently referred to as the plane of the vibrations. The direction of propagation OX is the direction of the rays of light along which the flow of energy occurs.

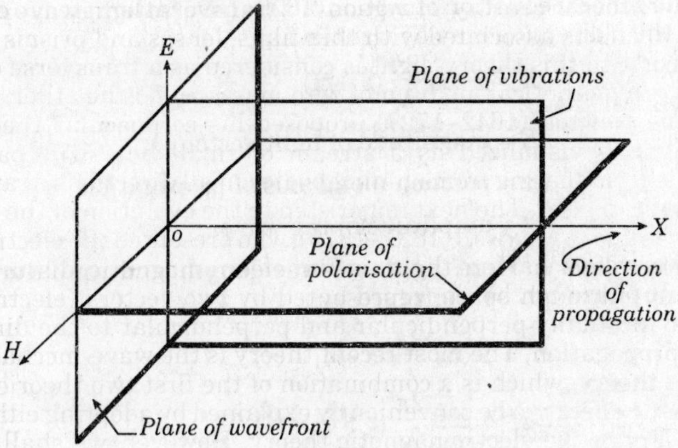

Fig. 7.1

(*a*) **Frequency and colour.** The frequency of a light vibration determines the colour of the light. The frequency is not affected by transmission of the light through any medium. The frequency is generally denoted by f (in Hz) or w (in radians per sec.) and $w = 2\pi f$ and is equal to the number of oscillations per second. Time period $T = 1/f$.

(*b*) **Velocity.** The velocity of light waves c of any frequency in a vacuum is 3×10^8 m/s, and it is sensibly the same in air. We shall denote this velocity by c. The velocity in all transparent liquids and solids is less than this value and varies from one medium to another. The ratio of the velocity of light in air to the velocity in the medium is called the refractive index of the medium and is denoted by n.

(*c*) **Wavelength.** The wavelength of any given frequency is the distance travelled during one complete vibration. We shall denote wavelength by λ and this is measured in angstroms ($1\ \text{Å} = 10^{-8}$ cm)

$$\lambda f = c$$

(*d*) **Amplitude.** This is a magnitude of the disturbance. The intensity of light may be taken as directly proportional to the square of the amplitude of the vibration.

(*e*) **Phase.** The phase of a vibration at any instant defines the stage of the cycle reached at that instant. The whole phenomenon of interference depends on it by which photoelastic effects are measured. Two particles on a wave separated by one or integral number of wavelengths are said to be in phase and when separated by half a wavelength or any odd number of half wavelengths are said to be out-of-phase. Phase difference may be linear or angular. Angular phase difference is $\frac{2\pi}{\lambda}$ times the linear phase difference.

The vector used to represent the light wave can be either the electric vector or the magnetic vector. The electric vector has been demonstrated to the active agent in interactions between light and a photographic plate and hence all discussions relating to the photoelastic effect will be associated with the electric vector.

The general equation of motion of a transverse light wave propagating in the z-direction may be written as

$$E = a \cos \frac{2\pi}{\lambda} (z - ct) \quad \text{...(7.1)}$$

where E = magnitude of light vector

z = position along axis of propagation

t = amplitude of the wave.

Two waves having the same wavelength and amplitude but a different phase can be expressed by :

$$E_1 = a \cos \frac{2\pi}{\lambda} (z + \delta_1 - ct)$$

$$E_2 = a \cos \frac{2\pi}{\lambda} (z + \delta_2 - ct) \quad \text{...(7.2)}$$

where δ_1 = initial phase of wave E_1

δ_2 = initial phase of wave E_2.

Linear phase difference between waves,

$$\delta = \delta_2 - \delta_1$$

is often referred to as a retardation.

Eq. (7.1) can be written as

$$E = a \cos (\phi - wt) \quad \text{...(7.3)}$$

where $\phi = \frac{2\pi}{\lambda} z$

is the phase angle associated with wave E at position z.

Hence the angular phase difference between two waves,

$$\Delta = \phi_2 - \phi_1 = \frac{2\pi\delta}{\lambda}.$$

When two plane waves superimpose, then it can be shown that the resulting wave has the same frequency as the original waves but a different amplitude and a different phase angle. However, when two linearly polarized light waves having the same frequency but mutually perpendicular planes of vibration interfere, the resulting light is elliptically polarized. When the amplitude of the two waves are equal and

$$\delta = \left(\frac{2n+1}{4}\right) \lambda, \; n = 0, 1, 2, \ldots\ldots,$$

then the resultant light is circularly polarized.

When the linear phase difference δ between the two waves is an integral number of half wavelength $\left(\delta = \frac{n\lambda}{2}, n = 0, 1, 2, \ldots\right)$, then the resulting light is plane or linearly polarized.

7.4 Natural Double Refraction

When a ray of light is incident on certain crystals like Calcite or iceland spar, it is split at entry into two components which in general are transmitted through the crystal in different directions with different velocities. This phenomenon is known as natural double refraction or birefringence. One of the rays is called the ordinary ray, which is not deviated and the other the extraordinary ray, which is always deviated from the original path. If the emergent rays are observed through an analyzer, it is found that they are plane-polarized in mutually perpendicular planes.

Any line which is equally inclined to the concurring edges at the two obtuse corners of the crystal is defined as the optic axis of the crystal. A plane normal to the optic axis is called the equatorial plane. Crystals having only one optic axis are called uniaxial crystals. Many crystals have two opitc axes and as such are known as biaxial crystals.

Now refractive index

$$n = \frac{\sin i}{\sin R} \quad \ldots(7.4)$$

where i = angle of incidence

R = angle of refraction.

According to Brewster's law of polarization

$$n = \tan i \quad \ldots(7.5)$$

Hence $$i + R = 90^\circ \quad \ldots(7.6)$$

which is the necessary condition for polarization by refraction.

The angle of incidence i corresponding to an angle of refraction $R = 90^\circ$ is defined as the critical angle. It is the limiting angle of incidence for which refraction will occur. Hence, the critical angle,

$$i_c = \sin^{-1} n \quad \ldots(7.7)$$

7.4.1 Production of Plane-Polarised Light

The following methods may be used to produce plane-polarized light:

1. **Blackened glass plate.** By reflecting a ray of light from a blackened glass plate upon its rear surface, plane polarized light may be produced. The angle of incidence i for glass is 57° for polarization.

2. **Pile of plates.** If ordinary light is made to pass through a pack of eight or ten thin plates of glass, it will emerge nearly completely polarized and the intensities of refracted and reflected beams will be nearly equal.

3. **Calcite Crystal.** Iceland spar or Calcite is a rhombohedral crystal bounded by six parallelograms, the angles of which are $101^\circ - 55'$ and $78^\circ - 5'$ respectively (Fig. 7.2). Solid angles at A and C are all obtuse and remaining six angles are bounded by one obtuse and two acute angle. The critical angle for iceland is $69^\circ - 57'$.

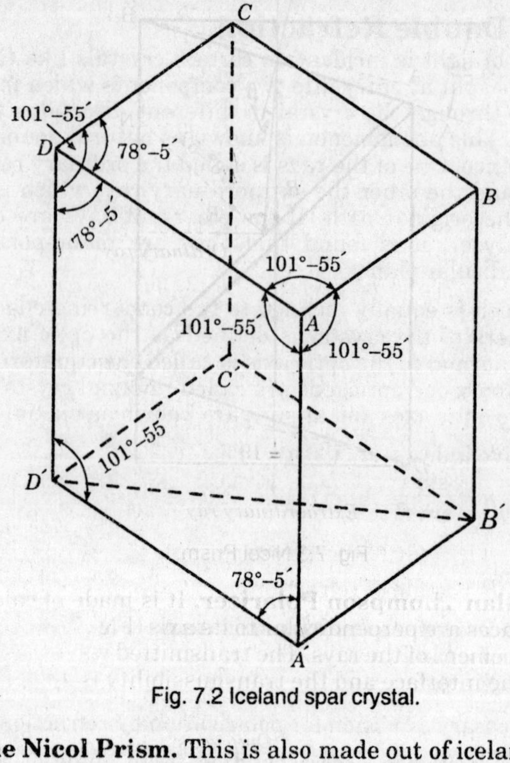

Fig. 7.2 Iceland spar crystal.

4. **The Nicol Prism.** This is also made out of iceland spar crystal whose natural angle of 19° is increased to 22° by grinding. Then the crystal is cut along a diagonal plane AC and cemented by canada balsam after polishing (Fig.7.3).

For ordinary ray,

$$1.65 = \frac{\sin 22^\circ}{\sin \beta}$$

or $$\sin \beta = 0.227$$

or $$\beta \approx 13^\circ - 8'$$

Hence $$R_0 = 90^\circ - (13^\circ - 8')$$

$$= (76^\circ — 52')$$

$$> (i_c = 69^\circ — 57')$$

Therefore, the ordinary ray is totally reflected and is absorbed by black paint on the long surface of Nicol. Extraordinary ray however passes through Canada balsam and is transmitted with no loss in intensity.

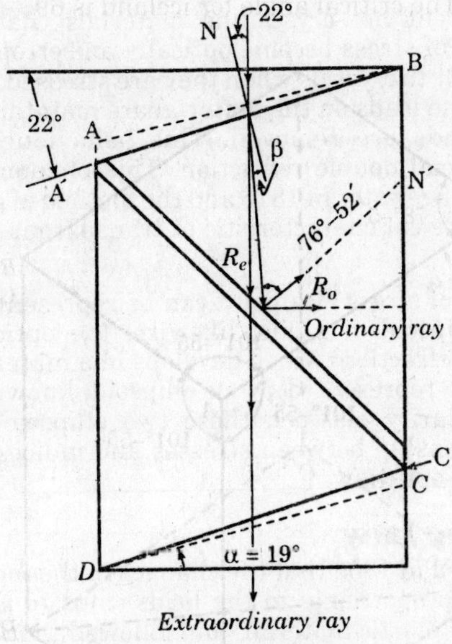

Fig. 7.3 Nicol Prism.

5. **The Glan Thompson Polarizer.** It is made of calcite and its transparent faces are perpendicular to its axis (Fig. 7.4). It is free from lateral displacement of the rays. The transmitted waves are parallel to the plane of the interface and the transmissibility is 40 percent.

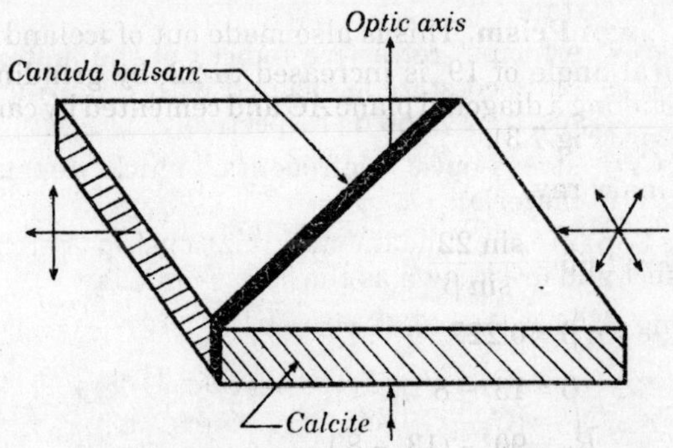

Fig. 7.4 Glan-Thompson polarizer.

6. **Ahrens Polarizer.** This is essentially a double Glan-Thompson prism in which, however, the ordinary ray is not stopped but emerges

from the prism and is eliminated by being diverted out of the regular cone of polarized rays. It has no lateral displacement.

7.5 Temporary Double Refraction

Many transparent non-crystalline materials that are optically isotropic when free of stress become optically anisotropic and display characteristics similr to crystals when they are stressed. These characteristics persist while loads on the material are maintained but disappear when the loads are removed. This behaviour is known as temporary or artificial double refraction. This phenomenon was observed by Sir David Brewster in 1816 and the method of photoelasticity is based on this physical characteristic of transparent noncrystalline materials.

Since the state of stress at a point can be represented by a stress ellipsoid or the ellipsoid of Lame, likewise, the optical anisotropy (temporary double refraction) which develops in a material as a result of stress can also be represented by an ellipsoid, known as the index ellipsoid. The similarity between these two ellipsoids suggest the presence of a relationship between stresses and indices of refraction, known as the stress-optic law.

7.6 Stress-Optic Law

Maxwell reported in 1853 that the changes in the indices of refraction were linearly proportional to the loads (thus to the stresses or strains for a linearly elastic material) and followed the relationship :

$$\left.\begin{aligned} n_1 - n_0 &= C_1\sigma_1 + C_2(\sigma_2 + \sigma_3) \\ n_2 - n_0 &= C_1\sigma_2 + C_2(\sigma_3 + \sigma_1) \\ n_3 - n_0 &= C_1\sigma_3 + C_2(\sigma_1 + \sigma_2) \end{aligned}\right\} \quad ...(7.8)$$

where $\sigma_1, \sigma_2, \sigma_3$ = principal stresses at the point

n_0 = index of refraction of material in the unstressed state.

n_1, n_2, n_3 = principal refractive indices of the material in the stressed state associated with the principal stresses, σ_1, σ_2 and σ_3 respectively.

C_1, C_2 = stress-optic coefficients, which depend on the material.

Equations (7.8) are the fundamental relationships between stress and optical effect and are known as the stress-optic law.

Eliminating n_0 from Eqs. (7.8), we get

$$\left.\begin{aligned} n_2 - n_1 &= (C_2 - C_1)(\sigma_1 - \sigma_2) = C(\sigma_1 - \sigma_2) \\ n_3 - n_2 &= (C_2 - C_1)(\sigma_2 - \sigma_3) = C(\sigma_2 - \sigma_3) \\ n_1 - n_3 &= (C_2 - C_1)(\sigma_3 - \sigma_1) = C(\sigma_3 - \sigma_1) \end{aligned}\right\} \quad ...(7.9)$$

where $C = C_2 - C_1$ is the relative or differential stress-optic coefficient expressed in terms of brewsters (1 brewster = 10^{-12} cm^2/dyn = 10^{-12} m^2/N).

Now the wave equation is,

$$E = a \cos \frac{2\pi}{\lambda} (z - ct)$$

$$= a \cos \phi$$

Angular phase shift between two waves,

$$\Delta = \phi_2 - \phi_1$$

Since the stressed photoelastic model behaves like temporary waveplate, hence

$$\phi_1 = \frac{2\pi h}{\lambda} (n_1 - n_0)$$

$$\phi_2 = \frac{2\pi h}{\lambda} (n_2 - n_0)$$

$$\therefore \quad \Delta = \phi_2 - \phi_1 = \frac{2\pi h}{\lambda} (n_2 - n_1) \quad ...(7.10)$$

Therefore, if a beam of plane-polarized light is passed through a slice of thickness h at normal incidence, the relative retardation Δ accumulated along each of the principal stress directions becomes,

$$\Delta_{12} = \frac{2\pi hC}{\lambda} (\sigma_1 - \sigma_2)$$

$$\Delta_{23} = \frac{2\pi hC}{\lambda} (\sigma_2 - \sigma_3)$$

$$\Delta_{31} = \frac{2\pi hC}{\lambda} (\sigma_3 - \sigma_1) \quad ...(7.11)$$

where $\Delta_{12}, \Delta_{23}, \Delta_{31}$ is the magnitude of the relative retardation developed between components of light beam propagating in the σ_3, σ_1, σ_2 directions respectively.

For two-dimensional or plane-stress problems ($\sigma_3 = 0$) and we get

$$\Delta = \frac{2\pi hC}{\lambda} (\sigma_1 - \sigma_2) \quad ...(7.12)$$

or $$\sigma_1 - \sigma_2 = \frac{N f_\sigma}{h} \quad ...(7.13)$$

where $$N = \frac{\Delta}{2\pi} \quad ...(7.14)$$

is the relative retardation in terms of a complete cycle of retardation and is termed the fringe order.

$$f_\sigma = \frac{\lambda}{C} \quad ...(7.15)$$

is a property of the model material for a given wavelength of light and is called the material fringe value in terms of normal stress and h is the model thickness.

Eq. (7.13) may be written as

$$\tau = \frac{\sigma_1 - \sigma_2}{2} = \frac{N f_\tau}{h} \qquad \text{...(7.16)}$$

where f_τ is the material fringe value in terms of shear and is equal to one-half of f_σ.

For a perfectly linear photoelastic material,

$$\varepsilon_1 = \frac{1}{E}(\sigma_1 - \nu\,\sigma_2)$$

$$\varepsilon_2 = \frac{1}{E}(\sigma_2 - \nu\,\sigma_1)$$

Thus $$\varepsilon_1 - \varepsilon_2 = \frac{1+\nu}{E}(\sigma_1 - \sigma_2)$$

Eq. (7.13) becomes

$$\left(\frac{E}{1+\nu}\right)(\varepsilon_1 - \varepsilon_2) = \frac{N f_\sigma}{h}$$

or $$\varepsilon_1 - \varepsilon_2 = \frac{N f_\varepsilon}{h} \qquad \text{...(7.17)}$$

where $$f_\varepsilon = \left(\frac{1+\nu}{E}\right) f_\sigma \qquad \text{...(7.18)}$$

is called the material fringe value in terms of strain Eq. (7.13) can also be written as

$$\sigma_1 - \sigma_2 = N F_\sigma \qquad \text{...(7.13a)}$$

where $F_\sigma = f_\sigma / h$ is the model fringe value in terms of stress.

Similarly Eq. (7.17) can be written as

$$\varepsilon_1 - \varepsilon_2 = N F_\varepsilon \qquad \text{...(7.17a)}$$

where $F_\varepsilon = \dfrac{f_\varepsilon}{h}$ is the model fringe value in terms of strain.

Eq. (7.12) states that in a transparent and isotropic model in which the stresses are two-dimensional, the angular phase difference between the two rectangular wave components travelling through the model is directly proportional to the difference of the principal stresses.

At those points in a stressed model where $\sigma_1 = \sigma_2$, the fringe order is zero and permanent black dots appear at these points. Such points are called *isotropic points.* If $\sigma_1 = \sigma_2 = 0$ then also the fringe order is zero at these points and permanent black dots appear. Such points are called *singular points.*

7.7 Basic Elements of a Polariscope

The polariscope is an optical instrument containing polaroids that utilizes the properties of polarized light in its operation. For photoelastic investigations two types of polariscopes are used :

1. Plane polariscope
2. Circular polariscope.

In the plane polariscope, plane-polarized light is used and in the circular polariscope, circularly polarized light is used. When the light is transmitted through the model then the polariscope is called of the transmission type. The polariscope may also be either of the lens type or diffused light type.

7.7.1 Plane polariscope

The basic arrangement of a lens type plane polariscope is shown in Fig. 7.5. Fig. 7.6 shows the set up for a diffused light polariscope.

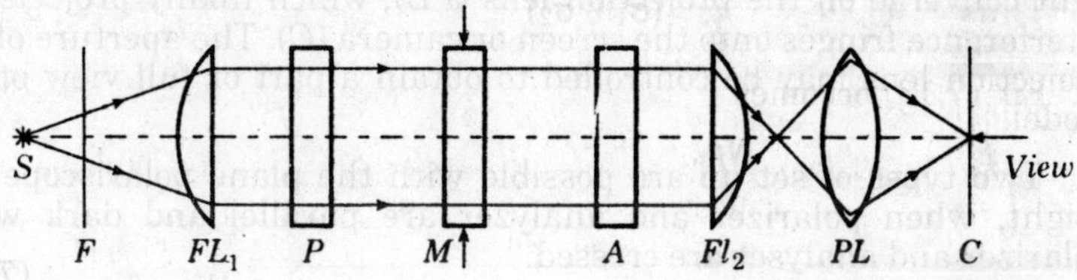

S = Light source
F = Filter
FL= Field lens
P = Polarizer
M = Model
A = Analyzer
PL = Projection lens
C= Camera or screen

Fig. 7.5 Lens type plane polariscope.

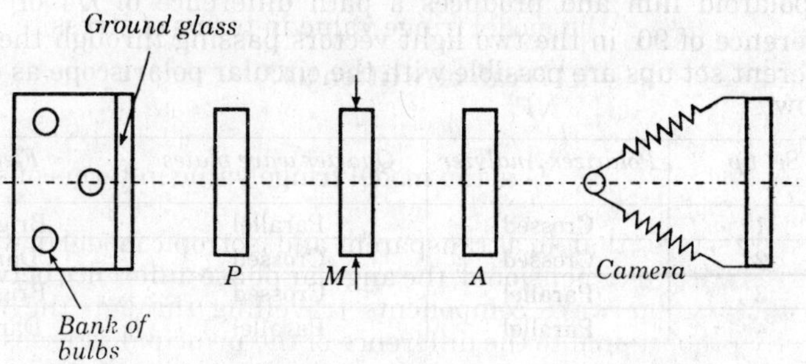

Fig. 7.6 Diffused light plane polariscope.

The light source may be a mercury or a sodium vapour lamp, an incandescent filament lamp or a bank of bulbs. Mercury or sodium vapour lamps are used as monochromatic light sources and incandescent filament lamp is used as a white light source, for the lens type polariscope. For the diffused light polariscope a bank of bulbs is used in an opaque box with a ground glass on one side to give diffused light. The filter F is generally a Wratten filter No. 77 to give a particular wavelength of 5461 Å (green) or 5893 Å (yellow).

The first field lens (FL_1) gives a parallel beam of light in the field of view.

The function of the polarizer (P) is to produce plane-polarized light. Polarizers are now-a-days made from thin sheets of polaroid.

The model M made out of a photoelastic material is loaded in a loading frame by which various types of loads can be applied. The load is applied either by means of dead weight through a lever or by means of a screw and measured by a spring balance.

The analyzer (A) is similar to the polarizer and is used to combined the two beams coming from the model. The polarizer and analyzer are generally coupled together by a flexible coupling to achieve their simultaneous rotation.

The second field lens (FL_2) is used to make the parallel beam of light converge on the projection lens (PL), which finally projects the interference fringes onto the screen or camera (C). The aperture of the projection lens may be controlled to obtain a part or full view of the model.

Two types of set up are possible with the plane polariscope, *i.e.* bright, when polarizer and analyzer are parallel and dark when polarizer and analyser are crossed.

7.7.2 Circular polariscope

In addition to all the elements of a plane polariscope, the circular polariscope has two more quarter wave plates (QWP), the first between the polarizer and model and the second between the model and the analyzer as shown in Fig. 7.7. The fast and slow axes of the QWP's are inclined at 45° with the polarizer or the analyzer. The QWP's are made of polaroid film and produces a path difference of $\lambda/4$ or a phase difference of 90° in the two light vectors passing through them. Four different set ups are possible with the circular polariscope as depicted below :

Set up	*Polarizer-Analyzer*	*Quarter wave plates*	*Field*
1	Crossed	Parallel	Bright
2	Crossed	Crossed	Dark
3	Parallel	Crossed	Bright
4	Parallel	Parallel	Dark

The crossed-crossed set up is called the standard set up of the circular polariscope. The first QWP converts plane polarized light into circularly polarized light and the second QWP converts circularly polarized light into plane polarized light.

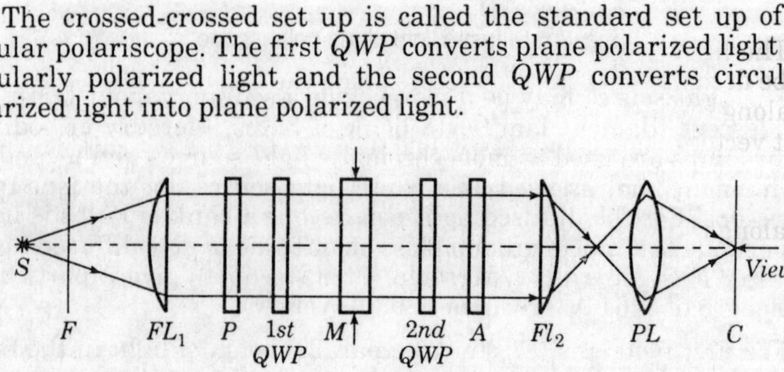

(*a*) Elements of lens type circular polariscope.

(*b*) Circular Polariscope.
Fig. 7.7

The diffused light plane polariscope can be easily converted into a circular polariscope by interposing two *QWP*'s as done for the lens polariscope. Diffused light polariscope is generally used for preliminary or rough work and lens type polariscope is used for more accurate work.

7.8 Effect of a Stressed Model in a Plane Polariscope

7.8.1 Dark-Field set up

Consider the dark-field set up of the plane polariscope (Fig. 7.8) when the polarizer and analyser are crossed. The plane polarized light beam emerging from the polarizer can be represented by

$$E = a \cos wt.$$

The light vector on entering the two dimensional stressed model will be decomposed into two vectors along the two principal directions, one along the fast (or σ_1) axis and the other along the slow (or σ_2) axis. Light vector (electric) along the fast axis on entering the model

$$E_{1e} = a \cos wt \cos \theta,$$

and along the slow axis

$$E_{2e} = a \cos wt \sin \theta$$

where θ is the angle between the axis of polarizer and maximum principal stress σ_1 and the subscript '*e*' stands for entering.

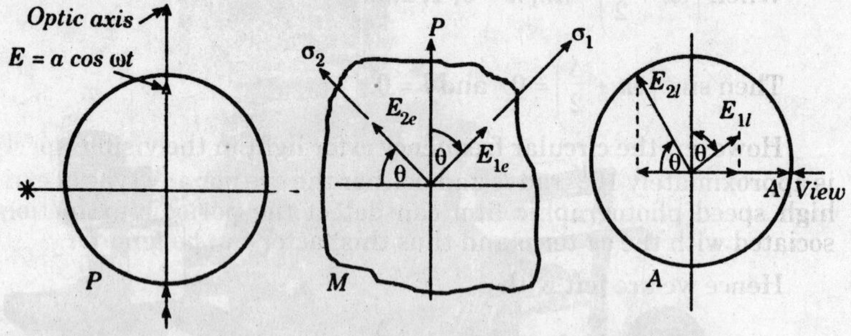

Fig. 7.8 Effects of a stressed model in a plane polariscope.

Since the light vector E_{1e} travels faster than E_{2e}, therefore, on emerging out from the model they develop a phase difference. Hence the light vector leaving along the fast axis of the model E_{1l} and falling on the analyzer becomes,

$$E_{1l} = a \cos(\omega t + \Delta) \cos\theta$$

Whereas the light vector leaving along the slow axis of the model and falling on the analyzer will be given by

$$E_{2l} = E_{2e} = a \cos \omega t \sin\theta$$

where the subscript l stands for leaving.

Since the axis of the analyzer is oriented at right angles to that of the polarizer, the light vector transmitted through the analyzer is

$$\begin{aligned} E_t &= E_{1l} \sin\theta - E_{2l}\cos\theta \\ &= a\cos(\omega t + \Delta)\cos\theta\sin\theta - a\cos\omega t\cos\theta\sin\theta \\ &= a\sin\theta\cos\theta\,[\cos(\omega t+\Delta) - \cos\omega t] \\ &= -a\sin 2\theta \sin\left(\omega t + \frac{\Delta}{2}\right)\sin\frac{\Delta}{2} \qquad \text{...(7.19)} \end{aligned}$$

Intensity of light I is proportional to the square of the amplitude E_t. Hence

$$\begin{aligned} I &\propto a^2 \sin^2 2\theta \sin^2\left(\omega t + \frac{\Delta}{2}\right)\sin^2\frac{\Delta}{2} \\ &= I_0 \sin^2 2\theta \,.\, \sin^2\left(\omega t + \frac{\Delta}{2}\right)\sin^2\frac{\Delta}{2} \qquad \text{...(7.20)} \end{aligned}$$

where I_0 = maximum transmitted light intensity.

Light intensity I will be zero or extinction can be obtained in the following three ways :

(a) Effect of frequency

When $\left(\omega t + \frac{\Delta}{2}\right) = n\pi$, $n = 0, 1, 2, ...$

Then $\sin^2\left(\omega t + \frac{\Delta}{2}\right) = 0$ and $I = 0$.

However, the circular frequency ω for light in the visible spectrum is approximately 10^{15} rad /s and neither the eye nor any type of existing high speed photographic film can detect the periodic extinction associated with the ωt term and thus this factor can be ignored.

Hence we are left with

$$I = I_0 \sin^2 2\theta \sin^2 \frac{\Delta}{2}$$

(b) Effect of principal stress directions.

When $2\theta = n\pi$, $n = 0, 1, 2, ...$ $\sin^2 2\theta = 0$ and $I = 0$.

Therefore, when one of the principal stress directions coincides with the axis of the polarizer, extinction occurs. When the entire model is viewed in the polariscope, a fringe pattern is observed ; the fringes are loci of points where the principal stress directions coincide with the axis of the polarizer. The fringe pattern formed by the $\sin^2 2\theta$ term is known as the *isoclinic* fringe pattern. These are the loci of points having constant stress directions. The isoclinic fringe patterns are employed to determine the principal stress directions in photoelastic model.

(c) Effect of principal stress difference.

When $\frac{\Delta}{2} = n\pi$, $n = 0, 1, 2, ...$, $\sin^2 \frac{\Delta}{2} = 0$

and extinction occurs. Therefore, when the principal stress difference is either zero ($n = 0$) or sufficient to produce an integral number of wavelengths of retardation ($n = 1, 2, 3, ..$), extinction occurs. When a complete model is viewed in the polariscope a fringe pattern is observed which are the loci of points exhibiting the same order of extinction ($n = 0, 1, 2, 3, ...$). The fringe pattern produced by the $\sin^2 \frac{\Delta}{2}$ term is known as the *isochromatic* (same colour) fringe pattern.

Now $\qquad \Delta = \frac{2\pi h C}{\lambda}(\sigma_1 - \sigma_2)$

Hence $\qquad \frac{\Delta}{2\pi} = \frac{hC}{\lambda}(\sigma_1 - \sigma_2)$

or $\qquad n = N = \frac{h}{f_\sigma}(\sigma_1 - \sigma_2)$, $n = 0, 1, 2, ...$ ...(7.21)

When a model is viewed with white light the isochromatic fringe pattern appears as a series of coloured bands. Thus we find that in a plane polariscope the isoclinic and isochromatic fringe patterns are obtained, superimposed on each other.

7.8.2 Bright-Field set up

In the bright-field set up the axis of the analyzer is parallel to that of the polarizer. Hence

$$E_t = E_{1l} \cos\theta + E_{2l} \sin\theta$$

$$= a \cos(\omega t + \Delta) + \cos^2\theta + a \cos\omega t \sin^2\theta$$

$$= a \cos(\omega t + \Delta)\left(\frac{1+\cos 2\theta}{2}\right) + a \cos\omega t\left(\frac{1-\cos 2\theta}{2}\right)$$

$$= \frac{a}{2}[\cos(\omega t + \Delta) + \cos\omega t] + \frac{a}{2}\cos 2\theta\, [\cos(\omega t + \Delta) - \cos\omega t]$$

$$= a \cos\left(\omega t + \frac{\Delta}{2}\right)\cos\frac{\Delta}{2} - a\cos 2\theta \sin\left(\omega t + \frac{\Delta}{2}\right)\sin\frac{\Delta}{2}$$

$$|E_t| = a\sqrt{\cos^2\frac{\Delta}{2} + \sin^2\frac{\Delta}{2}\cos^2 2\theta}$$

$$= a\sqrt{1 - \sin^2\frac{\Delta}{2}\sin^2 2\theta}$$

Hence
$$I \propto a^2\left(1 - \sin^2\frac{\Delta}{2}\sin^2 2\theta\right)$$

$$= I_0\left(1 - \sin^2\frac{\Delta}{2}\sin^2 2\theta\right) \quad ...(7.23)$$

$I = 0$ when $\sin^2 \Delta/2 \sin^2 2\theta = 1$ or the intensity I is maximum when $\sin^2 \Delta/2 \sin^2 2\theta = 0$. Therefore, the conditions for maximum intensity of the transmitted light are now the same as those for extinction for the dark field set up.

7.9 Effect of a Stressed Model in a Circular Polariscope

7.9.1 Dark-field set up

Consider the standard set up (crossed-crossed) of the circular polariscope as shown in Fig. 7.9. The light vector leaving the polarizer can be written as

$$E = a \cos\omega t$$

Components of light vector on entering the first QWP become

$$E_{1e} = a \cos\omega t \cos\frac{\pi}{2} = \frac{a}{\sqrt{2}}\cos\omega t$$

$$E_{2e} = a \cos\omega t \,.\, \sin\frac{\pi}{2} = \frac{a}{\sqrt{2}}\cos\omega t$$

The first QWP produces a phase deference of $\pi/2$ and converts plane polarized light into circularly polarized light. Components of light vector on leaving the first QWP become

$$E_{1l} = \frac{a}{\sqrt{2}} \cos\left(\omega t + \frac{\pi}{2}\right) = \frac{-a}{\sqrt{2}} \sin \omega t$$

$$E_{2l} = E_{2e} = \frac{a}{\sqrt{2}} \cos \omega t$$

If the principal axes of the model are inclined at angle θ with the axis of the first QWP, the components of light vector along the principal axis of the model on entering are

$$E_{ae} = E_{1l} \cos\theta - E_{2l} \sin\theta$$

$$= -\frac{a}{\sqrt{2}} \sin \omega t \cos\theta - \frac{a}{\sqrt{2}} \cos \omega t \sin\theta$$

$$E_{be} = E_{1l} \sin\theta + E_{2l} \cos\theta$$

$$= -\frac{a}{\sqrt{2}} \sin \omega t \sin\theta + \frac{a}{\sqrt{2}} \cos \omega t \cos\theta$$

The model introduces a phase difference of Δ. Thereofore, the components of light vector on leaving the model and entering the second QWP become,

$$E_{al} = -\frac{a}{\sqrt{2}} [\sin(\omega t + \Delta) \cos\theta + \cos(\omega t + \Delta) \sin\theta]$$

$$= -\frac{a}{\sqrt{2}} \sin(\omega t + \Delta + \theta)$$

$$E_{bl} = \frac{a}{\sqrt{2}} [-\sin \omega t \sin\theta + \cos \omega t \cos\theta]$$

$$= \frac{a}{\sqrt{2}} \cos(\omega t + \theta)$$

Now the second QWP is crossed to the first QWP. Therefore, the components of the light vector along the axes of the second QWP become,

$$E_{3e} = E_{al} \cos\theta + E_{bl} \sin\theta$$

$$= \frac{-a}{\sqrt{2}} [\sin(\omega t + \Delta + \theta) \cos\theta - \cos(\omega t + \theta) \sin\theta]$$

$$E_{4e} = E_{bl} \cos\theta - E_{al} \sin\theta$$

$$= \frac{a}{\sqrt{2}} [\cos(\omega t + \theta) \cos\theta + \sin(\omega t + \Delta + \theta) \sin\theta]$$

The second QWP also produces a phase difference of $\pi/2$. Therefore, the components of light vector on leaving the second QWP and entering the analyzer become

$$E_{3l} = E_{3e}$$

$$E_{4l} = \frac{a}{\sqrt{2}} \left[\cos\left(\omega t + \theta + \frac{\pi}{2}\right) \cos\theta + \sin\left(\omega t + \Delta + \theta + \frac{\pi}{2}\right) \sin\theta\right]$$

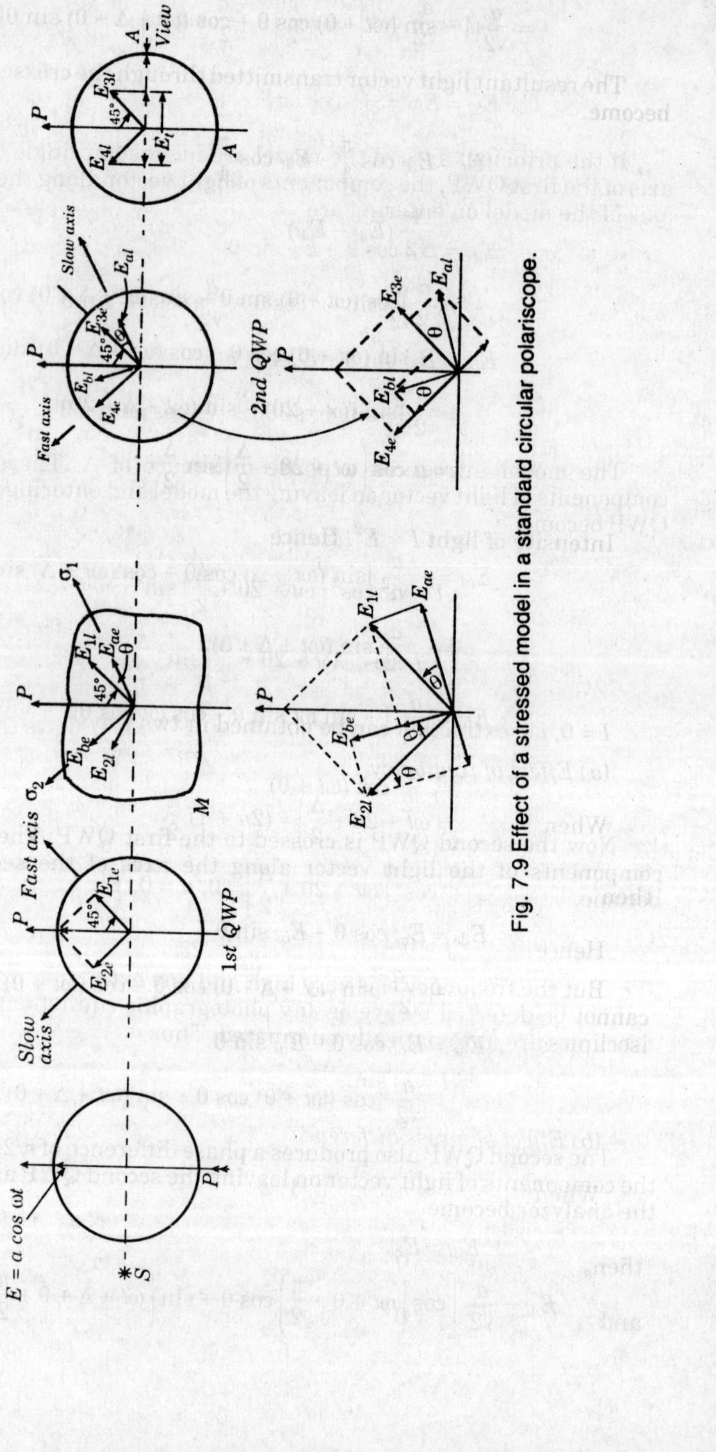

Fig. 7.9 Effect of a stressed model in a standard circular polariscope.

$$= \frac{a}{\sqrt{2}} [- \sin (\omega t + \theta) \cos \theta + \cos (\omega t + \Delta + \theta) \sin \theta]$$

The resultant light vector transmitted through the crossed analyzer become,

$$E_t = E_{3l} \cos \frac{\pi}{4} - E_{4l} \cos \frac{\pi}{4}$$

$$= \frac{1}{\sqrt{2}} (E_{3l} - E_{4l})$$

$$= \frac{a}{2} [\cos (\omega t + \theta) \sin \theta - \sin (\omega t + \Delta + \theta) \cos \theta$$

$$+ \sin (\omega t + \theta) \cos \theta - \cos (\omega t + \Delta + \theta) \sin \theta]$$

$$= \frac{a}{2} [\sin (\omega t + 2\theta) - \sin (\omega t + \Delta + 2\theta)]$$

$$= a \cos \left(\omega t + 2\theta + \frac{\Delta}{2} \right) \sin \frac{\Delta}{2} \qquad ...(7.24)$$

Intensity of light $I \propto E^2$. Hence

$$I \propto a^2 \cos^2 \left(\omega t + 2\theta + \frac{\Delta}{2} \right) \sin^2 \frac{\Delta}{2}$$

$$I = I_0 \cos^2 \left(\omega t + 2\theta + \frac{\Delta}{2} \right) \sin^2 \frac{\Delta}{2} \qquad ...(7.25)$$

$I = 0$, *i.e.* extinction can be obtained in two ways.

(*a*) *Effect of frequency.*

When $\left(\omega t + 2\theta + \frac{\Delta}{2} \right) = (2n + 1) \frac{\pi}{2}$

then $\cos^2 \left(\omega t + 2\theta + \frac{\Delta}{2} \right) = 0, n = 0, 1, 2,...$

Hence $I = 0$.

But the frequency ω is very high and any extinction produced by it cannot be detected by eye or any photographic equipment. Hence the isoclinics are automatically eliminated. Thus

$$I = I_0 \sin^2 \frac{\Delta}{2} \qquad ...(7.26)$$

(*b*) *Effect of stress difference.*

When $\frac{\Delta}{2} = n\pi, n = 0, 1, 2....$

then $\sin^2 \frac{\Delta}{2} = 0$

and $I = 0$

This type of extinction is identical with that for the plane polariscope and referred to as isochromatic fringe pattern.

Thus $$n = \frac{\Delta}{2\pi} = \frac{h}{f_\sigma}(\sigma_1 - \sigma_2)$$

or $$n = N = \frac{h}{f_\sigma}(\sigma_1 - \sigma_2) \quad \text{...(7.27)}$$

7.9.2 Bright Field Set Up

Consider the parallel-crossed set up in which the axes of polarizer and analyzer are parallel. Thus

$$E_t = E_{3l} \cos \frac{\pi}{4} + E_{4l} \cos \frac{\pi}{4}$$

$$= \frac{1}{\sqrt{2}}(E_{3l} + E_{4l})$$

$$= \frac{a}{2}[\cos(\omega t + \theta) \sin\theta - \sin(\omega t + \Delta + \theta)\cos\theta$$

$$- \sin(\omega t + \theta)\cos\theta + \cos(\omega t + \Delta + \theta)\cos\theta]$$

$$= \frac{a}{2}[-\sin\omega t - \sin(\omega t + \Delta)]$$

$$= -\frac{a}{2}\left[2\sin\left(\omega t + \frac{\Delta}{2}\right)\cos\frac{\Delta}{2}\right] \quad \text{...(7.28)}$$

$$I \propto a^2 \sin^2\left(\omega t + \frac{\Delta}{2}\right)\cos^2\frac{\Delta}{2}$$

$$I = I_0 \sin^2\left(\omega t + \frac{\Delta}{2}\right)\cos^2\frac{\Delta}{2} \quad \text{...(7.29)}$$

Neglecting the effect of frequency

$$I = I_0 \cos^2\frac{\Delta}{2} \quad \text{...(7.30)}$$

For extinction to occur

$$\frac{\Delta}{2} = (2n + 1)\frac{\pi}{2}, \; n = 0, 1, 2, \ldots.$$

$$\therefore \quad N = \frac{\Delta}{2\pi} = n + \frac{1}{2}$$

Hence the order of the first fringe observed in a light field polariscope is $\frac{1}{2}$ which corresponds to $n = 0$. The higher order fringes will be $\frac{3}{2}, \frac{5}{2}, \frac{7}{2}$..... etc. Therefore, by using dark and bright field set ups of the circular polariscope, it is possible to obtain the fringe order to the nearest $\frac{1}{2}$ order.

7.10 Double Exposure Photography in Photoelasticity

A pattern of isochromatics alone (without isoclinics) may be obtained with a plane polariscope by use of a doubly exposed photograph, first exposure being with the dark field set up and the second exposure with the polarizer and analyzer turned through 45°.

For the first exposure

$$I = I_0 \sin^2 2\theta \, . \, \sin^2 \frac{\Delta}{2}$$

and for the second exposure

$$I = I_0 \cos^2 2\theta \, . \, \sin^2 \frac{\Delta}{2}$$

For the doubly exposed film, the two intensities add to give the resultant intensity as

$$I = I_0 \sin^2 \frac{\Delta}{2} \qquad \text{...(7.31)}$$

Thus the resulting picture shows only isochromatics. This technique was first of all devised by Koch and Szego in 1954. By using this method they found that the isochromatics obtained were somewhat sharper than those obtained with a circular polariscope. This they attributed to the inevitable small imperfections in the QWP's of the circular polariscope.

7.11 Practical Problems in a Polariscope

1. **Intensity variation in the light source.** This problem may be eliminated by incorporating a monitor photomultiplier tube in the apparatus, which measures the source intensity as a function of time for the duration of the experiment. Intensity data from the polariscope can then be multiplied by the ratio of the monitor photomultiplier-tube voltage level during the test to the monitor level during the calibration procedure in order to obtain data corresponding to a constant source intensity.

2. **Polariscope imperfections.** When the analyzer of a perfect plane polariscope is rotated the intensity of light, I, which passes through the analyzer is governed by the equation,

$$I = I_l \sin^2 \beta \qquad \text{...(7.32)}$$

where β is the angle of rotation measured from the crossed (dark-field) orientation and I_l is the intensity of light which passes in the light-field orientation. In a real polariscope, the dark-field intensity I_d will not be zero. This result is significant when partial fringes are to be measured. When components of the electric vector of the light on the light and dark-field axes are recombined the intensity which passes at orientation β is found to be

$$I = I_l \sin^2 \beta + I_d \cos^2 \beta \qquad \text{...(7.33)}$$

Thus, the intensity I_c which would be measured in a perfect polariscope is determined from Eq. (7.32) and (7.33) with the use of a trigonometric identity as:

$$I_c = (I - I_d)/(1 - I_d/I_l) \quad ...(7.34)$$

Further simplification results by assuming $\frac{I_d}{I_l} \ll 1$. This relation can be used to correct measured intensity data before it is entered into equations which assume a perfect polariscope.

3. **Model imperfections.** Many model materials are not transparent perfectly. As a result the light passing through the polariscope is significantly attenuated. In addition, it is sometimes difficult to manufacture models which are free of initial birefringence. When the model has initial birefringence, the incidence plane or circularly polarized light emerges from the model elliptically polarized, which complicates the calibration procedure. These problems can be corrected by calibrating the polariscope with the model in place.

For the circular polariscope, in the light-field configuration, the intensity as a function of fringe order N is,

$$I_l = K_c \cos^2 \pi N \quad ...(7.35a)$$

while in the dark field configuration

$$I_d = K_c \sin^2 \pi N \quad ...(7.35b)$$

where K_c is a calibration constant.

Thus, if measurements are made with the model in place in both polariscope configurations with fixed initial fringe order N_i, the calibration constant K_c for the circular polariscope is

$$K_c = I_l + I_d \quad ...(7.36)$$

Once the calibration constant is known, either of Eqs. (7.35) can be solved for N.

In the plane polariscope, light enters the model plane polarized and emerges elliptically polarized and attenuated. The problem is to determine the intensity of the plane polarized light which would have emerged if the model had been free of initial birefringence. Light intensity is proportional to energy flux. If the light had emerged from the model plane polarized, all the energy flux would have been contained in one mode. The same total energy flux is contained in the elliptically polarized light in two orthogonal modes. Thus, if the analyzer is set at one arbitrary orientation and intensity in this mode, I_x, is measured and then the analyzer is rotated $\pi/2$ rad. and the intensity, I_y, in the orthogonal mode is measured, the total energy in the elliptically polarized light will be just the sum of the energies in these two independent modes. Thus for the plane polariscope

$$K_p = I_x + I_y \quad ...(7.37)$$

where I_x and I_y are intensities measured with the analyzer in any two orthogonal orientations.

7.12 Determination of Integral Fringe Orders

The stress optic law can be expressed as :

$$\sigma_1 - \sigma_2 = \frac{N\lambda}{Ch}$$

or
$$N = Ch\,(\sigma_1 - \sigma_2)\,\frac{1}{\lambda}$$

Now, if at the same point fringe orders are measured at two other wavelengths λ_1 and λ_2 then the respective fringe orders N_1 and N_2 are given by

$$N_1 = Ch\,(\sigma_1 - \sigma_2)\,\frac{1}{\lambda_1}$$

$$N_2 = Ch\,(\sigma_1 - \sigma_2)\,\frac{1}{\lambda_2}$$

Substracting, we get

$$N_1 - N_2 = Ch\,(\sigma_1 - \sigma_2)\left(\frac{1}{\lambda_1} - \frac{1}{\lambda_2}\right)$$

or
$$Ch\,(\sigma_1 - \sigma_2) = \frac{(N_1 - N_2)}{\left(\dfrac{1}{\lambda_1} - \dfrac{1}{\lambda_2}\right)}$$

Substituting in the stress-optic law, we get

$$N = \frac{1/\lambda}{(1/\lambda_1 - 1/\lambda_2)}\,(N_1 - N_2)$$

$$= K\,(N_1 - N_2) \qquad \text{...(7.38)}$$

where
$$K = \frac{\lambda_1\lambda_2}{\lambda\,(\lambda_2 - \lambda_1)}$$

Pant suggested that the value of K can be determined by using two different filters. Or a disc of the same material as that used for the model may be loaded diametrically and the fringe orders determined at the center successively with sodium light, white light with red filter and white light with green filter. Thus knowing N, N_1, N_2 the constant K can be determined.

Pant's analysis ignores the dependence of the stress-optic coefficient on λ and also is restricted to the case where the difference between the fringe orders associated with λ_1 and λ_2 is only a fraction *i.e.* the integral fringe orders associated with λ_1 and λ_2 are equal. Srinath and Sarma have shown how using two wavelengths, one can determine the integral values (and their multiplies) for both wavelengths, associated with the fractional fringe orders observed at any point.

7.13 Photoelastic Photography

For keeping a permanent record of photoelastic data, photographs are taken. Therefore it is essential to understand the basic principles of photography.

Certain silver halides when properly prepared and exposed to light undergo a latent change that can be seen and preserved by the photographic development process. The change is a darkening; caused by the formation of metallic silver and is the result of the successive action of light and development; the amount of darkening called density is indicated by tests in which the ability of the deposited silver to prevent transmission of light is measured; the amount of light, called exposure, is the product of light intensity and time.

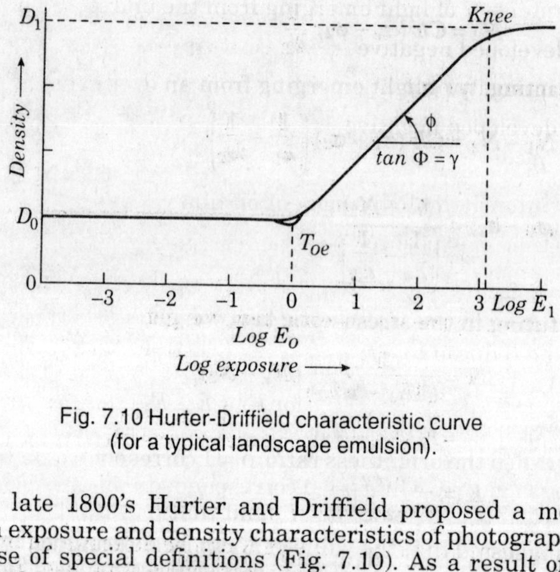

Fig. 7.10 Hurter-Driffield characteristic curve (for a typical landscape emulsion).

In the late 1800's Hurter and Driffield proposed a method for relating an exposure and density characteristics of photographic emulsions by use of special definitions (Fig. 7.10). As a result of plotting density as a function of the logarithm of the exposure, with a controlled chemical process and fixed type of emulsion, Hurter and Driffield were able to obtain characteristic curves of emulsions.

The curve presented in Fig. 7.10 defines four important characteristics of a photographic film, namely the fog density D_0, the exposure inertia E_0, the slope of the curve which establishes the gamma number of the film, and the maximum density D_1 which occurs with an exposure E_1. From this curve it is obvious that there is always a threshold or inertia exposure below which no increase in density over the unexposed or fog density can be detected. Threshold exposure is of much importance in photoelastic photography as it causes fringes which are narrow on the ground glass of the camera to produce as broad-bands on the negative. The usual landscape film incorporates an emulsion with $\gamma \approx 1$. This relatively low value of γ gives a wide range of exposure values over which the film emulsion will be effective in producing a satisfactory negative. For photoelastic photographs, film emulsions with a high γ (3 to 6) are often employed which gives a high contrast negative.

For the linear portion of the curve

$$D = \begin{cases} D_0 + \gamma(\log E - \log E_0) & \text{for } E_0 \le E \le E_1 \\ D_0 & \text{for } E \le E_0 \\ D_1 & \text{for } E \ge E_1 \end{cases} \qquad \text{...(7.39)}$$

where $D = \log (I_i/I_e)$

I_i = intensity of light incident upon developed negative

I_e = intensity of light emerging from developed negative

D_0 = fog density = $\log (I_i/I'_e)$

D_1 = maximum density = $\log (I_i/I''_e)$

I'_e = intensity of light emerging from the unexposed part of the developed negative

I''_e = intensity of light emerging from an over exposed part of developed negative

$E = It$

I = intensity of light incident on film

t = time of exposure

Thus $\quad \log \dfrac{I_i}{I_e} = \log \dfrac{I_i}{I'_e} + \gamma \log \dfrac{E}{E_0}$

which can be reduced to

$$\rho = \frac{I_c}{I'_e} = \left(\frac{E}{E_0}\right)^{-\gamma} \quad \text{for } E_1 \ge E \ge E_0 \qquad \text{...(7.40)}$$

where ρ is called the brightness ratio. $\rho = 1$ corresponds to the brightest area on the negative, while $\rho = 0$ corresponds to an opaque area. Note that $\rho = 1$ when $E \le E_0$ since $I_e = I'_e$ and that $\rho \to 0$ when $E \ge E_1$ since $I_e = I''_e$.

In photoelastic photography, at least theoretically, the limits of exposure have one zero value, however the emulsion records only values of the range of exposure above the threshold or inertia exposure. This is the cause of finite fringe width on a negative, when in theory it is a line. The maximum exposure alone can be controlled by the camera aperture and shuter. The fringe width must therefore be controlled by careful selection of the exposure ratio, which is the ratio of the maximum exposure E_p to the threshold or inertia exposure E_0.

Now for a standard circular polariscope

$$I = I_p \sin^2 \frac{\Delta}{2}$$

where I_p = uniform intensity of light entering the stressed model

I = light leaving the model.

The exposure for the dark-field negative will be

$$E = It = I_p \cdot t \sin^2 \frac{\Delta}{2} = E_p \sin^2 \frac{\Delta}{2} \qquad \text{...(7.41)}$$

Comparing Eqs. (7.40) and (7.41), we get

$$\rho = \begin{cases} \dfrac{1}{(E_p/E_0)^\gamma \sin^{2\gamma}(\Delta/2)} & \text{for } E_1 \geq E_p \sin^2 \dfrac{\Delta}{2} \geq E_0 \\ 1 & \text{for } E_p \sin^2 \dfrac{\Delta}{2} \leq E_0 \\ \to 0 & \text{for } E_p \sin^2 \dfrac{\Delta}{2} \geq E_1 \end{cases} \qquad \text{...(7.42)}$$

Increasing the exposure ratio E_p/E_0 reduces the fringe width and improves the contrast.

7.14 Fractional Fringe Photography

The dark-field and bright-field arrangement of a circular polariscope permit the determination of the fringes upto the nearest half fringe. In order to improve the accuracy of the determination of fractional fringe orders a photographic technique employing the mixed field may be used, which permit the determination of fringe orders upto the nearest one-fourth fringe.

Now for a dark-field circular polariscope

$$I_d = I_{pd} \sin^2 \frac{\Delta}{2}$$

and for the light-field

$$I_l = I_{pl} \cos^2 \frac{\Delta}{2}$$

Thus $\quad E_d = E_{pd} \sin^2 \dfrac{\Delta}{2},\ E_{pd} = I_{pd}\, t_d$

$$E_l = E_{pl} \cos^2 \frac{\Delta}{2},\ E_{pl} = I_{pl}\, t_l$$

From Eq. (7.42), which describe the brightness of a negative obtained with a dark-field polariscope,

$$\rho_d = \begin{cases} \dfrac{1}{(E_{pd}/E_0)^\gamma \sin^{2\gamma}(\Delta/2)} & \text{for } E_1 \geq E_{pd} \sin^2 \dfrac{\Delta}{2} \geq E_0 & \text{...(7.43}a) \\ 1 & \text{for } E_{pd} \sin^2 \dfrac{\Delta}{2} \leq E_0 & \text{...(7.43}b) \\ \to 0 & \text{for } E_{pd} \sin^2 \dfrac{\Delta}{2} \geq E_1 & \text{...(7.43c)} \end{cases}$$

Similarly for the light-field polariscope

$$\rho_l = \begin{cases} \dfrac{1}{(E_{pl}/E_0)^\gamma \cos^{2\gamma}(\Delta/2)} & \text{for } E_1 \geq E_{pl}\cos^2\dfrac{\Delta}{2} \geq E_0 \quad \text{...(7.44a)} \\ 1 & \text{for } E_{pl}\cos^2\dfrac{\Delta}{2} \leq E_0 \quad \text{...(7.44b)} \\ \to 0 & \text{for } E_{pl}\cos^2\dfrac{\Delta}{2} \geq E_1 \quad \text{...(7.44c)} \end{cases}$$

When the negatives are superimposed, there will be four distinct types of zones (Fig. 7.11) with the brightness ratio ρ_m of the mixed field, such that

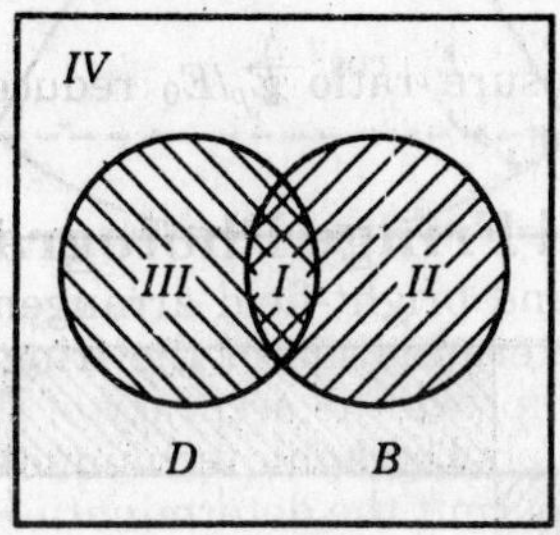

Fig.7.11 Formation of zones with different brightness ratio expressions due to superimposition of the negatives *D* and *B* are dark zones in the dark and light field negatives, respectively.

$$\rho_m = \rho_d\,\rho_l \quad \text{...(7.45)}$$

and given by

$$\rho_m = \begin{cases} \dfrac{1}{(E_{pd}/E_0)^\gamma (E_{pl}/E_0)^\gamma \sin^{2\gamma}(\Delta/2)\cos^{2\gamma}(\Delta/2)} & \text{from Eqs. (7.34a) and (7.44a), i.e. } (D \cap B) \\ \dfrac{1}{(E_{pl}/E_0)^\gamma \cos^{2\gamma}(\Delta/2)} & \text{from Eqs. (7.43b) and (7.44a), i.e. } (D \cap B) \\ \dfrac{1}{(E_{pd}/E_0)^\gamma \sin^{2\gamma}(\Delta/2)} & \text{from Eqs. 7.43 (a) and 7.44 (b), i.e. } (D \cap B) \\ 1 & \text{from Eqs. 7.43 (b) and 7.44 (b), i.e. } (\overline{D} \cap \overline{B}) \end{cases}$$

Assuming that the print replicates the pattern on the negative with exact black-white inversion, the so called mixed-field fringes will be formed in the areas where $\rho_m = 1$, *i.e.* where both the negatives are bright.

Since the fringe order in a negative is the locus of a point having an exposure equal to exposure inertia E_0, the fractional fringe orders n_d and n_l at the borders of the mixed-field fringe (Fig. 7.12) will be given by :

$$n_d = (1/\pi) \sin^{-1} (E_0/E_{pd})^{1/2} \qquad ...(7.47a)$$

and
$$n_l = (1/\pi) \cos^{-1} (E_0/E_{pl})^{1/2} \qquad ...(7.47b)$$

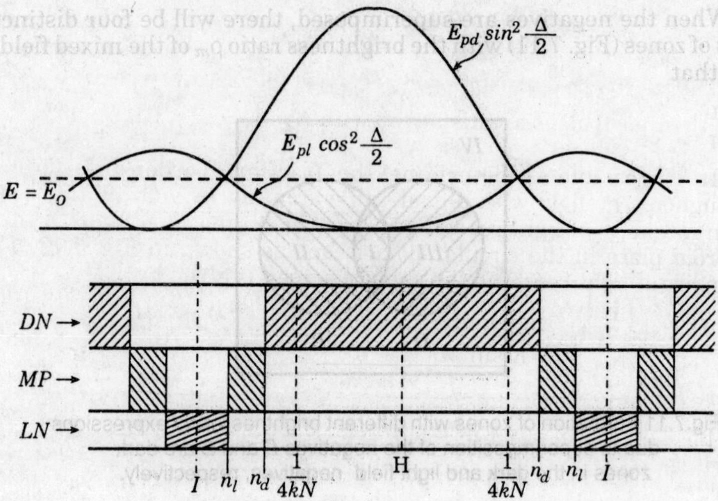

I = integer order fringe
H = half order fringe
DN = high exposure dark field negative
LN = low exposure light field negative
MP = mixed field point

Fig. 7.12 Mechanism of mixed field fringe formation.

It can be observed from Fig. 7.12 that, when the mixed field fringes are sufficiently thin, the orders of the fringes will be obtained from the solution of the equation,

$$E_{pd} \sin^2 \pi n = E_{pl} \cos^2 \pi n$$

or
$$n = (1/\pi) \tan^{-1} (E_{pl}/E_{pd})^{1/2} \qquad ...(6.48)$$

From Eq.(7.43), it can be seen that n will be equal to $1/(4\,kN)$ where $k = 1, 3, 5,..$ etc., only when

$$E_{pl} = E_{pd} \text{ or } I_{pl}\, t_l = I_{pd}\, t_d \qquad ...(7.49)$$

Note that $\rho_m = 1$ only in two regions where both

$$\cos^2 \frac{\Delta}{2} \leq \frac{E_0}{E_{pl}} \text{ and } \sin^2 \frac{\Delta}{2} \leq \frac{E_0}{E_{pd}} \qquad ...(7.50)$$

For
$$E_{pd} = E_{pl} = ME_0 \qquad ...(7.51)$$

where M is the exposure multiple. Combining Eq. (7.50) and (7.51) yields the condition $M \leq 2$ to obtain any region on the superimposed negative where $\rho_m = 1$. With $M = 2$, Eq. (7.50) become

$$\cos^2 \Delta/2 \leq \frac{1}{2}, \sin^2 \Delta/2 \leq \frac{1}{2} \quad ...(7.52)$$

Thus $\frac{\Delta}{2} = (2n+1)\frac{\pi}{4}$ where $n = 0, 1, 2,...$

and $$N = \frac{\Delta}{2\pi} = \frac{2n+1}{4} \quad ...(7.53)$$

Therefore, the superimposed negatives yield a fringe pattern where the $\frac{1}{4}$th order fringes are displayed with $N = \frac{1}{4}, \frac{3}{4},... \frac{5}{4},....$

It is possible to determine the fractional order interference throughout the field with considerable accuracy by varying the maximum intensity of light reaching the image of the camera with a third polaroid plate in the circular polariscope as shown in Fig. 7.13. The intensity of light reaching the camera screen is given by

$$I \propto a^2 \sin^2 n\pi \,.\, \cos^2 \alpha$$
$$= K \sin^2 n\pi \cos^2 \alpha \quad ...(7.54)$$

where K is a constant.

If $$n = N \pm n_f,\ 0 \leq n_f \leq \frac{1}{2} \quad ...(7.55)$$

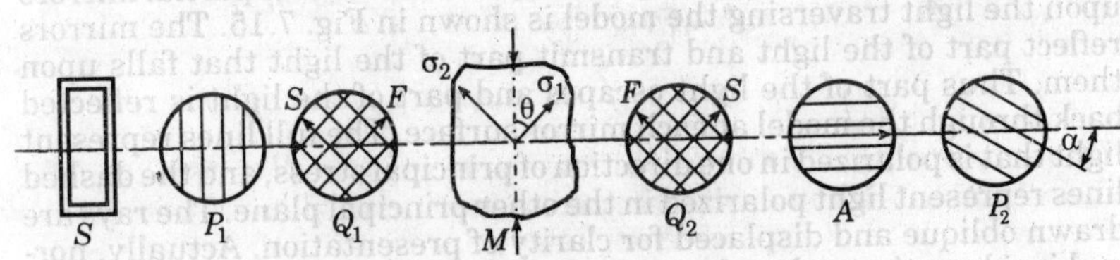

Fig.7.13 The polaroid polariscope.

where N is an integer, then n_f represents the fractional order interference at the point and Eq. (7.54) can be written as :

$$I = K \sin^2 \pi n_f \cos^2 \alpha \quad ...(7.56)$$

Now threshold exposure is defined as the exposure for which a point in the processed negative will have a density noticeable above the general background with density D_0. So a point on the processed negative will be :

$$\text{dark if } E \geq E_0;\ \text{bright if } E \leq E_0 \quad ...(7.57)$$

In other words, at the border of the isochromatic fringes in the processed negative

$$(It)_{border} = E_0 \quad ...(7.58)$$

If the fractional order interference n_f at the border of a fringe is represented by n_b, then from Eqs. (7.56) and (7.58) we have

$$(K \cos^2 \alpha \sin^2 \pi n_b)\, t = E_0 \quad ...(7.59)$$

or $$n_b = (1/\pi)\sin^{-1}[E_0/(K\cos^2\alpha \,.\, t)]^{1/2} \qquad ...(7.60)$$

Thus isochromatic photographs with different widths of fringes having different fractional-order interferences at the border can be obtained by varying either the exposure time t or angle α or both. However α can be varied conveniently and desired values of n_b can be obtained in the photograph by varying the angle. To eliminate the unknown factor E_0 in Eq. (7.60), a photograph of the fringes in a calibration specimen with $\alpha = 0$ may be taken. Keeping everything identical if n_b in the calibration negative is represented by n_{bc}, then

$$n_b = (1/\pi)\sin^{-1}(\sin n_{bc}\,\pi/\cos\alpha),\ \alpha \le \left(\frac{1}{2} - n_{bc}\right)\pi \qquad ...(7.61)$$

Similarly for the light-field set up

$$n_b = (1/\pi)\cos^{-1}\left[\cos\left(\frac{1}{2} - n_{bc}\right)\pi/\cos\alpha),\ \alpha \le \left(\frac{1}{2} - n_{bc}\right)\right]\pi \qquad ...(7.62)$$

The fringe border will have least fuzziness, when $n_b \approx 0.25$ and the corresponding value of α from Eq. (7.61) is

$$\alpha^* \approx \sqrt{2}\,\sin(n_{bc}\,\pi) \qquad ...(7.63)$$

7.15 Fringe Sharpening in Photoelasticity

To decrease the band width of the isochromatic fringes an ordinary circular polariscope is modified by inserting partial mirrors on both sides of the model and parallel to it. This technique was devised by D. Post in 1955 and is shown in Fig. 7.14. The effect of these partial mirrors upon the light traversing the model is shown in Fig. 7.15. The mirrors reflect part of the light and transmit part of the light that falls upon them. Thus part of the light escapes and part of the light is reflected back through the model at each mirror surface. The full lines represent light that is polarized in one direction of principal stress, and the dashed lines represent light polarized in the other principal plane. The rays are drawn oblique and displaced for clarity of presentation. Actually, normal incidence is employed and all the rays in Fig.7.15 are parallel and emerge from the same point.

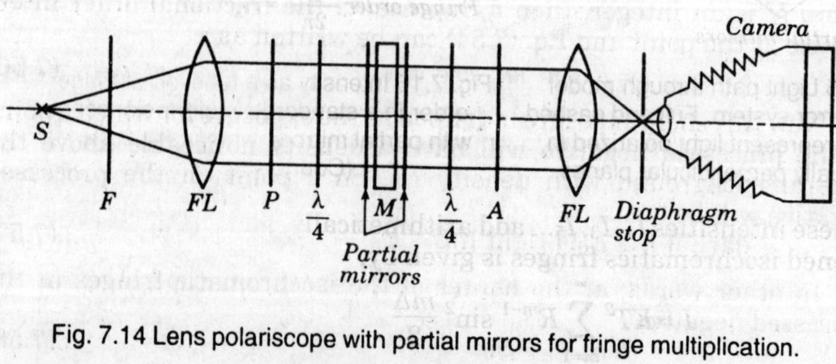

Fig. 7.14 Lens polariscope with partial mirrors for fringe multiplication.

For a standard circular polariscope $\quad I = K\sin^2\dfrac{\Delta}{2}$

The intensity of light is modified by the transmittance (T) and reflectance (R) coefficients of the mirrors. Consider ray 1, the intensity of light is lost by reflection from the partial mirrors at A and B, and the resultant intensity of light becomes,

$$I_1 = K(1-R)^2\sin^2\frac{\Delta}{2} = K.T^2\sin^2\frac{\Delta}{2}$$

Similarly the rays 3 and 3′ pass through the model three times and combine to yield the intensity

$$I_3 = KT^2R^2\sin^2 3(\Delta/2)$$

Following the same procedure, the intensity of the mth ray may be written as

$$I_m = KT^2R^{m-1}\sin^2\frac{m\Delta}{2},\ m = 1, 3, 5, 7,... \qquad ...(7.64)$$

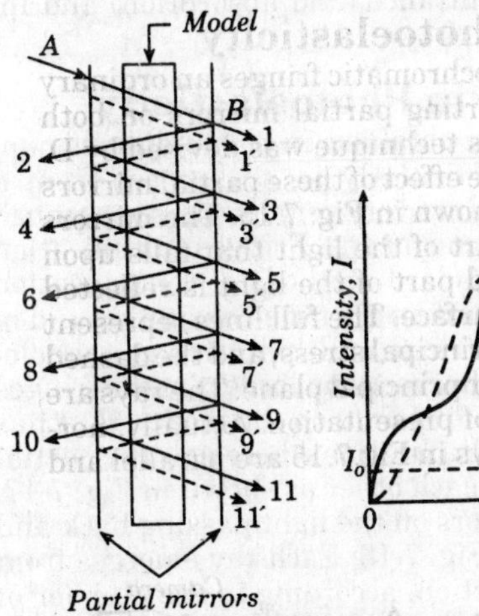

Fig. 7.15 Light path through model and mirror system. Full and dashed lines represent light polarized in mutually perpendicular planes.

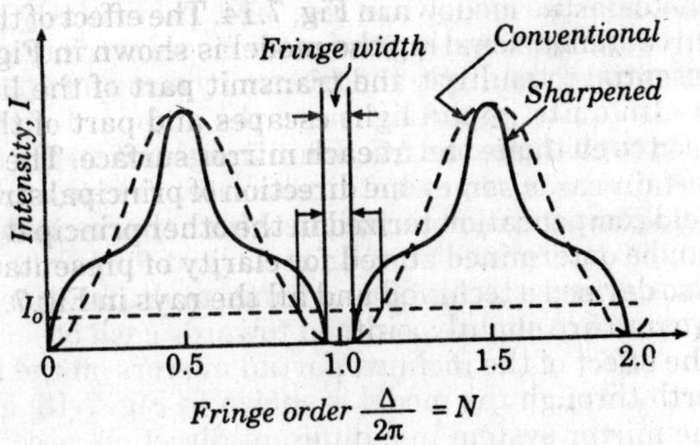

Fig. 7.16 Intensity as a function of fringe order in a standard circular polariscope with partial mirrors, whose $R = 0.85$ (Courtesy of D. Post)

These intensities I_1, I_3, I_5... add arithmetically, and the intensity of sharpened isochromatics fringes is given by,

$$I = KT^2\sum_{m=1}^{\infty} R^{m-1}\sin^2\frac{m\Delta}{2} \qquad ...(7.65)$$

If this relationship is expanded and plotted as a function of $N = \Delta/2\pi$, the intensity υ's fringe order plot as shown in Fig. 7.16 is obtained. A comparison with the conventional plot shows that the fringes are sharpened. The sharpened intensity system produces sharp peaks at integral fringe orders and at half fringe orders. It is obvious that the steep intensity gradients of the sharpened pattern permit much greater accuracy in locating the center of the fringe than the normal pattern. The intensity of the ray passing back and forth through the model decreases progressively as a result of which the peak intensity for the sharpened fringes is less than that for the normal isochromatics. If $T = 1 - R$, as is nearly obtainable with high reflectance dielectric coating (no absorption), the peak intensity reduces to

$$I_{max} = \left(\frac{T}{1+R}\right)K \quad ...(7.66)$$

Thus for $R = 0.85$, the peak intensity for the sharpened pattern is about 1/12 that of the normal peak intensity. For $R = 0.90$, the proportion is about 1/20. This decrease in fringe pattern intensity is not outside the range of comfort, and requires either a brighter light source or longer photographic exposure times, or both.

It should also be noted from Fig. 7.16 that the fringe peaks fall exactly upon the peaks of the normal isochromatic fringes, namely, at integral and half fringe order values. Thus the degree of fringe sharpening is independent of the transmittance (and absorption) and increases with increased reflectance.

7.16 Fringe Multiplication in Photoelasticity

Generally the number of fringes obtained in a two-dimensional photoelastic model are low and particularly in a slice cut from a three-dimensional stress frozen model are very very low, it is very much essential to multiply the fringes by some means. Fringe multiplication is also quite important since the standard methods of compensation used to evaluate the fractional fringe orders are time-consuming and in certain cases somewhat inaccurate. Fringe multiplication is a whole-field compensation technique where the fractional orders of the fringes can be determined simultaneously at all points on the model. Post has also devised a technique for fringe multiplication where now the partial mirrors are slightly inclined towards each other as shown in Fig. 7.17. The effect of the inclined partial mirrors on the light passing back and forth through the model is shown in Fig. 7.18. Each ray emerges from the mirror system in a different direction, according to the number of times the particular ray has traversed the model. Although the rays do not all pass through a unique point in the model, they do pass through points very close together.

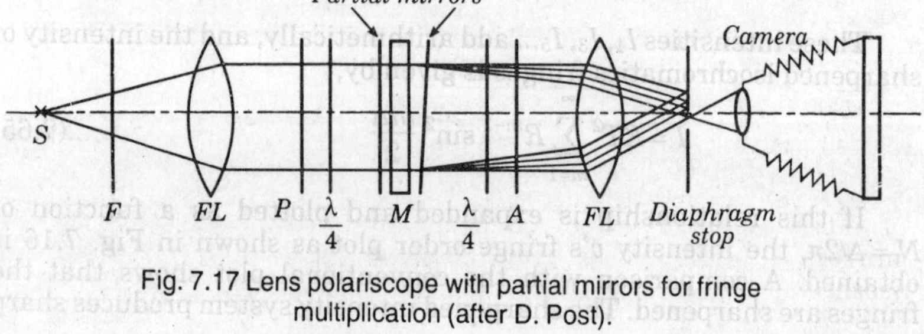

Fig. 7.17 Lens polariscope with partial mirrors for fringe multiplication (after D. Post).

The parallel beam of light that emerge from the mirror system at different angles, are converged to different points in the focal plane of the field lens. Then anyone of these beams can be observed by placing the eye or camera lens at the apex or the respective convergent light. Total isolation can be accomplished, and all the rays that traversed the model a given number of times can be observed without interference from other rays.

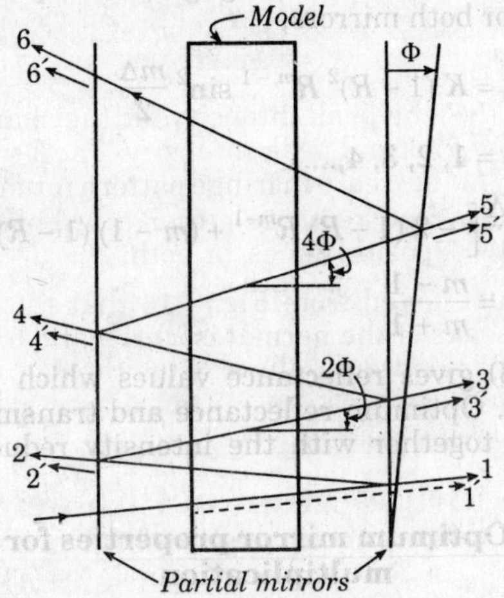

Fig. 7.18 Light path through model and slightly inclined mirror system. Full and dashed lines represent light polarized in mutually perpendicular planes.

As shown in Fig. 7.18, the rays traverse the model the same number of times as their ray number and emerge at angles ϕ, 2ϕ, 4ϕ and 6ϕ. The length of the line over which the photoelastic effect is averaged depends upon the angle of inclination ϕ, the ray number, and the separation distance between the mirrors. In practice, multiplication by factors of 5 to 7 can be achieved without introducing objectionable errors.

The intensity relationship for the mth ray can be obtained as follows :

$$I_1 = KT^2 \sin^2 \frac{\Delta}{2}$$

$$I_3 = KT^2R^2 \sin^2 3\frac{\Delta}{2} \qquad \text{...(7.67)}$$

$$I_5 = KT^2R^4 \sin^2 5\frac{\Delta}{2}$$

$$I_m = KT^2R^{m-1} \sin^2 \frac{m\Delta}{2}$$

It is assumed that the transmittance and reflectance for both mirrors is the same. The fringe shape is the same as that of ordinary isochromatics, but the number of fringes present with a given birefringent sample is m times that present in the ordinary isochromatic pattern.

Fringe multiplication by this method is accompanied by a considerable loss of light intensity. The intensity is decreased by $T^2 R^{m-1}$ compared to the intensity of ordinary isochromatics. The optimum mirror coefficient can be determined for given multiplication factors by maximizing the intensity. Then for negligible absorption $T + R = 1$, and equal reflectance for both mirrors,

$$I_m = K\,(1 - R)^2\, R^{m-1} \sin^2 \frac{m\Delta}{2}$$

$$m = 1, 2, 3, 4, \ldots\ldots$$

$$\frac{dI_m}{dR} = K \sin^2 \frac{m\Delta}{2} \left[-2\,(1 - R)\, R^{m-1} + (m-1)\,(1-R)^2 R^{m-2} \right] = 0$$

$$\therefore \quad R = \frac{m-1}{m+1} \qquad \ldots(7.68)$$

Equation (7.68) gives reflectance values which yield maximum resultant intensity. Optimum reflectance and transmittance is tabulated in Table 7.1 together with the intensity reduction coefficient $T^2 R^{m-1}$.

Table 7.1 Optimum mirror properties for fringe multiplication

Multiplication factor, m	*R*	*T*	*Intensity reduction coefficient, $T^2 R^{m-1}$*
1	0	1	1
3	0.500	0 500	0.0625
5	0.667	0.333	0.0219
7	0.750	0.250	0.0111
9	0.800	0.200	0.0067

Mirrors coated with low absorption dielectric films for reflectance of 75 to 85% would be well suited for general application of this technique. The length of the line over which the birefringence is averaged increases with distance between mirrors and with angular separation between mirrors, both of which should be made very small.

7.17 Mesnager's Theorem

According to this theorem the principal stresses tangent to a given stress trajectory are a maximum or minimum where an isoclinic cuts the stress trajectory at right angles. A stress trajectory, line of principal stress or isostatic is a line the tangents to which at every point coincides with the direction of one of the principal stresses. The Mesnager's theorem can be proved as follows :

Let S_1, S_2, S'_1 and S'_2 be the orthogonal stress trajectories as shown in Fig.7.19. Let ρ_1 and ρ_2 be the radii of S_1 and S_2 respectively. Then

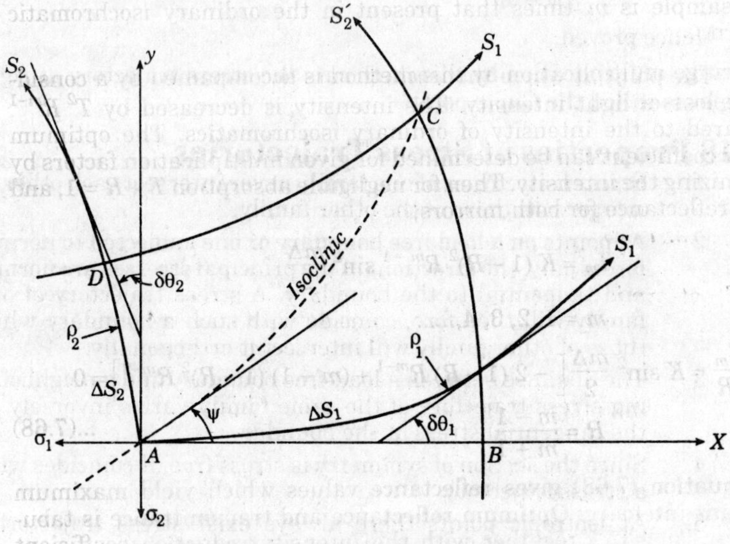

Fig. 7.19 Proving Mesnager's Theorem.

$$\delta\theta = \delta\theta_1 + \delta\theta_2 = \frac{\delta S_1}{\rho_1} + \frac{\delta S_2}{\rho_2}$$

Since points A and C lie on the isoclinic, hence $\delta\theta = 0$

Hence $$\frac{\delta S_1}{\rho_1} = -\frac{\delta S_2}{\rho_2}$$

or $$\frac{\delta S_2}{\delta S_1} = -\frac{\rho_2}{\rho_1}$$

Also $$\tan\psi = \frac{AD}{AB} = \frac{\delta S_2}{\delta S_1} = -\frac{\rho_2}{\rho_1}$$

where ψ is the angle between the isoclinic and the direction of σ_1 at A. Now Lame-Maxwell equations are

$$\frac{\partial\sigma_1}{\partial S_1} + \frac{\sigma_1 - \sigma_2}{\rho_2} = 0$$

$$\frac{\partial\sigma_2}{\partial S_2} + \frac{\sigma_1 - \sigma_2}{\rho_1} = 0$$

For σ_1 to be maximum or minimum,

$\frac{\partial\sigma_1}{\partial S_1} = 0$, which is possible from Lame-Maxwell equations,

when $\rho_2 = \infty$. Hence

$$\tan\psi = \infty$$

or $$\psi = 90^\circ$$

Hence proved.

The point at which the isoclinic cuts the stress trajectory at right angles is called the *Cupic* point.

7.18 Properties of Stress Trajectories

1. Stress trajectories of one family never intersect each other or merge with those of the other family.
2. At points on a load free boundary or one subjected to normal forces only, the directions of the principal stresses are normal and tangential to the boundary. A stress trajectory of one family will therefore, coincide with such a boundary while those of other family will intersect it orthogonally.
3. The distance between a load-free boundary and a neighbouring stress trajectory of the same family varies inversely as the tangential stress at the boundary.
4. Since the section of symmetry is stress free, it coincides with a stress trajectory.
5. At isotropic points there always exist stress trajectories which coincide with the direction of some isoclinics.
6. The stress along a stress trajectory reaches a maximum or a minimum value when the curvature of the intersecting stress trajectory is zero, *i.e.* the stress trajectory is straight or has a point of inflexion.
7. In doubly or multiply connected bodies the stress trajectories may form closed loops but not spirals.
8. The sign of $(\sigma_1 - \sigma_2)$ is constant along each stress trajectory.

7.19 Construction of Stress Trajectories

A stress trajectory, line of principal stress, or isostatic is a line such that its direction at any point coincides with that of one of the principal stresses at the point. Since the two principal stresses at any point of a two-dimensional stress system are mutually perpendicular, it follows that a system of stress trajectories will consist of two orthogonal families of curves. One of these families indicates the direction of the algebraically greater principal stress and the other those of the smaller principal stress. The following methods may be used for the construction of stress trajectories :

1. Let I_1, I_2, I_3 and I_4 be the given isoclinics of various parameters θ_1, θ_2, θ_3 and θ_4 respectively as shown in Fig. 7.20. At points on the isoclinics I_1, I_2 etc., small lines are drawn in a direction inclined to the reference direction at an angle equal to the parameters θ_1, θ_2, etc. of the respective isoclinics. The stress trajectories of one family are obtained by drawing smooth curves tangential to these lines. By drawing small lines in the perpendicular direction, the orthogonal family of stress trajectories can be obtained.

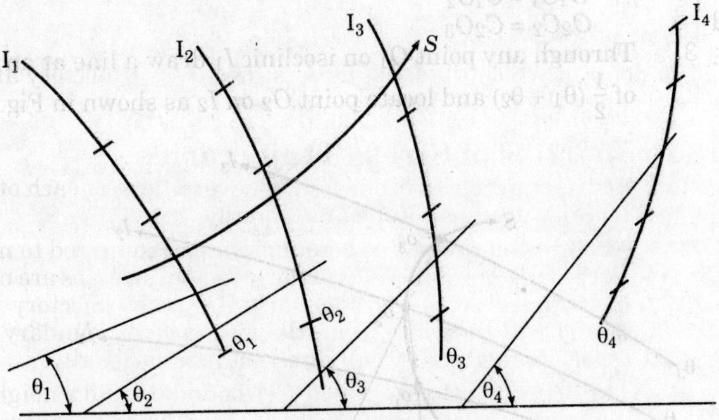

Fig. 7.20

2. When the isoclinics are more widely spaced then the method shown in Fig. 7.21 will produce more accurate results. From any point O_1 on the isoclinic I_1 of parameter θ_1, a straight line is drawn inclined at an angle $\frac{1}{2}(\theta_1 + \theta_2)$ to the reference direction to cut the isoclinic I_2 of parameter θ_2 at the point O_2. From O_2, a line is drawn at an inclination of $\frac{1}{2}(\theta_2 + \theta_3)$ to cut I_3 in O_3 and so on. Lines are then drawn through the points O_1, O_2, O_3, etc., at inclinations θ_1, θ_2, θ_3 respectively. The curve passing through the points O_1, O_2, O_3 tangential to the polygon formed by the second set of lines gives the stress trajectory of one family. The curved segments O_1O_2 and O_2O_3 of the stress trajectory S are assumed to be approximately circular in shape so that

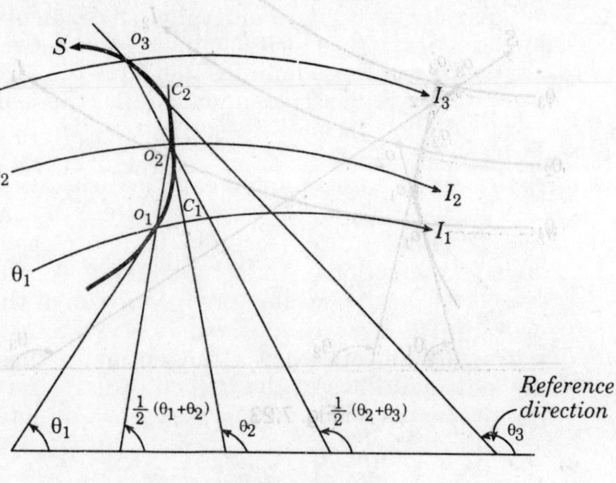

Fig. 7.21

$$O_1C_1 = C_1O_2$$

and $$O_2C_2 = C_2O_3$$

3. Through any point O_1 on isoclinic I_1 draw a line at an angle of $\frac{1}{2}(\theta_1 + \theta_2)$ and locate point O_2 on I_2 as shown in Fig. 7.22.

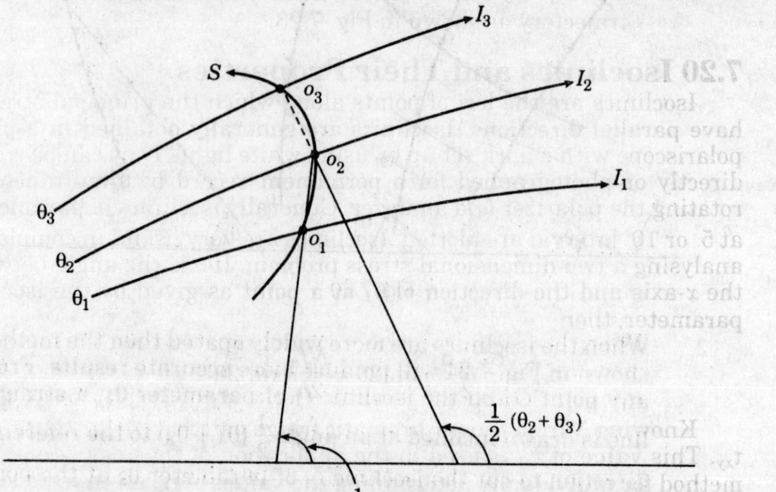

Fig. 7.22

Then draw the line from O_2 at the angle $\frac{1}{2}(\theta_2 + \theta_3)$ to locate O_3 in I_3 and so on. Join the points O_1, O_2, O_3 etc. by a free hand curve to obtain a stress trajectory of one family.

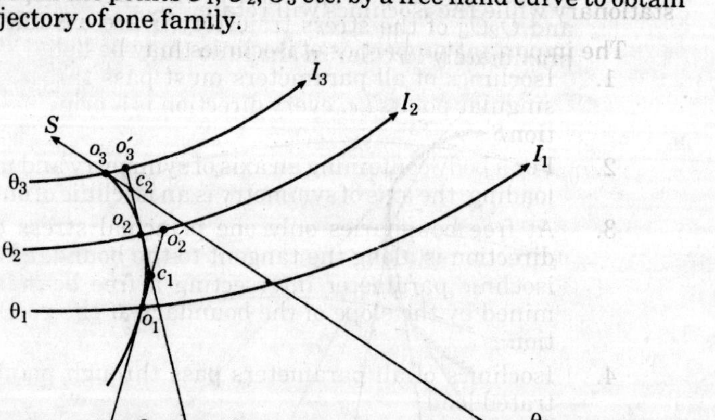

Fig. 7.23

4. At any point O_1 on I_1 draw a line at any angle of θ_1 with the reference line and produce to intersect I_2 at O'_2. Through C_1 draw a line at θ_2 to intersect I_2 at O_2 such that $O_1 C_1 = C_2 O_2$ and produce it to intersect I_3 at O_3. Through C_2 which bisects $O_2 O'_3$ draw a line at θ_3. Join the points O_1, O_2, O_3 etc. by a free hand curve to obtain the stress trajectory as shown in Fig. 7.23.

7.20 Isoclinics and Their Properties

Isoclinics are the loci of points along which the principal stresses have parallel directions. Isoclinics are generally obtained in a plane polariscope with a dark set up by using white light. They can be traced directly or photographed for a permanent record by simultaneously rotating the polarizer and analyzer. Generally isoclinics of parameters at 5° or 10° interval are plotted. Isoclinics are very useful in completely analysing a two-dimensional stress problem. If θ is the angle between the x-axis and the direction of θ_1 at a point as given by the isoclinic parameter, then

$$\tau_{xy} = \frac{\sigma_1 - \sigma_2}{2} \sin 2\theta = \frac{N f_\sigma}{2h} \sin 2\theta$$

Knowing N from the isochromatic fringe pattern, we can determine τ_{xy}. This value of τ_{xy} is used in the application of the shear difference method for individually determining the values of σ_1 and σ_2.

Generally it is easier to differentiate between the isoclinics and isochromatics in a plane polariscope using white light as a light source, as the isoclinics are the black bands crossing the multicoloured isochromatic fringes. Otherwise to ascertain the isoclinics, at a given load if the polarizer and analyzer are rotated simultaneously through the same angle in the same direction the isochromatics will remain stationary while the isoclinics will rotate.

The important properties of isoclinics may be listed as follows :

1. Isoclinics of all parameters must pass through isotropic or singular points *i.e.* every direction is a principal stress direction.
2. For a body containing an axis of symmetry and for symmetric loading, the axis of symmetry is an isoclinic of one parameter.
3. At free boundaries only one principal stress exists whose direction is along the tangent to the boundary and thus the isoclinic parameter intersecting a free boundary is determined by the slope of the boundary at the point of intersection.
4. Isoclinics of all parameters pass through points of concentrated load.
5. For isotropic points in the interior of the boundary, at least two isoclinics of different parameters should intersect.

6. Where an isoclinic cuts the stress trajectory at right angles, the principal stresses at that points are a maximum or minimum. (Mesnager's theorem).
7. The isoclinic parameter is independent of the magnitude of load applied and the fringe value of the material.
8. Isoclinics with parameters differing by 90°, 180°, etc. are identical.
9. At a point on a shear free boundary where the stress parallel to the boundary has a maximum or a minimum value, the isoclinic intersects boundary at right angles.

7.21 Fractional Fringe Order Determination

We can determine the isochromatic fringe order to the nearest $\frac{1}{2}$ order by using both the dark and bright-field arrangements of a polariscope. Further improvements on the accuracy of the fringe order determination can be achieved either by using the mixed-field patterns or by using Post's fringe multiplication method. In order to achieve higher accuracy, as is desirable in many applications, the following methods may be used :

1. Compensation techniques.
2. Colour matching techniques.
3. Equidensometry method.

7.21.1 Compensation Techniques

Compensation is a technique in which partial modification of relative retardation either by addition or subtraction is brought about so that the fractional fringe order at a point becomes integral. Then by knowing the amount of relative retardation added or substracted the actual fringe order at that point can be ascertained. The following methods for compensation techniques are most commonly used :

1. The Babinet compensation method.
2. The Babinet Soleil compensation method.
3. Tension or compression strip method.
4. Tardy method of compensation.
5. Senarmont method of compensation.
6. Photometric method.

1. The Babinet Compensation Method. The Babinet compensator uses two wedges of quarts, which is a naturally double refracting material. As shown in Fig. 7.24, one of the wedges is fixed in the instrument, while the other can be displaced relative to the first so as to alter combined thickness by means of a fine micrometer screw with graduated drum head. With micrometer screw at zero, the compensator is said to be in the neutral position. The compensator is placed in the polariscope in between the model and second quarter wave plate. The optic axis of the two wedges are orthogonal to each other. The polarized light beam is accelerated in one and retarded in the other wedge.

The relative retardation R produced when the two wedges have been displaced from their neutral position is given by,

$$R = \frac{K}{\lambda}(d - d_0)$$

$$= \frac{K}{\lambda}(t + d_0 - d_0)$$

$$= \frac{Kt}{\lambda} = \frac{K}{\lambda} x \tan \alpha \qquad \text{...(7.69)}$$

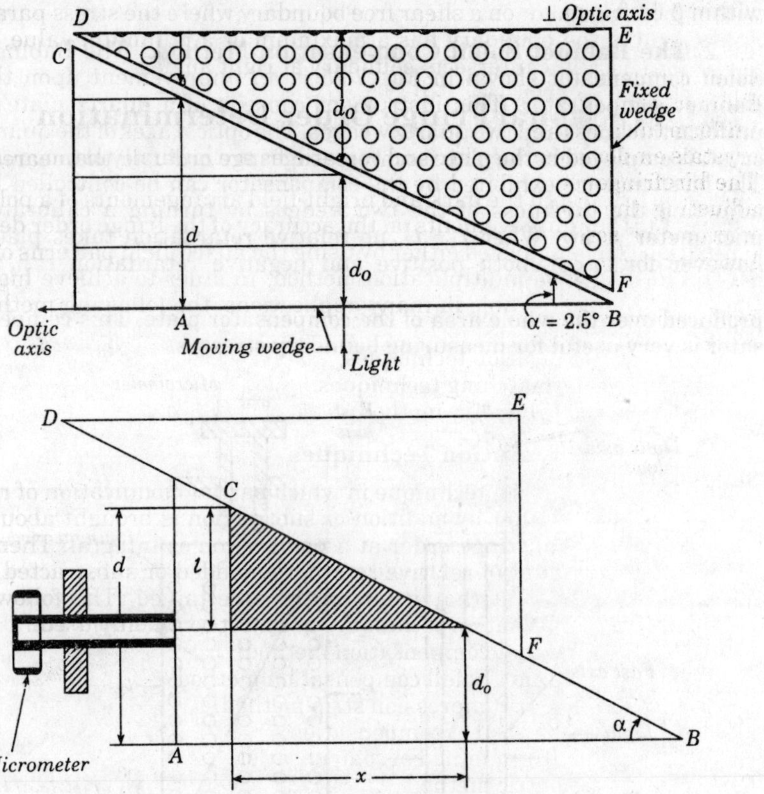

Fig. 7.24 The Babinet Compensator.

where $K = n_1 - n_2$

α = angle of wedge

$\approx 2.5^\circ$

x = horizontal displacement, which is equal to the micrometer reading

or

$$R = \left(\frac{K \tan \alpha}{\lambda}\right) . x$$

$$= C . x$$

where $C = \dfrac{K \tan \alpha}{\lambda}$ is a constant.

$$\text{Thus } R = \frac{m}{m_0} = \frac{\text{Micrometer reading}}{\left[\begin{array}{c}\text{Number of turns necessary to} \\ \text{produce a retardation of one} \\ \text{wavelength}\end{array}\right]} \quad ...(7.70)$$

The Babinet compensator allows fringe orders, to be determined to within 0.01 fringe.

2. **The Babinet Soleil Compensation Method.** The Babinet-Soleil compensator shown in Fig. 7.25 is an improvement upon the Babinet compensator. This instrument consists of a quartz plate of uniform thickness and two quartz wedges. The optical axes of the quartz crystals employed in the plate and the wedges are mutually orthogonal. The birefringence exhibited by the compensator can be controlled by adjusting the thickness of the two wedges by turning a calibrated micrometer screw. When $t_1 = t_2$, no relative retardation takes place, however for $t_2 \lessgtr t_1$, both positive and negative retardation can be produced over the whole area of the compensator plate. This compensator is very useful for measuring boundary stresses.

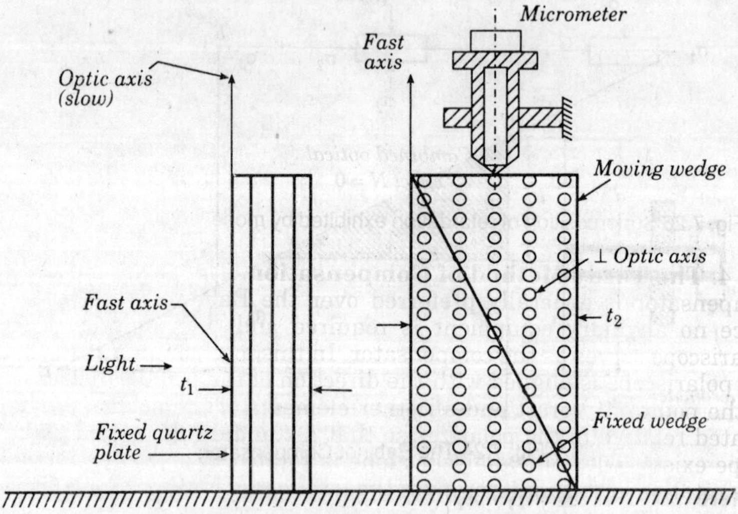

Fig. 7.25 The Babinet-Soleil Compensator.

In practice, a point is selected on the model where the fringe order is to be established precisely. Then isoclinic parameters are established for this point to give the direction of either σ_1 or σ_2. The compensator is then aligned with the principal stress direction and adjusted to cancel out the model retardation. The reading of the screw micrometer is proportional to the fringe order at that point. Like this fringe order at a point can be ascertained to within 0.001 fringe.

3. **Tension or Compression Strip Method.** In a standard circular polariscope, at an isotropic point the fringe order is always zero. Based upon this fact a method for the determination of $(\sigma_1 - \sigma_2)$ has been suggested by Wertheim and developed by Coker. In this method a pure tensile or compressive stress is superimposed over an arbitrary system of σ_1 and σ_2 in such a way as to convert the given stress system into one which is optically equivalent to an isotropic point. White light is exclusively used in this method.

Fig. 7.26 shows how the plane stress system at a point can be converted to an isotropic system plus a tension of $(\sigma_1 - \sigma_2)$. A tension compensator may be placed parallel to the minimum stress σ_2 and the compression compensator must be placed parallel to the maximum stress σ_1. The value of $(\sigma_1 - \sigma_3)$ equals numerically the stress in the compensator at extinction. If the fringe order at a point by placing a tension compensator increases, then that point is having tensile stress.

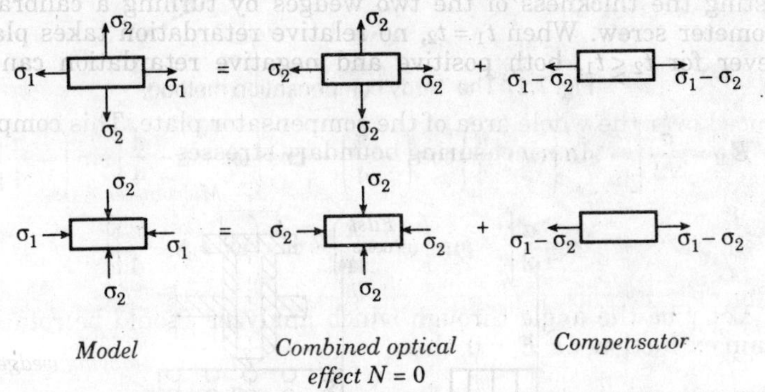

Fig. 7.26 Superposition of retardation exhibited by model and compensator.

4. **The Tardy Method of Compensation.** The Tardy method of compensator is generally preferred over the Babinet-Soleil method since no auxiliary equipment is required and the analyzer of the polariscope serves as the compensator. In this method the polarizer of the polariscope is aligned with the direction of the principal stress σ_1 at the point of interest and all other elements of the polariscope are rotated relative to the polarizer so that a standard dark-field polariscope exists. Then the analyzer alone is rotated to obtain extinction. The rotation of the analyzer gives the fractional fringe order.

As shown in Fig. 7.27, here $\theta = -\pi/4$ and the light vector emerging out from the second QWP becomes (see Art. 7.9.1).

$$E_{3l} = -\frac{a}{\sqrt{2}}\left[\sin\left(\omega t + \Delta - \frac{\pi}{4}\right)\cos\left(-\frac{\pi}{4}\right) - \cos\left(\omega t - \frac{\pi}{4}\right)\sin\left(-\frac{\pi}{4}\right)\right]$$

$$= -\frac{a}{2}\left[\sin\left(\omega t + \Delta - \frac{\pi}{4}\right) + \cos\left(\omega t - \frac{\pi}{4}\right)\right]$$

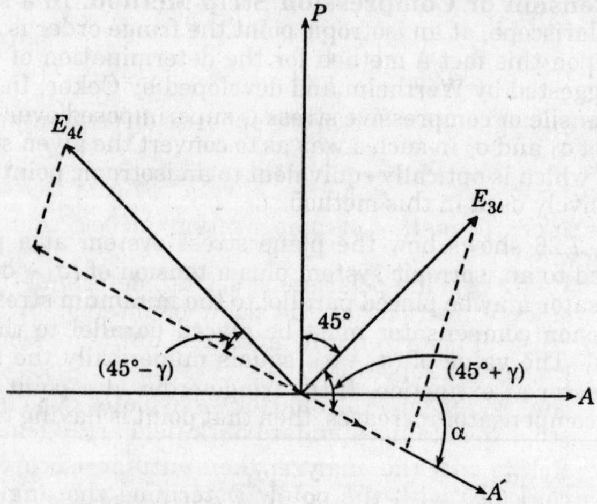

Fig. 7.27 The Tardy compensation method.

$$E_{4l} = \frac{a}{\sqrt{2}}\left[-\sin\left(\omega t - \frac{\pi}{4}\right)\cos\left(-\frac{\pi}{4}\right) + \cos\left(\omega t + \Delta - \frac{\pi}{4}\right)\sin\left(-\frac{\pi}{4}\right)\right]$$

$$= \frac{a}{2}\left[-\sin\left(\omega t - \frac{\pi}{4}\right) - \cos\left(\omega t + \Delta - \frac{\pi}{4}\right)\right]$$

Let γ be the angle through which analyzer should be rotated to obtain extinction, *i.e.* $E_t = 0$, then

$$E_t = E_{4l}\cos\left(\frac{\pi}{4} - \gamma\right) - E_{3l}\cos\left(\frac{\pi}{4} + \gamma\right)$$

$$= -\frac{a}{2}\left[\sin\left(\omega t - \frac{\pi}{4}\right) + \cos\left(\omega t + \Delta - \frac{\pi}{4}\right)\right]\cos\left(\frac{\pi}{4} - \gamma\right)$$

$$+ \frac{a}{2}\left[\sin\left(\omega t + \Delta - \frac{\pi}{4}\right) + \cos\left(\omega t - \frac{\pi}{4}\right)\right]\cos\left(\frac{\pi}{4} + \gamma\right)$$

Simplifying, we get

$$E_l = a\sin\left(\omega t + \frac{\Delta}{2}\right)\left\{\sin\left(\frac{\Delta}{2} - \gamma\right)\right\} = 0$$

Hence $\quad \sin\left(\frac{\Delta}{2} - \gamma\right) = 0$

or $\quad \frac{\Delta}{2} - \gamma = n\pi,\ n = 0, 1, 2, \ldots.$

or $\quad \frac{\Delta}{2} = n\pi + \gamma$

or $$N = \frac{\Delta}{2\pi} = n + \frac{\gamma}{\pi} \quad ...(7.71)$$

If the analyzer is rotated in the opposite direction, then

$$N = (n+1) - \frac{\gamma}{\pi} \quad ...(7.72)$$

Thus the Tardy method of compensation can be accomplished in the following way :

1. Using a plane-polariscope set up, determine the principal stress directions at the point of interest by rotating the crossed polarizer and analyzer until an isoclinic passes through that point.
2. Now rotate only the quarter wave plates of a circular polariscope to obtain a standard dark-field arrangement.
3. Rotate only the analyzer then until an isochromatic fringe coincides with the point. Determine the angle γ that the analyzer has rotated.
4. If the Nth order fringe moves to the point as the analyzer rotates through the angle γ, the fringe order N_0 at the point is

$$N_0 = N + \frac{\gamma}{\pi}$$

If the $(N+1)$st order fringe moves to the point as the analyzer rotates through the angle γ, the fringe order N_0 at the point is

$$N_0 = (N+1) - \frac{\gamma}{\pi}$$

To account for the finite fringe width, the following procedure, as illustrated in Fig. 7.28, may be followed :

1. The angle of anlayzed $r_a = 0$ [Fig. 7.28 (*a*)].
2. Rotate the analyzer until the fringe N just touches the boundary at the point of interest. This is angle r_b. [Fig. 7.28 (*b*)].

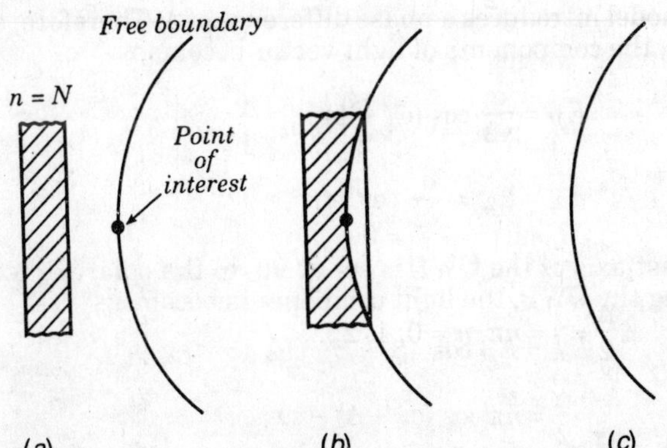

Fig. 7.28 Illustration of Tardy method of fringe order determination.

3. Continue to rotate the analyzer until N vanishes from the field of view. This is angle r_c. [Fig. 7.28 (*c*)].

Then the fringe order at the point of interest of the free boundary is

$$N_0 = N + \frac{r_b + r_c}{360}$$

This method is commonly referred to as the Tardy in-out method.

5. **The Senarmont Method of Compensation.**

(Friedel's Method)

The following steps are involved for this method :

1. Remove first quarter wave plate.
2. Rotate system of polarizer and analyzer so that their axes make angles of 45° with the principal directions in the modal at the point of interest.
3. Rotate second quarter-wave plate until one axis is parallel to the axis of the polarizer.
4. Rotate the analyzer until extinction is obtained at the point of interest.

The arrangement of the elements of the polariscope are shown in Fig. 7.29.

Let the light vector from the polarizer be given by

$$E = a \cos \omega t$$

Since the polarizer is set at 45° to the principal directions in the model hence on entering the model the light vector is resolved into two components, given by

$$E_{1e} = a \cos \omega t \,.\, \cos 45^\circ = \frac{1}{\sqrt{2}} a \cos \omega t$$

$$E_{2e} = a \cos \omega t \,.\, \sin 45^\circ = \frac{1}{\sqrt{2}} a \cos \omega t$$

The model introduces a phase difference of Δ. Therefore, on leaving the model, the components of light vector become,

$$E_{1l} = \frac{a}{\sqrt{2}} \cos (\omega t + \Delta)$$

$$E_{2l} = E_{2e} = \frac{a}{\sqrt{2}} \cos \omega t$$

The fast axis of the QWP is set at 90° to the polarizer axis. Hence on entering the QWP, the light components become

$$E_{ac} = E_{1l} \cos 45^\circ - E_{2l} \cos 45^\circ$$

$$= \frac{a}{2} [\cos (\omega t + \Delta) - \cos \omega t]$$

$$E_{bc} = E_{1l} \cos 45^\circ + E_{2l} \cos 45^\circ$$

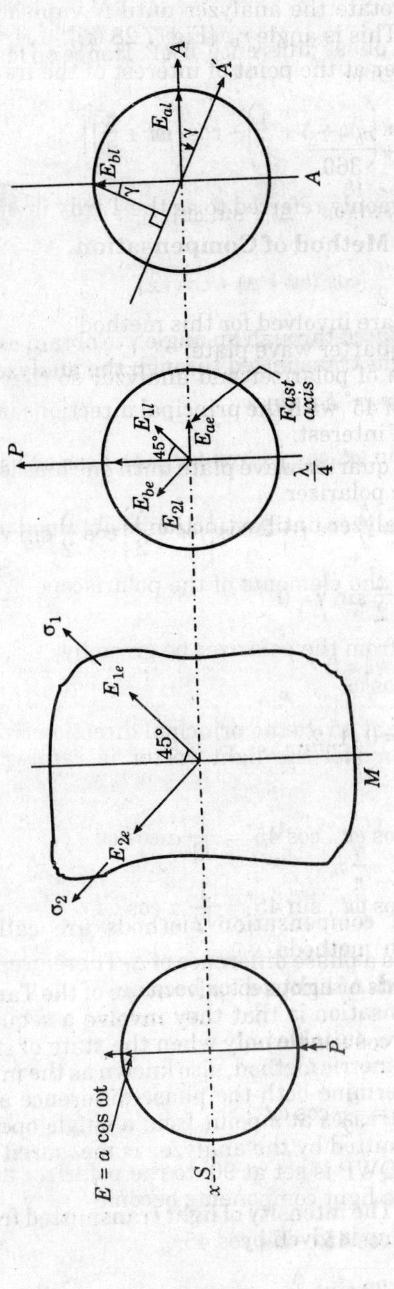

Fig. 7.29 Senarmont compensation method.

$$= \frac{a}{2} [\cos (\omega t + \Delta) + \cos \omega t]$$

The QWP introduces a phase difference of $\pi/2$. Hence on leaving the QWP, the light vectors become,

$$E_{al} = \frac{a}{2}\left[\cos\left(\omega t + \Delta + \frac{\pi}{2}\right) - \cos\left(\omega t + \frac{\pi}{2}\right)\right]$$

$$= \frac{a}{2} [-\sin (\omega t + \Delta) + \sin \omega t]$$

$$E_{bl} = E_{bc} = \frac{a}{2} [\cos (\omega t + \Delta) + \cos \omega t]$$

Now the analyzer is rotated through an angle γ to obtain extinction at the point of interest. Light transmitted through the analyzer is

$$E_t = E_{al} \cos \gamma - E_{bt} \sin \gamma$$

$$= -\frac{a}{2} [\{\sin (\omega t + \Delta) - \sin \omega t\} \cos \gamma + \{\cos (\omega t + \Delta) + \cos \omega t\} \sin \gamma]$$

$$= -\frac{a}{2}\left[2 \cos\left(\omega t + \frac{\Delta}{2}\right) \sin \frac{\Delta}{2} \cos \gamma + 2 \cos\left(\omega t + \frac{\Delta}{2}\right) \cos \frac{\Delta}{2} \sin \gamma\right] = 0$$

Hence $\sin \frac{\Delta}{2} \cos \gamma + \cos \frac{\Delta}{2} \sin \gamma = 0$

$$\sin\left(\frac{\Delta}{2} + \gamma\right) = 0$$

or

$$\frac{\Delta}{2} + \gamma = n\pi, \; n = 0, 1, 2, \ldots$$

$$\frac{\Delta}{2} = n\pi - \gamma$$

$$N = \frac{\Delta}{2\pi} = n - \frac{\gamma}{\pi} \qquad \ldots(7.73)$$

Tardy and Senarmont compensation methods are called the 'goniometric' or 'null location' methods.

6. **Photometric Method.** A serious disadvantage of the Tardy and Friedel's methods of compensation is that they involve a sequence of operations and are, therefore, suitable only when the state of stress is static. By means of the photometric method, also known as the intensity method it is possible to determine both the phase difference and the directions of the principal stresses at a point from a single operation. The intensity of light transmitted by the analyzer is measured with a photocell or photo-multiplier.

(*a*) **Plane polariscope.** The intensity of light transmitted from the analyzer for a dark-field set up is given by

$$I_1 \propto a^2 \sin^2 2\theta \sin^2 \frac{\Delta}{2}$$

and with the bright-field set up, we have

$$I_2 \propto a^2\left(1 - \sin^2 2\theta \sin^2 \frac{\Delta}{2}\right)$$

I_1 is maximum when $\theta = 45^\circ$ at which angle I_2 is minimum. Hence

$$I_{1\max} \propto \sin^2 \frac{\Delta}{2} \propto \frac{1}{2}(1 - \cos \Delta)$$

$$I_{2\min} \propto \left(1 - \sin^2 \frac{\Delta}{2}\right) \propto \cos^2 \frac{\Delta}{2} \propto \frac{1}{2}(1 + \cos \Delta)$$

$$\frac{I_{2\min}}{I_{1\max}} = \frac{1 + \cos \Delta}{1 - \cos \Delta}$$

or $$\cos \Delta = \frac{I_{2\min} - I_{1\max}}{I_{1\max} + I_{2\min}} \qquad \text{...(7.74)}$$

To apply the method, a travelling microscope is first focused at the desired point on the image of the model on the camera screen. The eyepiece of the microscope is then removed and photomultiplier head substituted in the eyepiece tube. Crossed polarizer and analyzer are now rotated until the intensity transmitted is maximum and the corresponding value of $I_{1\max}$ is noted. The analyzer is then rotated independently through 90° to obtain $I_{2\min}$. The phase difference is then obtained from Eq. (7.74). The directions of the principal stresses are at 45° to those of the axes of the polaroids. It is always advisable to use white light as it is not possible to determine the directions of the principal stresses with monochromatic light when the phase difference is a whole number of wavelength.

(*b*) **Circular polariscope.** For the standard circular polariscope with dark-field set up

$$I_1 \propto a^2 \sin^2 \frac{\Delta}{2} \propto \frac{a^2}{2}(1 - \cos \Delta)$$

and with bright-field set up

$$I_2 \propto a^2 \cos^2 \frac{\Delta}{2} \propto \frac{a^2}{2}(1 + \cos \Delta)$$

Hence, as for the plane polariscope, we have

$$\cos \Delta = \frac{I_{2\min} - I_{1\max}}{I_{1\max} + I_{2\min}} \qquad \text{...(7.75)}$$

In the circular polariscope the intensity transmitted is independent of the directions of the principal stresses in the model so that these cannot be determined. The phase difference, however, can be obtained with no movement at all of the elements of the polariscope. This method is, therefore, particularly suitable when the state of stress varies rapidly with time if the directions of the principal stresses is not required. The major sources of error of the method are :

(*i*) The intensity of light is measured over a finite area instead of at a point.
(*ii*) The effect of stray light.
(*iii*) Inaccuracies in the quarter-wave plates.

7.21.2 Colour Matching Technique

The isochromatics in a field of non-uniform stress field obtained with white light source vary in colour as the different constituent wavelengths are successively extinguished. The intensity transmitted of any given wavelength λ in the standard circular polariscope is proportional to $\sin^2 \Delta/2$ or $\sin^2 \pi R/\lambda$, where R is the relative retardation. Each wavelength or colour is extinguished in turn wherever $R = N\lambda$. The remaining colours are transmitted with different intensities depending on the wavelength and the colour observed is the complementary colour to that extinguished. Thus, any value of the retardation produces a characteristic colour of the transmitted light. Table 7.2 gives the visible spectrum.

Table 7.2 The Visible Spectrum

Wavelength range, Å	4000 to 4500	4500 to 4800	4800 to 5100	5100 to 5500	5500 to 5700	5700 to 5900	5900 to 6300	6300 to 7000
Colour	Violet	Blue	Blue-Green	Green	Yellow-Green	Yellow	Orange	Red

Table 7.3 Retardation Values and Colours Produced in a Dark Field White-light Source Polariscope

Colour	*Retardation,* Å	*Fringe order N*
Black	0	0
Gray	1600	0.28
White	2600	0.45
Yellow	3500	0.60
Orange	4600	0.79
Red	5200	0.90
Tint of passage 1*	5770	1.00
Blue	6200	1.06
Blue-Green	7000	1.20
Green-Yellow	8000	1.38
Orange	9400	1.62
Red	10500	1.81
Tint of passage 2*	11500	2.00
Green	13500	2.33
Green Yellow	14500	2.50
Pink	15500	2.67
Tint of passage 3*	17300	3.00

(*Table Contd...*)

Colour	*Retardation*, Å	*Fringe order N*
Green	18000	3.10
Pink	21000	3.60
Tint of passage 4*	23000	4.00
Green	24000	4.13

Note : * The tint of passage is a sharp dividing zone occupying between red and blue in the first-order fringe, red and green in the second order fringe and pink and green in the third, fourth, and fifth order fringes. Beyond five fringes, white light analysis is not adequate.

To use the method a simple tensile test is carried out and a table is then prepared of the colours observed and fringe order as the load is gradually increased for the light source used. Table 7.3 gives corresponding values of the retardation and the colour transmitted in a standard circular polariscope with a white light source giving continuous spectrum. This is an approximate method and depends upon the eye of the observer.

7.21.3 Equidensometry method

The compensation methods discussed so far are the point by point methods and the model is under load for a long time and subsequent rectification of errors may demand a repetition of the test set up. In the equidensity method, a number of photographs are taken with different exposure times or even a single photograph can provide a complete and permanent record which may be evaluated for fractional fringe orders at any later time.

A conventional black and white low contrast photograph of an isochromatic pattern exhibits continuous changes in density between the fringe centre lines. These changes can be quantified by various techniques of producing lines of constant density, so called equidensities, which represent constant fractional fringe orders.

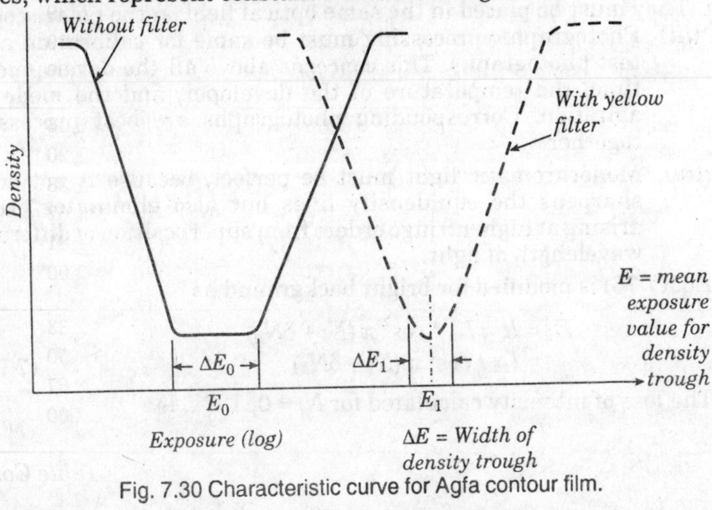

Fig. 7.30 Characteristic curve for Agfa contour film.

A conventional photographic film has a characteristic given by the Hurter-Driffield curve as shown in Fig. 7.10. A low contrast film with a moderate slope γ gives a wide range of half tones, a high contrast film with γ nearly 90° gives a sharp transition from black to white. Agfa contour film has combined descending and ascending characteristics as shown in Fig. 7.30.

In a monochromatic circularly polarized optical field with a loaded model and crossed polaroids, the exposure value for any point of the film is

$$E = It = I_o t \sin^2 \pi N = I_o t \sin^2 \pi (N_1 \pm \delta N) \quad ...(7.76)$$

where I = intensity of monochromatic light transmitted through a point in the model to the corresponding point on the film

t = exposure time

I_o = maximum transmitted intensity

N = exact fringe order value at the point in the model

N_i = 0, 1, 2,.., nearest integral fringe order.

$0 < \delta N < 0.5$, the fractional fringe order at the point.

As the developed film is transparent whenever $E = E_1$ (Fig. 7.30), transparent lines characterized by a particular pair of values $\pm\, \delta N$ will appear, one line on each side of the centre line of every integral fringe of order N_1. A change in exposure time t results in transparent lines for different values of $I = E_1/t$ and , hence, for a different pair of values of $\pm\, \delta N$. A change from dark to bright field also changes the values of δN for the transparent lines, except where $N = \pm\, 0.250$.

A number of conditions must be obeyed if this value is used for the calibration of δN in other equidensity photographs, as given below :

(*i*) I_o must be uniform over the field

(*ii*) I_o must be same for calibration piece and test model.

They must have the same thickness and the same transmission of light. They must be placed in the same optical field on the polariscope.

(*iii*) Photographic processing must be same for calibration and test photographs. This concerns above all the development time, the temperature of the developer, and the mode of agitation. Corresponding photographs are best processed together.

(*iv*) Monochromatic light must be perfect, because it not only sharpens the equidensity lines but also eliminates error arising at higher fringe orders from superposition of different wavelength of light.

Eq. (7.76) is modified for bright background as

$$E_1 = It = I_{oa}\, t \cos^2 \pi (N_i + \delta N_a)$$
$$= I_{ob}\, t \cos^2 \pi (N_i + \delta N_b) \quad ...(7.77)$$

The loss of intensity calculated for N_i = 0, 1, 2.., is

$$1-\frac{I_{ob}}{I_{oa}}=1-\frac{\cos^2 \pi\delta N_a}{\cos^2 \pi\delta N_b}=19\%.$$

Fractional fringe orders can also be obtained by a special photographic technique, known as *pseudo-solarization.* Pseudo-solarization or *Sabattier effect* is the "partial reversal" of the image obtained when the film is given a limited exposure to uniform light during development and when thus consequently the less exposed areas of the negative are preferentially darkened to a certain extent.

If a photographic material receives large differences in exposure over two adjacent areas and if the development is carried out without agitation, dark lines are formed just within the highly exposed areas in the developed image. These lines, which are in contrast with results expected from the characteristic curve of the material, are called *Mackie lines.*

In photoelasticity pseudo-solarization produces sharply defined equidensity lines or isochromatics of partial fringe order $N = N_i \pm \delta N$ with one line on either side of each integer or half order fringe N_i. The order N or partial orders δN of these sharp equidensity lines or isochromatics can be determined by suitable calibration so that the evaluation of the photoelastic pattern can be facilitated by recourse to additional isochromatic lines of fractional order without the need for additional equipment.

7.22 Calibration Techniques

The photoelastic material has to be calibrated to determine the material fringe value f_σ so as to convert the fringe orders into stresses. The following methods may be used to calibrate a photoelastic model.

1. **Simple tensile specimen.** If we prepare a simple tensile specimen as shown in Fig. 7.31 (*a*), whose width is w and thickness h, then under load P, the uniform stress in the test specimen is

$$\sigma_1 - \sigma_2 = P/wh, \sigma_2 = 0$$

Applying stress optic law, we get

$$\sigma_1 - \sigma_2 = \frac{Nf_\sigma}{h}$$

or
$$\frac{P}{wh} = \frac{Nf_\sigma}{h}$$

Hence
$$f_\sigma = \left(\frac{P}{N}\right)\frac{1}{w} \qquad \text{...(7.78)}$$

In the tensile specimen, we get escaping type of fringes, *i.e.* as the load is increased from zero, successive fringe appear in the field of view and disappear as the load is increased. Generally a graph is plotted between the load applied P and fringe order N as shown in Fig. 7.31 (*b*) and its slope is determined, which is substituted in Eq. (7.78) to determine f_σ. In this method the load P has to be adjusted to have a full fringe order in the field of view. In another technique, the Tardy method of compensation is used, where for a particular load P the extinction angles γ are plotted against the applied stress σ_1. Then by knowing the slope of the curve, we have

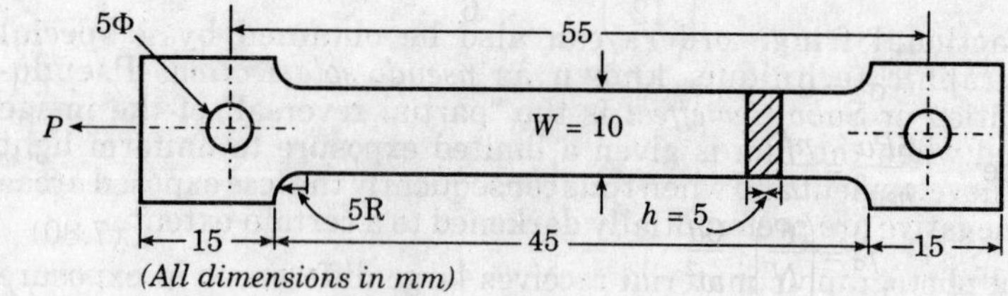

(a) Tensile calibration specimen.

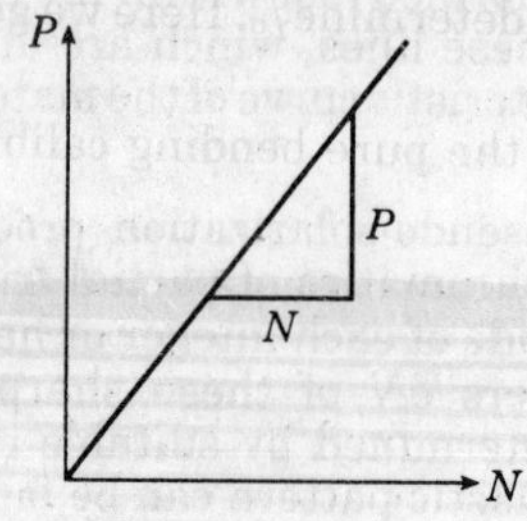

(b) Pv'sN curve.

Fig. 7.30

$$f_\sigma = \left(\frac{\sigma_1}{\gamma}\right) . h . 180^\circ \qquad ...(7.79)$$

In a similar way a compression test piece may also be used.

2. **Beam under pure bending.** A rectangular beam of thickness h and depth w as shown in Fig. 7.32 may be used and subjected to pure bending to determine f_σ. Pure bending in the beam may be produced by applying equal loads P at a distance 'a' from the ends of a beam of length l as shown. The uniform bending moment M in the middle portion of the beam is

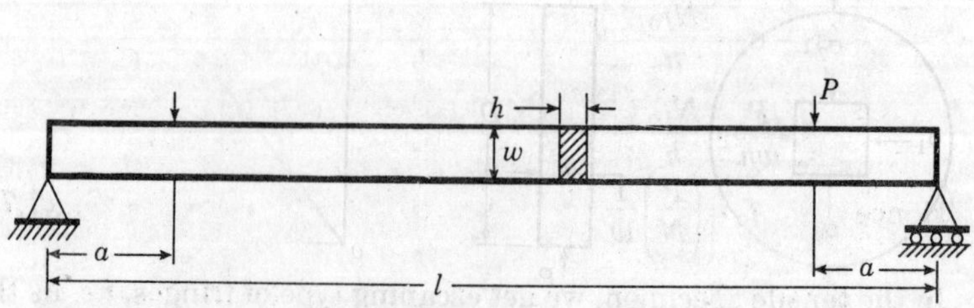

$l = 150,\ a = 25,\ h = 6,\ w = 20$ (*all mm*)

Fig. 7.32 Pure bending calibration specimen.

$$M = Pa$$

The stresses in the beam are

$$\sigma_1 = \frac{M}{I} \cdot y = \frac{Pa}{\left(\frac{hw^3}{12}\right)} \cdot \frac{w}{2} = \frac{Pa}{\frac{hw^2}{6}}$$

$$\sigma_2 = 0$$

Hence $$\frac{6Pa}{hw^2} = \frac{nf_\sigma}{h}$$

or $$f_\sigma = \left(\frac{P}{N}\right) \cdot \frac{6a}{w^2} \qquad \text{...(7.80)}$$

A graph is plotted between P and N and the slope of the curve is substituted in Eq. (7.80) to determine f_σ. Here we get non-escaping type of fringes.

The fringe pattern in the pure bending calibration specimen are shown in Fig. 7.33.

Fig. 7.33 Fringe patterns in pure bending.

3. Circular disc under diametral compression. For a circular disc diameter D and thickness h as shown in Fig. 7.34, when subjected to a diametral compressive load P, the stresses along the horizontal diameter are given by

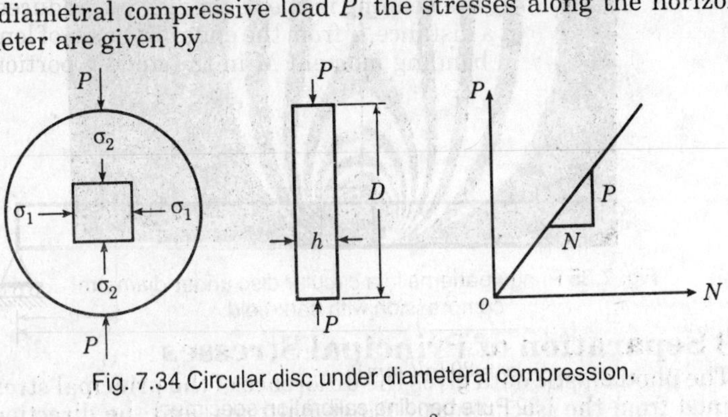

Fig. 7.34 Circular disc under diameteral compression.

$$\sigma_x = \sigma_1 = \frac{2P}{\pi hD}\left[\frac{D^2 - 4x^2}{D^2 + 4x^2}\right]^2$$

$$\sigma_y\ \sigma_2 = \frac{2P}{\pi hD}\left[\frac{4D^4}{(D^2+4x^2)^2} - 1\right] \quad \tau_{xy} = 0$$

Then $$\sigma_1 - \sigma_2 = \frac{8P}{\pi hD}\left\{\frac{[1-4\,(x/D)^2]}{[1+4\,(x/D)^2]^2}\right\}$$

$$= \frac{8P}{\pi hD}\, g\left(\frac{x}{D}\right) \qquad \text{...(7.81)}$$

At the centre, *i.e.* $x = 0$,

$$\sigma_1 = \frac{2P}{\pi hD} \text{ and } \sigma_2 = -\frac{6P}{\pi hD}. \text{ Hence}$$

$$\sigma_1 - \sigma_2 = \frac{8P}{\pi hD} = \frac{Nf_\sigma}{h}$$

$$\therefore \quad f_\sigma = \left(\frac{P}{N}\right)\left(\frac{8}{\pi D}\right) \qquad \text{...(7.82)}$$

By knowing the value of P for a particular fringe order N at the centre of the disc, a graph can be plotted, whose slope is substituted in Eq. (7.82) to determine the value of f_σ.

The fringe pattern in the circular disc are shown in Fig. 7.35 with dark-field set up.

Fig. 7.35 Fringe patterns in a circular disc under diametral compression with dark-field.

7.23 Separation of Principal Stresses

The photoelastic data gives the difference of the principal stresses, obtained from the isochromatic fringe patterns, and the directions of the principal stresses, obtained from the isoclinic fringe patterns. At free boundaries, one of the principal stresses which is normal to the boundary is zero, therefore, the isochromatic data yield directly the value of the other principal stress. At interior points of the model, individual values of the principal stresses cannot be determined from the isochromatic and isoclinic fringe patterns and, therefore, some supplementary methods have to be employed to separate the principal stresses. The following methods are generally used to separate the principal stresses :

1. Methods based on the equilibrium equations
   (*a*) The shear difference method
      (*i*) Graphical (*ii*) Numerical
   (*b*) Filon's method.
2. Methods based on the compatibility equations
   (*a*) Relaxation method
   (*b*) Analogous method
   (*c*) Analytic separation method.
3. Methods based on Hooke's law
   (*a*) Lateral extensometers
   (*b*) Optical interferometers.
4. Oblique incidence methods.

1. **Methods based on the equilibrium equations.** These methods are based on the equations of equilibrium and are thus independent of the elastic constants of the photoelastic material. The shear difference method is based on the graphical or numerical integration of the equilibrium equations whereas the Filon's method is based on the numerical integration of the Lame-Maxwell equations.

(*a*) **The Shear-difference method**

(*i*) *Graphical method.* In this method, the equilibrium conditions of elements cut parallel to Cartesian Co-ordinates are used. The shear stresses are registered by means of lines of constant shear stress. The values needed for plotting these lines are read from a nomogram, as shown in Fig. 7.36, in which, lines of constant shear stress are horizontal lines, while the isochromatics are circles, and the isoclinics are radial lines. The dimension of τ_{xy} is identical with that of the parameter of the isochromatics, *i.e.* fringe order, wavelength etc.

For determining the lines τ_{xy} = constant, the isochromatics and isoclinics are drawn, preferably in different colours, on one sheet of paper while another sheet of paper, a transparent one is placed on it. The lines of constant shear stress are registered on the latter, in a third colour. The parameters of isochromatics and isoclinics respectively, which correspond to a certain value of shear stress, can be read from the nomogram. So any line of constant shear stress can easily be traced.

The isoclinic of $\theta = 0^\circ$ is identical with the line $\tau_{xy} = 0$ and so are all vertical or horizontal load-free edges of the model. At intersections with the isoclinic $\theta = 45^\circ$, the line τ_{xy} = constant has the direction of the isochromatic. Its parameter is half of that of the isochromatic. A line τ_{xy} = const. will not cross the isochromatic which has twice its parameter but will be within that part of the field where the parameters of the isochromatics are higher

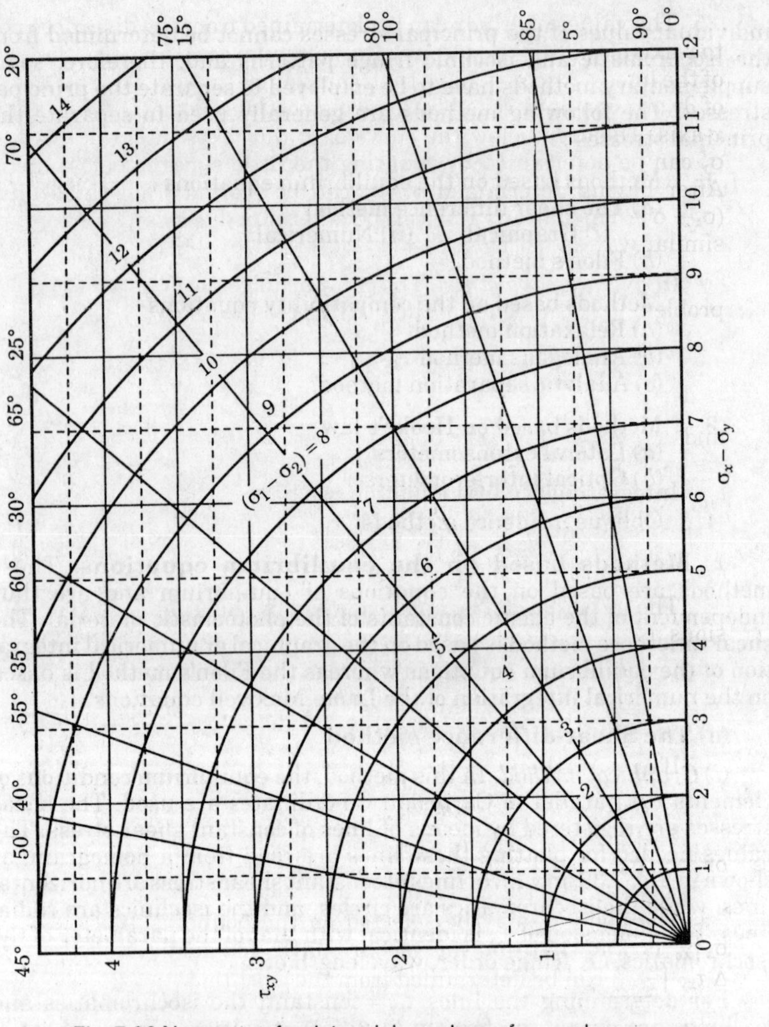

Fig. 7.36 Nomogram for determining values of τ_{xy} and $\sigma_x - \sigma_y$ from those of θ and $\sigma_1 - \sigma_2$.

As the parameters of the isochromatics are proportional to those of the line τ_{xy} = constant at intersections with a certain isoclinic, most of the lines τ_{xy} = constant can be drawn in a short time with these figures alone.

Using equilibrium equation

$$\frac{\partial \sigma_y}{\partial y} + \frac{\partial \tau_{xy}}{\partial x} = 0$$

$$\sigma_{y1} = -\int_0^1 \frac{\partial \tau_{xy}}{\partial x}\, dy + \sigma_{y0}$$

The values of $\partial\tau_{xy}/\partial x$ can be determined from the distances parallel to x-axis of the lines τ_{xy} = const. Its maximum occurs where the distances of the lines τ_{xy} = const. have their minimum. In case of doubt, the values of $\partial\tau_{xy}/\partial x$ can be checked by drawing sections of the hill parallel to the x-axis. The area below the curve of $\partial\tau_{xy}/\partial x$ is its integral, *i.e.* σ_y. Thus σ_y can be determined by counting the little squares below the curve. After having determined σ_y, σ_x can be plotted from this value and $(\sigma_x - \sigma_y)$. This latter value can be determined from the nomogram in a similar way as τ_{xy}. Then $\sigma_x = (\sigma_x - \sigma_y) + \sigma_y$.

(ii) Numerical method. The equilibrium equations for a plane stress problem in the absence of the body forces are

$$\frac{\partial\sigma_x}{\partial x} + \frac{\partial\tau_{xy}}{\partial y} = 0$$

and
$$\frac{\partial\tau_{xy}}{\partial x} + \frac{\partial\sigma_y}{\partial y} = 0$$

Integrating the first equation, we have

$$\int_{x_0}^{x_1} \frac{\partial\sigma_x}{\partial x}\, dx = -\int_{x_0}^{x_1} \frac{\partial\tau_{xy}}{\partial y}\, dx$$

The integrals can be approximated by the finite-difference expressions as

$$\sigma_x\big|_{x_1} - \sigma_x\big|_{x_0} = -\left.\frac{\Delta\tau_{xy}}{\Delta y}\right|_{\frac{x_0+x_1}{2}} .\ \Delta x$$

If $\Delta x = \Delta y$, then

$$\sigma_x\big|_{x_1} - \sigma_x\big|_{x_0} = -\,\Delta\,\tau_{xy}\big|_{\frac{x_0+x_1}{2}}$$

or
$$\sigma_x\big|_{x_1} = \sigma_x\big|_{x_0} - \Delta\,\tau_{xy}\big|_{\frac{x_0+x_1}{2}} = \sigma_x\big|_{x_0} - [(\tau_{xy})_a - (\tau_{xy})_b] \qquad ...(7.83)$$

The point x_0 may be selected on the boundary where the stress $\sigma_x\big|_{x_0}$ is known from the isochromatic fringe pattern. The stress $\Delta\,\tau_{xy}\big|_{\frac{x_0+x_1}{2}}$ can be determined from the isochromatic and isoclinic data at the points x_0 and x_1, since

$$\tau_{xy} = \frac{1}{2}(\sigma_1 - \sigma_2)\sin 2\theta$$

$(\sigma_1 - \sigma_2)$ can be known from the isochromatic passing through the point $\left(\frac{x_0 + x_1}{2}\right)$ and θ the angle between σ_1 and x-axis can be known from the isoclinic. Generally the term $\Delta\,\tau_{xy}$ is determined from the plot of the shear stress distributions along two auxiliary lines parallel to the line of interest and symmetrically located with respect to it (lines AB and

CD) as shown in Fig. 7.37. The area between the τ_{xy} curves between x_0 and x_1 represents the quantity $\Delta\tau_{xy}\,\Delta x$, where $\Delta x = x_1 - x_0$. Then $\Delta\tau_{xy}\,\Big|_{\frac{x_0 + x_1}{2}}$ = the above area divided by Δy. Thus in general the accumulated area between the origin and a point at a distance x from the origin x_0 along the line of interest can be used to compute $\sigma_x|_{x_1} - \sigma_x|_{x_0}$, simply by dividing by the distance Δy between the two auxiliary lines.

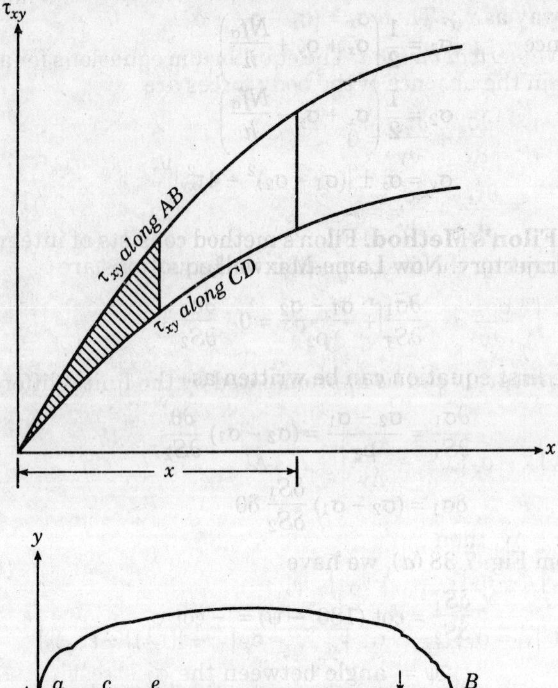

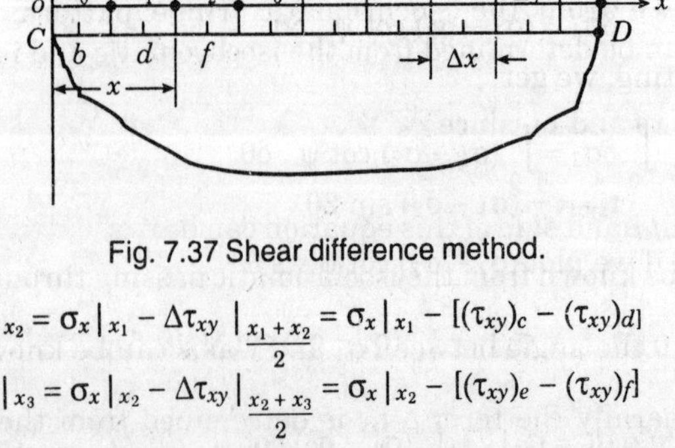

Fig. 7.37 Shear difference method.

$$\text{Thus } \sigma_x|_{x_2} = \sigma_x|_{x_1} - \Delta\tau_{xy}\,\Big|_{\frac{x_1 + x_2}{2}} = \sigma_x|_{x_1} - [(\tau_{xy})_c - (\tau_{xy})_d]$$

$$\sigma_x|_{x_3} = \sigma_x|_{x_2} - \Delta\tau_{xy}\,\Big|_{\frac{x_2 + x_3}{2}} = \sigma_x|_{x_2} - [(\tau_{xy})_e - (\tau_{xy})_f]$$

and so on.

When $\Delta x = \Delta y$ then $\Delta\tau_{xy} = \tau_{xy}|_{AB} - \tau_{xy}|_{CD}$

Once the value of σ_x is known at a given point, then σ_y can be computed from the expression

$$\sigma_y = \sigma_x - (\sigma_1 - \sigma_2)\cos 2\theta$$

$$= \sigma_x - \left(\frac{Nf_\sigma}{h}\right)\cos 2\theta \qquad ...(7.84)$$

Now $\quad \sigma_x + \sigma_y = \sigma_1 + \sigma_2$

and $\quad \sigma_1 - \sigma_2 = \dfrac{Nf_\sigma}{h}$

Hence $\quad \sigma_1 = \dfrac{1}{2}\left(\sigma_x + \sigma_y + \dfrac{Nf_\sigma}{h}\right)$

$$\sigma_2 = \frac{1}{2}\left(\sigma_x + \sigma_y - \frac{Nf_\sigma}{h}\right) \qquad ...(7.85)$$

and $$\sigma_y = \sigma_x \pm \left\{(\sigma_1 - \sigma_2)^2 - 4\tau_{xy}^2\right\}^{1/2} \qquad ...(7.86)$$

(*b*) **Filon's Method.** Filon's method consists of integration along a stress trajectory. Now Lame-Maxwell equations are :

$$\frac{\partial \sigma_1}{\partial S_1} + \frac{\sigma_1 - \sigma_2}{\rho_2} = 0 \quad \frac{\partial \sigma_2}{\partial S_2} + \frac{\sigma_1 - \sigma_2}{\rho_1} = 0$$

The first equation can be written as

$$\frac{\partial \sigma_1}{\partial S_1} = \frac{\sigma_2 - \sigma_1}{\rho_2} = (\sigma_2 - \sigma_1)\frac{\partial \theta}{\partial S_2}$$

or $$\delta\sigma_1 = (\sigma_2 - \sigma_1)\frac{\delta S_1}{\delta S_2}\delta\theta$$

From Fig. 7.38 (*a*), we have

$$\frac{\delta S_1}{\delta S_2} = \cot(180^\circ - \psi) = -\cot\psi$$

where $\quad \psi =$ angle between the σ_1 stress trajectory and the isoclinic of parameter $(\theta + \delta\theta)$

Hence $\quad \delta\sigma_1 = (\sigma_1 - \sigma_2)\cot\psi \,.\, \delta\theta$

Integrating, we get

$$\int_0^i \delta\sigma_1 = \int_0^i (\sigma_1 - \sigma_2)\cot\psi \,.\, \delta\theta$$

The right hand side of this equation can be evaluated by numerical integration, if we plot $(\sigma_1 - \sigma_2)\cot\psi$ v's θ.

$$\sigma_1|_i = \sigma_1|_0 + \int_0^i (\sigma_1 - \sigma_2)\cot\psi\, d\theta$$

Similarly $$\sigma_2|_i = \sigma_2|_0 + \int_0^i (\sigma_1 - \sigma_2)\cot\psi \,.\, d\theta \qquad ...(7.87)$$

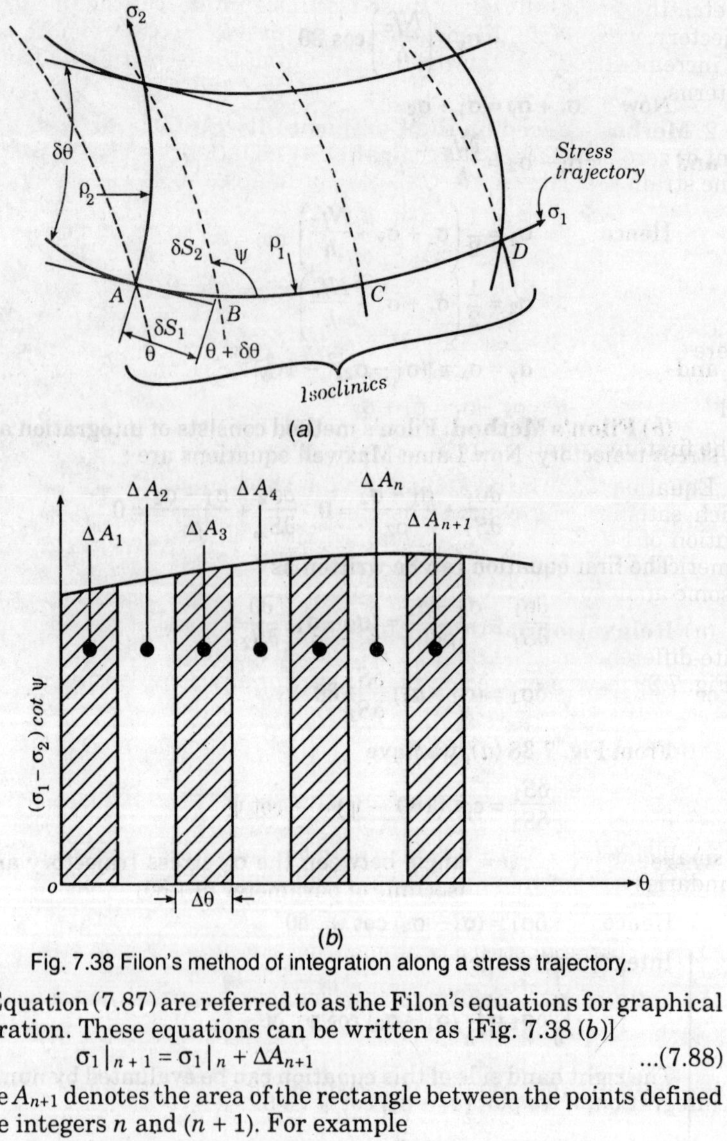

Fig. 7.38 Filon's method of integration along a stress trajectory.

Equation (7.87) are referred to as the Filon's equations for graphical integration. These equations can be written as [Fig. 7.38 (*b*)]

$$\sigma_1 |_{n+1} = \sigma_1 |_n + \Delta A_{n+1} \qquad ...(7.88)$$

where A_{n+1} denotes the area of the rectangle between the points defined by the integers n and $(n + 1)$. For example

$$\sigma_1 |_1 = \sigma_1 |_0 + \Delta A_1$$

$$\sigma_2 |_2 = \sigma_1 |_1 + \Delta A_2$$

and so on.

If the point A and stress trajectory σ_2 are on a free boundary, then $\sigma_1 = 0$ at A. By splitting up the stress trajectory into AB, BC, CD etc., into equal increments of isoclinic angle $\delta\theta$, and by determining ψ_A, ψ_B, ψ_C etc., the angles at which these isoclinics intersect the σ_1 stress trajectory, we can find the magnitude of σ_1 by successive summation of the increments $\delta\sigma_1$ by knowing $(\sigma_1 - \sigma_2)$ from the isochromatic fringe patterns.

2. **Methods Based on the Compatibility Equations.** With constant or zero body forces, the compatibility equation for plane stress or plane strain problems in Cartesian Co-ordinates can be expressed as :

$$\frac{\partial^2}{\partial x^2}(\sigma_x + \sigma_y) + \frac{\partial^2}{\partial y^2}(\sigma_x + \sigma_y) = 0$$

or $$\nabla^2 I = 0 \qquad \text{...(7.89)}$$

where $$\nabla^2 = \frac{\partial^2}{\partial x^2} + \frac{\partial^2}{\partial y^2}$$

and $$I = \sigma_x + \sigma_y = \sigma_1 + \sigma_2$$

is the first invariant of stress.

Equation (7.89) is the well-known Laplace's equation. Any function which satisfies this equation is called the harmonic function. The solution of Eq. (7.89) may be obtained either analytically or by some numerical technique like the four-point influence (relaxation) method or some analogous method like the electrical or membrane analogy.

(*a*) **Relaxation method.** Eq. (7.89) can be solved by using the finite-difference methods and the relaxation technique. A grid as shown in Fig. 7.39 (*a*) is prepared on the model. For any point 0,

$$(\nabla^2 I)_0 = \frac{I_1 + I_2 + I_3 + I_4 - 4I_0}{h^2} = 0$$

or $$I_0 = \frac{1}{4}(I_1 + I_2 + I_3 + I_4) \qquad \text{...(7.90)}$$

for small and non-zero value of h, where h is the grid size. For irregular boundaries as shown in Fig. 7.39 (*b*), we have

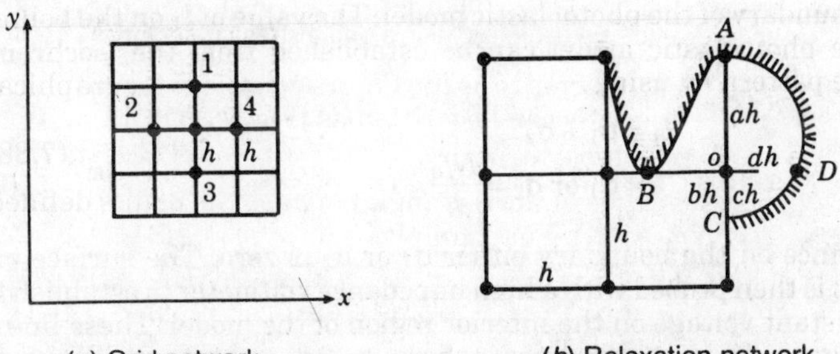

(*a*) Grid network (*b*) Relaxation network

Fig. 7.39 Relaxation method.

$$h^2 (\nabla^2 I)_0 = AI_A + BI_B + CI_C + DI_D - (E+F)\, I_0$$

or
$$(E+F)\, I_0 = AI_A + BI_B + CI_C + DI_D \qquad ...(7.91)$$

where
$$A = \frac{1}{a(a+c)},\ B = \frac{1}{b(b+d)}$$

$$C = \frac{1}{c(c+a)},\ D = \frac{1}{d(b+d)}$$

$$E = \frac{1}{ac},\ F = \frac{1}{bd}$$

Once the grid network has been established and the constants associated with each point evaluated, the known boundary values can be assigned to all points of intersection of the network with the boundary and estimated values or zero can be assigned to the interior points. The values are then improved by the relaxation technique. To save time and labour initially a coarse network may be selected to establish reasonable values for interior points and then a fine network may be selected to improve upon the values near selected regions like those of stress-concentration points.

(*b*) **Analogous method.** The electrical analogy method is the most commonly used analogous method for determining the sum of principal stresses. This method is based upon the fact that the voltage distribution in a uniformly conducting region enclosed by boundaries at known potential is governed by the Laplace equation in the same manner as the principal-stress sum in a plane stress situation. Because

$$\nabla^2 I_1 = 0$$

where
$$I_1 = \sigma_x + \sigma_y = \sigma_1 + \sigma_2$$

and
$$\nabla^2 V = 0$$

where V is the voltage.

Hence the two systems are analogous.

An electrical model of Teledeltos paper is made of the same geometry as the photoelastic model. Voltages applied to the boundary of the electrical model are proportional to the value of I_1 determined on the boundary of the photoelastic model. The value of I_1 on the boundary of the photoelastic model can be established from the isochromatic fringe pattern by using

$$I_1 = \sigma_1 + \sigma_2$$

$$= \sigma_1 \text{ or } \sigma_2 = \frac{Nf_\sigma}{h} \qquad ...(7.92)$$

Since on the boundary either σ_1 or σ_2 is zero. The surface of the model is then probed with a high impedance voltmeter to establish lines of constant voltage on the interior region of the model. These lines are analogous to isopachic lines, where $\sigma_1 + \sigma_2$ = constant. For further details refer to the chapter on analogous methods.

Table 7.4. Solution of $\nabla^2 H = 0$ in Various Co-ordinate Systems

Co-ordinate system		*Sequence of harmonic functions*	
Cartesian	$\dfrac{\partial^2 H}{\partial x^2} + \dfrac{\partial^2 H}{\partial y^2} = 0$	1 sinh kx sin ky x sinh kx cos ky y cosh kx sin ky xy cosh kx cos ky	sinh ky sin kx sinh ky cos kx cosh ky sin kx cosh ky cos kx
Polar	$x = r\cos\theta,\ y = r\sin\theta$ $\dfrac{\partial^2 H}{\partial r^2} + \dfrac{1}{r}\dfrac{\partial H}{\partial r} + \dfrac{1}{r^2}\dfrac{\partial^2 H}{\partial \theta^2} = 0$	1 r^n cos $n\theta$ $\ln r\, r^{-n}$ cos $n\theta$	r^n sin $n\theta$ r^{-n} sin $n\theta$
Bipolar	$x = \dfrac{C\sin\beta}{\cosh\alpha - \cos\beta},\ y = \dfrac{C\sinh\alpha}{\cosh\alpha - \cos\beta},\ \dfrac{\partial^2 H}{\partial \alpha^2} + \dfrac{\partial^2 H}{\partial \beta^2} = 0$	1 sinh $n\alpha$ sin $n\beta$ α sinh $n\alpha$ cos $n\beta$	cosh $n\alpha$ sin $n\beta$ cosh $n\alpha$ cos $n\beta$
Elliptic	$x = C\cosh u\cos v$ $y = C\sinh u\sin v$ $\quad \dfrac{\partial^2 H}{\partial u^2} + \dfrac{\partial^2 H}{\partial v^2} = 0$	1 sinh nu sin nv u sinh nu cos nv	cosh nu sin nv cosh nu cos nv
Spherical	$x = r\sin\phi\cos\theta,\ y = r\sin\phi\sin\theta,\ z = r\cos\phi$ $\dfrac{\partial^2 H}{\partial r^2} + \dfrac{2}{r}\dfrac{\partial H}{\partial r} + \dfrac{1}{r^2}\dfrac{\partial^2 H}{\partial \phi^2} + \dfrac{1}{r^2\tan\phi}\dfrac{\partial H}{\partial \phi} + \dfrac{1}{r^2\sin^2\phi}\dfrac{\partial^2 H}{\partial \theta^2} = 0$	$r^m P_m^n$ cos ϕ sin θ $r^{-m-1} P_m^n$ cos ϕ sin $n\theta$ where P is Legendre function	$r^m P_m^n$ cos ϕ cos $n\theta$ $r^{-m-1} P_m^n$ cos $n\theta$ cos ϕ

(*i*) *Analytic Separation Method.* The disadvantages of the supplementary numerical, graphical or experimental methods are that the auxiliary experiments are tedious to perform and the results obtained by these methods are not as accurate as the original photoelastic data. The analytic separation method is based on a harmonic series representation H of the first stress invariant I_1. It provides data for the sum of the principal stresses at interior points in the model which are as accurate as the photoelastic determination of the principal stress difference. A general harmonic series for H is obtained by solving Laplace's equation. Next, a finite number of these harmonic terms are selected to approximate H for a specific problem. The coefficient of each term retained in the series is then determined using either Fourier analysis or the method of least squares to match H to the prescribed boundary conditions. Once the coefficients for the series are evaluated, the value of H at any interior point can be determined. This information is then combined with the photoelastic data to obtain the value of the individual principal stresses at interior points. Solution for H referred to several co-ordinate systems are given in Table 7.4.

If the region of the model conforms to a regular co-ordinate system, determination of the proper coefficient for each function is considerably simplified. The sequence of functions when evaluated on the boundaries of the region reduces to a Fourier series. The unknown coefficients in these cases are the Fourier coefficients which are obtained by integrating the prescribed boundary values.

If the region of the model does not conform to a particular co-ordinate system. Fourier analysis cannot be employed to determine the coefficients which satisfy the prescribed boundary conditions. Instead, the method of least squares is used for the determination of the coefficients. A finite number of harmonic functions is first selected to appear in the series solution. Coefficients are then chosen such that the mean-square difference between the prescribed boundary values and the evaluation of the series along the boundaries is minimized. If N harmonic functions F_1, F_2 ,..., F_N are selected and the associated unknown coefficients are denoted as C_1, C_2... C_N, the series solution for the first stress invariant is

$$H = \sum_{n=1}^{N} C_n F_n \qquad \text{...(7.93)}$$

If S indicates a distance along the boundary of total length L, and if $I\,(S)$ represents the prescribed boundary values, the least-square method implies,

$$\int_0^L \left[I\,(S) - \sum_{n=1}^{N} C_n F_n \right]^2 ds = \text{Minimum} \qquad \text{...(7.94)}$$

The N unknown coefficients of the series are variables to be determined to minimize the integral shown above. This minimization process is accomplished by taking the partial derivative of the integral with respect to each coefficient and setting it equal to zero, as shown below

$$\frac{\partial}{\partial C_k}\int_0^L \left[I(S) - \sum_{n=1}^{N} C_n F_n \right]^2 ds = 0,\ k = 1, 2, ..., N \qquad ..(7.95a)$$

which can be reduced to

$$\sum_{n=1}^{N} C_n \int_0^L F_n\, F_k\, ds = \int_0^L I\,(S)\, F_k\, ds,\ k = 1, 2,..\ N \qquad ...(7.95b)$$

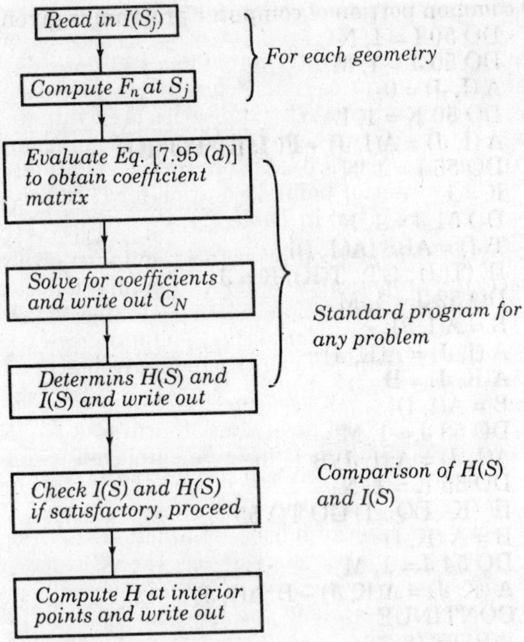

Fig. 7.40 Block diagram of computer program.

This result yields N simultaneous equations in terms of the N unknown coefficients. Solution of this set of equations gives the coefficients which result in the closest match of the boundary conditions possible with the N initially selected harmonic functions. By increasing the number of functions in the series for H, the least square fit can be made as accurate as the original photoelastic determination of $I\,(S)$.

Eq. (7.95a) can be written as :

$$\frac{\partial}{\partial\, C_k}\sum_{j=1}^{L} \left[I\,(S_j) - \sum_{n=1}^{N} C_n F_n \right]^2 = 0 \qquad ...(7.95c)$$

$$k = 1, 2, ..., N$$

or
$$\sum_{n=1}^{N} C_n \sum_{j=1}^{L} F_n F_k = \sum_{j=1}^{L} I(S_j) F_k \qquad k = 1, 2, \ldots, N \qquad \ldots(7.95d)$$

This yields N simultaneous equations in terms of the unknown coefficients.

A block diagram (Fig. 7.40) corresponding to the computer program to determine the unknown coefficients is shown below :

The common portion of computer program is given below :

```
40  DO 50 I = 1, N
    DO 50 J = 1, M
    A (I, J) = 0
    DO 50 K = 1, L
50  A (I, J) = A(I, J) + F( I, K)*F(J, K)
    DO 55 I = 1, N
    K = 1
    DO 51 J = 1, N
    T(J) = ABS (A(J, I))
51  IF (T(J) . GT . T(K)) K = J
    DO 52 J = 1, M
    B = A(I, J)
    A (I, J) = A(K, J)
52  A(K, J) = B
    B = A(I, I)
    DO 53 J = 1, M
53  A(I, J) = A (I, J)/B
    DO 55 K = 1, N
    IF (K . EQ . 1) GO TO 55
    B = A (K, I)
    DO 54 J = 1, M
54  A (K, J) = A(K, J) – B*A(I, J)
55  CONTINUE
    WRITE (8, 58)
    WRITE (8, 59) (A(I, M), I = 1, N)
    WRITE (8, 60)
    DO 57 K = 1, L
    B = 0
    DO 56 I = 1, N
56  B = B + A (1, M)*F(I, K)
57  WRITE (8, 61) K, F(M, K), B
58  FORMAT (13 H1 COEFFICIENTS //)
59  FORMAT (F 13.5 /)
60  FORMAT (21 H1 BOUNDARY VALUE 1 CHECK //)
61  FORMAT (13, 2F, 9.3)
    END
```

3. **Methods based on Hooke's law.** The strain in a direction perpendicular to the surface of a plane-stress model is given by

$$\varepsilon_z = \frac{\Delta h}{h} = -\frac{\nu}{E}(\sigma_1 + \sigma_2)$$

$$\therefore \qquad \Delta h = -\frac{\nu h}{E}(\sigma_1 + \sigma_2) \qquad \text{...(7.96)}$$

or
$$\sigma_1 + \sigma_2 = -\left(\frac{E}{\nu h}\right)\Delta h = -K\,\Delta h$$

where $K = E/\nu h$.

Thus the sum of principal stresses can be determined if the change in thickness of the model as a result of the applied loads, can be measured at the point of interest. The change in thickness can be measured precisely either by using a lateral extensometer or an optical interferometer. Lateral extensometers have been developed by Coker (mechanical type) and De-Forest and Anderson (electrical type). The optical interferometer of the reflected type was developed by Mesnager (1901) and of the transmission type by Post.

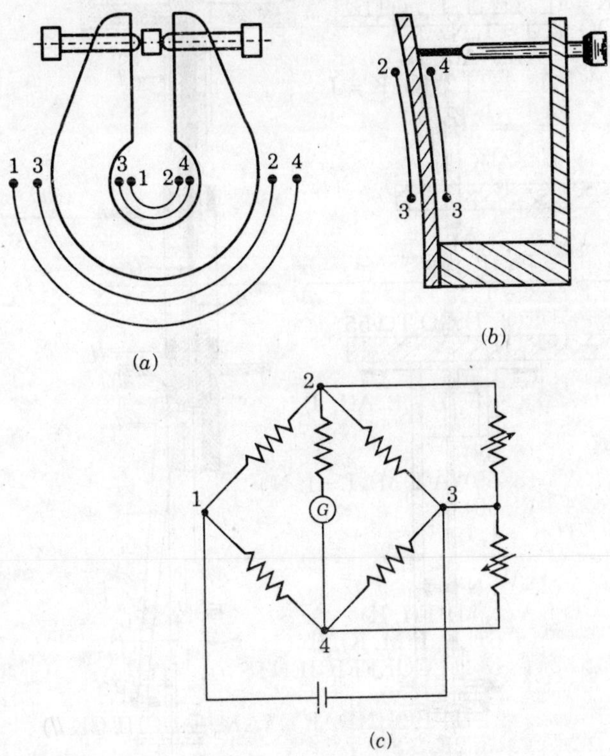

(a) U-frame (b) Compensator unit (c) Wiring diagram
Fig. 7.41 De-Forest extensometer.

(a) Lateral Extensometers

(i) *Electrical lateral extensometer.* The lateral extensometer of the electrical resistance strain gauges type as shown in Fig. 7.41 was developed by De-Forest and Anderson in 1941. The instrument comprises three units, a horse shoe-shaped gauge, a galvanometer and a compensator element housed in a metal cabinet. The cabinet also contains the necessary batteries and switches.

Four strain-sensitive elements are connected to the curved sections of the horse shoe gauge. When the gauge is clamped to the specimen with a light initial pressure, it can follow the change in thickness caused by application of the load. A change in thickness of the specimen introduces strains into the wire elements, with units 1-2 and 3-4 taking strains of opposite sign to units 1-4 and 2-3.

The strain-sensitive elements on the gauge act as arms of a Wheatstone bridge, and the strains are indicated by the deflection of the galvanometer.

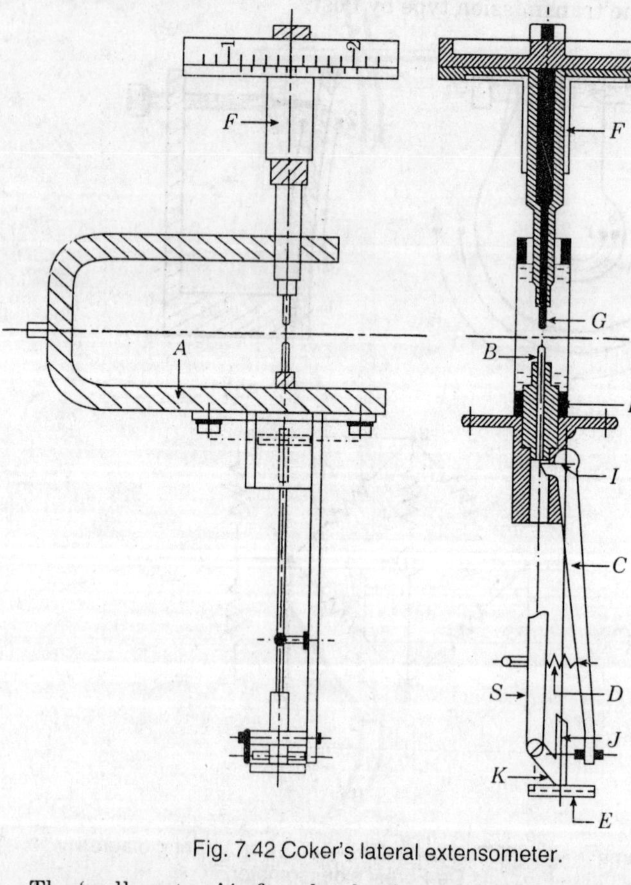

Fig. 7.42 Coker's lateral extensometer.

The 'null-system' is found to be the most accurate for strain measurements, and to accomplish this, a compensator element is introduced. The compensator is a steel cantilever spring, the bending of which is controlled by a micrometer screw. Strain-sensitive elements are located on either side of the cantilever, one side taking the opposite character to the other side.

In clamping the gauge to the specimen, the control switch is set to low sensitivity and the bridge is approximately balanced by adjusting the initial point pressure of the gauge. Final balance is made at high sensitivity with the micrometer. To measure lateral strain, one merely balances the bridge at zero load and again at final load, noting the micrometer readings. The difference in micrometer readings then gives the lateral strain. The extensometer can be calibrated by taking micrometer readings against strain or calibrate by a simple tension test to read sum of principal stresses. It has a very high degree of sensitivity, simplicity, stability and ruggedness.

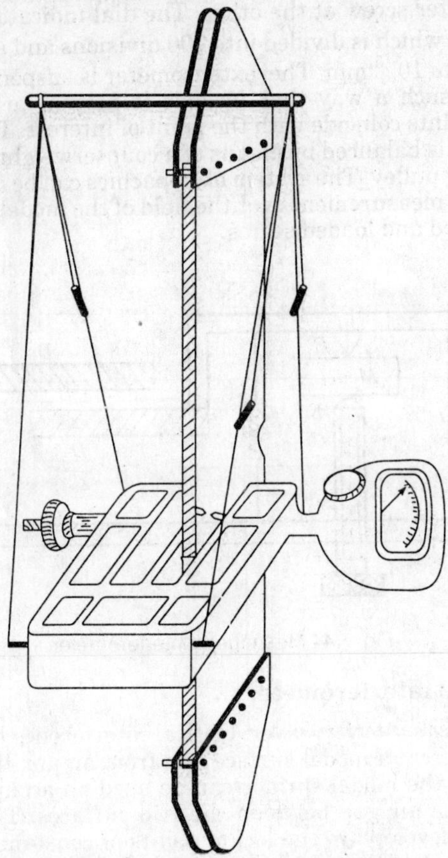

Fig. 7.43 Hiltscher lateral extensometer.

(*ii*) *Mechanical lateral extensometer*. A lateral extensometer of the mechanical-optical type was developed by Coker as shown in Fig. 7.42. It consists of a U-shaped frame A carrying a micrometer F in a friction tight grip and provided with a loose measuring needle G. A second similar needle *B* in line with the first is supported in a casing *H* and its outer end bears against the short arm of a bell-crank lever *C* pivoted at *I* and with the end of its longer arm kept in contact by a light spring with the projecting arm *J* of a mirror *E* pivoted at *K* to a member *S* of the frame *A*. Any displacement between the tips of the measuring needles causes a tilt of the mirror and serves to measure the lateral change produced in a stressed photoelastic model when set between them.

Hiltscher in 1962 developed one of the most simplest and successful form of the dial gauge-type mechanical lateral extensometer as shown in Fig. 7.43. This consists of a U-shaped frame carrying a precision measuring instrument on one side and a centre which can be adjusted by a micrometer screw at the other. The dial indicator has a range of 20×10^{-4} mm which is divided into 200 divisions and allow readings to be estimated to 10^{-5} mm. The extensometer is suspended by a system of chords in such a way that its axis is normal to the plate while measuring points coincide with the point of interest. The weight of the extensometer is balanced by means of a counterweight suspended over a free running pulley. The system of isopachics can be determined from point by point measurement over the field of the model of the thickness in the unloaded and loaded states.

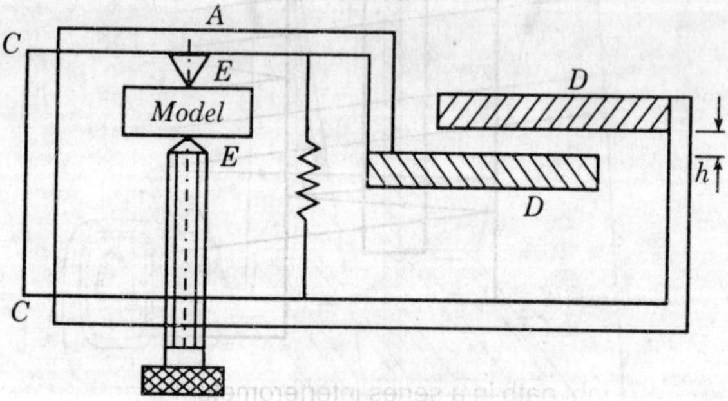

Fig. 7.44 Mesnager's interferometer.

(*b*) Optical interferometers

(*i*) *Mesnager's interferometer*. Optical interference between rays of light reflected from a model surface and from an auxiliary optical flat placed close to the model surface can be used an accurate, means for determining the air gap between the two surfaces. The interference fringes which develop are the loci of points of constant air-film thickness, which can be used to determine the changes in model thickness and hence the sum of principal stresses. An instrument of this type developed by Mesnager is shown in Fig. 7.44. Interference fringes will appear when $h = n\,(\lambda/2)$. This interferometer consists of two angular bars *A* and *B* attached to a flexible steel plate *CC*. At the right end the bars are equipped with optical flats *DD* separated by a small air gap *h*. The needle points *E-E* which move integrally with the bars are brought in contact with the model and transmit the change in thickness of the model to the optical flats in a some what magnified form. This deformation is measured by observing the movement of the interference fringes between the optical flats.

(*ii*) *Post's Series Interferometer*. This interferometer was developed by D. Post in 1954 to obtain the isopachic pattern by using transmitted light. The light path in this interferometer is shown in Fig. 7.45. The model M is placed between two of a system of three partial mirrors. Interference occurs between rays which have approximately the same lengths of optical path. If the optical path difference between the mirrors M_1 and M_2 (including that within the model M) is approximately equal to that between M_2 and M_3 interference will occur between rays which follow geometrically similar paths through the system. Interference will also occur between rays which have taken mutually similar paths involving multiple reflections. This can be eliminated by using an inclined mirror system.

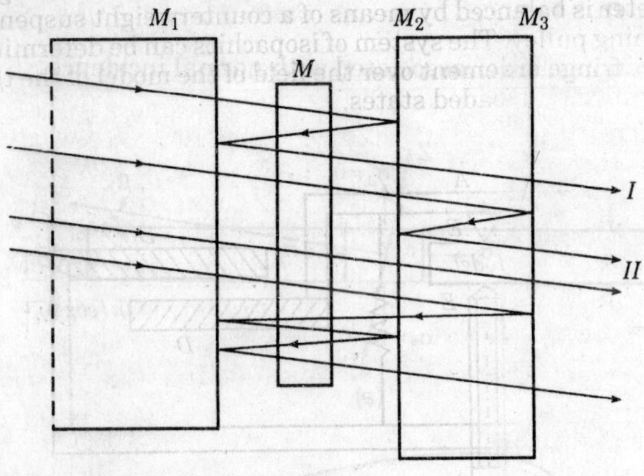

Fig. 7.45 Light path in a series interferometer (after D. Post)

Nisida and Saito have developed an interferometer of the Mach-Zehnder type and Favre and Schumann of the photometric type to obtain the isopachic patterns.

4. **Oblique-incidence Methods.** When the light passes through the model not at normal incidence, an oblique incidence fringe pattern may be obtained. This additional data along with the normal incidence data helps to separate the principal stresses. For oblique incidence the stress optic law is obeyed by the secondary principal stresses $\sigma_{1'}$ and $\sigma_{2'}$. The secondary principal stresses are the principal stresses on a plane which is perpendicular to the ray of light traversing the model. For example the secondary principal stresses for a ray of light traversing the model along the z-axis are :

$$\sigma'_{1,2} = \frac{1}{2}(\sigma_x + \sigma_y) + \frac{1}{2}\left\{(\sigma_x - \sigma_y)^2 + 4\tau_{xy}^2\right\}^{1/2}$$

Case 1. *Known principal stress directions.* Let us rotate the model about σ_1 axis by an amount θ as shown in Fig. 7.45. The light passes through the plane of the model obliquely and traverses a distance of $h/\cos\theta$ through the model. The secondary principal stresses for the light path shown in Fig. 7.46 (*a*) are σ_1 and σ'_2. Hence, applying stress optic law, we get

$$\sigma_1 - \sigma'_2 = \frac{N_\theta f_\sigma}{(h/\cos\theta)}$$

From Fig. 7.46 (*b*) we find that

$$\sigma'_2 = \sigma_2 \cos^2\theta$$

where N_θ = fringe order associated with oblique incidence angle θ.

$$\text{Hence } \sigma_1 - \sigma_2 \cos^2\theta = \frac{N_\theta f_\sigma \cos\theta}{h} \qquad ...(a)$$

Also for normal incidence

$$\sigma_1 - \sigma_2 = \frac{N_0 f_\sigma}{h} \qquad ...(b)$$

where N_0 = fringe order associated with normal incidence.

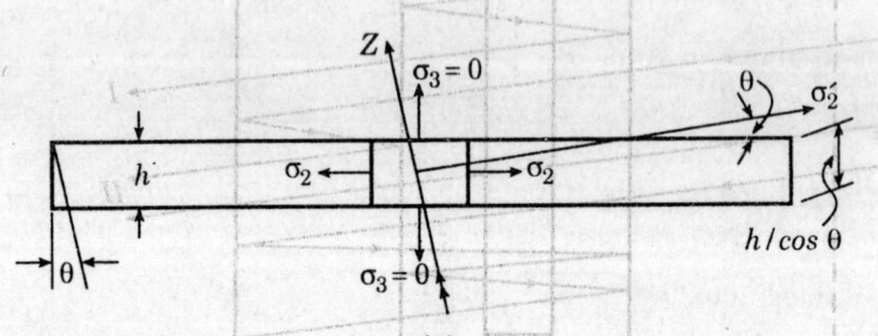

(*a*)

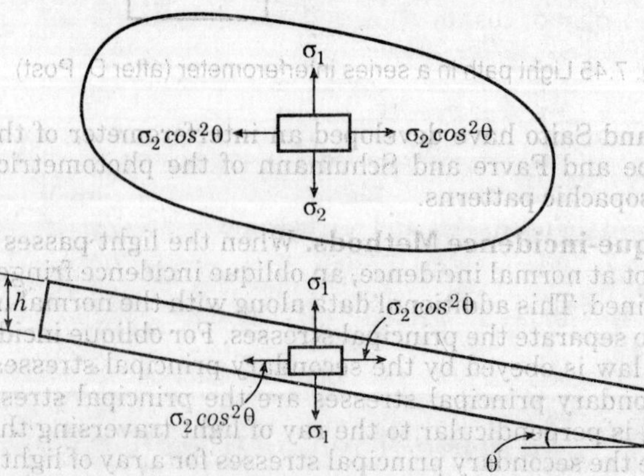

(*b*)

Fig. 7.46 Oblique incidence method.

Combining Eqs. (*a*) and (*b*), we get

$$\left.\begin{aligned}\sigma_1 &= \frac{f_\sigma \cos\theta}{h\sin^2\theta}(N_\theta - N_0\cos\theta)\\ \sigma_2 &= \frac{f_\sigma}{h\sin^2\theta}(N_\theta\cos\theta - N_0)\end{aligned}\right\} \quad ...(7.97)$$

Therefore, by employing two isochromatic fringe patterns, one from normal incidence and the other from oblique incidence, it is possible to separate the stresses.

Case 2. *Unknown directions of principal stresses.* In this case we obtain three isochromatic fringe patterns : normal incidence pattern, oblique incidence pattern for rotation about *ox*-axis, and oblique incidence pattern for rotation about *oy*-axis. For normal incidence, we have

$$\sigma_1 - \sigma_2 = \frac{N_0 f_\sigma}{h}$$

or

$$N_0 = \frac{h}{f_\sigma}(\sigma_1 - \sigma_2) = \frac{h}{f_\sigma}\left|(\sigma_x - \sigma_y)^2 + 4\tau_{xy}^2\right|^{1/2} \quad ...(c)$$

For rotation about *ox* axis

$$N_{\theta x} = \frac{h}{f_\sigma \cos\theta_x}\left|(\sigma_x - \sigma_y\cos^2\theta)^2 + 4\tau_{xy}^2\cos^2\theta\right|^{1/2} \quad ...(d)$$

For rotation about *oy* axis

$$N_{\theta y} = \frac{h}{\cos\theta y}\cdot\frac{\sigma'_1 - \sigma'_2}{f_\sigma}$$

where $\sigma'_1 - \sigma'_2 = \left|(\sigma'_x \quad \sigma'_y)^2 + 4\tau_{x'y'}^2\right|^{1/2}$

Now $\sigma_{x'} = \sigma_x \cos^2\theta y$

$$\sigma_{y'} = \sigma_y$$

$$\tau_{x'y'} = \tau_{xy}\cos\theta y$$

Thus $N_{0y} = \dfrac{h}{f_\sigma \cos\theta y}\left|(\sigma_x\cos^2\theta y - \sigma_y)^2 + 4\tau_{xy}^2\cos^2\theta y\right|^{1/2}$ ..(*e*)

If $\theta x = \theta y = \theta$ then Eqs. (*d*) and (*e*), become

$$\left.\begin{aligned}\left(\frac{N_{0x} f_\sigma\cos\theta}{h}\right)^2 &= (\sigma_x - \sigma_y\cos^2\theta)^2 + 4\tau_{xy}^2\cos^2\theta\\ \left(\frac{N_{0y} f_\sigma\cos\theta}{h}\right)^2 &= (\sigma_x\cos^2\theta - \sigma_y)^2 + 4\,\tau_{xy}^2\cos^2\theta\end{aligned}\right\} \quad ...(f)$$

Also Eq. (*c*) can be written as

$$\left(\frac{N_0 f_\sigma}{h}\right)^2 = (\sigma_x - \sigma_y)^2 + 4\tau_{xy}^2 \qquad ...(g)$$

Solving for x and y from Eqs. (f) and (g), we get

$$\left(\frac{\sigma_x h}{f_\sigma}\right)^2 = \frac{\cos^2\theta}{1-\cos^4\theta}\,[N_{\theta x}^2 + N_{\theta y}^2\cos^2\theta - N_0{}^2(1+\cos^2\theta)] \qquad ...(7.98)$$

$$\left(\frac{\sigma_y h}{f_\sigma}\right)^2 = \frac{\cot^2\theta}{1-\cos^4\theta}\,[N_{\theta y}^2 + N_{\theta x}^2\cos^2\theta - N_0{}^2(1+\cos^2\theta)]$$

σ_x and σ_y may be calculated from Eqs. (7.98), then

$$I_1 = \sigma_x + \sigma_y = \sigma_1 + \sigma_2$$

Hence the stresses can be separated.

7.24 Selection of Photoelastic Materials

An ideal photoelastic material should have the following properties :

1. Transparent to light used in the polariscope.
2. Easily machinable by conventional means.
3. It should have high optical sensitivity as indicated by low fringe values (f_σ or f_ε).
4. It should have linear characteristics with respect to stress-strain, stress-fringe order and strain-fringe order properties for model to prototype scaling.
5. It should be free from residual stresses.
6. It should have both mechanical and optical isotropy and homogeneity.
7. There should be absence of undue optical and mechanical creep.
8. It should have high modulus of elasticity, ultimate strength and hardness to avoid distortion and contact problems.
9. It should be free from time-edge effects.
10. The material fringe values f_σ or f_ε should remain constant during moderate temperature changes.
11. It should have moderate cost.
12. It should have high rigidity.

The meanings of some of the new terms are explained below.

Figure of Merit. In order to judge the ability of a material to resist distortion, the factor $\frac{1}{f_\varepsilon}$ or $\frac{E}{f_\sigma(1+\nu)}$ is used. A material will be more resistance to distortion if the value of $\frac{1}{f_\varepsilon}$ for the material is high or f_ε is low. Since Poisson's ratio for most of the photoelastic materials varies from 0.36 to 0.42 the ratio $Q = \frac{E}{f_\sigma}$ is used to evaluate the merit of the material. This factor E/f_σ is called the figure of merit.

Sensitivity Index. It is defined as

$$S = \frac{\sigma_{pl}}{f_\sigma}$$

where σ_{pl} = proportional limit for the model material

S = sensitivity index.

Time-Edge Effects. When a photoelastic material is machined and examined under a no load condition as a function of time. it is noted that a stress is induced on the boundary which produces a series of fringes, which are parallel to the boundary of the model. These fringes superimpose on the fringes obtained by applying load to the model and thus produce errors in the photoelastic data. This phenomenon is called time edge effects. It has been established that the time-edge effect is caused by diffusion of water vapour from the air into the plastic or from the plastic into the air.

7.25 Photoelastic Materials and Their Properties

1. **Epoxy Resins.** These are condensation products of epichlorohydrin and polyhydric phenol. Although they are available as a full polymerized material, usually in the form of flat sheets suitable for two-dimensional photoelastic work, epoxies are now-a-days supplied as a basic resin and hardener or curing agent. The finished resin is formed by the chemical reaction of basic resin and hardener.

In India the most commonly used epoxy resins are Araldite CY-230 and Hardener HY-951 (both liquids), which are of the cold-setting type and Araldite CT-200 (solid) and Hardener HT-901, which are of the hot setting type, and manufactured by Hindustan CIBA-Geigy Limited.

Epoxy resins possess good optical and mechanical properties, slightly susceptible to time edge effects and are available at comparatively low cost. They can be easily cast, machined, finished and cemented for making models of complicated shapes.

2. **Columbia Resin CR-39.** This is allyl diglycol carbonate which is produced by reacting phosgene with diethylene glycol to obtain a chloroformate, which is then esterified with allyl alcohol to yield a monomer. The monomer is polymerized by heating in the presence of catalyst (benzoyl peroxide) and the resultant sheet is a crystal-clear product. It is available in large sheets. It is brittle and cannot be machined but can be easily routed. It is less prone to time edge effect but suffers to some extent from creep. It has relatively low fringe value and sensitivity index.

3. **Castolite or Homolite 100.** It is a polyester resin which can be cast into sheet form between glass plates by adding a catalyst to the monomer and curing at about 93°C to complete polymerisation. The surfaces of the commercially available sheets are of optical quality, and the material is free of residual stresses. Models can be prepared by routing only. It is insensitive to time edge effect and is best suited for prolonged testing. The material exhibits both a low figure of merit and sensitivity index.

Table 7.5. Properties of photoelastic materials at room temperature

Material (1)	*Trade name* (2)	*Poisson's ratio* ν (3)	*Modulus of elasticity (GPa)* E (4)	*Propor-tional limit (MPa)* σ_{pl} (5)	*Stress** fringe value (N/mm)* f_σ (6)	*Strain fringe value (cm)* f_e (7)	*Figure of merit (1/cm)* Q (8)	*Sen-sitivity index (1/cm)* S (9)	*Remarks* (10)
Epoxy resin*	Araldite Cy-230 with 10% hardener	0.38	2.62	56	11.59	0.00061	2260	48.3	Good time edge effect, creep and machinability
	Araldite CT-200 with 25-30% hardener	0.36	2.94	56	10.52	0.00048	2794	53.2	
Allyldiglycol	CR-39	0.42	1.75	21	15.4	0.00125	1136	13.6	Poor time-edge effect, creep and machinability
Polymethacrylate	Perspex	0.36	2.1	38.5	125	0.004	168.25	3.08	Good time-edge effect and no creep, low optical sensitivity
	Plexiglass	0.37	2.8	35	135	0.006	207.4	2.59	
Polycarbonate	Makrolon	0.38	2.52	35	7.13	0.00039	3534	49.09	Excellent time-edge effect and creep and poor machinability

Table 7.5 (continued)

Castolite	Homolite-100	0.36*	3.8	42	24	0.008	1583	17.5	Excellent time-edge effect and creep and machinability
Bakelite	Catalin 61-893	0.365	4.3	49	15.37	0.00049	2797	31.88	Moderate creep. Exhibits time-edge effects
Polyurethane rubber	Photoflex Hysol 4485	0.46	31.5×10^{-4}	0.175	0.18	0.0008	175	9.72	Excellent time-edge effect and creep and poor machinability
Cellulose nitrate	Celluloid	0.33	2.1	28	30 to 300	0.0029 to 0.029	700 to 70	9.33 to 93.3	Prone to creep, used for complicated models
Gelatine	—	0.50	$(0.28 \text{ to } 2.8) \times 10^4$	—	0.03 to 0.09	0.160 to 1.60	9 to 31	—	Highly prone to time-edge effect, suitable for body force problems
Glass	—	0.25	70	60.9	142 and above	0.00025 and above	492.5	4.29	Difficult to machine. Very small optical sensitivity

*Values are given from the paper by Amba Rao published in Brit. J. Appl Phys., June 1956.

**For mercury green light 5461 Å.

4. **Polymethacrylate.** It is marketed under the trade name of Plexiglass (Germany and USA) and Perspex (U.K.). It is available in the form of flat sheets and round bars in a wide variety of sizes. The material is highly transparent, colourless and free from initial stress. It exhibits practically no creep or time edge effect. The optical sensitivity is very low.

5. **Bakelite (Catalin 61-893).** It is glyptal resin which is glycerine phthallic anhydride. Figure of merit and sensitivity index are quite high for bakelite. It is water clear, machinable with ordinary tools, not too brittle yet hard enough, isotropic, creeps moderately, unavailable in large sheets and exhibits time edge effect. It is now very rarely used for photoelastic work.

6. **Polycarbonate.** It is marketed under the trade name Makrolon (Europe) and Lexan (U.S.A.). It has very high optical sensitivity and figure of merit. It is free from time-edge effect and shows little creep at room temperature. Polycarbonate is a thermoplastic and is available in sheet form. Residual stresses produced during manufacturing may be removed by careful heat treatment. It can be routed by using water as a coolant.

7. **Polyurethane Rubber.** It is a rubber like plastic of very low elastic modulus and very high optical sensitivity. It is a highly transparent, amber coloured material and is practically free from time-edge effect. Optical and mechanical creep are negligible at room temperature. It is mainly used for demonstration purposes. It is available under the trade-name Photoflex (U.K.) and Hysol 4485 (U.S.A.). It is a popular material for dynamic photoelasticity and study of body force problems.

8. **Glass.** It is the first material to be used for photoelastic investigations. It is transparent, free from creep, insensitive to mild temperature changes, isotropic, homogeneous, inexpensive, difficult to machine and has low optical sensitivity.

9. **Gelatine.** The optical sensitivity of gelatine is very high as compared to any other photoelastic material. This is suitable for the investigation of stress problems in which the influence of self-weight is important, *e.g.* in determining the stress distribution in dams and around tunnels. It is highly susceptible to time-edge effect which can be decreased by adding glycerine. Models can be prepared by dissolving gelatine in water and moulding to the desired shape.

10. **Celluloid.** It is a colloidal mixture of nitrocellulose in camphor. It is susceptible to creep and is used for large and complicated models. Properties of photoelastic materials at room temperature are given in Table 7.5.

7.26 Quiz Questions

1. Define birefringence.
2. What is the photoelastic effect ?
3. Differentiate between temporary and permanent double refraction.
4. What is the nature of light ?

5. Differentiate between ordinary and monochromatic light.
6. What is a Nicol prism ?
7. Define stress optic law.
8. Define isoclinics, isochromatics and isopachics.
9. Differentiate between isotropic and singular points.
10. What is fog density of a photographic film ?
11. Draw the Hurter-Driffield curve.
12. What do you mean you compensation ?
13. Define Mesnager's theorem.
14. What is a stress trajectory ?
15. What is equidensometry ?
16. Differentiate between escaping and non-escaping type of fringes.
17. Define sensitivity index and figure of merit of a photoelastic material.
18. What is the necessity of calibration of a photoelastic material ?
19. Why Tardy method of compensation is preferred over all other methods ?
20. Who discovered the photoelastic effect and when ?

EXERCISES

7.1 State the stress optic law in two dimension and obtain an expression for the same.

7.2 Discuss the various methods of obtaining polarized light.

7.3 (*a*) Describe the basic elements of a plane polariscope.
(*b*) Derive an expression for the intensity of the emergent light from a plane polariscope with a stressed model and show how it enables us to determine the isoclinics and the isochromatics.

7.4 Describe the different methods for constructing stress trajectories from isoclinics.

7.5 Discuss the important properties of isoclinics. How isoclinics of various parameters can be obtained ?

7.6 Explain the effect of a stressed model in a standard circular polariscope.

7.7 Write short notes on the following :
(*i*) Double exposure photography in photoelasticity.
(*ii*) Practical problems in a polariscope.
(*iii*) Accurate determination of integral fringe order.

7.8 Describe the concepts of photoelastic photography. How fractional fringe order can be determined by the photographic method ?

7.9 What is the necessity of fringe sharpening and fringe multiplication in photoelasticity ? Describe the Post's methods for fringe sharpening and fringe multiplication.

7.10 State and prove Mesnager's theorem.

7.11 Discuss the various compensation techniques for obtaining fractional fringe order in brief.

7.12 Explain the Tardy's compensation method in detail. Why this method is preferred over other methods ?

7.13 Write short notes on
(*i*) Colour matching technique.
(*ii*) Isodensometry method.

7.14 Describe briefly the various methods used for the separation of principal stresses.

7.15 Explain the shear difference method for the separation of principal stresses in detail.

7.16 Write short notes on
(*i*) Filon's integration method along stress trajectories.
(*ii*) Analytic separation method.
(*iii*) Oblique incidence method.

7.17 Discuss briefly the various types of lateral extensometers in use.

7.18 What are the important properties of an ideal photoelastic material ? Discuss the important photoelastic materials.

7.19 Materials used in photoelasticity have the following properties using mercury light (λ = 5461 Å). Determine the number of fringes that can be shown by a model 6 mm thick of these materials and estimate the highest advisable number of fringes. If instead of mercury light, sodium light (λ = 5893 Å) is used, determine the corresponding fringe values.

Material	f_σ, *kN/m²/m/fringe*	*Breaking stress, MPa*
CR-39	17.5	25
Perspex	87.5	42.5
Glass	140	70

7.20 A model of CR-39, 0.6 cm thick shows six-fringes in sodium light and under a load of 100 N. Determine the stress under a load of 20 kN in a similar steel component 2.5 cm thick and twelve times larger in the plane of the plate than the model.

7.21 A photoelastic model in the shape of a beam 1.5 cm deep and 3 mm thick is stressed in pure bending. When a bending moment 7 N.m is applied, the ninth fringe just appears at the outer edge. Sketch the fringe distribution and calculate the fringe values of model and material.

7.22 A circular disc is of 75 mm diameter and 6 mm thick. Determine the material fringe value if a load of 2 kN produces a fringe order of 6 at the centre of the disc.

7.23 A photoelastic model in the shape of a long tension strip 2 cm wide, 0.35 cm thick, has a central hole 0.65 cm diameter and is subjected to a uniform tensile stress away from hole. A total force of 800 N applied at the ends of the strip produces a fringe of order 9 at a point A on the edge of the hole. If the material fringe value f_σ is 100 N/mm per fringe, calculate the stress at A, the ratio (σ_A/σ_0), and the stress concentration factor (σ_A/σ_m), where σ_m is the mean stress over the reduced cross-section at the hole.

7.24 A photoelastic beam 22.5 mm high, 6.25 mm thick is freely supported at the ends of a span of 7.5 cm and loaded by a concentrated force of 500 N acting at the mid portion of the beam. If the load produces 12 fringes at the most highly stressed point P of the bottom edge, calculate the fringe value of the material and its stress-optic coefficient in Brewsters. The light used is monochromatic of $\lambda = 5461$ Å. What fringe value would you expect on the neutral axis of bending just off the midplane of the model ?

7.25 Given a fringe order of 5, a model thickness of 6.25 mm, a fringe value of 160 N/cm^2/cm per fringe and an isoclinic parameter of 25° defining the angle between σ_1 and the x-axis, determine the shear stress τ_{xy}.

7.26 For the determination of the fractional fringe order at a certain point, a compensator is to be made of CR-39 (f_σ = 175 kN/m^2/m/fringe, maximum load 210 N/mm^2) with a constant width of 12.5 mm and tapering thickness or with a constant thickness of 12.5 mm and tapering width, calculate the required tension for 14 fringes to appear in each compensator. Indicate whether the tension axis of the compensator should be placed parallel with or normal to the edge of the model.

8

Three-Dimensional Photoelasticity

8.1 Introduction

Many stress analysis problems are three-dimensional in nature for which the two-dimensional photoelastic method cannot be employed. These problems, however, can be solved either by locking in the stresses in the model or a multilayer reflection technique may be used to determine the stresses at the inner layers of the body. Three-dimensional stress distribution in the body can also be determined by the scattered light method (refer to Chapter 11). In this chapter we shall discuss the locking-in method of stresses in three-dimensional models in detail and the multilayer reflection technique in brief.

The stresses in a three-dimensional model can be locked-in either by stress-freezing, by curing method, by creep method or by gamma-ray irradiation method. Out of these methods, the stress-freezing method is the most widely used. This method consists in loading the model at room temperature, heating at a specified slow rate above the critical temperature (at which the primary and secondary bonds break down), keeping at that temperature for few hours and then cooling to room temperature at a slow rate. The stresses thus frozen in the model can be analysed by slicing and viewing in a polariscope.

Maxwell in 1853, and Filon and Harris in 1923 had both obtained the stress-frozen effect accidentally, while Tuzi in 1927 and Solakian in 1935 both attempted to calculate the residual stresses and to relate them to the applied loads. None of these, however, fully appreciated the significance of the phenomenon, and it was Solakian who in 1935 and Oppel in 1936 first produced a quantitative solution of a three-dimensional problem, followed by He'tenyi, who in 1938 first established the strict proportionality of stresses. This discovery opened the way to the complete solution of the three-dimensional problems and resulted in a very sharp increase in activity in photoelastic research. Hetenyi, O' Rourke, Drucker and Mindlin, Drucker and Woodward, Frocht and Mindlin developed methods of measurement of the frozen stresses and Jessop in 1949 devised integration methods for determining the separate stresses. Jessop and Stableford in 1953 published an extension to three dimension of the Lame-Maxwell equations, which made it possible to determine the principal stresses along a stress trajectory in a plane of symmetry. The stress-freezing method of three-dimensional photoelasticity today is a practical instrument of stress analysis, particularly in complex structures.

8.2 Stress Locking-in Methods

The following methods may be used for locking-in stresses in three dimensional models :

1. The stress freezing method.
2. The curing method.
3. The creep method.
4. The gamma-ray irradiation method.

8.2.1 The Stress-Freezing Method

The stress-freezing method of locking in the model deformations due to an applied load is based on the diphase behaviour of many polymeric materials when they are heated. The polymeric materials are composed of long chain hydrocarbon molecules, cross-linked by chains of different molecular groups and it is assumed that when fully matured any mass of such a resin virtually consists of a number of very large, highly complex molecules, interlinked with one another and forming, in effect, one large deformable molecule. It is further assumed that at low temperature physical cohesion bonds operate between the molecular groups of the different chains forming a rigid mass which deforms under load like any ordinary elastic solid. However, as the temperature of the polymer is increased, the secondary bonds break down and the primary bonds in effect carry the entire applied load. The critical temperature corresponds to the melting point of the ordinary solid. It is the temperature at which the cohesive bonds break down. Since the secondary bonds constitute a very large portion of the polymer, the deflections which the primary bonds undergo are quite large, yet elastic in nature. If the temperature of the polymer is lowered to room temperature while the load is maintained on the model, the secondary bonds will reform between the highly elongated primary bonds and serve to lock them into their extended positions. When the load is removed, the primary bonds relax to a modest degree, but the main portion of their deformation is not recovered.

The primary and secondary molecular chains in a diphase polymer are shown in Fig. 8.1, where the full lines show liquid micelles (micromolecules) and dotted lines show liquid micelles. The phenomenon of stress freezing can be easily understood by the mechanical model shown in Fig. 8.2. Here the first phase (fluid) is represented by a material which is solid at room temperature but which melts at some temperature around 40°C. The second phase is represented by a spring. At room temperature, imposed loads will be carried by the solid phase with relatively small deformation. If a load is applied at a temperature above the melting point of the first phase, it will be carried entirely by the second phase, represented by the spring. The deformation for a given load will in this case be greater than at room temperature. If the system is cooled down with the load still acting it will be seen that the spring will be 'frozen' in its deformed state when the first phase again becomes solid and will remain deformed even when the load is removed. The spring is analogous to the primary bonds and the fluid to the secondary bonds.

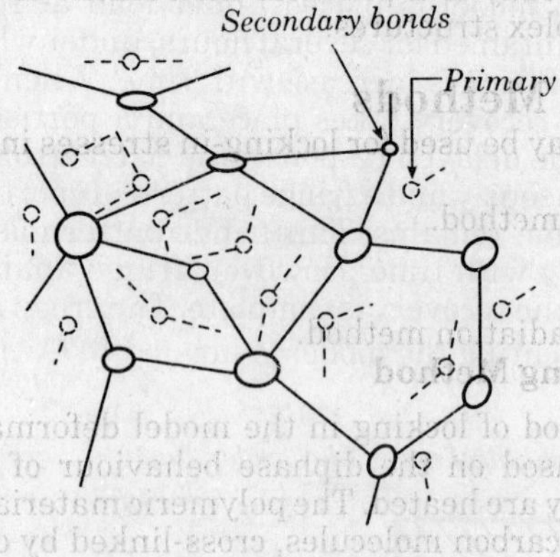

Fig. 8.1 Primary and secondary molecular chains in a diphase polymer.

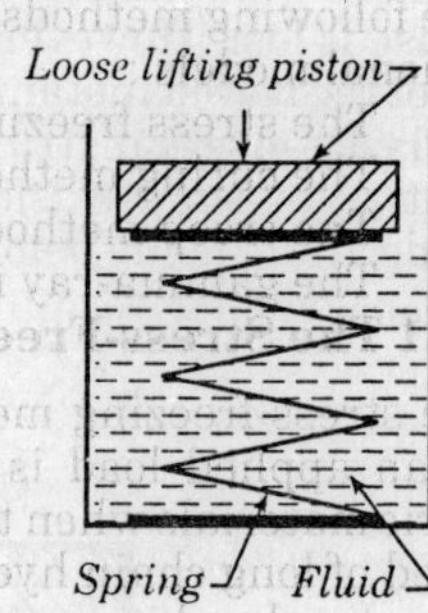

Fig. 8.2 Mechanical model of stress freezing method.

The following important facts are worth noting in connection with the stress freezing method :

1. The material fringe value of any material in the frozen state is different from that under cold loading and is much lower in value.
2. The Poisson's ratio in the frozen state or model material is very nearly 0.5.
3. The frozen stress patterns are not disturbed by careful cutting and machining provided that these operations are performed at reasonably low temperatures.

The following procedures may be followed for the stress freezing method :

1. Place the model in the stress freezing oven after applying the required loads.
2. Heat the model at the desired rate (2° to 5°C per hour) until the critical temperature is attained.
3. Soak the model at least 2 to 4 hours (depending upon the model thickness) until a uniform temperature throughout the model is obtained.
4. Cool the model slowly (2° to 5°C per hr) to the room temperature for temperature gradients to be minimized.
5. Remove the load and slice the model as desired.
6. View the slices in the polariscope for fringe order determinations.

The stress-freezing cycle is shown in Fig. 8.3.

8.2.2. The Creep Method

This method is based upon the fact that many plastics (phenolformaldehyde type) which creep exhibit a fringe pattern which remains directly proportional to the applied load even after considerable creep.

To employ the creep method, a model is placed under load at room temperature, and the load is maintained for several hours, under which the deformation and the order of fringes increase with time. When the load is removed, instantaneous recovery takes place and a portion of the response is lost. However, the delayed response due to creep of the model is not recovered instantaneously and a fringe pattern proportional to the elastic stress distribution remains. This fringe pattern is not permanent and decreases slowly with time. However, fringe analysis can be made after slicing before the recovery is complete. The creep rate can be accelerated by initially heating the model to about 140°C.

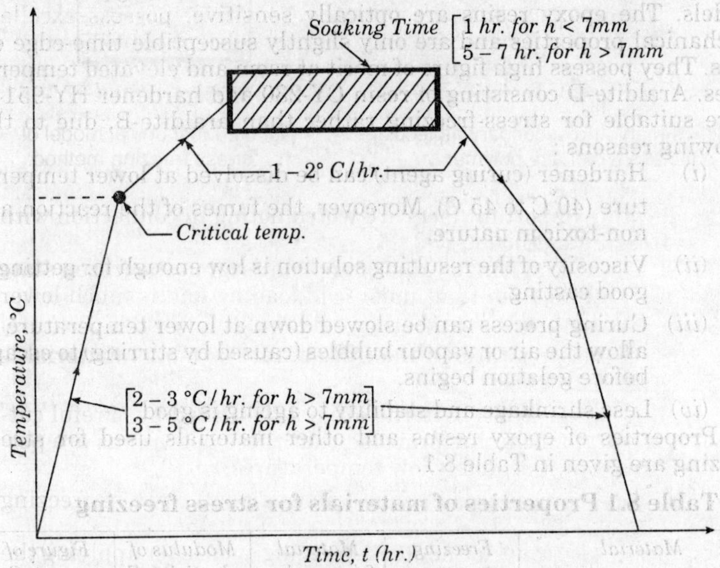

Fig. 8.3 Stress freezing cycle.

8.2.3 The Curing Method

Here the phenomena of stage curing is made use of, which is a typical behaviour of thermosetting resins. The load is applied to the model in state *B* and cured for a long time and resin advances to stage *C*, where it is hard and completely polymerized. During this period, new molecular bonds form about originally deformed bonds and lock them into their deformed state. On load removal the fringe pattern due to locked in deformation remains and can be studied for three-dimensional stress investigations.

8.2.4 The Gamma-Ray Irradiation Method

This method is similar to the curing method where the gamma rays are used to cure the model and provide complete retention of the fringe pattern associated with the load. This method has the advantages over the stress freezing method as the Poisson's ratio and modulus of elasticity of the model material do not change appreciably from those of their values at room temperature.

8.3 Material for the Models

The best photoelastic material will produce the greatest number of fringes upto the limit of stress strain-fringe proportionality and will cause least distortion. The material should also be homogeneous isotropic, with fringe coefficient insensitive to small temperature changes, resistant to mechanical and optical creep and time-edge effects, easily made by casting, bounding or machining without introducing residual stresses. To produce several fringes, the material must be capable of sustaining a high stress and it must have a long fringe-stress coefficients.

Epoxies are the most recent materials used for making photoelastic models. The epoxy resins are optically sensitive, possess excellent mechanical properties and are only slightly susceptible time-edge effects. They possess high figure of merit at room and elevated temperatures. Araldite-D consisting of resin CY-230 and hardener HY-951 is more suitable for stress-freezing rather than araldite-B, due to the following reasons :

(*i*) Hardener (curing agent) can be dissolved at lower temperature (40°C to 45°C). Moreover, the fumes of the reaction are non-toxic in nature.

(*ii*) Viscosity of the resulting solution is low enough for getting a good casting.

(*iii*) Curing process can be slowed down at lower temperature to allow the air or vapour bubbles (caused by stirring) to escape before gelation begins.

(*iv*) Less shrinkage and stability to ageing is good.

Properties of epoxy resins and other materials used for stress freezing are given in Table 8.1.

Table 8.1 Properties of materials for stress freezing

Material	*Freezing temperature, °C*	*Material fringe value, f_σ N/mm*	*Modulus of elasticity, E N/mm²*	*Figure of merit, Q 1/cm*
Araldite B CT-200 30 pph phthalic	140	0.23	12.95	563
Araldite D CY-230 6 pph HY-951	80	0.32	12.5	390
Araldite 6020 50 pph phthalic	162	0.415	35.7	860
Bakelite ERL-2774 50 pph phthalic	160	0.444	36.47	821
Bakelite (BT-61-893)	110	0.624	10.5	168
Columbia Resin CR-39	110	4.458	280	628
Castolite	118	1.480	28.4	192
Fosterite	87	0.686	16.2	236
Kriston	134	1.114	96.6	867
PLM-4B	120	0.392	17.5	446

8.4 Casting Technique for Models

The following technique for casting models out of araldite-D may be adopted.

The minimum amount of hardener HY-951, which can be added to resin CY-230, recommended by Ciba-Geigy is 5.5 percent by weight (p.b.w.) and the maximum amount is 10 p.b.w. The specific gravity of CY-230 is 1.15 and that of HY-951 is 1.0. Hence, depending upon the size of the model, these two quantities may be mixed together. Larger the casting, smaller should be the amount of hardener added, as the reaction is exothermic. Generally good casting can be obtained by adding 6 to 7 p.b.w. of hardener for three dimensional photoelastic work. As both the resin and the hardener are liquids, they can be conveniently measured by graduated jars. Before mixing, the resin alone may be heated in an oven from 80°C to 100°C for about two hours to remove all air bubbles and then cooled slowly to 40°C to 45°C. The resin should be filtered through a fine muslin cloth to remove all dirt particles. The measured quantity of hardener may then be added slowly and the mixture should be stirred for about ten minutes for thorough mixing. This mixture then should be poured in a mould box. Mould release agent QV-10 or LM-10 or Metroark-17 may be used. All joints of the mould should be made leak proof by using plastic clay. After pouring, the mixture should be allowed to polymerize at room temperature for about 48 hours. The models may then be placed for natural curing for about a week in a desiccator containing calcium chloride and copper sulphate to avoid time-edge effects. Test specimen of approximately 4 mm thickness may also be moulded from the same lot of mix for calibration purpose.

8.5 Machining and Heat Treatment of Models

Models of complicated shape may be made by cementing and simpler models may be made by machining. The models may be cut by a jig saw machine using small feeds and sharp tools and using air as a coolant. The models may then the machined using kerosene oil as a coolant on a milling machine or lathe. After machining the models may be ground and polished on a buffing machine.

During cutting and machining, residual stresses may be introduced in the model, which may be relieved by dipping the models in a liquid paraffin bath and slowly heating to about 100°C at the rate of 5°C per hour, soaking for about 4 hours and then cooling at the same rate. Before stress freezing the models should be observed in the polariscope to be free of any residual fringe pattern.

8.6 Stress Freezing Technique

A suitable loading fixture may be designed for the models. The models should be loaded applying suitable loads so that excessive deformations do not take place. Nigam has reported that by adding lowered quantities of hardener HY-951, the critical temperature of araldite-D may be as low as 60°C. Hence depending on the amount of hardener added, the critical temperature may be selected. The models are heated in an oven at the rate of 2° to 5°C per hour temperature rise, maintained at the critical temperature for 4 to 8 hours, depending upon the size of the model and then cooled at the same rate to room temperature. To decrease the heating and cooling rates, heavy cast iron blocks may be placed inside the heating oven. Heating ovens are nowadays available with thermostat temperature control or programmed temperature cycle. The calibration model has also to be stress frozen along with the test model.

8.7 Methods of Slicing

The slicing plan of any three-dimensional model depends upon what is to be investigated. The slices may be cut by a band saw of 1 mm blade thickness and using an abundant supply of kerosene oil as a coolant. The slices may then be rough ground on emery paper by hand and finished and polished on a polishing machine. The following methods may be used for slicing a three-dimensional model.

(*i*) *Plate method.* In this method, thin plates are actually sawed out of the model and each plate is examined in the polariscope.

(*ii*) *Difference method.* This method consists in removing a thick slice first and then gradually reducing the thickness and difference between the fringe orders at a point between successive patterns is taken to represent the fringe order or stress in a plate of thickness equal to that of the material removed. The results can be plotted and extrapolated for zero thickness to establish surface stresses.

8.8 Technique of Mixing Immersion Fluids

During machining and polishing of the slices cut from a stress-frozen photoelastic model, the stress pattern might be disturbed, if proper care is not taken ; due to heat generation. Fine machining and polishing of the slices could be avoided if the slices are placed in an immersion fluid for examination of fringe order in the polariscope. Photoelastic models have indices of refraction greater than unity. Hence, a parallel beam of light while passing through an irregular model (*i.e.* poorly machined and finished slice) will be refracted as a divergent beam. The most practical way to prevent this scatter and to obtain an unrefracted parallel beam and hence a reliable stress pattern is to immerse the slice in a fluid having substantially the same refractive index as the model.

A suitable immersion fluid is a mixture of α-bromonaphthalene (refractive index 1.66) and liquid paraffin (refractive index 1.44). Quite frequently photoelastic immersion fluids IMF 163 or Hallowax oil (RD 11-1) to which is added some mineral oil (Saybolt viscosity 125/135) to achieve the required refractive index is also used. Other immersion fluids like carbon disulphide and sodium thiosulphate have also been used.

In order to determine the required quantities of the two fluids to be mixed to be obtain the desired refractive index, some trial-and-error procedures have been presented by various research workers. The exact quantities to be mixed of the two fluids may be obtained from the following relationships :

$$p_1 = \frac{100\, d_1\, (n_2 - n)}{(n-1)\,(d_2 - d_1) - d_2\,(n_1 - 1) + d_1\,(n_2 - 1)} \qquad ...(8.1)$$

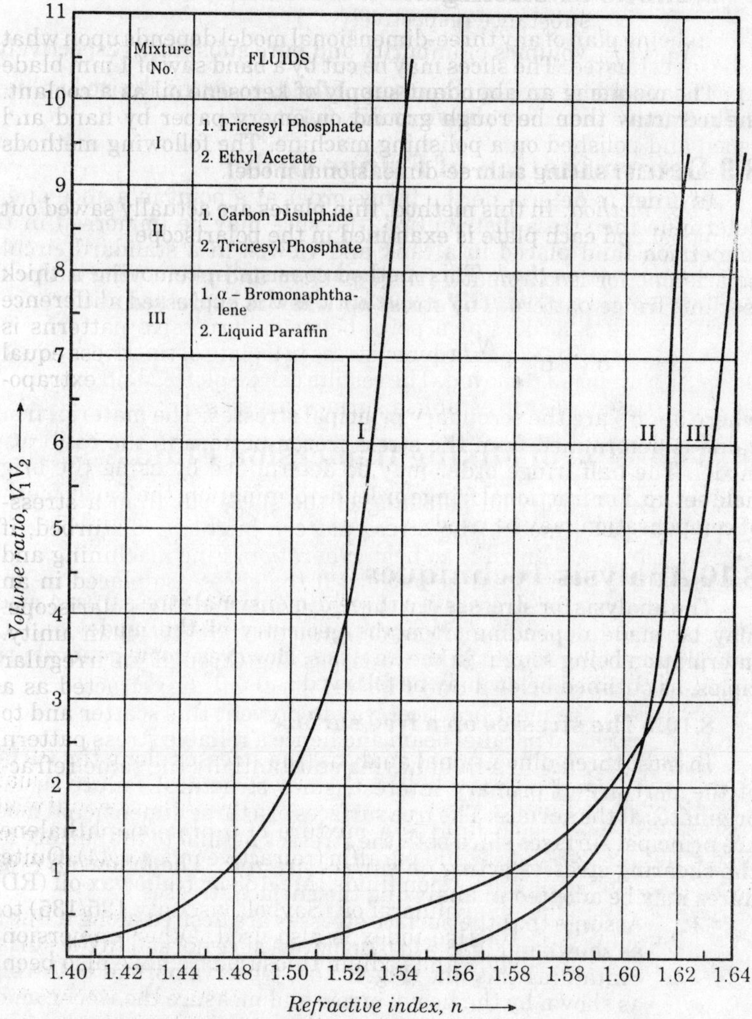

Fig. 8.4 Results of mixing three sets of fluids to obtain desired value of the refractive index.

...(8.1)

$$p_2 = 100\, p_1$$

$$V_1 = p_1/d_1,\ V_2 = p_2/d_2$$

where d_1, d_2 = densities of the impurity and pure substance respectively.

p_1, p_2 = percentage impurity and pure substance by weight in g per 100 g solution respectively.

n, n_1, n_2 = refractive indices of the mixture, impurity and pure substance respectively.

V_1, V_2 = volumes of impurity and pure substance respectively.

The results of mixing three sets of fluids to obtain desired value of the refractive index are shown in Fig. 8.4.

8.9 Determination of Fringe Order

In order to determine the fringe order at a point in a slice and to determine the stress distribution, the slice may be immersed in the immersion fluid placed in a tank and viewed in a standard circular polariscope for isochromatic fringe pattern and plane polariscope for isoclinic fringe pattern. The stress-optic law is expressed as :

$$\sigma'_1 - \sigma'_2 = \frac{N f_\sigma}{h} \quad ...(8.2)$$

where σ'_1, σ'_2 are the secondary principal stresses. The material fringe value is determined from the stress frozen pattern in the calibration model. The half fringe order may be determined by using the bright field set up. For fractional fringe order determination, the Tardy method of compensation may be used.

8.10 Analysis Techniques

The analysis for stresses of a three-dimensional stress frozen model may be made depending upon the geometry of the model and the information being sought in the analysis. However, some general principles, as outlined below may be followed :

8.10.1 The stresses on a free surface

In most three-dimensional analysis, the stresses along the surface of the part are of primary interest, since structural failure usually originates at the surface. The free surfaces of a three dimensional model are principal surfaces since both the stresses normal to the surface and the shearing stresses acting on surface are zero. The following procedures may be adopted in analyzing the surface stresses :

1. Assume that the surface stresses are desired along a line *s-s* as shown in Fig. 8.5 (*a*). Remove a slice normal to the surface containing this line (Fig. 8.5 *b*) ; Observe normal to the slice as shown by the heavy arrow and measure the isochromatic fringe order. Let σ_s and σ_n be the secondary principal stresses at the surface and since $\sigma_n = 0$, hence

$$\sigma_s - \sigma_n = \frac{N_t f_\sigma}{h_t} \text{ gives } \sigma_s = \frac{N_t f_\sigma}{h_t}$$

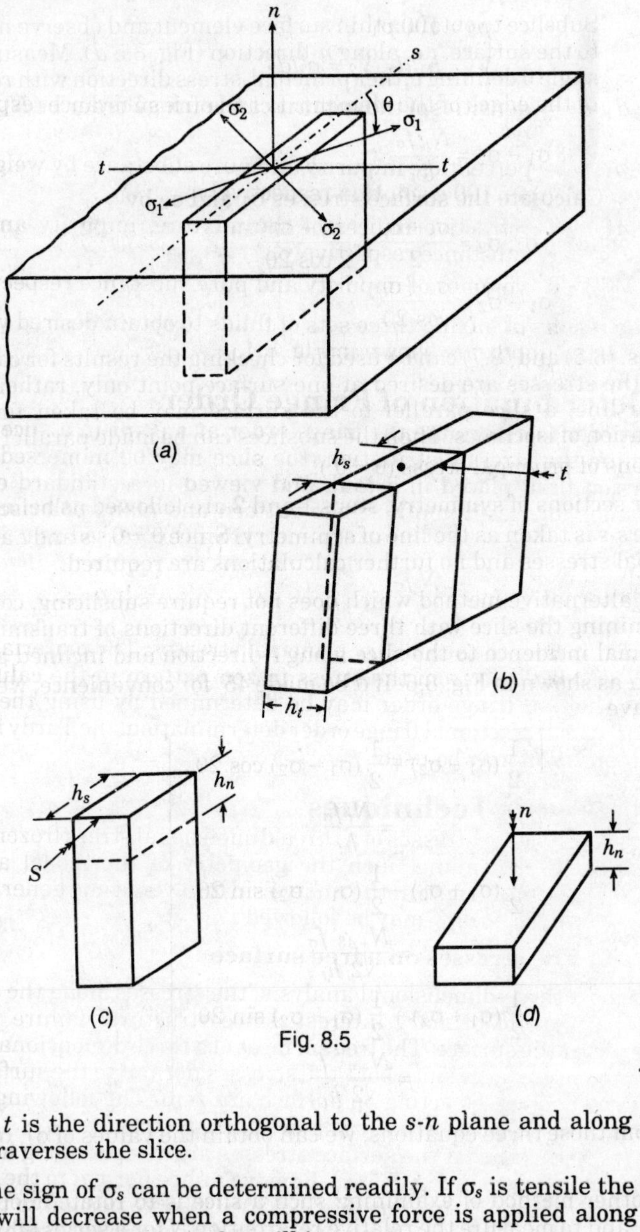

Fig. 8.5

...(8.3)

where t is the direction orthogonal to the s-n plane and along which light traverses the slice.

The sign of σ_s can be determined readily. If σ_s is tensile the fringe order will decrease when a compressive force is applied along s-s, if compressive, the fringe order will increase.

2. Subslice and measure the isochromatic fringe order in the perpendicular direction, *i.e.* direction s, as shown in Fig. 8.5 (c).

Now we have

$$\sigma_t = \frac{N_s f_\sigma}{h_s}$$

...(8.4)

3. Subslice to obtain a thin surface element and observe normal to the surface, *i.e.* along n-direction (Fig. 8.5 *d*). Measure the angle θ defining either principal-stress direction with respect to the edges of the element. Let the fringe order be N_n, then

$$\sigma_1 - \sigma_2 = \frac{N_n f_\sigma}{h_n} \quad ...(8.5)$$

4. Calculate the surface stresses σ_1 and σ_2 by

$$\sigma_1, \sigma_2 = \frac{\sigma_s + \sigma_t}{2} \pm \frac{\sigma_s - \sigma_t}{2 \cos 2\theta} \quad ...(8.6)$$

$$\therefore \quad \sigma_1 - \sigma_2 = \frac{\sigma_s - \sigma_t}{\cos 2\theta} \quad ...(8.7)$$

Eqs. (8.5) and (8.7) can be used for checking the results for cases in which the stresses are desired at one surface point only, rather than along a line, a slice parallel to the surface may be taken first for observation of isoclinics. Then the subslices can be made parallel to the directions of principal stress ($\theta = 0^\circ$).

For sections of symmetry, steps 1 and 2 are followed as before, but the line *s-s* is taken as the line of symmetry. Since $\theta = 0^\circ$, *s* and *t* are the principal stresses and no further calculations are required.

An alternative method which does not require subslicing, consists in examining the slice with three different directions of transmission, *i.e.* normal incidence to the slice along t-direction and inclined at $+\alpha$ and $-\alpha$ as shown in Fig. 8.6. If α be made 45° for convenience, we shall then have

$$\left.\begin{aligned} &\frac{1}{2}(\sigma_1 + \sigma_2) + \frac{1}{2}(\sigma_1 - \sigma_2)\cos 2\theta = \frac{N_t f_\sigma}{h_t} \\ &\frac{1}{2}(\sigma_1 + \sigma_2) - \frac{1}{2}(\sigma_1 - \sigma_2)\sin 2\theta = \frac{N_{+45^\circ} f_\sigma}{\sqrt{2}\, h_t} \\ &\frac{1}{2}(\sigma_1 + \sigma_2) + \frac{1}{2}(\sigma_1 - \sigma_2)\sin 2\theta = \frac{N_{-45^\circ} f_\sigma}{\sqrt{2}\, h_t} \end{aligned}\right\} \quad ...(8.8)$$

From these three equations, we can obtain the values of σ_1, σ_2 and θ.

Another method of examining such a slice is to rotate about the normal, and to measure the relative retardation N for a series of values of α and plot the values of $N \cos \alpha$. These will have a maximum or minimum when one of the principal stresses is in the plane of the wave front. The slice may then be set at the angles corresponding to maximum and minimum, and the values of the stresses are then measured directly.

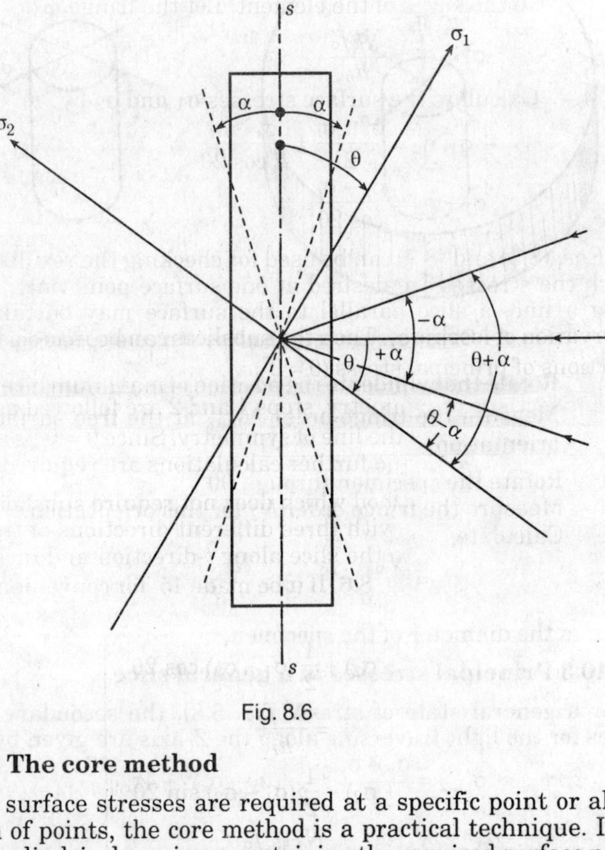

Fig. 8.6

8.10.2 The core method

When surface stresses are required at a specific point or along a succession of points, the core method is a practical technique. In this method, a cylindrical specimen containing the required surface point is cut from the three-dimensional model as shown in Fig. 8.7. A coring tool, which is a hollow end-milling tool, is used to cut the cylindrical surface with a generous flow of liquid coolant. The cylindrical specimen is then observed in a polariscope by immersing the specimen in a fluid contained in a tank, whose refractive index matches with that of the specimen, to prevent diffusion and refraction of light by the rough cylindrical surface of the specimen. A compensator is essential to determine the sign of stress as well as fringe order.

The specimen is rotated slowly while fringe order at the surface is observed. Since σ_1 is larger than any secondary principal stress in the surface and σ_3 is always zero, the orientation which yields a birefringence proportional to σ_1 is the orientation of maximum birefringence. Thus the core method employs the following simple procedure :

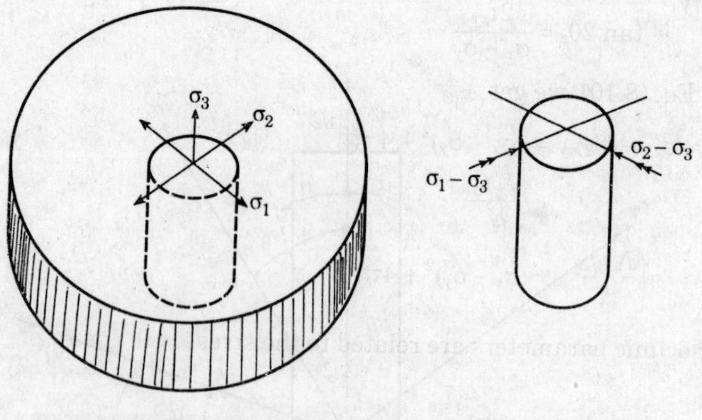

Fig. 8.7 Stress system at the surface of a core specimen.

1. Rotate the cylinder to the position of maximum birefringence.
2. Measure the fringe order N_{max} at the free surface for this orientation.
3. Rotate the specimen through 90°.
4. Measure the fringe order N_1 for this orientation.
5. Calculate,

$$\sigma_1 = \frac{N_{max} \cdot f_\sigma}{d}, \ \sigma_2 = \frac{N_1 \cdot f_\sigma}{d} \quad \text{...(8.9)}$$

where d is the diameter of the specimen.

8.10.3 Principal stresses in a general slice

For a general state of stress (Fig. 8.8), the secondary principal stresses for the light traversing along the Z-axis are given by

$$\sigma'_{1,2} = \frac{\sigma_x + \sigma_y}{2} \pm \frac{1}{2}\left\{(\sigma_x - \sigma_y)^2 + 4\tau_{xy}^2\right\}^{1/2} \quad \text{...(8.10)}$$

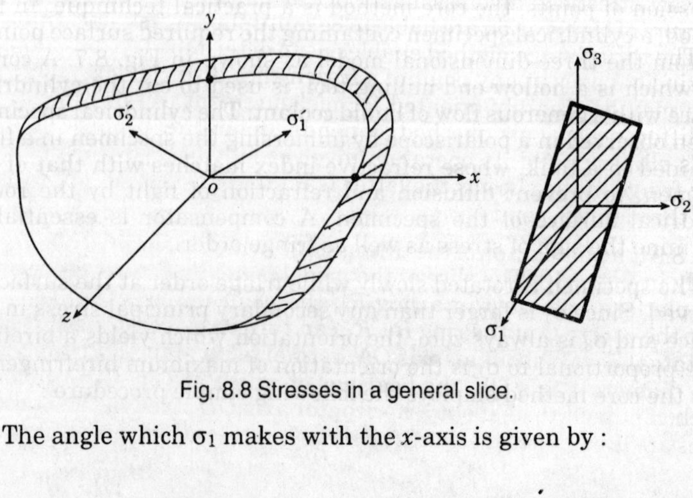

Fig. 8.8 Stresses in a general slice.

The angle which σ_1 makes with the x-axis is given by :

$$\tan 2\theta_z = \frac{2\tau_{xy}}{\sigma_x - \sigma_y} \qquad \text{...(8.11)}$$

From Eq. (8.10), we get

$$(\sigma'_1 - \sigma'_2)_{xy} = \left\{(\sigma_x - \sigma_y)^2 + 4\,\tau_{xy}^2\right\}^{1/2}$$

$$= \frac{N_z f_\sigma}{h}$$

or
$$\left(\frac{N_z f_\sigma}{h}\right)^2 = (\sigma_x - \sigma_y)^2 + 4\tau_{xy}^2 \qquad \text{...(8.12)}$$

The isoclinic parameters are related to the stresses in the xy plane by

$$\tan^2 2\theta_z = \frac{4\,\tau_{xy}^2}{(\sigma_x - \sigma_y)^2}$$

$$\cos^2 2\theta_z = \frac{(\sigma_x - \sigma_y)^2}{(\sigma_x - \sigma_y)^2 + 4\,\tau_{xy}^2}$$

$$\sin^2 2\theta_z = \frac{4\,\tau_{xy}^2}{(\sigma_x - \sigma_y)^2 + 4\,\tau_{xy}^2} \qquad \text{...(8.13)}$$

where θ_z is the angle between σ'_1 and the x-axis with the light passing through the model along the z-axis.

This method can enable us to find only the difference or normal stresses and shear stresses in a general slice. To determine the individual principal stresses, the shear-difference method in three dimensions has to be used.

8.10.4 The tilting stage method

The determination of the principal stresses or even of the principal stress-differences, by taking measurements of the relative retardations in arbitrary directions involves algebraic calculations in the course of which errors of observation are liable to be multiplied to an undesirable extent. The tilting stage method enables us to determine the directions of the principal axes at any point of a frozen slice directly, after which the slice may be suitably oriented for measurement of the principal stress-differences. This method depends upon the properties of Fresnel's ellipsoid, and its operation involves only observation of the isoclinic fringe in the slice as the latter is rotated about different axes passing through the point.

Fig. 8.9 is a photograph of the tilting stage, which is shown diagrammatically in Fig. 8.10. The slice of the model is held by spring clips on a glass platform mounted in a ring R_1, the point under examination being at the centre O of the ring R_1. R_1 can turn in a second ring R_2 so as to rotate the slice about an axis ON normal to its plane. R_2 can turn about a diametral axis OV, the bearings of which are on a third ring R_3 which can itself turn about a horizontal axis OH fixed in the stand S. Scales are provided to measure the three rotations. If desired, means may be provided for adjusting the plane of the platform relative to the plane of the axes so as to cater for slices of different thicknesses.

Fig. 8.9 The tilting stage.

The following sequence of operations may be followed to determine the principal stress directions at the point.

(*i*) Set all the scales at zero reading and place the slice in position with some reference line in it, oriented with regard to the scale on R_1. Place the stage in the immersion tank of the plane polariscope with dark field set up and focus the point O of the model on the cross-wires of the microscope, used in place of the camera.

(*ii*) Rotate the ring R_1 until an isoclinic fringe passes through the point O. The secondary principal axes in the plane of the slice will not be vertical and horizontal.

(*iii*) Perform a preliminary test by observing the effect of rotating the model about first the horizontal axis and then the vertical axis. If in either case no displacement of the fringe at O is observed, then that axis is one of the principal axes at O and the first part of the problem is solved.

(*iv*) Set the principal axis so found in the vertical position and then rotate the slice about OV until a position is reached at which the fringe is no longer displaced by rotating about OH. In this position two principal axes coincide with OV and OH, and all the axes are determined.

(*v*) If, in the preliminary test, rotation about both axes displaces the fringe, the following procedure is adopted :

(*a*) Give a small rotation about OH, which will displace the fringe from O.

(*b*) Bring back the fringe to O by a rotation of ring R_1 about the normal axis ON.

(*c*) Again displace the fringe, but now in the opposite direction, by a small rotation about *OH*.

(*d*) Bring back the fringe to *O* by a small rotation about the axis *OV*.

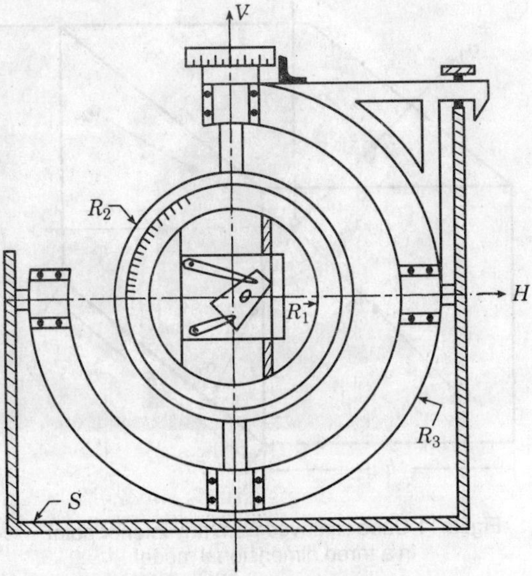

Fig. 8.10 The tilting stage.

(*vi*) Repeat the sequence of operations in (*v*) until a position is reached where rotation about *OH* produces no displacement of the fringe. *OH* is then the direction of one principal axis at *O*.

(*vii*) Return to the setting of (*ii*), repeat the operations of (*v*), but in the order *a*, *d*, *c*, *b* to find the direction of a second principal axis.

(*viii*) Return the stage to its original zero position setting and rotate the ring R_1 to an inclination differing from that of (*ii*) by 90°. An isoclinic fringe will again pass through *O*, but the secondary principal axes will have interchanged their positions.

(*ix*) Repeat the sequences now given in (*v*) and (*vii*).

8.11 Effective Stresses

The effective stress at a point in a three-dimensional model is given by

$$2\,\sigma_e^2 = (\sigma_1 - \sigma_2)^2 + (\sigma_2 - \sigma_3)^2 + (\sigma_3 - \sigma_1)^2 \qquad \text{...(8.14)}$$

The effective stress can be determined from a cube cut from a model at any random orientation as shown in Fig. 8.9. The cube is observed in normal incidence on its three mutually orthogonal faces, and the fringe orders N_x, N_y, N_z and the isoclinic parameters θ_x, θ_y and θ_z are recorded.

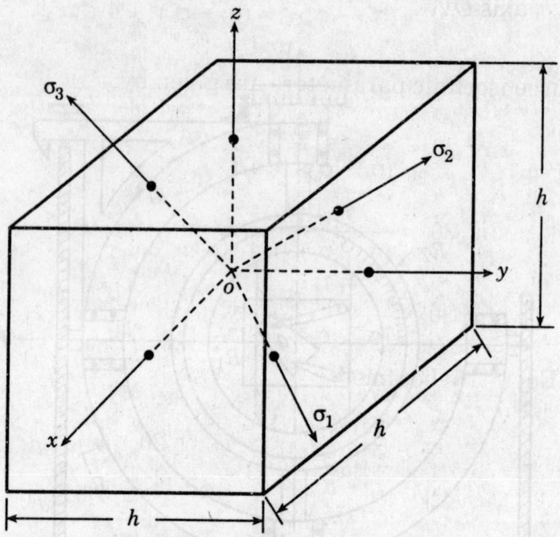

Fig. 8.11 Cube removed from any interior point in a three dimensional model.

Eq. (8.14) can be written as

$$\sigma_e^2 = (\sigma_1^2 + \sigma_2^2 + \sigma_3^2) - (\sigma_1\sigma_2 + \sigma_2\sigma_3 + \sigma_3\sigma_1)$$
$$= (I_1^2 - 2I_2) - I_2 = I_1^2 - 3I_2$$
$$= (\sigma_x + \sigma_y + \sigma_z)^2 - 3\,(\sigma_x\,\sigma_y + \sigma_y\sigma_z + \sigma_z\sigma_x - \tau_{xy}^2 - \tau_{yz}^2 - \tau_{xz}^2) \qquad ...(8.15)$$

Rearranging Eq. (8.15), we get

$$\sigma_e^2 = \frac{1}{4}\left[\left\{(\sigma_y - \sigma_z)^2 + 4\,\tau_{yz}^2\right\}\left\{2 + \frac{4\,\tau_{yz}^2}{(\sigma_y - \sigma_z)^2 + 4\,\tau_{yz}^2}\right\}\right.$$
$$+ \left\{(\sigma_x - \sigma_z)^2 + 4\,\tau_{xz}^2\right\}\left\{2 + \frac{4\,\tau_{xz}^2}{(\sigma_x - \sigma_z)^2 + 4\,\tau_{xz}^2}\right\}$$
$$\left. + \left\{(\sigma_x - \sigma_y)^2 + 4\,\tau_{xy}^2\right\}\left\{2 + \frac{4\,\tau_{xy}^2}{(\sigma_x - \sigma_y)^2 + 4\,\tau_{xy}^2}\right\}\right] \qquad ...(8.16)$$

From three fringe observations, we have

$$\left(\frac{N_x f_\sigma}{h}\right)^2 = (\sigma'_2 - \sigma'_3)^2 = (\sigma_y - \sigma_z)^2 + 4\,\tau_{yz}^2$$

$$\left(\frac{N_y f_\sigma}{h}\right)^2 = (\sigma'_1 - \sigma'_3)^2 = (\sigma_x - \sigma_z)^2 + 4\,\tau_{xz}^2$$

$$\left(\frac{N_z f_\sigma}{h}\right)^2 = (\sigma'_1 - \sigma'_2)^2 = (\sigma_x - \sigma_y)^2 + 4\,\tau_{xy}^2$$

The three isoclinic parameters are given by

$$\sin^2 2\theta_x = \frac{4\,\tau_{yz}^2}{(\sigma_y - \sigma_z)^2 + 4\,\tau_{yz}^2}$$

$$\sin^2 2\theta_y = \frac{4\,\tau_{xz}^2}{(\sigma_x - \sigma_z)^2 + 4\,\tau_{xz}^2}$$

$$\sin^2 2\theta_z = \frac{4\,\tau_{xy}^2}{(\sigma_x - \sigma_y)^2 + 4\,\tau_{xy}^2}$$

Thus Eq. (8.16) becomes

$$\sigma_e^2 = \frac{1}{4}\left[\left(\frac{N_x f_\sigma}{h}\right)^2 (2 + \sin^2 2\theta_x) + \left(\frac{N_y f_\sigma}{h}\right)^2 (2 + \sin^2 2\theta_y) + \left(\frac{N_z f_\sigma}{h}\right)^2 (2 + \sin^2 2\theta_z)\right] \quad \text{...(8.17)}$$

The effective stress calculated from Eq. (8.17) may be used as a criteria of plastic yielding for a wide variety of materials.

8.12 Oblique Incidence Method

In the three-dimensional problems it is not possible to determine the principal components of stress by pointwise photoelastic means alone. A hydrostatic pressure or tension has no effect on the relative retardation (Fig. 8.12) and therefore does not influence any photoelastic pattern. For this reason principal stress differences or maximum shearing stresses, can always be determined but generally not the principal stresses themselves.

For a general three dimensional state of stress, the retardation and isoclinic values for three incident directions are sufficient to calculate $\sigma_x - \sigma_z$, $\sigma_y - \sigma_z$, τ_{xy}, τ_{yz}, τ_{zx} and to provide a check.

Consider a slice cut from a three-dimensional stress frozen photoelastic model and take its middle plane as the *xy*-plane. The secondary principal stresses are given by

$$\sigma'_{1,2} = \frac{1}{2}(\sigma_x + \sigma_y) \pm \frac{1}{2}\left|(\sigma_x - \sigma_y)^2 + 4\,\tau_{xy}^2\right|^{1/2}$$

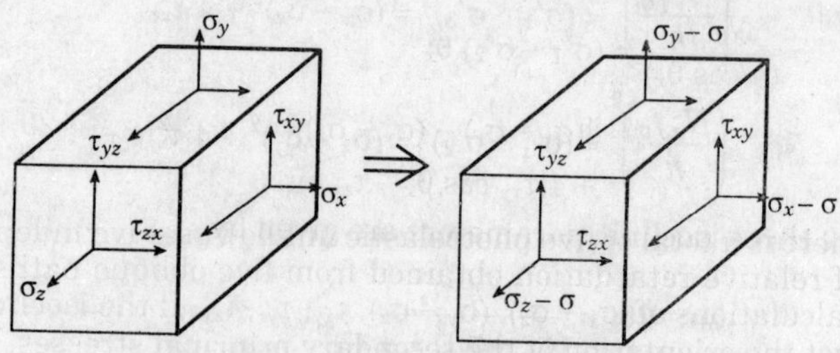

Fig. 8.12 Showing five photoelastic unknowns as the two stress states cannot be distinguished.

and $$\sigma'_1 - \sigma'_2 = \left(\frac{N_z f_\sigma}{h}\right) = \left\{(\sigma_x - \sigma_y)^2 + 4\,\tau_{xy}^2\right\}^{1/2} \qquad ...(8.18)$$

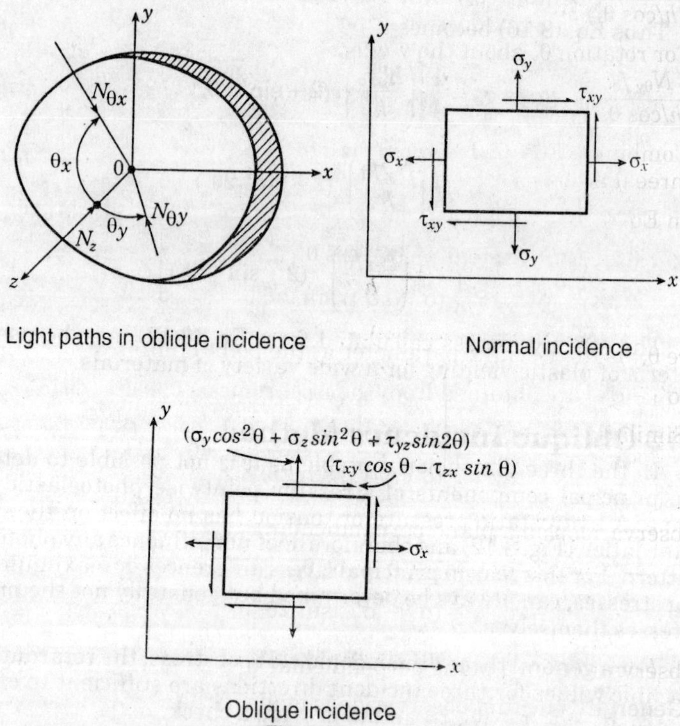

Light paths in oblique incidence

Normal incidence

Oblique incidence

Fig. 8.13.

Now let the slice be rotated about a horizontal axis, so that the wave normal makes an angle θ_x with the normal to the slice (Fig. 8.13). The stresses which cause the relative retardation are σ_x, $\sigma_y \cos^2\theta_x + \sigma_z \sin^2\theta_x + \tau_{yz} \sin^2\theta_x$, $\tau_{xy}\cos\theta_x - \tau_{zx}\sin\theta_x$ and the length of the light path has been increased to $h/\cos\theta$. Then

$$\frac{N_{\theta x} f_\sigma}{(h/\cos\theta_x)} = (\sigma'_1 - \sigma'_2)\,\theta_x$$
$$= \left\{[(\sigma_x - \sigma_z) - (\sigma_y - \sigma_z)\cos^2\theta_x - \tau_{yz}\sin 2\theta_x]^2 + 4[\tau_{xy}\cos\theta_x - \tau_{zx}\sin\theta_x]^2\right\}^{1/2} \quad ...(8.19)$$

So there is a total of five photoelastic unknowns. Five independent values of relative retardation obtained from five oblique paths would permit calculations of $(\sigma_x - \sigma_z)$, $(\sigma_y - \sigma_z)$, τ_{xy}, τ_{yz}, τ_{zx}. If the isoclinics are used to get the orientation of the secondary principal stresses, normal incidence plus oblique incidence in two perpendicular planes leads to comparatively straightforward computations.

For a principal slice in the xy-plane, τ_{yz} and τ_{xz} are zero at each point, and Eq. (8.19) becomes

$$\frac{N_{\theta x} f_\sigma}{(h/\cos\theta_x)} = \left\{[(\sigma_x - \sigma_z) - (\sigma_y - \sigma_z)\cos^2\theta_x]^2 + 4\tau_{xy}^2\cos^2\theta_x\right\}^{1/2} \quad ...(8.20)$$

For rotation θ_y about the y-axis

$$\frac{N_{\theta y} f_\sigma}{(h/\cos\theta_y)} = \left\{[(\sigma_y - \sigma_z) - (\sigma_x - \sigma_z)\cos^2\theta_y]^2 + 4\tau_{xy}^2\cos^2\theta_y\right\}^{1/2} \quad ...(8.21)$$

Combining Eqs. (8.18), (8.20) and (8.21) give us three equations for the three unknowns $(\sigma_x - \sigma_z)$, $(\sigma_y - \sigma_z)$ and τ_{xy}.

In Eq. (8.18), we have

$$\sigma_x - \sigma_y = (\sigma'_1 - \sigma'_2)\cos\theta_{xy}$$
$$\tau_{xy} = \frac{1}{2}(\sigma'_1 - \sigma'_2)\sin 2\,\theta_{xy} \quad ...(8.22)$$

where θ_{xy} is the isoclinic parameter at the point of interest.

$(\sigma'_1 - \sigma'_2)$ are obtained from the isochromatic parameter.

Similarly $\sigma_x - \sigma_z = (\sigma'_1 - \sigma'_3)\cos\theta_{xz}$

$$\tau_{zx} = \frac{1}{2}(\sigma'_1 - \sigma'_3)\sin 2\theta_{xz} \quad ...(8.23)$$

for observations on a plane perpendicular to y-axis.

$$\sigma_y - \sigma_z = (\sigma'_2 - \sigma'_3)\cos\theta_{yz}$$

and
$$\tau_{yz} = \frac{1}{2}(\sigma'_2 - \sigma'_3)\sin 2\theta_{yz} \quad ...(8.24)$$

for observations on a plane perpendicular to x-axis.

Generally, the first observation is made in the z-direction and Eqn. (8.22) are obtained from the isochromatic and isoclinic fringe patterns. A second observation is now made in a direction bisecting the angle between the x and z axes. Designating this direction as x' and the direction perpendicular to x' in the xz-plane by z', we get (Fig. 8.14 a).

$$(\sigma_y - \sigma'_z) = (\sigma'_1 - \sigma'_2)_{yz'}\cos 2\theta_{yz'}$$
$$\tau_{yz'} = \frac{1}{2}(\sigma'_1 - \sigma'_2)_{yz'}\sin 2\theta_{yz'} \quad ...(8.25)$$

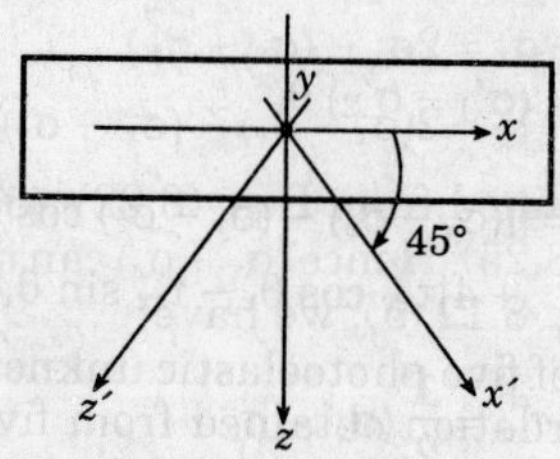

(*a*) Observation under normal and oblique incidence.

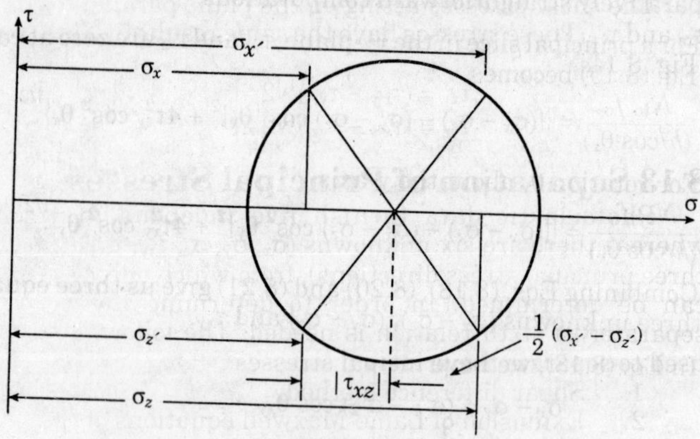

(*b*) Mohr's circle for stresses in the *xz*-plane.

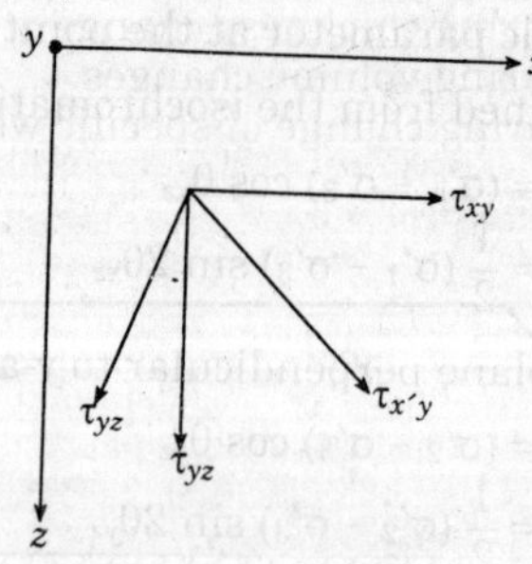

(*c*) Shear stresses parallel to the *xy*-plane.

Fig. 8.14

A third observation in the direction of z' gives

$$(\sigma'_x - \sigma_y) = (\sigma'_1 - \sigma'_2)_{x'y} \cos 2\theta_{x'y}$$

$$\tau_{xy} = \frac{1}{2}(\sigma'_1 - \sigma'_2)_{x'y} \sin 2\theta_{x'y} \qquad \text{...(8.26)}$$

Now $\sigma_x + \sigma_z = \sigma'_x + \sigma'_z$ as is seen from Fig. 8.14 (*b*).

Hence $\sigma_x - \sigma_z = 2\sigma_x - (\sigma_{x'} + \sigma_{z'})$

$$= 2(\sigma_x - \sigma_y) - (\sigma_{x'} - \sigma_y) + (\sigma_y - \sigma_{z'})$$

$(\sigma_x - \sigma_y)$ is obtained from Eqs. (8.22), $(\sigma_{x'} - \sigma_y)$ from Eq. (8.26) and $(\sigma_y - \sigma_{z'})$ from Eq. (8.25). Hence $(\sigma_x - \sigma_z)$ can be known. Also from Mohr's circle shown in Fig. 8.12 (*b*), we have

$$\tau_{xz} = \frac{1}{2}(\sigma_x' - \sigma_z')$$

$$= \frac{1}{2}[(\sigma'_x - \sigma_y) + (\sigma_y - \sigma_{z'})] \qquad ...(8.27)$$

The shear stresses acting on the plane parallel to the *xz*-plane are τ_{xz} and τ_{yz}. These stresses have the same resultant as $\tau_{x'z}$ and $\tau_{yz'}$, so that (Fig. 8.14*c*).

$$\left.\begin{aligned} \tau_{xy} &= (\tau_{x'y} - \tau_{yz'})/\sqrt{2} \\ \tau_{yz} &= (\tau_{x'y} - \tau_{yz'})/\sqrt{2} \end{aligned}\right\} \qquad ...(8.28)$$

8.13 Separation of Principal Stresses

Photoelastic data furnish five independent stress relations, whereas there are six unknowns ($\sigma_x, \sigma_y, \sigma_z, \tau_{xy}, \tau_{yz}, \tau_{xz}$ or $\sigma_1, \sigma_2, \sigma_3$ and three principal stress directions), from which only the principal shears can be determined. In order to determine the principal stresses separately a sixth relation is needed. The following methods may be used to separate the principal stresses :

1. Shear difference method.
2. Extension of Lame-Maxwell equations of three dimensions.
3. Solution of compatibility equation by relaxation method.
4. Experimental methods.
   (*a*) Measuring thickness change after annealing the slice.
   (*b*) Measuring volume changes.
   (*c*) Measuring change of specific weight.

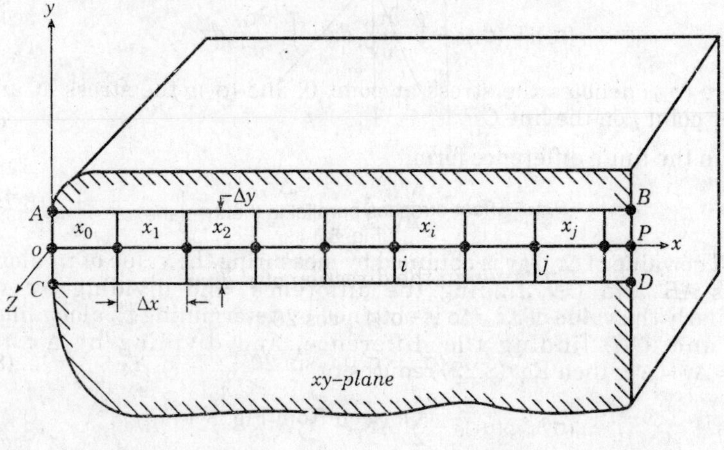

(*a*)

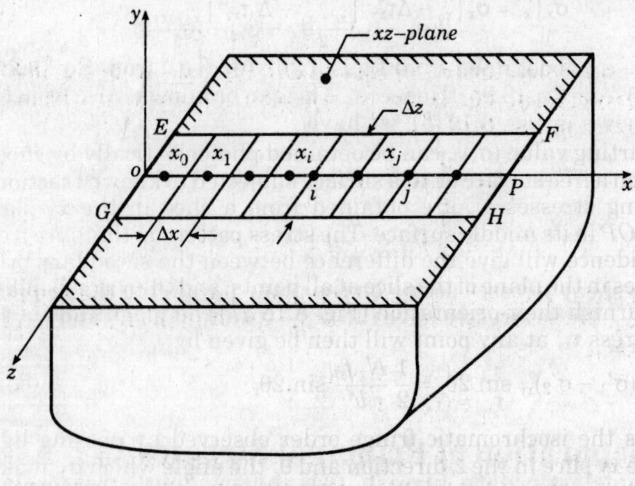

(b)

Fig. 8.15 Shear difference method illustrated about an arbitrary line *OP*.

1. **Shear Difference Method.** By the shear-difference method we can determine all the six stress components (*i.e.* σ_x, σ_y, σ_z, τ_{xy}, τ_{yz}, τ_{xz}) at a point separately. Consider an arbitrary loaded unsymmetrical model with the set of coordinate axes as shown in Fig. 8.15. Let a straight line *OP* be drawn through point *i* from boundary to boundary and let this line be taken as the *x*-axis. At any point along this line the first differential equation of equilibrium, with body forces neglected, is

$$\frac{\partial \sigma_x}{\partial x} + \frac{\partial \tau_{xy}}{\partial y} + \frac{\partial \tau_{xz}}{\partial z} = 0$$

and upon integration the stress at any point *j* is given by

$$(\sigma_x)_j = (\sigma_x)_0 - \int_0^j \frac{\partial \tau_{xy}}{\partial y}\, dx - \int_0^j \frac{\partial \tau_{xz}}{\partial z}\, dx$$

where $(\sigma_x)_0$ denotes the stress at point 0, and $(\sigma_x)_j$, the stress at any other point *j* on the line *OP*.

In the finite difference form,

$$(\sigma_x)_j = (\sigma_x)_0 - \frac{\Delta \tau_{xy}}{\Delta y}\, \Delta x \Big|_0^j - \frac{\Delta \tau_{xz}}{\Delta z} \cdot \Delta x \Big|_0^j \qquad \text{...(8.29)}$$

The value of $\Delta\tau_{xy}/\Delta y$ is obtained by measuring the value of τ_{xy} along lines *AB* and *CD*, finding the difference, and dividing by Δy. Similarly the value of $\Delta\tau_{xz}/\Delta z$ is obtained by determining τ_{xz} along lines *EF* and *GH*, finding the difference, and dividing by Δz. If $\Delta x = \Delta y = \Delta z$, then Eq. (8.29) reduces to

$$(\sigma_x)_j = (\sigma_x)_0 - \sum_0^j \Delta \tau_{xy} - \sum_0^j \Delta \tau_{xz} \qquad \text{...(8.30)}$$

in which $\Delta\tau_{xy}$ and $\Delta\tau_{xz}$ have the mean value in each interval.

Thus $\sigma_x |_{x_1} = \sigma_x |_{x_0} - \Delta\tau_{xy} \Big|_{\frac{x_0+x_1}{2}} - \Delta\tau_{xz} \Big|_{\frac{x_0+x_1}{2}}$

$$\sigma_x |_{x2} = \sigma_x |_{x1} - \Delta\tau_{xy} \Big|_{\frac{x_1+x_2}{2}} - \Delta\tau_{xz} \Big|_{\frac{x_1+x_2}{2}}$$

and so on.

The starting value $(\sigma_x)_0$, can be obtained photoelastically by choosing point 0 on a free surface or on a surface subjected to known tractions. The shearing stresses τ_{xy} are obtained from a slice in the *xy*-plane containing *OP* in its middle surface. The stress pattern of this slice from normal incidence will give the difference between the secondary principal stresses in the plane of the slice at all points, and the corresponding isoclinics furnish their orientation (Fig. 8.16 *a*). The magnitude of the shearing stress τ_{xy} at any point will then be given by

$$\tau_{xy} = \frac{1}{2}(\sigma'_1 - \sigma'_2)_{xy} \sin 2\theta_z = \frac{1}{2}\frac{N_z f_\sigma}{h} \sin 2\theta_z \qquad ...(8.31)$$

where N_z is the isochromatic fringe order observed by passing light through the *xy* slice in the *z*-direction and θ_z the angle which $\sigma_{1'}$ makes with the *x*-axis as provided by the isoclinic parameter.

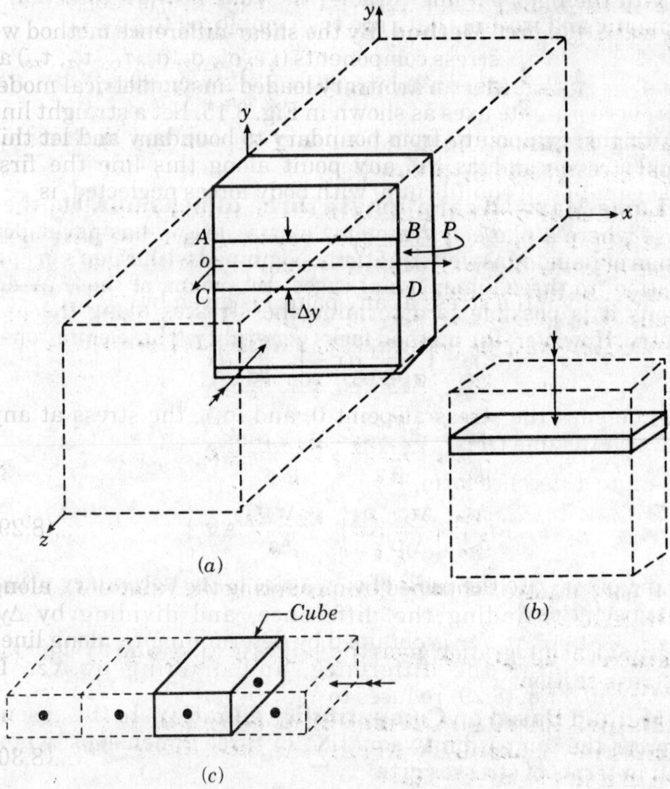

Fig. 8.16 Slicing plan and directions of light path for shear difference method.

Next a subslice is removed from the *xy* slice in the manner shown in Fig. 8.16 (*b*) and is observed with the light passing through the subslice in the *y*-direction. Isoclinic parameters and isochromatic fringe orders along lines *OP, EF* and *GH* give the shear stress τ_{xz} as

$$\tau_{xz} = \frac{1}{2}(\sigma'_1 - \sigma'_2)_{xz} \sin 2\theta_y = \frac{1}{2}\frac{N_y f_\sigma}{h} \qquad \text{...(8.32)}$$

where θ_y is the isoclinic parameter in the *xz*-slice.

Knowing τ_{xy} and τ_{xz}, σ_x can be obtained along *OP*.

Now from Mohr's circle, we have

$$(\sigma_y)_j = (\sigma_x)_j - [(\sigma'_1 - \sigma'_2)_{xy} \cos 2\theta_x]_j = (\sigma_x)_j - \left[\frac{N_z f_\sigma}{h} \cos 2\theta_z\right]$$

$$(\sigma_z)_j = (\sigma_x)_j - [(\sigma'_1 - \sigma'_2)_{xz} \cos 2\theta_y]_j = (\sigma_x)_j - \left[\frac{N_y f_\sigma}{h} \cos 2\theta_y\right]_j \qquad \text{...(8.33)}$$

To determine τ_{yz}, the subslice may be reduced to a series of cubes each containing an evaluation point x_1, x_2, x_3 etc. as its centre, as shown in Fig. 8.16 (*c*). The *yz* plane of these cubes is examined in the polariscope with the light passing through the cube in the *x*-direction. The isochromatic and isoclinic data are then employed to give τ_{yz}.

$$\tau_{yz} = \frac{1}{2}(\sigma'_1 - \sigma'_2)_{yz} \sin 2\theta_x = \frac{1}{2}\frac{N_x f_\sigma}{h} \sin 2\theta_x \qquad \text{...(8.34)}$$

Having known σ_x, σ_y, σ_z, τ_{xy}, τ_{yz} and τ_{xz}, we can determine the principal stresses and their directions.

2. **Lame-Maxwell equations in three-dimensions.** For the special case where a plane of symmetry exists, Jessop has developed an extension of Lame-Maxwell equations, combined with Filon's graphical integration, to three-dimensional cases. By means of these extended equations it is possible to determine the stresses along the axis of symmetry. However, the method lacks generality. These equations are:

$$\begin{aligned}
\frac{\partial \sigma_1}{\partial s_1} + \frac{\sigma_1 - \sigma_2}{\rho'_2} + \frac{\sigma_1 - \sigma_3}{\rho'_3} &= 0 \\
\frac{\partial \sigma_2}{\partial s_2} + \frac{\sigma_2 - \sigma_3}{\rho'_3} + \frac{\sigma_2 - \sigma_1}{\rho'_1} &= 0 \qquad \text{...(8.35)} \\
\frac{\partial \sigma_3}{\partial s_3} + \frac{\sigma_3 - \sigma_1}{\rho'_1} + \frac{\sigma_3 - \sigma_2}{\rho'_2} &= 0
\end{aligned}$$

where ρ'_1, ρ'_2, ρ'_3 are the radii of curvature of the secondary principal stress trajectories.

A graphical integration gives the values of σ_1, σ_2 and σ_3 at all points on the cross-section.

3. **Method Based on Compatibility equation.** In the absence of body forces the compatibility equation in three dimensions, when expressed in terms of stresses give

$$\left(\frac{\partial^2}{\partial x^2}+\frac{\partial^2}{\partial y^2}+\frac{\partial^2}{\partial z^2}\right)(\sigma_x+\sigma_y+\sigma_z)=0$$

or $$\nabla^2 I = 0 \qquad \text{...(8.36)}$$

where $$I = \sigma_x + \sigma_y + \sigma_z$$

Then $$I_\theta = \frac{I_1 + I_2 + I_3 + I_4 + I_5 + I_6}{6} \qquad \text{...(8.37)}$$

where I_0 is the sum of the three normal stresses at the centre of a cube while I_1 to I_6 are the sums of these stresses at the centres of the six faces of the cube. The stresses can then be determined by the relaxation method.

4. Experimental Methods

(*a*) *Strain measurement after annealing.* When slices cut from a model with frozen-in deformations are heated to the softening temperature of the model material, the frozen-in strains are released. By measuring this recovery, an additional independent experimental value is obtained which can be applied as the sixth value in conjunction with the five values determined optically to separate the stresses. Several mechanical and optical methods (*e.g.* comparators and interferometers respectively) have been suggested for determining the recovery of a frozen slice on reheating. The experimental methods suggested, however, suffer from the fact that Poisson's ratio comes very close to 0.5 with frozen in strain, which renders accuracy very poor as it can be read from the following.

Strain of a loaded body (measured in a certain direction, say x) is known to be

$$\varepsilon_x = \frac{1}{E}\left[\sigma_x - \nu\,(\sigma_y + \sigma_z)\right]$$

which may be written as

$$\varepsilon_x = \frac{1}{E}\left[\frac{(\sigma_x - \sigma_y) + (\sigma_x - \sigma_z)}{2} + (0.5 - \nu)\,(\sigma_y + \sigma_z)\right] \qquad \text{...(8.38)}$$

Thus, as the values of $(\sigma_x - \sigma_y)$ and $(\sigma_x - \sigma_z)$ are known (from the isochromatics and isoclinics), no additional information can be taken out of measuring ε_x if $\nu = 0.5$. Also, its accuracy and reliability will depend upon the amount by which ν differs from 0.5. Also when $\sigma_x = \sigma_y = \sigma_z$, *i.e.* for an isotropic stress system, and, in addition, $\nu = 0.5$, then

$$\varepsilon_x = \varepsilon_y = \varepsilon_z = 0$$

In other words, isotropic systems of stresses produce no strains. Hence, two stress systems differing by an arbitrary isotropic system produce the same strains. Thus, when $\nu = 0.5$ a given strain field does not determine a unique stress field. Strain measurements when $\nu = 0.5$ thus add nothing to the general solution of the three-dimensional problems.

(*b*) *Measurement of volume change.* Some attempts have also been made by various investigators to measure the small change of volume associated with the small amount by which the actual value of Poisson's ratio differs from 0.5. However, this difference in Poisson's ratio is much smaller so that such methods are impracticable.

(*c*) *Measurement of change of specific weight.* Kuske reported that the most accurate method to determine the change of volume is by measurement of change of specific weight. It was pointed out that directly measuring the stress sum without differences being involved obviously promises to be more reliable. The stress sum is proportional to the dilatation of an element. Suppressing terms of higher order, the dilatation e is

$$e = \varepsilon_x + \varepsilon_y + \varepsilon_z = \left(\frac{1-\nu}{E}\right) I_1 = \frac{I_1}{3K} \qquad ...(8.39)$$

where $I_1 = \sigma_x + \sigma_y + \sigma_z = \sigma_1 + \sigma_2 + \sigma_3$

$K = \dfrac{E}{3\,(1-\nu)}$ is the bulk modulus.

As the dilatation e causes a change of specific weight of $e.\gamma$ (where γ = specific weight), for separating principal stresses the following method of determining the specific weight was suggested by Kuske:

Small particles of a model (1 to 2 mm) are immersed into a liquid of suitable specific weight. Sinking or floating indicates their relative specific weight. Liquids of slightly differing specific weight which are needed in this method can easily be produced by varying the temperature or, in case of mixtures or solutions, by varying the concentration. Solution of sodium thiosulphate ($Na_2S_2O_3$) in water or trichlor-oethylene and methylalcohol, proves to be suited for this purpose. It is however difficult to determine the absolute values of the specific weights by these means. By comparing particles of unknown stress sum with those of known stress sum, however, the problem under consideration can be solved. Differences of specific weight of 10^{-5}, which would require extremely sensitive balances, could easily be determined by this method.

8.14 Multilayer Reflection Technique

The multilayer reflection technique utilizes a model fabricated from a series of cemented thin laminations of partially aluminized photoelastic plastic. The locations of the mirror coatings are arranged so that, in any area, observations may be made through at least two different thicknesses of the model. Data for a reconstruction of the three-dimensional isochromatic distribution can be obtained by a set of observations through the various thicknesses, for a given value of applied load. The technique is ideally suited for use with a model where the stress field is symmetric. Polarized light enters the model surface, passing through the layers of interest, is reflected and traverses the same layers again before leaving the model to pass to the analyzer. Such a double traverse doubles the sensitivity of the measurement since the photoelastic fringe order is twice that for a single passage.

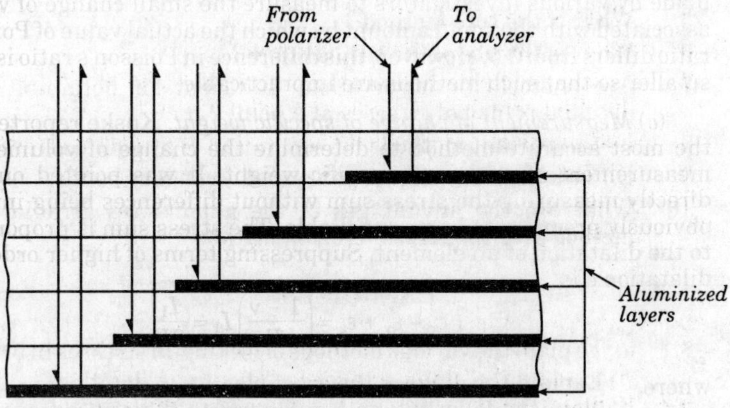

Fig. 8.17 Assembled multilayer model.

Fig. 8.17 shows an assembled multilayer mode and Fig. 8.18 shows the optical train schematically. This method may also prove to be very useful for the study of bending of thick plates.

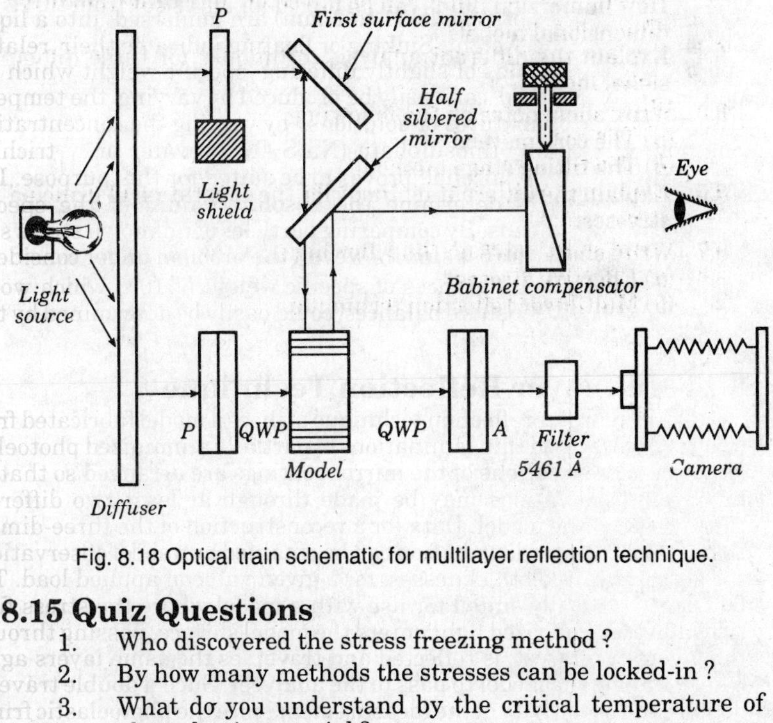

Fig. 8.18 Optical train schematic for multilayer reflection technique.

8.15 Quiz Questions

1. Who discovered the stress freezing method ?
2. By how many methods the stresses can be locked-in ?
3. What do you understand by the critical temperature of a photoelastic material ?

4. What is the necessity of an immersion fluid ?
5. What is the core method ?
6. What is the use of the tilting stage ?
7. Are photoelastic observations sufficient for obtaining individual principal stresses at a point ?
8. List important methods for separation of principal stresses.
9. Differentiate between primary and secondary bonds.
10. What are the advantages of the gamma ray irradiation method over the stress-freezing method ?

EXERCISES

8.1 (*a*) Explain the various methods of locking-in stresses in brief.
(*b*) Explain the diphase theory of plastics in detail.

8.2 Explain the following with reference to the stress-freezing method :
(*a*) Model materials,
(*b*) Casting technique, and
(*c*) Machining of models.

8.3 What is the necessity of an immersion fluid ?
How immersion fluids can be mixed for slices cut from three-dimensional models ?

8.4 Explain the different analysis techniques for three dimensional models.

8.5 Write short notes on the following :
(*a*) The core method
(*b*) The tilting stage method.

8.6 Explain the different methods for the separation of principal stresses.

8.7 Write short notes on the following :
(*a*) Effective stresses
(*b*) Multilayer reflection technique.

9

Photoelastic Coatings

9.1 Introduction

The method of photoelastic coatings also called the method of birefringent coatings or photostress, extends the well known photoelastic method to the measurement of surface strains in opaque bodies like steel, rock etc. It is one of the whole-field experimental methods that is suitable for two- and three-dimensional models. The coating is a thin layer of birefringent material, usually a polymer, that is bonded integrally to the flat or curved surface of the prototype being analyzed for stress. When the prototype is loaded, the surface strains are transmitted to the coating, reproducing the prototype strain field in the coating. To provide light reflection at the interface, the coating is bonded to the structure with a reflective cement. When viewed through a while light reflection polariscope, the strained coating exhibits black isoclinics and coloured isochromatic fringes. Isoclinic fringes provide directions of principal strains whereas isochromatic fringes, when viewed in normal incidence light, provide the difference of principal strains, when viewed in oblique incidence light, they permit the determination of the magnitude and sign of individual principal strains. Whole-field isochromatic and isoclinic patterns can be photographed in a reflection polariscope for subsequent analysis. The fringe pattern can also be analyzed on a point-by-point basis by using a compensator to determine the fringe order, with the magnitude of the strain being displayed on a digital readout device.

The concept of photoelastic coatings was first proposed by Mesnager in France in 1930. The method was re-examined during the period from 1932 to 1937 by Oppel in Germany. Mesnager tried to bond segments of glass to structures and Oppel used flat sheets of Bakelite. But much success could not be achieved due to the difficulties in machining glass, development of time-edge effect in Bakelite and the non-availability of a proper adhesive for bonding the coating to the structure. Not much work was done during the period from 1937 to 1953. With the availability of epoxy resins in the 1950's, the required high-strength adhesive and a photoelastic sheet relatively free of time-edge effect could be produced. The credit for obtaining the first practical result applicable to any shape and size of structural or machine part goes to the French scientists Fleury and Zandman (1954); D'Agostino, Drucker and Liu (1954) in the United States ; Kawata (1958) in Japan and Fessler and Heines (1958) in the United Kingdom.

Upto 1960, methods were developed to apply coatings to plain surfaces only. Zandman in 1960 developed the contour sheet procedure for applying a constant-thickness coating to curved surfaces without introducing residual birefringence. At the same time Zandman (1959) developed a portable reflection polariscope, making the method practicable for quantitative measurements under industrial conditions.

Photoelastic coatings have been successfully applied to study static, dynamic and transient stresses. Methods have been advanced for using the coatings in the analysis of plasticity, thermoelasticity, vibrations and wave and crack propagation. A wide variety of industrial design problems have been solved by this method. In this chapter we shall study this method of photoelastic coatings in detail.

9.2 Theory of Photoelastic Coatings

Photoelastic coatings are elastic bodies bonded to surfaces of other deformable bodies. On the application of the load to the deformable body, the surface displacements are transmitted to the coating through the adhesive. The exact determination of the distribution of the stresses and strains through the thickness of the coating is very complex problem. Considering both the coating and the specimen to be subjected to a state of plane stress where the strains are uniformly distributed through the thickness of the coating, it is possible to introduce the relations between the stresses in the coating and the specimen.

9.2.1 Stresses and Strains in the Coating

Consider a plane specimen with a thin coating as shown in Fig. 9.1. The geometry of the specimen is assumed such that the loading produces a state of plane stress. The state of stress and strain fields in the specimen may be described as :

$$\left.\begin{aligned} \sigma_x^s &= \sigma_x^s\,(x, y)\ ;\ \varepsilon_x^s = \varepsilon_x^s\,(x, y) \\ \sigma_y^s &= \sigma_y^s\,(x, y)\ ;\ \varepsilon_y^s = \varepsilon_y^s\,(x, y) \\ \tau_{xy}^s &= \tau_{xy}^s\,(x, y)\ ;\ \varepsilon_z^s = \varepsilon_z^s\,(x, y) \\ \tau_{xz}^s &= \tau_{yz}^s = \sigma_z^s = 0\ ;\ \gamma_{xy}^s = \gamma_{xy}^s\,(x, y) \\ &\qquad\qquad\qquad \gamma_{xz}^s = \gamma_{yz}^s = 0 \end{aligned}\right\} \qquad ...(9.1)$$

Since the strains in the specimen are constant with respect to z, it is assumed that they are transmitted to the coating through the adhesive without loss or amplification and that they are also constant with respect to z through the thickness of the coating.

Thus
$$\begin{aligned} \varepsilon_x^c\,(x, y) &= \varepsilon_x^s\,(x, y) \\ \varepsilon_y^c\,(x, y) &= \varepsilon_y^s\,(x, y) \end{aligned} \qquad ...(9.2)$$

where the superscripts c and s refer to the coating and the specimen respectively.

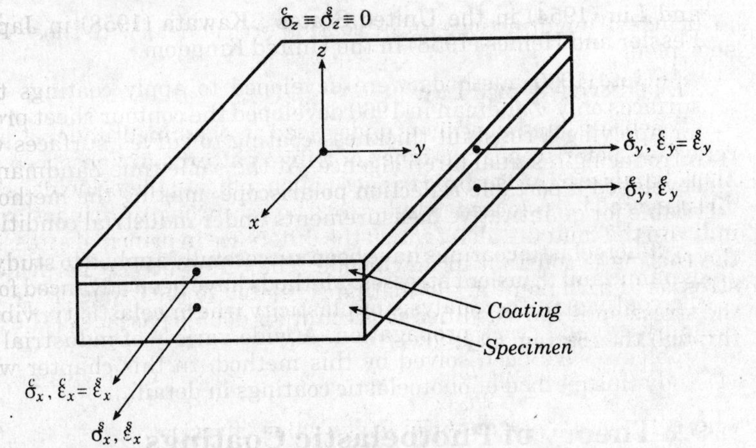

Fig. 9.1 Stresses and strains in the coating and specimen.

Because the coating is relatively thin, it is assumed that a state of plane stress also exists in the coating, from which

$$\sigma_z^c = \sigma_z^s = 0 \qquad \text{...(9.3)}$$

These foregoing assumptions amount to neglecting the influence of,

(*i*) the coating reinforcement on the specimen behaviour.

(*ii*) any mismatch in Poisson's ratio between the specimen and the coating, and

(*iii*) the strain ε_z^s normal to the plane of the specimen.

The stresses in the coating can be expressed as functions of the stresses in the specimen as follows :

$$\left.\begin{aligned} \varepsilon_1^s &= \frac{1}{E_s}(\sigma_1^s - \nu_s \sigma_2^s) = \varepsilon_1^c = \frac{1}{E_c}(\sigma_1^c - \nu_c \sigma_2^c) \\ \varepsilon_2^s &= \frac{1}{E_s}(\sigma_2^s - \nu_s \sigma_1^s) = \varepsilon_2^c = \frac{1}{E_c}(\sigma_2^c - \nu_c \sigma_1^c) \end{aligned}\right\} \qquad \text{...(9.4)}$$

where the subscripts 1 and 2 refer to the principal directions.

Solving for principal stresses, we get

$$\left.\begin{aligned} \sigma_1^c &= \frac{E_c}{E_s(1-\nu_c^2)}[(1-\nu_c\nu_s)\sigma_1^s + (\nu_c - \nu_s)\sigma_2^s] \\ \sigma_2^c &= \frac{E_c}{E_s(1-\nu_c^2)}[(1-\nu_c\nu_s)\sigma_2^s + (\nu_c - \nu_s)\sigma_1^s] \end{aligned}\right\} \qquad \text{...(9.5)}$$

or $$\sigma_1^c - \sigma_2^c = \left(\frac{E_c}{E_s}\right)\left[\frac{1+\nu_s}{1+\nu_c}\right](\sigma_1^s - \sigma_2^s) \qquad \text{...(9.6)}$$

and $$\varepsilon_1^c - \varepsilon_2^c = \varepsilon_1^s - \varepsilon_2^s \qquad \text{...(9.7)}$$

Thus the stresses in the coating are linearly related to the stresses in the specimen, with the elastic constants of both materials entering into the proportionality coefficients. Further, the principal stress and principal strain directions in the coating are colinear with those in the specimen.

9.2.2 Stress-Optic Law

When a coated specimen under load is examined under a plane reflection polariscope, two types of fringe patterns are observed. The black bands are the isoclinic fringes which indicate the principal stress directions. The coloured bands are the isochromatic fringes which indicate the contours along which the difference in principal stresses in the coating is constant in magnitude. The difference in the principal stresses at each point in the coating is related to the fringe order N by the stress-optic law, modified to account for double passage of the light through the coating, as follows,

$$\sigma_1^c - \sigma_2^c = \frac{Nf_\sigma}{2h_c} \quad ...(9.8)$$

where f_σ = material fringe value (stress), (MPa-mm/fringe) ...(9.9)

h_c = coating thickness, (mm).

Combining Eqs. (9.6) and (9.8), we get

$$\sigma_1^s - \sigma_2^s = \left(\frac{E_s}{E_c}\right)\left[\frac{1+\nu_c}{1+\nu_s}\right]\left(\frac{Nf_\sigma}{2h_c}\right) \quad ...(9.10)$$

Similarly the strain-optic law can be expressed as,

$$\varepsilon_1^s - \varepsilon_2^s = \varepsilon_1^c - \varepsilon_2^c = \frac{Nf_\varepsilon}{2h_c} \quad ...(9.11)$$

where f_ε = material fringe value (strain), (mm/fringe).

Equation (9.11) can be written as,

$$\varepsilon_1^s - \varepsilon_2^s = \varepsilon_1^c - \varepsilon_2^c = \left(\frac{N}{2h_c}\right)\left(\frac{\lambda}{K}\right) \quad ...(9.12)$$

where λ = wavelength of the light used for viewing of fringes.

K = optical sensitivity constant.

For a perfectly elastic photoelastic material, f_σ, f_ε and K are related as follows :

$$f_\sigma = \left(\frac{E_s}{1+\nu_c}\right)\left(\frac{\lambda}{K}\right)$$

$$f_\varepsilon = \left(\frac{1+\nu_c}{E_c}\right) f_\sigma$$

$$f_\varepsilon = \frac{\lambda}{K} \quad ...(9.13)$$

The shear strain γ_{xy} in the coating is given by

$$\gamma_{xy}^c = \gamma_{xy}^s = (\varepsilon_1^c - \varepsilon_2^c) \sin 2\theta \quad ...(9.14)$$

where θ is the isoclinic parameter defining the angle between σ_1 and the x-axis.

Using Eq. (9.11), we get

$$\gamma_{xy}^{s} = \left(\frac{Nf_z}{2h_c}\right)\sin 2\theta \qquad \text{...(9.15)}$$

Also $\tau_{xy}^{s} = G_s\, \gamma_{xy}^{s}$

Hence $\tau_{xy}^{s} = \left(\frac{G_s\, Nf_\varepsilon}{2h_c}\right)\sin 2\theta$

$$= \left(\frac{E_s}{E_c}\right)\left(\frac{1+\nu_c}{1+\nu_s}\right)\frac{Nf_\sigma}{4h_c}\sin 2\theta \qquad \text{...(9.16)}$$

9.2.3 Coating Sensitivity

The stress-sensitivity index S_σ of a coating is defined as :

$$S_\sigma = \frac{N}{(\sigma_1^s - \sigma_2^s)} = \left(\frac{2h_c}{f_\sigma}\right)\left(\frac{E_c}{E_s}\right)\left(\frac{1+\nu_s}{1+\nu_c}\right) \qquad \text{...(9.17)}$$

Thus S_σ represents the number of fringes which can be obtained in a coating per unit applied stress to the specimen on which the coating is cemented.

Substituting Eqs. (9.10) and (9.13), we get

$$S_\sigma = \left(\frac{2h_c}{f_\varepsilon}\right)\left[\frac{1+\nu_s}{E_s}\right] = C_c C_s \qquad \text{...(9.18)}$$

where $C_s = \frac{2h_c}{f_\varepsilon}$, the coating coefficient of sensitivity

$C_s = \frac{1+\nu_s}{E_s}$, the specimen coefficient of sensitivity.

Thus we find that the optical response depends upon coating parameters embodied in C_s and on the elastic constants of the specimen material as reflected in C_s.

Similarly the coating strain-sensitivity is defined as

$$S_\varepsilon = \frac{N}{\varepsilon_1^s - \varepsilon_2^s} = \frac{2h_c}{f_\varepsilon} = \frac{2h_c}{f_\sigma}\left(\frac{E_c}{1+\nu_c}\right) \qquad \text{...(9.19)}$$

Figure of merit

$$Q = \left(\frac{E_c}{1+\nu_c}\right)\frac{1}{f_\sigma} = \frac{1}{f_\varepsilon} \qquad \text{...(9.20)}$$

The figure of merit of the coating can be employed effectively to rate the suitability of available polymeric materials for birefringent applications. The figure of merit for various materials suitable for coatings is given in Table 9.1.

Table 9.1 Figure of merit for various materials suitable for coatings

Material	f_ε^*, *cm / fringe*	$Q = \frac{1}{f_\varepsilon}$, *fringe / cm*
Epoxy CIBA 6020 (50 parts per 100 phthalic anhydride)	4.52×10^{-4}	2212
Catalin 61-893	4.85×10^{-4}	2061
Photostress 'S'	6.55×10^{-4}	1526
Castolite	7.72×10^{-4}	1295
CR-39	12.77×10^{-4}	78
Glass	4.82×10^{-4}	2072

*For λ = 5461 Å.

9.2.4 Law of Failure of Stress Coat

If $\overset{s}{\sigma}_2 < 0$ and the material follows the Tresca yield condition, the maximum difference in principal stresses at yielding is

$$(\overset{s}{\sigma}_1 - \overset{s}{\sigma}_2)_{\max} = \overset{s}{\sigma}_0 \qquad \text{...(9.21)}$$

where $\overset{s}{\sigma}_0$ = specimen material yield strength.

The corresponding maximum fringe order becomes

$$N_{\max} = C_c\, C_s\, \overset{s}{\sigma}_0 = \left(\frac{2h_s}{f_\varepsilon}\right)\left[\frac{1+\nu_s}{E_s}\right]\overset{s}{\sigma}_0 \qquad \text{...(9.22)}$$

when $\overset{s}{\sigma}_1 = 0$, then $\overset{c}{\sigma}_1 = \dfrac{E_c\,(\nu_c - \nu_s)}{E_s\,(1-\nu_c^2)}\overset{s}{\sigma}_2$

Thus $\overset{c}{\sigma}_1 = f\,(\nu_c - \nu_s)$ ...(9.23)

If $\nu_c > \nu_s$ then $\overset{c}{\sigma}_1$ and $\overset{c}{\sigma}_2$ are of the same sign. Hence for pure compression both principal stresses in the coating are compressive, although one of the strains in the specimen is tensile. Also when $\overset{s}{\sigma}_1 = 0$, then

$$\overset{c}{\varepsilon}_z = -\frac{\nu_c\,(1-\nu_s)}{E_s\,(1-\nu_c)}\overset{c}{\sigma}_2 \qquad \text{...(9.24)}$$

It can be seen from Eq. (9.22) that the maximum achievable fringe order in the photoelastic coating is a function of three parameters $\overset{s}{\sigma}_0$, C_c and C_s. Typical values of the maximum achievable fringe order are given in Table 9.2 for a wide range of materials.

Table 9.2 Typical values of N_{max}

Material	ν_s	E_s GPa	σ_0^s MPa	C_s $(m^2/N) \times 10^{12}$	N^*_{max} Fringes
Aluminium	0.32	70	245	18.86	2.04
Steel					
C 15	0.30	208	240	6.25	0.664
C 35	0.30	206	310	6.31	0.866
C 60	0.30	204	920	6.37	1.184
Cast iron, tension	0.28	98	150	13.06	0.867
Phosphor-Bronze	0.34	105	180	12.76	0.102
Polycrystal glass	0.25	88	140	14.20	0.880
Glass reinforced plastic	0.42	10.55	70.3	130.6	4.187
Concrete (compression)	15	25	25	640	7.079

$*C_c = \frac{2h_c}{f_\varepsilon}$. For $h_c = 1$ mm and $f_\varepsilon = 4.52 \times 10^{-4}$ cm/fringe,

$C_c = 442.48$ fringes. $\lambda = 5461$ Å green mercury light.

9.3 Procedures for Fringe Measurement

The method to be adopted to measure the fringe order depends upon the response of the coating and the accuracy or resolution, required in the analysis. If the response of the coating in large (*e.g.* four or more fringes), monochromatic light can be used and by using dark and bright set up of the polariscope, fringe order can be interpolated or extrapolated to the nearest 0.2 fringe. For fringe patterns with two to four fringes it is usually advantageous to use white light source giving coloured fringes. By adopting colour matching technique the fringe orders can be ascertained to within about 0.1 fringe. When the highest fringe order is less than two, compensation techniques can be used. For compensation either tension or compression strip or Babinet Soleil compensator may be used. Fringes within 0.01 fringe order can be achieved with the Babinet Soleil compensator. Compensation can also be achieved optically by using Tardy method of compensation. Fringe orders can be estimated to within 0.02 fringe with this method. Likewise Senarmont compensation method may also be used. The reader may refer to Chapter 7 for complete description of these methods of fringe measurement.

9.4 Stress-Separation Methods

From the reflection polariscope with normal incidence we obtain the difference of the principal stresses. To separate the principal stresses the following methods can be used :

(*i*) Oblique incidence method
(*ii*) Strip coatings
(*iii*) Graphical integration
(*iv*) Strain gauges
(*v*) Summation gauge.

9.4.1 Oblique incidence method

To determine the individual principal stresses the normal and oblique incidence fringe measurements are combined.

From Eq. (9.11), the normal-incidence fringe order is given by

$$N_0 = \frac{2h_c}{f_\varepsilon}(\varepsilon_x - \varepsilon_y) \qquad ...(9.25)$$

where superscripts on the strain terms have been omitted since it is assumed that the coating and specimen strains are identical. The x and y directions of principal strains are established from isoclinic determination. If an oblique-incidence measurement $N_{\theta x}$ is made by rotating the direction of observation about σ_x by an angle θ_x as shown in Fig. 9.2, the fringe order is expressed by,

$$N_{\theta x} = \frac{2h_c}{\varepsilon_x \cos\theta_x}(\varepsilon_x - \varepsilon_y') \qquad ...(9.26)$$

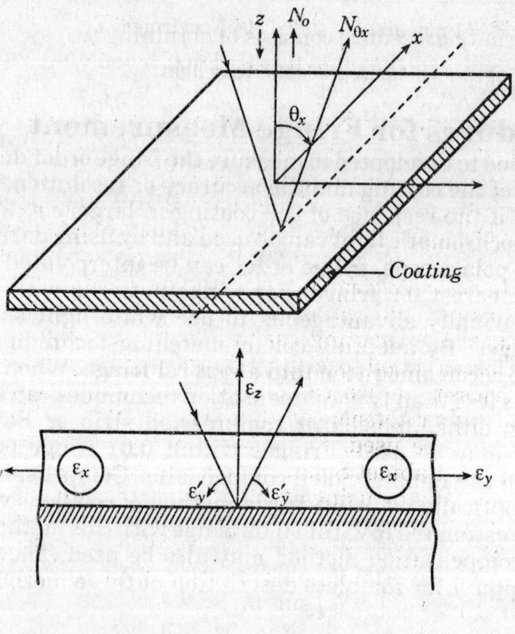

Fig. 9.2 Co-ordinates for oblique-incidence measurements.

where ε_y' is the secondary principal strain in planes normal to the incident reflected light rays.

Now,
$$\varepsilon_y' = \varepsilon_y \cos^2\theta_2 + \varepsilon_z \sin^2\theta_x \qquad ...(9.27)$$

As the coating is under a plane state of stress, hence

$$\varepsilon_z = -\left(\frac{\nu_c}{1-\nu_c}\right)(\varepsilon_x + \varepsilon_y) \qquad ...(9.28)$$

Substituting Eqs. (9.27) and (9.28) in Eq. (9.26), we get

$$N_{\theta x} = \frac{1}{(1-\nu_c)\cos\theta_x}\left[\varepsilon_x (1-\nu_c)\cos^2\theta_x - \varepsilon_y(\cos^2\theta_x - \nu_c)\right] \quad ...(9.29)$$

Similarly for a rotation around σ_y, we get

$$N_{\theta y} = \frac{2h_e}{f_\varepsilon}\,\frac{1}{(1-\nu_e)\cos\theta_y}\left[\varepsilon_y (1-\nu_c\cos^2\theta_y) - \varepsilon_x(\cos^2\theta_y - \nu_e)\right] \quad ...(9.30)$$

Solving Eqs. (9.25) and (9.29) simultaneously for ε_x and ε_y, we get

$$\varepsilon_x = \frac{f_\varepsilon}{2h_e}\,\frac{1}{(1+\nu_e)\sin^2\theta_x}\left[N_{yx}(1-\nu_e)\cos\theta_x - N_0(\cos^2\theta_x - \nu_c)\right] \quad ...(9.31)$$

$$\varepsilon_y = \frac{f_\varepsilon}{2h_e}\,\frac{1}{(1+\nu_c)\sin^2\theta_x}\left[N_{\theta x}(1-\nu_c)\cos\theta_x - N_0(1-\nu_c\cos^2\theta_x)\right].$$

An alternate procedure consists of obtaining two measurements in oblique incidence so that $\theta_x = \theta_y = 0$. Thus by solving Eqs. (9.29) and (9.30) simultaneously, we get

$$\varepsilon_x = \frac{f_\varepsilon}{2h_c}\,\frac{\cos\theta}{(1+\nu_c)(1-\cos^4\theta)}\left[N_{\theta x}(1-\nu_c\cos^2\theta) + N_{\theta y}(\cos^2\theta - \nu_c)\right] \quad ...(9.32)$$

$$\varepsilon_y = \frac{f_\varepsilon}{2h_c}\,\frac{\cos\theta}{(1+\nu_c)(1-\cos^4\theta)}\left[N_{\theta x}(\cos^2\theta - \nu_c) + N_{\theta y}(1-\nu_c\cos^2\theta)\right]$$

Eq. (9.31) can be written into a general form

$$\varepsilon_x = \left(\frac{f_\varepsilon}{2h_c}\right)(A\,N_{\theta x} - BN_0)$$

$$\varepsilon_y = \left(\frac{f_\varepsilon}{2h_c}\right)(AN_{\theta x} - CN_0) \quad ...(9.33)$$

where $$A = \left(\frac{1-\nu_c}{1+\nu_c}\right)\frac{\cos\theta_x}{\sin^2\theta_x}$$

$$B = \left(\frac{1}{1+\nu_c}\right)\left(\frac{\cos^2\theta_x - \nu_c}{\sin^2\theta_x}\right)$$

$$C = \left(\frac{1}{1+\nu_x}\right)\left(\frac{1-\nu_c\cos^2\theta_x}{\sin^2\theta_x}\right)$$

Since the physical properties of the coating material are not always known, it is customary to establish A, B and C by calibration, measuring N_0, $N_{\theta x}$ and $N_{\theta y}$ on a specimen, where ε_x and ε_y are known.

Solving A, B and C in terms of ε_y, ε_y and N_0, $N_{\theta x}$, $N_{x\theta}$, gives

$$\left.\begin{aligned} A &= \left(\frac{\varepsilon_x + \varepsilon_y}{\varepsilon_x - \varepsilon_y}\right)\left(\frac{N_0}{N_{\theta x} + N_{\theta y}}\right) \\ B &= \frac{1}{2}\left(\frac{\varepsilon_x + \varepsilon_y}{\varepsilon_x - \varepsilon_y}\right)\left(\frac{N_{\theta x} - N_{\theta y}}{N_{\theta x} + N_{\theta y}}\right) - \frac{1}{2} \\ C &= B + 1 \end{aligned}\right\} \quad \text{...(9.34)}$$

The individual principal stresses then are given by

$$\left.\begin{aligned} \sigma_1^s &= \frac{E_s}{1 - \nu_s^2}(\varepsilon_1 + \nu_s\,\varepsilon_2) \\ \sigma_2^s &= \frac{E_s}{1 - \nu_s^2}(\varepsilon_2 + \nu_s\,\varepsilon_1) \end{aligned}\right\} \quad \text{...(9.35)}$$

Substituting Eq. (9.31), we get

$$\left.\begin{aligned} \sigma_1^s &= \frac{E_s\,f_\varepsilon}{2h_c\,(1 + \nu_c)\sin^2\theta}(F_3\cos\theta\,N_{\theta 1} - F_2\cos^2\theta\,N_0) \\ \sigma_2^s &= \frac{E_s\,f_\varepsilon}{2h_c\,(1 + \nu_c)\sin^2\theta}(F_3\cos\theta\,N_{\theta 1} - F_1\,N_0) \end{aligned}\right\} \quad \text{...(9.36)}$$

where $$F_1 = \left(\frac{1}{1 - \nu_s^2}\right)[1 - \nu_c\nu_s - (\nu_c - \nu_s)\cos^2\theta]$$

$$F_2 = \left(\frac{1}{1 - \nu_s^2}\right)[1 - \nu_c\nu_s - (\nu_c - \nu_s)/\cos^2\theta]$$

$$F_3 = \left(\frac{1 - \nu_c}{1 - \nu_s}\right)$$

If $\nu_c = \nu_s$,

then $F_1 = F_2 = F_3$.

Sign determination in oblique incidence method. A tensile specimen possessing the same strain-optical strain relationship as the coating is loaded in tension and oriented along the y-axis in oblique incidence as shown in Fig. 9.3. If the fringe order decreases, $(\varepsilon_x - \varepsilon_y')$ is positive. If however, the tensile specimen causes the fringe order to increase then $(\varepsilon_x - \varepsilon_y')$ is negative. The strains are given by,

$$\varepsilon_x = \frac{f_\varepsilon}{2h_c}\left[\frac{(1 - \nu_c)\cos\theta_x}{(1 + \nu_c)\sin^2\theta_x}(\pm N_{\theta x}) - \frac{(\cos^2\theta x - \nu_c)\,N_0}{(1 + \nu_c)\sin^2\theta_x}\right] \quad \text{...(9.37)}$$

$$\varepsilon_y = \frac{f_\varepsilon}{2h_c}\left[\frac{(1-\nu_c)\cos\theta_x}{(1+\nu_c)\sin^2\theta_x}(\pm N_{\theta x}) - \frac{(1-\nu_c)\cos^2\theta_x N_0}{(1+\nu_c)\sin^2\theta_x}\right]$$

where $\varepsilon_x - \varepsilon_y = \dfrac{f_\varepsilon}{2h_c} N_0$

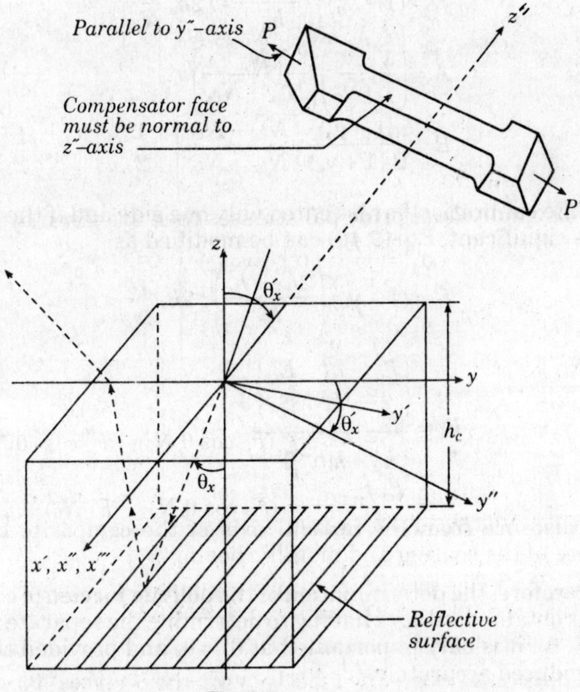

Fig. 9.3

Normally the positive signs are used, except when it is determined that $(\varepsilon_x - \varepsilon_y)$ is negative then negative sign should be used. Oblique incidence angle in air θ_x' is given by

$$\theta_x' = \sin^{-1}(n_c \sin\theta_x) \qquad \text{...(9.38)}$$

where n_c = relative index of refraction of coating.

New method for the determination of oblique-incidence coefficients. To determine the values of f_ε, A and B as required in Eq. (9.33). Any convenient calibration device for which values of ε_x and ε_y are known can be used. Generally, a fixed-deflection-type metallic cantilever beam is employed. Let h_a, E_a and ν_a represent respectively the thickness, Young's modulus and Poisson's ratio of the metallic beam. When the thickness of the photoelastic coating is h_c and if the neutral axis shift in the metallic beam is negligible, the axial strain in the mid-plane of the coating is

$$\varepsilon_x = \frac{h_a + h_c}{h_a} \varepsilon_a \quad ...(9.39)$$

where ε_a is the strain on the surface (interface of coating and metal beam) of the metallic beam. ε_a can be easily computed. The values of A, B and f_ε may be expressed as

$$f_\varepsilon = (1 + \nu_a)\left(\frac{h_a + h_c}{h_a}\right) . 2h_c \frac{\varepsilon_a}{N_o} \quad ...(9.40)$$

$$A = \left(\frac{1 - \nu_a}{1 + \nu_a}\right)\left(\frac{N_o}{N_{\theta x} + N_{\theta y}}\right) \quad ...(9.41)$$

$$B = \frac{(1 - \nu_a)}{2\,(1 + \nu_a)}\left[\frac{N_{\theta x} - N_{\theta y}}{N_{\theta x} + N_{\theta y}}\right] - \frac{1}{2} \quad ...(9.42)$$

If the calibration bar is coated only one side and if the neutral axis shift is significant, Eq. (9.40) can be modified as

$$f_\varepsilon = (1 + \nu_a)\left(\frac{2h_1 + h_c}{h_a}\right) . 2h_e \frac{\varepsilon_a}{N_o} \quad ...(9.43)$$

where $$h_1 = \frac{\left(\frac{h_a^2}{2} - \frac{h_c^2}{2} . \frac{E_c}{E_a}\right)}{\left(h_a + h_c . \frac{E_c}{E_a}\right)}$$

is the distance from the neutral axis of the composite beam to the interface of the coating and metallic beam.

Therefore, the determination of the oblique incidence coefficients A and B is obtained without having to determine the separate magnitudes of ν_c, θ_x, θ_y, it is only important that $\theta_x = \theta_y$ and provided that this can be reproduced accurately.

Causes of errors. The following are the possible causes of error in the oblique incidence method :

1. Change in sign of the oblique incidence fringe order number.
2. Inability to determine the oblique angle θ.
3. Although it is quite accurate to establish the oblique-incidence angle θ' in the air, the angle θ in the plastic will vary from one coating to another, since the relative index of refraction varies.

9.4.2 Strip coatings

Photoelastic coatings method gives the difference of principal stresses. In order to obtain the stresses individually, shear difference, oblique incidence and numerical integration methods of Laplace equation are used. These methods are more difficult and time-consuming than the initial experiment. The photoelastic strip method is an alternative to the above technique. A photoelastic strip coating is composed of closely spaced parallel (Fig. 9.4) strips which are cemented to the surface of a structure in the same manner as the continuous coating. These strips are sensitive only to the longitudinal strain parallel to their axes, thus this strain can be determined for the entire surface. Hence, two straight forward experiments—one using a continuous coating and the other using photoelastic strips—enable one establish the state of stress on the surface of a structure.

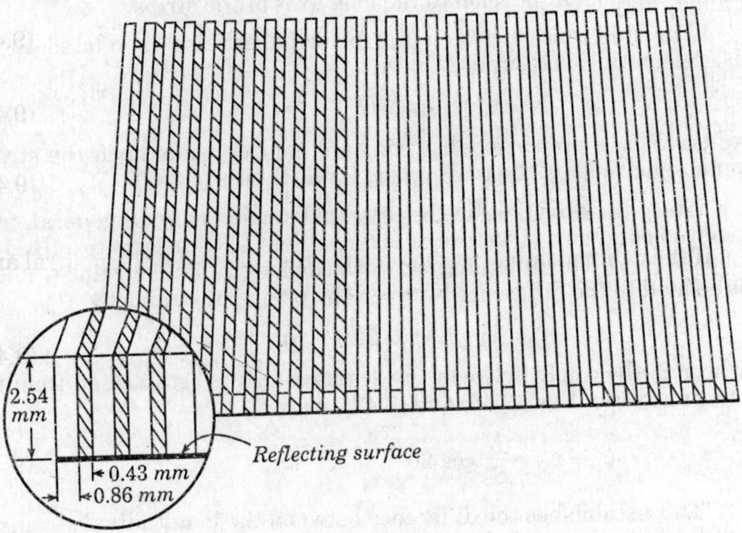

Fig. 9.4 Details for photoelastic strip coatings.

To understand the principle of coating, consider the strain-optic law for a single strip oriented in the x-direction.

$$N_s = S_a\, \varepsilon_x + S_t\, \varepsilon_y + S_s\, \gamma_{xy} \quad ...(9.44)$$

where N_s = fringe order exhibited by the strip

S_a = axial-strain sensitivity of the strip

S_t = transverse-strain sensitivity

S_s = shear-strain sensitivity.

The values of the strain sensitivities depend upon the geometric proportions of the strip, *i.e.* width w, height h_c, if the strip length is large as compared to the cross-section. Strips with a large w/h_c ratio approach continuous coatings, and for this case $S_a = -S_t = S_s = 2h_c/f_\varepsilon$. However, when $(w/h_c) \ll 1$, $S \to 2h_e/f_\varepsilon$, and S_t and S_s tend to vanish because the transverse and shear strains in the specimen are not transmitted into the coating. Thus for strips with sufficiently small w/h_c ratio, S_a and S_t can be neglected, and the strain-optic law can be written as

$$N_s = S_a\, \varepsilon_a \quad ...(9.45)$$

where $S_a = 2h_c/f_c$ and ε_a is the axial (normal) strain parallel to the strips. If the strips are positioned close together, the regions of extinction in adjacent strips blend together and appear to form continuous fringes. As a result the strip coatings provide whole-field data for the normal strain component parallel to the long axes of the strips.

The difference between the principal strains is related to the isochromatic fringe order N by

$$N = S_a\,(\varepsilon_1 - \varepsilon_2) \qquad ...(9.46)$$

where S_a = a proportionality constant that depends upon the strain-optic sensitivity of the coating and its thickness $= 2h_c/f_\varepsilon$.

Since the directions of the principal strains vary, in general, from point to point on a structure, it is convenient to transform to a fixed set of axes (x, y). The difference between the longitudinal strains ε_x and ε_y is related to the difference between the principal strains by

$$(\varepsilon_x - \varepsilon_y) = (\varepsilon_1 - \varepsilon_2)\cos 2\theta \qquad ...(9.47)$$

where θ, the angle between the ε_1 and x-axis is established from the isoclinic. From Eqs. (9.46) and (9.47), we get

$$(\varepsilon_x - \varepsilon_y) = \frac{N}{S_a}\cos 2\theta \qquad ...(9.48)$$

This establishes the difference between the longitudinal strains in terms of the observed photoelastic data.

From the continuous coating, the shear strain, γ_{ay} can also be established in terms of the observed photoelastic data. Now

$$\gamma_{xy} = \frac{1}{2}(\varepsilon_1 - \varepsilon_2)\sin 2\theta \qquad ...(9.49)$$

Hence

$$\gamma_{xy} = \frac{N}{2S_a}\sin 2\theta \qquad ...(9.50)$$

It is seen that the continuous coating gives the difference between the longitudinal strains $(\varepsilon_x - \varepsilon_y)$ and the shear strain γ_{xy}. The photoelastic strips will provide ε_x or ε_y directly and, consequently, the complete state of strains will be known.

As the photoelastic strips are very nearly insensitive to shear strain, the optical response to strain must depend upon extensional strains only, and can be written in the form

$$N_s = S_x\,\varepsilon_x - S_y\,\varepsilon_y \qquad ...(9.51)$$

where N_s represents the fringe order and S_x and S_y are the strain-optic coefficients. The x-direction is considered to be parallel to the axes of the strips and the y-direction is perpendicular to these axes. Further $S_x \gg S_y$ which indicates that the fringe order depends upon the extensional strain parallel to the axes of the strips very nearly. Eq. (9.51) can now be written more simply as

$$N_s = S_x\,\varepsilon_x \qquad ...(9.52)$$

or

$$\varepsilon_x = \frac{N_s}{S_x} \qquad ...(9.53)$$

From Eqs. (9.48) and (9.52), we get

$$\varepsilon_y = \frac{N_s}{S_x} - \frac{N}{S_x}\cos 2\theta,\ S_x = S_a,\ S_y = S_t \qquad ...(9.54)$$

Also $$\gamma_{xy} = \frac{N_s}{2S_x}\sin 2\theta \qquad ...(9.55)$$

where N, θ are determined from the continuous coating and N_s from the photoelastic strips. Eq. (9.53) to (9.55) give the state of strain at a point in terms of the photoelastic data there.

The mapping and measurement of isoclinics can be avoided by performing three experiments in which the photoelastic strips are oriented in different directions on the surface of the structure. If photoelastic strips are applied successively in some prescribed directions x, y and at 45°, ε_x and ε_y are obtained directly. The shear strain is

$$\gamma_{xy} = \frac{2N_{45^\circ} - N_x - N_y}{S_x} \qquad ...(9.56)$$

Strip coatings can be applied in three different ways to establish the individual values of the principal stresses in the specimen.

1. Three different strip coatings are used to measure the strains ε_A, ε_B and ε_C, with the A, B and C directions defined as shown in Fig. 9.5, similar to a strain-gauge rosette. The conventional rectangular-rosette equations can then be used to compute the principal strains and stresses.

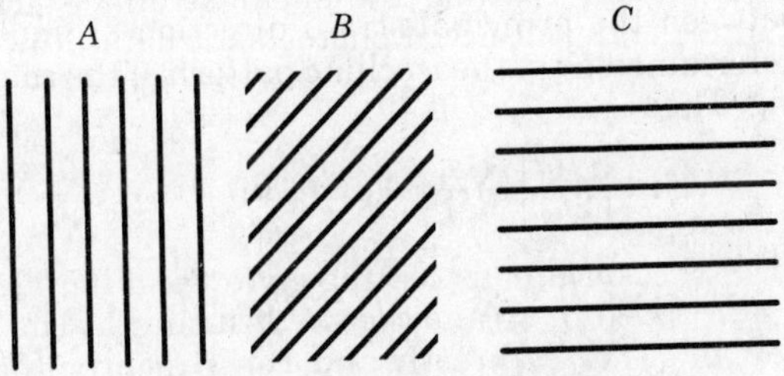

Fig. 9.5 Three strip coatings.

$$\sigma_1^s = E_s\left[\frac{\varepsilon_A + \varepsilon_C}{2(1-\nu_s)} + \frac{1}{2(1+\nu_s)}\left\{(\varepsilon_A - \varepsilon_C)^2 + (2\,\varepsilon_B - \varepsilon_A - \varepsilon_C)^2\right\}^{1/2}\right]$$

$$\sigma_2^s = E_s\left[\frac{\varepsilon_A + \varepsilon_C}{2(1-\nu_s)} - \frac{1}{2(1+\nu_s)}\left\{(\varepsilon_A - \varepsilon_C)^2 + (2\,\varepsilon_B - \varepsilon_A - \varepsilon_C)^2\right\}^{1/2}\right]$$

and $$\tan 2\theta_1 = \frac{2\,\varepsilon_B - \varepsilon_A - \varepsilon_C}{\varepsilon_A - \varepsilon_C} \qquad ...(9.57)$$

$$\varepsilon_{1,2} = \frac{\varepsilon_A + \varepsilon_C}{2} \pm \frac{1}{2}\left\{(\varepsilon_A - \varepsilon_C)^2 + (2\,\varepsilon_B - \varepsilon_A - \varepsilon_C)^2\right\}^{1/2} \qquad ...(9.58)$$

2. Two strip coatings are used to measure the orthogonal strains ε_x and ε_y and a continuous coating to measure $(\varepsilon_1 - \varepsilon_2)$. For this case

$$\varepsilon_x + \varepsilon_y = \varepsilon_1 + \varepsilon_2 = \frac{f_\varepsilon}{2h_c}(N_{sx} + N_{sy}) \quad ...(9.59)$$

where N_{sx} and N_{sy} are the fringe orders measured from the strip coatings in the x and y directions respectively. Assuming that f_ε and h_c are identical for all three coatings and solving Eqs. (9.11) and (9.58) simultaneously, for the principal strains, we get

$$\left.\begin{aligned} \varepsilon_1 &= \left(\frac{f_\varepsilon}{4h_c}\right)(N_{sx} + N_{sy} + N_0) \\ \varepsilon_2 &= \left(\frac{f_\varepsilon}{4h_c}\right)(N_{sx} - N_{sy} - N_0) \end{aligned}\right\} \quad ...(9.60)$$

The principal stresses in the specimen then become

$$\left.\begin{aligned} \sigma_1^s &= \frac{E_s f_\varepsilon}{2h_c}\left[\frac{N_{sx} + N_{sy}}{2(1-\nu_s)} + \frac{N_0}{2(1+\nu_s)}\right] \\ \sigma_2^s &= \frac{E_s f_\varepsilon}{2h_c}\left[\frac{N_{sx} + N_{sy}}{2(1-\nu_s)} - \frac{N_0}{2(1+\nu_s)}\right] \\ \text{and} \quad \cos 2\theta_1 &= \frac{N_{sx} - N_{sy}}{N_0} \end{aligned}\right\} \quad ...(9.61)$$

3. In a third method a strip coating is used to measure ε_x and a continuous coating is used to measure $(\varepsilon_1 - \varepsilon_2)$. The angle between the principal-strain direction ε_1 and the x-axis is determined from the isoclinic pattern of the continuous coating. Then

$$\left.\begin{aligned} \varepsilon_1 &= \left(\frac{f_\varepsilon}{2h_c}\right)(N_{cx} + N_0 \sin^2\theta_1) \\ \varepsilon_2 &= \left(\frac{f_\varepsilon}{2h_c}\right)(N_{sx} - N_0 \cos^2\theta_1) \end{aligned}\right\} \quad ...(9.62)$$

The principal stresses then become

$$\left.\begin{aligned} \sigma_1^s &= \frac{E_s f_\varepsilon}{2h_c}\left[\frac{N_{sx}}{1-\nu_s} + \frac{N_0(\sin^2\theta_1 - \nu_s\cos^2\theta_1)}{1-\nu_s^2}\right] \\ \sigma_2^s &= \frac{E_s f_\varepsilon}{2h_c}\left[\frac{N_{sx}}{1-\nu_s} - \frac{N_0(\cos^2\theta_1 - \nu_s\sin^2\theta_1)}{1-\nu_s^2}\right] \end{aligned}\right\} \quad ...(9.63)$$

9.4.3 Numerical Integration

The Lame-Maxwell equilibrium equations are

$$\begin{aligned} \frac{\partial\sigma_1^c}{\partial s_1} + \frac{\sigma_1^c - \sigma_2^s}{\rho_2} &= 0 \\ \frac{\partial\sigma_2^c}{\partial s_2} + \frac{\sigma_1^c - \sigma_2^c}{\rho_1} &= 0 \end{aligned} \quad ...(9.64)$$

where s_1 and s_2 are the curvilinear co-ordinates and ρ_1, ρ_2 are their radii of curvature.

Stepwise integration of these equations gives

$$[\sigma_1^c]_{s_1} = [\sigma_1^c]_{s_0} + \left.\frac{\sigma_1^c - \sigma_2^c}{\rho_2}\right|_{\frac{s_0+s_1}{2}} \Delta s$$

$$[\sigma_1^c]_{s_2} = [\sigma_1^c]_{s_1} + \left.\frac{\sigma_1^c - \sigma_2^c}{\rho_2}\right|_{\frac{s_1+s_2}{2}} . \Delta s$$

$$\ldots \quad \ldots \quad \ldots \quad \ldots \quad \ldots \quad \ldots$$

$$[\sigma_1^c]_{sn} = [\sigma_1^c]\, s_{n-1} + \left.\frac{\sigma_1^c - \sigma_2^c}{\rho_2}\right|_{\frac{s_{n-1}+s_n}{2}} \Delta s \qquad \ldots(9.65)$$

where s_0 = coordinate of the boundary points where σ_1^c is known

$s_1, s_2 \ldots. s_x$ = coordinates of closely spaced points along the isotatic.

$\Delta s = s_x - s_{x-1}$

When ρ_1 or ρ_2 goes to infinity, then

$\dfrac{\partial \sigma_1^c}{\partial s_1} = 0$ or $\dfrac{\partial \sigma_2^c}{\partial s_2} = 0$ over the region considered. When

$\rho_1 \to \infty$, then σ_1^c is a maximum or a minimum along s_1 ; and if

$\rho_1 \to \infty$, then σ_2^c is a maximum or a minimum along s_2.

9.4.4 Electrical-resistance strain gauges

In this case the isochromatic and isoclinic data for the coating yield $(\varepsilon_1 - \varepsilon_2)$ and θ_1 over the entire strain field. The points of interest are selected and a single element strain-gauge is mounted at each such point along the ε_1 direction. This strain gauge indicates the principal strain $\varepsilon_1 = \varepsilon_{sg}$. Then

$$\varepsilon_2 = \varepsilon_{sg} - N \frac{f_c}{2h_c} \qquad \ldots(9.66)$$

The principal stresses then can be determined from

$$\left.\begin{aligned} \sigma_1 &= E_s \left[\frac{\varepsilon_{sg}}{1 - \nu_s} - \frac{\nu_s N f_\varepsilon}{2h_c (1 - \nu_s^2)} \right] \\ \sigma_2 &= E_s \left[\frac{\varepsilon_{sg}}{1 - \nu_s} - \frac{N f_\varepsilon}{2h_c (1 - \nu_s^2)} \right] \end{aligned}\right\} \qquad \ldots(9.67)$$

9.4.5 Summation Gauge

As seen in art. 9.4.1, a normal-incidence photoelastic coating measurement (N_0) provides the difference in principal strains at the test point. If the sum of the principal strains can be measured at the same point, then the separate principal strains are obtainable by simply adding and subtracting the two measurements. It is evident from the Mohr's circle of strain (Fig. 9.6) that the centre of the circle corresponds to $\frac{1}{2}(\varepsilon_1 + \varepsilon_2)$. However the centre also corresponds to $\frac{1}{2}(\varepsilon_x + \varepsilon_y)$. Thus, for any point P on the coating surface (Fig. 9.7), the sum $(\varepsilon_x + \varepsilon_y)$ is constant, independent of the angle β, and equal to the sum $(\varepsilon_1 + \varepsilon_2)$. As a result, it is not necessary to measure the sum of the principal strains as such, but only the sum of any two perpendicular strains at that same location.

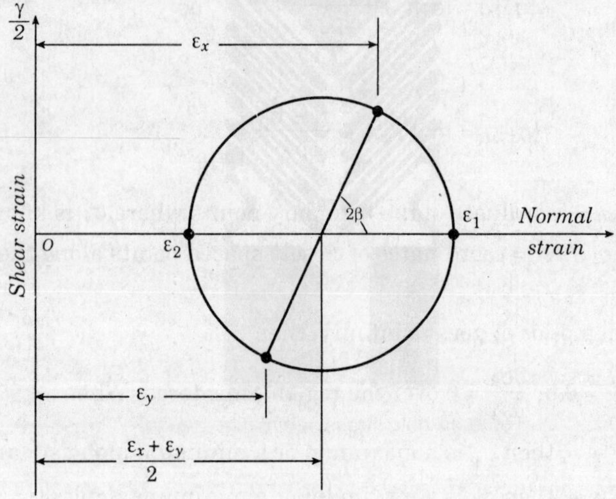

Fig. 9.6 Mohr's circle of strain, illustrating the equivalence of $(\varepsilon_x - \varepsilon_y)/2$ and $(\varepsilon_1 + \varepsilon_2)/2$.

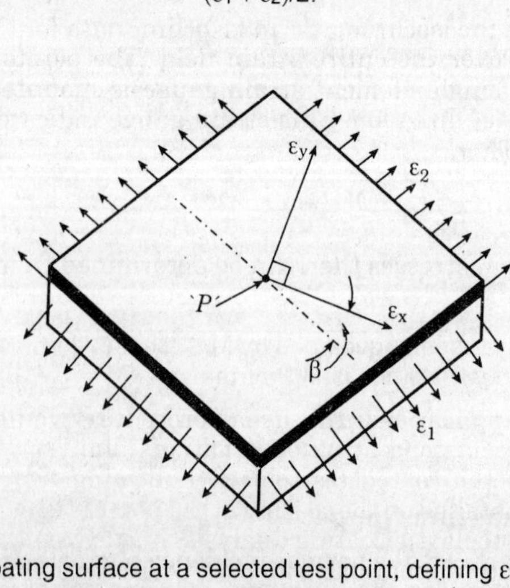

Fig. 9.7 Coating surface at a selected test point, defining ε_x, ε_y, ε_1, ε_2.

The summation gauge is based on this fundamental principle of mechanics. As shown in Fig. 9.8, the gauge grid consists of two perpendicular elements (for sensing ε_x and ε_y) connected in series. The indicated strain from the gauge then corresponds to $\frac{1}{2}(\varepsilon_x + \varepsilon_y)$, and thus to $\frac{1}{2}(\varepsilon_1 + \varepsilon_2)$, regardless of the gauge orientation on the test surface. Representing the summation-gauge output signal by the symbol S_G,

Fig. 9.8 Photo stress summation gauge.

$$S_G = \frac{1}{2}(\varepsilon_x + \varepsilon_y) = \frac{1}{2}(\varepsilon_1 + \varepsilon_2) \qquad ...(9.68)$$

and $$2\,S_G = \varepsilon_1 + \varepsilon_2 \qquad ...(9.69)$$

Adding and subtracting with

$$\varepsilon_1 - \varepsilon_2 = \frac{N_0 f_\varepsilon}{2h_c} \text{ gives}$$

$$\varepsilon_1 = S_G + \frac{N_0 f_\varepsilon}{4h_c} \qquad ...(9.70)$$

and $$\varepsilon_2 = S_G - \frac{N_0 f_\varepsilon}{4h_c} \qquad ...(9.71)$$

Such a gauge has been developed by M/s Measurements Group, Inc. (U.S.A). The gauge resistance is 200-ohms.

In practical applications, the usual procedure would be to first complete all photoelastic-coating observations and normal-incidence measurements on the coated test object. Following this, summation gauges would be installed on the coating at the potentially critical points established by photoelastic-coating analysis. Loads would be reapplied to the test object and summation strains $(\varepsilon_1 + \varepsilon_2)$ determined. Individual principal strains would then be calculated from Eqs. (9.70) and (9.71). Local reinforcement of the photoelastic coating by the strain gauge is automatically compensated by setting the gauge-factor control of the strain indicator at the effective value. The possible reinforcement effects of the coating on the test object can be accounted for by applying corrections. The correction for plane stress C_{ps} can be expressed as

$$C_{ps} = 1 + E^* h^* \qquad ...(9.72)$$

where $E^* = \dfrac{E_c}{E_s}$ and $h^* = \dfrac{h_c}{h_s}$.

The corresponding correction for bending C_B is

$$C_B = [1 + E^* (4h^* + 6h^{*2} + 4h^{*2}) + E^{*2} h^{*4}]/[1 + h^*] \qquad ...(9.73)$$

The relationships given in Eqs. (9.72) and (9.73) are plotted in Fig. 9.9.

The correction factor for strain gauge reinforcement effect for plane stress is the same as that for the fringe order, namely

$$K_{ps} = C_{ps} = 1 + E^* h^* \qquad ...(9.74)$$

The correction factor for strain gauge reinforcement effect for bending is

$$K_B = \frac{1 + E^* (4h^* + 6h^{*2} + 4h^{*3}) + E^{*2} h^{*4}}{1 + 2h^* + E^* h^{*2}} \qquad ...(9.75)$$

Eqs. (9.74) and (9.75) are plotted in Fig. 9.10.

After correcting both the measured fringe order and the indicated strain, the adjusted values of N_0 and $(\varepsilon_1 + \varepsilon_2)$ are substituted in Eqs. (9.70) and (9.71) to obtain the separate principal strains. The separate principal stresses are then calculated from

$$\sigma_1 = \frac{E_s}{1 - \nu_s^2} (\varepsilon_1 + \nu_s \varepsilon_2) \qquad ...(9.76)$$

$$\sigma_2 = \frac{E_s}{1 - \nu_s^2} (\varepsilon_2 + \nu_2 \varepsilon_1) \qquad ...(9.77)$$

Example 9.1 *A coating of photostress—S is bonded to a steel specimen. Determine the stress-sensitivity index for the coating for the following data :*

$E_s = 2.04 \times 10^6$ *kg/cm*^{2}, $\quad \nu_c = 0.30$

$E_c = 0.03 \times 10^6$ *kg/cm*^{2}, $\quad \nu_c = 0.36$

$f_\sigma = 13.87$ *kg/cm*^{2}*/cm/fringe* $\quad h_c = 0.25$ *cm.*

Also calculate the strain-sensitivity index and the figure of merit.

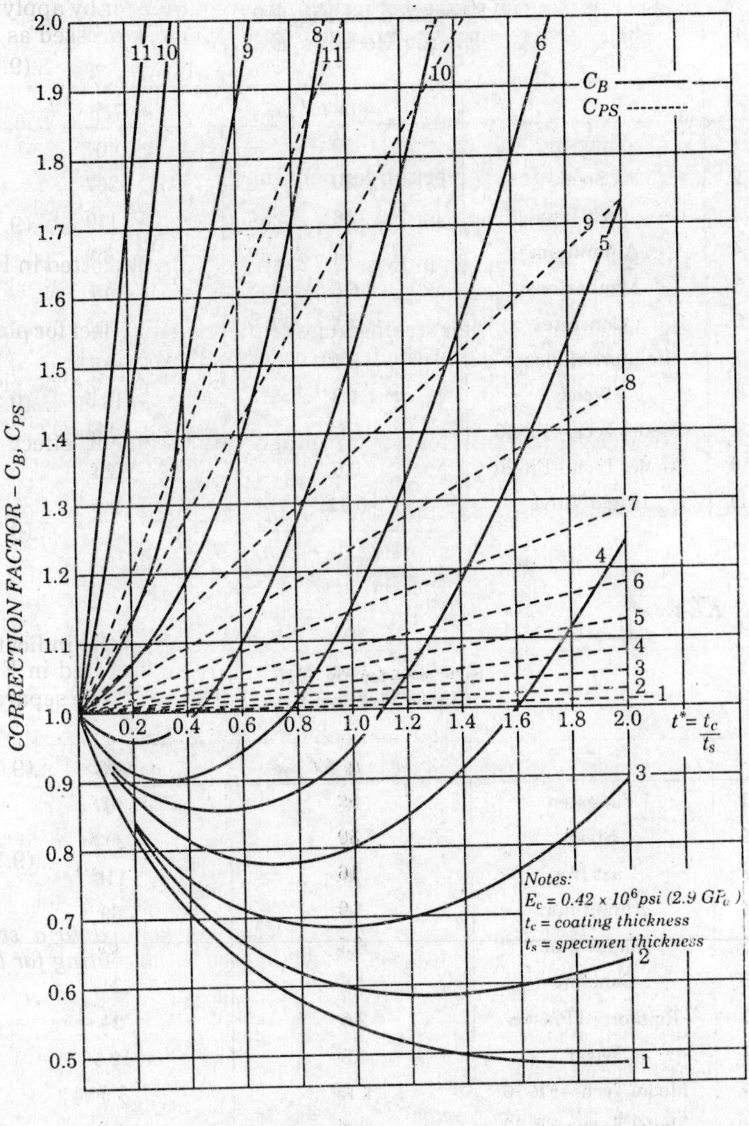

Fig. 9.9 Correction factor C_B (bending) and C_{PS} (plane stress) or photoelastic-coatings. Multiply the observed birefringence by the appropriate factor to obtain the corrected fringe order.

KEY :

Specimen for Fig. 9.9
Elastic Modulus, E_S

		in 10^4 psi	in GPa
1.	Tungsten	59	407
2.	Steel	30	207
3.	Cast Iron	16	110
4.	Aluminium	10	69
5.	Magnesium	6.5	45
6.	Concrete	4.5	31
7.	Reinforced Plastic	3.0	21
8.	Wood	1.8	12.5
9.	Model Tech—FR-10	1.15	7.9
10.	Model Tech—FR-20	0.6	4.1
11	Rigid Vinyl	0.42	2.9

KEY :

Specimen for Fig. 9.10
Elastic Modulus, E_S

		in 10^4 psi	in GPa
1.	Tungsten	59	407
2.	Steel	30	207
3.	Cast Iron	16	110
4.	Aluminium	10	69
5.	Magnesium	6.5	45
6.	Concrete	4.5	31
7.	Reinforced Plastic	3.0	21
8.	Wood	1.8	12.5
9.	Model Tech—FR-10	1.15	7.9
10.	Model Tech—FR-20	0.6	4.1
11.	Rigid Vinyl	0.42	2.9

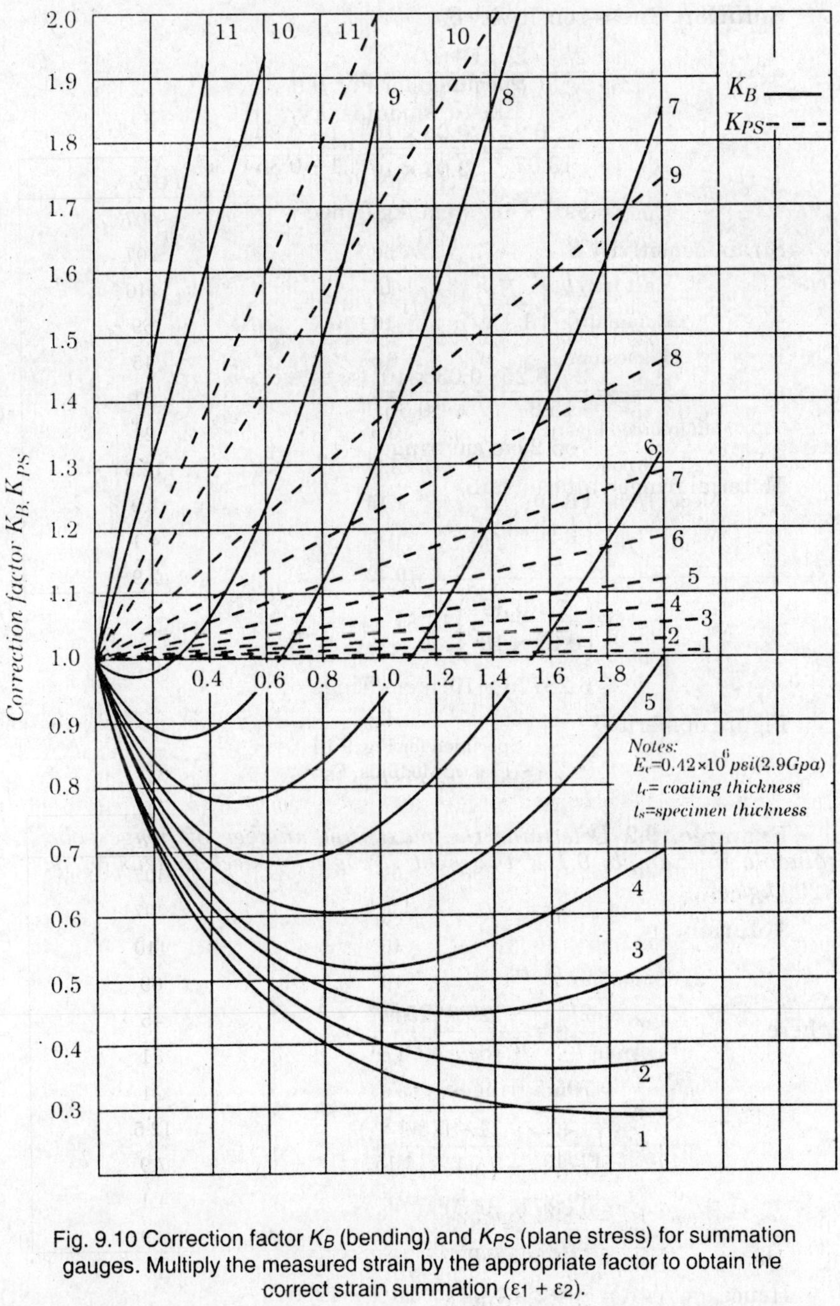

Fig. 9.10 Correction factor K_B (bending) and K_{PS} (plane stress) for summation gauges. Multiply the measured strain by the appropriate factor to obtain the correct strain summation ($\varepsilon_1 + \varepsilon_2$).

Solution. Stress-sensitivity S_σ

$$= \frac{2h_c}{f_\sigma} \cdot \frac{E_c}{E_s}\left(\frac{1+\nu_s}{1+\nu_c}\right)$$

$$= \frac{2 \times 0.25}{13.87} \times \frac{0.03 \times 10^6}{2.04 \times 10^6}\left(\frac{1+0.30}{1+0.36}\right)$$

$$= 3.07 \times 10^{-4} \text{ cm}^2\text{/kg/fringe}$$

Strain-sensitivity S_ε

$$= \frac{2h_c}{f_\sigma}\left(\frac{E_c}{1+\nu_c}\right)$$

$$= \frac{2 \times 6.25}{15.87}\left(\frac{0.03 \times 10^6}{1+0.36}\right)$$

$$= 795.2 \text{ cm/cm/fringe}$$

Material fringe value (strain)

$$f_\varepsilon = \left(\frac{1+\nu_c}{E_c}\right) f_\sigma$$

$$= \left(\frac{1+0.36}{0.03 \times 10^6}\right) 13.87$$

$$= 6.28773 \times 10^{-4} \text{ cm/fringe}$$

Figure of merit Q

$$= \frac{1}{f_\varepsilon} = 1590.4 \text{ fringes/cm.}$$

Example. 9.2 *Determine the maximum number of fringes obtainable in example 9.1 if the yield strength of steel in tension is 4200 kg/cm².*

Solution.

$$N_{\max} = C_c\, C_s\, \sigma_0^s$$

where $$C_c = \frac{2h_c}{f_\varepsilon} = \frac{2 \times 0.25}{6.2877 \times 10^{-4}}$$

$$= 795.2 \text{ fringes}$$

$$C_s = \frac{1+\nu_s}{E_s} = \frac{1+0.30}{2.04 \times 10^6}$$

$$= 0.637 \times 10^{-6} \text{ cm}^2\text{/kg}$$

$$\sigma_0^s = 4200 \text{ kg/cm}^2$$

Hence $$N_{\max} = 795.2 \times 0.637 \times 10^{-6} \times 4200$$

$$= 2.128 \text{ fringes.}$$

Example 9.3 *A photoelastic coating CR-39 having material fringe value 17.2 kg/cm²/cm/fringe, thickness $h_c = 2$ mm, $\nu_c = 3.5$ and modulus of elasticity $E_c = 2 \times 10^4$ kg/cm² is used to measure stresses on aluminium for which $E_s = 0.7 \times 10^6$ kg/cm², $\nu_s = 0.32$. At a point of interest the normal incidence gave the fringe order to be 4.25 and an isoclinic of 30° passed through that point. Oblique incidence measurements by a rotation about the maximum principal stress axis by 15° gave the fringe order to be 4.05. Determine the principal stresses at this point.*

Solution. $$\sigma_1^s = \frac{E_s f_\varepsilon}{2h_c(1+\nu_c)\sin^2\theta}(F_3 \cos\theta N_{\theta 1} - F_2 \cos^2\theta N_0)$$

$$\sigma_2^s = \frac{E_s f_\varepsilon}{2h_c(1+\nu_c)\sin^2\theta}(F_3 \cos\theta N_{\theta 1} - F_1 N_0)$$

where $$F_1 = \left(\frac{1}{1-\nu_s^2}\right)[1 - \nu_c \nu_s - (\nu_c - \nu_s)\cos^2\theta]$$

$$F_2 = \left(\frac{1}{1-\nu_s^2}\right)[1 - \nu_c \nu_s - (\nu_c - \nu_s)/(\cos^2\theta)]$$

$$F_3 = \frac{1-\nu_c}{1-\nu_s}$$

Here $$f_\varepsilon = \left(\frac{1+\nu_c}{E_c}\right) f_\sigma = \left(\frac{1+0.35}{2\times 10^4}\right)\times 17.2$$

$$= 11.61 \times 10^{-4} \text{ cm/fringe}$$

$$N_0 = 4.05$$

$$N_{s1} = 4.25$$

$$\theta = 15^\circ$$

$$F_1 = \frac{1}{1-(0.32)^2}[1 - 0.32\times 0.35 - (0.35 - 0.32)\cos^2 15^\circ]$$

$$= 0.958$$

$$F_2 = \frac{1}{1-(0.32)^2}[1 - 0.32\times 0.35 - (0.35 - 0.32)/\cos^2 15^\circ]$$

$$= 0.953$$

$$F_3 = \frac{1-0.35}{1-0.32} = 0.956$$

$$\sigma_1^s = \frac{0.7\times 10^6 \times 11.61\times 10^{-4}}{2\times 0.2\,(1+0.35)\times 0.06698}[0.956\times 0.96592$$

$$\times 4.25 - 0.953 \times 0.953 \times 4.05]$$

$$= 1457.87 \text{ kg/cm}^2$$

$$\sigma_2^s = \frac{0.7 \times 10^6 \times 11.61 \times 10^{-4}}{2 \times 0.2\,(1 + 0.35) \times 0.06698} [0.956 \times 0.96592 \times 4.25 - 0.958 \times 4.05]$$

$$= 1002.86 \text{ kg/cm}^2.$$

Example 9.4 *A photoelastic coating of epoxy resin araldite-D having material fringe value $f_\sigma = 10.3$ kg/cm²/cm/fringe was used to determine stresses at a point in aluminium subjected to biaxial state of stress. The fringe order at the point with normal incidence was obtained as 3.28 and with oblique incidence by rotation about the σ_1 axis by 25° the fringe order was found to be 3.85. To determine the stresses separately a calibration strip made of aluminium of size 2.5 cm × 6 mm × 30 cm was used. A photoelastic coating of araldite-D of thickness 2 mm was bonded to aluminium strip at 25 cm from the loaded end. When a load of 2 kg was applied at the free end of the calibration strip, 2.52 fringe order was observed with normal incidence and 2.65 and 2.35 with oblique incidence by rotation by the same angle about the x and y-axes respectively. Determine the stresses at the point. Assume $E_s = 0.7 \times 10^6$ kg/cm², $\nu_s = 0.32$ and $E_c = 3.15 \times 10^4$ kg/cm².*

Solution. From Eq. (9.43), we have

$$f_\varepsilon = (1 + \nu_a)\left[\frac{2h_1 + h_c}{h_a}\right] 2h_c \frac{\varepsilon_a}{N_0}$$

$$h_1 = \frac{\left(\frac{h_a^2}{2} - \frac{h_c^2}{2} \cdot \frac{E_c}{E_a}\right)}{\left(h_a + h_c \frac{E_c}{E_a}\right)}$$

Here $h_a = 0.6$ cm, $h_c = 0.2$ cm

$$E_a = 0.7 \times 10^6 \text{ kg/cm}^2$$

$$E_c = 3.15 \times 10^4 \text{ kg/cm}^2$$

$$h_1 = \frac{\left[\frac{(0.6)^2}{2} - \frac{(0.2)^2}{2} \times \frac{3.15 \times 10^4}{0.7 \times 10^6}\right]}{\left(0.6 + 0.2 \times \frac{3.15 \times 10^4}{0.7 \times 10^6}\right)}$$

$$= 0.294 \text{ cm}.$$

Bending moment in the calibration strip at the coating location,

$$M = 2 \times 25 = 50 \text{ kg-cm}$$

$$\varepsilon_a = \frac{\sigma_a}{E_a} = \frac{M_y}{IE_a}$$

$$= \frac{50 \times 0.3}{\frac{2.5 \times (0.6)^2}{12} \times 0.7 \times 10^6}$$

$$= 476.19 \times 10^{-6}$$

$$\text{Hence } f_\varepsilon = (1 + 0.32)\left[\frac{2 \times 0.294 + 0.2}{0.6}\right] \times 2 \times 0.2 \times \frac{476.19 \times 10^{-6}}{2.52}$$

$$= 131.035 \times 10^{-6} \text{ cm/fringe}$$

$$A = \left(\frac{1 - \nu_a}{1 + \nu_a}\right)\left(\frac{N_o}{N_{\theta x} + N_{\theta y}}\right)$$

$$= \left(\frac{1 - 0.32}{1 + 0.32}\right)\left(\frac{2.52}{2.65 + 2.35}\right)$$

$$= 0.2596$$

$$B = \frac{1}{2}\left(\frac{1 - \nu_a}{1 + \nu_a}\right)\left(\frac{N_{\theta x} - N_{\theta y}}{N_{\theta x} + N_{\theta y}}\right) - \frac{1}{2}$$

$$= \frac{1}{2}\left(\frac{1 - 0.32}{1 + 0.32}\right)\left(\frac{2.65 - 2.35}{2.65 + 2.35}\right) - \frac{1}{2}$$

$$= -0.4845$$

$$C = B + 1$$

$$= 0.5155$$

$$\varepsilon_1 = \frac{f_\varepsilon}{2h_c}(AN_{\theta x} - BN_o)$$

$$= \frac{131.035 \times 10^{-6}}{2 \times 0.2}[0.2596 \times 3.85 - (-0.9845 \times 3.28)]$$

$$= 848 \times 10^{-6}$$

$$\varepsilon_2 = \frac{f_\varepsilon}{2h_c}(AN_{\theta x} - CN_0)$$

$$= \frac{131.035 \times 10^{-6}}{2 \times 0.2}(0.2596 \times 3.85 - 0.5155 \times 3.28)$$

$$= -226.48 \times 10^{-6}$$

$$\sigma_1^s = \frac{E_s}{1 - \nu_s^2}(\varepsilon_1 + \nu_s\, \varepsilon_2)$$

$$= \frac{0.7 \times 10^6}{1 - (0.32)^2}(848 - 0.32 \times 226.48) \times 10^{-6}$$

$$= 604.8 \text{ kg/cm}^2$$

$$\sigma_2^s = \frac{E_s}{1-\nu_s^2}(\varepsilon_2 + \nu_s\,\varepsilon_1)$$

$$= \frac{0.7\times 10^6}{1-(0.32)^2}\,(-226.48 + 0.32\times 848)\,10^{-6}$$

$$= 35\ \text{kg/cm}^2.$$

9.5 Coating Materials and Selection

The physical properties of an ideal photoelastic coating material are listed below :

1. High optical sensitivity constant K to maximize the number of fringes per unit of strain for a given coating thickness.
2. Low modulus of elasticity to minimize reinforcing effects.
3. High resistance to both optical and mechanical stress relaxation for maximum stability of the fringe indication with time.
4. Linear strain optic response for ease of data reduction.
5. Good bondability to engineering materials for ensuring perfect strain transmission at the interface with the coated object.
6. Strain-optic coefficient independent of temperature for minimizing problems in interpreting and correcting for temperature effects.
7. Negligible moisture absorption to eliminate birefringence caused by humidity changes.
8. Freedom from initial birefringence.
9. Good machinability for ease in fubricating complex configurations.
10. Conformability to curved surfaces.

Numerous birefringent materials are available which can be used as photoelastic coatings. Usually all those materials which are suitable for photoelastic work can be used as photoelastic coatings. The more commonly used coating materials are polycarbonate, epoxy resins, catalin, photostress, castolite, columbia resin and glass. Polycarbonate generally displays a superior combination of properties. It is available only in sheet form and can not be applied to curved surfaces. Epoxy photoelastic-coating materials have comparatively high strain optic coefficients and are readily conformable and bondable to plane and curved surfaces. For measuring large and post-yield strains, modified expoxies are usually used. In application involving very large strains polyurethane rubber can be used. Typical properties of various coating materials are given in Table 9.3.

After the type of coating is selected, the thickness must be specified along with the coating sensitivity. The coefficient of coating sensitivity $C_c = \dfrac{2h_c}{f_\varepsilon}$ varies linearly with the coating thickness and increases as h_c increases. However, as h_c is increased, the coating reinforcement effects become significant and require corrections.

Table 9.3 Properties of coating materials

Material	*Modulus of Elasticity E, MPa*	*Sensitivity, K*	*Strain limit %*
Polycarbonate	2240	0.16	—
PS-1	2520	0.15	10
Epoxy anhydride	3325	0.12	2
Epoxy-amine	3150	0.09	3
PS-2	3150	0.13	3
Polyester	2800	0.04	1.5
Modified epoxy	21	0.02	15
PS-3	210	0.02	30
Polyurethane	3.5	0.008	100
PS-4	7	0.009	150
Glass	70,000	0.14	0.10

Another factor of equal importance is the accuracy with which the fringe order N can be measured. The absolute error between the principal strains can be written as :

$$\Delta\,(\varepsilon_1^c - \varepsilon_2^c) = \left(\frac{f_\varepsilon}{2h_c}\right)\Delta N = \frac{\Delta N}{C_c} \qquad \text{...(9.78)}$$

where ΔN = error in measuring N.

Equation (9.78) indicates that increasing the coating thickness decreases the absolute error $\Delta\,(\varepsilon_1^c - \varepsilon_2^c)$. Thus error also decreases as ΔN decreases. ΔN is of the order of $\pm$ 0.1 fringe for the full field coloured fringes and $\pm$ 0.01 fringe for the point-by-point compensation methods. The relative error 'e' can be expressed as

$$e = \Delta\,(\varepsilon_1^c - \varepsilon_2^c)/(\varepsilon_1^c - \varepsilon_2^c)\ \max \qquad \text{...(9.79)}$$

where $(\varepsilon_1^c - \varepsilon_2^c)_{max}$ = maximum principal-strain difference.

Combining Eqs. (9.78) and (9.79), we get

$$e = \left(\frac{f_\varepsilon\,\Delta N}{2h_c}\right)\Big/(\varepsilon_1^c - \varepsilon_2^c)_{max}$$

$$= C_c\,\Delta N/(\varepsilon_1^c - \varepsilon_1^c)_{max} \qquad \text{...(9.80)}$$

or

$$h_c = \left(\frac{f_\varepsilon\,\Delta N}{2e}\right)\Big/(\varepsilon_1^c - \varepsilon_2^c)_{max} \qquad \text{...(9.81)}$$

Generally the coating thickness should not be less than 0.05 mm and more than 2.5 mm to avoid error due to variation in thickness or reinforcing effects.

Example 9.5 *A photoelastic coating of epoxy anhydride having sensitivity $K = 0.12$ is used to analyze stresses on aluminium and using mercury light (λ = 5461 Å) for viewing of fringes. The maximum error in measuring principal strain difference should be less than 0.005. The error in measuring fringe order $\Delta N = \pm\, 0.01$ and the relative error is to be less than 2.5 per cent. Determine the coating thickness.*

Solution. Material fringe value (strain)

$$f_\varepsilon = \frac{\lambda}{K}$$

$$= \frac{5461 \times 10^{-8}}{0.12}$$

$$= 455.08 \times 10^{-6} \text{ cm/fringe}$$

Coating thickness $h_c = \left(\dfrac{f_\varepsilon \, \Delta N}{2e}\right) / (\varepsilon_1^e - \varepsilon_2^e)_{max}$

$$= \frac{455.08 \times 10^{-6} \times 0.01}{2 \times 0.025 \times 0.005}$$

$$= 0.182 \text{ mm.}$$

9.6 Coating Application Procedures and Cements

The coating application procedures can be classified into two categories depending upon whether the surface of the specimen is plane or curved.

1. **Plane surface.** Photoelastic coatings to plane surfaces can be applied most readily and economically by cementing flat, procured sheets of material to the surface. Preparation of the specimen surface consists of removal of all foreign matter, sanding and finally cleaning with a suitable chemical agent and solvents. The flat sheet of coating is machined to size, cleaned, properly located and aligned relative to the specimen and then bonded. At the edges of the coating it is a normal practice to bevel the edge or to provide a fillet formed with cement to eliminate high stress concentration. The coating boundary must be precisely matched to the specimen boundary. The cement should be evenly spread over the specimen surface. All air bubbles should be removed. The cement should be allowed to the cure for 24 hours and its thickness then should be 0.08 to 0.25 mm. Pressure to the sheet is generally avoided while cement is curing.

2. **Curved surfaces.** While applying photoelastic coating to a curved surface, contoured sheet technique may be used. This technique consists of four steps, as explained below :

(*i*) A sheet of flexible epoxy is cast in an open face mould, which is a Teflon-covered surface plate carefully levelled to ensure a uniform thickness of the cast sheet.

(*ii*) While the sheet is still soft and pliable, it is stripped from the open-face mould and then contoured to fit the curved surface of the test specimen. The contoured sheet is allowed to polymerize fully.

(*iii*) The fully polymerized sheet is now removed, cleaned and trimmed to size as required.

(*iv*) The contoured sheet is then cemented back in place on the curved surface of the specimen.

The success of the photoelastic coating method depends to a large extent to the cemented bond. An adequate cement should have the following characteristics :

1. Long pot life to allow sufficient time for application.
2. Low viscosity, permitting excess adhesive to flow from under the applied sheet.
3. Short total curing time at room temperature.
4. Low stress-relaxation tendency after cure.
5. Sufficient strain capability to transmit strains upto the maximum elongation of the coating.
6. Uniform and high reflectivity.
7. Modulus of elasticity greater than or at least equal to that of the coating.

Generally amine-cured epoxies can be formulated to meet the above requirements. 10 to 30 per cent of a aluminium powder by weight is added to the cement to obtain a good reflecting bonding layer. Modified epoxies and polyurethane coatings should be bonded by cements which can sustain large strains. Liquid coatings can be applied directly to the specimen surface by dipping, spreading, brushing or spraying. The specimen surface should be preheated to 50° to 60°C to obtain a good bond.

3. **Large strains.** For application of birefringent coatings to metal surfaces which are to undergo large plastic strains, the following procedure may be adopted :

The metal surface to be coated is cleansed using 220, 300, 400 and 600 grades of silicon-carbide paper flooded with water. The surface is thoroughly washed in a strong soap and water solution to remove surface dirt and grease and, to ensure chemical cleanliness, is later rinsed in methanol. The metal surface is dried using a hot-air blower and then the coating is applied. By this method strains upto 10% can be measured.

9.7 Parameters Influencing the Analysis of Data

Upto now we have made the following simplifying assumptions to analyze the coating behaviour.

(*i*) The strain in the coating is assumed to be uniformly distributed through the thickness of the coating.

(*ii*) The test conditions are isothermal.
(*iii*) The coating material is elastic and linear.
(*iv*) The state of stress is static.

In the analysis of actual structures these parameters may become significant and affect the behaviour of the coating. The important parameters affecting the coating behaviour are :

(*i*) Coating thickness, which results in (*a*) the average strain in the coating does not equal the strain at the interface, (*b*) a strain gradient exists through the thickness of the coating and (*c*) the coating reinforces the specimen.

(*ii*) Poisson's ratio mismatch.
(*iii*) Thermal fields.
(*iv*) Dynamic response.
(*v*) Large plastic strains.

9.7.1. Reinforcing effects

(*a*) **Plane stress problems.** Consider the structural part with a birefringent coating in a state of plane stress and let Fig. 9.11 represent an infinitesimal element taken from the member. The influence of load carried by the coating can be determined by equating the forces acting on the composite element to the forces acting on the same element in the uncoated structure.

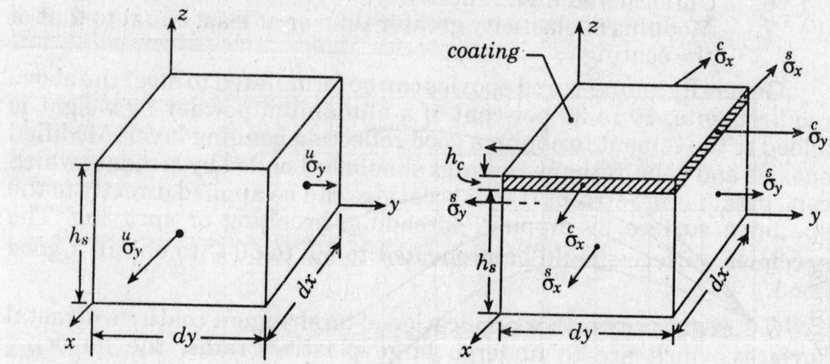

(*a*) Uncoated specimen (*b*) Coated specimen

Fig. 9.11 Principal element taken from a plane stress specimen.

Thus $\sigma_x^u\ h_s\ dy = \sigma_x^s\ h_s\ dy + \sigma_x^c\ h_c\ dy$

$$\sigma_y^u\ h_s\ dx = \sigma_y^s\ h_s\ dx + \sigma_s^c\ h_c\ dx \qquad \text{...(9.82)}$$

where superscript u stands for uncoated specimen. Strains are independent of z and equal at the interface between structure and coating, accordingly,

$$\sigma_x^c = \sigma_x^s,\ \sigma_y^c = \sigma_y^s$$

Also from Hooke's law for plane stress case

$$\sigma_x = \frac{E}{1-\nu^2}(\varepsilon_x + \nu\ \varepsilon_y)$$

$$\sigma_y = \frac{E}{1-\nu^2}(\varepsilon_y + \nu\ \varepsilon_x)$$

Substituting in Eqs. (9.82), we get

$$\varepsilon_x^u - \varepsilon_y^u = (\varepsilon_x^c - \varepsilon_y)^\upsilon \left[1 + \frac{h_c}{h_s}\ \frac{E_c}{E_s}\ \frac{1+\nu_s}{1+\nu_c}\right] \qquad \text{...(9.83)}$$

$$= \frac{1}{C_1}(\varepsilon_x^c - \varepsilon_y^s)$$

where $$\frac{1}{C_1} = 1 + \frac{h_c E_c}{h_s E_s}\left(\frac{1+\nu_s}{1+\nu_c}\right)$$

C_1 represents the correction factor required to convert measured strains into strains, that would be developed on the uncoated structural part. The factor

$$\left(\frac{1+\nu_s}{1+\nu_c}\right) \approx 1$$

When $\nu_c \approx \nu_s$ and consequently

$$\frac{1}{C_1} = 1 + \frac{h_c\, E_c}{h_s h_s} \qquad ...(9.84)$$

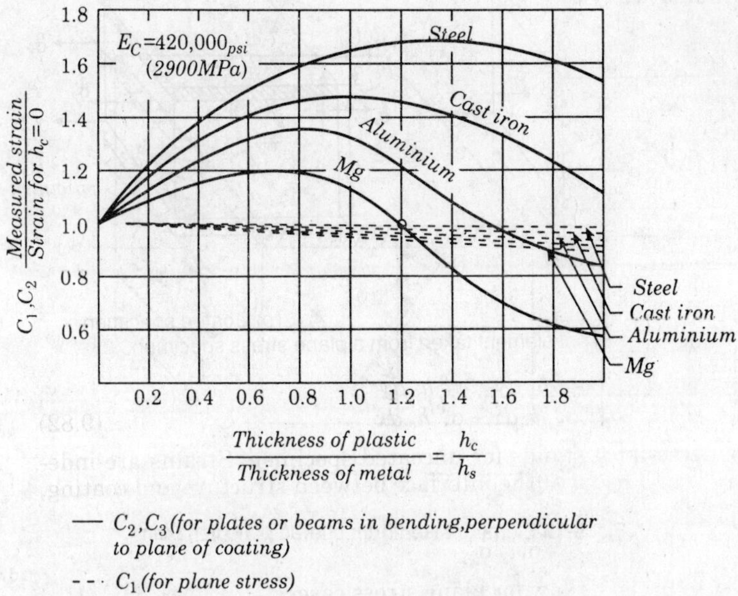

Fig. 9.12 Reinforcing correction factors C_1 and C_2 as a function of h_c/h_s for different specimen materials.

The following assumptions were made in the foregoing analysis :

(*i*) Structure and coating are isotropic elastic materials.

(*ii*) Identical deformation of structure and coating exists at the interface.

(*iii*) Plane stress prevails in structure and coating.

The correction factor C_1 is shown as a function of h_c/h_s in Fig. 9.12 for commonly used materials with E_c = 2900 MPa and ν_c = 0.36. From the figure it can be seen that the reinforcing effect is quite small. The effect is significant only in cases where coating are employed on materials of low elastic modulus or on very thin specimens.

(*b*) **Flexure of plates.** An analysis of birefringent-coating behaviour is very important for flexure problems, since large correction factors are possible in this case. Besides the reinforcing effect resulting from the bending moments carried by the coating, two additional factors must be considered, namely, gradient of strain through the coating thickness and displacement of the neutral plane in the member if the coating is applied on one side of the plate.

Consider a plate coated on one side with a photoelastic plastic and subjected to any system of bending moments acting in planes perpendicular to the coated surface. Let Fig. 9.13 represent an infinitesimal element in the plate such that x and y are principal axes. It is well known that a straight line normal to the neutral surface remains a straight line after flexure and also that normal strains are inversely proportional to the radius of curvature of the neutral surface. This is expressed mathematically by

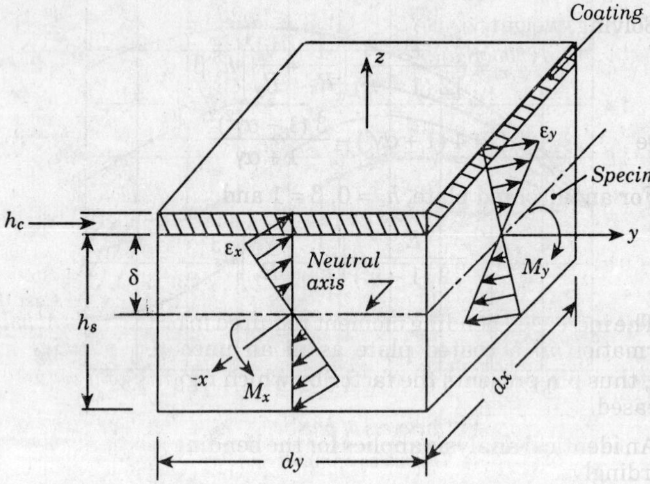

Fig. 9.13 Element taken from coated plate in flexure.

$$\varepsilon_x = \frac{z}{R_x}, \ \varepsilon_y = \frac{z}{R_y} \qquad ...(9.85)$$

where z is the measured from the neutral surface.

Since the neutral surface is displaced by the presence of the coating, its position should be determined in terms of coating thickness and material properties. Equilibrium of forces acting on element dy wide requires that

$$\int_{\delta - h_s}^{\delta} \sigma_x^s \, dx + \int_{\delta}^{\delta + h_c} \sigma_x^c \, dz = 0$$

Substituting stresses in terms of strains and using Eqs. (9.85), we get

$$\delta = \frac{h_s^2 - \alpha h_c^2}{2h_s + 2\alpha h_c} = \frac{h_s}{2}\left(\frac{1 - \alpha\gamma^2}{1 + \alpha\gamma}\right) \qquad ...(9.86)$$

where $\gamma = \dfrac{h_c}{h_s}$

and
$$\alpha = \frac{E_c\,(1-\nu_s^2)\left[\dfrac{1}{R_x}+\dfrac{\nu_c}{R_y}\right]}{E_s\,(1-\nu_c^2)\left[\dfrac{1}{R_x}+\dfrac{\nu_s}{R_y}\right]} \quad \text{...(9.87)}$$

The reinforcement caused by the presence of the coating can now be calculated. The bending moment per unit width acting on the *yz* face of the element is

$$M_{x\,(s,\,c)} = \int_{\delta - h_s}^{\delta} \sigma_x^s\, z\, dx + \int_{\delta}^{\delta + h_c} \sigma_x^c\, z\, dz \quad \text{...(9.88)}$$

Solving, we get

$$M_{x\,(s,\,c)} = \frac{E_s}{12\,(1-\nu_s^2)}\left(\frac{1}{R_x}+\frac{\nu_s}{R_y}\right) h_s^3\, \beta \quad \text{...(9.89)}$$

where
$$\beta = 4\,(1+\alpha\gamma^3) - \frac{3\,(1-\alpha\gamma^2)^2}{1+\alpha\gamma} \quad \text{...(9.89a)}$$

For an uncoated plate, $h_c = 0$, $\beta = 1$ and

$$M_x^u = \frac{E_s}{12\,(1-\nu_s^2)}\left(\frac{1}{R_x}+\frac{\nu_s}{R_y}\right) h_s^3 \quad \text{...(9.90)}$$

The increased bending moment required in order to obtain the same deformation in a coated plate as in an uncoated plate is given by $\beta\, M_x^u$, thus β represents the factor by which rigidity of a coated plate is increased.

An identical analysis applies for the bending moment on the *xz* face. Accordingly

$$M_{x\,(s,\,c)} = \frac{E_s}{12\,(1-\nu_s^2)}\left(\frac{1}{R_y}+\frac{\nu_s}{R_x}\right) h_s^3\, \beta \quad \text{...(9.91)}$$

and
$$M_y^u = \frac{E_s}{12\,(1-\nu_s^2)}\left(\frac{1}{R_y}+\frac{\nu_s}{R_x}\right) h_s^3 \quad \text{...(9.92)}$$

From Eq. (9.85)

$$\varepsilon_x = \varepsilon_y = z\left(\frac{1}{R_x}-\frac{1}{R_y}\right) \quad \text{...(9.93)}$$

From Eqs. (9.89) and (9.91), we get

$$\left(\frac{1}{R_x}-\frac{1}{R_y}\right) = \frac{12\,(1+\nu_s)}{E_s\, h_s^3\, \beta}\,[M_{x\,(s,\,c)} - M_{y\,(s,\,c)}] \quad \text{...(9.94)}$$

Since the measured birefringence is proportional to the average value of $(\varepsilon_x - \varepsilon_y)$ through the coating thickness, the difference of principal strains will be determined at $z = \delta + \dfrac{h_c}{2}$. Thus from Eqs. (9.93) and (9.94), birefringence measurements yield

$$(\varepsilon_x^c - \varepsilon_y^c)_{avg} = \left(\delta + \frac{h_c}{2}\right) \frac{12\,(1 + \nu_s)\,[M_x\,(s, c) - M_y\,(s, c)]}{E_s\, h_s^3\, \beta} \quad ...(9.95)$$

Similarly for an uncoated plate by using Eqs. (9.90), (9.92) and (9.93), we get

$$\varepsilon_x^u - \varepsilon_y^u = \frac{h_s}{2}\; \frac{12\,(1 + \nu_s)}{E_s\, h_s^3}\,(M_x^u - M_y^u) \quad ...(9.96)$$

Thus $$\varepsilon_x^u - \varepsilon_y^u = \frac{h_s\,\beta}{2\delta + h_c}\,(\varepsilon_x^c - \varepsilon_y^c)_{avg}. \quad ...(9.97)$$

$$= \frac{1}{C_2}\,(\varepsilon_x^c - \varepsilon_y^c)_{avg}. \quad ...(9.97\,a)$$

where $$\frac{1}{C_2} = \frac{h_s\,\beta}{2\delta + h_c} = \frac{h_s}{2\delta + h_c}\left[4\,(1 + \alpha\gamma^3) - \frac{3\,(1 - \alpha\gamma^2)^2}{1 + \alpha\gamma}\right] \quad ...(9.98)$$

and C_2 = correction factor required to convert strains determined by birefringence measurements into strains that would be developed in an uncoated part when subjected to the same loads.

For $\nu_c = \nu_s, \quad \alpha = \dfrac{E_c}{E_s}$

Since in practical problems $\nu_c \approx \nu_s$ and $E_c \ll E_s$, hence $\alpha \ll 1$. Therefore Eq. (9.98) is not highly sensitive to small variations in α and for all practical purposes the approximation $\alpha = \dfrac{E_c}{E_s}$ is valid. Thus

$$\delta = \frac{h_s}{2}\left[\frac{1 + \dfrac{E_c}{E_s}\left(\dfrac{h_c}{h_s}\right)^2}{1 + \dfrac{E_c}{E_s}\left(\dfrac{h_c}{h_s}\right)}\right] \quad ...(9.99)$$

$$\frac{1}{C_2} = \frac{h_s}{2\delta + h_c}\left[4\left\{1 + \frac{E_c}{E_s}\left(\frac{h_c}{h_s}\right)^3\right\} - \frac{3\left\{1 + \dfrac{E_c}{E_s}\left(\dfrac{h_c}{h_s}\right)^2\right\}^2}{1 + \dfrac{E_c}{E_s}\left(\dfrac{h_c}{h_s}\right)}\right] \quad ...(9.100)$$

In practical applications $h_c \ll h_s$ and $\delta \to \dfrac{h_s}{2}$ then

$$\frac{1}{C_2} = \frac{h_s}{h_s + h_c} \quad ...(9.101)$$

If the effect of Poisson's ratio is accounted for then Eq. (9.100) becomes

$$\frac{1}{C_3} = \frac{h_s}{2\delta + h_c}\left[4\left\{1 + \frac{E_c}{E_s}\left(\frac{1-\nu_s^2}{1-\nu_c^2}\right)\left(\frac{h_c}{h_s}\right)^3\right\} - \frac{3\left\{1 - \dfrac{E_c}{E_s}\left(\dfrac{1-\nu_s^2}{1-\nu_c^2}\right)\left(\dfrac{h_c}{h_s}\right)^2\right\}^2}{1 + \dfrac{E_c}{E_s}\left(\dfrac{1-\nu_s^2}{1-\nu_c^2}\right)\dfrac{h_c}{h_s}}\right] \quad ...(9.102)$$

where
$$\delta = \frac{h_s}{2}\left[\frac{1 - \dfrac{E_c}{E_s}\left(\dfrac{1-\nu_s^2}{1-\nu_c^2}\right)\left(\dfrac{h_c}{h_s}\right)^2}{1 + \dfrac{E_c}{E_s}\left(\dfrac{1-\nu_s^2}{1-\nu_c^2}\right)\dfrac{h_c}{h_s}}\right]$$

Factors C_2 and C_3 for the bending of a beam are shown in Fig. 9.7 and the factor C_3 for a wide plate is shown in Fig. 9.14.

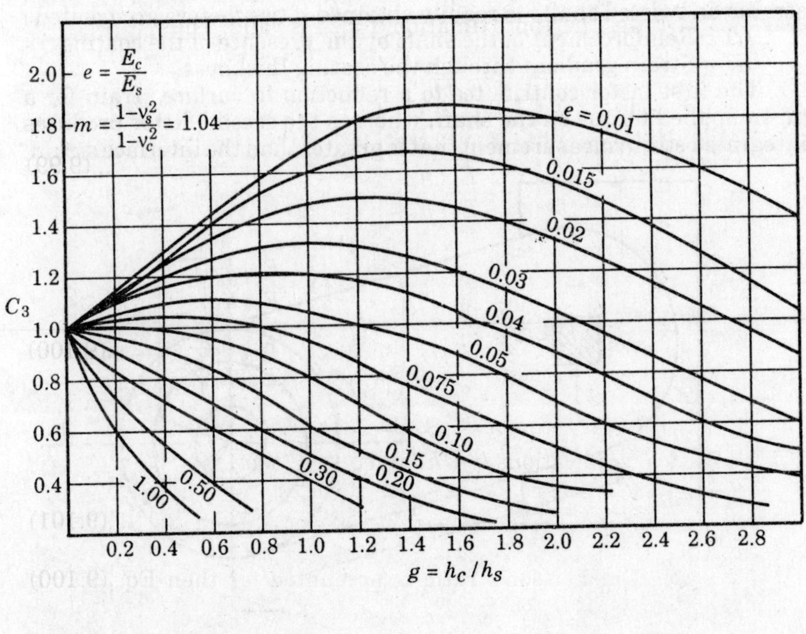

Fig. 9.14 Correction factor C_3 for bending of wide plates.

(*c*) **Combined plane and flexural loads.** Problems in combined plane and flexural loading can be approached by one of the methods described below, depending upon the individual situation.

(*i*) In some problem, the proportionate effects of each type of loading is known. In that case respective corrections can be applied individual to the two components of total strain and corrections are thereby properly weighted. This procedure depends only upon the principle of superposition, which must be applicable for elastic systems.

(*ii*) In general a coating thickness can be chosen so as to yield correction factors that are lower than the required accuracy of the test. This usually prescribes thin coatings however, thick coatings may be chosen so that the correction factors C_1 and C_2 are small.

(*iii*) For combined plane stress and bending a coating thickness can always be found such that $C_1 = C_2$. This value of h_c is determined by equating the right hand side of Eqs. (9.84) and (9.100).

(*iv*) As an alternate method for thin plates, a coating of any convenient thickness might first be applied to examine the general distribution of strains and to locate high strain regions. Then the coating can be stripped off and replaced in the critical regions of high strain by a thin coating.

(*d*) **Torsion of circular shafts.** Faithful prediction of surface strains on twisted shafts is readily obtained if two factors are treated :

(*i*) Reinforcement of the shaft by the presence of the coating.

(*ii*) Strain gradient through the coating thickness.

The first factor contributes to a reduction in surface strain for a given applied torque on the shaft, whereas the second factor produces integrated strain measurement that is greater than the interface strain.

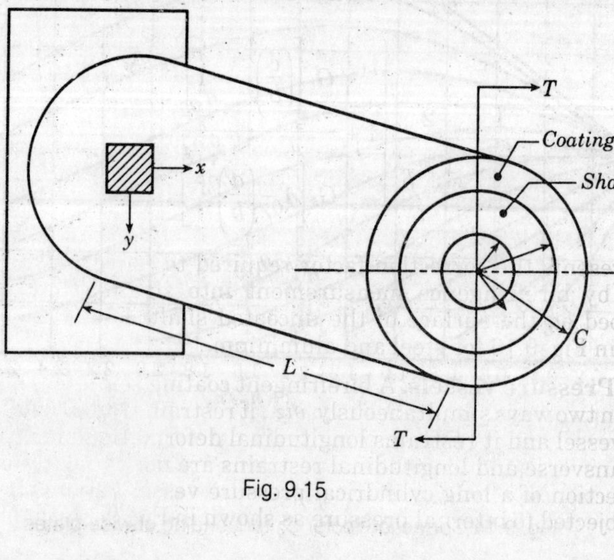

Fig. 9.15

Consider the general case of a hollow circular shaft in torsion as shown in Fig. 9.15. For the uncoated shaft, we have

$$\frac{T^u}{J_s} = \frac{G_s\,\theta^u}{L} \qquad \text{...(9.103)}$$

where $J_s = \frac{\pi}{2}(b^4 - a^4)$

For the coated shaft

$$\frac{T_{s,c}}{\theta_{s,c}/L} = \frac{T_s}{\theta_{s,c}/L} + \frac{T_c}{\theta_{s,c}/L} = J_s\,G_s + J_c\,G_c \qquad \text{...(9.104)}$$

where $J_c = \frac{\pi}{2}(c^4 - b^4)$

For equal torque carried by coated and uncoated shaft $T^u = T_s$ and ratio of angles of twist is

$$\frac{\theta^u}{\theta_{s,c}} = 1 + \frac{J_c\,G_c}{J_s\,G_s} \qquad \text{...(9.105)}$$

Also $\varepsilon_x - \varepsilon_y = \frac{\rho\theta}{L}$ ...(9.106)

Birefringent coating measurement yield the average strain through the coating thickness, corresponding to the strain at $\rho = \frac{1}{2}(b + c)$ and this must be compared to the strain at $\rho = b$ in the uncoated part. Accordingly from Eq. (9.105) and (9.106)

$$\varepsilon_x^u - \varepsilon_y^u = \left(\frac{2b}{b+c}\right)\left(1 + \frac{J_c\,G_c}{J_s\,G_s}\right)(\varepsilon_x^c - \varepsilon_y^c)_{avg}. \qquad \text{...(9.107)}$$

$$= \frac{1}{C_4}(\varepsilon_x^c - \varepsilon_y^c)_{avg} \qquad \text{...(9.107)}$$

where

$$\frac{1}{C_4} = \frac{2}{1 + \frac{c}{b}}\left\{1 + \frac{G_c\left[\left(\frac{c}{b}\right)^4 - 1\right]}{G_s\left[1 - \left(\frac{a}{b}\right)^4\right]}\right\} \qquad \text{...(9.108)}$$

C_4 represents the correction factor required to convert strains determined by birefringence measurement into strains that would be developed on the surface of the uncoated shaft. Factor C_4 has been shown in Fig. 9.16 for steel and aluminium.

(*e*) **Pressure vessels.** A birefringent coating reinforces a pressure vessel in two ways simultaneously, *viz.*, it restrains radial displacement of the vessel and it restrains longitudinal deformation of the member. The transverse and longitudinal restrains are not equal. Consider the cross-section of a long cylindrical pressure vessel having closed ends and subjected to internal pressure as shown in Fig. 9.17. Radial forces, denoted as pressure q are developed at the cylinder-coating interface as a result of the radial expansion of the pressurized vessel. The stresses in the cylinder are :

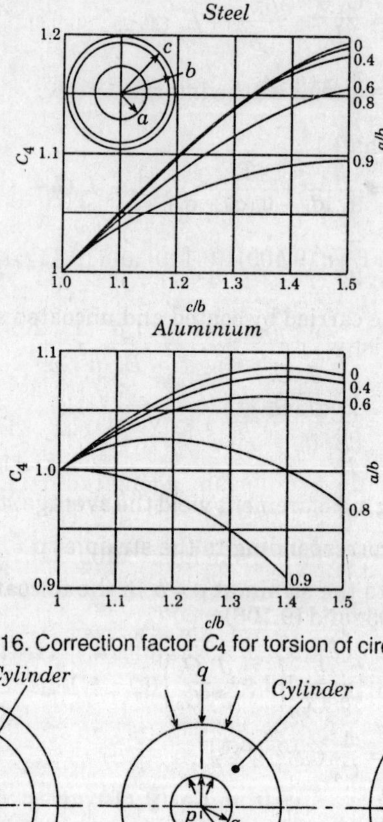

Fig. 9.16. Correction factor C_4 for torsion of circular shafts.

Fig. 9.17 Cross-section of a coated pressure vessel.

$$\sigma_r^s = \frac{pa^2 - qb^2}{b^2 - a^2} - \frac{(p-q)\, a^2\, b^2}{(b^2 - a^2)\, r^2}$$

$$\sigma_\theta^s = \frac{pa^2 - qb^2}{b^2 - a^2} + \frac{(p-q)\, a^2 b^2}{(b^2 - a^2)\, r^2} \qquad \text{...(9.109)}$$

$$\sigma_z^s = 2\, \nu_s \left(\frac{pa^2 - qb^2}{b^2 - a^2} + E_s\, \varepsilon_z \right)$$

Similarly for the coating

$$\sigma_r^c = \frac{qb^2}{c^2 - b^2} - \frac{qb^2\, c^2}{(c^2 - b^2)\, r^2}$$

$$\sigma_\theta^c = \frac{qb^2}{c^2 - b^2} + \frac{qb^2c^2}{(c^2 - b^2)\, r^2} \quad ...(9.110)$$

$$\sigma_z^c = 2\nu_c \left(\frac{qb^2}{c^2 - b^2} \right) + E_c\, \varepsilon_z$$

For the bonded coating, at the interface $r = b$

$$\varepsilon_\theta^s = \varepsilon_\theta^c \quad ...(9.111)$$

By Hooke's law,

$$\varepsilon_\theta = \frac{1}{E} [\sigma_\theta - \nu\, (\sigma_r + \sigma_z)] \quad ...(9.112)$$

By substituting Eqs. (9.109), (9.110) and (9.112) in Eq. (9.111), we get

$$q \left[\frac{(1 + \nu_c) \{b^2 (1 - 2\nu_c) + c^2\}}{E_c\, (c^2 - b^2)} + \frac{(1 + \nu_s) \{b^2 (1 - 2\nu_s) + a^2\}}{E_s\, (b^2 - a^2)} \right]$$

$$= \frac{2pa^2 (1 - \nu_s^2)}{E_s\, (b^2 - a^2)} + \varepsilon_z\, (\nu_c - \nu_s) \quad ...(9.113)$$

For closed ends, the equilibrium of longitudinal forces give

$$pa^2 = \sigma_z^s\, (b^2 - a^2) + \sigma_z^c\, (c^2 - b^2) \quad ...(9.114)$$

Substituting for σ_z^s and σ_z^c from Eqs. (9.109) and (9.110) respectively, we get

$$\varepsilon_z = \frac{pa^2 (1 - 2\nu_s) - 2qb^2\, (\nu_c - \nu_s)}{E_s\, (b^2 - a^2) + E_c\, (c^2 - b^2)} \quad ...(9.115)$$

For a cylindrical pressure vessel

$$\varepsilon_\theta - \varepsilon_z = \frac{1 + \nu}{E} (\sigma_\theta - \sigma_z)$$

Substituting for stresses from Eq. (9.110) gives

$$\varepsilon_\theta^c - \varepsilon_z^c = \frac{1 + \nu_c}{E_c} \left[\frac{qb^2}{c^2 - b^2} \left(1 + \frac{c^2}{r^2} - 2\nu_c \right) - E_c\, \varepsilon_z \right] \quad ...(9.116)$$

Since the normal incidence birefringence measurements yield the integrated value of the principal strain difference through the coating thickness, the mean value is required, thus

$$(\varepsilon_\theta^c - \varepsilon_s^c)_{avg} = \frac{1}{(c - b)} \int_b^c (\varepsilon_\theta^c - \varepsilon_z^c)\, dr$$

$$= (1 + \nu_c) \left[\frac{qb^2}{E_c\, (c^2 - b^2)} \left(1 + \frac{c}{b} - 2\nu_c \right) - \varepsilon_z \right] \quad ...(9.117)$$

For the uncoated closed vessel at $r = b$

$$\left.\begin{aligned}\sigma_\theta^u &= \frac{2pa^2}{b^2-a^2},\ \sigma_r^u = 0\\ \sigma_s^u &= \frac{pa^2}{b^2-a^2}\end{aligned}\right\}\qquad ...(9.118)$$

and
$$\varepsilon_\theta^u - \varepsilon_z^u = \frac{1+\nu_s}{E_s}\left(\frac{pa^2}{b^2-a^2}\right)\qquad ...(9.119)$$

$$= \frac{1}{C_5}\,(\varepsilon_\theta^c - \varepsilon_z^c)_{avg}\qquad ...(9.119\ a)$$

where
$$C_5 = \frac{1+\nu_c}{1+\nu_s}\left[\frac{2\,(1-2\nu_c+c/b)\,(1-\nu_s)}{\dfrac{1+\nu_c}{1+\nu_s}\left(1-2\nu_c+\dfrac{c^2}{b^2}\right)+\alpha\left(\dfrac{c^2-b^2}{b^2-a^2}\right)\left(1-2\nu_s+\dfrac{a^2}{b^2}\right)} - \frac{1-2\nu_s}{1+\alpha\left(\dfrac{c^2-b^2}{b^2-a^2}\right)}\right]\qquad ...(9.120)$$

For $\nu_c \approx \nu_s = \nu$

$$C_5 = \frac{2\,(1-2\nu+c/b)\,(1-\nu)}{\left(1-2\nu+\dfrac{c^2}{b^2}\right)+\alpha\left(\dfrac{c^2-b^2}{b^2-a^2}\right)\left(1-2\nu+\dfrac{a^2}{b^2}\right)} - \frac{1-2\nu}{1+\alpha\left(\dfrac{c^2-b^2}{b^2-a^2}\right)}\qquad ...(9.121)$$

Factor C_5 is plotted in Fig. 9.18.

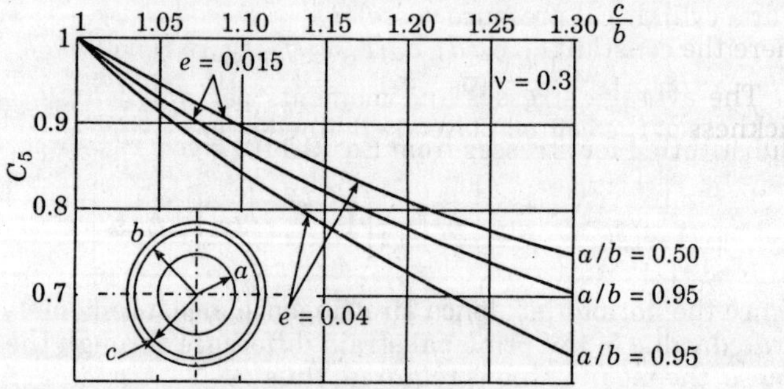

Fig. 9.18 Correction factor C_5 for thick-walled closed-end pressure vessels.

(*f*) **Flat annular plate.** Consider a flat annular plate coated with photoelastic material as shown in Fig. 9.19. The stresses acting on both the plate and coating as shown in Fig. 9.20 may be assumed of the form

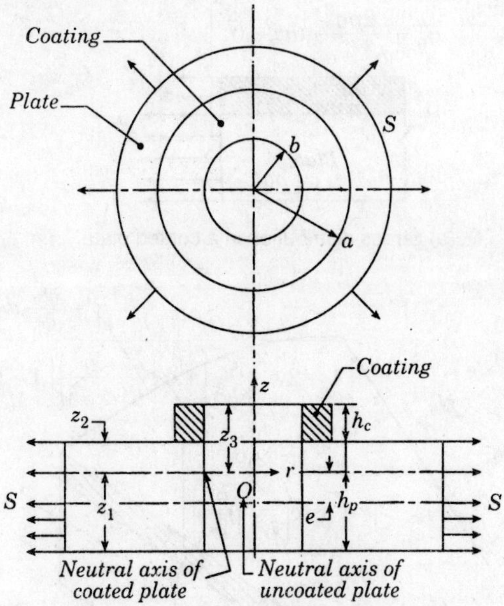

Fig. 9.19 A circular plate with birefringent coating.

$$\left.\begin{aligned} \sigma_r^p &= c_1 z + d_1 \\ \sigma_\theta^p &= c_2 z + d_2 \\ \sigma_r^c &= e_1 z + f_1 \\ \sigma_\theta^c &= e_2 z + f_2 \end{aligned}\right\} \qquad ...(9.122)$$

where the constant $c_1, c_2, d_1, d_2, e_1, e_2, f_1, f_2$ are functions of r.

The average stresses and moments per unit length through the thickness of the coated plate are defined respectively as :

$$\left.\begin{aligned} N_r &= \frac{1}{h_p + h_c}\left[\int_{-z_1}^{z_2} \sigma_r^p \, dz + \int_{z_2}^{z_3} \sigma_r^c \, dz\right] \\ N_\theta &= \frac{1}{h_p + h_c}\left[\int_{-z_1}^{z_2} \sigma_\theta^p \, dz + \int_{z_2}^{z_3} \sigma_\theta^c \, dz\right] \end{aligned}\right\} \qquad ...(9.123)$$

and

$$\left.\begin{aligned} M_r &= \int_{-z_1}^{z_2} \sigma_r^2 \, zdz + \int_{z_2}^{z_3} \sigma_r^o \, zdz \\ M_\theta &= \int_{-z_1}^{z_2} \sigma_\theta^p \, zdz + \int_{z_2}^{z_3} \sigma_\theta^c \, zdz \end{aligned}\right\} \qquad ...(9.124)$$

The equations of equilibrium and corresponding boundary conditions are :

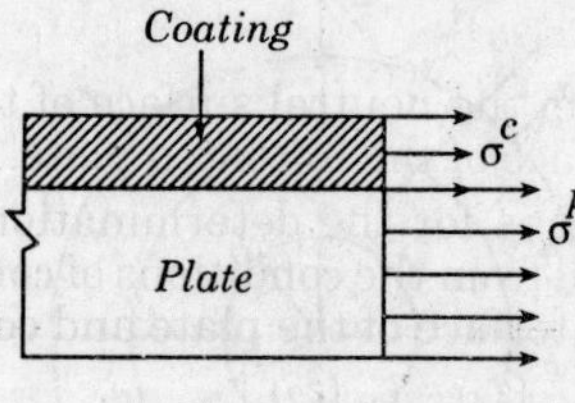

(*a*) Stress distribution in a coated plate.

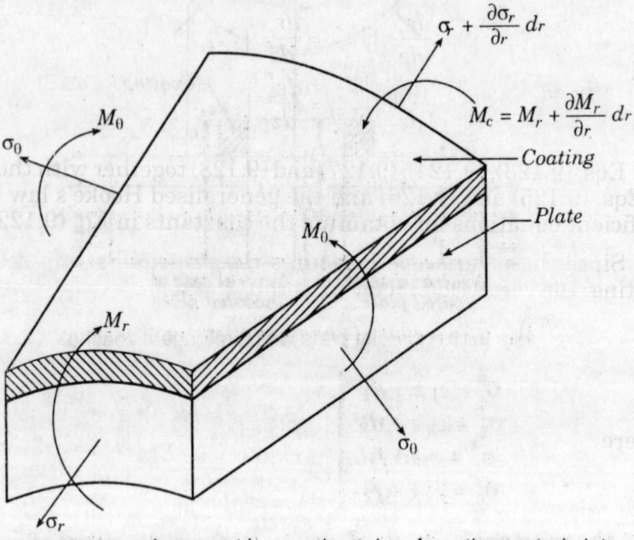

(*b*) Average stress and moment in a wedge taken from the coated plate.

Fig. 9.20

$$\left.\begin{aligned} &\frac{N_r - N_\theta}{r} + \frac{dN_r}{dr} = 0 \\ &N_r(a) = \frac{S}{h_c + h_p} \\ &N_r(b) = 0 \end{aligned}\right\} \quad \text{...(9.125)}$$

and

$$\left.\begin{aligned} &r\frac{dM_r}{dr} + M_r - M_\theta = 0 \\ &M_r(a) = Se \\ &M_r(b) = 0 \\ &w(a) = 0 \end{aligned}\right\} \quad \text{...(9.126)}$$

where e = distance from the neutral surface of the coated plate to the neutral surface of the uncoated plate.

Four other conditions for the determination of constants of Eqs. (9.122) may be obtained from the conditions of continuity of strains and then gradient at the interface of the plate and coating, *i.e.*,

$$\left.\begin{aligned} \varepsilon_r^p (z_2) &= \varepsilon_r^c (z_2) \\ \varepsilon_\theta^p (z_2) &= \varepsilon_\theta^c (z_2) \end{aligned}\right\} \qquad ...(9.127)$$

and

$$\left.\begin{aligned} \frac{d\varepsilon_r^p}{dz}\Big|_{z=z_2} &= \frac{d\varepsilon_r^c}{dz}\Big|_{z=z_2} \\ \frac{d\varepsilon_\theta^p}{dz}\Big|_{z=z_2} &= \frac{d\varepsilon_\theta^c}{dz}\Big|_{z=z_2} \end{aligned}\right\} \qquad ...(9.128)$$

Eqs. (9.123), (9.124), (9.127) and (9.128) together with the solutions of Eqs. (9.125) and (9.126) and the generalised Hooke's law constitute sufficient equations for obtaining the constants in Eq. (9.122).

Since the polariscope measures the principal strain difference in coating, the correction factor C_6 is thus defined as

$$C_6 = \frac{(\varepsilon_r^p - \varepsilon_\theta^p)}{(\varepsilon_r^c - \varepsilon_\theta^c)} \qquad ...(9.129)$$

where
$$\varepsilon_r^p - \varepsilon_\theta^p = \left[\frac{-2a^2b^2}{a^2 - b^2}\right]\left(\frac{S}{r^2}\right)\left(1 + \frac{\nu_p}{h_p E_p}\right)$$

$$\varepsilon_r^c - \varepsilon_\theta^c = \frac{1}{h_p}\int_{z_2}^{z_3} (\varepsilon_r^c - \varepsilon_\theta^c)\, dz$$

Making use of the Eqs. (9.122) and (9.129), we get

$$C_6 = \frac{1 + 4\left(\frac{E_c}{E_p}\right) + 6\left(\frac{E_c}{E_p}\right)\left(\frac{h_c}{h_p}\right)^2}{1 + 6\left(\frac{E_c}{E_p}\right)\left(\frac{e}{h_p}\right)\left(\frac{h_c}{h_p}\right)} \qquad ...(9.130)$$

Assuming $\nu_p = \nu_c$ and neglecting higher order terms.

$$e = \frac{E_c h_c (h_p + h_c)}{2 (E_p h_p + E_c h_c)} \qquad ...(9.131)$$

Also
$$\varepsilon_r^p - \varepsilon_\theta^p = \frac{\lambda N}{2Kh_c} \times \text{Correction factor } C_6 \qquad ...(9.132)$$

where K = Coating sensitivity.

9.7.2 Effect of Poisson's ratio mismatch

In plane stress problems the errors due to coating reinforcement, strain gradients and curvature are usually negligible. However, as ν_c is usually greater than ν_s, this difference in Poisson's ratio produces a distortion of the displacement field through the thickness of the coating. This effect is particularly more significant at the boundaries as shown in Fig. 9.21. If we assume that the strains ε_1 tangent to the boundary are transmitted without loss or amplification so that $\varepsilon_1^c = \varepsilon_1^s$ then this implies that the distortion of the strain field occurs only in the transverse direction due to the difference in Poisson's ratio. At the interface $\varepsilon_1^c = \varepsilon_2^s = -\nu_s \varepsilon_1^s$. Whereas at the free surface of the coating

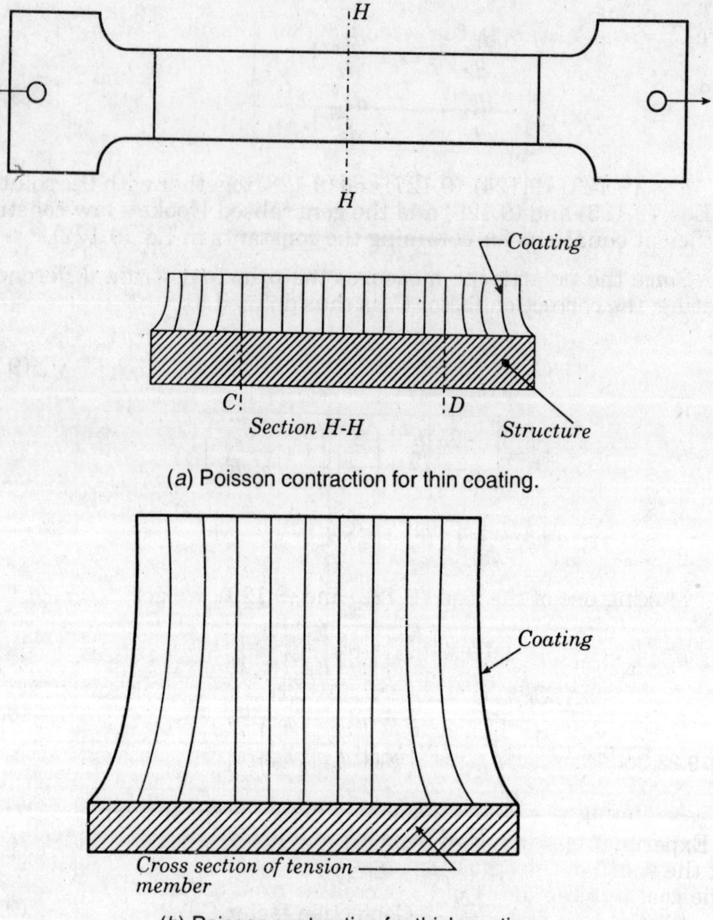

(a) Poisson contraction for thin coating.

(b) Poisson contraction for thick coating.

Fig. 9.21 Effect of Poisson's ratio.

$$\varepsilon_2^c = -\nu_c \varepsilon_1^c = -\nu_s \varepsilon_1^s.$$

Thus the fringe order response of the coating at the free boundary is bounded by

$$\varepsilon_1^s (1 + \nu_s)/F_\varepsilon < N < \varepsilon_2^s (1 + \nu_c)/F_\varepsilon$$

where $F_\varepsilon = \dfrac{f_\varepsilon}{2h_c}$.

Therefore the magnitude of the strain distortion is determined by the Poisson's ratio mismatch parameter $(1 + \nu_c)/(1 + \nu_s)$. The relationship between the observed fringe order and the strain in a tension specimen can be expressed as :

$$N = [1 + \nu_s + C_\nu (\nu_c - \nu_s)] (\varepsilon_1^s / F_\varepsilon) \quad \text{...(9.133)}$$

where C_ν = a correction factor accounting for mismatch effect.

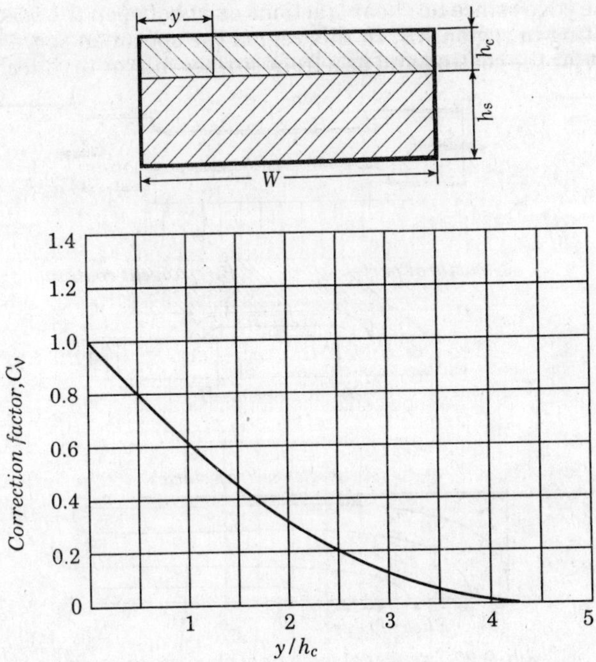

Fig. 9.22 Correction factor C_V as a function of position y/h_c across the transition zone.

Experiments, conducted by Dally and Alfirevich on GFRP indicate that the width of the transition zone is about four times the thickness of the coating. The value of C_ν decreases from 1.0 at the boundary to zero at a distance of $4h_c$ from the boundary as shown in Fig. 9.22. For metallic specimens, $\nu_c - \nu_s$ is usually less than 0.06, which is relatively small as compared to $1 + \nu_s = 1.30$, and the Poisson's ratio mismatch can often be neglected.

9.7.3. Effect of Strain Gradients

In general the forces must be transferred from the structure to the coating by shear forces (Fig. 9.23) developed in the interface. However, the state of stress or strain at a point in the coating depends upon the continuity of this elastic member as well as upon the shear tractions.

Stress trajectories through the thickness of the coating are shown in a tensile specimen in Fig. 9.23. The deformation of the coating is introduced by the action of the shear forces near the ends of the coating. A concentration of shear stress is developed near the discontinuity of the coating layer. This is a local concentration however and shears diminish to zero a small distance from the discontinuity. The sections at which the shear tractions vanish are designated *A* and *B*. Within zone *AB*, both the structure and coating are in a state of plane stress. The photoelastic coating behaves as an independent member subjected to the same axial displacement as the specimen between *A* and *B*. This implies that the strain field in the coating depends only on the bond near the edges since no shear tractions exist between the specimen and the coating in region *AB*. In this region the specimen serves only as a support for the coating and as a front surface mirror to reflect the light.

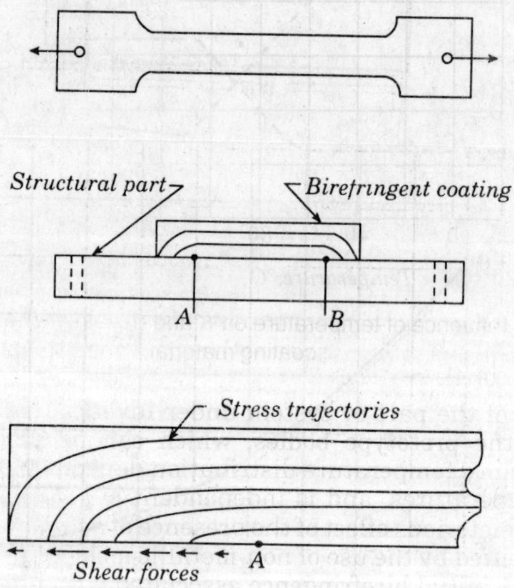

Fig. 9.23 Transfer of force from structure to coating.

Usually the in-plane strain gradients do not affect the accuracy of the coating indication in any analysis of a structure subjected to plane stress. However, there remains an error due to a mismatch in Poisson's ratio, which is less than 5% for metallic test specimens.

9.7.4 Effect of Thermal Fields

The photoelastic coating method is potentially very useful for measurement of stresses in structures subjected to variable temperature conditions. An ideal coating material would exhibit the following qualities :

1. Thermal conductivity equal to that of the workpiece.
2. Coefficient of thermal expansion equal to that of the structure.
3. Strain optical sensitivity invariable with temperature.

Photoelastic coating materials can be utilized successfully to measure strains from – 45°C to 200°C by applying corrections for temperature changes (Fig. 9.24). Existing photoelastic coatings are relatively good thermal insulators, while metallic structural parts feature higher thermal conductivity. As a consequence, the presence of the coating may alter the temperature distribution in the coated part. This would be a deleterious effect for those cases in which a strain field under investigation is a direct result of the temperature gradients along the surface.

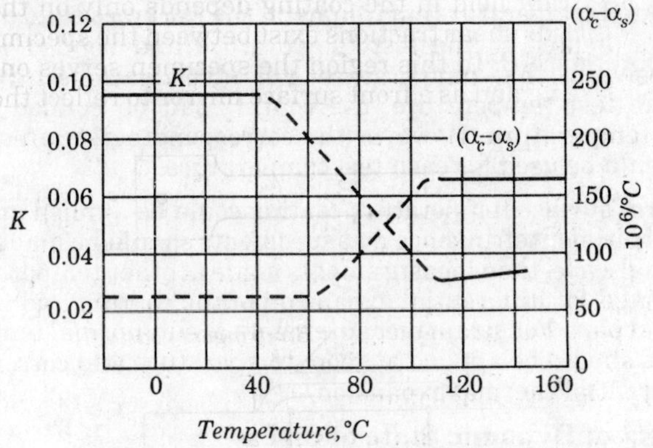

Fig. 9.24 Influence of temperature on K and $(\alpha_c - \alpha_s)$ for a typical epoxy coating material.

Models of the part or system under investigation can be utilized instead of the prototype bodies, which can be made of insulating materials, since temperature distribution depends upon geometry and surface temperatures, and is independent of conductivity. Thus, the otherwise deleterious effect of the presence of an insulating coating can be circumvented by the use of non-metallic model. Corrections must be made for the initial birefringence associated with differential thermal expansion of the work-piece and coating. The differential expansion merely introduces an increase of birefringence of N_α and principal directions or isoclinic parameter remains unaltered. Thus

$$N_{corrected} = N_{measured} - N_\alpha \quad ...(9.134)$$

where $$N_\alpha = 2h_c K_f \left(\frac{1+\nu_c}{1-\nu_c}\right) \frac{\sin^2\theta}{\cos\theta} \int_{T_i}^{T_f} (\alpha_s - \alpha_c)\, dT \quad ...(9.135)$$

θ = angle of incidence

α_s, α_c = coefficients of linear thermal expansion for the specimen and coating respectively.

T = temperature

$N_\alpha \to 0$ if $\theta = 0$. For any temperature T_f, N_α is constant.

If material properties are also taken into account then

$$N\alpha = 2h_cK_f \int_{T_i}^{T_f} (\alpha_s - \alpha_c)\, dT\, [g\,(\nu, \beta)] \qquad ...(9.136)$$

It is recommended that in all cases involving elevated temperature tests, the coating be applied at the highest temperature expected, or that the coating be applied at room temperature and one complete temperature cycle performed before taking measurements. Otherwise tests may be performed on model materials similar to the photoelastic coating material so that the corrections for differential thermal expansion are not in cases where the workpiece experiences external loading in a fixed elevated temperature environment, the workpiece and coating should both be heated to the test temperature and bonded with a suitable adhesive at that temperature. For investigations involving more than one test temperature, the coating can be bonded at an intermediate temperature. However the corresponding strain-optical coefficient should be used for each test temperature.

For uniform surface temperature coating could be applied at room temperature. Initial birefringence measurements should be made after the first thermal cycle, then measurements made at other temperatures must be corrected for differential expansion of the coating and underlying structural part. For strain measurements at sub-normal temperatures, coatings should be applied at room temperature and corrections made for differential thermal expansion.

9.7.5 Effect of Dynamic State of Stress

The use of photoelastic coatings to study dynamic states of stress requires that the coating have a sufficiently high-frequency response to follow the changes that occur in the stress field with time. A bonded strip can be used as a very effective means to study dynamic stresses created by wave propagation. The frequency response f_r of a coating is given by

$$f_r = \frac{1}{T_R} = \frac{C_t}{10h_s} \qquad ...(9.137)$$

where T_R = the period of response

C_t = transverse velocity of wave propagation.

Thus the frequency response of the coating increases as the coating thickness is decreased. For $C_t = 1 \times 10^3$ m/s, $h_c = 2.5$ mm, $f_r = 40$ kHz. This value is sufficiently high that photoelastic coatings can be employed in most dynamic-stress-analysis problems. For photoelastic coatings to be used on vibrating members having low damping energy, the results should be verified with strain gauges. If the inherent damping in the structure is large and the exciting forces are not near the natural frequency of the structure, the additional damping introduced by the coating is not significant, and the results obtained with stroboscopic reflected light are quite accurate.

9.8 Calibration Methods

Two methods are generally used to calibrate the coating to determine the strain-optic sensitivity.

(*a*) **Cantilever Beam in Bending.** A cantilever beam of aluminium or steel of 25 mm × 6 mm × 300 mm size with coating cemented on one side is used for calibration purpose. The coating size may be 20 mm × 2 mm × 100 mm approximately. It is generally cemented at a distance of 200 mm from the free end where load is applied. At a distance x from the free end of the cantilever, the bending moment due to force F is $M = Fx$. Then

$$\varepsilon_1^s - \varepsilon_2^s = \frac{6\,(1+\nu_s)\,Fx}{h_s\,h_s^2\,E_s}$$

or for specified deflection δ of the free end of the cantilever,

$$\varepsilon_1^s - \varepsilon_2^s = \frac{3\,(1+\nu_s)\,h_s\,x\,\delta}{2l_s^3}$$

where b_s, h_s and l_s are the width, height and effective length of the beam respectively (Fig. 9.25).

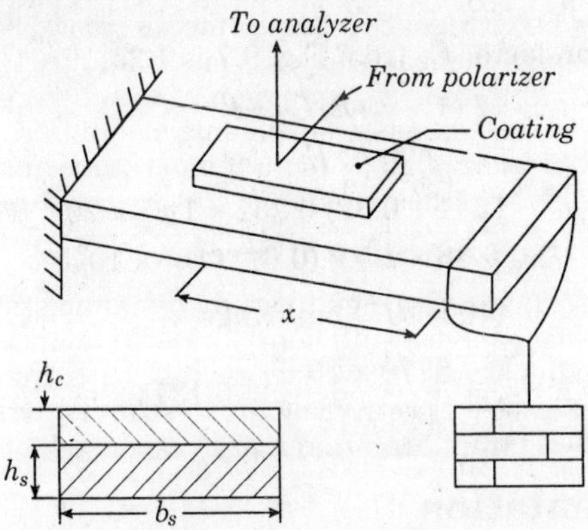

Fig. 9.25 Calibrating a photoelastic coating.

Applying correction factor C_2 for coating thickness effect

$$(\varepsilon_1^c - \varepsilon_2^c)_{avg.} = C_2\,(\varepsilon_1^s - \varepsilon_2^s)$$

Hence $$f_\varepsilon = \frac{\lambda}{K} = \frac{12\,(1+\nu_s)\,h_c\,C_2\,xF}{Nb_s\,h_s^2\,E_s} \qquad ...(9.138)$$

or $$f_\varepsilon = \frac{3\,(1+\nu_s)\,h_c\,C_2\,h_s\,x\delta}{Nl_s^3} \qquad ...(9.139)$$

A point is marked centrally on the coating and fringe order N is measured accurately by using Tardy method with a reflection polariscope. Generally a graph of F v's. N is plotted and a best fit straight line is constructed through the data points or the value of δ/N is accurately established. This method is preferred for high sensitivity coating material like the polycarbonates.

(*b*) **Tension Specimen.** The coating is bonded to a tensile specimen. The fringe order is measured with a reflection polariscope and the axial strain is measured with an extensiometer. Then

$$f_\varepsilon = 2\,(1 + \nu_c)\, h_s \left(\frac{\varepsilon_1^c}{N}\right) \quad \text{...(9.140)}$$

Example 9.6. *A calibration beam 25 mm × 300 mm is fabricated from aluminium having* $\nu_s = 0.32$, $E_s = 0.7 \times 10^6$ *kg/cm*^{2}. *A coating of thickness 2.52 mm is cemented to the beam at a distance of 20 cm from the free end. The fringe order N was measured with a reflection polariscope as the load F was increased in steps. The slope of the Fv's N curve was found to be 0.36 fringes/kg. Determine the sensitivity of the coating.* $\lambda = 5770$ *Å.*

Solution. Here

$$\frac{h_c}{h_s} = \frac{2.52}{6} = 0.42$$

The correction factor C_2 from Fig. 9.7 is 1.25.

Now
$$f_\varepsilon = \frac{12\,(1 + \nu_s)\, h_s\, C_2\, x\, F}{N b_s\, h_s^2\, E_s}$$

$$= \frac{12\,(1 + 0.32)\, 0.252 \times 1.25 \times 20}{0.36 \times 2.5 \times (0.6)^2 \times 0.7 \times 10^6}$$

$$= 440 \times 10^{-6} \text{ cm/fringe}$$

$$K = \frac{\lambda}{f_\varepsilon} = \frac{5770 \times 10^{-8}}{440 \times 10^{-6}} = 0.1311.$$

9.9 Instrumentation

The measuring instrument used with a photoelastic coating is the reflection polariscope. With normal light incidence and plane polariscope arrangement, both the isochromatics and isoclinics are obtained. Oblique light incidence helps in determining the stresses separately.

A number of arrangement can be used for the reflection polariscope. The two commonly used arrangements are shown in Fig. 9.26. Arrangement (*a*) permits perfect normal incidence of light. But this arrangement is not preferred as the fringe contrast is degraded and the ellipticity of polarization is altered due to the presence of the partial mirror. The arrangement (*b*) is generally preferred. However, the light incidence is not perfectly normal, but the error introduced is less than 1 per cent for angles of incidence less than 4°. This type of polariscope may also be equipped with a magnifying arrangement. For field use the polariscope may be mounted on a tripod stand as shown in Fig. 9.27.

For making oblique incidence measurement the arrangement as shown in Fig. 9.28 may be used. Fig. 9.28 (*a*) represents a special purpose unit based upon an equilateral glass prism and employs a 45° angle of incidence. In this case the index of refraction of the glass is matched to that of the coating. A drop of oil between the glass and the coating provides the necessary optical continuity. This design is used for fringe-order measurements on flat or slightly concave surfaces. This system is rather inconvenient in practice and introduces errors due to its self-weight.

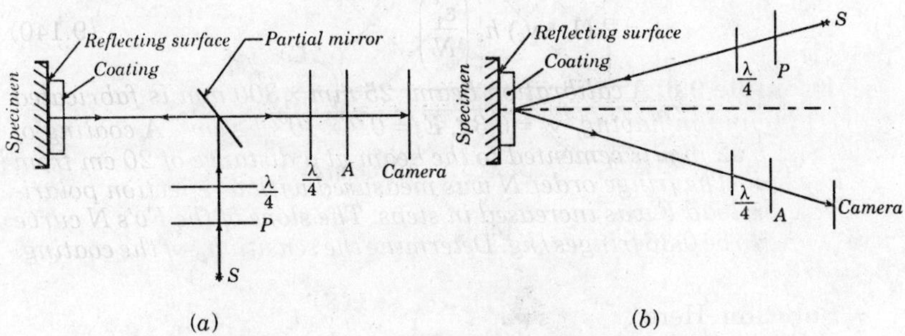

Fig. 9.26 Arrangements for a reflection polariscope.

Fig. 9.27 Reflection polariscope fitted on a tripod stand. (*Courtesy*: Photoelastic Inc.).

The system shown in Fig. 9.28 (*b*) is usually preferred. This is simply an attachment to the conventional normal incidence reflection polariscope. The maximum angle of incidence obtainable by the method is given by

$$\sin \theta_{max} = \frac{1}{n_0}$$

which yields $\theta_{max} = 39^\circ$ for $n_0 = 1.6$.

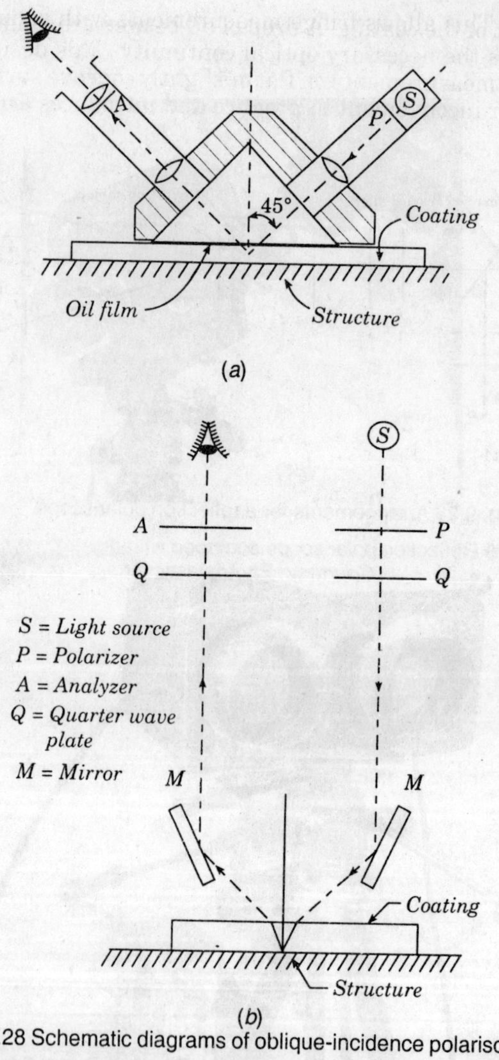

Fig. 9.28 Schematic diagrams of oblique-incidence polariscopes.

For handling large data a reflection polariscope equipped with a digital compensator and auxiliary instrumentation, as shown in Fig. 9.29, may be used. Static records of fringe patterns may be obtained by a camera. For dynamic recording stroboscopic lighting (Fig. 9.30) or motion picture records may be obtained. For recording very low static or dynamic birefringence or for high resolution measurements photoelectric recording may be used. In this system a photocell is placed behind the analyzer of the polariscope and an appropriate optical system is arranged to project the image of the point under study onto the photocell grid. Changes in birefringence produce changes in the light intensity, which in turn changes the photoelectric current. The current is conducted to an oscilloscope or oscillograph for observation or recording. This allows fringe measurements with sensitivities to a 0.0001 fringe.

Fig. 9.29 Reflection polariscope equipped with digital compensator. (*Courtesy*: Photoelastic Inc.)

Fig. 9.30 Reflection polariscope equipped with stroboscope lighting. (*Courtesy*: Photoelastic Inc.)

To observe the fringe patterns continuously, closed-circuit television can be used very effectively, with the television camera mounted behind the analyzer.

9.10 Fringe Multiplication Techniques

When the sensitivity of the coating is quite low and the fringe order obtained is also low, then a fringe multiplication technique can be used. Fig. 9.31 shows an optical set up for fringe multiplication. When a fringe multiplication mirror (partially silvered) is placed in the path of a light beam projected onto a back-silvered birefringent coating, the reflected light from the coating will again be reflected back onto the coating. This reflection occurs many times in succession, thus increasing the optical path and hence the briefringence without increase of the actual thickness of the coating. In order to isolate the multi-reflected light according to the number of reflections, the fringe multiplication mirror should be obliquely inclined so that the multireflected light will be projected in directions of progressively increasing inclinations. A focusing lens which collects these obliquely inclined light beams onto a screen will then produce a succession of focal points. By placing an aperture at this focal plane, any particular image of a multi-reflected light can be isolated for projection on an observation screen.

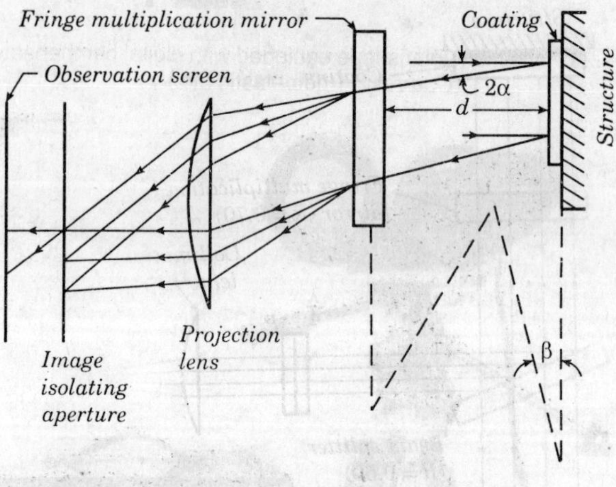

Fig. 9.31 Optical set-up for fringe multiplication.

Since the direction of the reflected light changes progressively with the number of multi-reflections, the light does not enter nor exit the coating at the same point. Rather, these incident and exit points move along the surface of the coating as the number of multiplications increases. The resultant birefringence observed after fringe multiplication is then the average birefringence over a small but finite area. This averaging effect is one of the inaccuracies in the fringe multiplication technique. This effect can be minimized by decreasing either the incident angle of light α, the inclination of the fringe multiplication mirror, β or the mirror distance d.

Any slight irregularity in the reflective surface of the coating will scatter the multi-reflected light and cause the focal points to become an irregular shaped area of finite size. In order to separate these finite-sized focal points, α and β must be increased, which results in averaging effect of birefringence over a large area. The intensity of reflected light is given by

$$I_n = I_o T_m^2 R_p^{n/2} R_m^{(n-2)/2} \qquad \text{...(9.141)}$$

where I_n = intensity of reflected light

I_0 = intensity of incident light

T, R = transmissibility and the reflectivity of the mirror respectively

n = number of times the light passes through the coating

m, p = subscripts indicating fringe multiplication mirror and back-silvered surface coating respectively.

Fig. 9.32 shows the schematic arrangement for fringe multiplication.

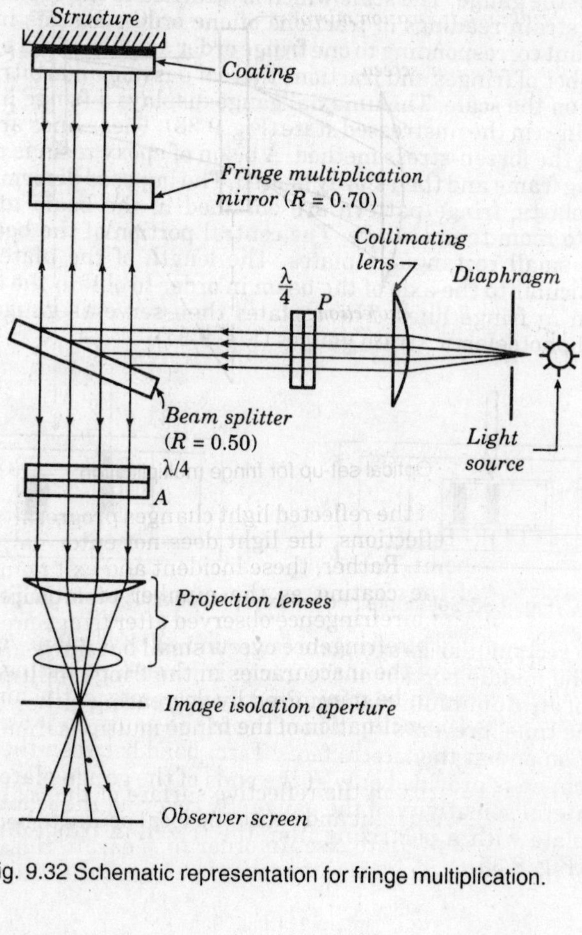

Fig. 9.32 Schematic representation for fringe multiplication.

9.11 Photoelastic Gauges

9.11.1 Photoelastic Strain Gauge

A photoelastic strain gauge consists essentially of a thin, small plate made of an optical strain-sensitive material which indicates variations in strain by changes in number and in position of interference fringes. The plate is glued or otherwise rigidly fixed to the surface of the structural part to be tested and then subjected to static or dynamic loading. The fringe in the gauge plate become visible when observing the gauge in polarized light. For this purpose, a polarizing film is incorporated in the gauge or positioned in the path of the light. Therefore, common light is the only power source required for obtaining strain reading. Various types of gauges can be obtained by shaping and preparing the gauge plate in different manners.

(*a*) **Uniaxial photoelastic strain gauge.** The uniaxial photoelastic-strain gauge indicates changes in strain by displacements of fringes visible in the gauge. The scale which is attached to the top of the gauge permits strain readings of fractions of one order. Strains in excess of the amount corresponding to one fringe order are measured by counting the number of fringes and fractions thereof passing an arbitrary picked location on the scale. The uniaxial gauge displays a fringe line or a set of such lines in the unstressed state (Fig. 9.33). These lines are obtained by using the forzen-stress method. A beam of epoxy resin is placed into a bending frame and then slowly heated. The imposed deformations and a photoelastic fringe pattern are obtained in the beam after slowly cooling to room temperature. The central portion of the beam is then cut into small rectangular plates. The length of the plates is taken perpendicular to the axis of the beam in order to obtain the desired set of frozen in fringe lines. These plates then serve as gauge plates of uniaxial photoelastic strain gauges (Fig. 9.34).

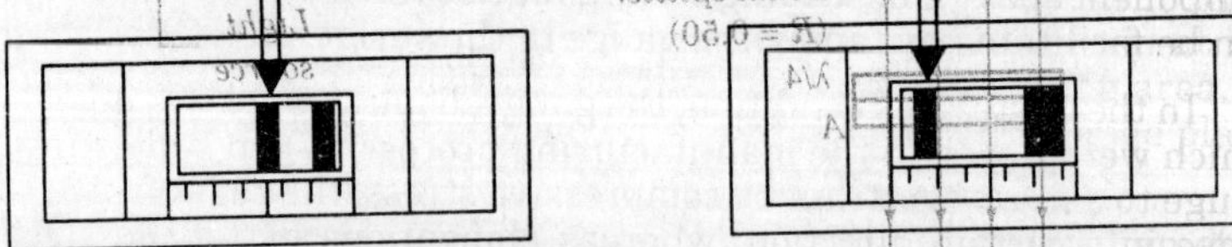

Fig. 9.33 Self-contained uniaxial photoelastic strain gauge.

The rectangular gauge plate is ground to have plane and parallel faces. The middle portion of the gauge is given a reflecting surface by means of an aluminium coating. Plastic tape protects the mirror and at the same time, prevents rigid bonding of the gauge to the specimen in this region and at the lateral faces. Firm bond between the gauge and the specimen is provided only at the ends of the gauge plate in order to avoid lateral sensitivity of the gauge. By covering the front face of the gauge plate with a polarizing film, the frozen-in fringe lines become visible (Fig. 9.35).

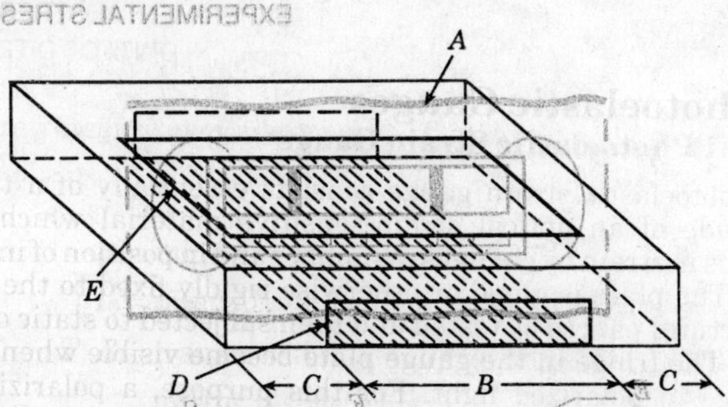

(*a*) Uniaxial gauge. Schematic design diagram A—gauge plate, B—reflecting rear face, C—gluing area, D—rubber sheet, E—polarizing film.

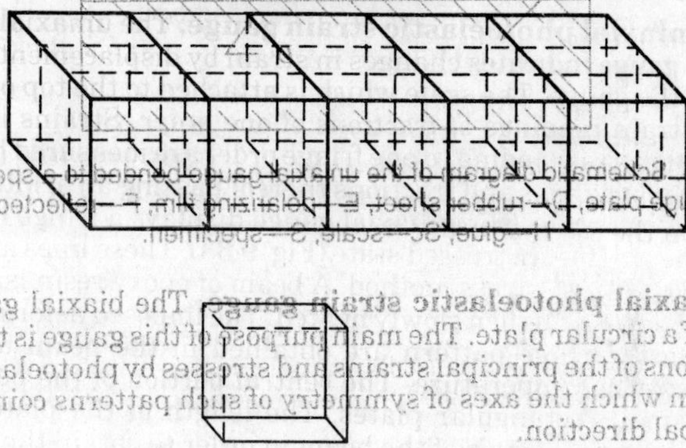

(b) Method of cutting a gauge plate

Fig. 9.34 Uniaxial strain gauge.

The gauge commonly is attached to the specimen by means of a two component epoxy glue. Gluing of the gauge at vertical or sloped surfaces can be facilitated by taping the gauge to the surface of the specimen.

In the unstrained condition, the gauge displays a set of fringe lines, which were frozen in the manufacturing process. When subjecting the gauge to a negative strain by compressive stress, the set of fringe lines move in a certain direction, whereas elongations by tensile stresses cause displacements of the fringe lines in the opposite direction. In this manner, positive and negative strains are distinguishable. Lines of higher or of lower order may enter the field of observation when increasing the load. However, the distances between the lines remain constant. The fringe movement is directly proportional to the longitudinal deformation of the gauge and, therefore, to the directional strain of the part to which the gauge is bonded. The uniaxial photoelastic strain gauge is suited as a tool for exact strain determination and that the gauge displays a constant gauge factor and a strong linear strain optical behaviour.

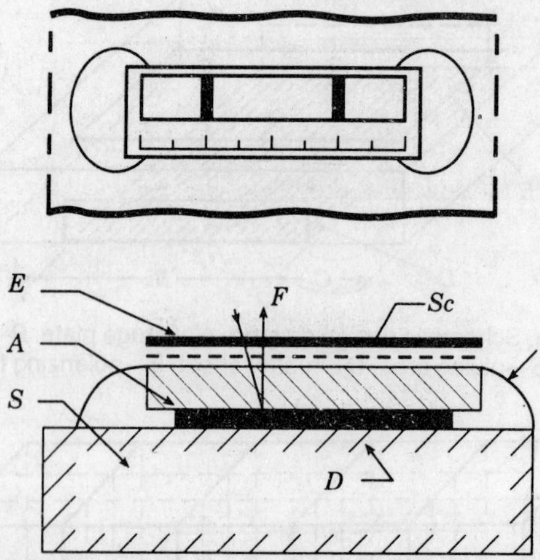

Fig. 9.35. Schematic diagram of the uniaxial gauge bonded to a specimen. A—gauge plate, D—rubber sheet, E—polarizing film, F—reflected light, H—glue, Sc—scale, S—specimen.

(*b*) **Biaxial photoelastic strain gauge.** The biaxial gauge is in the form of a circular plate. The main purpose of this gauge is to indicate the directions of the principal strains and stresses by photoelastic fringe patterns, in which the axes of symmetry of such patterns coincide with the principal direction.

The biaxial gauge (Fig. 9.36) consists of a circular gauge plate (A) of uniform thickness having a circular hole at the centre. The hole acts as a stress raiser and causes a stress concentration effect in its surroundings. A rubber shear (D) covers the central part (B) of the gauge plate and prevents the gauge from being rigidly bonded to the structural part in this region. The gauge plate is, therefore, free to deform at its hole. The boundary (C) of the gauge plate serves as the gluing area. A circular polarizing film (E) attached to the front face of the gauge plate renders a self-contained biaxial photoelastic strain gauge.

If the outer diameter of the gauge is equal to four times the diameter of the circular hole, then the gauge will undergo at the boundary the same deformations as the structural part. The gauge will read as its hole like a large plate with a hole. The gauge will indicate strains and stresses acting in the region of the structural part to which the gauge is bonded.

The advantages of the photoelastic strain gauge are :

1. These gauges do not require any complicated and expensive or troublesome additional equipment for conducting strain measurements.

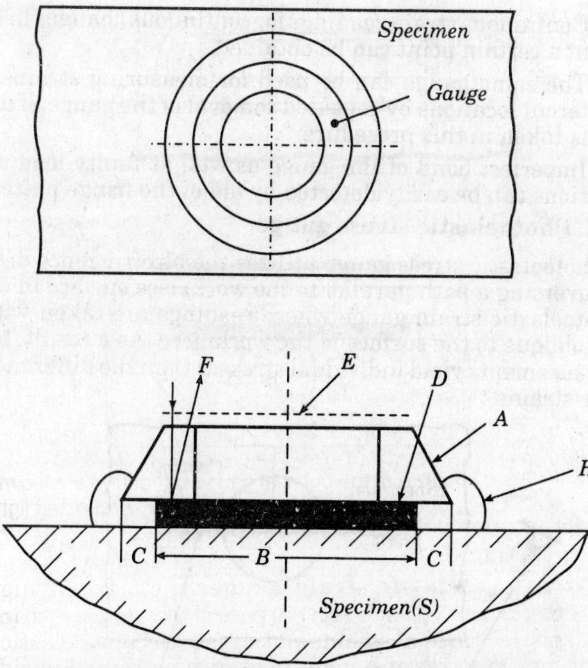

A—circular gauge, B—silvered area, C—gluing area, D—rubber sheet, E—polarising film, F—reflected light, H—glue.
Fig. 9.36 Biaxial photoelastic strain gauge.

2. The gauge provides quick information.
3. The magnitude of the strain can be read directly from a scale attached to the uniaxial gauge.
4. The changes in strain are indicated practically without any inertia effect.
5. A number of gauges can be observed or photographed at the same time.
6. The variation in strain in a structural part due to periodic loading can be observed if a stroboscopic light source is used.
7. They can be used in explosive atmosphere where high-voltage equipment is not permissible.
8. Telemetering of strain sensed is possible in an explosive atmosphere since the telemetering device can be completely encased.
9. The ease of setting up results in considerable saving of time over measurements with other types of strain gauges.
10. They can withstand rough handling without being disturbed.

11. Continuous strain readings for continuous changes in loading at a certain point can be obtained.
12. The same gauge can be used for measuring strains at different locations by repeated removal of the gauge, if due care is taken in this procedure.
13. Imperfect bond of the gauge as well as faulty load applications can be easily detected by aid of the fringe pattern.

9.11.2. Photoelastic stress gauge

The photoelastic stress gauge utilizes the birefringence developed in light traversing a path parallel to the workpiece surface in contrast to the photoelastic strain gauge where readings are taken with light normal or oblique to the surface of the workpiece. As a result, birefringence measurements yield individual stresses than the difference of the stresses or strains.

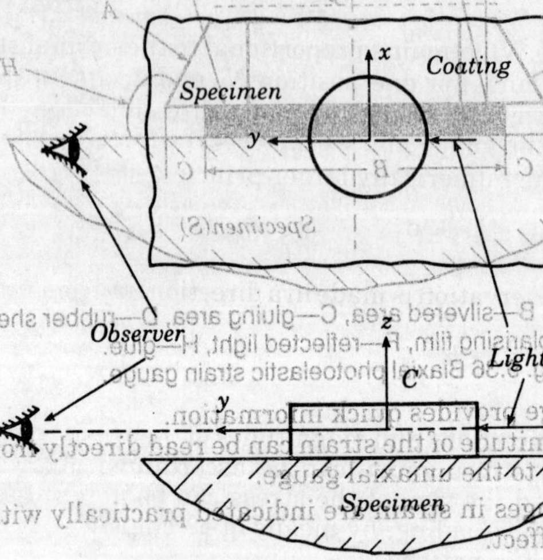

Fig. 9.37 Circular stress gauge.

Let a disc *C*, having substantially lower stiffness than the workpiece, be securely bonded to the workpiece before the stress system is applied as shown in Fig. 9.37. When stressed, the surface strains in the workpiece are transmitted to the disc by the bonding medium, thus introducing a state of stress in the disc that it is related to the surface stresses in the workpiece so that

$$\sigma_x^c = \sigma_x^s \left\{ \frac{E_c}{E_s} \left(\frac{1-\nu_s^2}{1+\nu_c^2} \right) \left(\frac{\varepsilon_x + \nu_c\, \varepsilon_y}{\varepsilon_x + \nu_s\, \varepsilon_y} \right) \right\}$$

or
$$\sigma_x^s = \frac{\sigma_x^c}{\alpha}$$

Where
$$\alpha = \frac{E_c}{E_s} \left(\frac{1-\nu_s^2}{1-\nu_c^2} \right) \left(\frac{\varepsilon_x + \nu_c\, \varepsilon_y}{\varepsilon_y + \nu_s\, \varepsilon_y} \right)$$

Thus $\sigma_x^c \propto \sigma_x^s$

If $\nu_c = \nu_s = \nu$

then $\alpha = \frac{E_c}{E_s}$

Let the disc be a photoelastic material, viewed in a direction parallel to the interface as shown in Fig. 9.37. The birefringence in a stressed photoelastic material is proportional to the difference of secondary principal stresses in the plane normal to the direction of observation. In the absence of shear stresses τ_{xz}, the secondary principal stresses are σ_x^c and σ_z^c and since $\sigma_z^c = 0$, the birefringence is directly proportional to σ_x^c. Thus the observed birefringence, or photoelastic fringe order is related to the stress developed in the gauge by

$$N_x = \pm \frac{h_c \sigma_x^c}{f_\sigma} = \pm \frac{1+\nu_c}{E_c} K h_c \sigma_x^c$$

The birefringence, N_x, remains proportional to the normal stress σ_x, for all azimuth positions. For one position N_x and σ_x attain their largest magnitudes and this azimuth defines the direction of one of the principal stresses in the gauge and workpiece. If the x-axis coincides with the direction of the numerically larger principal stress σ_1^c, then

$$N_{max} = \pm \frac{h_c}{f_\sigma} \sigma_1^c \qquad ...(9.142)$$

Similarly if the observation is made in a direction 90° from this direction, then

$$N_\perp = \pm \frac{h_c}{f_\sigma} \sigma_2^c \qquad ...(9.143)$$

Accordingly the directions and magnitudes of the two principal stresses developed in the stress gauge can be ascertained directly from the circular gauge and the sign of the stress can be determined from the known conditions of loading, by means of a compensator, or by use of gauge with an initial pattern.

Since along the line of observation—the diameter—there is no component of shear tractions acting in the xz-plane, thus Eqs. (9.142), (9.143) are unaffected by the shear forces developed near the periphery of the gauge. In general, components of shear tractions do exist in the xz-plane for other directions of observation. However, the influence of these tractions can be made negligibly small as the stress gauge thickness to diameter ratio decreases.

For the workpiece

$$\sigma_1^s = \pm \frac{f_\sigma}{h_c \alpha} N_{max}$$

$$\sigma_2^s = \pm \frac{f_\sigma}{h_c \alpha} N_\perp \qquad ...(9.144)$$

and the directions of principal stresses are determined when the direction N_{max} is established

when $\nu_c \neq \nu_s$ then

$$\alpha = \frac{E_c}{AE_s} \quad ...(9.145)$$

where
$$A = \frac{1 - \nu_c \nu_s - (\nu_c - \nu_s)\,\beta \dfrac{N_y}{N_x}}{1 - \nu_s^2} \quad ...(9.146)$$

and $\beta = +1$ when σ_x and the σ_y are of the same sign and -1 when σ_x and σ_y are of different signs.

The correction factor A varies with the direction of observation of the stress gauge relative to the principal directions. If the arbitrary x-axis is aligned with the direction of σ_1, combination of Eqs. (9.144) and (9.145) yields,

$$\sigma_1^s = \pm \frac{f_\sigma E_s}{h_c E_c} A_1 N_{max} \quad ...(9.147)$$

and
$$\sigma_2^s = \pm \frac{f_\sigma E_s}{h_c E_c} A_2 N_\perp$$

where
$$A_1 = \frac{1 - \nu_c \nu_s - (\nu_c - \nu_s)\,\beta \dfrac{N_\perp}{N_{max}}}{1 - \nu_s^2}$$

$$A_2 = \frac{1 - \nu_c \nu_s - (\nu_c - \nu_s)\,\beta \dfrac{N_{max}}{N_\perp}}{1 - \nu_s^2} \quad ...(9.148)$$

When the photoelastic stress gauge is used in a non-uniform plane stress field, the stresses in portion of the gauge and interface are shown in Fig. 9.38.

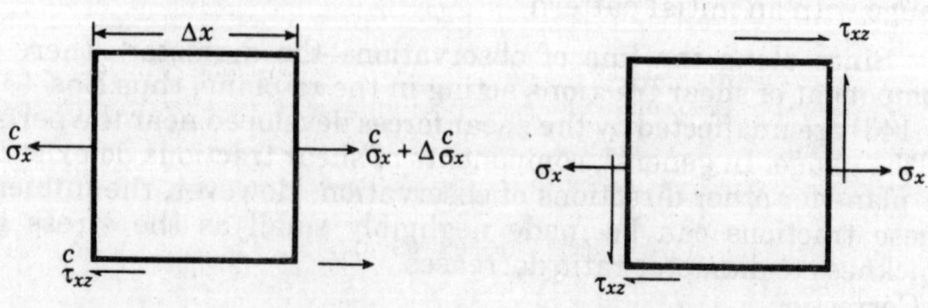

Fig. 9.38

In a non-uniform plane stress field, shear tractions τ_{xz}^c are developed at the interface to maintain continuity between workpiece and gauge.

These shear tractions increase with stress gradient and with gauge thickness. As a first approximation, let

$$\tau_{xz}^c = \frac{h \,.\, \Delta\, \sigma_x^c}{\Delta\, x}$$

If $\quad \Delta\, x = h$, then

$$\tau_{xz}^c = \Delta \sigma_x^c$$

In the absence of shear traction, photoelastic observation would yield the secondary principal stress difference ($\sigma_x - 0$). In the presence of the shear traction, however birefringence yields the difference of secondary principal stresses as $\left\{\sigma_x^2 + 4\tau_{xz}^2\right\}^{1/2}$. Thus the error δ is introduced in the determination of σ_x in the amount

$$\delta = \frac{\left\{\sigma_x^2 + 4\tau_{xz}^2\right\}^{1/2} - \sigma_x}{\sigma_x} \qquad ...(9.149)$$

If $\delta \not> 5\%$ then $\tau_{xz} \le 0.16\, \sigma_x$. In general, the effective gauge length of the circular stress gauge is too large for application in regions of strong stress gradients. The linear gauge as shown in Fig. 9.39 is better suited for such regions. This gauge is normally applied along an axis of principal stress so that there will be no components of shear tractions associated with the lateral strain in the xz-plane. The birefringence introduced into light traversing the strip in the y-direction is proportional to σ_x. All the relations derived for the circular gauge apply equally to the linear gauge.

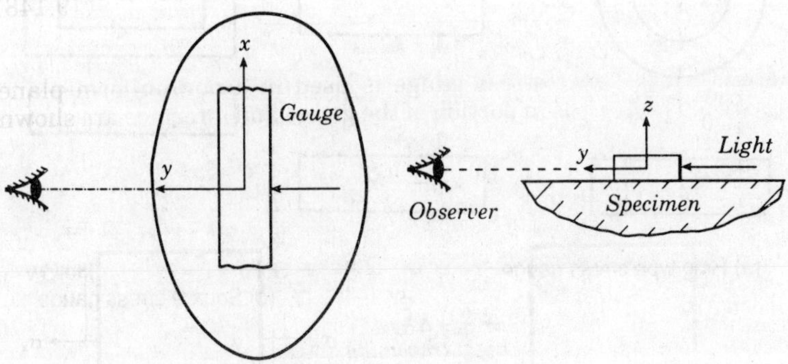

Fig. 9.39 Linear stress gauge.

Correction for the effect of τ_{xz} is possible with linear gauge and is given by

$$\delta = \frac{\left\{\sigma_x^2 + 4h^2\left(\frac{\Delta\, \sigma_x}{\Delta\, x}\right)^2\right\}^{1/2} - \sigma_x}{\sigma_x}$$

Since $\sigma_x \propto N$

$$\therefore \quad \delta = \frac{\left\{N^2 + 4h^2\left(\dfrac{\Delta N}{\Delta x}\right)^2\right\}^{1/2} - N}{N} \qquad \text{...(9.150)}$$

Thus the magnitude of the error δ, can be ascertained by measurement of the rate of change of N along the x-axis. The presence of shear stress always increases the birefringence. For the specimen

$$\sigma_x^s = \pm \frac{f_\sigma N}{h_c \alpha B} \qquad \text{...(9.151)}$$

$$= \pm \frac{f_\sigma}{h_c\, \alpha} \frac{N^2}{\left\{N^2 + 4h^2\left(\dfrac{\Delta N}{\Delta x}\right)^2\right\}^{1/2}} \qquad \text{...(9.151a)}$$

where $$B = 1 + \delta = \frac{1}{N}\left\{N^2 + 4h^2\left(\frac{\Delta N}{\Delta x}\right)^2\right\}^{1/2} \qquad \text{...(9.152)}$$

Other configurations used for the photoelastic stress gauge are shown in Fig 9.40.

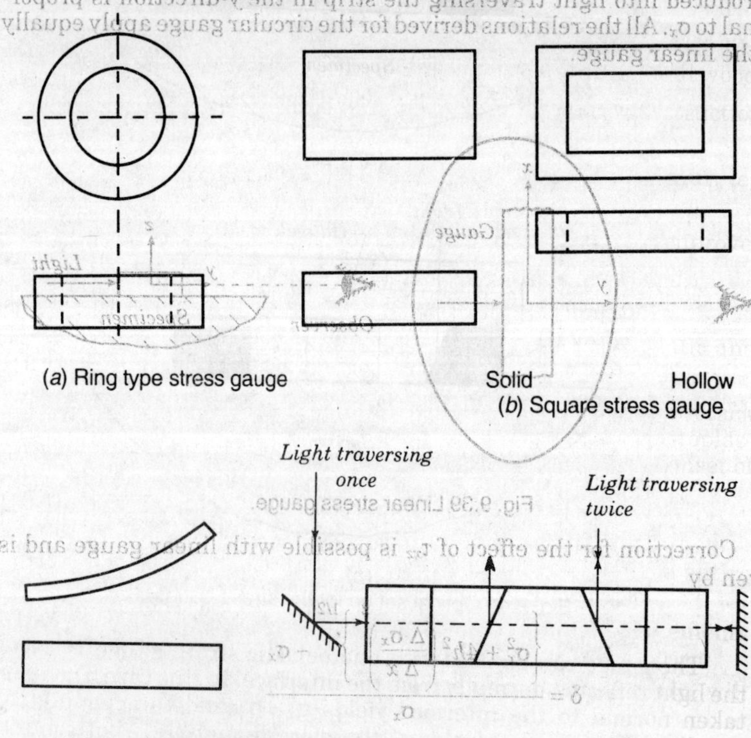

(*a*) Ring type stress gauge

(*b*) Square stress gauge

(*c*) Curved stress gauge

(*d*)

Fig. 9.40 Stress gauge configurations.

Ring type stress gauges are suitable for low stress gradients and square gauges can be used where directions of principal stresses are known. The curved stress gauge is used for applying along curved stress trajectories.

The set up for the stress gauge is shown in Fig. 9.41. This consists of a conical mirror, immersion oil and a cover plate containing a circular polarizer. The immersion oil should have the index of refraction, matching that of the gauge and adhesive cement, so as to eliminate reflections and refractions at the unpolished edge of the gauge and at the cement fillet. For gauge with unpolished edges immersion oil may not be necessary. Birefringence readings should be taken at the inside surface of the gauge. Fringe order is defined as the number of fringes that pass a given point in the pattern in going to the stressed condition from zero. For linear stress gauge, plane mirrors are used in place of the conical and cylindrical mirrors.

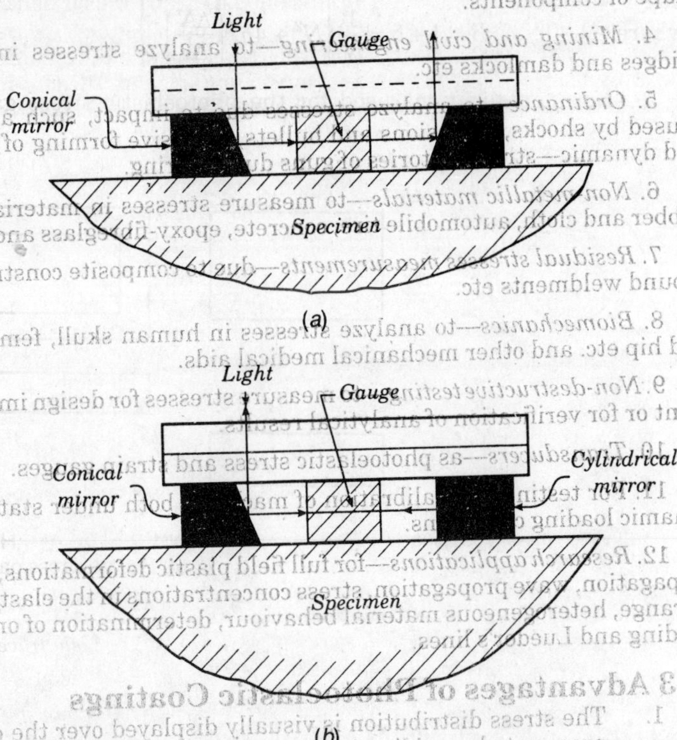

Fig. 9.41 Optical set up for the stress gauge.

The gauge can be used as a photoelastic strain gauge by viewing the light reflected normally from the interface. In this case, the reading taken normal to the interface yields $\sigma_1 - \sigma_2$ and the reading taken parallel to the interface yields σ_1, therefore, σ_1 and σ_2 are both obtained.

In the event of bending perpendicular to the plane of the interface, axial stress will vary through the thickness of the stress gauge. The interface birefringence remains proportional to the interface stress, and the slope of the fringes can be used to establish the location of the neutral surface for the bending action.

9.12 Applications

Photoelastic coatings have been used widely to analyze stresses in many industrial and research problems. Some of the important applications are :

1. *Aircraft industry*—to analyze stresses in airplane wing and window frame under both static and flight conditions. Stresses in the landing gear, compressor blades and aircraft body.

2. *Pressure vessels*—to analyze stresses at regions of discontinuity around branch connections and openings.

3. *Automotive industry*—for design changes and optimization of shape of components.

4. *Mining and civil engineering*—to analyze stresses in rocks, bridges and damlocks etc.

5. *Ordinance*—to analyze stresses due to impact, such as those caused by shocks, explosions and bullets, explosive forming of metals and dynamic—stress histories of guns during firing.

6. *Non-metallic materials*—to measure stresses in materials like rubber and cloth, automobile tire, concrete, epoxy-fibreglass and wood.

7. *Residual stresses measurements*—due to composite construction around weldments etc.

8. *Biomechanics*—to analyze stresses in human skull, femur, leg and hip etc. and other mechanical medical aids.

9. *Non-destructive testing*—to measure stresses for design improvement or for verification of analytical results.

10. *Transducers*—as photoelastic stress and strain gauges.

11. For testing and calibration of machines both under static and dynamic loading conditions.

12. *Research applications*—for full field plastic deformations, crack propagation, wave propagation, stress concentrations in the elastoplastic range, heterogeneous material behaviour, determination of onset of yielding and Lueder's lines.

9.13 Advantages of Photoelastic Coatings

1. The stress distribution is visually displayed over the entire area coated providing important design information.
2. The gauge length is zero permitting accurate measurements regardless of gradients.
3. Yielding is easily detected, since the stress pattern will remain visible after the loads are removed.
4. Assembly stresses can be measured.

5. Combined effect of various load conditions can be observed and measured.
6. Dynamic analysis can be performed.
7. The overall cost of testing is greatly reduced.

9.14 Limitations of Photoelastic Coatings

1. Stress or strain measurement can be made in areas accessible by light only.
2. The strain sensitivity of the coating is affected by temperature changes.
3. Reinforcing effects due to coating thickness and Poisson's ratio mismatch have to be accounted for.
4. In the case of oblique incidence, the gauge length is not zero as in normal incidence but is dependent on the coating thickness.

9.15 Quiz Questions

1. What do you understand by the photostress method ?
2. What are the various assumptions made in the photoelastic coatings analysis ?
3. What is the significance of figure of merit of the photoelastic coating ?
4. On which factors the sensitivity of the photoelastic coating depends ?
5. What is the effect of Poisson's ratio of the coating on its strain sensitivity ?
6. How do you determine the sign in the oblique incidence method ?
7. What are the various causes of errors in the oblique incidence method ?
8. What are strip coatings ?
9. List the various coating materials.
10. If the fringe order is of the order of 5, how would you determine the fractional fringe order ?
11. To how much accuracy the fringe order can be established by the Tardy method of compensation ?
12. What do you understand by "thickness effects" of photoelastic coatings ?
13. Under which circumstances the reinforcing effect of photoelastic coatings is appreciable ?
14. What is the effect of Poisson's ratio mismatch ? Is this effect appreciable ?
15. Is the effect of strain gradients appreciable on photoelastic coating data ?
16. How the effect of thermal fields can be minimized ?

17. Why a circular disc under diametral compression is not preferred for the calibration of photoelastic coating ?
18. What are the limitations on the angle of incidence in the oblique incidence method ?
19. What is the basic principle of the photoelastic gauge ?
20. List the limitations of photoelastic coatings.

EXERCISES

9.1. What are photoelastic coatings ? What are their uses and limitations ?

9.2. Explain how stresses and strains can be determined by photoelastic coatings. List the various assumptions made.

9.3. What is the stress-optic law for photoelastic coatings ? Determine the relationship between the stress and strain material fringe values.

9.4. Write short notes on the following :
(a) Coating sensitivity
(b) Figure of merit
(c) Law of failure of stress coat.

9.5. What are the various methods usually followed for fringe measurements ? Give their uses and limitations.

9.6. What are the various methods used for stress separation ? Explain the oblique incidence method in detail.

9.7. What are strip coatings ? How strip coatings can be used to separate the principal stresses ?

9.8. An epoxy coating is bonded to an aluminium specimen. Determine the stress and strain-sensitivity indices for the coating for the following data :

$E_s = 0.7 \times 10^6$ kg/cm^2, $\nu_s = 0.32$, $E_c = 3.15 \times 10^4$ kg/cm^2

$\nu_c = 0.36$, $f_\sigma = 10.3$ kg/cm^2/cm/fringe, $h_c = 2.54$ mm.

9.9. Determine the maximum number of fringes obtainable in exercise 9.8 if the yield strength of aluminium in tension is 245 kg/cm^2.

9.10. A photoelastic coating of epoxy resin having material fringe value 10.3 kg/cm^2/cm/fringe, thickness 2 mm, $\nu_c = 0.35$ and $E_c = 2.5 \times 10^4$ kg/cm^2 is used to measure stresses on steel for which $E_c = 2 \times 10^6$ kg/cm^2, $\nu_s = 0.30$. At a point of interest the normal incidence gave the fringe order to be 3.5. Oblique incidence measurements by a rotation about the maximum principal stress axis by 20° gave the fringe order to be 3.68. Determine the principal stresses at this point.

9.11. A photoelastic coating of epoxy resin having material fringe value f_σ = 10.3 kg/cm^2/cm/fringe was used to determine stresses at a point in aluminium subjected to biaxial state of stress. The fringe order at the point with normal incidence was found to be 4.25 and with oblique incidence by rotation about the σ_1 axis by 30° the fringe order was 4.35. To determine the stresses separately a calibration strip made of aluminium of size 25 mm × 6 mm × 300 mm was used. A photoelastic coating of epoxy resin 2.25 mm thick was bonded to the aluminium strip at 200 mm from the free end. When a load of 2.5 kg was applied at the free end of the calibration strip, 2.45 fringe order was observed with normal incidence and 2.55 and 2.25 with oblique incidence by rotation by the same amount of 20° about the x and y-axes respectively. Determine the stresses at the point. Neglect the effect of coating thickness and assume $E_s = 0.7 \times 10^6$ kg/cm^2, $\nu_s = 0.33$.

9.12. What are the various factors to be considered while selecting a photoelastic coating? Which are the various materials used for photoelastic coatings?

9.13. (*a*) How do you decide the thickness of the coating? (*b*) A photoelastic coating of epoxy amine having sensitivity $K = 0.09$ is used to analyze stresses on aluminium and using white light with λ = 5770 Å for viewing of fringes. The maximum error in measuring principal-strain difference should be less than 0.004. The error in measuring fringe order $\Delta N = \pm\, 0.012$ and the relative error is to be less than 3 per cent. Determine the coating thickness.

9.14. (*i*) Explain the procedure of applying coatings to (*a*) Plane surfaces (*b*) Curved surfaces and (*c*) For measuring large strains.

(*ii*) What are the characteristics of a good cement for photoelastic coatings?

9.15. What are the various parameters influencing the analysis of data by photoelastic coatings? Determine the correction factor for plane stress problems.

9.16. Determine the correction factors due to reinforcement of coating for (*a*) flexure of beams and plates, (*b*) combined plane and flexural loads and (*c*) torsion of circular shafts.

9.17. Determine the correction factors due to reinforcement of coating for (*a*) pressure vessels, (*b*) flat annular plate.

9.18. Discuss the effect of the following on coating analysis:

(*a*) Poisson's ratio mismatch

(*b*) Strain gradients

(*c*) Thermal fields

(*d*) Dynamic state of stress.

9.19. Explain the two usual methods of calibrating a photoelastic coating.

9.20. A cantilever beam made of aluminium, 6 mm thick and 25 mm wide is coated with a strip of 2 mm thick photoelastic plastic bonded to the top surface of the beam. With a Babinet-Soleil compensator, the fringe value 150 mm from the point of loading is found to be 1.54 after a 9 kg weight is applied to the end of the beam. Determine the fringe constant for the coating. The material constants for aluminium are :

$$E_a = 0.7 \times 10^6 \text{ kg/cm}^2, \; \nu_a = 0.33.$$

9.21. Explain the various set-ups usually used for the reflection polariscope. How these set-ups can be modified for oblique incidence measurements ?

9.22. What is the necessity of fringe multiplication while using birefringent coatings ? Explain the method of fringe multiplication in brief.

9.23. Write short notes on :

(*a*) Photoelastic strain gauge
(*b*) Photoelastic stress gauge
(*c*) Summation gauge.

9.24.(*a*) List the various applications of photoelastic coatings.
(*b*) What are the advantages and limitations of photoelastic coatings ?

9.25. For a coating with $h_c = 1.5$ mm and $f_\varepsilon = 0.80$ μm/fringe, determine the maximum fringe order N which could be developed in the following materials :

(*a*) Steel, $\sigma_0 = 900$ MPa, $C_s = 6.2$ pm^2/N
(*b*) Aluminium, $\sigma_0 = 500$ MPa, $C_s = 19.3$ pm^2/N
(*c*) Glass, $\sigma_0 = 21$ MPa, $C_s = 18.1$ pm^2/N.

9.26. Specify a coating, *i.e.* material and thickness, to use for the analysis of the following steel ($E_s = 200$ GPa, $\nu_s = 0.30$) structures :

(*a*) A curved beam where $\sigma_{max} = 150$ MPa.
(*b*) A spherical shell with radius $R = 3$ m and wall thickness 15 mm subjected to a pressure of 1530 kPa.
(*c*) A cylindrical shell with radius of 1500 mm and wall thickness 15 mm subjected to a pressure of 5 MPa.

9.27. At an interior point on a steel specimen with a polycarbonate coating ($h_c = 4$ mm and $f_\varepsilon = 5.10$ μm/fringe) a value of $N = 1.85$ and $\theta_1 = 27°$ is measured. $E_s = 2 \times 10^6$ kg/cm^2, $\nu_s = 0.30$. Describe the state of stress in the specimen at this point.

9.28. A birefringent coating ($E_c = 2.50$ GPa, $\nu_c = 0.36$) is used on a plane-stress tensile specimen fabricated from glass-reinforced plastic ($E_s = 27.5$ GPa and $\nu_s = 0.20$) to measure the stress concentration factor resulting from a centrally located hole. If $N_{max} = 4.5$ on the boundary of the hole and $N_o = 1.00$ at an interior point well removed from the hole, determine the stress-concentration factor due to the hole.

9.29. Determine the principal stresses at a point in a steel specimen if $f_\varepsilon = 5.10$ μm/fringe and $h_c = 2$ mm when $N_0 = 2.64$ and $N_{\theta 1} = 1.32$, $\theta_1 = 45^\circ$, $\nu_c = 0.36$.

10

Brittle Coatings

10.1 Introduction

The brittle-coating or stress coat method is a qualitative whole-field technique where a brittle-lacquer is sprayed on the part to be analysed, dried overnight, then loaded in a static, dynamic or impact mode. The brittle lacquer will crack perpendicular to the direction of maximum principal stress first, in the most highly stressed area. As the load increases the crack pattern enlarges as the area of high stress becomes larger. By knowing the stresses in the coating the stresses in the specimen can be ascertained. Stresses to an accuracy of ± 15 percent can be obtained quantitatively by this method. In this chapter we shall study this method in detail.

The first brittle coatings to be employed were those coatings which naturally formed on structural members, such as mill scale on hot-rolled steel and oxides on heated surfaces. These brittle coatings failed by flaking or cracking when the base material yielded under load and excessive strains were produced. To improve the visibility of the crack patterns, the structural members were often coated with whitewash. The cracking and flaking of the coating produced dark lines which were readily visible against the white back ground.

The first artificially produced brittle coating was a mixture of shellac and alcohol used by Sauerwald and Wieland in 1925 to indicate regions of plastic strain. This coat was an improvement over the whitewash technique, but the strains required for the coating to fail were still in the yield region of the base material. In order to reduce the strain sensitivity, Dietrich and Lehr in Germany in 1932 developed brittle coatings for the indication of strains within the elastic range. This lacquer appears to have begun to crack at stresses from 500 to 2000 kg/cm^2. This work and that of Cymboliste and Portevin (1934) in France, resulted in the process becoming more popular. Although further efforts were made to improve upon these lacquers, no substantial improvement was achieved until Ellis in 1937, while working for his M. Tech. thesis at Massachusetts Institute of Technology (USA) developed a series of lacquers. These lacquers were suitable under a wide range of humidity and temperature conditions. Later Ellis, while working with the Magnaflux Corporation, made his resin-based coating commercially available in 1941, which became popular with the trade name : 'Stress-Coat'. These lacquers were capable of recording dynamic strain also. However, these coatings are susceptible to temperature and humidity changes.

In 1952 the Magnaflux Corporation introduced their stress coat All-Temp, a ceramic based coating usable from − 45° to 315°C with sensitivities ranging from 200 to 1800 μ cm/cm. Singdale in 1954 developed a porcelain-enamel coating which, when applied to metals, will fail by cracking at predetermined stress levels. Recently a new brittle lacquer under the trade name Tens-Lac has been marketed by Photo-lastic Inc (USA). This lacquer is highly sensitive, non-inflammable and odourless. Strain sensitivity of 500 μ cm/cm can be easily achieved by this lacquer. Hickson in England in 1965 developed a glass lacquer which consists of a mixture of lithium hydroxide, boric acid and water, dries at room temperature and is similar to resin based coatings.

To facilitate quantitative measurements, Durelli and Dewolf (1948) and Durelli and Tsao (1953) postulated the law of failure of stresscoat, which acted as a breakthrough in the coating analysis. To determine the threshold strain for the coating, *i.e.* the strain at which cracks will just appear, either the calibration strips under static loading or the method devised by Brown and Cunningham (1962) by impact loading may be adopted. A number of investigations have been carried out by various researchers to determine the properties of stresscoat under static and dynamic loading conditions. To predict the strain sensitivity of brittle coating Dally and Durelli (1955) have suggested a statistical regression technique. A number of parameters affect the properties of brittle coatings for which detailed investigations have been carried out by Dally and Durelli (1959).

Brittle coatings have been used on plastics, wood, paper, rubber, glass, bones and metals to investigate stresses under static, dynamic and impact loads. They have been used to test parts in the laboratory as well as out-of-doors under field conditions. Stresses around weldments, on pressure vessels, gas turbine blades, reactor head closure, and turbo-super charger impeller have been successfully analysed.

10.2 Coating Stresses

The brittle coating method of stress analysis generally gives two types of information : the directions of the principal stresses which are perpendicular to the cracks (isostatic) and the estimated magnitude of the larger principal stress by means of the isoentatics (loci of crack ends). For a more complete solution of the problem the magnitude of the smaller principal stress must also be estimated. The brittle coating fails when the maximum tensile stress in the coating reaches a critical value.

The following assumptions are made in the analysis :

1. A state of plane stress is assumed to exist.
2. Perfect adhesion between the coating and the specimen is assumed so that $\varepsilon^c = \varepsilon^s$ and the principal direction of strains in the coating coincides with that of the specimen.

3. Maximum principal stress theory is assumed to govern the failure of the coating.
4. When the brittle coating fractures, the crack is perpendicular to the principal stress concerned.
5. Brittle coating fails when the maximum tensile strain reaches a critical value called the threshold strain.
6. Residual stresses in the calibration strip and specimen are the same.

Consider the coating and the specimen as shown in Fig. 10.1. By Hooke's law

$$\left.\begin{aligned} E_s\,\varepsilon_1^s &= \sigma_1^s - \nu_s\,\sigma_2^s \\ E_s\,\varepsilon_2^s &= \sigma_2^s - \nu_s\,\sigma_1^s \\ E_c\,\varepsilon_1^c &= \sigma_1^c - \nu_c\,\sigma_2^c \\ E_c\,\varepsilon_1^c &= \sigma_1^c - \nu_c\,\sigma_2^c \\ E_c\,\varepsilon_2^c &= \sigma_2^c - \nu_c\,\sigma_1^c \end{aligned}\right\} \qquad ...(10.1)$$

Since there is perfect adhesion between the coating and the surface of the specimen, hence

$$\left.\begin{aligned} \varepsilon_1^c &= \varepsilon_1^s \\ \varepsilon_2^c &= \varepsilon_2^s \end{aligned}\right\} \qquad ...(10.2)$$

Thus, we get

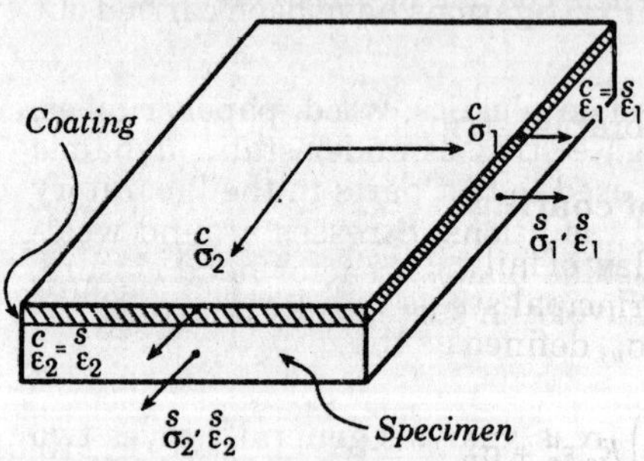

Fig. 10.1 Stresses and strains in the coating and the specimen before any crack is opened.

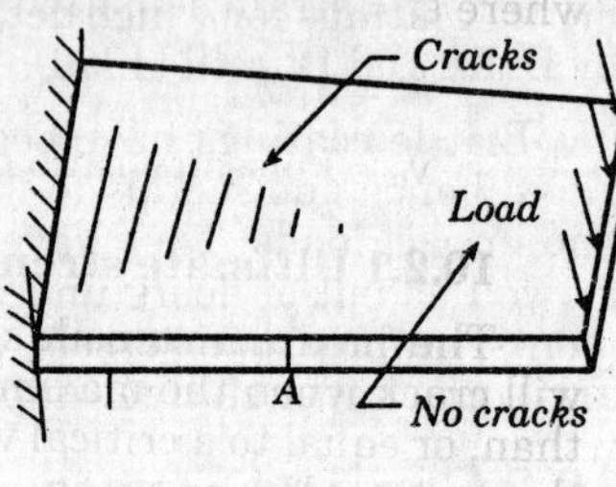

Fig. 10.2 Calibration strip.

$$\left.\begin{aligned} \sigma_1^c &= \frac{E_c}{E_s\,(1-\nu_c^2)}\left[(1-\nu_c\,\nu_s)\,\sigma_1^s + (\nu_c - \nu_s)\,\sigma_2^s\right] \\ \sigma_2^c &= \frac{E_c}{E_s\,(1-\nu_c^2)}\left[(1-\nu_c\,\nu_s)\,\sigma_2^s + (\nu_c - \nu_s)\,\sigma_1^s\right] \\ \sigma_1^c - \sigma_2^c &= \frac{E_c}{E_s}\left(\frac{1+\nu_s}{1+\nu_c}\right)(\sigma_1^s - \sigma_2^s) \end{aligned}\right\} \qquad ...(10.3)$$

From Eq. (10.3) it is evident that $(\sigma_1^c - \sigma_2^c)$ always has the same sign as $(\sigma_1^s - \sigma_2^s)$. In other words σ_1^c is always greater then σ_2^c. Further σ_1^c is parallel to σ_1^s and σ_2^c parallel to σ_2^s.

Now $$\frac{\sigma_1^c}{E_c} = \left(\frac{1-\nu_c\nu_s}{1-\nu_c^2}\right)\left(\frac{\sigma_1^s}{E_s}\right) + \left(\frac{\nu_c-\nu_s}{1-\nu_c^2}\right)\left(\frac{\sigma_2^s}{E_s}\right)$$

which represents a straight line for any particular value of σ_1^c/E_c.

To calibrate the coating a cantilever calibration strip as shown in Fig. 10.2 is used to determine the strain sensitivity. The strain at 'A' where the cracks start appearing is called the *strain-sensitivity* of the coating or the *threshold strain*. The stresses at 'A' in the coating produced by the external load are found by setting $\sigma_2^s = 0$ in Eqs. (10.3). Thus

$$\left.\begin{aligned} \sigma_1^c &= \left(\frac{1-\nu_c\,\nu_a}{1-\nu_c^2}\right)\sigma_1^s\,\frac{E_c}{E_a} \\ &= \left(\frac{1-\nu_c\,\nu_a}{1-\nu_c^2}\right)E_c\,\varepsilon_s^d \\ \sigma_2^c &= \left(\frac{\nu_c-\nu_a}{1-\nu_c^2}\right)E_c\,\varepsilon_s^d \end{aligned}\right\} \quad ...(10.4)$$

where ε_s^d = strain sensitivity of brittle coating in direct loading

$= \sigma_1^s/E_a$

ν_a = Poisson's ratio of calibration strip.

10.2.1 Ultimate strength of coating

The maximum tensile stress law of failure assumes that the coating will crack when the maximum principal stress in the coating is larger than, or equal to a critical value σ_u, defined as the ultimate strength of the coating. Hence

$$\sigma_u = \left(\frac{1-\nu_c\nu_a}{1-\nu_c^2}\right)E_c\,\varepsilon_s^d + \sigma_R^c \quad ...(10.5)$$

where σ_R^c = residual hydrostatic tension existing in the coating before the external load is put on and before refrigeration, if any.

10.2.2. Analysis of coating data

(*a*) **Cracks perpendicular to σ_1^s by direct loading.** The coating will crack when the value of σ_1^c as calculated from Eq. (10.3) is larger than or equal to $(\sigma_u - \sigma_R^c)$. Hence cracks perpendicular to σ_1^s will appear when

$$\frac{E_c}{E_s\,(1-\nu_c^2)}\,[(1-\nu_c\,\nu_s)\,\sigma_1^s + (\nu_c-\nu_s)\,\sigma_2^s] \geq (\sigma_u - \sigma_R^c) \quad ...(10.6)$$

σ_R^c is assumed same on the specimen and calibration strip.

Eq. (10.6) gives the relation between the applied stresses σ_1^s, σ_2^s and σ_u of the coating when cracks are impending.

By definition σ_0^d is the minimum σ_1^s required to crack the coating when σ_2^s is zero. Hence by Eq. (10.6), we get

$$\frac{E_c}{E_s(1-\nu_c^2)}(1-\nu_c\,\nu_s)\,\sigma_0^d = (\sigma_u - \sigma_R^c) \qquad ...(10.7)$$

Eliminating $(\sigma_u - \sigma_B^c)$ from Eqs. (10.5) and (10.7), we get

$$\sigma_0^d = \left(\frac{1-\nu_c\nu_a}{1-\nu_c\,\nu_s}\right) E_s\,\varepsilon_s^d \qquad ...(10.8)$$

(*b*) For relaxation loading strain at '*A*' in the calibration strip is denoted by ε_s^r, defined as the strain sensitivity of the coating in relaxation loading. The Eqs. (10.5) and (10.8) can be written as :

$$\sigma_u = \left(\frac{1-\nu_c\nu_a}{1-\nu_c^2}\right) E_c\,\varepsilon_s^r + \sigma_R^c \qquad ...(10.9)$$

$$\sigma_0^r = \left(\frac{1-\nu_c\nu_a}{1-\nu_c\nu_s}\right) E_s\,\varepsilon_s^r \qquad ...(10.10)$$

where σ_0^r is the minimum value of σ_1^s required to crack the coating in the relaxation loading test when $\sigma_2^s = 0$. It is also assumed that in the relaxation loading the coating used has the same Poisson's ratio as the coating used in direct loading. In the special case when $\nu_a = \nu_s$, then Eqs. (19.8) and (10.10) reduce to,

$$\sigma_0^d = E_s\,\varepsilon_s^d$$
$$\sigma_0^r = E_s\,\varepsilon_s^r \qquad ...(10.12)$$

Eliminating $(\sigma_u - \sigma_R^c)$ between Eqs. (10.6) and (10.7), we get

$$\frac{\sigma_1^s}{\sigma_0^d} + \left(\frac{\nu_c - \nu_s}{1-\nu_c\,\nu_s}\right)\frac{\sigma_2^s}{\sigma_0^d} \geq 1 \qquad ...(10.13)$$

Eq. (10.13) gives the relation between σ_1^s, σ_2^s and σ_0^d when a crack in the coating perpendicular to σ_1^s is impending. At that instant the stress σ_1^c in the coating will be equal to or larger than the maximum stress which the coating can take and cracks perpendicular to σ_1^s will appear. Eq. (10.13) is called the *Biaxiality equation*.

(*c*) **Cracks perpendicular to σ_2^s by direct loading.** Immediately after the coating is cracked in the direction perpendicular to σ_1^s, ε_1^c becomes less than ε_1^s. For any point at the edge cracks (point *P* or P_1 and P_2) as shown in Figs. 10.3 and 10.4, both the residual stress σ_R^c and the applied stress σ_1^c in the direction of σ_1^s are reduced to zero. For any point not at the edge of the cracks (point *Q*), these stresses are also reduced but not to zero. Further increase of load may cause the stress

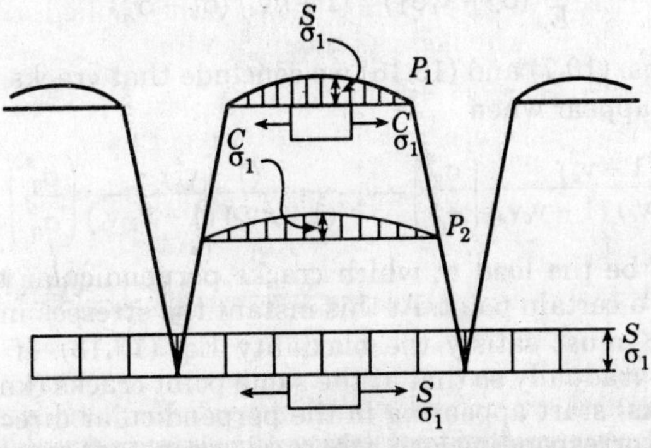

Fig. 10.3 Distribution of σ_1^c after the coating is cracked perpendicular to σ_1^s.

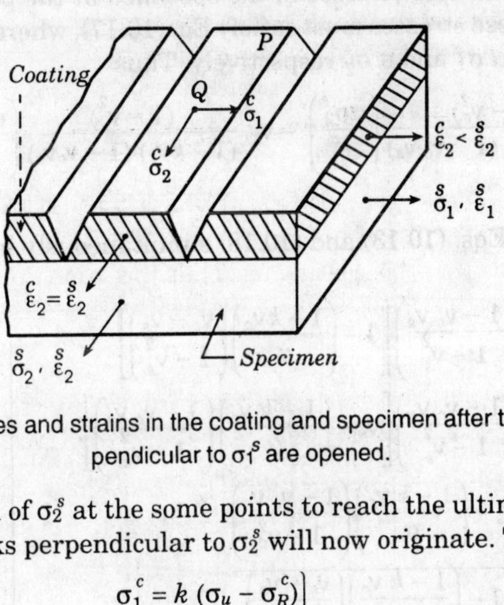

Fig. 10.4 Stresses and strains in the coating and specimen after the cracks perpendicular to σ_1^s are opened.

in the direction of σ_2^s at the some points to reach the ultimate strength σ_u, where cracks perpendicular to σ_2^s will now originate. Then

$$\left.\begin{aligned} \sigma_1^c &= k\,(\sigma_u - \sigma_R^c) \\ \sigma_2^c &= (\sigma_u - \sigma_R^c) \\ \varepsilon_1^c &< \varepsilon_1^s \\ \varepsilon_2^c &= \varepsilon_2^s \end{aligned}\right\} \quad \text{...(10.14)}$$

where k represents the ratio of σ_1^c to $(\sigma_u - \sigma_R^c)$ when the cracks perpendicular to σ_2^s just appear. Due to the opening up of primary cracks, the residual stress would have become reduced, but this is taken care of by the experimental value of k. The value of k may not be a constant but may be dependent on the thickness of the coating and other factors.

From the second and fourth of Eqs. (10.1) and the first and last of Eqs. (10.14), we get

$$\sigma_2^c = k\nu_c\,(\sigma_u - \sigma_R^c) + \frac{E_c}{E_s}\,(\sigma_2^s - \nu_s\,\sigma_1^s) \quad \text{...(10.15)}$$

From Eq. (10.15) and second of Eq. (10.14), we get

$$\frac{E_c}{E_s}(\sigma_2^s - \nu_s\sigma_1^s) = (1 - k\nu_c)(\sigma_u - \sigma_R^c) \quad ...(10.16)$$

By Eqs. (10.7) and (10.16) we conclude that cracks perpendicular to σ_2^s will appear when

$$\frac{(1-\nu_c^2)}{(1-k\nu_c)(1-\nu_c\nu_s)}\left(\frac{\sigma_2^s}{\sigma_0^d}\right) - \nu_s\frac{(1-\nu_c^2)}{(1-k\nu_c)(1-\nu_c\nu_s)}\left(\frac{\sigma_1^s}{\sigma_0^d}\right) \geq 1 \quad ...(10.17)$$

Let P be the load at which cracks perpendicular to σ_1^s begin to appear at a certain point. At this instant the stresses in the specimen σ_1^s and σ_2^s must satisfy the biaxiality Eq. (10.13). If the load P is increased gradually so that at the same point cracks (known as secondary cracks) start appearing in the perpendicular direction, then, let αP be the corresponding load, where α is a constant greater than unity. Hence the principal stresses in the specimen at the point will be $\alpha\,\sigma_1^s$ and $\alpha\sigma_2^s$. These stresses must satisfy Eq. (10.17), wherein σ_1^s and σ_2^s are replaced by $\alpha\,\sigma_1^s$ and $\alpha\,\sigma_2^s$ respectively. Thus

$$\frac{(1-\nu_c^2)}{(1-k\nu_c)(1-\nu_c\nu_s)}\left(\frac{\alpha\sigma_2^s}{\sigma_0^d}\right) - \nu_s\frac{(1-\nu_c^2)}{(1-k\nu_c)(1-\nu_c\nu_s)}\left(\frac{\alpha\,\sigma_1^s}{\sigma_0^d}\right) = 1 \quad ...(10.18)$$

Solving Eqs. (10.13) and (10.18) simultaneously for σ_1^s and σ_2^s, we get

$$\left.\begin{aligned}
\frac{\sigma_1^s}{\sigma_0^d} &= \left(\frac{1-\nu_c\nu_s}{1-\nu_s^2}\right)\left[1-\left(\frac{1-k\nu_c}{\alpha}\right)\left(\frac{\nu_c-\nu_s}{1-\nu_s^2}\right)\right]\\
\frac{\sigma_2^s}{\sigma_0^d} &= \left(\frac{1-\nu_c\nu_s}{1-\nu_s^2}\right)\left[\nu_s+\left(\frac{1-k\nu_c}{\alpha}\right)\left(\frac{1-\nu_c\nu_s}{1-\nu_c^2}\right)\right]\\
\frac{\sigma_2^s}{\sigma_1^s} &= \frac{\nu_s+\left(\frac{1-k\nu_c}{\alpha}\right)\left(\frac{1-\nu_c\nu_s}{1-\nu_c^2}\right)}{1-\left(\frac{1-k\nu_c}{\alpha}\right)\left(\frac{\nu_c-\nu_s}{1-\nu_c^2}\right)}
\end{aligned}\right\} \quad ...(10.19)$$

(*d*) **Cracks produced by Relaxation.** Relaxation loading is merely a reversed loading. Here the coating is sprayed and dried while the maximum load P is maintained on the specimen, so that only a hydrostatic residual stress σ_R^c is present in the coating while the specimen is under load P. When this maximum load P is later completely released, the induced stresses in the brittle coating are identical to those induced by a load P on the specimen. Similarly, the stresses induced in the brittle coating due to a partial release of the initial high load P to the final low load $(P - \beta P)$ will be identical to those caused by a loading of $-\beta P$ in the specimen. If $\beta = 1$, the initial load is completely released.

Suppose that a coating of sensitivity ε_s^d starts to crack in a direction perpendicular to σ_1^s when the load is P. The stresses σ_1^s and σ_2^s in the specimen corresponding to P must satisfy the biaxiality Eq. (10.13). This cracked coating is then removed and a new coating of a different sensitivity ε_s^r is applied and dried. If this new coating starts to crack at the same point in a direction perpendicular to the first under the relaxation load $-\beta P$, then the stresses are $-\beta\sigma_1^s$ and $-\beta\sigma_2^s$. These being primary cracks must satisfy the biaxiality Eq. (10.130). But now the major principal stress is $-\beta\sigma_2^s$. The uniaxial stress σ_0^r required to crack the coating is now $\left(\dfrac{1-\nu_c\,\nu_a}{1-\nu_c\,\nu_s}\right) E_s\,\varepsilon_s^r$ as given by Eq. (10.10). We have called σ_1^s, σ_2^s and σ_0^d the major principal stress, the minor principal stress and the minimum uniaxial tensile stress in the specimen required to crack the coating used in the direct loading test, so that $-\beta\,\sigma_2^s$, $-\beta\,\sigma_1^s$ and $\sigma_0^r = \varepsilon_s^r/\varepsilon_s^d$. σ_0^d will be the major principal stress, the minor principal stress and the minimum uniaxial tensile stress in the specimen required for cracking the coating used in the relaxation loading. Substituting these new values σ_1^s, σ_2^s and σ_0^d in Eq. (10.13), we get

$$\frac{-\beta\varepsilon_s^d}{\varepsilon_s^r}\left(\frac{\sigma_2^s}{\sigma_0^d}\right)+\left(\frac{\nu_c-\nu_s}{1-\nu_c\,\nu_s}\right)\left(\frac{-\beta\,\varepsilon_s^d}{\varepsilon_s^r}\right)\left(\frac{\sigma_1^s}{\sigma_0^d}\right)=1 \qquad \text{...(10.20)}$$

Solving Eqs. (10.13) and (10.20) simultaneously, we get

$$\left.\begin{aligned}\frac{\sigma_1^s}{\sigma_0^d}&=\frac{(1-\nu_c\,\nu_s)^2}{(1-\nu_c^2)\,(1-\nu_s^2)}\left[1+\frac{\varepsilon_s^r}{\beta\,\varepsilon_s^d}\left(\frac{\nu_c-\nu_s}{1-\nu_c\,\nu_s}\right)\right]\\ \frac{\sigma_2^s}{\sigma_0^d}&=\frac{-(1-\nu_c\,\nu_s)^2}{(1-\nu_c^2)\,(1-\nu_s^2)}\left[\frac{\varepsilon_s^r}{\beta\,\varepsilon_s^d}+\left(\frac{\nu_c-\nu_s}{1-\nu_c\,\nu_s}\right)\right]\end{aligned}\right\} \qquad \text{...(10.21)}$$

where σ_0^d is given by Eq. (10.8). The coating in relaxation loading is assumed to have the same Poisson's ratio as the coating used in direct loading. β may be defined as the ratio of minimum relaxation load required to crack the coating in the direction perpendicular to σ_2^s to the minimum direct load required to crack the coating perpendicular to σ_1^s.

(*e*) **Apparent stress.** If an assumption is made that $\sigma_2^s = 0$, then the biaxiality Eq. (10.13) will give $\sigma_1^s = \sigma_0^d$ so that Eq. (10.8) becomes :

$$\sigma_1^s=\sigma_0^d=\left(\frac{1-\nu_c\,\nu_a}{1-\nu_c\,\nu_s}\right)E_s\,\varepsilon_s^d \qquad \text{...(10.22)}$$

This stress σ_1^s calculated from Eq. (10.22) is called 'apparent stress'. When σ_2^s/σ_0^d is known to be small as compared with unity, the apparent stress represents a good estimate of the true stress. From brittle coating data, σ_1^s is not determined exactly, but an approximation to it is obtained, called apparent stress. Using the apparent stress, σ_2^s may be found by graphical integration of the Lame-Maxwell equations of equilibrium. Using this value of σ_2^s an improved value of σ_1^s may be found by an iteration procedure.

10.2.3. Effect of Refrigeration

In a large portion of the surface of the specimen even under the highest possible load no cracks may be obtained. The stresses in these regions may not be large enough to cause the coating to crack. In such cases, if it is desired to find the stresses in these regions, refrigeration, dye-etching or both the techniques may be used. In the refrigeration technique, first the specimen is loaded until the stress in the critical region is just below the yield stress, then the coating is subjected to a rapid temperature drop while under load. The effect of refrigeration is two fold. It lowers the ultimate strength of the coating and secondly induces a hydrostatic tension $\overset{c}{\sigma}_H$. If σ_u^0 is the ultimate strength of the coating at test temperature t_0 and σ_u^r at the lowered temperature t_r, then the contraction per unit length of the coating due to temperature drop is $\gamma_c\ (t_0 - t_r)$ and that of the specimen $\gamma_s\ (t_0 - t_s)$.

where γ_c, γ_s = coefficients of linear expansion for the coating and specimen respectively

t_s = temperature of the specimen after refrigeration.

The expansion per unit of the coating due to the hydrostatic tension $\overset{c}{\sigma}_H$ at temperature t_r is given by the corresponding hydrostatic strain $(1 - \nu_c)\ \overset{c}{\sigma}_H/E_c^r$, where E_c^r is the modulus of elasticity of the coating at temperature t_r. The contraction of the test specimen due to the hydrostatic compression is so small that it can be neglected. Assuming perfect adhesion, we have

$$\gamma_c\ (t_0 - t_r) - \gamma_s\ (t_0 - t_s) = (1 - \nu_s)\ \frac{\overset{c}{\sigma}_H}{E_c^r}$$

or $$\overset{c}{\sigma}_H = \frac{E_c^r}{(1 - \nu_c)}\ [\gamma_c\ (t_0 - t_r) - \gamma_s\ (t_0 - t_s)] \qquad \text{...(10.23)}$$

This relative expansion in the coating produced by refrigeration can be thought of as if it were produced by a hydrostatic tension in the specimen $\overset{s}{\sigma}_H$. This fictitious hydrostatic tension in the specimen $\overset{s}{\sigma}_H$ which would induce the same amount of stress in the coating as refrigeration, can be obtained by substituting E_c^0 for E_c, $\overset{c}{\sigma}_H$ for $\overset{c}{\sigma}_1$, $\overset{s}{\sigma}_H$ for both $\overset{s}{\sigma}_1$ and $\overset{s}{\sigma}_2$ in the first of Eqs. (10.3).

Thus $$\overset{c}{\sigma}_H = \frac{E_c^0}{E_s\ (1 - \nu_c^2)}\ [1 - \nu_c\ \nu_s + \nu_c - \nu_s]\ \overset{s}{\sigma}_H$$

or $$\overset{s}{\sigma}_H = \frac{E_s}{E_c^0} \left(\frac{1 - \nu_c}{1 - \nu_s}\right) \overset{c}{\sigma}_H \qquad \text{...(10.24)}$$

where E_c^0 is the modulus of elasticity of the coating at temperature t_0. Once the constants σ_u^0, σ_u^r, γ_c, γ_s and ν_s and determined for the particular coating and test specimen used, the effect of refrigeration can be evaluated.

10.2.4 Load required to produce secondary cracks when stress ratio is 2 : 1

Let $\quad \sigma_x^s = \sigma_1$

$$\sigma_y^s = \frac{1}{2}\sigma_1$$

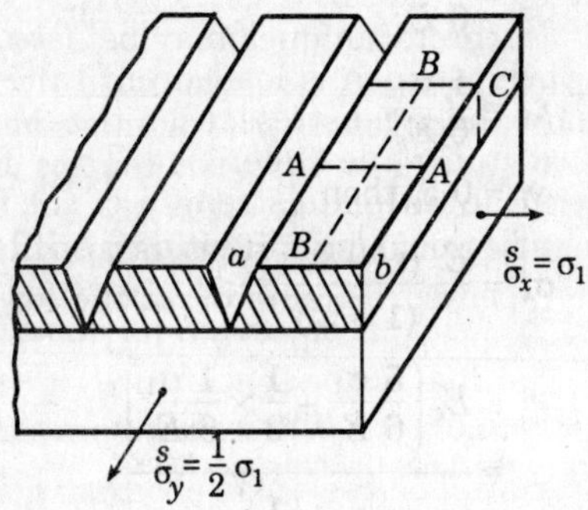

(a)

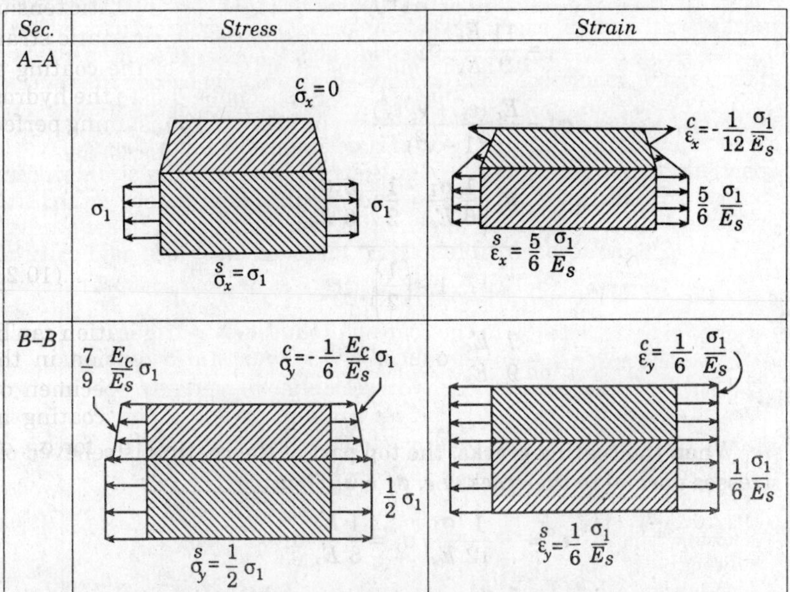

Fig. 10.5 (*b*) Stresses and strains in coating after failure of the coating.

If Poisson's ratio for the specimen $\nu_s = \frac{1}{3}$, then strains in the specimen will be (Fig. 10.5).

$$\varepsilon_x^s = \frac{1}{E_s}(\sigma_x - \nu\,\sigma_y)$$

$$= \frac{1}{E_s}\left[\sigma_1 - \frac{1}{3}\times\frac{1}{2}\sigma_1\right] = \frac{5}{6}\frac{\sigma_1}{E_s}$$

$$\varepsilon_y^s = \frac{1}{E_s}(\sigma_y - \nu\,\sigma_x)$$

$$= \frac{1}{E_s}\left[\frac{1}{2}\sigma_1 - \frac{1}{3}\sigma_1\right] = \frac{1}{6}\frac{\sigma_1}{E_s}$$

Hence $\varepsilon_x^c = \frac{5}{6}\frac{\sigma_1}{E_s}$

$$\varepsilon_y^c = \frac{1}{6}\frac{\sigma_1}{E_s}$$

If $\nu_c = 0.5$, then

$$\sigma_x^c = \frac{E_c\,(\varepsilon_x^c + \nu_c\,\varepsilon_y^c)}{(1-\nu_c^2)}$$

$$= \frac{E_c\left(\frac{5}{6}\frac{\sigma_1}{E_s} + \frac{1}{2}\times\frac{1}{6}\frac{\sigma_1}{E_s}\right)}{1-\left(\frac{1}{2}\right)^2}$$

$$= \frac{11}{9}\frac{E_c}{E_s}\,\sigma_1$$

$$\sigma_y^c = \frac{E_c\,(\varepsilon_y^c + \nu_c\,\varepsilon_x^c)}{(1-\nu_c^2)}$$

$$= \frac{E_c\left(\frac{1}{6}\frac{\sigma_1}{E_s} + \frac{1}{2}\times\frac{5}{6}\frac{\sigma_1}{E_s}\right)}{1-\left(\frac{1}{2}\right)^2}$$

$$= \frac{7}{9}\frac{E_c}{E_s}\,\sigma_1$$

When the coating cracks, the top part of the coating is relieved of stresses normal to the cracks *i.e.* $\sigma_x^c = 0$. Then

$$\varepsilon_x^c = -\frac{1}{12}\frac{\sigma_1}{E_s},\ \sigma_y^c = \frac{1}{6}\frac{E_c}{E_s}\sigma_1$$

$$\varepsilon_y^c = \frac{1}{6}\frac{\sigma_1}{E_s}.$$

$$\text{Thus} \qquad \frac{\sigma_y^c}{\sigma_x^c} = \frac{\frac{1}{6}}{\frac{11}{9}} = 1 : 7.33 \qquad \text{...(10.26)}$$

Therefore a load of 7.33 times as great as the one producing the first set of cracks would be required to crack the coating again in the perpendicular direction when the ratio of specimen stresses is 2 : 1.

10.3 Crack Patterns

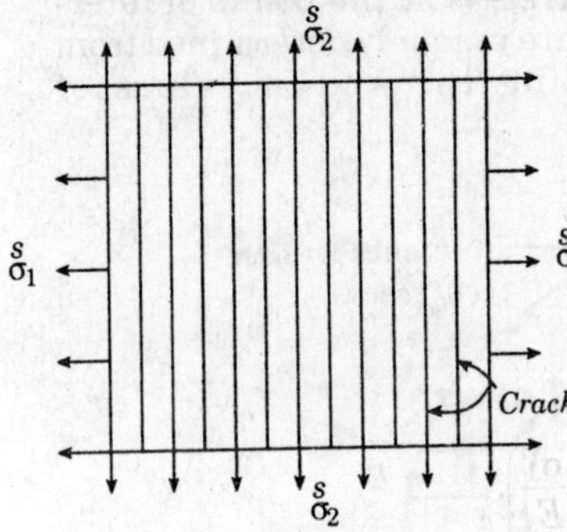

Fig. 10.6 Crack pattern for $\sigma_1^s > 0, \sigma_3^s < 0$ and $\sigma_s^s = 0$.

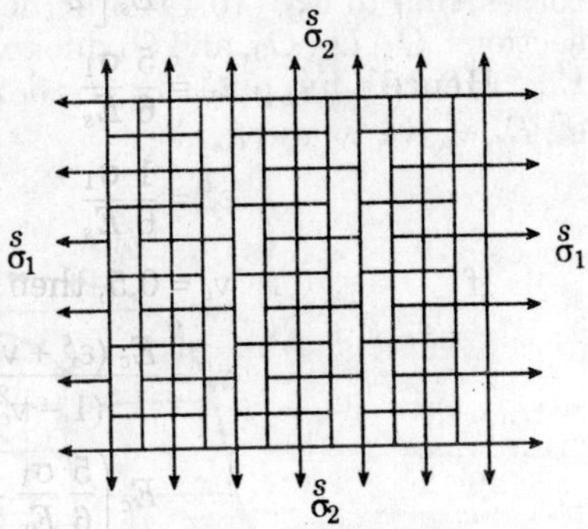

Fig. 10.7. Crack patterns for $\sigma_1^s > \sigma_2^s > 0, \sigma_3^s = 0$.

10.3.1 Direct loading

(*a*) $\sigma_1^s > 0, \sigma_2^s < 0, \sigma_3^s = 0$. In this case, only one set of cracks forms and they are perpendicular to σ_1^s as shown in Fig. 10.6. These cracks indicate the principal stress directions of σ_2^s and as a consequence, the cracks represent stress trajectories or isostatics.

(*b*) $\sigma_1^s > \sigma_2^s > 0, \sigma_3^s = 0$. In this case, two families of cracks can form. The first set of cracks due to σ_1^s forms perpendicular to σ_1^s and parallel to σ_2^s. When the stress level of σ_2^s becomes sufficiently high, a second family of cracks will form perpendicular to σ_2^s and parallel to σ_1^s as shown in Fig. 10.7. When both families of cracks are produced, a complete set of isostatics or stress trajectories is obtained.

(*c*) $\sigma_1^s = \sigma_2^s > 0, \sigma_3^s = 0$. This is an isotropic stress system and every direction is a principal direction. If the values of σ_1^s and σ_2^s are sufficiently high, the coating will fail, however the crack pattern produced will be random in character (Fig. 10.8),

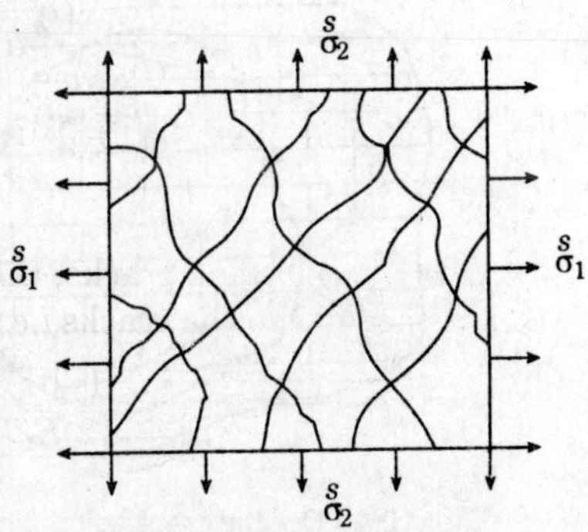

Fig. 10.8 Random crack patterns for $\sigma_1^s = \sigma_2^s > 0, \ \sigma_1^3 = 0$.

called craze patterns. Crack patterns of this type occur when pressure vessels with hemispherical head closures are tested.

Fig. 10.9 shows a doubly cracked coating. When cracks are opened up, the locus of their ends is called the *isoentatic*. Let ABC be the isoentatic for the load P and DEF for load $2P$. At this load, cracks perpendicular to σ_2^s also appear. Let GHI and LMN be the isoentatics for the secondary cracks for loads $2P$ and $3P$ respectively. Then the stresses at A, B and C due to the load P and the stresses at D, E and F under the load $2P$ must correspond to the biaxiality Eq. (10.13). The stresses at G, H, I due to load $2P$ and at L, M, N due to load $3P$ must correspond to Eq. (10.17). Further, the stresses at the points of intersections, O_1, O_2, O_3, and O_4 due to load P are uniquely determined from Eq. (10.19) by putting $\alpha = 3$ and using the known values of ε_s^d, E_s, ν_a, ν_s, ν_c and k.

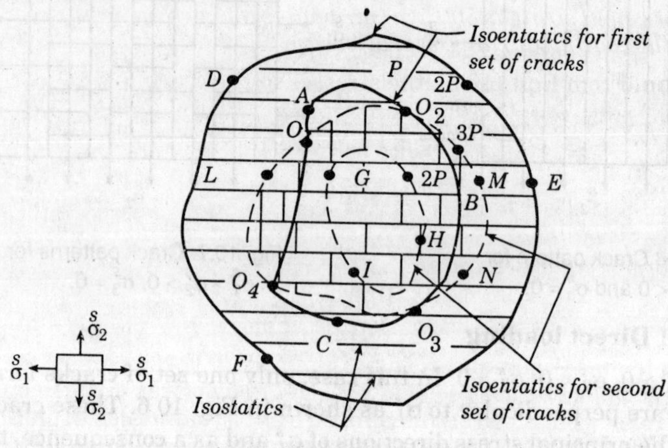

Fig. 10.9 Doubly cracked coating.

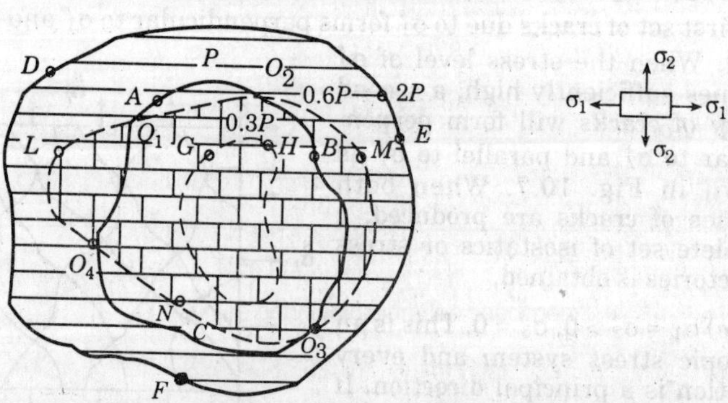

Fig. 10.10 Doubly cracked coating by direct and relaxation loading.

10.3.2. Relaxation Loading

Fig. 10.10 shows the crack pattern when the coating cracked in one direction by a direct load and later cracked at the same point in a direction perpendicular to the first one by a relaxation load. *ABC* and *DEF* are the isoentatics due to direct loading for load *P* and 2*P* respectively. *GHI* and *LMN* are the isoentatics due to relaxation loading of –0.3*P* and –0.6*P* respectively. Stresses at points O_1, O_2, O_3 and O_4 due to direct load *P* are determined from Eq. (10.21) by putting $\beta = 0.6$ and using known values of ε_s^d, ε_s^r, E_s, ν_a, ν_c and ν_s.

Example 10.1 *Determine the stresses in a brittle coating applied to a component made of steel for which $E_s = 200$ GPa, $\nu_s = 0.30$, when the specimen stresses are $\sigma_1^s = 210$ MPa and $\sigma_2^s = -140$ MPa (a) for a resin based coating with $E_c = 1.40 \times 10^{-3}$ MPa and $\nu_c = 0.42$ and (b) for a ceramic based coating with $E_c = 70 \times 10^3$ MPa and $\nu_c = 0.25$.*

If the threshold strain is 500 μ m / m, what is the corresponding state of stress in the coating during calibration ?

Solution. From Eqs. (10.3), the stresses in the coating are :

$$\sigma_1^c = \frac{E_c}{E_s\,(1 - \nu_c^2)}\,[(1 - \nu_c\,\nu_s)\,\sigma_1^s + (\upsilon_c - \upsilon_s)\,\sigma_2^s]$$

$$\sigma_2^c = \frac{E_c}{E_s\,(1 - \nu_c^2)}\,[(1 - \nu_c\,\nu_s)\,\sigma_2^s + (\nu_c - \nu_s)\,\sigma_1^s]$$

(*a*) *For a resin based coating*

$$\sigma_1^c = \frac{1.40 \times 10^3}{2 \times 10^5\,[1 - (0.42)^2]}\,[(1 - 0.42 \times 0.30)\,2100 + (0.42 - 0.30)\,(-1400)]$$
$$= 1.417 \text{ MPa}$$

$$\sigma_2^c = \frac{1.40 \times 10^3}{2 \times 10^5\,[1 - (0.42)^2]}\,[(1 - 0.42 \times 0.30)\,(-1400) + (0.42 - 0.30)\,2100]$$
$$= -0.826 \text{ MPa}$$

(*b*) *For a ceramic based coating*

$$\sigma_1^c = \frac{70 \times 10^3}{2 \times 10^5\,[1 - (0.25)^2]}\,[(1 - 0.25 \times 0.30)\,2100 + (0.25 - 0.30)\,(-1400)]$$
$$= 9.865 \text{ MPa}$$

$$\sigma_2^c = \frac{70 \times 10^3}{2 \times 10^5\,[1 - (0.25)^2]}\,[1 - (0.25 \times 0.30)\,(-1400) + (0.25 - 0.30)\,(2100)]$$
$$= -8.754 \text{ MPa}$$

Now threshold strain $\varepsilon_s^d = 500\ \mu$ cm/cm. Assuming material of the calibration strip to be the same as that of the component, *i.e.* steel so that $\nu_a = \nu_s = 0.30$, we have from Eqs. (10.4).

$$\sigma_1^c = \left(\frac{1 - \nu_s\,\nu_a}{1 - \nu_c^2}\right) E_c\,\varepsilon_s^d$$

$$\sigma_2^c = \left(\frac{\nu_c - \nu_a}{1 - \nu_c^2}\right) E_c\,\varepsilon_s^d$$

For the resin based coating, the stresses in the coating on the calibration strip are :

$$\sigma_1^c = \left[\frac{1 - 0.42 \times 0.30}{1 - (0.42)^2}\right] 1.40 \times 10^3 \times 500 \times 10^{-6}$$

$$= 0.743 \text{ MPa}$$

$$\sigma_2^c = \left[\frac{0.42 - 0.30}{1 - (0.42)^2}\right] 1.40 \times 10^3 \times 500 \times 10^{-6}$$

$$= 0.102 \text{ MPa}$$

For the ceramic based coating, the stresses in the coating on the calibration strip are :

$$\sigma_1^c = \left[\frac{1 - 0.25 \times 0.30}{1 - (0.25)^2}\right] 70 \times 10^3 \times 500 \times 10^{-6}$$

$$= 34.533 \text{ MPa}$$

$$\sigma_2^c = \left[\frac{0.25 - 0.30}{1 - (0.25)^2}\right] 70 \times 10^3 \times 500 \times 10^{-6}$$

$$= -1.866 \text{ MPa.}$$

Example 10.2 *At a certain point A of an aluminium specimen, cracks in one direction begin to appear when the external load is 5 kN. At the same point A, cracks perpendicular to the above mentioned cracks begin to appear when the load reaches 10 kN. The strain sensitivity ε_s^d of the coating as obtained from the aluminium cantilever calibration strip is 600 μ m/m, $\nu_a = \nu_s = 0.32$, $\nu_c = 0.42$, $E_s = 70$ GPa, $k = 0.5$. Find the principal stresses when the external load is 4 kN. Assume maximum tensile stress law of failure.*

Solution. From Eq. (10.8), the minimum value of σ_1^s required to crack the coating when $\sigma_2^s = 0$ is given by

$$\sigma_0^d = \left(\frac{1 - \nu_c\,\nu_a}{1 - \nu_c\,\nu_s}\right) E_s\,\varepsilon_s^d$$

Here $\nu_a = \nu_s$

hence $\sigma_0^d = E_s\,\varepsilon_s^d = 70 \times 10^9 \times 600 \times 10^{-6} = 42$ MPa

$$\alpha = \frac{10}{5} = 2$$

From Eqs. (10.19), we have

$$\frac{\sigma_1^s}{\sigma_0^d} = \left(\frac{1 - \nu_c \nu_s}{1 - \nu_s^2}\right)\left[1 - \left(\frac{1 - k\nu_c}{\alpha}\right)\left(\frac{\nu_c - \nu_s}{1 - \nu_c^2}\right)\right]$$

$$= \left[\frac{1 - 0.42 \times 0.32}{1 - (0.32)^2}\right]\left[1 - \left(\frac{1 - 0.5 \times 0.42}{2}\right) \times \left(\frac{0.42 - 0.32}{1 - (0.42)^2}\right)\right]$$

$$= 0.952$$

$$\frac{\sigma_2^s}{\sigma_0^d} = \left(\frac{1 - \nu_c \nu_s}{1 - \nu_s^2}\right)\left[\nu_s + \left(\frac{1 - k\nu_c}{\alpha}\right)\left(\frac{1 - \nu_c \nu_s}{1 - \nu_c^2}\right)\right]$$

$$= \left[\frac{1 - 0.42 \times 0.32}{1 - (0.32)^2}\right]\left[0.32 + \left(\frac{1 - 0.5 \times 0.42}{2}\right) \times \left(\frac{1 - 0.42 \times 0.32}{1 - (0.42)^2}\right)\right]$$

$$= 0.415$$

Hence $\sigma_1^s = 0.952 \times 42 = 39.984$ MPa

$\sigma_2^s = 0.415 \times 42 = 17.430$ MPa

At 4 kN load, the stresses become

$$\sigma_1^s = 39.984 \times \frac{4}{5} = 31.987 \text{ MPa}$$

$$\sigma_2^s = 17.430 \times \frac{4}{5} = 13.944 \text{ MPa}.$$

Example 10.3 *At a certain point A of a steel specimen cracks in one direction began to appear when the external load was 5 kN, $\varepsilon_s^d = 600\ \mu$ m/m. This coating was removed, a new coating was applied and cured while a load of 12 kN was maintained on the specimen. On the partial release of the 12 kN load to 55 kN, cracks perpendicular to those observed in the first set began to appear at the same point A. $\varepsilon_s^r = 700\ \mu$ m/m, $\nu_a = 0.32$, $\nu_c = 0.42$, $\nu_s = 0.30$, $E_s = 200$ GPa. Find the principal stresses at point A when the external load is 4 kN. Assume maximum tensile stress law of failure.*

Solution. From Eq. (10.8), we have

$$\sigma_0^d = \left(\frac{1 - \nu_c\, \nu_a}{1 - \nu_c\, \nu_s}\right) E_s\, \varepsilon_s^d$$

$$= \left(\frac{1 - 0.42 \times 0.32}{1 - 0.42 \times 0.30}\right) 2 \times 10^5 \times 600 \times 10^{-6}$$

$$= 118.85 \text{ MPa}$$

From Eq. (10.21), we have for relaxation loading

$$\frac{\sigma_1^s}{\sigma_0^d} = \frac{(1 - \nu_c\, \nu_s)^2}{(1 - \nu_c^2)\,(1 - \nu_s^2)}\left[1 + \frac{\varepsilon_s^r}{\beta\, \varepsilon_s^d}\left(\frac{\nu_c - \nu_s}{1 - \nu_c\, \nu_s}\right)\right]$$

Here $\beta = \dfrac{550}{500} = 1.1$

$$\frac{\sigma_1^s}{\sigma_0^d} = \frac{(1 - 0.42 \times 0.30)^2}{[1 - (0.42)^2]\,[1 - (0.30)^2]}\left[1 + \frac{700}{1.1 \times 600} \times \left(\frac{0.42 - 0.30}{1 - 0.42 \times 0.30}\right)\right]$$

$$= 1.16763$$

$$\sigma_1^s = 138.77 \text{ MPa}$$

$$\frac{\sigma_2^s}{\sigma_0^d} = \frac{-(1 - \nu_c\, \nu_s)^2}{(1 - \nu_c^2)\,(1 - \nu_s^2)}\left[\frac{\varepsilon_s^r}{\beta\, \varepsilon_s^d} + \left(\frac{\nu_c - \nu_s}{1 - \nu_c\, \nu_s}\right)\right]$$

$$= \frac{-(1 - 0.42 \times 0.30)^2}{[1 - (0.42)^2]\,[1 - (0.30)^2]}\left[\frac{700}{1.1 \times 600} + \left(\frac{0.42 - 0.30}{1 - 0.42 \times 0.30}\right)\right]$$

$$= -1.22092$$

$$\sigma_2^s = -145.1 \text{ MPa}$$

At 400 kg load, the specimen stresses are

$$\sigma_1^s = 138.77 \times \frac{4}{5} = 111.01 \text{ MPa}$$

$$\sigma_2^s = -145.1 \times \frac{4}{5} = -116.0 \text{ MPa.}$$

10.4 Refrigeration Techniques

In low stress regions it is possible to obtain coating cracks by employing refrigeration techniques. First, the specimen is loaded until the stresses in the critical region is just below the yield stress, then, the coating is subjected to a rapid temperature drop while under load. The rapid temperature drop produces a state of hydrostatic tension in the coating which is superimosed on the existing stresses in the coating due to the load. The combined load and thermal stresses are usually sufficient to produce coating failure and a crack pattern. The direction of the resultant cracks is coincident with one of the principal stresses due to the load since the isothermal thermal stresses have no preferential directions.

In order to reduce the temperature of the coating two methods are employed :

1. Ice water is sponged over the area of the coating which has not previously responded. This method is not very much successful.
2. A stream of compressed air is passed through a box containing dry ice and then it is directed into the surface of the coated model. The stream of very cold air can be accurately directed and the resulting crack patterns can be closely controlled.

10.5 Load Relaxation for Compressive Stresses

A brittle coating does not respond to compressive loads. In order to overcome this difficulty, a relaxation technique is applied. A load is applied to the coated specimen before it has had the opportunity to dry. The load is maintained on the coated specimen until drying is complete. Under these conditions the coating is stress free, while the specimen is highly stressed in compression. If a portion of this load is relieved, the specimen will stretch, since it was previously compressed and tensile stresses will develop in the coating which are sufficiently high to indicate regions of compressive specimen stress.

10.6 Crack Detection Methods

When the coating fails, very fine V-shaped cracks with a depth equal to the coating thickness and a width of approximately 0.05 mm to 0.075 mm appear. These cracks are generally not visible to the naked eye. In order to observe these cracks the following methods may be used:

1. In order to visually observe these fine cracks, a focussed light source must be directed at oblique incidence to the surface and normal to the cracks. For observing small areas this is a good method. However, this method is a very much time consuming.

2. **Statiflux method.** This is a form of electrified particle inspection method. This method consists in applying a special statiflux penetrant to the coated test piece, the surface is then superficially dried, leaving the penetrant in the coating cracks and finally an ionized statiflux powder is blown over the part. The powder particles, which have obtained an electrostatic charge in being blown from a special gun, are electrically attracted to the cracks. When dynamic strains are being studied or when coatings with high threshold strains are used, it will often be necessary to apply the statiflux penetrant before initiating the test and to keep the coating wet with the penetrant during the test. Upon completion of the test, the part is dried and the statiflux powder applied in the normal manner. Statiflux does not destroy the sensitivity of the coating for further testing. The powder forms small, white mounds over the cracks and provides an excellent means of locating the crack pattern and recording the crack patterns for a permanent record. The disadvantages of this method is that the non-uniform application of the statiflux penetrant will probably result in a temperature gradient due to differential evaporation rates.

3. **Dye-Etching method.** Red dye-etchant can be used to increase the visibility of the crack patterns for photographic purposes. The

dye-etchant is a mixture containing turpentine, machine oil and red dye. This method consists in applying a small amount of dye-etchant solution on the coated part leaving, the dye-etchant on the coated portion for about five minutes after it is removed by an emulsifying agent (soap + water). Removal of the dye-etchant can be facilitated if the surface of the part is kept wet with that solution during the period of etching activity. The coating cracks will appear as dark red lines which are easily photographed. Dye-etchant can also show cracks which have closed due to plastic flow in the coating. This method must be used only after all tests have been completed, since the dye-etchant destroys the sensitivity of the coating.

10.7 Types of Brittle Coatings

The following types of coatings are available :

1. **Resin based coating—'Stress coat'.** This consists of about one-third zinc resinate as a base dissolved in about two-third carbon disulphide with a small amount of plasticizer. Dibutyl phthalate is used as a plasticizer to vary the degree of brittleness of the coating, which increases with its increase. The strain sensitivity of this coating varies from 0.0003 to 0.0030. It can be applied to the test specimen by a spraying method. This coating can be used upto 60°C and absorbs water and oil. The thickness of this coating can be made varying from 0.10 to 0.15 mm and can be used for macro and micro applications. Stresscoat has been employed widely and can be applied to all materials. Synthetic resin dissolved in trichloroethylene or benzene and phenolic resin mixed with titanic white and dissolved in a mixture of benzene, toluene and xylene have also been used as brittle lacquers.

2. **Ceramic based coating—'All Temp'.** It consists of finely ground ceramic particles suspended in a solvent. It can be sprayed by conventional means onto the specimen. Upon drying at room temperature the coating presents a chalklike appearance and is not suitable for use. In order to make the coating effective, it must be fired at about 540°C until the ceramic particles melt and coalesce. When fired, the coating is glasslike in appearance and brown in colour. These coatings are relatively insensitive to minor changes in temperature. They can be used upto 370°C and are not influenced by the presence of oil and water. Their disadvantages include the high temperature of 537.7°C required to fire the coating which produces detrimental effect on components fabricated from aluminium, magnesium, plastics and highly heat-treated steels. Their visual inspection for cracks is not possible and statiflux method must be resorted to. Strain sensitivity of these coatings range from 0.0002 to 0.0020. Porcelain enamel coatings are also available, whose properties are similar to ceramic based coatings, but can be used at all temperatures.

3. **Tens-Lac Brittle Lacquer.** This is a new, high sensitivity, non-flammable, odorless and of low toxicity brittle lacquer. This lacquer can be applied by spraying on test specimens. The nominal threshold strain for Tens-Lac is 500 μ cm/cm. This lacquer requires a reflective

under coating if the test surface is dark. Tens-Lac is available in eleven grades from TL-500-40 to TL-500-100, were 500 indicates the strain sensitivity and the last number (*e.g.* 40 and 100) indicates the temperature of use in F° to obtain the strain sensitivity of 500 μ cm/cm. The best thickness of the coating is 0.075 mm.

Table 10.1 gives the relative comparison of these lacquers.

Table 10.1 Comparison of Brittle Coatings

S.No.	*Property*	*Stress-coat*	*All-Temp*	*Tens-Lac*
1.	Minor changes in temperature	Very sensitive	Insensitive	Sensitive
2.	Limiting temperature	37.7°C (100°F)	– 45°C to 370°C (– 50°F to 700°F)	37.7°C (100°F)
3.	Effect of oil and water	Influenced	Not influenced	Influenced
4.	Firing of coating	Not required	Very high temperature of 537.7°C (1000°F) is required for 15 minutes	Not required
5.	Visual observation	Possible	Not possible	Possible
6.	Strain sensitivity	300 to 3000 μ cm/cm	200 to 2000 μ m/m	500 μ m/m at the specified temperature
7.	Suitable for	All materials	Except those having melting point less than 537.7°C	All materials

10.8 Evaluation of the Coating

The following characteristics are used to evaluate the coating :

1. *Strain sensitivity*. This is the threshold strain which is defined as the minimum strain necessary to crack the coating in a uniaxial state of stress. Coating sensitivity is the inverse of strain sensitivity. Strain sensitivity of a coating can be determined by a calibration technique.

2. *Continuous crack*. This is defined as the first crack extending from one boundary of the calibration beam to the other boundary.

3. Crazing or failure by shrinkage and by thermal and humidity effects, without loading the specimen.

4. Closing of cracks after unloading.

5. Crack density.

6. Flaking.

10.9 Basic Brittle Lacquer Technique

The following basic steps are involved in the brittle lacquer method:

1. Preparation of the test specimen surface by cleaning and spraying with a reflective coating like aluminium.
2. Selection of appropriate lacquer for the expected test conditions.
3. Application of the lacquer to the test specimen and calibration strip.
4. Curing the lacquer.
5. Loading the test specimen and observing the cracks.
6. Loading the calibration strip to determine the strain corresponding to incipient cracking, *i.e.* threshold strain.
7. Treating with dye etchants or statiflux for improved crack visibility when desired.

10.10 Lacquer Selection

From temperature-humidity charts for the brittle coatings as shown in Figs. 10.11 to 10.13, select the coating number by knowing dry and wet bulb temperatures from a sling phychrometer. If the strains are expected to be low, one can select a higher lacquer number than that indicated. When the lacquer is tested at a temperature and humidity lower than the one for which it is designed, the coating cracks occur at a correspondingly lower strain, then also higher coat number may be selected.

Stress-coat coating grades ranging from 1202 to 1210 are quite sufficient for temperatures ranging from 60°F to 90°F. For outdoor use during the cold months, the coatings in the 1100 series are often employed. According to Magnaflux Corporation the variation in the threshold strain is approximately 100 μ cm/cm for a unit change in the coating number. A decrease in the coating number by 1 increases the value of threshold strain by 100 μ cm/cm and *vice versa*. A more precise method of selecting stresscoat number is based on two statistically derived equations which express the threshold strain as a function of the coating number, curing temperature, testing temperature, relative humidity and thickness. These two formulae are given below :

$$\varepsilon_s^d = 70{,}833 - 59.50\ (\text{St. No.}) + 25.4\ (\text{TT}) + 1.48\ (\%\ \text{RH}) - 3.85\ (\text{CT}) - 12.9\ (h) \quad \ldots(10.26)$$

for stress coat numbers between 1200 and 1210 and testing temperature between 60°F and 105°F,

$$\text{and } \varepsilon_s^d = 98{,}360 - 83.45\ (\text{St. No.}) + 55.6\ (\text{TT}) - 15.00\ (\%\text{RH}) - 3.17\ (\text{CT}) - 42.3\ (h) \quad \ldots(10.27)$$

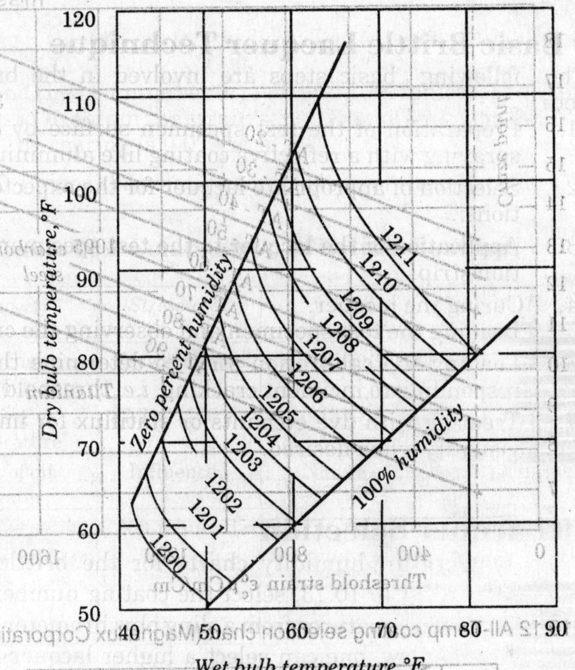

(a)

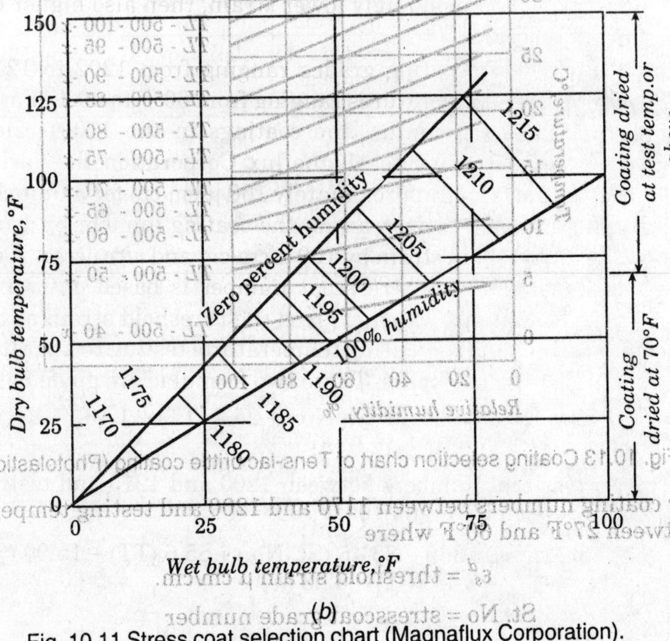

(b)

Fig. 10.11 Stress coat selection chart (Magnaflux Corporation).

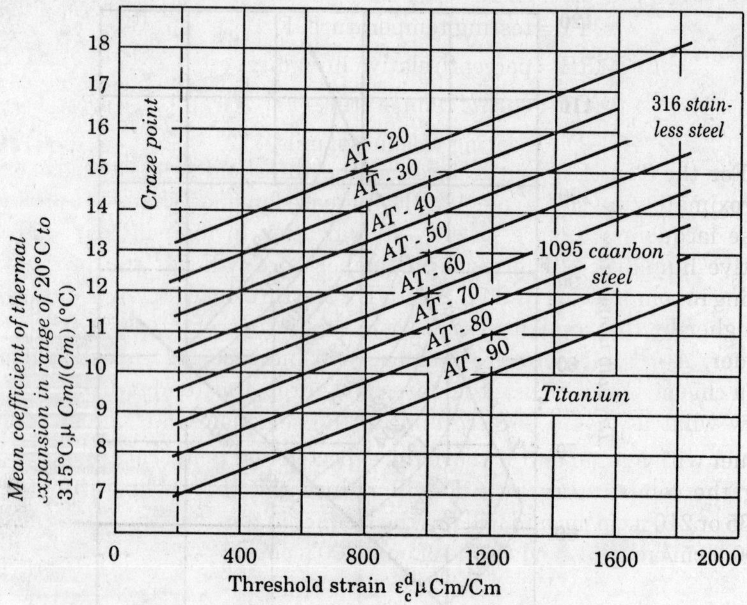

Fig. 10.12 All-Temp coating selection chart (Magnaflux Corporation).

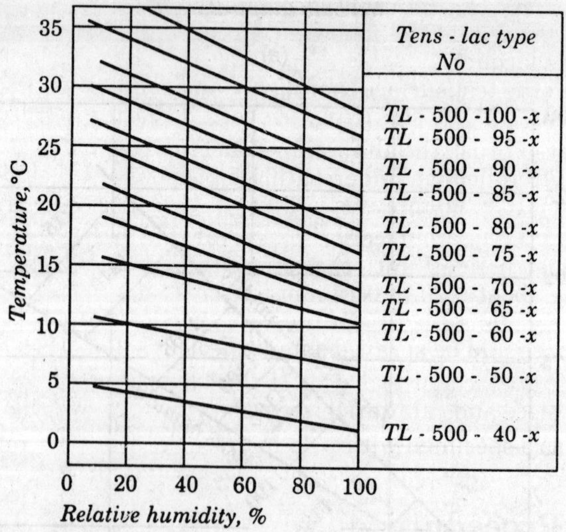

Fig. 10.13 Coating selection chart of Tens-lac brittle coating (Photolastic, Inc.).

for coating numbers between 1170 and 1200 and testing temperatures between 27°F and 60°F where

$$\varepsilon_s^d = \text{threshold strain } \mu \text{ cm/cm.}$$

St. No = stresscoat grade number

TT = testing temperature, F°

%RH = percent relative humidity

CT = curing temperature, F°

h = coating thickness, mils.

For the Tens-Lac brittle lacquer, the threshold strain increases approximately 5 μ cm/cm per 1% RH, increase for small changes in RH. These lacquers are more sensitive to variation in temperature than relative humidity. An increase in temperature will put the lacquer coating in compression by 35 μ cm/cm F°. The threshold strain will then be higher by this amount to overcome the initial compression in the lacquer. A 6°F temperature increase will increase the threshold to 700 μ cm/cm. To decrease the threshold, drop the temperature 5°F below what it should be according to the selection chart, or pick a lacquer with a number 5°F above the expected test temperature. Dropping the temperature by 6°F will reduce the threshold strain by 6 × 35 or 210 μ cm/cm and will put the lacquer in tension, thus changing a 500 μ cm/cm threshold to one of only 300 μ cm/cm.

10.11 Lacquer Application Method

Brittle lacquers can be used successfully on all metal surfaces, glass, plastics and wood. The following procedure may be followed to apply the brittle lacquer :

1. Clean the test surface thoroughly and decrease by a suitable solvent.
2. Spray or brush the aluminium reflective paint, for stress coat or U-10 reflective undercoating for Tens-Lac and allow it to dry for 10 to 20 minutes.
3. Spray the brittle lacquer in several thin coats according to the instructions, until the correct thickness is obtained, this being about 0.10 to 0.15 mm for stresscoat and about 0.076 mm for Tens-Lac. Both the test specimen and calibration beam should be sprayed simultaneously.
4. Allow the lacquer to dry for 15 to 24 hours before loading the test piece and calibration strip.
5. Test the specimen within 48 hours.

10.12 Test Procedure

The determination of the load for first cracking of the lacquer is an important object of the test and to maintain the strain sensitivity of the lacquer as constant as possible throughout, the best loading technique is an incremental one called the return to zero technique with an incremental step of 25 per cent or less of the preceding total load. The rate of loading should be kept as constant as possible for each loading. The following procedure may be followed for applying the load :

1. Load is applied to a predetermined small value, is held constant only long enough to check for cracks and is then dropped to zero. The load should not be held too long or the lacquer will creep excessively and so become less sensitive.
2. The parts are rested at zero load for two to five times the total time of the preceding load cycle to allow the lacquer to creep back to its original state of stress in order to maintain a constant value of threshold strain.
3. The parts are loaded and unloaded to higher increments in a similar fashion until the full analysis has been completed.
4. Calibration is performed throughout the whole test period in an incremental way.
5. The boundaries of the cracks should be marked at each load increments.
6. Analyse the coating data.

For compressive stresses, relaxation technique may be used. For dynamic loads, some crack intensification technique may be used. With cyclic loading the member can be viewed under stroboscopic light which will make the cracks appear to persist.

10.13 Calibration Method

To determine the strain sensitivity or threshold strain for the coating, the coating has to be calibrated. The static method may be adopted to calibrate the coating, as described below :

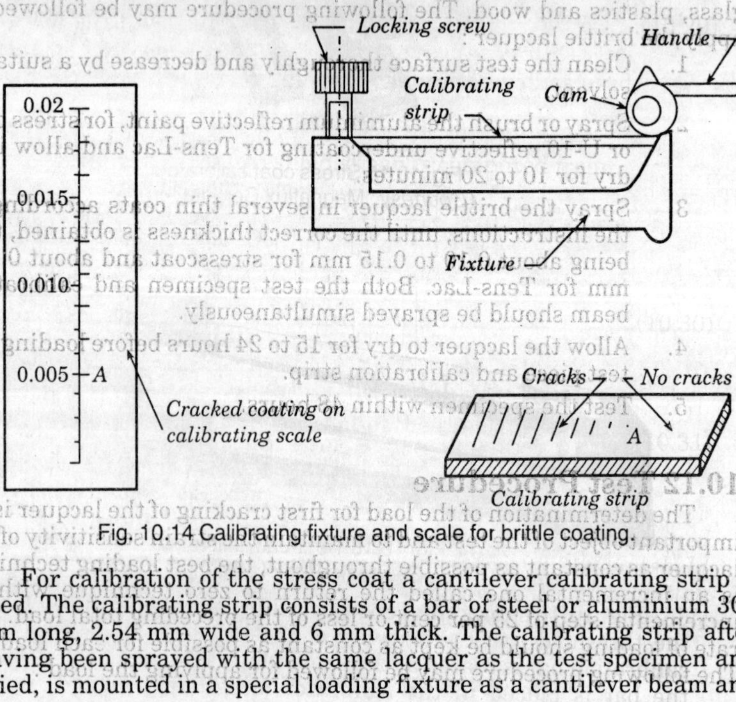

Fig. 10.14 Calibrating fixture and scale for brittle coating.

For calibration of the stress coat a cantilever calibrating strip is used. The calibrating strip consists of a bar of steel or aluminium 300 mm long, 2.54 mm wide and 6 mm thick. The calibrating strip after having been sprayed with the same lacquer as the test specimen and dried, is mounted in a special loading fixture as a cantilever beam and subjected to a fixed deformation at its free end as shown in Fig. 10.14. The lacquer should be scraped from the calibrating strip at the end which is to be clamped in the loading fixture and at the point of contact with the cam. When clamping the strip in the calibrating fixture, the locking screw should be tightened until the strip just touches the bottom of the loading cam to ensure consistency of strain between the calibrating fixture and the calibrating scale. The load is applied to the calibrating strip in the same length of time as that used in loading the test specimen. The point on the strip at which the cracks commence is marked and represents the section where the strains are equal to the strain sensitivity of the lacquer.

The calibrating strip can then be removed from the loading fixture and placed alongside a calibrated scale, from which the incipient cracking strain can be read. Fig. 10.15 is a photograph of the stress coat calibrator and strain scale manufacturer by Magnaflux Corporation.

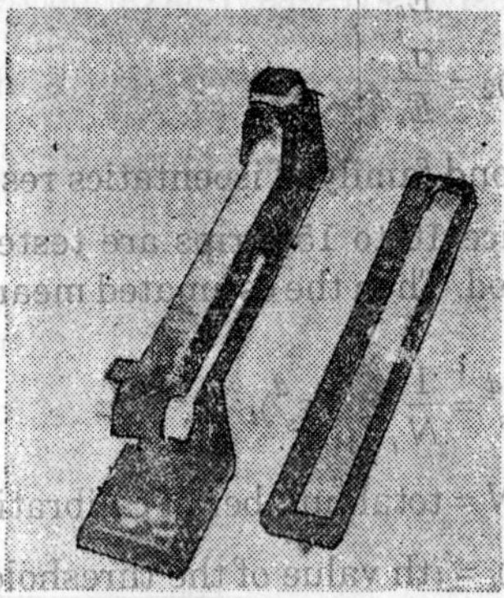

Fig. 10.15 Stress coat calibrator.
(*Courtesy*: Magnaflux Corporation)

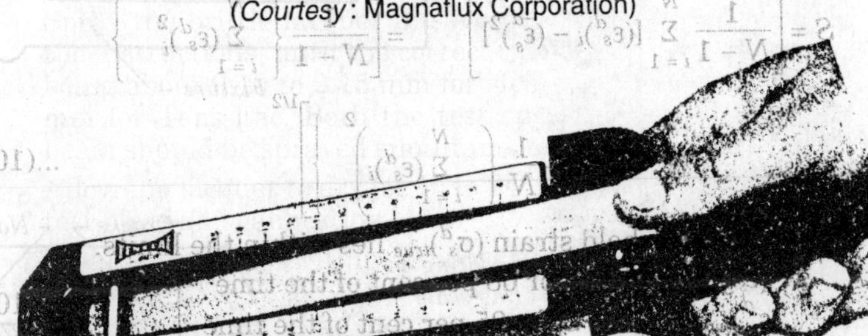

Fig. 10.16 Tens-Lac calibrator.
(*Courtesy*: Photolastic Inc.)

Fig. 10.16 shows the Tens-Lac calibrator which is used to measure the threshold crack sensitivity of the brittle coating. In this case a calibration bar is coated at the same time as the test part. After drying, the bar is placed in the calibrator and simply loaded with thumb pressure at its free end. Cracks will appear in the coating and threshold strain value (μ cm/cm) is read directly from a scale built in the calibrator. The Tens-Lac calibrator is available with twelve calibration bars.

For a biaxial state of stress two strain gauges are mounted on an isoentatic line, the first perpendicular to the isostatics and the second parallel to the isostatics and their readings are taken. Then

$$\sigma_1^s = \frac{E_s}{1 - \nu_s^2} (\varepsilon_1^s + \nu_s \varepsilon_2^s)$$

and

$$\sigma_2^s = \frac{E_s}{1 - \nu_s^2} (\varepsilon_2^s + \nu_s \varepsilon_1^s)$$

The threshold strains are computed from

$$\left.\begin{aligned} (\varepsilon_s^d)_1 &= \frac{\sigma_1^s}{E_s} \\ (\varepsilon_s^d)_2 &= \frac{\sigma_2^s}{E_s} \end{aligned}\right\} \qquad ...(10.28)$$

for the first and second family of isoentatics respectively.

In actual practice 10 to 15 strips are tested so that a number of ε_s^d values are obtained. Then the estimated mean value of the threshold strain becomes

$$\bar{\varepsilon}_s^d = \frac{1}{N} \sum_{i=1}^{N} (\varepsilon_s^d)_i \qquad ...(10.29)$$

where N = total number of calibration values used

$(\varepsilon_s^d)_i$ = ith value of the threshold strain.

Standard deviation of threshold strain is computed from

$$S = \left[\frac{1}{N-1} \sum_{i=1}^{N} [(\varepsilon_s^d)_i - (\bar{\varepsilon}_s^d)^2]\right]^{-1/2} = \left[\frac{1}{N-1}\left\{ \sum_{i=1}^{N} (\varepsilon_s^d)_i^2 - \frac{1}{N}\left(\sum_{i=1}^{N} (\varepsilon_s^d)_i\right)^2 \right\}\right]^{1/2} \qquad ...(10.30)$$

The true threshold strain $(\sigma_s^d)_{true}$ lies within the limits.

$$\left.\begin{aligned} (\varepsilon_s^d)_{true} &= \bar{\varepsilon}_s^d \pm S \text{ for 68 per cent of the time} \\ (\varepsilon_s^d)_{true} &= \bar{\varepsilon}_s^d \pm 2\,S \text{ for 95 per cent of the time} \end{aligned}\right\} \qquad ...(10.31)$$

Example 10.4 *In an experiment 12 calibration values were obtained for the threshold strain. The arithmetic mean value of the threshold strain was found to be 503 μ m / m and the estimated standard deviation was 34.5 μ m/m. Determine the error introduced by the variable threshold strain.*

Solution. Error in threshold strain is given by

$$\pm \frac{S}{\bar{\varepsilon}_s^d} \text{ for 68 per cent of the time}$$

and $$\pm \frac{2S}{\bar{\varepsilon}_s^d} \text{ for 95 per cent of the time}$$

The error $$= \pm \frac{34.5}{503}$$

$$= \pm 6.85 \text{ per cent for 68 per cent of the time}$$

and $$= \pm \frac{2 \times 34.5}{503}$$

$$= \pm 13.71 \text{ for 95 per cent of the time.}$$

Example 10.5 *In order to determine the threshold strain for a brittle lacquer an aluminium calibration strip of size 300 mm × 25 mm × 6 mm was sprayed with the lacquer, dried and loaded at the free end. When the load was 40 N the incipient cracks were found to appear at a distance of 150 mm from the loaded end. If $E_a = 70$ GPa, determine the threshold strain.*

Solution. Bending moment in the calibration strip at the location of the incipient cracks

$$M = 40 \times 0.15 = 6 \text{ N.m}$$

Stress in the strip at this location

$$\sigma = \frac{My}{I} = \frac{6 \times 3 \times 10^{-3} \times 12}{25 \times 6^3 \times 10^{-12}} = 40 \text{ MPa}$$

$$\text{Threshold strain} = \frac{\sigma}{E_a} = \frac{40}{70 \times 10^3} = 571.43 \times 10^{-6}$$

$$= 571.43 \text{ μ m/m.}$$

10.14 Variables Influencing the Coating Behaviour

There are many variables which influence the behaviour of the coating. For stresscoat, Durelli, Phillips and Tsao have listed 37 of these variables. However, the influence of these variables can be minimised if proper precautions are taken as per the manufacturer's instructions. Some of the important variables are discussed below :

1. **Number and type of coating.** For stresscoat and All-Temp brittle lacquers, the strain sensitivity increases as the coating code number increases. However, the strain-sensitivity of Tens-Lac is 500 μ cm/cm at the specified temperature. If the quantity of plasticizer is increased in stresscoat then the threshold strain increases. Coatings made from old liquid are more sensitive.

2. **Effect of spraying unit.** Water vapours in the spraying air causes large bubbles in the coating, which should be avoided by using a filter. The pressure of the spraying unit should also be as specified by the manufacturer. Greater the pressure, the 'dustier' is the appearance

of the coating because there is more air to evaporate the solvent in the liquid and consequently some of the lacquer reaches the surface of specimen in solid form.

3. **Effect of coating application method.** The distance of the gun from the test specimen should be 75 to 100 mm. The speed of spraying traverse should be 1.5 m/s to 2 m/s. Coating should be applied by spraying uniform thicknesses in a number of passes until the specified thickness is obtained. The coating strain sensitivity decreases with coating thickness. It has been found that cross-spraying gives a more uniform coating thickness than parallel spraying. The spraying passes should be made after at least 5 seconds, and should not be more than about 40 seconds.

4. **Influence of heat treatment.** To improve the strain-sensitivity of the coating by a heat-treatment technique, the time between spraying and heating should be at least 5 minutes. Strain sensitivity of stresscoat at approximately 107°F is higher than that for the same coating thickness at 75°F. At any given temperature over approximately 90°F, strain sensitivity increases with decreasing thickness. At higher rate of cooling, crazing occurs. Higher humidity during curing increases the strain sensitivity. As outer layers of the coating dry first they have a higher modulus of elasticity than the inner layers.

5. **Testing conditions.** The strain sensitivity of all coatings increase with the increase in testing temperature and decreases with the increase in relative humidity. The coating should be tested within 48 hours after spraying. Virgin coatings have higher threshold strain than coatings that have been loaded once or twice previously upto the same load. Loads should be applied slowly enough. Static loads should be applied for 2 seconds or more and dynamic loads for about 3 or 4 milli seconds. After 15 seconds the changes in sensitivity are negligible. Therefore calibration and loading time for static tests should be standardized at 15 seconds. Waiting time between successive applications of load should be four times the loading time to eliminate the influence of creep.

6. **Effect of stress conditions.** If the strain gradients perpendicular to the cracks in the test specimen are appreciably different from that of the calibration strip, then the corrected strain sensitivity is given by,

$$(\varepsilon_s^d)_{corrected} = \varepsilon_s^d - \frac{2980\,(2 \times 10^{-4} - x^2)}{(\varepsilon_s^d - 68 \times 10^{-5})^{1/9} + 1.1} \quad \text{...(10.32)}$$

where x = strain gradient at the investigated point, cm/cm/2.54 cm.

The coating behaviour is also influenced by the biaxiality of stress and hydrostatic pressure. Near free boundaries the coating is thicker than inside the field. Residual stresses may be produced by shrinkage in the coating, when it passes from the liquid to the solid state or by change in temperature.

7. **Effect of refrigeration and dye-etchant.** The strain sensitivity of the coating decreases with a sudden drop in temperature. The coating sensitivity increases with the application of dye-etchant.

10.15 Advantages of Brittle Coatings

1. It provides whole field data for both magnitude and direction of principal stresses and does not require a tedious point-by-point method.
2. It does not require the construction of a model and can usually be applied to a prototype of the actual machine component being studied.
3. There is no load simulation problem.
4. The data analysis is simple.

However the accuracy of the method depends upon a number of variables as discussed in the previous article, whose knowledge is very essential.

10.16 Brittle Coating Applications

Brittle coating technique may be employed in the following applications :

1. Determination of residual stresses in conjunction with the hole-drilling method.
2. Determination of compressive strains by using relaxation technique.
3. Determination of dynamic strains.
4. Determination of strains at high temperatures upto 370°C.
5. Determination of yield and plastic strains.
6. For outdoor operations.
7. For operations under water and hydrostatic pressure.
8. Determination of strains on very thin components.

10.17 Brittle Lacquer Technique for GFRP

When a brittle lacquer is applied to an anisotropic structure, the analysis proceeds on the same lines as in the case of the isotropic structure : the principal strain directions for the structure and for the coating are assumed to be the same, and the strains are assumed to be transmitted faithfully from the structure to the coating. The plane state of stress produced in the coating by the plane state of stress acting on the surface of the composite structure can be represented by

$$\left.\begin{aligned} \sigma_x^c &= \frac{E_c}{(1-\nu_c^2)}\left[\sigma_x^s (A + B\nu_c) + \sigma_y^s (B + D\nu_c)\right] \\ \sigma_y^c &= \frac{E_c}{(1-\nu_c^2)}\left[\sigma_x^s (A\nu_c + B) + \sigma_y^s (B\nu_c + D)\right] \end{aligned}\right\} \quad \ldots(10.33)$$

where

$$\left.\begin{aligned} A &= \overline{S}_{11} - \frac{\overline{S}_{16}}{\overline{S}_{66}}\overline{S}_{26} \\ B &= \overline{S}_{12} - \frac{\overline{S}_{16}}{\overline{S}_{66}}\overline{S}_{26} \\ D &= \overline{S}_{22} - \frac{\overline{S}_{16}}{\overline{S}_{66}}\overline{S}_{26} \end{aligned}\right\} \quad \ldots(10.34)$$

and $\overline{S}_{11}$, $\overline{S}_{12}$,..... etc., are the composite compliances transformed to the principal strain axes, making an angle θ with the material symmetry axes.

If the brittle coating calibration is performed in the usual manner on beams prepared from the same composite material as the structure, with the angle between the beam axis and the direction of major reinforcement varied from zero to 90 deg., we can write

$$\sigma_{x'}^{s} = \varepsilon_{x'}^{s} / \overline{S}'_{11}, \quad \sigma_{y'}^{s} = 0 \quad \text{and} \quad \varepsilon_{x'}^{s} = \varepsilon_{s}^{d} \qquad ...(10.35)$$

where 1 stands for the calibration beam axes.

Substituting Eqs. (10.35) in (10.33), the coating stresses in the calibration beam are given by :

$$\left\{\begin{aligned} \sigma_x^c &= \frac{E_c}{(1-\nu_c^2)}\,[(A + B\nu_c)\,\sigma_x^d] \\ \sigma_y^c &= \frac{E_c}{(1-\nu_c^2)}\,[(A\,\nu_c + B)\,\sigma_x^d] \end{aligned}\right\} \qquad ...(10.36)$$

The principal strains and principal stresses for the composite are not in the same direction, except when the beam axis coincides with one of the material symmetry axes. Therefore, the cracks in the brittle coating will be inclined at an angle $\left(\frac{\pi}{2} - \phi\right)$ with the beam axis, instead of π/2, as shown in Fig. 10.17,

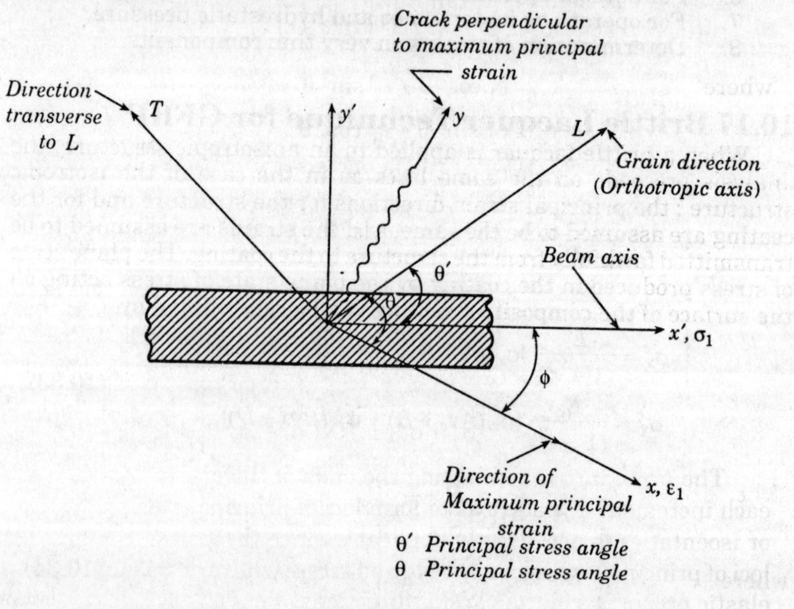

Fig. 10.17

where $$\tan 2\phi = \frac{\overline{S}'_{16}}{(\overline{S}'_{11} - \overline{S}'_{12})} \quad ...(10.37)$$

The failure of the coating in a biaxial stress field can be investigated by employing the Mohr theory of failure. For the case of biaxial tension ($\sigma_x^c \geq \sigma_y^c \geq 0$), the failure equation can be obtained as :

$$\frac{\sigma_x^s}{\sigma_x^d} + \frac{\sigma_y^s}{\sigma_x^d}\left(\frac{B + D\,\nu_c}{A + B\,\nu_c}\right) \geq 1 \quad ...(10.38)$$

For the case of tension-compression ($\sigma_x^c \geq 0 \geq \sigma_y^c$),

$$\frac{\sigma_x^s}{\sigma_x^d}\left[1 - \frac{A\,\nu_c + B}{K(A + B\,\nu_c)}\right] + \frac{\sigma_y^s}{\sigma_x^d}\left[\frac{B + D\nu_c}{A + B\nu_c} - \frac{B\nu_c + D}{K\,(A + B\nu_c)}\right] \geq 1 \quad ...(10.39)$$

The failure condition for the case of biaxial compression ($0 \geq \sigma_x^c \geq \sigma_y^c$) is given by

$$-\left[\frac{\sigma_x^s}{\sigma_x^d}\left(\frac{A\nu_c + B}{A + B\nu_c}\right) + \frac{\sigma_y^s}{\sigma_x^d}\left(\frac{B\nu_c + D}{A + B\nu_c}\right)\right] \geq K \quad ...(10.40)$$

where K is the ratio of compressive strength of brittle coating to its tensile strength.

$$\text{Now} \quad \left\{\begin{aligned} \theta' &= -\frac{1}{2}\tan^{-1}\left(\frac{2\,\tau_{xy}^s}{\sigma_x^s - \sigma_y^s}\right) \\ \theta &= -\frac{1}{2}\tan^{-1}\left(\frac{\gamma_{xy}^s}{\varepsilon_x^s - \varepsilon_y^s}\right) \end{aligned}\right. \quad ...(10.41)$$

where
$$\varepsilon_x^s = \varepsilon_1^s \cos^2\theta + \varepsilon_2^s \sin^2\theta$$
$$\varepsilon_y^s = \varepsilon_2^s \sin^2\theta + \varepsilon_1^s \cos^2\theta$$
$$\gamma_{xy}^s = (\varepsilon_2^s - \varepsilon_1^s)\sin 2\theta$$
$$\sigma_x^s = \frac{E_x^s}{1 - \nu^s\,\nu_{xy}^s\,\nu_x}\,[\varepsilon_x^s + \nu_{xy}^s\,\varepsilon_y^s]$$
$$\sigma_y^s = \frac{E_y^s}{1 - \nu_{xy}^s\,\nu_{yx}^s}\,[\varepsilon_y^s + \nu_{xy}^s\,\varepsilon_x^s]$$
$$\tau_{xy}^s = G_{sxy}\,\gamma_{xy}^s$$
$$\sigma_2^s = \frac{1}{2}(\sigma_x^s + \sigma_y^s) \pm \frac{1}{2}\sqrt{(\sigma_x^s - \sigma_y^s)^2 + 4\,\tau_{xy}^{s\,2}}$$

The procedure of connecting the ends of the cracks together after each increment of load so as to form loci of principal stress magnitude or isoentatics is not directly applicable since these are at best simply loci of principal strain magnitude and stress will vary depending on the elastic properties in the various directions.

In the inverse operation, knowing the direction of the principal stress, determine in which direction the principal strains will act. Even when the principal stress acts at a very small angle to the direction of the grain, a large shift in the direction of the principal strain occurs.

Thus it is seen that the failure of the brittle coating is influenced by the biaxiality of the stress field in the composite structure that is being determined. An exact analysis is much more difficult as the failure envelope is different for each angle of fiber orientation. However, the approximate analysis, based on the equation,

$$\sigma_1^s = E_s \, \varepsilon_s^d , \; \sigma_2^s = 0, \; \varepsilon_2^s = -\nu_s \, \varepsilon_1^s$$

can be used and the accurate information regarding the principal strain directions can be used in conjuction with other experimental methods, such as strain gauges.

10.18. Quiz Questions

1. What do you understand by the brittle-lacquer method ?
2. What do you understand by threshold strain ?
3. What is the direction of the cracks when the coating fails ?
4. How much is the accuracy of the brittle-lacquer method ?
5. What is the biaxiality equation ?
6. What do you understand by the relaxation method ?
7. What is the apparent stress ?
8. What is the necessity of the refrigeration technique ?
9. Draw crack patterns for $\sigma_1^s = \sigma_2^s > 0$.
10. What are the various crack detection methods ?
11. What are the various types of coatings available ?
12. What are the various methods to evaluate the coating ?
13. What are the temperature limits for the brittle lacquers available ?
14. How do you select a particular brittle lacquer ?
15. Explain the returned-to-zero-load method.
16. How do you calibrate the coating for a biaxial state of stress ?
17. What is the effect of the code number of the coating on its strain-sensitivity ?
18. What is the effect of relative humidity on strain-sensitivity of the coating ?
19. What is the effect of dye-etchant on strain-sensitivity of the coating ?
20. What is the effect of refrigeration on coating strain-sensitivity ?

EXERCISES

10.1. Explain the brittle coating method in brief. What are the advantages and limitations of this method ?

10.2. What are the assumptions made while analysing brittle coatings ? Derive expressions for coating stresses.

10.3. Derive the biaxiality equation for direct loading. What are the advantages of this equation ?

10.4. Derive expressions to determine the specimen stresses when cracks perpendicular to the smaller principal stress also start appearing.

10.5. When do we use relaxation loading method to analyse brittle coating data ? How specimen stresses can be determined by this method?

10.6. Explain briefly the refrigeration technique used for brittle lacquers. What are the effects of this technique on brittle lacquers ?

10.7. Discuss the crack patterns which can be obtained under various combinations of stresses. Illustrate your answer by giving sketches.

10.8. Determine the stresses in a brittle coating applied to a component made of aluminium for which $E_s = 70$ GPa, $\nu_s = 0.33$, when the specimen stresses are $\sigma_1^s = 70$ MPa and $\sigma_2^s = 25$ MPa and $\nu_c = 0.36$, $E_c = 0.7$ GPa.

If the threshold strain is 740 μ m/m, what is the corresponding state of stress in the coating during calibration ?

10.9. At a certain point *O* of a steel specimen, cracks in one direction begin to appear when the external load is 10 kN. At the same point *O*, cracks perpendicular to the above mentioned cracks begin to appear when the load reaches 18 kN. The strain sensitivity of the coating as obtained from the aluminium calibration strip is 700 μ m/m, $\nu_a = 0.33$, $\nu = 0.30$, $\nu_c = 0.42$, $E_s = 200$ GPa, $k = 0.6$. Find the principal stresses when the external load is 8 kN. Assume maximum tensile stress law of failure.

10.10. At a certain point *O* of an aluminium specimen cracks in one direction began to appear when the external load was 6 kN. The threshold strain in direct loading for the brittle coating was 650 μ m/m. This coating was removed, a new coating was applied and cured, while a load of 14 kN was maintained on the specimen. On the partial release of the 14 kN load to 7 kN, cracks perpendicular to those observed in the first set began to appear at the same point *O*. The threshold strain for this coating in relaxation loading was 700 μ m/m, $\nu_a = 0.33$, $\nu_c = 0.42$, $\nu_s = 0.33$, $E_s = 70$ GPa. Determine the principal stresses at point *O* when the external load is 5 kN. Assume maximum tensile stress law of failure.

10.11. Write short notes on the following :

(*i*) Relaxation method (*ii*) Refrigeration techniques

(*iii*) Crack detection methods.

10.12. What are the various types of brittle coatings available ? Discuss their important features.

10.13. What are the various characteristics used to evaluate a brittle coating? Discuss the various applications of brittle coatings.

10.14. Discuss the brittle lacquer method with special reference to:

(*a*) lacquer selection, (*b*) lacquer application method,

(*c*) testing procedure.

10.15. Describe the calibration method generally used for brittle coatings. How true threshold strains can be determined by this method?

10.16. In an experiment 12 calibration values as given below were obtained for the threshold strain. Calculate the standard deviation, true threshold strain and percentage error for 95 per cent confidence level.

Test No.	1	2	3	4	5	6	7	8	9	10	11	12
Threshold strain, μ m/m	490	495	500	505	503	502	498	504	495	502	504	505

10.17. In order to determine the threshold strain for a brittle lacquer a perspex calibration strip of size 300 mm × 25 mm × 10 mm was sprayed with the brittle lacquer, dried and loaded at the free end. When the load was 5 N the incipient cracks were found to appear at a distance of 150 mm from the loaded end. If $E_a = 3$ GPa, determine the threshold strain.

10.18. Discuss briefly the various variables influencing the coating behaviour.

10.19. A pressure vessel is sprayed with a brittle coating having a threshold strain of 500 μ m/m. The vessel is then pressurized and the first cracks of the coating occur at a specific location at a pressure of 0.7 MPa. The pressure is then increased, and similar cracks continue to occur at other locations. At a pressure of 1.05 MPa a second set of cracks form perpendicular to the first set of cracks and at the same location. Both stresses at this location are obviously tensile. Assuming that $\sigma_1 = k_1 p$ and $\sigma_2 = k_2 p$, where k_1 and k_2 are constants and p is the pressure, estimate the values of k_1 and k_2. $E_s = 200$ GPa, $\nu_s = 0.29$.

10.20. Describe qualitatively how the state of stress in the coating on a calibration beam changes after the coating fails by cracking.

10.21. A horizontal round bar is coated with brittle lacquer and then statically loaded in combined tension and in vertical bending.

(*a*) As the loading is increased, where would the initial coating cracks probably occur ?

(*b*) Make a sketch showing the general direction of coating cracks on the top side and bottom surface.

10.22. A steel machine frame with a small hole at point *O* as shown in Fig. 10.18 (*a*) is first subjected to stresscoat testing ; then electric resistance strain gauge measurements are made in directions *a*—*a* and *b*—*b*. Data are given below :

(*a*) What does the stresscoat test indicate the maximum normal stress to be at 50 kN load ?

(*b*) What does the resistance strain gauge test indicate the maximum normal stress to be at 50 kN load ?

(*c*) What is the maximum shear stress at this point ?

Stresscoat data : Load-returned-to-zero method used, with load applied over a 5 s interval each time. $\varepsilon_{cal} = 950$ μ m/m was obtained from test bars loaded over a 5 s interval. This value was approximately constant throughout the test.

Strain gauge data :

Gauge resistance = 500 ohms

Gauge constant = 3.5

(*a*) What does the stresscoat test indicate the maximum normal stress to be at 50 kN load ?

(*b*) What does the resistance strain gauge test indicate the maximum normal stress to be at 50 kN load ?

(*c*) What is the maximum shear stress at this point ?

Stresscoat data : Load-returned-to-zero method used, with load applied over a 5 s interval each time. ε_{cal} = 950 μ m/m was obtained from test bars loaded over a 5 s interval. This value was approximately constant throughout the test.

Strain gauge data :

Gauge resistance = 500 ohms
Gauge constant = 3.5
Fixed resistant = 500 ohms
Meter resistance = 200 ohms
Voltage = 22.5 volts

I_m for *a*—*a* = 2.5×10^{-5} amps
I_m for *b*—*b* = 1.0×10^{-5} amps.

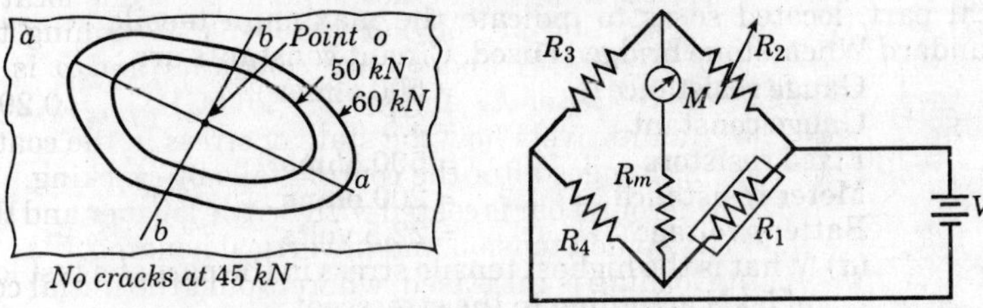

(*a*) (*b*)

Fig. 10.18

Readings at 5*t* load :

10.23. A steel machine part is first subjected to stresscoat testing, then metal strain-gauge measurements are made in directions *a*, *b* and *c* as shown in Fig. 10.19.

Stresscoat data :

ε_{cal} = 600 μ m/m ; crack patterns are as shown.

Strain-gauge data : (Standard wheatstone bridge circuit)

Resistance of fixed resistors, dummy gauge and active gauge ohms 500 each.

Gauge constant = 3.5
Meter resistance = 200 ohms
Voltage = 22.5 volts.

Readings when test part is subjected to 25 kN load :

I_m when *a* is the active gauge = 2.5×10^{-5} amps.
I_m when *b* is the active gauge = 1.0×10^{-5} amps.

(*a*) What are the maximum normal stress and maximum shear stress at this location when the load is 25 kN ?

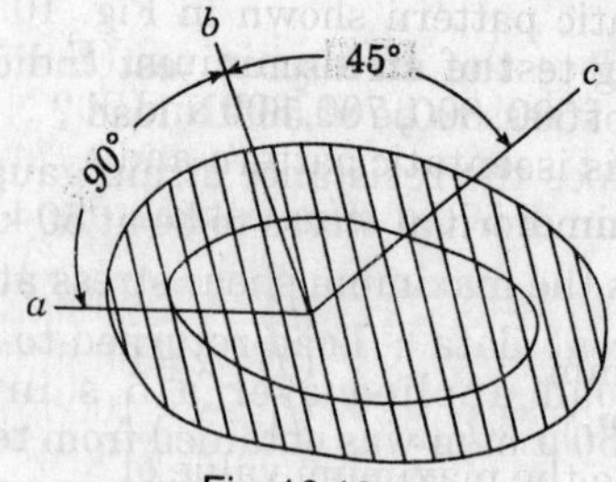

Fig. 10.19

(b) Loading data for the stresscoat test were lost and strain-gauge c failed to work (i) At what load roughly did the first stress-coat cracks probably occurs ? What value of I_m should have been obtained when c was the active gauge ?

10.24. A steel part (E_s = 200 GPa, ν = 0.30, σ_u = 700 MPa) is coated with stresscoat and loaded to produce a crack pattern. It was observed that the first very small cracks occured at a test load of 5 kN. At the same time it was observed that the stresscoat had a calibration strain of ε_{cal} = 700 μ m/m. Next a single strain gauge is mounted on an identical part, located so as to indicate the maximum tensile stress. A standard Wheatstone bridge is used. Circuit constants are :

Gauge resistance	= 500 ohms
Gauge constant	= 3.5
Fixed resistors	= 500 ohms
Meter resistance	= 200 ohms
Battery voltage	= 22.5 volts

(a) What is the highest tensile stress in the part at a test load of 5 kN according to the stresscoat.

(b) Estimate the metre reading which will be obtained.

10.25. The maximum normal stress theory of failure for brittle coatings indicates that cracks will form whenever

$$\sigma_1^c \geq \sigma_{ut}, \quad \sigma_2^c \geq \sigma_{ut}$$

where σ_{ut} is the ultimate tensile strength of the coating. Show that the failure equations for the coating in terms of the stresses applied to the specimen are :

$$\frac{\sigma_1^s}{\sigma_0^d} + \frac{(\nu_c - \nu_s)\,\sigma_2^s}{(1 - \nu_c\nu_s)\,\sigma_0^d} \geq 1, \qquad \frac{\sigma_2^s}{\sigma_0^d} + \frac{(\nu_c - \nu_s)\,\sigma_1^s}{(1 - \nu_c\,\nu_s)\,\sigma_0^d} \geq 1.$$

10.26. At a certain point on a steel specimen, cracks begin to appear when the load is raised to 5 kN. The corrected calibration threshold strain for the coating at this time is 500 μ m/m.

The load is increased in increments, and at a level of 20 kN cracks perpendicular to the first set begin to appear at the same point. The corrected calibration threshold strain for the second family of cracks is 600 μ m/m. Determine the two principal stresses in the specimen at a load level of 5 kN by assuming that the coating cracks according to the maximum normal stress theory. Assume that the coating is resin based with E_c = 1.4 GPa, ν_c = 0.42.

10.27. The isoentatic pattern shown in Fig. 10.20 was produced during a direct loading test of an aluminium (E = 70 GPa, ν = 0.33) specimen. Load levels of 500, 600, 700, 800 and 900 N were used during the test. Using only this isoentatic pattern and a corrected calibration value of threshold strain of 570 μ m/m, estimate the distribution of σ_1^s along the lines:

(a) $y = 0$, (b) $y = 20$ mm,
(c) $y = -20$ mm, (d) $x = 60$ mm,
(e) $x = 80$ mm, (f) $x = 100$ mm,
(g) Determine the maximum value of σ_1^s.

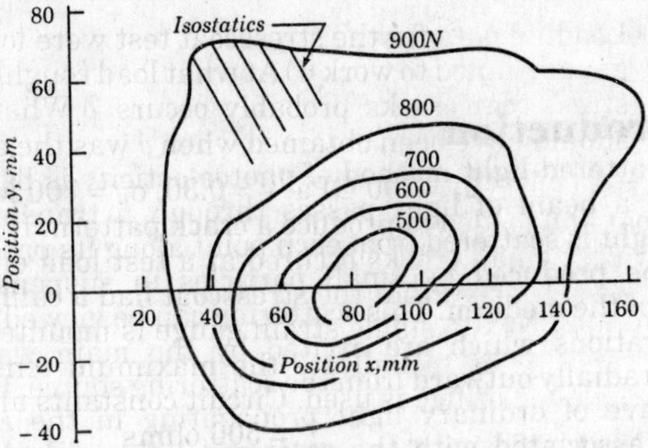

Fig. 10.20

10.28. The relaxation loading method was used to obtain the isostatic and isoentatic patterns associated with σ_2^s as shown in Fig. 10.21 on an aluminium specimen (E = 70 GPa, ν = 0.33). The corrected calibration value of threshold strain was 620 μ m/m. Estimate the distribution of σ_2^s along the lines :
(a) $y = 0$, (b) $y = 20$ mm, (c) $y = -20$ mm (d) $x = 60$ mm, (e) $x = 80$ mm, (f) $x = 100$ mm, (g) Determine the maximum value of σ_2^s.

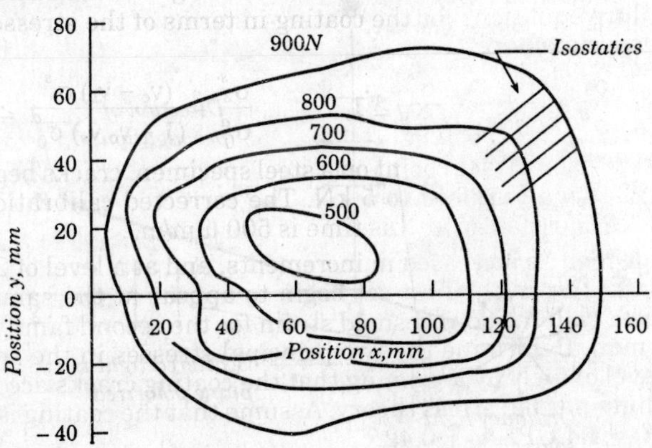

Fig. 10.21

11

Scattered Light Photoelasticity

11.1 Introduction

The scattered-light method of photoelasticity is based on the fact that when a beam of light passes through a transparent isotropic medium, light is scattered from each point along its path. This scattering may be produced by small particles in suspension or by the molecules of the medium. This scattering can be viewed as a secondary set of vibrations which are excited by the main wave and which propagate radially outward from the scattering source. For example for a main wave of ordinary light propagating in the z-direction, the vibrations associated with the scattered light will all lie in planes normal to the z-axis. Thus, when the scattered light is viewed along any ray which is normal to the z-axis, it will be plane-polarized as shown in Fig. 11.1 (a). Along any other direction, which is not normal to the z-axis, the degree of polarization decreases as coincidence with the z-axis is approached. The intensity of the ordinary light scattered from any point is the same in all directions within the plane normal to the axis of propagation of the primary beam while that of the polarized light in any direction is proportional to the square of the component of amplitude of the primary vibration in the perpendicular direction [Fig. 11.1 (b)], called the apparent amplitude.

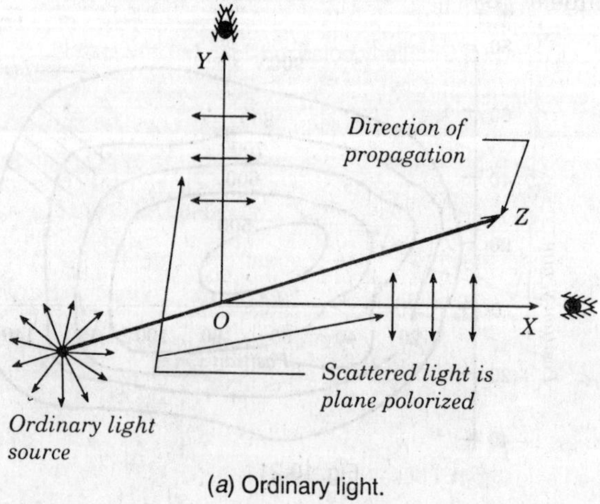

(a) Ordinary light.

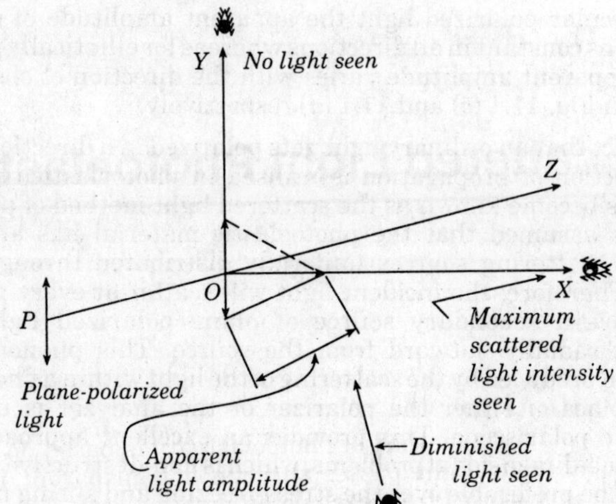

(*b*) Plane-polarized light.

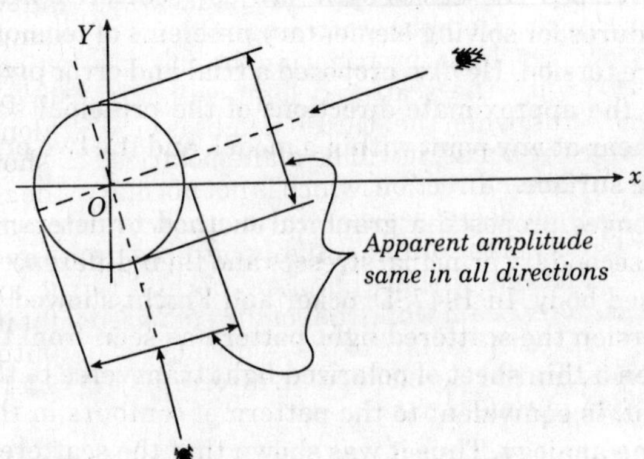

(*c*) Circularly polarized light.

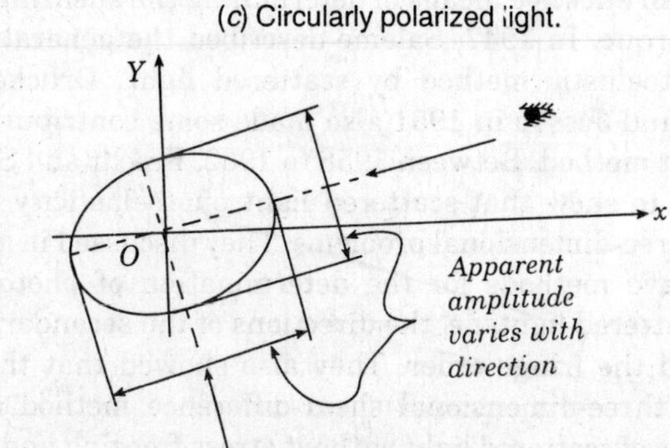

(*d*) Elliptically polarized light.

Fig. 11.1

For circular polarized light the apparent amplitude of scattered light remains constant in all directions whereas for elliptically polarized light the apparent amplitude varies with the direction of observation as shown in Fig. 11.1 (*c*) and 11.1 (*d*) respectively.

This fact that an ordinary light gets polarized in a direction normal to the direction of propagation is utilised in photoelasticity and the method has become known as the scattered light method of photoelasticity. It is assumed that the photoelastic material has an infinite number of scattering sources uniformly distributed throughout the material. Therefore, the incident light will scatter at every point and will produce a secondary source of plane polarized light which propagates radially outward from the source. This phenomenon of polarization produced by the scattering of the light within a photoelastic model in place of either the polarizer or the analyzer is used in a photoelastic polariscope. This provides an excellent approach to the general three-dimensional problems, which is non-destructive in nature and should be preferable over the stress-freezing and slicing method of exploring three-dimensional stresses.

The use of scattered light in photoelasticity was poineered by Weller in 1938. He developed the stress-optic law for scattered light and suggested procedures for solving elementary problems of tension, pure bending and pure torsion. He also proposed a trial and error procedure for determining the approximate directions of the principal stresses, the maximum shear at any point within a model, and the two principal stresses at a free surface.

In 1940, Menges proposed a graphical method to determine the directions of the secondary principal stresses and their difference at any point in a stressed body. In 1947, Drucker and Frocht showed that in Saint Venant torsion the scattered light pattern as seen from the end of the shaft, when a thin sheet of polarized light transverse to the axis passes through it, is equivalent to the pattern of contours in the well known membrane analogy. Thus it was shown that the scattered light pattern provides an effective means of determining the shearing stresses for a given torque. In 1947, Saleme described the general three-dimensional photoelastic method by scattered light. Drucker and Mindlin in 1940 and Jessop in 1951 also made some contributions to the scattered light method. Between 1958 to 1962, Frocht and Srinath published papers to show that scattered light photoelasticity can be used in general three-dimensional problems. They discussed in general principles and gave methods for the determination of photoelastic parameters in scattered light, *i.e.* the directions of the secondary principal stresses and the fringe order. They also showed that the data required for the three-dimensional shear-difference method can be obtained by means of scattered light without stress freezing and consequently slicing the model, thereby providing a non-destructive method for three-dimensional photoelasticity.

11.2 Preliminary Optics

(*a*) **Light Ellipse.** When a wave of light traversing a material medium of uniform dielectric constant, meets a particle with different dielectric constant, the particle acts as a source of secondary electric energy and light is emitted from the particle or obstacle in every direction. Consider a ray of plane polarized-light travelling through a stressed medium and meeting such an obstacle at a point *o* as shown in Fig. 11.2. The component vibrations in the directions of the secondary principal axes *ou* and *ov* in the incident wavefront are :

$$u = a \cos \omega t$$
$$v = b \cos (\omega t + \psi) \qquad \text{...(11.1)}$$

where ψ = relative phase difference in radians between these two vibrations.

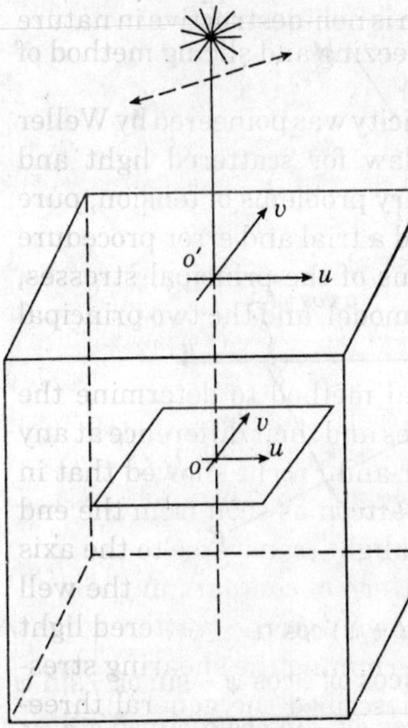

Fig. 11.2 Transmission of plane-polarized light through stressed model.

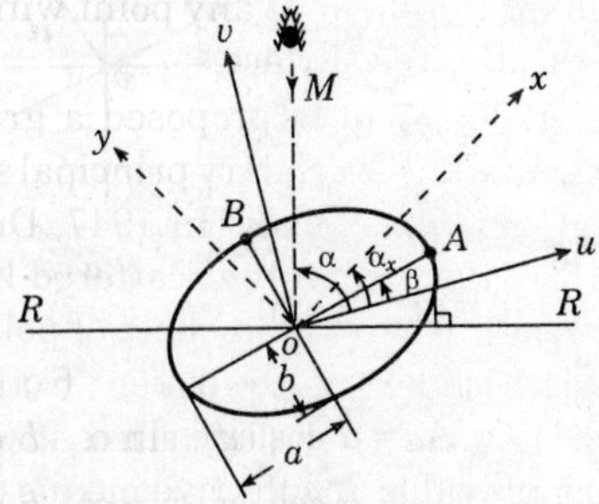

Fig. 11.3 Light ellipse showing direction of observation *oM*, plane *RR* normal to *oM* and the two arbitrary axes *ox* and *oy*.

The light at point *o* is elliptically polarized in the plane of the incident wave front and the equation of this ellipse is

$$\frac{u^2}{a^2} + \frac{v^2}{b^2} - \frac{2uv}{ab} \cos \psi = \sin^2 \psi \qquad \text{...(11.2)}$$

where *a* and *b* are the semi-major and semi-minor axes of the ellipse respectively. The axes of this light ellipse are oriented at angles β and $\left(\beta + \frac{\pi}{2}\right)$ to the *u*-axis (Fig. 11.3), such that

$$\tan 2\beta = \left(\frac{2ab}{a^2 - b^2}\right)\cos\psi \qquad ...(11.3)$$

From Eqs. (11.1) to (11.3), it is observed that when $\psi = 2m\pi$ or $(2m-1)\pi$; $m = 0, 1, 2, 3, ...$, the light is plane polarized and the light vector is inclined at an angle $\pm\beta_1$ to the u-axis, such that $\tan\beta_1 = \pm b/a$, *i.e.* the light ellipse degenerates into straight lines oriented at an angle $\pm\beta_1$ to the u-axis.

(*b*) **Intensity of scattered light.** For directions of observations normal to the incident light, *i.e.* normal to the axis of propagation $o'o$ (Fig. 11.1) the intensity of scattered light is proportional to the square of the apparent amplitude, *i.e.* the amplitude of the vibration normal to the line of observation. This is obtained from the projections of u and v on a line RR normal to the line of observation OM. The amplitude along RR becomes (Fig. 11.4).

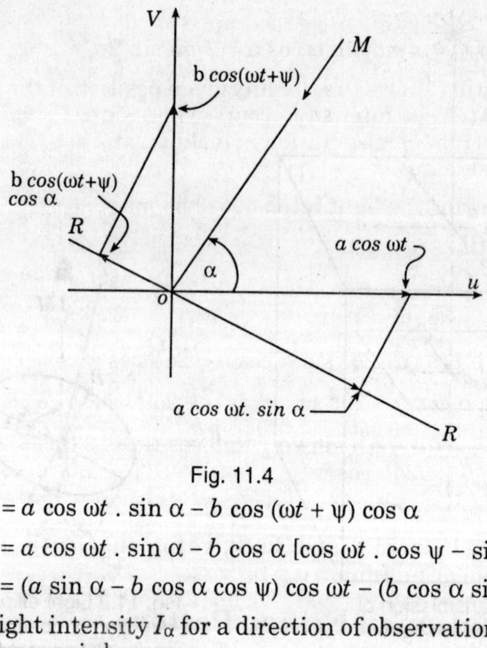

Fig. 11.4

$$A_\alpha = a\cos\omega t \,.\, \sin\alpha - b\cos(\omega t + \psi)\cos\alpha$$

$$= a\cos\omega t \,.\, \sin\alpha - b\cos\alpha\,[\cos\omega t \,.\, \cos\psi - \sin\omega t \,.\, \sin\psi]$$

$$= (a\sin\alpha - b\cos\alpha\cos\psi)\cos\omega t - (b\cos\alpha\sin\psi)\sin\omega t$$

Thus the light intensity I_α for a direction of observation making an angle α with the u-axis becomes

$$I_\alpha \propto (a\sin\alpha - b\cos\alpha\cos\psi)^2 + (b\cos\alpha\sin\psi)^2$$

$$\propto a^2\sin^2\alpha + b^2\cos^2\alpha\cos^2\psi - 2ab\sin\alpha\cos\alpha\cos\psi$$

$$+ b^2\cos^2\alpha\sin^2\psi$$

$$\propto a^2\sin^2\alpha + b^2\cos^2\alpha - 2ab\sin\alpha\cos\alpha\cos\psi$$

$$I_\alpha = \gamma\,(a^2\sin^2\alpha + b^2\cos^2\alpha - 2ab\sin\alpha\cos\alpha\cos\psi) \qquad ...(11.4)$$

where γ is a constant depending upon the scattering properties of the material.

$$I_{(90^\circ + \alpha)} = \gamma\,(a^2\cos^2\alpha + b^2\sin^2\alpha + 2ab\cos\alpha\sin\alpha\cos\psi) \qquad ...(11.5)$$

Hence

$$I_\alpha + I_{(90^\circ + \alpha)} = \gamma\,(a^2 + b^2) = I_0 \qquad \text{...(11.6)}$$

where I_0 is the total intensity of scattered light.

The intensity of light will vary from point to point as α varies. The light intensity will be a maximum when the direction of observation is along the minor axis of the light ellipse and is a minimum when the direction of observation is along the major axis, *i.e.* the intensity is a maximum or a minimum for directions of observations $\alpha = \beta$ given by Eq. (11.13).

For $\quad \psi = 2m\pi$

$$(I_\alpha)_{\min} = \gamma\,(a \sin\alpha - b \cos\alpha)^2$$

and for $\quad \psi = (2m - 1)\,\pi$

$$(I_\alpha)_{\max} = \gamma\,(a \sin\alpha + b \cos\alpha)^2$$

thus we have

$$(I_\alpha)_{\max} - (I_\alpha)_{\min} = 4\gamma ab \sin\alpha \cos\alpha = 2\gamma ab \sin 2\alpha \qquad \text{...(11.7)}$$

This equation shows that for any given position of the polarizer, the greatest variation of intensity occurs when $\sin 2\alpha = 1$, *i.e.* $\alpha = 45^\circ$ or when the direction of observation is inclined at 45° to the directions of the principal stresses.

Otherwise, for the light intensity to be maximum or minimum,

$$\frac{dI_\alpha}{d\alpha} = 0$$

which gives

$$\gamma\,(2a^2 \sin\alpha \cos\alpha - 2b^2 \sin\alpha \cos\alpha - 2ab \cos\psi \cos 2\alpha) = 0$$

$$2a^2 \sin\alpha \cos\alpha - 2b^2 \sin\alpha \cos\alpha - 2\,ab \cos\psi \cos 2\alpha = 0$$

$$(a^2 - b^2) \sin 2\alpha = 2ab \cos\psi \cos 2\,\alpha$$

$$\tan 2\alpha = \frac{2ab \cos\psi}{a^2 - b^2} \qquad \text{...(11.8)}$$

Comparing Eqs. (11.3) and (11.8), we find that for the light intensity to be maximum or minimum $\alpha = \beta$.

11.3 Formation of Fringe Pattern

From Eq. (11.4) we find that for any fixed direction of observation, the intensity of scattered light varies from a maximum to a minimum depending upon the value of ψ. When α is less than π/2, the intensity is a minimum (although not necessarily zero) when $\psi = 2m\pi$ and becomes a maximum when $\psi = (2m - 1)\,\pi$. When α is more than π/2, the condition for maximum and minimum will be reversed. Except for special cases, ψ will vary from point to point along the axis of propagation and in general, will assume the values necessary for a maximum and a minimum light intensity. This gives rise to a sequence of bright and dark regions which forms the scattered light fringe pattern. Eq. (11.3) shows that for approximately equal amplitudes a and b, the axes of the light ellipse are at 45° to the directions of the secondary principal stresses and therefore this direction gives a pattern of sharpest contrast.

At the point of entrance, the relative retardation is zero for an initially plane polarized beam of light and Eq. (11.4) shows that if α is less than $\pi/2$, the initial point will be dark. The dark fringes in the pattern will represent relative retardations of an integral number of wavelength. Conversely, if α is greater than $\pi/2$, the initial point will be bright and the successive dark fringes in the pattern will represent relative retardations of odd multiples of half wavelengths.

11.4 Stress-Optic Law

Before stating the stress-optic law we shall explain the meaning of secondary principal stresses. The secondary principal stresses are the stresses which lie on a plane perpendicular to the direction of propagation of the light wave. For the light travelling along the z-direction, the secondary principal stresses, for example, are

$$\sigma'_{1,2} = \frac{\sigma_x + \sigma_y}{2} \pm \frac{1}{2}\left\{(\sigma_x - \sigma_y)^2 + 4\tau_{xy}^2\right\}^{1/2}$$

We first consider the case in which the secondary principal stresses maintain constant directions along the axis of propagation. Since the light scattered within a photoelastic model at right angles to the direction of the incident beam is plane-polarized, it can be used as either a polarizer or an analyzer.

11.4.1 The scattering property used as a polarizer

Consider a beam of unpolarized light which enters through the model at point P as shown in Fig. 11.5. As the incident light beam passes through the model, each point along the beam acts as a source of plane-polarized light, the direction of vibration being mutually perpendicular to the direction of observation and the incident beam.

At an interior point Q the polarized light scattered from the stressed model is resolved into two components along the directions of the secondary principal stresses σ'_1 and σ'_2. As the light travels outwards along QR, a phase difference develops between the two components. This phase difference or relative retardation can be measured by inserting an analyser between point R and the camera. Thus

$$N_{QR} = \frac{h}{f_\sigma}(\sigma'_1 - \sigma'_2)_{avg\,.\,QR} \qquad \text{...(11.9)}$$

where $(\sigma'_1 - \sigma'_2)_{avg}$ is the average value of $(\sigma'_1 - \sigma'_2)$ over the distance QR if rotational effects are ignored and $h = QR$. Similarly the relative retardation from an adjacent point Q' will be given by

$$N_{Q'R} = \frac{(h + \Delta h)}{f_\sigma}(\sigma'_1 - \sigma'_2)_{avg.\,Q'R}$$

$$= \frac{1}{f_\sigma}[h\,(\sigma'_1 - \sigma'_2)_{avg.\,QR} + \Delta\,h\,(\sigma'_1 - \sigma'_2)_{avg.}\,\Delta h] \qquad \text{...(11.10)}$$

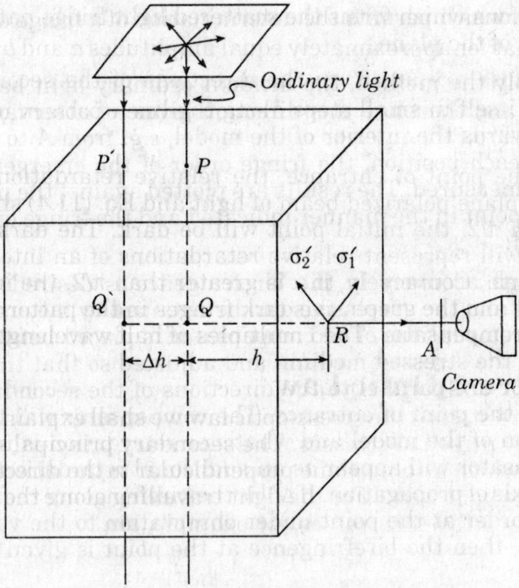

Fig. 11.5 Arrangement for using the scattering property as a polarizer.

$$\text{Thus} \qquad \Delta N = N_{Q'R} - N_{QR} = \frac{1}{f_\sigma}\left[\Delta h\,(\sigma'_1 - \sigma'_2)_{avg}\,\Delta h\right]$$

$$\text{or} \quad (\sigma'_1 - \sigma'_2)_{avg.}\,\Delta h = f_\sigma \frac{\Delta N}{\Delta h} \approx f_\sigma\left(\frac{N_2 - N_1}{\Delta h}\right) \qquad \text{...(11.11)}$$

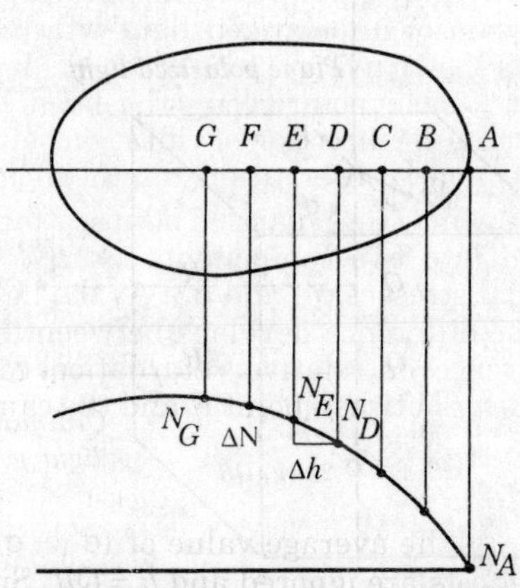

Fig. 11.6 Method of determining the fringe order gradient.

where N_2 and N_1 denote the fringe orders at two neighbouring points Δh apart and $\Delta N/\Delta h$ is the fringe order gradient. By determining, ΔN and measuring Δh it is possible to measure $(\sigma'_1 - \sigma'_2)$ over a centralized plane of observation of thickness Δh without slicing the model. In practice, a sheet of light is used to illuminate a plane in the model rather than a line, which permits the determination of a fringe order over the whole field of the plane.

To apply the method, the incident ordinary light beam is moved parallel to itself in small steps along the line of observation from the surface towards the interior of the model, *e.g.* from *A* to *B, C, D* (Fig. 11.6). For each position, the fringe order of the emergent light components is measured. The results are plotted against the position of the scattering point in the manner indicated and the fringe order gradient determined.

If a high accuracy in the birefringence is desired than that of obtainable from the graph, this can be obtained by means of a Babinet or similar compensator. The compensator is placed between the light source and the stressed medium and adjusted so that the axes of the compensator are parallel to the directions of the secondary principal stresses at the point of entrance. The compensator will then act as a continuation of the model and whatever retardation is introduced by the compensator will appear as an additional retardation at all points along the axis of propagation. If ΔN is the birefringence required to raise the fringe order at the point under observation to the value N of the next fringe, then the birefringence at the point is given by $(N - \Delta N)$. Then

$$\sigma'_1 - \sigma'_2 = f_\sigma\left(\frac{(\Delta N_1 - \Delta N_2)}{\Delta h}\right) \quad ...(11.12)$$

11.4.2 The scattering property used as an analyser

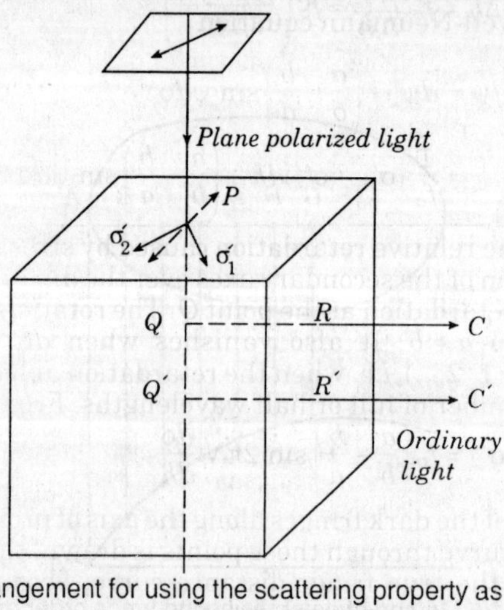

Fig. 11.7 Arrangement for using the scattering property as an analyzer.

Consider Fig. 11.7 where an incident beam of plane-polarized light is resolved as it enters the model into two components along the secondary principal axes associated with σ'_1 and σ'_2. These two components travel with different velocities along the secondary principal planes, and in traversing the distance PQ they acquire a certain relative retardation. The scattering source located at point P acts as an analyzer since the scattered light is polarized. The resulting image observed along line QC will have an intensity dependent upon the relative retardation acquired over the path PQ. If the line of observation is moved to $Q'C'$, the relative retardation varies, depending upon the additional retardation acquired over the distance QQ'. Since $QQ' = \Delta h$ and the additional retardation acquired over the distance Δh is ΔN, the ratio $\Delta N/\Delta h$ is the gradient of retardation in successive planes normal to the incident light beam, and is related to the difference in secondary principal stresses $(\sigma'_1 - \sigma'_2)$ lying in the plane normal to the incident light by

$$(\sigma'_1 - \sigma'_2)_{avg.\ \Delta h} = f_\sigma \frac{\Delta N}{\Delta h} \quad \text{...(11.13)}$$

Eq. (11.11) and (11.13) are identical. However Eq. (11.11) requires two scattered-light photographs whereas Eq. (11.13) requires only a single scattered-light photograph since the magnitude of the stresses will be proportional to the space gradient of the fringes.

Of the two options for use of scattered light, the scattering is usually used to provide a temporary analyzer. A sheet of light is used to illuminate a given plane in the model, and the light scattered from this plane is photographed to give a whole field fringe pattern.

11.4.3. Effect of rotation of secondary principal stresses

When the directions of the secondary principal stresses vary the relative retardation of $d\psi$ acquired by the wave components over dh is given by Maxwell-Neumann equation

$$d\psi = d\psi^* + \left(\frac{a}{b} - \frac{b}{a}\right) \sin \psi d\phi \quad \text{...(11.14)}$$

$$= \frac{1}{f_\sigma}(\sigma'_1 - \sigma'_2)dh + \left(\frac{a}{b} - \frac{b}{a}\right) \sin \psi d\phi$$

where $d\psi^*$ is the relative retardation caused by stresses alone, $d\phi$ is the angle of rotation of the secondary axes over the distance dh and ψ is the total existing retardation at the point Q. The rotational effect obviously vanishes when $a = b$. It also vanishes when $d\phi$ is zero, or when $\psi = m\pi$ ($m = 0, 1, 2,...$), *i.e.* when the retardation at a point Q consists of an integral number of full or half wavelengths. From Eq. (11.14),

$$\sigma'_1 - \sigma'_2 = f_\sigma \left(\frac{a}{b} - \frac{b}{a}\right) \sin 2\pi N \frac{d\phi}{dh} \quad \text{...(11.15)}$$

If the position of the dark fringes along the axis of propagation is plotted and a smooth curve through these points is drawn, then this curve does not represent the true fringe-distance curve, because as Eq. (11.14) shows, the slope of this curve must have periodic changes and the positions of the dark fringes alone are not sufficient to give any indications about these changes. It has been observed that there is a marked diminution in the sharpness of the fringes when the secondary axes rotate by more than 10° or 12°, so that if we observe about two or three fringes sharply defined over a certain length, it may be assumed that, over this distance the secondary axes could not have rotated by more than the above limit and that the error in the values of N from a smooth curve drawn through these points is negligible. The rotational effect can be eliminated by measuring the birefringence with a compensator and bringing the retardation at the point to a full or a half wavelength with the result that the second term in Eq. (11.15) becomes zero. The value of $(\sigma_1' - \sigma_2')$ will then be given by Eq. (11.12).

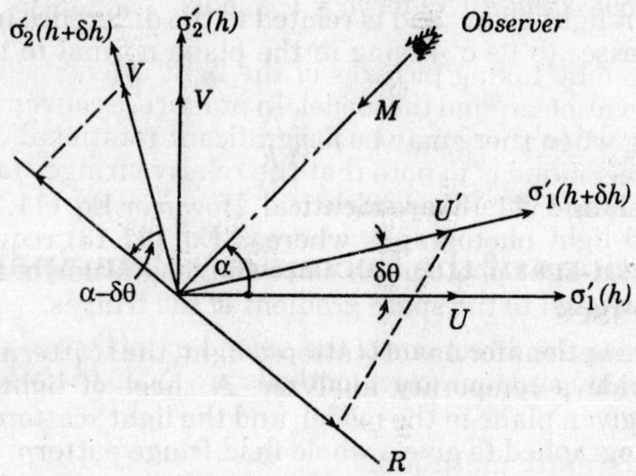

Fig. 11.8 Scattered light resultant.

If the secondary principal stresses rotate by $\delta\theta$ between h and $h + \delta h$ of the material, then the expression for scattered-light intensity as derived by Aderholdt et. al. is given by (Fig. 11.8),

$$I_\alpha = \gamma\,[a^2 \sin^2(\alpha - \delta\theta) - 2ab\cos(\psi + \delta\psi) \times \cos(\alpha - \delta\theta)\sin(\alpha - \delta\theta) + b^2\cos(\alpha - \delta\theta)] \quad ...(11.16)$$

A relative fringe is defined as any point along the light path where I_α reaches a relative minimum value but not zero ; an absolute fringe is defined as any point along the light path where I_α becomes zero.

First, consider a stressed birefringent medium with continuous rotation of the secondary principal axes and set $a = b$. Eq. (11.16) reduces to

$$I_\alpha = \gamma a^2\,[1 - \cos(\psi + \delta\psi)\sin 2(\alpha - \delta\theta)] \quad ...(11.17)$$

Considering this equation, absolute fringes can occur only if $\cos(\psi + \delta\psi) = 1$ and $\sin 2(\alpha - \delta\theta) = 1$. Therefore, if the observation angle is rotated such that

$$(\alpha - \delta\theta) = (2m - 1)\frac{\pi}{4},\ m = 1, 2, 3.... \quad ...(11.18)$$

as the observer moves along the light path, absolute fringes will occur as a result of the difference in secondary principal stresses at points where

$$\psi + \delta\psi = 2n\pi,\ n = 1, 2, 3.... \quad ...(11.19)$$

Since only $(\psi + \delta\psi)$ determines where along the light path absolute fringes occur, the spacing dN/dh will not be altered by rotation of the secondary principal axes. Thus, the difference in the secondary principal stresses can be correctly expressed by

$$\sigma'_1 - \sigma'_2 = f_\sigma \frac{dN}{dh} \qquad ...(11.20)$$

The difficulty of moving the observation point along h and rotating such that

$$(\alpha - \delta\theta) = (2m - 1)\frac{\pi}{4} \text{ for } m = 1, 2, 3.....$$

can be overcome by taking pictures of the light intensity at different angles of observation around the model. In practice, a convenient means of determining when there may be a significant rotational error and a need for this technique is to note that the relative fringes fade as they are observed along h at a fixed angle α.

11.5 Directions of the Secondary Principal Stresses

To determine the directions of the secondary principal stress axes, three approximate and four exact methods are available, which may be listed as follows :

(*a*) **Approximate methods**
1. Displaced pattern method.
2. Sharpest contrast method.
3. Minimum intensity method.

(*b*) **Exact methods**
1. Constant intensity method.
2. Zero intensity method.
3. Intensity variation method.
4. Absolute intensity method.

11.5.1 Approximate methods

The approximate locations of the secondary principal axes can be readily found by visual observation without a compensator or a photometer.

1. **Displaced pattern method.** When looking along either one of the two secondary principal axes the center of the local scattered light pattern is of uniform brightness, and the fringes on opposite sides of this region become displaced relative to each other by half a fringe. The discontinuity in the fringes arises because for a direction of observation on one side of the uniform region α is less than $\pi/2$ and on the other side it is greater than $\pi/2$. Therefore the same retardation $2\,m\pi$ will produce dark fringes on one side and bright fringes on the other.

2. **Sharpest contrast method.** This method consists in rotating the model until the scattered light stress pattern appears of sharpest contrast to the naked eye when viewed along the line of vision of the photometer. In this position the secondary principal axes are approximately at ±45° to the line of vision of the photometer.

3. **Minimum intensity method.** This method rests on the fact that for circularly polarized light the axes of the light ellipse are independent

of the birefringence and are always inclined at ± 45°, approximately, to the directions of the secondary principal stresses. Hence, the determination of one of the axes of the ellipse also determines the directions of the secondary principal stresses. The direction of the major axis of the ellipse can be readily and accurately located with a photometer, as the intensity of the light is minimum for observations along the major axis.

11.5.2 Exact methods

In the exact methods the observations are made by means of a compensator and a photometer.

1. **The constant intensity method.** This method is based on the assumption that, for directions of observations along the principal axes, the intensity of scattered light is independent of the retardation. Hence, by varying the birefringence at any point by a suitably placed compensator at the entrance, one can hunt for the direction along which the scattered light intensity remains constant. This assumption is equivalent to saying that the amplitudes of the light vectors along the principal axes remain constant when the birefringence at that point is changed, and that the light ellipse would rotate inside a rectangle with sides $2a$ and $2b$. However, when rotation is present, the amplitudes a and b changes as follows :

$$\frac{da}{dh} = b \cos \psi \frac{d\phi}{dh}$$
$$\frac{db}{dh} = -a \cos \psi \frac{d\phi}{dh} \qquad ...(11.21)$$

Since, in general, the rate of rotation of the secondary axes $d\phi/dh \neq 0$, the amplitudes do change with the retardation. The light ellipse would still rotate since the values of ψ, a and b all change, but it would no longer be bound inside the original rectangle. The total intensity, however, would remain constant, since, from Eqs. (11.21)

$$a\,da + b\,db = 0$$
or
$$a^2 + b^2 = \text{const.} \qquad ...(11.22)$$

when $d\phi/dh$ is small, these changes are negligible and the photometer shows no variation in light intensity.

2. **The zero intensity method.** This method is based on the fact that whenever $\psi = 2\,m\pi$ or $(2m - 1)\,\pi$, the ellipse generates into a line ellipse and the intensity of scattered light is zero for a direction of observation along this line. To achieve this the compensator is adjusted so that for a given direction of observation, α, the intensity becomes a minimum or a maximum. For $\alpha < \pi/2$, the intensity will be a minimum when $\psi = 2\,m\pi$ and a maximum when $\psi = (2m - 1)\,\pi$. If $\alpha > \pi/2$ then these conditions are reversed. This method is valid only when a and b do not change with ψ. When $\psi = 2\,m\pi$, the line is inclined at an angle $\beta_1 = \tan^{-1}(b/a)$ and when $\psi = (2m - 1)\,\pi$ the line is inclined at an angle $\beta_1 = \tan^{-1}(-b/a)$ to the u-axis. The intensities of scattered light for observations along these lines will be zero.

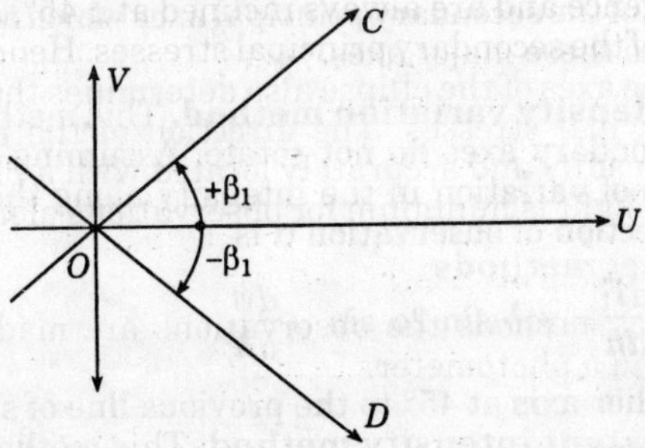

Fig. 11.9 The possible positions of line ellipse *OC* and *OD*.

We begin by adjusting the compensator to make the intensity at a point a minimum for an arbitrary direction of observation such as *OM* in Fig. 11.2. Assuming α to be less than $\pi/2$, ψ will then have assumed a value $2\,m\pi$ and the light ellipse will have become a straight line *CO* (Fig. 11.9), making an angle $\beta_1 = \tan^{-1} b/a$ with the *u*-axis. This line can be located with a photometer. Next, keeping approximately the same direction of observation *OM*, we adjust the compensator to give the maximum light intensity. This time the light ellipse will have become once again a straight line *OD*, inclined at an angle $\beta_1 = \tan^{-1}\left(\frac{-b}{a}\right)$ to the *u*-axis. This line is also located with a photometer. The directions *CO* and *DO*, are equally inclined with respect to $\sigma'_1 - \sigma'_2$.

$$\text{Now } \frac{dI_\alpha}{d\psi} = \left\{\left(\frac{da}{d\psi}\right)[2ab \cot 2\alpha + (b^2 - a^2)\cos\psi] - ab^2 \sin\psi\right\} \times \left(-\frac{\gamma}{b}\sin 2\alpha\right) \quad \text{...(11.23)}$$

If I_α were to reach a maximum or a minimum, $\psi = 2m\pi$ or $(2m-1)\pi$, only if $da/d\psi = 0$. If $da/d\psi \neq 0$, the condition for $dI_\alpha/d\psi$ to be zero would be

$$\cos^2\psi\left[\left(\frac{da}{d\psi}\right)^2(b^2 - a^2) + a^2 b^4\right] + \cos\psi\left[\left(\frac{da}{d\psi}\right)^2 (b^2 - a^2)\, 4ab \cot 2\alpha\right] + \left[\left(\frac{da}{d\psi}\right)^2 4a^2b^2 \cot^2 2\alpha - a^2 b^4\right] = 0 \quad \text{...(11.24)}$$

The above equation will give two values for ψ one of which will make I_α a minimum and the other a maximum. In both of these cases, the light ellipse will have become very close to line ellipses and for lines of sight along their major axes, the light intensity will be minimum and very nearly equal to zero. Location of these major axes will determine the directions of the secondary principal axes which are equally inclined with respect to these major axes.

3. **The intensity variation method.** This method is strictly valid when the secondary axes do not rotate. Assuming no rotation of the axes, the rate of variation in the intensity along the wave normal for any given direction of observation α is

$$\frac{dI_1^*}{dh} = \gamma ab \sin 2\alpha \sin \psi \frac{d\psi}{dh}$$

choosing another axis at 45° to the previous line of sight

$$\frac{dI_2^*}{dh} = \gamma ab \cos 2\alpha \sin \psi \frac{d\psi}{dh}$$

Dividing we get

$$(dI_1^*/dh)/(dI_2^*/dh) = \tan 2\alpha \qquad ...(11.25)$$

The effect of rotation of axes may be eliminated if one starts with a circularly polarized light such that $a \approx b$ at any point and the retardation ψ is made equal to an odd multiple of half wavelength.

4. **The absolute intensity method.** This method is also called the 'dual observation method' and depends upon the measurement of light intensities along two directions 45° apart. Instead of measuring dI/dh as in the intensity variation method, this method compares the light intensities before and after loading. This method is strictly valid for the case when the secondary axes do not rotate. Neglecting completely the rotation of secondary axes, the intensities of scattered light for two directions of observation 45° apart are given by

$$I_1 = \frac{1}{2}\gamma A^2 (1 + \cos 2\alpha \sin \psi)$$

$$I_2 = \frac{1}{2}\gamma A^2 (1 + \sin 2\alpha \sin \psi)$$

From these $\alpha = \tan^{-1}\left(\dfrac{I_2 - \gamma A^2}{I_1 - \gamma A^2}\right)$ ...(11.26)

and $$\psi = \sin\left[\frac{2}{\gamma A^2}\left\{\left(I_1 - \frac{1}{2}\gamma A^2\right)^2 + \left(I_2 - \frac{1}{2}\gamma A^2\right)^2\right\}\right]$$

where $\gamma A^2 = I_0$ is the total intensity of scattered light before the load is applied and circularly polarized light is assumed to traverse the model.

Using finite differences, Eq. (11.25) can be written as

$$\tan 2\alpha = \frac{(I_1)_{h+dh} - (I_1)_h}{(I_2)_{h+dh} - (I_2)_h} \qquad ...(11.27)$$

Due to the inherent difficulties in the measurement of the absolute intensity of scattered light, such as varying absorption over different optical paths, this method is not practicable.

In addition to these methods another 'Mini-max Method' has been proposed by Srinath. Assuming α less than $\pi/2$, the maximum and minimum intensities of scattered light are given by

$$(I_\alpha)_{max} = \gamma\,(a \sin \alpha + b \cos \alpha)^2 = \mu_1^2$$

$$(I_\alpha)_{min} = \gamma\,(a \sin \alpha - b \cos \alpha)^2 = \mu_2^2$$

$$\text{Hence } I_\alpha = \frac{1}{2}\left\{(I_\alpha)_{max} + (I_\alpha)_{min} - \cos \psi\,[(I_\alpha)_{max} - (I_\alpha)_{min}]\right\}$$

or
$$\cos \psi = -\frac{2I_\alpha + [(I_\alpha)_{max} + (I_\alpha)_{min}]}{(I_\alpha)_{max} - (I_\alpha)_{min}}$$

$$= \frac{2I_\alpha + (\mu_1 + \mu_2)}{(\mu_1 - \mu_2)}$$

Further if α and β are two directions of observations 90° apart then

$$(I_\beta)_{max} = \gamma\,(a \cos \alpha + b \sin \alpha)^2 = \mu_3^2$$

$$(I_\beta)_{min} = \gamma\,(a \cos \alpha - b \sin \alpha)^2 = \mu_4^2$$

From these

$$\tan \alpha = \frac{\mu_1 + \mu_2}{\mu_3 + \mu_4} \qquad ...(11.28)$$

This method has the advantage that the rotational effect is removed since the ratio of μ is involved and absolute values of ab do not appear in the final equation. As the light intensities are used in their maximum and minimum magnitudes, the error are also reduced.

11.6 Solution of General Three Dimensional Problems

In the case of a general three-dimensional problem where all the six rectangular stress components are present, the scattered light method gives the values of $(\sigma_x - \sigma_y)$, $(\sigma_y - \sigma_z)$, $(\sigma_z - \sigma_x)$, τ_{xy}, τ_{yz} and τ_{zx} in the following manner :

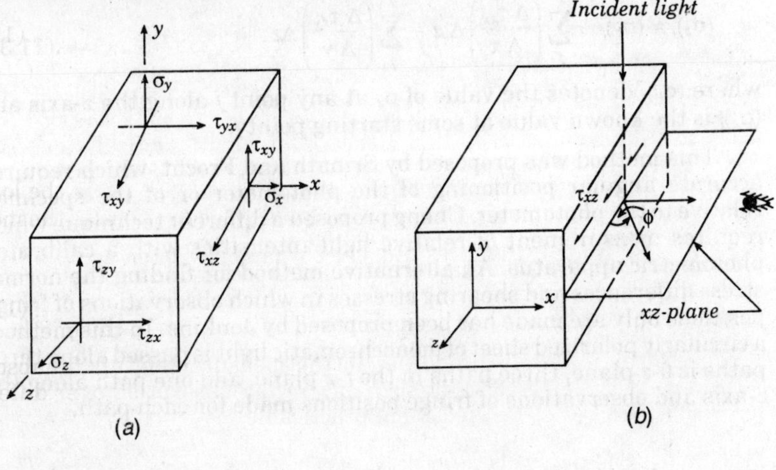

(a) (b)

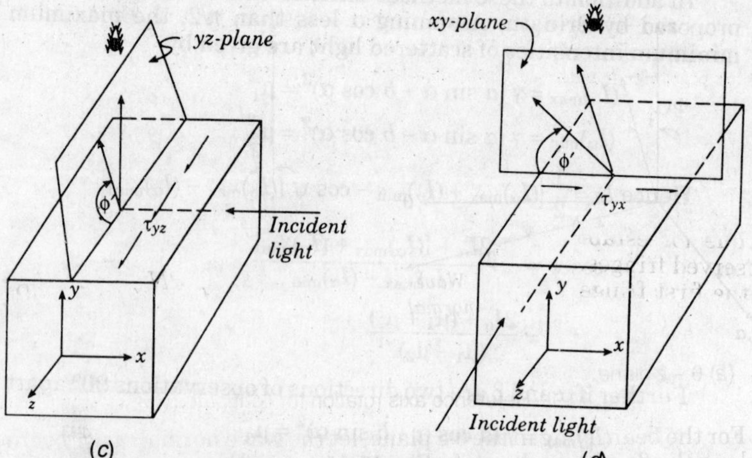

Fig. 11.10 Method for determining the three shears.

By sending the incident light beam in a direction parallel to y-axis (Fig. 11.10 *b*), and making scattered light observations in the XZ plane one can get the secondary principal stress difference $(\sigma'_1 - \sigma'_2)$ in the xz-plane and also the directions of σ'_1 and σ'_2. If ϕ' is the orientation of the σ'_1 stress with respect to the z-axis, then

$$\tau_{xy} = \frac{\sigma'_1 - \sigma'_2}{2} \sin 2\phi'$$

and $$(\sigma_z - \sigma_x) = (\sigma'_1 - \sigma'_2) \cos 2\phi' \qquad ...(11.29)$$

Similarly, by sending the light beam along the x-direction (Fig. 11.10 *c*), and making scattered light observations in the yz-plane one can determine τ_{yz} and $(\sigma_y - \sigma_z)$. Lastly by sending the incident light beam in the z-direction (Fig. 11.10 *d*), we can determine τ_{xy} and $(\sigma_x - \sigma_y)$. The individual normal stresses can be found by means of the shear difference method. For example, along the z-axis

$$(\sigma_z)_j \approx (\sigma_z)_f - \sum_f^j \left(\frac{\Delta \tau_{zx}}{\Delta x}\right) \Delta z - \sum_f^j \left(\frac{\Delta \tau_{xy}}{\Delta y}\right) \Delta z \qquad ...(11.30)$$

where $(\sigma_z)_j$ denotes the value of σ_z at any point j along the z-axis and $(\sigma_z)_f$ is the known value at some starting point f.

This method was proposed by Srinath and Frocht, which requires accurate angular positioning of the photometer or of the specimen relative to the photometer. Cheng proposed a different technique which requires measurement of relative light intensities with a calibrated photometric apparatus. An alternative method for finding the normal stress differences and shearing stresses in which observations of fringe positions only are made has been proposed by Jenkins. In this method, a circularly polarized sheet of monochromatic light is passed along three paths is θ-z plane, three paths in the r-z plane, and one path along the z-axis and observations of fringe positions made for each path.

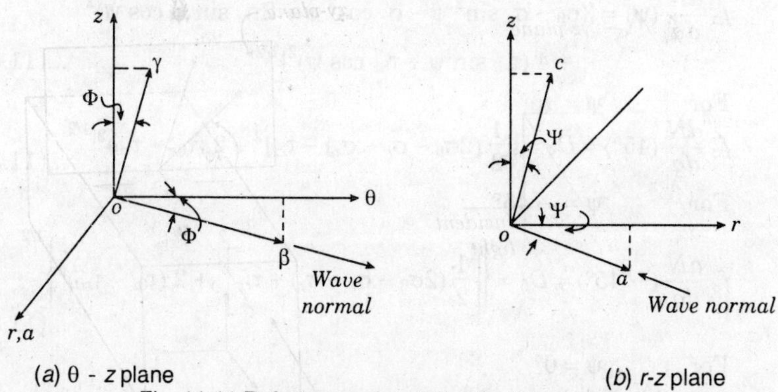

Fig. 11.11 Reference axis rotation for light paths.

For the beam lying in the θ-*z* plane, let the wave normal of the beam be along the β-axis, as shown in Fig. 11.11 (*a*), in the positive direction of the axis. Then

$$\left\{(\sigma_\alpha - \sigma_\gamma)^2 + 4\tau_{\alpha\gamma}^2\right\}^{1/2} = f_\sigma \frac{dN}{d\beta} \qquad ...(11.31)$$

The three-dimensional stress transformation equations give the stresses in the rotated set of axes in terms of the stresses in the original set of axes as follows

$$\left.\begin{aligned} \sigma_\alpha &= \sigma_r \\ \tau_{\alpha\gamma} &= \tau_{r\theta} \sin\phi + \tau_{rz}\cos\phi \\ \sigma_\gamma &= \sigma_\theta \sin^2\phi + \sigma_z\cos^2\phi + 2\,\tau_{\theta z}\sin\phi\cos\phi \end{aligned}\right\} \qquad ...(11.32)$$

Substituting in Eq. (11.31), we get

$$f_\sigma \frac{dN}{d\beta}(\phi) = [(\sigma_r - \sigma_\theta\sin^2\phi - \sigma_z\cos^2\phi - 2\tau_{\theta z}\sin\phi\cos\phi)^2 + 4\,(\tau_{r\theta}\sin\phi + \tau_{rz}\cos\phi)^2]^{1/2} \qquad ...(11.33)$$

Eq. (11.33) applies for any angle ϕ. Three convenient paths on directions of the wave normal are selected.

If $\phi = 45°$, then

$$f_\sigma \frac{dN}{d\beta}(45°) = D_1 = \left\{[\frac{1}{2}(2\sigma_r - \sigma_\theta - \sigma_z) - \tau_{\theta z}]^2 + 2\,(\tau_{rz} + \tau_{r\theta})^2\right\}^{1/2} \qquad ...(11.34)$$

and if $\phi = -45°$

$$f_\sigma \frac{dN}{d\beta}(-45°) = D_4 = \left\{[\frac{1}{2}(2\sigma_r - \sigma_\theta - \sigma_z) + \tau_{\theta z}]^2 + 2\,(\tau_{rz} - \tau_{r\theta})^2\right\}^{1/2} \qquad ...(11.35)$$

when $\phi = 0°$, then

$$f_\sigma \frac{dN}{d\beta}(0°) = D_3 = \left\{(\sigma_r - \sigma_z)^2 + 4\tau_{rz}^2\right\}^{1/2} \qquad ...(11.36)$$

Now let the beam lie in the *r*-*z* plane and let the wave normal be along the *a*-axis in the negative *a*-direction as shown in Fig. 11.11 (*b*). Following the same procedure as above, we get

$$f_\sigma \frac{dN}{da}(\psi) = [(\sigma_\theta - \sigma_r \sin^2\psi - \sigma_z \cos^2\psi + 2\tau_{rz} \sin\psi \cos\psi)^2 + 4(\tau_{r\theta} \sin\psi + \tau_{\theta z} \cos\psi)^2]^{1/2} \quad ...(11.37)$$

For $\psi = 45°$

$$f_\sigma \frac{dN}{da}(45°) = D_4 = \left\{\left[\frac{1}{2}(2\sigma_\theta - \sigma_r - \sigma_z) - \tau_{rz}\right]^2 + 2(\tau_{\theta z} + \tau_{r\theta})^2\right\}^{1/2} \quad ...(11.38)$$

For $\psi = -45°$

$$f_\sigma \frac{dN}{da}(-45°) = D_5 = \left\{\left[\frac{1}{2}(2\sigma_\theta - \sigma_r - \sigma_z) + \tau_{rz}\right]^2 + 2(\tau_{\theta z} - \tau_{r\theta})^2\right\}^{1/2} \quad ...(11.39)$$

For $\psi = 0°$

$$f_\sigma \frac{dN}{da}(0°) = D_6 = [(\sigma_\theta - \sigma_z)^2 + 4\tau_{\theta z}^2]^{1/2} \quad ...(11.40)$$

and for $\psi = 90°$

$$f_\sigma \frac{dN}{da}(90°) = D_7 = [(\sigma_r - \sigma_\theta)^2 + 4\tau_{r\theta}^2]^{1/2} \quad ...(11.41)$$

In Eq. (11.41) the wave normal is along the z-axis in the positive direction.

By algebraic manipulation we find that

$$\pm(\sigma_z - \sigma_\theta) = [-D_1^2 - D_2^2 + D_3^2 + \frac{1}{2}(D_6^2 + D_7^2]^{1/2} \quad ...(11.42)$$

$$\pm\tau_{\theta z} = \frac{1}{2}[D_1^2 + D_2^2 - D_3^2 + \frac{1}{2}D_6^2 - D_7^2]^{1/2} \quad ...(11.43)$$

$$\pm(\sigma_z - \sigma_r) = \left[\frac{1}{2}D_3^2 - D_4^2 - D_5^2 + D_6^2 + D_7^2\right]^{1/2} \quad ...(11.44)$$

$$\pm\tau_{rz} = \frac{1}{2}\left[\frac{1}{2}D_3^2 + D_4^2 + D_5^2 - D_6^2 - D_7^2\right]^{1/2} \quad ...(11.45)$$

$$(\sigma_r - \sigma_\theta) = (\sigma_z - \sigma_\theta) - (\sigma_z - \sigma_r) \quad ...(11.46)$$

$$\pm\tau_{\theta r} = \frac{1}{2}(D_7^2 - (\sigma_r - \sigma_\theta)^2]^{1/2} \quad ...(11.47)$$

When the r-z plane is a plane of symmetry, the shearing stresses $\tau_{r\theta} = \tau_{\theta z} = 0$ and σ_θ is a principal stress. When the circularly polarized beam of thin sheet of light lies in the r-z plane. Eqs. (11.45) to (11.47) become,

$$f_\sigma \frac{dN}{da}(45°) = \frac{1}{2}(2\sigma_\theta - \sigma_r - \sigma_z) - \tau_{rz} \quad ...(11.43)$$

$$f_\sigma \frac{dN}{da}(-45°) = \frac{1}{2}(2\sigma_\theta - \sigma_r - \sigma_z) + \tau_{rz} \quad ...(11.49)$$

$$f_\sigma \frac{dN}{da}(0°) = \sigma_\theta - \sigma_z \quad ...(11.50)$$

Since only $\sigma_z - \sigma_\theta$, $\sigma_r - \sigma_\theta$ and τ_{rz} are non-zero quantities, observations for these three light paths are sufficient. Solving Eqs. (11.48) to

(11.50) for the unknown normal stress differences and the shearing stresses gives

$$\sigma_r - \sigma_\theta = D_6 - D_4 - D_5 \qquad ...(11.51)$$

$$\tau_{rz} = \frac{1}{2}(D_5 - D_4)$$

11.7 Establishing the Boundary Retardation

Aderholdt and Swinson (1971) proposed a technique for establishing the boundary retardation with respect to the observed fringes. In general problem, it is uncertain as to which value the first fringe takes without carefully analyzing the entering light for a given polariscope and model material. However, it is possible to assign the first observed fringe a number with respect to the boundary and thus utilize the boundary as an extra data point.

In most instances, the light source for the scattered light polariscope is a laser and the plane of the polarization is easily noted, which can be used as a reference for angle measurements and calibration of the polariscope arrangement for a given model material. All angles will be measured using the "right hand screw-rule" with the thumb along the propagating light path, the fingers will point in the positive direction of angle measurement. To circularize the light, set the maximum axis of the *QWP* at +45° to the plane of polarization, so that the light component emerging from the *QWP* along this axis leads by 90° the component along the other axis, the minimum axis. When the light component along the maximum secondary principal stress axis of the model is leading the minimum component, then it can be shown that (Fig. 11.12).

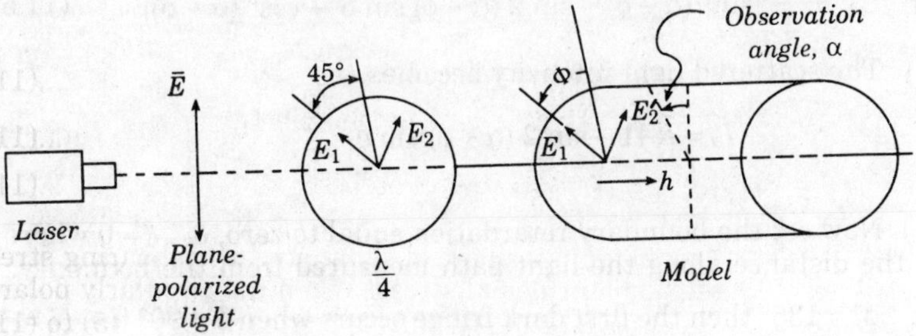

Fig. 11.12. Light components.

$$\left.\begin{aligned} E'_1 &= \frac{A}{\sqrt{2}} \cos\left(\omega t + \frac{\pi}{4} - \phi\right) \\ E'_2 &= -\frac{A}{\sqrt{2}} \sin\left(\omega t + \frac{\pi}{4} - \phi + \delta\right) \end{aligned}\right\} \qquad ...(11.52)$$

where E'_1 = component along maximum secondary principal stress axis.

E'_2 = component along minimum secondary principal stress axis.

ϕ = angle between plane of polarization and maximum secondary principal stress axis.

δ = retardation.

A = maximum magnitude of the linear polarized light vector before entering *QWP*.

The resultant scattered light amplitude observed from an angle α is

$$E_s = E'_1 \cos(\alpha - \phi) - E'_2 \sin(\alpha - \phi) \quad \text{...(11.53)}$$

or
$$E_s = \frac{A}{\sqrt{2}} \left[\{\cos(\alpha - \phi) + \sin(\alpha - \phi) \sin \delta\} \cos\left(\omega t + \frac{\pi}{4} - \phi\right) + \{\sin(\alpha - \phi) \cos \delta\} \sin\left(\omega t + \frac{\pi}{4} - \phi\right)\right] \quad \text{...(11.54)}$$

Eq. (11.54) is of the form

$$E_s = -C_1 \sin \xi \sin\left(\omega t + \frac{\pi}{4} - \phi\right) + C_1 \cos \xi \cos\left(\omega t + \frac{\pi}{4} - \phi\right) \quad \text{...(11.55)}$$

or
$$E_s = C_1 \cos\left(\omega t + \frac{\pi}{4} - \phi + \xi\right) \quad \text{...(11.56)}$$

where $-C_1 \sin \xi = \frac{A}{\sqrt{2}} \sin(\alpha - \phi) \cos \delta$

$$C_1 \sin \xi = \frac{A}{\sqrt{2}} [\cos(\alpha - \phi) + \sin \delta \sin(\alpha - \phi)]$$

or
$$C_1^2 = \frac{A^2}{2} [\sin^2(\alpha - \phi) + \sin 2(\alpha - \phi) \sin \delta + \cos^2(\alpha - \phi)] \quad \text{...(11.57)}$$

The scattered light intensity becomes

$$I_\alpha = K [1 + \sin 2(\alpha - \phi) \sin \delta] \quad \text{...(11.58)}$$

Now set the boundary retardation equal to zero, $\delta_{h=0} = 0$ where h is the distance along the light path measured from the boundary. If $(\alpha - \phi) = 135°$ then the first dark fringe occurs when $\delta = 90°$ (*i.e.* $N = \frac{1}{4}$). If $(\alpha - \phi) = 45°$, then the first dark fringe occurs when $\delta = \frac{3\pi}{2}$ (*i.e.* $N = \frac{3}{4}$). Hence, if $(\alpha - \phi) = 135°$, the boundary retardation is $\frac{1}{4}$ of a fringe less than the first observed fringe, while if $(\alpha - \phi) = 45°$, then the boundary retarding is $\frac{3}{4}$ of a fringe less than the first observed fringe. With this information, the retardation on the boundary can be used as data which improves the accuracy in determining the fringe spacing.

11.8 Scattered Light Technique for Two Dimensional Problems

When a plane-polarized beam of light enters a stressed birefringent medium, it is resolved into components along the secondary principal-stress directions of the plane perpendicular to the direction of light propagation. As these components traverse the model, they acquire a relative retardation which is proportional to the difference in these secondary principal stresses and fringes are formed. The fringes are related to the secondary principal stresses by the stress-optic law

$$\sigma'_1 - \sigma'_2 = f_\sigma \frac{\partial N}{\partial x}$$

where x is the direction of light propagation. For the case of plane stress where light propagates in plane of the model, the stress-optic law becomes,

$$\sigma_y = f_\sigma \frac{\partial N}{\partial x} \qquad ...(11.59)$$

where σ_y is the stress acting normal to the x-direction, and direct separation of the stresses is obtained. Integrating σ_y on the domain $i(y) \le x \le v(y)$, where $x = i(y)$ describes the entrance boundary of a model and $x = v(y)$ describes some arbitrary fringes (Fig. 11.13), it follows that

$$\int_{i(y)}^{v(y)} f_y \, dx = \text{const.} \qquad ...(11.60)$$

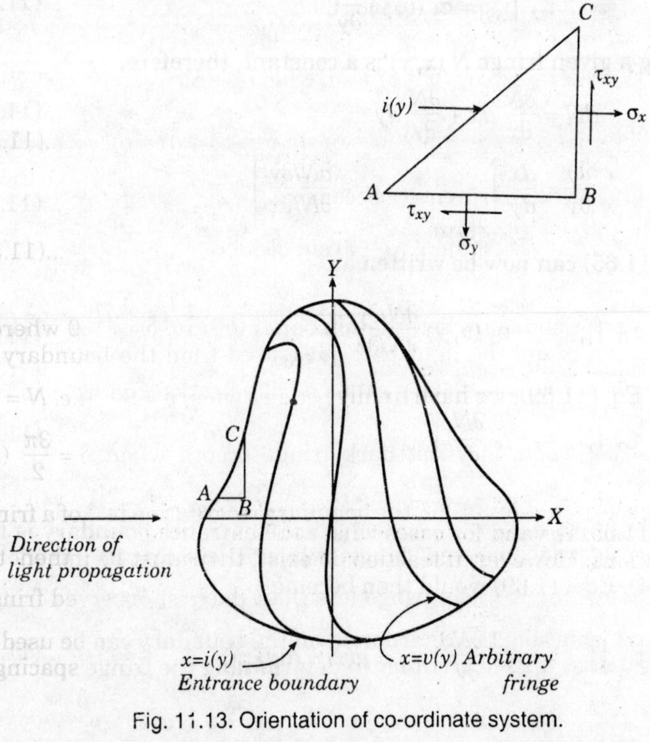

Fig. 11.13. Orientation of co-ordinate system.

Multiplying this expression by model thickness shows that the total vertical load acting on a cross-section from the boundary to a given fringe is constant all along the fringe. Differentiating Eq. (11.60) w.r.t. y yields

$$\frac{\partial}{\partial y}\left[\int_{i(y)}^{v(y)} \sigma_y \, dx\right] = \int_{i(y)}^{v(y)} \frac{\partial \sigma_y}{\partial y} dx + \sigma_y(v, y)\frac{\partial v}{\partial y} - \sigma_y(i, y)\frac{\partial i}{\partial y} = 0 \qquad ...(11.61)$$

From the equilibrium equation in the y-direction, we have

$$\frac{\partial \sigma_y}{\partial y} = -\frac{\partial \tau_{xy}}{\partial x} \qquad ...(11.62)$$

Substituting Eq. (11.62) into the first term of Eq. (11.61) and integrating yields,

$$\tau_{xy}\,\big|_{v(y)} - \tau_{xy}\,\big|_{i(y)} = \sigma_y(v, y)\frac{\partial v}{\partial y} - \sigma_y(i, y)\frac{\partial i}{\partial y} \qquad ...(11.63)$$

By considering the equilibrium in the y-direction of the small element ABC of Fig. 11.13 on the traction free boundary, $x = i(y)$, we have

$$\tau_{xy}\,\big|_{i(y)} = \sigma_y(i, y)\frac{\partial i}{\partial y} \qquad ...(11.64)$$

Thus Eq. (11.63) becomes

$$\tau_{xy}\,\big|_{v(y)} = \sigma_y(v, y)\frac{\partial v}{\partial y} \qquad ...(11.65)$$

Along a given fringe $N(x, y)$ is a constant, therefore,

$$dN = \frac{\partial N}{\partial x} dx + \frac{\partial N}{\partial y} dy \qquad ...(11.66)$$

or

$$\frac{\partial v}{\partial y} = \frac{dx}{dy}\bigg|_{x = v(y)} = -\frac{\partial N/\partial y}{\partial N/\partial x}\bigg|_{x = v(y)} \qquad ...(11.67)$$

Eq. (11.65) can now be written as

$$\left|\ \tau_{xy}\,\big|_{v(y)} = -\sigma_y(v, y)\frac{\partial N/\partial y}{\partial N/\partial x}\ \right|_{x = v(y)} \qquad ...(11.68)$$

With Eq. (11.59), we have finally

$$\tau_{xy}\,\big|_{v(y)} = -f_\sigma \frac{\partial N}{\partial y}\,\Big|_{v(y)} \qquad ...(11.69)$$

Eq. (11.69) is valid for cases where the entrance boundary is free from tractions. However, if traction do exist, they must be included in Eq. (11.64). Eq. (11.69) would then become

$$\tau_{xy}\,\big|_{v(y)} = -f_\sigma \frac{\partial N}{\partial y}\,\Big|_{v(y)} + g(y) + h(y)\frac{\partial i}{\partial y} \qquad ...(11.70)$$

where $g(y)$ and $h(y)$ are the shearing and normal stresses respectively on the entrance boundary. By differentiating Eq. (11.69) and applying the equilibrium equation

$$\frac{\partial \sigma_x}{\partial x} + \frac{\partial \tau_{xy}}{\partial y} = 0$$

we have $$\frac{\partial \sigma_x}{\partial x} = f_\sigma \frac{\partial^2 N}{\partial y^2} \text{ or } \sigma_x = f_\sigma \frac{\partial N}{\partial y} \qquad ...(11.71)$$

Thus $$\sigma_x + \sigma_y = \sigma_1 + \sigma_2 = f_\sigma (\partial N/\partial x + \partial N/\partial y) \qquad ...(11.72)$$

Eqs. (11.59), (11.69) and (11.71) supply the relationship necessary to determine the complete state of stress in a model where the entrance boundary is free from tractions. Thus, in the ideal situation, all information is obtainable from one photograph.

Eq. (11.65) describes the significance of the slope of the fringes, namely τ_{xy}/σ_y. Therefore, points where the fringe slope becomes vertical lie along the same isoclinic path. Isoclinics can also be determined from Eq. (11.69).

Calibration of the model material may be accomplished from the same photograph as follows :

Multiplying Eq. (11.59) by the model thickness and integrating along a path for which the resultant vertical stress is known, gives

$$\int_1^2 h\, \sigma_y\, dx = \int_1^2 f_\sigma h \frac{\partial N}{\partial x} dx \qquad ...(11.73)$$

or $$F = f_\sigma h (N_2 - N_1)$$

Hence $$f_\sigma = \frac{F}{h (N_2 - N_1)} \qquad ...(11.74)$$

where F = resultant vertical force across the section.

11.9 The Scattered Light Polariscope

Fig. 11.14 shows schematically the optical system of a scattered light polariscope. Light from the laser passes through a condenser C and is brought to a focus on the aperature of an iris diaphragm D. The light then passes through a collimator L after which it is projected vertically downwards by means of an inclined mirror M. It then passes through a polarizer P, quarter-wave plate Q, monochromatic filter F and adjustable slit S and finally through the model contained in a tank having immersion fluid whose refractive index is matched with that of the model. Provision is made to allow rotational and translational movement of the model in the tank. It is also sometimes desirable to locate a compensator in the light path forward of the model.

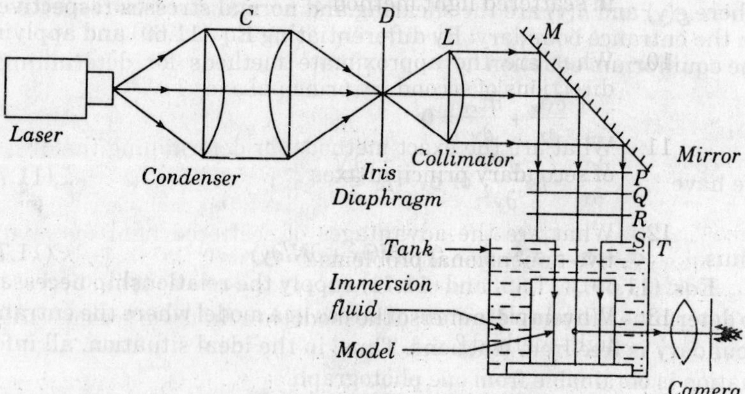

Fig. 11.14 A schematic illustration of scattered light polariscope.

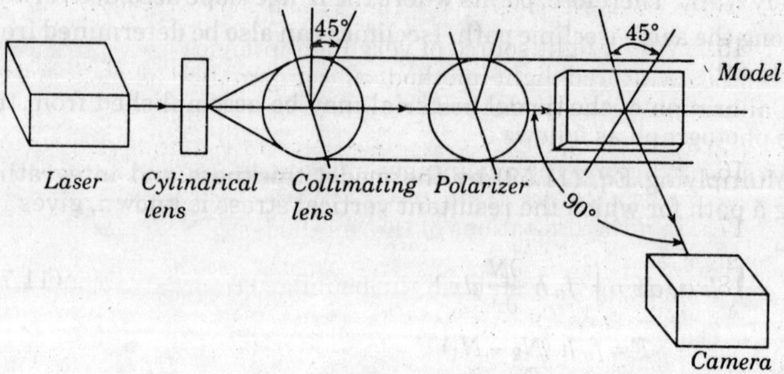

Fig. 11.15 Two-dimensional scattered light polariscope.

Fig. 11.15 shows a scattered light polariscope arrangement used by Hemann and Becherer for two-dimensional analysis.

11.10 Quiz Questions

1. What do you mean by scattering of light ?
2. What do you mean by apparent amplitude of light ?
3. How does the intensity of scattered light varies for (*a*) ordinary light, (*b*) plane polarized light, (*c*) circularly polarized light and (*d*) elliptically polarized light.
4. Who pioneered the use of scattered light in photoelasticity ?
5. How fringes are formed in scattered-light photoelasticity ?
6. What do you unerstand by secondary principal stresses ?
7. State the stress-optic law for scattered light.
8. Of the two options for use of scattered light, which one is generally preferred ?

9. What is the effect of rotation of secondary principal stresses in scattered light method ?

10. What are the approximate methods for determining the directions of secondary principal axes ?

11. What are the exact methods for determining the directions of secondary principal axes ?

12. What are the advantages of scattered light for analysing two-dimensional problems ?

13. Why do we immerse the model in a fluid while using scattered light method ?

14. Along which axis of the light ellipse the intensity of light is maximum ?

15. Why a light source of very high intensity is required for the scattered light method as compared to the conventional photoelastic method ?

16. What are the advantages of the scattered light method ?

17. List the limitations of this method.

18. How do you establish the boundary retardation ?

EXERCISES

11.1 Describe briefly the scattered-light method of photoelastic stress analysis. Discuss the advantages and limitations of this method.

11.2 Derive an expression for the intensity of scattered light for an arbitrary angle of observation. Determine conditions for the light intensity to be maximum or minimum.

11.3 Discuss the stress-optic law for scattered-light method. How does this law differs from the conventional stress-optical law for photoelasticity ?

11.4 Explain briefly the effect of rotation of secondary principal stresses in scattered light photoelasticity. How this effect can be minimised ?

11.5 Discuss briefly the various methods of determining the directions of the secondary principal stresses.

11.6 How the solution to general three-dimensional problems can be obtained by the scattered-light method ? Discuss the simplifications possible in this method.

11.7 Explain briefly how the boundary retardations can be established in the scattered light method.

11.8 Discuss the scattered-light method for two-dimensional problems. What are the advantages of this method over the conventional two-dimensional photoelastic method ?

11.9 Describe the set-up of a scattered light polariscope bringing out the salient features.

12

Grid Method

12.1 Introduction

This is one of the oldest methods of strain analysis, which is whole-field in nature. In order to determine displacements or strain components at given points of arbitrarily shaped surfaces a grid can be engraved on the surface to be studied. This grid acts as a reference element and the changes that the grid experiences from the undeformed to the deformed condition can be utilized to determine either displacements or strains. Two main difficulties are encountered which limit the use of grids for measuring deformations. Firstly, the strains to be measured are usually very small, and in most cases the displacement readings are difficult to make with sufficient accuracy. This is particularly true in elastic stress analysis. However, this method is very much suitable for the study of plastic deformation of rubber like materials. For this method to be applied conveniently the strains must be more than 5 per cent. Particularly when the strains are more than 20 to 33 per cent then only the grid or moire methods may be used. Secondly, when the photographs of the grid network are magnified by a micrometer-microscope or optical comparator, the images of the grid lines are usually poorly defined introducing appreciable errors into the displacement readings. This method has the advantages that a photographic record of deformations covers the entire field of the specimen. This record can be obtained for either static, dynamic, elastic or plastic deformations. The strain is also measured directly.

12.2 Principle of the Method

This method requires placement of a grid of a sufficiently small pitch on the specimen surface and taking photographs before and after loading to obtain negatives which will show that distortion of the grid. Then the strain may be measured from either of the following ways :

$$\text{Lagrangian strain } \varepsilon^L = \frac{l_f - l_i}{l_i} \quad \text{...(12.1)}$$

$$\text{Eulerian strain } \varepsilon^E = \frac{l_f - l_i}{l_f} \quad \text{...(12.2)}$$

$$\text{Natural strain } \bar{\varepsilon} = \ln \frac{l_f}{l_i} \quad \text{...(12.3)}$$

where l_f and l_i are the gauge lengths after and before deformations.

An orthogonal grid consisting of two series of parallel lines will give the strain components over the entire-field. The strain ε_x in the horizontal direction is obtained by comparing the distances between the vertical grid lines before and after deformation ; ε_y from the distance between the horizontal grid, lines and the $\varepsilon_{45°}$ component of strain can be obtained from measurements across the diagonal if the grid array is square.

12.3 Strain-Displacement Relations for Large Strains

Since the grid method is very much suitable for measuring large strains so we present below the large strain-displacement relations. These relations can be either expressed in Lagrangian description or Eulerian description. In the Lagrangian description as shown in Fig. 12.1 the initial line is parallel to x-axis whereas in the Eulerian description (Fig. 12.2) the displaced line is parallel to x-axis.

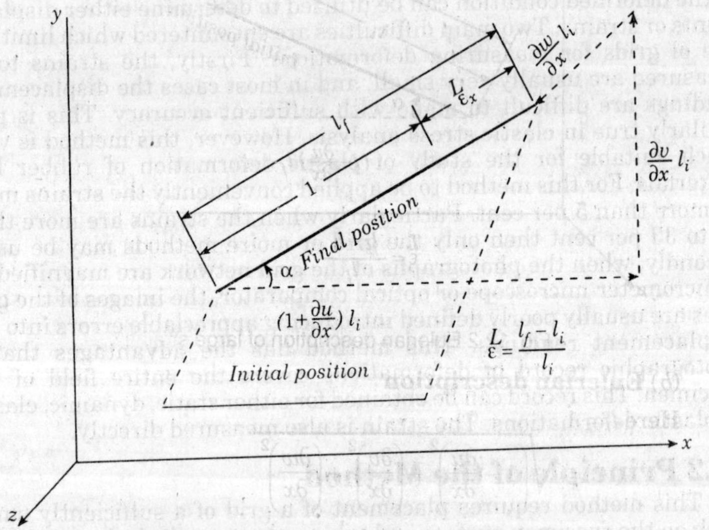

Fig. 12.1 Lagrangian description of large strains.

12.3.1 Normal Strains

(*a*) **Lagrangian description.** If u, v, w are the displacement components along the x, y and z axes respectively, then

$$l_f = \sqrt{\left(1 + \frac{\partial u}{\partial x}\right)^2 + \left(\frac{\partial v}{\partial x}\right)^2 + \left(\frac{\partial w}{\partial x}\right)^2} \qquad ...(12.4)$$

Assuming $l_i = 1$

$$\varepsilon_x^L = \sqrt{1 + 2\frac{\partial u}{\partial x} + \left(\frac{\partial u}{\partial x}\right)^2 + \left(\frac{\partial v}{\partial x}\right)^2 + \left(\frac{\partial w}{\partial x}\right)^2} - 1 \quad \text{...(12.5)}$$

Similarly, $$\varepsilon_y^L = \sqrt{1 + 2\frac{\partial v}{\partial y} + \left(\frac{\partial u}{\partial y}\right)^2 + \left(\frac{\partial v}{\partial y}\right)^2 + \left(\frac{\partial w}{\partial y}\right)^2} - 1 \quad \text{...(12.6)}$$

$$\varepsilon_z^L = \sqrt{1 + 2\frac{\partial w}{\partial z} + \left(\frac{\partial u}{\partial z}\right)^2 + \left(\frac{\partial v}{\partial z}\right)^2 + \left(\frac{\partial w}{\partial z}\right)^2} - 1 \quad \text{...(12.7)}$$

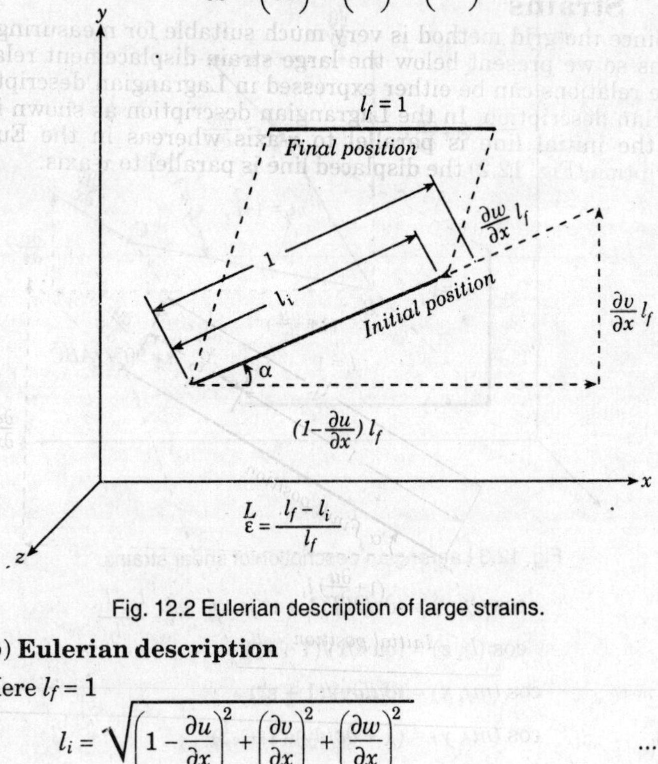

Fig. 12.2 Eulerian description of large strains.

(*b*) Eulerian description

Here $l_f = 1$

$$l_i = \sqrt{\left(1 - \frac{\partial u}{\partial x}\right)^2 + \left(\frac{\partial v}{\partial x}\right)^2 + \left(\frac{\partial w}{\partial x}\right)^2} \quad \text{...(12.8)}$$

$$\varepsilon_x^E = 1 - \sqrt{1 - 2\frac{\partial u}{\partial x} + \left(\frac{\partial u}{\partial x}\right)^2 + \left(\frac{\partial v}{\partial x}\right)^2 + \left(\frac{\partial w}{\partial x}\right)^2} \quad \text{...(12.9)}$$

Similarly

$$\varepsilon_y^E = 1 - \sqrt{1 - 2\frac{\partial v}{\partial y} + \left(\frac{\partial u}{\partial y}\right)^2 + \left(\frac{\partial v}{\partial y}\right)^2 + \left(\frac{\partial w}{\partial y}\right)^2} \quad \text{...(12.10)}$$

$$\varepsilon_z^E = 1 - \sqrt{1 - 2\frac{\partial w}{\partial z} + \left(\frac{\partial u}{\partial z}\right)^2 + \left(\frac{\partial v}{\partial z}\right)^2 + \left(\frac{\partial w}{\partial z}\right)^2} \quad \text{...(12.11)}$$

12.3.2 Shear strain

In Lagrangian description as shown in Fig. 12.3, we have

$$\gamma^L = 90 - \angle ABC$$

$$\sin \gamma^L = \sin (90° - \angle ABC) = \cos \angle ABC$$

$$\cos (l_f, x) = \left(1 + \frac{\partial u}{\partial x}\right) \Big/ (1 + \varepsilon_x^L)$$

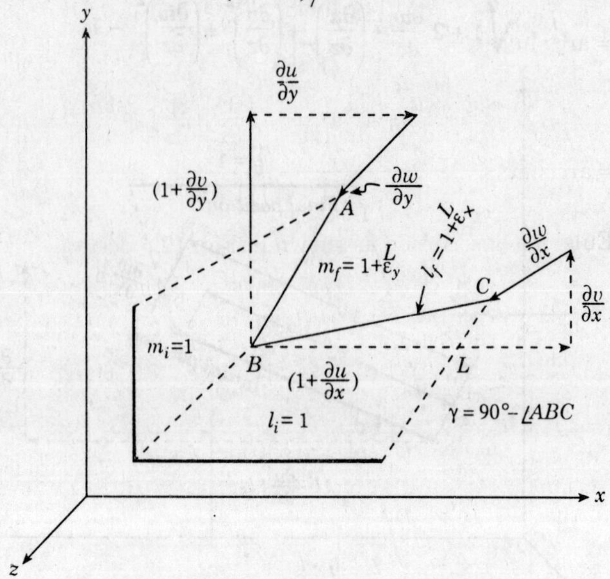

Fig. 12.3 Lagrangian description of shear strains.

$$\cos (l_f, y) = (\partial v/\partial x)/(1 + \varepsilon_x^L)$$

$$\cos (l_f, z) = (\partial w/\partial x)/(1 + \varepsilon_x^L)$$

$$\cos (m_f, x) = (\partial u/\partial y)/(1 + \varepsilon_y^L)$$

$$\cos (m_f, y) = (1 + \partial v/\partial y)/(1 + \varepsilon_y^L)$$

$$\cos (m_f, z) = (\partial w/\partial y)/(1 + \varepsilon_y^L)$$

$$\gamma_{xy}^L = \text{arc sin} \left\{ \left(1 + \frac{\partial u}{\partial x}\right)\left(\frac{\partial u}{\partial y}\right) \Big/ (1 + \varepsilon_x^L)(1 + \varepsilon_y^L) + \left(\frac{\partial v}{\partial x}\right)\left(1 + \frac{\partial v}{\partial y}\right) \Big/ (1 + \varepsilon_x^L)(1 + \varepsilon_y^L) + \left(\frac{\partial w}{\partial x}\right)\left(\frac{\partial w}{\partial y}\right) \Big/ (1 + \varepsilon_x^L)(1 + \varepsilon_y^L) \right\}$$

$$= \text{arc sin}\left[\frac{\frac{\partial u}{\partial y}+\frac{\partial v}{\partial x}+\left(\frac{\partial u}{\partial x}\right)\left(\frac{\partial u}{\partial y}\right)+\left(\frac{\partial v}{\partial x}\right)\left(\frac{\partial v}{\partial y}\right)+\left(\frac{\partial w}{\partial x}\right)\left(\frac{\partial w}{\partial y}\right)}{(1+\varepsilon_x^L)\,(1+\varepsilon_y^L)}\right]$$

Similarly

$$\gamma_{yz}^L = \text{arc sin}\left[\frac{\frac{\partial v}{\partial z}+\frac{\partial w}{\partial y}+\left(\frac{\partial u}{\partial y}\right)\left(\frac{\partial u}{\partial z}\right)+\left(\frac{\partial v}{\partial y}\right)\left(\frac{\partial v}{\partial z}\right)+\left(\frac{\partial w}{\partial y}\right)\left(\frac{\partial w}{\partial z}\right)}{(1+\varepsilon_z^L)\,(1+\varepsilon_z^L)}\right]$$

$$\gamma_{zx}^L = \text{arc sin}\left[\frac{\frac{\partial w}{\partial x}+\frac{\partial u}{\partial z}+\left(\frac{\partial u}{\partial x}\right)\left(\frac{\partial u}{\partial z}\right)+\left(\frac{\partial v}{\partial x}\right)\left(\frac{\partial v}{\partial z}\right)+\left(\frac{\partial w}{\partial x}\right)\left(\frac{\partial w}{\partial z}\right)}{(1+\varepsilon_z^L)\,(1+\varepsilon_x^L)}\right] \quad \text{...(12.12)}$$

In Eulerian description as shown in Fig. 12.4, we have

$$\gamma^E = \angle DEF - 90°$$

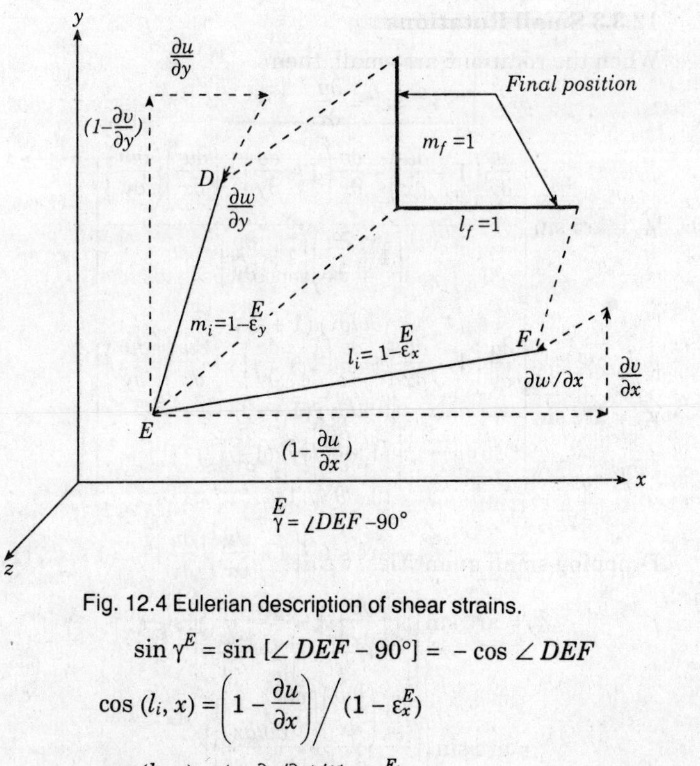

Fig. 12.4 Eulerian description of shear strains.

$$\sin \gamma^E = \sin\,[\angle DEF - 90°] = -\cos \angle DEF$$

$$\cos\,(l_i, x) = \left(1 - \frac{\partial u}{\partial x}\right)\Big/ (1 - \varepsilon_x^E)$$

$$\cos\,(l_i, y) = (-\,\partial v/\partial x)/(1 - \varepsilon_x^E)$$

$$\cos\,(l_i, z) = (-\,\partial w/\partial x)/(1 - \varepsilon_x^E)$$

$$\cos(m_i, x) = (-\partial u/\partial y)/(1 - \varepsilon_y^E)$$

$$\cos(m_i, y) = (-\partial v/\partial y)/(1 - \varepsilon_y^E)$$

$$\cos(m_i, z) = (-\partial w/\partial y)/(1 - \varepsilon_y^E)$$

$$\gamma_{xy}^E = \text{arc sin}\left[\frac{\dfrac{\partial u}{\partial y} + \dfrac{\partial v}{\partial x} - \left(\dfrac{\partial u}{\partial x}\right)\left(\dfrac{\partial u}{\partial y}\right) - \left(\dfrac{\partial v}{\partial x}\right)\left(\dfrac{\partial v}{\partial y}\right) - \left(\dfrac{\partial w}{\partial x}\right)\left(\dfrac{\partial w}{\partial y}\right)}{(1 - \varepsilon_x^E)\,(1 - \varepsilon_y^E)}\right]$$

$$\gamma_{yz}^E = \text{arc sin}\left[\frac{\dfrac{\partial v}{\partial z} + \dfrac{\partial w}{\partial y} - \left(\dfrac{\partial u}{\partial y}\right)\left(\dfrac{\partial u}{\partial z}\right) - \left(\dfrac{\partial v}{\partial y}\right)\left(\dfrac{\partial v}{\partial z}\right) - \left(\dfrac{\partial w}{\partial y}\right)\left(\dfrac{\partial w}{\partial z}\right)}{(1 - \varepsilon_y^E)\,(1 - \varepsilon_z^E)}\right]$$

$$\gamma_{zx}^E = \text{arc sin}\left[\frac{\dfrac{\partial w}{\partial x} + \dfrac{\partial u}{\partial z} - \left(\dfrac{\partial u}{\partial z}\right)\left(\dfrac{\partial u}{\partial x}\right) - \left(\dfrac{\partial v}{\partial z}\right)\left(\dfrac{\partial v}{\partial x}\right) - \left(\dfrac{\partial w}{\partial z}\right)\left(\dfrac{\partial w}{\partial x}\right)}{(1 - \varepsilon_z^E)\,(1 - \varepsilon_x^E)}\right] \quad \text{...(12.13)}$$

12.3.3 Small Rotations

When the rotations are small, then

$$\varepsilon_x^L = \varepsilon_x^L = \frac{\partial u}{\partial x} \quad \text{...(12.14)}$$

$$\gamma_{xy}^L = \text{arc sin}\left[\frac{\dfrac{\partial u}{\partial y}\left(1 + \dfrac{\partial u}{\partial x}\right) + \dfrac{\partial v}{\partial x}\left(1 + \dfrac{\partial v}{\partial y}\right) + \left(\dfrac{\partial w}{\partial x}\right)\left(\dfrac{\partial w}{\partial y}\right)}{\left(1 + \dfrac{\partial u}{\partial x}\right)\left(1 + \dfrac{\partial v}{\partial y}\right)}\right]$$

$$\gamma_{xy}^E = \text{arc sin}\left[\frac{\dfrac{\partial u}{\partial y}\left(1 - \dfrac{\partial u}{\partial x}\right) + \dfrac{\partial v}{\partial x}\left(1 - \dfrac{\partial v}{\partial y}\right) - \left(\dfrac{\partial w}{\partial x}\right)\left(\dfrac{\partial w}{\partial y}\right)}{\left(1 - \dfrac{\partial u}{\partial x}\right)\left(1 - \dfrac{\partial v}{\partial y}\right)}\right]$$

Dropping small quantities, we get

$$\gamma_{xy}^L = \text{arc sin}\left[\left(\frac{\partial u/\partial y}{1 + \dfrac{\partial v}{\partial y}}\right) + \left(\frac{\partial v/\partial x}{1 + \dfrac{\partial u}{\partial x}}\right)\right] \quad \text{...(12.15)}$$

$$\gamma_{xy}^E = \text{arc sin}\left[\left(\frac{\partial u/\partial y}{1 - \dfrac{\partial v}{\partial y}}\right) + \left(\frac{\partial v/\partial x}{1 - \dfrac{\partial u}{\partial x}}\right)\right] \quad \text{...(12.16)}$$

12.3.4 Small strains

From Eqs. (12.5) and (12.9), we get

$$(\varepsilon_x^L + 1)^2 = 1 + 2\frac{\partial u}{\partial x} + \left(\frac{\partial u}{\partial x}\right)^2 + \left(\frac{\partial v}{\partial x}\right)^2 + \left(\frac{\partial w}{\partial x}\right)^2$$

$$(\varepsilon_x^E - 1)^2 = 1 - 2\frac{\partial u}{\partial x} + \left(\frac{\partial u}{\partial x}\right)^2 + \left(\frac{\partial v}{\partial x}\right)^2 + \left(\frac{\partial w}{\partial x}\right)^2$$

When the strains are small, then

$$\varepsilon_x^L = \frac{\partial u}{\partial x} + \frac{1}{2}\left[\left(\frac{\partial u}{\partial x}\right)^2 + \left(\frac{\partial v}{\partial x}\right)^2 + \left(\frac{\partial w}{\partial x}\right)^2\right] \quad ...(12.17)$$

$$\varepsilon_x^E = \frac{\partial u}{\partial x} - \frac{1}{2}\left[\left(\frac{\partial u}{\partial x}\right)^2 + \left(\frac{\partial v}{\partial x}\right)^2 + \left(\frac{\partial w}{\partial x}\right)^2\right] \quad ...(12.18)$$

If $(\varepsilon_x)^2 \ll \varepsilon_x$, which requires that $\varepsilon_x \ll 1$, then $(1 + \varepsilon_x) \approx 1$. Hence Eq. (12.12) becomes

$$\gamma_{xy}^L = \text{arc sin}\left[\frac{\partial u}{\partial y} + \frac{\partial v}{\partial x} + \left(\frac{\partial u}{\partial x}\right)\left(\frac{\partial u}{\partial y}\right) + \left(\frac{\partial v}{\partial x}\right)\left(\frac{\partial v}{\partial y}\right) + \left(\frac{\partial w}{\partial x}\right)\left(\frac{\partial w}{\partial y}\right)\right]$$

If $(\gamma_{xy})^2 \ll \gamma_{xy}$ then taking $\sin \gamma_{xy} \approx \gamma_{xy}$, we get

$$\gamma_{xy}^L = \frac{\partial u}{\partial y} + \frac{\partial v}{\partial x} + \left(\frac{\partial u}{\partial x}\right)\left(\frac{\partial u}{\partial y}\right) + \left(\frac{\partial v}{\partial x}\right)\left(\frac{\partial v}{\partial y}\right) + \left(\frac{\partial w}{\partial x}\right)\left(\frac{\partial w}{\partial y}\right) \quad ...(12.19)$$

Similarly from Eqs. (12.13), we get

$$\gamma_{xy}^E = \frac{\partial u}{\partial y} + \frac{\partial v}{\partial x} - \left(\frac{\partial u}{\partial x}\right)\left(\frac{\partial u}{\partial y}\right) - \left(\frac{\partial v}{\partial x}\right)\left(\frac{\partial v}{\partial y}\right) - \left(\frac{\partial w}{\partial x}\right)\left(\frac{\partial w}{\partial y}\right) \quad ...(12.20)$$

12.3.5 Small rotations and small strains

When $\left(\frac{\partial v}{\partial x}\right)^2 \ll \frac{\partial u}{\partial x}, \left(\frac{\partial w}{\partial x}\right)^2 \ll \frac{\partial u}{\partial x}$

$$\left(\frac{\partial v}{\partial x}\right)^2 \ll \varepsilon_x, \left(\frac{\partial w}{\partial x}\right)^2 \ll \varepsilon_x$$

and $(\varepsilon_x)^2 \ll \varepsilon_x$, then

$$\varepsilon_x = \frac{\partial u}{\partial x} \quad ...(12.21)$$

$$\gamma_{xy} = \frac{\partial u}{\partial y} + \frac{\partial v}{\partial x} \quad ...(12.22)$$

Similar expressions can be written for other strain terms.

12.4 Application of Grid

The grid can be applied to the test specimens by the following methods :

1. **Hand-writing or scribing.** The grids can be made on the specimens by hand or can be scribed by a sharp pointed needle. To calculate the strains in the specimen at all points each element of the grid will have to be measured before and after straining. This method can be used for relatively soft transparent materials like plastics.

2. **Machine scribing.** Grids can be scribed by machine using ruling engines for flat and cylindrical surfaces. The individual elements in the grid may be identical and measurements need be made only after straining. Machine scribed grids are used only when tests are to be carried upto rupture.

3. **Ink drawing.** Grids can be drawn with ink on models like rubber. The thickness of lines should be as small as possible to obtain more accuracy.

4. **Rubber threads.** For soft porous materials, thin rubber threads of 0.2 mm diameter can be glued by latex and strain measurements may be made after loading.

5. **Embedded rubber threads.** Test models can also be prepared by embedding grids of thin extruded rubber threads which have been stretched to reduce their original diameter from 0.2 mm to 0.1 mm. The grid is threaded in the appropriate array through the sides of the plate mould and transparent rubber is cast about it. On curing, the sheet of transparent rubber contains the embedded grid and can be machined to the model geometry. This model then can be analysed for strain and stress distribution. This method is very useful in three-dimensional, dynamic and plastic deformation studies, inelastic and axial strains.

6. **Photogrid method.** Grids can be applied photographically by painting a light sensitive emulsion on the surface of the test specimen, covering the surface with a master grid negative, exposing to strong light, and developing the resultant print in the usual manner. This is called a photogrid.

The master grid negative may be prepared by drawing the grid to a very large scale and then photographically reducing to obtain the desired grid spacing and accuracy. More commonly, master grid negatives are made by contact printing from master grid on glass plates which are machine ruled.

To apply the photogrid the surface is cleaned and slightly roughened to receive the grid. The emulsion is prepared by mixing by weight 4 parts photoengraving glue, 28 parts water, 1 part ammonium bichromate and $\frac{1}{4}$ part ammonia water. This solution is then mixed with water and alcohol in the proportion of one part of the solution to 113 g of water and 11 g of alcohol (Preservative). This emulsion is applied by spraying the stock solution on to the surface of the specimen. For best results four or five light coats are applied. The specimens should be kept out of light between sprayings and provision should be made for fume removal. After drying, the coupons are placed in a vacuum printing frame with the master glass negative and exposed. Exposure requires 5 to 7 minutes, 90 cm distance from a 35 ampere arc light. A vacuum printing frame must be used to secure maximum clarity of the lines.

Following exposure, the coupon is dipped in cold water to remove the unexposed portions of the emulsion. It is then placed in a hot solution of Diamond dye of the desired colour. For toughening it may be dipped in formaldehyde solution and then dried in air.

7. **Replica method.** This is modification of the photogrid method for determining static strains which eliminates the requirement for accurate placement of a grid array on the specimen. This method was developed by Hickson in 1959. With this method, a family of parallel scratches of uneven spacing and thickness is applied to a polished region of a specimen by drawing fine abrasive paper along the edge of a template. Lines equivalent to those produced by the best engraving techniques are frequently present in such a scratch pattern. A second pattern, applied perpendicular to the first, produces the rectangular array of grid lines. A coarse pattern of broad reference lines is scribed over the scratch pattern to serve as datum lines and to help identify specific scratch lines being used for measurements.

To facilitate strain measurements a replica technique is used to record the scratch patterns before and after loading. The replicas are made by using a thin film of fusible alloy on a stiffening platen. The alloy is capable of reproducing the finest detail in the scratch pattern.

Displacement measurements are made by comparing a pair of replicas, taken before and after loading. The identification of lines being used for strain determinations is simplified by use of the reference grid and the random nature of the lines in the scratch pattern.

12.5 Displacement Measurement Method

The distance between the grid lines on the model is measured by a micrometer microscope by keeping the magnification of the microscope same before and after loading. More often, photographs are taken before and during test and measurements are made afterwards by a micrometer-microscope or an optical comparator.

In the Fischer's method the x-components of displacement are measured for points which originally lie along a straight line parallel to the x-axis, these displacements are plotted against the original positions of the points. If a smooth curve is drawn through these plotted points, then the slope of this displacement position curve at any point is equal to ε_x for that point. This strain can be ascertained for any point along the line with considerable accuracy even in regions of large strain gradients.

12.6 Quiz Questions

1. How much is the minimum strain limit for the grid method to be applied efficiently ?
2. Differentiate between Lagrangian and Eulerian strain description.
3. How do you calculate $\varepsilon_{45°}$ strain component ?
4. When machine scribing is preferred for applying grids ?

5. When embedded rubber threads are used for applying grids?
6. What is a photogrid ?
7. What is the replica method ?
8. How do you measure the displacements ?
9. What is the Fischer's method ?
10. Which grid application method you would suggest for steel ?

EXERCISES

12.1 Explain the grid method of strain analysis in brief. What are the limitations and advantages of this method ?

12.2 Derive the strain-displacement relations for large strains. Reduce these relations for small strain and small rotations.

12.3 Explain the various methods for application of grid to test specimens. How displacement measurements are generally made ?

12.4 Write short notes on :
(*a*) Photogrid method.
(*b*) Replica Technique.
(*c*) Fischer's method.

13

Moire's Fringe Methods

13.1 Introduction

One of the problems of experimental mechanics is the determination of displacements or strain components at given points of arbitrary shaped surfaces. A possible solution of this problem is the Moire's methods. The word Moire's is the French name for a fabric known as watered or wavy silk, which exhibits patterns of light and dark bands. The Moire's effect occurs whenever two similar but not quite identical arrays of equally spaced lines or dots are arranged so that one array can be viewed through the other.

The phenomenon of Moire's fringes was first described by Lord Rayleigh in 1874. Ronchi in 1925 studied the case of the Moire's patterns created by the superposition of a line and a circular grating. Tollenaar in 1945 gave an interpretation of the Moire's phenomenon based on geometric optics. In 1952 Kaczer and Kroupa applied for the first time the properties of Moire's fringes to determine the strain components in a two-dimensional strain field. In 1960 Morse, Durelli and Sciammarella presented a complete analysis of the geometry of Moire's fringes in strain analysis. A second method of analysis of Moire's fringe patterns was presented by Wéller and Shepard in 1948, describing an application in which Moire's fringes were used to measure displacements. Dantu in 1954 followed the same approach and introduced the interpretation of the Moire's patterns in terms of the components of the displacements. Dantu's presentation was limited to the field of small strains and deformations. Sciammarella and Durelli in 1961, 1962 extended this approach into the region of large strains.

The shadow Moire's method introduced by Theocaris in 1964 has been used to measure out-of-plane displacements and the reflection Moire's method by Ligtenbérg in 1954 to measure slope and moment distribution in flat slabs. Durelli and Daniel in 1960 has used the Moire's method to measure displacements in structural models.

Methods have been devised by Post (1967, 1968) to sharpen and multiply Moire's fringes to increase the sensitivity of the method.

In this chapter we shall study the Moire's methods by restricting our study to linear gratings. Both the geometrical and the displacement field approaches to Moire's fringe analysis will be followed.

13.2 Fundamental Properties of the Moire's Fringes

The arrays used to produce Moire's fringes may be a series of straight parallel lines, a series of radial lines emanating from a point, a series of concentric circles, or a pattern of dots. Arrays consisting of straight parallel lines having opaque bars with transparent interspaces of equal width are the most commonly used for experimental work. Such arrays are called grids, gratings or grills. Coarse arrays having upto about 4 lines per cm are generally called grids and arrays having from 20 to 400 lines per cm are called gratings. Two mutually perpendicular line arrays are termed as cross grating. Gratings having upto 200 lines per cm are most commonly used.

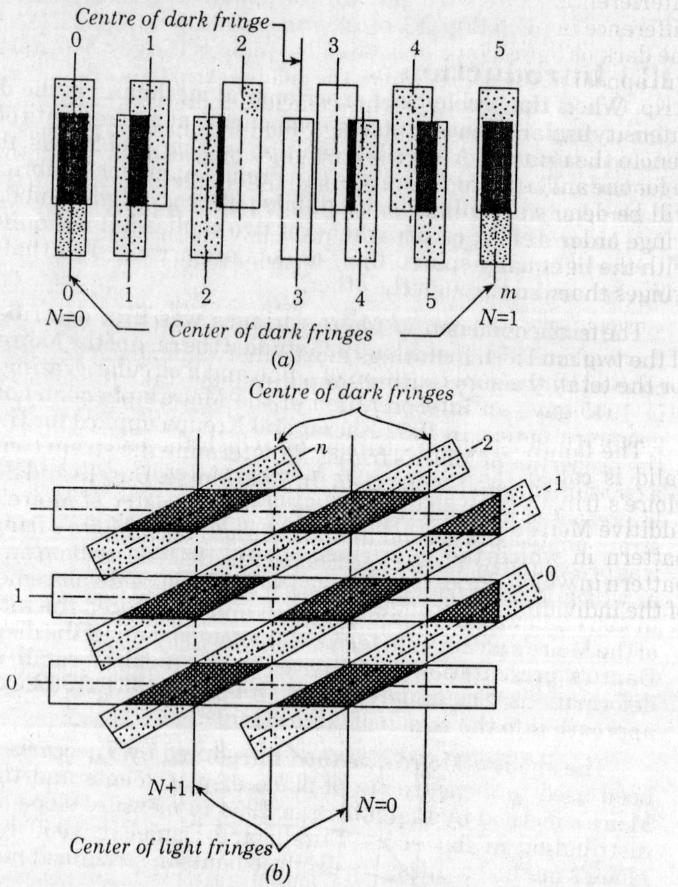

Fig. 13.1 Moire's fringes (*a*) difference in pitch (*b*) difference in orientation.

Two line gratings used in the strain analysis are, the model or specimen grating and the master or reference grating. Model grating can be either applied by coating the specimen with a photographic emulsion and contact printing through the master grating or by bonding, ruling or etching. The model grating deforms along with the test specimen whereas the master grating does not deform during the test. The distance between the master grating lines is called the pitch and is denoted by p. The pitch may be visualized as the reciprocal of the density of the lines in a grating. The centre-to-centre distance on the model grating after deformation will be denoted by p'. By interference of the two gratings a pattern of fringes is produced. The distance between fringes is called "fringe spacing" and is denoted by δ. Any line perpendicular to the master grating lines will be called the principal direction and a line parallel to the master grating lines a secondary direction.

When the gratings are superimposed one against another, the interference Moire's fringes are the result of either their having a difference in pitch [Fig. 13.1 (*a*)] or in orientation [Fig. 13.1 (*b*)]. Either the dark or light bands may be called Moire's fringes. The dark fringes will appear at the points where the opaque strip falls over a transparent strip. When two opaque strips coincide, there is a maximum of light intensity and one has a light fringe. For identification purpose, we shall denote the centre lines of the dark lines of gratings with numbers 0 to m for one and 0 to n for the other, and the center lines of the light fringes will be denoted by the number 0 to N (N an integer), where N is the fringe order. It may be noted that we have associated the fringe order with the light fringes as it is much easier to identify the centre of light fringes than dark ones.

The fringe order N and the parameters m and n identifying the lines of the two interfering gratings must satisfy an indicial equation which, for the totality of two grating simple systems, take the form

$$m \pm n = N \qquad \text{...(13.1)}$$

The family of Moire's fringes for which the equation $m - n = N$ is valid is called the subtractive Moire's pattern, while the family of Moire's fringes for which the equation $m + n = N$ is valid is called the additive Moire's pattern. The effective or visible Moire's pattern is the pattern in which the interfringe spacing is the longest, that is the pattern in which the Moire's fringes coincide with the shortest diagonals of the individual quadrangles (Fig. 13.2).

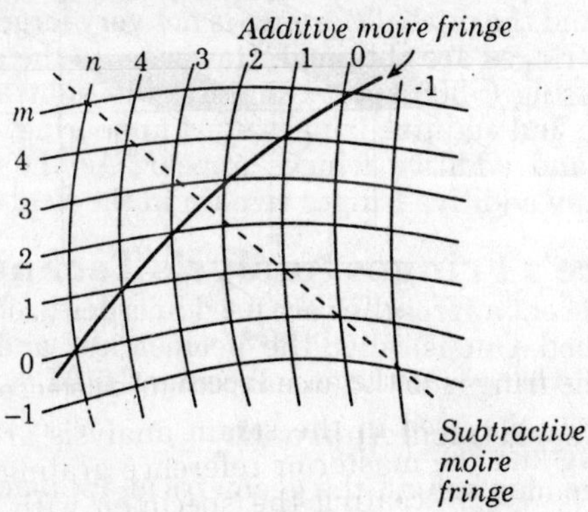

Fig. 13.2

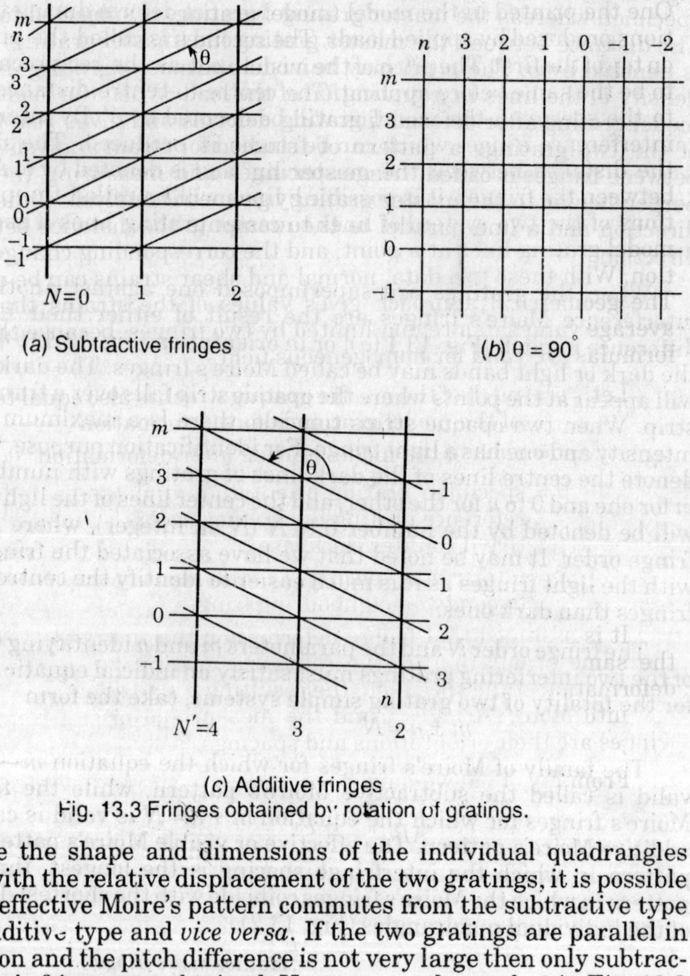

(a) Subtractive fringes (b) θ = 90°

(c) Additive fringes

Fig. 13.3 Fringes obtained by rotation of gratings.

Since the shape and dimensions of the individual quadrangles change with the relative displacement of the two gratings, it is possible that the effective Moire's pattern commutes from the subtractive type to the additive type and *vice versa*. If the two gratings are parallel in orientation and the pitch difference is not very large then only subtractive Moire's fringes are obtained. However, as the angle θ in Fig. 13.3 starts increasing (>30° approximately) the subtractive fringes start disappearing and additive fringes start appearing. At θ = 90° both the subtractive and additive fringes appear. As the angle θ is further increased, only additive fringes remain in the field of view.

13.3 Moire's Fringes Analysis Techniques

Two different approaches are used in order to obtain strains by the Moire's method. One is called the 'geometrical' and the other consists in relating the fringes to the 'displacement' field.

13.3.1 Geometrical Approach

The basic idea behind the geometrical approach is the following : Moire's fringes are formed by two interfering lines screens or gratings.

One the printed in the model (model grating) is subjected to deformations produced by applied loads. The second (master grating) is applied on top of the first. The pitch of the model and master gratings is assumed to be the same before application of the load. When the load is applied to the specimen the model grating deforms and gives rise to Moire's interference fringes which can be studied for strain analysis. Knowing the distance between the master lines and measuring the distance between the fringes, it is possible by geometric analysis of the intersections of the two system of lines to compute the distance between the model grating lines at a point, and the corresponding change in direction. With these two data, normal and shear strains can be computed. The geometrical approach gives values of the strains that are the average values in a region limited by two fringes, because the applied formulas are valid for homogeneous field.

Let p = pitch of the master grating which is also equal to the pitch of the model grating before deformation

p' = pitch of the model grating after deformation

θ = specimen grating orientation angle measured from the reference grating line to the specimen grating line ; positive if counter clockwise

δ = interfringe spacing, *i.e.* the perpendicular distance between two neighbouring fringes.

It is assumed that before deformation the specimen grating have the same orientation as the reference grating, *i.e.* $\theta = 0$. After the deformation of the specimen, the resulting p' and θ manifests themselves into Moire's fringes ; and the measurable properties of Moire's fringes are their orientations and spacings.

From Fig. 13.4, we have

$$AB = \frac{p}{\cos\left(\phi - \frac{\pi}{2}\right)} = \frac{p}{\sin\phi}$$

$$= \frac{p'}{\cos\left(\phi - \frac{\pi}{2} - \theta\right)}$$

$$= \frac{p'}{\sin(\phi - \theta)}$$

Hence
$$p' = \frac{p\sin(\phi - \theta)}{\sin\phi} \quad \text{...(13.2)}$$

where ϕ is the angle of the light fringe orientation measured from the reference grating lines.

Solving for the angle ϕ in terms of the pitch p of the master grating, pitch p' of specimen grating and θ, we get

$$\tan\phi = \frac{p\sin\theta}{p\cos\theta - p'}$$

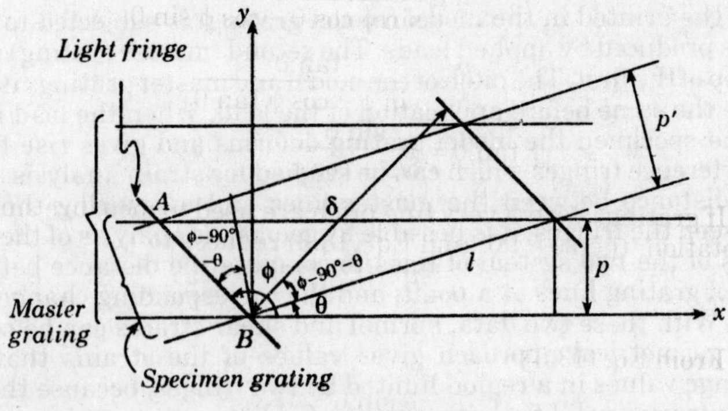

Fig, 13.4 Fringe orientation and spacing as a function of interfringe gratings.

or $$\phi = \tan^{-1}\left(\frac{p \sin \theta}{p \cos \theta - p'}\right) \quad \text{...(13.3)}$$

Also $$l = \frac{p}{\sin \theta}$$

and $$\delta = l \cos\left(\phi - \frac{\pi}{2} - \theta\right)$$

$$= l \sin(\phi - \theta)$$

$$= \frac{p \sin(\phi - \theta)}{\sin \theta} \quad \text{...(13.4)}$$

Combining Eqs. (13.2) and (13.4), we get

$$\delta = \frac{p' \sin \phi}{\sin \theta} \quad \text{...(13.5)}$$

From Eq. (13.3), we can deduce that

$$\sin \phi = \frac{p \sin \theta}{\sqrt{p^2 \sin^2 \theta + (p \cos \theta - p')^2}} \quad \text{...(13.6)}$$

Substituting in Eq. (13.5), we get

$$\delta = \frac{pp'}{\sqrt{p^2 \sin^2 \theta + (p \cos \theta - p')^2}} \quad \text{...(13.7)}$$

Hence for given values of p, p' and θ, the fringe orientation ϕ and fringe spacing δ can be determined from Eqs. (13.6) and (13.7) respectively.

Conversely, for a given reference grating pitch p and from the measured quantities ϕ and δ, we can determine the pitch and orientation of the deformed specimen grating.

From Eq. (13.4), we have

$$\frac{p}{\sin \theta} = \frac{\delta}{\sin(\phi - \theta)}$$

$$= \frac{\delta}{\sin\phi\cos\theta - \cos\phi\sin\theta}$$

or
$$\frac{p}{\delta} = \frac{\tan\theta}{\sin\phi - \cos\phi\tan\theta}$$

or
$$\tan\theta = \frac{\sin\phi}{\delta/p + \cos\phi} \qquad ...(13.8)$$

If gratings with a very fine pitch are used to measure small angles of rotation, then $\phi \approx 90°$ and Eq. (13.8) reduces to

$$\theta = \frac{p}{\delta} \qquad ...(13.9)$$

From Eq. (13.5)

$$p' = \frac{\delta\sin\theta}{\sin\phi}$$

Also
$$\sin\theta = \frac{\tan\theta}{\sqrt{1+\tan^2\theta}}$$

Using Eq. (13.8), we get

$$\sin\theta = \frac{\sin\phi}{\sqrt{\left(\frac{\delta}{p} + \cos\phi\right)^2 + \sin^2\phi}}$$

$$= \frac{\sin\phi}{\sqrt{1 + \left(\frac{\delta}{p}\right)^2 + 2\frac{\delta}{p}\cos\phi}}$$

Hence
$$p' = \frac{\delta}{\sqrt{1 + \left(\frac{\delta}{p}\right)^2 + 2\frac{\delta}{p}\cos\phi}} \qquad ...(13.10)$$

when $\theta = 0$, it is seen from Eq. (13.3) that $\phi = 0$, *i.e.* the fringes are parallel to the grating lines and their spacing from Eq. (13.7) becomes

$$\delta = \frac{p\,p'}{p - p'} \qquad ...(13.11)$$

Eq. (13.11) indicates that the larger the pitch difference between the gratings, the smaller the fringe spacing and *vice versa*. When θ is very small then Eq. (13.3) can be written as :

$$\phi = \tan^{-1}\left(\frac{p\theta}{p - p'}\right) \qquad ...(13.12)$$

and Eq. (13.7) becomes

$$\delta = \frac{p\,p'}{\sqrt{(p\theta)^2 + (p - p')^2}} \qquad ...(13.13)$$

Once the deformed specimen pitch p' has been determined the component of normal strain in a direction perpendicular to the lines of the master grating can be computed as :

$$\varepsilon = \frac{p' - p}{p} \quad ...(13.14)$$

The two commonly used descriptions of strain are the Lagrangian (or engineering) description and the Eulerian description. The Lagrangian strain is based on the initial length and the Eulerian strain is based on the final length. Thus, we may define

$$\varepsilon^L = \frac{l_f - l_i}{l_f} \quad ...(13.15)$$

l is the gauge length

and $$\varepsilon^E = \frac{l_f - l_i}{l_f} \quad ...(13.16)$$

The shearing strain

$$\gamma^L = \gamma^E$$

is the same in both the descriptions.

The two descriptions of strain can be related as

$$\varepsilon^E = \frac{\varepsilon^L}{1 + \varepsilon^L}, \ \varepsilon^L = \frac{\varepsilon^E}{1 - \varepsilon^E} \quad ...(13.17)$$

In the application of the Moire's methods, the coordinates are usually measured off from a deformed body, it is then natural to use the Eulerian description. If the deformation is small, the difference between the two descriptions is negligible. Thus

$$\left.\begin{aligned} |\varepsilon^E| &= \left|\frac{l_f - l_i}{l_f}\right| = \left|\frac{p' - p}{p'}\right| = \frac{p}{\delta} \\ \text{and} \quad \varepsilon^L &= p/(\delta - p) \end{aligned}\right\} \quad ...(13.18)$$

To orientation of the reference and specimen gratings to determine normal strains is shown in Fig. 13.5 (*a*). For the determination of simple shearing strain, specimen grating should be so oriented that its principal direction is parallel to the direction of shear as shown in Fig. 13.5 (*b*). Thus

$$\gamma = \theta = p/\delta \quad ...(13.19)$$

13.3.2 Displacement Approach

Geometrical approach is quite suitable for measuring uniaxial homogeneous in plane normal strain and simple shearing strain. For measuring general two-dimensional strains, it is more convenient to describe Moire's fringes as contours of displacement component—the so called isothetics.

The uniaxial view point is shown in Fig. 13.6. The observable fringes are the substractive one and the fringe order is given by

$$N = m - n$$

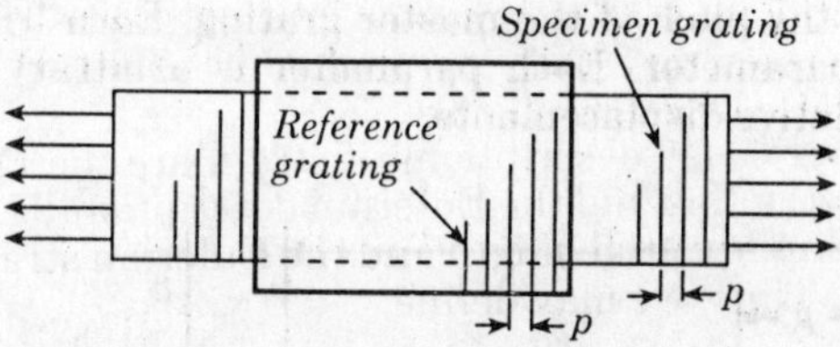

(*a*) Determination of uniaxial normal strain.

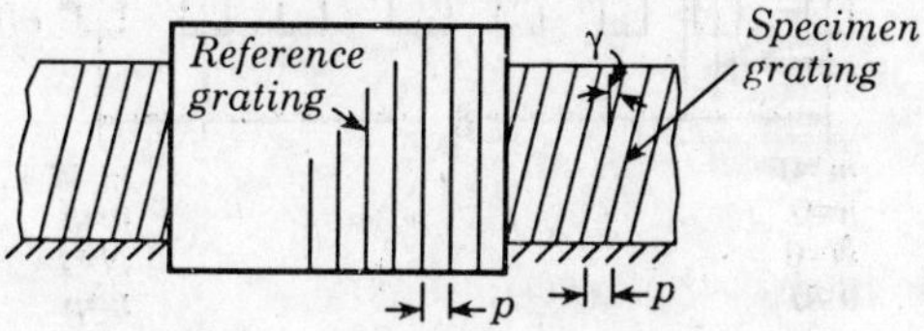

(*b*) Determination of simple shearing strain.

Fig. 13.5

If it is assumed the the model grating is the one with the largest pitch, a point P in the undeformed state has undergone a displacement equal to the pitch p of the master grating and is now at P'. Then the centre line of the first light fringe indicates a displacement in the direction of the principal section equal to p ; if the centre of the light fringe is considered to the right of the first one, the displacement is equal to $2p$, and for the Nth fringe, the displacement is N_p. It can be concluded that the Moire's pattern gives the relative displacement in the direction of the principal section referred to the final or deformed shape of the body. The pattern indicates the point P' in the deformed state of the model has undergone a displacement p. If we denote the displacement as u we have then

$$u = Np, N = 0, 1, 2,... \qquad ...(13.20)$$

Similarly, we can write that

$$v = N'p, N' = 0, 1, 2, \qquad ...(13.21)$$

where N' is the fringe order of the v-field fringe pattern. In a general two-dimensional deformation, the specimen grating experiences rotation as well as change of pitch with magnitudes varying from point to point. As shown in Fig. 13.7, the Moir's fringes are again the substractive fringes, represented by $N = m - n$. As shown in Fig. 13.7, the Moire's fringes are the loci of the points representing the same relative displacement in the direction normal to the master grating. Call zero the first fringe to the right of Fig. 13.7, one the second fringe and so on. Assuming that the points of fringe zero do not experience any displacement, the fringe one is produced by the displacement p of the points of the model grating in the direction of the principal section, fringe two is produced by the displacement $2p$ and the Nth fringe by the displacement Np. Then the Moire's fringes are the loci of points with a relative displacement in the direction of the principal section which is equal to an integer number times the pitch of the master grating. Each fringe is characterized by a parameter. Each parameter is arbitrary since we are considering relative displacements.

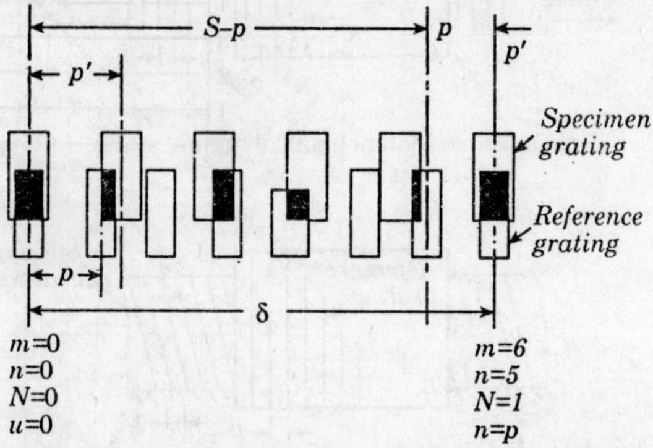

Fig. 13.6 Formation of fringes in a tensile specimen (Unidirectional case).

In order to obtain both the u and v components of displacement either a cross-grating (two lines gratings intersecting at right angles) may be used as the model reference gratings or the reference line grating may be turned by 90° after one family of fringes is obtained. While using a cross grating it becomes difficult to distinguish which fringe belongs to which family. In this case one can use the technique of optical spatial filtering to separate the two families of fringes. For purpose of analysis, the Moire's fringe pattern can be visualized as a displacement surface where a height of a point on the surface above a plane of reference represents the displacement of the point in a direction perpendicular to the lines of the master grating.

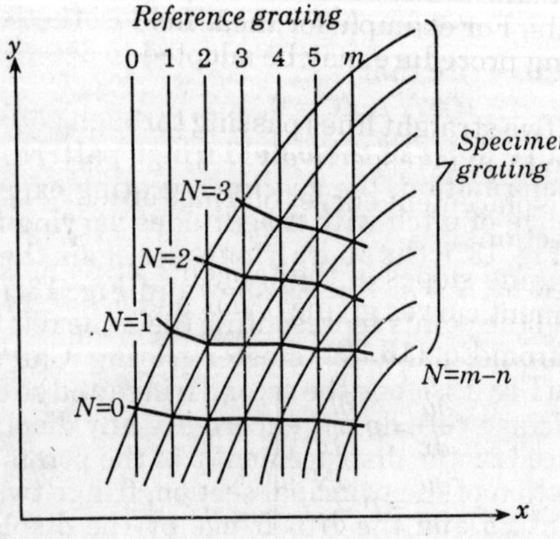

Fig. 13.7 Formation of Moire's fringes in a biaxial tensile specimen.

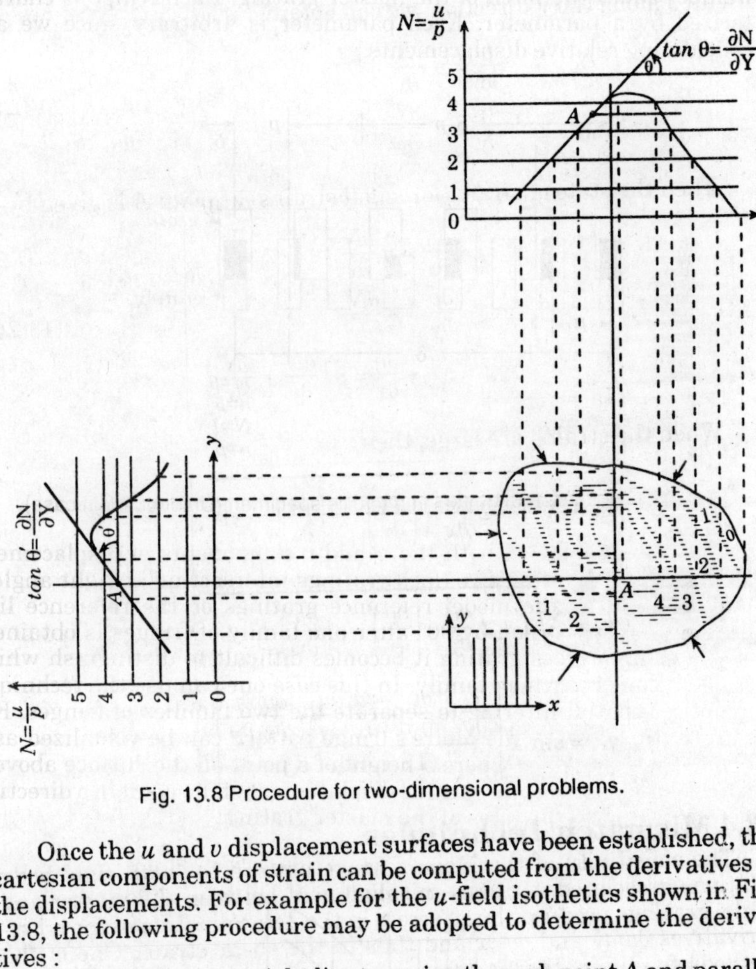

Fig. 13.8 Procedure for two-dimensional problems.

Once the u and v displacement surfaces have been established, the cartesian components of strain can be computed from the derivatives of the displacements. For example for the u-field isothetics shown in Fig. 13.8, the following procedure may be adopted to determine the derivatives :

1. Draw two straight lines passing through point A and parallel to x and y axis respectively.
2. Plot displacement curves of fringe order v's position along the two sections.
3. Determine slopes of the tangents at point A from both displacement curves giving $\partial N/\partial x$ and $\partial N/\partial y$, respectively.
4. Then from Eq. (13.20)

$$\left.\begin{aligned}\frac{\partial u}{\partial x} &= p\,\frac{\partial N}{\partial x}\\ \frac{\partial u}{\partial y} &= p\,\frac{\partial N}{\partial y}\end{aligned}\right\} \qquad \text{...(13.22)}$$

Similarly, from the v-field Moire's fringe pattern obtained under the identical load but with the principal direction of the gratings oriented along the y-direction, we can obtain

$$\left.\begin{aligned}\frac{\partial v}{\partial x} &= p\,\frac{\partial N'}{\partial x}\\ \frac{\partial v}{\partial y} &= p\,\frac{\partial N'}{\partial y}\end{aligned}\right\} \qquad ...(13.23)$$

Then the state of strain (for small strains) at point A is given by

$$\left.\begin{aligned}\varepsilon_x &= \frac{\partial u}{\partial x} = p\,\frac{\partial N}{\partial x}\\ \varepsilon_y &= \frac{\partial v}{\partial y} = p\,\frac{\partial N'}{\partial y}\\ \gamma_{xy} &= \frac{\partial u}{\partial y} + \frac{\partial v}{\partial x} = p\left(\frac{\partial N}{\partial y} + \frac{\partial N'}{\partial x}\right)\end{aligned}\right\} \qquad ...(13.24)$$

When the strains are large, then

$$\left.\begin{aligned}\varepsilon_x &= \sqrt{1 + 2\,\frac{\partial u}{\partial x} + \left(\frac{\partial u}{\partial x}\right)^2 + \left(\frac{\partial v}{\partial x}\right)^2} - 1\\ \varepsilon_y &= \sqrt{1 + 2\,\frac{\partial v}{\partial y} + \left(\frac{\partial v}{\partial y}\right)^2 + \left(\frac{\partial u}{\partial y}\right)^2} - 1\\ \gamma_{xy} &= \sin^{-1}\left[\frac{\dfrac{\partial u}{\partial y} + \dfrac{\partial v}{\partial x} + \dfrac{\partial u}{\partial x}\,\dfrac{\partial u}{\partial y} + \dfrac{\partial v}{\partial x}\,\dfrac{\partial v}{\partial y}}{(1+\varepsilon_x)\,(1+\varepsilon_y)}\right]\end{aligned}\right\} \qquad ...(13.25)$$

13.4 Mismatch Techniques

The sensitivity of the Moire's fringe pattern to small rigid body rotations associated with any misalignment between the master and model gratings produces large errors in the determination of the cross-derivatives $\partial u/\partial y$ and $\partial v/\partial x$ and thus in the shear strain. One of the methods to eliminate this error is to use cross-gratings on both the specimen and the master. But this method is not recommended because of the interweaving between the two families of fringes. Alternately to decrease the shear-strain errors the mismatch techniques may be used. The mismatch technique also helps in increasing the number of the data points for plotting the displacement curve. The mismatch may be either the initial difference in pitch between the two gratings, called the linear mismatch or the initial difference in orientation, called the rotational mismatch. The resulting fringes are called linear mismatch and rotational mismatch fringes respectively.

13.4.1 Linear Mismatch Method

Let the pitch of specimen grating = p

and pitch of master grating = $p\,(1 + \lambda)$

where λ is small compared with unity. The initial apparent strain

$$\varepsilon_i = \lambda = \frac{p}{\delta_i} \qquad \text{...(13.26)}$$

where δ_i = initial fringe spacing.

The displacements introduced by subsequent specimen deformation are then added to this initial displacement. On loading the specimen normal to the grating lines, we obtain a new fringe spacing δ_m ($\delta_m < \delta_i$ for tensile strains), and the true strains will be given by

$$\varepsilon = \varepsilon_m - \varepsilon_i = p\left(\frac{1}{\delta_m} - \frac{1}{\delta_i}\right) \qquad \text{...(13.27)}$$

This technique, while relatively simple, is only really suitable for analysis of symmetrical systems where only the normal components of strain are required.

13.4.2 Moire's-Grid-Analyzer Method

Using an analyzer of identical pitch to that of the specimen grating, and giving it an initial small rotation produces a system of fringes which bisect the angle made by perpendiculars to the two sets of grating lines as shown in Fig. 13.1 (*b*). Fig. 13.9 shows a pair of *y*-grids with the analyzer rotated anti-clockwise through an angle θ_x. If the specimen grating is subjected to a principal strain ε_2 such as to change its pitch from p_0 to p_y, then the fringe system will be displaced from the initial angle ϕ_{x1} to an angle ϕ_{x2}. With θ_x anti-clockwise, an extensional strain ε_2 will cause the fringe system to rotate clockwise, so that sign of ε_2 is readily determined.

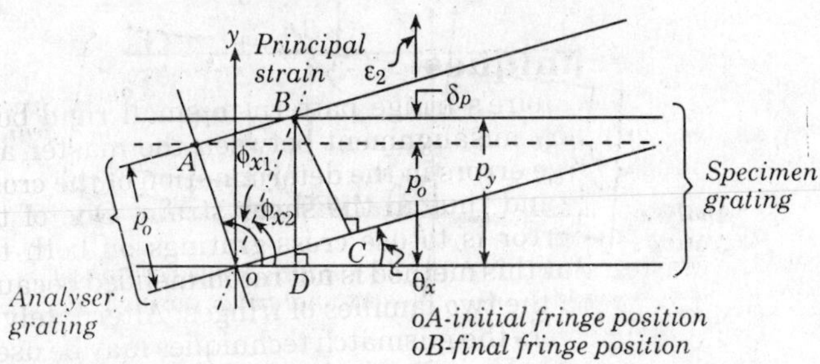

Fig. 13.9 Formation of Moire's fringes by analyser rotation.

From Fig. 13.9, we have

$$OB = \frac{BD}{\sin \phi_{x_2}}$$

$$= \frac{BC}{\sin (\phi_{x_2} - \theta_x)}$$

so that $$\frac{BD}{BC} = \frac{p_y}{p_0}$$

$$= \frac{\sin \phi_{x_2}}{\sin (\phi_{x_2} - \theta_x)}$$

Thus the engineering strain

$$\varepsilon_2 = \frac{p_y - p_0}{p_0} = \frac{\sin \phi_{x_2}}{\sin (\phi_{x_2} - \theta_x)} - 1 \quad ...(13.28)$$

Equation (13.28) is much more sensitive to changes in ϕ_{x_2} than θ_x. Selecting a small constant value of $\theta_x = \pm 1°$ or $2°$, the strain magnitudes at a given point may be obtained from the changes in fringe inclination produced by deformation of the specimen grating.

If the strain ε_2 is a normal strain ε_y rather than a principal strain, then there will be a shear induced rotation α of the specimen grating lines. In that case as shown in Fig. 13.10, we have

$$OB = \frac{BD}{\sin (\phi_{x_2} - \alpha)} = \frac{BC}{\sin (\phi_{x_2} - \theta_x)}$$

so that $$\frac{BD}{BC} = \frac{\sin (\phi_{x_2} - \alpha)}{\sin (\phi_{x_2} - \theta_x)}$$

Thus the normal strain

$$\varepsilon_y = \frac{p_y - p_o}{p_o} = \frac{\sin (\phi_{x_2} - \alpha)}{\sin (\phi_{x_2} - \theta_x)} - 1 \quad ...(13.29)$$

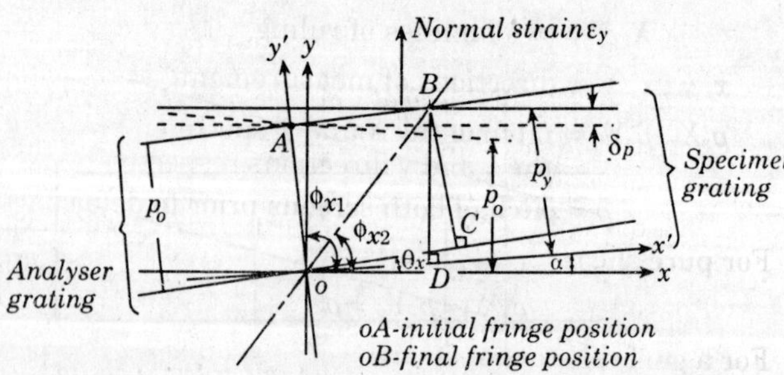

Fig. 13.10 Formation of Moire's fringes by analyser rotation.

By selecting two values of analyzer rotation, say $\theta_x = \pm 2°$, and measuring the corresponding fringe inclinations, both ε_y and α may be determined from the resulting simultaneous equations. Repeating the process with a set of x-gratings will give us values of ε_x and shear rotation β. Thus the complete state of strain ε_x and ε_y and $\gamma_{xy}(= \alpha + \beta)$ can be determined. However this method is unsuitble for large field measurements.

13.4.3 Combined Linear and Rotational Mismatch

In this method orthogonal gratings are used for both specimen and analyzer and the method consists in combining pitch mismatch and analyzer rotation so that an initial pattern of two orthogonal sets of parallel, closely packed Moire's fringes, oriented at 45° to the co-ordinate axes, covers the whole area to be anlayzed. The initial pattern is arranged so that the largest strains to be measured do not deflect the Moire's fringes from their 45° orientation by too great an amount. The 45° orientation of both sets of fringes ensures that there are always an adequate number of fringes available for graphical determination of $\partial u/\partial x$, $\partial v/\partial y$, $\partial u/\partial y$ and $\partial v/\partial x$. The initial pattern effectively presents the inter-weaving of the two sets of fringes, and it also eliminates uncertainties in the assignment of fringe orders throughout the field. Because orthogonal gratings are used for both specimen and analyzer, any errors in computing shear strains due to analyzer misalignment are automatically cancelled, and the effects of rigid body rotation of elements within the specimen are also eliminated in the calculations.

The X and Y families of fringes are readily distinguished because their inclination depends on the sign of λ and the direction of analyzer rotation.

Using a right hand (x, y) co-ordinate system and positive λ (*i.e.* line density in analyzer grating is greater than specimen grating), a clockwise analyzer rotation $(+\theta)$ produces positive slope of the X-fringes and negative slope of the Y-fringes. The same applies when both λ and θ are negative. When λ or θ is negative, X fringes have negative slope and Y fringes positive slope.

Let s, a = subscripts for specimen and analyzer

X, Y = two families of ruling

$x, y\,;\,x', y'$ = directions of measurement

p_sX_x, p_sY_y = pitch of the X and Y specimen gratings (screens) in the x and y directions respectively.

p = pitch of both screens prior to deformation.

For pure shear

$$p_sX_y = p_sY_y = p$$

For a general state of strain

$$p_sX_x = p\,(1 + \varepsilon_x)$$

$$p_xY_y = p\,(1 + \varepsilon_y)$$

Super-impose the analyzer upon the specimen with rulings approximately parallel to the specimen rulings, and then rotate the analyzer to produce the desired gradient of initial Moirs fringes of rotation. Define the rotation relative to the orthogonal x' and y' axes by angle θ, positive for clockwise rotation of the analyzer. The super position of these screens produces two families of straight uniformly spaced Moire's fringes.

Let m_{sx}, m_{sy} designate numerically to every line of the specimen and analyzer screens for both the X and Y screens. Let the numerical index increase in the positive x and y directions and for convenience, let $m_s = m_a = 0$ at the origin. As the Moire's method manifests itself as a mechanical subtraction process, hence

$$\left.\begin{aligned} N_x &= m_{ax} - m_{sx} \\ N_y &= m_{ay} - m_{sy} \end{aligned}\right\} \qquad ...(13.30)$$

Since γ is small, therefore, x' and y' axes are indistinguishable from the x, y axes and at any point the gradient of Moire's fringes in x and x' directions may be considered identical. Let δ = inter-fringe spacing. Then considering only the X screen, at any point on the x' axis (Fig. 13.11),

$$N_X \, \delta_{X_{x'}} = m_{sx} \, p_s \, X_{x'} = m_{ax} \, p_a \, X_{x'} \qquad ...(13.31)$$

Hence
$$\frac{1}{\delta X_{x'}} = \frac{1}{p_a \, X_{x'}} - \frac{1}{p_s \, X_{x'}} \qquad ...(13.32)$$

where
$$p_a X_{x'} = \frac{p}{(1 + \lambda) \cos \theta} \qquad ...(13.33)$$

For small γ,

$$p_s X_{x'} = p_s X_x = p \, (1 + \varepsilon_x) \qquad ...(13.34)$$

The x displacement at any point is

$$u = p_x N_x \qquad ...(13.35)$$

$$\frac{\partial u}{\partial x'} = \frac{p}{\delta x \, x'} \qquad ...(13.36)$$

where u is the total displacement, introduced by screen rotations, analyzer mismatch and specimen strain.

From Eqs. (13.32), (13.33), (13.34) and (13.36), we get

$$\varepsilon_x = 1 - (1 + \lambda) \cos \theta + \frac{\partial u}{\partial x'} \qquad ...(13.37)$$

By Eq. (13.35),

$$\varepsilon_x = 1 - (1 + \lambda) \cos \theta + p \, \frac{\partial N_x}{\partial x'} \qquad ...(13.38)$$

and similarly
$$\varepsilon_y = 1 - (1 + \lambda) \cos \theta + p \, \frac{\partial N_y}{\partial y'} \qquad ...(13.39)$$

Now
$$p_s X_{y'} = \frac{2p \, (1 + \varepsilon_x)}{\gamma} \qquad ...(13.40)$$

and for the analyzer

$$p_a X_y = \frac{p}{(1 + \lambda) \sin \theta} \qquad ...(13.41)$$

Let positive shear γ, be defined at the angular change resulting in an acute angle between the x and y axes. Then positive shear of the specimen screen increases the frequency of Moire's fringe in the y' direction, whereas positive rotation of the analyzer has the opposite effect. Accordingly

$$\frac{1}{\delta X_{y'}} = \frac{1}{p_s \, X'_y} - \frac{1}{p_a X_{y'}} \qquad ...(13.42)$$

Again, for small strains, displacement per Moire's fringe is p, and

$$\frac{\partial u}{\partial y'} = \frac{p}{\delta_{Xy'}} \qquad \text{...(13.43)}$$

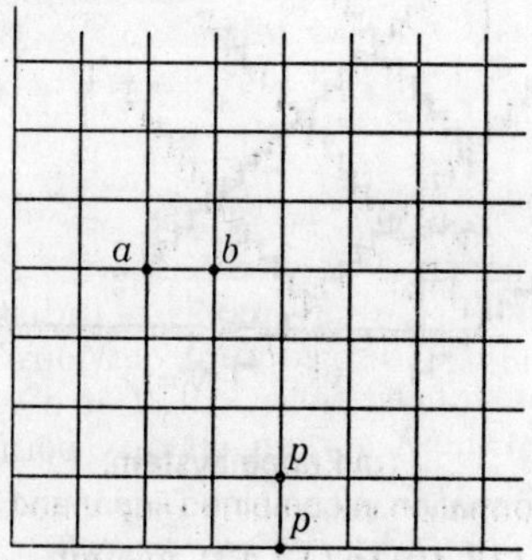

(*a*) Undeformed specimen grid.

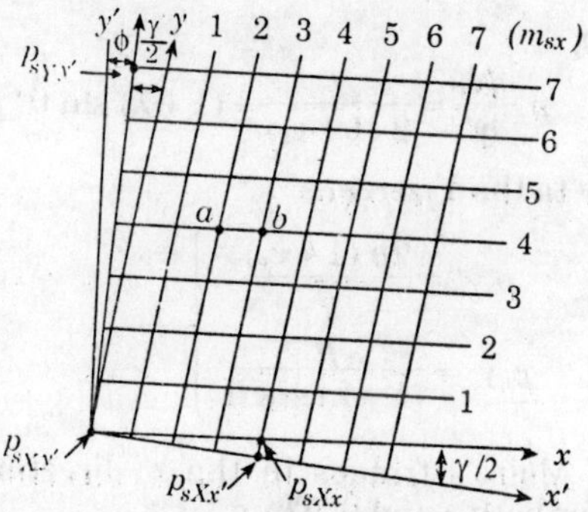

(*b*) Deformed specimen grid.

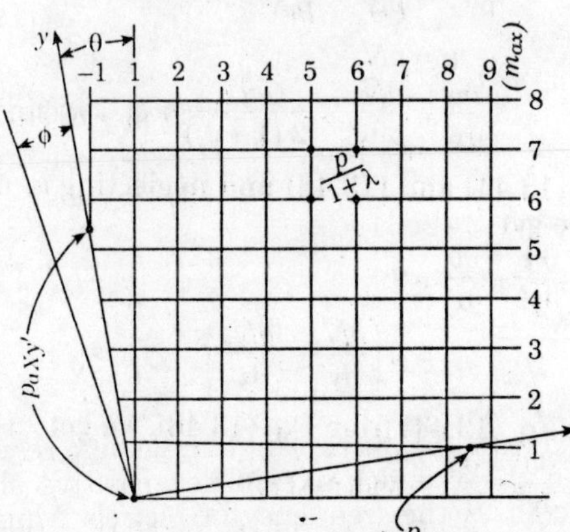

(*c*) Analyser grid.

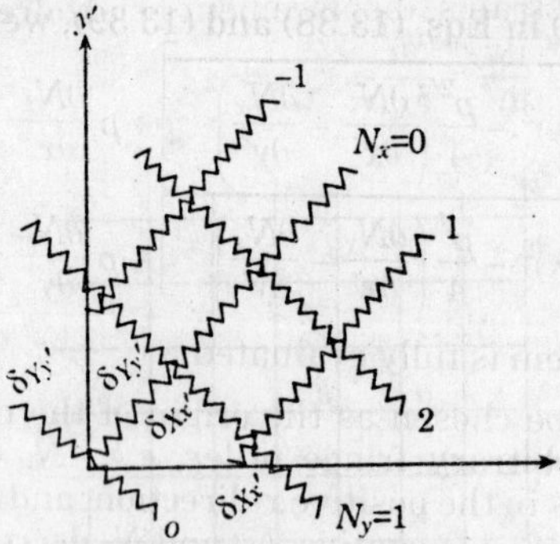

(*d*) Fringe system.

Fig. 13.11 Fringe formation in combined linear and rotational mismatch.

Combining Eqs. (13.40) to (13.43), we get

$$\frac{\partial u}{\partial y'} = \frac{\gamma}{2\,(1+\varepsilon_x)} - (1+\lambda)\sin\theta \qquad ...(13.44)$$

and by Eq. (13.36),

$$p\,\frac{\partial N_x}{\partial y'} = \frac{\gamma}{2\,(1+\varepsilon_x)} - (1+\lambda)\sin\theta \qquad ...(13.45)$$

Referring now to the *Y*-screens

$$\left.\begin{aligned} p_{sY_{x'}} &= \frac{2p\,(1+\varepsilon_y)}{\gamma} \\ p_{aY_{x'}} &= \frac{p}{(1+\lambda)\sin\theta} \end{aligned}\right\} \qquad ...(13.46)$$

The frequency of Moire's fringes in the x' direction increases with positive rotation for both γ and θ. Thus

$$\frac{1}{\delta_{Y_{z'}}} = \frac{1}{p_{sY_{x'}}} + \frac{1}{p_{aY_{x'}}} \qquad ...(13.47)$$

Since $\qquad v = pN_y$

$$\frac{\partial v}{\partial x'} = \frac{\partial N_y}{p\partial x'} = \frac{\gamma}{2\,(1+\varepsilon_y)} + (1+\lambda)\sin\theta \qquad ...(13.48)$$

Adding Eqs. (13.44) and (13.48) and neglecting ε_x and ε_y as compared to unity, we get

$$\frac{\partial u}{\partial y'} + \frac{\partial v}{\partial x'} = \gamma \qquad ...(13.49)$$

or

$$\gamma_{xy} = p\left(\frac{\partial N_x}{\partial y'} + \frac{\partial N_y}{\partial x'}\right) \qquad ...(13.50)$$

Substracting Eq. (13.44) from Eq. (13.48), we get

$$\frac{\partial v}{\partial x'} - \frac{\partial u}{\partial y'} = 2\,(1+\lambda)\sin\theta \qquad ...(13.51)$$

Thus

$$\theta = \sin^{-1}\left[\frac{p}{2\,(1+\lambda)}\left(\frac{\partial N_y}{\partial x'} - \frac{\partial N_x}{\partial y'}\right)\right] \qquad ...(13.52)$$

Subtracting for θ in Eqs. (13.38) and (13.39), we get

$$\varepsilon_x = \left[1 - \sqrt{(1+\lambda)^2 - \frac{p^2}{4}\left(\frac{\partial N_y}{\partial x'} - \frac{\partial N_x}{\partial y'}\right)^2}\right] + p\,\frac{\partial N_x}{\partial x'} \qquad \text{...(13.53)}$$

$$\varepsilon_y = \left[1 - \sqrt{(1+\lambda)^2 - \frac{p^2}{4}\left(\frac{\partial N_y}{\partial x'} - \frac{\partial N_x}{\partial y'}\right)^2}\right] + p\,\frac{\partial N_y}{\partial y'} \qquad \text{...(13.54)}$$

Thus the strain system is fully evaluated.

Any point may be chosen as the origin of the co-ordinate system and assigned an arbitrary fringe order, *e.g.*, $N_x = N_y = 100$. If λ is positive, N_x increases in the positive x-direction, and N_y increases in the positive y-direction. If λ is negative, N_x and N_y decrease in the positive x and y directions respectively. With Moire's fringe orders established throughtout the field, their gradient and thus the strains can be determined at any or every point.

13.5 Fringe Ordering

The order of a fringe may be either absolute or relative. The absolute fringes represent absolute displacement values of N_p from the zero point. In general, it is very difficult or impossible to identify absolute fringe orders. Therefore, it is a common practice to order fringes with relative fringe orders. There are two reasons for this,

(*i*) it is usually the derivative of the fringe order that is of use.

(*ii*) a displacement curve can be shifted to fit the boundary conditions if they exist.

The following procedure may be adopted to assign the fringe orders:

1. Start with a very large number so that it will not become zero or negative, so as to avoid possible confusion.
2. Set up an x-y coordinate system on the pattern with one of the axes coinciding with the principal direction of the gratings.
3. Assign fringe order with increasing orders along the positive principal direction if the fringes are positive, and decreasing orders if negative, and this can be done starting from different regions.
4. When the fringes meet, smooth out the difference so that the orders are consecutive.
5. Two neighbouring fringes can be of the same order, if they are on the opposite side of a hill or valley of fringe orders.

13.6 Sign Determination

A fringe is said to be positive if $\partial N/\partial\delta > 0$ and negative if $\partial N/\partial\delta < 0$, where δ is the distance along the principal direction of the reference grating. The fringes can also be neutral as produced due to rotation alone for which $\partial N/\partial\delta = 0$. A single fringe may be used for determination of fringe sign.

1. **Linear mismatch method.** In this method a small change is imposed in the pitch of the reference grating and the resulting change

of the Moire's fringe spacing is observed. Now the fringe spacing is given by

$$\delta = \frac{pp'}{p - p'}$$

If p is changed to $p + dp$, the resulting fringe spacing is

$$\delta' = \delta + d\delta = \frac{(p + dp)\,p'}{(p + dp) - p'} \approx \frac{pp'}{(p - p) + dp}$$

Thus for $dp > 0$, we have

$$\delta' < \delta, \text{ if } (p - p') > 0 \qquad \text{...(13.55)}$$

and

$$\delta' > \delta, \text{ if } (p - p') < 0 \qquad \text{...(13.56)}$$

Since difference of pitch is a measure of normal strain which is directly proportional to $\partial N/\partial \delta$, for positive dp we have negative fringes, or

$$\frac{\partial N}{\partial \delta} < 0 \text{ if } \delta' < \delta \qquad \text{...(13.57)}$$

and positive fringes, or

$$\frac{\partial N}{\partial \delta} > 0 \text{ if } \delta' > \delta \qquad \text{...(13.58)}$$

The reverse will hold if a negative dp is imposed.

2. **Rotational mismatch method.** In this method the sign of fringes is determined by rotating the reference (or specimen) grating slightly and observing the resulting rotation of the fringes. For a small rotation, the fringe orientation is given by

$$\tan \phi = \frac{p\theta}{p - p'}$$

Differentiating by keeping p and p' constant, we get

$$\sec^2 \phi d\phi = \left(\frac{p}{p - p'}\right) d\theta \qquad \text{...(13.59)}$$

Therefore for a given $d\theta$, the sign of $d\phi$ is determined by the sign of $(p - p')$, *i.e.*, the normal strain. The following rule may be formulated to determine the sign of fringes :

Upon the imposition of a small rotation to the reference grating, the Moire's fringes will rotate in the same direction if they are positive, and in the opposite direction if negative.

If the rotation is applied to the specimen grating, the rule as stated above is reversed.

The sign of the shear strain γ_{xy} can be determined by using the following table :

$\varepsilon_{x,y}$	*X-grating*	*Y-grating*	γ_{xy}
+	+	−	−
+	−	+	+
−	+	−	+
−	−	+	−

13.7 Sensitivity of Moire's Fringes

Now $$\varepsilon = \frac{p}{\delta}$$

Differentiating, we get

$$d\varepsilon = -\frac{p}{\delta^2}\,d\delta = -\frac{\varepsilon}{\delta}\,d\delta$$

Hence $$\frac{d\delta}{\delta} = -\frac{d\varepsilon}{\varepsilon} \quad \text{...(13.60)}$$

Eq. (13.60) gives us a simple means of determining the sensitivity of the Moire's technique.

13.8 Moire's Gap Effect and Fringe Shifting

The main drawback of the Moire's method is lack of sensitivity. Sensitivity can be increased by increasing the line density of the grating but practical difficulties have limited this density to about 400 lines per cm. Several methods to increase the sensitivity of the method have been suggested in the literature. One of the simplest method is the technique of fringe shifting by either shifting the reference grating or the model grating.

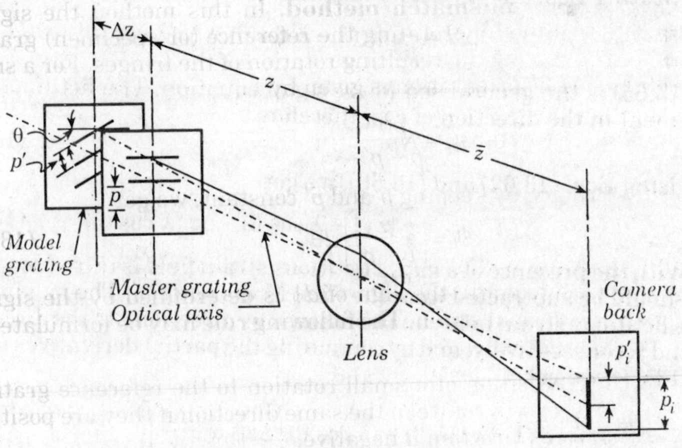

Fig. 13.12 Optical set up for the observation of Moire's gap effect.

13.8.1 Generalised Moire's Gap Equation

If two gratings with a gap between them are placed in front of the camera whose optical axis is perpendicular to the plane of the master grating and camera is focused on the master grating, they will appear at the image plane of the camera as shown in Fig. 13.12. Let p and p' denote the pitches of the master grating and model grating, respectively, $\lambda = p/p'$ denote the linear mismatch, and θ $(0 \le \theta \le \pi/2)$ denote the rotational mismatch, it is easily seen that the effective pitch, before the imaging process, of the model grating in the direction normal to the master-grating lines is given by

$$\frac{p'}{\cos\theta} = \frac{p}{\lambda\cos\theta} \qquad ...(13.61)$$

After going through the camera lens, the pitch of the master grating at the image plane is given by

$$p_i = p\,\frac{\bar{z}}{z} \qquad ...(13.62)$$

in which z and $\bar{z}$ are the object and image distances respectively. And the effective pitch of the model grating at the image plane is given by

$$p_i' = \frac{p}{\lambda\cos\theta}\cdot\frac{\bar{z}}{z+\Delta z} \qquad ...(13.63)$$

The relative displacement in terms of Moire's fringe order is then

$$N = \left(\frac{1}{p_i} - \frac{1}{p_i'}\right) r \qquad ...(13.64)$$

where r is the distance measured from the optical axis along the direction normal to master grating lines (*i.e.* the principal direction). Because of the axial symmetric property of a lens, the principal directions can be oriented arbitrary in a plane normal to the optical axis. Substituting Eqs. (13.62) and (13.63) into (13.64), we get

$$N = \frac{r}{p\bar{z}}\,[z\,(1-\lambda\cos\theta) - \Delta z(\lambda\cos\theta)] \qquad ...(13.65)$$

Eq. (13.65) is the generalised Moire's-gap equation. The fictitious displacement in the direction of r is, therefore,

$$u_r = Np_i \qquad ...(13.66)$$

Using Eqs. (13.62) and (13.66), we get

$$u_r = \frac{r}{z}\,[z\,(1-\lambda\cos\theta) - \Delta z\,(\lambda\cos\theta)] \qquad ...(13.67)$$

With the presence of a gap, a fictitious strain field is introduced and this should be subtracted from the final Moirs pattern. The magnitude of the fictitious strain field can be obtained by direction r to the direction of x and y, consecutively, and by computing the partial derivatives using Eq. (13.67), we get

$$\varepsilon_x = \frac{\partial u}{\partial x} = \frac{1}{z}\left[z\,(1-\lambda\cos\theta) - (\lambda\cos\theta)\left(\Delta z + x\,\frac{\partial\Delta z}{\partial x}\right)\right] \qquad ...(13.68)$$

$$\varepsilon_y = \frac{\partial v}{\partial y} = \frac{1}{z}\left[z\,(1-\lambda\cos\theta) - (\lambda\cos\theta)\left(\Delta z + y\,\frac{\partial\Delta z}{\partial y}\right)\right] \qquad ...(13.69)$$

$$\gamma_{xy} = \frac{\partial u}{\partial y} + \frac{\partial v}{\partial x} = -\frac{1}{z}\,(\lambda\cos\theta)\left(x\,\frac{\partial\,\Delta z}{\partial y} + y\,\frac{\partial\Delta z}{\partial x}\right) \qquad ...(13.70)$$

When λ, θ, Δz are constants, Eq. (13.65) becomes

$$N = -kr \qquad ...(13.71)$$

in which k is the constant of proportionality.

When $\lambda = 1$ and $\theta = 0$ then

$$N = -\frac{\Delta zr}{zp} \qquad ...(13.72)$$

With $k = \frac{\Delta z}{zp}$, differentiating Eq. (13.72), we get

$$dN = -kdr \qquad ...(13.73)$$

Eq. (13.73) states that the change of the position of optical axis (dr) is directly proportional to the change of fringe order (dN) with opposite sign.

Thus when a gap exists between the master and model gratings, it can be used advantageously to read fractional fringe orders. This is done by shifting the optical axis of the recording camera. The change in fringe order is directly proportional to the change of position of optical axis but with opposite sign. This phenomena can also be used for the determination of sign of the Moire's fringes. The fringe movement will be in the same direction as the shift of the optical axis if the local strain is compressive, and in the opposite direction if the local strain is tensile.

13.8.2 Mechanism of Fringe Shifting

Fringe positions are functions of the intersection points of the two gratings as shown in Fig. 13.13, where master grating has been shifted one quarter of its pitch in the direction normal to the lines. The fringe positions have changed accordingly. The same amount of movement of the fringe can be obtained if the master grating is held fixed a proper shift is given to the specimen grating. However, in general, this is less practical. From Fig. 13.13 it can be seen that the ratio k can be defined from similar triangles AFC and DEF such that

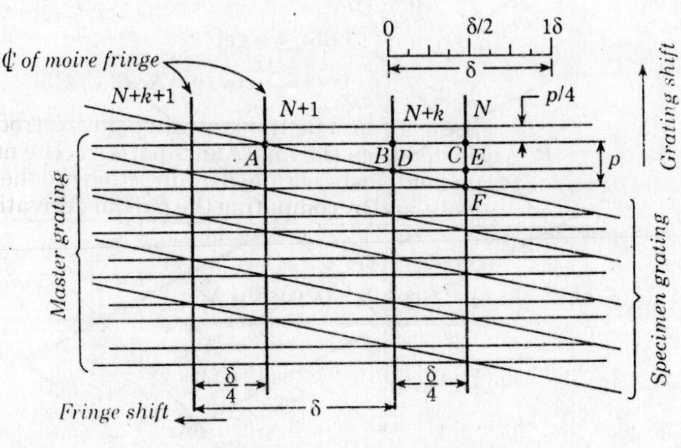

Fig. 13.13 Moire's fringe shift method.

$$\frac{EF}{CF} = \frac{BC}{AC} = k \qquad ...(13.74)$$

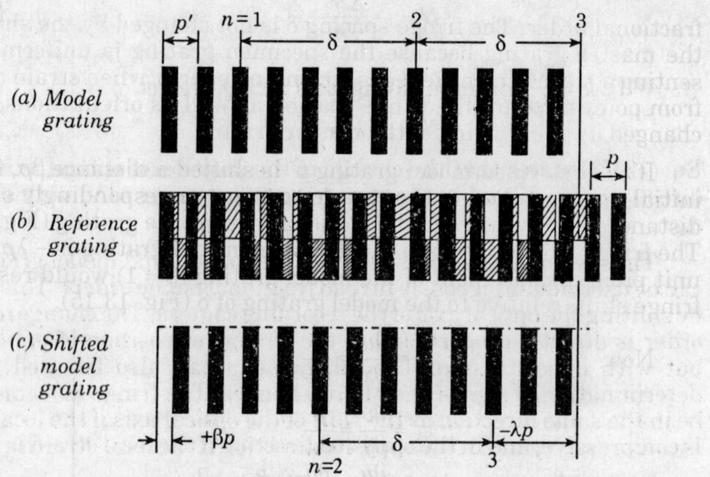

Fig. 13.14 Grid and fringe shifts.

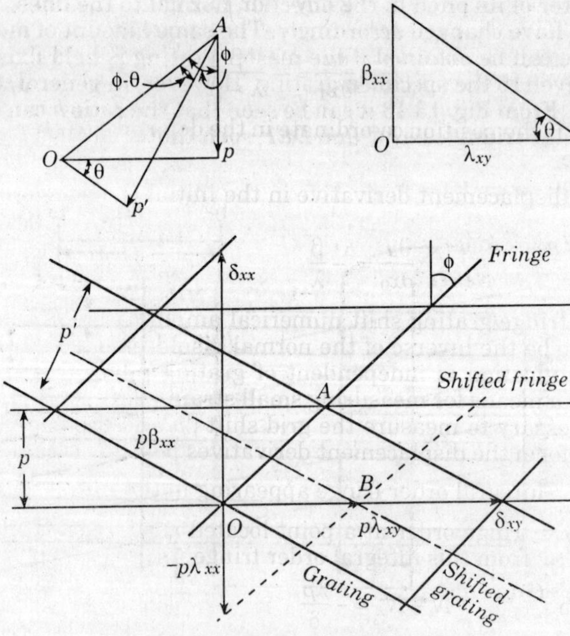

Fig. 13.15 Grid shift geometry.

Therefore, the new positions now occupied by the fringes are of the order $(N + k)$ and $(N + 1) + k$, respectively. Since k can be varied continuously, it is evident that we can shift the fringes continuously across the field. Thus, we can use the technique of fringe shifting to read fractional order. The fringe spacing δ is not changed by the shifting of the master grating because the specimen grating is uniform, representing a state of homogeneous strain. In general, when strain changes from point to point, the fringe spacing as well as orientations, will be changed by the shifting of the master grating.

If the deformed model grating p' is shifted a distance βp, from its initial position, the interference fringes are correspondingly shifted a distance $-\lambda p$, relative to the stationary reference grating (Fig. 13.14). The fringe shift relative to the displaced model grating is $-\lambda p + \beta p$. A unit pitch displacement of the model grating ($\beta = 1$) would result in a fringe shift, relative to the model grating of δ (Fig. 13.15).

Now
$$\left.\begin{aligned} \varepsilon_x &= \frac{\partial u}{\partial x} = \frac{p}{\delta_{xx}} \\ \varepsilon_y &= \frac{\partial v}{\partial y} = \frac{p}{\delta_{yy}} \\ \gamma_{xy} &= \frac{\partial u}{\partial y} + \frac{\partial v}{\partial x} = \frac{p}{\delta_{xy}} + \frac{p}{\delta_{yx}} \\ \text{Rotation} \quad w &= \frac{1}{2}\left(\frac{\partial u}{\partial y} - \frac{\partial v}{\partial x}\right) = \frac{1}{2}\left(\frac{p}{\delta_{xy}} - \frac{p}{\delta_{yx}}\right) \end{aligned}\right\} \qquad ..(13.75)$$

Thus
$$\frac{p}{\delta} = \frac{\partial u}{\partial x_1} = -\frac{\beta}{\lambda - \beta} \qquad ...(13.76)$$

where x_1 is the position co-ordinate in the deformed (Eulerian) frame of reference.

The displacement derivative in the initial (Lagrangian) reference is

$$\frac{\partial u}{\partial x_0} = -\frac{\beta}{\lambda} \qquad ...(13.77)$$

The fringe/grating shift numerical amplification is seen from Eq. (13.77) to be the inverse of the normal displacement derivative. Since the amplification is independent of grating pitch, this phenomenon provides a means for measuring small strain with coarse gratings. It is only necessary to measure the grid shift βp and the fringe shift λp in order to form the displacement derivatives point by point.

If N = integral order fringe appearing in the initial pattern

N_λ = fringe order at a point located λ reference grating pitches from this integral order fringe.

Then
$$N - N_\lambda = -\frac{\lambda p}{\delta} \qquad ...(13.78)$$

Substituting Eq. (13.76) in (13.78), we obtain

$$N_\lambda = N - \beta\left(\frac{\lambda}{\lambda - \beta}\right) \qquad ...(13.79)$$

Using Eq. (13.79) and measuring β for a number of different λ, the fringe order can be determined at as many as δ/p positions between integral fringes.

By proportion

$$\frac{\beta_{xx}\, p}{p} = \frac{p\,(\beta_{xx} - \lambda_{zx})}{\delta_{xx}}$$

from which, and referring to Eq. (13.75)

$$\frac{p}{\delta_{xx}} = \frac{\partial u}{\partial x_1} = -\frac{\beta_{xx}}{\lambda_{xx} - \beta_{xx}} \qquad \text{...(13.80)}$$

The u-fringe shift in the y-direction is governed by somewhat more complex relationships. From Fig. 13.15, we see that

$$\sin \theta = \frac{\beta_{xr}}{(\lambda_{xy}^2 + \beta_{xx}^2)^{1/2}} = \frac{p'}{\delta_{xy}}$$

or

$$\frac{p}{\delta_{xy}} = \frac{\partial u}{\partial y_1} = \frac{p}{p'}\, \beta_{xx}\, (\lambda_{xy}^2 + \beta_{xx}^2)^{1/2} \qquad \text{...(13.81)}$$

$$OA = \frac{p}{\sin\left(\dfrac{\pi}{2} - \phi\right)}$$

$$= \frac{p'}{\sin\left(\dfrac{\pi}{2} - \phi + \theta\right)}$$

from which

$$\frac{p}{p'} = \frac{\cos \phi}{\cos (\phi - \theta)} \qquad \text{...(13.82)}$$

Substituting Eq. (13.82) in (13.81), we get

$$\frac{\partial u}{\partial y_1} = \frac{\beta_{xx} \cos \phi}{\cos (\phi - \theta)}\, (\lambda_{xy}^2 + \beta_{xx}^2)^{-1/2} \qquad \text{...(13.83)}$$

where

$$\theta = \tan^{-1}\left(\frac{\beta_{xx}}{\lambda_{xy}}\right) \qquad \text{...(13.84)}$$

and

$$\phi = \tan^{-1}\left(\frac{\lambda_{xy}}{-\lambda_{xx}}\right)$$

Similarly for orthogonal v-displacement set of gratings

$$\frac{\partial v}{\partial y_1} = \frac{-\beta_{yy}}{\lambda_{yy} - \beta_{yy}} \qquad \text{...(13.85)}$$

$$\frac{\partial v}{\partial x_1} = \frac{\beta_{yy} \cos \phi}{\cos (\phi - \theta)}\, (\lambda_{yx}^2 + \beta_{yy}^2)^{-1/2} \qquad \text{...(13.86)}$$

where now

$$\theta = \tan^{-1}\left[\frac{\beta_{yy}}{\lambda_{yx}}\right]$$

and

$$\phi = \tan^{-1}\left[\frac{\lambda_{yx}}{-\lambda_{yy}}\right]$$

For moderate rotation

$$\frac{p}{p'} = 1 - \varepsilon_x$$

and $\beta_{xx} \ll \lambda_{xy}$

then

$$\left.\begin{aligned}\frac{\partial u}{\partial y_1} &= \left(\frac{\beta_{xx}}{\lambda_{xy}}\right)\left(\frac{\lambda_{xx}}{\lambda_{xx} - \beta_{xx}}\right)\\ \frac{\partial v}{\partial x_1} &= \left(\frac{\beta_{yy}}{\lambda_{yx}}\right)\left(\frac{\lambda_{yy}}{\lambda_{yy} - \beta_{yy}}\right)\end{aligned}\right\} \quad \ldots(13.87)$$

13.9 Sharpening the Multiplication of Moire's Fringes

For analysis of small strains, the basic Moire's method is inadequate, as its sensitivity is low, and auxiliarly means to enhance its accuracy are required. Both the geometrical and displacement field approaches to Moire's fringe analysis require accurate determination of either the fringe spacings or the fringe gradients at the point of interest of the specimen. With the line density of the gratings limited to about 400 lines per cm, only a few fringes are normally present. Therefore, the spacings or gradients cannot be established with the required accuracy. To increase the sensitivity of the Moire's method, fringe sharpening and fringe multiplication techniques have been developed for use with the coarse gratings.

13.9.1 Fringe Sharpening

For identical model and master gratings before deformation and the opaque and clear bands of the gratings being of equal width, the emergent light perpendicular to the Moire's fringes varies with position according to the triangular distribution as shown in Fig. 13.16. The maximum intensity is that which emerges from one grating in the absence of the other, and the minimum is zero. The analyzer, or reference grating, will always consist of opaque and transparent basis. The ratio of black-line width to white line width will be denoted by R. Transmittance (T) of a grating is defined as the ratio of the white area to the total area of grating or $T = \frac{1}{1+R}$. Fringe sharpening can be achieved by the following methods.

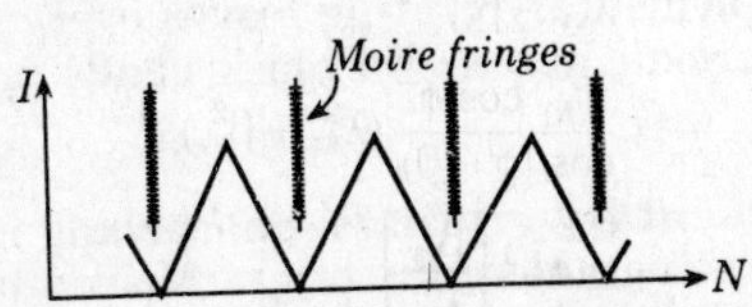

Fig. 13.16 Variation of light intensity with Moire's fringe order.

(*a*) **With Complementary gratings.** Post has shown that Moire's fringes can also be formed when the opaque bars and the clear spaces in the gratings do not have equal width. Moire's fringe sharpening is achieved by the superposition of two similar gratings in which the width of clear and opaque lines are complementary, *i.e.*, the ratio of R of one of the gratings is the reciprocal of the other. Thus if $R = A$ for one grating, $R = 1/A$ for the complementary grating. The details of fringes formation are shown in Fig. 13.17. Moire's fringes are formed along the vertical dashed lines, and average intensity, I, of emergent light along lines perpendicular to Moire's fringes is shown in the graph. With complementary gratings, extinction is complete along the centre of dark Moire's fringes. The average intensity increases rapidly to its maximum value, remains constant for an appreciable portion of the distance δ between the fringes and again drops rapidly to zero. Since the average intensity varies linearly, the effective width of the dark fringe may be taken as the width at $\frac{1}{2} I_{max}$ as designated by w in Fig. 13.17. The relationship between fringe spacing is readily derived as

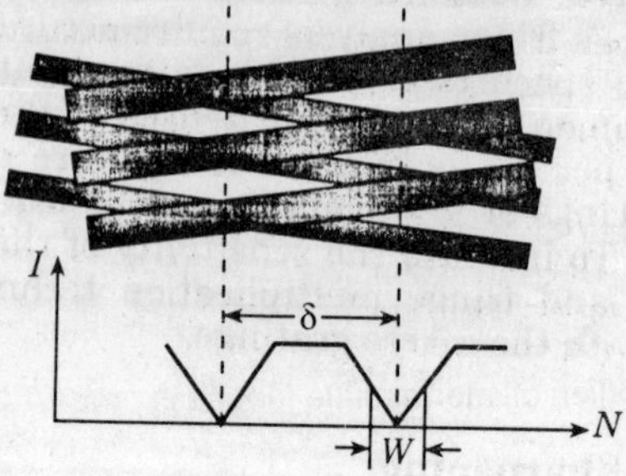

Fig. 13.17 Formation of sharpened fringes by complementary gratings.

$$\frac{w}{\delta} = \frac{1}{R+1} = T \qquad ...(13.88)$$

where $R > 1$, *i.e.* where R and T pertain to the darker screen. Thus Moire's fringe sharpness increases as the black to white ratio in the complementary gratings increasingly depart from unity.

(*b*) **Dashed fringes.** When every nth white band in the grating of greater transmittance is blackened, whereas in the mating complementary grating, every nth black band is absent, dashes Moire's fringes are obtained. The result is a pattern of sharpened Moire's fringes in which the condition of complementary grating leaves every nth fringe continuous, while the periodic absence of black bands produces dashed intermediate fringes.

(*c*) **Non-complementary gratings.** Sharpening is also achieved with $R > 1$ for both gratings. Here the bright Moire's bands are sharpened, but the intensity of the Moire's pattern is drastically diminished. This method is seldom used for fringe sharpening.

13.9.2 Fringe Multiplication

(*a*) **Geometrical methods.** Moire's patterns are typically formed by gratings of approximately the same frequency, *e.g.*,

$$f_a = (1 + \lambda) f_s \qquad \text{...(!3.89)}$$

where f = frequency of grating in lines per unit width

λ = analyser mismatch

a, s = subscripts for analyzer and specimen gratings.

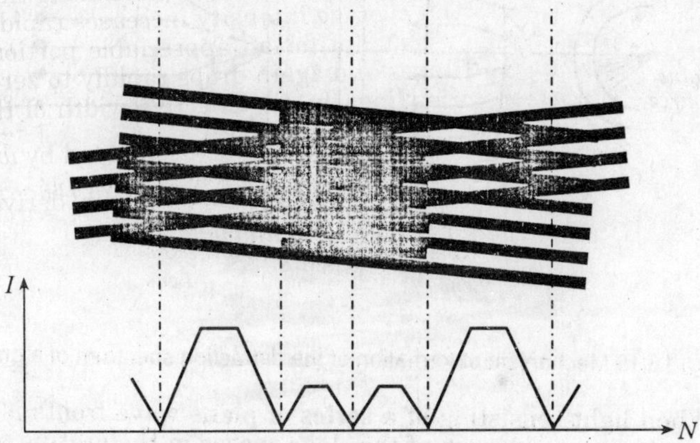

Fig. 13.18 Formation of intermediate fringes in fringe multiplication.

The phenomenon is also recognized when the frequency of the analyzer is increased by an integral factor, such that

$$f_a = \beta\,(1 + \lambda) f_s \qquad \text{...(13.90)}$$

where β is designated the fringe multiplication factor.

Moire's fringe multiplication is accomplished by introducing additional lines in the lighter grating of a complementary pair as shown in Fig. 13.18. The sharpened Moire's fringes of complementary gratings are evident in the end section of the pattern. By insertion of one extra line is each broad space of the lighter grating, one intermediate Moire's fringe is formed. The intensity distribution graph shows that the multiplied fringes are sharpened but diminished in intensity. The Moire's pattern formed by such a pair of gratings will then have several times as many fringes as the pattern formed by the original complementary pairs of gratings.

The specifications for gratings for fringe multiplication is Eq. (13.90) combined with

$$R_s = R_a = \beta \qquad \text{...(13.91)}$$

Fringe multiplication can also be achieved by using dashed gratings.

(*b*) **Optical methods.** The methods described above for fringe sharpening and fringe multiplication are the geometrical methods. Other methods of fringe sharpening and fringe multiplication by

Holister, Post, Sciammarella and Chiang utilize the diffraction effects associated with light passage through the gratings.

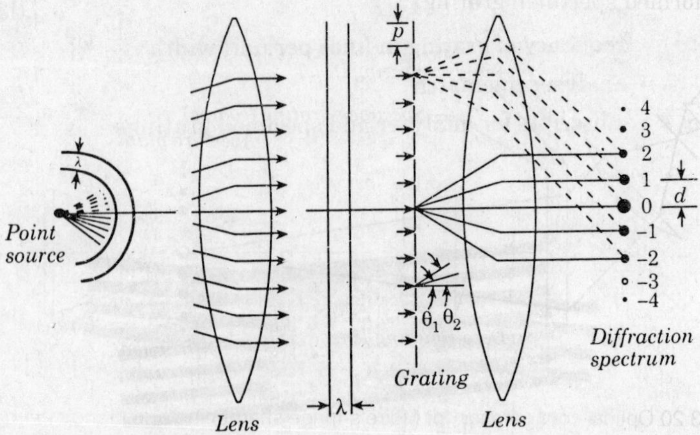

Fig. 13.19 Mechanism of formation of the diffraction spectrum of a grating.

When light consisting of a series of plane wave fronts is used to illuminate a grating, each of the clear spaces in the grating acts as a slit, and in accordance with Huygen's principle, emits light in the form of a series of secondary cylindrical wavelets. A surface which is tangent to these wavelets will be a wavefront in the region beyond the grating. A number of wavefronts are possible and are referred to as the different diffraction orders. Fig. 13.19 shows the diffraction of a plane wave front by a grating. The image formed by collecting all the diffraction orders from the grating with a lens is known as the diffraction spectrum of grating. Since the wavelets forming the first order beam are out of phase by one wavelength, the angle θ_1 can be determined from the expression

$$\sin \theta_1 = \theta_1 = \frac{\lambda}{p}$$

In general,

$$\sin \theta_n = \theta_n = \frac{n\lambda}{p} \qquad \text{...(13.92)}$$

The distance d between any two dots is

$$d = f\,\theta_1 = f\frac{\lambda}{p} \qquad \text{...(13.93)}$$

where f is the focal length of the decollimating lens.

One of the optical methods used to produce Moire's fringe sharpening and Moire's fringe multiplication based upon the simple diffraction phenomena is shown in Fig. 13.20. Light is diffracted first by the fine analyzer grating and then by the coarse specimen grating (or replica thereof). A pair of beams that emerge essentially parallel to the optical axis is converged by the decollimating lens and admitted through the aperture plate into the camera. They combine and form a two beam interference pattern—or Moire's pattern—depicting displacements in the deformed specimen grating.

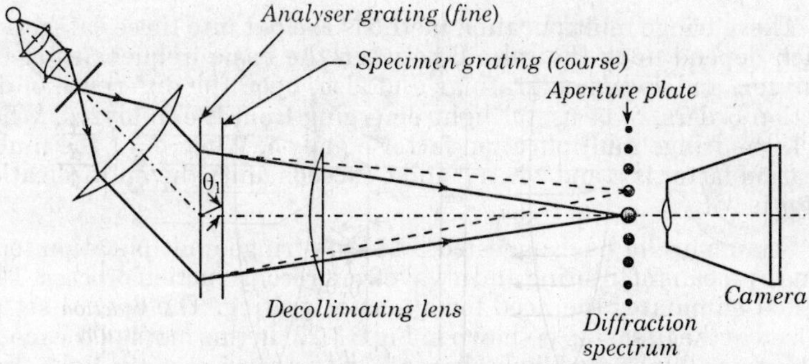

Fig. 13.20 Optical configuration for Moire's-fringe sharpening and Moire's-fringe multiplication by the diffraction method.

This configuration offers the important advantage that the Moire's fringes measure in plane displacements alone, out-of-plane displacements, manifest as variations of the distance between the specimen grating and analyzer grating, are not sensed. In addition, for a given multiplication, fringe formation is accomplished with the lowest possible diffraction orders. The Moire's fringes are basically two-beam interference fringes of high contrast. The Moire's pattern is viewed at or near normal emergence, thus avoiding distortion of the specimen geometry. Sensitivity is proportional to the frequency of rulings in the fine analyzer grating and independent of the specimen grating. This method can also be used for on-homogeneous strain fields.

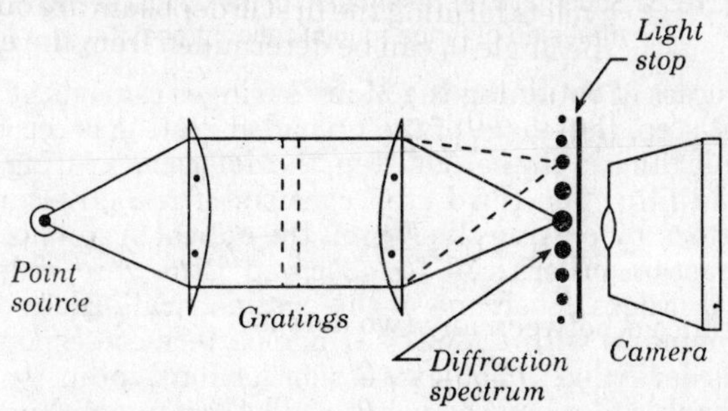

Fig. 13.21 Basic optical system for Moire's fringe multiplication.

Another method for Moire's-fringe sharpening and Moire's-fringe multiplication is shown in Fig. 13.21. The light stop or aperture is used to isolate the particular diffraction order being permitted to enter the camera lens. The experimental data may be obtained in the form of a deformed grating on a transparent plate. This grating may be (*i*) a photograph, (*ii*) a contact print or (*iii*) a replica of the specimen grating in the deformed state. The specimen grating is usually of the amplitude type, in the form of a grid, although phase gratings are also possible. The deformed specimen grating is mated with an analyzer, which may be amplitude or phase grating.

These fringe multiplication methods are put into three categories, which depend upon the ratio β between the basic frequencies of the analyzer, and specimen gratings and also, upon the difference of diffraction orders, δ, of useful light emerging from the analyzer. When β = 1, the fringe multiplication factor equals δ. When δ = 1 the multiplication factor is β and when β and δ exceeds unity the multiplication factor is βδ.

Sciammarella has suggested a Moire's-fringe multiplication technique by means of filtering and a wavefront reconstruction process. This method eliminates the need for a master grating. The optical set up utilised in the first step is shown in Fig. 13.22. In this method the model grating is illuminated by coherent and monochromatic light, and produces in a given plane P_1 a Fraunhofer diffraction pattern.

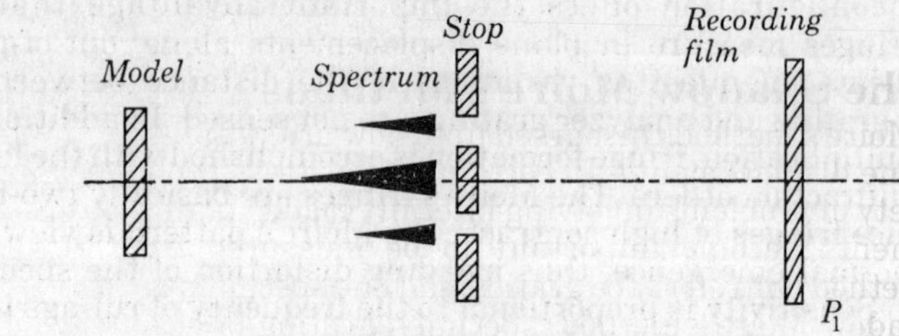

Fig. 13.22 Schematic representation of the optical set up in the first step of fringe multiplication process..

The process of obtaining the Moire's fringes consists of three steps ; in the first step, the image of the unloaded grating is recorded on the photographic film. In the second step, the deformed grating is recorded on the same film. The third step consists of the observation of the Moire's pattern by putting the film in the optical system of Fig. 13.23. Three diffraction orders can be observed ; the zero order and two symmetrical orders. Each one of the symmetrical orders contains an image of the model with a Moire's fringe pattern corresponding to the fractional order fringes. The expression for total intensity of light on the photographic film has been obtained by Sciammarella as :

$$I = I_0 + I_1 \cos 2\pi x \left[\frac{1}{p_2(x)/2n} - \frac{1}{p_1/2n}\right] \quad ...(13.94)$$

where $I_0 = 2A_0^2$

$I_1 = A_0^2$

A_0 = amplitude resulting in the reconstruction process

n = diffraction order

p_1 = pitch of undeformed grating

$p_2(x)$ = pitch of the deformed grating

x = distance between the objective lens L_2 and image plane.

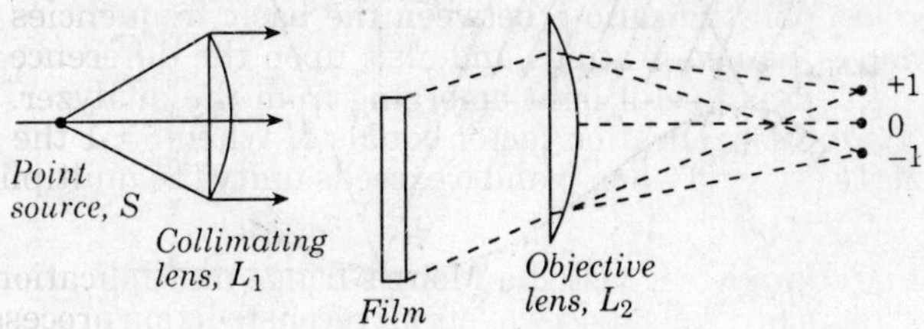

Fig. 13.23 Optical system utilized in the wave front reconstruction process.

Eq. (13.94) shows that $2n$ times as many fringes are obtained as in the fundamental pattern. Consequently, two successive image superpositions can be made equivalent to the simultaneous superposition of two gratings.

13.10 The Shadow Moire's Methods

The Moire's methods discussed upto now are suitable for determining in plane displacements. In certain plane-stress problems and in a wide variety of problems involving laterally loaded plates, out-of-plane displacements become important to be measured. In the general Moire's method one reference grating and one specimen grating is used. In the shadow Moire's method, specimen grating is not used, but the shadow of the reference grating as cast on the surface of the structure (thus the name shadow Moire's) is used as the specimen grating. The shadow grating will be distorted by the out-of-plane depth of the surface, and when it is viewed together with the reference grating by eye or a camera, Moire's fringes are created which represent the topology of the surface. This method was first of all developed by Theocaris and later modified by Chiang and Marasco. Depending upon the complexity of the arrangement and its application, the shadow Moire's method may be categorized into the following three types.

1. **Parallel illumination and parallel receiving.** Fig. 13.24 shows the arrangement of shadow-Moire's method of this kind. A beam of collimated light impinges upon the reference grating of pitch p at an angle α from the normal to the grating plane. The shadow of the reference grating is cast on the surface of the specimen. The shadow grating together with the reference grating are viewed at infinity by camera whose axis makes an angle β from the normal to the grating plane. Moire fringes form as a result of interference between the lines of the reference and the shadows. The lines contained in AB of the reference grating occupy the distance AE on the surface of the structure. However, since point E coincides with point D at the image plane of the

viewing camera, the lines contained in AD will interfere with the lines in AE to form Moire's fringes. Assuming AD and AB have m and n lines respectively, we have

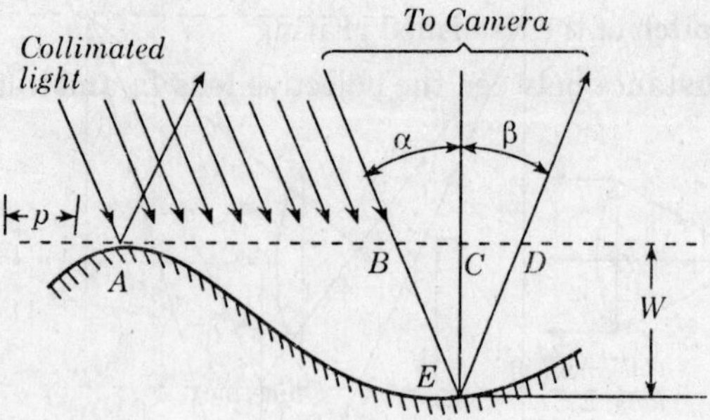

Fig. 13.24 Shadow Moire's method with parallel illumination and parallel receiving.

$$AD = mp, AB = np$$

and $$BD = AD - AB = (m - n)p = Np \quad ...(13.95)$$

where N is the fringe order at point D. But

$$BD = w\ (\tan \alpha + \tan \beta) \quad ...(13.96)$$

where w = vertical distance from the grating plane to point E

Substituting Eq. (13.96) into Eq. (13.95), we get

$$w = \frac{Np}{\tan \alpha + \tan \beta} \quad ...(13.97)$$

Eq. (13.97) is the field equation of this method. The Moire's fringes are contours of equal depth measured from the grating plane. For normal incidence, $\beta = 0$ and we get

$$w = \frac{Np}{\tan \alpha} \quad ...(13.98)$$

The assumption of the camera being at infinity can be closely approximately if the structure (model) is small and the camera is at sufficiently far distance away.

13.10.2 Use of curved grating in Shadow-Moire's

When both the light source and the camera are at a finite distance away from the structure, both the light source and the aperture of the camera lens may be approximated by a point. It will also be assumed that the point light source and the camera lens are located at the same distance away from the grating plane as shown in Fig. 13.25. If we assume that a fringe of order N is observed at point f on the surface through point d of the grating, it is the result of interference between the lines contained in ad of the reference grating and the liens in ab, as projected onto af, of the shadow-specimen grating. If the number of lines are m and n respectively, then

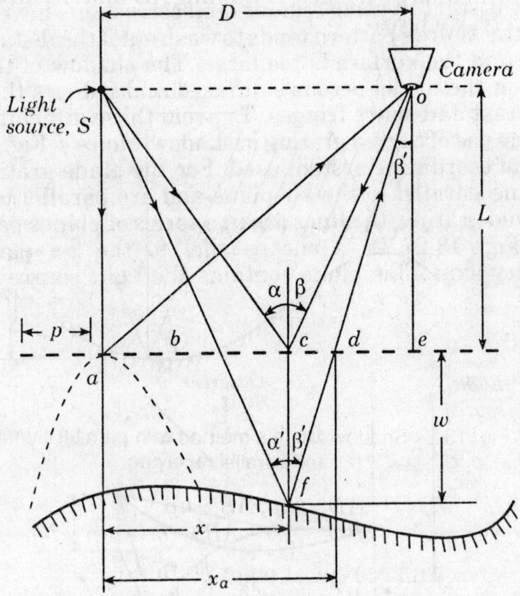

Fig. 13.25 Shadow-Moire's method with point illumination and point receiving.

$$ad = mp, \quad ab = np$$

and $$bd = ad - ab = (m - n)p = Np$$

But $$bd = w\,(\tan \alpha' + \tan \beta')$$

Thus $$w = \frac{Np}{\tan \alpha' + \tan \beta'}$$

$$= \frac{Np}{\dfrac{x}{L+w} + \dfrac{D-x}{L+w}} = \frac{Np\,(L+w)}{D} \quad \text{...(13.99)}$$

where D = distance (horizontal) between light and camera

L = distance of light source and camera from the grating plane.

Eq. (13.99) can be written as :

$$w = \frac{Np}{\dfrac{D}{L} - \dfrac{Np}{L}} \quad \text{...(13.100)}$$

when $D \gg Np$ and noting that

$$\frac{D}{L} = \tan \alpha + \tan \beta$$

we get $$w = \frac{Np}{\tan \alpha + \tan \beta}$$

which is identical with Eq. (13.97).

For large structures a plane grating used on a curved surface will be relatively distant in some regions, and corrections have to be made. In addition the Moire's pattern tends to wash out if the distance between the grating and the surface is too large. The shadow of the reference rating cast on the model becomes diffused and reduces the possibility of good contrast and sharp fringes. To avoid these difficulties Marasco suggested the use of curved grating in shadow-Moire's. Fig. 13.26 shows the system of coordinate system used. For the plane grating the lines are in a plane parallel to the *x-y* plane and are parallel to the *y*-axis. For the curved grating, the lines are in a series of planes parallel to the *y-z* plane. Fig. 13.27 is a cut parallel to the *x-z* plane at $y = b$, the symmetry axis. This plane contains the light source and the observer.

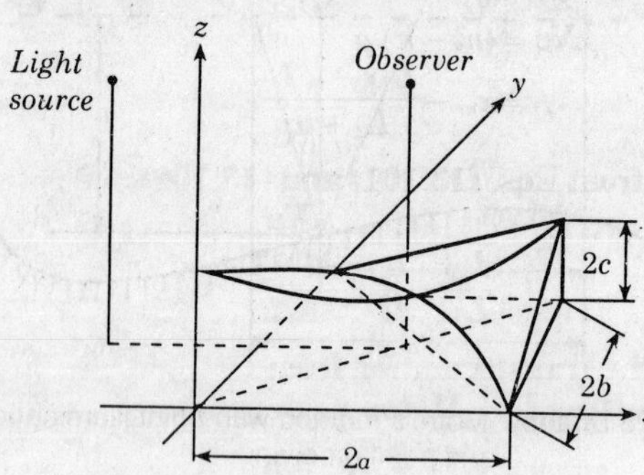

Fig. 13.26 Definition of coordinate axes.

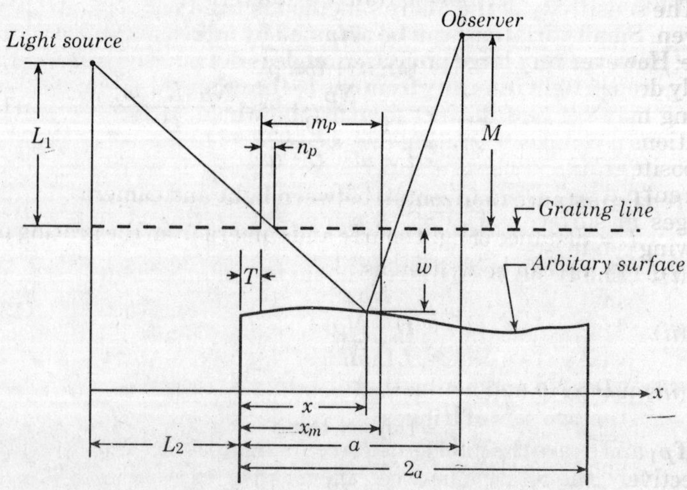

Fig. 13.27 Plane grating cut parallel to the *x-z* plane at $y = b$.

In order to determine w, the Moire's fringes are measured in the grating plane ; the point (x, b) is measured at (x_m, b). From Fig. 13.27, from similar triangles

$$x = x_m + \frac{w}{M}(x_m - a) \qquad ...(13.101)$$

Also $$\frac{L_2 + T + np}{L_1} = \frac{L_2 + x}{L_1 + w}$$

or $$np = \frac{L_1 x - wL_2}{L_1 + w} - T$$

Now $$np = x_m - T$$

If a Moire's fringe of order N is observed at x_m, it follows that

$$Np = (m - n)p$$

$$= x_m - \frac{L_1 x - wL_2}{L_2 + w} \qquad ...(13.102)$$

Eliminating x from Eqs. (13.101) and (13.102), we get

$$w = \frac{Np}{\dfrac{L_2}{L_1} + \dfrac{a}{M} + \dfrac{M - L_1}{ML_1} x_m - \dfrac{Np}{L_1}} \qquad ...(13.103)$$

Once w is known, the transformation from x_m to x is accomplished with Eq. (13.101). For setting $L_1 = M$, the x_m dependence vanishes.

Further $$y = y_m + \frac{w}{M}(y_m - b) \qquad ...(13.104)$$

13.10.3 Shadow-Moire's method with two discrete sensitivities

The sensitivity of the Moire's method is fixed once a grating pitch is given. Small variations can be obtained by increasing the projection angle. However very large projection angle is not advised because of the steady drop in light intensity from one to the other. Also sometimes one grating may not be sufficient to map the whole surface. In such like situations a composite grating may be used as proposed by Chiang. A composite grating consists of superimposed gratings with two discretely different pitches. This grating can effectively map small as well as large changes in surface variation. A composite grating should fulfil the following conditions :

(*i*) The two sets of fringes should not interfere with each other spatially.

(*ii*) They should be distinctly observable as individual fringes as well as two different families.

(*iii*) There should be a simple relationship between the orders of the two sets of fringes.

If p_1 and p_2 are the pitches of the coarser and finer element gratings respectively, the relation between them can be expressed as :

$$p_1 = kp_2, k > 2 \qquad ...(13.105)$$

The condition of k larger than 2 is imposed for avoiding linear mismatch fringes. In the case of shadow-Moire's fringes, it is necessary that the zero-order fringes for both families coincide, therefore, one can write

$$N_2 = kN_1,\ k > 2 \text{ and } N_1, N_2 \geq 0 \qquad \text{...(13.106)}$$

in which N_1 and N_2 are the absolute fringe orders for the coarser and finer elements gratings, respectively. In order to have both families of fringes distinctively observable and non-interfering, k should not be an irrational or a fractional number, because otherwise there will be regions where two-fringes from different families are situated too closely together to be distinguishable. In the cases where k involves half, the bright fringes of one family will at places, coincide with the dark fringes of the other. This may also create confusion and difficulty in observation. Therefore, the only allowable constants are integers. It is also necessary to have the width of the grating lines equal to one half of the pitch. Otherwise, there will be irregular spacings creating which tend to generate irregularity in the resulting fringe pattern. Furthermore, best visibility fringes also desires, the line-width to space ratio to be one. These considerations lead to the exclusion of k being even numbers as well. Therefore, the only permissible combinations of grating are such that

$$p_1 = kp_2,\ \ k = 3, 5, 7, 9,.. \qquad \text{...(13.107)}$$

In this way there will be k integral subfringes in between any two broad fringes and they can be considered as fractional fringes interpolating the coarser set with the following orders :

$$N_1 + \frac{r}{k},\ r = 0, 1, 2..., k \qquad \text{...(13.108)}$$

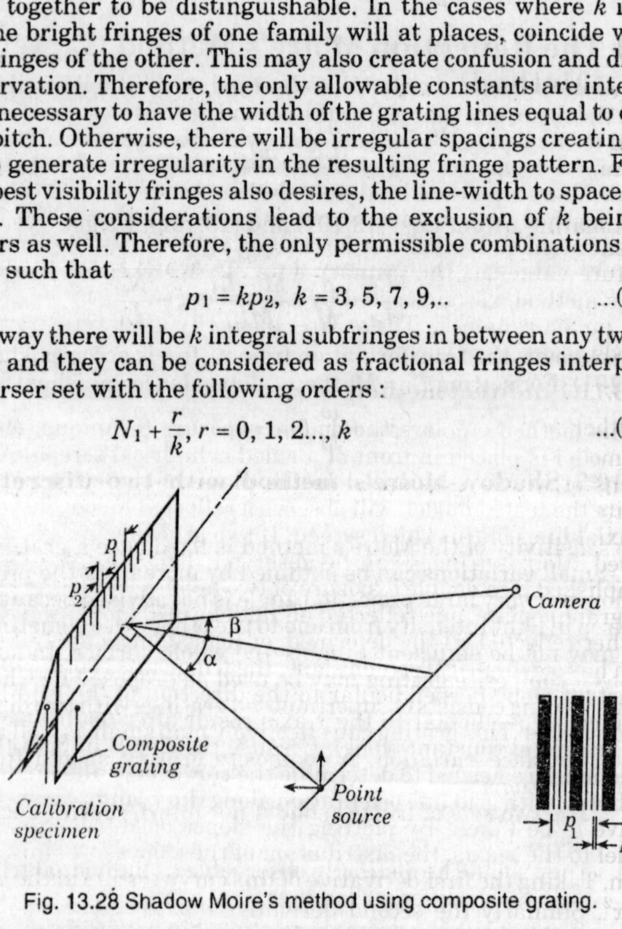

Fig. 13.28 Shadow Moire's method using composite grating.

The shadow-Moire's with composite gratings consists of wedge gap behind a composite grating with lines running along the wedge as shown in Fig. 13.28. It is illuminated by a point source of light and viewed by a camera. The centre of the camera lens is located on a line from the light source running parallel to the grating plane, but perpendicular to the grating lines. The field equation of the resulting shadow Moire's pattern as modified for the composite grating is given by

$$w = \frac{\left(N_1 + \frac{r}{k}\right)p_1}{\tan\alpha + \tan\beta - \frac{\left(N_1 + \frac{r}{k}\right)p_1}{L}}, \; r = 0, 1, 2,.., k \qquad ...(13.109)$$

13.11 The Reflection Moire's Method (Ligtenberg Method)

In the flexure of thin plates the second derivatives of deflection are related to the bending moments and twist. Second derivatives may be determined from the out-of-plane displacements obtained by the Shadow-Moire's method by differentiating twice. This is a very inaccurate method and serious errors may be introduced. To limit the differentiation to the first order only it is desirable to have slope or curvature values as the primary data. To achieve this the reflective Moire's method was suggested by Ligtenberg in 1954 for out-of-plane slope measurements. There are basically two reflection-Moire's methods as discussed below.

13.11.1 Indirect method

This method employs the double exposure technique. A reflected plate model is placed in front of a ruled cylindrical screen. A camera, the lens of which is mounted in the plane of the cylindrical screen opposite the tested model, will observe a reflected image of the equidistant axial lines of this ruled screen. If two grid-line images are superimposed, Moire's fringes can be observed. This superposition can be accomplished by a double exposure of two images on the same negative photographic plate, one reflected off undeformed, or unloaded, model ; the other reflected off the deformed, or loaded, model. Since the ruled screen has a cylindrical screen slope, the fringe lines obtained are lines of constant slope perpendicular to the direction of the grid lines (*e.g.* grid lines perpendicular to the x-axis result after double exposure in $\partial w/\partial x$ fringes of constant slope). Because the slopes in both the x- and y-directions are needed to determine the curvatures and angle of twist, two photos, with grid line orientation along the y- and x-axis respectively, have to be taken. By plotting the slopes $\partial w/\partial x$ along any section parallel to the x-axis, the distribution of the slopes over this section is known. Taking the first derivative of this curve results in the curvature $\partial^2 w/\partial x^2$. Similarly the second derivative $\partial^2 w/\partial y^2$ can be determined. Plotting the distribution of the $\partial w/\partial x$ slopes along a section parallel to the y-direction and evaluating the first derivative of this curve (in the y-direction) will result in the angle of twist $\partial^2 w/\partial x \partial y$. An identical result is reached if the first derivatives of $\partial w/\partial y$ slope distribution along a section parallel to the x-axis is determined. Then the stresses in the plate can be obtained from.

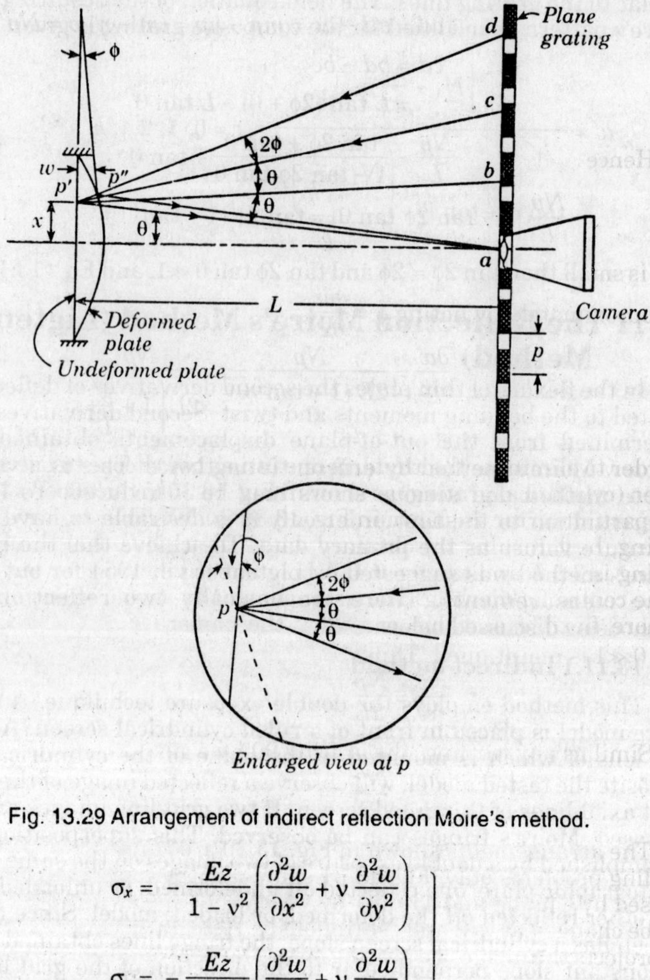

Fig. 13.29 Arrangement of indirect reflection Moire's method.

$$\left.\begin{aligned}\sigma_x &= -\frac{Ez}{1-\nu^2}\left(\frac{\partial^2 w}{\partial x^2}+\nu\frac{\partial^2 w}{\partial y^2}\right)\\ \sigma_y &= -\frac{Ez}{1-\nu^2}\left(\frac{\partial^2 w}{\partial y^2}+\nu\frac{\partial^2 w}{\partial x^2}\right)\\ \tau_{xy} &= -\frac{Ez}{1-\nu}\,\partial^2 w/\partial x\partial y\end{aligned}\right\} \qquad ...(13.110)$$

The optical arrangement of this method is shown in Fig. 13.29. If a fringe order N is observed at the image plane, it is due to the superposition of points c and d on the grating via points P' and P'' on the undeformed and deformed plates. For small deflection of the plate, points P' and P'' can be approximated by a single point P as shown in the enlarged view. If the slope of the plate along the x-direction changes from zero to ϕ, the light ray turns an angle 2ϕ. If m and n are the number of lines contained in ad and ac respectively then

$$cd = ad - ac = mp - np = (m - n)\,p = Np$$

and
$$cd = bd - bc$$
$$= L \tan(2\phi + \theta) - L \tan\theta$$

Hence
$$\frac{Np}{L} = \frac{\tan 2\phi + \tan\theta}{1 - \tan 2\phi \tan\theta} - \tan\theta$$

or
$$\frac{Np}{L}(1 - \tan 2\phi \tan\theta) = \tan 2\phi\,(1 + \tan^2\theta) \qquad \text{...(13.111)}$$

If 2ϕ is small then $\tan 2\phi \approx 2\phi$ and $\tan 2\phi \tan\theta \ll 1$, and Eq. (13.111) can be approximately by noting $\phi = \frac{\partial w}{\partial x}$,

$$\frac{\partial w}{\partial x} = \frac{Np}{2L\,(1 + \tan^2\theta)} = \frac{Np}{2L\left(1 + \frac{x^2}{L^2}\right)} \qquad \text{...(13.112)}$$

In order to eliminate the *x/L* term one can either choose to use a curved screen (cylindrical grating) as show in Fig. 13.30 (*a*) or to bend the light by a partial mirror as shown in Fig. 13.30 (*b*). While using a cylindrical grating, best results are obtained when the radius of the cylindrical grating is 3.5 L and $\tan\theta \approx 0.4$. A hole has to be drilled in the grating at the centre for viewing. The arrangement as shown in Fig. 13.30 (*b*) is more flexible and one can vary the camera position as long as $\tan^2\theta \ll 1$ is maintained. Thus

$$\frac{\partial w}{\partial x} = \frac{Np}{2L} \qquad \text{...(13.113)}$$

Similarly by turning, the grating 90°, we get

$$\frac{\partial w}{\partial y} = \frac{N'p}{2L} \qquad \text{...(13.114)}$$

The arrangements shown in Fig. 13.30 are suitable for static plate bending problems only. Fig. 13.31 shows another optical arrangement devised by Chiang and Treiber by which the sensitivity of the method can be changed at will and continuously. Here an ordinary slide projector projects the image of a grating on to a large ground glass. This image is then transmitted *via* a 45° oriented partial mirror to the model (flexed plate) and reflected back to a recording camera whose optical axis is perpendicular to the original plate plane. With this arrangement, the line density of the grating can be changed continuously and at will without disturbing any other component of the system, either optically or by using gratings of different line densitities in the projector. Further advantages are that the gratings used are very small as compared to the full size gratings required in the Ligtenberg method, and different types of gratings (*e.g.* circular, radial or crossed) may be used to best suit the particular problem.

Chiang and Bailangadi have also applied the reflective Moire's method to determine the deflection of flexed plates. The experimental set up is shown in Fig. 13.32. Here the grating plane is at an angle from the optical axis of the recording camera. The illumination is assumed to be from a diffused light source surrounding the model. Thus a point

P on the model collects a ray along the path DP and sends it to the camera along the path PA. Then

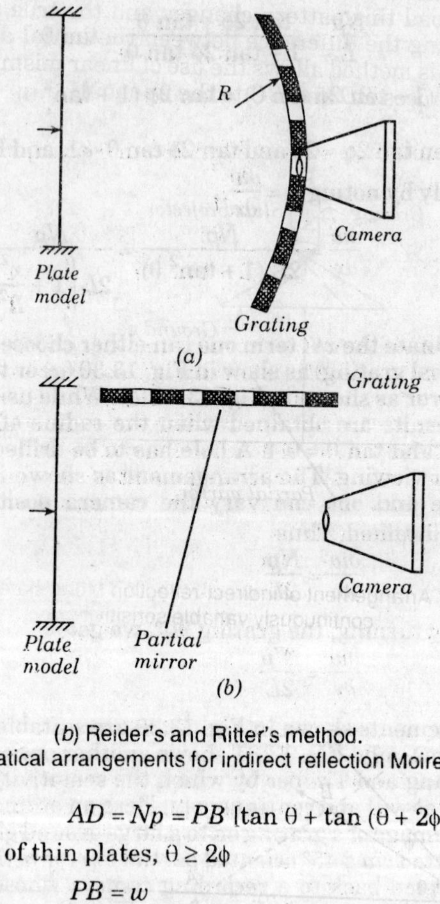

(b) Reider's and Ritter's method.
Fig. 13.30 Pratical arrangements for indirect reflection Moire's method.

$$AD = Np = PB\ [\tan\theta + \tan(\theta + 2\phi)]$$

For bending of thin plates, $\theta \geq 2\phi$

With $PB = w$

$$w = \frac{Np}{2\tan\theta} \quad \text{...(13.115)}$$

For $\theta = 45°,\ w = \dfrac{Np}{2}$

For $\theta = 0°,\ w = 0$ ...(13.116)

13.11.2 Direct method

Fig. 13.33 shows the arrangement for the direct method. Before loading the distance BC and BD are maintained equal so that the model and the reference mirror are images of each other. Two gratings are seen by the camera, one coming from the reference mirror and the other from the model. Under load specimen grating will be distorted and interferes with the reference grating to give reflection Moire's fringes directly. Thus the Moire's fringes can be observed in real time and can be recorded with a high-speed camera in a continuous fashion. This method is thus also best suited for plate vibration problems. Initial non-flatness of the model plate if any will be shown as initial Moire's fringes. Under load this pattern changes and the true deformation is obtained by taking the difference between the initial and final Moirś patterns. Also this method allows the use of linear mismatch fringes by making the distances BD and BC to the unequal.

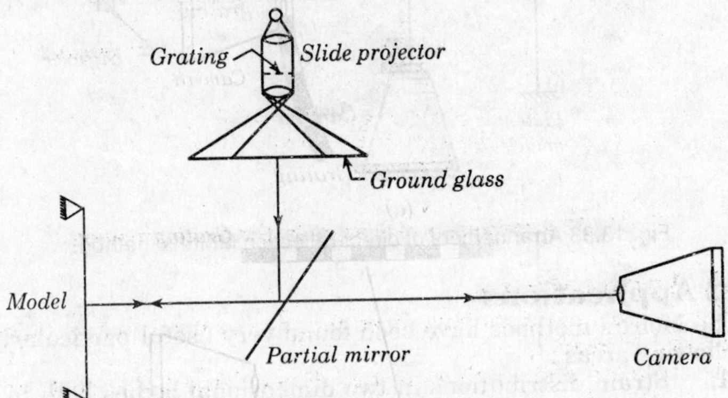

Fig. 13.31 Arrangement of indirect-reflection Moire's method with continuously variable sensitivity.

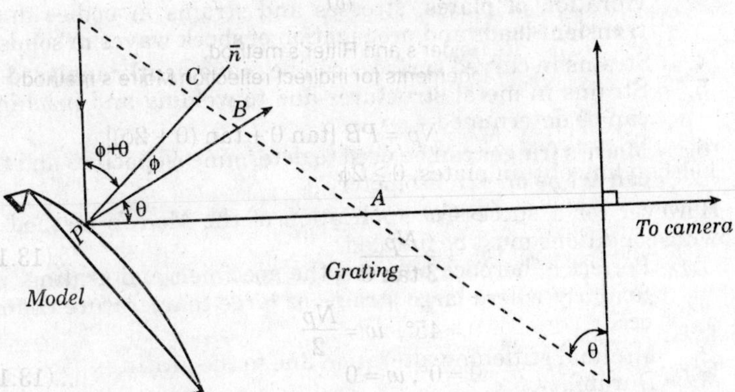

Fig. 13.32 Experimental set up for image Moire's method for the bending of plate.

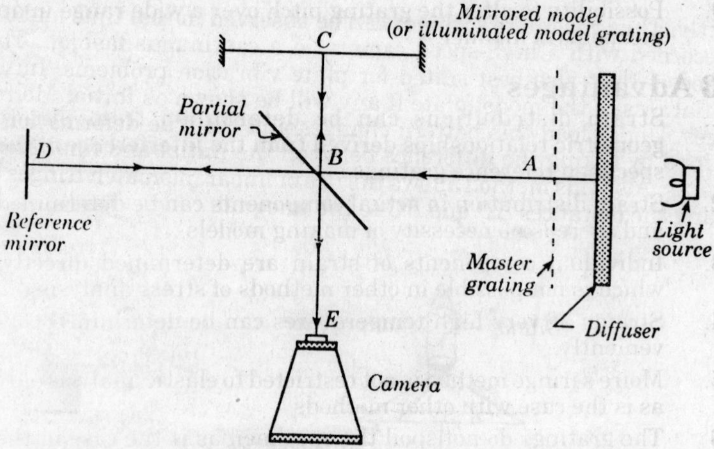

Fig. 13.33 Arrangement of direct-reflection Moire's method.

13.12 Applications

The Moire's methods have been found very useful particularly in the following areas :

1. Strain distributions in two dimensional bodies both in the elastic and elastoplastic states can be determined conveniently, particularly around sharp corners.
2. In plane and out-of-plane displacements and slopes can be determined easily.
3. Moire's methods can be used to study dynamic problems, *e.g.*, vibration of plates, stresses and strains in bodies due to transient loads and propagation of shock waves in solids.
4. Strains in curved surfaces can be conveniently analysed.
5. Strains in metal structures due to welding and machinery can be determined.
6. Moire's fringes can be used to determine isopachics and thus can act as an extensometer.

However for a successful application of the Moire's method the following conditions must be fulfilled.

1. Perfect adherence between the specimen and grating, particularly where large strains or large temperature changes occur.
2. Minimal stiffening alteration due to the grating.
3. Durability.
4. Easy and economical application of grating to specimen.
5. Easy removal of unsuccessfully applied grating without damaging the surface of the specimen.
6. Minimal initial distortion.
7. Sufficiently high contrast.
8. Sufficiently small pitch of the grating.

9. Possibility to alter the grating pitch over a wide range in an inexpensive manner.

13.13 Advantages

1. Strain distributions can be determined from purely geometric relationships derived from the interference of the specimen reference gratings.
2. Strain distribution in actual components can be determined and there is no necessity of making models.
3. Individual components of strain are determined directly, which is not possible in other methods of stress analysis.
4. Strains at very high temperatures can be determined conveniently.
5. Moire's fringe method is not restricted to elastic analysis only as is the case with other methods.
6 The gratings do not spoil the specimen as is the case in the brittle lacquer and strain-gauge methods.
7. It does not require any sophisticated equipment as is needed in other experimental methods.

13.14 Quiz Questions

1. What is a grating ?
2. Differentiate between a model and master grating.
3. What is the pitch of a grating ?
4. Define 'line density' and 'fringe spacing'.
5. Differentiate between primary and secondary directions.
6. Do you associate the fringe order to the dark or ling fringes?
7. Differentiate between additive and subtractive Moire's patterns.
8. Define the Eulerian and Lagrangian strains.
9. What do you mean by the mismatch technique ?
10. Differentiate between linear and rotational mismatch.
11. What are the advantages of combined linear and rotational mismatch ?
12. Why it is a common practice to order fringes with relative fringe orders ?
13. When a fringe order is said to be positive or negative ?
14. What are neutral fringes ?
15l Define sensitivity of Moire's fringes.
16. What is the use of fringe shifting ?
17. What are complementary gratings ?
18. What are dashed fringes ?
19. What is the shadow Moire's method ?
20. What is a composite grating ?
21. Which method would you suggest for the bending of plates ?
22. How much is the optimum radius of the cylindrical grating ?

EXERCISES

13.1 Explain the Moire's method in brief and discuss the fundamental properties of the Moire's fringes.

13.2 What are the two techniques used for Moire's-fringe analysis? Discuss the displacement approach in detail.

13.3 Discuss the geometric approach of Moire's-fringe strain analysis.

13.4 Discuss the mismatch technique of Moire's-strain analysis.

13.5 Write short notes on the following :
(*a*) Fringe ordering
(*b*) Sign determination of Moire's fringes.

13.6 Explain the Moire's gap effect. How this method helps in increasing the sensitivity of the Moire's method ?

13.7 Explain the technique utilized for Moire's-fringe sharpening and fringe multiplication.

13.8 Describe the shadow Moire's method in detail and give its uses.

13.9 Describe the Ligtenberg method to solve plate bending problems.

13.10 Discuss briefly the applications and advantages of the Moire's method of strain analysis. What are the limitations of this method ?

14

Similarity and Model Laws

14.1 Introduction

A model is a device which stimulates the functions of the prototype. The model may be smaller or larger in size than the prototype. Model analysis of machine members and structural components may be used for one of the following reasons :

(*i*) The mathematical analysis of the problem encountered is virtually impossible.

(*ii*) The mathematical analysis is so complex and tedious that the model analysis offers an advantageous short cut.

(*iii*) The importance of the problem is such that verification of the mathematical solution by model test is warranted.

The construction and testing of models for the purpose of predicting stresses, deformations etc. requires the knowledge of similarity and model laws. The flow chart for model analysis is shown in Fig. 14.1. In this chapter we shall study the model laws with special reference to photoelastic analysis.

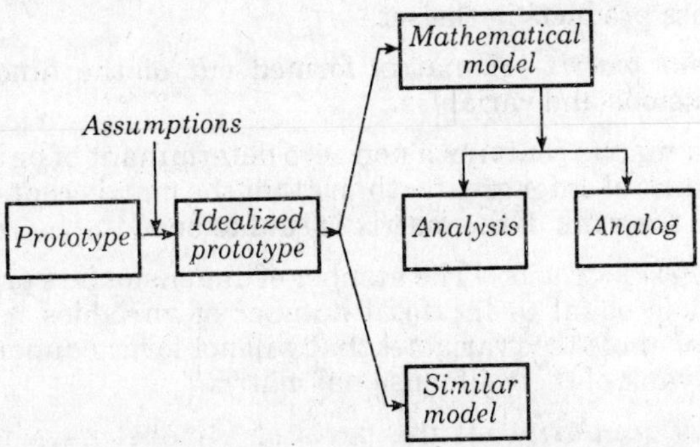

Fig. 14.1 Flow chart for model analysis.

14.2 Theory of Similitude and Modeling

Two methods commonly used for establishing similarity relationships between a model and prototype are based on (*a*) an analysis of the characteristic equation of the system and (*b*) dimensional analysis. If the former method is used, the system is first described in terms of a mathematical model and then the scaling laws, model-design conditions, or similarity requirements are developed from this model. If it is extremely difficult to obtain closed-form solutions, then it is necessary to obtain a solution experimentally using a similar model.

14.2.1 Characteristic equation method

The characteristic equations describing physical problems are frequently differential equations and these equations, combined with the initial and boundary conditions, describe the problem. Essentially, the method of determining similarity requirements from the characteristic equations consists of reviewing the characteristic equations in dimensionless form, and determining from the transformed equation the conditions under which the behaviour of two systems will be similar. In many problems, the characteristic equations are more numerous and complicated or even unknown and this method cannot be readily used.

14.2.2 Dimensional analysis

The principal purpose of dimensional analysis from the engineering point of view is the arrangement of the variables of a physical relation, so that, without destroying the generality of the relationship, it may be more easily determined experimentally. The method is particularly valuable when the number of variables is so great (usually four or more) that the data cannot be plotted conveniently using a co-ordinate axis for each variable. By dimensional analysis it is possible to arrange the variables into a less number of dimensionless groups which can be represented on co-ordinate axes. By doing so it is also possible to determine an analytical formula for the general function.

(*a*) Basic Concepts

Complete set—A set of dimensionless products of given variables is complete if each product in the set is independent of the others, and every other dimensionless product of the variables is a product of powers of dimensionless products in the set.

Dimensional matrix—A matrix formed out of the fundamental physical dimensions and variables.

Rank—If a matrix contains a non zero determinant of order r, and if all determinants of order greater than r that the matrix contains have the value zero, the rank of the matrix is said to be r.

Dimensionless products—The number of dimensionless products in a complete set is equal to the total number of variables minus the maximum number of these variables that will not form a dimensionless product or the rank of their dimensional matrix.

Geometrical similarity—If the parts of a model have the same shapes as the corresponding parts of the prototype, the two systems are said to be geometrically similar.

Distorted models—In a distorted model, the horizontal lengths and the vertical lengths are reduced by different scales. The prototype of a distorted model is a 'dilatation' of the model or *vice versa*.

Homologous points—Two points that correspond to each other are called homologous.

Complete similarity—The model and the prototype are said to be completely similar, provided that the independent dimensionless variables have the same values for the model as for the prototype. Complete similarity is impossible without geometric similarity.

Scale ratio (factor)—It is the ratios of the lengths of the model to the prototype. If the model is geometrically similar to the prototype then all the three scale factors are equal.

Kinematic similarity—The motions of two systems are similar, if homologous particles lie at homologous points at homologous times.

Dynamic similarity—Two systems are said to be dynamically similar if homologous parts of the systems experience similar net forces.

Function concept—A variable Q_1 is said to be a function of the variables Q_2, Q_3, Q_4..., Q_n, if for some values of Q_2, Q_3, Q_4.., Q_n there correspond values of Q_1. In symbolic form

$$Q_1 = f(Q_2, Q_3, Q_4, \ldots, Q_n) \qquad \ldots(14.1)$$

Once such a function is established or assumed, then a function will still exist even after the variables are intermultiplied in any manner whatsoever.

Principle of dimensional Homogeneity—This principle states that each and every term of a correct physical equation must have the same dimensions. Hence if Eq. (14.1) is a correct physical relation and the left hand side is made dimensionless in any manner, the right hand side must also become dimensionless, which means that each variable of the right hand side is combinable with other variables of the equation to form a dimensionless product. Thus by the foregoing process of intermultiplication, Eq. (14.1) can be written in the non-dimensionless form as symbolized by

$$\pi_1 = \phi(\pi_2, \pi_3, \pi_4, \ldots, \pi_n) \qquad \ldots(14.2)$$

If in any assumed physical relation Q is not combinable with any other Q's to form a dimensionless product, then that Q cannot appear in the original function. In such cases the corresponding π in Eq. (14.2) would be zero.

The greatest advantage of the method lies in the fact that through its use it is not necessary to write out $n\pi$'s, one for each variable of the original function, but only $i\pi$'s, where $i \angle n$, unless the Q's are all dimensionless, where upon $i = n$, Eq. (14.2) then becomes

$$\pi_1 = \phi(\pi_2, \pi_3, \pi_4, \ldots, \pi_i) \qquad \ldots(14.3)$$

(*b*) **The Buckingham Pi Theorem.** Any secondary quantity S_i is expressible in terms of the primary quantities in the form

$$S_i = L^a T^b M^c X^d Y^e$$

where L = length, T = time, M = mass and X, Y,... are other basic dimensions such as temperature and electric charge etc.

In a given problem, there are usually several variables, $Q_1, Q_2, \ldots, Q_n$, required to describe the phenomenon of interest. A number of dimensionless products of these variables can be formed by combining the variables in the form ;

$$Q_1^{x_1}\, Q_2^{x_2} \ldots Q_n^{x_n}$$

where the exponents $x_1, x_2, \ldots, x_n$ are selected so that the resulting product is dimensionless. Thus, if we let any one of variables, say Q_i, have the basic dimension

$$Q_i = L^{a_i}\, T^{b_i}\, M^{c_i}\, X^{d_i}\, Y^{e_i}$$

We can express the product as :

$$(L^{a_1}\, T^{b_1}\, M^{c_1}\, X^{d_1}\, Y^{e_1})^{x_1}\, (L^{a_2}\, T^{b_2}\, M^{c_2}\, X^{d_2}\, Y^{e_2})^{x_2} \ldots$$
$$\ldots\ldots (L^{a_n}\, T^{b_n}\, M^{c_n}\, X^{d_n}\, Y^{e_n})^{x_n}$$

In order that the product be dimensionless, the exponent of the various basic dimensions must be combined to give a zero value for each basic dimension. Thus

$$\left.\begin{aligned} a_1x_1 + a_2x_2 + \ldots.. + a_nx_n &= 0 \\ b_1x_1 + b_2x_2 + \ldots.. + b_nx_n &= 0 \\ c_1x_1 + c_2x_2 + \ldots.. + c_nx_n &= 0 \\ d_1x_1 + d_2x_2 + \ldots.. + d_nx_n &= 0 \\ e_1x_1 + e_2x_2 + \ldots.. + e_nx_n &= 0 \end{aligned}\right\} \quad \ldots(14.4)$$

We note that there will be as many equations as basic dimensions, say m in number, and n unknown x's, where n is equal to the number of original variables in the problem. From the theory of equations, it is known that there are $n - r$ linearly independent solutions to Eq. (14.4), where r is the rank of the matrix of coefficients.

$$\begin{Bmatrix} a_1 & a_2 \ldots\ldots & a_n \\ b_1 & b_2 \ldots\ldots & b_n \\ c_1 & c_2 \ldots\ldots & c_n \\ d_1 & d_2 \ldots\ldots & d_n \\ e_1 & e_2 \ldots\ldots & e_n \end{Bmatrix}$$

This matrix is called the dimensional matrix. Since the rank of a matrix is the highest order non-zero determinant contained in the matrix, it is apparent that the rank cannot exceed the number of equations but may be smaller. Thus, the number of independent dimensionless products that can be formed is equal to the number of original variables, n, minus the rank, r, of the coefficient matrix. Such a set of dimensionless products is called a complete set. Once a complete set of dimensionless products is found, all other possible dimensionless combinations can be formed as products of powers of the products contained in the complete set. Thus the well known Buckingham—P_i Theorem can be stated as follows :

"If an equation involving n variables is dimensionally homogeneous, it can be reduced to a relationship among $(n - r)$ independent dimensionless products, where r is the rank of the dimensional matrix."

Example 14.1 *Determine the scaling laws for the deflection of a cantilever beam shown in Fig. 14.2.*

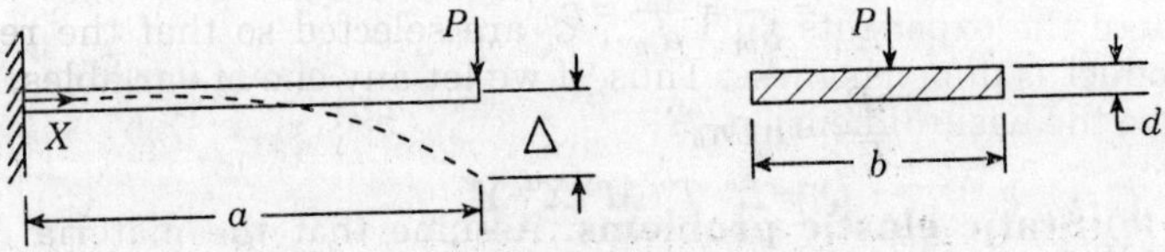

Fig. 14.2

Solution. For the cantilever beam shown in Fig. 14.2. Let

Δ = end deflection, L

a = length of beam, L

b = width of beam, L

d = depth of beam, L

P = load, F

E = modulus of elasticity, FL^{-2}

Application of the P_i-theorem reveals that, since there are six variables expressible in terms of two basic dimensions, four dimensionless parameters are required to describe this problem. One possible set is

$$\frac{\Delta}{a} = f\left(\frac{b}{a}, \frac{d}{a}, \frac{P}{Ea^2}\right)$$

It now follows that, if

$$\left.\begin{aligned} \frac{b}{a} &= \frac{b_m}{a_m} \\ \frac{d}{a} &= \frac{d_m}{a_m} \\ \frac{P}{Ea^2} &= \frac{P}{E_m a_m^2} \end{aligned}\right\} \qquad ...(a)$$

for the two systems, ...en

$$\frac{\Delta}{a} = \frac{\Delta_m}{a_m} \qquad ...(b)$$

Eqs. (a) are the similarity requirements for this problem and Eq. (b) is the prediction equation between the model and prototype. Since there are two basic dimensions in this problem, two 'scales' can arbitrarily be selected, *e.g.* let

$$\frac{a}{a_m} = n_a$$

where n_a is the 'length scale' and
where n_p is the force scale.

The scales for all other variables are then fixed, *i.e.*

$$\frac{\Delta}{\Delta_m} = \frac{b}{b_m} = \frac{d}{d_m} = n_a$$

and $$\frac{E}{E_m} = n_p\, n_a^{-2}$$

(*c*) **Static elastic problems.** Assume that the material obey's Hooke's law and can be described by Young's modulus E and Poisson's ratio ν. In addition any stress component, σ, at some point, x_i will be a function of the geometry of the system as characterized by some length l, and other required lengths, λ_i. The subscript, i, will be used to designate a set of variables. The loading may be specified with the loads, P and P_i, and any prescribed boundary displacements by η_i. The stresses can, therefore, be expressed in the functional form :

$$\sigma = \phi\,(x_i, l, \lambda_i, P, P_i, \eta_i, E, \nu) \quad \text{...(14.5)}$$

We now apply dimensional analysis to this set of variables to obtain

$$\frac{\sigma l^2}{P} = f\left(\frac{x_i}{l}, \frac{\lambda_i}{l}, \frac{\eta_i}{l}, \frac{P}{El^2}, \frac{P_i}{P}, \nu\right) \quad \text{...(14.6)}$$

Therefore, geometrical similarity requires

$$\left.\begin{aligned} \left(\frac{x_i}{l}\right)_p &= \left(\frac{x_i}{l}\right)_m \\ \left(\frac{\lambda_i}{l}\right)_p &= \left(\frac{\lambda_i}{l}\right)_m \\ \left(\frac{\eta_i}{l}\right)_p &= \left(\frac{\eta_i}{l}\right)_m \end{aligned}\right\} \quad \text{...(14.7)}$$

The loading scale is established from the relationship

$$\frac{P}{El^2} = \frac{P_m}{E_m l_m^2}$$

or $$\frac{P}{P_m} = \frac{E}{E_m}\,\frac{l^2}{l_m^2}$$

$$\frac{P_i}{P_{im}} = \frac{P}{P_m} \quad \text{...(14.8)}$$

$\frac{P}{El^2}$ is called Hooke's non-dimensional value.

The last p_i-term imposes the similarity requirement that Poisson's ratio must be equal for the model and the prototype. Of course, if the model and prototype are constructed of the same material, this condition is satisfied. For plane-strain or plane-stress problems involving simply connected bodies, for which the body forces are zero, constant or vary linearly with position, the stress distribution is independent of Poisson's ratio. Similar problems involving multiply connected bodies containing holes can also be modelled without regard to Poisson's ratio if the resultant force acting on the boundary of the hole is zero. However, if these conditions are not met and if different materials are used, the Poisson's ratio condition will not in general be satisfied and for this case a judgment must be made with respect to the significance of Poisson's ratio for the specific problem under consideration.

If all the above design conditions are satisfied then it follows that

$$\frac{\sigma l^2}{P} = \frac{\sigma_m l_m^2}{P_m}$$

or $$\frac{\sigma}{\sigma_m} = \frac{P}{P_m}\frac{l_m^2}{l^2} = \frac{E}{E_m} \qquad ...(14.9)$$

Since any displacement component, u, or strain component ε, will be a function of the same variables, it follows that the same model design conditions are required for displacements and strains as for stresses. The corresponding prediction equations become

$$\frac{u}{l} = \frac{u_m}{l_m}$$

or $$\frac{u}{u_m} = \frac{l}{l_m} \qquad ...(14.10)$$

and $$\varepsilon = \varepsilon_m$$

(*d*) **Reduced similarity requirements.** For small deformations, the stress, strain and displacement are linear functions of applied loads. Therefore, $\sigma l^2/P$ should be independent of P/El^2, since σ must depend linearly on P. Hence

$$\frac{\sigma l^2}{P} = f\left(\frac{x_i}{l}, \frac{\lambda_i}{l}, \frac{\eta_i}{l}, \frac{P_i}{P}, \nu\right) \qquad ...(14.11)$$

and $$\frac{u}{l} = \frac{P}{El^2} f_1\left(\frac{x_i}{l}, \frac{\lambda_i}{l}, \frac{\eta_i}{l}, \frac{P_i}{P}, \nu\right) \qquad ...(14.12)$$

$$\varepsilon = \frac{P}{El^2} f_2\left(\frac{x_i}{l}, \frac{\lambda_i}{l}, \frac{\eta_i}{l}, \frac{P_i}{P}, \nu\right) \qquad ...(14.13)$$

The principle of superposition applies for small deformation problems and, if desired, the model may be tested with a series of loads rather than applying all loads simultaneously.

(*e*) **Dynamic elastic problems.** For dynamic loading, an additional material property, the mass density ρ, must be included in the analysis. Now

$$\frac{p}{p_0} = \psi\left(\sqrt{\frac{E}{\rho}}\cdot\frac{t}{l}\right) \qquad ...(14.14)$$

where $l\sqrt{\dfrac{\rho}{E}}$ has the dimension of time and can be combined with time t to form a dimensionless time variable and

$$\varepsilon = \phi\,(x_i, l, \lambda_i, E, \nu, \rho, p_0, t)$$

$$= f\left(\frac{x_i}{l}, \frac{\lambda_i}{l}, \nu, \frac{p_0}{E}, \sqrt{\frac{E}{\rho}}\frac{t}{l}\right) \qquad \text{...(14.15)}$$

where $f\left(\dfrac{x_i}{l}, \dfrac{\lambda_i}{l}, \nu\right)$ represents geometrical similarity

$$\frac{p_0}{E} = \frac{p_{om}}{E_m} \text{ is pressure scale}$$

or
$$\frac{p_o}{p_{om}} = \frac{E}{E_m} \qquad \text{...(14.16)}$$

The time scale is

$$\sqrt{\frac{E}{\rho}}\cdot\frac{t}{l} = \sqrt{\frac{E_m}{\rho_m}}\cdot\frac{t_m}{l_m}$$

or
$$\frac{t}{t_m} = \sqrt{\frac{E_m}{E}\frac{\rho}{\rho_m}}\;\frac{l}{l_m} \qquad \text{...(14.17)}$$

If all similarity requirements are met, it follows that

$$\varepsilon = \varepsilon_m$$

where the strain in the model and prototype are measured at corresponding times based on the time scale.

(*f*) **Distorted models.** If $\pi_2 \neq \pi_{2m}$ then $\pi_1 \neq \pi_{1m}$ and the model is said to be distorted. Possible procedures for handling distorted models include :

(*i*) Neglect certain variables that may be only slightly significant but lead to the distortion.

(*ii*) Determine the effect of the distortion analytically.

(*iii*) Determine the effect of distortion empirically.

(*iv*) Consider a phenomenon that is governed by three p_i terms so that

$$\pi_1 = f\,(\pi_2, \pi_3) \qquad \text{...(14.19)}$$

Assume that the value of the model *pi* term π_{3m} is distorted by an amount β so that

$$\pi_{2m} = \pi_2,\ \pi_{3m} = \beta\,\pi_3$$

It then follows that

$$\pi_1 = \delta\,\pi_{1m}$$

where δ is a prediction factor required to correct for the distortion of π_{3m}. If the manner in which π_3 influences π_1 can be determined, the relationship between δ and β can be determined.

$$\delta = \frac{\pi_1}{\pi_{1m}} = \frac{f(\pi_2, \pi_3)}{f(\pi_{2m}, \pi_{3m})}$$
$$= f_1(\beta, \pi_2, \pi_3) \quad ...(14.20)$$

which shows that δ can be a function not only of β but also of π_2 and π_3. However, in certain special cases, where the distorted p_i term is separable, and expressible in the form

$$\pi_1 = \pi_3^{\alpha} f_2(\pi_2) \quad ...(14.21)$$

it follows that $\delta = \beta^{-\alpha}$ ...(14.22)

(*i*) Consider a problem in which four p_i terms are involved, *i.e.*

$$\pi_1 = f(\pi_2, \pi_3, \pi_4)$$

and the required design condition $\pi_2 = \pi_{2m}$ cannot be met although the other two design conditions $\pi_3 = \pi_{3m}$ and $\pi_4 = \pi_{4m}$ are satisfied. By running a series of model experiments the value of π_{2m} and π_2 can be correlated.

(*g*) **Extended similarity.** If a mathematical relation between two dimensional values and, therefore, between two non-dimensional values can be combined to one 'extended nondimensional value' by using the mathematical correlation, then the number of nondimensional values of the problem is decreased by one. The resulting law is called 'extended similarity'. This means one series of experiments less.

(*h*) **Approached similarity.** In most cases, a regular relation between two non-dimensional values, which leads to putting up an 'extended similarity law' is only valid in a certain region or perhaps only approximately, then one speaks of 'approached similarity. The incorrectness of the similarity conditions at approached similarity causes errors by transferring the results from model to prototype, usually called, scale errors.

14.3 Scaling Errors in Photoelasticity

In the analysis of photoelastic model fabricated from a polymeric material, the presence of the elastic constants in the field equations and boundary conditions of elastostatic complicates the work of the analyst as well as of the experimentalist when the stresses as measured from the model are to be correlated to the prototype, because the elastic constants of the photoelastic model are greatly different from those of the metallic prototype. For a plane stress problem we have the biharmonic equation in the presence of body force field.

$$\nabla^4 \phi = (1 - \nu) \nabla^2 \Omega \quad ...(14.23)$$

and for the case of plane-strain the stress-compatibility equation is :

$$\nabla^2 (\sigma_x + \sigma_y) = -(1 - \nu)\left(\frac{\partial F_x}{\partial x} + \frac{\partial F_y}{\partial y}\right) \quad ...(14.24)$$

where $F_x = -\frac{\partial \Omega}{\partial x}$, $F_y = -\frac{\partial \Omega}{\partial y}$ are the body force intensities and Ω is the body force potential. If the body forces are zero, *i.e.* $\nabla^2 \Omega = 0$, then biharmonic equation becomes,

$$\nabla^4 \phi = 0 \quad ...(14.25)$$

where ϕ is the Airy's stress function such that the stresses are given by

$$\left.\begin{aligned}\sigma_x &= \frac{\partial^2 \phi}{\partial y^2}\\ \sigma_y &= \frac{\partial^2 \phi}{\partial x^2}\\ \tau_{xy} &= \frac{\partial^2 \phi}{\partial x \partial y}\end{aligned}\right\} \qquad ...(14.26)$$

Examination of Eqs. (14.25) and (14.26) show that ϕ and thereby σ_x, σ_y and τ_{xy} are independent of the elastic constants. This condition is very important in two dimensional photoelasticity since it indicates that the stresses obtained from a photoelastic model are identical to those in a metal prototype if the body is singly connected and subject to zero or a uniform body force field. Difference in the values of the modulus of elasticity and Poisson's ratio between the model and the prototype do not influence the results for stresses.

Now if we examine Eq. (14.25), then we see that the compatibility equation is independent of the modulus of elasticity and thus shows that the value of the model modulus of elasticity does not influence the stress distribution. The influence of Poisson's ratio depends on the nature of the body force distribution. If $\frac{\partial F_x}{\partial x} + \frac{\partial F_y}{\partial y} = 0$ in Eq. (14.24) then the stress distribution is independent of Poisson's ratio. Thus, there will be no influence of Poisson's ratio, when

(*i*) the body forces are zero, *i.e.* $F_x = F_y = 0$,

(*ii*) the body force field is uniform, *i.e.*, $F_x = C_1$ and $F_y = C_2$, and

(*iii*) the body force field is linear in x and y, *i.e.* $F_x = C_1 x$ and $F_y = -C_1 y$.

If the two-dimensional photoelastic model is multiply connected then Eqs. (14.23) and (14.24) do not apply and the effect of Poisson's ratio will depend upon the nature of the loading on the boundary of the hole. For such cases the Michell's theorem asserts that :

"When a homogeneous and isotropic elastic body is in a state of either plane strain or generalised plane stress induced by prescribed surface tractions the in-plane stresses do not depend on the elastic constants of the material, provided there are no net forces transmitted by closed contours lying in the body."

Mathematically, this can be written as

$$\oint T_x ds = \oint T_y ds = 0 \qquad ...(14.27)$$

where T_x and T_y are the boundary tractions along x and y direction respectively. The closed contours may transmit couples. If condition (14.27) is violated then the stresses depend on Poisson's ratio.

For the plane problems of a body strained by specifying displacements or mixed conditions at the surface, no comparable results are available. For such problems the surface tractions required to produce the specified displacements and consequently the whole stress field depend on Poisson's ratio in a quite complicated manner.

Another difficulty may arise when the photoelastic model undergoes appreciable distortion under the action of the applied load. These model distortions can be minimized by selecting a model material with a high figure of merit and reducing the applied load to the lowest value consistent with adequate model response.

Now Eq. (14.9) can be written as

$$\frac{\sigma}{\sigma_m} = \frac{P}{P_m} \cdot \frac{h_m}{h} \cdot \frac{l_m}{l} \qquad \text{...(14.28)}$$

Therefore the modulus of elasticity is not a consideration in determining stresses unless the loading is such that model deformations change the load distribution as in contact stresses. Further dimensional analysis cannot bring out complete similarity between the stresses in the model and the prototype until and unless the Poisson's ratio is the same.

Coker and Filon have indicated a technique which can be followed if the influence of Poisson's ratio on the stress distribution in multiply connected plates is to be accounted for. When the body is subjected to tractions then on converting a mutliply connected body to a singly-connected body by making a cut we introduce a system of barriers called dislocations. For any stress (normal or shear) at any point in a given geometric shape subjected to given boundary stress conditions, the following conditions apply :

$$[\sigma_p]_{\text{load}} = [\sigma_m]_{load} + [\sigma_m]_{dislocation} \qquad \text{...(14.29)}$$

where for any load there is a unique dislocation of a particular type and magnitude. According to Filon, the magnitude of the dislocation when the angle between the two cut faces is preserved, is given by

$$\alpha_1 + i\alpha_2 = [(X + iY)/E_m]\,(\nu_p - \nu_m) \qquad \text{...(14.30)}$$

Thus

$$\alpha_1 = -(Y/E_m)\,\Delta\nu$$

$$\alpha_2 = -(X/E_m)\,\Delta\nu \qquad \text{..(14.31)}$$

where $\Delta\nu = \nu_p - \nu_m$

For a plate model with a single hole loaded by a pin at the hole, Coker and Filon have shown that

$$\sigma_p = \sigma_m + \alpha\sigma_d \qquad \text{...(14.32)}$$

where $\alpha = -\dfrac{P\,(\nu_p - \nu_m)}{E_m h_m t}$

where h is the width of the cut and P is the force applied at the hole. For a plate having many holes,

$$\sigma_p = \sigma_m + \sum_{i=1}^{n} \alpha_i\sigma_{di},\ n = 1, 2, 3 \qquad \text{...(14.33)}$$

where σ_{di} denotes the stress components due to the dislocations at the ith hole.

Table 14.1 Model Analysis Equations

	To find prototype stresses	*To find prototype strains*	*To find prototype deflection*
If moments are given	$\sigma_p = \sigma_m \dfrac{M_p}{M_m}\left(\dfrac{l_m}{l_p}\right)^2$	$\epsilon_p = \epsilon_m \dfrac{M_p}{M_m}\dfrac{E_m}{E_p}\left(\dfrac{l_m}{l_p}\right)^2$	$\delta_p = \delta_m \dfrac{M_p}{M_m}\dfrac{E_m}{E_p}\left(\dfrac{l_m}{l_p}\right)^2$
If concentrated loads are given	$\sigma_p = \sigma_m \dfrac{P_p}{P_m}\left(\dfrac{l_m}{l_p}\right)^2$	$\epsilon_p = \epsilon_m \dfrac{P_p}{P_m}\dfrac{E_m}{E_p}\left(\dfrac{l_m}{l_p}\right)^2$	$\delta_p = \delta_m \dfrac{P_p}{P_m}\dfrac{E_m}{E_p}\dfrac{l_m}{l_p}$
If loads per unit length are given	$\sigma_p = \sigma_m \dfrac{Q_p}{Q_m}\dfrac{l_m}{l_p}$	$\epsilon_p = \epsilon_m \dfrac{Q_p}{Q_m}\dfrac{E_m}{E_p}\dfrac{l_m}{l_p}$	$\delta_p = \delta_m \dfrac{Q_p}{Q_m}\dfrac{E_m}{E_p}$
If loads per unit surface area are given	$\sigma_p = \sigma_m \dfrac{R_p}{R_m}$	$\epsilon_p = \epsilon_m \dfrac{R_p}{R_m}\dfrac{E_m}{E_p}$	$\delta_p = \delta_m \dfrac{R_p}{R_m}\dfrac{E_m}{E_p}\dfrac{l_p}{l_m}$
If loads per unit volume are given	$\sigma_p = \sigma_m \dfrac{S_p}{S_m}\dfrac{l_p}{l_m}$	$\epsilon_p = \epsilon_m \dfrac{S_p}{S_m}\dfrac{E_m}{E_p}\dfrac{l_p}{l_m}$	$\delta_p = \delta_m \dfrac{S_p}{S_m}\dfrac{E_m}{E_p}\left(\dfrac{l_p}{l_m}\right)^2$

However, in most practical cases the corrections to the stress distribution produced by a different Poisson's ratio are negligible.

Dundurs studied the influence of Poisson's ratio on stresses theoretically in plane elasticity for multiply connected regions. He concluded that for a body subjected to given surface tractions, stresses can be found for any Poisson's ratio provided that it is known for two specific values of this ratio. Then the stresses at any point in the prototype can be known from the stresses at the same points in the model by means of linear inter or exprapolation.

In stress freezing method, Poisson's ratio has a value of 0.5. Therefore, in contrast to the plane photoelasticity one has to accept in three-dimensional experiments bigger scale errors, which are caused by non-observance of Poisson's model law, which, moreover, is nearly always required by the similarity analysis of three-dimensional model experiments. Corrective measurements are, of course, even more impossible, than in the plane photo-elasticity. Besides these measurements are of little use because the second source of scale errors, the application of deformations which are too large, is also to greater weight in spatial procedures than in plane ones, and the amount of these second errors is presumably higher than the errors caused by Poisson's ratio.

14.3.1 Structural similarity

For those two-dimensional problems in which the Poisson's ratio influence is negligible, the translation of model stresses, strains and deflecations into prototype stresses, strain and deflections can be determined by using the formulas given in Table 14.1.

14.4 Directional Analysis

Dimensional analysis is based on the assumption that equations representing physical phenomena have to be dimensionally homogeneous. Dimensionally homogeneous means any equation in which the fundamental quantities or dimensions appear with the same exponents in all the terms of both members of the equation.

Directional analysis is based on the assumption that in equations with terms representing vectorial entities both members must have resultants not only of the same magnitude but also with the same direction. The individual terms in each member need not have same direction.

In dimensional analysis directions are ignored and vectorial entities dealt with as if they were scalar. Available information on the directions of vectorial entities involved is ignored. The scope of directional analysis is to put to use the available information concerning the directions of vectorial entities and the influence of distortion, anisotropy and heterogeneity on the magnitude and direction of vectorial entities to be represented in a model. Since stress is a tensor quantity with both magnitude and direction, it is more accurate to use directional analysis in the design of models and in the interpretation of experiments. Table 14.2 gives the dimensions in directional analysis of normal and tangential stresses.

Table 14.2
Dimensions in Directional Analysis of Normal and Tangential Stresses

	Component parallel to *OX*	Component parallel to *OY*	Component parallel to *OZ*
Normal stress	$[MXY^{-1}Z^{-1}T^{-2}]$ 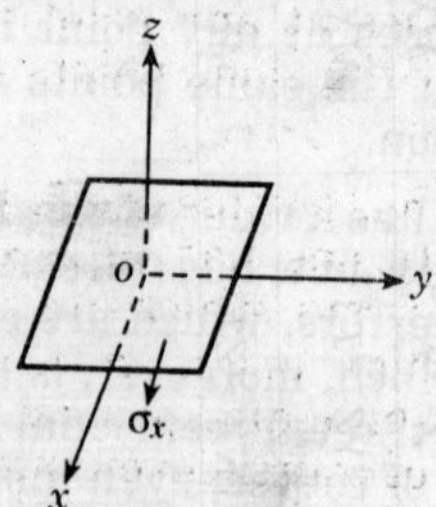	$[MX^{-1}YZ^{-1}T^{-2}]$ 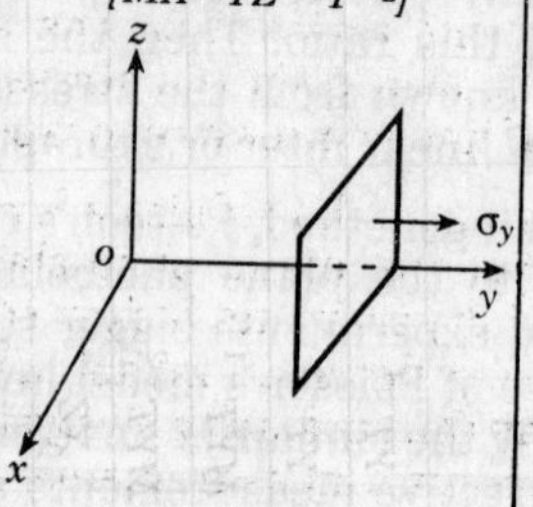	$[MX^{-1}Y^{-1}ZT^{-2}]$ 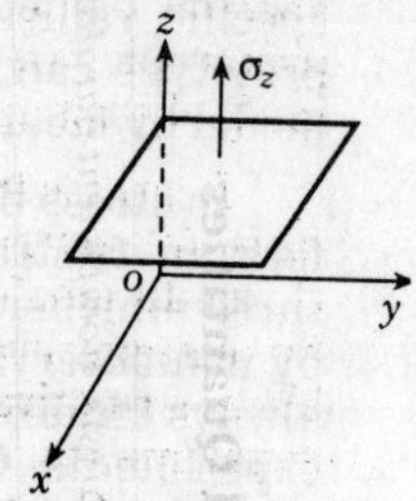
Tangential stress on plane normal to *OX*	–	$[MZ^{-1}T^{-2}]$ 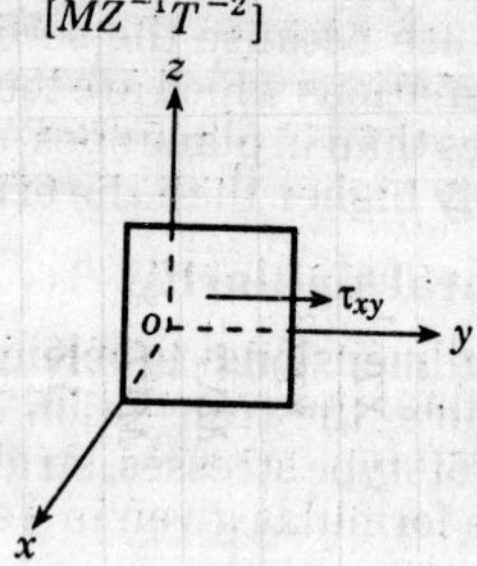	$[MX^{-1}T^{-2}]$ 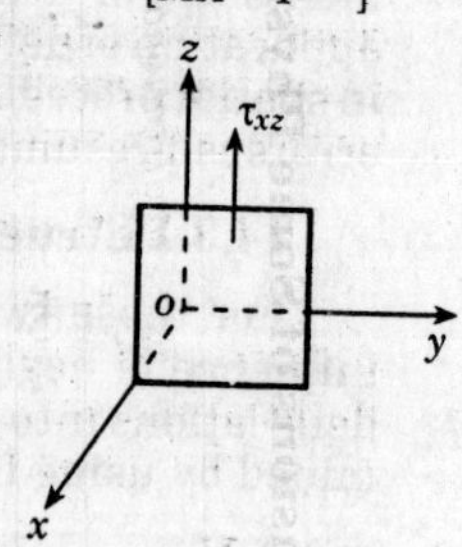
OY	$[MZ^{-1}T^{-2}]$ 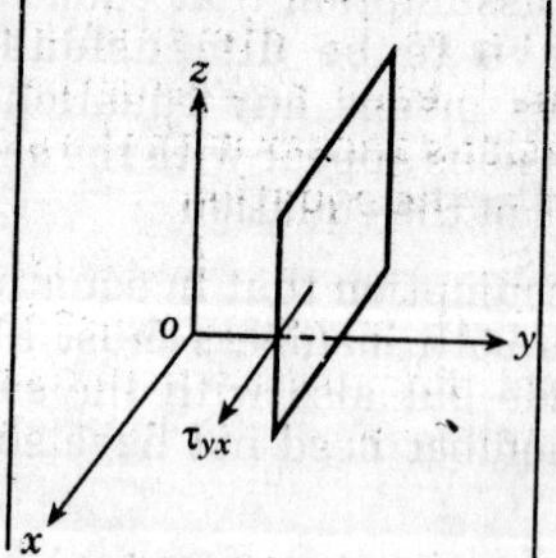	–	$[MX^{-1}T^{-2}]$ 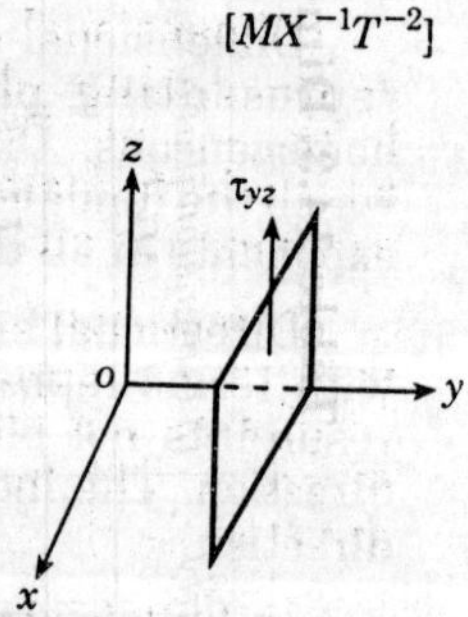
OZ	$[MY^{-1}T^{-2}]$ 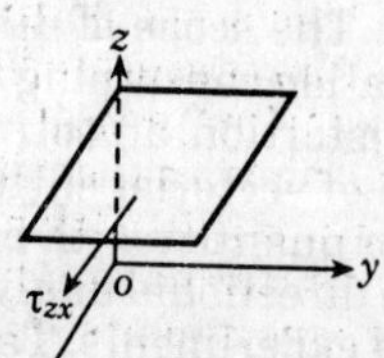	$[MX^{-1}T^{-2}]$ 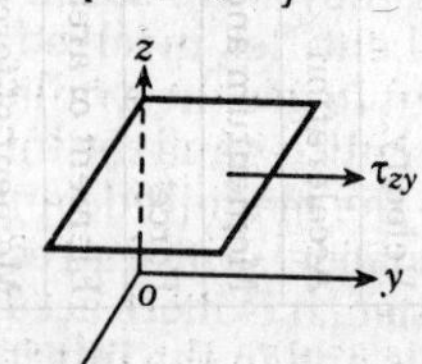	

Table 14.3. Dimensions of Some Physical Quantities

Physical quantity	*In dimensional analysis MLT*	*In directional analysis. Component parallel to*		
		OX	OY	OZ
Vectors of position, displacement	L	X	Y	Z
Velocity	LT^{-1}	XT^{-1}	YT^{-1}	ZT^{-1}
Acceleration	LT^{-2}	XT^{-2}	YT^{-2}	ZT^{-2}
Momentum and Impulse	MLT^{-1}	MXT^{-1}	MYT^{-1}	MZT^{-1}
Force	MLT^{-2}	MXT^{-2}	MYT^{-2}	MZT^{-2}
Element of area	L^2	YZ	XZ	XY
Moment of force	ML^2T^{-2}	$MYZT^{-2}$	$MXZT^{-2}$	$MXYT^{-2}$
Pressure gradient	$ML^{-2}T^{-2}$	$MY^{-1}Z^{-1}T^{-2}$	$MX^{-1}Z^{-1}T^{-2}$	$MX^{-1}Y^{-1}T^{-2}$
Normal stress, Modulus of elasticity	$ML^{-1}T^{-2}$	$MXY^{-1}Z^{-1}T^{-2}$	$MX^{-1}YZ^{-1}T^{-2}$	$MX^{-1}Y^{-1}ZT^{-2}$
Compressibility	$M^{-1}LT^2$	$M^{-1}X^{-1}YZT^2$	$M^{-1}XY^{-1}ZT^2$	$M^{-1}XYZ^{-4}T^2$

Thus in directional analysis in addition to dimensional homogeneity equations must also be directionally homogeneous. The dimensions of some physical quantities are given in Table 14.3.

In the design of distorted models the choice of six fundamental dimensions F_x, F_y, F_z, X, Y, Z will be found to be of advantage. For the study of some problems the use of cylindrical or spherical coordinates, or even of more general frames of reference, will certainly be found more adequate. For indefinite direction in a surface, *e.g.*, *xy*, the symbol *LXY* etc. should be used.

Example 14.2 *A half scale photoelastic model is made to represent a prototype design. A single force of 1 kN will be applied to the proposed prototype :*

(*a*) *The model is loaded to 1 kN, and the maximum stress is found to be 7 MPa. Determine the maximum stress in the prototype when loaded to 10 kN.*

(*b*) *If the modulus of elasticity of the model is 3.5×10^3 MPa and the modulus of the prototype is 70×10^3 MPa, estimate the total deflection of the prototype if the total deflection of the model is 5 mm.*

Solution. (*a*) $\dfrac{\sigma_p}{\sigma_m} = \dfrac{P_p}{P_m}\dfrac{l_m^2}{l_p^2}$

$$\sigma_p = \sigma_m \frac{P_p}{P_m}\frac{l_m^2}{l_p^2}$$

$$= 7 \times \frac{10}{1} \times \left(\frac{1}{2}\right)^2$$

$$= 17.5 \text{ MPa}$$

(*b*) $$\frac{\delta_p}{\delta_m} = \frac{P_p}{P_m}\frac{l_m}{l_p}\frac{E_m}{E_p}$$

$$\delta_p = 5 \times \frac{10}{1} \times \frac{1}{2} \times \frac{3.5 \times 10^3}{70 \times 10^3}$$

$$= 1.25 \text{ mm}$$

Example 14.3 *A simply supported steel beam 3 m long of rectangular cross section 75 mm wide and 150 mm deep is to carry a uniform load of 6 kn / m along a section of the span (E_s = 200 GPa). A photoelastic scale model 500 mm long is to be constructed of a material with a modulus of elasticity of 20 GPa.*

(*a*) *Determine the cross section of the model.*

(*b*) *To assume that the stresses in the model do not go beyond the elastic limit of the material, it was decided to use a uniform load of 250 N / m on the model. Determine every scale factor.*

(*c*) *The following data were recorded for the model :*

Maximum bending stress = 1.5 MPa

Maximum deflection = 0.05 mm.

Estimate the corresponding values associated with prototype.

Solution. (*a*) Length scale ratio

$$= \frac{l_p}{l_m} = \frac{3000}{500} = 6$$

For geometrical similarity, the scale ratio along the width and depth should also be 6. Hence width of model

$$= \frac{75}{6} = 12.5 \text{ mm}$$

Depth of model

$$= \frac{150}{6} = 25 \text{ mm}$$

(*b*) Now $Q_p = 6$ kN/m

$Q_m = 250$ N/m

$E_p = 200$ GPa

$E = 20$ GPa

$$\text{Force scale } = \frac{Q_p}{Q_m}\frac{l_p}{l_m} = \frac{6000}{250} \times 6 = 144$$

$$\text{Stress scale } = \frac{\sigma_p}{\sigma_m} = \frac{Q_p}{Q_m}\frac{l_m}{l_p} = \frac{24}{6} = 4$$

$$\text{Modulus scale } = \frac{E_p}{E_m} = \frac{200}{20} = 10$$

Moment scale

$$= \frac{M_p}{M_m} = \frac{Q_p}{Q_m}\left(\frac{l_p}{l_m}\right)^2$$

$$= 24 \times 36 = 864$$

$$\text{Strain scale} = \frac{\varepsilon_p}{\varepsilon_m} = \frac{Q_p}{Q_m}\frac{E_m}{E_p}\frac{l_m}{l_p}$$

$$= \frac{24}{10} \times \frac{1}{6} = \frac{2}{5}$$

Deflection scale

$$= \frac{\delta_p}{\delta_m} = \frac{Q_p}{Q_m}\frac{E_m}{E_p} = \frac{24}{10} = 2.4$$

(*c*)
$$\sigma_p = \sigma_m \frac{Q_p}{Q_m}\frac{l_m}{l_p}$$

$$= 1.5 \times 24 \times \frac{1}{6} = 6 \text{ MPa}$$

$$\delta_p = \delta_m \frac{Q_p}{Q_m}\frac{E_m}{E_p}$$

$$= 0.05 \times 24 \times \frac{1}{10} = 0{:}120 \text{ mm}$$

Example 14.4 *In a test model of a thick walled disc loaded by diametrically opposing concentrated forces, the tangential strain at a point was found to be 300 μ m / m after a load of 100 kN / m was applied to the disc (E_m = 70 GPa, ν_m = 0.34).*

(*a*) *Determine the tangential stress in the model.*

(*b*) *If the prototype is steel and 4 times larger than the model and the applied load is 1000 kN / m, determine the tangential stress at the same point (E_P = 200 GPa, ν_P = 0.29).*

Solution. (*a*) Tangential stress in the model

$$\sigma_m = E_m \, \varepsilon_m$$

$$= 70 \times 10^9 \times 300 \times 10^{-6}$$

$$= 21 \text{ MPa}$$

(*a*)
$$\sigma_p = \sigma_m \frac{Q_p}{Q_m} \frac{l_m}{l_p}$$

$$= 21 \times \frac{1000}{100} \times \frac{1}{4}$$

$$= 525 \text{ MPa}$$

14.5 Quiz Questions

1. What is the necessity of model analysis ?
2. Prepare a flow chart for model analysis.
3. What is the principal purpose of dimensional analysis ?
4. What do you understand by a complete set ?
5. Differentiate between geometrical similarity and complete similarity ?
6. Differentiate between distorted model and distortion factor.
7. What is the principle of dimensional similarity ?
8. State the Buckingham's P_i theorem.
9. Differentiate between extended and approached similarity.
10. What is the main scaling error in photoelasticity ?
11. How do you account for the effect of Poisson's ratio for multiply connected bodies ?
12. Why the effect of Poisson's ratio is not very serious in three dimensional photoelastic problems ?
13. Write the expression for obtaining stresses in the prototype from the model.
14. How dislocation can be created in photoelastic models which are multiply connected ?
15. What is the basic difference between dimensional and directional analysis ?

EXERCISES

14.1 Which are the methods commonly used for establishing similarity relationships between the model and the prototype ? Explain these methods briefly giving their limitations.

14.2 Explain the principle of dimensional homogeneity. How this principle helps us in dimensional analysis ?

14.3 Explain and state the Buckingham's P_i Theorem. What are the advantages of this theorem ?

14.4 Determine the model laws for static elastic problems. How these laws are modified for dynamic problems ?

14.5 What do you understand by a distorted model ? Explain the possible procedures for handling distorted models.

14.6 What is the effect of material constants in scaling stresses from model-to-prototype in singly and multiply connected bodies ? How do you account for these effects in photoelastic models ?

14.7 Explain the various advantages of directional analysis over dimensional analysis ? How model laws can be obtained by this method ?

15

Analogous Methods

15.1 Introduction

For many cases when the geometry and boundary conditions are simple, the boundary-value problems can be solved directly by the principles of theory of elasticity. In many cases for which the differential equation cannot be solved, numerical analysis or experimental methods are used. The most common experimental methods used are analogous methods. When the characteristics of two or more apparently different physical phenomena can be expressed in identical mathematical form, then the two physical systems are said to be analogous. The most popular analogous methods are :

Conducting sheet electrical analogy, membrane or soap film analogy, plate analogy, hydrodynamic analogy, electro-optic analogy and electrical network analogous method. The following steps are involved for the analogous method.

1. Conversion of the original physical system to mathematical form.
2. Conversion of the analogous physical system to mathematical form.
3. Identification of the two mathematical expressions.
4. Physical realization of the analogous system.
5. Measurement of quantities in the analogous system.

The advantages of the analogues methods are :

1. It is only necessary to study one out of the two analogous systems in order to gain insight into both.
2. Improvements in the technique of solving problems in one field are automatically improvements in the analogous fields.
3. Specific solution of boundary value problems are often directly applicable to several analogous physical systems.
4. An analogy helps in obtaining a mental grasp of the essential features of a complicated system.
5. The analogous system may serve as a calculating machine for solving the equations governing the original system.

15.2 Membrane Analogy

Consider a homogeneous membrane under a uniform tension T per unit of length and subjected to a normal pressure p per unit of surface area. If the slope of the membrane relative to a plane x, y is everywhere small, the ordinate z of the membrane surface, is governed by the differential equations :

$$\nabla^2 z = \frac{\partial^2 z}{\partial x^2} + \frac{\partial^2 z}{\partial y^2} = -\frac{p}{T} \qquad ...(15.1)$$

If there is no pressure exerted against the membrane, then Eq. (15.1) reduces to

$$\nabla^2 z = \frac{\partial^2 z}{\partial x^2} + \frac{\partial^2 z}{\partial y^2} = 0 \qquad ...(15.2)$$

Eq. (15.1) is the Poisson's equation and Eq. (15.2) is the Laplace equation.

15.2.1 Membrane analogy for torsion

For the pure torsion of a prismatic bar

$$\nabla^2 \phi = -2G\theta \qquad ...(15.3)$$

where ϕ = stress function

G = modulus of rigidity

θ = angle of twist per unit length

and $\phi_{ci} = k_i \ (i = 0, 1, 2, ...n)$ ...(15.4)

$$\int_{c_i} \frac{\partial \phi}{\partial n}\, ds = 2\, G\, \theta\, A_i \ (i = 1, 2, 3 \ ....n) \qquad ...(15.5)$$

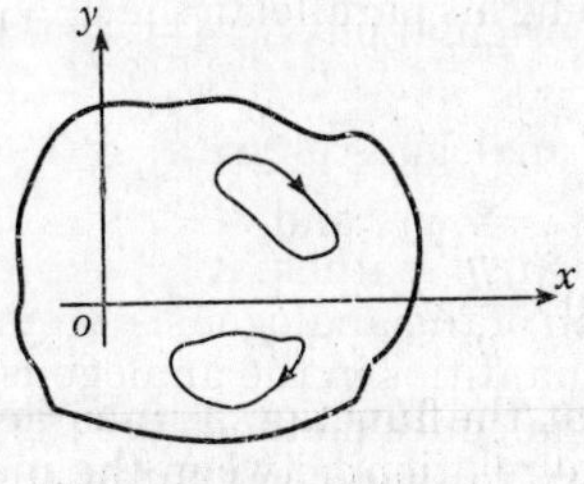

Fig. 15.1. Positive direction along boundaries of a multiply connected section.

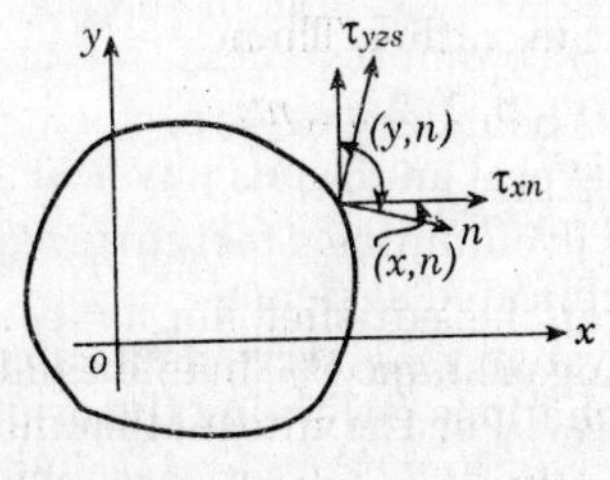

Fig. 15.2. Components of stress at a point on a contour of constant shear.

$$\text{Torque } M_z = 2\iint_R \phi\, dxdy - 2k_0 A_0 + 2\sum_{i=1}^{n} k_i A_i \qquad ...(15.6)$$

where A_0 is the area of the gross cross-section. It is seen that the torque is equal to twice the volume enclosed by the surface $\phi = \phi(x, y)$ and the portions of $n + 1$ planes bounded by the $n + 1$ curves C_i at levels $\phi_{ci} = k_i$, where k_i is a constant (Fig. 15.1). The torsional rigidity C of the bar is defined as the ratio of the torque to the angle of twist per unit of length.

$$C = \frac{M_z}{\theta} \qquad ...(15.7)$$

The resultant shearing stress at any point acts along the tangent to the contour ϕ = const. through that points. Component of shearing stress along the normal n is (Fig. 15.2)

$$\tau_{yz}\cos(y, n) + \tau_{xz}\cos(x, n)$$

$$= \frac{\partial\phi}{\partial x}\frac{dx}{ds} + \frac{\partial\phi}{\partial y}\frac{dy}{ds} = \frac{\partial\phi}{\partial s} = 0$$

The magnitude of the resultant shearing stress at any point P is

$$\tau = \tau_{yz}\cos(x, n) - \tau_{xz}\cos(y, n)$$

$$= -\frac{\partial\phi}{\partial x}\frac{dx}{dn} - \frac{\partial\phi}{\partial y}\frac{dy}{dn}$$

$$= -\frac{\partial\phi}{\partial n} \qquad ...(15.8)$$

= maximum slope of the surface at the point.

Let the linear geometrical scale ratio of lengths parallel to the x, y plane of the prototype to lengths parallel to the x_1, y_1 plane of the model by λ.

Then, setting

$$x = \lambda x_1,\ y = \lambda y_1 \quad \text{and}$$

$$\phi = 2G\,\theta\,\lambda^2 \frac{T}{p} z \qquad ...(15.9)$$

In Eq. (15.3), we find that the function z, thus defined satisfies Eq. (15.1). Eq. (15.9) gives the relation between the membrane ordinates and the function ϕ. Now we specify the shapes of the boundaries C'_i of the membrane to be geometrically similar to the boundaries C_i of the section of the bar, with scale ratio λ. Then

$$z'_{Ci} = k_i' \ (i = 0, 1, 2, ..., n) \qquad ...(15.10)$$

where $$k_i' = \frac{p}{2G\,\theta\,\lambda^2 T} k_i \qquad ...(15.11)$$

This requirement can be satisfied for $i = 0$, by stretching the membrane over an opening of shape C'_0, in a flat plate whose elevation above the x_1, y_1 plane is k_0'. For the internal boundaries, discs whose edges are the curves C_i' (i = 1, 2, 3, ..., n) are placed, in the proper positions over the opening, with their edges at elevations k_i' above the x_1, y_1 plane.

To determine the elevations k_1', we substitute Eq. (15.9) in (15.5) and get

$$T\oint_{C_i} \frac{\partial z}{\partial n_1} ds_1 = pA_i', (i = 1, 2, ..., n) \qquad ...(15.12)$$

where $$n_1 = \frac{n}{\lambda}, s_1 = \frac{s}{\lambda}, A_i' = \frac{A_i}{\lambda^2} \qquad ...(15.13)$$

in which A_i' is the area of the ith disc.

For small membrane slopes, the quantity on the left side of Eq. (15.12) is the total force, in the z_1 direction, exerted by the membrane on the ith disc. The right hand side of Eq. (15.12) is the resultant of the pressure p on the ith disc. Thus each disc must be in equilibrium under these two forces alone. This may be accomplished by balancing out the gravitational force on each disc, leaving it acted on only by the membrane tension and the applied pressure, and restricting its motion to pure displacement in the z_1 direction as shown in Fig. 15.3.

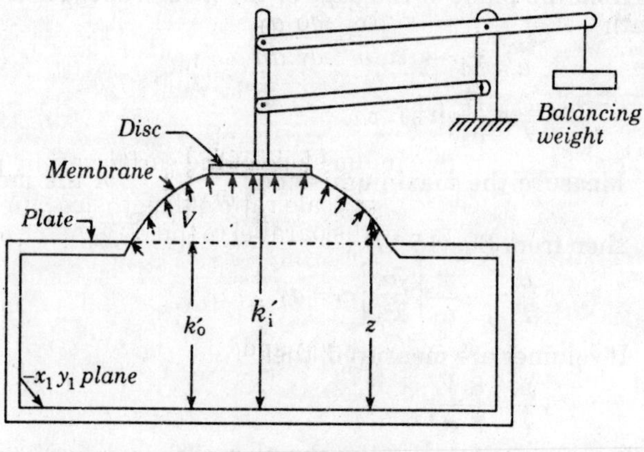

Fig. 15.3 Section of a multiply connected membrane under pressure.

The resultant shearing stress at any point is

$$\tau = -\frac{2G\theta\lambda T}{p}\frac{\partial z}{\partial n_1}$$

$$= \left(-\frac{2G\theta\lambda T}{p}\right) \times |\text{maximum slope of membrane at that point}$$

The torsional rigidity of the bar is

$$C = \frac{4G\lambda^4 T}{p}\left[\iint_{R_1} z dx_1 dy_1 - k'_0 A'_0 + \sum_{i=1}^{n} k'_i A'_i\right]$$

$$= \frac{4G\lambda^4 T}{p} \cdot V \qquad ...(15.15)$$

where V is the volume enclosed by the membrane, the n discs and the plane of the hole in the plate. If the bar is solid, V is simply the volume bounded by the membrane and the plane of the plate over which it is stretched.

The resultant shear stress can also be expressed as :

$$\tau = -\frac{M_z}{2\lambda^2 V} \frac{\partial z}{\partial n_1} \qquad ...(15.16)$$

Now for the torsion of a solid circular shaft of radius 'a'

$$\phi = \frac{G\theta}{2}(a^2 - r^2) \qquad ...(15.17)$$

where $r^2 = x^2 + y^2$ and k_0 has been taken equal to zero. The measurement of p/T ratio can be avoided by performing an auxiliary experiment in which a membrane is stretched over a circular opening of radius a, and the same tension T and pressure p are used as in the main experiment. One of the following techniques may be used to determine the p/T ratio.
(*a*) Measure the ordinate $[z]_{r1=0}$ of the highest point of the membrane, reckoned from the plane of the edge of the membrane. Then from Eq. (15.17) with

$$a = \lambda a_1$$

$$\frac{p}{T} = \frac{4}{a_1^2}[z]_{r1=0} \qquad ...(15.18)$$

(*b*) Measure the maximum slope $\left[\frac{\partial z}{\partial r_1}\right]_{r_1 = a_1}$ of the membrane, then from Eq. (15.17),

$$\frac{p}{T} = -\frac{2}{a_1}\left[\frac{\partial z}{\partial r_1}\right] r_1 = a_1 \qquad ...(15.19)$$

(*c*) If volumes are measured, then

$$\frac{p}{T} = \frac{8}{\pi}\frac{V_c}{\sigma_1^4} \qquad ...(15.20)$$

where V_c is the volume enclosed between the membrane and the plane of the circular opening of radius a_1.

In order to minimise errors due to excessive slopes of the membrane surface the slope of the membrane should be limited to about 15°. The important results of membrane analogy are : (Fig. 15.4)

(*i*) The tangent to the contour line at any point of the deflected membrane gives the direction of the shearing stress, at the corresponding point in the cross-section of the twisted bar.

(*ii*) The maximum slope of the membrane at any point is proportional to the magnitude of the shearing stress at the corresponding point in the twisted bar.

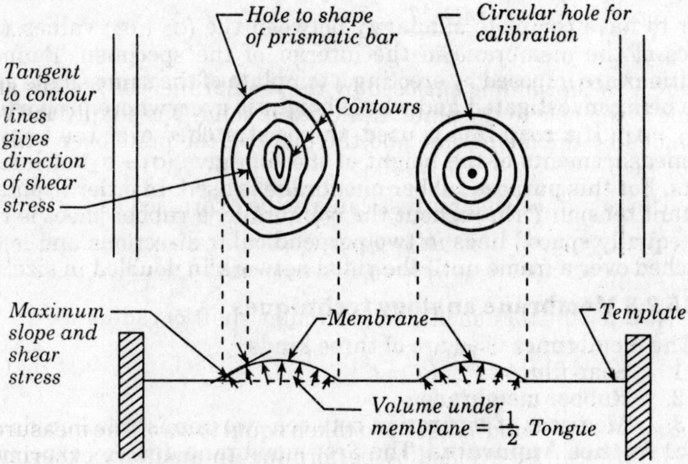

Fig. 15.4 Results of membrane analogy.

(*iii*) The volume included between the surface of the deflected membrane and the plane of the template is proportional to the torque of the twisted bar.

15.2.2 Membrane Analogy Supplementing Photoelasticity

Membrane analogy may be used in conjunction with photoelasticity to determine the principal stresses separately. Due to the fact that at the unloaded boundaries of the specimen, one of the principal stresses disappear, it is possible from a photoelastic photograph to evaluate $(\sigma_1 + \sigma_2)$ along all free boundaries since $(\sigma_1 - \sigma_2)$ equals $(\sigma_1 + \sigma_2)$. Now it so happens that the equation of the small ordinates of a membrane stressed with a constant tension and having the same pressure on both sides is the same as the equation defining the distribution of $(\sigma_1 + \sigma_2)$. This differential equation of Laplace is written for the two cases as follows :

$$\frac{\partial^2 z}{\partial x^2} + \frac{\partial^2 z}{\partial y^2} = 0 \qquad \text{...(15.21)}$$

for the ordinate z of the membrane

and $$\frac{\partial^2 (\sigma_1 + \sigma_2)}{\partial x^2} + \frac{\partial^2 (\sigma_1 + \sigma_2)}{\partial y^2} = 0 \qquad \text{...(15.22)}$$

for the distribution of $(\sigma_1 + \sigma_2)$, provided that the slopes and deflections of the sheet are small and that gravitational forces on the sheet are negligible.

In order to have complete similarity it is only necessary to satisfy the same boundary conditions. Since the boundary values of $(\sigma_1 + \sigma_2)$ can be obtained from photoelasticity, we have only to make the boundary ordinates of the membrane proportional to the $(\sigma_1 + \sigma_2)$ values in order to have complete similarity between the $(\sigma_1 + \sigma_2)$ values and z values of the membrane in the interior of the specimen. Boundary conditions are imposed by erecting a template of the same shape as the plate being investigated and whose height is everywhere proportional to $(\sigma_1 + \sigma_2)$. If a soap film is used, this is stretched over the template and measurements of the height of the film give $(\sigma_1 + \sigma_2)$ at internal points. For this purpose rubber membrane is used. In order to obtain a constant tension T throughout the membrane, a rubber sheet is ruled with equally spaced lines in two perpendicular directions and is then stretched over a frame until the ruled network in doubled in size.

15.2.3 Membrane analogy techniques

The membranes used are of three kinds

1. Soap film
2. Rubber membrane
3. Meniscus of separation between two immiscible liquids.

(*a*) **Anthes Apparatus.** The first membrane analogy experiment was performed by Anthes in 1906 to solve torsion problems. In this apparatus, the soap film is stretched over an opening in the vertical side of a rectangular box. The film is pressurized by introducing a measured amount of air displaced from a glass tube. The quantity of air is controlled by elevating a flask of water joined to the tube by a flexible connection.

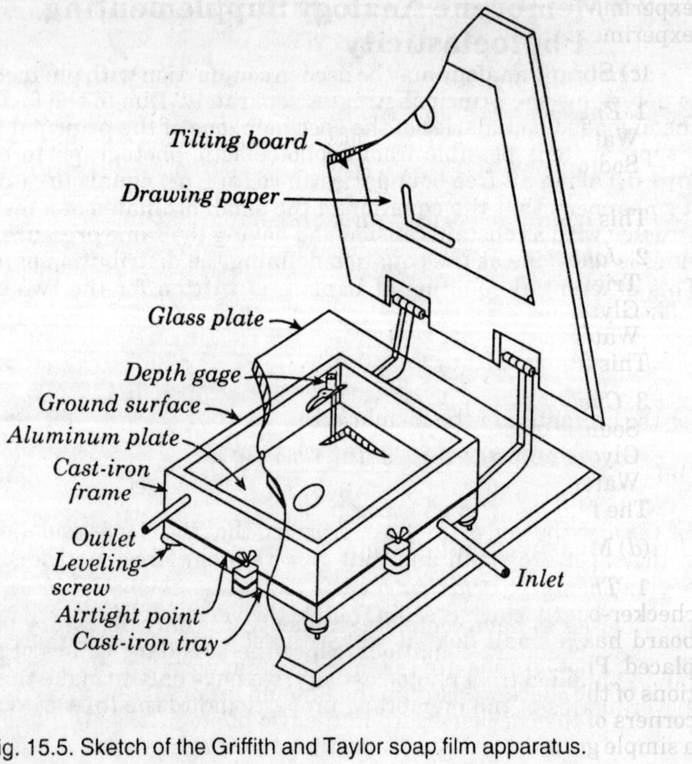

Fig. 15.5. Sketch of the Griffith and Taylor soap film apparatus.

(*b*) **Griffith and Taylor apparatus.** The Griffith and Taylor apparatus developed in 1917 is shown in Fig. 15.5. The circular test hole and the experimental hole are cut from a flat aluminium plate 1.25 mm thick and beveled on the upper side of the opening to an angle of 45°. The aluminium plate is clamped between two parts of a square cast iron box, the lower part of which is a 6 mm deep tray supported on levelling screws and the upper part of which is a square frame. The inside of the tray is blackened, and the inside of the frame is enameled white. The two parts are clamped together and the joint is made tight by means of grease or thick oil which must be wiped out carefully in order to avoid contact with the films. The lower part is connected with a flask of water or soap solution, by means of a rubber tube and a three way cock, the upper part communicates with the outer air by means of a plain tube through the wall of the frame.

A glass plate 6 mm thick, slides freely on the edges of the upper frame and has fixed to it a depth micrometer, the lower end of which is made to touch the film. A drawing board, pivoted on a horizontal axis, can be swung down so as to touch a pencil point on the upper end of the micrometer, thus recording the position in the $x_1 - y_1$ plane, of the point being measured. The largest linear dimension of the experimental hole is of the order of 25 to 75 mm, while the radius of the circular hole is chosen equal to twice the ratio of the area to the perimeter of the experimental hole, in order to make the average boundary slope of the experimental hole equal to the slope at the edge of the circle.

(*c*) **Soap solutions**

1. *Englemann*

Water	= 45 parts
Sodium oleate	= 5 parts (by weight) plus a little sugar.

This membrane dries without breaking.

2. *Johnston*

Triethynolamine oleate	= 10%
Glycerine	= 30%
Water	= 60% (by weight)

This film lasts 3 to 4 days.

3. *Cushman*

Sodium oleate	= 2 g
Glycerine	= 30 ml
Water	= 1 litre

The film lasts for 25 hours.

(*d*) **Measurement of slope**

1. *The anthes checker board.* This consists of a black and white checker-board which is set in front of the vertical film. The centre of the board has a small hole at which the objective lens of the camera is placed. Photographs are taken of the undistorted and distorted reflections of the checker-board in the flat and inflated film. The shifts of the corners of the checker-board in the two photographs give, by means of a simple graphical construction, the values of the slopes at these points.

2. *Griffith and Taylor Autocollimator.* In this instrument (Fig. 15.6) a collimated bundle of light rays from a small source is directed on the surface of the film. The collimation axis is rotated about a horizontal axis until the reflected ray coincides with the incident ray. The angle between the collimation axis and the vertical measures the slope of the film. The accuracy obtained is 2 to 4 per cent.

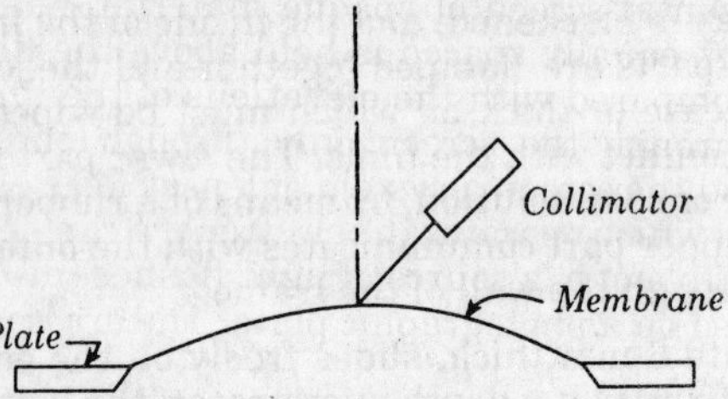

Fig. 15.6 Griffith and Taylor autocollimator.

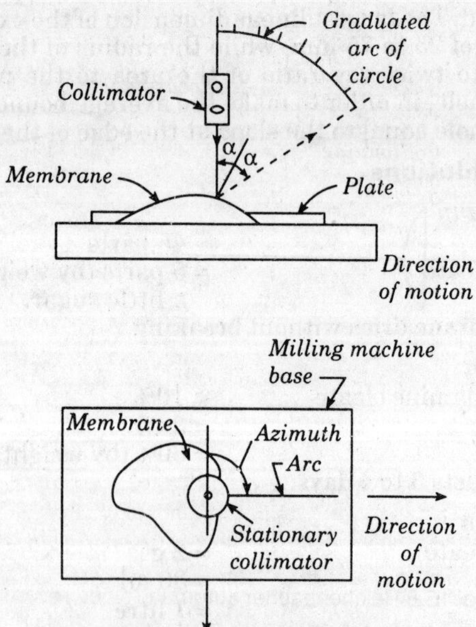

Fig. 15.7 Quest collimator.

3. *Quest collimator.* In this the incident ray is vertical, and the refracted ray makes an angle 2α with the vertical (Fig. 15.7). An arc of a circle, made of two steel angles and graduated in degrees swings around the collimation axis of the apparatus until the ray refracted from the film is intercepted. The azimuth of the arc being indicated on a horizontal graduation, both the maximum slope α and its direction are measured at the same time. The box carrying the soap films is mounted

on a milling-machine base, while the collimator is stationary. In this way the coordinates of the point whose slope is being measured can be accurately fixed and the slope can be evaluated point by point.

4. *Reichenbacher automatic slope recorder.* In this instrument (Fig. 15.8), a horizontal ray of light is reflected vertically downward by a 45° mirror, strikes the film, and is reflected at an angle of 2α to the vertical. A horizontal screen of opaque material, with ten concentric annular openings equally spaced is held above the film at a distance which is large compared with the elevations of the film. The reflected ray can pass through the screen only through one of the annular openings. Beyond the screen a system of lenses focuses the source on a photoelectric cell which operates the shutter of a camera. Whenever the slope α is a multiple of β, a source of light flashes into the camera and a dash is recorded on a photographic plate. The error is 3 to 4 per cent.

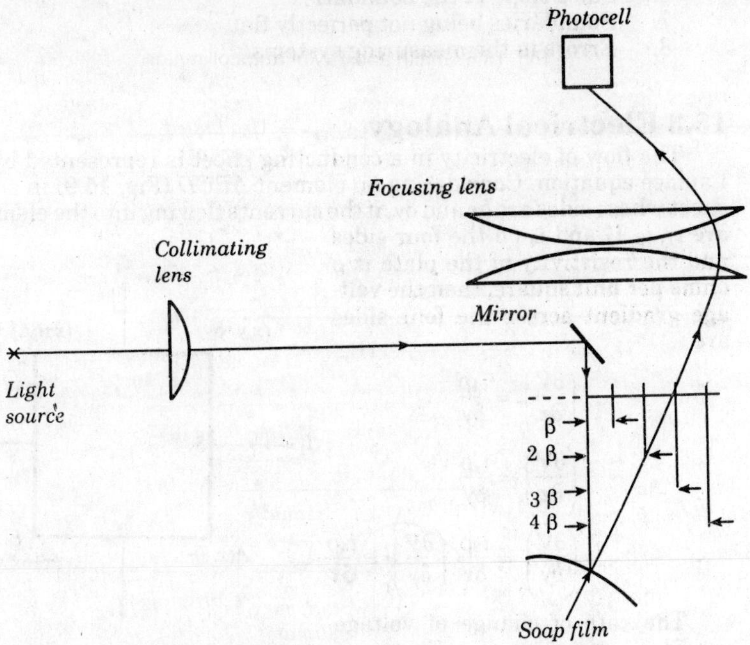

Fig. 15.8 Reichenbacher automatic slope recorder.

5. *Photogrammetric method.* In order to photograph transparent soap films, lycopodium powder is sprinkled on the film and slope can be determined by graphical or numerical method from the map.

(*e*) Measurement of Volume

1. Contours can be plotted by spherometer, and volume can be computed by graphical or numerical methods.

2. *The black-spot method.* After a long time the solution in soap film starts moving down, and a black dot appears at the highest level when

the thickness of the film becomes less than the wavelength of light. Photographs of the dots can be taken and volume computed.

3. *Integration method.* After knowing the slopes another graphical integration gives the volume after plotting the equally spaced sections of the membrane.

4. *Direct measurements.* By knowing the amount of air used in blowing the bubble.

15.2.4 Sources of error

The following sources of error are inherent in the method :

1. Approximate instead of rigorous equation of the film surface.
2. Weight of film.
3. Vibration of the film.
4. Change of volume due to temperature.
5. Change of pressure.
6. False slope at the boundaries.
7. Boundaries being not perfectly flat.
8. Errors in the measuring systems.

15.3 Electrical Analogy

The flow of electricity in a conducting sheet is represented by the Laplace equation. Considering an element *ABCD* (Fig. 15.9) in such a sheet whose sides are δx and δy, if the currents flowing into the elements are i_1, i_2, i_3 and i_4 on the four sides and the resistivity of the plate is ρ ohms per unit square, then the voltage gradient across the four sides are :

$$\left(\frac{\partial V}{\partial x}\right)_1 = \frac{i_1\rho}{\delta y},$$

$$\left(\frac{\partial V}{\partial x}\right)_2 = \frac{i_2\rho}{\delta y}$$

$$\left(\frac{\partial V}{\partial y}\right)_3 = \frac{i_3\rho}{\delta x}, \left(\frac{\partial V}{\partial y}\right)_4 = \frac{i_4\rho}{\delta x}$$

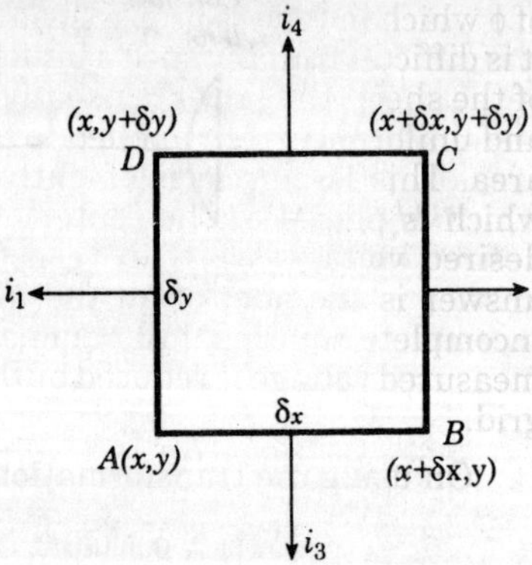

Fig. 15.9

The rate of change of voltage gradient is thus

$$\frac{\partial^2 V}{\partial x^2} = \underset{\delta x \to 0}{Lt} \frac{\left(\frac{\partial V}{\partial x}\right)_2 - \left(\frac{\partial V}{\partial x}\right)_1}{\delta x}$$

$$\frac{\partial^2 V}{\partial y^2} = \underset{\delta y \to 0}{Lt} \frac{\left(\frac{\partial V}{\partial y}\right)_4 - \left(\frac{\partial V}{\partial y}\right)_3}{\delta y}$$

Adding we get

$$\frac{\partial^2 V}{\partial x^2} + \frac{\partial^2 V}{\partial y^2} = \frac{\rho}{\delta x \delta y}(i_1 - i_2 + i_3 - i_4)$$

By Kirchoff's law,

$$i_1 - i_2 + i_3 - i_4 = 0$$

Hence $$\frac{\partial^2 V}{\partial x^2} + \frac{\partial^2 V}{\partial y^2} = 0 = \nabla^2 V \quad ...(15.23)$$

i.e. the voltage distribution in a conducting sheet is described by Laplace's equation.

If another current i is fed into the element, then we get Poisson's equation,

$$\nabla^2 V = -\rho i \quad ...(15.24)$$

15.3.1 Electrical analogy for torsion

St. Venant torsion problem of bars of prismatic cross-section is

$$\nabla^2 \phi = -2G\theta \quad ...(15.25)$$

For simply connected regions, $\phi = 0$ on the boundary. Such a problem may be solved by the conducting sheet analog method if a constant current (uniformly distributed over the surface of the model) is applied to the surface and the boundary of the sheet is held at a constant potential by means of a busbar shaped to fit the boundary such that the voltage distribution obeys Eq. (15.24). The analogy between Eqs. (15.24) and (15.25) is obvious. The desired shear stress is equal to the gradient of ϕ which in turn is proportional to the gradient of the voltage V. Since it is difficult to apply such a uniformly distributed current to the surface of the sheet, the latter is usually divided into a grid of appropriate size and uniform current applied to the centre of gravity of each element of area. This is most conveniently done with one current supply probe which is placed at the center of gravity of each square in turn. The desired voltage are then read for each probe position and the final answer is the sum of all the individual voltage readings. In case of incomplete squares, full value of current is applied and the resultant measured voltage is reduced by the ratio of this area to that of the square grid.

On using the transformation

$$\psi = \phi + G\theta \frac{r^2}{2} \quad ...(15.26)$$

where $r^2 = x^2 + y^2$, Eq. (15.25) becomes

$$\nabla^2 \psi = 0 \quad ...(15.27)$$

with $$\psi = G\theta \frac{r^2}{2} \text{ on the boundary} \quad ...(15.28)$$

To utilize the conducting-sheet analogy here, one need only set up a voltage distribution on the boundary that correspond to Eq. (15.28) and measure the voltage distribution over the surface of the sheet corresponding to ψ. The shear stress is then

$$\tau = \frac{\partial \phi}{\partial n} = \frac{\partial \psi}{\partial n} - G\theta_r \frac{\partial r}{\partial n} \quad ...(15.29)$$

where n denotes the direction normal to the shear stress. The gradient of ψ is determined from the analog at any point by careful measurement of the potential V. If $V = \lambda G\theta (x^2 + y^2)/2$. On the boundary and the dimensions of the conducting sheet X are related to those of the actual section of interest by a factor μ such that $X = \mu x$, then $V = \lambda\mu$ and it follows that

$$\tau = \frac{\mu \partial V}{\lambda \partial n} - \frac{G\theta_r}{\mu} \frac{\partial r}{\partial n} \qquad \text{...(15.30)}$$

The required boundary voltage specified by Eq. (15.28) can be approximated by applying the voltage in discrete steps along the

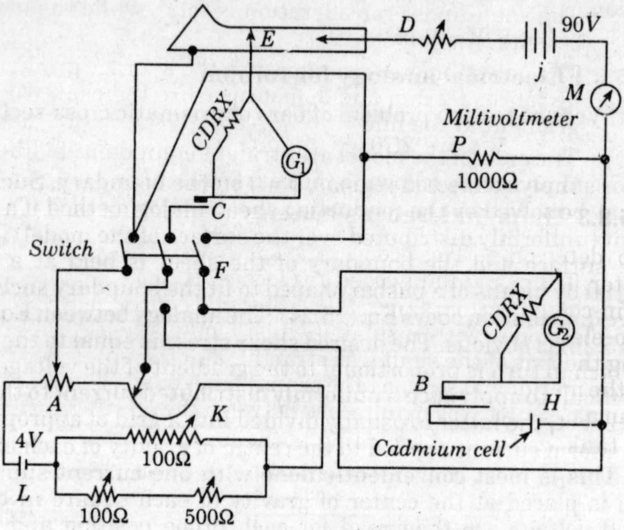

Fig. 15.10 Wiring diagram for conducting sheet analogy for torsion.

boundary and a voltage divider used to set voltages corresponding to the positions of the electrodes. The experimental set up used by Waver and Soroka is illustrated in Fig. 15.10.

15.3.2 Jacobsen's analogy

To determine the stress-concentration factor for circular shafts of two diameters connected by a circular fillet Jacobsen proposed the electrical analogy in 1925.

Jacobsen model (Fig. 15.11) is made of a steel plate with one surface flat and the other curved to cylindrical shape $h = c \times 3$. Since it is impractical to make the side $x = 0$ of the model of zero thickness, the steel plate is cut at a distance from the x-axis equal to one-eighth of the largest width of the model. The plate thus represents the meridional section

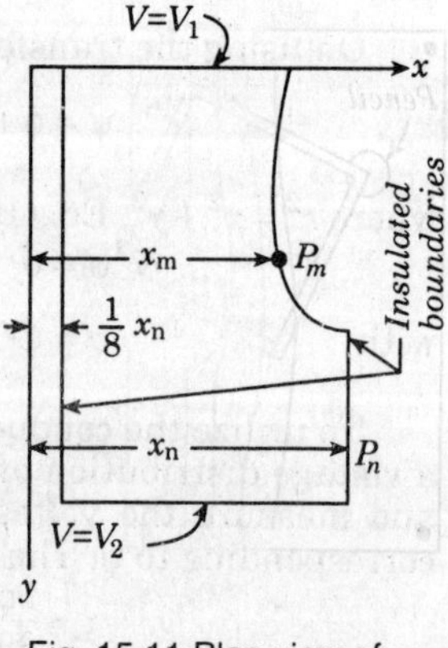

Fig. 15.11 Plan view of Jacobsen's model.

of a hollow shaft. To the two ends of the model, straight and perpendicular to the sides, are soldered copper electrodes. These are kept at a constant potential difference. The potential gradient along the external side of the model, is measured by means of a sensitive galvanometer, whose terminals are connected to two needles kept 2 mm apart by embedding them in a block of hard rubber.

The ratio of the radius of the bar times the gradient, at the point (P_m) of maximum gradient, to the value of the same product at a point (P_n) distant from the fillet, is the stress-concentration factor.

This method has the following causes of error :

1. The shaft under consideration is solid, while the model represents a hollow shaft.
2. The galvanometer readings give the average gradient over a distance of 2 mm and do not measure the peak value of the gradient at the fillet.
3. The ends of the model are straight equipotential lines rather than curves following the equiangular lines of the prototype.

15.3.3 Thum and Bautz's analogy

To determine stress-concentration factors in shafts of varying diameter, Thum and Bautz used an electrolytic tank made of wood with paraffin-coated bottom (Fig. 15.12). The sides of the tank were formed by two electrodes with insulated ends. One of the electrodes, representing the axis of the shaft was straight, and the other curved according to the meridional section to be examined. A fixed potential difference from an a.c. source was maintained between the electrodes. The bottom of the tank was curved according to the law $h = c/x^3$ upto a distance X

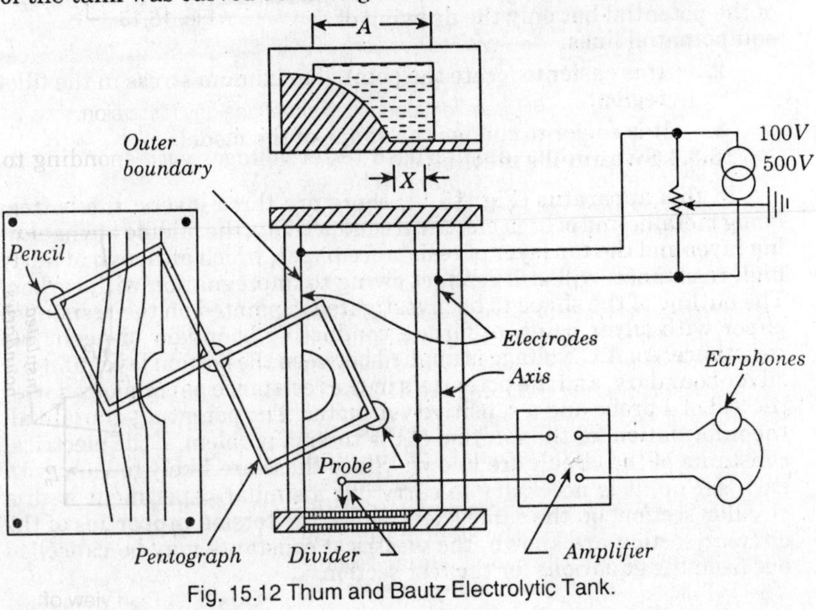

Fig. 15.12 Thum and Bautz Electrolytic Tank.

from the side representing the axis of the shaft and was flat from $x = 0$ to $x = X$. X should be at least one-third of the maximum width of the plate. The tank is filled with tap water. The equipotential lines were plotted by exploring the field with a point electrode connected to one of the terminals of an earphone. The other terminal of the earphone was connected to a voltage divider and bridge as shown in Fig. 15.12. The absence of noise in the earphone indicated that the potential of the field was equal to the previously set unbalance of the bridge. The position of the exploring electrode was located on a piece of paper by means of a pantograph. Thus, by moving the electrode so as to keep the earphone noise at a minimum, a contour of constant potential was traced.

To determine the stress-concentration factor the normal distances D_m and D_n between two equipotential lines at their point of closer approach P_m and at a point P_n, where they are practically parallel to the sides of the model, are measured, as well as the radii x_m and x_n (Fig. 15.13). The stress concentration factor K_t is obtained by plotting the curve.

$$\alpha = \frac{x_n^2 D_m}{x_m^2 D_n} \text{ v's } x_m$$

and extrapolating to the boundary. The advantages of this method over the Jacobsen's method are :

1. It does not require a measure of the potential but only the drawing of equipotential lines.
2. It is easier to locate the point of maximum stress in the fillet region.
3. It is easier to change the shape of the model.

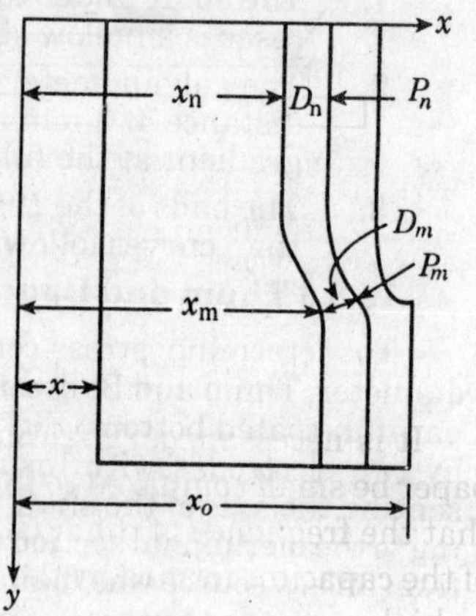

Fig. 15.13

15.3.4 Swannell's method

In this apparatus (Fig. 15.14) there are three layers, the bottom being metallic and of high electrical conductivity, the middle an insulating layer and the top layer of resistance paper, which although of fairly high resistance, will still conduct owing to impregnation with carbon. The outline of the shape to be investigated is painted on the resistance paper with silver paint, to form a conducting boundary of negligible resistance. An A.C. voltage is applied between the bottom layer and the silver boundary, and the potentials in the resistance paper plotted with the aid of a probe and a sensitive voltmeter. The potentials contain all the information for the solution of the torsion problem, if the electrical constants of the circuit are known. Since these are likely to vary with each set up, it is necessary to carry out a similar experiment with a circular section, on the same sheet. Since the torsion properties of the circular section are known, the electrical constants may be cancelled out from the equations for the test section.

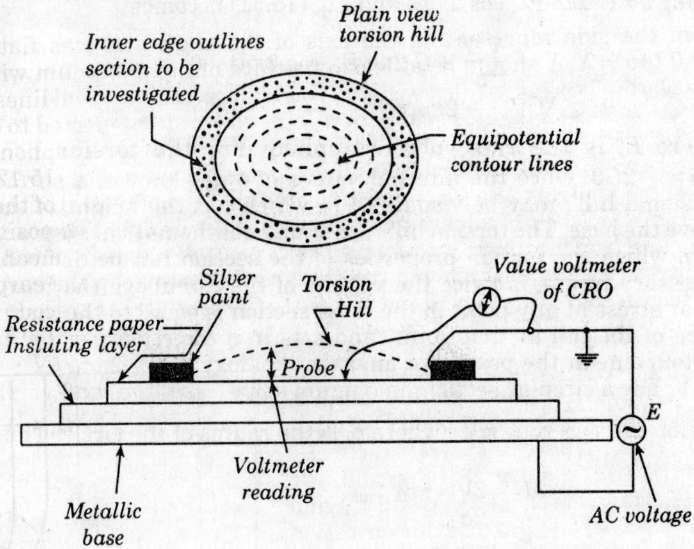

Fig. 15.14 Layout of apparatus for Swannell's method.

It is necessary for accuracy that the variation in potential in the paper be small compared to the applied voltage. This in practice means that the frequency of the A.C. should be low enough for the impedance of the capacitor formed by the resistance paper and the bottom sheet to be high compared to the resistance of the paper.

If the resistance across unit area of the semiconducting sheet is R and current leakage into the paper is E/R per unit area then the differential equation for local voltage becomes,

$$\frac{\nabla^2 V}{\rho} + \frac{E}{R} = 0 \qquad ...(15.31)$$

Where the potential applied is A.C. and the conducting layer is replaced by an insulator. The quantities i and V will vary with time and hence there will be a leakage current across the insulating layer, which will act as the dielectric of a capacitor formed by the resistance paper and the metal base. If q is the charge per unit area of this plate capacitor, then

$$q = CE$$

where C is the capacity of the capacitor, and the current per unit area flowing into the paper from the base is $i = dq/dt = C\ dE/dt$. If the applied potential is of frequency n, then

$$E = E_m \sin 2\pi\, nt$$

giving $i = C\, 2\pi n\, E_m \cos 2\pi\, nt$ and Eq. (15.31) becomes

$$\frac{\nabla^2 V}{\rho} + C\, 2\pi n\, E_m \cos 2\pi nt = 0$$

or $$\nabla^2 V = -\,2\pi n\rho CE' \qquad ...(15.32)$$

where E' is the rms voltage applied. For the torsion problem $\nabla^2\phi = -\,2G\theta$. Once the internal values of ϕ are known, a surface, or 'torsional hill', may be visualized in which ϕ is the height of the hill above the base. The torsion hills are simply mathematical abstractions, from which the torsion properties of the section can be derived. The necessary torque is twice the volume of the hill above the base. The shear stress at any point in the cross-section is equal to the maximum slope of the hill at that point and acts in a direction parallel to the contour line at the point. For an exact analogy $2G\theta = 2\pi n\rho\, CE'$, when $\phi = V$. For a circular section, maximum slope $= 2\phi_{max}/r_0$ and volume of torsion hill $= \frac{1}{2}\,\phi_{max}\,\pi r_0^2$; where r_0 is the radius of the circle. Thus

$$M_z = 2V = \pi r_0^2\, \phi_{max}$$

$$\tau_{max} = \frac{2\phi_{max}}{r_0} \qquad ...(15.33)$$

$$\theta = \frac{M_z}{GJ} = 2\phi_{max}/Gr_0^2$$

By painting silver paint over the area occupied by holes, thus forming areas of constant potential, this method can be applied to hollow sections also.

15.3.5 Conducting sheet analogy for Laplace Equation

Stokey and Hughes in 1955 developed the conducting sheet analogy for determining isopachic lines. Theocaris used this technique in 1956 for the separation of principal stresses along stress trajectories and in 1958 deermined stress concentration produced in perforated strips under tension.

In a two-dimensional stress field, the principal stresses σ_1 and σ_2 satisfies the Laplace equation

$$\nabla^2\,(\sigma_1 + \sigma_2) = 0$$

which is identical with the Eq. (15.23), $\nabla^2 V = 0$. Hence the analogy is complete.

In the Stokey and Hughes apparatus, a sheet of conducting paper is cut to the outlines of the test pieces, but with a margin of about 10 mm outside the true boundary (Fig. 15.15). If the test piece is symmetrical the sheet may be cut along the axes of symmetry, but in this case leaving no margin. A line 2 to 6 mm in width is then drawn round the boundaries about 1.5 mm from the line representing the true boundaries with resistance paint of the type used for printed electronic circuits. This line should have a resistance of 400 to 1600 ohms/cm depending on whether voltage connections are widely or closely spaced.

The actual value is not critical, but must be uniform and considerably lower than the resistance of the adjoining paper. It will be noted that edges lying along axes of symmetry are not painted in this way, and no voltage connections are made to them because no current will flow across such lines. Boundaries which are at constant potential are edges with a high conductivity paint.

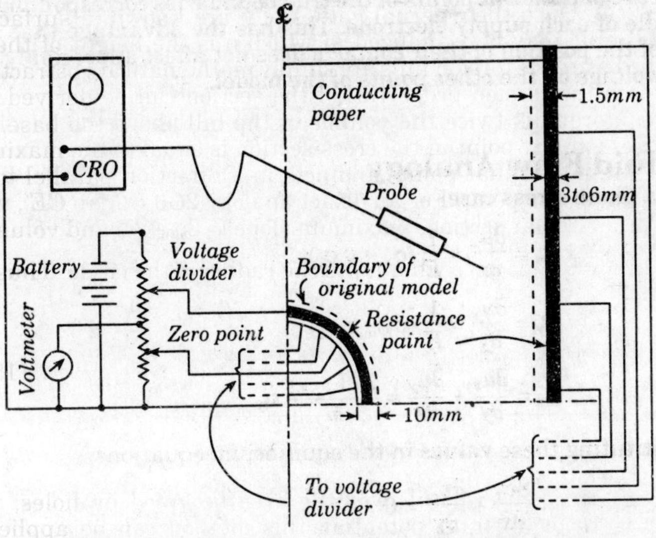

Fig. 15.15 Conducting sheet analogy for Laplace equation.

Having prepared the conducting sheet in this way, the next step is to apply the necessary boundary voltages from a simple voltage divider. This may consist of a wire about 4 m in length having a resistance of about 30 ohms. Connections are tapped off at appropriate points along the wire with crocodile clips and connected to the boundary line with silver conducting paint. With resistance of the order mentioned above, the connection of successive clips will have no appreciable effect on those already set. The spacing of connections on the boundary is related to the gradient of the boundary voltage ; if this is small, connections may be 5 cm, to 7.4 cm apart, reducing, to, say 3 mm where the boundary stresses are changing rapidly.

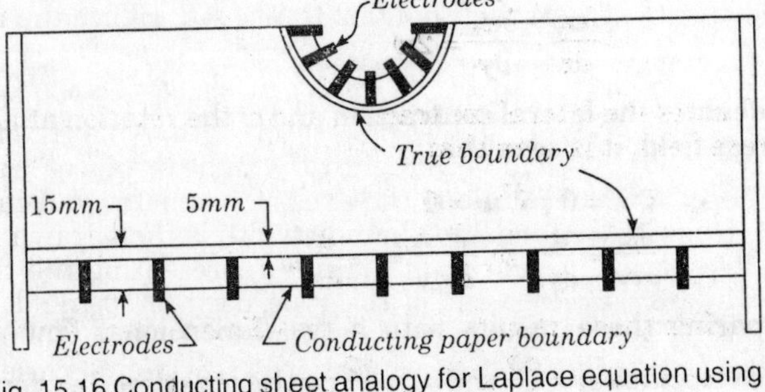

Fig. 15.16 Conducting sheet analogy for Laplace equation using copper foil electrodes.

Instead of using resistance paint copper foil electrodes may be struck along the margin as shown in Fig. 15.16, with their edges 5 mm from the lines representing the true boundaries. The sliding contact of each resistance is then connected by copper wire with the corresponding electrode in model. By proper positioning of these contacts, the desired voltages are obtained at points of the true boundaries corresponding to the middle of each supply electrode. This has the advantage that any change of the position of their contacts does not affect appreciably the applied voltage on the other points of the model.

15.4 Fluid Flow Analogy

For a plane stress case

$$\varepsilon_x = \frac{\partial u_x}{\partial x} = \frac{1}{E}(\sigma_x - \nu\,\sigma_y)$$

$$\varepsilon_y = \frac{\partial u_y}{\partial y} = \frac{1}{E}(\sigma_y - \nu\,\sigma_x)$$

$$\gamma_{xy} = \frac{\partial u_x}{\partial y} + \frac{\partial u_y}{\partial x} = \frac{2\,(1+\nu)}{E}\,\tau_{xy}$$

Substituting these values in the equilibrium equations.

$$\frac{\partial \sigma_x}{\partial x} + \frac{\partial \tau_{xy}}{\partial y} = 0$$

$$\frac{\partial \sigma_y}{\partial y} + \frac{\partial \tau_{xy}}{\partial x} = 0$$

We have

$$\frac{2}{1-\nu}\frac{\partial}{\partial x}\left(\frac{\partial u_x}{\partial x} + \frac{\partial u_y}{\partial y}\right) - \frac{\partial}{\partial y}\left(\frac{\partial u_y}{\partial x} - \frac{\partial u_x}{\partial y}\right) = 0$$

$$\frac{2}{1-\nu}\frac{\partial}{\partial y}\left(\frac{\partial u_x}{\partial x} + \frac{\partial u_y}{\partial y}\right) + \frac{\partial}{\partial x}\left(\frac{\partial u_y}{\partial x} - \frac{\partial u_x}{\partial y}\right) = 0$$

Putting $\frac{\partial u_x}{\partial x} + \frac{\partial u_y}{\partial y} = (1-\nu)\,\frac{\lambda}{\nu}$

$$\frac{\partial u_y}{\partial x} - \frac{\partial u_x}{\partial y} = 2w$$

where λ denotes the lateral contraction and w the rotation at any point of the stress field, it is seen that

$$\nabla^2\lambda = 0\ ;\ \nabla^2 w = 0$$

while $$\frac{\partial \lambda}{\partial x \nu} = \frac{\partial}{\partial y}\,.\,w,\ \frac{\partial}{\partial y}\frac{\lambda}{\nu} = -\frac{\partial}{\partial x}\,w \qquad ...(15.34)$$

Comparing these results with a two-dimensional flow problem where the velocities $v_x = \frac{\partial \phi}{\partial x}$ and $v_y = \frac{\partial \phi}{\partial y}$ can be considered as derivatives of a velocity potential ϕ, the conditions of a source free and irrotational flow can be written as

$$\frac{\partial v_x}{\partial x} + \frac{\partial v_y}{\partial y} = 0$$

and $\frac{\partial v_y}{\partial x} - \frac{\partial v_x}{\partial y} = 0$ respectively.

Since the relations between the stream function ψ and the velocity potential ϕ are :

$$\frac{\partial \phi}{\partial x} = \frac{\partial \psi}{\partial y}\,;\ \frac{\partial \phi}{\partial y} = -\frac{\partial \psi}{\partial x} \qquad ...(15.35)$$

in addition to $\nabla^2\phi = 0,\ \nabla^2\psi = 0$.

Comparing Eqs. (15.34) and (15.35) it is seen that the relationship between ϕ and ψ is the same as that found between λ/ν and w. Hence the equipotential and stream lines of a flow pattern can always be considered as lines of equal lateral contractions (isopachics) and lines of equal rotations in a corresponding plane stress system.

If $\quad u_x = kv_x = k\frac{\partial \psi}{\partial y}\,;\ u_y = k\,v_y = -k\frac{\partial \psi}{\partial x}$

then the equilibrium equations in terms of displacements are satisfied, where k is a constant. Hence the velocities of a potential flow can be considered as displacements in a plane stress system. This is called displacement-velocity analogy. Some of the important conclusions of fluid flow analogy are :

1. The orthogonal system of the equipotential and strain lines in a flow problem is equivalent of a system of stress trajectories.
2. In any plane stress system the variable distance between the unloaded boundary and the principal stress trajectory is inversely proportional to the boundary stress value.
3. Only an isometric set of stress trajectories can be considered as a set of potential and stream lines of a flow problem.
4. In case of viscous flow the lines of constant thicknesses (isopachics) in the stress problem will correspond to lines of constant vorticity in the flow field and the lines of constant rotations, being orthogonal trajectories of the isopachics, will be equivalent to the lines of constant fluid pressure in the flow problem.

15.5 Hydrodynamic Analogy

This analogy is based on the fact that the stress function ϕ for the torsion problems is identical with the stream function of a certain irrotational motion of ideal fluid contained in a vessel of the same cross-section as the twisted bar.

Now $\qquad v_x = \frac{\partial \psi}{\partial y},\ v_y = \frac{\partial \psi}{\partial x}$

where ψ is the stream function and continuity equation for incompressible fluids is

$$\frac{\partial v_x}{\partial x} + \frac{\partial v_y}{\partial y} = 0$$

$$\text{Also vorticity } 2w = \frac{\partial v_x}{\partial y} - \frac{\partial v_y}{\partial x}$$

$$\text{Hence} \quad \nabla^2\psi = -2\,w$$
$$\text{Also} \quad \nabla^2\phi = 2G\theta \qquad ...(15.36)$$

If $w = G\theta$ these equations are identical. The stresses are analogous to the velocities of the fluid flow. This analogy is very useful in determining stress-concentration factors in shafts under torsion.

15.6 Electro-Optic Analogy

In the electro-optic analog, a small tank is constructed which contains an organic dye that has a high electro-optic coefficient. The boundaries are either electrodes, where the values of the potential function are constants, and insulating surfaces on which the normal derivative of this function is zero. When the fluid is viewed between crossed polaroids, a birefringent pattern is seen when there is a potential difference between electrodes. The fringe order depends upon the magnitude of the potential gradient at each point of the region. The direction of gradient can be determined from isoclinics, as is done in photoelasticity. Once this information is available, the potential can be determined easily everywhere in the region.

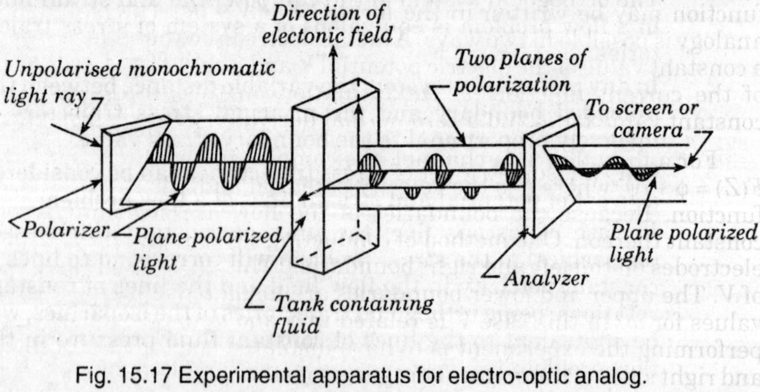

Fig. 15.17 Experimental apparatus for electro-optic analog.

The electro-optic effect may be explained as follows. When an organic dye (1.5% Milling Yellow NGS in distilled water) is subjected to an electric field, the molecules tend to line up in the direction of the field, and the fluid becomes optically anisotropic. Linearly polarized light, passing through the fluid, is split into two components one is parallel and the other is perpendicular to the field (Fig. 15.17). The propagation velocities of these components are different and the emerging light is elliptically polarized. When the light is viewed through an analyzer with its polarization axis perpendicular to a polarizer, extinction of light occurs, if (*a*) the direction of the electric field is parallel to the axis of either of the polarizing elements or (*b*) the relative retardation between the two components passing through the fluid is an integral number of wavelengths. Extinction of light associated with the direction of the electric field gives isoclinics from which the direction of the field can be determined throughout a region. The extinction caused by the magnitude of the electric field give isochromatic fringes from which this magnitude can be determined. Circularly polarized light can be used instead of linearly polarized light to eliminate the isoclinics.

In the electro-optic fluid, the conduction current vector j is related to the electrical potential V by the equation,

$$j = -\sigma \text{ grad. } V \qquad \text{...(15.37)}$$

where σ = conductivity. Because there are no current sources or sinks in the fluid, div. $j = 0$ and div. (σ grad V) = 0. For constant conductivity

$$\text{div. (grad } V) = \nabla^2 V = 0. \qquad \text{...(15.38)}$$

This steady current field satisfies Laplace's equation, hence it can be used as an analogue for all physical problems which satisfy the same equation. Associated with V, there exists a current function w, which is the complex conjugate of V. This function, which also satisfies Laplace's equation is defined by

$$dw = -\sigma \frac{\partial V}{\partial n} ds = \sigma \left(\frac{\partial V}{\partial y} dx - \frac{\partial V}{\partial x} dy \right) \qquad \text{...(15.39)}$$

Physically dw is interpretable as the current flux between points of the region separated by a distance ds. Lines of constant w represent current flow and they are orthogonal to equipotential lines. The complex function may be written in the form $G(Z) = V + iw$. The electro-optic analogy is possible in two ways. A metal electrode on the boundary gives a constant value of the electric potential V and a zero normal derivative of the current function w. An insulation on the boundary gives a constant value for w and a zero normal derivative for V.

For a fluid flow in a channel, the complex potential for the flow is $F(Z) = \phi + i\psi$, where ϕ is the velocity potential and ψ is the stream line function. Because the boundaries of the flow are streamlines, ψ is constant thereon. One method of conducting the experiment is to place electrodes on the left and right boundaries. This gives a constant value of V. The upper and lower boundaries are insulated and give constant values for w. In this case V is related to ψ and w to ϕ. Another way of performing the experiment is to have insulated boundaries on the left and right sides of the origin. This gives constant values for w. The upper and lower boundaries are electrodes which gives constant values for V. In this latter case, V is related to ϕ and w to ψ.

$$\text{Fringe order, } N = \left(\text{Ctnh } a - \frac{1}{a} \right) = AL(a) \qquad \text{...(15.40)}$$

where A depends upon concentration and 'a' depends upon both voltage gradient and temperature.

$$\left(\text{Ctnh } a - \frac{1}{a} \right) = \text{Langevin function, } L(a)$$

An empirical formula is

$$N = A\,(1 - e^{-k|\nabla V|}) \qquad ...(15.41)$$

where A depends upon concentration and thickness of tank containing the fluid and k depends upon temperature.

$$N = 14.3\,(1 - e^{-0.01693\,\nabla V})$$
$$= 14.3\,L\,(0.0470\,\nabla V) \qquad ...(15.42)$$

15.7 Plate Analogy

When body forces are absent or constant, the compatibility equation in terms of Airy stress function ϕ for a homogeneous isotropic elastic body in a state of plane stress or plane strain is $\nabla^2 . \nabla^2 \phi = 0$. When a plate is subjected to lateral forces and the moments at the edges only and the deflections are small in comparison with thickness, then $\nabla^2 . \nabla^2 w = 0$, where w = deflection of plate. In 1905 A. Timpe first observed and mentioned the analogy between these two cases. According to this analogy, the stresses in the x and y directions at points in an elastic body in a state of plane stress or plane strain, when body forces are absent or constant, are proportional to the curvatures in planes parallel to yz and xz-planes respectively, at corresponding points on the surface of a plate which is slightly deflected by lateral edge loadings.

The biharmonic equation when the body forces are absent or constant is given by

$$\frac{\partial^4 \phi}{\partial x^4} + \frac{2\partial^4 \phi}{\partial x^2 \partial y^2} + \frac{\partial^4 \phi}{\partial y^4} = \nabla^2 . \nabla^2 \phi = 0 \qquad ...(15.43)$$

where $$\nabla^2 = \frac{\partial^2}{\partial x^2} + \frac{\partial^2}{\partial y^2}$$

and $$\sigma_x = \frac{\partial^2 \phi}{\partial y^2},\ \sigma_y = \frac{\partial^2 \phi}{\partial x^2},\ \tau_{xy} = -\frac{\partial^2 \phi}{\partial x \partial y} \qquad ...(15.44)$$

The normal and shear stresses at a point in a direction at an angle θ with the x-axis are

$$\sigma_n = \sigma_x \cos^2\theta + \sigma_y \sin^2\theta$$
$$\tau_{nt} = \frac{1}{2}(\sigma_x - \sigma_y)\sin 2\theta \qquad ...(15.45)$$

Thus at any point in the elastic body, the difference of the principal stresses is equal to twice the maximum shearing stress and the sum of normal stresses at right angle is invariant in any direction.

For a plate of uniform thickness subjected to moments and lateral forces at the edges only, we have

$$\frac{\partial^4 w}{\partial x^4} + \frac{2\partial^4 w}{\partial x^2 \partial y^2} + \frac{\partial^4 w}{\partial y^4} = \nabla^2 . \nabla^2 w = 0 \qquad ...(15.46)$$

For small deflections

$$\frac{1}{R_x} = -\partial^2 w/\partial x^2$$

$$\frac{1}{R_y} = -\partial^2 w/\partial y^2 \qquad \text{...(15.47)}$$

$$\frac{1}{R_{xy}} = \partial^2 w/\partial x \partial y$$

where $\frac{1}{R_x}, \frac{1}{R_y}$ = curvatures of the middle plane of the plate in sections parallel to xz and yz-planes.

$\frac{1}{R_{xy}}$ = twist of surface w.r.t. x and y axes

If $\frac{1}{R_x}$ and $\frac{1}{R_y}$ are the principal curvatures at point '*a*' of a deflected plate, then the curvature in any direction $\overline{n}$ at an angle θ to the x-axis and the twist of surface w.r.t. a-n and a-t are respectively,

$$\frac{1}{R_n} = \frac{1}{R_x}\cos^2\theta + \frac{1}{R_y}\sin^2\theta$$

$$\frac{1}{R_{nt}} = \frac{1}{2}\left(\frac{1}{R_x} - \frac{1}{R_y}\right)\sin 2\theta \qquad \text{...(15.48)}$$

Thus the difference of the principal curvatures at a point is equal to twice the maximum twist and the sum of curvatures of planes at right angles is invariant in any direction.

The correlation between Eqs. (15.43) and (15.46) suggests the possibility of solving two dimensional stress problems experimentally. The stress function ϕ is a function of x and y. If we imagine vertical lines of magnitude $\phi(x, y)$ erected at corresponding points (x, y), the end points of these lines will form a surface which may be called a stress surface. The equation of stress surface is $z = (x, y)$. According to Eq. (15.44), the stress at a point in the x-direction is equal to the curvature in a plane parallel to the yz-plane at a corresponding point on the stress surface, and similarly the stress at a point in the y-direction is equal to the curvature in a plane parallel to the xz-plane. If we apply moments and lateral forces to the edges of a thin plate of the same shape as the xy plane of the elastic body, so that the boundary conditions of the plate are the same as those of the stress surface, the surface of the deflected plate will be virtually the stress-surface. The boundary conditions of the stress surface can be readily determined from the boundary conditions of the elastic body as follows :

The boundary forces in terms of stress function ϕ are :

$$\left.\begin{aligned} X &= \frac{\partial^2\phi}{\partial y^2}\cdot\frac{dy}{ds} + \frac{\partial^2\phi}{\partial x\partial y}\frac{dx}{ds} \\ -Y &= \frac{\partial^2\phi}{\partial x^2}\frac{dx}{ds} + \frac{\partial^2\phi}{\partial x\partial y}\frac{dy}{ds} \end{aligned}\right\} \qquad \text{...(15.49)}$$

Integrating along the boundary from an arbitrary point $P_0(x_0, y_0)$ to any point $P(x, y)$, we have

$$\int_{(x_0, y_0)}^{(x, y)} X\, ds = \int_{P_0\,(x_0, y_0)}^{P\,(x, y)} d\left(\frac{\partial\phi}{\partial y}\right) = \left(\frac{\partial\phi}{\partial y}\right)_P - \left(\frac{\partial\phi}{\partial y}\right)_{P_0}$$

$$\int_{(x_0, y_0)}^{(x, y)} Y\, ds = \int_{P_0\,(x_0, y_0)}^{P\,(x, y)} d\left(\frac{\partial\phi}{\partial x}\right) = -\left(\frac{\partial\phi}{\partial x}\right)_P + \left(\frac{\partial\phi}{\partial x}\right)_{P_0}$$

or

$$\left.\begin{aligned} \frac{\partial\phi}{\partial x} &= -\int_{(x_0, y_0)}^{(x, y)} Y\, ds + C_1, \text{ where } C_1 = \left(\frac{\partial\phi}{\partial x}\right)_{P_0} \\ \frac{\partial\phi}{\partial y} &= \int_{(x_0, y_0)}^{(x, y)} X\, ds + C_2, \text{ where } C_2 = \left(\frac{\partial\phi}{\partial y}\right)_{P_0} \end{aligned}\right\} \quad \text{...(15.50)}$$

From the above equations, the slopes, both in the x and y directions at any point on the boundary of the analogous deflected plate may be calculated, if the X and Y components of the forces acting on the boundary of the elastic body are known. The stress at any point in any direction in the elastic body can be determined by measuring the curvature at a corresponding point on the surface of a deflected plate in a plane perpendicular to the direction of the stress.

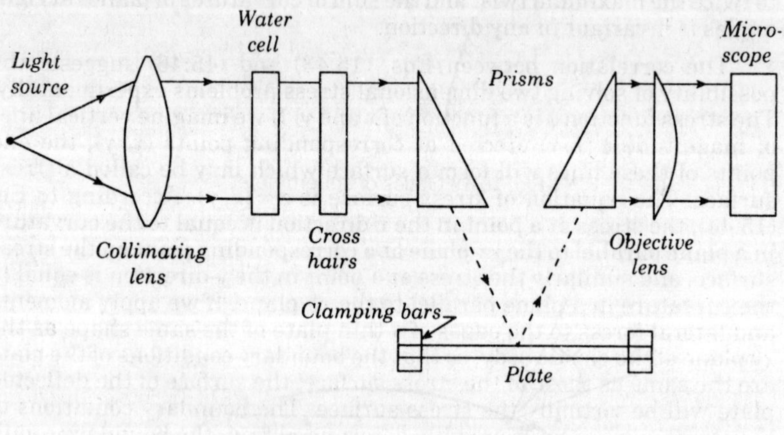

Fig. 15.18 Optical set up for measuring curvature.

The optical system for measuring the curvature of the plate is shown in Fig. 15.18. With reference to Fig. 15.19, a light source S is collimated by a lens L_1. The rays are reflected from the plate P, and an image of the source is brought to focus by a lens L_2 distant C from the plate. If the plate were plane, the image would be at a distance from lens L_2 equal to its focal length f since the source appears at infinity.

If the plate is convex, the apparent source comes in from infinity to a distance x from the plate, and the lens L_2 brings the image to focus at $f + d$, where

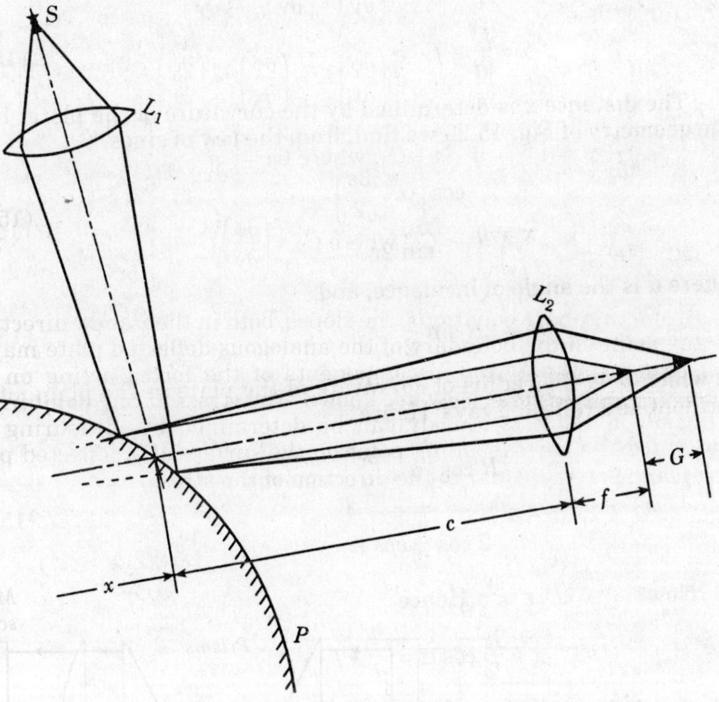

Fig. 15.19 Optics of spherometer.

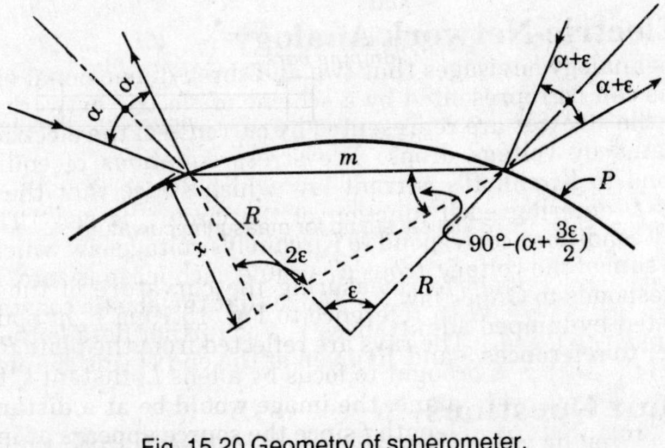

Fig. 15.20 Geometry of spherometer.

$$\frac{1}{c+x}+\frac{1}{f+d}=\frac{1}{f} \quad ...(15.51)$$

or

$$x=\frac{f^2}{d}+f-c \quad ...(15.52)$$

The distance x is determined by the curvature of the plate. From the geometry of Fig. 15.20 we find, from the law of sines,

$$x=m\frac{\cos\left(\alpha+\frac{3\varepsilon}{2}\right)}{\sin 2\varepsilon} \quad ...(15.53)$$

where α is the angle of incidence, and

$$m=2R\sin\frac{\varepsilon}{2} \quad ...(15.54)$$

in which R is the radius of curvature of the plate in the plane of the incident and reflected rays. Hence,

$$x=\frac{R\cos\left(\alpha+\frac{3\varepsilon}{2}\right)}{2\cos\frac{\varepsilon}{2}\cos\varepsilon} \quad ...(15.55)$$

Now $\varepsilon \ll \alpha$ Hence

$$x\approx\frac{R}{2}\cos\alpha=\frac{f^2}{d}+f-c$$

and

$$R=\frac{2f^2}{d\cos\alpha}+\frac{2(f-c)}{\cos\alpha}$$

$$=\frac{2f^2}{d}+2(f-c) \text{ as } \alpha \text{ is small and } \cos\alpha=1 \quad ...(15.56)$$

15.8 Electric-Network Analogy

This analogy envisages that two and three-dimensional elasticity problems can be represented by a scheme of electric network. In this analogy the stresses are represented by currents in the electric circuit and strains by voltage drops. The stress equations of equilibrium correspond to Kirchhoff's current law which states that the sum of currents I, entering each junction of the circuit, is zero. The compatibility conditions correspond to Kirchhoff's voltage law which states that the sum of the voltage drops E, around each mesh is zero. Hooke's law corresponds to Ohm's law $I = YE$, so that the elastic constants are represented by lumped admittances Y. For further details the reader may refer to references 9 and 10 given at the end of this chapter.

15.9 Quiz Questions

1. What do you understand by an analogous method ?
2. What are the various steps involved for the analogous method ?

3. What are the advantages of the analogous method ?
4. How do you estimate torque by the membrane analogy ?
5. How do you determine the magnitude and direction of shear stress in torsion by membrane analogy ?
6. How membrane analogy helps in separating the principal stresses ?
7. Out of rubber membrane and soap film, which one is preferred and why ?
8. Name the various soap solutions used for the soap film analogy.
9. Name the various instruments used for measuring the slope of the membrane.
10. How do you measure the volume of the membrane ?
11. List the sources of error in the membrane analogy.
12. Write the analogous formulae for torsion and membrane analogy ?
13. What is Kirchhoff's law ?
14. How do you determine stress-concentration factor by Jacobsen's analogy ?
15. What are the causes of error in the Jacobsen's analogy ?
16. What are the advantages of Thum and Bautz's analogy over Jacobsen's analogy ?
17. What is the advantage of using electrodes, over continuous resistance paint in the conducting sheet analogy ?
18. Name the conducting paper generally used for the conducting sheet analogy.
19. Write the analogous equations for fluid flow and plane stress elasticity problems.
20. What are the various analogous quantities in the hydrodynamic analogy ?
21. What is electro-optic analogy ?
22. Write the analogous formulae and quantities for the plate analogy.
23. How do you determine stresses by the plate analogy ?
24. Write the analogous quantities in the electric network analogue.
25. When do we resort to analogous methods ?

EXERCISES

15.1 What do you understand by an analogous method ? What are the various analogous methods used for separating principal stresses ? Give their advantages and limitations.

15.2 Describe the membrane analogy for torsion. How, this analogy is modified for hollow cross-sections ?

How do you avoid the measurement of the ratio p/T, where p is the pressure and T the tension in the membrane.

15.3 Describe the membrane analogy for separating the principal stresses. What are the advantages of this method ?

15.4 Describe the Griffith and Taylor apparatus for membrane analogy for torsion. How do you measure slope and volume ?

15.5 Give a brief account of the electrical analogy for torsion. Illustrate your answer by a suitable sketch.

15.6 Write short notes on the following :
(*i*) Jacobsen's analogy
(*ii*) Thum and Bautz's analogy.

15.7 Describe the conducting sheet analogy for Laplace equation. How do you determine stress-concentration factors in a thin plate with a circular hole under tension ?

15.8 (*a*) Write the important results of the fluid flow analogy.
(*b*) Describe briefly the hydrodynamic analogy. What is the main advantage of this analogy ?

15.9 What is electro-optic effect ? How this effect can be used in determining stresses in plane stress problems ?

15.10 Discuss the plate analogy in brief. What are the limitations of this analogy ?

16

Numerical Methods

16.1 Introduction

When it is difficult to solve the elasticity equations directly, then some numerical technique may be used to obtain an approximate solution. The well known numerical techniques are the finite-difference method (FDM) and the finite-element method (FEM). A less known numerical technique is the method of lines, which is a new technique of solving elasticity problems. This technique is in between the exact and approximate methods. In this chapter we shall study these methods in brief.

16.2 Finite Difference Method

This method is based on a technique in which the continuum is reduced to a system with finite number of degrees of freedom. The basis of the method is that the derivatives of functions at a point can be approximated by algebraic expression consisting of the value of the function at the point and at several nearby points. Thus the governing equations are reduced to finite difference equations. This set of simultaneous algebraic equations can be solved by relaxation techniques.

The points at which finite difference approximations are expressed is called pivotal points and the points at which the function is defined are called grid points. The finite differences may be expressed either forward, backward and central. Central difference expressions are more accurate than either forward or backward difference expressions for a given spacing of grid points.

Now the stress function ϕ is a function of both x and y. Taking $\Delta x = \Delta y = h$ and dividing the domain into a square mesh as shown in Fig. 16.1, at a point O, we obtain

$$\frac{\partial \phi}{\partial x} \approx \frac{1}{2h} [(\phi (x+h, y) - \phi (x-h, y)]$$

$$= \frac{1}{2h} (\phi_1 - \phi_3)$$

$$\frac{\partial \phi}{\partial y} \approx \frac{1}{2h} (\phi (x, y+h) - \phi (x, y-h)]$$

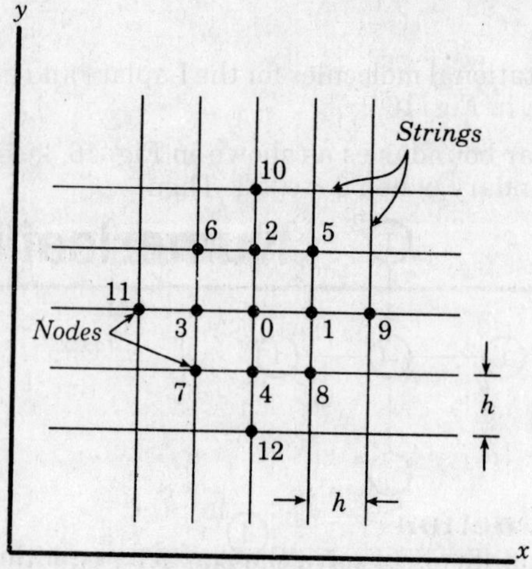

Fig. 16.1

$$= \frac{1}{2h}(\phi_2 - \phi_4)$$

$$\frac{\partial^2 \phi}{\partial x^2} \approx \frac{1}{h^2}[\phi(x+h, y) - 2\phi(x, y) + \phi(x+h, y)]$$

$$= \frac{1}{h^2}(\phi_1 - 2\phi_0 + \phi_3)$$

$$\frac{\partial^2 \phi}{\partial y^2} \approx \frac{1}{h^2}[\phi(x, y+h) - 2\phi(x, y) + \phi(x-h, y)]$$

$$= \frac{1}{h^2}(\phi_2 - 2\phi_0 + \phi_4)$$

Hence $\nabla^2 \phi = \frac{\partial^2 \phi}{\partial x^2} + \frac{\partial^2 \phi}{\partial y^2}$

$$= \frac{1}{h^2}(\phi_1 + \phi_2 + \phi_3 + \phi_4 - 4\phi_0)$$

and the Laplace equation $\nabla^2 \phi = 0$ becomes

$$\phi_1 + \phi_2 + \phi_3 + \phi_4 - 4\phi_0 = 0 \qquad ...(16.1)$$

If the governing equation is of the Poisson type

$$\nabla^2 \phi = -2$$

then the corresponding finite difference equation is

$$\phi_1 + \phi_2 + \phi_3 + \phi_4 - 4\phi_0 = -2h^2 \qquad ...(16.2)$$

Similarly the finite difference form of biharmonic equation $\nabla^4 \phi = 0$ can be written as

$$\frac{1}{h^2}\left[20\phi_0 - 8\sum_{i=1}^{4}\phi_i + 2\sum_{i=5}^{8}\phi_i + \sum_{i=9}^{12}\phi_i\right] = 0$$

...(16.3)

The computational molecules for the Laplace and biharmonic equations are shown in Fig. 16.2.

For irregular boundaries as shown in Fig. 16.3, consider a node B close to the boundary, when $0 < \alpha < 1$. Then

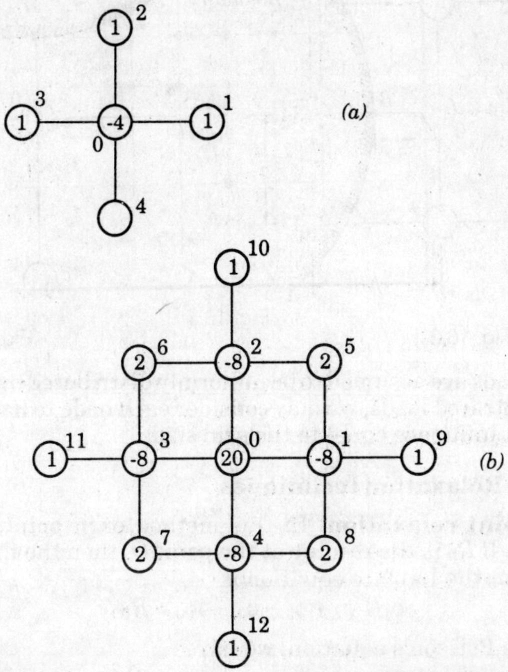

(a) Laplace (b) Biharmonic

Fig. 16.2 Computational molecules for Laplace and Biharmonic operators.

$$\left[\frac{\partial^2 \phi}{\partial x^2}\right]_0 = \frac{2}{h^2 \, . \, \alpha(1+\alpha)} \left[(\phi_B - \phi_0) + \alpha\,(\phi_3 - \phi_0)\right] \quad ...(16.4)$$

Similarly for a node C, where $0 < \beta < 1$, we have (Fig. 16.4)

$$\left[\frac{\partial^2 \phi}{\partial y^2}\right]_0 = \frac{2}{h^2 \beta\,(1+\beta)} \left[(\phi_C - \phi_0) + \beta(\phi_4 - \phi_0)\right] \quad ...(16.5)$$

Hence $h^2\,(\nabla^2\phi)_0 = A\phi_B + B\phi_C + C\phi_3 + D\phi_4 - (E+F)\,\phi_0$ ...(16.6)

where $A = \dfrac{2}{\alpha\,(1+\alpha)},\ B = \dfrac{2}{\beta\,(1+\beta)},\ C = \dfrac{2}{(1+\alpha)}$

$$D = \frac{2}{(1+\beta)},\ E = \frac{2}{\alpha},\ F = \frac{2}{\beta}$$

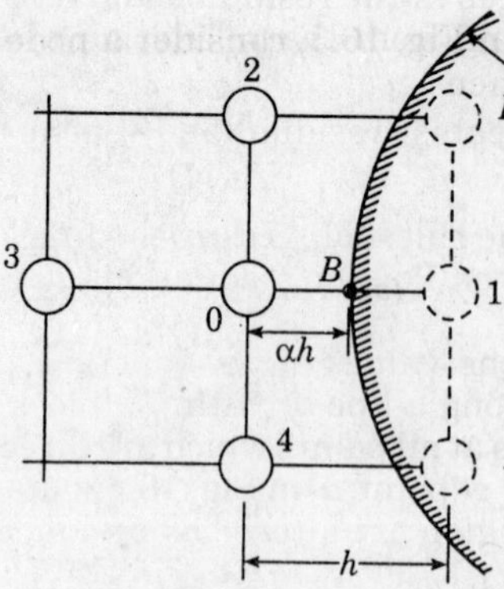

Fig. 16.3

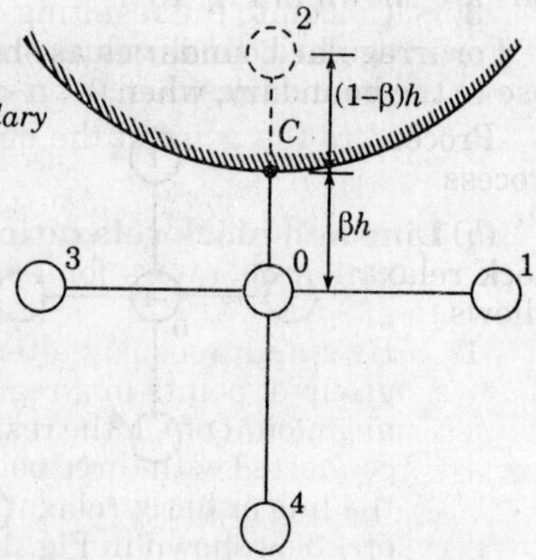

Fig. 16.4

The loads are assumed to be uniformly distributed over the domain. For concentrated loads, we may consider each node to have a surrounding zone of influence equal to the grid size.

16.2.1 Relaxation techniques

(*a*) **Point relaxation.** In this method each point is relaxed individually. If R_0 is the residue at the point *O*, then the finite-difference equation for the Laplace equation is

$$\phi_1 + \phi_2 + \phi_3 + \phi_4 - 4\phi_0 = R_0 \qquad \text{...(16.7)}$$

and for the Poisson's equation, we have

$$\phi_1 + \phi_2 + \phi_3 + \phi_4 - 4\phi_0 + 2h^2 = R_0 \qquad \text{...(16.8)}$$

If the values ϕ_1, ϕ_2, ϕ_3, ϕ_4 and ϕ_0 are the correct ones then the residue R_0 is equal to zero, otherwise R_0 does not vanish. The exact solution of Laplace or Poisson's equation may be said to consist of such adjustments in the initial values of ϕ which would make the residues zero. When the residual R_0 vanishes the point is said to be relaxed. The unit relaxation pattern for the Laplace operator is shown in Fig. 16.5. A set of five residuals at a point *O* which satisfies the expression

$$R_1 = R_2 = R_3 = R_4 = \frac{R_0}{4}$$

is called a vanishing set. The following procedure may be adopted for the point relaxation method.

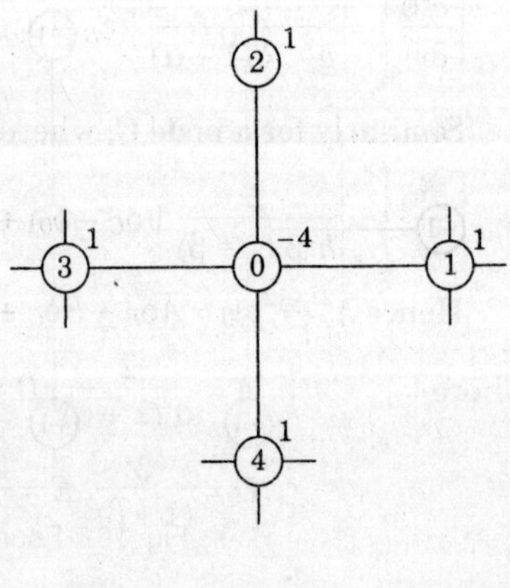

Fig. 16.5 Unit relaxation pattern.

1. Calculate and record all residuals in the net work.
2. Select the point at which the residual is numerically the greatest and relax it.
3. Calculate the resulting changes in the residuals and as well as their final values, resulting from the relaxation of the greatest residual.

Proceed to the point of the next greatest residual and repeat the process.

(b) **Line and block relaxation.** The rules for writing the line and block relaxation operators for Laplace or Poisson's equations are as follows :

1. By simultaneously altering the values of the function at a group of points in a region along a line or within a block by an amount of + 1, the residuals at all points which are directly connected with three points (*e.g.* point '*a*' in Fig. 16.6) outside the line or block relaxation region are altered by an amount of – 3 as shown in Fig. 16.6.

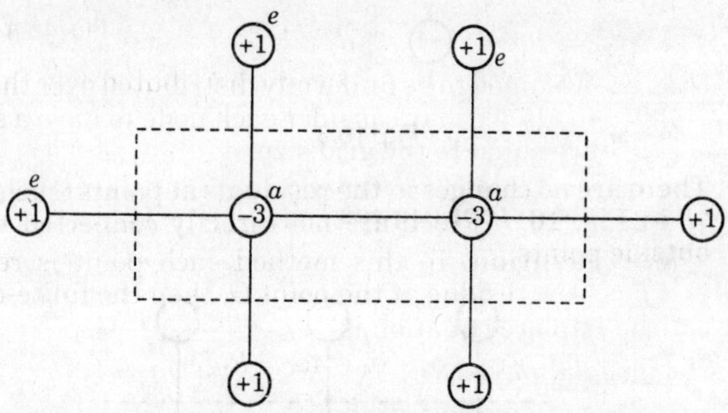

Fig. 16.6 Two point line operator.

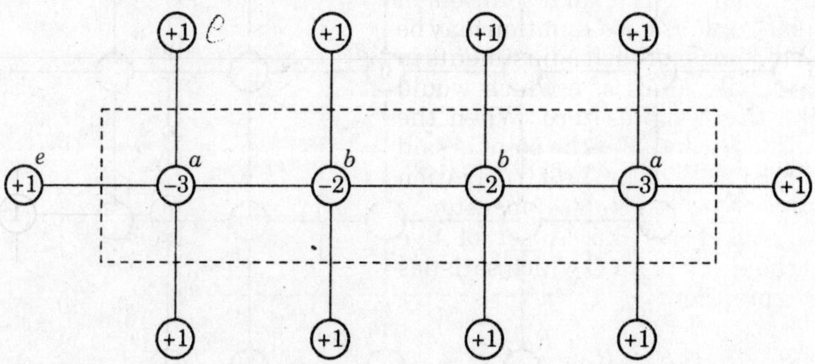

Fig. 16.7 Four point line operator.

2. The residuals at all points which are connected with two outside points (*e.g.* point '*b*' in Fig. 16.7) are altered by an amount of –2.
3. The residual at a point which is connected with one outside point (*e.g.* point *C* in Fig. 16.8) alters by an amount of –1.

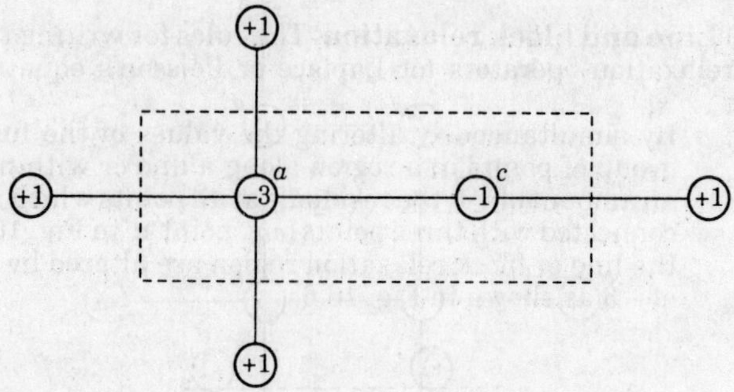

Fig. 16.8

4. There are no changes in the residuals at points (such as point '*d*' in Fig. 16.9) which are not directly connected with any outside points.

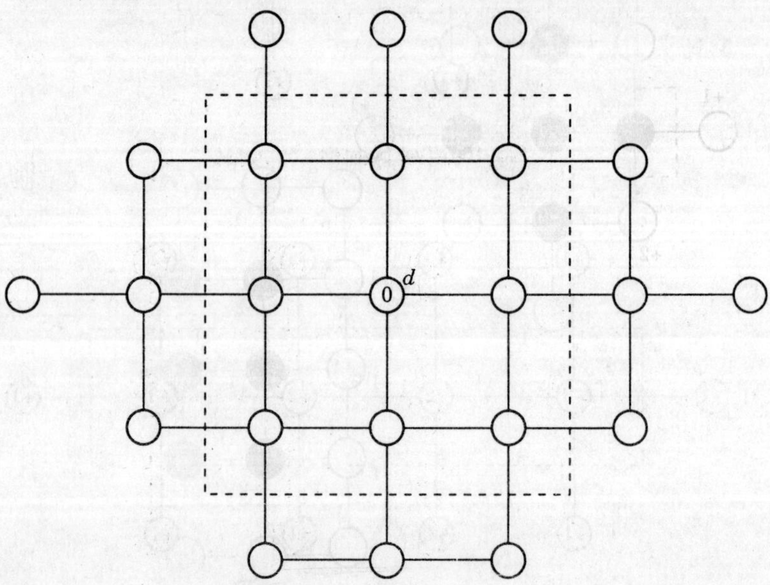

Fig. 16.9

5. The residuals at points like e, which are outside the line or block-relaxation region but directly connected to one point within the region are altered by +1.
6. The residual at any outside point (such as point f in Fig. 16.10) which is directly connected to two outside points is altered by +2.

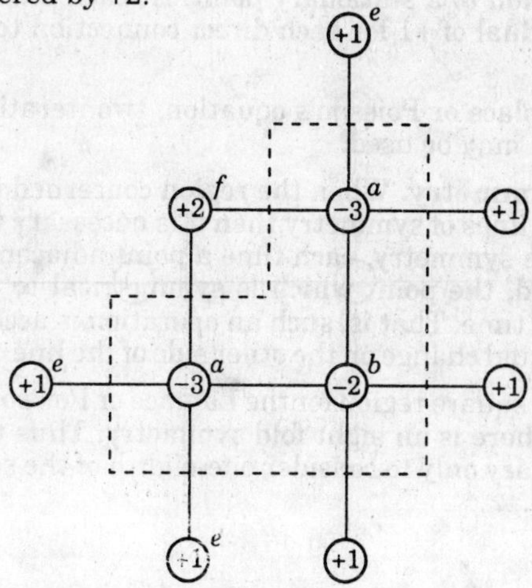

Fig. 16.10

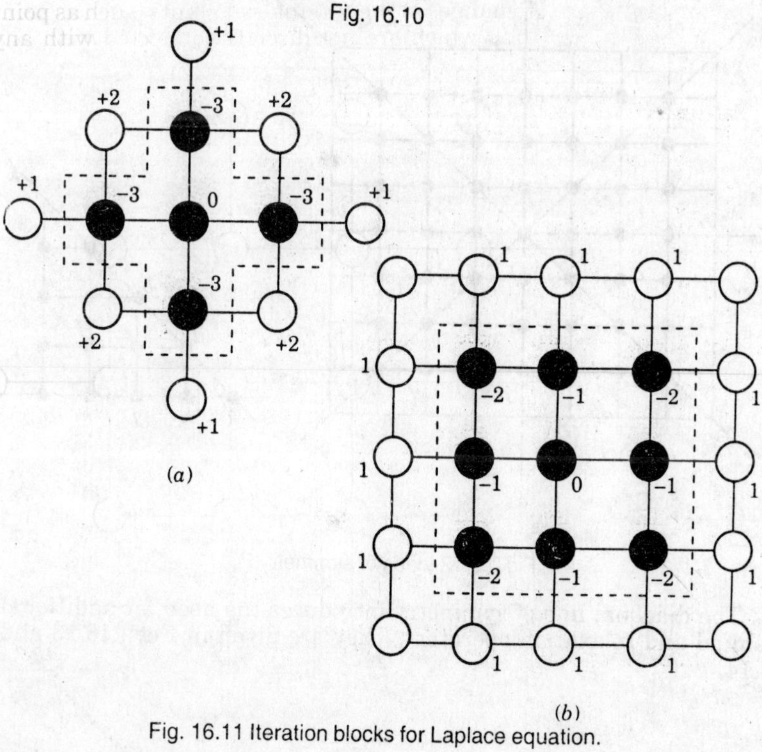

Fig. 16.11 Iteration blocks for Laplace equation.

Thus by making a judicious choice of a block for relaxation, much of the iteration time or "washing back" of residuals can be prevented. The points outside the line or block are called *stationary* points. The following general rule may be formulated for the relaxation operators.

"At each point that is displaced there will be a residual of –1 for each direct connection to a stationary point. At each stationary point there will be a residual of +1 for each direct connection to a displaced point."

For solving Laplace or Poisson's equation, two iteration blocks as shown in Fig. 16.11 may be used.

(*c*) **Lines of Symmetry.** When the region concerned in a problem exhibit one or more lines of symmetry then it is necessary to remember that to preserve the symmetry, each time a point adjacent to a line of symmetry is altered, the point which is symmetrical to this point is altered at the same time. That is, such an operation is accompanied by an automatically equal change on the other side of the line of symmetry.

If we consider a square region for the Laplace or Poisson's equation, then we find that there is an eight fold symmetry. Thus to obtain the solution it is necessary only to consider one-eighth of the square region as shown in Fig. 16.12.

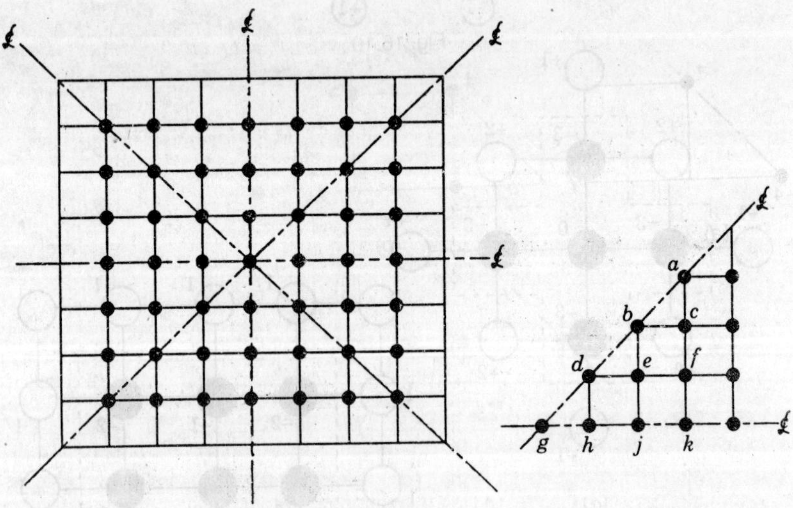

(*a*) (*b*)

Fig. 16.12 Lines of symmetry.

The diagonal line of symmetry introduces the need for additional residual and relaxation operators. They are given in Figs. 16.13 and 16.14.

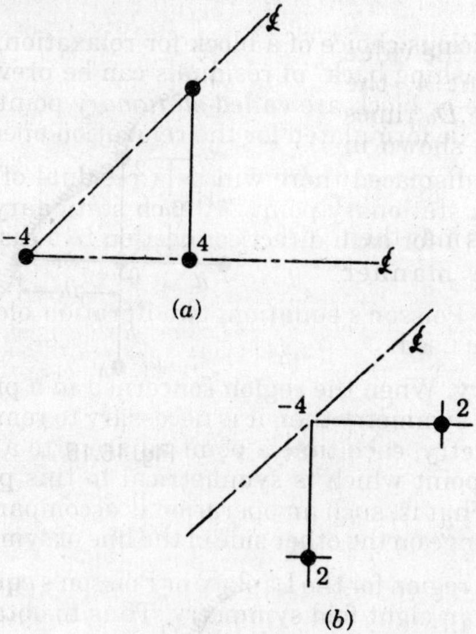

Fig. 16.13 Residual operators.

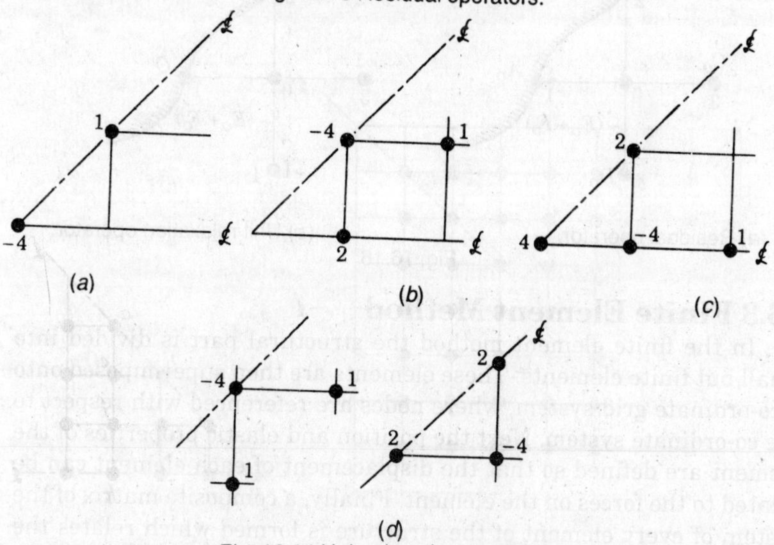

Fig. 16.14 Unit relaxation operators.

(*d*) **Curved Boundaries.** For a curved boundary Eq. (16.6) may be written as (Fig. 16.15) :

$$h^2\,(\nabla^2\,\phi)_0 = A\phi_1 + B\phi_2 + C\phi_3 + D\phi_4 - (E + F)\,\phi_0 \qquad \ldots(16.9)$$

The residual and unit relaxation operators have been shown in Fig. 16.16. If the value of the function is altered by +1 at point 0, the residual there is altered by $-(E_0 + F_0)$. At the same time at positions 3 and 4, the residual alters by +1. No residual are recorded at the boundary points 1 and 2. If we alter the value of the function at point 4, the residual at O will change D_0 times the value altered at 4 as shown in Fig. 16.17.

The relaxation process may then be carried out in the manner described earlier.

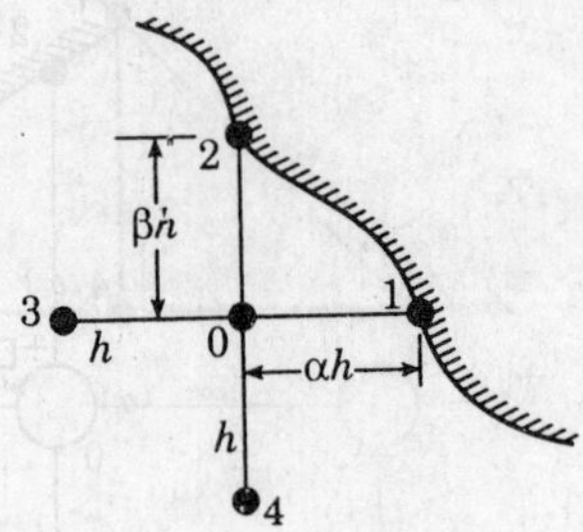

Fig. 16.15

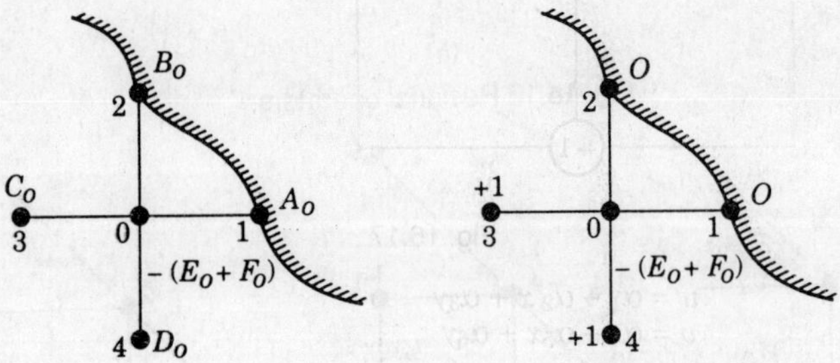

(*a*) Residual operator. (*b*) Unit relaxation operator.

Fig. 16.16

16.3 Finite Element Method

In the finite element method the structural part is divided into small but finite elements. These elements are then superimposed onto a co-ordinate grid system, where nodes are referenced with respect to the co-ordinate system. Next the position and elastic properties of the element are defined so that the displacement of each element can be related to the forces on the element. Finally, a composite matrix of the system of every element of the structure is formed which relates the displacements of the nodel points of each element to the external forces on the structure. Once the displacement field is determined, the strains can then be evaluated using the strain-displacement relations, and finally stresses are evaluated using the stress-strain relations.

If we restrict our study to two-dimensional problems only, the first step is to characterize the displacement behaviour. Assuming that the displacements are a linear function of position within the structure, the displacements within each element in the x and y directions are respectively given by

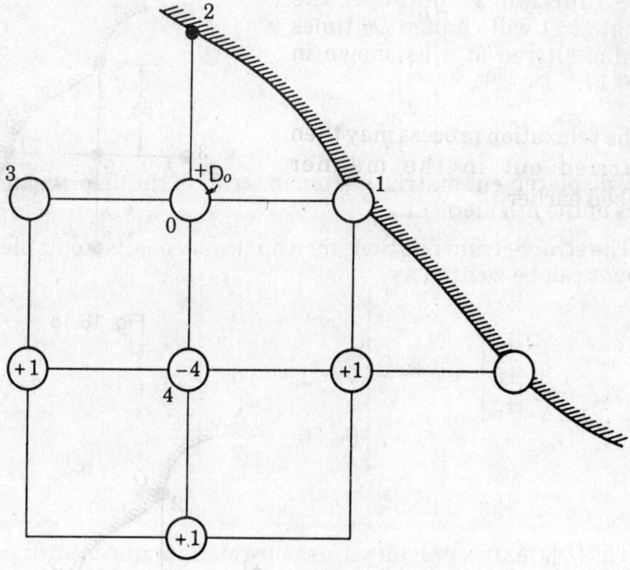

Fig. 16.17

$$u = \alpha_1 + \alpha_2 x + \alpha_3 y$$
$$v = \alpha_4 + \alpha_5 x + \alpha_6 y \qquad \text{...(16.10)}$$

The six constants α_1 to α_6 are found by substituting the coordinates of each nodal point of the element. The next step is to determine the strains using the two-dimensional strain-displacement relations. This results in

$$\left.\begin{aligned} \varepsilon_x &= \frac{\partial u}{\partial x} = \alpha_2 \\ \varepsilon_y &= \frac{\partial v}{\partial y} = \sigma_6 \\ \gamma_{xy} &= \frac{\partial u}{\partial y} + \frac{\partial v}{\partial x} = \alpha_3 + \alpha_5 \end{aligned}\right\} \qquad \text{...(16.11)}$$

The constants α_i will be functions of the geometric size of the element and the positions of each node. In matrix form, this can be expressed as :

$$\{\varepsilon\}_n = [B]_n \{\delta\}_n \qquad \text{...(16.12)}$$

where $\qquad \{\varepsilon\}_n = \begin{Bmatrix} \varepsilon_x \\ \varepsilon_y \\ \gamma_{ay} \end{Bmatrix}_n$

and $[B]_n$ is the matrix term due to the geometric size of nth element predicted by the node locations, and $$\{\delta\}_a = \begin{Bmatrix} u_1 \\ v_1 \\ u_2 \\ v_2 \\ \vdots \end{Bmatrix}_n$$

is the displacement matrix written in terms of the displacements of the nodes of the nth element.

The stress-strain relations for a homogeneous, isotopic plane-stress element can be written as :

$$\begin{Bmatrix} \sigma_x \\ \sigma_y \\ \tau_{xy} \end{Bmatrix}_n = \frac{E_n}{1-\nu_n^2} \begin{bmatrix} 1 & \nu & 0 \\ \nu & 1 & 0 \\ 0 & 0 & \frac{1-\nu}{2} \end{bmatrix}_n \begin{Bmatrix} \varepsilon_x \\ \varepsilon_y \\ \gamma_{xy} \end{Bmatrix}_n \quad ...(16.13)$$

or $$\{\sigma\}_n = [D]_n \{e\}_n \quad ...(16.14)$$

The $[D]_n$ matrix provides a measure of the material stiffness properties of the nth element. Substituting Eq. (16.12) in (16.14), we get

$$\{\sigma\}_n = [D]_n [B]_n \{\delta\}_n \quad ...(16.15)$$

which provides the relationship between the stress in the element and its nodal displacements.

The final step is to relate the forces on each nodal point to the stress on the element. In general the nodal forces can be related to the nth element stresses as

$$\{f\}_n = [A]_n \{\sigma\}_n \quad ...(16.16)$$

where $$\{f\}_n = \begin{Bmatrix} f_{1x} \\ f_{1y} \\ f_{2x} \\ f_{2y} \\ \vdots \end{Bmatrix}$$

are the internal forces in the x and y directions at each node. The $[A]_n$ matrix is related to the element shape and size, as is the $[B]_n$ matrix, and hence the two matrices are related. Substituting Eq. (16.15) in (16.16), we get

$$\{f\}_n = [A]_n [D]_n [B]_n \{\delta\}_n \quad ...(16.17)$$

$$= [k]_n \{\delta\}_n \quad ...(16.18)$$

where $$[k_n] = [A]_n [D]_n [B]_n \quad ...(16.19)$$

is the stiffness matrix of the nth element. Finally, the stiffness matrices of each element are compiled into a system matrix equation. This can be represented by

$$\{F\}_{sys} = [K] \{\delta\}_{sys} \quad ...(16.20)$$

where $\{F\}_{sys}$ = array of total external forces F_{xi}, F_{yi} at each node.

$[K]$ = master stiffness matrix.

$\{\delta\}_{sys}$ = array of displacements u_i, v_i

of each node in system of elements.

Thus $\{\delta\}_{sys} = [K]^{-1}\{F\}_{sys}$ ...(16.21)

The inverse matrix $[K]^{-1}$ is evaluated considering boundary conditions. The matrix $\{\delta\}_{sys}$, fields the displacements of each node within the system, from which the strains and stresses are determined by using Eqs. (16.12) and (16.15). For further details of this method, the reader may refer to the references 7 to 10 given at the end of this chapter.

16.4 Method of Lines

The line method lies midway between completely analytical and discrete methods. The basis of this technique is the substitution of finite differences for the derivatives with respect to all the independent variables except one for which the derivatives are retained. This approach replaces a given partial differential equation with a system of simultaneous ordinary differential equations whose solutions can then be obtained in closed form. These equations describe the dependent variable along lines which are parallel to the co-ordinates in whose direction the derivatives were retained. Application of the line method is most useful when the resulting ordinary differential equations are linear and have constant coefficients.

An inherent advantage of the line method over other numerical methods is that good results are obtained from the use of relatively coarse grids. This use of a coarse grid is permissible because parts of the solutions are obtained in terms of continuous functions. Additional accuracy in normal stress distributions is derived from the fact that they are expressed as first-order derivatives of the displacements and these derivatives can be analytically evaluated. The disadvantage of the method lies in the increased amount of computation necessary. For further details refer to references 11 and 12.

14.5 Quiz Questions

1. When do we seek numerical solutions for elasticity problems?
2. Why do we prefer central differences over forward and backward differences ?
3. Write the finite-difference equation for Laplace equation ?
4. Write the finite-difference form of biharmonic equation ?
5. Draw the computational molecules for Laplace and Biharmonic operators.
6. What is a vanishing set ?
7. Differentiate between a displaced and a stationary node.
8. State the general rule for the relaxation operators.

9. What is the basic difference between finite-difference and finite-element methods ?
10. What are the advantages of the method of lines over the finite-difference and finite-element methods.

EXERCISES

16.1 Explain briefly how the finite-difference method can be used to obtain the sum of principal stresses in two-dimensional elasticity problems.

16.2 Describe the finite-difference method in brief for solving the biharmonic equation.

16.3 Discuss the relaxation techniques with special reference to lines of symmetry and curved boundaries.

16.4 Explain the finite-element method for solving plane stress problems.

16.5 Give the basic principle of the method of lines for solving elasticity problems. What are the advantages of this method over the other numerical methods ?

16.6 Determine the stress concentration factor in an infinite plate with a circular hole under uniaxial tension by the finite element method.

16.7 Determine the stress distribution in a cantilever having end load by the finite element method.

16.8 Determine the stress distribution in a circular disc under diametral compression by the finite difference method.

17

Photo-Holo-Elasticity

17.1 Introduction

Holography is a relatively now process in which one records the electro-magnetic field that has been reflected from the same object scene, both amplitude and phase, whereas in conventional photography, only the variations in the intensity of the light across the object can be recorded. In holography the wave is recorded in such a way that a subsequent illumination of this record serves to reconstruct the original object wave, even in the absence of the original object. In effect, these light waves are "frozen" in the emulsion of the photographic plate and on illumination they are 'unfrozen".

In this chapter we shall study briefly the basic concepts of holography, hologram inter-ferometry and their applications in photoelasticity, which has become known by the term "photo-holo-elasticity".

17.2 Historical Developments

The idea of holography was first of all conceived by a British research scientist, Dennis Gabor in 1948. The idea remained dormant for a couple of years because of the relatively low spatial coherence of the available light sources at that time. It is only in the past few years, however, that the method has become widely known and used. The modern renaissance in holography had to await the general availability of the laser with the great temporal and spatial coherence of its light. Schawlow and Towns constructed the first laser in 1960, both in gaseous and solid states. Helium-Neon laser was developed in 1960 shortly after the Ruby laser was discovered by Maiman. With the invent of laser, interest began reviving in the field when Leith and Upatneiks demonstrated further details and informations about this method and introduced the concept of diffuse illumination and off-axis holography.

Hologram interferometry may be defined as the study and applications of the interference effects in the fields diffracted from holograms, which exhibit optical path differences in the recording interferometers. The name hologram was given to the recording by D. Gabor, a Greek word (holos) which means "self-record" and sums up what holography is all about. The use of hologram for interferometry was introduced by Horman (1965). Later on Burch (1965), Haines and Hilderbrand (1966) used it for measurement on diffuse surface. Stetson and Powell (1965) introduced the use of hologram interferometry for vibrating objects.

The application of holography in experimental stress analysis has been stimulated by hologram interferometry particularly. Taylor et. al. in 1966 introduced the applications of lasers to static and dynamic photoelasticity. The use of holography to photoelasticity was introduced by Hovanesian (1967), as he called it "Stress-Holo Interferometry". Fourney and Mate (1968), first demonstrated the application of double exposure interference holography to photoelasticity. In this paper no mathematical treatment of the subject was presented and the isopachic fringes were not interpreted properly. A more correct interpretation was given by Hovanesian et al (1968) and presented a mathematical description by considering only the interference generated during the hologram formation process. Based on this analysis they obtained the same governing equation as derived by Nisida and Saito (1964) for a Mach-Zehnder interferometer. A more thorough analytical description was presented by Fourney and Mate (1970) by including the effects of the reconstruction process also, thus deriving the correct result for the observed intensity. While the result obtained by Fourney and Mate differed from that of Hovanesian et. al., all of them concluded that the observed interference fringe pattern consisted of the independent super-position of the isopachic and isochromatic fringe patterns with half-order fringe shifts in the isopachic fringes that intersect the isochromatics.

Upto now the analytical descriptions of the hologram process presented so far treated the polarized light as if it were a scalar wave, when in fact, the electric field is a vector wave with two polarization components, both with amplitude and phase. This fact was recognised by Lohman (1965), who qualitatively described the influence of each of the polarization components on the holographic process. By taking into account the polarization effects in holography. Rose et al (1970) concluded that reconstructed image brightness is greatest when the electric vectors of the object and reference fields are perpendicular to the plane containing their axes of propagation, and further more when the electric vector of the illuminating beam is perpendicular to the plane containing the illumination and reconstructed axes. Durelli and Sanford (1970) made analytical treatments to account for the vector nature of the light by treating each of the two components separately and then coherently adding them at some appropriate point. They concluded that the observed interference patterns cannot, in general, be interpreted as simply the independent superposition of the isochromatics and isopachics as has been previously assumed. For the more common situation in which the spatial frequency of the isopachics is greater than that of the isochromatics, this assumption is valid only when the fringes are nearly orthogonal. Conversely, when the two families of fringes are parallel, the interaction of the isochromatics and isopachics is the most pronounced. It was demonstrated that the isochromatic does not appear as a distinct minimum whenever the slopes of the isochromatic and isopachic functions are of opposite sign at an isochromatic fringe location. It was further shown, when the isochromatic is visible, the isopachic fringe order changes by one and one-half orders upon crossing the isochromatics and when it does not appear, the isopachic fringe order changes by only one-half of an order on either side of the point at which the isochromatic would be located.

In order to avoid situations when it becomes difficult to interpret the isochromatic and isopathic fringe patterns, Dudderar and O' Regan (1971) developed an interferometer by making use of real time holography by means of which the isochromatic and isopachic fringe patterns may be obtained simultaneously but recorded separately. Further developments to record these fringes simultaneously and separately have been presented by Holloway et. al. (1972), Assa and Betser (1973, 1974), Chatelaine (1973), Hovanesian (1971, 1974), Sanford (1973), Ebbeni et. al. (1976) and Gasvik (1976).

17.3 Laser Optics

The most common and a suitable light source for holography is the gas laser. Gas lasers generate beams which spread over a much smaller range of wavelengths, which make them particularly suitable for applications in holography. Laser (Light Amplification by Stimulated Emission of Radiation) works on the "stimulated emission" principle. Here an atom in the excited state is exposed to a photon of electromagnetic radiation which moves the atom to the lower state with the accompanying release of a photon to radiation of the same frequency and in phase with the radiation. Thus the released radiation adds to the incident radiation effecting an amplification of the latter. This is monochromatic and spatially coherent emission. The two released photons give four and this cascading effect soon amplifies the incident photon tremendously. In order to have the lasing phenomenon built up, it is necessary to have the probability of a photon striking an excited atom greater than the probability of its striking an atom in the ground state. When the number of excited atoms are greater than the atoms at the ground state, then the condition is called population inversion".

Of the many types of gas lasers presently available, the He-Ne laser is the one used for most of the hologram work being performed today. The He-Ne laser emits light radiations at 6328Å wave-length. The output from a He-Ne laser is nearly 100 percent linearly polarised with the electric vector perpendicular to the plane containing the optic axis. The linearly polarized light can be converted into a circularly polarized light by using a polarizer and a quarter wave plate as and when desired. Fig. 17.1 shows the arrangement for obtaining circularly polarized light from a continuous wave (CW) Helium-Neon laser.

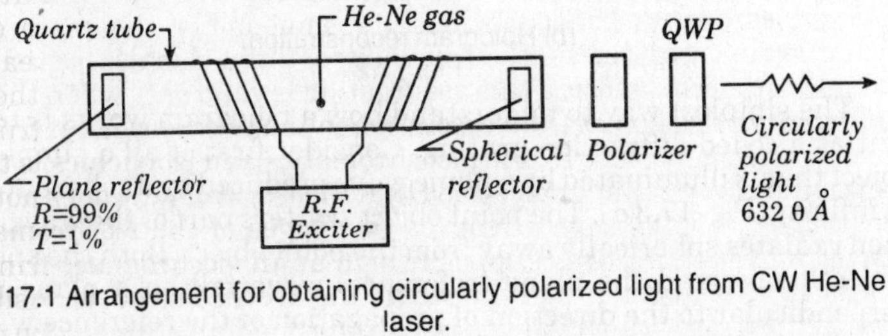

Fig. 17.1 Arrangement for obtaining circularly polarized light from CW He-Ne laser.

17.4 Fundamentals of Holography

Optical holography, sometimes called the wavefront reconstruction process, became practical with the development of laser which provides an intense light source whose waves are coherent or in unison. An optical hologram is formed by directing a laser beam at an object and recording at a photographic plate the interference patterns produced when the light waves reflected from the object interact with a portion of the undisturbed laser radiation, which serves as a reference beam as shown in Fig. 17.2 (*a*). The hologram produced in this fashion contains in coded form all the information the eye would intercept if it were located at the position of the photographic plate. The code can be broken by illuminating the hologram with another laser beam, which reconstructs the original scene as shown in Fig. 17.2 (*b*). The hologram formed in this fashion and reconstructed is known as the single-exposure holography.

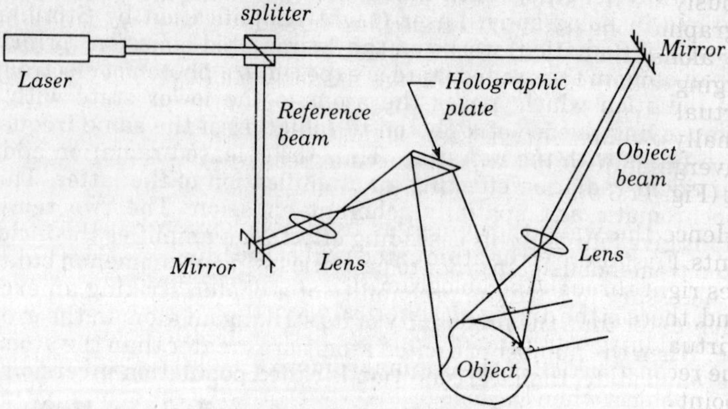

(*a*) Hologram formation.

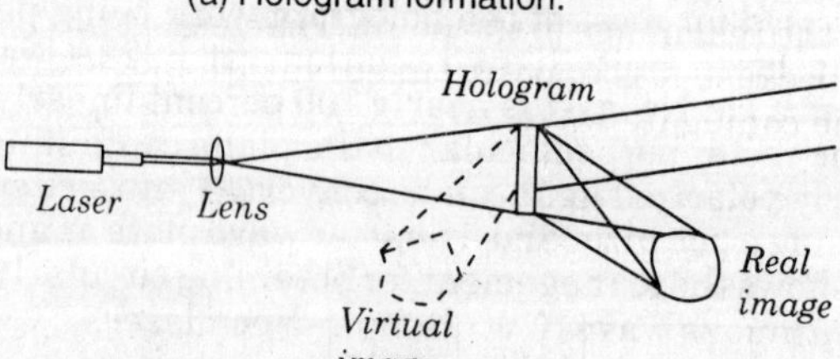

(*b*) Hologram reconstrution.

Fig. 17.2

The simplest way to understand how a hologram works is to think of it as a coded diffraction grating. Consider first of all a simple point object that is illuminated by a plane wave produced by a coherent source at infinity (Fig. 17.3 *a*). The point object scatters part of the wave, which then radiates spherically away from the point object. Both the spherical (object) wave and the plane (reference) wave fall on a plane that is perpendicular to the direction of propagation of the reference wave. At some points on the plane the object wave is in phase with the reference wave, so that the two waves constructively interfere with each other and are therefore added together to increase the wave amplitude. At other points on the plane the object wave is out of phase with the reference wave, so that the two waves destructively interfere, thereby cancelling each other and decreasing the wave amplitude. If we record the amplitude (intensity) in the plane as variations of density on a photographic plate, the resulting pattern will be a continuous set of concentric circles centered on the point on the plane that is obtained by projecting a line from the light source through the point object onto the plane. This pattern closely resembles a Fresnel Zonal Plate, an optical device in which a round bull's eye is surrounded by concentric rings of regularly decreasing thickness. In the point-object hologram however, the density of the ring varies outward from the center in a sine-wave pattern, and simultaneously the frequency of the sine-wave decreases.

A well-known property of a zone-plate is that the diffraction effects of the rings will cause the plate to act as a lens. When illuminated when a wave, the zone-plate will focus the wave. However, it acts simultaneously as if it were both a positive and a negative lens. If the holographic zone-plate pattern is illuminated by the plane (reference) wave alone, the negative lens effect of the zone-plate will cause a diverging spherical wave to emerge from the plate, thereby producing a "virtual" (true) image of the point in the same position the point object originally occupied. At the same time the positive lens effect will creat a converging wave that will produced a "real" (conjugate) image of the point (Fig. 17.3 *b*).

Hence the wave that emerges from a hologram has three components. First there is the attenuated part of the illuminating wave that passes right through the hologram. This is called the zero order wave. Second, there is the diverging spherical wave that appears to come from the virtual image of the point. This is a first order diffracted wave, that is true reconstruction of the original spherical wave that radiated from the point object when the hologram recording was made ; it is called the true reconstructed wave. Third, there is the converging spherical wave that forms the real image of the point. This too is a first-order diffracted wave, but because it is opposite in curvature to the diverging wave, it is called the conjugate wave.

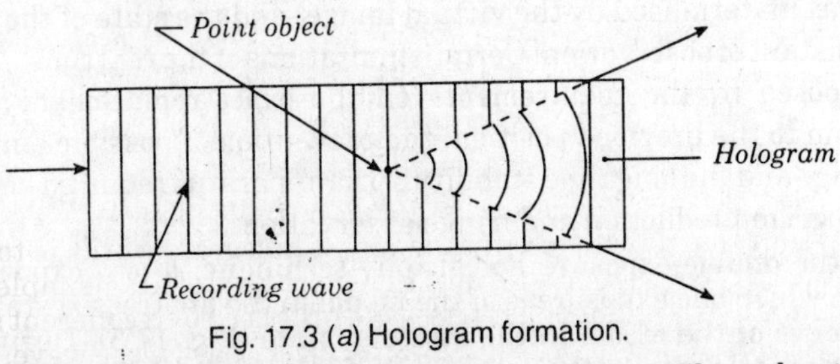

Fig. 17.3 (*a*) Hologram formation.

The holography of complicated objects, can be easily understood by thinking of their complicated surfaces as being made up of a large number of point objects. Each point on the surface of the complicated object forms its own hologram zone-plate patterns from all the other points on the object. The resulting hologram then has the appearance of an unintelligible mass of broken fringes and grainy blocks, but in reality each zone-plate component acts independently of all the others in the reconstruction process to produce its individual point on the surface of the object image.

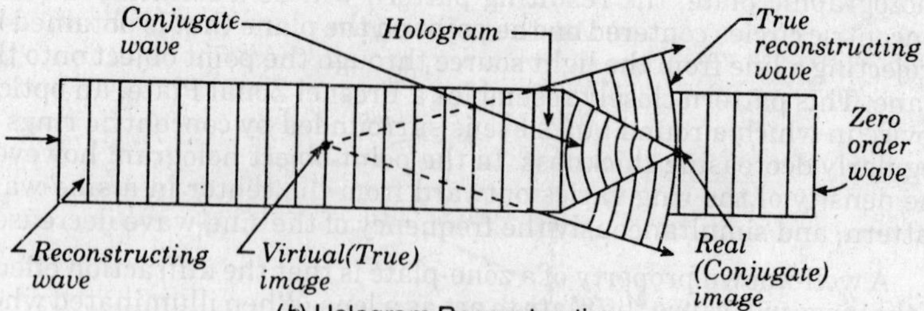

(b) Hologram Reconstruction.

Fig. 17.3 Formation of optical hologram of a point.

17.5 Hologram Interferometry

Hologram interferometry is an extension of holography. The following procedures have been proposed to accomplish this :

1. Real time holographic interferometry.
2. Double exposure holographic interferometry.
3. Time average holographic interferometry.

Real time hologram interferometry (Fig. 17.4) consists of taking a single-exposure hologram of an object in a given state and time, processing the emulsion, replacing the hologram exactly into the position in which it was recorded, illuminating the object with the same coherent light as during the recording , and using the coherent reference beam as the illuminating beam for the hologram. The virtual image reconstructed by the hologram then appears exactly superimposed onto the object behind the hologram. However, one can make a set of interference fringes cover the object (*i.e.* the virtual image) by causing the object to be suitably displaced with respect to the "superimposed" virtual image. The system of interference fringes gas results, in effect, from the interferometric comparison between the original state of the object (as materialised by the virtual image) and the state of the object at the instant of observation. Certain limitations of the real time method are imposed by the requirements on the exact replacement of the hologram to the previous position, the prevention of possible emulsion shrinkage and the long time stability of the apparatus required between the hologram production and fringe observation.

In the double-exposure holography technique, a two exposure is made in which one exposure is of the model in the unstressed state and the other is of the model in the stressed state (Fig. 17.5). During the reconstruction process, the wavefronts from the model with stressed and unstressed state are reconstructed simultaneously.

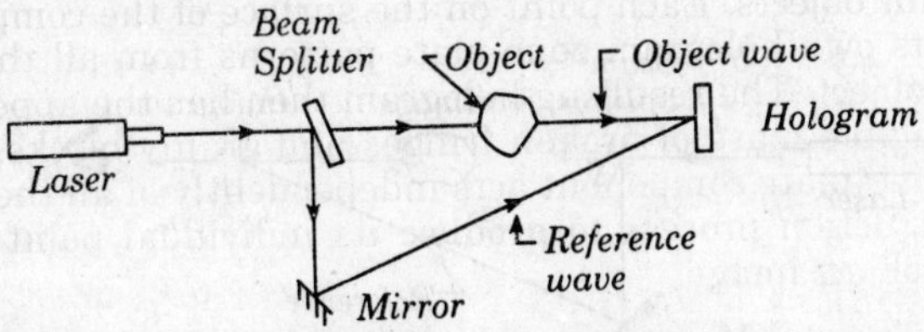

(a) Make at rest hologram.

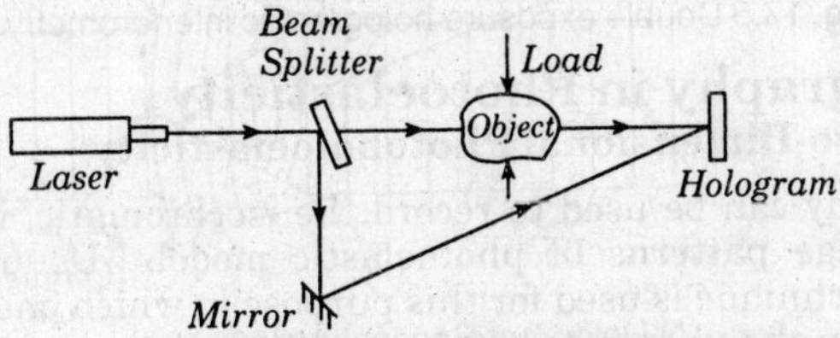

(b) View object under test load.

Fig. 17.4 Real-time holographic interferometry.

The reconstructed wavefront from the unstressed model is used as a reference to which the reconstructed wave front from the stressed model is compared. The two wave fronts interfere resulting in a set of isochromatic and isopachic fringe patterns superimposed on the reconstructed image of the model. This technique is of much use in photoelasticity.

In time average holography a time exposure of vibrating object is made and the hologram is viewed simultaneously as the reconstruction with the reference beam is going on. This technique is of much use in vibration analysis.

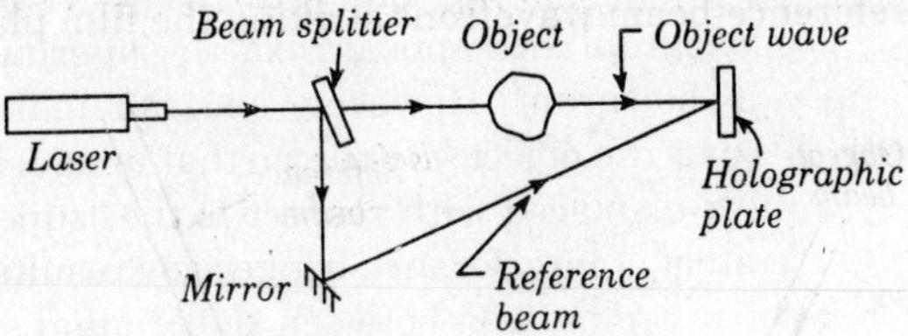

(a) Record at rest hologram.

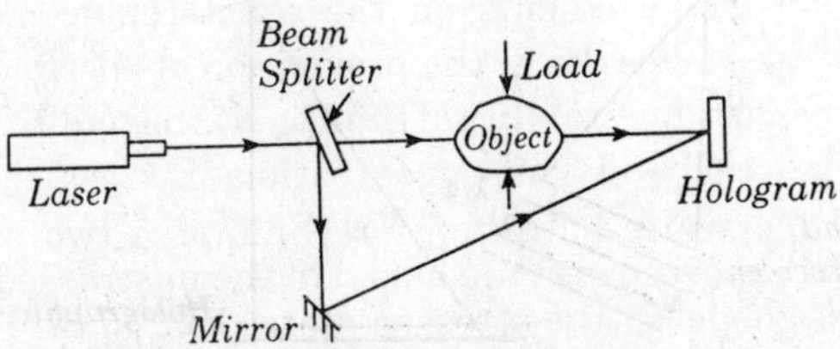

(b) Record test hologram.

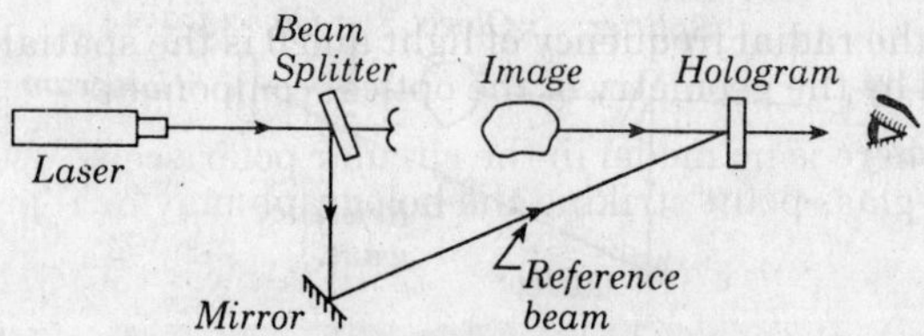

(*c*) View double-exposure hologram.

Fig. 17.5 Double exposure holographic interferometry.

17.6 Holography in Photoelasticity

17.6.1 Two-Dimensional Photoholoelasticity

Holography can be used to record the isochromatic, isoclinic and isopachic fringe patterns of photoelastic models. Double-exposure-holography technique is used for this purpose in which one exposure is of the model in the unstressed state, and the other is of the model in the stressed state. During the reconstruction process, the wavefronts from the model in the stressed and unstressed states are reconstructed simultaneously. The reconstructed wave-front from the unstressed model is used as a reference to which the reconstructed wave front from the stressed model is compared. The two wavefronts interfere resulting in a set of isochromatic and isopachic fringe patterns superimposed on the reconstructed image of the model. From these patterns, the sum and difference of the principal stresses may be determined.

The experimental arrangement (Fig. 17.6) using a plane-polarized light is like a standard circular polariscope except that the reference beam acts as the analyzer. The quarter-wave plates are oriented to give a light field when the polariscope is viewed through an analyzer with the same orientation as the polarization of the reference beam.

Let the reference-beam wavefront striking the film plate be given by

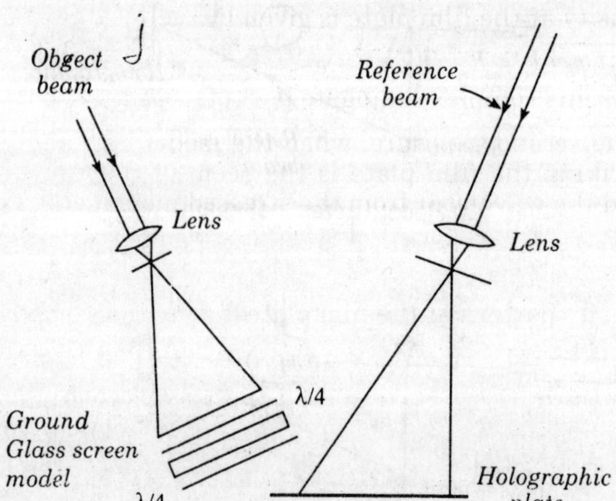

Fig. 17.6 Experimental arrangement for two dimensional photo-holoelasticity.

where ω is the radial frequency of light and θ is the spatial phase actor determined by the geometry of the optical components.

When there is no model in the circular polariscope, the wave-front the ground-glass point striking the holograph may be represented by

$$e^{i}\,(\omega t + \varphi)\hat{i}$$

where φ is the spatial phase factor that depends on the geometry of the ground glass and the two quarter-wave plates. The unit vector $\hat{i}$ indicates that the reference beam wavefronts have the same polarization orientation.

However, when the model is placed in the light path, the phase of the ground glass wavefront is altered by the optical properties of the model. Let this change be denoted by α of the model is in the unstressed state and by α′ and α″ for the stressed state in the directions parallel to the principal stresses σ_1 and σ_2. Thus for the unstressed model, the wavefront striking the holograph is given by :

$$e^{i}\,(\omega t + \varphi + \alpha)\,\hat{i}$$

For the stressed state as shown in Fig. 17.7, the wavefront can be written as :

$$\frac{1}{2}\,[e^{i\,(\omega t + \varphi + \alpha')} + e^{i\,(\omega t + \varphi + \alpha'')}]\,\hat{i}$$

The $\hat{j}$ component to this wavefront, which exists too, is here ignored, because it has been assumed that the polarization of the reference beam is in the $\hat{i}$ direction.

During the first exposure, the model is unstressed and the total wavefront striking the holograph is the sum of the reference-beam wavefront and the wavefront from the unstressed model,

$$\overline{E}_1 = [e^{i\,(\omega t + \varphi + \alpha)} + e^{i\,(\omega t + \theta)}]\,\hat{i} \qquad \text{...(17.1)}$$

The intensity at the film plate is given by

$$I_1 = \overline{E}_1 \,.\, \overline{E}_1^{*} = 2 + e^{i\,(\varphi + \alpha - \theta)} + e^{i\,(\varphi + \alpha - \theta)} \qquad \text{...(17.2)}$$

where * represents complex conjugate part of.

During the second exposure, when the model is loaded, the total wavefront striking the film plate is the seem of the reference-beam wavefront and the wavefront from the stressed model.

$$\overline{E}_2 = [e^{i\,(\omega t + \theta)} + \frac{1}{2}\,e^{i\,(\omega t + \varphi + \alpha')} + \frac{1}{2}\,e^{i\,(\omega t + \varphi + \alpha'')}]\,\hat{i} \qquad \text{...(17.3)}$$

The intensity pattern at the film plate during the second exposure is

$$\begin{aligned} I_2 = \frac{3}{2} &+ \frac{1}{2}\,e^{i\,(\varphi + \alpha' - \theta)} + \frac{1}{2}\,e^{-i\,(\varphi + \alpha' - \theta)} \\ &+ \frac{1}{2}\,e^{i\,(\varphi + \alpha'' - \theta)} + \frac{1}{2}\,e^{-i(\varphi + \alpha'' - \theta)} \\ &+ \frac{1}{4}\,e^{i\,(\alpha' - \alpha'')} + \frac{1}{4}\,e^{-i(\alpha' - \alpha'')} \end{aligned} \qquad \text{...(17.4)}$$

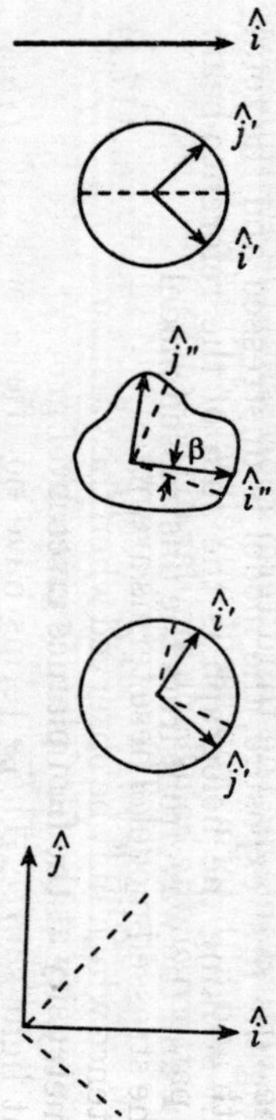

Incident beam $\hat{i}$ polarization

$$e^{i\varphi}\,\hat{i}$$

first λ/4 plate $\hat{i}'$ and $\hat{j}'$ principal axes

$$\frac{1}{\sqrt{2}}\left[e^{i\varphi}\,\hat{i}' + e^{i(\varphi+\pi/2)}\,\hat{j}'\right]$$

model's principal stress axes are $\hat{i}''$ and $\hat{j}''$

$$\frac{1}{\sqrt{2}}\left[\cos\beta\, e^{i(\varphi+\alpha')} + \sin\beta\, e^{i(\varphi+\pi/2+\alpha')}\right]\hat{i}''$$

$$\frac{1}{\sqrt{2}}\left[\cos\beta\, e^{i(\varphi+\pi/2+\alpha'')} - \sin\beta\, e^{i(\varphi+\alpha'')}\right]\hat{j}''$$

2nd λ/4 plate $\hat{i}'$ and $\hat{j}'$ principal axes

$$\frac{1}{\sqrt{2}}\left[\begin{array}{l}\sin\beta\cos\beta\, e^{i(\varphi+\alpha')} + \sin^2\beta\, e^{i(\varphi+\pi/2+\alpha')}\\ +\cos^2\beta\, e^{(\varphi+\pi/2+\alpha'')} - \cos\beta\sin e^{i(\varphi+\alpha'')}\end{array}\right]\hat{i}$$

$$\frac{1}{\sqrt{2}}\left[\begin{array}{l}\cos^2\beta\, e^{i(\varphi+\alpha'+\pi/2)} + \cos\beta\sin\beta\, e^{i(\varphi+\alpha'+\pi)}\\ -\sin\beta\cos\beta\, e^{i(\varphi+\alpha''+\pi)} + \sin^2\beta\, e^{i(\varphi+\alpha''+\pi/2)}\end{array}\right]\hat{j}$$

Wavefront striking holograph.

$$\frac{1}{2}\left[e^{i(\varphi+\alpha'+\pi/2)} + e^{i(\varphi+\alpha''+\pi/2)}\right]\hat{i}$$

$$\left[\begin{array}{l}\dfrac{1}{2}\sin^2\beta\left[e^{i(\varphi+\alpha')} + e^{i(\varphi+\alpha'')}\right] -\\ \dfrac{1}{2}\cos^2\beta\left[e^{i(\varphi+\pi/2+\alpha')} - e^{i(\varphi+\pi/2+\alpha'')}\right]\end{array}\right]\hat{j}$$

Fig. 17.7 Changes in phase of wavefront through the various optical components used in interferometric holography.

After processing, the interference pattern recorded on the film (hologram) acts as a transmission diffraction grating. The transmission factor T of the diffraction grating or hologram depends on the total exposure. Since there are two exposures, T is proportional to the sum of I_1 and I_2.

$$T = k\,[I_1 + I_2] \qquad \text{...(17.5)}$$

where k is a constant.

In the reconstruction process, the holograph is returned to its original location and illuminated by the reference beam. The grating pattern on the holograph attenuates the reference beam as it passes through the holograph. The amplitude of the transmitted wavefront emerging from the backside of the holograph is given by the product of the incident wavefront and the transmission factor of holograph.

$$\overline{E}_I = T\, e^{i\,(\omega t + \theta)}\,\hat{i} \qquad \text{...(17.6)}$$

By substituting Eqs. (17.2), (17.4) and (17.5) into (17.6), we get

$$\begin{aligned}\overline{E}_T &= K\,[I_1 + I_2]\, e^{i\,(\omega t + \theta)}\,\hat{i}\\ &= K_1\, e^{i\,(\omega t + \theta)}\,\hat{i} + K_2\, e^{i\,(\omega t + \varphi)}\,[e^{i\alpha} + \frac{1}{2}\, e^{i\alpha'} + \frac{1}{2}\, e^{i\,x''}]\,\hat{i}\\ &\quad + K_3\, e^{i\,(\omega t - \varphi + 2\theta)}\,[e^{-i\alpha} + \frac{1}{2}\, e^{-i\alpha'} + \frac{1}{2}\, e^{i\alpha''}]\,\hat{i} \qquad \text{...(17.7)}\\ &\quad + K_4\,\frac{1}{4}\, e^{i\,(\omega t + \theta + x' - \alpha'')}\,\hat{i} + K_5\,\frac{1}{4}\, e^{i\,(\omega t + \theta - \alpha' + \alpha'')}\,\hat{i}\end{aligned}$$

The first term of the wavefront emerging from the holograph is the undiffracted reference beam. The second term represents the wavefront of the virtual image. The third term represents the real image. The fourth and fifth terms represent wavefronts diffracted by a transmission pattern on the holograph similar to the isochromatic pattern seen on the stressed model. These terms are noted only to acknowledge their existence which may be observed when the variations of the equipment geometry are used, for instance instead of ground glass to apply one point light source. These terms have no effect on the reconstructed virtual image.

The virtual image is represented by the second set of terms

$$\overline{E}_v = e^{i\,(\omega t + \varphi)}\left[e^{i\alpha} + \frac{1}{2}\, e^{i\alpha'} + \frac{1}{2}\, e^{i\alpha''}\right]\hat{i} \qquad \text{...(17.8)}$$

where the constant K_2 is chosen as unity for convenience.

The intensity pattern of this image is then

$$\begin{aligned} I &= \overline{E}_v \,.\, \overline{E}_v^{*}\\ &= \frac{3}{2} + \cos(\alpha - \alpha') + \cos(\alpha - \alpha'') + \frac{1}{2}\cos(\alpha' - \alpha'') \qquad \text{...(17.9)}\end{aligned}$$

Now the relationship between the principal stresses and the isopachic-isochromatic fringe pattern on the reconstructed image can now be developed.

The phase changes due to the model are given by

$$\alpha = \frac{2\pi}{\lambda} n_0 t$$
$$\alpha' = \frac{2\pi}{\lambda} [n_1 t' + n (t - t')] \quad ...(17.10)$$
$$\alpha'' = \frac{2\pi}{\lambda} [n_2 t' + n(t - t')]$$

where n = index of refraction of ambient air.

n_0 = index of refraction of unstressed model.

n_1, n_2 = index of refraction of the stressed model in the direction of the principal stresses σ_1 and σ_2.

t = initial thickness of model.

t' = final thickness of model.

λ = wave length of the laser.

The Maxwell-Neumann stress-optic law gives

$$n_1 - n_0 = A\sigma_1 + B\sigma_2$$
$$n_2 - n_0 = B\sigma_1 + A\sigma_2 \quad ...(17.11)$$

where A and B are the material constants of the model. Since the model is in a state of plane stress, the thickness under stress is given by

$$t' = t - \frac{\nu}{E} (\sigma_1 + \sigma_2)\, t \quad ...(17.12)$$

Substituting Eqs. (17.10), (17.11) and (17.12) into Eq. (17.9), we get after neglecting small-order terms :

$$I = 1 + 2 \cos \frac{\pi t}{\lambda} C (\sigma_1 - \sigma_2) \left\{\frac{\nu}{E} (\sigma_1 + \sigma_2) - 1\right\}$$
$$\times \cos \frac{\pi t}{\lambda} (\sigma_1 + \sigma_2) \left\{\frac{\nu}{E} (A + B) (\sigma_1 + \sigma_2) - (A' + B')\right\}$$
$$+ \cos^2 \frac{\pi t}{\lambda} C (\sigma_1 - \sigma_2) \left\{\frac{\nu}{E} (\sigma_1 + \sigma_2) - 1\right\} \quad ...(17.13)$$

$$\approx 1 + 2 \cos \frac{\pi t}{\lambda} C (\sigma_1 - \sigma_2) \cos \frac{\pi t}{\lambda} (A' + B') (\sigma_1 + \sigma_2)$$
$$+ \cos^2 \frac{\pi t}{\lambda} C (\sigma_1 - \sigma_2) \quad ...(17.14)$$

where
$$A' = A - \frac{\nu}{E} (n_0 - n)$$
$$B' = B - \frac{\nu}{E} (n_0 - n) \quad ...(17.15)$$
$$C = A' - B' = A - B$$

The intensity pattern depends on both the sum and difference of the principal stresses, *i.e.* the isochromatic pattern in modulated by the isopachic pattern. The locus of points

where $\frac{\pi}{\lambda} C (\sigma_1 - \sigma_2)\, t = m\pi$, m = integer ...(17.16) usually corresponds to a light isochromatic fringe in a standard light-field pattern. But here, the light isochromatic is modulated by the isopachic pattern, giving

$$I = 2 \pm 2 \cos \frac{\pi}{\lambda} (A' + B')(\sigma_1 + \sigma_2)\, t \qquad \text{...(17.17)}$$

At points where

$$\frac{\pi}{\lambda} C (\sigma_1 - \sigma_2) = (2m + 1) \frac{\pi}{2} \qquad \text{...(17.18)}$$

usually corresponding to a dark isochromatic pattern, the intensity is

$$I = 1 \qquad \text{...(17.19)}$$

Thus, the fringes corresponding to the dark isochromatics are the half-tone gray fringes curving through the isopachic lines. Furthermore, as isopachic lines intersect the isochromatic lines, their intensities reverse from light to dark and *vice versa*.

Thus, Fourney and Mate concluded that the entire intensity pattern consists of two independent families of fringes, one family determined by $\sigma_1 + \sigma_2$ and the other family by $\sigma_1 - \sigma_2$, which are sufficient to solve plane problems. If N_c and N_p are the fringe orders of an isochromatic fringe and an isopachic fringe, respectively, then the sum and difference of the principal stresses are :

$$\sigma_1 + \sigma_2 = \frac{\lambda N_p}{(A' + B')\, t}$$

$$|\sigma_1 - \sigma_2| = \frac{\lambda N_c}{Ct} \qquad \text{...(17.20)}$$

A generalisation of the Eq. (17.14) is necessary in order to incorporate the ratio of the intensities of the two exposures, a factor which has a considerable influence on the final intensity pattern. The generalised expression for a light field intensity pattern in double-exposure holographic photoelasticity has been obtained by Holloway and Johnson as :

$$I = 1 + 2\eta^2 \cos\alpha \cos\beta + \eta^4 \cos^2\alpha \qquad \text{...(17.21)}$$

where $\alpha = \frac{\pi t}{\lambda} (A - B)(\sigma_1 - \sigma_2)$

$$\beta = \frac{\pi t}{\lambda} (A' + B')(\sigma_1 + \sigma_2)$$

$$\eta^2 = \frac{\text{Exposure with model stressed}}{\text{Exposure with model unstressed}}$$

when $\eta^2 = 1$ then Eq. (17.21) reduces to Eq. (17.14).

The examination of Eq. (17.21) reveals several important items. The intensity pattern obviously depends on the quantities $(\sigma_1 - \sigma_2)$ and $(\sigma_1 + \sigma_2)$. Because Eq. (17.21) consists of a constant a function of $(\sigma_1 - \sigma_2)$, and a function of both $(\sigma_1 - \sigma_2)$ and $(\sigma_1 + \sigma_2)$, the minima of Eq. (17.21) do not correspond to the minima of the individual terms. Also, due to the effect of η^2, both the contrast and position of the fringes can be changed by either making the first exposure more intense than the second or *vice-versa*. The fringes resulting from Fig. (17.21) are called conditional isochromatic and isopachic fringes. Holloway and Johnson verified that as η^2 is increased the positions of the conditional isochromatics of Eq. (17.21) approach the standard values established by Eq. (17.20). The closest agreement between the conditional isopachics and the standard isopachics occur when $\eta^2 = 1$. In order to eliminate the effect of the exposure ratio, materials with similar isochromatic and isopachic fringe constants should be avoided.

Durelli and Sanford made an exhaustive study to investigate the phenomenon of superposition of isochromatics and isopachics by taking the electric field as a vector wave with two polarization components. They obtained the following expression for the ratio of the intensity of the virtual image to the reconstructed image.

$$\frac{I_v}{I_{R_c}} \propto 1 + 2\cos\frac{\pi t'}{\lambda}(A' + B')(\sigma_1 + \sigma_2)\,.\,\cos\frac{\pi t'}{\lambda}C(\sigma_1 - \sigma_2) + \cos^2\frac{\pi t'}{\lambda}C(\sigma_1 - \sigma_2) \qquad \text{...(17.22)}$$

This is essentially the same result as obtained by Fourney and Mate in Eq. (17.14), with the exception of the value of the thickness which, in Eq. (17.22) is the thickness of the loaded model. When the exposure times are not equal, then Eq. (17.22) may be written as :

$$\frac{I_v}{I_{R_c}} \propto \frac{t_1}{t_2} + 2\cos\frac{\pi t'}{\lambda}(A' + B')(\sigma_1 + \sigma_2)\,.\,\cos\frac{\pi t'}{\lambda}C(\sigma_1 - \sigma_2) + \frac{t_2}{t_1}\cos^2\frac{\pi t'}{\lambda}C(\sigma_1 - \sigma_2) \qquad \text{...(17.23)}$$

where t_1, t_2 are the exposure times of the unloaded and loaded model, respectively. In the second term

$$\cos\frac{\pi t'}{\lambda}(A' + B')(\sigma_1 + \sigma_2) \equiv \text{isopachic function} \qquad \text{...(17.24)}$$

depends only on the sum of the principal stresses, and the other function

$$\cos\frac{\pi t'}{\lambda}C(\sigma_1 - \sigma_2) \equiv \text{isochromatic function} \qquad \text{...(17.25)}$$

depends only on the difference of the principal stresses Durelli and Sanford pointed that it is erroneous to assume that these two fringe patterns consist of the independent superposition of the isopachics and isochromatics, since the fringes correspond to local minima of the intensity expression and not to the minima of any particular term in the expression. Results of Durelli and Sanford can be summarized as follows :

When the slope of the isopachic function and the isochromatic function are of the same sign at the point where the isochromatic function equal zero, the interference pattern has a fringe associated with the isochromatic. On the other hand, if these functions are of opposite slope, there is no fringe associated with the isochromatic and isopachics on either side may be shifted in position. In those regions in which a minimum associated with the isochromatic exists, the isopachic fringe order changes by one and a half fringe orders upon crossing the isochromatic. However, the regions in which the isochromatic minimum fails to exist, the isopachic fringe order changes by only one half of an order.

17.6.2 Three Dimensional Photoholoelasticity

The intensity of the reconstructed virtual image from a double exposure hologram of a transparent birefringent model for its unstressed and stressed condition is given by Eq. (17.9) as :

$$I = \text{const.}\left[\frac{3}{2} + \cos(\alpha - \alpha') + \cos(\alpha - \alpha'') + \frac{1}{2}\cos(\alpha' - \alpha'')\right]$$

This equation does not place any restriction on the method of application of load. It therefore also applies to any arbitrary slice from a stress frozen photoelastic model where the second exposure of the hologram is made after annealing the slice. In this case, however, α' and α'' would be along the directions of the secondary principal stresses. If care is taken to have the slice occupy essentially the same spatial position between the two exposures, the fringes in the reconstructed image would be directly related to the stresses in the slice.

Then

$$\left.\begin{aligned} \alpha - \alpha' &= \frac{2\pi}{\lambda}\,[n_1 t - n_0 t - n\,(t' - t)] \\ \alpha - \alpha'' &= \frac{2\pi}{\lambda}\,[n_2 t' - n_0 t - (t' - t)] \end{aligned}\right] \qquad \text{...(17.26)}$$

The stress optic law for any arbitrary slice is

$$\left.\begin{aligned} n_1 - n_0 &= A\sigma'_1 + B\,(\sigma'_2 + \sigma'_3) \\ n_2 - n_0 &= A\sigma'_2 + B(\sigma'_1 + \sigma'_3) \\ n_3 - n_0 &= A\sigma'_3 + B(\sigma'_1 + \sigma'_2) \end{aligned}\right] \qquad \text{...(17.27)}$$

where σ'_1, σ'_2, and σ'_3 are the secondary principal stresses. Substituting Eqs. (17.26) and (17.27) in (17.9), we get

$$I = \text{Const.}\,(1 + 2\cos X \cos Y + \cos^2 Y) \qquad \text{...(17.28)}$$

where

$$\begin{aligned} X &= \frac{nt}{\lambda}\left\{\frac{1}{E}\,[(A + B)\,(\sigma'_1 + \sigma'_2) + 2\,B\sigma'_3] \right. \\ &\quad \times [\sigma'_3 - \nu\,(\sigma'_1 + \sigma'_2)] + \left[A + B + \frac{2\nu}{E}\,(n - n_0)\right] \\ &\quad \left. \times (\sigma'_1 + \sigma'_2) + \left[2B - \frac{2}{E}\,(n - n_0)\right]\sigma'_3\right\} \\ &\approx \frac{\pi t}{\lambda}\left\{\left[A + B + \frac{2\nu}{E}\,(n - n_0)\right](\sigma'_1 + \sigma'_2)\right. \\ &\quad \left. + \left[2B - \frac{2}{E}\,(n - n_0)\right]\sigma'_3\right\} \end{aligned}$$

$$Y = \frac{\pi t}{\lambda}\left\{(A - B)(\sigma'_1 - \sigma'_2) + \left[\frac{1}{E}(A - B)(\sigma'_1 - \sigma'_2)\right.\right.$$
$$\left.\left.\times [\sigma'_3 - \nu(\sigma_1 - \sigma'_2)]\right]\right\}$$
$$\approx \frac{\pi t}{\lambda}(A - B)(\sigma'_1 - \sigma'_2)$$

At the locus of the points where

$$Y = \frac{\pi t}{\lambda}(A - B)(\sigma'_1 - \sigma'_2) = m\pi,\ m = 0, 1, 2, \ldots$$

which corresponds to a light isochromatic fringe in a bright-field polariscope, the intensity is given by

$$I = \text{Const. } (2 \pm 2 \cos X) \qquad \ldots(17.29)$$

At the points where

$$Y = \frac{\pi t}{\lambda}(A - B)(\sigma'_1 - \sigma'_2) = (2m + 1)\frac{\pi}{2},\ m = 0, 1, 2, \ldots.$$

which corresponds to a dark isochromatic fringe, the intensity would be

$$I = \text{Const.} \qquad \ldots(17.30)$$

Thus the fringes corresponding to the dark isochromatic are the half-tone fringes, and the other family of fringes which is discontinuous across these half-tone fringes, would be the locus of the points defined by

$$X = \frac{\pi t}{\lambda}\left[\left\{A + B + \frac{2\nu}{E}(n - n_0)\right\}(\sigma'_1 + \sigma'_2)\right.$$
$$\left. + \left\{2B - \frac{2}{E}(n - n_0)\right\}\sigma'_3\right] = n\pi$$
$$n \quad 0, 1, 2, \ldots. \qquad \ldots(17.31)$$

The above fringes would be dark whenever m is odd and n is even or m is even and n is odd.

Several experimental difficulty is encountered in obtaining the fringe pattern of Eq. (17.31) for a three dimensional analysis, *e.g.* annealing the slice within the holographic set up between the two exposures, the motion of the slice during annealing, the temperature gradient etc. However, the slice may not be optically flat.

Dhir and Peterson pointed out that annealing of the slice may be avoided by placing the slice in an immersion tank containing fluid whose refractive index matches with that of the slice material. The first exposure is made of the immersion tank alone. Then the stress frozen slice is placed in the tank and the second exposure made. For this arrangement Eq. (17.26), reduces to

$$\alpha - \alpha' = \frac{2\pi t}{\lambda}(n_1 - n_0)$$
$$\alpha - \alpha'' = \frac{2\pi t}{\lambda}(n_2 - n_0) \qquad \ldots(17.32)$$

where n_0 now refers to the refractive index of the tank fluid and slice material. Substituting Eqs. (17.27) and (17.32) in Eq. (17.9), we get

$$I = \text{conts. } (1 + 2 \cos X \,.\, \cos Y + \cos^2 Y) \qquad ...(17.33)$$

where

$$X = \frac{\pi t}{\lambda} [(A + B)(\sigma'_1 + \sigma'_2) + 2B\sigma'_3]$$

$$Y = \frac{\pi t}{\lambda} [(A - B)(\sigma'_1 - \sigma'_2)]$$

In this case Eq. (17.31) reduces to

$$X = \frac{\pi t}{\lambda} [(A + B)(\sigma'_1 + \sigma'_2) + 2B\sigma'_3]$$
$$= n\pi, n = 0, 1, 2,..... \qquad ...(17.34)$$

which is the necessary equation for a complete three-dimensional stress analysis.

For two dimensional problems, Eq. (17.34) becomes

$$X = \frac{\pi t}{\lambda} (A + B)(\sigma_1 + \sigma_2)$$
$$= n\pi, n = 0, 1, 2,.... \qquad ...(17.35)$$

17.7 Separation of Isochromatic and Isopachic Fringe Patterns

When a photoelastic model is subjected to a load, it not only shows birefringence (piezo-optic effects) but also variations in size which lead to interference phenomena is non-polarized light. In two dimensional holographic interferometry two different families of fringes are observed simultaneously when the model is stressed. One family represents the conventional isochromatic fringe pattern yielding the difference of the principal stresses and the second one represent the isopachic fringe pattern yielding the sum of the principal stresses. Theoretically, from these complementary patterns, the magnitudes of the principal stresses can be determined. However, these fringe patterns are superimposed and intersect in such a way that their analysis and interpretation are extremely complex.

The combination of photoelastic method to determine isochromatics and the interferometric method to determine the isopachics, and hence to separated the principal stresses was introduced by Favre in 1929 and extended to the full field by Post in 1956. In 1964 Nisida and Saito developed an interferometric method which gives $(\sigma_1 - \sigma_2)$ and $(\sigma_1 + \sigma_2)$ simultaneously over the whole field. In 1968, Fourney and Hovanesian. Breic and Powell were among the first to apply holography to full photoelastic analysis. Fourney and Mate later is 1970 derived the equation relating the light intensity to the stresses in the model. Chau in 1968 obtained only the isopachics by using a holographic system incorporating a light rotator. O'Regan and Dudderar in 1971 used a system similar to Chau's and suggested diverting part of the object beam to record the isochromatics. Holloway, Ranson and Taylor in 1972 introduced a reflection technique and applied it along with the suggested technique of O'Regan and Dudderar to the dynamic range.

In the method of O'Regan and Dudderar and of Holloway, Ranson and Taylor, the two patterns are recorded simultaneously, though separately; that is, the isopachics are recorded on the hologram, while the isochromatics are recorded by a separate camera. Assa and Betser in 1974 have suggested a technique for separate recording of isopachic and isochromatic fringe patterns which does not need the separate camera for recording the isochromatics. Chatelain in 1973 described a method, by which a simple holographic recording of a photoelastic object under stress allows the isochromatics to be observed. The isopachics are obtained by double exposure interferometery : a second traverse of the wavefront through the object after a 90° rotation of its polarization by a Faraday cell eliminates the unwanted isochromatics.

Recently, Hovanesian (1974) have shown the depolarizing properties of some materials able to be used as a diffuser. Ebbeni, Coenen and Hermanne in 1976 assumed this type of diffuser, Opalin glass or tracing paper, represent a random birefringence, equivalent of the sum of a single birefringent and a rotatory power. This permitted the perparation of an interferometer without particular preparation of the surface front of the model and without any addition of optical elements or special arrangements for applying the loads. Thus they were successful in simultaneous but independent recording of the fringe pattern related to the difference of the principal stresses by conventional means, and one or more fringe patterns related to the sum of the principal stresses by interferometry. Gasvik in 1976 have suggested a technique to separate the isochromatic and isopachic fringe patterns by passing the object beam twice through the model.

In this article we shall study these techniques briefly to separate the isochromatic and isopachic fringe patterns. For a full treatment of these techniques, the reader may refer to the original papers as listed in the references.

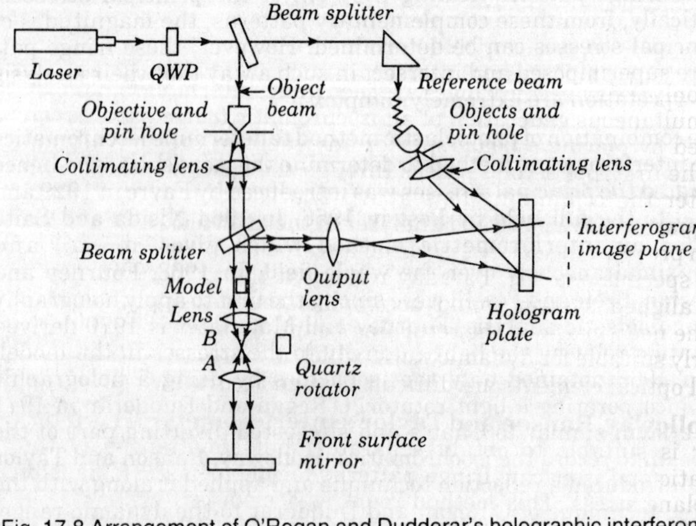

Fig. 17.8 Arrangement of O'Regan and Dudderar's holographic interferometer.

(*a*) **O'Regan and Dudderar's Interferometer.** Fig. 17.8 shows the diagram of the O'Regan and Dudderar's interferometer. The plane polarized light from the He-Ne laser is changed to circularly polarized light by the quarter-wave plate. It next passes through a beam splitter, where it is divided into a reference beam and an object beam, whose path lengths are nearly equal. The object beam passes through an objective, pin hole and collimatting lens.

The collimated beam passes through the unloaded model and passes through the lens system shown. The front surface mirror, used to return the object beam for a second pass through the specimen, is placed in the image plane of the specimen and aligned so that an image of the specimen is superimposed on the specimen itself. The collimating lens at *A* has been positioned slightly off axis, so that the focal point at *B* for the return pass is slightly shifted from its position for the first pass. At the focal point, a passive rotator is inserted in the beam which intercepts one of the passes. Adjustment of the position of the rotator crystal to produce a 90° rotation of the polarization ellipse of the object beam on the return pass effectively reverses the roles of the first and second light vectors. As a consequence, each vector retraces the initial path of the other on its second pass through the specimen. The total changes in phase angle are given by :

$$\begin{aligned} \partial\alpha' &= k\,[(n_1+n_2)t - 2\,(t-t_0) - 2n_0\,t_0] \\ \partial\alpha'' &= k\,[(n_1+n_2)t - 2\,(t-t_0) - 2n_0\,t_0] \end{aligned} \qquad \text{...(17.36)}$$

where $k = \pi/\lambda$

As both waves now experience identical phase changes, $(\delta\alpha' - \delta\alpha'')$ disappears through the field and $(\delta\alpha' + \delta\alpha'')$ is twice as sensitive. Thus system is completely insensitive to $(\sigma_1 - \sigma_2)$ and twice as sensitive to $(\sigma_1 + \sigma_2)$. The light intensity equation becomes

$$I = 2\left[1 + \cos\left\{\frac{\pi}{\lambda}\,C_1\,(\sigma_1+\sigma_2)\,t\right\}\right] \qquad \text{...(17.37)}$$

where $C_1 = A' + B'$.

Thus only the isopachic fringes are seen in the interferogram image plane. Simultaneous generation of an isochromatic fringe pattern can be achieved by placing a beam splitter anywhere in the object beam between the first and second passes through the specimen (most efficiently after the collimating lens at *A*). The addition of a properly oriented quarter-wave plate and analyzer in the diverted portion of the beam then provides the desired isochromatics, on a separate film plane. For thick specimens a 45°, Faraday rotator at the focal point *B* in a perfectly aligned system would accomplish the necessary rotation without the need to askew the returning beam. This interferometer is particularly suitable for dynamic work, which is more complex and the additional optical elements are difficult to align accurately.

(*b*) **Holloway, Ranson and Taylor's Interferometer.** This interferometer is suitable to obtain separately but simultaneously the isochromatic and isopachic fringe patterns for photoelastic models in state of plane stress. This method requires a model with a partially reflecting front surface. Isopachics, which are proportional to the thickness change, are recorded using holographic interferometry from the reflected light. The isochromatics are obtained from the transmitted light by conventional means. This interferometer can be either used for static or dynamic work. The expression for the intensity of light may be obtained as :

$$I = K\left[1 + \cos\frac{2\pi}{\lambda}\left\{-\frac{\nu t}{E}(\sigma_1 + \sigma_2)\cos\xi\right\}\right] \quad ...(17.38)$$

where ξ is the angle of incidence of light on the partially coated aluminium layer on the model.

The intensity will be a minimum when

$$\left.\frac{2\pi}{\lambda}\left[-\frac{\nu t}{E}(\sigma_1 + \sigma_2)\cos\xi\right] = (2n-1)\pi,\right\} \quad ..(17.39)$$

or

$$\left[\begin{array}{l}\dfrac{\nu t}{E}(\sigma_1 + \sigma_2)\cos\xi = \pm N_p, \\ N_p = \dfrac{1}{2}, \dfrac{3}{2}, \dfrac{5}{2}\end{array}\right] \quad ...(17.40)$$

Now material fringe constant

$$f_p = \frac{\lambda E}{\nu},$$

hence from Eq. (17.40), we get

$$\sigma_1 + \sigma_2 = \pm\frac{N_p f_p}{t\cos\xi} \quad ...(17.41)$$

The schematic sketch for the interferometer is shown in Fig. 17.9.

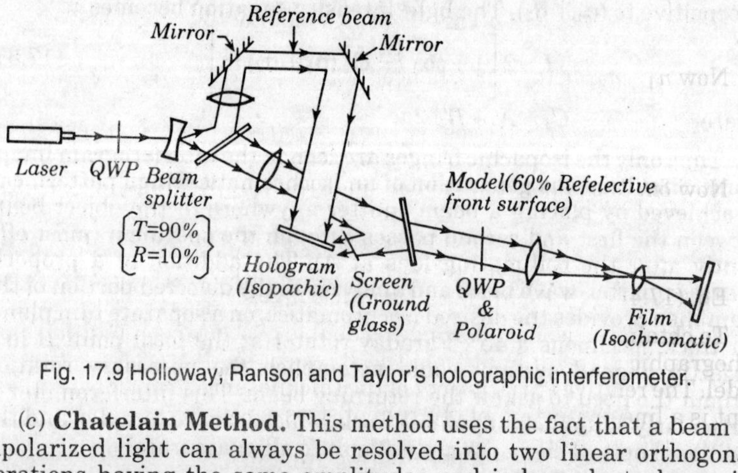

Fig. 17.9 Holloway, Ranson and Taylor's holographic interferometer.

(*c*) **Chatelain Method.** This method uses the fact that a beam of unpolarized light can always be resolved into two linear orthogonal vibrations having the same amplitudes and independent phases irrespective of the orientation of the axes along which they have been resolved. If circularly polarized light is used, the resolution into two orthogonal vibrations of equal amplitude is still valid.

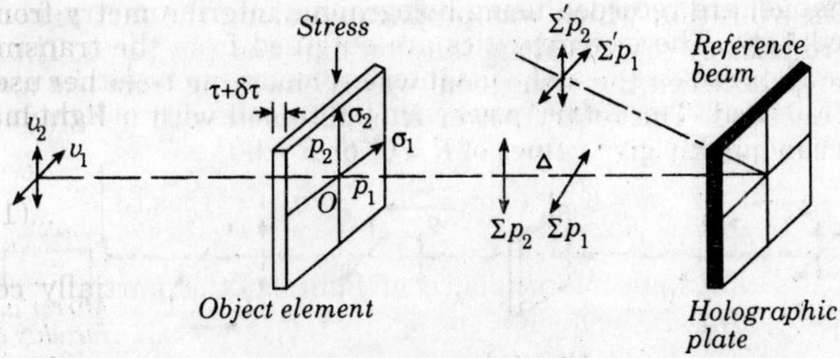

Fig. 17.10 Arrangement for obtaining isochromatic fringes.

The light incident upon the model can thus be resolved into two orthogonal linear vibrations parallel respectively to the principal axes of stress op_1 and op_2 at a point o on the model as shown in Fig. 17.10. The emergent vibration Σ_{p1} and Σ_{p2} has a phase difference between them given by

$$\phi_1 - \phi_2 = \frac{2\pi}{\lambda}(n_1 - n_2)(t + \delta t) \qquad \text{...(17.42)}$$

The reference vibration Σ_R can also be resolved into two vibrations Σ_{p1R} and Σ_{p2R} which are independent and orthogonal. In the plane of the holographic plate, interference occurs between Σ_{p1} and Σ_{p1R} on the one hand and between Σ_{p2} and Σ_{p2R} on the other. The intensity in the field of observation becomes

$$I = |\Sigma_{p1} + \Sigma_{p2}|^2 \propto |e^{ip_1} + e^{1p_2}|^2$$

$$= 2\,[1 + \cos(\phi_1 - \phi_2)]$$

$$= 1 + \cos\left[\frac{2\pi}{\lambda}(n_1 - n_2)(t + \delta t)\right]$$

Now $n_1 - n_2 = c\,(\sigma_1 - \alpha_2)$, hence

$$I = 1 + \cos\left[\frac{2\pi c}{\lambda}(\sigma_1 - \sigma_2)(t + \delta t)\right]$$

Now $\delta t/t$ is comparatively very small, hence

$$I = 1 + \cos\left[\frac{2\pi}{\lambda}c\,(\sigma_1 - \sigma_2)\,t\right] \qquad \text{...(17.43)}$$

Eq. (17.43) represents isochromatic fringes.

To obtain the isopachic fringes a double exposure is made on same orthographic plate, of light from the stressed and then the unstressed model. The relative variation $\delta t/t$ of the thickness of the model at a given point is a linear function of the sum of stresses at this point.

$$\frac{\delta t}{t} = -\frac{\nu}{E}(\sigma_1 + \sigma_2) = c'\,(\sigma_1 + \sigma_2) \qquad \text{...(17.44)}$$

As the model is birefringent, both the isochromatics and isopachics are obtained. In order to remove the birefringent effect, the light beam (Fig. 17.11) is made to traverse the model twice, but after the first passage the vibration direction is subjected to an optical rotation of 90°. The vibration which was propagated along the fast axis on the outward journey returns along the slow axis and *vice versa*. The phase difference between the orthogonal waves emerging from the model is thus cancelled. The rotary power R is obtained with a Faraday cell, which can quickly give values of $R = 0°$ or $R = 90°$

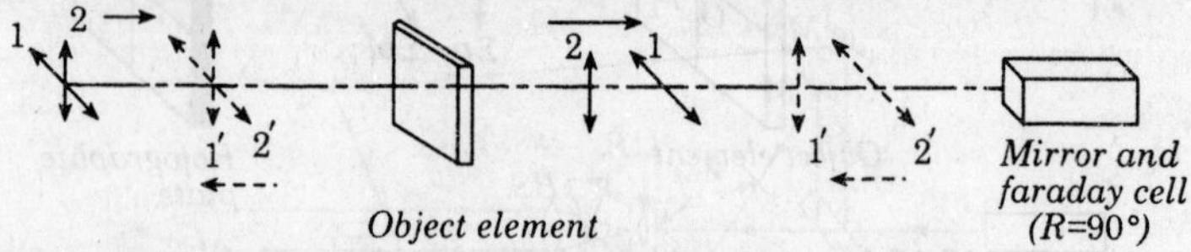

Fig. 17.11 Arrangement for obtaining isopachic fringes.

During the initial exposure (unstressed model $R = 90°$), the hologram of a wave Σ_0 is recorded ;

$$\Sigma_0 \propto e^{i\phi_0}$$

During the second exposure (stressed model $R = 90°$), the incoherent superposition of two holograms corresponding to the two waves Σ_{p1} and Σ_{p2} polarized parallel to the principal axes is recorded.

$$\Sigma_{p1} \propto \frac{1}{\sqrt{2}} e^{i\phi_1}$$

$$\Sigma_{p2} \propto \frac{1}{\sqrt{2}} e^{i\phi_2}$$

with $\phi_1 - \phi_2 = 0$. During reconstruction the three waves Σ_0, Σ_{p1} and Σ_{p2}, which are now coherent, interfere. In the first order of the diffraction pattern from the holographic plate, the intensity of the reconstructed image at the point under consideration is thus given by :

$$I \propto |e^{i\phi_0} + e^{i\phi_1}| = 2\,[1 + \cos(\phi_1 - \phi_0)]$$

Now $$\phi_1 - \phi_0 = \frac{2\pi}{\lambda}(n_1 + n_2 - 2n_0)t + (n_1 + n_2 - 2)\,\delta t$$

$$\approx \frac{2\pi}{t}(n_1 + n_2 - 2n_0)$$

where $$\frac{\delta t}{t} \ll 1.$$

Also from Maxwell-Neumann law

$$(n_1 + n_2 - 2n_0) = c''\,(\sigma_1 + \sigma_2)$$

where c'' is photoelastic constant characteristic of the material. Thus

$$I \propto 1 + \cos\,(c''\,(\sigma_1 + \sigma_2)\,t] \qquad \text{...(17.45)}$$

Eq. (17.45) represents isopachic fringes.

(*d*) **Assa and Betser Multiplexing Technique.** As shown in Fig. 17.12, the plane polarized light beam passes through a glass block beam splitter. The front and rear surface reflected waves serve as the reference waves. These two collimated, circularly polarized reference waves strike the hologram plate at different angles, the difference being large enough to ensure spatial separation of the diffracted waves during reconstruction. The beam transmitted by the glass block is expanded and collimated and serves as the object beam. Both the reflecting mirror and the ground glass are in the image plane of the model.

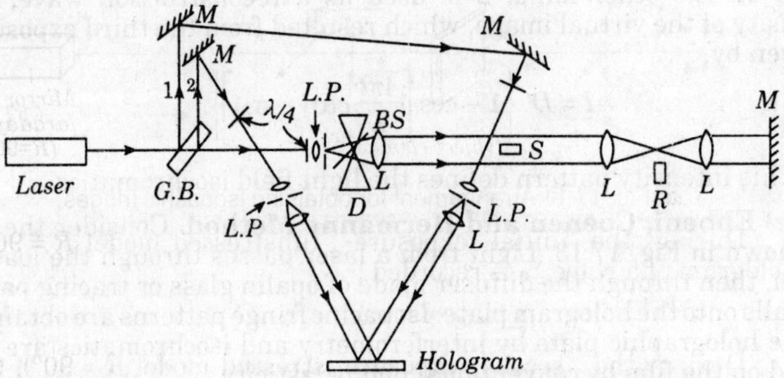

M = mirror
L = Biconvex lens
λ/4 = Q WP
D = Diffuses
B.S. = Beam splitter
L.P. = Lens-pinhole
G.B. = Glass block
R = Rotator
S = specimen.

Fig. 17.12 Holographic system for recording independent isochromatics and isopachic fringe patterns.

For the first two exposures, only one reference wave is used, say 1. Reference wave 2 is blocked and the system is set to record the isopachics. That is, the light rotator is set so that the outgoing object wave does not pass through it, but the reflected wave, which is slightly displaced, does. Thus the reflected wave obtains a 90° rotation of its planes of polarization before repassing through the model.

For the first exposure, the unstressed model causes a uniform retardation of the object wave, denoted as 2 ϕ_0. The model is then loaded and the plate exposed a second time. Because of the action of the rotator, each polarization component of the object wave receives a retardation ($\phi_1 + \phi_2$), where ϕ_1 and ϕ_2 are the retardations-associated with the principal stresses σ_1 and σ_2 respectively. Between the second and third exposures, reference wave 1 is covered, 2 uncovered, and the light rotator is removed from the system. Thus the two components of the object wave retain their polarization directions for both passes through the model, receiving retardations $2\phi_1$ and $2\phi_2$ respectively. The hologram is now processed and, for construction, a wave similar to 1 is first used. Assuming the geometry of the system has been correctly arranged, the waves associated with the virtual image from the first two exposures can be isolated and viewed separately from the other defracted waves. The intensity of the virtual image in this case can be shown to be

$$I = D\left\{1 + \cos\left[\frac{2\pi t}{\lambda}(A+B)(\sigma_1+\sigma_2)\right]\right\} \quad ...(17.46)$$

where A, B and D are constants. This intensity pattern defines the isopachics.

If on the other hand, 2 is used as a reconstruction wave, the intensity of the virtual image, which resulted from the third exposure, is given by,

$$I = D'\left\{1 - \cos\left[\frac{4\pi t}{\lambda}c(\sigma_1-\sigma_2)\right]\right\} \quad ...(17.47)$$

This intensity pattern defines the light field isochromatics.

(*e*) **Ebbeni, Coenen and Hermanne Method.** Consider the set up shown in Fig. 17.13. Light from a laser passes through the loaded model, then through the diffuser made of opalin glass or tracing paper and falls onto the hologram plate. Isopachic fringe patterns are obtained on the holographic plate by interferometry and isochromatics are obtained on the film by conventional photoelasticity.

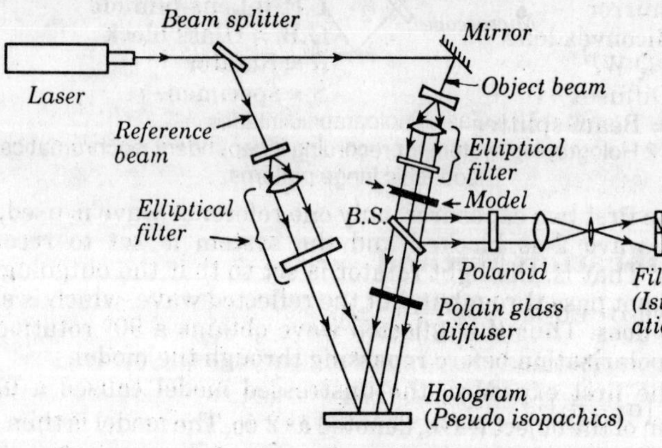

Fig. 17.13 Ebbeni, Coenen and Hermanne interferometer.

(*f*) **Gasvik Method.** In order to separate the isochromatics and isopachics the object beam may be passed twice through the model. The arrangement as shown in Fig. 17.14 has been suggested by Gasvik to achieve this. The beam incident on the model on its first passage converges slightly to a point where the polarizing element is placed. As a polarizing element Gasvik applied the method with two $\lambda/2$ plates in tandem. This is executed by placing a $\lambda/2$ plate with a small hole in the centre at the point of convergence after the first pass followed by a $\lambda/4$ plate with its fast axis inclined at 45° to that of the $\lambda/2$ plate. The light passes twice through the $\lambda/4$ plate which, therefore, acts effectively as a $\lambda/2$ plate. At points 1 and 2 before the microscope objectives in the object and reference beam paths, two $\lambda/4$ plates are placed to make the originally linearly polarized laser light circularly polarized.

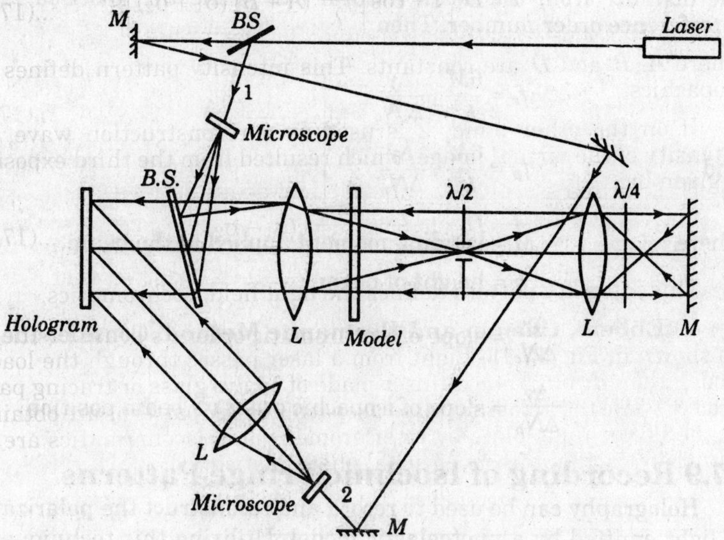

Fig. 17.14 Gasvik holographic interferometer.

17.8 Calibration Method

We have $\sigma_1 + \sigma_2 = \dfrac{\lambda N_p}{(A' + B')t}$

and $|\sigma_1 - \sigma_2| = \dfrac{\lambda N_c}{Ct}$

Let $f_p = \dfrac{\lambda}{A' + B'}$

= isopachic -stress fringe material value

$f_c = \dfrac{\lambda}{C}$

= isochromatic -stress fringe material value

Then $\sigma_1 + \sigma_2 = \dfrac{f_p N_p}{t}$

$|\sigma_1 - \sigma_2| = \dfrac{f_c N_c}{t}$

A calibration beam subjected to pure bending is used and both the isopachic the isochromatic fringe patterns are recorded simultaneously and separately.

Then a graph is plotted with the ordinate of the paper representing the distance from the beam natural axis while the abscissa is the interference order number. Then

$$\left.\begin{aligned} f_c &= \frac{6M}{h^3} \cdot \frac{\Delta y}{\Delta N_c} \\ \text{and} \qquad f_p &= \frac{6M}{h^3} \cdot \frac{\Delta y}{\Delta N_p} \end{aligned}\right] \qquad \text{...(17.48)}$$

where M = bending moment applied to the beam.

h = height of beam.

$\frac{\Delta y}{\Delta N_c}$ = slope of isochromatic order v's beam position.

$\frac{\Delta y}{\Delta N_p}$ = slope of isopachic order v's beam position.

17.9 Recording of Isoclinic Fringe Patterns

Holography can be used to record and reconstruct the polarization of light emitted by a photoelastic model. Utilizing this technique, an observer viewing the hologram may determine the entire family of isoclinics a posteriori. This requires that the state of polarization of the photoelastic model be recorded. Lohman suggested that two orthogonally polarized reference beams might be used in order to produce a holograph that would reconstruct the polarization of light scattered by an object. Later, Bryngdahl pointed out that the reconstruction geometry must be arranged so that the crosstalk images do not overlap. The crosstalk images are those images which arise in the reconstruction process due to the diffraction of one of the polarized reference beams by the interference pattern formed by the other orthogonal reference beam. Fourney, Waggoner and Mate demonstrated that the technique could be applied to the study of photoelastic models by reconstructing both the light and dark-field isochromatic pattern.

The schematic diagram of the optical arrangement for recording the isoclinics is shown in Fig. 17.15. Each beam produces an interferences pattern in the holograph plane with the similarly polarized component of light scattered by the object. The two interference patterns are superimposed and recorded simultaneously by the hologram. If the hologram is illuminated by the original reference beams, the reference wavefronts are diffracted by the hologram and combined vectorially to reproduce the polarization of light emitted by the object. It is necessary to maintain the polarization the location of the reference beams with respect to each other and with respect to the holograph from formation to reconstruction. To reconstruct the object's polarization, the phase relationship must be maintained. For mathematical treatment refer to the paper by Fourney and Mate.

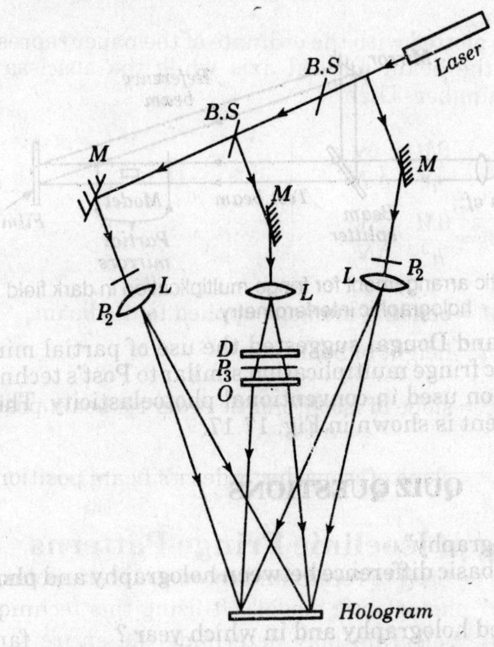

B.S. = beam splitter P_1, P_2, P_3 = Polarizers

M = Mirror D = Diffuser

O = Object L = Lens.

Fig. 17.15 Schematic arrangement for recording isoclinics.

17.10 Fringe Multiplication Methods

Kalestynski in 1973 developed a technique for holographic multiplication in one exposure by the use of a multi beam reference beam as shown in Fig. 17.16. The method consists of forming a hologram of one object using a set of reference beams whose sources can be suitably distributed in space. A multi beam reference field is produced by laser lighting a collection of microlenses distributed in a programmed way in a flat or spiral mask.

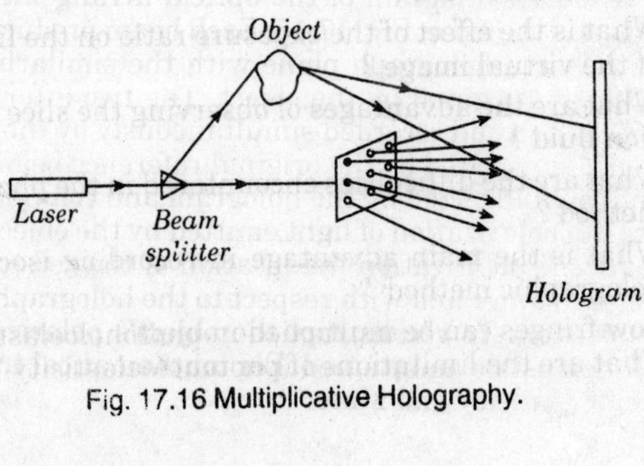

Fig. 17.16 Multiplicative Holography.

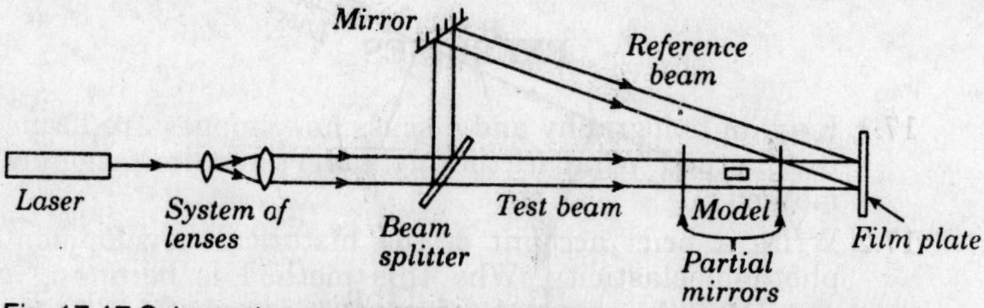

Fig. 17.17 Schematic arrangement for fringe multiplication in dark field holographic interferometry.

Weigl, Friedric'، and Dougal suggested the use of partial mirrors in 1969 for holographic fringe multiplication similar to Post's technique for fringe multiplication used in conventional photoelasticity. The experimental arrangement is shown in Fig. 17.17.

QUIZ QUESTIONS

1. Define "holography".
2. What is the basic difference between holography and photography ?
3. Who invented holography and in which year ?
4. What are the advantages of holographic photoelasticity over conventional photoelasticity ?
5. Define "Laser".
6. What do you understand by stimulated emission ?
7 What do you mean by population inversion ?
8. Explain spatial and temporal coherence.
9. Which type of laser is generally preferred for holographic work ?
10. Differentiate between object beam and reference beam.
11. Differentiate between true and conjugate images.
12. Define hologram interferometry.
13. What are the various schematics for hologram interferometry ?
14. Which type of holographic interferometry is used for photoelastic work ?
15. What is the effect of the exposure ratio on the light intensity of the virtual image ?
16. What are the advantages of observing the slice in an immersion fluid ?
17. What are the difficulties encountered in the photoholoelastic method ?
18. What is the main advantage in recording isoclinics by the holographic method ?
19. How fringes can be multiplied in photoholoelasticity ?
20. What are the limitations of photoholoelasticity ?

EXERCISES

17.1 Explain holography and discuss how images are formed by this method. What are the advantages and limitations of this method ?

17.2 Write a brief account of the historical developments in photoholoelasticity. Why this method is becoming more popular ?

17.3 Discuss the various schematic arrangements used for hologram interferometry bringing clearly their field of applications.

17.4 Derive the light-intensity equation as obtained by Fourney and Mate. Explain how isochromatic and isopachic fringe patterns can be obtained from this equation.

17.5 Explain how photo-holo-elasticity can be used for solving three-dimensional problems. How this technique can be simplified ?

17.6 Explain the following holographic interferometers.
(*a*) O'Regan and Dudderar interfermeter.
(*b*) Holloway, Ranson and Taylor interferometer.

17.7 How isochromatic and isopachic fringe patterns can be separated by the following methods ?
(*a*) Chatelain method
(*b*) Assa and Betser multiplexing technique.

17.8 Explain the working of the following interferometers :
(*a*) Ebbeni, Coenen and Hermanne interferometer.
(*b*) Gasvik interferometer.

17.9 Explain the method of recording isoclinics by holographic method. What are the advantages of this method ?

17.10 Write short notes on the following :
(*a*) Fringe multiplication methods.
(*b*) Calibration method.

18

Photo-Orthotropic Elasticity

18.1 Introduction

Composite materials and standwich construction are replacing most of the conventional materials. These materials are orthotropic in nature and as such the usual laws governing the photoelastic investigations cannot be applied straight away and some modifications have to be made. In this chapter we shall study the various approaches used to analyse the stresses in composite materials by the photoelastic method, which has become popular under the name "photo-orthotropic elasticity".

18.2 Historical Developments

Composite materials are ideal for structural applications where high strength-to-weight and stiffness-to-weight ratios are required. Aircraft and space craft are typical weight-sensitive structures in which composite materials are cost-effective. The most important class of composite materials is fiber reinforced and these materials exhibit anisotropic properties which must be accounted for in any stress analysis technique. Some efforts have been made to extend photoelastic methods of stress analysis for applications involving composite materials. One approach, outlined by Dally and Alfirevic (1969), is to employ isotropic birefringent coatings bonded to the composite. In this case, the strain field is determined from the coating using a reflection polariscope together with conventional methods of photoelastic analysis established for isotropic materials. Brittle coating method for the analysis of composite materials has been suggested by Agarwal and Chaturvedi (1978) and Prabhakaran (1979).

Because of its whole field character, the use of photoelasticity would be obviously very advantageous for the evaluation of the stresses in composite materials. In recent years, there has been a considerable effort to develop a stress-optic or strain-optic relationship for fiber-reinforced composite materials. The most promising approach, the use of the transmission polariscope, was pioneered by Pih and Knight in 1969 and Sampson in 1970. They utilized a composite model fabricated with glass-fiber reinforcement and a polymeric matrix. Research work in this area has been primarily devoted to establishing the calibration constants for unidirectionally reinforced material and developing stress-optic laws to relate the photoelastic response to the applied stresses. Pih and Knight developed the stress-optic law based upon a stress-proportioning technique whereas Sampson formulated a stress-optic law which hypothesized the concept of a Mohr's circle of birefringence. In addition, Sampson introduced the concept that three photoelastic constants are required in order to characterize these new materials photoelastically. Dally and Prabhakaran (1971) have developed simple methods for the fabrication of the fiber-reinforced birefringent material and successfully applied the stress-proportioning concept in order to predict the three fundamental photoelastic constants based upon properties of the constituents. Their predictions agreed closely with experimental results and with those obtained by Sampson, but their approach seemed to fail if the isoclinic parameter was to be predicted. Pih and Knight observed that the optical isoclinic angle differed considerably from the physical isoclinic angle and Sampson lately suggested that the optical isoclinic angle is one half the angle between the fiber direction and the direction of the principal component of birefringence as determined by Mohr's circle.

Bert (1972) applied Bhagavantam's theory of photoelectricity for an orthorhombic crystalline system in order to develop a general theory of photo-ortho-elasticity. His results do not differ from those obtained by Sampson. Bert has shown that the concept of a Mohr's circle of birefringence as proposed by Samson, is a direct result of tensorial nature of birefringence.

Pipes and Dalley (1973) recently noticed that the isoclinic parameter is stress dependent. They suggested that this could be caused by residual birefringence but they made no attempt to correlate their experimental results with theory.

Cerņosek (1975) using the theory of the unitary system of retarders has shown that two seemingly different theories of photo-elasticity put forward by Sampson and Dally and Prabhakaran are identical if the heterogeneous nature of the composites is respected. Further it is shown that the optical isoclinic parameter can be accurately predicted even if the initial birefringence is present in the unloaded specimen.

Prabhakaran (1975) has examined the Sampson's stress-optic law for orthotropic materials subjected to biaxial-stress fields. This law has been simplified for the special cases where the material is balanced or the principal-stress directions and the principal materials axes are identical. The stress optic law was verified experimentally for a unidirectionally reinforced circular disc by employing strain gauges. While the verification was satisfactory for the case of transverse loading, the validity of the approximation involved in applying the simplified stress-optic law to the case of 45-deg, loading was doubtful. It is shown that the three independent material fringe values can be found from measurements of the fringe order and the strains at the centre of the disc for the three cases of loading, perpendicular, parallel and at 45 deg. to the reinforcement direction.

Pipes and Rose in 1974 proposed a strain-optic law for a certain class of birefringent fiber-reinforced composite materials which requires both mechanical and optical characterization of the material.

The strain-optic law requires only a single strain-optic coefficient, coupled with four independent mechanical material properties, for prediction of the optical response of a birefringent anisotropic material. Experimental results are found to have good agreement with the developed strain optic relation. The isoclinic angle for this class of birefringent composite materials (collimated S-glass fibers embedded in an epoxy matrix) has been hypothesized to be equal to the principal-strain direction of an equivalent homogeneous anisotropic medium.

Prabhakaran (1975) has shown that the strain-optic law need not be restricted to composites with low-fiber-volume fractions and that an orthotropic model material can be treated as optically isotropic. However this simplification leads to errors of the order of 20 per cent, which decreases as the fiber reinforcement decreases.

Prabhakaran (1976) has shown that Sampson's prediction for the optical isoclinic parameter is good, both for uniaxial and biaxial stress fields. As an approximation, the principal-strain angles are closer compared to the principal-stress angles.

Agarwal (1983) has derived an approximate method of orthotropic photoelastic analysis. Prabhakaran (1982) and Chaturvedi (1983) have extended the oblique incidence method to photo-orthotropic elasticity.

18.3 Stress-strain Relations for Orthotropic Materials

For an orthotropic material there are two orthogonal planes of material property symmetry, and symmetry will exist relative to a third mutually orthogonal plane. The stress-strain relations in coordinates aligned with principal material directions are :

$$\begin{Bmatrix} \sigma_1 \\ \sigma_2 \\ \sigma_3 \\ \tau_{23} \\ \tau_{31} \\ \tau_{12} \end{Bmatrix} = \begin{bmatrix} C_{11} & C_{12} & C_{13} & 0 & 0 & 0 \\ C_{12} & C_{22} & C_{23} & 0 & 0 & 0 \\ C_{13} & C_{23} & C_{33} & 0 & 0 & 0 \\ 0 & 0 & 0 & C_{44} & 0 & 0 \\ 0 & 0 & 0 & 0 & C_{55} & 0 \\ 0 & 0 & 0 & 0 & 0 & C_{66} \end{bmatrix} \begin{Bmatrix} \varepsilon_1 \\ \varepsilon_2 \\ \varepsilon_3 \\ \gamma_{23} \\ \gamma_{31} \\ \gamma_{12} \end{Bmatrix} \qquad \text{...(18.1)}$$

There are 9 independent constants in the stiffness matrix.

Conversely

$$\begin{Bmatrix} \varepsilon_1 \\ \varepsilon_2 \\ \varepsilon_3 \\ \gamma_{23} \\ \gamma_{31} \\ \gamma_{12} \end{Bmatrix} = \begin{bmatrix} S_{11} & S_{12} & S_{13} & 0 & 0 & 0 \\ S_{12} & S_{22} & S_{23} & 0 & 0 & 0 \\ S_{13} & S_{23} & S_{33} & 0 & 0 & 0 \\ 0 & 0 & 0 & S_{44} & 0 & 0 \\ 0 & 0 & 0 & 0 & S_{55} & 0 \\ 0 & 0 & 0 & 0 & 0 & S_{66} \end{bmatrix} \begin{Bmatrix} \sigma_1 \\ \sigma_2 \\ \sigma_3 \\ \tau_{23} \\ \tau_{31} \\ \tau_{12} \end{Bmatrix} \qquad \text{...(18.2)}$$

where S_{ij} is the compliance matrix defined by the inverse of the stress-strain relations. For the orthotropic material,

$$[S_{ij}] = \begin{bmatrix} \frac{1}{E_1} & -\frac{\nu_{21}}{E_1} & -\frac{\nu_{31}}{E_3} & 0 & 0 & 0 \\ -\frac{\nu_{12}}{E_1} & \frac{1}{E_2} & -\frac{\nu_{32}}{E_3} & 0 & 0 & 0 \\ -\frac{\nu_{13}}{E_1} & -\frac{\nu_{23}}{E_2} & \frac{1}{E_3} & 0 & 0 & 0 \\ 0 & 0 & 0 & \frac{1}{G_{23}} & 0 & 0 \\ 0 & 0 & 0 & 0 & \frac{1}{G_{31}} & 0 \\ 0 & 0 & 0 & 0 & 0 & \frac{1}{G_{12}} \end{bmatrix} \qquad ...(18.3)$$

where E_1, E_2, E_3 = Young's moduli in 1, 2 and 3 directions respectively.

ν_{ij} = Poisson's ratio for transverse strain in the j-direction when stressed in the i-direction.

$= -\frac{\varepsilon_j}{\varepsilon_i}$, for $\sigma_i = \sigma$ and all other stresses are zero.

G_{23}, G_{31}, G_{12} = Shear moduli in the 2—3, 3—1, and 1—2 planes respectively.

Now $\quad S_{ij} = S_{ji}$

Hence $\quad \frac{\nu_{ij}}{E_j} = \frac{\nu_{ji}}{E_j} \qquad ...(18.4)$

The relationship between the stiffness and compliance matrices can be obtained as :

$$C_{11} = \frac{S_{22}\,S_{33} - S_{23}^2}{S},\ C_{12} = \frac{S_{13}\,S_{23} - S_{12}\,S_{33}}{S}$$

$$C_{22} = \frac{S_{33}\,S_{11} - S_{13}^2}{S},\ C_{13} = \frac{S_{12}\,S_{23} - S_{13}\,S_{22}}{S}$$

$$C_{33} = \frac{S_{11}\,S_{22} - S_{12}^2}{S},\ C_{23} = \frac{S_{12}\,S_{13} - S_{23}\,S_{11}}{S}$$

$$C_{44} = \frac{1}{S_{44}},\ C_{55} = \frac{1}{S_{55}},\ C_{66} = \frac{1}{S_{66}}$$

where $S = S_{11}\,S_{22}\,S_{33} - S_{11}\,S_{23}^2 - S_{22}\,S_{13}^2 - S_{33}\,S_{12}^2 + 2\,S_{12}\,S_{23}\,S_{13}$ ...(18.5)

In terms of the engineering constants,

$$C_{11} = \frac{1 - \nu_{23}\,\nu_{32}}{E_2 E_3 \Delta},\ C_{12} = \frac{\nu_{21} + \nu_{31}\,\nu_{23}}{E_2 E_3\,\Delta}$$

$$C_{13} = \frac{\nu_{31} + \nu_{21}\,\nu_{32}}{E_2 E_3 \Delta},\ C_{22} = \frac{1 - \nu_{13}\,\nu_{31}}{E_1 E_3 \Delta}$$

$$C_{23} = \frac{\nu_{32} + \nu_{12}\,\nu_{31}}{E_1 E_3 \Delta},\ C_{33} = \frac{1 - \nu_{12}\,\nu_{21}}{E_1 E_2 \Delta}$$

$$C_{44} = G_{23},\ C_{55} = G_{31},\ C_{66} = G_{12}$$

where $$\Delta = \frac{1 - \nu_{12}\,\nu_{21} - \nu_{23}\,\nu_{32} - \nu_{31}\,\nu_{13} - 2\nu_{21}\,\nu_{32}\,\nu_{13}}{E_1 E_2 E_3} \qquad ...(18.6)$$

For the plane stress case, $\sigma_3 = \tau_{23} = \tau_{31} = 0$ and Eqs. (18.2) become.

$$\begin{Bmatrix} \varepsilon_1 \\ \varepsilon_2 \\ \gamma_{12} \end{Bmatrix} = \begin{bmatrix} S_{11} & S_{12} & 0 \\ S_{12} & S_{22} & 0 \\ 0 & 0 & S_{66} \end{bmatrix} \begin{Bmatrix} \sigma_1 \\ \sigma_2 \\ \tau_{12} \end{Bmatrix} \qquad ...(18.7)$$

where $$S_{11} = \frac{1}{E_1},\ S_{12} = -\frac{\nu_{12}}{E_1}$$

$$S_{22} = \frac{1}{E_2},\ S_{66} = \frac{1}{G_{12}}$$

Conversely

$$\begin{Bmatrix} \sigma_1 \\ \sigma_2 \\ \tau_{12} \end{Bmatrix} = \begin{bmatrix} Q_{11} & Q_{12} & 0 \\ Q_{12} & Q_{22} & 0 \\ 0 & 0 & Q_{66} \end{bmatrix} = \begin{Bmatrix} \varepsilon_1 \\ \varepsilon_2 \\ \gamma_{12} \end{Bmatrix} \qquad ...(18.8)$$

where $$Q_{11} = \frac{S_{22}}{S_{11}S_{22} - S_{12}^2} = \frac{E_1}{1 - \nu_{12}\,\nu_{21}}$$

$$Q_{12} = \frac{-S_{12}}{S_{11}\,S_{22} - S_{12}^2} = \frac{\nu_{12}\,E_2}{1 - \nu_{12}\,\nu_{21}}$$

$$Q_{22} = \frac{S_{11}}{S_{11}\,S_{22} - S_{12}^2} = \frac{E_2}{1 - \nu_{12}\,\nu_{21}}$$

$$Q_{66} = \frac{1}{S_{66}} = G_{12} \qquad ...(18.9)$$

For a lamina of arbitrary orientation,

$$\begin{Bmatrix} \sigma_x \\ \sigma_y \\ \tau_{\sigma y} \end{Bmatrix} = \begin{bmatrix} C^2 & S^2 & -2CS \\ S^2 & C^2 & 2CS \\ CS & -CS & C^2 - S^2 \end{bmatrix} \begin{Bmatrix} \sigma_1 \\ \sigma_2 \\ \tau_{12} \end{Bmatrix} \qquad ...(18.10)$$

where $C = \cos\theta$, $S = \sin\theta$, and θ is the angle from the x-axis to the 1-axis.

Similarly

$$\begin{Bmatrix} \varepsilon_x \\ \varepsilon_y \\ \dfrac{\gamma_{xy}}{2} \end{Bmatrix} \begin{bmatrix} C^2 & S^2 & -2CS \\ S^2 & C^2 & 2CS \\ CS & -CS & C^2 - S^2 \end{bmatrix} \begin{Bmatrix} \varepsilon_1 \\ \varepsilon_2 \\ \dfrac{\gamma_{12}}{2} \end{Bmatrix} \qquad ...(18.11)$$

A specially orthotropic lamina is one whose principal material axes are aligned with the natural body axes for the problem, for the example

$$\begin{Bmatrix} \sigma_x \\ \sigma_y \\ \tau_{yx} \end{Bmatrix} = \begin{Bmatrix} \sigma_1 \\ \sigma_2 \\ \tau_{12} \end{Bmatrix} = \begin{bmatrix} Q_{11} & Q_{12} & 0 \\ Q_{12} & Q_{22} & 0 \\ 0 & 0 & Q_{66} \end{bmatrix} \begin{Bmatrix} \varepsilon_1 \\ \varepsilon_2 \\ \gamma_{12} \end{Bmatrix} \quad ...(18.12)$$

when the principal material directions do not coincide with the natural directions of the body, then

$$\begin{Bmatrix} \sigma_x \\ \sigma_y \\ \tau_{xy} \end{Bmatrix} = \begin{bmatrix} \overline{Q}_{11} & \overline{Q}_{12} & \overline{Q}_{16} \\ \overline{Q}_{12} & \overline{Q}_{22} & \overline{Q}_{26} \\ \overline{Q}_{16} & \overline{Q}_{26} & \overline{Q}_{66} \end{bmatrix} \begin{Bmatrix} \varepsilon_x \\ \varepsilon_y \\ \gamma_{xy} \end{Bmatrix} \quad ...(18.13)$$

where
$$\overline{Q}_{11} = Q_{11}C^4 + 2(Q_{12} + 2Q_{66})S^2C^2 + Q_{22}S^4$$
$$\overline{Q}_{12} = (Q_{11} + Q_{22} - 4Q_{66})S^2C^2 + Q_{12}(S^4 + C^4)$$
$$\overline{Q}_{22} = Q_{11}S^4 + 2(Q_{12} + 2Q_{66})S^2C^2 + Q_{22}C^4$$
$$\overline{Q}_{16} = (Q_{11} - Q_{12} - 2Q_{66})SC^3 + (Q_{12} - Q_{22} + 2Q_{66})S^3C$$
$$\overline{Q}_{26} = (Q_{11} - Q_{12} - 2Q_{66})S^2C + (Q_{12} - Q_{22} + 2Q_{66})SC^3$$
$$\overline{Q}_{66} = (Q_{11} + Q_{22} - 2Q_{12} - 2Q_{66})S^2C^2 + Q_{66}(S^4 + C^4)$$

Similarly

$$\begin{bmatrix} \varepsilon_x \\ \varepsilon_y \\ \gamma_{xy} \end{bmatrix} = \begin{bmatrix} \overline{S}_{11} & \overline{S}_{12} & \overline{S}_{16} \\ \overline{S}_{12} & \overline{S}_{22} & \overline{S}_{26} \\ \overline{S}_{16} & \overline{S}_{26} & \overline{S}_{66} \end{bmatrix} \begin{bmatrix} \sigma_x \\ \sigma_y \\ \tau_{xy} \end{bmatrix} \quad ...(18.14)$$

where
$$\overline{S}_{11} = S_{11}C^4 + (2S_{12} + S_{66})C^2S^2 + S_{22}S^4$$
$$\overline{S}_{12} = S_{12}(S^4 + C^4) + (S_{11} + S_{22} - S_{66})S^2C^2$$
$$\overline{S}_{22} = S_{11}S^4 + (2S_{12} + S_{66})S^2C^2 + S_{22}C^4$$
$$\overline{S}_{16} = (2S_{11} - 2S_{12} - S_{66})SC^3 - (2S_{22} - 2S_{12} - S_{66})S^3C$$
$$\overline{S}_{26} = (2S_{11} - 2S_{12} - S_{66})S^3C - (2S_{22} - 2S_{12} - S_{66})SC^3$$
$$\overline{S}_{66} = 2(2S_{11} + 2S_{22} - 4S_{12} - S_{66})S^2C^2 + S_{66}(S^4 + C^4)$$

18.4 Determination of Elastic Constants

The elastic moduli of a fiber-reinforced composite are determined in terms of the properties of the fibers and the matrix and in terms of the relative volumes of fibers and matrix.

$$C_{ij} = C_{ij}(E_f, \nu_f, V_f, E_m, \nu_m, V_m)$$

where the subscripts f and m stand for the fiber and matrix respectively and V represents the volume ratio of the fibers or matrix to the total volume of composite.

The strength of a fiber-reinforced composite is also determined in terms of the strengths of the fibers and the matrix and their relative volumes. Thus

$$\sigma_i = \sigma_i\,(\sigma_{if}, V_f, \sigma_{im}, V_m)$$

where $\quad \sigma_i = \sigma_L, \sigma_T, \tau_{LT}$ = composite strengths

$$\sigma_{if} = \sigma_{L_f}, \sigma_{T_f}, \tau_{LT_f} = \text{Fiber strengths}$$

$$\sigma_{im} = \sigma_{L_m}, \sigma_{T_m}, \tau_{LT_m} = \text{Matrix strengths}$$

L, T and *LT* represents longitudinal (along the fiber axis), transverse and shear strengths respectively.

The lamina is assumed to be microscopically homogeneous, linearly elastic, microscopically orthotropic, initially stress free ; the fibers are homogeneous, linearly elastic, isotropic, regularly spaced, perfectly aligned and the matrix is homogeneous, linearly elastic and isotropic. Further it is assumed that no voids can exist in the fibers or matrix or in between them.

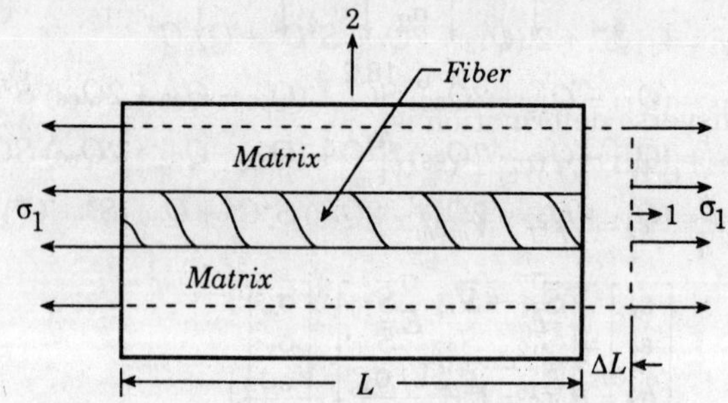

Fig. 18.1

(*a*) **Determination of E_1.** As shown in Fig. 18.1, for loading in the fiber direction, the strain ε_1 in the composite is

$$\varepsilon_1 = \frac{\Delta L}{L}$$

Also $\quad \sigma_f = E_f\,\varepsilon_1$

$$\sigma_m = E_m \varepsilon_1$$

The resultant force on the element of composite material is :

$$P = \sigma_1 A = \sigma_f A_f + \sigma_m A_m$$

where A_f, A_m represents the area of the fibers and matrix respectively.

Now $\quad \sigma_1 = E_1 \varepsilon_1$

Hence $\quad E_1 = E_f \frac{A_f}{A} + E_m \frac{A_m}{A}$

Also $\quad V_f = \frac{A_f}{A}, V_m = \frac{A_m}{A}$

Thus $\quad E_1 = E_f V_f + E_m V_m \qquad \text{...(18.15)}$

(*b*) **Determination of E_2.** The apparent Young's modulus E_2 in the direction transverse to the fibers can be obtained as follows (Fig. 18.2),

$$\varepsilon_f = \frac{\sigma_2}{E_f}$$

$$\varepsilon_m = \frac{\sigma_2}{E_m}$$

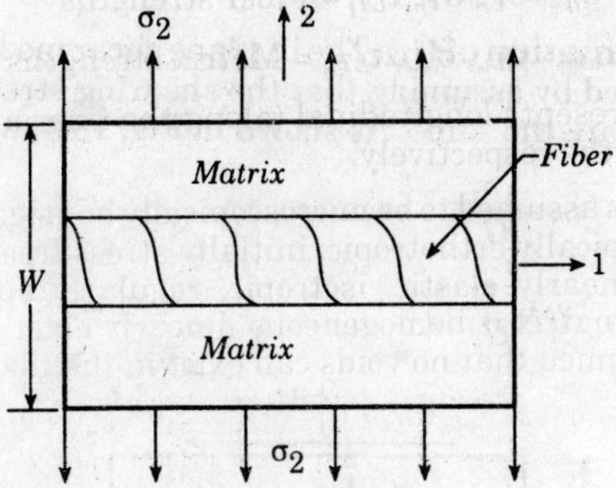

Fig. 18.2

Total transverse deformation is

$$\varepsilon_2 W = V_f W \varepsilon_f + V_m W \varepsilon_m$$

or $$\varepsilon_2 = V_f \varepsilon_f + V_m \varepsilon_m$$

$$= V_f \frac{\sigma_2}{E_f} + V_m \frac{\sigma_2}{E_m}$$

But $$\sigma_2 = E_2 \varepsilon_2 = E_2 \left(\frac{V_f \sigma_2}{E_f} + \frac{V_m \sigma_2}{E_m} \right)$$

Hence $$E_2 = \frac{E_f E_m}{V_m E_f + V_f E_m} \quad \text{...(18.16)}$$

(*c*) **Determination of ν_{12}.** The major Poisson's ratio is defined as:

$$\nu_{12} = -\frac{\varepsilon_2}{\varepsilon_1}$$

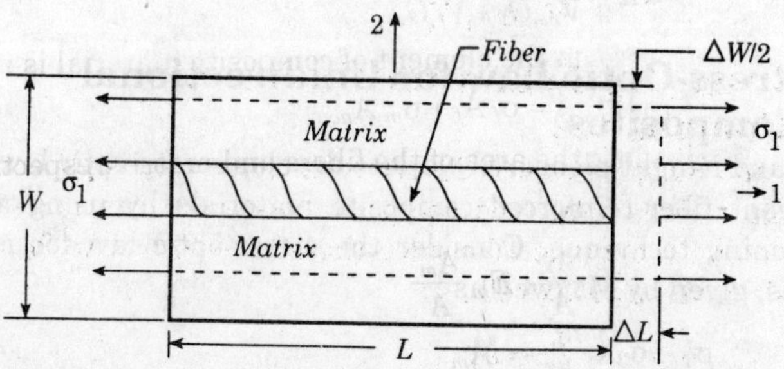

Fig. 18.3

for the stress state $\sigma_1 = \sigma$ and all other stresses are zero. The deformations are shown in Fig. 18.3. The transverse deformation ΔW is

$$\Delta W = -W\varepsilon_2 = W\nu_{12}\,\varepsilon_1$$

Also $\Delta W = \Delta_m W + \Delta_f W$

Approximately $\Delta_m W = WV_m\, \nu_m \varepsilon_1$

$$\Delta_f W = WV_f\, \nu_f\, \varepsilon_1$$

Thus
$$\nu_{12} = V_m\, \nu_m + V_f\, \nu_f \qquad ...(18.17)$$

(*d*) **Determination of G_{12}.** The in-plane shear modulus of a lamina, G_{12} is determined by assuming that the shearing stresses on the fiber and the matrix are the same. As shown in Fig. 18.4, we thus have

$$\gamma_m = \frac{\tau}{G_m}$$

$$\gamma_f = \frac{\tau}{G_f}$$

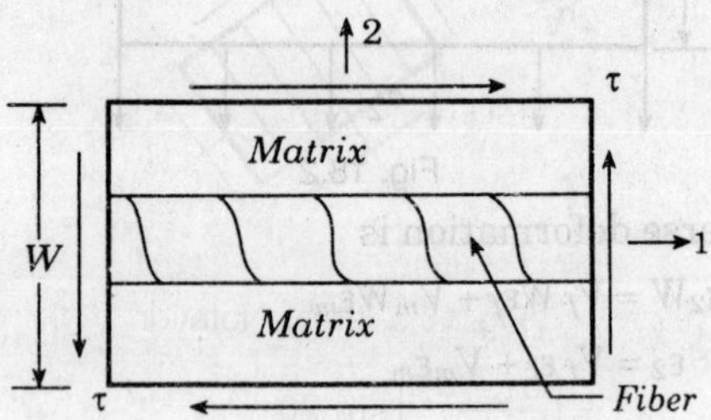

Fig. 18.4

The total shearing deformation is defined as :

$$\Delta = \gamma W = \Delta_m + \Delta_f$$

$$= V_m\, W\gamma_m + V_f W\, \gamma_f$$

Hence
$$\gamma = V_m\, \gamma_m + V_f\, \gamma_f$$

or
$$\frac{\tau}{G_{12}} = V_m \cdot \frac{\tau}{G_m} + V_f \frac{\tau}{G_f}$$

or
$$G_{12} = \frac{G_m G_f}{V_m\, G_f + V_f\, G_m} \qquad ...(18.18)$$

18.5 Stress-Optic Law for Unidirectional Composites

Pih and Knight pioneered work to develop stress-optic law for the birefringent fiber-reinforced composite materials by using a stress proportioning technique. Consider the stress-optic law for isotropic materials, given by Maxwell as :

$$\sigma_1 - \sigma_2 = \frac{nf}{h} = Nf \qquad ...(18.19)$$

where n is the fringe order and N the fringe order per unit thickness, f is the stress optic coefficient.

But $$\sigma_1, \sigma_2 = \frac{1}{2}(\sigma_x + \sigma_y) \pm \sqrt{\left(\frac{\sigma_x - \sigma_y}{2}\right)^2 + \tau_{xy}^2} \quad ...(18.20)$$

Combining Eqs. (18.19) and (18.20) yields,

$$N^2 = \left(\frac{\sigma_x}{f} - \frac{\sigma_y}{f}\right)^2 + \left(\frac{2\tau_{xy}}{f}\right)^2 \quad ...(18.21)$$

where $$\sigma_x = \sigma_1 \cos^2\theta + \sigma_2 \sin^2\theta$$

$$\sigma_y = \sigma_1 \sin^2\theta + \sigma_2 \cos^2\theta$$

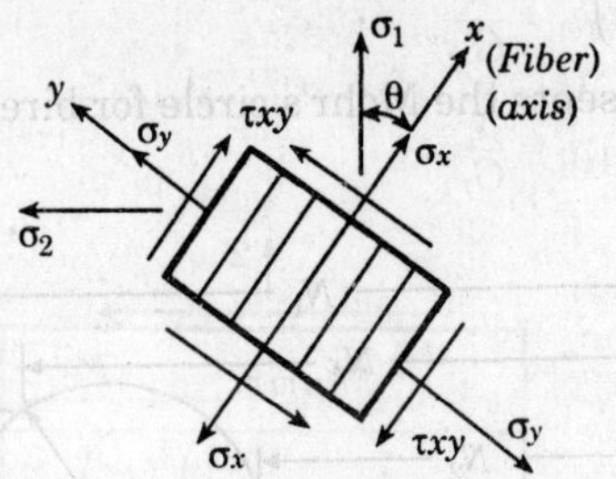

Fig. 18.5 Stress Notation.

$$\tau_{xy} = \left(\frac{\sigma_1 - \sigma_2}{2}\right)\sin 2\theta$$

as shown in Fig. 18.5.

Sampson reasoned that the anisotropic stress-optic law should be of the same form as Eq. (18.21), but defined three independent stress-optic coefficients, f_x, f_y and f_{xy}.

Defining $N_x = \frac{\sigma_x}{f_x}$, $N_y = \frac{\sigma_y}{f_y}$, $N_{xy} = \frac{\tau_{xy}}{f_{xy}}$, Eq. (18.21) can be written as :

$$N = \left\{\left(\frac{\sigma_x}{f_x} - \frac{\sigma_y}{f_y}\right)^2 + \left(\frac{2\tau_{xy}}{f_{xy}}\right)^2\right\}^{1/2} \quad ...(18.22)$$

$$N = \frac{\sigma_1}{f_x}\left\{\left[\left(\cos^2\theta + \frac{\sigma_2}{\sigma_1}\sin^2\theta\right) - \left(\sin^2\theta + \frac{\sigma_2}{\sigma_1}\cos^2\theta\right)\frac{f_x}{f_y}\right]^2 + \left[\frac{f_x}{f_{xy}}\left(1 - \frac{\sigma_2}{\sigma_1}\right)\sin 2\theta\right]^2\right\}^{\frac{1}{2}} \quad ...(18.23)$$

or $$N = \sqrt{(N_x - N_y)^2 + (2N_{xy})^2} \quad ...(18.24)$$

Also, $$N_{1,2} = \frac{1}{2}(N_x + N_y) \pm \frac{1}{2} N \qquad ...(18.25)$$

$$N_x - N_y = N \cos 2\theta' \qquad ...(18.26)$$

and $$\sin 2\theta' = \frac{2N_{xy}}{N} \qquad ...(18.27)$$

where θ' = angle between the axis of the major principal components of birefringence N_1 and the x-direction.

$$\tau_{xy} = \frac{f_{xy}}{2} N \sin 2\theta' \qquad ...(18.28)$$

$$\left(\frac{\sigma_x}{f_x} - \frac{\sigma_y}{f_y}\right) = N \cos 2\theta' \qquad ...(18.29)$$

Fig. 18.6 represents the Mohr's circle for birefringence.

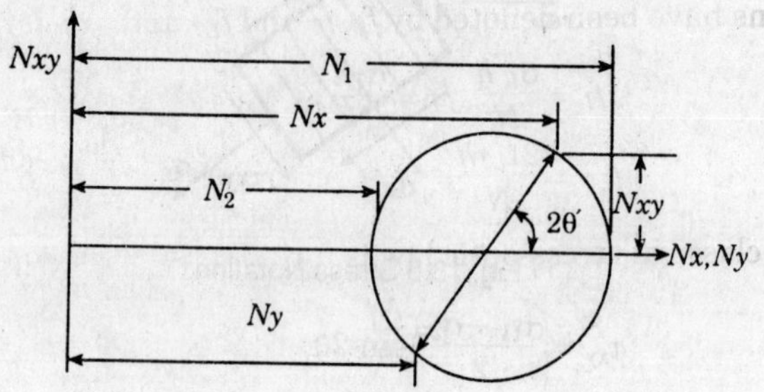

Fig. 18.6 Mohr's Circle for birefringence.

The stress σ_x at any point along that line is found by the shear-difference method from the relation

$$\sigma_x = \sigma_{x,0} - \int_0^x \frac{\partial \tau_{xy}}{\partial y} dx \qquad ...(18.30)$$

As shown in Fig. 18.7, we have

$$\frac{\partial \tau_{xy}}{\partial y} \approx \frac{\tau_{xy}^B - \tau_{xy}^A}{\Delta y}$$

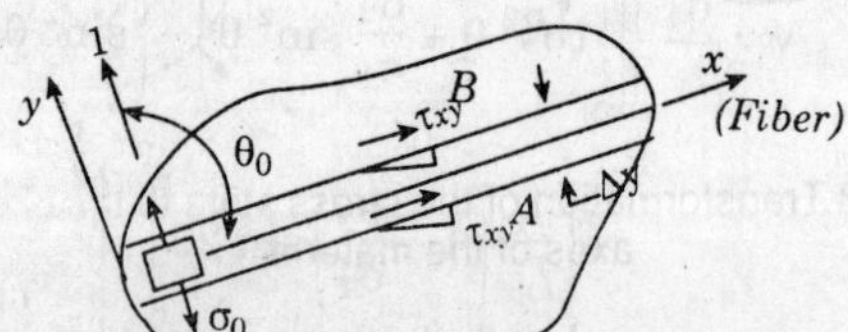

Fig. 18.7 Shear-difference stress separation.

In general $\sigma_{x,0} \neq 0$
but rather $\sigma_{x,0} = \sigma_0 \cos 2\theta_0$ ...(18.31)

where σ_0 and θ_0 are the boundary values of the tangent stress and the physical isoclinic, respectively.

Then $\sigma_y = \dfrac{f_y}{f_x}(\sigma_x - f_x N \cos 2\theta')$ ...(18.32)

Dally and Prabhakaran pointed out that in the general case, the directions of the stresses applied to a undirectional composite may not coincide with the axes of material symmetry and the simplified form of the stress optic law must be modified. It is necessary to transform the principal stresses σ_1 and σ_2 into a state of stress σ_L, σ_T and τ_{LT} which coincides with the principal elastic axes of the model material as shown in Fig. 18.8. The three stress components are treated individually by considering the fundamental models for photoelastic calibration depicted in Fig. 18.9.

The photoelastic constants for these three fundamental stress conditions have been denoted by f_L, f_T and f_{LT} and are defined as :

$$f_L = \frac{\sigma_L h}{N}, \; f_T = \frac{\sigma_T h}{N};$$

$$f_{LT} = \frac{2\tau_{LT} h}{N} \quad \text{...(18.33)}$$

The classical stress-optic law is

$$S = \sigma_1 - \sigma_2 = \frac{Nf}{h}$$

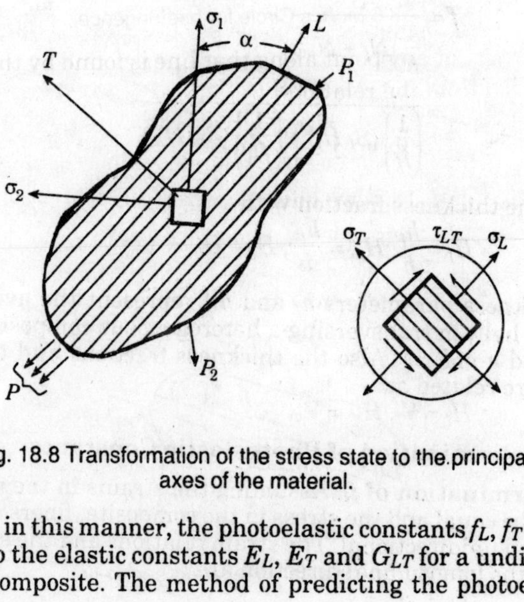

Fig. 18.8 Transformation of the stress state to the principal axes of the material.

Defined in this manner, the photoelastic constants f_L, f_T and f_{LT} are analogous to the elastic constants E_L, E_T and G_{LT} for a undirectionally rainforced composite. The method of predicting the photoelastic constants of the composite from the properties of the two constituents is similar in nature to the procedure used to predict the elastic constants. Stress-strain models for each fundamental stress condition are prescribed and the applied stress proportional between the glass fibers and the matrix. The optical response in terms of fringe order due to each constituent is algebraically summed to give the total retardation as :

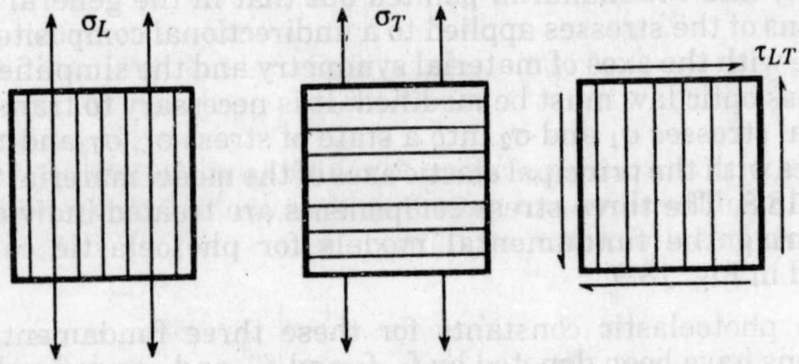

Fig. 18.9 Fundamental stress conditions for photoelastic calibration.

$$N = N_f + N_m \qquad ...(18.34)$$

This algebraic summing neglects any influence of the changing direction of the principal stresses as the light propagates through the heterogeneous composite. Treating the composite and the constituents each as a homogeneous material, we get the photoelastic constant f associated with the composite

$$f = \frac{S}{\frac{1}{h}(N_f + N_m)} = \frac{S}{\left(\frac{1}{f_f}\right)(S_f H_f) + \left(\frac{1}{f_m}\right)(S_m H_m)} \qquad ...(18.35)$$

where H is the thickness fraction with

$$H_f = \frac{h_f}{h}, H_m = \frac{h_m}{h}, H_f + H_m = 1 \qquad ...(18.36)$$

The thickness parameters h_f and h_m represent the average path length of the light in transversing a heterogeneous composite containing fibers and a matrix. Also the thickness fractions and the volume fractions V are related as :

$$H_f = V_f, H_m = V_m \qquad ...(18.37)$$

18.5.1 Determination of Photoelastic Constants

(*a*) **Determination of f_l.** Assuming the strains in the matrix and the fibers to be equal and the stress in the composite, fibers and matrix are considered unidirectional. The strain relations and the equilibrium condition in the longitudinal direction are

$$\varepsilon_{L_f} = \varepsilon_{L_m} = \varepsilon_L \qquad ...(18.38)$$

$$\sigma_L = \sigma_{L_f} V_f + \sigma_{L_m} V_m$$

where the subscript L refers to the direction of the stress or strain. Substituting Eq. (18.37) into Eq. (18.35) and using the principal-stress differences, we get the following expression for the longitudinal material-fringe value f_L.

$$f_L = \frac{\left[V_f + \left(\frac{E_m}{E_f}\right) V_m\right] f_f f_m}{V_f f_m + V_m f_f \left(\frac{E_m}{E_f}\right)} \qquad ...(18.39)$$

For a biaxial state of stress in the fibers and matrix and assuming the strains in the fiber and matrix to be equal both in the longitudinal and transverse directions, we have

$$\left\{\begin{array}{l} \varepsilon_{L_f} = \varepsilon_{L_m} = \varepsilon_L \\ \varepsilon_{T_f} = \varepsilon_{T_m} \\ \sigma L = \sigma_{L_f} V_f + \sigma_{L_m} V_m \\ \sigma_T = \sigma_{T_f} V_f + \sigma_{T_m} V_m = 0 \end{array}\right\} \qquad ...(18.40)$$

Solution of Eqs. (18.40), together with the biaxial form of the stress-strain relations gives the stress components as :

$$\begin{aligned} \sigma_{L_f} &= A_{f1}\, \sigma_L \\ \sigma_{L_m} &= A_{m1}\, \sigma_L \\ \sigma_{T_f} &= B_{f1}\, \sigma_L \\ \sigma_{T_m} &= B_{m1} \sigma_L \end{aligned} \qquad ...(18.41)$$

where the proportionality constants are given by

$$A_{f1} = \frac{\frac{V_m}{V_f}(\nu_m \nu_f - 1) + \frac{E_f}{E_m}(\nu_m^2 - 1)}{a}$$

$$A_{m1} = \frac{\frac{E_m}{E_f} \cdot \frac{V_m}{V_f}(\nu_f^2 - 1) + (\nu_m \nu_f - 1)}{a}$$

$$B_{f1} = \frac{\frac{V_m}{V_f}(\nu_m - \nu_f)}{a}$$

$$B_{m1} = \frac{(\nu_f - \nu_m)}{a}$$

and $\quad a = 2\, V_m (\nu_m \nu_f - 1) + \frac{E_f V_f}{E_m}(\nu_m^2 - 1) + \frac{E_m}{E_f} \frac{V_m^2}{V_f}(\nu_f^2 - 1)$

Proceeding as before, we get

$$f_L = \frac{\left[V_f + V_m \dfrac{E_m}{E_f}\left(\dfrac{1+\nu_f}{1+\nu_m}\right)\right] f_f f_m}{V_f f_m + V_m f_f \dfrac{E_m}{E_f}\left(\dfrac{1+\nu_f}{1+\nu_m}\right)} \qquad \text{...(18.42)}$$

Eq. (18.42) gives better agreement with the experimental results than Eq. (18.39) as shown in Fig. 18.10.

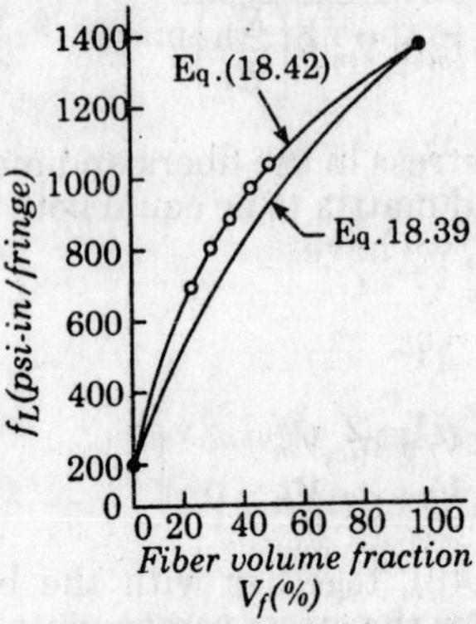

Fig. 18.10 Longitudinal material fringe f_L value as a function of V_f.

(*b*) **Determination of f_T.** Assuming equal stresses in the transverse direction and no stresses in the longitudinal direction, we have

$$\sigma_T = \sigma_{T_f} = \sigma_{T_m} \qquad \text{...(18.43)}$$

Substituting Eqs. (18.43) are (18.37) into (18.35), we get

$$f_T = (f_f f_m)/(V_f f_m + V_m f_f) \qquad \text{...(18.44)}$$

From Fig. 18.11, it is evident that the predicted values of f_T are significantly lower than the experimental values. It appears that the simple series model under estimates the reinforcing effect of the glass fibers when they are oriented in the transverse direction.

To improve upon the effect of glass fibers, the requirement of equal strains in the longitudinal direction was added to the condition of equal stresses in the transverse direction. Thus

$$\varepsilon_L = \varepsilon_{L_f} = \varepsilon_{L_m} \qquad \text{...(18.45)}$$

Combining Eqs. (18.43) and (18.45) with the biaxial form of the stress-strain relations and using Eqs. (18.37) and (18.35),

$$f_T = \frac{1 + \left(\dfrac{E_m}{E_f}\right)\left(\dfrac{V_m}{V_f}\right)}{\left\{\left(\dfrac{1}{f_f}\right)\left[(V_f + \nu_m V_m) + \left(\dfrac{E_m}{E_f}\right) V_m (1-\nu_f)\right] + \left(\dfrac{1}{f_m}\right) \times \left[V_m (1-\nu_m) + \left(\dfrac{E_m}{E_f}\right)\left(\dfrac{V_m}{V_f}\right) + (V_m + \nu_f V_f)\right]\right\}} \qquad \text{...(18.46)}$$

As shown in Fig. 18.11, Eq. (18.46) gives better agreement with experimental observations than Eq. (18.44).

Further improvements can be achieved by proportioning the stresses between the fibers and the matrix. This method is based upon a monofilament laminate which has been subdivided into elements with thickness small relative to the fiber diameter. Following this method, we have

$$E_L = E_f V_f + E_m V_m$$

$$E_T = E_f^* V_f^* + E_m^* V_m^*$$

$$G_{LT} = G_f^* V_f^* + G_m^* V_m^*$$

where

$$E_m^* = E_m/(1 - \nu_m^2)$$

$$G_m^* = G_m/[1 - 2\nu_m^2/(1 - \nu_m)]$$

$$E_f^* = \frac{E_m^* + 2V_f^* (E_f - E_m^*)}{1 + [2V_f^* (1 - 2V_f^*)/E_m^* E_f] [(E_f - E_m^*)^2 - (\nu_m E_f - \nu_f E_m^*)^2]}$$

$$G_f^* = G_m^* G_f/[G_f + 2 V_f^* (G_m^* - G_f)]$$

$$V_f^* = \sqrt{V_f/\pi}$$

$$V_m^* = 1 - V_f^* \qquad \text{...(18.47)}$$

E_f^* and V_f^* may be assumed as fictitious modulus and fictitious volume fraction respectively which depend strongly on the actual fiber content V_f. If the strains in the T direction for the matrix and the fictitious fibers are equated, then we get

$$f_T = \frac{[V_f^* + (E_m^*/E_f^*) V_m^*] f_f f_m}{V_f f_m + V_m f_f (E_m^*/E_f^*)} \qquad \text{...(18.48)}$$

where the fictitious fiber volume V_f^* was used to proportion the stresses, but the actual fiber volume V_f was used in accounting for the photoelastic response. Fig. 18.11 shows that Eq. (18.48) compare very well with the experimental results. The match can be made almost perfect by requiring equal strains in both the L and T directions. Using the fictitious fibers in the transverse direction, we have

$$\sigma_{L_f} = A_{f2}\, \sigma_T$$

$$\sigma_{L_m} = A_{m2}\, \sigma_T$$

$$\sigma_{T_f} = B_{f2}\, \sigma_T$$

$$\sigma_{T_m} = B_{m2}\, \sigma_T \qquad \text{...(18.49)}$$

where the proportionality constants are given by

$$A_{f2} = \frac{\dfrac{V_m^*}{V_f^*} (\nu_m - \nu_f)}{a^*}$$

$$A_{m2} = \frac{\nu_f - \nu_m}{a^*}$$

$$B_{f2} = \frac{\frac{V_m^*}{V_f^*}(\nu_m \nu_f - 1) + \frac{E_f^*}{E_m^*}(\nu_m^2 - 1)}{a^*}$$

$$B_{m2} = \frac{\frac{E_m^*}{E_f^*}\frac{V_m^*}{V_f^*}(\nu_f^2 - 1) + (\nu_m \nu_f - 1)}{a^*}$$

and $a^* = 2\, V_m^* (\nu_m \nu_f - 1) + \frac{E_f^* V_f^*}{E_m^*}(\nu_m^2 - 1) + \frac{E_m^* V_m^{*2}}{E_f^* V_f^*}(\nu_f^2 - 1)$

The transverse material-fringe value is

$$f_T = \frac{\left[V_f^* + V_m^* \frac{E_m^*}{E_f^*}\left(\frac{1+\nu_f}{1+\nu_m}\right)\right] f_f f_m}{V_f f_m + V_m f_f \frac{E_m^*}{E_f^*}\left(\frac{1+\nu_f}{1+\nu_m}\right)} \quad ...(18.50)$$

Eq. (18.50) compare quite closely to the experiment observations as shown in Fig. 18.11.

Pih and Knight utilized an over-simplified procedure for stress proportioning and assumed

$$S_{Tj} = \frac{\sigma_T}{2V_f}$$

$$S_{Tm} = \frac{\sigma_T}{2\,V_m} \quad ...(18.51)$$

so that $\qquad f_T = 2f_f f_m/(f_f + f_m) \qquad ...(18.52)$

This result does not adequately account for the effect of V_f on f_T.

(*c*) **Determination of f_{LT}.** The shear material-fringe value f_{LT} relates the photoelastic-fringe order observed in a composite material

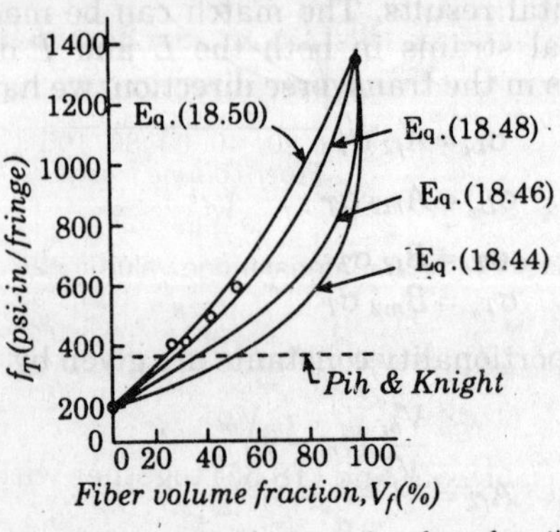

Fig. 18.11 Transverse material fringe value f_T as function of V_f.

subjected to a state of pure shear stress. A state of pure shear is created by orienting the fibers in the specimen at a 45° angle to the axis of loading as shown in Fig. 18.12. Assuming a simple series model where the shear stresses in the fibers and the matrix are equal, we have

$$\tau_{LT} = \tau_f = \tau_m \quad ...(18.53)$$

This method of proportioning leads to the following relation for

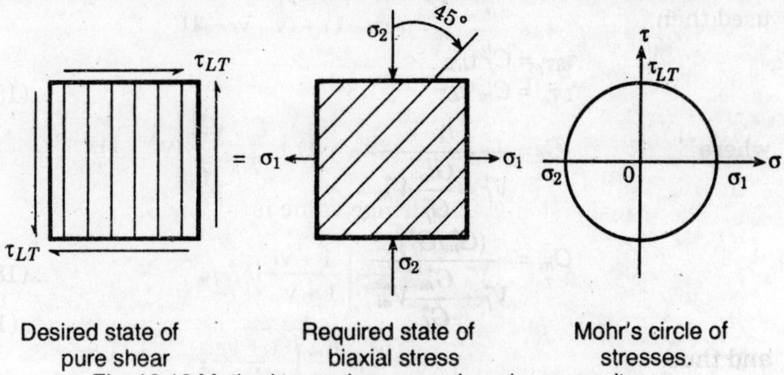

Fig. 18.12 Method to produce pure shear in composites.

f_{LT} :

$$f_{LT} = f_f\, f_m/(V_f f_m + V_m\, f_f) \quad ...(18.54)$$

As shown in Fig. 18.13, this model is quite inadequate.

In the next stress-strain model, the shear strains in the fibers and matrix are equated and equilibrium considered to give :

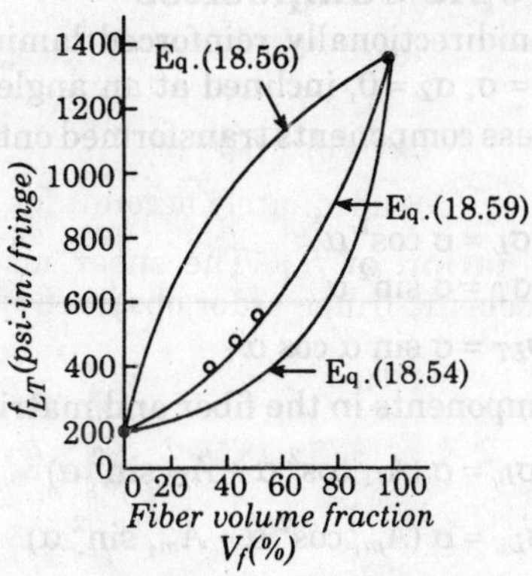

Fig. 18.13 Shear material fringe value f_{LT} as a function of V_f.

$$\gamma_{LT} = \gamma_f = \gamma_m \quad ...(18.55)$$

$$\gamma_{LT} = \tau_f\, V_f + \tau_m V_m$$

Using Eqs. (18.55) and (18.35) together with $\tau = G\gamma$, we get

$$f_{LT} = \frac{\left[V_f + \frac{G_m}{G_f} V_m\right] f_f f_m}{V_f f_m + V_m f_f \frac{G_m}{G_f}} \qquad \text{...(18.56)}$$

From Fig. 18.13 it may be seen that Eq. (18.56) over estimates the results. If the modified moduli G_m^* and G_f^* as defined in Eq. (18.47) are used then

$$\tau_{LT_f} = C_f \tau_{LT}$$
$$\tau_{LT_m} = C_m \tau_{LT} \qquad \text{...(18.57)}$$

where
$$C_f = \frac{1}{V_f^* + \frac{G_m^*}{G_f^*} V_m^*}$$
$$C_m = \frac{(G_m^*/G_f^*)}{V_f^* + \frac{G_m^*}{G_f^*} V_m^*} \qquad \text{...(18.58)}$$

and thus
$$f_{LT} = \frac{[V_f^* + (G_m^*/G_f^*) V_m^*] f_f f_m}{V_f f_m + V_m f_f (G_m^*/G_f^*)} \qquad \text{...(18.59)}$$

The results for f_{LT} from Eq. (18.59) compare very closely with the experimental observations as shown in Fig. 18.13.

18.6 Stress-optic Law for Orthotropic Composites

Consider a unidirectionally reinforced laminate with a uniaxial state of stress $\sigma_1 = \sigma$, $\sigma_2 = 0$, inclined at an angle α to the direction of the fibers. The stress components transformed onto the axes of material symmetry are :

$$\sigma_L = \sigma \cos^2 \alpha$$
$$\sigma_T = \sigma \sin^2 \alpha \qquad \text{...(18.60)}$$
$$\sigma_{LT} = \sigma \sin \alpha \cos \alpha$$

The stress components in the fiber and matrix are :

$$\sigma_{L_f} = \sigma (A_{f1} \cos^2 \alpha + A_{f2} \sin^2 \alpha)$$
$$\sigma_{L_m} = \sigma (A_{m_1} \cos^2 \alpha + A_{m_2} \sin^2 \alpha)$$
$$\sigma_{T_f} = \sigma (B_{f_1} \cos^2 \alpha + B_{f2} \sin^2 \alpha)$$
$$\sigma_{T_m} = \sigma (B_{m1} \cos^2 \alpha + B_{m2} \sin^2 \alpha)$$
$$\tau_{LT_f} = C_f \sigma \sin \alpha \cos \alpha$$
$$\tau_{LT_m} = C_m \sigma \sin \alpha \cos \alpha \qquad \text{...(18.61)}$$

The principal stress differences S_f and S_m may be expressed as :

$$S_f = \sigma\,[(A_f \cos^2\alpha - B_f \sin^2\alpha)^2 + C_f^2 \sin^2 2\alpha]^{1/2}$$
$$S_m = \sigma\,[(A_m \cos^2\alpha - B_m \sin^2\alpha)^2 + C_m^2 \sin^2 2\alpha]^{1/2} \quad \text{...(18.62)}$$

where $A_f = A_{f1} - B_{f1},\ B_f = B_{f2} - A_{f2}$

$$A_m = A_{m1} - B_{m1},\ B_m = B_{m2} - A_{m2}$$

Substituting Eqs. (18.62) in Eq. (18.35), we get the following expression for the material fringe value.

$$\frac{1}{f_\alpha} = \frac{V_f}{f_f}[(A_f \cos^2\alpha - B_f \sin^2\alpha)^2 + C_f^2 \sin^2 2\alpha]^{1/2} + \frac{V_m}{f_m}[(A_m \cos^2\alpha - B_m \sin^2\alpha)^2 + C_m^2 \sin^2 2\alpha]^{1/2} \quad \text{...(18.63)}$$

This result predicts the optical response of a unidirectional orthotropic material by the simple relation

$$N = \frac{\sigma h}{f_\alpha}.$$

According to Pih and Knight

$$A_f = 1/[V_f + (E_m/E_f)]\,V_m,$$
$$B_f = 1/2V_f$$
$$A_m = (E_m/E_f)/[V_f + (E_m/E_f)\,V_m]$$
$$B_m = \frac{1}{2\,V_m}$$
$$C_f = \frac{1}{2\,V_f},\ C_m = \frac{1}{2\,V_m} \quad \text{...(18.64)}$$

The values of f_α predicted by using these constants has been found to be signifcantly lower than the experimental results. Dally and Prabhakaran modified Sampson's components of birefringence as :

$$N_L = \frac{\sigma_L h}{f_L},\ N_T = \frac{\sigma_T h}{f_T}$$
$$N_{LT} = \frac{2\tau_{LT} h}{f_{LT}} \quad \text{...(18.65)}$$

By using the Mohr's circle of birefringence leads to

$$N^2 = (N_L - N_T)^2 + (N_{LT})^2 \quad \text{...(18.66)}$$

Combining Eqs. (18.60), (18.65) and (18.66) with the relation

$$N = \frac{\sigma h}{f_\alpha}$$

leads to Sampson's result for uniaxial loading

$$\left(\frac{1}{f_\alpha}\right)^2 = \left(\frac{\cos^2\alpha}{f_L} - \frac{\sin^2\alpha}{f_T}\right)^2 + \frac{\sin^2 2\alpha}{f_{LT}^2} \quad \text{...(18.67)}$$

It has been found that Eqs. (18.63) and (18.67) are in close proximity. The difference between the results obtained from Sampson's analogy and stress proportioning can be written as :

$$\left(\frac{1}{f_\alpha}\right)^2_{(18.67)} (1+\eta) = \left(\frac{1}{f_\alpha}\right)^2_{(18.63)} \qquad \text{...(18.68)}$$

where subscripts indicate equation number and η is a difference term. Eq. (18.68) can also be expressed as :

$$\left(\frac{1}{f_\alpha}\right)^2_{(18.63)} = \left(\frac{1}{f_\alpha}\right)^2_{(18.67)} + R \qquad \text{...(18.69)}$$

where R is a correction term given by

$$R = \left(\frac{2\,V_m\,V_f}{f_f\,f_m}\right)\Big\{\sin^2\alpha\cos^2\alpha\,(A_m B_f + A_f B_m) - A_m A_f \cos^4\alpha - B_m B_f \sin^4\alpha - C_m C_f \sin^2 2\alpha + [(A_f\cos^2\alpha - B_f\sin^2\alpha)^2 + C_f^2\sin^2 2\alpha]^{1/2}\,[(A_m\cos^2\alpha - B_m\sin^2\alpha)^2 + C_m^2\sin^2 2\alpha]^{1/2}\Big\} \qquad \text{...(18.70)}$$

and

$$\eta = \frac{R}{\left(\frac{1}{f_\alpha}\right)^2_{(18.87)}} \qquad \text{...(18.71)}$$

The error introduced by using Sampson's simple relation is generally low and may be used for all practical purposes.

For bidirectional laminates also Sampson's stress-optic law can be used by choosing the L-axis to coincide with the warp direction and T axis along the fill direction.

Example 18.1 *Calculate the material fringe values for a composite material the properties of whose constituents are given below :*

Material	*Material fringe value, f kNm²/m/fringe*	*Modulus of elasticity, E GPa*	*Modulus of rigidity, G GPa*	*Poisson's ratio, ν*
Fibers (E-glass)	*38*	*72*	*30*	*0.20*
Matrix (Polyester)	*5.4*	*4.05*	*1.5*	*0.35*

$$V_f = 0.40,\ \alpha = 30°.$$

Solution. Longitudinal material-fringe value

$$f_L = \frac{\left[V_f + V_m \dfrac{E_m}{E_f}\left(\dfrac{1+\nu_f}{1+\nu_m}\right)\right] f_f f_m}{V_f f_m + V_m f_f \dfrac{E_m}{E_f}\left(\dfrac{1+\nu_f}{1+\nu_m}\right)}$$

$$= \frac{\left[0.4 + 0.6\,\dfrac{4.05}{72}\left(\dfrac{1+0.20}{1+0.35}\right)\right] 38 \times 5.4 \times 10^6}{0.4 \times 5.4 \times 10^3 + 0.6 \times 38 \times 10^3 \times \dfrac{4.05}{72}\left(\dfrac{1+0.20}{1+0.35}\right)}$$

$$= 26.745 \text{ kN/m}^2\text{/m/fringe}$$

Transverse material-fringe value

$$f_T = \frac{\left[V_f^* + V_m^* \dfrac{E_m^*}{E_f^*}\left(\dfrac{1+\nu_f}{1+\nu_m}\right)\right] f_f f_m}{V_f f_m + V_m f_f \dfrac{E_m^*}{E_f^*}\left(\dfrac{1+\nu_f}{1+\nu_m}\right)}$$

where $$E_m^* = \frac{E_m}{(1-\nu_m^2)} = \frac{4.05}{1-(0.35)^2}$$

$$= 4.6154 \text{ GPa}$$

$$E_f^* = \frac{E_m^* + 2V_f^*\,(E_f - E_m^*)}{1 + [2V_f^*\,(1-2V_f^*)/E_m^*\,E_f]\,[(E_f - E_m^*)^2 - (\nu_m E_f - \nu_f E_m^*)^2]}$$

$$V_f^* = \sqrt{V_f/\pi} = \sqrt{\frac{0.4}{\pi}} = 0.3568$$

$$V_m^* = 1 - V_f^* = 0.6432$$

$$E_f^* = \frac{4.6154 + 2 \times 0.3568\,(72 - 4.6154)}{1 + \left[\dfrac{2 \times 0.3568\,(1 - 2 \times 0.3568)}{4.6154 \times 72}\right][(72 - 4.6154)^2 - (0.35 \times 72 - 0.2 \times 4.6154)^2]}$$

$$= 15.3644 \text{ GPa}$$

$$f_T = \frac{\left[0.3568 + 0.6432 \times \dfrac{4.6154}{15.3644}\left(\dfrac{1+0.20}{1+0.35}\right)\right] 28 \times 5.4 \times 10^6}{0.4 \times 5.4 \times 10^3 + 0.6 \times 38 \times 10^3 \times \dfrac{4.6154}{15.3644}\left(\dfrac{1+0.20}{1+0.35}\right)}$$

$$= 13.15 \text{ kN/m}^2\text{/m/fringe}$$

Shear material fringe values

$$f_{LT} = \frac{\left[V_f^* + \frac{G_m^*}{G_f^*} V_m^*\right] f_f f_m}{V_f f_m + V_m f_f \frac{G_m^*}{G_f^*}}$$

$$G_m^* = G_m/[1 - 2\nu_m^2/(1 - \nu_m)]$$
$$= 1.5/[1 - 2(0.35)^2/(1 - 0.35)]$$
$$= 2.4074 \text{ GPa}$$

$$G_f^* = G_m^* G_f/[G_f + 2V_f^* (G_m^* - G_f)]$$
$$= \frac{2.4074 \times 30}{[30 + 2 \times 0.3568 (2.4074 - 30)]}$$
$$= 7.0051 \text{ GPa}$$

$$f_{LT} = \frac{\left[0.3568 + \frac{2.4074}{7.0051} \times 0.6432\right] 38 \times 5.4 \times 10^6}{\left(0.4 \times 5.4 + 0.6 \times 38 \times \frac{2.4074}{7.0051}\right) \times 10^3}$$

$$= 11.86 \text{ kN/m}^2\text{/m/fringe}$$

According to Sampson

$$\left(\frac{1}{f_\alpha}\right)^2 = \left(\frac{\cos^2\alpha}{f_L} - \frac{\sin^2\alpha}{f_T}\right)^2 + \frac{\sin^2 2\alpha}{f_{LT}^2}$$
$$= \left(\frac{0.75}{26.745} - \frac{0.25}{13.15}\right)^2 + \frac{0.75}{(11.86)^2}$$
$$= 5.67027 \times 10^{-3}$$
$$f_\alpha = 13.28 \text{ kN/m}^2\text{/m/fringe}$$

According to Dally and Prabhakaran

$$\frac{1}{f_\alpha} = \frac{V_f}{f_f} [(A_f \cos^2\alpha - B_f \sin^2\alpha)^2 + C_f^2 \sin^2 2\alpha]^{1/2}$$
$$+ \frac{V_m}{f_m} [(A_m \cos^2\alpha - B_m \sin^2\alpha)^2 + C_m^2 + \sin^2 2\alpha]^{1/2}$$

$$A_{f1} = \left[\frac{V_m}{V_f} (\nu_m \nu_f - 1) + \frac{E_f}{E_m} (\nu_m^2 - 1)\right] \Big/ a$$

$$a = 2V_m (\nu_m \nu_f - 1) + \frac{E_f V_f}{E_m} (\nu_m^2 - 1) + \frac{E_m}{E_f} \frac{V_m^2}{V_f} (\nu_f^2 - 1)$$

$$= 2 \times 0.6\,(0.35 \times 0.20 - 1) + \frac{72 \times 0.4}{4.05}\,[(0.35)^2 - 1] + \frac{4.05}{72} \times \frac{0.36}{0.4}\,[(0.2)^2 - 1]$$

$$= -6.4002$$

$$A_{f1} = \left[\frac{0.6}{0.4}\,(0.35 \times 0.2 - 1) + \frac{72}{4.05}\,\{(0.35)^2 - 1\}\right] \Big/ (-6.4002)$$

$$= 2.6554$$

$$A_{m1} = \left[\frac{E_m}{E_f} \cdot \frac{V_m}{V_f}\,(\nu_f^2 - 1) + (\nu_m \nu_f - 1)\right] \Big/ a$$

$$= \left[\frac{4.05}{72} \times \frac{0.6}{0.4}\,\{(0.2)^2 - 1 + (0.35 \times 0.2 - 1)\right] \Big/ (-6.4002)$$

$$= 0.1579$$

$$B_{f1} = \left[\frac{V_m}{V_f}\,(V_m - \nu_f)\right] \Big/ a$$

$$= \left[\frac{0.6}{0.4}\,(0.35 - 0.2)\right] \Big/ (-6.4002)$$

$$= -0.0351$$

$$B_{m1} = (\nu_f - \nu_m)/a$$

$$= (0.20 - 0.35)/(-6.4002)$$

$$= 0.0234$$

$$C_f = \frac{1}{V_f^* + \dfrac{G_m^*}{G_f^*}\,V_m^*}$$

$$= \frac{1}{0.3568 + \dfrac{2.4074}{7.0051} \times 0.6432} = 1.7305$$

$$C_m = \frac{G_m^*/G_f^*}{V_f^* + \dfrac{G_m^*}{G_f^*}\,V_m^*}$$

$$= \frac{2.4074/7.0051}{0.3568 + \dfrac{2.4074}{7.0051} \times 0.6432}$$

$$= 0.5947$$

$$A_f = A_{f1} - B_{f1} = 2.6554 + 0.0351 = 2.6905$$

$$A_m = A_{m1} - B_{m1} = 0.1579 - 0.0234 = 0.1345$$

$$a^* = 2V_m^* (\nu_m \nu_f - 1) + \frac{E_f^* V_f^*}{E_m^*} (\nu_m^2 - 1) + \frac{E_m^* V_m^{*2}}{E_f^* V_f^*} (\nu_f^2 - 1)$$

$$= 2 \times 0.6432 (0.35 \times 0.20 - 1) + \frac{15.3644}{4.6154}$$

$$\times 0.3568 [(0.35)^2 - 1] + \frac{4.6154}{15.3644} \times \frac{(0.6432)^2}{0.3568} \times (-0.96)$$

$$= -2.1193$$

$$A_{f2} = \left[\frac{V_m^*}{V_f^*} (\nu_m - \nu_f) \right] \Big/ a^*$$

$$= \left[\frac{0.6432}{0.3568} (0.35 - 0.20) \right] \Big/ (-2.1193)$$

$$= -0.1276$$

$$A_{m2} = \frac{\nu_f - \nu_m}{a^*} = \frac{0.20 - 0.35}{-2.1193} = 0.0708$$

$$B_{f2} = \left[\frac{V_m^*}{V_f^*} (\nu_m \nu_f - 1) + \frac{E_f^*}{E_m^*} (\nu_m^2 - 1) \right] \Big/ a^*$$

$$= \left[\frac{0.6432}{0.3568} (0.35 \times 0.2 - 1) + \frac{15.3644}{4.6154} (10.35)^2 - 1 \right] \Big/ (-2.1193)$$

$$= 2.1694$$

$$B_{m_2} = \left[\frac{E_m^*}{E_f^*} \times \frac{V_m^*}{V_f^*} (\nu_f^2 - 1) + (\nu_m \nu_f - 1) \right] \Big/ a^*$$

$$= \left[\frac{4.6154}{15.3644} \times \frac{0.6432}{0.3568} \{(0.2)^2 - 1\} + (0.35 \times 0.2 - 1) \right] (-2.1193)$$

$$= 0.6841$$

$$B_f = B_{f2} - A_{f2} = 2.1694 + 0.1276 = 2.2970$$

$$B_m = B_{m2} - A_{m2} = 0.6841 - 0.0708 = 0.6133$$

$$\frac{1}{f_\alpha} = \frac{0.4}{38} [(2.6905 \times 0.75 - 2.2970 \times 0.25)^2 + (1.7305)^2 \times 0.75]^{1/2}$$

$$+ \frac{0.6}{5.4} [(0.1345 \times 0.75 - 0.6133 \times 0.25)^2 + (0.5947)^2 \times 0.75]^{1/2}$$

$$f_\alpha = 12.59 \text{ kN/m}^2\text{/m/fringe}$$

18.7 Stress Optic Law for Orthotropic Materials in Biaxial Stress Fields

Sampson has proposed the general stress-optic law in the form

$$N = \frac{\sigma_1}{f_L}\left[\left\{\left(\cos^2\alpha + \frac{\sigma_2}{\sigma_1}\sin^2\alpha\right) - \left(\sin^2\alpha + \frac{\sigma_2}{\sigma_1}\cos^2\alpha\right)\right.\right.$$

$$\left.\left.\times \frac{f_L}{f_T}\right\}^2 + \left\{\frac{f_L}{f_{LT}}\left(1 - \frac{\sigma_2}{\sigma_1}\right)\sin 2\alpha\right\}^2\right]^{1/2} \qquad ...(18.72)$$

Regrouping the terms, we get

$$N = \frac{\sigma_1}{f_L}\left[\left\{\left(\cos^2\alpha - \frac{f_L}{f_T}\sin^2\alpha\right) + \frac{\sigma_2}{\sigma_1}\left(\sin^2\alpha - \frac{f_L}{f_T}\cos^2\alpha\right)\right\}^2\right.$$

$$\left. + \left\{\frac{f_L}{f_{LT}}\sin 2\alpha - \frac{\sigma_2}{\sigma_1}\frac{f_L}{f_{LT}}\sin 2\alpha\right\}^2\right]^{1/2} \qquad ...(18.73)$$

For uniaxial stress field $\sigma_2 = 0$ and the material fringe value corresponding to the α – direction can be written as

$$f_\alpha = f_L\left\{\left(\cos^2\alpha - \frac{f_L}{f_T}\sin^2\alpha\right)^2 + \left(\frac{f_L}{f_{LT}}\sin 2\alpha\right)^2\right\}^{-1/2} \qquad ...(18.74)$$

Replacing α by $\left(\frac{\pi}{2} - \alpha\right)$, we get

$$f\left(\frac{\pi}{2} - \alpha\right) = f_L\left[\left(\sin^2\alpha - \frac{f_L}{f_T}\cos^2\alpha\right)^2 + \left(\frac{f_L}{f_{LT}}\sin 2\alpha\right)^2\right]^{-1/2} \qquad ...(18.75)$$

Further regrouping the terms in Eq. (18.73) and making use of eqs. (18.74) and (18.75), we get

$$N = \frac{\sigma_1}{f_L}\left[\frac{f_L^2}{f_\alpha^2} + \frac{f_L^2}{f^2\left(\frac{\pi}{2} - \alpha\right)}\cdot\frac{\sigma_2^2}{\sigma_1^2} + 2\frac{\sigma_2}{\sigma_1}\left[\left(\cos^2\alpha - \frac{f_L}{f_T}\times\sin^2\alpha\right)\right.\right.$$

$$\left.\left.\left(\sin^2\alpha - \frac{f_L}{f_T}\cos^2\alpha\right) - \left(\frac{f_L}{f_{LT}}\sin 2\alpha\right)^2\right]\right]^{1/2} \qquad ...(18.76)$$

Rewriting Eq. (18.76) as

$$N = \frac{\sigma_1}{f_L}\left[\frac{f_L^2}{f_\alpha^2} + \frac{f_L^2}{f^2\left(\frac{\pi}{2} - \alpha\right)}\cdot\frac{\sigma_2^2}{\sigma_1^2} + \frac{2\sigma_2}{\sigma_1}\right.$$

$$\left.\times\left\{\frac{f_L^4}{f_\alpha^2 f^2\left(\frac{\pi}{2} - \alpha\right)} - \left(\frac{f_L}{f_{LT}}\sin 2\alpha\right)^2\left(1 - \frac{f_L}{f_T}\right)^2\right\}^{-12}\right]^{\frac{1}{2}} \qquad ...(18.77)$$

For $\frac{f_L}{f_T} = 1$, as in the case of balanced composites, we get

$$N = \frac{\sigma_1}{f_\alpha} \pm \frac{\sigma_2}{f_{\left(\frac{\pi}{2} - \alpha\right)}}$$

The minus sign is valid as the fringe order is considered always positive. Hence

$$N = \frac{\sigma_1}{f_\alpha} - \frac{\sigma_3}{f_{\left(\frac{\pi}{2} - \alpha\right)}} \quad \text{...(18.79)}$$

The following important conclusions can be drawn :

1. For a balanced composite, Eq. (18.79) is valid and in addition

$$f_\alpha = f_{\left(\frac{\pi}{2} - \alpha\right)}$$

$$N = \frac{1}{f_\alpha} (\sigma_1 - \sigma_2) \quad \text{...(18.80)}$$

Therefore the isochromatic fringe order gives the difference in the principal stresses. Further the zero order isochromatic indicates anisotropic state of stress.

2. For an unbalanced composite, when the principal stress directions and the principal material axes coincide :

(*a*) Eq. (18.79) is valid and the isochromatic fringe order gives a linear function of the principal stresses and not their difference.

(*b*) The zero order isochromatic corresponds to points where the ratio of the principal stresses is equal to the ratio of the corresponding material fringe values.

3. For balanced as well as unbalanced composites in general, Eq. (18.72) is valid and for an isotropic state of stress reduces to

$$N = \sigma_1 \left(\frac{1}{f_L} - \frac{1}{f_T}\right) \quad \text{...(18.81)}$$

which indicates that the fringe order is independent of the angle α.

Example 18.2 *Determine the ratio of the principal stresses in example 8.1 which corresponds to zero order isochromatic fringe. Also calculate* $f_{\left(\frac{\pi}{2} - \alpha\right)}$.

Solution. From Eq. (18.72), we have

$$N = \frac{\sigma_1}{f_L}\left[\left[\left\{\left(\cos^2 \alpha + \frac{\sigma_2}{\sigma_1}\sin^2 \alpha\right) - \left(\sin^2 \alpha + \frac{\sigma_2}{\sigma_1}\cos^2 \alpha\right)\frac{f_L}{f_T}\right]^2 + \left\{\frac{f_L}{f_{LT}}\left(1 - \frac{\sigma_2}{\sigma_1}\right)\sin 2\alpha\right\}^2\right]^{1/2}$$

$$0 = \frac{\sigma_1}{26.745}\left[\left\{(0.75 + x \times 0.25) - (0.25 + x \times 0.75)\,\frac{26.745}{13.15}\right\}^2 + \left\{\frac{26.745}{11.86}\,(1-x)\,\frac{\sqrt{3}}{2}\right\}^2\right]^{1/2}$$

where $\qquad x = \sigma_2/\sigma_1$

or $\qquad x = 0.68$

$$f_{\left(\frac{\pi}{2}-\alpha\right)} = f_L\left\{\left(\sin^2\alpha - \frac{f_L}{f_T}\cos^2\alpha\right)^2 + \left(\frac{f_L}{f_{LT}}\sin 2\alpha\right)^2\right\}^{1/2}$$

$$= 26.745\left\{\left(0.25 - \frac{26.745}{13.15}\times 0.75\right)^2 + \left(\frac{26.745}{11.86}\times\frac{\sqrt{3}}{2}\right)^2\right\}^{-1/2}$$

$$= 11.47 \text{ kN/m}^2\text{/m fringe}$$

18.8 Interpretation of Isoclinics

In the case of orthotropic model materials, the isochromatic-fringe order does not directly give the difference in principal stresses but only a certain linear function involving them. The separation of the principal stresses may be necessary to obtain sufficient data for design purposes and the information provided by isoclinics may be important.

(*a*) **Uniaxial Stress Fields.** It has been recognised by Pih and Knight as well as Sampson, that the isoclinic fringes under uniaxial loading conditions do not represent the principal stress directions. According to Pih and Knight (Fig. 18.14)

$$\tan 2\theta' = \frac{f_L \sin 2\theta}{f_{LT}\left(\cos^2\theta - \dfrac{f_L}{f_T}\sin^2\theta\right)} \qquad \text{...(18.82)}$$

where $\qquad \theta'$ = angle between the direction of the major principal component of birefringence and the L-direction.

For uniaxial loading ($\sigma_2 = 0$), the strain components referred to the L-T axes are given by

$$\varepsilon_1 = \frac{\sigma_1}{E_1} \qquad \text{...(18.83)}$$

$$\varepsilon_2 = -\frac{\nu_{12}}{E_1}\sigma_1 \qquad \text{...(18.84)}$$

$$\gamma_{12} = -\frac{m_1}{E_L}\sigma_1 \qquad \text{...(18.85)}$$

where $\dfrac{1}{E_1} = \dfrac{\cos^4\theta}{E_L} + \dfrac{\sin^4\theta}{E_T} + \dfrac{1}{4}\sin^2 2\theta\left(\dfrac{1}{G_{LT}} - \dfrac{2\nu_{LT}}{E_L}\right)$

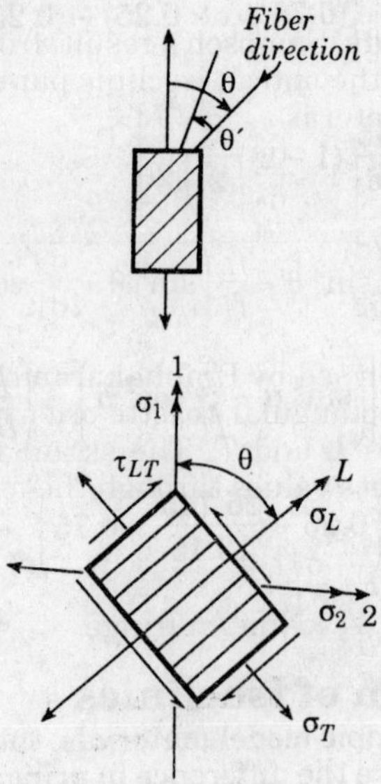

θ′ = optical isoclinic parameter.
θ = physical isoclinic.
Fig. 18.14 Co-ordinate axes and stress notation.

$$m_1 = \sin 2\theta \left[\nu_{LT} + \frac{E_L}{E_T} - \frac{E_L}{2G_{LT}} - \cos^2\theta \left(1 + 2\,\nu_{LT} + \frac{E_L}{E_T} - \frac{E_L}{G_{LT}} \right) \right]$$

$$\nu_{12} = \frac{E_1}{E_L} \left[\nu_{LT} - \frac{1}{4}\sin^2 2\theta \left(1 + 2\nu_{LT} + \frac{E_L}{E_T} - \frac{E_L}{G_{LT}} \right) \right]$$

The angle between the major principal strain and the L-axis, θ_ε is given by

$$\tan 2\theta_\varepsilon = \frac{m_1 \varepsilon_1}{E_L(1 + \nu_{12})} \qquad ...(18.86)$$

It has been found that the principal strain angles are a closer approximation to the optical isoclinic parameters than the principal stress angles. This has promoted some investigations to propose that the isoclinics represent the principal strain directions in the composite model.

The angle between the major principal stress or strain in the fibers and the L-axis, θ_f is given by

$$\tan 2\theta_f = \frac{C_f \sin 2\theta}{(Af_1 - Bf_1)\cos^2\theta + (Af_2 - Bf_2)\sin^2\theta} \qquad ...(18.87)$$

and the corresponding angle for the matrix, θ_m is given by

$$\tan 2\theta_m = \frac{C_m \sin 2\theta}{(A_{m_1} - B_{m_1})\cos^2\theta + (A_{m_2} - B_{m_2})\sin^2\theta} \qquad ...(18.88)$$

where A_{f1}, B_{f1}, etc. are the constants as defined in Art. 8.5.

(*b*) **Biaxial Stress Fields.** Sampson's result, from the Mohr circle of birefringence concept for the optical isoclinic parameter in terms of the physical isoclinic parameter is

$$\tan 2\theta' = \frac{f_L\left(1-\frac{\sigma_2}{\sigma_1}\right)\sin 2\theta}{f_{LT}\left[\cos^2\theta+\frac{\sigma_2}{\sigma_1}\sin^2\theta-\frac{f_L}{f_T}\left(\sin^2\theta+\frac{\sigma_2}{\sigma_1}\cos^2\theta\right)\right]} \quad ...(18.89)$$

Experiments were performed by Prabhakaran on a reinforced circular disc by cementing a rectangular rosette oriented with respect to the material symmetry axes L and T. The strain readings could be directly connected to the stress values through the following equations

$$\varepsilon_L = \frac{\sigma_L}{E_L} - \frac{\nu_{LT}}{E_T}\sigma_T$$

$$\varepsilon_T = \frac{\sigma_T}{E_T} - \frac{\nu_{LT}}{E_T}\sigma_L$$

$$\gamma_{LT} = \frac{\tau_{LT}}{G_{LT}} \quad ...(18.90)$$

It was seen that Sampson's predictions for the optical isoclinic parameter is good for the case of biaxial stress fields also.

18.9 Strain Optic Law

The classical strain-optic law for isotropic photoelastic materials is

$$\varepsilon_1 - \varepsilon_2 = \frac{nf_\varepsilon}{h} = Nf_\varepsilon \quad ...(18.91)$$

The principal strains may be expressed in terms of the strain components in an arbitrary co-ordinate system $x - y$.

$$\varepsilon_{1,2} = \frac{\varepsilon_x+\varepsilon_y}{2} \pm \sqrt{\left(\frac{\varepsilon_x-\varepsilon_y}{2}\right)^2 - \left(\frac{\gamma_{xy}}{2}\right)^2} \quad ...(18.92)$$

Hence $\quad \varepsilon_1 - \varepsilon_2 = \sqrt{(\varepsilon_x-\varepsilon_y)^2+\gamma_{xy}^2} \quad ...(18.93)$

The fringe order N can, therefore, be expressed as a function of the general strain components

$$N = \frac{1}{f_\varepsilon}\sqrt{(\varepsilon_x-\varepsilon_y)^2+\gamma_{xy}^2} \quad ...(18.94)$$

or $$N^2 = \left(\frac{\varepsilon_x-\varepsilon_y}{f_\varepsilon}\right)^2 + \left(\frac{\gamma_{xy}}{f_\varepsilon}\right)^2 \quad ...(18.95)$$

For an isotropic material subjected to a state of plane stress, the stress-strain relationship is

$$\varepsilon_x = S_{11}\,\sigma_x + S_{12}\,\sigma_y + S_{16}\,\tau_{xy}$$

$$\varepsilon_y = S_{12}\,\sigma_x + S_{22}\,\sigma_y + S_{26}\,\tau_{xy}$$

$$\gamma_{xy} = S_{16}\,\sigma_x + S_{26}\,\sigma_y + S_{66}\,\tau_{xy} \quad ...(18.96)$$

When the medium possesses a plane of elastic symmetry, S_{16} and S_{26}, the shear-coupling compliance terms, vanish. Therefore

$$(\varepsilon_x - \varepsilon_y)^2 = [(S_{11} - S_{12})\,\sigma_x - (S_{22} - S_{12})\sigma_y]^2 \qquad \text{...(18.97)}$$

$$\gamma_{xy}^2 = (S_{66}\,\tau_{xy})^2 \qquad \text{...(18.98)}$$

Combining Eqs. (18.95), (18.97) and (18.98) yields the new strain-optic law

$$N^2 = \left[\frac{(S_{11} - S_{12})}{f_\varepsilon}\,\sigma_x - \frac{(S_{22} - S_{12})}{f_\varepsilon}\,\sigma_y\right]^2 + \left[\frac{S_{66}\,\tau_{xy}}{f_\varepsilon}\right]^2 \qquad \text{...(18.99)}$$

The stress-optic law is given by

$$N^2 = (N_x - N_y)^2 + N_{xy}^2$$
$$= \left[\frac{\sigma_x}{f_x} - \frac{\sigma_y}{f_y}\right]^2 + \left[\frac{2\tau_{xy}}{f_{xy}}\right]^2 \qquad \text{...(18.100)}$$

Comparing Eqs. (18.99) and (18.100), we find that

$$f_x = \frac{f_\varepsilon}{(S_{11} - S_{12})}$$

$$f_y = \frac{f_\varepsilon}{(S_{22} - S_{12})}$$

$$f_{xy} = \frac{2f_\varepsilon}{S_{66}} \qquad \text{...(18.101)}$$

Now $\quad S_{11} = \dfrac{1}{E_1}\quad S_{12} = -\dfrac{\nu_{12}}{E_1}$

$$S_{12} = \frac{1}{E_2}\quad S_{66} = \frac{1}{G_{12}} \qquad \text{...(18.102)}$$

where $\quad E_1$ = Young's modulus in the fiber direction

E_2 = Young's modulus perpendicular to fiber direction

ν_{12} = Poisson's ratio in fiber direction

G_{12} = Shear modulus

$$= \frac{E_{45^\circ}}{2(1 + \nu_{45^\circ})}$$

At an arbitrary fiber orientation α,

$$\left(\frac{1}{f_x}\right)^2 = \left(\frac{\cos^2\alpha}{f_x} - \frac{\sin^2\alpha}{f_y}\right)^2 + \left(\frac{\sin 2\alpha}{f_{xy}}\right)^2 \qquad \text{...(18.103)}$$

For $\quad \alpha = 45^\circ$, we get

$$\left(\frac{1}{f_{xy}}\right)^2 = \left(\frac{1}{f_{45°}}\right)^2 - \left(\frac{1}{2f_{0°}} - \frac{1}{2f_{90°}}\right)^2 \qquad ...(18.104)$$

Prabhakaran has proposed that

$$f_{\varepsilon_L} = \frac{1 - \nu_{LT}\,\nu_{TL}}{\dfrac{E_L}{f_L} - E_T\dfrac{\nu_{LT}}{f_T}}$$

$$f_{\varepsilon_T} = \frac{1 - \nu_{LT}\,\nu_{TL}}{\dfrac{E_T}{f_T} - E_L\dfrac{\nu_{TL}}{f_L}}$$

$$f_{\gamma LT} = \frac{f_{LT}}{2G_{LT}} \qquad ...(18.105)$$

So that the strain-optic law can be expressed that

$$N = \frac{\varepsilon_1}{f\varepsilon_L}\left\{\left[\left(\cos^2\beta + \frac{\varepsilon_2}{\varepsilon_1}\sin^2\beta\right) - \left(\sin^2\beta + \frac{\varepsilon_2}{\varepsilon_1}\cos^2\beta\right)\frac{f\varepsilon_L}{f\varepsilon_T}\right]^2 + \left[\left(1 - \frac{\varepsilon_2}{\varepsilon_1}\right)\frac{f\varepsilon_L}{f_{\gamma LT}}\sin^2\beta\right]^2\right\}^{1/2} \qquad ...(18.106)$$

where β = angle between the major principal strain and L-direction.

The principal strain direction for isotropic materials is given by

$$\tan 2\phi = \frac{\gamma_{xy}}{\varepsilon_x - \varepsilon_y} \qquad ...(18.107)$$

The stress-strain relation for orthotropic materials in an arbitrary co-ordinate system is

$$\begin{bmatrix}\varepsilon_x\\ \varepsilon_y\\ \gamma_{xy}\end{bmatrix} = \begin{bmatrix}S'_{11} & S'_{12} & S'_{16}\\ S'_{12} & S'_{22} & S'_{26}\\ S'_{16} & S'_{26} & S'_{66}\end{bmatrix}\begin{bmatrix}\sigma_x\\ \sigma_y\\ \tau_{xy}\end{bmatrix} \qquad ...(18.108)$$

where $\sigma_x = \sigma$ and $\sigma_y = \tau_{xy} = 0$ then

$$\varepsilon_x = S'_{11}\,\sigma$$
$$\varepsilon_y = S'_{12}\,\sigma \qquad ...(18.109)$$
$$\gamma_{xy} = S_{16}'\,\sigma$$

Hence the principal strain direction is given by

$$\tan 2\phi = \frac{S'_{16}}{(S'_{11} - S'_{12})} \qquad ...(18.110)$$

where

$$S'_{11} = S_{11}C^4 + (S_{66} + 2S_{12})\,C^2S^2 + S_{22}\,S^4$$

$$= \frac{C^4}{E_1} + \left(-\frac{2\,\nu_{12}}{E_1} + \frac{1}{G_{12}}\right)C^2S^2 + \frac{S^4}{E_2}$$

$$S'_{12} = (S_{11} + S_{22} - S_{66})\,C^2S^2 + S_{12}\,(C^2 + S^2)$$

$$= -\frac{\nu_{12}}{E_1}(C^4 + S^4) + \left(\frac{1}{E_1} + \frac{1}{E_2} + \frac{1}{G_{12}}\right) C^2 S^2$$

$$S'_{16} = (2\,S_{11} - 12\,S_{12} - S_{66})\,SC^3 - (2\,S_{22} - 2\,S_{12} - S_{66})\,S^3C$$

$$= \left(\frac{2}{E_1} - \frac{2\,\nu_{12}}{E_1} - \frac{1}{G_{12}}\right) SC^3 - \left(\frac{2}{E_2} + \frac{2\,\nu_{12}}{E_1} - \frac{1}{G_{12}}\right) S^3C$$

where $C = \cos\theta$

$S = \sin\theta$

Thus $$\tan 2\phi = \frac{A}{B} \qquad \text{...(18.111)}$$

where $A = \left(\frac{1}{E_1} + \frac{2\,\nu_{12}}{E_1} - \frac{1}{G_{12}}\right) SC^3 - \left(\frac{2}{E_2} + 2\,\nu_{12} - \frac{1}{G_{12}}\right) S^3C$

$$B = \frac{C^2}{E_1}(C^2 - S^2) + \frac{\nu_{12}}{E_1}(C^2 - S^2)^2 + \frac{S^2}{E_2}(S^2 - C^2) + \frac{2\,C^2\,S^2}{G_{12}}$$

If $\theta = 45°$

then $C = S = \frac{1}{\sqrt{2}}$ and

$$S'_{11} = \frac{S_{11}}{4} + \frac{S_{66}}{4} + \frac{S_{12}}{2} + \frac{S_{22}}{4}$$

$$S'_{12} = \frac{S_{11}}{4} - \frac{S_{66}}{4} + \frac{S_{12}}{2} + \frac{S_{22}}{4}$$

Subtracting, we get

$$S_{66}' = 2\,(S'_{11} - S'_{12})$$

$$S'_{66} = \frac{1}{G_{12}}$$

$$S'_{11} = \frac{1}{E_{45°}}$$

$$S'_{12} = -\frac{\nu_{45°}}{E_{45°}}$$

$$G_{12} = \frac{E_{45°}}{2\,(1 + \nu_{45°})}$$

Thus, we find that the strain-optic law requires only a single strain-optic coefficient as compared to three in the stress-optic law.

18.9.1 Approximate Strain-optic Law

Agarwal and Chaturvedi have proposed the exact strain-optic law as follows :

$$N = \left[\left(\frac{\varepsilon_L}{f\varepsilon_L} - \frac{\varepsilon_T}{f\varepsilon_T}\right)^2 + \left(\frac{\gamma_{LT}}{f_{\gamma LT}}\right)^2\right]^{1/2} \qquad \text{...(18.112)}$$

and isoclinic angle

$$\phi = \frac{1}{2}\tan^{-1}\left[\frac{\gamma_{LT}/f_{\gamma LT}}{\varepsilon_L/f_{\varepsilon L} - \varepsilon_T/f_{\varepsilon T}}\right] \qquad ...(18.113)$$

Now $\qquad \varepsilon_L = \varepsilon_1 \cos^2\theta + \varepsilon_2 \sin^2\theta$

$$\varepsilon_T = \varepsilon_1 \sin^2\theta + \varepsilon_2 \cos^2\theta$$

$$\gamma_{LT} = (\varepsilon_1 - \varepsilon_2)\sin 2\theta \qquad ...(18.114)$$

where θ is the angle between ε_1 and L axis.

Substituting Eqs. (18.114) in Eqs. (18.112) and (18.113), we get

$$N = \frac{1}{f\varepsilon_L}\left\{\left[\left(\varepsilon_1 - \frac{f\varepsilon_L}{f\varepsilon_T}\varepsilon_2\right) - \sin^2\theta\,(\varepsilon_1 - \varepsilon_2)\left(1 + \frac{f\varepsilon_L}{f\varepsilon_T}\right)\right]^2 + \left[(\varepsilon_1 - \varepsilon_2)\frac{f\varepsilon_L}{f_{\gamma LT}}\sin 2\theta\right]^2\right\}^{1/2} \qquad ...(18.115)$$

$$\phi = \frac{1}{2}\tan^{-1}\left[\frac{(\varepsilon_1 - \varepsilon_2)\dfrac{f\varepsilon_L}{f_{\gamma LT}}\sin 2\theta}{\left(\varepsilon_1 - \dfrac{f\varepsilon_L}{f\varepsilon_T}\varepsilon_2\right) - \sin^2\theta\,(\varepsilon_1 - \varepsilon_2)\left(1 - \dfrac{f\varepsilon_L}{f\varepsilon_T}\right)}\right] \qquad ...(18.116)$$

We find that the principal strains appear as their difference except in one term where ε_2 is multiplied by $f\varepsilon_L/f\varepsilon_T$. If this term is also assumed equal to the principal strain difference, then Eqs. (18.115) and (18.116) can be written as :

$$N = \frac{\varepsilon_1 - \varepsilon_2}{f\varepsilon_L}\left\{\left[1 - \sin^2\theta\left(1 + \frac{f\varepsilon_L}{f\varepsilon_T}\right)\right]^2 + \left(\frac{f\varepsilon_L}{f_{\gamma LT}}\sin 2\theta\right)^2\right\}^{1/2} \qquad ...(18.117)$$

$$\phi = \frac{1}{2}\tan^{-1}\left[\frac{(f_{\varepsilon L}/f_{\gamma LT})\sin 2\theta}{1 - \sin^2\theta\left(1 + \dfrac{f_{\varepsilon L}}{f_{\varepsilon T}}\right)}\right] \qquad ...(18.118)$$

This approximation amounts to assuming $f_{\varepsilon L} = f_{\varepsilon T}$ in one of the terms of these equations. If this approximation is used in the second term also, then

$$N = \frac{\varepsilon_1 - \varepsilon_2}{f_{\varepsilon L}}\left[\cos^2 2\theta + \left(\frac{f_{\varepsilon L}}{f_{\gamma LT}}\right)^2 \sin^2 2\theta\right]^{1/2} \qquad ...(18.119)$$

$$\tan 2\phi = \frac{f_{\varepsilon L}}{f_{\gamma LT}}\tan 2\theta \qquad ...(18.120)$$

18.10 Composite Materials

There are three types of composite materials :

1. Fibrous composites—which consist of fibers in a matrix.
2. Laminated composites—which consist of layers of various materials.
3. Particulate composites—which are composed of particles in a matrix.

Fibrous composites consist of long fibers in various forms embedded in a matrix. The fibers are inherently much stiffer and stronger than the same material in bulk form. The fibers having different properties from the bulk form is due to the more perfect structure of a fiber. The crystals are aligned in the fiber along the fiber axis. Typical properties of commonly used fibers are given in Table 18.1.

Table 18.1 Properties of Fibers and Wires

Fiber or wire	*Density kg/cm³ (kN/m³)*	*Modulus of Elasticity kg/cm² × 10⁻⁶ (GN/m²)*		*Tensile strength kg/cm² × 10⁻³ (GN/m²)*		*Poisson's Ratio*	*Material fringe value kg/cm² /cm/fringe*
Aluminium	0.00268 (26.3)	0.742	(73)	6.3	(1.62)	0.33	
Titanium	0.00469 (46.1)	1.169	(115)	19.6	(1.9)		
Steel	0.0078 (76.6)	2.1	(207)	42	(4.1)	0.30	
E-glass	0.00254 (25.0)	0.735	(72)	35	(3.4)	0.20	38
S-glass	0.00248 (24.4)	0.875	(86)	49	(4.8)	0.17	
Carbon	0.00141 (13.8)	1.89	(190)	17.5	(1.7)		
Beryllium	0.00185 (18.2)	3.08	(300)	17.5	1.7		
Boron	0.00257 (25.2)	4.2	(400)	35	(3.4)		
Graphite	0.00141 (13.8)	2.59	(250)	17.5	(1.7)		

The fibers are bound together to take the form of a structural element which can take loads. The binder material is usually called a matrix. The purpose of the matrix is manifold : support, protection, stress transfer etc. The matrix is of considerably lower density, stiffness and strength than the fibers. The combination of fibers and matrix can have very high strength and stiffness, yet still have low density. Commonly used matrix materials are, epoxy resins and polyesters.

Laminated composites consist of layers of at least two different materials that are bonded together. Laminated fibrous composites are a hybrid class of composites involving both fibrous composites and lamination techniques, commercially known as laminated fiber reinforced composites.

Particulate composites consist of particles of one or more materials suspended in a matrix of another material. This types of composites have become popular under the trade name "Model Tech".

Typical mechanical properties of some composites are given in Table 18.2.

Table 18.2 Properties of Composite Materials

Property	*Glass / epoxy*	*Boron / epoxy*	*Graphite / epoxy*
E_1, GPa	54.6	210	210
E_2, GPa	18.2	21	5.25
ν_{12}	0.25	0.30	0.25
G_{12}, GPa	9.1	7	2.625

A "lamina" is a flat arrangement of unidirectional fibers or woven fibers in a matrix. A "laminate" is a stack of laminate with various orientations of principal material directions in the laminal.

18.11 Manufacture of Composite Materials

The application of photo-orthotropic-elasticity to stress analysis of structures fabricated from composite materials involves the developement of a model which is sufficiently transparent for light to be transmitted in the polariscope. Also, the model material must exhibit the required degree of anisotropy and show an adequate degree of birefringence. The two principal steps in the manufacture of laminated fiber-reinforced composite materials are layup and curing. Layup is the arranging of fibers in laminate and laminae in layers of laminates. Curing is the drying, or polymerization, of the resinous material to form a permanent bond between fibers and between laminae.

There are three principal layup processes for laminated fiber-reinforced composite materials : winding and laying, moulding, and continuous lamination. Winding and laying operations include filament winding, tape laying and cloth winding or wrapping. Filament winding consists of passing a fiber through a liquid resin and then winding it on a mandrel. The fibers are wrapped at different orientations on a mandrel to yield many layers and hence strength and stiffness in many directions. Subsequently, the entire assembly, including the mandrel, is cured after which the mandrel is removed. Tape laying starts with a tape consisting of fibers in a preimpregnated form held together by a removable backing material. The tape is unwound to form the desired shape in the desired orientations of tape layers. Cloth winding or laying begins with preimpregnated cloth which is unrolled and deposited in the desired form and orientation. Cloth winding or laying is more inflexible and inefficient than filament winding or tape laying in achieving specified strength and stiffness.

Moulding operations, which are less commonly used, begin with hand or automated deposition of preimpregnated fibers in layers. Subsequently, the layers are compressed under elevated temperature to form the final laminate.

Continuous lamination involves the bonding of sheets of laminae with subsequent application of pressure by rolling.

Pih and Knight produced orthotropic model materials with Epon 815 resin and modified E-glass fibers (w-1) by employing wet filament winding with vacuum impregnation. Sampson used HTS glass roving and Dow 332 epoxy resin and employed dry-filament winding followed by immersion in a resin bath under vacuum. Dally and Prabhakaran has described a procedure to produce large sheets of material with either unidirectional or bidirectional reinforcement, which is sufficiently transparent for photoelastic applications. Glass fabric, style 7500, containing E-glass fibers with a Volan finish was used for reinforcement and Paraplex P444A was used as a base resin which could be blended with styrene from 10 to 60 per cent to produce a matrix material with a range of refractive index between 1.529 to 1.570. The refractive index of E-Glass is 1.548 ± 0.003. A blending containing 30 percent styrene (with n = 1.548) was cured with 0.5 percent benzoyl peroxide and 0.5 per cent methyl ethyl ketone peroxide to provide the matrix material.

After removing the fill fibres the glass fabric was soaked in a resin bath to obtain impregnation. A laminate was formed by aligning several plies of fabric and then this wet layup was sandwiched between two sheets of mylar film. The laminate was rolled to carefully remove all of the entrapped air and placed between heavy plates to prevent air from reentry. The laminate was initially cured in a platen press at 10 psi for 2 hr at 67°C and then the temperature was increased to 100°C for 4 hrs to complete the cure.

An orthotropic model in the form of a plate can be made by casting epoxy resin (Araldite Cy-230, 100 pbw + Hardener Hy-951, 10 pbw) around glass fibres unidirectionally arranged and stretched between the two edges of a frame. The resin matrix is selected to provide a matching refractive index for the glass fibers used (n = 1.55 ± 3%). The volume of fibres going into the composite can be determined by recovering the fibres from the specimen by burning off the resin at around 500°C.

18.12 Numerical Method for Separation of Stresses

Chandrashekhara and Jacob have developed an experimental numerical hybrid technique for obtaining the stress distribution in an orthotropic composite body. This method requires that only boundary stresses are to be obtained experimentally and the interior stresses can be obtained using a numerical method. The numerical solution of two-dimensional orthotropic-compatibility equation can be used for separation of stresses in photo-orthotropic elasticity. The solution of this equation provides a linear relation between normal stresses, whereas the photoelastic data provide another relation between normal stress components and the shear stress.

The basic equations of elasticity as applied to two-dimensional orthotropic composites are :

(*i*) the equilibrium equations

$$\frac{\partial \sigma_x}{\partial x} + \frac{\partial \tau_{xy}}{\partial y} = 0$$

$$\frac{\partial \tau_{xy}}{\partial x} + \frac{\partial \sigma_y}{\partial y} = 0 \qquad \text{...(18.121)}$$

(*ii*) the compatibility equation

$$\frac{\partial^2 \varepsilon_x}{\partial y^2} + \frac{\partial^2 \varepsilon_y}{\partial x^2} = \frac{\partial \gamma_{xy}}{\partial x \partial y} \qquad ...(18.122)$$

The stress-strain relation can be written as

$$\varepsilon_x = \frac{\sigma_x}{E_x} - \frac{\nu_x}{E_y}\sigma_y$$

$$\varepsilon_y = -\frac{\nu_y}{E_x}\sigma_x + \frac{1}{E_y}\sigma_y$$

$$\gamma_{xy} = \frac{1}{G_{xy}}\tau_{xy} \qquad ...(18.123)$$

Due to the symmetry of stress-strain matrix

$$\nu_x E_x = \nu_y E_y \qquad ...(18.124)$$

Eq. (18.122) can be written in terms of stresses in the form

$$\left(\frac{\partial^2}{\partial x^2} + K_1^2 \frac{\partial^2}{\partial y^2}\right)(\sigma_y + K_2^2\sigma_x) = 0 \qquad ...(18.125)$$

where $K_1^2 + K_2^2 = \dfrac{E_y}{G_{xy}} - 2\nu_x$

and $K_1^2 \,.\, K_2^2 = E_y/E_x$ ...(18.126)

When the orthotropic constants $K_1 = K_2 = 1$, Eq. (18.125) represents the isotropic case.

The compatibility Eq. (18.125) can be written as :

$$\left(\frac{\partial^2}{\partial x^2} + K_1^2 \frac{\partial^2}{\partial y^2}\right) S = 0 \qquad ...(18.127)$$

where S is the stress parameter given by

$$S = \sigma_y + K_2^2 \sigma_x \qquad ...(18.128)$$

Eq. (18.127) can be put in finite difference form using the standard procedure. The recurring relation for S at any interior mesh point 0 (i, j) as shown in Fig. 18.15 becomes

$$S_{i,j} = [S_{i+1,j} + S_{i-1,j} + (S_{i,j+1} + S_{i,j-1})K_1^2]/2(1 + K_1^2) \qquad ...(18.129)$$

Along the free boundaries, the photoelastic data give the value of the principal stresses. On loaded boundaries, one of the principal stresses is known and, hence, from the photo-elastic data, the stress components can be calculated. The boundary value of S can be calculated using Eq. (18.128). Now Eq. (18.129) can be used to calculate the value of S in the interior, with the help of an iteration program. The photoelastic data will provide a relation between the normal stresses as

$$\frac{\sigma_x}{f_x} - \frac{\sigma_y}{f_y} = N\cos 2\theta' \qquad ...(18.130)$$

where θ' is the optical (observed) isoclinic

or $K\sigma_x - \sigma_y = Nf_y \cos 2\theta'$ ...(18.131)

where $\quad K = f_y / f_x$

Now, the values of σ_x and σ_y can be calculated knowing the value of S from

$$\sigma_x = \frac{S + N f_y \cos 2\theta'}{K_2^2 + K} \qquad \text{...(18.132)}$$

and
$$\sigma_y = S - K_2^2 \sigma_x \qquad \text{...(18.133)}$$

$$\tau_{xy} = \frac{N f_{xy}}{2} \sin 2\theta' \qquad \text{...(18.134)}$$

The isochromatics are measured along the boundaries and along the axes of symmetry if any. Along load free boundaries, one of the principal stresses is zero and the other is calculated from the isochromatic-fringe order. This is done using the formula

$$\sigma_\alpha = N f_\alpha \qquad \text{...(18.135)}$$

where f_α is given by

$$\left(\frac{1}{f_\alpha}\right)^2 = \left(\frac{\cos^2 \alpha}{f_x} - \frac{\sin^2 \alpha}{f_y}\right)^2 + \frac{\sin^2 2x}{(f_{xy})^2} \qquad \text{...(18.136)}$$

and α indicates the direction of stresses with respect to the principal axes of orthotropy. Where the boundaries are parallel to the principal axes of orthotropy, the boundary stresses are calculated from

$$\sigma_x = N f_x \text{ and } \sigma_y = N f_y \qquad \text{...(18.137)}$$

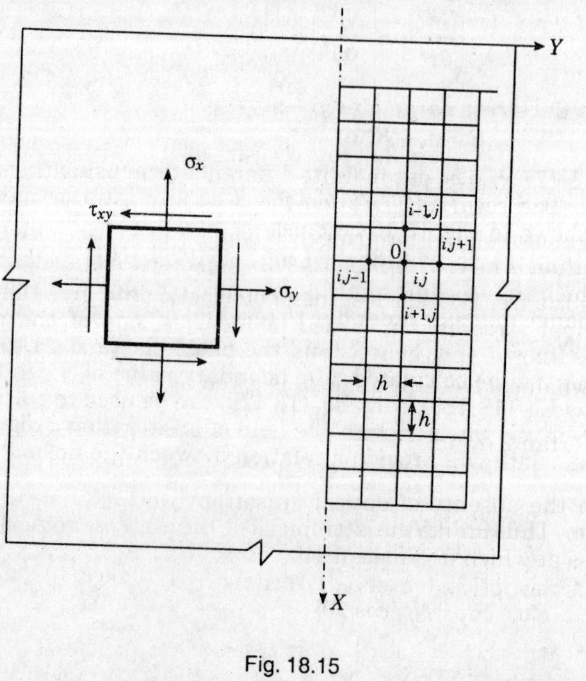

Fig. 18.15

On loaded portion of boundary, one of the normal stresses is known from the loading and the other is calculated using Eq. (18.131).

Along the axes of symmetry, the following conditions are made use of :

$$\left.\begin{array}{l}\text{Along the axis } x = 0,\ S_{i,j-1} = S_{i,j+1} \\ \text{and, along the axis } y = 0,\ S_{i-1,j} = S_{i+1,j}\end{array}\right] \quad ...(18.138)$$

18.13 Effect of Residual Birefringence

Residual birefringence is produced in the fabrication of fibre reinforced materials. This is attributed to different optical and thermal characteristics of matrix and reinforcements. Pipes and Dally have discussed the qualitative effect of residual birefringence on the isoclinic angle. Mittal has presented a linear strain or stress birefringence law, based on Toupin's theory of deformable dielectrics and including residual birefringence. According to Mittal, the fringe order N_α for a uniaxial state of stress σ, inclined at an angle α with the reinforcement direction is given by :

$$N_\alpha = \sigma \left[\left\{ \frac{N_r}{\sigma} + \frac{\cos^2 \alpha}{(f_\sigma)_x} - \frac{\sin^2 \alpha}{(f_\sigma)_y} \right\}^2 + \left(\frac{\sin 2\alpha}{(f_\sigma)_{xy}} \right)^2 \right]^{1/2} \quad ...(18.139)$$

where N_r is the residual birefringence. This formula is similar to Sampson's result provided $\frac{N_r}{\sigma}$ is small compared to other terms.

The isoclinic angle, by considering residual birefringence becomes

$$\tan 2\alpha_n = \pm \left[\frac{1}{(f_\sigma)_{xy}} \sin 2\alpha \right] \left[\frac{N_r}{\sigma} + \frac{\cos^2 \alpha}{(f_\sigma)_x} - \frac{\sin^2 \alpha}{(f_\sigma)_y} \right]^{-1} \quad ...(18.140)$$

when σ is large, then

$$\tan 2\alpha_n = \pm \frac{\sin 2\alpha}{(f_\sigma)_{xy}} \left[\frac{\cos^2 \alpha}{(f_\sigma)_x} - \frac{\sin^2 \theta}{(f_\sigma)_y} \right]^{-1}$$

The effect of residual birefringence is more pronounced when the fiber orientation is near 0° or 90°. This discrepancy is dependent on the stress at which the isoclinic angle is measured, and is wider at lower stresses. Change in fringe order due to residual birefringence is within $+N_r$ and $-N_r$.

The mechanical isoclinic angle α_ε is given by

$$\tan 2\alpha_\varepsilon = \pm \frac{2\varepsilon_{xy}}{\varepsilon_{xx} - \varepsilon_{yy}} - \frac{S_{66} \sin 2\alpha}{S_{11} \cos^2 \alpha - S_{22} \sin^2 \alpha - S_{12} \cos 2\alpha}$$

Only in the absence of optical anisotropy and residual birefringence, $\alpha_n = \alpha_\varepsilon$. Thus unlike the isotropic case, the isoclinic angle depends on the stress at which it is measured.

18.14 Experimental Determination of the Material Fringe Values

To determine the longitudinal, transverse and shear material fringe values f_L, f_T and f_{LT} respectively for the composite material, a circular disc of approximately 75 mm diameter and 4 mm thick is prepared. Strain gauges in the form of a rectangular rosette are cemented on the disc along the diameter parallel to the reinforcement direction and at 45° as shown in Fig. 18.16. The fringe order and strain gauges output is measured at the centre of disc as a function of load, which is applied in transverse, parallel and 45° direction to the reinforcement direction.

Then for transverse loading

$$\frac{\sigma_L}{f_L} - \frac{\sigma_T}{f_T} = N$$

or $$\frac{1}{f_L}\left(\frac{\sigma_L}{N}\right) - \frac{1}{f_T}\left(\frac{\sigma_T}{N}\right) = 1$$

and for parallel loading

$$\frac{\sigma_T}{f_T} - \frac{\sigma_L}{f_L} = N$$

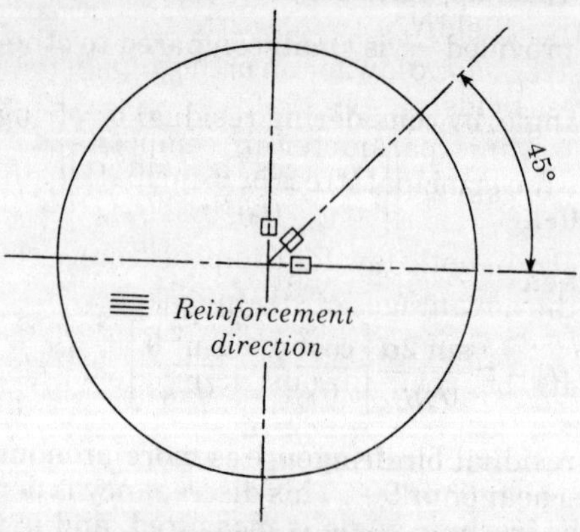

Fig. 18.16

or $$\frac{1}{f_T}\left(\frac{\sigma_T}{N}\right) - \frac{1}{f_L}\left(\frac{\sigma_L}{N}\right) = 1$$

σ_L and σ_T are computed from the strain values by means of the orthotropic stress strain relations. Thus f_L and f_T can be calculated.

Assuming $f_{LT} \approx f_{45^\circ}$, we can determine the shear material-fringe value from 45° loading, as

$$N = \frac{1}{f_{45^\circ}}(\sigma_1 - \sigma_2)$$

Thus $$f_{45^\circ} = \left(\frac{\sigma_1 - \sigma_2}{N}\right)$$

By knowing the stress difference and fringe order at the centre of the disc, f_{45° can be calculated.

QUIZ QUESTIONS

1. Differentiate between a lamina and a laminate.
2. What do you understand by a composite material ?
3. Differentiate between GFRP and CFRP.
4. When do we prefer composite materials over conventional materials ?
5. What are the various experimental methods used for the analysis of stresses in composite materials ?
6. What do you understand by an orthotropic material ?
7. How many independent elastic constants are there for an orthotropic material ?
8. How many stress-optic constants are there for an orthotropic material ?
9. Which techniques are generally followed to determine the material-fringe values for an orthotropic material ?
10. Write the stress-optic law for an orthotropic composite under uniaxial stress fields.
11. Write the stress-optic law for an orthotropic composite under biaxial stress fields.
12. Does the isoclinic parameter in composite materials corresponds to the principal stress or principal strain directions? Comment.
13. Write the strain-optic law for composite materials.
14. What are the advantages of strain-optic law over the stress-optic law ?
15. Differentiate between fibrous, laminated and particulate composites.
16. Why the strength of a composite material is much greater than its constituents ?
17. What is the function of the matrix in a composite material?
18. How do you manufacture a composite material ?
19. How do you estimate the volume fractions of the fibers and matrix ?
20. Explain the experimental numerical hybrid technique for stress analysis.

EXERCISES

18.1 Give a brief account of the historical developments in photo-orthotropic elasticity.

18.2 Describe the stress-strain relations for composite materials.

18.3 Explain the procedure of determining the elastic constants for an orthotropic material.

18.4 Derive an expression for the stress-optic law for orthotropic composites.

18.5 Calculate the material fringe value for a composite material the properties of whose constituents are given below :

Material	*Material fringe value, f* $kN/m^2/m/fringe$	*Modulus of Elasticity, E GPa*	Modulus of Rigidity, GPa	*Poisson's Ratio,* ν
Fibers (glass-microspheres)	228	70	30	0.205
Matrix (Polyester)	39	4	1.5	0.345

$V_f = 0.35$, $\alpha = 25°$.

18.6 Derive an expression for the stress-optic law under biaxial stress fields. Discuss the isochromatics obtained by this law.

18.7 How do you interpret the isoclinic parameter in orthotropic materials under uniaxial and biaxial stress fields ?

18.8 Derive an expression for the strain-optic law for composite materials. Why this law is preferred over the stress-optic law?

18.9 How composite materials are manufactured for photoelastic investigations ? Describe briefly.

18.10 Explain the experimental-numerical technique for separation of principal stresses in composite materials. Discuss the advantages of this method.

18.11 Describe the experimental technique to determine the longitudinal, transverse and shear material-fringe values.

18.12 In exercise 8.5, determine the ratio of principal stresses which correspond to zero fringe order.

References

1. Cernosek, J., *"On photoelastic response of composites,"* Exp. Mech., Vol. 15, No. 9, 1975, pp. 354-357
2. Dally, J.W. and Prabhakaran, R., *"Photo-orthotropic elasticity,"* Proc. SESA, Vol. 28, No. 2, 1971, pp. 346-356.
3. Pih, H. and Knight, C.E., *"Photoelastic analysis of an isotropic fiber-reinforced composites,"* J. Comp. Matl., Vol. 3, 1969, p. 94.
4. Pipes, R.B. and Rose, J.L., *"Strain-optic law for a certain class of birefringent composites,"* Proc. SESA, Vol. 31, No. 2, 1974, pp. 355-360.
5. Prabhakaran, R., *"The interpretation of isoclinics in photo-orthotropic elasticity,"* Exp. Mech., Vol. 16, No. 1, 1976, pp. 6-10.
6. Prabhakaran, R., *"On the stress-optic law for orthotropic model materials in biaxial stress fields,"* Exp. Mech., Vol. 15, No. 1, 1975, pp. 29-34.
7. Prabhakaran, R., *"Stress-strain models for photo-orthotropic elasticity,"* J. Aeron. Soc. India.
8. Sampson, R.C., *"A stress-optic law for photoelastic analysis of orthotropic composites"*, Proc. SESA, Vol. 27, No. 1, 1970, pp. 210-215.
9. Sathikh. S. and Prabhakaran, R., *"Discussion of strain-optic law for a certain class of birefringent composites"*, Exp. Mech., Vol. 15, No. 10, 1975, pp. 392-393.
10. Bert, C.W., *"Theory of photoelasticity for birefringent filamentary composites"*, Fiber Science and Technology, Vol. 5, 1972, pp. 165-171.
11. Broutman, L.J. and Krock, R.J., *"Modern composite Materials"*, Addison-Wesley Publishing Co., Reading Mass., (1967).
12. Dally, J.W. and Alfirevic, I., *"Application of Birefringent coating to glass-fiber-reinforced plastic"*, Exp. Mech., Vol. 9, No. 3, March 1969, pp. 97-102.
13. Pipes, R.B. and Dally, J.W., *"On the fiber-reinforced birefringent composite materials,"* Exp. Mech., Vol. 13, No. 8, 1973, pp. 348-349.
14. Calcote, L.R., *"The analysis of laminated Composite structures"*, Van Nostr and Reinhold Company, New York (1969).

15. Prabhakaran, R., *"A strain-optic law for orthotropic model materials"*, AIAA J., Vol. 13, No. 6, 1975, p. 723.
16. Prabhakaran, R., *"Photoelastic analysis of an orthotropic ring under diametral compression"*, AIAA Jnl.. Vol. 11 No. 6, June 1973, pp. 777-778.
17. Jones, R.M., *"Mechanics of Composite Materials,"* McGraw-Hill Kogakusha, Ltd. (1975).
18. McCullough, R.L., *"Concepts of Fiber-Resin Composites"*, Marcel Dekker, New York (1971).
19. Schwartz, R.T. and Schwartz,, H.S. (eds.), *"Fundamental Aspects of Reinforced Plastic Composites"*, Wiley Interscience, (1968).
20. Chaturvedi, S.K. and Agarwal, B.D., *"Brittle coating studies on fibrous composites"*, Strain, Vol. 14, No. 4, Oct. 1978, pp. 131-136.
21. Agarwal, B.D. and Chaturvedi, S.K., *"Improved birefringent composites assessment of photoelastic theories"*, Fibre Science and Technology, Vol. II, No. 6, Nov. 1978, pp. 399-412.
22. Prabhakaran, R., *"Application of brittle coatings to orthotropic materials"*, Fibre Science and Technology, Vol. 12, No. 1, Jan. 1979, pp. 11-19.
23. Lekknitskii, S.G., *"Theory of Elasticity of an Anisotropic Elastic Body"*, Holden—Day, San Francisco, (1963).
24. Knight, C.E., Jr. and Pih, H., *"Shear difference method and application in orthotropic photoelasticity"*, ASME Paper No. 76-Mat-e 1976.
25. Aderholdt, R.W. and Berghaus, D.G., *"Model design and fabrication for stress analysis in multilaminar composites"*, Exp. Mech., Vol. 16, No. 1976, pp. 32-37.
26. Hancock, J., *"Residual streses in the photoelastic analysis of composite materials"*, Strain, Vol. 11, No. 4, Oct. 1975, pp. 174-175.
27. Knight, C.E., Jr. and Pih, H., *"Orthotropic stress-optic law for plane stress photoelasticity of composite materials"*, Fibre Sci., and Tech. Vol. 9, No. 4, Oct. 1976, pp. 297-313.
28. Daniel, I.M., *"Photoelastic investigation of composites"*, Composite Materials, Vol. 2, 1974, pp. 433-439.
29. Berghaus, D.G. and Aderholdt, R.W., *Photoelastic analysis of interlaminar matrix stresses in fibrous composite models"*, Exp. Mech., Vol. 15, No. 11, Nov. 1975, pp. 409-417.

30. Tyson, W.R. and Davies, G.J., *"A photoelastic study of the shear stresses associated with the transfer of stress during fiber reinforcement"*, Brit J. Appl. Phys., Vol. 16, 1965, pp. 199-205.

31. MacLaughlin, T.F., *"A photoelastic analysis of fiber discontinuities in composite materials"*, J. Comp. Material, Vol. 2, 1968, pp. 44-55.

32. Marloff, R.H. and Daniel, I.M., *"Three dimensional photoelastic analysis of a fiber-reinforced model"*, Exp. Mech., Vol. 9, No. 4, 1969, pp. 156-162.

33. Rose, J.L., *"On the use of photoelastic composite models"*, Exp. Mech., Vol. 13, No. 2, 1973, pp. 59-63.

34. Daniel, I.M. and Rowlands, R.E., *"Experimental stress analysis of composite materials"*, ASME Paper No. 72—DE—6, 1972.

35. Greszczuk, L.B., *"Theoretical and experimental studies on properties and behaviour of filamentary composites"*, Proc. 21st Arm. Tech. Conf., SPI Reinforced Plastics Div., Soc. of the Plastics Ind., Inc., Section 8-A. Feb. 1966.

36. Jacob, K.A. and Chandrashekhar, K., *"Photoelastic analysis of composite prism subjected to partial compression"*, J. Appl. Mech., Trans ASME, Vol. 45, No. 2, June 1978, pp. 436-440.

37. Prabhakaran, R., *"Application of brittle coatings to graphite fiber-reinforced plastics"*, AIAA Journal, Vol. 17, No. 1, 1979, pp. 110-112.

38. Prabhakaran, R. and Dally, J.W., *"The application of photo-orthotropic elasticity"*, J. Strain Analysis, Vol. 7, No. 4, 1972, p. 253.

39. Knight, C.E., J.R., *"Orthotropic photoelastic analysis of residual stresses in filament wound rings"*, Exp. Mech., Vol. 12, No. 2, 1972, pp. 107-112.

40. Chandrashekhara, K. and Abraham, Jacob, K., *"An experimental numerical hybrid technique for stress analysis of orthotropic composites"*, Development in Composite Materials, G.S. Holister, ed., Allied Publishers (1979).

41. Chandrashekhara, K. and Abraham Jacob, K., *"A numerical method for separation of stresses in photo-orthotropic elasticity"*, Exp. Mech, Vol. 18 No. 2, 1978, pp. 61-66.

42. Kedward, K.T. and Hindle, G.R., *"Analysis of strain in fiber reinforced materials"*, J. Strain Analysis, Vol. 5, No. 4, 1970, p. 39.

43. Sabodh, K.G. Vytas, S. and Gerald, A.G., *"Analysis of structural composite materials"*, Marcel Dekkar, Inc., New York (1973).
44. Richard, T.G. and Young, W.C., *"The birefringent response of a potential photoelastic material with variable elastic properties"*; Exp. Mech., Vol. 15, No. 6, June 1975, pp. 226-229.
45. Netrebko, V.P., *"Photoelastic method of investigating the state of stress of anisotropic bodies"*, Izv. ANSSR Mekhanika Tverdogo Tela, Vol. 6, No. 1, 1971, p. 94.
46. Mittal, R.K., *"On the effect of residual birefringence in anisotropic photoelastic materials"*, Strain, Vol. 11, No. 2, April 1975, pp. 55-57.
47. Stone, D.E.W., *"A contribution to the application of photoelasticity to the micromechanics of composite materials"*, J. Strain Analysis, Vol. 4, No. 2, 1969, p. 88.
48. Doyle, J.F., *"A unified approach to optical constitutive relations"*, Proc. SESA, Vol. 35, No. 2, 1978, pp. 416-420.
49. Chandrashekhara, K., Abraham Jacob, K. and Prabhakaran, R., *"Towards stress freezing birefringent orthotropic composites models"*, Exp. Mech., Vol. 17, No. 8, 1977, pp. 317-320.
50. Prabhakaran, R., *"Model materials for photo-orthotropic elasticity"*, Fibre Sci. Tech., Vol. 13, No. 1 Jan.-Feb., 1980, pp. 1-11.
51. Doyle, James, F., *"Constitute relations in photomechanics"*, Int. J. Mech Sec. Vol. 22, No. 1, 1980, pp. 1-8.
52. Agarwal, B.D., *"An approximate method of orthotropic photoelastic analysis"*, Exp. Mech., Vol. 23, No. 3, March 1983, pp. 55-58.
53. Chaturvedi, S.K., *"A rational theory of oblique incidence and its extension to stress-separation in birefringent composites"*, Exp. Mech., Vol. 23, No. 3, March 1983, pp. 36-41.
54. Prabhakaran, R., *"Extension of oblique-incidence method to photo-orthotropic elasticity"*, Exp. Mech., Vol. 22, No. 12, Dec. 1982, pp. 462-467.
55. Agarwal, B.D. and Chaturvedi, S.K., *"Exact and approximate strain optic laws for orthotropic photelastic materials"*, Polymer Composites, Vol. 3, No. 3, Juiy 1982, pp. 146-151.
56. Prabhakaran, R., *"Fabrication of birefringent anisotropic model materials"*, Exp. Mech., Vol. 20, No. 9, Sept. 1980, p. 320-321.

Suggested Readings

1. *Ajovalasit, A. and Tscninke, M.,* 'Photoelasticity in Theory and Practice', 2nd ed., Springer-Verlag (1974).
2. *Coker, E.G. and Filon, L.N.G.,* 'A Treatise on Photoelasticity', Cambridge University Press, Cambridge, England (1931).
3. *Dally, J.W. and Riley W.F.,* 'Experimental Stress Analysis', 2nd ed., McGraw-Hill, New York (1978).
4. *Dove, R.C. and Adams, P.H.,* 'Experimental Stress Analysis and Motion Measurements', Prentice-Hall of India (Pvt.) Ltd., New Delhi (1965).
5. *Durelli, A.J.,* 'Applied Stress Analysis', Prentice-Hall, Inc., Englewood Cliffs, N.J. (1967).
6. *Durelli, A.J. and Park, V.J.,* 'Moire Analysis of Strain', Prentice-Hall, Inc., Englewood Cliffs, N.J. (1970).
7. *Durelli, A.J. Phillips, E.A. and Tsao, C.H.,* 'Introduction to the Theoretical and Experimental Analysis of Stress and Strain', McGraw-Hill, New York (1958).
8. *Durelli, A.J. and Riley W.F.,* 'Introduction to Photomechanics', Prentice-Hall, Inc., Englewood Cliffs, N.J. (1965).
9. *Frocht, M.M.,* 'Photoelasticity', Vol. I and II, John Wiley & Sons, Inc., New York (1966).
10. *Hendry, A.W.,* 'Photoelastic Analysis', Pergamon Press (1966).
11. *Hendry, A.W.,* 'Elements of Experimental Stress Analysis', Pergamon Press (1977).
12. *Hetenyi, M.,* 'Handbook of Experimental Stress Analysis', John Wiley & Sons, Inc., New York (1980).
13. *Heywood, R.B.,* 'Designing by Photoelasticity', Chapman Hall, Ltd., London (1952).
14. *Holister, G.S.,* 'Experimental Stress Analysis', Cambridge University Press, Cambridge (1967).
15. *Holister, G.S.,* 'Developments in Stress Analysis', Allied Science Publishers, London (1979).
16. *Jessop, H.T.,* 'Photoelasticity in Handbook of Physics', Vol. VI, Ed. by Flugge, S., Berlin-Goettingen-Heidelberg, Springer (1958).
17. *Kuske, A. and Robertson, G.,* 'Photoelastic Stress Analysis', John Wiley & Sons (1974).
18. *Lee, G.H.,* 'An Introduction to Experimental Stress Analysis', John Wiley and Sons, Inc., New York (1950).
19. *Leven, M.M.,* 'Photoelasticity : The Selected Scientific Papers of M.M. Frocht', Pergamon Press (1969).

20. 'Manual on Experimental Stress Analysis', 3rd. ed., Edited by Kobayashi, A.S., SESA, Saugatuck, Westport (1979).
21. *Neubert, H.K.P.*, 'Strain Gauges : Kinds and Uses', McMillan, London (1967).
22. *Perry, C.C. and Lissner, H.R.*, 'The Strain Gauge Primer', 2nd ed., McGraw-Hill Book Co., Inc., New York (1962).
23. *Potma, T.*, 'Strain Gauges : Theory and Applications', Philips Paperbacks, London (1967).
24. *Singh, S.*, 'Applied Stress Analysis', Khanna Publishers, Delhi 1979.
25. *Theocaris, P.S.*, 'Moire Fringes in Strain Analysis', Pergamon Press, New York (1969).
26. *Zienkiewicz, O.C. and Holister, G.S.*, 'Experimental and Numerical Methods of Stress Analysis', John Wiley, New York (1965).
27. *Zandman, F., Redner, S. and Dally, J.W.*, 'Photoelastic Coatings', The Iowa State University Press, Amer, Iowa and SESA, Westport, Connecticut (1977).

Subject Index

S

T

U

V

W